Lecture Notes in Computer Science 1644

Edited by G. Goos, J. Hartmanis and J. van Leeuwen

Springer

Berlin
Heidelberg
New York
Barcelona
Hong Kong
London
Milan
Paris
Singapore
Tokyo

Jiří Wiedermann ⌐ Peter van Emde Boas
Mogens Nielsen (Eds.)

Automata, Languages and Programming

26th International Colloquium, ICALP'99
Prague, Czech Republic, July 11-15,1999
Proceedings

 Springer

Series Editors

Gerhard Goos, Karlsruhe University, Germany
Juris Hartmanis, Cornell University, NY, USA
Jan van Leeuwen, Utrecht University, The Netherlands

Volume Editors

Jiří Wiedermann
Institute for Computer Science, Academy of Sciences of the Czech Republic
Pod vodarenskou vezi 2, 182 07 Prague 8 - Liben, Czech Republic
E-mail: wieder@uivt.cas.cz

Peter van Emde Boas
ILLC-WINS-University of Amsterdam
Plantage Muidergracht 24, 1018 TV Amsterdam, The Netherlands
E-mail: peter@wins.uva.nl

Mogens Nielsen
BRICS, Department of Computer Science, University of Aarhus
Ny Munkegade, Bldg. 540, DK-8000 Aarhus C, Denmark
E-mail: mn@brics.dk

Cataloging-in-Publication data applied for

Die Deutsche Bibliothek - CIP-Einheitsaufnahme

Automata, languages and programming : 26th international colloquium ;
proceedings / ICALP '99, Prague, Czech Republik, July 11 - 15, 1999. Jiří
Wiedermann ... (ed.). - Berlin ; Heidelberg ; New York ; Barcelona ; Hong Kong
; London ; Milan ; Paris ; Singapore ; Tokyo : Springer, 1999
(Lecture notes in computer science ; Vol. 1644)
ISBN 3-540-66224-3

CR Subject Classification (1998): F,D, C.2-3, G.1-2

ISSN 0302-9743
ISBN 3-540-66224-3 Springer-Verlag Berlin Heidelberg New York

This work is subject to copyright. All rights are reserved, whether the whole or part of the material is
concerned, specifically the rights of translation, reprinting, re-use of illustrations, recitation, broadcasting,
reproduction on microfilms or in any other way, and storage in data banks. Duplication of this publication
or parts thereof is permitted only under the provisions of the German Copyright Law of September 9, 1965,
in its current version, and permission for use must always be obtained from Springer-Verlag. Violations are
liable for prosecution under the German Copyright Law.

© Springer-Verlag Berlin Heidelberg 1999
Printed in Germany

Typesetting: Camera-ready by author
SPIN: 10703537   06/3142 – 5 4 3 2 1 0   Printed on acid-free paper

Foreword

ICALP – the International Colloquium on Automata, Languages, and Programming – is a series of annual conferences of the European Association for Theoretical Computer Science (EATCS). ICALP'99 was organized by the Institute of Computer Science of the Academy of Sciences of the Czech Republic in cooperation with the Action M Agency. Stimulated by the positive experience from previous meetings, the guiding idea of the ICALP'99 organization was to keep and to enhance the idea of a parallel two–track conference with invited plenary talks.

Similarly to the two parts of the journal Theoretical Computer Science, Track A of the meeting is devoted to *Algorithms, Automata, Complexity, and Games*, and Track B to *Logic, Semantics, and Theory of Programming*. The Program Committee was structured along these same lines. As a further innovation, ICALP'99 was coordinated with the European Symposium on Algorithms (ESA'99) in such a way that both conferences took place in the same location with the former immediately followed by the latter.

ICALP'99 was the 26th in the series of ICALP colloquia. Previous colloquia were held in Paris (1972), Saarbrücken (1974), Edinburgh (1976), Turku (1977), Udine (1978), Graz (1979), Amsterdam (1980), Haifa (1981), Aarhus (1982), Barcelona (1983), Antwerp (1984), Nafplion (1985), Rennes (1986), Karlsruhe (1987), Tampere (1988), Stresa (1989), Warwick (1990), Madrid (1991), Vienna (1992), Lund (1993), Jerusalem (1994), Szeged (1995), Paderborn (1996), Bologna (1997), and Aalborg (1998). In the year 2000 ICALP will be held in Geneva.

The Program Committee selected 56 papers from a total of 126 submissions. Authors of submitted papers came from 20 countries. Each paper was reviewed by at least four Program Committee members who were often assisted by subreferees. The Program Committee meeting took place in Prague, on March 13–14, 1999. This volume contains all accepted papers and ten invited papers plus the abstract of the keynote address by Juris Hartmanis.

It is our pleasure to announce that at the opening of the conference, Jan van Leeuwen from Utrecht University, the Netherlands, received the Bolzano Honorary Medal of the Academy of Sciences of the Czech Republic for his contribution to the development of computer science in general and his long–term, fruitful co-operation with Czech computer scientists in particular. At this occasion he gave an acceptance speech entitled "Embedded Computations".

We thank all Program Committee members and the subreferees who assisted them in their work. A special thanks goes to Vladimiro Sassone who created the WWW software used for electronic submission and reviewing. The secretary of the Program Committee, Martin Beran, deserves our special gratitude for running and extending the above mentioned software, for realizing and maintaining the conference web page, and, last but not least, for his preparing the electronic version of the proceedings for Springer-Verlag.

We gratefully acknowledge the support from the European Research Consortium in Informatics and Mathematics (ERCIM), the Grant Agency of the Czech Republic (GAČR), Deloitte&Touche and the Institute of Computer Science of the ASČR.

The cooperation with Springer-Verlag and the local arrangement by Action M was, as usual, excellent.

May 1999   Jiří Wiedermann, Peter van Emde Boas, Mogens Nielsen

Invited Speakers

Miklos Ajtai
N.G. de Bruijn
Luca Cardelli
Kevin Compton; Scott Dexter

Karl Crary; Greg Morrisett

Felipe Cucker
Abbas Edalat; Marko Krznaryč
Juris Hartmanis (keynote address)
Grzegorz Rozenberg; Arto Salomaa

Jeff Vitter

Osamu Watanabe

IBM Research, Alamden, USA
Eindhoven University of Technology, NL
Microsoft Research, Cambridge, UK
BRICS, DK; City University
of New York, USA
Carnegie Mellon University;
Cornell University, USA
City University of Hong Kong, CHI
Imperial College, London, UK
Cornell University, Ithaca, NY, USA
Leiden University, NL;
Turku University, FI
Duke University, USA; INRIA
Sophia Antipolis, FR
Tokyo Institute of Technology, JP

Program Committee[1]

Jiří Wiedermann, *conference chair* •
Academy of Sciences of the CR,
Prague, CZ

Track A:

Peter van Emde Boas, *chair* •
Max Garzon
Ricard Gavalda •
Jan van Leeuwen •
Alberto Marchetti–Spaccamela •
Chris Meinel •
Jaroslav Nešetřil
Prabhakar Raghavan
Branislav Rovan •
Dan Roth
Wojciech Rytter
Miklos Santha •
Hava Siegelmann
Michael Sipser
Paul Spirakis •
Michiel Smid •

University of Amsterdam, NL
University of Memphis, US
University of Catalania, Barcelona, ES
Utrecht University, NL
University of Rome, IT
University of Trier, DE
Charles University, Prague, CZ
IBM, San Jose, US
Comenius University, Bratislava, SK
University of Illinois, Urbana/Champaign, US
Warsaw University, PL
LRI, Paris, FR
Technion, Haifa, IL
MIT, Cambridge, US
CTI, Patras, GR
University of Magdeburg, DE

---

[1] Members marked with • participated in the PC meeting.

Track B:

Mogens Nielsen, *chair* •
Stephen Brookes
Manfred Broy
Roberto Gorrieri
Thomas Henzinger
Mojmír Křetínský •
Johann Makowsky •
Dale Miller
Vincent van Oostrom
Fernando Orejas
Davide Sangiorgi •
Don Sannella
Wolfgang Thomas
Igor Walukiewicz •

BRICS, Aarhus, DK
CMU, Pittsburgh, US
University of Munich, DE
University of Bologna, IT
University of California, Berkeley, US
Masaryk University, Brno, CZ
Technion, Haifa, IL
The Pennsylvania State University, US
CWI, Amsterdam, NL
University of Catalania, Barcelona, ES
INRIA, Sophia-Antipolis, FR
University of Edinburgh, UK
University of Aachen, DE
University of Warsaw, PL

Organizing Committee

Jiří Wiedermann, *chair*

Daniela Bakrlíková
Martin Beran
Hana Klímová
Roman Neruda
Jiří Šíma
Arnošt Štědrý
David Štrupl
Lucie Váchová
Milena Zeithamlová

List of Referees

L. Aceto, J.-P. Allouche, H. Alt, C. Alvarez, F. d'Amore, M. Andreou, A. Avron, P. Baldan, C. Bazgan, M. von der Beeck, M. Beemster, A. Ben-Hur, J. F. A. K. van Benthem, T. Berger-Wolf, P. Berman, G. M. Bierman, D. A. Bini, L. Birkedal, P. van Emde Boas, H. L. Bodlaender, H. Bordihn, J. Bradfield, M. Breitling, F. van Breugel, L. Brim, S. Brookes, H. M. Buhrman, N. Busi, I. Caragiannis, I. Cerna, F. Corradini, B. Courcelle, K. Crary, M. Crochemore, A. Czumaj, V. Dalmau, I. Damgaard, C. Damm, P. Degano, N. Dershowitz, D. Dubashi, B. Durand, C. Durr, P. Efraimidis, J. Engelfriet, J. Erickson, P. Fatourou, G. Ferrari, A. Filinski, M. Flammini, R. Fleischer, D. Fotakis, P. Fraigniaud, N. Francez, S. Frschle, M. Furer, J. Gabarro, V. Galpin, M. Garzon, R. Gavalda, D. Giammarresi, N. Gilboa, R. van Glabbeek, U. Goltz, R. Gorrieri, F. C. A. Groen, J. F. Groote, I. Guessarian, D. Guijarro, L. Gurvits, J. Hannan, T. Harju, M. Hasegawa, T. Henzinger, Y. Hirshfeld, C. Hofmann, J. Hromkovic, M. Di Ianni, C. S. Iliopoulos, A. Itai, P. Jancar, D. Janin, S. Jha, S. Jukna, M. Jurdzinski, S. Kahrs, K. Kalorkoti, M. Kaminski, J. Karhumäki, J. Karhumaki, M. Karpinski, D. Konopnicki, S. C. Kontogiannis, M. van Kreveld, M. Křetínský, A. Kučera, O. Kupferman, E. Kushilevitz, D. Kuske, M. Kutylowski, D. Lapoire, C. Lautemann, J. van Leeuwen, H.-P. Lenhof, M. Lenisa, J. K. Lenstra, S. Leonardi, J. Levy, J. Longley, Z. Lukasiak, B. Luttik, T. Mailund, J. A. Makowsky, A. Marchetti-Spaccamela, D. Marchignoli, R. Maron, C. Martínez, O. Matz, G. Mauri, R. Mayr, J. Mazoyer, P.-A. Mellies, M. Merro, M. Mihail, D. Miller, M. Mislove, F. Moller, O. Mueller, M. Mukund, M. Mundhenk, W. Naraschewski, M. Nielsen, S. Nikoletseas, T. Nipkow, D. Niwinski, E. Ochmanski, D. von Oheimb, V. van Oostrom, F. Orejas, C. Palamidessi, E. Papaioannou, G. Pentaris, A. Petit, F. Pfenning, J. Philipps, G. Michele Pinna, G. Pirillo, M. Pistore, W. Plandowski, A. Poigne, B. Poizat, S. Prasad, A. Proskurowski, P. Quaglia, F. van Raamsdonk, A. Rabinovich, P. Raghavan, J. F. Raskin, H. Reichel, E. Reingold, K. Reinhardt, M. Reniers, J. Reynolds, A. Roiterstein, L. Rosaz, A. Rosen, D. Roth, B. Rovan, B. Rumpe, P. Ruzicka, W. Rytter, H. Sack, J. Sakarovitch, K. Salomaa, R. Sandner, D. Sangiorgi, V. Sassone, B. Schätz, B. Schieder, A. Schubert, T. Schwentick, H. Seidl, H. Shachnai, J. F. Sibeyn, H. Siegelmann, A. Simpson, M. Sipser, C. Skalka, M. Skoviera, P. M. A. Sloot, M. Smid, K. Spies, P. Spirakis, J. Srba, L. Staiger, I. Stark, P. Stevenhagen, P. Stevens, J. Stribrna, J. Sturc, R. Szelepcsenyi, T. Tamir, S. Tan, S.-H. Teng, S. A. Terwijn, W. Thomas, L. Torenvliet, J. Tromp, W. Unger, Y. S. Usenko, S. Varricchio, R. Virga, P. M. B. Vitanyi, J. Voege, F.-J. de Vries, I. Walukiewicz, E. Wattel, M. Wehr, P. Weil, C. Weise, T. Wilke, G. Winskel, K. Xatzis, F. Xhafa, A. Yakovlev

Table of Contents

Invited Talks

Contributed Papers

Generating Hard Instances of the Short Basis Problem

Miklós Ajtai

IBM Almaden Research Center, CA 95120, USA

Abstract. A class of random lattices is given, in [1] so that (a) a random lattice can be generated in polynomial time together with a short vector in it, and (b) assuming that certain worst-case lattice problems have no polynomial time solutions, there is no polynomial time algorithm which finds a short vector in a random lattice with a polynomially large probability. In this paper we show that lattices of the same random class can be generated not only together with a short vector in them, but also together with a short basis. The existence of a known short basis may make the construction more applicable for cryptographic protocols.

1. Introduction. Most of the well-known, hard computational problems, (e.g. factoring), are worst-case problems, while for cryptographic applications we need hard average-case problems. The reason is that any random instance of a hard average case problem is also hard with a positive probability, while there is no known way that would create a hard instance of a hard worst-case problem. Using lattice problems it is possible to create average-case problems which are just as difficult as certain well-known worst-case problem. For a more detailed description of the worst-case, average-case connection and for cryptographic applications see e.g. [1], [2], [4], [5], [6], [7] or the survey paper [3]. (Further references are given in [3].) One of the worst-case lattice problems used in [1] is the following:

(P) *Find a basis $b_1, ..., b_n$ in the n-dimensional lattice L whose length, defined as $\max_{i=1}^n \|b_i\|$, is the smallest possible up to a polynomial factor.*

We will refer to this problem as the short basis problem. It is proved in [1] that if (**P**) has no polynomial time solution then a random lattice L can be generated in polynomial time (with a suitably chosen distribution), together with a vector shorter than $\sqrt{n}$ in it, so that, for any algorithm $\mathcal{A}$ the probability that $\mathcal{A}$ finds in L a vector shorter than $\sqrt{n}$, if L is given as an input, is smaller than n^{-c} (for any fixed $c > 0$ if n is sufficiently large). That is, using the assumption that the worst-case short basis problem is hard, we are able to create a hard instance of the short vector problem with a known solution. In this paper we show that instead of the short vector problem we may use the short basis problem in the conclusion of the theorem as well, in the strong sense that we construct the random lattice together with a short basis, but to find even a short vector in it is difficult. This last property will be a consequence of the fact that we are using the same random class of lattices as in [1], we only modify the way as a random lattice is generated, without changing it's distribution (by more than an exponentially small error). (These type of random lattices where a short basis is known for the person who generates the lattice, but nobody else can find even a short vector, seem to be more suitable for cryptographic applications, than the ones generated together with a single short vector. We intend to return to this question in a separate paper. The public-key crypto-system of Goldreich, Goldwasser and Halevi described in [6] is based on the availability of a short basis. However the size of a basis is defined in a different way, so our random lattice together with the generated basis probably does not meet the requirements of their system.) The dimension of the lattice for the average-case problem is larger than for the corresponding worst-case problem. If the dimension of the lattice in the worst-case problem is n, then the dimension of the lattice in the average case problem is $c'n \log n$ for a suitably chosen constant $c' > 0$. We will use the same construction for a random lattice as was used in [1], (more precisely the distance of the distributions of the random lattices used in the two papers is exponentially small in n). To give an exact formulation of our result we recall the definition of the random lattice form [1] with a somewhat modified notation. (n will denote now the dimension of the random lattice.)

Assume that the positive integers q, r, n, $r < n$ are fixed. (The results of [1] hold if $r^{c_1} < q < 2r^{c_1}$ and $r^{c_3} > n \geq c_2 r \log r$ for some suitably chosen absolute constants c_1, c_2, c_3.) Let I_i^j be the set of all j dimensional vectors whose coordinates are from the set $\{0, 1, ..., i-1\}$. First we pick a random sequence $u_0, ..., u_{n-1}$ independently and with uniform distribution from the set I_q^r. The random lattice L will consist of all sequences of integers $h_0, ..., h_{n-1}$ so that

$$\sum_{i=0}^{n-1} h_i u_i \equiv 0 \pmod{q}$$

The distribution of L will be denoted by Γ_n.

This definition gives an explicit way of generating lattices in the random class. In [1], with a slight modification of this definition, we were able to generate almost the same distribution (with an exponentially small error) together with a short vector in L. Namely, first we randomize only $u_0, ..., u_{n-2}$ independently and with uniform distribution from I_q^r and independently from that a random $0, 1$ sequence $\delta_0, ..., \delta_{n-2}$, with uniform distribution on the set of all $0, 1$ sequences of length $n-1$. Let u_{n-1} be the smallest nonnegative residue modulo q of

$$-\sum_{i=0}^{n-2} \delta_i u_i$$

(where we take the residue of each component of the vector). This way we have defined the sequence $u_0, ..., u_{n-1}$ and from this we can define the lattice the same way as in the original definition. The distribution of this lattice will be denoted by Γ_n'. The sequence $v = \langle \delta_0, ..., \delta_{n-2}, 1 \rangle$ will be in the lattice and its length is at most $\sqrt{n}$. (It is shown in [1] that if (**P**) has no polynomial time solutions, then such a short vector cannot be found in polynomial time with a polynomially large probability, provided that the sequence $u_0, ..., u_{n-1}$ is given as an input.) We define the distance of two probability dstributions P_1 and P_2 on the same σ-algebra X as $\max\{|P_1(A) - P_2(A)| + |P_1(B) - P_2(B)| \mid A, B \in X, A \cap B = \emptyset\}$

Theorem 1. *There is a $c > 0$ so that for each positive integer n there is a distribution Φ_n on the set of n dimensional lattices so that the distance of the distributions Γ_n and Φ_n is at most 2^{-cn}, moreover a random lattice L according to the distribution Φ_n, can be generated in polynomial time together with a basis in it whose length, (that is, the maximum of the lengths of it's elements) is at most $n^3\sqrt{n}$.* $\quad\square$

Remark. The results of [1] imply that if there is no polynomial time solution for (**P**), then there is no algorithm which finds a vector shorter than $\sqrt{n}$ in a random L (according to the distribution Γ_n) with a probability greater then $n^{-c'}$, for any $c' > 0$ if n is sufficiently large. Since the distance of the distributions Γ_n, Φ_n is exponentially small this holds for the distributions Φ_n as well. That is, as we claimed earlier, we are able to generate a random lattice together with a short basis, so that it is hard to find even a short vector in the random latttice, if only the lattice is given as an input, provided that the worst-case problem (**P**) is hard.

2. The proof of the theorem. In the proof of our theorem we will use the following lemma from [1]. (There the lemma is used in the proof of the fact that the distance of Γ_n and Γ_n' is exponentially small in n.)

Lemma A. *There exists a $c > 0$ so that if A is a finite Abelian group with n elements and k is a positive integer and $b = \langle b_1, ..., b_k \rangle$ is a sequence of length k whose elements are chosen independently and with uniform distribution from A, then with a probability of at least $1 - 2^{-ck}$ the following holds:*

Assume that b is fixed and we randomize a $0, 1$-sequence $\delta_1, ...\delta_k$, where the numbers δ_i are chosen independetly and with uniform distribution from $\{0, 1\}$. For each $a \in A$ let $p_a = P(a = \sum_{i=1}^{k} \delta_i b_i))$. Then

(a) $\sum_{a \in A}(p_a - |A|^{-1})^2 \leq 2^{-2ck}$ *and*

(b) $\sum_{a \in A}|p_a - |A|^{-1}| \leq |A|^{\frac{1}{2}}2^{-ck}$.

If $A = I_q^r$ (with the modulo q addition) then this lemma shows that for almost all fixed values of $u_0, ..., u_{n-2}$ if $\delta_0, ..., \delta_{n-2}$ is picked at random then the distribution of

$$\sum_{i=0}^{n-2} \delta_i u_i = -u_{n-1}$$

is almost uniform on I_q^r.

This construction gives a single short vector v in L. We want to modify it so that we get a short basis of L. Short will mean now that the Euclidean norm of each basis vector is at most $n^3\sqrt{n}$.

To make our construction simpler we assume that q is odd. (We will prove the independence of the constructed vectors by showing that their determinant is odd.) Instead of generating a short basis of L we will generate first only n linearly independent vectors and then from them we can get a basis of L while we increase their length only by a factor of n. (See [1])

There is an easy way to generate the random lattice L together with more than one short vector. Namely we randomize only $u_0, ..., u_{n-1-s}$ for some fixed s and define the remaining $u_{n-s}, ..., u_{n-1}$ as their linear combinations with random $0, 1$ coefficients. If $n - s > c \log |A| = c \log(q^r) = c'r \log r$ then Lemma A remains applicable and we get s linearly independent vectors. Although this cannot be improved further, we keep the idea of randomizing certain vectors u_i and get the other ones as their random linear combinations in our final construction. (The coefficients in this construction will not be $0, 1$ and their distribution will not be uniform.) More precisely we will get the random sequence $u_0, ...u_{n-1}$ in the following way:

We randomize first only r vectors $u_0, ..., u_{r-1}$ independently and with uniform distribution from I_q^r. Let Y be an n by r matrix whose first r rows are $u_0, ..., u_{r-1}$ and the remaining entries are variables. Let T be the set of these variables. We will define a random n by n matrix A' (with integer entries) depending on the vectors $u_0, ..., u_{r-1}$. The distribution of the matrix A' is the crucial part of the definition; we will give it later. Assume that A' has been chosen. A will be the matrix consisting of the first $n-r$ rows of A'. Consider that equation $AY = 0$. We will define A' so that this equation has a unique rational solution for the variables in T, moreover this solution assigns integer values for all of these variables. Substituting these values into Y and then taking their least nonnegative residue modulo q we get a matrix Y'. The rows of Y' will be $u_0, ..., u_{n-1}$. We will show that $A'Y' \equiv 0 \pmod{q}$. The rows of A' will be short linearly independent elements of L. The congruence $A'Y' \equiv 0 \pmod{q}$ imples that that the rows of A' are indeed elements of L. Using the definition of A' we will show that they are short and linearly independent.

We define A' in two parts. First we define only A, an $n - r$ by n matrix. A will be the first $n - r$ rows of A'. Then separately we define the last r rows of A'. A together with $u_0, ..., u_{r-1}$ will already determine the sequence $u_0, ..., u_{n-1}$.

The first r columns of the matrix A forms an $n - r$ by r matrix this will be denoted by A_1. The remaining columns form a square ($n - r$ by $n - r$) matrix A_2. Let $\mu = [\log_r q] + 2$

We will start the numbering of the rows and columns of each matrix with 0. That is, an i by j matrix D has rows $0, 1, ..., i - 1$ and columns $0, 1, ..., j - 1$. If $D = \{d_{s,t}\}_{s=0,...,i-1, t=0,...j-1}$ then we say that $d_{s,t}$ is the tth elements of the sth row. When we say "the first k rows of the matrix D" we refer to rows $0, 1, ..., k-1$.

Definition of A_1. The ith element of the μith row is 1 for $i = 0, ..., r - 1$, all of the other entries are 0.

Definition of A_2. We will define A_2 as $A_2 = BC$ where B, C are $n - r$ by $n - r$ matrices.

Later we will give a concise but technical definition of the matrices B and C. Now we give a more easily understandable but longer definition, together with the motivating ideas. Let X be an $n - r$ by r matrix, consisting of the last $n - r$ rows of Y, that is containing only the variables, and let U be an $n - r$ by r matrix whose $i\mu$th row is u_i for $i = 0, ..., r$ and all other rows have all 0 entries. The definition of A_1 implies that the equation $AY = 0$ is equivalent to the equation $A_2 X = -U$. We we want to define the matrix $A_2 = BC$ in a way that will make it easy to get an explicit description of the solution of the equation $BCX = -U$. B will be a lower triangular matrix with integer entries and 1s in the main diagonal. C will be an upper triangular matrix with integer entries and 1s in the main diagonal. This already implies that the equation $BCX = -U$ has a unique solution in X with integer entries. Since $X = -C^{-1}B^{-1}U$ we first define B in a way that we will have a clear description of $B^{-1}U$. $-B^{-1}U$ is the solution of the equation $-BZ = U$ where Z is an n by r matrix whose entries are variables. Let $\xi_1, ..., \xi_n$ be the rows of Z. If B is given, then using the fact that B is lower triangular we can determine the value of ξ_i by recursion on i. Each ξ_i will be a linear combination of the rows of $-U$ where the coefficients are determined by B. Since each row of U is an u_j, $j = 0, 1, ..., r - 1$ or 0, we have that each ξ_i will be a linear combination of the vectors $u_0, ..., u_{n-1}$. Recall that the $j\mu$th row of U is u_j, for $j = 0, 1, ..., r - 1$ and the other rows are 0. By definition the $j\mu$th row of B will contain a sigle 1 in the main diagonal and all of its other enries will be 0, that is, $b_{j\mu, j\mu} = 1$ and $b_{j\mu, k} = 0$ for all $j = 0, 1, ..., r - 1$ and $k \neq j\mu$, where $B = \{b_{s,t}\}$. This implies that $\xi_{j\mu} = -u_j$ for $j = 0, 1, ..., r - 1$. E.g. $\xi_0 = -u_0$. We want ot define B so that $\xi_2 = -ru_0, ..., \xi_j = -r^j u_0$ for $j = 0, 1, ..., \mu - 1$. We can attain this if we put $b_{j,j-1} = -r$ for $j = 2, ..., m - 1$ and $b_{j,t} = 0$ for all $t \neq j$, $t \neq j - 1$, $j = 1, ..., \mu - 1$. (That is the jth row will contain exactly two nonzero entries, in the main diagonal and immediately left from it.) Determining ξ_i by recursion on i we get the required values. The motivation for this definition is the following: as an integer linear combination of the integers $r^j u_0$, $j = 0, ..., r - 1$ we can express any integer of the from bu_0 where b is a integer in the interval $[0, q) \subseteq [0, r^\mu)$. Therefore if we choose the further coefficients of B in a suitable way then we may force ξ_s for some $s > \mu$ take any value of the form bu_0. Since we want to do the same thing for $u_1, ... u_{r-1}$ as well we define the first $r\mu$ rows of B in the following way

$b_{i,i} = 1$ for all $0 = 1, ..., n - r - 1$.

For all $j = \mu i + k$, $i = 0, ..., r - 1$, $k = 1, ..., \mu - 1$ we have $b_{j,j-1} = -r$.

All of the other entries in the first μr rows of B are 0.

The definition so far implied that

(B1) $\xi_{i\mu+j} = -r^j u_i$ for $i = 0, ..., r - 1$, $j = 0, ..., \mu - 1$.

The next r rows, that is, rows $r\mu + k$, $k = 0, 1, ..., r - 1$ have a special role. The definition of these rows will guarantee that

(B2) $2\xi_{r\mu+k} \equiv -u_k \pmod{q}$ for $k = 0, ..., r - 1$.

To get this, first we take an integer z with $0 < z < q$ so that $2z \equiv 1 \pmod{q}$. Let

$$z = \sum_{s=0}^{\mu-1} \alpha_s r^s$$

where $0 \le \alpha_s < r$ are integers for $s = 0, ..., \mu - 1$.

For all $j = \mu r + k$, $k = 0, ..., r - 1$ and $i = 0, 1, ..., \mu - 1$ we put $b_{j,k\mu+i} = -\alpha_i$, and $b_{j,j} = 1$. All of the other entries of these rows are 0. This definition and (B1) implies (B2).

We want to define the remaining rows in a way that

(B3)   for any fixed $u_0, ..., u_{r-1}$, if $u_0, ..., u_{r-1}$ are linearly independent modulo q, then the distribution of $\xi_{(r+1)\mu}, \xi_{(r+1)\mu+1}, ..., \xi_{n-r-1}$ (with respect to the randomization of B), is uniform modulo q on the set of all r dimensional vector sequences of length $n - r - (r+1)\mu$.

To attain this, first we define a random variable η whose values are sequences of integers $x_0, x_1, ..., x_{\mu-1}$ so that $0 \le x_i < r$ for all $i = 0, ..., \mu - 1$, moreover we choose η so that the number $\sum_{i=0}^{\mu-1} x_i r^i$ has uniform distribution on the interval $[0, q-1]$. (Such an η can be efficiently generated by randomizing first the value of $\sum_{i=0}^{\mu-1} x_i r^i$ and then determining the unique values of the numbers x_i.)

Now we can define row j for all $j \ge (\mu + 1)r$. For all $j \ge (\mu + 1)r$ $b_{j,j} = 1$ for and $i = 0, ..., r - 1$ the sequence of the entries $b_{j,\mu i}, b_{j,\mu i+1}, ..., b_{j,\mu i+\mu-1}$ will be a random value of the random variable η. (For all of the possible numbers j the values of the random variable η are taken independently.) All of the other entries in these rows are 0.

(B1) and the definition of μ implies that for each $i \in [(r+1)\mu, n-r]$, ξ_i is the linear combination of the vectors $u_0, ..., u_{r-1}$, where the coefficients are taken at random and with uniform distribution modulo q, moreover these coefficients are independent for different values of i and for different elements of the sequence $u_0, ..., _{r-1}$. This implies (B3).

This completes the definition of B. We repeat the definiton below in a more concise form.

Definition of B. For the definition of B, first we define a random variable η whose values are sequences of integers $x_0, x_1, ..., x_{\mu-1}$ so that $0 \le x_i < r$ for all $i = 0, ..., \mu - 1$. We choose η so that the number $\sum_{i=0}^{\mu-1} x_i r^i$ has uniform distribution on the interval $[0, q-1]$.

We will denote by $b_{i,j}$ the element of B in the ith row and jth column for $i = 0, ..., n - r - 1$, $j = 0, ..., n - r - 1$.

$b_{i,i} = 1$ for all $0 = 1, ..., n - r - 1$.

For all $j = \mu i + k$, $i = 0, ..., r - 1$, $k = 1, ..., \mu - 1$ we have $b_{j,j-1} = -r$.

For all $j = \mu r + k$, $k = 0, ..., r - 1$ and $i = 0, 1, ..., \mu - 1$ we have $b_{j,k\mu+i} = -\alpha_i$ where $\sum_{s=0}^{\mu-1} \alpha_s (r)^s = z$, $0 \le z < q$ and $2z \equiv 1 \pmod{q}$ and $0 \le \alpha_s < r$ are integers for $s = 0, ..., \mu - 1$.

For all $j \ge (\mu + 1)r$ and $i = 0, ..., r - 1$ the sequence of the entries $b_{j,\mu i}, b_{j,\mu i+1}, ..., b_{j,\mu i+\mu-1}$ will be a random value of the random variable η. (For all of the possible j and i the values of the random variable η are taken independently.)

All of the other entries of B are 0s.

The definition of C is simpler so we start with the formal definition.

Definition of C. $c_{i,j}$ will denote the jth element of the ith row in the matrix C for $i = 0, ..., n - r - 1$, $j = 0, ..., n - r - 1$.

$c_{i,i} = 1$ for all $i = 0, 1, ..., n - r - 1$.

The entries $c_{i,j}$, $i \leq [\frac{n-r}{2}]$, $j > [\frac{n-r}{2}]$ are taken independently and with uniform distribution from the set $\{0, 1\}$.

All of the other entries of C are 0s.

Clearly we have that

(C1) C is an upper triangular matrix with 1's in the main diagonal.

This implies that we can compute the $(n - r - 1 - j)$th row of $C^{-1}(B^{-1}U)$ by recursion on j. Assume that the rows of the unique solution of $C^{-1}(-B^{-1}U)$ are the r-dimensional integer vectors $\rho_0, ..., \rho_{n-r-1}$.

Let $\kappa = [\frac{n-r}{2}]$. Since the rows of $B^{-1}U$ are $\xi_0, ..., \xi_{n-r-1}$ the definition of C implies that

(C2) $\rho_i = \xi_i$ for all $i = \kappa + 1, ..., n - r - 1$.

and

(C3) $\rho_i = - \sum_{j=\kappa+1}^{n-r-1} c_{i,j} \rho_j = - \sum_{j=\kappa+1}^{n-r-1} c_{i,j} \xi_j$ for all $i = 0, 1, ..., \kappa$.

(The second equality is a consequence of (C2)). With a probability exponentially close to one for the randomization of $u_0, ..., u_{r-1}$, the sequence $u_0, ..., u_{r-1}$ is linearly independent modulo q. Assume now that such a sequence $u_0, ..., u_{r-1}$ is fixed. (B3) implies that the distribution of the sequence $\xi_\kappa, ..., \xi_{n-r-1}$ is uniform modulo q on the set of all sequences of length $n - r - 1 - \kappa$ consisting of r-dimensional vectors. Therefore we may apply Lemma A for the sum in (C3) so that I_q^r with the addition modulo q is the Abelian group. We get that

(C4')   *for almost all fixed $u_0, ..., u_{r-1}$, and for allmost all fixed $\xi_0, ..., \xi_{n-r-1}$ (according to the distribution of B), the distribution of $\rho_0, ..., \rho_\kappa$ is almost uniform modulo q on the set of all r dimensional vector sequences of length $\kappa + 1$.*

More precisely we have the following:

(C4)   *There is a $c_4 > 0$ so that for all sufficiently large n if we randomize $u_0, ..., u_{r-1}$ and B, then with a probability of at least $1 - 2^{-c_4 n}$ we get a sequence $u_0, ..., u_{r-1}, \xi_\kappa, ..., \xi_{n-r}$, so that for the randomization of C the distance of the distribution of the sequence $\rho_0, ..., \rho_\kappa$ from the uniform distribution is at most $2^{-c_4 n}$.*

This thogether with (C2) and (B3) implies that:

(C5)   *There is a $c_5 > 0$ so that for all sufficiently large n and for the randomization of both B and C the distance of the distribtuion of the sequence $\rho_0, ..., \rho_{n-r-1}$ from the uniform distribtuion is at most $2^{-c_5 n}$.*

The definition of C also implies that every entry of C is small which will be useful when we estimate the length of the constructed linearly independent vectors. More precisely

(C6)   each entry of C in the main diagonal is 1 and all of the other entries belong to the set $\{0, 2\}$.

Now we return to the equation $AY = 0$. The definitions of A_1, U, $\rho_0, ..., \rho_{n-r-1}$ imply that if S is an n by r matrix whose rows are $u_0, ..., u_{r-1}, \rho_0, ..., \rho_{n-r-1}$ then $AS = 0$. Therefore we may define the random lattice L by $u_{r+i} = \rho_i$ for $i = 0, ..., n-r-1$. That is, L is the set of integer vectors $h_0, ..., h_{n-1}$ with $\sum_{i=0}^{n-1} h_i u_i \equiv 0 \pmod{q}$. This definition together with (C6) implies that the distance of Γ_n and Φ_n is ineed at most 2^{-cn} for a suitably chosen constant $c > 0$ as claimed in the theorem. To complete the proof of the theorem we have to show only that using B and C we may construct n linearly independent elements of L each with length at most $n^2 \sqrt{n}$.

$AS = 0$ implies that the rows of A are elements of L. They are clearly linearly independent since the submatrix $A_2 = BC$ has determinant 1. We have to construct r more linearly independent elements of L. We will add r new rows to the matrix A, the new matrix will be A'. The jth new row for some fixed $j = 0, ..., r-1$ is defined in the following way:

The $(n-r-1+j)$th row of A' is a sequence of length n that we get by the concatenation of the jth unit vector and the $(r\mu + j)$th row of C multiplied by two.

If we multiply this row by the matrix S then we get $u_j + 2(\rho_{r\mu+j} + \sum_{i=\kappa+1}^{n-r-1} c_{r\mu+j,i}\rho_i)$. By (C3) this is equal to $u_j + 2\xi_{r\mu+j}$. According to (B2) $2\xi_{r\mu+j} \equiv -u_j \pmod{q}$ and so the product is 0 modulo q. This shows that $A'S \equiv 0 \pmod{q}$ and so all of the rows of A' are elements of L. We have to prove that the rows are linearly independent (over the rationals). We show that the determinant of the matrix A' is an odd integer so it is not 0 which implies the required independence. Every element of A' is an integer (by definition of A'). We compute the determinant of A' modulo 2. A' consists of 4 submatrices A_1, A_2, A_3, A_4 where A_1, A_2 have been already defined; A_3 consist of those entries of A' which are in the last r rows and first r columns, A_4 consists of those entries of A' which are in the last r rows and last $n-r$ columns. Every entries of A_4 is even that is A_4 is zero modulo 2. Therefore the determinant of A' modulo 2 is equal to the products of the determinants of A_3 and A_2 modulo 2. A_3 is an r by r identity matrix so its determinant is 1. $A_2 = BC$. B is a lower triangular matrix C is an upper triangular matrix both have 1s in their main diagonal thefore the determinant of A_2 is 1. These imply that the determinant of A' is congruent to 1 modulo 2.

Finally we estimate the absolute values of the entries of A'. Each entry of A' outside A is $0, 1$ or 2. $A = BC$. The absolute value of each entry of C is ethier 0 or 1. Every entry of B is an integer in the interval $[0, r]$. Therefore each entry of A is an integer in the interval of $[-r(n-r), r(n-r)]$ and so this is true for the entries of A' as well. This implies that the Euclidean norm of our basis vectors is at most $(n(r(n-r))^2)^{\frac{1}{2}} = n^{\frac{1}{2}}r(n-r) \leq n^2\sqrt{n}$. (If we take into account that in each row of B the number of nonzero entries is relatively small, then we can improve this upper bound.)

References

1. M. Ajtai, Generating Hard Instances of Lattice Problems, Proceedings of the 28th Annual ACM Symposium on Theory of Computing, 1996, or Electronic Colloquium on Computational Complexity, 1996, http://www.eccc.uni-trier.de/eccc/
2. M. Ajtai and C. Dwork, A Public-Key Cryptosystem with Worst-Case/Average-Case Equivalence, Proceedings of the 29th Annual ACM Symposium on Theory of Computing, 1997, or
3. J-Y Cai, Some Recent Progress on the Complexity of Lattice Problems, Electronic Colloquium on Computational Complexity, 1999, http://www.eccc.uni-trier.de/eccc/, to appear in the Proceedings of the IEEE Conference of Computational Complexity, 1999.
4. J-Y Cai, A. Nerurkar. An Improved Worst-Case to Average-Case Connection for Lattice Problems. In Proc. 38th IEEE Symposium on Foundations of Computer Science, 1997, 468-477.
5. O. Goldreich, S. Goldwasser, S. Halevi, Collision-free hashing from lattice problems, Electronic Colloquium, on Computational Complexity, 1996, http://www.eccc.uni-trier.de/eccc/
6. O. Goldreich, S. Goldwasser, S. Halevi, Public-key cryptosystems from lattice reduction problems, In *Advances in Cryptology-Crypto'97*, Burton S. Kaliski Jr. (Ed.), Lecture Notes in Computer Science, 1294:112-131, Springer-Verlag, 1997.
7. O. Goldreich, S. Goldwasser, S. Halevi, Eliminating decryption errors in the Ajtai-Dwork cryptosystem, In *Advances in Cryptology-Crypto'97*, Burton S. Kaliski Jr. (Ed.), Lecture Notes in Computer Science, 1294:105-111, Springer-Verlag, 1997.

Wide Area Computation

Luca Cardelli

Microsoft Research

Abstract. The last decades have seen the emergence of the *sea of objects* paradigm for structuring complex distributed systems on workstations and local area networks. In this approach, applications and system services are composed of and communicate among themselves through reliable and transparently accessible object interfaces, leading to the interaction of hundred or thousands of unstructured objects.

This approach has lead to major progress in software composability and reliability. Unfortunately, it is based on a number of assumptions that do not hold on wide area networks. There, access to resources is intrinsically unreliable (because of failure, congestion, voluntary disconnected operation, etc.) and not transparent (because of variations in latency and bandwidth, hardware and software mobility, and the presence of firewalls). These characteristics are so radically different from the current computational norm that they amount to a new model of computation.

We discuss the challenges of computation on wide area networks. Our approach reflects the intuition that, to function satisfactorily on a wide area network, the *sea of objects* must be partitioned and made hierarchical, internally mobile, and secure. This paper is an abridged version of [3].

1 Introduction

The Internet and the World-Wide-Web provide a computational infrastructure that spans the planet. It is appealing to imagine writing programs that exploit this global infrastructure. Unfortunately, the Web violates many familiar assumptions about the behavior of distributed systems, and demands novel and specialized programming techniques. In particular, three phenomena that remain largely hidden in local area network architectures become readily observable on the Web:

- *(A) Virtual locations*. Because of the presence of potential attackers, barriers are erected between mutually distrustful administrative domains. Therefore, a program must be aware of where it is, and of how to move or communicate between different domains. The existence of separate administrative domains induces a notion of virtual locations and of virtual distance between locations.

- *(B) Physical locations*. On a planet-size structure, the speed of light becomes tangible. For example, a procedure call to the antipodes requires at least 1/10 of a second, independently of future improvements in networking technology. This absolute lower bound to latency induces a notion of physical locations and physical distance between locations.

- *(C) Bandwidth fluctuations*. A global network is susceptible to unpredictable congestion and partitioning, which result in fluctuations or temporary interruptions of bandwidth. Moreover, mobile devices may perceive bandwidth changes as a consequence of physical movement. Programs need to be able to observe and react to these fluctuations.

These features may interact among themselves. For example, bandwidth fluctuations may be related to physical location because of different patterns of day and night network utilization, and to virtual location because of authentication and encryption across domain boundaries. Virtual and physical locations are often related, but need not coincide.

In addition, another phenomenon becomes unobservable on the Web:

- **(D) Failures.** On the Web, there is no practical upper bound to communication delays. In particular, failures become indistinguishable from long delays, and thus undetectable. Failure recovery becomes indistinguishable from intermittent connectivity. Furthermore, delays (and, implicitly, failures) are frequent and unpredictable.

These four phenomena determine the set of *observables* of the Web: the events or states that can be in principle detected. Observables, in turn, influence the basic building blocks of computation. In moving from local area networks to wide area networks, the set of observables changes, and so does the computational model, the programming constructs, and the kind of programs one can write. The question of how to "program the Web" reduces to the question of how to program with the new set of observables provided by the Web.

At least one general technique has emerged to cope with the observables characteristic of a wide area network such as the Web. *Mobile computation* is the notion that running programs need not be forever tied to a single network node. Mobile computation can deal in original ways with the phenomena described above:

- **(A) Virtual locations.** Given adequate trust mechanisms, mobile computations can cross barriers and move between virtual locations. Barriers are designed to impede access, but when code is allowed to cross them, it can access local resources without the impediment of the barriers.

- **(B) Physical locations.** Mobile computations can move between physical locations, turning remote calls into local calls, and thus avoiding the latency limit.

- **(C) Bandwidth fluctuations.** Mobile computations can react to bandwidth fluctuations, either by moving to a better-placed location, or by transferring code that establishes a customized protocol over a connection.

- **(D) Failures.** Mobile computations can run away from anticipated failures, and can move around presumed failures.

Mobile computation is also strongly related to recent hardware advances, since computations move implicitly when carried on portable devices. In this sense, we cannot avoid the issues raised by mobile computation: more than an avant-garde software technique, it is an existing hardware reality.

2 Three Mental Images

We begin by comparing and contrasting three *mental images*; that is, three abstracted views of distributed computation. From the differences between these mental images we derive the need for new approaches to global computation.

2.1 Local Area Networks

The first mental image corresponds to the now standard, and quickly becoming obsolete, model of computation over local area networks.

When workstations and PCs started replacing mainframes, local networks were invented to connect autonomous computers for the purpose of resource sharing. A typical local area network consists of a collection of computers of about the same power (within a couple of hardware generations) and of network links of about the same bandwidth and latency. This environment is not always completely uniform: specialized machines may operate as servers or as engineering workstations, and specialized subnetworks may offer special services. Still, by and large, the structure of a LAN can be depicted as the uniform network of nodes (computers) and links (connections) in Mental Image 1:

Administrative Domain

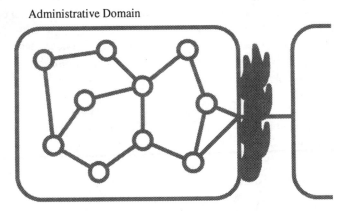

Mental Image 1: Local Area Network

A main property of such a network is its predictability. Communication delays are bounded, and processor response times can be estimated. Therefore, link and process failures can be detected by time-outs and by "pinging" nodes.

Another important property of local area networks is that they are usually well-administered and, in recent times, protected against attack. Network administrators have the task of keeping the network running and protect it against infiltration. In the picture, the boundary line represents an *administrative domain*, and the flames represent the protection provided by a *firewall*. Protection is necessary because local area networks are rarely completely disconnected: they usually have slower links to the outside world, which are however enough to make administrators nervous about infiltration.

The architecture of local area networks is very different from the older, highly centralized, mainframe architecture. This difference, and the difficulties implied by it, resulted in the emergence of novel distributed computing techniques, such as remote-procedure-call, client-server architecture, and distributed object-oriented programming. The combined aim and effect of these techniques is to make the programming and application environment stable and uniform (as in mainframes). In particular, the network topology is carefully hidden so that any two computers can be considered as lying one logical step apart. Moreover, computers can be considered immobile; for example, they usually preserve their network address when physically moved.

Even in this relatively static environment, the notion of mobility has gradually acquired prominence, in a variety of forms. Control mobility, found in RPC (Remote Procedure Call) and RMI (Remote Method Invocation) mechanisms, is the notion that a thread of control moves (in principle) from one machine to another and back. Data mobility is achieved in RPC/RMI by linearizing, transporting, and reconstructing data across machines. Link mobility is the ability to transmit the end-points of network channels, or remote object proxies. Object mobility is the ability to move objects between different servers, for example for load balancing purposes. Finally, in Remote Execution, a computations can be shipped for execution to a server (this is an early version of code mobility, proposed as an extension of RPC [13]).

In recent years, distributed computing has been endowed with greater mobility properties and easier network programming. Techniques such as Object Request Brokers have emerged to abstract over the location of objects providing certain services. Code mobility has emerged in Tcl and other scripting languages to control network applications. Agent mobility has been pioneered in Telescript [14], aimed towards a uniform (although wide area) network of services. Closure mobility (the mobility of active and connected entities) has been investigated in Obliq [4].

In due time, local area network techniques would have smoothly and gradually evolved towards deployment on wide area networks, e.g. as was explicitly attempted by the CORBA effort. But, suddenly, a particular wide area network came along that radically changed the fundamental assumptions of distributed computing and its pace of progress: the Web.

2.2 Wide Area Networks

Global computing evolved over the span of a few decades in the form of the Internet. But it was not until the emergence of the Web that the peculiar characteristics of the Internet were exposed in a way that anybody could verify with just a few mouse clicks. For clarity and simplicity we will refer to the Web as the primary global information infrastructure, although it was certainly not the first one.

We should remember that the notions of a global address space and of a global file system have been popular at times as extensions of the mainframe architecture to wide area networks. The first obvious feature of the Web is that, although it forms a global computational resource, it is nothing like a global mainframe, nor an extension of it. The Web does not support a global (updatable) file system and, although it supports a global addressing mechanism, it does not guarantee the integrity of addressing. The Web has no single reliable component, but it also has no single failure point; it is definitely not the centralized all-powerful mainframe of 1950's science fiction novels that could be shut off by attacking its single "brain".

The fact that the Web is not a mainframe is not a big concern; we have already successfully tackled distributed computing based on LANs. More distressing is the fact that the Web does not behave like a LAN either. Many proposals have emerged along the lines of extending LAN concepts to a global environment; that is, in turning the Internet into a distributed address space, or a distributed file system. However, since the global environment does not have the stability properties of a LAN, this can be achieved only by introducing redundancy (for reliability), replication (for quality of service), and scalability (for management) at many different levels. Things might have evolved in this direction, but this is not the way the Web came to be. The Web is, almost by definition, unreliable, unpredictable, and unmanageable as a whole, and was not designed with LAN-like guarantees of service.

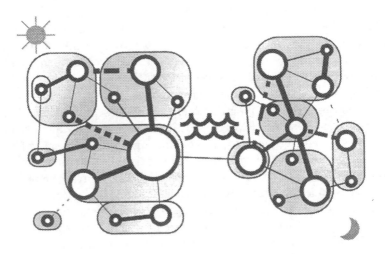

Mental Image 2: Wide Area Network (for example, the Web)

Therefore, the main problem with the Web is that it is not just a big LAN, otherwise, modulo issues of scale, we would already know how to deal with it. There are several ways in which the Web is not a big LAN, and we will describe them shortly. But the fundamental reason is that, unlike a LAN, the Web is not centrally administered. Instead, it is a dynamic collection of countless independent administrative domains, all widely different and mutually distrustful. This is represented in Mental Image 2.

In that picture, computers differ greatly in power and availability, while network links differ greatly in capacity and reliability. Large physical distances have visible effects, and so do time zones. The architecture of a wide area network is yet again fundamentally different from that of a local area network. Most prominently, the network topology is dynamic and non-trivial. Computers become intrinsically mobile: they require different addressing when physically moved across administrative boundaries. Techniques based on mobility become more important and sometimes essential. For example, mobile Java applets provided the first disciplined mechanism for running code able to (and allowed to) systematically penetrate other people's firewalls. Countless projects have emerged in the last few years with the aim of supporting mobile computation over wide areas, and are beginning to be consolidated.

At this point, our architectural goal might be to devise techniques for managing computation over an unreliable collection of far-flung computers. However, this is not yet the full picture. Not only are network links and nodes widely dispersed and unreliable; they are not even liable to stay put, as we discuss next.

2.3 Mobile Computing

A different global computing paradigm has been evolving independently of the Web. Instead of connecting together all the LANs in the world, another way of extending the reach of a LAN is to move individual computers and other gadgets from one LAN to another, dynamically.

We discussed in the Introduction how the main characteristics of the Web point towards mobile comput*ation*. However, that is meant as mobile computation over a fixed (although possibly flaky) network. A more interesting picture emerges when the very components of the network can move about. This is the field of mobile comput*ing*. Today, laptops and personal organizers routinely move about; in the future entire networks will go mobile (as in IBM's Personal Area Network). Existing examples of this kind of mobility include: a smart card entering a network computer slot; an active badge entering a room; a wireless PDA or laptop entering a building; a mobile phone entering a phone cell.

We could draw a picture similar to Mental Image 1, but with mobile devices moving within the confines of a single LAN. This notion of a dynamic LAN is a fairly minor extension of the basic LAN concepts, and presents few conceptual problems (wireless LANs are already common). A much more interesting picture emerges when we think of mobile gadgets over a WAN, because administrative boundaries and multiple access pathways then interact in complex ways, as anybody who travels with a laptop knows all too well.

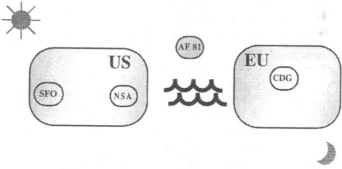

Mental Image 3: Mobile Computing

Mental Image 3 focuses on two domains: the United States and the European Union, each enclosed by a political boundary that regulates the movement of people and computers. Within a political boundary, private companies and public agencies may further regulate the flow of people and devices across their doors. Over the Atlantic we see a third domain, representing Air France flight 81 travelling from San Francisco to Paris. AF81 is a very active mobile computational environment: it is full of people working with their laptops and possibly connecting to the Internet through airphones. (Not to mention the hundreds of computers that control the airplane and let it communicate with a varying stream of ground stations.)

Abstracting a bit from people and computation devices, we see here a hierarchy of boundaries that enforce controls and require permissions for crossing. Passports are required to cross political boundaries, tickets are required for airplanes, and special clearances are required to enter (and exit!) agencies such as the NSA. Sometimes, whole mobile boundaries cross in and out of other boundaries and similarly need permissions, as the mobile environment of AF81 needs permission to enter an airspace. On the other hand, once an entity has been allowed across a boundary, it is fairly free to roam within the confines of the boundary, until another boundary needs to be crossed.

2.4 General Mobility

We have described two different notions of mobility. The first, *mobile computation*, has to do with virtual mobility (mobile software). The second, *mobile computing*, has to do with physical mobility (mobile hardware). These two fields are today almost disconnected, the first dominated by a software community, and the second dominated by a hardware community. However, the borders between virtual and physical mobility are fuzzy, and eventually we will have to treat all kinds of mobility in a uniform way. Here are two examples where the different forms of mobility interact.

The first example is one of virtual mobility achieved by physical means. Consider a software agent in a laptop. The agent can move by propagating over the network, but can also move by being physically transported with the laptop from one location to another. In the first case, the agent may have to undergo security checks (e.g., bytecode verification) when it crosses administrative domains. In the second case the agent may have to undergo security checks (e.g., virus detection) when the laptop is physically allowed inside a new administrative domain. Do we need two completely separate security infrastructures for these two cases, or can we somehow find a common principle? A plausible security policy for a given domain would be that a physical barrier (a building door) should provide the same security guarantees as a virtual barrier (a firewall).

The second example is one of physical mobility achieved by virtual means. Software exists that allows remote control of a computer, by bringing the screen of a remote computer on a local screen. The providers of such software may claim that this is just as good as moving the computer physically, e.g. to access its local data. Moreover, if the remote computer has a network connection, this is also equivalent to "stringing wire" from the remote location, since the remote network is now locally accessible. For example, using remote control over a phone line to connect from home to work where a high-bandwidth Internet connection is available, is almost as good as having a high-bandwidth Internet connection brought into the home.

The other side of the coin of being mobile is of becoming disconnected or intermittently connected. Even barring flaky networks, intermittent connectivity can be caused by physical movement, for example when a wireless user moves into some form of Faraday cage. More interestingly, intermittent connectivity may be caused by virtual movement, for example when an agent moves in and out of an administrative domain that does not allow communication. Neither case is really a failure of the infrastructure; in both cases, lack of connectivity may in fact be a desirable security feature. Therefore, we have to assume that intermittent connectivity, caused equivalently by physical or virtual means, is an essential feature of mobility.

In the future we should be prepared to see increased interactions between virtual and physical mobility, and we should develop frameworks where we can discuss and manipulate these interactions.

2.5 Barriers and Action-at-a-Distance

The unifying difficulty in both mobile computing and mobile computation is the proliferation of barriers, and the problems involved in crossing them. This central difficulty implies that we must regard barriers as fundamental features of our computational models. This seems contrary to the usual trend.

Access barriers have arisen many times in the history of computing, and one of the main tasks of computer science has been to "abstract them away", often by the proverbial additional level of indirection. For example, physical memory boundaries are circumvented by virtual memory; address space boundaries are circumvented by network proxies; firewall boundaries are circumvented by secure tunnels and agent sandboxing. Unfortunately, when barriers are not purely technological it is not possible to completely abstract them away. The crossing of administrative barriers must be performed by bureaucratic operations, such as exhibiting equipment removal passes and export licences.

Therefore, administrative barriers constitute a fundamental change to the way we compute. Let's review some historical scenarios that, because of barriers, have now become unrealizable computing utopias.

In the early days of the Internet, any computer could talk to any other computer by knowing its IP number. We can now forget about flat IP addressing and transparent routing: routers and firewalls effectively hide certain IP addresses from view and make them unreachable by direct means.

In the early days of programming languages, people envisioned a universal address space in which all programs would live and share data, possibly with world-wide garbage-collection, and possibly with strong typing to guarantee the integrity of pointers. We can now forget about universal addressing: although pointers are allowed across machines on a LAN (by network proxies), they are generally disallowed across firewalls. Similarly, we can forget about transparent distributed object systems: some network objects will be kept well hidden within certain domains, and reaching them will require effort.

In the early days of mobile agents, people envisioned agents moving freely across the network on behalf of their owners. We can now forget about this kind of free-roaming. If sites do not trust agents they will not allow them in. If agents do not trust sites to execute them fairly, they will not want to visit them.

In general, we can forget about the notion of *action-at-a-distance computing*: the idea that resources are available transparently at any time, no matter how far away. Instead, we have to get used to the notion that movement and communication are step-by-step activities, and that they are visibly so: the multiple steps involved cannot be hidden, collapsed, or rendered atomic.

The action-at-a-distance paradigm is still prevalent within LANs, and this is another reason why LANs are different from WANs, where such an assumption cannot hold.

2.6 Why a WAN is not a big LAN

We have already discussed in the Introduction how a WAN exhibits a different set of observables than a LAN. But could one emulate a LAN on top of a WAN, restoring a more familiar set of observables, and therefore a more familiar set of programming techniques? If this were possible, we could then go on and program the Internet just like we now program a LAN.

To turn a WAN into a LAN we would have to hide the new observables that a WAN introduces, and we would have to reveal the observables that a WAN hides. These tasks ranges from difficult, to intolerable, to impossible. Referring to the classification in the Introduction, we would have to achieve the following.

(A) Hiding virtual locations. We would have to devise a security infrastructure that makes navigation across multiple administrative domains painless and transparent (when legitimate). Although a great deal of cryptographic technology is available, there might be impossibility results lurking in some corners. For example, it is far from clear whether one can in principle guarantee the integrity of mobile computations against hostile or unfair servers [12]. (This can be solved on a LAN by having all computers under physical supervision.)

(B) Hiding physical locations. One cannot "hide" the speed of light; techniques such as caching and replication may help, but they cannot fool processes that attempt to perform long-distance real-time control and interaction. In principle, one could make all delays uniform, so that programs would not behave differently in different places. Ultimately this can be achieved only by slowing down the entire infrastructure, by embedding the maximal propagation delay in all communications. (This would be about 1/10 of a second on the surface, but would grow dramatically as the Web is extended to satellite communication, orbital stations, and further away.)

(C) Hiding bandwidth fluctuations. It is possible to introduce service guarantees in the networking infrastructure, and therefore eliminate bandwidth fluctuations, or reduce them below certain thresholds. However, in overload situations this has the only effect of turning network congestion into access failures, which brings us to the next point.

(D) Revealing failures. We would have to make failures as observable as on a LAN. This is where we run into fundamental trouble. A basic result in distributed systems states that we cannot achieve distributed consensus (such as agreeing on which nodes have failed) in a system consisting of a collection of asynchronous processes [10]. The Web is such a system: we can make no assumption about the relative speed of processors (they may be overloaded, or temporarily disconnected), about the speed of communication (the network may be congested or partitioned), about the order of arrival of messages, or even about the number of processes involved in a computation. In these circumstances, it is impossible to detect the failure of processors or of network nodes or links: any consensus algorithm can be delayed indefinitely. The common partial solutions for this unsolvable problem are to dictate some degree of synchrony and failure detection. These solutions work well on a LAN, but they seem unlikely to apply to WANs simply because individual users may arbitrarily decide to turn off their processors without warning, or take them into unreachable places. Other partial solutions involve multiple-round broadcast-based probabilistic algorithms [2] which might be expensive on a WAN in terms of communication load, and would be subject to light-speed delays. Moreover, it is difficult to talk about the failure of processors that are invisible because they are hidden behind firewalls, and yet take part in computations. Therefore, it seems unlikely that techniques developed to deal with asynchrony in op-

erating systems and LANs can be successfully applied to a WAN such as the Web in full generality. The Web is an inherently asynchronous system, and the impossibility result of [10] applies with full force.

In summary: task (A) may be unsolvable for mobile code; in any case, a non-zero amount of bureaucracy will always be required; task (B) is only solvable (in full) by introducing unacceptable delays; task (C) can be solved in a way that reduces it to (D); task (D) is unsolvable in principle, and probabilistic solutions run into tasks (A) and (B).

2.7 WAN Postulates

We summarize this section by a collection of postulates that capture the main properties of the reality we are interested in modeling:

- *Separate locations exist.*

- *Different locations have different properties, hence both people and programs will want to move between them.*

- *Barriers to mobility will be erected to preserve the properties of certain locations.*

- *Some people and some programs will still need to cross those barriers.*

The point of these postulates is to stress that mobility and barrier crossing are inevitable requirements of our current and future computing infrastructure.

The observables that are characteristic of wide area networks have the following implications:

- Distinct virtual locations are observed because of the existence of distinct administrative domains, which are produced by the inevitable existence of attackers. Distinct virtual locations preclude the unfettered execution of actions across domains, and require a security model.

- Distinct physical locations are observed, over large distances, because of the inevitable latency limit given by the speed of light. Distinct physical locations preclude instantaneous action at a distance, and require a mobility model.

- Bandwidth fluctuations (including hidden failures) are observed because of the inevitable exercise of free will by network users, both in terms of communication and movement. Bandwidth fluctuations preclude reliance on response time, and require an asynchronous communication model.

3 Modeling Wide Area Computation

Section 2 was dedicated to showing that the reality of mobile computation over a WAN does not fall into familiar categories. Therefore, we need to invent a new model that can help us in understanding and eventually in taking advantage of this reality.

3.1 Barriers

We believe that the most fundamental new notion is that of barriers; this is the most prominent aspect of post-LAN computing environments.

Many of the basic features of WANs have to do with barriers: **Locality** (the existence of different virtual or physical locations, and the notion of being in the same or different locations) is induced by a topology of barriers. *Mobility* is barrier crossing. *Security* has to do with the ability or inability to cross barriers. *Communication* is partitioned by barriers: local communication happens within barriers, while long-distance communication is a combination of local communication and movement across barriers. *Action at a distance* (immediate interaction across many barriers) is forbidden.

We have chose barriers as the most important feature of an abstract model of computation for wide area networks, the Ambient Calculus [7], which we briefly outline.

3.2 Ambients

The current literature on wide area network languages can be broadly classified into agent-based languages (e.g., Telescript [14]), and place-based languages (e.g., Linda [8]). An ambient is a generalization of both notions. Like an agent, an ambient can move across places (also represented by ambients) where it can interact with other agents. Like a place, an ambient supports local undirected communication, and can receive messages (also represented by ambients) from other places. Ambients can be arbitrarily nested, generalizing the limited place-agent-data nesting of most agent languages, and the nesting of places allowed in some Linda dialects.

Briefly, an *ambient* is a place that is delimited by a boundary and where multithreaded computation happens. Each ambient has a *name*, a collection of local *processes*, and a collection of *subambients*. Ambients can move in and out of other ambients, subject to *capabilities* that are associated with ambient names. Ambient names are unforgeable, this fact being the most basic security property.

In further detail, an ambient has the following main characteristics.

- An ambient is a *bounded* place where computation happens.

  If we want to move computations easily we must be able to determine what parts should move. A boundary determines what is inside and what is outside an ambient, and therefore determines what moves. A boundary implies some flexible addressing scheme that can denote entities across the boundary; examples are symbolic links, URLs (Uniform Resource Locators) and Remote Procedure Call proxies. Flexible addressing is what enables, or at least facilitates, mobility. It is also, of course, a cause of problems when the addressing links are "broken".

- Ambients can be nested within other ambients, forming a tree structure.

  As we discussed, administrative domains are (often) organized hierarchically. Mobility is represented as navigation across a hierarchy of ambients. For example, if we want to move a running application from work to home, the application must be removed from an enclosing (work) ambient and inserted in a different enclosing (home) ambient.

- Each ambient has a collection of local running processes.

  A local process of an ambient is one that is contained in the ambient but not in any of its subambients. These "top level" local processes have direct control of the ambient, and in particular they can instruct the ambient to move. In contrast, the local processes of a subambient have no direct control on the parent ambient: this helps guaranteeing the integrity of the parent.

- Each ambient moves as a whole with all its subcomponents.

The activity of a single local process may, by causing movement of its parent, influence the location, and therefore the activity, of other local processes and subambients. For example, if we move a laptop and reconnect it to a different network, then all the threads, address spaces, and file systems within it move accordingly and automatically, and have to cope with their new surrounding. Agent mobility is a special case of ambient mobility, since agents are usually single-threaded. Ambients, like agents, automatically carry with them a collection of private data as they move.

- Each ambient has a name.

The name of an ambient is used to control access (entry, exit, communication, etc.). In a realistic situation the true name of an ambient would be guarded very closely, and only specific capabilities based on the name would be handed out.

3.3 Ideas for Wide Area Languages

Ambients represent our understanding of the fundamental properties of mobile computation over wide area networks. Our final goal, though, is to program the Internet in some convenient high-level language. Therefore, we aim to find programming constructs that are semantically compatible with the ambient principles, and consequently with wide area networks.

These compatibility requirements include (A) *WAN-soundness*: a wide area network language cannot adopt primitives that entail action-at-a-distance, continued connectivity, global consensus, or security bypasses, and (B) *WAN-completeness*: a wide area network language must be able to express the behavior of web surfers and of mobile agents and users, and of any other entities that routinely roam those networks.

More specifically, we believe the following are necessary ingredients of wide area languages.

- *Naming*. Names are symbolic ways of referring to entities across a barrier. Names are detached from their corresponding entities; one may possess a name without having immediate access to any entity of that name. To enable mobility and disconnected operation, all entities across a barrier should be denoted by names, not by "hard" pointers.

- *Migration*. Active hardware and software components should be able to migrate. Migration of certain active hardware components is possible today, but the ability to automatically disconnect and reconnect those components to surrounding (possibly multiple) networks is not currently available. Migration of active software components is even harder, typically for lack of system facilities for migrating live individual threads and groups of threads.

- *Dynamic connectivity*. A wide area network cannot be started or stopped all at once. Therefore, it is necessary to dynamically connect components. This is contrary to the current prominence in programming languages of static binding, static module composition, and static linking. The ambient calculus provides an example of a novel mixture of ordinary static scoping of names (which enables typechecking) with dynamic binding of operations to names (which enables dynamic linking).

- *Communication*. Communication on wide area networks must in general be asynchronous. However, local communication (within or even across a single barrier) can usefully be synchronous. Moreover, in the presence of mobility, it is necessary to have some level of synchronization between communication and movement operations. This remains an interesting design area for mobile languages.

- *Security*. Security abstractions should be provided at the programming-language level, that is, above the fundamental cryptographic primitives. Programmers need to operate with reliable high-level abstractions, otherwise subtle security loopholes can creep in. We believe that barriers are one such high-level security abstraction, which can be supported by programming constructs that can be mechanically analyzed (e.g., via type systems [6]).

Summary

The ambient semantics naturally suggests unusual programming constructs that are well-suited for wide area computation. The combination of mobility, security, communication, and dynamic binding issues has not been widely explored yet at the language-design level, and certainly not within a unifying semantic paradigm. We hope our unifying foundation will facilitate the design of such new languages.

3.4 Wide Area Challenge: A Conference Reviewing System

We conclude with the outline of an ambitious wide area application. The application described here does not fit well with simple-minded Web-based technology because of the complex flow of active code and stateful information between different sites, and because of an essential requirement for disconnected operation. The application fits well within the agent paradigm, but also involves the traversal of multiple administrative domains, and has security and confidentiality requirements.

This is meant both as an example of an application that could be programmed in a wide area language, and as a challenge for any such language to demonstrate its usability. We hope that a language based on ambients or similar notions would cope well with this kind of situation.

- Description of the problem. The problem consists in managing a virtual program committee meeting for a conference. The basic architecture was suggested to me by comments by Richard Connors, as well as by my own experience with organizing program committee meetings and with using Web-based reviewing software developed for ECOOP and other conferences.

In the following scenario, the first occurrence of each of the principals involved is shown in boldface.

- Announcement. A **conference** is announced, and an electronic **submission form**, signed by the **conference chair**, is publicized.

- Submission. Each **author** fetches the submission form, checks the signature of the conference chair, and activates the form. Once activated, the form actively guides most of the reviewing process. Each author fills an instance of the form and attaches a **paper**. The form checks that none of the required fields are left blank, electronically signs the paper with a signature key provided by the author, encrypts the attached paper, and finds its way to the **program chair**. The program chair collects the submissions forms,

and gives them a decryption key so that they can decrypt the attached papers and verify the signatures of the authors. (All following communications are signed and encrypted; we omit most of these details from now on.)

- *Assignment.* The program chair then assigns the submissions to the **committee members**, by instructing each submission form to generate a **review forms** for each assigned member. The review forms incorporate the paper (this time signed by the program chair) and find their way to the appropriate committee members.

- *Review.* Each committee member is a **reviewer**, and may decide to review the paper directly, or to send it to another reviewer. The review form keeps tracks of the chain of reviewers so that it can find its way back when either completed or refused, and so that each reviewer can check the work of the subreviewers. Eventually a review is filled. The form performs various consistency checks, such as verifying that the assigned scores are in range and that no required fields are left blank. Then it finds its way back to the program chair.

- *Report generation.* Once the review forms reach the program chair, they become **report forms**. The various report forms for each paper merge with each other incrementally to form a single report form that accumulates the scores and the reviews. The program chair monitors the report form for each paper. If the reviews are in agreement, the program chair declares the form an **accepted paper report form**, or a **rejected paper review form**.

- *Conflict resolution.* If the reports are in disagreement, the program chair declares the form an **unresolved review form**. An unresolved review form circulates between the reviewers and the program chair, accumulating further comments, until the program chair declares the paper accepted or rejected.

- *Notification.* The report form for an accepted or rejected paper finds its way back to the author (minus the confidential comments), with appropriate congratulations or regrets.

- *Final versions.* Once it reaches the author, an accepted paper report form spawns a **final submission form**. In due time, the author attaches to it the final version of the paper and signs the copyright release notice. The completed final submissions form finds its way back to the program chair.

- *Proceedings.* The final submission forms, upon reaching the program chair, merge themselves into the **proceedings**. The program chair checks that all the final versions have arrived, sorts them into a conference schedule, attaches a preface, and lets the proceedings find their way to the conference chair.

- *Publication.* The conference chair files the copyright release forms, signs the proceedings, and posts them to public sites.

In summary, in this example, interactions between various parts of the system happen over a wide area network. The people involved may be physically moving during or between interaction. As they move, they may transport without warning active parts of the system. At other times, active parts of the system move by their own initiative and must find a route to the appropriate principals wherever they are.

4 Conclusions

The global computational infrastructure has evolved in fundamental ways beyond standard notions of sequential, concurrent, and distributed computational models. The notion of *ambients* captures the structure and properties of wide area networks, of mobile computing, and of mobile computation. The ambient calculus [7] formalizes these notions simply and powerfully. It supports reasoning about mobility and security, and has an intuitive graphical presentation in terms of a folder calculus [3]. On this foundation, we can envision new programming methodologies, libraries and languages for wide area computation.

5 Acknowledgments

Andrew D. Gordon is a coauthor of several related papers.

References

[1] Bharat, K. and L. Cardelli: **Migratory applications**, *Proc. of the ACM Symposium on User Interface Software and Technology '95*. 133-142. 1995.

[2] Bracha, G. and S. Toueg, **Asynchronous consensus and broadcast protocols**. *J.ACM* **32**(4), 824-840. 1985.

[3] Cardelli, L., **Abstractions for Mobile Computation**, in *Secure Internet Programming: Security Issues for Distributed and Mobile Objects*, Jan Vitek and Christian Jensen (Eds.). Springer. 1999. (To appear.)

[4] Cardelli, L., **A language with distributed scope**. *Computing Systems,* **8**(1), 27-59. MIT Press. 1995.

[5] Cardelli, L. and R. Davies. **Service combinators for web computing.** *Proc. of the First Usenix Conference on Domain Specific Languages, Santa Barbara.* 1997.

[6] Cardelli, L., G. Ghelli, and A.D. Gordon, **Mobility Types for Mobile Ambients**, *Proc. ICALP'99.*

[7] Cardelli, L. and A.D. Gordon, **Mobile ambients**, in *Foundations of Software Science and Computational Structures*, Maurice Nivat (Ed.), Lecture Notes in Computer Science 1378, Springer, 140-155. 1998.

[8] Carriero, N. and D. Gelernter, **Linda in Context**. *Communications of the ACM*, **32**(4), 444-458. 1989.

[9] Chandra, T.D., S.Toueg, **Unreliable failure detectors for asynchronous systems.** *ACM Symposium on Principles of Distributed Computing*, 325-340. 1991.

[10] Fischer, M.J., N.A. Lynch, and M.S. Paterson, **Impossibility of distributed consensus with one faulty process.** *J.ACM* **32**(2), 374-382. 1985.

[11] Milner, R., J. Parrow and D. Walker, **A calculus of mobile processes, Parts 1-2**. *Information and Computation*, **100**(1), 1-77. 1992

[12] Sander, A. and C. F. Tschudin, **Towards mobile cryptography**, *ICSI technical report 97-049*, November 1997. *Proc. IEEE Symposium on Security and Privacy*, Spring 1998.

[13] Stamos, J.W. and D.K. Gifford, **Remote evaluation**. *ACM Transactions on Programming Languages and Systems* **12**(4), 537-565. 1990.

[14] White, J.E., **Mobile agents**. In *Software Agents*, J. Bradshaw, ed. AAAI Press / The MIT Press. 1996.

Proof Techniques for Cryptographic Protocols

Kevin J. Compton[1] and Scott Dexter[2]

[1] BRICS, University of Aarhus, DK - 8000 Aarhus C, Denmark and
EECS Dept., University of Michigan, Ann Arbor, MI 48109-2122, USA
kjc@umich.edu

[2] Department Of Computer and Information Science, Brooklyn College, City
University of New York, Brooklyn, New York 11210 USA
sdexter@sci.brooklyn.cuny.edu

Abstract. We give a general introduction to cryptographic protocols and the kinds of attacks to which they are susceptible. We then present a framework based on linear logic programming for analyzing authentication protocols and show how various notions of attack are expressed in this framework.

1 Introduction

Cryptographic protocols provide the framework for secure communication in email programs, browsers, remote login facilities, electronic commerce, and many other applications. Not surprisingly, many researchers have worked on providing a rigorous mathematical framework for reasoning about cryptographic protocols. Central to their efforts is the notion of an *attack* on a cryptographic protocol. We give general introduction to cryptographic protocols and the kinds of attacks to which they are susceptible. We illustrate these ideas with four well known protocols. We then present a straightforward method for formalizing protocols within a logic programming framework and argue that linear logic provides a foundation for easily expressing various kinds of attacks. Attacks are easily discovered (or security proved, if there are no attacks) by means of a resolution theorem prover that combines ideas from linear logic programming and equational theorem proving.

2 Related Work

Researchers have employed tools from a variety of areas, including logic, algebra, and complexity theory, to analyze cryptographic protocols.

Logics of belief have played an important role, first with the development of BAN logic [11], and then its successors (e.g. [18, 43, 41]). These logics reason about the evolution of belief in the agents participating in authentication and key exchange protocols. Criticisms (e.g. [28, 39, 40]) of these logics center on an informal "idealization" step in which the protocol is modified, the reliance on belief, and the semantics of the logic.

The idea of using algebraic specifications for security protocols is due to Dolev and Yao [16]. In their model, there is an intruder from whose perspective the protocol is a machine for producing words in some language. Symbols in these words correspond to encryption and decryption operations.

Meadows [30] based her work (the "Analyzer") on that of Dolev and Yao. She noted two limitations of Dolev and Yao's work: first, that their analysis is limited to a restrictive class of protocols; and second, that adversaries may do more than just discover secret information; many protocols are "broken" when the intruder convinces an agent that information in the intruder's possession has a certain function, e.g. when the intruder successfully introduces a bogus session key. This method is an extremely powerful tool and has been used to find flaws in a variety of protocols, but it is not designed for proving positive results about security since it does not do a complete search of the search space. We remark that even though the search engine is logic programming based, it is quite different from the logic programming search presented in this paper.

Woo and Lam [45] present an algebraic system in which the specification is given in terms of the protocol each agent follows (rather than in terms of an intruder's state). Each protocol is a sequence of actions that the agent takes. The authors assert that their model is sufficiently formal to address precisely issues of soundness and completeness, although this is deferred as a question about specific analysis techniques. It is unclear what proofs in this system actually entail, as the correctness assertions need to be proved for all possible executions.

Bolignano [6] has developed a method that has been described [29] as occupying an intermediate position between the techniques of Woo & Lam and Meadows. In this framework, the intruder's state is represented by the words it can derive, while the agents' states are simply denoted by program counters. While Bolignano states that his goal is simple and concise proofs (rather than automatability, for example), the proof process becomes unwieldy and must be customized for each protocol. In a later paper [7] some of these problems are rectified.

The process algebra CSP [20] has served as the foundation for a number of investigations of modeling protocols as communicating processes. In [24], the public key variant of the Needham-Schroeder protocol is modeled as a set of CSP processes; this model is tested using FDR, a model checker for CSP. Ryan and Zakiuddin [38] present a summary of methods of formalizing security properties in CSP notation. Bryans and Schneider [9] present a CSP-based analysis of a recursive protocol presented in [10] (and also analyzed in [36]). While all of these analyses benefit from the wide usage CSP enjoys it is also clear that the state space limitations incurred by model-checking sharply affect the quality of the results, although research in this area is ongoing.

Bellare and Rogaway [4, 3, 5] present a complexity-theoretic model of cryptographic protocols that does away entirely with issues of agents' knowledge, belief, and trust and instead places the intruder at the center. In this model, the intruder is the means by which the players communicate; all messages are sent to the intruder, who may intercept and alter them, or not, as she pleases. While the framing of this model is very rigorous and produces provably secure protocols, the proofs themselves and the techniques used within them are not easy to automate. Moreover, this technique is designed solely for proving *security*; there is no mechanism for uncovering protocol flaws.

The logic-based approach has proven to be particularly well-suited for automation. Millen's Interrogator [22] is a Prolog-based search engine that searches for instantiations of a predicate signifying the intruder's knowledge of specified data via some sequence of messages to an insecure goal state. While the Interrogator has successfully found protocol flaws fairly quickly, search time may vary significantly depending on the precise format of the protocol specification and the amount of information provided about the insecure goal states. Additionally, search heuristics may prevent some flaws from being noticed.

Paulson [34, 35] has developed a model that is tailored for use with Isabelle, an ML-based theorem prover. In his model an intruder can read all messages and send new messages; it can also act as an "honest" agent using its own long-term key. Protocols are modeled by defining the set of possible utterances (both by the honest agents and, possibly, by the intruder), then inductively defining the set of possible protocol traces. Protocol specifications are sets of rules for extending a protocol trace, including a rule describing what the intruder may send. Protocol analysis then consists of proving properties (regularity, uniqueness, secrecy, etc.) of all possible traces.

Marrero *et al.* [29] produced a *model checker* for security protocols. Like Paulson's work, this approach involves reasoning about all possible protocol traces, but rather than reason about the logical properties of these traces, the model checker performs a state space search and tests the properties of each trace. Security is defined in terms of *secrecy* and *correspondence* properties – each protocol specification includes a list of terms which the intruder must not learn and a mapping between protocol runs of distinct agents.

In this paper we propose linear logic as a framework for security proofs. Mitchell [31] and Cervasato *et al.* [13] have also started applying linear logic in this area.

Much of the recent activity in protocol analysis has focused on defining and characterizing attacks on cryptographic protocols; see [37, 8, 26, 25].

3 Protocols and Attacks

A protocol is a script for the exchange of information between two or more individuals or *principals*. The goal of a cryptographic protocol is to allow principals to send information over an open channel with a guarantee of secrecy and authenticity. *Secrecy* means that an intruder with the ability to intercept, alter, and redirect messages will not have access to information the principals wish to protect. *Authenticity* means that the receiver's assumption about the originator of a message is correct. There may be other goals as well.

Cryptographic protocols may use either a *private* (or *symmetric*) *key* cryptosystem or a *public key* cryptosystem.

In a private key cryptosystem, the same key is used both for encryption and decryption. $\{M\}_K$ will denote the encryption of message M using private key K. Thus, $\{\{M\}_K\}_K = M$. (In some systems encryption and decryption are different functions, but here we will assume they are the same.) Usually, a trusted server S shares a private key K_A (called a *long lived key*) with each principal A. This simplifies key management, since a system with n principals requires only n long lived keys, and the addition of a new principal requires the distribution of just one long lived key. The drawback is *key distribution* between a group of two or more principals must take place before they can communicate. Key distribution is often the goal of a cryptographic protocol.

In a public key cryptosystems, each principal A has a public key K_A^+ which is generally known and by which anyone can send encrypted messages to A, and a private key K_A^- which is known only to A. Obtaining K_A^- from K_A^+ should be infeasible. These keys are inverses in the sense that $\{\{M\}_{K_A^+}\}_{K_A^-} = \{\{M\}_{K_A^-}\}_{K_A^+} = M$.

3.1 The Needham-Schroeder Protocol

The (private key) Needham-Schroeder protocol [32] is the canonical example of a flawed protocol.

(1) $A \rightarrow S$: A, B, N_i
(2) $S \rightarrow A$: $\{N_i, B, K_i, \{K_i, A\}_{K_B}\}_{K_A}$
(3) $A \rightarrow B$: $\{K_i, A\}_{K_B}$
(4) $B \rightarrow A$: $\{M_i\}_{K_i}$
(5) $A \rightarrow B$: $\{M_i - 1\}_{K_i}$
(A) $A \rightarrow B$: $\{P_i\}_{K_i}$
(B) $B \rightarrow A$: $\{Q_i\}_{K_i}$

The principals are A, B, and S. A wishes to establish a private communication with B on an open channel, but A and B do not share a key. Since this protocol may be run many times and by many different principals, we designate a session number i which is used as an index for all information particular to the session.

In step (1), A sends a message to the S indicating that A wishes to initiate communication with B. A includes a nonce N_i. A *nonce* is a string of random bits, usually freshly generated, sent a principal with a message in the expectation that the nonce will accompany a response. In step (2), S responds with a message encrypted under the key K_A. This message contains A's nonce, the new session key K_i, and a message that A will forward to B. In (3), A forwards this message to B. This message, encrypted under K_B, contains the K_i and indicates that it is to be used to communicate with A. The next two messages are a *handshake* indicating that the parties have received the new key: B sends a new nonce M_i to A, encrypted under the new key; A then decrypts the message and replies with $M_i - 1$ encrypted under the new key. One of the implicit assumptions about the cryptosystem is that only the possessor of K_i could make such a reply. The principals then proceed with their session. We assume that the session key will be used at some point by either or both agents to encrypt secret information: we model this information explicitly as P_i and Q_i in steps (A) and (B). Strictly speaking, these steps are not part of the protocol and do not appear in most presentations. We include them here and subsequent examples as a convenience.

The Denning-Sacco attack [14] on this protocol assumes that an intruder I has obtained a message of the form $\{k, A\}_{K_B}$ and knows k, perhaps by anlayzing an old session. (This is an example of a *replay attack*.) I masquerades as A by sending this message to B, who will interpret this as the third message in the protocol. Since I knows k, he can trick B into completing the "handshake", and B will believe he has mutually authenticated with A. B then divulges the secret Q_i. Here is the description of the attack. I initiates a bogus session α. We will write I_A to indicate that I is masquerading as A.

(3α) $I_A \rightarrow B$: $\{k, A\}_{K_B}$
(4α) $B \rightarrow I_A$: $\{M_i\}_k$
(5α) $I_A \rightarrow B$: $\{M_i - 1\}_k$
$(A\alpha)$ $B \rightarrow I_A$: $\{Q_i\}_k$

I then knows Q_i.

3.2 The Public Key Needham-Schroeder Protocol

In this protocol principals A and B use a public key cryptosystem to share a secret which could be used, for example, as a shared private key. The secret is a pair of nonces N_i and M_i generated by A and B, respectively.

(1) $A \rightarrow B$: $\{A, N_i\}_{K_B^+}$
(2) $B \rightarrow A$: $\{N_i, M_i\}_{K_A^+}$
(3) $A \rightarrow B$: $\{M_i\}_{K_B^+}$
(A) $A \rightarrow B$: $\{P_i\}_{[N_i, M_i]}$
(B) $B \rightarrow A$: $\{Q_i\}_{[N_i, M_i]}$

Lowe [24] found the following *man-in-the-middle* attack. A, unaware that I is malicious, begins a protocol session with I.

(1α) $A \rightarrow I$: $\{A, n\}_{K_I^+}$

I decrypts this message with his private key, encrypts it with the public key of B, and begins a masquerade as A.

(1β) $I_A \rightarrow B$: $\{A, n\}_{K_B^+}$
(2β) $B \rightarrow I_A$: $\{n, M_i\}_{K_A^+}$

I now returns to the original session with A.

(2α) $I \rightarrow A$: $\{n, M_i\}_{K_A^+}$
(3α) $A \rightarrow I$: $\{M_i\}_{K_I^+}$

I then returns to the protocol session with B, completing the masquerade.

(3β) $I_A \rightarrow B$: $\{M_i\}_{K_B^+}$
$(B\beta)$ $B \rightarrow I_A$: $\{Q_i\}_{[n, M_i]}$

3.3   The Wide Mouthed Frog Protocol

This intriguingly named protocol first appeared in [11]. It incorporates a novel combination of techniques to achieve its small size. For example, A rather than S generates the session key K_i. Freshness is guaranteed by use of *timestamps* T_1 and T_2. Timestamps are common in cryptographic protocols. Usually the duration a timestamped message is valid is several hours, so clock synchronization is not a problem.

(1) $A \rightarrow S$: $A, \{T_1, B, K_i\}_{K_A}$
(2) $S \rightarrow B$: $\{T_2, B, K_i\}_{K_B}$
(A) $A \rightarrow B$: $\{P_i\}_{K_i}$
(B) $B \rightarrow A$: $\{Q_i\}_{K_i}$

Lowe [24] proposed an attack in which I eavesdrops on a session above and later sends another copy of message 2.

(2α) $I_S \rightarrow B$: $\{T_2, B, K_i\}_{K_B}$

Is this really an attack? In contrast to the previous attacks, messages P_i an Q_i have not been compromised, and there is no indication that I could send a bogus message R_i masquerading as one of the principals. However, in session α, B believes he has successfully completed a (second) session of the protocol, but he has not.

Lowe presents several attacks using essentially the same idea. These attacks can usually be thwarted by adding a handshake.

3.4   The Bellare-Rogaway 3PKD Protocol

This protocol [5] uses a cryptographic hash to reduce the size. A principal A may authenticate a message M to B by sending an encryption $\{M\}_K$, where K is a key shared between A and B. However, it may not be important that $\{M\}_K$ be decipherable; in some situations M may have been been sent as clear text and $\{M\}_K$ is simply a *message authentication code*, a kind of signature. In these cases computing a *keyed hash function* $\langle M \rangle_K$ may be much easier to implement and much faster. Given a key K and message M, it should be easy to compute the hash value, but without K it should be infeasible.

(1) $A \rightarrow B$: A, N_i
(2) $B \rightarrow S$: A, B, N_i, M_i
(3) $S \rightarrow A$: $\{K_i\}_{K_A}, \langle A, B, N_i, \{K_i\}_{K_A}\rangle_{K_A}$
(4) $S \rightarrow B$: $\{K_i\}_{K_B}, \langle A, B, N_i, \{K_i\}_{K_B}\rangle_{K_B}$
(A) $S \rightarrow A$: $\{P_i\}_{K_i}$
(B) $B \rightarrow A$: $\{Q_i\}_{K_i}$

Bellare and Rogaway prove that this protocol secure using a "partner function" definition of security. Notice, though, that the protocol is susceptible to the same kind of attack as we saw for the Wide Mouthed Frog Protocol.

(1α) $I_A \to B$: A, N_i
(2α) $B \to S$: A, B, N_i, M_i
(3α) $S \to I_A$: $\{K_i\}_{K_A}, \langle A, B, N_i, \{K_i\}_{K_A}\rangle_{K_A}$
(4α) $S \to B$: $\{K_i\}_{K_B}, \langle A, B, N_i, \{K_i\}_{K_B}\rangle_{K_B}$

B now believes that he has successfully completed the protocol with A, but he has not.

4 Formalizing Protocol Analysis

In this section we develop a formalism for describing protocols and proving them correct. The goal, as we have seen in the examples of the previous section, is to give a definition of attack that is simple, easy to verify, and takes into account the attacks proposed in the literature.

4.1 The Vocabulary of a Protocol Session

From the examples above we see that there are various subtypes partitioning the type **Messages**.

- **Names** of principals (A, B, etc.) are public and *session independent* (*i.e.*, not subscripted).
- **Keys** may either be private and session independent or private and session dependent.
- **Secrets** include nonces and messages such as P_i and Q_i. Secrets are session dependent and private.
- **Timestamps** are used to restrict the availability of information to a particular time interval.

We build complex messages from simpler messages using various operations.

- The *encryption operation* $E(K, M) = \{M\}_K$.
- The long lived key operation $K(A) = K_A$. For public key protocols there are two operations $K^+(A)$ and $K^-(A)$.
- The *handshake operation* $F(M)$.
- The *tupling operation* applied to a sequence of messages $M_1, \ldots, M_k$ (with $k \geq 0$), produces a list $[M_1, \ldots, M_k]$.
- The *keyed hash function* $H(K, M) = \langle M\rangle_K$.
- The bitwise exclusive-or function $X(N, M)$, which was not used in any of the protocols discussed here, but does appear often in protocols.

We may specify a vocabulary of constant and function symbols for a particular session i of a protocol. In the Needham-Schroeder protocol the constant symbols are A, B, S of type **Names**; K_A, K_B, K_i of type **Keys**; and N_i, M_i, P_i and Q_i of subtype **Secrets**. The unary function symbols are K of type **Names** $\to$ **Keys** and F of type **Secrets** $\to$ **Secrets**. The only binary function symbol is E of type **Keys** $\times$ **Secrets** $\to$ **Secrets**. The tupling function is of type **Messages*** $\to$ **Secrets**.

4.2 The Equational Theory of a Cryptosystem

The equational theory Γ for private key crytosystems contains the axiom

$(\Gamma1)$ $E(k, E(k, x)) = x$

Free variables in axioms are assumed to be universally quantified. When we model a public key cryptosystem or use the exclusive-or operation, other axioms are needed.

Since Γ is an equational theory, it has an *initial structure* $\mathbf{A}_\Gamma$ (see [27]); *i.e.*, there is a unique structure $\mathbf{A}_\Gamma \models \Gamma$ such that for every $\mathbf{B} \models \Gamma$, there is a unique homomorphism from $\mathbf{A}_\Gamma$ to $\mathbf{B}$. Furthermore, $\mathbf{A}_\Gamma$ is a *term structure*: every element is interpreted by some closed term. Let $\mathbf{A}$ be the set of all closed terms over the vocabulary (sometimes this is called the *Herbrand universe*) and $\sim$ be the equivalence relation holds between closed terms t_1 and t_2 if and only if $\Gamma \vdash t_1 = t_2$. Then $\mathbf{A}_\Gamma$ is the quotient structure $\mathbf{A}/\sim$. We will refer to $\mathbf{A}_\Gamma$ as the *message universe* of the protocol. Our methods assume *strong encryption*: distinct elements of the message universe represent items of information not easily computable from one another. This is a difficult property to verify, but one made implicitly not only in security proofs, but even in the design of protocols. For example, the Needham-Schroeder handshake assumes that $\{M\}_K$ and $\{M - 1\}_K$, represented as distinct elements $E(K, M)$ and $E(K, F(M))$ in the message universe, are not easily computed from each other.

4.3 The Horn Theory of the Passive Intruder

Intruder-based methods for verifying protocol security reason about the information that an intruder can gain. An intruder can gain information by passive means, such as eavesdropping and using public information, or by active means such as manipulating the flow of information, impersonating other agents, and using old information from other sessions. The passive means by which an intruder can gain information can be written as a universal Horn theory Δ describing a unary relation I representing the information accessible to the intruder. In anticipation of the theorem proving techniques we will be using, we express the universal Horn sentences in a logic programming syntax. (Lower case letters are variables and are universally quantified.)

$(\Delta1)$ $I(E(k, x)) \leftarrow I(k), I(x)$
$(\Delta2)$ $I([x_1, \ldots, x_k]) \leftarrow I(x_1), \ldots, I(x_k)$ for every $k \geq 0$.
$(\Delta3)$ $I(x_i) \leftarrow I([x_1, \ldots, x_k])$ for every $k \geq i \geq 1$.
$(\Delta4)$ $I(x) \leftarrow I(K(x))$
$(\Delta5)$ $I(x) \leftarrow I(F(x))$
$(\Delta6)$ $I(F(x)) \leftarrow I(x)$

In addition, under the label $(\Delta0)$ we include trivial axioms $I(A)$, $I(B)$, and $I(S)$, since names are public. Notice that in the private key framework, the Horn sentence $I(x) \leftarrow I(x), I(E(k, x))$ follows from $(\Gamma1)$ and $(\Delta1)$. If the keyed hash function H is used in the protocol, it is also necessary to include the axiom

$(\Delta 7)$ $I(H(k,x)) \leftarrow I(k), I(x)$

$\Gamma \cup \Delta$ can be regarded as a logic program (with equations) whose least fixpoint semantics (see [23]) on the message universe defines a relation I representing the intruder's passive knowledge. Inductive definability is a recurrent theme in protocol security proofs. For example, logics of knowledge and belief operate on the principle that a principal's knowledge is inductively defined, and Paulson [2, 34–36] bases his method on inductively defined relations.

4.4 Linear Logic and the Active Intruder

We now have a fairly clear picture of the passive means by which the intruder can obtain information. The active means involve manipulating the network and sending false messages. For example, in steps (3) and (4) of the Needham-Schroeder protocol, B receives a message $\{K_i, A\}_{K_B}$ and sends a message $\{M_i\}_{K_i}$. Now B really has no idea who sent this message. If the intruder sends a message of the form $\{k, A\}_{K_B}$, B will reply $\{M_i\}_k$. Later, in steps (5) and (B), if the intruder sends a message of the form $\{M_i - 1\}_k$, B will reply $\{Q_i\}_k$. It seems that we need two more Horn sentences.

(B1) $I(E(k, M_i)) \leftarrow I(E(K(B), [k, A]))$
(B2) $I(E(k, Q_i)) \leftarrow I(E(K(B), [k, A])), I(E(k, F(M_i)))$

Notice that the second sentence says that the intruder cannot trick B into responding unless it can supply both of the messages B expects to receive in previous steps of the protocol.

There are several problems here. We do not know that k in the first sentence is the same k as in the second sentence. The first sentence may be used several times in a proof. Thus, from $E(K(B), [k, A])$ the intruder may learn $E(k, M_i)$ and from $E(K(B), [k', A])$ the intruder may learn $E(k', M_i)$. This is not correct. The second time the rule is used, B generates a new nonce M_j and replies $E(k', M_j)$. It is possible to express this distinction using first-order logic, but the analysis becomes much more complicated. Instead, we observe that from the intruder's viewpoint, agents' responses are limited resources: the appropriate logic to describe limited resources is linear logic [17]. Mitchell *et al.* [31] observed that linear logic is a useful tool to reason about cryptographic protocols. We will a familiarity with the basics of linear logic for the remainder of the paper.

To see how linear logic pertains to security, take the conjunction of the Horn formulas describing how the intruder can derive information from a given principal, preface with ! and then universally quantify. In the traditional linear logic syntax we would obtain the following from (B1) and (B2) above.

$$\forall k! \, (I(E(K(B), [k, A])) \multimap I(E(k, M_i)) \otimes$$
$$(I(E(K(B), [k, A])) \otimes I(E(k, F(M_i))) \multimap I(E(k, Q_i))))$$

Reasoning about this linear logic sentence more accurately reflects how the intruder obtains information. Recall how the left $\forall$-introduction rule works in linear logic.

$$\frac{\Sigma, \psi(k \leftarrow t) \vdash \Pi}{\Sigma, \forall k\, \psi(k) \vdash \Pi}$$

We assume that Σ and Π are multi-sets of linear logic formulas, k is a variable, and t is a term. Also, $\psi(k \leftarrow t)$ is formed by substituting t for free occurrences of k in ψ (subject to the usual condition that variable occurrences in t must be free wherever t is substituted). When we work our backward through a linear logic proof, we see that the variable k in $\psi(k)$ *can be instantiated only once.* This instantiation determines the information the intruder requires to send a bogus message to B and receive replies.

Consequently, we should view (B1) and (B2) as as a unit (Λ_B) rather than separate Horn sentences. Such units will be called *definite program templates.* We will give a precise definition in the next section, but first we present the other definite program templates derived from the Needham-Schroeder protocol. Template (Λ_A) consists of the following Horn sentences.

(A1) $\ I([A, B, N_i]) \leftarrow$
(A2) $\ I(y) \leftarrow I(E(K(A), [N_i, B, k, y]))$
(A3) $\ I(E(k, F(m))) \leftarrow I(E(K(A), [N_i, B, k, y])), I(E(k, m))$
(A4) $\ I(E(k, P_i)) \leftarrow I(E(K(A), [N_i, B, k, y])), I(E(k, m))$

Template (Λ_S) consists of the following Horn sentence.

(S1) $\ I(E(K(a), [n, b, k, E(K(b), [k, a])])) \leftarrow I([a, b, n])$

4.5 Linear Logic Programming

We first extend the usual logic programming terminology. These definitions could be somewhat more general, but they will suffice for security proving applications.

A (linear) *definite program clause* is of the form $\psi \leftarrow \varphi_1, \ldots, \varphi_k$, where $\varphi_1, \ldots, \varphi_k, \psi$ are non-equational atomic formulas. Formula ψ is the *head* of the clause and formula sequence $\varphi_1, \ldots, \varphi_k$ is the *body* of the clause. A (linear) *definite template* is a set of definite program clauses. A *definite program* is a set of equations, definite program clauses, and definite templates. A (linear) *goal clause* is of the form $\varphi_1, \ldots, \varphi_k$, where $\varphi_1, \ldots, \varphi_k$ are non-equational atomic formulas.

Given a substitution σ mapping variables to terms we denote by $E\sigma$ (where E is either a term, definite clause, or definite template) the result obtained by replacing variables with their images under σ. Substitution σ is a *unifier* for expressions E and F if $E\sigma$ and $F\sigma$ are syntactically identical; σ is the *most general unifier* (written $mgu(E, F)$) if, in addition, whenever θ is a unifier of E and F, there is a substitution ρ such that $\theta = \sigma\rho$

As we have seen, cryptographic protocols can be translated directly into definite programs.

When equations are incorporated into logic programs, different mechanisms may be added to SLD-resolution to obtain a complete theorem proving system.

Many of these use modifications of the *paramodulation* rule (see [33] for a discussion). There are also many logic programming theorem provers for fragments of linear logic [1, 12, 19, 21, 42, 44]. The following resolution theorem prover combines ideas from these two areas and is a complete theorem proving system for the fragment of linear logic used here. It is easier to state as a nondeterministic process which can then be transformed into a backtracking resolution search (as found, for example, in pure Prolog). Without loss of generality we assume that initially the variables in each definite template are unique to that template.

> **Given:** Definite program Π and goal clause γ
> **Find:** Substitution σ such that $\Pi \vdash \gamma\sigma$
>
> Initialize $\sigma =$ identity substitution
> **Repeat** until γ is empty
> > **Choose** one:
> > > Equation $s = t$ or $t = s$ from Π:
> > > > **Choose** subterm u of γ unifiable with t
> > > > Let $\gamma = \delta(x \leftarrow u)$ and $\rho = mgu(t, u)$
> > > > Replace γ with $(\delta(x \leftarrow s))\rho$
> > > Definite clause $\varphi \leftarrow \psi_1, \ldots, \psi_k$ from Π or a template:
> > > > **Choose** subformula ϑ of γ unifiable with φ
> > > > Let $\gamma = \beta \cup \{\vartheta\}$ and $\rho = mgu(\varphi, \vartheta)$
> > > > Replace γ with $(\beta \cup \{\psi_1, \ldots, \psi_k\})\rho$
> > > Replace each definite template Λ with $\Lambda\rho$
> > > Replace σ with $\sigma\rho$

The novelty is that the definite templates are modified as the proof proceeds; i.e., the logic program modifies itself. This reflects the linear logic philosophy that a formula is a proof resource and is modified whenever it is used.

5 Defining Attack

We conclude the paper by describing how the resolution theorem prover above finds the attacks on protocols in the previous sections.

If we run the resolution theorem prover above on the definite program Π for the Needham-Schroeder with the goal $I(Q_i)$, we do not find (as we might have hoped) a proof corresponding to the Denning-Sacco attack. In fact, if we add some obvious heuristics to prune infinite branches in the resolution search process, we discover that $I(Q_i)$ does not follow from Π: the intruder should not be able to learn Q_i.

To see what goes wrong, use the attack (steps (3α), (4α), (5α) and $(A\alpha)$ in section 3.1) to guide the nondeterministic choices made by the theorem prover. The result is pictured as a tree in Figure 1. Each node is labeled by a formula. For each formula ϑ on an internal node, a definite clause $\varphi \leftarrow \psi_1, \ldots, \psi_k$ is chosen, $\rho = mgu(\varphi, \vartheta)$ is computed, and the children of the node are labeled $\psi_1\rho, \ldots, \psi_k\rho$. The problem is apparent: this is not a complete proof. The leaves

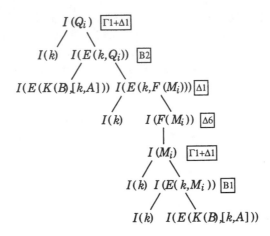

Fig. 1. Proof giving the Denning-Sacco Attack

the tree should have empty labels, but here they are labeled either by $I(k)$ or $I(E(K(B), [k, A]))$. This is to be expected since we assume that I knows k and $\{k, A\}_{K_B}$. In fact, Figure 1 shows that $\Pi, I(k), I(E(K(B), [k, A])) \vdash I(Q_i)$. This suggests that the key to finding replay attacks it to use some condition other than goal clause emptiness to terminate the resolution process. Examining the this resolution proof and the ones that results from the Public Key Needham-Schroeder Protocol and other protocols, we see a pattern. Formulas at the leaves of the tree contain no session dependent information: there are no occurrences of the session number index i. Replay attacks are discovered by changing the loop termination condition to session independence of γ. Since the intruder can mount uninteresting attacks by stealing long lived keys, our definition of *session independence* excludes formulas of the form $I(K(A))$ as well formulas containing session subscripted information.

To formalize protocols with timestamps we introduce a predicate $C(T)$ indicating that the timestamp T is current. In this case we say that a goal clause is *time independent* if, whenever it contains a formula $C(T)$, it contains no other occurrences of T except perhaps the formula $I(T)$ (since I can always produce a current timestamp). The termination condition in the resolution theorem prover now requires both session and time independence of the goal.

We now have a general framework for defining and finding attacks. As we have seen, we find violations of *secrecy* by setting the goal to be either $I(P_i)$ or $I(Q_i)$, where P_i and Q_i are messages sent by A and B with the distributed key.

Violations of *authenticity* are more subtle. Consider the Needham-Schroeder definite program. To show that I can originate a message which B thinks came from A, we add a new program clause $I(R_i)$ and set γ to be $I(E(k, Q_i)), I(E(k, R_i))$. The first formula ensures that B has successfully completed the protocol and and accepted k. The second formula says that I can encrypt a known message with k. In this kind of situation we say that *weak key authenticity* has been violated.

Authenticity might be violated in another way. I might send B a message encrypted with the distributed key, but not know the message. In that case, the goal should be $I(E(k, Q_i)), I(E(k, m))$. This goal is satisfied by any protocol that succeeds in distributing a session key. I simply transmits messages sent out by the principals to the proper receivers and at the conclusion $m = Q_i$. However, if there is another value that satisfies the goal, the theorem prover will find it. In this kind of situation we say that *strong key authenticity* has been violated

Observe that the definite templates have been modified during the resolution process and that when the process terminates, the templates describe the information each principal has received and sent. For example, at the end of the Denning-Sacco attack, substitutions will have been made in the variables of template Λ_B to match the goal variables. (Recall that initially the variables in a template are unique to that template.) However, the variables in Λ_A are unchanged, indicating that the attack was played without the participation of A.

We can use the same idea to uncover Lowe's attack on the Wide Mouthed Frog Protocol. Set γ to be $I(E(k, Q_i))$. Again, since the protocol succeeds in distributing a key, the goal will be satisfied. However, for some proofs, the variables in Λ_A are unchanged, indicating that A did not initiate a prtocol session, even though B believes she did. The same kind of analysis uncovers the attack we described on the Bellare-Rogaway 3PKD protocol.

We have implemented a limited version of the resolution theorem prover described here and tested secrecy and weak key authenticity for many protocols [15]. This system provides a straightforward conversion from conventional informal protocol specifications to formal specifications and allows us to perform fast automated analysis. As we have seen, another advantage is that it should be easily adaptable to find other kinds protocol attacks. The system uses heuristics to prune infinite resolution searches and is therefore capable of proving security as well as finding attacks. Since the heuristics pertain only to the program clauses in Γ and Δ, they do not have to be tailored to a particular protocol. The system has taken less than one second of CPU time on every protocol we have given it, and has always produced an answer – either by displaying an attack or certifying security of the protocol.

References

1. J.-M. Andreoli. Logic programming with focusing proofs in linear logic. *Journal of Logic and Computation*, 2(3), 1992.
2. G. Bella and L. C. Paulson. Using Isabelle to prove properties of the Kerberos authentication system. In *Proceedings of the DIMACS Workshop on Formal Verification of Cryptographic Protocols*, September 1997.
3. M. Bellare and P. Rogaway. Entity authentication and key distribution. In *Advances in Cryptology — Crypto '93 Proceedings*, 1993.
4. M. Bellare and P. Rogaway. Random oracles are practical: A paradigm for designing efficient protocols. In *Proceedings of the First ACM Conference on Computer and Communications Security*, 1993.

5. M. Bellare and P. Rogaway. Provably secure session key distribution — the three party case. In *Proceedings of the 27th ACM Symposium on the Theory of Computing*, 1995.

6. D. Bolignano. An approach for the formal verification of cryptographic protocols. In *Proceedings of the Third ACM Conference on Computer and Communications Security*, pages 106–118. ACM Press, 1996.

7. D. Bolignano. Towards a mechanization of cryptographic protocol verification. In *Proceedings of the 9th International Computer-Aided Verification Conference*, June 1997.

8. C. Boyd. Towards extensional goals in authentication protocols. Preprint.

9. J. Bryans and S. Schneider. CSP, PVS, and a recursive authentication protocol. In *Proceedings of the DIMACS Workshop on Formal Verification of Cryptographic Protocols*, September 1997.

10. J. A. Bull and D. J. Otway. The authentication protocol. Technical Report CSM/436-04/03, Defence Research Agency, Malvern, UK, 1997.

11. M. Burrows, M. Abadi, and R. Needham. A logic of authentication. *ACM Transactions on Computer Systems*, 8, February 1990.

12. S. Cerrito. Herbrand methods in sequent calculi: Unification in LL. In K. Apt, editor, *Logic Programming: Proceedings of the Joint International Conference and Symposium on Logic Programming*, pages 607–621. The MIT Press, 1992.

13. I. Cervesato, N. A. Durgin, P. D. Lincoln, J. C. Mitchell, and A. Scedrov. A meta-notation for protocol analysis. Preprint.

14. D. E. Denning and G. M. Sacco. Timestamps in key distribution protocols. *Communications of the ACM*, 24(8):533–536, 1981.

15. S. D. Dexter. *An Adversary-Centric Logic of Security and Authenticity*. PhD thesis, University of Michigan, 1998.

16. D. Dolev and A. C. Yao. On the security of public key protocols. *IEEE Transactions on Information Theory*, IT-29(2):198–208, March 1983.

17. J.-Y. Girard. Linear logic. *Theoretical Computer Science*, 50:1–102, 1987.

18. L. Gong, R. Needham, and R. Yahalom. Reasoning about belief in cryptographic protocols. In *Proceedings of the IEEE Computer Society Symposium on Security and Privacy*, pages 234–248. IEEE, May 1990.

19. J. Harland and D. Pym. A uniform proof-theoretic investigation of linear logic programming. *Journal of Logic and Computation*, 4(2), April 1994. 175–207.

20. C. A. R. Hoare. *Communicating Sequential Processes*. Prentice-Hall, 1985.

21. J. S. Hodas and D. Miller. Logic programming in a fragment of intuitionistic linear logic. *Journal of Information and Computation*, 110(2):327–365, May 1994.

22. R. Kemmerer, C. Meadows, and J. Millen. Three systems for cryptographic protocol analysis. *Journal of Cryptology*, 7:79–130, 1994.

23. J. W. Lloyd. *Foundations of Logic Programming*. Spinger-Verlag, second extended edition edition, 1993.

24. G. Lowe. Breaking and fixing the Needham-Schroeder public key protocol using CSP and FDR. In T. Margaria and B. Steffen, editors, *Tools and Algorithms for the Construction and Analysis of Systems Second International Workshop, TACAS '96*, volume 1055 of *Lecture Notes in Computer Science*, pages 147–166. Springer-Verlag, 1996.

25. G. Lowe. A hierarchy of authentication specification. In *Proceedings of the 10th IEEE Computer Security Foundations Workshop*, June 1997.

26. G. Lowe. Some new attacks upon security protocols. In *Proceedings of the 9th IEEE Computer Security Foundations Workshop*, pages 162–169, 1997.

27. J. A. Makowsky. Why Horn formulas matter in computer science: Initial structures and generic examples. *Journal of Computer and System Sciences*, 34:266–292, 1987.
28. W. Mao and C. Boyd. Development of authentication protocols: Some misconceptions and a new approach. In *Proceedings of the Computer Security Foundations Workshop VII*, pages 178–186. IEEE, 1994.
29. W. Marrero, E. Clarke, and S. Jha. Model checking for security protocols. Technical Report CMU-CS-97-139, School of Computer Science, Carnegie Mellon University, May 1997.
30. C. Meadows. The NRL protocol analyzer: an overview. *The Journal of Logic Programming*, pages 113–131, 1996.
31. J. C. Mitchell. Analysis of security protocols. Slides for a talk at CAV '98, available at http://www.stanford.edu/jcm, July 1998.
32. R. M. Needham and M. D. Schroeder. Using encryption for authentication in large networks of computers. *Communications of the ACM*, 21(12):993–999, 1978.
33. P. Padawitz. *Computing in Horn clause theories*. Springer-Verlag, Berlin, 1988.
34. L. C. Paulson. Proving properties of security protocols by induction. Technical Report TR-409, Computer Laboratory, University of Cambridge, 1996.
35. L. C. Paulson. Mechanized proofs for a recursive authentication protocol. In *Proceedings of the 10th IEEE Computer Security Foundations Workshop*, pages 84–95, June 1997.
36. L. C. Paulson. Mechanized proofs of security protcols: Needham-Schroeder with public keys. Unpublished manuscript, January 1997.
37. A. W. Roscoe. Modelling and verifying key exchange protocols using CSP and FDR. In *Proceedings of the Computer Security Foundations Workshop VIII*, volume 8, pages 98–107. IEEE, 1995.
38. P. Ryan and I. Zakiuddin. Modelling and analysis of security protocols. In *Proceedings of the DIMACS Workshop on Formal Verification of Security Protocols*, September 1997.
39. E. Snekkenes. Exploring the BAN approach to protocol analysis. In *Proceedings of the IEEE Computer Society Symposium on Security and Privacy*, pages 171–181, May 1991.
40. P. Syverson. The use of logic in the analysis of cryptographic protocols. In *Proceedings of the 1991 IEEE Computer Society Symposium on Research in Security and Privacy*, pages 156–170. IEEE, May 1991.
41. P. Syverson and P. van Oorschot. On unifying some cryptographic protocol logics. In *Proceedings of the IEEE Symposium on Research in Security and Privacy*, pages 14–28, 1994.
42. T. Tammet. Proof strategies in linear logic. *Journal of Automated Reasoning*, 12:273–304, 1994.
43. P. C. van Oorschot. Extending cryptographic logics of belief to key agreement protocols (extended abstract). In *Proceedings of the First ACM Conference on Computer and Communications Security*, pages 232–243, November 1993.
44. M. Winikoff and J. Harland. Some applications of the linear logic programming language lygon. In *Proceedings of the Australasian Computer Science Conference*, pages 262–271, February 1996.
45. T. Y. C. Woo and S. S. Lam. A semantic model for authentication protocols. In *Proceedings of the Symposium on Research in Security and Privacy*, pages 178–194. IEEE, May 1993.

Type Structure for Low-Level Programming Languages

Karl Crary[1] and Greg Morrisett[2]

[1] Carnegie Mellon University, Pittsburgh, PA 15213
[2] Cornell University, Ithaca, NY 14850

Abstract. Providing type structure for extremely low-level programming languages, such as assembly language, yields a number of important benefits for compiler and systems projects, where reliability and security are crucial concerns. We discuss some of the issues involved in designing type systems for low-level languages, and identify some general principles that simplify constructing a proof of soundness.

1 Introduction

Over the past twenty years, there has been tremendous progress in the design and foundations of type systems for high-level programming languages culminating in the design of such languages as Modula-3, Standard ML, Haskell, and Java. The goal of much of the research was to strengthen the logic of a type system so that a richer class of abstractions and invariants could be stated and yet enforced automatically.

Recently, we (and others) have been exploring the design, applications, and foundations of type systems for extremely *low-level* languages. In particular, we have concentrated on the design and implementation of a statically *typed assembly language* (TAL) [14], suitable for execution on realistic machines. Our TAL consists of low-level instructions and data that correspond to a conventional, untyped assembly language, but augmented with annotations that support *static* type-checking. Once a program has been type-checked, the type annotations can be erased and the program can then be directly executed on a machine without fear that the program will violate the abstractions of the type system.

We have also been studying the benefits and drawbacks of compiling high-level languages in a type-preserving fashion to a typed assembly language. In a type-preserving compiler, high-level linguistic abstractions, such as variables, modules, closures, or objects, as well as abstractions introduced by the compiler, such as activation records or calling conventions, must be encoded using typing abstractions provided by TAL.

In our work thus far, we have found that using a typed assembly language within the framework of a type-preserving compiler has a number of compelling benefits:

- Compilers can use type information to support many optimizations. For instance, many code-motion transformations, such as loop invariant removal, require accurate information about whether two variables may contain aliases to the same data structure. A compiler based on TAL can easily determine that two variables do not alias if the types of the variables are incompatible.

- It is easy to find and eliminate a wide class of compiler bugs if the compiler emits TAL code. The reason is that at least some compilation bugs will manifest themselves as type-errors in the output code and be caught by the TAL type-checker. In practice, we have found that indeed, *most* bugs are caught by the checker. For instance, in the implementation of our Safe-C code generator [10], only one bug was not caught by type-checking.

- A current trend in systems software is to allow untrusted extensions to be installed in services, relying upon safe language technology to protect the integrity of the service. For example, Web browsers rely upon the type-safety of the Java Virtual Machine Language (JVML) to protect users from faulty or malicious applets. Because the JVML is not a real machine language, it cannot be directly executed; rather, a trusted interpreter or compiler must be used. The former costs performance, whereas the latter introduces a complicated component into the trusted computing base. By basing an extensible system on TAL, both drawbacks can be avoided.

While imposing a type structure on an assembly language has many benefits, designing the type system involves a number of complicated tradeoffs. On the one hand, we desire a very expressive type system so that we can encode more source-level abstractions, more compiler invariants, and more security properties. On the other hand, to realize the advantages of compiler debugging and security, we need decidable and relatively efficient algorithms for type-checking.

We have discovered that perhaps the most difficult aspect of the design is constructing a suitable formal model of the language and its type system so that we may easily establish a proof of soundness. On the one hand, the model should accurately capture the relevant low-level details of realistic machines. On the other hand, the model should abstract from as many low-level details as possible so that a rigorous proof of soundness is tractable.

Fundamentally, there is no optimal, general solution to these tradeoffs and therefore, we expect that different type systems will be needed in different contexts. It is therefore crucial that we identify general principles in the design of type systems for low-level languages, and useful proof techniques that simplify the construction of the model and the proof of soundness.

In this paper, we discuss some of the general principles that have emerged from our experience with designing, implementing, and using TAL. In particular, we discuss the rewriting model used for TAL, and how its syntactic structure is used to provide a faithful model of realistic machine states, and yet abstract enough details that we may use largely standard proof techniques, developed primarily for high-level languages, to establish soundness. We also state a general principle regarding types for memory states, and show how the type structure of TAL applies this principle in three different ways to achieve a desired level of flexibility. For the sake of brevity and clarity, we omit many of the technical

```
l_fact:    Λ[ρ].code{r1 : int, sp : ρ, ra : ∀[]. code{r1 : int, sp : ρ}}.
           bnz  r1,l_nzero[ρ]  % if n ≠ 0 goto l_nzero
           mov  r1,1           % result is 1
           jmp  ra             % return
l_nzero:   Λ[ρ].code{r1 : int, sp : ρ, ra : ∀[]. code{r1 : int, sp : ρ}}.
           sub  sp,sp,2        % allocate stack space for n and the return address
           st   sp(0),r1       % save n
           st   sp(1),ra       % save return address
           sub  r1,r1,1        % set argument to n − 1
           mov  ra,l_cont[ρ]   % set return address to l_cont
           jmp  l_fact[int :: ∀[]. code{r1 : int, sp : ρ} :: ρ] % recursive call
l_cont:    Λ[ρ].code{r1 : int, sp : int :: ∀[]. code{r1 : int, sp : ρ} :: ρ}.
           ld   r2,sp(0)       % restore n
           ld   ra,sp(1)       % restore return address
           add  sp,sp,2        % deallocate stack space
           mul  r1,r2,r1       % n × (n − 1)!
           jmp  ra             % return
```

Fig. 1. TAL Factorial Example

details in our discussion and refer the interested reader to our more detailed reports [14, 11].

2 Basic Design

Figure 1 gives a simple example of TAL code that represents a recursive factorial function. The code consists of three labels, l_fact, l_nzero, and l_cont. Each of the labels is followed by a code-type annotation that is used during type-checking. Informally, the annotation specifies a typing pre-condition that must be satisfied before control may be transferred to the corresponding label. For example, the l_fact pre-condition requires that register r1 contain an integer value (the argument to the function), and register ra contains a valid return address that itself expects an integer value in r1 (the return value of the function). As we will discuss later, the pre-condition is polymorphic in the shape of the control stack. That is, the function may be called with any number and any type of values placed upon the stack. Furthermore, upon return, the size of the stack and indeed the values that were on the stack will remain unchanged.

In this example, all of the instructions are standard, RISC-style assembly language instructions with register, integer immediate, or label operands. However, some operands require typing annotations to support type-checking. For example, the operand of the jmp instruction in the basic block labelled by l_nzero is an explicit instantiation of the polymorphic label l_fact.

Whereas the example shown here uses only RISC-style instructions, in practice, we need a few unconventional instructions in order to simplify the type system. In our implementation, we implement these instructions as macros that are expanded at assembly time into real machine instructions. For example, to heap-allocate a data structure such as a record or tuple in TAL, a programmer must use the `malloc` macro instruction. The macro expands into a call to a runtime routine that allocates memory of the appropriate size and returns a pointer to the data. In this case, the macro is necessary because the type of the allocation routine is dependent upon the integer value passed as an argument, but the type system of TAL does not support such dependent types.

Thus, the designer of a typed assembly language does have some latitude in introducing new terms as macros in order to provide some abstraction and to simplify the type system. The price paid is that the macro terms must be translated before the code can be executed. Furthermore, the failure to expose the underlying primitive instructions prevents inter-macro optimizations such as instruction scheduling. It is therefore a delicate task to decide whether to add a new "instruction" or to add new typing constructs.

In the rest of this section, we further motivate and explain the design of the TAL language, and describe the model we use for the semantics of the language.

2.1 Programs and Values

In order to state and prove a type-soundness theorem for TAL code, we must construct a model of program evaluation that is faithful to the semantics of a real machine. We choose to model evaluation using a rewriting system that maps abstract machine states to abstract machine states in a fashion similar to the λ_{gc} machine [12, 13]. This style of abstract machine provides syntactic structure that reflects the intended abstractions provided by a type system, making it easy to state and prove soundness. For example, we draw a syntactic distinction between integer values and pointers. The abstract machine supports arithmetic on integers, but becomes "stuck" if we attempt to perform arithmetic upon pointers, because this would violate the intended abstraction. Thus, we can state that the type system is sound if it prevents programs from entering stuck states.

Though our model abstracts much of the inner workings of a real machine, we must make explicit more details than machines such as λ_{gc}. For example, we must distinguish between data that are stored in a register and data that are stored in memory, because the instructions for accessing data in these locations is quite different. In addition, for typing reasons that will become manifest later, we have found that it is profitable to break memory into two abstract areas: the heap and the control stack. Consequently, the syntax of the TAL abstract machine makes each of these stores explicit.

More formally, a state of the TAL abstract machine (which we sometimes refer to as a "program") is a quadruple, (H, S, R, I), consisting of an abstract heap, stack, register file, and sequence of instructions. The first three correspond to memory components of a real machine; the last is a sequence of instructions to be executed by the machine and thus represents the machine's program counter. (To simplify the discussion, we will neglect the stack until Section 3.3.)

register names	$r ::= \texttt{r1} \mid \texttt{r2} \mid \texttt{r3} \mid \cdots$
word values	$w ::= i \mid \ell$
heap values	$h ::= \langle w_1, \ldots, w_n \rangle$
small values	$v ::= r \mid w$
heaps	$H ::= \{\ell_1 \mapsto h_1, \ldots, \ell_n \mapsto h_n\}$
register files	$R ::= \{r_1 \mapsto w_1, \ldots, r_n \mapsto w_n\}$
instruction sequences	$I ::= \epsilon \mid \iota; I$
instructions	$\iota ::= \texttt{mov } r_d, v \mid \texttt{bnz } r, v \mid \texttt{add } r_d, r_s, v \mid \texttt{ld } r_d, r_s[i]$
	$\mid \texttt{st } r_d[i], r_s \mid \cdots$
programs	$P ::= (H, R, I)$

Fig. 2. Basic Syntax

The syntax includes strictures ensuring that each store contains only abstract values of appropriate size. In particular, registers may only contain word-sized values, whereas the heap may contain values of arbitrary size. Thus, the syntax makes a distinction between *word values* and *heap values*. Word values include integers (i) and labels (ℓ) (also referred to as pointers). Heap values include tuples and code blocks. Tuples are ordered pairs of word values, whereas code blocks are sequences of primitive instructions, prefixed with a typing annotation.

With these syntactic distinctions established, a heap is defined to be a finite mapping of labels (ℓ) to heap values (h), and a register file is defined to be a finite mapping of register names (r) to word values (w). Thus, if register r1 is to "contain" the tuple $\langle 3, 4 \rangle$, the register file would map r1 to some label ℓ, and the heap would map ℓ to $\langle 3, 4 \rangle$. These points are summarized in Figure 2.

Certain instructions, such as **mov**, may be used either with a register or literal operand. This gives rise to a third class of values called *small values* (v), which are either registers or word values. Thus the syntax for an instruction to move a small value v into a register r is **mov** r, v; the move's destination must be a register, but the source may be a register or a literal value. The distinction between word and small values must be drawn (instead of simply including register names among word values) because a register cannot contain another register.

It is worth noting that this syntactic structure is intentionally designed to be limiting. In particular, by viewing the heap as an abstract mapping of pointers to heap values, we hide additional structure that is present in a conventional machine, such as the relative locations of values in the heap. It is possible to expose such low-level details, but doing so makes it more difficult to state and reason about many properties relevant to type safety, compilers, or security. For example, in the contexts of both garbage collection and address-space isolation, it is crucial that we can easily identify or limit those heap objects that are "reachable" from the current program state. In our framework, doing so is trivial because pointers are abstract and do not admit operations such as pointer arithmetic. In other contexts, it might be necessary to expose lower-level details.

2.2 Types and Code

As stated earlier, the ultimate goal of the type system is to prevent the abstract machine from entering a "bad" or "stuck" state. In order to do so, the type system must track, at all program points, the types of all accessible data objects and prevent control from reaching an instruction that potentially violates the intended abstraction. For the most part, all accessible data objects are reached (directly or indirectly) through registers.[1]

Consequently, the primary burden of the type system is to track the types of the contents of every register. All this information is collected in a *register file type* (Γ), which is a finite mapping of register names to (ordinary) types. We say that the register file $R = \{r_1 \mapsto w_1, \ldots, r_m \mapsto w_m\}$ has type $\Gamma = \{r_1{:}\tau_1, \ldots, r_n{:}\tau_n\}$, if $m \geq n$ and w_i has type τ_i (for every $1 \leq i \leq n$). Note that we permit the forgetting of registers in order to match a register file type.

In a high-level programming language, an expression is type-checked relative to some context that specifies the types of its free variables. In TAL, registers serve the function of free variables, so the instructions of a code block are checked relative to a register file type. Thus, the judgement for instructions is of the form $\Gamma_1 \vdash \iota : \Gamma_2$ which reads informally as, given a register file satisfying the typing pre-condition Γ_1, execution of the instruction ι yields a register file satisfying the typing post-condition Γ_2.[2] For example, the rule instance:

$$\frac{\Gamma(r_1) = \texttt{int} \qquad \Gamma(r_2) = \texttt{int}}{\Gamma \vdash \texttt{add } r_d, r_1, r_2 : \Gamma\{r_d : \texttt{int}\}}$$

specifies that we may execute the add instruction in any context where registers r_1 and r_2 contains integer values, and that after the instruction is executed, the register file type will remain unchanged except that register r_d will contain an integer.

Type-checking a sequence of instructions is achieved by using the post-condition of a previous instruction as the pre-condition for the next instruction. The judgement that a sequence of instructions I is valid is written $\Gamma \vdash I$. Note that in this judgement the sequence I is assigned no result type (*i.e.*, no post-condition). This is because all sequences are required to end with an unconditional control transfer (*i.e.*, jump or return). This aspect of TAL is similar to high-level functional languages that require programs to be written in *continuation-passing style* (CPS) [3, 15, 5].

---

[1] The exception to this, preallocated data objects in the heap, are handled by means very similar to those we now describe, as discussed in Morrisett *et al.* [14].

[2] In this paper we will deal with only a few of the TAL judgements and those only informally; full details appear in Morrisett *et al.* [14, 11]. In particular, the code validity judgement as formalized in Morrisett *et al.* includes other context components in addition to the register file type.

heap values	$h ::= \cdots \mid \mathsf{code}\,\Gamma.I$	

types	$\tau ::= \mathsf{int} \mid \mathsf{code}\,\Gamma$	
register file types	$\Gamma ::= \{r_1{:}\tau_1, \ldots, r_n{:}\tau_n\}$	

Fig. 3. Type Syntax

The CPS nature of low-level code is important to understand the types that are assigned to code blocks. Because well-formed blocks end with an unconditional jump, control will never fall off the end of the block. Thus, logically speaking, the post-condition could specify *any* type for the registers since control will never reach that point.[3] We therefore omit the post-condition on well-formed blocks of code.

Within the abstract machine, each code block that is bound to a label must is prefixed with its typing pre-condition, written $\mathsf{code}\,\Gamma.I$. If I is valid assuming that register file type on entry (*i.e.*, if $\Gamma \vdash I$), then we say that the code block has type $\mathsf{code}\,\Gamma$. The new syntactic constructs are summarized in Figure 3. (For convenience we assume that code blocks are located in the heap. Types for tuples are omitted from the figure; they are the subject of Section 3.2.)

For example, in a high-level language such as ML, the factorial function would have type $\mathsf{int} \to \mathsf{int}$. In a CPS-based functional language, the type would be $(\mathsf{int} * (\mathsf{int} \to \mathsf{void})) \to \mathsf{void}$, reflecting the fact that the integer-accepting continuation is passed as a second argument. Similarly, in TAL the type of the function would be $\mathsf{code}\{r1{:}\mathsf{int}, r2{:}\mathsf{code}\{r1{:}\mathsf{int}\}\}$ (assuming the argument and result are passed in $r1$ and the return address in $r2$).

2.3 Quantified Types

In order to support polymorphism and data abstraction, TAL supplies universal and existential [9] types. This is important so that TAL may serve as a target language for compilers of high-level languages with these features, of course, but even monomorphic features of high-level languages often implicitly require type quantification. For example, existential types arise in objects [1] and closures [8], and universal types arise in stacks [11].

For simplicity, universal quantification is limited to code, since that is where the intended use of universal types lies. The introduction form (and the type) allows for the simultaneous abstraction of a series of type variables $\alpha_1, \ldots, \alpha_n$, collectively written Δ. Note that the elimination form, the instantiation of a value at a type (written $w[\tau]$ or $v[\tau]$), is considered a value, rather than a function call. This is permissible because we interpret TAL in a manner consistent with type erasure. That is, types are never relevant to execution and may be erased, and consequently there is no run-time difference between w and $w[\tau]$.

---

[3] Equivalently, we could use "false" (*i.e.*, a void or empty type) for the post-condition.

$$\begin{array}{llll}
\textit{word values} & w & ::= & \cdots \mid w[\tau] \mid \mathsf{pack}[\tau, w] \text{ as } \exists \alpha.\tau' \\
\textit{heap values} & h & ::= & \cdots \mid \Lambda[\Delta]. \mathsf{code}\, \Gamma.I \\
\textit{small values} & v & ::= & \cdots \mid v[\tau] \mid \mathsf{pack}[\tau, v] \text{ as } \exists \alpha.\tau' \\
\\
\textit{types} & \tau & ::= & \cdots \mid \alpha \mid \forall[\Delta]. \mathsf{code}\, \Gamma \mid \exists \alpha.\tau \\
\textit{tyvar series} & \Delta & ::= & \epsilon \mid \Delta. \alpha
\end{array}$$

Fig. 4. Universal and Existential Types

The type-erasure interpretation makes TAL more faithful to real machines (which, of course, do not compute using types), and it makes some aspects of compilation substantially simpler, such as closure conversion [14]. Others, however, it makes more complicated, such as intensional polymorphism [6, 2]. An extensive discussion of type erasure, and of how type-passing languages may be compiled to type-erasure languages such as TAL, appears in Crary *et al.* [2].

Because of the type-erasure interpretation, the introduction form for existential types (written $\mathsf{pack}[\tau, w]$ as $\exists \alpha.\tau'$ or $\mathsf{pack}[\tau, v]$ as $\exists \alpha.\tau'$) is also considered a value. The elimination form for existential types is the instruction $\mathsf{unpack}[\alpha. r], v$. The type variable α is bound in the remainder of the instruction sequence. When v contains the pack value $\mathsf{pack}[\tau, w]$ as $\exists \alpha.\tau'$, the unpack instruction executes by moving w into r and substituting τ for α is the remainder of the instruction sequence. Under the type-erasure interpretation, this is implementable at run-time as a simple move.

2.4 Scope and Alpha-Conversion

An important observation is the status of scope and alpha-conversion in TAL. So far we have seen three forms of "variable": type variables, register names, and pointers. Binding occurrences of type variables within code are introduced at the beginning of polymorphic code block or within an **unpack** instruction, and the scope of the variable extends to the end of the ensuing instruction sequence. As usual, we consider code blocks (and types) to be equivalent up to alpha-conversion of bound type variables.

Register names, however, do not alpha-convert; the purpose of making them explicit in the language is to be able to identify particular registers for calling conventions and for data placement. Nevertheless, there is ample evidence that variable names should not be important in well-behaved programming languages.

These two facts are reconciled by observing that registers are not really variables. Consider the code block $\mathsf{code}\{\mathsf{r1}:\mathsf{int}\}. \mathsf{mov}\ \mathsf{r2}, \mathsf{r1}; \mathsf{mov}\ \mathsf{r3}, \mathsf{r1}; \ldots$ The argument to this code is not really the integer in $\mathsf{r1}$, it is the *entire register file*. The register file is essentially a linear record [4, 17, 18]; each instruction consumes the register file and produces a new one. In essence the code amounts to the following representation with explicit register files:

$$\lambda rf : \{\mathsf{r1}:\mathsf{int}\}. \mathsf{let}\ rf' = (\mathsf{mov}\ \mathsf{r2}, \mathsf{r1})(rf)\ \mathsf{in}$$
$$\mathsf{let}\ rf'' = (\mathsf{mov}\ \mathsf{r3}, \mathsf{r1})(rf')\ \mathsf{in}\ \ldots$$

Any of these register files names can be alpha-varied as usual. However, since the invariant holds that at every point there is exactly one register file available, we simply elide any mention of register files by name.

For pointers there is an open choice: we can make them alpha-vary, or we can view the entire memory as an enormous linear object as we did with the register file. Without a compelling case for the latter, we decide to make them alpha-vary for technical convenience. This means that when allocating memory, we need not specify the strategy for generating a new address; we may simply choose any unused pointer. However, as a consequence, it is impossible to perform any operations on pointers such as hashing them. Under some circumstances these operations may be useful, but it can also be argued that they often violate important abstraction properties: given objects of abstract type, it should be impossible to determine any properties about them, but it will sometimes be possible in the presence of pointer operations.

3   Memory and Aliasing

The most delicate aspect of the design of TAL lies in the way its type system handles data in memory. As we observed in Section 2.2, for the type system to work, it must track the types of all accessible data objects. As this applies to memory, it means that at every program point, the type system must have an accurate view of the contents of all accessible memory locations. An immediate consequence of this is that the type system cannot permit access to any memory location of which it does not have a view. In other words, arbitrary, unrestricted memory accesses are fundamentally incompatible with the type system.

Given that the type system permits memory accesses only to locations of which it has a view, a more subtle and important issue arises. The type system must ensure the invariant that its view of every accessible memory location is accurate. In the presence of aliasing, this invariant is not trivial to maintain: Suppose a memory location is accessible via two different paths, and the program, using one of those paths, modifies the memory location so that its type changes. It is easy enough to modify the view of that memory corresponding to the access path that was used, but to maintain the type system's invariants, we must also modify the view of that location along the other, aliasing, access path. Unfortunately, it is very difficult to determine statically whether two paths alias, and even harder to find statically all aliases of a given path.

The basic principle to be observed then is: *Any change to a memory location must not invalidate the type system's view of that location along any usable access path.* In the remainder of this section, we discuss several memory type mechanisms that adhere to this principle, each one being suitable for different problems.

3.1   Registers

The simplest possible means to track aliasing is to prevent it from happening. One common mechanism to do this is to use linear types [4, 17, 18], which prevents there from being multiple access paths to any piece of data. An even more draconian mechanism is to disallow any indirect access to data at all, allowing only a single, unit-length access paths. However, this mechanism is entirely appropriate for machine registers, which cannot be accessed indirectly anyway. Thus, registers can be modified freely, updating their types in the register file type, without fear that any aliases to those registers would be given an inaccurate view.

3.2 The Heap

The heavy-handed mechanism that works for registers is clearly unacceptable for the heap, where it is essential to permit multiple access paths to data objects. Nevertheless, it is impractical to track aliasing in the heap. Instead, we assume that any memory location may have any number of unknown aliases, and employ a typing regime in which a modification cannot invalidate the type system's view of any of those aliases.

This regime works as follows: When a memory location is first allocated, it is stamped with a type. From that point on, stores into the memory location may only write values of the type with which the location is stamped. Since the stamping occurs when the memory location is first allocated, all aliases will view the memory location as stamped in the same way. Therefore, any stores will write only values appropriate to what is expected along other access paths.

This mechanism is familiar as the typing regime for references in Standard ML [7] and other ML dialects. However, a complication arises in TAL because when first allocated, memory locations are uninitialized and conceptually contain junk. In contrast, in Standard ML an initial value is provided for references, so an uninitialized state is avoided.

An attractive alternative is to give uninitialized memory locations a *nonsense* type and refine that type when it is initialized. But this mechanism is barred by the solution to the aliasing problem. (This mechanism will be suitable in the next section when dealing with stacks.)

The solution we have adopted to this problem is to flag every memory location with its initialization state. Suppose a two-word block is allocated, intended to contain a pair of integers. The newly allocated location is given the type $\langle \text{int}^0, \text{int}^0 \rangle$. The 0 flags indicate that both fields of the tuple are uninitialized and may not be read from. When a field of a tuple is initialized, the flag is changed to a 1, indicating that it is permissible to read from the field. Thereafter, interference [16] is possible, in that an initialized field may be changed using alternative access paths, but any such changes can only write integers, so all views of that field remain valid.

One form of inaccurate view can arise in this regime: it is possible for a field to be initialized using one access path while another path still believes it to be uninitialized. However, this sort of inaccuracy is benign; it does no harm for an alias to believe it may not read from a field that happens to be initialized. Thus, a better way to read the "0" flag is that the corresponding field is *possibly* uninitialized.

types $\quad\quad\quad\quad \tau ::= \cdots \mid \langle \tau_1^{\varphi_1}, \ldots, \tau_n^{\varphi_n} \rangle$

initialization flags $\quad \varphi ::= 0 \mid 1$

Fig. 5. Heap Typing Mechanisms

There are two essential limitations on TAL code that make the above mechanism work. First, it is not permissible to reuse a memory location at a different type. Once memory is allocated, it remains stamped with the same type until it is reclaimed by the garbage collector (at which point the collector has verified that there are no access paths to that memory).

Second, we cannot expose the internal workings of the memory allocation process. Instead, memory allocation is viewed as an atomic operation that finds the needed memory and stamps it with a type. In the semantics, allocation is performed by a primitive `malloc` instruction; in practice the `malloc` instruction macro-expands (after typechecking) to an appropriate fixed code sequence. This limitation is necessary because any finer view of the memory allocation process would expose that allocated space is drawn from a pool of untyped memory. Our approach for dealing with aliasing depends essentially on the fact that no location ever exists (as far as the type system is concerned) without being typed.

3.3 The Stack

To supports stacks in Typed Assembly Language, we must consider a third approach to dealing with the aliasing problem. The typing regime discussed in the previous section for heap-allocated space is unsuitable for stack-allocated space, because the pattern of access to the stack is quite different than to the heap. For the heap we made the significant restriction that no space could ever be re-used at a different type. This restriction is unacceptable for stack space: the entire purpose of the stack is to re-use space repeatedly during dynamic growing and shrinking of the stack.

Recall that the basic principle to observe is that any change to a memory location must not invalidate the type system's view of that location along any *usable* access path. For the heap we adopted a regime ensuring no change could invalidate the view along any path. For the stack we take a different approach: it will be possible to invalidate the view of a stack slot along some access paths, but such paths will become unusable.

Before we can discuss the regime that enforces this, we must begin with some preliminaries. First, we introduce the notion of a *stack type*, which describes the shape of the stack. Stack types are either `nil`, indicating that the stack is empty, or $\tau::\sigma$, indicating that the first value on the stack has type τ and the remainder is described by σ. The stack is accessed by an identified stack pointer register (`sp`), and the register file type accordingly assigns `sp` a stack type, rather than a regular type. This is summarized in Figure 6.

The type system maintains the invariant that the stack type assigned to `sp` by the current register file type is always correct. For example, allocating

$$
\begin{array}{lll}
\textit{types} & \tau ::= \cdots \mid \texttt{ns} \\
\textit{stack types} & \sigma ::= \texttt{nil} \mid \tau :: \sigma \\
\textit{register file types} & \Gamma ::= \{\texttt{sp}:\sigma, r_1:\tau_1, \ldots, r_n:\tau_n\} \\
\\
\textit{stacks} & S ::= \texttt{nil} \mid w :: S \\
\textit{programs} & P ::= (H, S, R, I)
\end{array}
$$

Fig. 6. Stack Typing Mechanisms

$$
\begin{array}{lll}
\textit{word values} & w ::= \cdots \mid \texttt{ptr}(i) \\
\textit{types} & \tau ::= \cdots \mid \texttt{ptr}(\sigma)
\end{array}
$$

Fig. 7. Stack Indirection

one word of space on the stack (in practice performed by subtracting the word size from the stack pointer) when **sp** has type σ, changes sp's type to $\texttt{ns} :: \sigma$, indicating that the top stack word is nonsense (garbage), and the remainder of the stack is as before. Unlike the regime for heaps, we may store a value of any type into any stack slot, and the type of **sp** will change accordingly. Thus, if the sp has type $\texttt{int} :: \texttt{ns} :: \sigma$, then storing an integer into the second stack slot (*e.g.*, $\texttt{mov sp}(1), 12$) results in the type $\texttt{int} :: \texttt{int} :: \sigma$.

To this point, we have trivially avoided any aliasing problems by providing only a single access path into the stack, through **sp**. We now wish to consider what happens we add pointers into the stack. Syntactically, we represent pointers into the stack by $\texttt{ptr}(i)$, which points to the ith word of the stack. Pointers into the stack are indexed from the bottom, so they need not change when the stack grows or shrinks. The type of a pointer into the stack is given by $\texttt{ptr}(\sigma)$, which describes the segment of the stack lying below that pointer. This is summarized in Figure 7.

A pointer into the stack is first obtained by copying the stack pointer into another register. At that point, that register has type $\texttt{ptr}(\sigma)$, where σ is the type of **sp**. However, further computation may change the stack's type, and this will not be reflected in the type of the copy (to do so would require tracking of aliasing). For example:

```
;; begin with sp : ⟨int¹⟩ :: σ
mov r1, sp      ;; r1 : ptr(⟨int¹⟩ :: σ)
mov sp(0), 12   ;; sp : int :: σ, but still r1 : ptr(⟨int¹⟩ :: σ)
```

After the second line, the type for **r1** is no longer consistent with what it points to. If the type system permits loading from **r1**, the resulting value will be believed to have the tuple type $\langle \texttt{int}^1 \rangle$, but in fact will be the integer 12.

The problem is that the store to $\texttt{sp}(0)$ has invalidated the view of the stack held by **r1**. To solve this problem, we disallow loading from any pointer whose view has been invalidated. It is easy to determine statically when such an invali-

$$
\begin{aligned}
\textit{word values} \quad & w ::= \cdots \mid w[\sigma] \\
\textit{small values} \quad & v ::= \cdots \mid v[\sigma] \\
\\
\textit{stack types} \quad & \sigma ::= \cdots \mid \rho \mid \sigma_1 \cdot \sigma_2 \\
\textit{tyvar series} \quad & \Delta ::= \cdots \mid \Delta, \rho
\end{aligned}
$$

Fig. 8. Stack Hiding Mechanisms

dation has occurred because sp's type is ensured always to be valid. Thus, when loading from a pointer into the stack, that pointer's type is compared against sp's type and the load is rejected if the pointer's type is inaccurate.

Stack Polymorphism The problem with the type discipline discussed to this point is that stack types always fully describe the shape of the stack. In practice, however, it is extremely important to be able to ignore irrelevant portions of the stack. Typically, nearly all the stack is irrelevant. Recall that a function with type code{sp:σ,...} can only be called with stacks described by σ. If σ fully describes the stack, then calls to that function are limited to cases in which the stack has the indicated depth and components. One of many negative consequences of this is that recursion is impossible.

We settle this problem by adding stack type variables (ρ) and polymorphism over stack types. Thus, if the only relevant element of the stack is the top value (say, an integer argument), then we might use the type $\forall[\rho]$. code{sp:int::ρ,...}. By a suitable instantiation of ρ, this function could be called with any stack whose top element is an integer.

This mechanism allows us to ignore all of the stack after some initial segment. However, it is also often useful to ignore a non-terminal segment of the stack. For instance, we might care about some material at the top of the stack and some in the middle, but none in between. This often happens with exception handlers or displays placed amidst the stack. To support this, we add a facility for concatenating stack types. Thus, (ns :: nil) · (int :: nil) is equivalent to ns :: int :: nil. These mechanisms are summarized in Figure 8.

Stack concatenation is useful in conjunction with stack type variables. Suppose we are interested in a value with type τ located amidst the stack, but are not interested in any other part. Then we may specify the stack to have type $\rho_1 \cdot (\tau :: \rho_2)$, where ρ_1 and ρ_2 are universally quantified. By suitable instantiation of ρ_1 and ρ_2, this type will apply to any stack that contains a τ value.

Note that since the length of ρ_1 is unknown, there is no way to locate the τ value of interest. It is in this setting that it is important to support pointers into the middle of the stack, raising the aliasing issues discussed above. Thus, a function that wished to receive a τ value passed in the middle of the stack would be given a type such as $\forall[\rho_1, \rho_2]$. code{sp:$\rho_1 \cdot (\tau :: \rho_2)$, r1:ptr($\tau :: \rho_2$)}. This type typically arises when τ is the type of an exception handler and r1 is the exception register [11].

Limitations The principal limitation of this approach to typing stacks is that an undesirable amount of information must be explicitly specified. Although polymorphism can be used to hide portions of the stack that are irrelevant, all stack components that are of interest must be specified in the stack's type, even when those components are accessed using a pointer. In contrast, when data is stored on the heap, only a well-typed heap pointer is necessary.

Another limitation is that when the stack contains multiple values of interest, the stack type must specify their relative order, if not their precise locations. This difficulty can be ameliorated by adding intersection types to provide multiple views of the same stack. For example, when the stack contains two interesting values (with types τ_1 and τ_2) in no particular order, the stack could be given type $(\rho_1 \cdot \tau_1 :: \rho_1') \wedge (\rho_2 \cdot \tau_2 :: \rho_2')$. We have not yet explored all the ramifications of this enhancement, as experience has not yet demonstrated a convincing need for it.

A third limitation stems from having two different type systems, one for heaps and one for stacks. Since the data in the heap are given different types than data in the stack (tuple types versus `ptr` types), interfaces must specifically state in which their data will lie. Because of this, and because of the limitations of stacks discussed above, programmers prefer to keep data on the heap unless there is a particular reason to place it on the stack. In practice, then, TAL stacks are not really a first-class storage medium.

4 Conclusion

There are a number of difficult but interesting tradeoffs in the design of type systems for low-level languages and, in all likelihood, there is no "ultimate" type system. Rather, a language designer must weigh the costs and benefits of expressiveness versus simplicity. In the design of TAL, we opted for the latter when reasonable.

In this paper, we have stated a general principle regarding types for memory locations that is useful in the design of any programming language. In essence, the principle states that we may change the contents of a location in memory, as long as we track the changes in the type system along all accessible paths. Within the context of Typed Assembly, we showed how this principle is used in three different ways to achieve some needed expressiveness while retaining as much simplicity as possible. In particular, we argued that a linear discipline was appropriate for register files, but was too inflexible for heaps and stacks. Similarly, we argued that the standard reference discipline of high-level languages is appropriate for most heap objects, but that a validation approach may be more appropriate for objects allocated on the stack.

References

1. Kim B. Bruce, Luca Cardelli, and Benjamin C. Pierce. Comparing object encodings. In *Theoretical Aspects of Computer Software*, Sendai, Japan, September 1997.

2. Karl Crary, Stephanie Weirich, and Greg Morrisett. Intensional polymorphism in type-erasure semantics. In *1998 ACM International Conference on Functional Programming*, pages 301–312, Baltimore, September 1998. Extended version published as Cornell University technical report TR98-1721.

3. M.J. Fischer. Lambda calculus schemata. In *ACM Conference on Proving Assertions About Programs, SIGPLAN Notices 7(1)*, pages 104–109, 1972.

4. Jean-Yves Girard. Linear logic. *Theoretical Computer Science*, 50:1–102, 1987.

5. Robert Harper and Mark Lillibridge. Explicit polymorphism and CPS conversion. In *Twentieth ACM Symposium on Principles of Programming Languages*, pages 206–219, January 1993.

6. Robert Harper and Greg Morrisett. Compiling polymorphism using intensional type analysis. In *Twenty-Second ACM Symposium on Principles of Programming Languages*, pages 130–141, San Francisco, January 1995.

7. Robin Milner, Mads Tofte, Robert Harper, and David MacQueen. *The Definition of Standard ML (Revised)*. The MIT Press, Cambridge, Massachusetts, 1997.

8. Yasuhiko Minamide, Greg Morrisett, and Robert Harper. Typed closure conversion. In *Twenty-Third ACM Symposium on Principles of Programming Languages*, pages 271–283, St. Petersburg, Florida, January 1996.

9. John C. Mitchell and Gordon D. Plotkin. Abstract types have existential type. *ACM Transactions on Programming Languages and Systems*, 10(3):470–502, July 1988.

10. Greg Morrisett, Karl Crary, Neal Glew, Dan Grossman, Richard Samuels, Frederick Smith, David Walker, Stephanie Weirich, and Steve Zdancewic. TALx86: A realistic typed assembly language. In *Second Workshop on Compiler Support for System Software*, Atlanta, May 1999. To appear.

11. Greg Morrisett, Karl Crary, Neal Glew, and David Walker. Stack-based typed assembly language. In *Second Workshop on Types in Compilation*, volume 1473 of *Lecture Notes in Computer Science*. Springer-Verlag, March 1998. Extended version published as CMU technical report CMU-CS-98-178.

12. Greg Morrisett, Matthias Felleisen, and Robert Harper. Abstract models of memory management. In *Conference on Functional Programming Languages and Computer Architecture*, pages 66–77, La Jolla, California, June 1995.

13. Greg Morrisett and Robert Harper. Semantics of memory management for polymorphic languages. In A. D. Gordon and A. M. Pitts, editors, *Higher Order Operational Techniques in Semantics*. Cambridge University Press, 1997.

14. Greg Morrisett, David Walker, Karl Crary, and Neal Glew. From System F to typed assembly language. *ACM Transactions on Programming Languages and Systems*, 1999. To appear. An earlier version appeared in 1998 Symposium on Principles of Programming Languages.

15. John C. Reynolds. Definitional interpreters for higher-order programming languages. In *Conference Record of the 25th National ACM Conference*, pages 717–740, Boston, August 1972.

16. John C. Reynolds. Syntactic control of interference. In *Fifth ACM Symposium on Principles of Programming Languages*, pages 39–46, Tucson, Arizona, 1978.

17. Philip Wadler. Linear types can change the world! In *IFIP Working Conference on Programming Concepts and Methods*, Sea of Galilee, Israel, April 1990. North-Holland.

18. Philip Wadler. A taste of linear logic. In *Mathematical Foundations of Computer Science*, volume 711 of *Lecture Notes in Computer Science*. Springer-Verlag, 1993.

Real Computations with Fake Numbers

Felipe Cucker

Department of Mathematics, City University of Hong Kong
83 Tat Chee Avenue, Kowloon, HONG KONG
macucker@math.cityu.edu.hk

Abstract. During the last few years a theory of computation over the real numbers developed with the aim of laying theoretical foundations for the kind of computations performed in numerical analysis. In this paper we describe the notions playing major roles in this theory —with special emphasis on those which do not appear in discrete complexity theory— and review some of its results.

1   Please, give me one Turing machine and two PRAMs

Models of computation are not sold in hardware stores (or in any other store, for that matter). They are abstract devices designed to model computations in the real world and set a formal framework in which the power and limitations of computation can be rigorously proved. Real world computations, however, depend on too many parameters and the consideration of all of them would make the abstract model too cumbersome and therefore useless. For instance, when computing the gcd of two positive integers a number of features, besides the choice of the two particular integers taken as input, determine the speed of the computation: the computer at hand, the programming language of choice, its compiler's version, etc. However, all these features are somehow contingent and their consideration in the formal model would only complicate matters unnecessarily.

The key question is how does one select a set of features to be considered in the formal model. In this and the next section we shall try to motivate one such choice (with two main variants) for a model of computation over the real numbers.

Early computers in the 40's and 50's represented real numbers as either fixed point or floating point numbers. According to Knuth [13], fixed point arithmetic was favored originally since floating point was harder to implement with electronic tubes. Eventually, however, floating point arithmetic prevailed and is today synonymous with implementation of real number arithmetic.

A distinctive feature of all these machine implementations of real number arithmetic is that there is no notion of *varying size* of a real number and that, consequently, all real numbers are assumed to have *unit* size. This assumption somehow involves the fact that a real number is considered as an indivisible entity, much as it is in everyday mathematical thought. This contrasts with, for instance, the consideration of rational numbers in a Turing machine. A rational number in this context is not an entity in itself. Rather, a representative is required (4/5 not being the same as 280/350) and the representative is in turn not an entity in itself but it is encoded as a string of more elementary objects: bits.

Another consequence of the assumption that all numbers have unit size is that arithmetic operations between real numbers have a *fixed* (which we can set to unit) cost. Sometimes, one may consider multiplications and divisions as much more expensive than additions and subtractions and disregard the latter (by assigning them cost zero) but this does not turn out to be a crucial issue.

In a sense unit cost real arithmetic is so natural that it should come as no surprise that as early as 1948, unit cost was already considered as a complexity measure for real number computations.

> It is convenient to have a measure of the amount of work involved in a computing process, even though it be a very crude one. [...] In the case of computing with matrices most of the work consists of multiplications and writing down numbers, and we shall therefore only attempt to count the number of multiplications and recordings. For this purpose, a reciprocation will count as a multiplication. This is purely formal. A division will then count as two multiplications; this seems a little too much, and there may be other anomalies, but on the whole substantial justice should be done.

One may wonder whether in 1948, with the Turing machine firmly established as a formal model of computation, the consideration of unit cost arithmetic was a sensible choice. It is then perhaps reasuring to know that the quote above was written by Turing himself [32].

Turing's (and von Neumann's and Wilkinson's) consideration of a unit cost arithmetic for computing with real numbers did not lead to the definition of a formal model of computation. The design of algorithms within the numerical tradition, as we remarked in the preceding section, had been a well developed practice and there was little need of further elaboration on models for the analysis of particular algorithms. This is no longer true if one is interested in *lower* bounds. In this case, the bound should hold for *all* possible algorithms and proving such bounds requires a formal definition of algorithm.

An early instance of a lower bound problem was posed by Ostrowski who, in [15], conjectured the optimality of Horner's rule for evaluating univariate polynomials. This optimality was with respect to a certain formal model of computation —the arithmetic circuit— which used the unit cost arithmetic we discussed above. In [16] Pan proved Ostrowski's conjecture. The arithmetic circuit is a *non-uniform* model of computation which takes its inputs from some Euclidean space $\mathbb{R}^n$. So all inputs have a fixed size n. This, and other non-uniform models, have been the building blocks around which the study of lower bounds evolved into what is known today as *Algebraic Complexity Theory*, a subject whose maturity is apparent in the monograph [4].

But in order to build a complexity theory over the reals with similar achievements as those of discrete complexity theory one needs a uniform model of computation. A number of such models have been used in the last decades with definitions of varying degree of formality. To the best of our knowledge, the first steps towards a complexity theory over the reals as described above was given by Blum, Shub and Smale in [3]. The machine model introduced there —in the sequel the BSS machine— takes its inputs from $\mathbb{R}^\infty$, the disjoint union of $\mathbb{R}^n$ for $n \geq 1$, and returns as outputs elements in this space. During the computation it performs arithmetic operations and comparisons and has the ability to "move" information (i.e. real numbers) between different coordinates of its state space (roughly, its tape). This last feature, equivalent to the addressing instructions on a RAM, allows for some form of management. The *size* of a point $x \in \mathbb{R}^\infty$ is the unique $n \in \mathbb{N}$ such that $x \in \mathbb{R}^n$. Running time, which is defined as the number of operations, comparisons and movements, is then considered as a function of the input size.

2 Errare humanum est

But we are not alone in erring. Computers also err (at least when dealing with real numbers) and their errors are called *round-off errors*. Actually, digital computers do not really work with real numbers but with a finite set of numbers $\mathbb{F} \subset \mathbb{R}$ wich are called *floating point* numbers along with a function $r : \mathbb{R} \to \mathbb{F}$ which *rounds* each real number to a floating point number "close" to it.

The problem with round-off errors is that they accumulate during the computation yielding, in some cases, meaningless results. The desire of minimizing this accumulated error will affect the choice of an algorithm as much as the desire of minimizing its running time does.[1]

Again, the exact way the set $\mathbb{F}$ is selected and the function r operates varies with the programming language and the computer brand. And again, a few common features are selected to model the pair $(\mathbb{F}, r)$. Besides removing the assumption that $\mathbb{F}$ is finite (much as we assume the tape of a Turing machine to be infinite) the only property we require of $(\mathbb{F}, r)$ is the existence of a number $u \in \mathbb{R}$, $0 < u < 1$ such that, for all $x \in \mathbb{R}$, $x \neq 0$,

$$\left| \frac{x - r(x)}{x} \right| \leq u.$$

The number u is called the *unit round-off* or the *machine precision*.

---

[1] This was already noted by Gauss.

Since none of the numbers we take out from logarithmic or trigonometric tables admit of absolute precision, but are all to a certain extent approximate only, the results of all calculations performed by the aid of these numbers can only be approximately true. [...] It may happen, that in special cases the effect of the errors of the tables is so augmented that we may be oblidged to reject a method, otherwise the best, and substitute another in its place.

Carl Friedrich Gauss, *Theoria Motus* (cited in [10] p. 258).

It is easy to modify the BSS model to allow for round-off errors. One may even distinguish between `integer` and `float` data, the first being free of round-off errors (but having varying size and cost, as oposed to unit size and cost for the second). This has been done in [6].[2] We will call this model *round-off BSS*.

Round-off machines are obviously more realistic than exact BSS machines. There are two reasons, however, to consider a complexity theory build upon the exact BSS model. Let us briefly discuss them.

(1) The way we solve a computational problem over the reals passes normally through two different stages. Firstly, we design an algorithm which solves the problem. At this stage, we may evaluate its complexity and compare it with those of other algorithms solving the same problem. Secondly, we study how "stable" the algorithm is, i.e., rougly speaking, how much the accuracy of the final result is affected by round-off errors. At the end of this stage we may again compare our algorithm with others, and finally settle on one using a mix of complexity and stability reasons.

For the first stage of this two-stage procedure (which is implicit in Gauss' quotation above) the consideration of round-off errors is unnecessary. So, one may perfectly well use the exact BSS model. In this way, in addition, the machine models the way we *think* about the algorithm (and not only the way the computer performs it).

(2) Complexity theory deals mainly with lower bounds i.e., with the search for inherent limits to our capacity to solve a given problem. And a lower bound for the exact model should be considered as a lower bound for the round-off one. For instance, if we know that a certain problem can not be solved with less than $\Omega(n^3)$ operations in the exact model, then the consideration of round-off errors will not allow us to find an algorithm with complexity, say, $\mathcal{O}(n^2)$.

A possible analogy with a common idealization in discrete complexity theory is the consideration of models for parallel computation. Most of these models (uniform families of circuits, PRAMs, ...) are defined allowing an "all to all" connectivity between processors. This is certainly not possible in real life but makes the model simpler. It is upon these simpler models that the theory of classes such as NC is built. And this theory has provided us a deep insight into the realm of computations below polynomial time, both in the form of lower bounds and in the form of NC algorithms. The design of NC algorithms follows a two-stage process similar to the one above. In the first stage a problem, say in P, is shown to be in NC via a parallel algorithm in which intricacy of interconnection is, for the most part, ignored. In a later stage, interconnection topologies are considered. When comparing parallel algorithms, the topologies of interconnecting processors appearing in the different algorithms are taken into account to ultimately select an algorithm on a mixed basis of complexity

---

[2] The model of round-off described in this paper deals with absolute errors and therefore corresponds to fixed point rather than floating point. A version dealing with relative errors can be defined in a straightforward manner.

(running time and number of processors) and feasibility of interconnection. On the other hand, these topologies are rarely considered when proving lower bounds for parallel time, just as in (2) above.

In the next section we will review some results of complexity theory for the exact model. We will then discuss issues related with round-off.

3   Complexity

We remarked in Section 1 that the breakthrough towards a complexity theory over the reals was the publication of [3]. Probably the most important result in this paper is the existence of NP-complete problems over the reals (and other rings as well). The P = NP question had been at the core of research in discrete complexity theory and a specific goal of [3] was to extend this question to computations involving real numbers.

Recall that a set S is *decidable in polynomial time*, or in the class P, if there is a machine M deciding S whose running time is bounded, for all inputs of size n, by a polynomial function of n. Classically, S is a set of strings over a finite alphabet. Over the reals, the same definition can be made by considering S a set of elements in $\mathbb{R}^\infty$. In this case we write $P_\mathbb{R}$ instead of P. In the same manner, a function $\varphi : \mathbb{R}^\infty \to \mathbb{R}^\infty$ is *computable in polynomial time* if there is a machine M computing $\varphi(x)$, for each input $x \in \mathbb{R}^\infty$, in time bounded by a polynomial in size(x).

The definition of the class NP over $\mathbb{R}$ is a bit more elaborate and can be done in several ways. Here we modify the machine model and endow it with the ability to guess points $y \in \mathbb{R}^\infty$ (with cost n if $y \in \mathbb{R}^n$). We call such extended machine *nondeterministic*.

A set S (of elements in $\mathbb{R}^\infty$) is in $NP_\mathbb{R}$ if there exists a nondeterministic machine M satisfying the following:

1. For all $x \in \mathbb{R}^\infty$ the running time of M with input x is bounded by a polynomial in size(x).
2. For all $x \in \mathbb{R}^\infty$, $x \in S$ if and only if there exists a guess $y \in \mathbb{R}^\infty$ such that the computation of M with input x and guess y ends in an accepting state (or, equivalently, returns 1).

Example 1. Fix $d \geq 1$ and let f be a polynomial of degree d in n variables. We can encode f by its list of coefficients, which contains $\mathcal{O}(n^d)$ elements. Consider the set d-FEAS of those polynomials f having a real zero (FEAS for "feasibility"). The set d-FEAS is in $NP_\mathbb{R}$.

To prove this, consider the algorithm which, with input f, checks that f encodes a polynomial of degree d in n variables and, if so, guesses $y \in \mathbb{R}^n$ and accepts if $f(y) = 0$. All this can be performed in time polynomial in n and therefore polynomial in size(f) = $\mathcal{O}(n^d)$.

Example 2. As above, fix $d \geq 1$ and let $f_1, \ldots, f_m, g_1, \ldots, g_p, h_1, \ldots, h_q$ be polynomials of degree d in n variables. Let d-SAS be the set of those collections which are satisfiable in the sense that there exists $x \in \mathbb{R}^n$ such that

$$\begin{aligned}
f_i(x) &= 0 \text{ for } i = 1, \ldots, m \\
g_j(x) &\geq 0 \text{ for } j = 1, \ldots, p \\
h_k(x) &> 0 \text{ for } k = 1, \ldots, q
\end{aligned}$$

(SAS for semi-algebraic satisfiability). Again, for all $d \geq 1$, d-SAS is in $\text{NP}_\mathbb{R}$.

In the same way, define SAS to be the same problem without the restriction on the degree, i.e. letting d vary. The problem SAS also belong to $\text{NP}_\mathbb{R}$.

The systems $\psi = (f, g, h)$ as in Example 2 are called *semi-algebraic systems* and their sets of solutions *semi-algebraic sets*. The design of algorithms to solve geometric problems related to semi-algebraic sets is important in a number of disciplines, from robotics to computer graphics and from data-base searching to economic theory. The satisfiability problem of Example 2 is an instance of these problems. We will meet some more later in this paper.

Immediate questions raised by the definition of the class $\text{NP}_\mathbb{R}$ are the existence of complete problems as well as finding deterministic upper bounds for problems in the class. Regarding the first question recall that a function $\varphi : \mathbb{R}^\infty \to \mathbb{R}^\infty$ is said to be a *polynomial time reduction* from A to B $(A, B \subseteq \mathbb{R}^\infty)$ if ψ is computable in polynomial time and, for all $x \in \mathbb{R}^\infty$, $x \in A$ if and only if $\varphi(x) \in B$. A set $S \in \text{NP}_\mathbb{R}$ is $\text{NP}_\mathbb{R}$-*complete* if for every set $T \in \text{NP}_\mathbb{R}$ there exists a polynomial time reduction from T to S.

Theorem 1 ([3]). *The set SAS and the sets d-SAS, for all $d \geq 2$, are $\text{NP}_\mathbb{R}$-complete. For all $d \geq 4$ the set d-FEAS is $\text{NP}_\mathbb{R}$-complete.*

It is interesting to note that for $d = 1, 2, 3$ the sets d-FEAS are in $\text{P}_\mathbb{R}$ (cf. [31]). The set 1-SAS, however, is not known to be in $\text{P}_\mathbb{R}$. Actually, this problem is essentially linear programming over the reals. And real linear programming is known to be in $\text{NP}_\mathbb{R}$ but is not known to be in $\text{P}_\mathbb{R}$ or to be $\text{NP}_\mathbb{R}$-complete. This contrasts with integer programming which is NP-complete (in the Turing model) and with rational linear programming which is known to be in P (also in the Turing model). Notice how the choice of ground ring affects the complexity of linear programming.

While there are several examples of problems in $\text{NP}_\mathbb{R}$, there are relatively few known examples of $\text{NP}_\mathbb{R}$-complete sets. Besides the two mentioned in Theorem 1 the following is worth noting.

Theorem 2 ([14]). *The problem of deciding, given as input a semi-algebraic system system ψ and a positive integer D, whether the semi-algebraic set of points satisfying ψ has dimension at least D is $\text{NP}_\mathbb{R}$-complete.*

Concerning the second question above, i.e., finding deterministic upper bounds for problems in the class $\text{NP}_\mathbb{R}$, a series of papers (e.g. [11, 17, 1]) locate $\text{NP}_\mathbb{R}$ just as in the classical case.

Theorem 3. *One has*

$$NP_{\mathbb{R}} \subseteq PAR_{\mathbb{R}} \subset EXP_{\mathbb{R}}.$$

Here $PAR_{\mathbb{R}}$ denotes the class of sets decidable in parallel polynomial time and $EXP_{\mathbb{R}}$ the class of those decidable in exponential time.

Unlike the classical case, however, it can be proved that the second inclusion in the theorem above is strict (cf. [5]).

The publication of [3] was followed by a flow of papers building different aspects of a complexity theory over the reals. An account of much of this work is presented in [2]. Later in this paper we will review some of these results. Meanwhile we turn our attention to round-off issues.

4 Conditioning and Perturbation

A first approach to dealing with round-off errors considers the simple case in which errors only occur while reading the input and the computation is otherwise exact. This amounts to study, for the computed function φ and a point x in its domain, how sensitive φ is to small perturbations of x. In the picture below, how much large is $\varphi(x + \Delta x) - \varphi(x)$ compared to Δx.

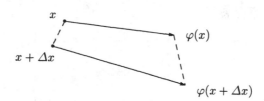

There are a number of reasons to begin considering this specific simplification.

1. We can delay algorithmic considerations regarding the computation of φ since we are assuming that all algorithms compute φ exactly. The problem of measuring the sensitivity of φ to small perturbations of x depends on φ and x only, and is thus purely mathematical.
2. In some cases, we can take advantage of an existing body of knowledge (known as perturbation theory) which grew independently of round-off analysis.
3. Perturbation happens in practice (e.g., while doing exact computations over $\mathbb{Q}$ with input data obtained by measuring (and rounding) some physical quantities).
4. As we shall see, a main character of our play first appears in this perturbation analysis.
5. Eventually, the round-off analysis of an important class of algorithms translates more general round-off errors into perturbation (we will return to this in the next section).

To gently introduce concepts, let us consider a classical example. Let A be an invertible $n \times n$ real matrix and $b \in \mathbb{R}^n$. We are interested in solving the system

$$Ax = b$$

and want to study how the solution x is affected by perturbations in the vector b. Let Δb be such that the perturbed vector is $b + \Delta b$ and Δx such that

$$A(x + \Delta x) = (b + \Delta b).$$

Then, the relative errors for b and x satisfy the relation

$$\frac{\|\Delta x\|}{\|x\|} \leq \kappa(A) \frac{\|\Delta b\|}{\|b\|} \tag{1}$$

where $\| \ \|$ denotes the Euclidean norm,

$$\kappa(A) = \|A\| \|A^{-1}\|$$

and $\|A\|$ denotes the operator norm of A defined by

$$\|A\| = \max_{x \text{ s.t. } \|x\|=1} \|A(x)\|.$$

Here is the argument

$$\frac{\|\Delta x\|}{\|x\|} = \frac{\|\Delta x\|}{\|b\|} \frac{\|b\|}{\|x\|} = \frac{\|(A^{-1}\Delta b)\|}{\|b\|} \frac{\|Ax\|}{\|x\|} \leq \|A\| \|A^{-1}\| \frac{\|\Delta b\|}{\|b\|} = \kappa(A) \frac{\|\Delta b\|}{\|b\|}.$$

Moreover, it is easily seen that there are vectors b and Δb such that

$$\frac{\|\Delta x\|}{\|x\|} = \kappa(A) \frac{\|\Delta b\|}{\|b\|}$$

where $x = A^{-1}b$ and $\Delta x = A^{-1}(b + \Delta b) - x$. So $\kappa(A)$ is a sharp worst-case estimate of the relative error in x as a function of the relative error in b.[3]

If we allow errors in both A and b it is possible to prove that

$$\frac{\|\Delta x\|}{\|x\|} \leq \frac{\kappa(A)}{1 - \kappa(A)\frac{\|\Delta A\|}{\|A\|}} \left(\frac{\|\Delta A\|}{\|A\|} + \frac{\|\Delta b\|}{\|b\|} \right).$$

Notice that the factor $\frac{\kappa(A)}{1-\kappa(A)\frac{\|\Delta A\|}{\|A\|}}$ is close to $\kappa(A)$ when $\|\Delta A\|$ is small enough. Also, we remark that this bound is no longer sharp in the sense above but it is optimal in the sense that it becomes sharp for infinitesimal perturbations.

We see that the number $\kappa(A)$ measures exactly what we are interested in, the sensitivity of the problem to small perturbations or, in other words, how well conditioned the input is with respect to the problem. This idea of *conditioning* is already present in the paper of Turing quoted in Section 1, which we quote again.

---

[3] Taking the base 2 log of equation 1 we see that if b has m bits of relative accuracy, then x has $m - \log \kappa(A)$ bits of accuracy. Therefore $\log \kappa(A)$ measures the loss of precision of the computation.

We should describe the equations (8.2) as an *ill-conditioned* set, or, at any rate, as ill-conditioned when compared with (8.1). It is characteristic of ill-conditioned sets of equations that small percentage errors in the coefficients given may lead to large percentage errors in the solution.

In this same paper Turing introduced the name *condition number* for $\kappa(A)$.

When A is not invertible its condition number is not well defined. However, we can extend its definition by setting $\kappa(A) = \infty$ if A is singular. Matrices A with $\kappa(A)$ small are said to be *well-conditioned*, those with $\kappa(A)$ large are said to be *ill-conditioned*, and those with $\kappa(A) = \infty$ *ill-posed*.

Note that the set Σ of ill-posed problems has measure zero in the space $\mathbb{R}^{n^2}$. The distance of a matrix A to this set is closely related to $\kappa(A)$.

Theorem 4 (Condition Number Theorem, [9]). *For any $n \times n$ real matrix A one has*

$$d_F(A, \Sigma) = \frac{\|A\|}{\kappa(A)}.$$

Here d_F means distance in $\mathbb{R}^{n^2}$ with respect to the Frobenius norm, $\|A\|_F = \sqrt{\sum a_{ij}^2}$.

The factor $\|A\|$ in the theorem above appears to scale as $d_F(A, \Sigma)$. This makes sense since by definition $\kappa(A)$ is homogeneous of degree 0.

We have by now a reasonably clear picture of conditioning for a specific problem (linear equation solving). How can this be extended to other problems? Let $\varphi : \mathbb{R}^n \to \mathbb{R}^m$ be the restriction to $\mathbb{R}^n$ of the function we are computing. For $x \in \mathbb{R}^n$ the *relative condition number* $\mu(x)$ is defined by

$$\mu(x) = \lim_{\delta \to 0} \sup_{\|\Delta x\| \le \delta} \left(\frac{\|\varphi(x + \Delta x) - \varphi(x)\|}{\|\varphi(x)\|} \cdot \frac{\|x\|}{\|\Delta x\|} \right). \tag{2}$$

If φ is differentiable we can express $\mu(x)$ in terms of the Jacobian $J(x)$ of φ at x,[4]

$$\mu(x) = \frac{\|J(x)\|}{\|\varphi(x)\|/\|x\|}.$$

While this definition is very useful in many problems (e.g. polynomial evaluation, matrix multiplication, computation of determinants) it does not fit problems in which, for instance, φ is not a well-defined function or has a finite set of values. An example of the first case is to compute a *single* solution of a system of non-linear equations. Since the system may have several solutions and we do not require any one in particular, φ is not a well-defined function. An example of the second case is any decision problem.

A possible solution for multiple-defined φ is to consider the condition number $\mu(x, y)$ for a pair (x, y) with $x \in \mathbb{R}^n$ and $y \in \mathbb{R}^m$ being one of the possible values

---

[4] A similar definition can be done for the *absolute condition number* μ_{abs}. In the differentiable case it yields $\mu_{\text{abs}}(x) = \|J(x)\|$.

of $\varphi(x)$. Then, one may define the condition number $\mu(x)$ in terms of the worst conditioned solution y, i.e.,

$$\mu(x) = \max_{y \in S(x)} \mu(x, y)$$

where $S(x)$ denotes the set of possible values for $\varphi(x)$. An example is root finding for complex systems of polynomials. This problem, which we will see as a computational version of Bézout's Theorem, was dealt with in the series of papers [21–23, 25, 24].

Let $d = (d_1, \ldots, d_n) \in \mathbb{N}^n$ and $\mathcal{H}_{(d)}$ denote the set of polynomial systems $f = (f_1, \ldots, f_n)$ where f_i is a complex homogeneous polynomial of degree d_i in $x_0, \ldots, x_n$ (as well as the system $(0, 0, \ldots, 0)$). Under addition of n-tuples, $\mathcal{H}_{(d)}$ can be regarded as a vector space, so let $\mathbb{P}(\mathcal{H}_{(d)})$ be the complex projective space associated to $\mathcal{H}_{(d)}$. The problem at hand is: given $f \in \mathbb{P}(\mathcal{H}_{(d)})$, find $\xi \in \mathbb{P}(\mathbb{C}^{n+1})$ such that $f(\xi) = 0$. For each sytem f and each root $\xi \in \mathbb{P}(\mathbb{C}^{n+1})$ one may consider the condition number $\mu(f, \xi)$ for the pair $(f, \xi) \in \mathbb{P}(\mathcal{H}_{(d)}) \times \mathbb{P}(\mathbb{C}^{n+1})$ defined as in (2).[5] In [21] Shub and Smale gave a closed form for $\mu(f, \xi)$ from which a characterization of Σ', the set of ill-posed pairs (f, ξ) follows. More precisely,

$$\Sigma' = \{(f, \xi) \mid f(\xi) = 0 \text{ and } \ker(Df(\xi)) \neq 0\},$$

i.e., Σ' is the set of pairs (f, ξ) such that ξ is a degenerate zero of f. Shub and Smale then proved a Condition Number Theorem as follows. Let

$$V_\xi = \{f \in \mathbb{P}(\mathcal{H}_{(d)}) \mid f(\xi) = 0\}$$

and $d_\xi((f, \xi), \Sigma')$ denote the distance in $V_\xi \times \{\xi\}$ from (f, ξ) to Σ'. Then

$$\mu(f, \xi) = \frac{1}{d_\xi((f, \xi), \Sigma')}.$$

To obtain a condition number for f only, Shub and Smale define

$$\mu(f) = \max_{\xi \mid f(\xi) = 0} \mu(f, \xi).$$

The condition number of a polynomial system is that of its worst conditioned zero. The set Σ of ill-posed systems is then the set of all systems having a degenerate zero. Defining

$$\rho(f) = \min_{\xi \mid f(\xi) = 0} d_\xi((f, \xi), \Sigma')$$

one gets $\mu(f) = \rho(f)^{-1}$. This is not a Condition Number Theorem for $\mu(f)$ since $\rho(f)$ is not the distance from f to Σ but it is akin to one. A simplified account

---

[5] Projective spaces are the natural setting for Bézout's Theorem. Their consideration in Shub and Smale's series of papers gave to the latter a great conceptual coherence. It introduced however some technical difficulties. For instance, projective spaces are no longer vector spaces and thus, the norm in equation (2) needs to be replaced by a Riemannian distance. These technical difficulties are not relevant for our exposition.

of this is presented in Chapter 12 of [2]. In closing this example, note that some ideas behind $\mu(f)$ go back to the work of Wilkinson [34] and Woźniakowski [36].

A completely different problem arises when considering conditioning for decision problems. Let $S \subseteq \mathbb{R}^\infty$ be a decision problem and let $S_n \subseteq \mathbb{R}^n$ be its subset of points with size n. Restricted to $\mathbb{R}^n$ the function φ we are computing is the characteristic function of S_n,

$$\varphi(x) = \begin{cases} 1 \text{ if } x \in S_n \\ 0 \text{ if } x \notin S_n \end{cases}$$

Let Σ_n be the boundary of S_n. We can naturally think of Σ_n as the set of ill-posed inputs (of size n). For, given a point $x \in \Sigma_n$, there are points $y \in \mathbb{R}^n$ arbitrarily close to x such that $|\varphi(x) - \varphi(y)| = 1$. Thus, the relative error in the output is infinitely larger than the relative error in the input and the condition number of $x \in \Sigma_n$ is ∞. But for points outside Σ_n the definition of conditioning is less clear. If $x \notin \Sigma_n$, for points y sufficiently close to x we have $\varphi(x) = \varphi(y)$ and therefore, $\mu(x) = 0$. One may say that all points outside Σ_n are well-conditioned but this is not satisfying.

We will return to decision problems in Section 6.

5 Conditioning and Round-off

We proceed now to the case of arbitrary round-off errors. So, consider a round-off machine M and denote by $\tilde{\varphi}$ and φ the functions computed by M with and without round-off errors respectively. We want to evaluate, for an input $x \in \mathbb{R}^\infty$, a bound for the *forward-error* $\|\varphi(x) - \tilde{\varphi}(x)\|$, or for the *relative forward-error*

$$\frac{\|\varphi(x) - \tilde{\varphi}(x)\|}{\|\varphi(x)\|}.$$

A clever idea, which is already implicit in [33, 32] and was strongly advocated by Wilkinson (cf. his 1970 SIAM's John von Neumann Lecture [35]), is what is known today as *backward-error analysis*. Roughly, it consist on looking for a Δx such that $\varphi(x + \Delta x) = \tilde{\varphi}(x)$. That is, we look for a perturbed input $x + \Delta x$ whose image under φ coincides with the outcome of the round-off computation with input x.

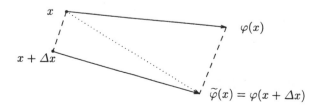

The smallest Δx (in norm) is called the *backward-error* (the *relative backward-error* is obtained dividing by $\|x\|$).

Notice that both backward and forward errors depend, not only on φ and the input x, but also on the algorithm at hand and the unit round-off u defined in Section 2.

If we are able to estimate a bound for the backward-error and we know the condition number $\mu(x)$ of x we can bound the forward-error as well. This is because the relative forward-error is approximately bounded by the relative backward-error times the condition of the input, i.e.,

$$\frac{\|\varphi(x) - \tilde{\varphi}(x)\|}{\|\varphi(x)\|} \lesssim \mu(x)\frac{\|\Delta x\|}{\|x\|}$$

The "approximately" can be explained by the use of infinitesimals in the definition of $\mu(x)$ and is harmless if the unit round-off u is small enough. The relation above is a bona fide inequality for the problems of linear algebra we saw in the preceding section and the condition number $\kappa(A)$.

We can actually use $\kappa(A)$ and linear algebra to give a first example of bakward-error analysis. A classical way to solve the system $Ax = b$ is to use Gaussian elimination (with partial pivoting) to compute an LU factorization of A (cf. [12]), $A = LU$, and then solve $LUx = b$ taking advantage of the special structure of L (a unit lower triangular matrix) and U (an upper triangular matrix). A backward-error analysis of this method yields the bound (cf. [12] Theorem 9.4[6])

$$(A + \Delta A)\tilde{x} = b, \qquad \|\Delta A\| \leq n^3 \frac{3nu}{1 - 3nu}\rho_n\|A\| \tag{3}$$

where ρ_n, the growth factor, is defined by

$$\rho_n = \frac{\|U\|_{\max}}{\|A\|_{\max}}.$$

Here, $\|A\|_{\max} = \max|a_{ij}|$. If u is small compared with $3n$ we have $\|\Delta A\| \leq 3n^4 u\rho_n\|A\|$.

Therefore, the relative forward-error satisfies the bound

$$\frac{\|x - \tilde{x}\|}{\|x\|} \leq 3n^4 u\rho_n \frac{\kappa(A)}{1 - \kappa(A)\frac{\|\Delta A\|}{\|A\|}} \leq 3n^4 u\rho_n \frac{\kappa(A)}{1 - \kappa(A)3n^4 u\rho_n}.$$

In addition, if u is sufficiently small, our preceding bound for the relative error in x reduces to

$$\frac{\|x - \tilde{x}\|}{\|x\|} \leq 3n^4 u\rho_n\kappa(A).$$

---

[6] Actually, the backward error-analysis in this reference is stated in terms of the infinity norm. The bound we state here, slightly weaker, is an immediate consequence of that in [12].

The growth factor ρ_n is bounded by 2^{n-1} for all matrices A but appears to be much smaller in practice and can be proved to be so for some classes of structured matrices (e.g., upper Hessenberg matrices have $\rho_n \leq n$).

There are problems and algorithms for which it is not possible to do a backward-error analysis. A simple example is polynomial evaluation. For some polynomial functions f and some evaluation algorithms, if x is a global minimum of f, we may not be able to find the Δx above. The reason is that if $\widetilde{f}(x) < f(x)$ there is no Δx such that $f(x + \Delta x) < f(x)$. For these kind of problems, bounds for the forward-error need to be found by direct methods.

What can be a desirable result for a backward-error analysis of a given algorithm? A good one is certainly $\frac{\|\Delta x\|}{\|x\|} = \mathcal{O}(u)$. We can not expect a relative error smaller than u since this error may be produced merely by reading the input. For many algorithms we do not achieve such a nice bound but the backward-error is nevertheless small. An algorithm with a small backward-error is said to be *backward-stable*. Of course, the meaning of "small" is context dependent.

Remark 1. It is possible to give formal definitions of backward-stability (one such definition is given in [7]). One may, for instance, say that an algorithm is polynomialy backward-stable if the backward-error is polynomial in u and $\text{size}(x)$ for every input x. However, this is not the tradition in numerical analysis. The word "stable" is not used like the word "tractable" in complexity theory (which is synonymous with polynomial time) but rather like the word "fast". An algorithm with a complexity $\mathcal{O}(n^{100})$ is said to be tractable but is certainly not fast. The exact threshold for a polynomial time algorithm to be considered fast is not a fixed exponent and depends on the problem at hand.

Remark 2. The exponential dependence on n in the worst-case error analysis for Gaussian elimination makes this algorithm, according to our definitions, unstable. Even for matrices with $\rho_n = 1$, the n^4 factor may imply a loss of all the precision for modestly sized matrices. Why then is Gaussian elimination so popular in practice? Because, in practice, Gaussian elimination is stable, and faster than other methods which are worst-case stable. This suggests an *average-case* error analysis as oposed to the worst-case analysis of the bound (3). A first step toward such analysis is [30].

An algorithm is *forward-stable* if it produces forward-errors similar in magnitude to those produced by a backward-stable algorithm. As we already remarked, for some algorithms this is the best we can get.

6 Conditioning and Decision Problems

We saw in Section 4 that, for a decision problem S, a direct application of equation (2) yields a condition number which is ∞ on the boundary of S and 0 elsewhere. In some sense this is not satisfying. For instance, it is hard to see how such a condition number may be helpful in round-off analysis (even if by now we have not specified which form this analysis will take). One wants a condition number which varies continuously and, if possible, for which some form of Condition Number Theorem holds.

One possible solution is to use the Condition Number Theorem itself to define more general condition numbers. Thus, one may define, for $x \in \mathbb{R}^n$,

$$\mu(x) = \frac{\|x\|}{d(x, \Sigma_n)}.$$

This has been done, for instance, by Renegar in [18–20] for linear programming. A standard feasibility form of this problem requires one to decide whether there exists an $x \in \mathbb{R}^n$ satisfying

$$Ax = b$$
$$x \geq 0.$$

Here A is an $m \times n$ real matrix and $b \in \mathbb{R}^m$.

Let $\mathcal{F}_{m,n}$ denote the set of feasible pairs (A, b) (i.e. those for which a solution x exists) and let $\Sigma_{m,n}$ be its boundary. Renegar defined

$$C(A, b) = \frac{\|(A, b)\|}{d((A, b), \Sigma_{m,n})}.$$

He then used this condition number to obtain several complexity results (we will mention some of them in Example 6 in the next section).

Another solution is possible in the case that the decision problem has a natural functional problem associated to it. As an example, consider the problem SAS of Example 2. A "functional" problem associated to it is, given input ψ, compute a point $x \in \mathbb{R}^n$ satisfying ψ. The quotes above are due to the fact that if φ denotes this function, φ may have multiple values (even infinitely many) in some cases and no value at all in some others (for infeasible systems ψ). As in the case of complex polynomial systems we discussed in Section 4 we may define a condition number $\mu^*(\psi, x)$ for the pair (ψ, x) with x satisfying ψ. In [6] a condition number $\mu^*(\psi)$ is defined by then taking the minimum of $\mu^*(\psi, x)$ over the set of x satisfying ψ. If ψ is infeasible, $\mu^*(\psi)$ is defined differently. The resulting $\mu^*(\psi)$ varies continuously with ψ. One may see $\mu^*(\psi)$ as a far reaching generalization of $\kappa(A)$ which extends the ideas we mentioned in Section 4 concerning condition numbers for non-linear problems.

Which kind of round-off analysis can we do with these condition numbers? A model result would state that, for a certain algorithm deciding a set $S \subset \mathbb{R}^\infty$, if the unit round-off u satisfies some bound in terms of $\mu(x)$ and $\text{size}(x)$

$$u \leq \text{Expression}(\mu(x), \text{size}(x))$$

for all inputs $x \in \mathbb{R}^\infty$ then the algorithm output is correct. We will give an instance of this kind of result in Example 7 in the next section.

7 Conditioning and Complexity

Although its enormous importance in numerical analysis, linear equation solving is not the paradigm of numerical computation. The reason is that it is a problem admitting exact solutions. The majority of the problems in numerical analysis can not be solved exactly. An approximation, up to some predetermined ε, is sought instead and the algorithm proceeds by iterating some basic step until this approximation is reached. This kind of algorithms, called *iterative*, is ubiquitous in numerical analysis. Its complexity, in contrast with the so called *direct* methods whose complexity depends only on the input size, may depend on ε and on the input itself.

The above applies for exact machines as well as for round-off machines. An interesting point is that more often than not the complexity of iterative algorithms appears to depend on the condition of the input, no matter whether the machine is exact or not. To illustrate this, we now briefly review some examples. Unless otherwise stated, all machines are exact.

Example 3. Even for linear equation solving one may consider the use of iterative methods. One such method is the conjugate gradient (cf. [8, 29]). It begins with a candidate solution $x_0 \in \mathbb{R}^n$ of the system $Ax = b$, A a real symmetric positive definite matrix. Then, it constructs a sequence of iterates $x_0, x_1, x_2, \ldots$ converging to the solution x^* of the system and satisfying

$$\|x_j - x^*\|_A \leq 2 \left(\frac{\sqrt{\kappa(A)} - 1}{\sqrt{\kappa(A)} + 1} \right)^j \|x_0 - x^*\|_A.$$

Here the A-norm $\|v\|_A$ of a vector v is defined as $\|v\|_A = (v^T A v)^{1/2}$. One concludes that for

$$j = \mathcal{O}\left(\sqrt{\kappa(A)} \log \frac{1}{\varepsilon} \right)$$

one has $\|x_j - x^*\|_A \leq \varepsilon \|x_0 - x^*\|_A$. Notice the dependence of the number of iterations on both $\kappa(A)$ and ε.

Example 4. The Fundamental Theorem of Algebra. A common computational form of this theorem consists of, given $\varepsilon > 0$ and a polynomial

$$f = x^d + a_1 x^{d-1} + \ldots + a_d$$

with $a_i \in \mathbb{C}$, find $z \in \mathbb{C}$ such that $|f(z)| \leq \varepsilon$. In [2] an algorithm (whose basic idea goes back to [26]) is described doing so with running time

$$\mathcal{O}\left(d^2 \left(d + \ln \frac{1}{\varepsilon} + d \ln b \right) \right)$$

where $b = \max(|a_i|^{1/i}, 1)$.

This algorithm proceeds by selecting a point $z_0 \in \mathbb{C}$ and then constructing a sequence of iterates $z_0, z_1, z_2, \ldots, z_k$. The element z_k satisfies the desired condition $|f(z_k)| \leq \varepsilon$ provided

$$k \geq 26\mu(f, z_0) \left(\log \frac{|f(z_0)|}{\varepsilon} + 1 \right)$$

where $\mu(f, z_0)$ is a certain quantity akin to a condition number. An analysis of $\mu(f, z_0)$ shows, in addition, that if one takes $4d$ points z uniformly distributed in the circumference of radius R (for a R well-defined in terms of f), one of them has small $\mu(f, z)$. The algorithm then considers the k corresponding to this well-conditioned point z and repeats k iterates for all the $4d$ initial points until for one of them the corresponding z_k is the desired approximate zero. This leads to the complexity bound above, independent of z_0.

Example 5. Bézout's Theorem. Let us consider again the problem of, given $f \in \mathbb{P}(\mathcal{H}_{(d)})$, find $\xi \in \mathbb{C}^{n+1}$, $\xi \neq 0$, such that $f(\xi) = 0$.

Consider an initial pair (f_0, ξ_0) with $f_0 \in \mathbb{P}(\mathcal{H}_{(d)})$ and $\xi_0 \in \mathbb{P}(\mathbb{C}^{n+1})$ satisfying $f_0(\xi_0) = 0$. Define, for $t \in [0, 1]$, the function $f_t = tf + (1 - t)f_0$. In general, when t varies from 0 to 1, the pair (f_0, ξ_0) varies continuosly yielding a curve $\mathcal{C}$ of pairs (f_t, ξ_t) with $f_t(\xi_t) = 0$ in the product space $\mathbb{P}(\mathcal{H}_{(d)}) \times \mathbb{P}(\mathbb{C}^{n+1})$. Since $f_1 = f$, ξ_1 is the point we are looking for. The homotopy algorithm in [21] produces a sequence of pairs (f^i, ξ^i) which "follows" this curve and whose endpoint (f^k, ξ^k) is a good approximation of (f, ξ) (in the sense that Newton's method for f with initial point ξ^k converges quadratically to ξ from the first iteration) provided

$$k = \mathcal{O}(D^2 \mu(\mathcal{C})^2 L_f).$$

Here $D = \max\{d_1, \ldots, d_n\}$, L_f is the length of the curve $\{f_t \mid 0 \leq t \leq 1\}$ in $\mathbb{P}(\mathcal{H}_{(d)})$ and $\mu(\mathcal{C})$ is a condition number for $\mathcal{C}$ (thus depending on f, f_0 and ξ_0) defined by

$$\mu(\mathcal{C}) = \max_{t \in [0,1]} \mu(f_t, \xi_t).$$

In some sense $\mu(\mathcal{C})$ is measuring how close is $\mathcal{C}$ to the set Σ' (and thus introducing the scent of a Condition Number Theorem).

We remark here that the choice of a good initial pair (f_0, ξ_0) is an open problem. The last paper of the Bézout series, [24], provides the state of the art for this issue under the form of a non-uniform, average polynomial time algorithm.

Example 6. Consider the following linear programming problem. Given the pair (A, b) with A an $m \times n$ real matrix and $b \in \mathbb{R}^m$ find $x \in \mathbb{R}^n$ satisfying

$$Ax = b$$
$$x \geq 0$$

or prove that no such x exists.

The simplex method, despite its good performance in practice may require exponential time for some inputs. The ellipsoid and interior point methods, in contrast, iteratively approximate a desired solution. When the input's coordinates are rational numbers one can "jump" to an exact solution of the problem after k iterations for a k which is bounded by a polynomial in n, m and L, the largest bit-size of the input's coordinates.

Renegar used the condition number $C(A, b)$ defined in Section 6 to bound, for an interior-point method, the number of iterations necessary to ε-approximate a solution of the problem (in the feasible case). Actually, this number of iterations is polynomially bounded in $n, m, \log C(A, b)$ and $|\log \varepsilon|$.

Example 7. The last example we review in this section is the problem SAS of Example 2.

We saw in Section 3 that SAS is $NP_{\mathbb{R}}$-complete. Moreover, we mentioned the existence of algorithms solving SAS in exponential time. These are direct algorithms; their complexities are functions of the size of the input ψ only. In contrast, their behavior under round-off errors seems to be very poor. A simple reason of this is that these algorithms need eventually to do linear algebra with matrices of size exponentialy large in size(ψ).

In [6] we described another algorithm to solve SAS which has a much better behavior with respect to round-off since it avoids large matrices and works instead with a large number of small matrices which can be dealt with independently. The algorithm is iterative and its complexity is bounded by

$$(\mathcal{O}(\mu^*(\psi)^2 d^3 (n + p + q)))^n.$$

Here, we recall, $\psi = (f, g, h)$, d is a bound for the degrees of the polynomials in ψ, p is the number of gs and q the number of hs. In addition $\mu^*(\psi)$ is a condition number for ψ (which we already mentioned in Section 6). Note that M may not halt on inputs ψ such that $\mu^*(\psi) = \infty$.

About half of [6] is devoted to a round-off analysis of the algorithm. This has been done with an absolute error machine model instead of the relative error model we described in Section 2 (but an analysis for a relative error machine model can be derived easily). Let

$$\delta = \frac{1}{(\mu(\psi)\text{size}(\psi))^{c_1(m+p+q)^2} 2^{c_2(m+p+q)^3}}$$

with c_1, c_2 universal constants and m the number of fs. In [6] we proved that if all the round-off errors are smaller in absolute value than δ, then the machine M answers correctly. Notice that this implies a bound for the necessary number of correct digits after the decimal point which is polynomial in size(ψ) and in $\log \mu^*(\psi)$.

The above examples suggest, maybe too briefly, how conditioning may affect the complexity of iterative algorithms in numerical analysis. A paper which elaborates more on this is [28].

We close this section with a remark on conditioning and reductions. Complete problems in a complexity class capture the complexity of the class in a precise sense. An algorithm for a complete problem (with respect to polynomial time reductions) implies an algorithm with the same complexity (modulo a polynomial slow-down) for any problem in the class. This does not carry over with regard to round-off. And the reason is that reductions do not necessarily respect conditioning.

As an example, when reducing SAS to 4-FEAS one first reduces ψ to a system of equations, then to a system of quadratic equations $q_1, \ldots, q_s$ and finally to a single polynomial of degree 4 namely, $f = q_1^2 + \cdots + q_s^2$. If the original ψ is feasible, so is f. However, there exist arbitrarily small perturbations of f, e.g. those of the form $f + \varepsilon$ with $\varepsilon > 0$, which are infeasible. This means that well-conditioned systems are mapped to ill-posed polynomials. We conclude that, while finding an exponential (resp. polynomial) time algorithm for 4-FEAS is enough to prove that any problem in $NP_{\mathbb{R}}$ has exponential (resp. polynomial) time algorithms, finding a stable algorithm for 4-FEAS will not necessarily yield stable algorithms for SAS.

References

1. S. Basu, R. Pollack, and M.-F. Roy. On the combinatorial and algebraic complexity of quantifier elimination. *Journal of the ACM*, 43:1002–1045, 1996.
2. L. Blum, F. Cucker, M. Shub, and S. Smale. *Complexity and Real Computation*. Springer-Verlag, 1998.
3. L. Blum, M. Shub, and S. Smale. On a theory of computation and complexity over the real numbers: NP-completeness, recursive functions and universal machines. *Bulletin of the Amer. Math. Soc.*, 21:1–46, 1989.
4. P. Bürgisser, M. Clausen, and A. Shokrollahi. *Algebraic Complexity Theory*. Springer-Verlag, 1996.
5. F. Cucker. $P_{\mathbb{R}} \neq NC_{\mathbb{R}}$. *Journal of Complexity*, 8:230–238, 1992.
6. F. Cucker and S. Smale. Complexity estimates depending on condition and round-off error. To appear in *Journal of the ACM*, 1997.
7. L.S. de Jong. Towards a formal definition of numerical stability. *Numer. Math.*, 28:211–219, 1977.
8. J.W. Demmel. *Applied Numerical Linear Algebra*. SIAM, 1997.
9. C. Eckart and G. Young. The approximation of one matrix by another of lower rank. *Psychometrika*, 1:211–218, 1936.
10. H.H. Goldstine. *A History of Numerical Analysis from the 16th through the 19th Century*. Springer-Verlag, 1977.
11. J. Heintz, M.-F. Roy, and P. Solerno. Sur la complexité du principe de Tarski-Seidenberg. *Bulletin de la Société Mathématique de France*, 118:101–126, 1990.
12. N. Higham. *Accuracy and Stability of Numerical Algorithms*. SIAM, 1996.
13. D. Knuth. *The Art of Computer Programming*, volume 2, Seminumerical Algorithms. Addison-Wesley, 2 edition, 1981.
14. P. Koiran. The real dimension problem is $NP_{\mathbb{R}}$-complete. To appear in *Journal of Complexity*, 1997.
15. A.M. Ostrowski. On two problems in abstract algebra connected with Horner's rule. In *Studies in Mathematics and Mechanics presented to Richard von Mises*, pages 40–48. Academic Press, 1954.

16. V.Ya. Pan. Methods of computing values of polynomials. *Russian Math. Surveys*, 21:105–136, 1966.

17. J. Renegar. On the computational complexity and geometry of the first-order theory of the reals. Part I. *Journal of Symbolic Computation*, 13:255–299, 1992.

18. J. Renegar. Some perturbation theory for linear programming. *Mathematical Programming*, 65:73–91, 1994.

19. J. Renegar. Incorporating condition measures into the complexity theory of linear programming. *SIAM Journal of Optimization*, 5:506–524, 1995.

20. J. Renegar. Linear programming, complexity theory and elementary functional analysis. *Mathematical Programming*, 70:279–351, 1995.

21. M. Shub and S. Smale. Complexity of Bezout's theorem I: geometric aspects. *Journal of the Amer. Math. Soc.*, 6:459–501, 1993.

22. M. Shub and S. Smale. Complexity of Bezout's theorem II: volumes and probabilities. In F. Eyssette and A. Galligo, editors, *Computational Algebraic Geometry*, volume 109 of *Progress in Mathematics*, pages 267–285. Birkhäuser, 1993.

23. M. Shub and S. Smale. Complexity of Bezout's theorem III: condition number and packing. *Journal of Complexity*, 9:4–14, 1993.

24. M. Shub and S. Smale. Complexity of Bezout's theorem V: polynomial time. *Theoretical Computer Science*, 133:141–164, 1994.

25. M. Shub and S. Smale. Complexity of Bezout's theorem IV: probability of success; extensions. *SIAM J. of Numer. Anal.*, 33:128–148, 1996.

26. S. Smale. The fundamental theorem of algebra and complexity theory. *Bulletin of the Amer. Math. Soc.*, 4:1–36, 1981.

27. S. Smale. Some remarks on the foundations of numerical analysis. *SIAM Review*, 32:211–220, 1990.

28. S. Smale. Complexity theory and numerical analysis. In A. Iserles, editor, *Acta Numerica*, pages 523–551. Cambridge University Press, 1997.

29. L.N. Trefethen and D. Bau III. *Numerical Linear Algebra*. SIAM, 1997.

30. L.N. Trefethen and R.S. Schreiber. Average-case stability of Gaussian elimination. *SIAM J. Matrix Anal. Appl.*, 11:335–360, 1990.

31. E. Triesch. A note on a theorem of Blum, Shub, and Smale. *Journal of Complexity*, 6:166–169, 1990.

32. A.M. Turing. Rounding-off errors in matrix processes. *Quart. J. Mech. Appl. Math.*, 1:287–308, 1948.

33. J. von Neumann and H.H. Goldstine. Numerical inverting matrices of high order. *Bulletin of the Amer. Math. Soc.*, 53:1021–1099, 1947.

34. J. Wilkinson. *Rounding Errors in Algebraic Processes*. Prentice Hall, 1963.

35. J. Wilkinson. Modern error analyis. *SIAM Review*, 13:548–568, 1971.

36. H. Woźniakowski. Numerical stability for solving non-linear equations. *Numer. Math.*, 27:373–390, 1977.

A Model for Associative Memory, a Basis for Thinking and Consciousness

N.G. de Bruijn

Eindhoven University of Technology
Dept. of Mathematics and Computing Science
PO Box 511, 5600MB Eindhoven, The Netherlands
`wsdwnb@win.tue.nl`

Abstract. The paper presents a model for associative memory, based on the idea of a roaming random set. It is very robust, at the expense of quite some redundancy.

Thinking, consciousness and various features of memory can be interpreted in terms of the memory model. Like in the von Neumann computer the larger part of operational routines can be stored in the same memory they operate on.

The modeling does not directly build on what is actually known from cell biology and biochemistry, but was certainly inspired by it. The author believes that it is not entirely impossible that it presents an overall description of the mind of biological systems like ourselves.

1   Introduction

The basic attitude of this paper is that the human mind is a gigantic parallel machine, built around a big associative memory. Yet we have to admit that no simple uniform model can describe the whole body-mind system. It is very hybrid, reflecting the extensions it went through in the course of the evolution. It is also a multimedia system, having particular kinds of hardware for the various input and output organs. Nevertheless one can have the feeling that there is a more or less uniform central part that gives the human being its memory of what happened before (or, rather, of interpretations of what happened) and gives it the habits it has taught itself. It is for that central part of the memory that the models of this paper are mainly intended[1].

1.1   What Mathematics and Computer Science Can Contribute

Many people feel that the mind-body problem is a matter of practical sciences like psychology and physiology (including biochemistry), and that, as long as there is nothing to be calculated, abstract sciences like mathematics or computer science have nothing to contribute. This is foolish, of course: the problem has

---

[1] In this paper the emphasis will be mainly on the model itself; earlier presentations (like [1, 2]) gave more attention to interpretations.

always been a big mystery, and one can never predict where solutions will come from. Many of the tools, ideas and methodologies of the abstract sciences have hardly penetrated in the practical sciences. Some points are mentioned here (in this list "we" is short for "mathematicians and computer scientists").

1. We have experience in model-building, and we are used to handle models for complex practical situations without claiming them to represent the *truth* (we are much more modest than other people think). We like our models if they show some resemblance to reality, and we hope to learn how to adapt them by asking critical questions, getting closer to reality all the time.

2. A substantial part of the mind-body problem is about information processing, an area in which we may have useful suggestions.

3. In particular we know about languages, and we are able to keep them apart from metalanguages.

4. We don't know precisely what thinking is, but we know about mathematical thinking, and we are aware that our ordinary practice is very different from complete formalization. We do not necessarily feel the need to describe a brain as a logical machine.

5. In its details, the human brain does not look very much like a modern computer, but the similarities in *architecture* can be striking. In particular, multimedia computers have many trends in common with the mind-body system.

6. A very important architectural feature is von Neumann's idea of stored programming, which makes it possible to see a computer as a machine that does little more than memory storage and retrieval.

7. We have some experience in handling the notion of probability.

This paper illustrates these points. In particular the idea of a roaming random set and the idea of thinking soup would not easily present themselves if the mind-body problem is approached from either psychology or physiology. In the abstract sciences problems are often better attacked by starting somewhere in the middle, without direct experimental validation.

1.2 Basic Ideas

The central idea is the roaming random set: an ever changing set of brain cells (or of other local stations like local neural networks). At any moment the cells of this set are awake, ready to store as well as to retrieve memory items. Main features of this system are:

1. There is no addressing system: the central processors do not know to which cells the information is sent, neither which cells answers come from.

2. The memory capacity of the system is roughly the capacity of a single cell multiplied by the square root of the number of cells. The effect of the roaming random set system is that one can easily memorize about 10^4 as much as a single cell can do.

3. The memory of the system is very much more dependable than the memory of a single cell can be.

4. The system is very *robust*: it is possible to damage or to remove a large number of cells without any loss in memory performance.

5. The roaming random set system models a major feature of consciousness: the fact that our contact with the present is so much stronger than with past memories. Most of cells to which we send information are still awake a tenth of a second later. But the number of cells which have got the information and are able to report about it as well, is dropping dramatically in a second. That number is the sum of an exponentially decreasing function plus a small constant. The exponential part may drop from 10^6 to zero, and the constant may be of the order of 10^2.

6. Several other features of what is called consciousness and thinking can be understood from the point of view of von Neumann's idea of stored programming (see sections 6 and 8.2).

2   Roaming Random Set

We consider a finite set S, to be called the *base space* and a real variable t which will be referred to as the *time*. The values of t will be called *moments*. The number of elements of S will be called M.

The term *moving subset* will denote a function of t whose values are subsets of S. So if A is such a function, then $A(t)$ is a subset of S at every moment t.

If s is an element of S, then it depends on time whether $s \in A(t)$. The behavior is described by a function of t taking values 0 and 1 only. The value at moment t will be called the *state* of s at moment t. It is 1 if $s \in A(t)$, and 0 if $s \notin A(t)$. Equivalently, we say that s is ON if the state is 1 and OFF if it is 0.

The term *roaming random set* (the word "roaming" suggests gradual random variations in the course of time) will be used if the moving subset is produced in a particular random fashion, controlled by positive constants a and b. It will have the effect that for every element s there is a collection of disjoint time intervals in which s is ON; in the remaining intervals s is OFF. The average length of the ON-intervals will turn out to be b^{-1}, the one of the OFF-intervals a^{-1}.

The random behavior of the state of s is a simple case of what is called a stationary Markov process (see [3,5]. It will be presented here in a slightly informal style, the way Euler would have done it, using infinitesimal positive time increments dt.

If at moment t the state is OFF then with probability $a{\cdot}dt$ it switches to ON in the period from t to $t + dt$; if at moment t the state is ON then with probability $b{\cdot}dt$ it switches to OFF between t and $t + dt$.

This gives the behaviour of a single s. In order to describe the behavior of the random subset $A(t)$, it suffices to stipulate that the processes of the different elements of S are completely independent, all with the same values of the parameters a and b.

Consider two moments t_0 and t_1, where $t_0 \leq t_1$. We want to know the conditional probability of the state of s at moment t_1 if the state at time t_0 is given. Let i and j be numbers, both either 0 or 1. Since the process is stationary, the conditional probability that the state is j at moment t_1 under the condition that it was i at moment t_0 only depends on the difference $t_1 - t_0$. So it can be written as $f_{ij}(t_2 - t_1)$, if $f_{ij}(t)$ is (for $t \geq 0$) the conditional probability that the state is j at moment t under the condition that it was i at moment 0.

If t and dt are positive, the value of $f_{i1}(t + dt)$ can be expressed in terms of $f_{i0}(t)$ and $f_{i1}(t)$ by splitting the interval from 0 to $t + dt$ into the one from 0 to t and the one from t to $t + dt$. The state has passed through moment t either as 0 or as 1. In the first case there is a probability $a \cdot dt$ that it switched to 1 in the interval from t to $t + dt$, in the second case there is a probability $b \cdot dt$ that it switched to 0 in that interval (the length of that interval being infinitesimally small, the cases of more than one switch in that interval can be ignored). So the probability that the state is 1 at moment $t + dt$ is

$$f_{i1}(t + dt) = f_{i0}(t) \; a \; dt + f_{i1}(t) \; (1 - b \; dt) \; .$$

By virtue of $f_{i0}(t) + f_{i1}(t) = 1$ we get the differential equation

$$f'_{i1} = a - (a + b)f_{i1} \; .$$

Because of the initial conditions $f_{01}(0) = 0$, $f_{11}(0) = 1$ the solution is

$$f_{01}(t) = (a - ae^{-(a+b)t})/(a + b), \; f_{11}(t) = (a + be^{-(a+b)t})/(a + b) \; . \quad (1)$$

Assuming that the system has been working infinitely long already, we use this result for showing that at any moment t the probability that the state is 1 equals $a/(a+b)$. Let $p(u)$ be the probability for the state to be 1 at moment u. If $u \leq v$ we have

$$p(v) = (1 - p(u))f_{01}(v - u) + p(u)f_{11}(v - u) \; .$$

Making $u \to -\infty$ and keeping v fixed, then by (1) both $f_{01}(v - u)$ and $f_{11}(v - u)$ tend exponentially to $a/(a+b)$, whence $p(v) = a/(a+b)$. So $p(t) = a/(a+b)$ for all values of t.

Now take two moments t and $t + x$ ($t \geq 0, x \geq 0$). The probability that the state is 1 both at t and at $t + x$ is the product $p(t)f_{11}(x)$:

$$a(a + b)^{-1}(a + be^{-(a+b)x})/(a + b) \; ,$$

which only depends on the difference x of $t + x$ and t. So when writing

$$H(x) = a(a + be^{-(a+b)x})/(a + b)^2 \quad (2)$$

we have proved that the probability of the state being 1 both at t and at $x + t$ equals $H(x)$.

The result for f_{11} can also be used to determine the average length of the intervals where the state of s is ON. Just take $a = 0$, which means that the transition from ON to OFF still has the same probability $b \cdot dt$ but that there are no transitions at all from OFF to ON. Once OFF, it will be OFF forever. If the state is ON at moment 0, it will still be ON at moment t with probability e^{-bt} (the value of f_{11} in the case $a = 0$, according to (1). From this it can be derived that the expectation of the length of an ON-interval starting at 0 is b^{-1}.

In a similar way the average length of the OFF-intervals turns out to be a^{-1}.

Thus far we discussed the behavior of a single element s of the set S. As said before, the random processes controlling the behavior of the M elements of S are completely independent.

At any moment t, the subset $A(t)$ is the set of all s which have state 1. Therefore, the expectation of the number of elements of $A(t)$ is M times the probability that a single element s has state 1, so the expectation of the size of $A(t)$ equals

$$Ma/(a + b) .\tag{3}$$

Next take two moments, t and $t+x$, where $x \geq 0$. We consider the intersection $A(t) \cap A(t + x)$, and ask for its expected size. An s belongs to that intersection if and only if it has state 1 both at t and at $t + x$. The probability for this event was shown to be $H(x)$ (see (2)). It follows that the expectation of the size of the intersection $A(t) \cap A(t + x)$ equals $MH(x)$. This function of x is the sum of a constant and an exponentially decreasing function. At the start we have $x = 0$, where the expectation is $Ma/(a + b)$, and the asymptotic value for $x \to \infty$ is

$$Ma^2/(a + b)^2 .\tag{4}$$

3   Signals and Associative Memory Stations

We consider a kind of *signals*. One might think of words written in Morse code, or of bar codes, or of short melodies.

A *signal pair* is an ordered pair of signals. If the pair is (p, q), where p and q are signals, then p is called the first, and q the second component of the pair.

An *associative memory station* (AMS) is a machine that can receive a number of signal pairs, with the effect that it gets permanently into a state in which it is able to reply to certain interrogations. If p is any signal, if the question is asked "What followed p?", and the AMS previously received at least one pair with first component p, then it is supposed to reply with the second component of one of those pairs. If it never received any pair starting with p, then it does not reply at all.

An AMS has a certain *capacity*: a number γ such that it can handle at most γ pairs. And it has a certain *unreliability* φ. It means that if an AMS gets a question "What followed p?", and it is in possession of a suitable pair, then there is still a probability φ that it fails to give a correct answer. In particular one might assume, pessimistically, that if the number of pairs offered to an AMS exceeds the capacity γ then it stops answering questions at all.

An AMS does not record the *time* at which it received the pairs, and not even the order: if in the past it received both (p,q) and (u,v), it does not remember which one of the two pairs came first.

And an AMS is not necessarily able to do its work reversely, i.e., to handle the question whether any q ever occurred as the second component of a pair.

In all this, it is not required that the answer to the interrogation is always unique: an AMS might have received more than one pair with the same first component.

4   Roaming Random Set as Associative Memory

We take set S, every element of which is an AMS. Moreover we fix positive constants a and b, and take S as a base space for a roaming random set with parameters a and b, according to section 2.

There is some agent, let us call it CPU (for Central Processing Unit) that delivers signal pairs. A signal pair issued at time t is received by an AMS if and only if that station is ON at that moment. For simplicity, we assume that the signal pairs are infinitely short; therefore a pair falls either entirely inside or entirely outside such an ON-interval.

At any moment the CPU can ask a question: "What followed p?". We assume that the question is received by all the AMS's which are ON at that moment, and that the CPU receives all the answers, correct or not. Let us take it for granted that every AMS gives at most one answer.

The CPU can get a number of answers this way. It takes the answer that occurs most often as the valid answer, and ignores all others (if there are several answers with the same maximal number of occurrences, then it selects one of them at random).

In this way the system turns into a big AMS itself. It receives a number of signal pairs, and answers to interrogations in the same way as the original AMS's, which we now call the small ones. Only, the capacity of the big one can be much bigger than γ, and its unreliability can be much smaller than φ.

For the time being, let us make two extra simplifying assumptions. The first one is that the signal pairs have been distributed evenly over the AMS's (this is quite realistic if the actions of the CPU are spread over a period of time which is very long compared to the length of the ON and OFF periods). The effect of this even distribution is that overflow failure of individual AMS's plays no role until the time that most of the AMS's are loaded almost to their capacity.

The second simplifying assumption is that every signal has occurred at most *once* in a pair, and that a small AMS never gives a wrong answer. That is, if a pair (p,q) has ever been issued, then an AMS answers the question about what followed p either by q or it does not answer at all. In cases where it did receive (p,q) and did get the question, it can still fail to answer, with a probability φ.

Under these assumptions we investigate the unreliability and the capacity of the big AMS. Assume that the pair (p, q) was presented by the CPU at time t, which means that it was received by all small AMS's which were ON at that moment. At some later moment $t + x$ the CPU tries to retrieve q by asking what ever followed p. The question is given to all AMS's which are ON at time $t + x$. What is the probability that the CPU gets the answer q at least once?

According to (2) the probability that a given small AMS received the pair as well as the question is at least $a^2/(a + b)^2$. Abbreviating $(a + b)/a = P$ we infer that the probability that one particular AMS answers q is at least $(1 - \varphi)/P^2$. The probability that *all* the M small AMS's *fail* to give the answer q is therefore at most

$$\varphi^* = (1 - (1 - \varphi)/P^2)^M . \tag{5}$$

This is the unreliability of the big AMS.

Let us now get an idea about the capacity γ^*, i.e., the total number of signal pairs that the CPU can get accepted by the system. If the CPU issues a series of γ^* pairs then an individual small AMS will pick up about γ^*/P of them, since it is ON only about one P-th of the time (note that the average ON-interval is b^{-1} and the average OFF-interval a^{-1}, and that $(a^{-1} + b^{-1})/b^{-1} = P$). Assuming that with the total input of γ^* pairs all the small AMS's are loaded to their capacity, we conclude that $\gamma^* = P\gamma$.

The effect is more or less optimal if M is somewhat larger than the square of P. Let us take a positive number K, and $M = 2P^2K$, $\varphi = 0.5$. According to (5) the unreliability of the big AMS is at most about $(1 - 1/(2P^2))^M$, which is about e^{-K}. If, for example, $K = 20$, then the big AMS is incredibly reliable. And its capacity is about $P\gamma$.

Let us illustrate this in a particular example that does not seem to be unrealistic in the application to a biological brain. We take

$$M = 36.10^9, \ \gamma = 10^4, \ a^{-1} = 15000, \ b^{-1} = 0.5, \ \varphi = 0.5 ,$$

and recall here what these stand for. M is the number of AMS's, γ the capacity of a small AMS. Next, a and b the parameters of the Markov process; a^{-1} and b^{-1} are the average length of the OFF periods and ON periods, respectively; the unit of time for a^{-1} and b^{-1} is the second. Finally, φ is the unreliability of a small AMS, i.e., the probability that it fails to do what it should.

Now P is about 30000. The unreliability of the big AMS is at most e^{-20}, and its capacity is about 30000 times the one of a small AMS.

It is only the *ratio* of a and b that plays a role in the matter of capacity and reliability of the system. The actual values of a and b themselves are related to the *speed* of the system.

5 Fibers, Ropes and Cables in Associative Memory

A big AMS like the roaming random set memory is able to memorize strings of signals.

In the course of time the CPU can emit a long string of signals $p_1, \ldots, p_m$ and expect that small AMS's build the pairs (p_1, p_2), (p_2, p_3), $\ldots$, (p_{m-1}, p_m).

At any later moment, the CPU may repeat one of the signals of the string, with the question what followed it. The big AMS will reply with the next signal, then the CPU asks what followed that one, etc. So the whole string, from the first-mentioned signal onward, can unfold itself, at least with a very high probability. But of course, the CPU can stop asking at any moment it pleases.

Note that each one of the small AMS's may help in the reconstruction of the sequence with isolated portions only; it is the action of the CPU that keeps the string together.

But there is more. Simultaneously with the sequence $p_1, \ldots, p_m$, the CPU can issue a second sequence $q_1 \ldots, q_r$. Or it may issue a bunch of such sequences. And there might not be single CPU, but a collection of CPU's, and each one may be able to dig up what its colleagues had planted. In such cases the small AMS's have not registered from which CPU their knowledge originated; nevertheless they conscientiously carry out their humble tasks.

There can be extensive interaction between the memorized sequences. With such interaction the associative memory will be called a *sisal memory*, because of the metaphor of heavy cables used by tugboats towing large vessels. A cable consists of a number of intertwined thinner cables, those ones consist of inter-twined ropes, the ropes consist of intertwined thinnest fibers. For simplicity we mention only three stages (cable, rope, fiber), but there may be more. In case of sisal, the fibers may be less than one foot long, and the forces they execute are passed on to their neighbors just by the friction caused by the intertwining. Millions of tiny short fibers form a strong long cable.

Back to the roaming random set memory. By the cooperation of the small AMS's, sequences like $p_1, \ldots, p_m$ can be memorized. These are to be compared to the tiniest fibers of the cable. The various fibers can support one another. If two sequences, like the p's and q's are issued simultaneously, either by the same CPU or by different ones, then the small AMS's may also build pairs consisting of one p and one q. If, for example, p_{318} is issued *almost* at the same time as q_{72}, then an AMS that receives both signals may build (p_{318}, q_{72}) or (q_{72}, p_{318}). So later, if some CPU asks what followed p_{318}, it might get either p_{319} or q_{72} as a reply. And asking what followed a particular q may be replied either by some p or by some q. This process of mutual support of p's and q's corresponds to the friction that keeps the fibers of the cable together.

The process of recalling a single fiber can trigger the reappearance of the rest of the cable. Errors in the fibers of that cable can be tolerated because of the continuing interplay between neighbors.

6 Big Associative Memory as a Thinking Machine

Around 1945, von Neumann's stored programming idea (see [4,6]) was quite a revolution in computer architecture.

The core of the computer, what we might call CPU, the central processing unit, used to play the role of an intelligent being. It was supposed to know programs and to know how to execute them. During the execution of a program it needed some unintelligent assistance in the form of a large memory for numbers. The CPU kept track of where it had stored those numbers and knew how to retrieve them. No intelligence could be attributed to the memory. Of course, the CPU had a kind of extra memory to represent the program and the operating system, but that could be considered as *part* of the CPU. The computer was not able to change them. Operating system and input-output protocols were fixtures, and the program was set by hand by means of wires and plugs, possibly supported by things like punched cards.

Stored programming changed all this. Programs, operating systems, protocols could all go into one and the same big memory for all sorts of *words*. All the intelligence of the CPU was reduced to a simple protocol for handling memory, addresses, input and output. This went on: the memory could be used for program source texts, compilers, and many things more, but whatever was added, the CPU could always suffice with the same simple protocol. The von Neumann revolution turned the CPU from a superintelligent brain into an unintelligent accurate bureaucrat. Almost all the knowledge, all the abilities and habits went into the memory.

This describes what we might call a pure von Neumann computer. Today's practice is slightly different: we embed quite some software (like the one for floating point arithmetic) into the CPU. But this is a matter of economy only, making things faster or cheaper. If we wish, we could easily undo it: machines would become slower, but that would not run into exponential explosion.

It is a standard question whether a big pure von Neumann computer can *think*. The answer very much depends on the interpretation of the word "thinking". It has to be admitted that the computer can do a lot of things that people always used to call thinking. That is, if one provides the computer with suitable programs for it. Quite a different matter is whether the machine can discover and develop such programs itself (but one should not forget that few *people* ever discover anything themselves).

Usually one thinks of a von Neumann computer as a machine that organizes its memory by means of addresses, but if, instead of that, we use an associative memory, we can do the same things at least as easily. After all, address organization can be emulated in an associative system, just by associating every memory item with a different integer, to be called the address. Conversely, associative memory can be implemented in an address machine too, but that may take more trouble and more time.

7   Connecting the Memory Model to Physiology

This section cannot be much more than a fantasy. Not just because the author is a layman, but also because the whole field is so miraculous, with new discoveries all the time. What we write today will be outdated in the near future.

Part of the mystery of *life* is the chemistry inside a cell. The thinking soup model, to be explained below, suggests that the *mind* uses that same chemical machinery. How this works in detail can hardly be expected to be detectable. Biochemistry of brain functions may have even bigger secrets than biochemistry of life, where most phenomena can be expected to happen on a large scale in almost identical copies. In the thinking soup model every cell can play its own little chemistry game, partly depending on the experiences of the individual it is working for.

Physiology does not live under the pressure of having to explain everything in detail, starting from first principles, like in physics. One may be able to read the codes expressed in molecules, but there is little hope that the biological effect can ever be computed from those codes. One may understand that chemical communication in a lump of cells eventually results in the formation of an eye or a finger, but that is very far from calculation. Those marvels just happen.

It is not too bold to assume that such untractable chemical marvels happen in the brain's information processing too. This section describes a bowl of thinking soup as computer, and in particular as an AMS.

The thinking soup model is about information-carrying molecules and about catalyzers, all floating in a soup of all kinds of pieces from which those molecules can be built. The information carriers may be molecules in the form of long strings of relatively few different components. In section 7.1 the strings will be called proteins, but they might also be pieces of DNA or of anything else. The catalyzers may fall under the category of enzymes: big molecules that provoke changes in other molecules without changing themselves. Their output is not necessarily entirely composed of parts of the input molecules: they can also pick fragments floating around in the soup. Those fragments may have been remainders of protein molecules that died by falling to pieces.

We just talk about proteins, enzymes, forgetting about any other biochemical structures that might play a role.

The phrase 'protein molecule' will be used for an individual object, the word 'protein' stands for a class of identical protein molecules.

7.1 Thinking Soup

A computer can be constructed from components like transistors. Each one has two input wires A and B and an output wire C. The function of the transistor is that whenever there is sufficient electric activity on *both* A and B, electrical activity on C will be generated. The transistors are arranged in a large network, where output wires are linked to input wires of other transistors. Add a few things, like clock pulses, and we have a machine for all sorts of logical tasks.

There is a simple analogy with what can be imagined to happen in a brain cell. That is a bowl of soup, containing many different proteins. And there may be many different emzymes; each enzyme is able to do just one reaction of the type $A + B \rightarrow C$. That is, if the enzyme molecule receives protein molecules A and B simultaneously, it begins to produce a protein molecule C. In a cell this means that if at a certain moment the proteins A and B have sufficient concentration, then protein C gets a reasonable concentration too. So an enzyme is the analog of a transistor, the proteins correspond to wires, and sufficient concentration corresponds to sufficient electric activity.

This is the idea of a *thinking soup computer*. Every brain cell is a computer, and the brain becomes a very big computer network. To give an idea of the size: it is not unrealistic to think that each cell can contain 10^4 different proteins, which might be compared to a computer with 10^4 wires. And there may be 10^{11} cells. The speed does not have to be a problem, since zipper-like chemical reactions might do their elementary steps in nanoseconds.

It sounds great, but it is hard to conceive how such a computer would ever come into being. How would it build itself, how would it be able to program itself? Both abilities would be essential for the evolutionary success of such biological miracles.

7.2 Cell as Chemical AMS

Fortunately, there can be success on a simpler level. One can imagine a soup bowl computer with just two different enzymes, a *storing enzyme* and a *retrieving enzyme*, able to handle associative memory. They are not dedicated to particular proteins.

The action of the storing enzyme is that if at a certain moment some protein A comes up, and the protein B immediately after that, then the enzyme builds a protein C that carries the information of both A and B. One might think of A and B as strings of amino acids, and of C as the concatenation of these strings, provided with some extra separation marks. Let us write that C as $A * B$. The A and B are very weak, and vanish almost immediately, before new proteins come in, but $A * B$ is quite resistant. One might imagine that the cell is subject to all sorts of signals, coming from outside, not necessarily chemical ones, and that at the cell-wall each signal gives rise to the production of a protein that somehow bears the information contained in the signal. So a series of proteins emerge in the cell, and they do not live much longer than the time between two consecutive signals. The storing enzyme builds concatenation proteins like the $A * B$ mentioned above. The A's and B's vanish rapidly, but each $A * B$ remains as a long-lasting witness of an association between an A and a B (and therefore, between the two consecutive signals that gave rise to those proteins).

There has to be a mechanism that prevents the enzyme from building $B * A$ too: we only want $A * B$. It might use the fact that A and B are degrading rapidly, A being almost dead when B comes up. The mechanism would be that the enzyme only wants to couple a dying A to a fresh B, in that order.

The action of the retrieving enzyme is as follows. At the cell-wall there arrives a signal p that previously gave rise to the production of protein A. This time an extra piece is added to the signal, to be called a question mark, so let us write the incoming signal as $p^?$. At the cell-wall there now emerges protein $A^?$. In the soup there are still copies of some $A * B$ bearing the information of the concatenation of A and B. The retrieving enzyme takes $A^?$ and C as inputs and gives $B^!$, i.e., B provided with an exclamation mark. At the cell-wall this $B^!$

leads to an output signal $q!$, if q had been the incoming signal that had caused B in the past.

There is, of course, the possibility that storage and retrieval actions need no enzymes at all. The work might be done by the influence of extra marks on the proteins. At the retrieval stage the $A^?$ tries to check all molecules it meets, asking whether they start as $A*$.

So the cell has got associative memory, and has become a small AMS in the sense of section 3.

In order to account for what we seem to know about human memory, one might try to assume some extras in this chemical memory machine. One might think that the $A * B$'s are not so stable at all, that they steadily degrade into weaker forms, and possibly vanish entirely on the long run, but that in cases where they really get to work (i.e., where an $A * B$ is confronted with an $A^?$), they turn into a more resistant form, possibly even multiplying themselves. Some more attention to this was given in [1, 2].

7.3   Memory Stations in the Form of Neural Nets

The idea of the thinking soup puts all the associative memory in the cells. But one can also imagine that groups of cells form neural networks with associative memory capacity. For the matter of the cooperation of a large set of small AMS's it makes no differences whether these are cells of local networks.

It is quite possible that for very frequently occurring memory tasks a group of cells begins to build a neural net that does them faster, this way getting to local neural networks doing the same work as associative memory proteins, and possibly also the work of the enzymes. It is not easy to imagine how this would take place, but the finger telephone (section 7.4) may do such a thing. After all, the finger telephone network will have many portions with strong mutual local connections.

Apart from the neural nets formed in the brain by some kind of learning, there can be other nets that have been produced genetically. And one can think of matrix nets, the elements of which can be filled in by learning.

But seen from the point of evolution, the cell chemistry was there first. Multicellular individuals were preceded by unicellular ones, and these had to have a kind of brain too. It is even reasonable to think there was life before membranes were formed: there was living soup before there were bowls. Memory processes may be similar to other aspects of life, so why not assume that there was chemical memory even before there were cells?

7.4   Implementing the Roaming Random Set

The roaming random set was described in section 2. Each one of the small AMS's, either cells or local neural nets, was assumed to have its own random generator for switching between ON and OFF.

An attractive possibility for the implementation is the *finger telephone* (see [1, 2]). It is a machinery that takes care of two things at the same time: the signal transmission between CPU and AMS, and the ON-OFF switching. Let us describe it in a few words for the case that the AMS's are brain cells.

Brain cells have long tails with many fingers they can put on other cells. For every finger it is a matter of chance which cell is touched, and when. And the grip can be lost at random too. The fingers can transmit messages from cell to cell in both directions. So at each moment a number of cells is connected to CPU. Messages are passed on from cell to cell in a tree-shaped arrangement. The remotest parts of the brain might be reached in something of the order of ten steps, so it is attractive to postulate that the finger telephone is able to transport messages quickly and reliably over that distance. The so-called 'height' of the tree is limited, but because of the enormous number of fingers the tree can be very wide; it can easily contain a million cells. These are the cells to be considered as being ON at that moment.

In this picture the Markov processes are not really independent, and not all cells are treated equally. Cells closest to CPU have the best chance of getting connected. And fingers of cells close to the CPU have much more influence than some of the others. They can change big parts of the tree: large groups of cells are switching simultaneously.

Nevertheless it is not unreasonable to expect that the main randomness effects will be roughly the same as for completely independent random processes.

The finger telephone network is a kind of big neural net. It may be able to learn too: fingers may like to keep their grip if they have important messages to transmit.

8 Connecting the Memory Model to Psychology

The roaming random set memory model has a number of properties that can be compared to what we know about the human mind.

In the first place it is realistic that the model is about *associative* memory. It is *forward associativity*. The suggested chemical mechanism (see section 7.2) could easily be modified so as to cater for *backward associativity* as well, but it seems that Nature has not implemented it for us. For survival it is important to predict the effect of a given cause; scientific interest in the causes of a given effect is a later concern.

Next there is the roaming behavior of the set of active cells (instead of cell one may read, more generally: small AMS, and "active" means; connected to the CPU). That active set is our *window*, floating over our entire memory, just like our computer screen flows over the text of a file, at any moment showing a piece we can operate on. At time $t + x$ we are trying to find an association that was stored at time t. Let us use the word *response* for the number of cells that can give the right answer. According to the end of section 2 it can be expected to be $MH(x)$, so let us think about a response like

$$10^2 + 10^6 e^{-5x} . \tag{6}$$

If x is small, less than a fifth of a second, the response is of the order of a million, and the CPU is able to have repeated memory contact with that large number of cells, storing and retrieving all the time. Within a few seconds, however, the response drops down to 100, and it becomes much harder to pick up the associations. This small number may often be insufficient, and we may have to roam quite some time to find what we want. But once there is the beginning of an answer, things may improve: the sisal structure produces more and more associations, strengthening the grip on one or more ropes of the cable.

The intense contact with our present window gives the strong difference between what we are experiencing *now* in contrast to our weak memories of the past. It is the *remembered present* that is kept alive for a split-second. But in its turn, this remembered present fades away according to (6). This is the *transiency* of our momentary experiences.

Another thing that the model may explain is that memory improves by being consulted. If the CPU gets an answer about some past event, that answer is available to the whole present window, so during a short period the memory may become as clear as if things are happening right here. And this substantially increases the number of cells that know about the point in question.

But there may be more. Improving the memory by consulting, and loosing it by not consulting, may also happen in the small AMS's themselves. For example, in the case of the chemical protein associations sketched in section 7.2, one might assume that the effect of $A^?$ on $A * B$ is not just $B^!$, but as some modification of $A * B$, more resistant than the old one (more about this in [1, 2]). One reason for assuming such a machinery is that so many trivialities are remembered quite well for hours and even days, and then (fortunately) vanish for ever. Formula (6) would not explain such a thing.

8.1 Thinking

The ability of human beings to *think* is often overrated, as well as the role of language in it. Much more fundamental is *pattern recognition*. A large number of signals, forming a pattern, is sent to the memory. If a similar pattern comes up later, it may be compared with the pattern in the memory. Animals can recognize friends and enemies by vision, hearing and smell.

Once pattern recognition is available, the way is open to all other intellectual abilities. For humans, the ability to compare different sounds is the root of spoken language, the ability to compare written symbols is the root of reading and writing, etc. In general, pattern recognition is essential for our ability to *imitate*, and imitation is indispensable for our intelligence. It is not just the social imitation, but also the imitation of our own actions as far as they were successful in the past.

We probably have no inborn hardware for reasoning. Most of it is jigsaw puzzling applied to sentences (or pictures), and therefore based on pattern recognition. The essence of logic and mathematics is that there do exist formal rules by which correctness can be established. Such rules are the fitting rules for the jigsaw pieces. Solving the puzzle is a matter of trial and error, verifying the correctness is a mechanical affair. One should not think that these fitting rules began as formal rules. They were just habits, acquired by trial and error. Once we begin to work with pencil and paper, a more formal new set of fitting rules may evolve, and we begin to believe that they express what we did ourselves in the first place.

8.2 Consciousness

People use the word "consciousness" in various situations. Rather than inspecting a list of aspects to be modeled, we start here from the model, and describe a number of its possibilities in the realm of consciousness.

The most important thing is the transiency effect, described in the beginning of section 8.

A further consciousness item lies in the von Neumann architecture (see section 6). Thoughts, in particular those expressed by means of language, are stored the same way as observations. And procedures for *handling* thoughts can be stored too. Thoughts can be recalled and can become subject of further thoughts, these thoughts can be stored again, etc. The memory has transient observations about the real world, connected to it by many associations. These are strong in particular since so much of that real world hardly changes. But the memory also stores fantasies with much fewer realistic associations. So when recalling memories, the CPU has information about whether it was fact or fantasy. It may learn to use that information in order to see the distinction. The machine can observe the thoughts it just had, and is able to know that it went through the process of thinking. This *awareness* can be stored again; remembering the awareness of a moment ago might be called *introspection*. Needless to say, the matter is quite complex, and can have social aspects too (part of thinking may be preparing answers to other people's possible questions).

People are doing a lot of intellectual work *without* being aware of it. Awareness is work too, and it is hard to do two strenuous things at the same time.

What about the dichotomy consciousness-subconsciousness? In section 7.3 it was pointed out that frequently repeated tasks can be taken over by fast neural nets whose actions require hardly any consultation of the remembered present. One might call their work subconscious. Once a task is taken over by neural nets, it is no longer available to introspection, and can hardly be done consciously any more.

Subconsciousness and unconsciousness may also be related to having more than one CPU. Let us say that there are two, the Realist and the Dreamer, the latter one being hardly connected to the input and output organs. It is doing fantasies, day-dreaming. It may be so active that it takes control, and lets the Realist keep working unconsciously, even talking and writing, without any awareness. One might say that awareness is always dedicated to just one task in just one CPU. Only a small part of the system's activities is open to introspection (and that is one of the reasons why psychology is so hard).

8.3 Feelings

Some people say to admit that a machine like a computer can do some thinking, but to deny that it can have emotions. They may be right, as long as the machine is only a *mind* and does not have a *body*. Thoughts are software, feelings are much more a matter of hardware.

A simplified vision on feelings is the following. In some situations (like alarm) the brain sends a message, possibly via nerves, to a particular gland somewhere in the body. That one begins to eject chemical messengers (like hormones) into the blood stream, with an effect on some other organs in the body, but possibly also on the brain. In terms of our model, these messengers may alter the parameters a and b of section 2, they may change the working of enzymes, or may close down some of the CPU's. And the effect on the brain is sometimes noticeable by introspection.

The messengers do not carry information the way proteins do: it is just their concentration that matters.

It seems that the blood vessels in the brain are much less porous than in other parts of the body, and that they do no admit the passage of molecules with extensive information. After all, this may turn out to be the only leftover of the old ideas about separation of mind and body!

References

1. de Bruijn, N.G.: A model for information processing in human memory and consciousness, Nieuw Archief voor Wiskunde (4), Vol 12, pp. 35-48 (1994).
2. de Bruijn, N.G.: Can people think? Journal of Consciousness Studies, Vol. 3, 1996, pp. 425-447 (1996).
3. Chung, K.L.: Markov Chains with Stationary Transition Probabilities. Springer-Verlag (1960)
4. Goldstine, H.H. The Computer from Pascal to von Neumann. Princeton University Press, 1972.
5. Norris, J.R., Markov Chains. Cambridge University Press (1997).
6. Savage, J.E., Magidson, S., Stein, A.M., The Mystical Machine. Issues and Ideas in Computing. Addison-Wesley Publishing Company, 1986.

Numerical Integration with Exact Real Arithmetic[*]

Abbas Edalat and Marko Krznarić

Department of Computing, Imperial College
180 Queen's Gate, London SW7 2BZ, UK
ae@doc.ic.ac.uk, marko@doc.ic.ac.uk

Abstract. We show that the classical techniques in numerical integration (namely the Darboux sums method, the compound trapezoidal and Simpson's rules and the Gauss–Legendre formulae) can be implemented in an exact real arithmetic framework in which the numerical value of an integral of an elementary function is obtained up to any desired accuracy without any round–off errors. Any exact framework which provides a library of algorithms for computing elementary functions with an arbitrary accuracy is suitable for such an implementation; we have used an exact real arithmetic framework based on linear fractional transformations and have thereby implemented these numerical integration techniques. We also show that Euler's and Runge–Kutta methods for solving the initial value problem of an ordinary differential equation can be implemented using an exact framework which will guarantee the convergence of the approximation to the actual solution of the differential equation as the step size in the partition of the interval in question tends to zero.

1 Introduction

In numerical methods for integration of a real–valued function, such as in the Darboux sums method, the trapezoidal method, Simpson's rule or the Gauss–Legendre formulae, the value of an integral $If = \int_a^b f(x)dx$ is approximated by a sum $Q_n f = \sum_{i=0}^{n} c_i f(x_i)$, where the x_i's are the integration nodes and the c_i's are the corresponding integration weights. In each method, an upper bound for the error can be obtained in terms of the number n of the integration nodes and an upper bound for a higher derivative of the integrand. Mathematically, this error always tends to zero as n tends to infinity. However, when any of these methods is implemented in floating point, one obtains an extra round–off error in the computation of $Q_n f$ and, as n tends to infinity, the computed values of $Q_n f$ may fail to converge to the value of the integral [4]. This same problem occurs in the floating point implementation of the Euler's and Runge–Kutta methods for the numerical computation of the solution of an initial value problem for an ordinary differential equation.

This undesirable situation can be overcome in exact real arithmetic. Simpson [21] has developed a theoretical setting for the exact computation of integrals

---

[*] This work is supported by EPSRC.

using higher order functions. However, the resulting algorithms are intractable. This is even more so in the earlier work of Edalat and Escardó [7] which defines integration in an extension of the theoretical language PCF.

We show here that one can use any of the above methods of integration to obtain the numerical value of the integral of any elementary function up to any desired accuracy ϵ, provided that we have: (i) a set of algorithms for the computation of elementary functions with arbitrary accuracy, and, (ii) an upper bound for the corresponding higher derivative of the integrand. This is achieved by first writing $\epsilon = \epsilon_m + \epsilon_r$ with $\epsilon_m, \epsilon_r > 0$. Then, for a given integration method, we determine the number of nodes such that $Q_n f$ differs from the integral by at most ϵ_m; finally $Q_n f$ is evaluated using the exact real arithmetic framework up to precision ϵ_r, which means the result differs from the integral by at most ϵ as desired. We also show that by using such an exact framework, one can obtain a convergent sequence of approximations with the Euler's and Runge–Kutta methods as the number of nodes tends to infinity.

We actually use the exact real arithmetic framework based on linear fractional transformations (LFTs) as developed by Edalat and Potts [8, 6, 20] based on the work of Gosper [12], Vuillemin [22] and Kornerup and Nielsen [19] on the one hand and Di Gianantonio [5] and Escardó [11] on the other. Using the complexity results of Heckmann [13] for computing elementary functions in the LFT framework, we obtain, as an example, the complexity of integrating the exponential function in the Darboux sums method, the trapezoidal method and in Simpson's rule in this framework. A number of examples for numerical integration using the above different methods and for the initial value problem using the Euler's and Runge–Kutta methods are presented.

2 Numerical Integration

We will deal with the numerical integration of a real–valued bounded function f over a finite closed interval $[a, b]$:

$$\mathrm{I}f = \int_a^b f(x)dx.$$

The simplest way to approximate the value $\mathrm{I}f$ is by a linear combination $Q_n f$ of the values of f:

$$\mathrm{I}f \approx Q_n f$$
$$= c_0 f(x_0) + c_1 f(x_1) + \ldots + c_n f(x_n).$$

Some integration methods are employed on specific intervals (e.g. Gauss–Legendre formula is given for the interval $[-1, 1]$). In order to apply such methods on another interval, we have to transform an integral over an arbitrary interval $[a, b]$ to an integral over $[-1, 1]$:

$$\int_a^b f(x)dx = \frac{b-a}{2} \int_{-1}^1 f\left(\frac{b-a}{2}x + \frac{a+b}{2}\right) dx.$$

We summarize four integration formulae; more details about these methods can be found in any book about numerical integration (see, for example [16, 4]):

Darboux sums For a bounded function $f : [a, b] \to \mathbb{R}$, and an equipartition $\mathcal{P} = \{x_0, x_1, \ldots, x_n\}$ of $[a, b]$, the lower Darboux sum is given by $\underline{S}(f; \mathcal{P}) = \frac{b-a}{n} \sum_{k=1}^{n} m_k$, where m_k is the minimum value of f on the subinterval $[x_{k-1}, x_k]$. If additionally f is a monotone function, then the minimum m_k is obtained at one of the end–points of the subinterval $[x_{k-1}, x_k]$, while n can be obtained as the least integer n which satisfies $\frac{b-a}{\epsilon} |f(b) - f(a)| < n$, where $\epsilon > 0$ is the required accuracy.

Closed Newton–Cotes formulae The compound trapezoidal and Simpson's rules are constructed by dividing $[a, b]$ into n subintervals by an equipartition $\mathcal{P} = \{x_0, x_1, \ldots, x_n\}$ and approximating f on each subinterval by polynomials of degree one and two respectively. These two rules are respectively given by:

$$Q_1^n f = \frac{b-a}{2n} \left[f(x_0) + 2 \sum_{k=1}^{n-1} f(x_k) + f(x_n) \right], \tag{1}$$

$$Q_2^n f = \frac{b-a}{6n} \left[f(x_0) + 2 \sum_{k=1}^{n-1} f(x_k) + 4 \sum_{k=0}^{n-1} f(x_{k+\frac{1}{2}}) + f(x_n) \right], \tag{2}$$

where $x_{k+\frac{1}{2}} = (x_k + x_{k+1})/2$. We may obtain an approximation which differs from If by at most $\epsilon > 0$, provided that f is smooth enough ($f \in C^2[a, b]$ for the trapezoidal rule, and $f \in C^4[a, b]$ for Simpson's rule). This is done by taking $\frac{B(b-a)^3}{12\epsilon} < n^2$ and $\frac{C(b-a)^5}{2880\epsilon} < n^4$ for the trapezoidal and Simpson's rules respectively. B and C are upper bounds for $|f^{(2)}|$ and $|f^{(4)}|$ respectively on the interval $[a, b]$. For given n, the number of integration nodes for the trapezoidal rule is $(n + 1)$, while for Simpson's rule is $(2n + 1)$.

Gauss–Legendre formulae In the formulae above, the choice of the integration nodes (equipartition of $[a, b]$), does not guarantee the maximum possible degree of accuracy[1]. The Gauss formulae, however, guarantee this accuracy. Here, we discuss the Gauss–Legendre formula, with the roots of Legendre polynomials as the integration nodes. The error of the formula is given by:

$$\int_{-1}^{1} f(x)dx - \sum_{k=1}^{n} c_k f(x_k) = \frac{2^{2n+1}(n!)^4}{(2n+1)[(2n)!]^3} f^{(2n)}(\xi), \tag{3}$$

for some $\xi \in (-1, 1)$, provided f has a continuous $(2n)$th derivative.

The Darboux (or any Riemann) sums method is the most general but the least efficient technique. The number of subintervals required for a given accuracy is usually huge compared with the other formulae described here. On the other

---

[1] The degree of accuracy of integration formula Qf, is the greatest integer d such that Qf integrates exactly all polynomials of degree less than or equal to d.

hand, if the Riemann integral exists, this method can always be applied whereas the other methods may fail. Gauss formulae are commonly used because of their accuracy, despite the fact that it may be difficult to obtain an upper bound for the $(2n)$th derivative of f.

3 Numerical Methods for Solving the Initial Value Problem of Ordinary Differential Equations

The initial value problem of the ordinary differential equation may be written in the form:

$$y' = f(t, y), \qquad t \geq a, \qquad y(a) = y_0, \tag{4}$$

where $f : [a, \infty) \times \mathbb{R}^d \to \mathbb{R}^d$, and y_0 is an initial condition. The usual requirement is that f satisfies a Lipschitz condition[2], which is sufficient for the initial value problem (4) to have a unique solution $y(t)$. Usually, the problem is to compute a numerical solution of (4) at a point $b > a$. Numerical methods fit such a problem well, because using them we actually do not obtain a continuous approximation of $y(t)$, but calculate the solution $y_0, y_1, \ldots, y_n$ at points $a = t_0 < t_1 < \ldots < t_n = b$, called mesh points, of the compact interval $[a, b]$. In the following we outline Euler's and Runge–Kutta methods, where the mesh points make an equidistant partition of $[a, b]$ ($h = t_{j+1} - t_j = \frac{b-a}{n}$, $j = 0 \ldots (n - 1)$).

Euler's method Using a Taylor's expansion of y about t_{j+1}, $j = 0 \ldots (n - 1)$ we can write $y(t_{j+1}) \approx y(t_j) + (t_{j+1} - t_j) y'(t_j)$, which gives us:

$$y_{j+1} = y_j + h f(t_j, y_j), \qquad j = 0, \ldots, (n - 1), \tag{5}$$

where h is the step size. The error of this method is given by

$$\|e_j^h\| = \|y_j - y(t_j)\| \leq \frac{Bh}{\lambda} (e^{(b-a)\lambda} - 1), \tag{6}$$

where λ is a Lipschitz constant in a given norm $\| \cdot \|$, and B is an upper bound of $\|y''\|$ over the interval $[a, b]$ (since all norms are equivalent in finite dimensional spaces, the choice of the vector norm is not relevant).

Runge–Kutta methods Integrating the differential equation given in (4) over $[t_j, t_{j+1}]$, we obtain $y(t_{j+1}) = y(t_j) + \int_{t_j}^{t_{j+1}} f \, dt$. Using various numerical integration methods to calculate the last integral, we obtain the Runge–Kutta methods. For example, using the trapezoidal rule we obtain the second–order Runge–Kutta method (RK2), while Simpson's rule is used in the construction of the third and the fourth–order Runge–Kutta methods (RK3 and RK4 respectively). These methods are summarized in Table 1.

All of these methods are convergent, i.e. $\|e_j^h\| \to 0$ when $h \to 0$ [14].

---

[2] A function $f : [a, \infty) \times \mathbb{R}^d \to \mathbb{R}^d$ is said to satisfy a Lipschitz condition in the variable y, if there exists a constant $\lambda > 0$ such that

$$\|f(t, x) - f(t, y)\| \leq \lambda \|x - y\|,$$

whenever $(t, x), (t, y) \in [a, \infty) \times \mathbb{R}^d$, where $\| \cdot \|$ is a given vector norm.

Table 1. Runge–Kutta methods

	RK2	RK3	RK4
k_1	$hf(t_j, y_j)$	$hf(t_j, y_j)$	$hf(t_j, y_j)$
k_2	$hf(t_{j+1}, y_j + k_1)$	$hf\left(t_j + \frac{1}{2}h, y_j + \frac{1}{2}k_1\right)$	$hf\left(t_j + \frac{1}{2}h, y_j + \frac{1}{2}k_1\right)$
k_3		$hf\left(t_{j+1}, y_j - k_1 + 2k_2\right)$	$hf\left(t_j + \frac{1}{2}h, y_j + \frac{1}{2}k_2\right)$
k_4			$hf(t_{j+1}, y_j + k_3)$
y_{j+1}	$y_j + \dfrac{1}{2}[k_1 + k_2]$	$y_j + \dfrac{1}{6}[k_1 + 4k_2 + k_3]$	$y_j + \dfrac{1}{6}[k_1 + 2k_2 + 2k_3 + k_4]$

4 Exact Real Arithmetic Using LFTs

By an exact real arithmetic framework we mean any set of algorithms for computing elementary function up to any required accuracy. One example is Boehm and Cartwright's framework [1, 2], developed and implemented by Ménissier–Morain, [17], which uses B–adic numbers. Another example, which uses linear fractional transformations, is based on the work of Gosper, Vuillemin, Kornerup and Nielsen, and has been developed and implemented on the special base interval $[0, \infty]$ by Edalat and Potts, [8, 20]. Recently, Heckmann [13] has considered the base interval $[-1, 1]$. In this section we summarize the representation of real numbers and functions using LFTs, based on the special base interval $[-1, 1]$.

We work in $\mathbb{R}^* = \mathbb{R} \cup \{\infty\}$, the one–point compactification of $\mathbb{R}$ (as in [22]) identified with the unit circle in the plane as in Fig.1.

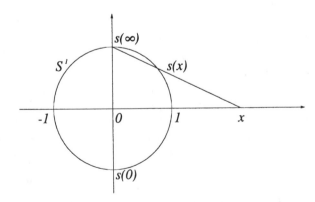

Fig. 1. The stereographic projection

Let us denote the set of vectors, matrices and tensors with integer coefficients respectively by:

$$\mathbb{V} = \left\{ \begin{pmatrix} a \\ b \end{pmatrix} \mid a, b \in \mathbb{Z} \right\}, \qquad \mathbb{M} = \left\{ \begin{pmatrix} a & c \\ b & d \end{pmatrix} \mid a, b, c, d \in \mathbb{Z} \right\},$$

$$\mathbb{T} = \left\{ \begin{pmatrix} a & c & e & g \\ b & d & f & h \end{pmatrix} \mid a, b, c, d, e, f, g, h \in \mathbb{Z} \right\}.$$

Vectors, matrices and tensors induce respectively 0–dimensional LFTs (a fraction in $\mathbb{R}^*$), 1–dimensional LFTs (a function from $\mathbb{R}^*$ to $\mathbb{R}^*$) and 2–dimensional LFTs (a function from $\mathbb{R}^* \times \mathbb{R}^*$ to $\mathbb{R}^*$), which are given by:

$$\Theta \begin{pmatrix} a \\ b \end{pmatrix} = \frac{a}{b}, \qquad \Theta \begin{pmatrix} a & c \\ b & d \end{pmatrix} (x) = \frac{ax + c}{bx + d},$$

$$\Theta \begin{pmatrix} a & c & e & g \\ b & d & f & h \end{pmatrix} (x, y) = \frac{axy + cx + ey + g}{bxy + dx + fy + h}.$$

We can identify an LFT $\Theta(K)$ with K, where K is vector, matrix or tensor. This identification is unique up to scaling: $\Theta(K) = \Theta(kK)$ for any non–zero integer k. The composition of two 1–dimensional LFTs corresponds to matrix multiplication. A non–singular matrix M maps an interval to an interval: the interval $[p, q]$ is mapped to $[Mp, Mq]$ for $\det M > 0$ and $[Mq, Mp]$ for $\det M < 0$. One can verify that for any two intervals with rational end–points, there exists an LFT M such that $M[p, q] = [r, s]$. We say that a matrix M is bounded, respectively refining, on base interval $[-1, 1]$ if $M[-1, 1] \subseteq \mathbb{R}$, respectively $M[-1, 1] \subseteq [-1, 1]$. Similarly, we say that a tensor T is bounded, respectively refining, if $T([-1, 1], [-1, 1]) \subseteq \mathbb{R}$, respectively $T([-1, 1], [-1, 1]) \subseteq [-1, 1]$. The sets of all refining vectors, matrices and tensors with integer coefficients are denoted by $\mathbb{V}^+$, $\mathbb{M}^+$ and $\mathbb{T}^+$ respectively. It is easy to check that for $M, N \in \mathbb{M}$, we have $MN[-1, 1] \subseteq M[-1, 1] \Leftrightarrow N \in \mathbb{M}^+$. A signed normal product (snp), an unsigned normal product (unp), a signed expression tree (sext) and an unsigned expression tree (uext) are respectively defined by the following recursive relations:

$$snp := V \mid M(unp), \qquad sext := V \mid M(uext) \mid T(uext, uext),$$
$$unp := V^+ \mid M^+(unp), \qquad uext := V^+ \mid M^+(uext) \mid T^+(uext, uext),$$

where $V \in \mathbb{V}$, $M \in \mathbb{M}$, $T \in \mathbb{T}$, $V^+ \in \mathbb{V}^+$, $M^+ \in \mathbb{M}^+$ and $T^+ \in \mathbb{T}^+$.

A real number, x, is represented as a shrinking sequence of nested closed intervals with rational end–points, $\{x\} = \bigcap_n [p_n, q_n]$, or using the facts above, as a signed normal product, $\{x\} = \bigcap_n M_n[-1, 1]$. By analogy with the usual representation of real numbers, the first matrix of the normal product, $M_0 \in \mathbb{M}$, is called the sign matrix, while the matrices $M_n \in \mathbb{M}^+$, $n > 0$, are called digit matrices. Edalat and Potts in [6, 8] proposed a standard form, called exact floating form, where the first matrix is one of the four sign matrices S_∞, S_-, S_0, S_+:

$$S_\infty = \begin{pmatrix} 1 & 1 \\ -1 & 1 \end{pmatrix}, \ S_- = \begin{pmatrix} 0 & 1 \\ -1 & 0 \end{pmatrix}, \ S_0 = \begin{pmatrix} 1 & -1 \\ 1 & 1 \end{pmatrix}, \ S_+ = \begin{pmatrix} 1 & 0 \\ 0 & 1 \end{pmatrix}.$$

The matrices M_n, $n > 0$ belong to the finite set of digit matrices in base $r > 0$:
$$A_k^r = \begin{pmatrix} 1 & k \\ 0 & r \end{pmatrix}, \ |k| < r.$$

One can perform some simple functions, such as $x \mapsto x - 1$, $x \mapsto \frac{1}{2x}$, over real numbers using 1–dimensional LFTs. The computation is done by a sequence of emissions and absorptions. A transformation $M \mapsto N_1(N_1^* M)$ is called an emission of a matrix N_1 from a matrix M. Here N_1^* denotes an integer inverse of N_1 (recall that N_1^* is unique up to scaling). In the exact floating form, the first emitted matrix of any expression is one of sign matrices S_σ, $\sigma \in \{\infty, -, 0, +\}$, while the subsequent emitted matrices are digits matrices. On the other hand, by absorption we mean a transformation $M N_2 \mapsto (M N_2)$. Here, matrix M consumes a matrix N_2. Let $S_\sigma D_1 D_2 \ldots$ be an exact floating point representation of a real number x. In order to compute the exact floating expression of $M(x) = \frac{ax+c}{bx+d}$ we first emit a sign matrix $S_{\sigma'}$ and then digit matrices A_k^r from M until the required accuracy is attained. Whenever no emission is possible one has to absorb further digits from x.

While matrices may be used in representation of real numbers by normal product, tensors are used to represent functions by an expression tree. Basic arithmetic operations over two arguments are easily represented by suitable tensors. For example, multiplication xy is represented by $\frac{1xy+0x+0y+0}{0xy+0x+0y+1}$. Furthermore, Edalat and Potts in [8, 20] gave an expression tree representation of a number of elementary functions like sine, cosine, tangent, exponential, logarithm. Their expression tree representation is given in the form as shown in Fig.2. Tensors may emit a matrix in the same way as matrices. But tensors may absorb digits from both of their arguments. These absorptions are called left and right absorption. For more details see [20], where Potts studies various emission and absorption strategies. We say that a tensor T is made of two matrices $T = (T_0, T_1)$, and a matrix M is made of two vectors $M = (M_0, M_1)$. T^T denotes the transpose of a tensor T, obtained by swapping the two middle columns of T. Then, right absorption, $\bullet_R$, and left absorption, $\bullet_L$ are given by:

$$(T_0, T_1) \bullet_R M = (T_0 M, T_1 M), \qquad T \bullet_L M = (T^T \bullet_R M)^T$$

We define, as in [13], the contractivity and the expansivity of a bounded matrix M by $\mathrm{con} M = \sup_{x \in [-1,1]} |M'(x)|$, $\exp M = \inf_{x \in [-1,1]} |M'(x)|$ respectively. For a bounded tensor T, the right contractivity is defined as $\mathrm{con}_R T = \sup_{x \in [-1,1]} \mathrm{con}(T|_x)$, where for fixed x, the 1–dimensional LFT $(T|_x)$ is given by $(T|_x) := (y \mapsto T(x,y))$. Similarly, the left contractivity of T is defined by $\mathrm{con}_L T = \sup_{y \in [-1,1]} \mathrm{con}(T|^y)$. If $\widetilde{T}$ is a result of emission of a digit matrix in base r from a bounded tensor T, then $\mathrm{con}_R \widetilde{T} = r \, \mathrm{con}_R T$ and $\mathrm{con}_L \widetilde{T} = r \, \mathrm{con}_L T$. If, on the other hand, the tensor $\widetilde{T}$ is the result of an absorption of a digit matrix from the right, we have $\mathrm{con}_R \widetilde{T} \leq \frac{1}{r} \mathrm{con}_R T$ and $\mathrm{con}_L \widetilde{T} \leq \mathrm{con}_L T$. Similarly, in the case of absorption from left we have $\mathrm{con}_R \widetilde{T} \leq \mathrm{con}_R T$ and $\mathrm{con}_L \widetilde{T} \leq \frac{1}{r} \mathrm{con}_L T$.

Heckmann in [13] studies the problem of how many input digits in exact floating point form are needed from an argument to produce the required number

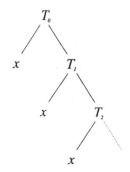

Fig. 2. $f(x)$ represented by an expression tree

of output digits (input complexity). Here we outline some relevant results that we need in order to study the complexity of numerical integration later in this paper. In order to emit k digits in base r of $M(x)$, where M is a refining matrix applied to an argument $x \in [-1, 1]$, at least $k + \lceil \log_r(\exp M) \rceil$ and at most $k + \lceil \log_r(2\mathrm{con}M) \rceil$ digits from x have to be absorbed. If the tensor T takes two arguments $x, y \in [-1, 1]$, and produces the result in the same interval (refining tensors belong to this class), then in order to produce k digits of $T(x, y)$ in base r, at most $k + \lceil \log_r(4\mathrm{con}_L T) \rceil$ and $k + \lceil \log_r(4\mathrm{con}_R T) \rceil$ digits are needed from x and y respectively.

5 Numerical Integration in Exact Framework

Given an exact real arithmetic framework, to calculate a numerical value of an integral $\mathrm{I}f$ with error not greater than $\epsilon > 0$, we first split ϵ into two parts: $\epsilon = \epsilon_\mathrm{m} + \epsilon_\mathrm{r}$. The number of the integration nodes is obtained by the error ϵ_m of the numerical integration method. Then we compute the approximation $\mathrm{Q}_n f$ which is the value of an elementary function up to ϵ_r accuracy in the exact arithmetic framework.

For example, the number of integration nodes of the compound trapezoidal rule (1) and the compound Simpson's rule (2) are respectively obtained as the integer n such that

$$\frac{B(b-a)^3}{12\epsilon_\mathrm{m}} < n^2 \quad \text{and} \quad \frac{C(b-a)^5}{2880\epsilon_\mathrm{m}} < n^4. \tag{7}$$

We then calculate $\mathrm{Q}_1^n f$ by the trapezoidal rule and Q_2^n by Simpson's rule up to precision ϵ_r. Here B and C represent upper bounds of $|f^{(2)}|$ and $|f^{(4)}|$ over $[a, b]$ respectively, and do not have to be calculated exactly.

The computation of the lower Darboux sum for a monotone function f is straightforward; for $\epsilon_\mathrm{m} > 0$ we find an integer n such that $\frac{b-a}{\epsilon_\mathrm{m}} |f(b) - f(a)| < n$, and calculate the Darboux sum up to precision ϵ_r. This can be easily extended to a piecewise monotone function if the local minima and maxima of the function are computable. We split the integration region into, say, k subintervals on each of which f is monotonic. We then calculate the integral on each of the subintervals and add them up. The error ϵ_m is split into $\epsilon_1, \ldots, \epsilon_k$, and each of these errors is used in order to calculate one of the k integrals. The points where f reaches its k peaks may be obtained by calculating the k roots of f' using the trisection algorithm described by Edalat and Rico in [9].

Comparing the error term of the Gauss–Legendre formula (3) with ϵ_m, we can obtain the number of integration nodes required for such accuracy. Therefore, if $f^{(2n)}$ vanishes for some n, the Gauss formulae with n integration nodes will integrate the function f with no error. For example, any polynomial of degree m will be integrated exactly using the Gauss formula with $n \geq \frac{m+1}{2}$. In this case our only concern is the error of the representation ϵ_r. We have tabulated the integration nodes (the zeros of Legendre polynomials of degree n) and weights of some Gauss–Legendre integration formulae in the binary sign form in Table 2.

Table 2. The integration nodes and weights of Gauss–Legendre formulae in the binary sign form

n	Integration Nodes	Integration Weights
2	$\bar{1}111\bar{1}111\bar{1}\bar{1}\bar{1}111\bar{1}\bar{1}\bar{1}111\bar{1}\ldots$ $11\bar{1}\bar{1}1\bar{1}\bar{1}11111\bar{1}\bar{1}11\bar{1}\bar{1}\bar{1}\bar{1}1\ldots$	$111111111111111111111\ldots$ $111111111111111111111\ldots$
3	$\bar{1}\bar{1}\bar{1}111\bar{1}\bar{1}111\bar{1}11\bar{1}\bar{1}\bar{1}\bar{1}\bar{1}\ldots$ $\bar{1}11111111111111111111\ldots$ $111\bar{1}\bar{1}\bar{1}11\bar{1}\bar{1}\bar{1}11\bar{1}\bar{1}111111\ldots$	$100101\bar{1}100100\bar{1}0010010\ldots$ $11100100\bar{1}00100\bar{1}0010\bar{1}\ldots$ $100101\bar{1}100100\bar{1}0010010\ldots$
4	$\bar{1}\bar{1}\bar{1}11\bar{1}\bar{1}1\bar{1}111\bar{1}\bar{1}1\bar{1}11\bar{1}\bar{1}1\bar{1}\ldots$ $\bar{1}\bar{1}1\bar{1}1\bar{1}1\bar{1}\bar{1}11111\bar{1}11111\bar{1}\bar{1}\ldots$ $1\bar{1}1\bar{1}1\bar{1}111\bar{1}\bar{1}\bar{1}\bar{1}1\bar{1}11\bar{1}111\ldots$ $111\bar{1}1111\bar{1}\bar{1}\bar{1}111\bar{1}\bar{1}11\bar{1}111\ldots$	$1\bar{1}10\bar{1}01\bar{1}000101\bar{1}\bar{1}0001\ldots$ $11\bar{1}010\bar{1}1000\bar{1}010\bar{1}0000\ldots$ $11\bar{1}010\bar{1}1000\bar{1}01\bar{1}10000\ldots$ $1\bar{1}10\bar{1}01\bar{1}00010\bar{1}1\bar{1}0000\ldots$

6   Numerical Integration Using LFTs

Using the LFT framework, we have implemented numerical integration methods and numerical methods for solving the initial value problem of ODEs in C and in the functional programming language Haskell. Here we describe our implementation of numerical integration and give some examples.

All the integration methods described in this work use linear combinations of values of f. Thus for ϵ_m, we determine the number of subintervals n and construct an expression tree which represents the nth integration formula $Q_n f$. Computing the expression tree up to precision ϵ_r we obtain the value of the integral If within $\epsilon = \epsilon_m + \epsilon_r$ accuracy. The expression tree for $Q_n f$ is shown in Fig.3, where the number p is given by $p = \lceil \log_2(n+1) \rceil$. Here T_+ is the addition tensor, i.e. $T_+(x,y) = x + y$, while the values $f(x_0), \ldots, f(x_n)$ are as in Fig.2. For the Darboux sums method and the closed Newton–Cotes formulae, the integration coefficients $c_0, \ldots, c_n$ are rational numbers and are represented by a single matrix. In the case of the compound trapezoidal rule, for example, we have $c_0 = c_n = A$, $c_1 = \ldots = c_{n-1} = B$, where A and B are given by:

$$A = \begin{pmatrix} 1 & 0 \\ 0 & n \end{pmatrix}, \qquad B = \begin{pmatrix} 2 & 0 \\ 0 & n \end{pmatrix}.$$

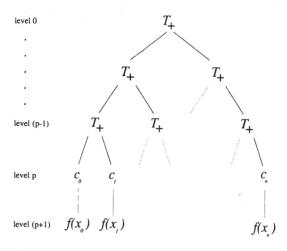

Fig. 3. The expression tree representation of $Q_n f$

6.1 Case Study: $\int_{-1}^{1} \exp x \, dx$

In this section we determine how many LFT operations (emissions and absorptions) we need to calculate the value of $\int_{-1}^{1} \exp x \, dx$ within the given precision $\epsilon = \epsilon_m + \epsilon_r$.

Potts in [20] has given expression tree representation of all basic transcendental functions including the exponential function, which can be represented, for $x \in [-1, 1]$, by the following infinite product:

$$\exp x = S_\infty \prod_{j=0}^{\infty} T_j |_x \quad \text{where} \quad T_j = \begin{pmatrix} 0 & 1 & 0 & 0 \\ 1 & 0 & 0 & 4j + 2 \end{pmatrix}.$$

We also use results in [13] in order to determine how many input digits are required to produce, say, k output digits. For example, to produce k output digits in base 2 of $\exp x$ we need in total $\frac{3}{4}k^2 + \frac{13}{2}k + 9$ LFT operations. Provided that

$x + y \in [-1, 1]$ T_+ needs $k + 2$ digits from each argument in order to produce k output digits in base 2, therefore giving $3k + 4$ LFT operations in total. Without loss of generality, we may assume that the result of any addition in Fig.3 is in $[-1, 1]$. (Since $\int_{-1}^{1} \exp x \, dx < 6$, we can multiply the integration weights by $\frac{1}{6}$. Of course, the final result has to be multiplied by 6.) For $n > 3$, in order to produce k output digits in base 2, matrices A and B do not require more than k input digits, giving in total $2k$ LFT operations.

Since digit matrices in base r are refining with contractivity $1/r$, in order to calculate If with precision $\epsilon = \epsilon_m + \epsilon_r$, we obtain the number of subintervals n, construct the expression tree as shown in Fig.3 and emit $k = \lceil 1 - \log_2 \epsilon_r \rceil$ digits in base 2. Table 3 gives the upper bound of LFT operations necessary at each level.

Table 3. Number of LFT operations

level	LFT	digits to emit	total LFT operations	copies
0	T_+	k	$3k + 4$	1
1	T_+	$k + 2$	$3k + 10$	2
$\vdots$	$\vdots$	$\vdots$	$\vdots$	$\vdots$
$(p-1)$	T_+	$k + 2(p-1)$	$3k + 6(p-1) + 4$	$\leq 2^{(p-1)}$
p	c_j	$k + 2p$	$2k + 4p$	$n + 1$
$(p+1)$	$f(x_j)$	$k + 2p$	$\frac{3}{4}(k + 2p)^2 + \frac{13}{2}(k + 2p) + 9$	$n + 1$

We then use these results to determine the upper bound for the total number of LFT operations required to calculate $Q_n f$. For the for Darboux sums method, the trapezoidal rule and Simpson's rule, these are respectively of order:

$$\mathcal{O}\left(\frac{1}{\epsilon_m} \cdot \left(\log_2^2 \frac{1}{\epsilon_m} + \log_2^2 \frac{1}{\epsilon_r}\right)\right)$$
$$\mathcal{O}\left(\sqrt{\frac{1}{\epsilon_m}} \cdot \left(\log_2^2 \frac{1}{\epsilon_m} + \log_2^2 \frac{1}{\epsilon_r}\right)\right)$$
$$\mathcal{O}\left(\sqrt[4]{\frac{1}{\epsilon_m}} \cdot \left(\log_2^2 \frac{1}{\epsilon_m} + \log_2^2 \frac{1}{\epsilon_r}\right)\right).$$

6.2 Examples

Example 1. In the first two examples, the required precision is divided into two equal parts, $\epsilon_m = \epsilon_r = \frac{1}{2}\epsilon$. As expected, Simpson's rule requires the least number of subintervals. Note that the Gauss formula is very accurate with significantly less integration nodes. First we calculate $\int_{-1}^{1} \exp x \, dx$ with the precision $\epsilon = 2^{-14}$ ($\epsilon_m = \epsilon_r = 2^{-15}$):

method	n	number of nodes	value
Darboux sums	154036	154036	N/A
trapezoidal rule	244	245	0.235041e1
Simpson's rule	6	13	0.235041e1
Gauss formula	5	5	0.2350402386e1
correct value			0.2350402387e1

Example 2. For $\epsilon = 2^{-10}$ the approximation values of $\int_{-\frac{1}{2}}^{1} \tan x \, dx$ are given in the table below:

method	n	number of nodes	value
Darboux sums	6463	6463	N/A
trapezoidal rule	79	80	0.4851e0
Simpson's rule	17	35	0.4850e0
Gauss formula	5	5	0.48503e0
correct value			0.48504e0

Example 3. By increasing ϵ_m and hence decreasing ϵ_r, the number of subintervals required may fall. But, then we have to emit more digits from the expression. Vice versa, with decreasing ϵ_m and increasing ϵ_r. Using Simpson's rule, we integrate $f(x) = \exp x$, over the interval $[-1, 1]$, with constant precision $\epsilon = 2^{-20}$, but with different values ϵ_m and ϵ_r.

ϵ_m	ϵ_r	n	number of nodes	digits required
$63 \cdot 2^{-26}$	2^{-26}	14	29	33
$31 \cdot 2^{-25}$	2^{-25}	14	29	32
$15 \cdot 2^{-24}$	2^{-24}	14	29	31
$7 \cdot 2^{-23}$	2^{-23}	14	29	30
$3 \cdot 2^{-22}$	2^{-22}	15	31	29
2^{-21}	2^{-21}	16	33	28
2^{-22}	$3 \cdot 2^{-22}$	19	39	28
2^{-23}	$7 \cdot 2^{-23}$	23	47	28
2^{-24}	$15 \cdot 2^{-24}$	27	55	28
2^{-25}	$31 \cdot 2^{-25}$	32	65	28
2^{-26}	$63 \cdot 2^{-26}$	38	77	27

7   Initial Value Problem in Exact Framework

In non–exact frameworks, round–off errors play a significant role in the choice of the step size h. As h becomes smaller, more computation is needed and round–off errors may have more influence on the final result. Furthermore, for sufficiently small h, the error will not decrease, but will become larger, i.e. the method will not converge to the exact solution. Fortunately, in exact frameworks we do not have such a problem. We can solve the initial value problem of ODEs in an exact framework following the same idea as in the numerical integration methods described in the previous section. To obtain the numerical value of the solution $y(b)$ with a given accuracy $\epsilon = \epsilon_m + \epsilon_r$, we use the error term of Euler's method given by relation (6). Provided that we have a Lipschitz constant λ and an upper bound B for $\|y''\|$, we calculate an integer n such that:

$$n \geq \frac{B(b-a)(e^{(b-a)\lambda} - 1)}{\lambda \epsilon_m}.$$

The step size, given by $h = (b-a)/n$, will guarantee that the global error is smaller than ϵ_m. We calculate the value y_n, which is an approximation of $y(b)$, up to precision ϵ_r. Unfortunately, very often this error is too conservative to be exploited. For example, to calculate $y(1)$ with accuracy $\epsilon_m = 10^{-3}$, where y is the solution of the initial value problem $y' = -100y$, $y(0) = 1$, we have $h < 10^{-48}$.

7.1 Examples

Example 4. In this example we use Euler's method and Runge–Kutta methods (RK2, RK3, RK4), implemented in exact framework using LFTs, to obtain $y(1)$, where y is the solution of the initial value problem given by:

$$y' = y^2 \left(\frac{1}{x^2} - 1\right), \quad y\left(\frac{1}{2}\right) = \frac{2}{7}.$$

The step size is $h = \frac{1}{20}$, and the exact solution is given by $y = \frac{x}{x^2+x+1}$.

x	Euler's	RK2	RK3	RK4	exact value
0.50	0.2857143	0.2857143	0.2857143	0.2857143	0.2857143
0.55	0.2979592	0.2969544	0.2968981	0.2968962	0.2968961
0.60	0.3081945	0.3062298	0.3061259	0.3061226	0.3061225
0.65	0.3166375	0.3137789	0.3136355	0.3136310	0.3136309
0.70	0.3234896	0.3198163	0.3196401	0.3196349	0.3196347
0.75	0.3289354	0.3245333	0.3243303	0.3243245	0.3243243
0.80	0.3331431	0.3281000	0.3278753	0.3278691	0.3278688
0.85	0.3362646	0.3306666	0.3304247	0.3304181	0.3304179
0.90	0.3384361	0.3323659	0.3321103	0.3321035	0.3321033
0.95	0.3397794	0.3333144	0.3330484	0.3330414	0.3330412
1.00	0.3404031	0.3336144	0.3333406	0.3333336	0.3333333

Example 5. We use RK4 over the interval $[0, 2]$ with step size $h = \frac{1}{5}$ to obtain approximations of the initial value problem:

$$y' = -y + x^2 + 2x, \quad y(0) = 1.$$

The exact solution of the problem is $y = e^{-x} + x^2$.

x	RK4	exact value	error
0.0	1.000000000000000000	1.000000000000000000	0.000000000000000000
0.2	0.858739999999999999	0.858730753077981858	0.000009246922018141
0.4	0.830336395999999999	0.830320046035639300	0.000016349964360699
0.6	0.908833418618399999	0.908811636094026432	0.000021782524373567
0.8	1.089354880936838026	1.089328964117221591	0.000025916819616435
1.0	1.367908486185687187	1.367879441171442321	0.000029045014244865
1.2	1.741225607923094956	1.741194211912202096	0.000031396010892859
1.4	2.206630112726901943	2.206596963941606476	0.000033148785295466
1.6	2.761930960959938851	2.761896517994655408	0.000034442965283443
1.8	3.405334275436600602	3.405298888221586538	0.000035387215014064
2.0	4.135371349109126133	4.135335283236612691	0.000036065872513441

Acknowledgements

We would like to thank Lindsay Errington for his C implementation of exact reals using LFTs. The second author would like to thank Marko Vrdoljak for discussions.

References

1. Boehm, H. J., Cartwright, R.: Exact Real Arithmetic: Formulating Real Numbers as Functions. In Turner, D., editor, Research Topics in Functional Programming, Addison–Wesley (1990) 43–64.
2. Boehm, H. J., Cartwright, R., Riggle, M., O'Donnell, M. J.: Exact Real Arithmetic: A Case Study in Higher Order Programming. ACM Symposium on Lisp and Functional Programming (1986).
3. Collatz, L.: The Numerical Treatment of Differential Equations. Springer-Verlag, Berlin Heidelberg New York Tokyo (1966).
4. Davis, P. J., Rabinowitz, P.: Methods of Numerical Integration. Academic Press, London New York (1975).
5. Di Gianantonio, P.: A functional approach to real number computation. PhD Thesis, University of Pisa (1993).
6. Edalat, A.: Domains for Computation in Mathemetics, Physics and Exact Real Arithmetic. Bulletin of Symbolic Logic, Vol. 3 (1997).
7. Edalat, A., Escardó, M. H.: Integration in Real PCF. Eleventh Annual IEEE Symposium on Logic in Computer Science (LICS) (1996).
8. Edalat, A., Potts, P. J.: A New Representation for Exact Real Numbers. Electronic Notes in Theoretical Computer Science, Proceedings of Mathematical Foundations of Programming Semantics 13 (1997).
9. Edalat, A., Rico, F.: Two Algorithms for Root Finding in Exact Real Arithmetic. Third Real Numbers and Computers Conference (1998) 27-44.
10. Engels, H.: Numerical Quadrature and Cubature. Academic Press, London New York (1980).
11. Escardó, M. H.: PCF extended with real numbers. Theoretical Computer Science, 162(1):79–115 (1996).

12. Gosper, W.: Continued Fraction Arithmetic. HAKMEM Item 101B, MIT Artificial Intelligence Memo 239, MIT (1972).
13. Heckmann, R.: How Many Argument Digits are Needed to Produce n Result Digits? To appear ENTCS (1999).
14. Iserles, A.: A First Course in the Numerical Analysis of Differential Equations. Cambridge Texts in Applied Mathematics, Cambridge University Press (1996).
15. Krommer, A. R., Ueberhuber, C. W.: Numerical Integration on Advanced Computer Systems. LNCS, Vol. 848, Springer-Verlag, Berlin Heidelberg New York Tokyo (1994).
16. Krylov, V. I.: Approximate Calculation of Integrals. Macmillan, New York London (1962).
17. Ménissier–Morain, V.: Arbitrary Precision Real Arithmetic: Design and Algorithms. Submitted to the Journal of Symbolic Computation (1996).
18. Nakamura, S.: Applied Numerical Methods with Software. Prentice Hall, Englewood Cliffs, New Jersey (1991).
19. Nielsen, A., Kornerup P.: MSB–First Digit Serial Arithmetic. Journal of Univ. Comp. Science, 1(7):523–543 (1995).
20. Potts, P. J.: Exact Real Arithmetic Using Möbius Transformations. PhD Thesis, University of London, Imperial College (1998).
21. Simpson, A. K.: Lazy Functional Algorithms for Exact Real Functionals. Mathematical Foundations of Computer Science, Springer LNCS 1450:456–464 (1998).
22. Vuillemin, J. E.: Exact Real Computer Arithmetic with Continued Fractions. IEEE Transactions on Computers, 39(8):1087–1105 (1990).

Observations about the Nature and State of Computer Science (Keynote Address)

Juris Hartmanis

Cornell University, Ithaca, NY, USA

Abstract. Observations about computer science, after two years in Washington as an Assistant Director of the National Science Foundation for Computer and Information Science and Engineering . This talk will assess the state of computer science, the expanding research horizons, the shaping of the new "Information technology for the Twenty First Century " initiative, and the role of theoretical computer science in this setting.

DNA Computing: New Ideas and Paradigms

Grzegorz Rozenberg[1] and Arto Salomaa[2]

[1] Leiden Institute of Advanced Computer Science (LIACS)
Leiden University, Niels Bohrweg 1, 2333 CA Leiden, The Netherlands
rozenber@wi.leidenuniv.nl
Department of Computer Science, University of Colorado at Boulder
Campus Box 430, Boulder, Colorado 80309, U.S.A.
[2] Turku Centre for Computer Science, Lemminkäisenkatu 14A
20520 Turku, Finland
asalomaa@utu.fi

Abstract. DNA computing is one of the most exciting new developments in computer science, from both technological and theoretical point of view. We begin by observing how the structure of DNA molecules and the technics available for manipulating them are very suitable for computing. We then establish a link with certain fairly old results from computability theory which essentially explain why the main feature of DNA molecules, the Watson-Crick complementarity, gives rise to the Turing-universality of DNA computations. Selected areas of DNA computing, interesting from a theoretical point of view but offering also practical potential, will be briefly examined.

1 Computer hardware of a new kind

We begin by investigating the suitability of DNA molecules for computing: can one speak of computer hardware of a new kind? In our estimation the answer is positive, at least potentially, after adequate advances in DNA technology.

DNA molecules appear both as single strands and double strands, the familiar helix being a double strand. Two *complementary* single strands anneal to form a double strand. By encoding information in a clever way on single strands, one can make far-reaching conclusions from a mere reading of the resulting double strands. Such an encoding will be illustrated in a moment. It is also present in Adleman's famous experiment, [1]. Thus, in each specific task, let us visualize a certain way of encoding information on single strands. The method of encoding should guarantee that annealing (formation of double strands) takes place only under specific conditions encoded in the original information. Consequently, the formation history of the double strands tells us that the specific conditions mentioned are satisfied – we may infer results from the mere existence of double strands.

Our discussion so far concerns only one step in a DNA computation: the formation of double strands from single strands. However, the *massive parallelism* of DNA computations can be present in this single step. Moreover, the following state of affairs, also present in this single step, can be viewed as a new paradigm of computing. The end result of the computation (or rather the end result of a specific computation step) is a physical object, a DNA double-stranded molecule. Since the process is massively parallel, there may be enormously many such objects. If we are interested in specific ones among the end results, such as the shortest paths in a graph (satisfying some conditions), we only have to sort out the physical objects, which in most cases is doable by present lab techniques. Another basic observation is that the computing activity of DNA, the formation of double strands, is provided "for free": complementary single strands anneal under appropriate conditions – this is an example of a self-assembly.

We wanted to enter in this paper directly in medias res of DNA computing: the Watson-Crick complementarity and massive parallelism. The former constitutes the basic "computing activity", whereas the later is the main source of high hopes about the practical significance of DNA computing. Our discussion has so far been in very general terms. Let us now be more specific and present the ideas in terms of an example. The example follows the lines of Adleman's experiment.

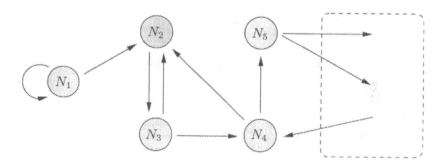

Fig. 1. An arbitrary directed graph

Consider the directed graph in Fig. 1. The dotted area indicates that the graph might actually be much bigger. However, all arrows emanating from and leading to the five specific nodes N_1 – N_5 have been marked down. Typical questions we might want to answer are the following: (i) Is there a path from the node N to the node N'? (ii) Are any two nodes connected by a path? (iii) Is there a path involving every node? (iv) Is there a path involving every node exactly once (that is, a Hamiltonian path)?

Such questions can be answered using the following method. First encode the nodes as binary strings, that is, strings consisting of zeros and ones. The strings have to be long if the total number of nodes is large; we don't want to encode two nodes in the same way. For the sake of readability, we make the encodings shorter and take care of only the "visible" part of the graph. For reasons becoming obvious below, we also want to keep the two halves of the encodings different among themselves. Thus, we consider the following encodings of length 8:

$$0\;0\;1\;1\;0\;1\;1\;0 \qquad 1\;0\;0\;0\;0\;0\;1\;0 \qquad 0\;1\;0\;0\;0\;0\;0\;1$$
$$N_1 \qquad\qquad\qquad N_2 \qquad\qquad\qquad N_3$$

$$0\;1\;1\;1\;1\;1\;0\;1 \qquad 1\;0\;1\;1\;1\;1\;1\;0$$
$$N_4 \qquad\qquad\qquad N_5$$

We call the first (resp. last) four bits of each node the *incoming* (resp. *outgoing*) half.

Next we turn to the arrows and catenate the outgoing half of the source with the incoming half of the sink, in this order:

$$\bar 0\;\bar 1\;\bar 1\;\bar 0\;\bar 0\;\bar 0\;\bar 1\;\bar 1 \qquad \bar 0\;\bar 1\;\bar 1\;\bar 0\;\bar 1\;\bar 0\;\bar 0\;\bar 0 \qquad \bar 0\;\bar 0\;\bar 1\;\bar 0\;\bar 0\;\bar 1\;\bar 0\;\bar 0$$
$$N_1 \longrightarrow N_1 \qquad\qquad N_1 \longrightarrow N_2 \qquad\qquad N_2 \longrightarrow N_3$$

$$\bar 0\;\bar 0\;\bar 0\;\bar 1\;\bar 1\;\bar 0\;\bar 0\;\bar 0 \qquad \bar 0\;\bar 0\;\bar 0\;\bar 1\;\bar 0\;\bar 1\;\bar 1\;\bar 1 \qquad \bar 1\;\bar 1\;\bar 0\;\bar 1\;\bar 1\;\bar 0\;\bar 0\;\bar 0$$
$$N_3 \longrightarrow N_2 \qquad\qquad N_3 \longrightarrow N_4 \qquad\qquad N_4 \longrightarrow N_2$$

$$\bar 1\;\bar 1\;\bar 0\;\bar 1\;\bar 1\;\bar 0\;\bar 1\;\bar 1 \qquad \bar 1\;\bar 1\;\bar 1\;\bar 0 \qquad\qquad \bar 0\;\bar 1\;\bar 1\;\bar 1$$
$$N_4 \longrightarrow N_5 \qquad\qquad N_5 \longrightarrow ? \qquad\qquad ? \longrightarrow N_4$$

With DNA double strands and complementarity in mind, we have provided the bits 0 and 1 with bars. The details will be clear in a moment.

In this way, all the information in the original graph has been encoded in two levels that might be called the object level and relational level. We now look for matches between the two levels. The significance of such matches is obvious, from our method of encoding information: the matches indicate paths in the graph.

The arrows act as splints. For instance, the match between the two levels

$$0\;0\;1\;1\;0\;1\;1\;0\;1\;0\;0\;0\;0\;0\;1\;0\;0\;1\;0\;0\;0\;0\;0\;1$$
$$\bar 0\;\bar 1\;\bar 1\;\bar 0\;\bar 1\;\bar 0\;\bar 0\;\bar 0\;\bar 0\;\bar 0\;\bar 1\;\bar 0\;\bar 0\;\bar 1\;\bar 0\;\bar 0$$

indicates that there is a path from N_1 to N_2 to N_3. On the other hand, if we begin with

$$1\;0\;0\;0\;0\;0\;1\;0\;0\;1\;1\;1\;1\;1\;0\;1$$

we can find no matching block for the second level. This tells us that there is no arrow from N_2 to N_4, although there is a path from N_2 to N_4 via N_3:

$$1\;0\;0\;0\;0\;0\;1\;0\;0\;1\;0\;0\;0\;0\;0\;1\;0\;1\;1\;1\;1\;1\;0\;1$$
$$\bar 0\;\bar 0\;\bar 1\;\bar 0\;\bar 0\;\bar 1\;\bar 0\;\bar 0\;\bar 0\;\bar 0\;\bar 1\;\bar 0\;\bar 1\;\bar 1\;\bar 1$$

To summarize: Strands of our 8-bit-long node blocks represent proper paths exactly in case they can be splinted together with perfectly matching arrow blocks.

Imagine now that large quantities of each of our blocks swim together in a molecular soup and, moreover, have a strong tendency for forming double strands in which each bit must match with its barred version. We pick up a double strand. If we then observe the encoding of the sequence of nodes $N_1 N_1 N_2 N_3 N_2 N_3 N_4 N_2 N_3 N_4 N_5$ on one of the strands, we know that the sequence constitutes a path in the graph. As such, a double strand contains the same information as a single strand: repeating the same binary sequence in a barred version cannot produce anything new. However, the *knowledge of the history of double strands (that is, the knowledge of the simple strands present in the initial soup) gives essentially new information*: the proper paths. This is guaranteed by our method of encoding: double strands are formed only if a proper path exists between the nodes. The formation rule of the double strands (complementarity) did the actual computation for us. Our method of encoding enabled us to make our conclusions because, by their formation rule, the double strands could not have come into being without our conclusions (about the existence of proper paths) being valid. We got the actual computation step, the formation of double strands, "for free".

This simple example contains the central ideas of DNA computing. DNA consists of polymer chains, referred to as *DNA strands*. A chain is composed of four nucleotides uniquely determined by their bases: A (adenine), G (guanine), T (thymine), and C (cytosine). The familiar double helix of DNA arises by the bondage of two complementary strands. The base A always bonds with T, and C with G. This phenomenon, known as the *Watson-Crick complementarity*, can be depicted as in Fig. 2.

Coming back to our example, we can of course use the alphabet $\{A, G\}$ instead of the binary alphabet by setting $0 = A$ and $1 = G$. The complementary bits are denoted by bars: $\bar{0} = T$ and $\bar{1} = C$. Thus, the five nodes get the following representations as DNA simple strands: AAGGAGGA, GAAAAAGA, AGAAAAAG, AGGGGGAG, GAGGGGGA. The encoding of the arrow $N_4 \longrightarrow N_2$ gets now the form CCTCCTTT, and the encodings of the other arrows are changed similarly.

Because of our original binary encoding, the nodes are encoded using only A and G, whereas only T and C appear in the encodings of the arrows. In DNA strands this is by no means necessary: we could use all four bases in both encodings. Thus, with DNA we have the leeway of a four-letter alphabet. However, everything we say below about Turing-universality remains valid even if we use the bases as in the example: A and G for one class of strands, and T and C for the other. The significance of this additional flexibility and leeway in DNA remains to be investigated both from the theoretical and practical points of view. The additional leeway could be the source of augmented reliability and greater efficiency.

In fact, our exposition above also describes the essentials of Adleman's experiment, [1]. Adleman encodes the nodes of a graph by DNA single strands

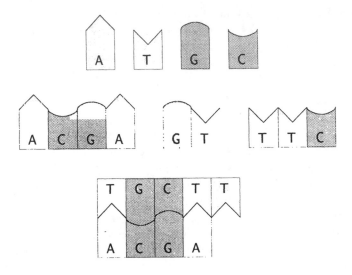

Fig. 2. The complementarity of the four bases

(oligonucleotides) and the arrows exactly as above, using complements of out-going and incoming halves. After the annealing has produced double strands, many encodings of proper paths are present: results of the computation exist as physical objects. Questions such as (i)-(iv) mentioned earlier can now be an-swered using suitable screening procedures. Strands can be filtered, for instance, according to the length or appearance of a specific substring. (We refer to [5] for details of screening precedures, as well as for other details omitted here, such as the orientation of strands and the precautions to prevent the formation of somehow "wrong" double strands.)

Apart from the Watson-Crick complementarity, Adleman's experiment makes essential use of the massive parallelism: all paths are formed simultaneously. The experiment constitutes the first proof of principle of DNA computing. It is also of great didactic values in demonstrating the correspondence between molecular operations and steps of computation.

We still add a few remarks concerning the two fundamental features of DNA computing, massive parallelism and complementarity.

Most of the famous computationally intractable problems can be solved by an exhaustive search through all possible solutions. (The history of such "perebor" algorithms is surveyed in [9] or recently in [10].) However, the unsurmountable difficulty lies in the fact that such a search is too vast to be carried out by the present technology. On the other hand, such a search could be possible if it could be done in parallel. The density of information stored in DNA strands and the ease of replicating them might render such searches possible. A typical example is the cryptanalysis of a ciphertext: All possible keys could be tried out simultaneously.

Watson-Crick complementarity is a phenomenon provided us "for free" by nature. When bondage takes place (under ideal conditions) between two single strands, we know that the bases opposite each other are complementary. This information is "free"; there is no need to check it in any way. As such, there is nothing great in knowing that the two strands in a bondage are complementary. Essentially, both strands repeat the same information. However, conclusions can be made from the history of a double strand, from the knowledge of how it came into being. If we know how information was encoded on the DNA strands subjected to bondage, we may learn much from the fact that bondage has actually taken place.

2 Déjà vu: universality is not surprising

Various theoretical models of DNA computing have been proposed – many of them are treated in [5]. While the models are based on different principles, complementarity is somehow present in a computation or derivation step in all of them. This is of course natural, in view of the central role of complementarity in DNA computing. Essentially, a model of DNA computing consists of augmenting a computational aspect of complementarity with some input-output format.

A property shared by most of the models is that they produce all recursively enumerable sets, that is, are universal in the sense of Turing machines. This property seems to be completely independent, for instance, of a model being grammatical or a machine model. Complementarity, augmented with sufficient input-output facilities, guarantees universality.

We now establish a link with certain fairly old results from computability theory, with the purpose of showing that it is not surprising that complementarity is a source of universality. Complementarity is a powerful tool because it brings, in a certain sense, the universal *twin-shuffle language* to the computing scene.

Consider the *DNA-alphabet* $\Sigma_{\text{DNA}} = \{A, G, T, C\}$ and define the letter-to-letter morphism $h_{\text{w}} : \Sigma_{\text{DNA}}^* \longrightarrow \Sigma_{\text{DNA}}^*$ by

$$h_{\text{w}}(A) = T, \quad h_{\text{w}}(G) = C, \quad h_{\text{w}}(T) = A, \quad h_{\text{w}}(C) = G.$$

The morphism h_{w} will be called the *Watson-Crick morphism*. Clearly, the square of h_{w} is the identity mapping. Words over Σ_{DNA} can be viewed as single strands. Two single strands x and y are complementary (and, thus, subject to bondage) if $x = h_{\text{w}}(y)$ or, equivalently, $y = h_{\text{w}}(x)$. The morphism h_{w} is denoted also by an upper bar: $h_{\text{w}}(x) = \overline{x}$. Thus, in this notation, the double bar will be the identity: $\overline{\overline{x}} = x$. Moreover, the DNA-alphabet can be viewed as the extended binary alphabet $\{0, 1, \overline{0}, \overline{1}\}$, with the conventions:

$$A = 0, \quad G = 1, \quad T = \overline{0}, \quad C = \overline{1}.$$

(This also agrees with the bar notation for the Watson-Crick morphism.) A generalization of the DNA-alphabet (and the extended binary alphabet) is the

DNA-like alphabet

$$\Sigma_n = \{a_1, a_2, \ldots, a_n, \bar{a}_1, \bar{a}_2, \ldots, \bar{a}_n\}, \quad n \geq 2.$$

The letters in the unordered pairs $(a_i, \bar{a}_i)$, $1 \leq i \leq n$, are called *complementary*, and also now the morphism mapping each letter to its complementary one is called and denoted as before.

The *twin-shuffle language*, TS, consists of all words over the extended binary alphabet $\{0, 1, \bar{0}, \bar{1}\}$, obtained in the following fashion. Take an arbitrary word w over $\{0, 1\}$, its complementary word $\bar{w}$, and shuffle the two in an arbitrary way. (Here we are using the customary language-theoretic shuffle operation, analogous to the shuffling of two decks of cards. Thereby, the order of letters in w and $\bar{w}$ remains unchanged.) For instance, each of the words

$$0\bar{0}00\bar{1}1\bar{0}0, \quad \bar{0}0\bar{1}00010, \quad 000\bar{1}00\bar{1}0$$

is in TS, whereas $000\bar{0}11\bar{0}1\bar{0}1$ is not. All words in TS are of an even length and contain equally many barred and nonbarred letters.

The *generalized twin-shuffle language* TS_n over the DNA-like alphabet Σ_n is defined exactly as TS except that now w ranges over the words over the alphabet $\{a_1, a_2, \ldots, a_n\}$. We need also the *reverse twin-shuffle language* RTS, defined as TS except that the words w and $\bar{w}^R$ are shuffled, where $\bar{w}^R$ is the reverse (also called mirror image) of $\bar{w}$.

The *universality* of the language TS is based on the following *representation result* for recursively enumerable languages or, equivalently, for languages accepted by Turing machines. For every recursively enumerable language L, a gsm-mapping g such that

$$L = g(TS) \tag{$*$}$$

can be effectively constructed.

The representation $(*)$ was established in [2]. For various proofs and history of this result, the reader is referred to [7]. The result shows why TS is universal: It remains the same in all representations. Only the mapping g (that can be viewed to constitute the input-output format) has to be specified differently according to each particular L, in other words, according to the needs of each particular task. The result $(*)$ is highly invariant, and remains valid also if RTS is taken instead of TS. This is important because, at least in some cases and certainly in nature, DNA double strands are read according to their orientation, which leads to words in RTS.

A further analysis of the mapping g in $(*)$ leads to various strengthnings of the result. Such strengthenings are called for in various contexts. We mention the following one, particularly suitable for models of DNA computing. Every recursively enumerable language L can be represented in the form

$$L = p(TS_n \cap R), \tag{$*$}'$$

for some $n \geq 2$, regular language R, and projection p. (By a projection we mean a morphism mapping some letters into themselves, in this case the letters of L, and erasing all the other letters.)

We refer to [7] for the proof of $(*)'$. Again the items R, p, n are effectively constructable, provided L is effectively given. The representation $(*)'$ is stronger than $(*)$ because $(*)'$ tells us that we may restrict the attention to a particular kind of gsm-mapping, namely, the product of the three mappings resulting from the operations p, $\cap R$, and the transition from TS to TS_n.

The interconnection between TS and Watson-Crick complementarity is rather obvious. We use the extended binary alphabet $\{0, 1, \bar{0}, \bar{1}\}$ to replace the DNA-alphabet, in the way indicated above. Then the DNA double strands are of the form

$$
z = \frac{x_1\ x_2\ \cdots\ x_n}{\bar{x}_1\ \bar{x}_2\ \cdots\ \bar{x}_n}
$$

where each x_i is one of the letters $0, 1, \bar{0}, \bar{1}$. (Recall that $\bar{\bar{x}} = x$.)

There are several natural ways of writing such a z as a word over the alphabet $\{0, 1, \bar{0}, \bar{1}\}$. They all lead to words either in TS or RTS. For instance, we may take the letters alternatively from upper and lower strands. In this way a word in TS results. We may also follow the orientation of the double strands, obtaining the word

$$
x_1 x_2 \ldots x_n \bar{x}_n \ldots \bar{x}_2 \bar{x}_1
$$

which is in RTS. (It is irrelevant that neither the whole TS nor RTS is obtained in this fashion.)

Conversely, the words in TS or RTS can be written as double strands in a natural way. Consider a word u in TS. It is of an even length $2m$ and, moreover, the scattered subword u' (resp. u'') of u consisting of unbarred (resp. barred) letters is of length m. If, for $1 \leq i \leq m$, we denote by x_i' (resp. x_i'') the ith letter of u' (resp. u''), then the unordered pair (x_i', x_i'') always equals either $(0, \bar{0})$ or $(1, \bar{1})$. A double strand can now be written, where the pair (x_i', x_i'') appears in the ith position and, moreover, the letter in the upper strand is the one of the two letters x_i' and x_i'' that occurs more to the left in u. Thus, for instance, the double strand

$$
\frac{\bar{1}\ \ \bar{0}\ \ 0}{1\ \ \ 0\ \ \bar{0}} = \frac{\text{C T A}}{\text{G A T}}
$$

results in this fashion from both of the words $\bar{1}\bar{0}00\bar{0}$ and $\bar{1}01000$ in TS.

The interconnection between the twin-shuffle language and Watson-Crick complementarity forms, together with representation results such as $(*)$ and $(*)'$, a basis for the universality of (models of) DNA computing. The main task is to make the input-output features (that is, the realization of the gsm-mapping) feasible, in order to fully apply the computational universality provided by the Watson-Crick complementarity. As we have already pointed out, there is quite a lot of leeway within the theoretical framework. For instance, the universality results are not affected if one assumes that one of the strands in the double strands contains only A's and G's.

3   A case study: a machine model of DNA computing

We now describe a simple machine model, where universality is realized in a straightforward way. Our *Watson-Crick finite automata* work on double-stranded sequences of symbols, similar to DNA molecules. Indeed, the essential difference between these automata and the customary ones lies in the data structures they handle: double strands versus linear strings.

Consider the DNA-like alphabet Σ_n defined in Section 2. By definition, *double strands* over Σ_n are concatenations of ordered pairs of the forms $(a_i, \bar{a}_i)$ and $(\bar{a}_i, a_i)$, $1 \leq i \leq n$. Instead of the pair notation, we have in the sequel in mind our costumary notation for double strands. A *Watson-Crick finite automaton* is a quintuple

$$\mathcal{A} = (\Sigma_n, Q, q_0, F, \delta),$$

where Q, q_0, F are exactly as in an arbitrary finite automaton (state set, initial state, final state set) and δ is a finite set of quadruples (q, x_u, x_l, q') with $q, q' \in Q$ and $x_u, x_l \in \Sigma_n^*$.

Intuitively, the automaton $\mathcal{A}$ consists of a control box, being at any moment in one of finitely many possible states, and two read-only heads H_u and H_l, moving independently of each other from left to right (see Fig. 3). The inputs are double strands over Σ_n, and the overall behaviour is nondeterministic.

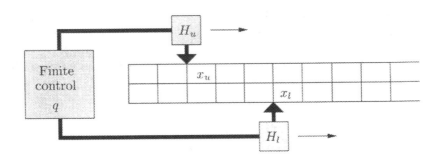

Fig. 3. The Watson-Crick automaton

Consider a quadruple (q, x_u, x_l, q'). Assume that $\mathcal{A}$ is in the state q and that x_u (resp. x_l) appears in the upper (resp. lower) strand of the input, immediately to the right of the position scanned by H_u (resp. H_l). Then it is possible for $\mathcal{A}$ to pass H_u (resp H_l) over x_u (resp. x_l) and go to the state q'. (Because $\mathcal{A}$ is nondeterministic, it might have other possible behaviours in the same configuration. In particular, it is possible that x_u and/or x_l is empty and, thus, at most one strand is read during a computation step.)

A double strand is *accepted* by $\mathcal{A}$ if the following computation is possible, using the quadruples of δ in the way described above. Initially, $\mathcal{A}$ is in the state

q_0 and the head H_u (resp. H_l) is positioned to the left of the whole upper (resp. lower) strand. At the end of the computation, $\mathcal{A}$ is in a state belonging to F and the head H_u (resp. H_l) is positioned to the right of the whole upper (resp. lower) strand.

The language *accepted* by $\mathcal{A}$ consists of all upper strands of the double strands accepted by $\mathcal{A}$. A language is termed a *Watson-Crick language* if and only if it is accepted by some Watson-Crick finite automaton.

The following universality result is fundamental. Every recursively enumerable language is a projection (that is, the morphic image obtained by a projection) of a Watson-Crick language.

The proof of this result, [5], is based on the representation $(*)'$. Indeed, the twin-shuffle language encodes a derivation in two different ways, and the projection picks up a terminal word. The intersection with a regular language is needed to exclude wrong derivations. On the other hand, the intersection can be directly checked by the Watson-Crick finite automaton, whereas TS_n is present in its data structures.

The latter observation is important also because of the following reason. As mathematical objects, Watson-Crick finite automata are almost identical with ordinary finite automata having two independent one-way reading heads. Obviously, a strand and its complementary strand contain the same information as a single strand read twice. What makes the difference is the history, the knowledge about how the double strands came into being. This fact was emphasized already earlier in our article, and is also apparent in the proof of the universality result concerning Watson-Crick languages: the two encoded versions of a derivation match only if the total double strand is correct. It is also interesting to note that, in spite of its simplicity, no result analogous to this universality result has been presented in the literature for ordinary finite two-head automata.

4 Operational complementarity and L systems

Our last topic originates from DNA computing in the sense that it studies the idea of complementarity from an operational point of view. Moreover, it is closely linked with another area of theoretical computer science, *Lindenmayer systems*, arising originally from biological considerations, [6].

Complementarity can be viewed as a language theoretic operation. As such h_w is only a morphism of a special kind. However, the operational complementarity can be considered also as a tool in a developmental model: undesirable conditions in a string *trigger* a transition to the complementary string. One assumes that the class of "bad" strings is somehow specified. Whenever a bad string x is about to be produced by a generative process, the string $h_w(x)$ is taken instead of x. If the generative process produces a unique sequence of strings, the sequence continues from $h_w(x)$. The class of bad strings is supposed to satisfy the following condition of *soundness*: whenever x is bad, then $h_w(x)$ is not bad. This condition guarantees that no bad strings are produced.

While the operational complexity can be investigated with any generative process for words, it seems particularly suitable for *Lindenmayer systems* which themselves model biological development. The simplest L system, the $D0L$ *system*, has been thoroughly investigated, [6]. A $D0L$ system generates a sequence of words. When it is augmented with a *trigger* for complementarity transitions, as described above, the resulting sequence contains no bad words. Such *Watson-Crick D0L systems*, [4,8], have opened new views in the theory of L systems. Some aspects will now be briefly outlined.

Consider a $D0L$ system $G = (\Sigma_n, g, w_0)$ over the DNA-like alphabet Σ_n. Thus, $w_0 \in \Sigma_n^*$ and $g : \Sigma_n^* \longrightarrow \Sigma_n^*$ is an endomorphism. (The morphism g is often defined in terms of *productions*, indicating the image of each letter.)

Let h_w be the Watson-Crick morphism on Σ_n^* and $TR \subseteq \Sigma_n^*$ be a recursive set such that, whenever $x \in TR$, then $h_w(x) \notin TR$. Assume, further, that $w_0 \notin TR$. Then the pair $G_w = (G, TR)$ is referred to as a *Watson-Crick D0L system* and the set TR as its *trigger*. The system G_w generates the *word sequence* $w_0, w_1, w_2, \ldots$ with

$$
w_{i+1} = \begin{cases} h_w(g(w_i)), & \text{if } g(w_i) \in TR, \\ g(w_i), & \text{otherwise,} \end{cases}
$$

for all $i \geq 0$. The *language and growth function* of G_w are defined as for ordinary $D0L$ systems: the language consists of all words in the sequence, and the growth sequence gives the word lengths. The *Watson-Crick road* associated to G_w is the infinite binary word $b_1 b_2 \ldots$ such that, for all i, $b_i = 0$ (resp. $b_i = 1$) if $w_i = g(w_{i-1})$ (resp. $w_i = h_w(g(w_{i-1}))$). (The term "road" refers to a finite graph, resulting from G_w and a morphic equivalence on Σ_n^*, [8].) We may now define the *sequence, language, growth* and *road equivalence problems* for Watson-Crick $D0L$ systems in a natural fashion.

Properties of the trigger TR are of course important, especially from the point of view of decidability. For adequately general triggers, problems become undecidable. The subset of Σ_n^*, consisting of words, where the barred letters form a strict majority, constitutes a very natural trigger. (This subset is a context-free nonregular language.) Watson-Crick $D0L$ systems having this trigger are referred to as *standard*.

We take an example from [4]. Although very simple, the standard Watson-Crick $D0L$ system defined by the axiom $a_1 a_2 \bar{a}_3$ and productions

$$a_1 \longrightarrow a_1, \ a_2 \longrightarrow a_2, \ a_3 \longrightarrow a_3, \ \bar{a}_1 \longrightarrow \bar{a}_1 \bar{a}_2, \ \bar{a}_2 \longrightarrow \bar{a}_2, \ \bar{a}_3 \longrightarrow \bar{a}_3^3$$

has quite remarkable properties. The beginning of its word sequence looks as follows, where bold characters indicate that a complementarity transition has taken place:

$$
\begin{aligned}
&a_1 a_2 \bar{a}_3, \quad \bar{a}_1 \bar{a}_2 a_3^4, \quad \bar{a}_1 \bar{a}_2^2 a_3^4, \quad a_1 a_2^3 \bar{a}_3^3, \quad \bar{a}_1 \bar{a}_2^3 a_3^9, \quad \bar{a}_1 \bar{a}_2^4 a_3^9, \\
&\bar{a}_1 \bar{a}_2^5 a_3^9, \quad \bar{a}_1 \bar{a}_2^6 a_3^9, \quad \bar{a}_1 \bar{a}_2^7 a_3^9, \quad \bar{a}_1 \bar{a}_2^8 a_3^9, \quad a_1 a_2^9 \bar{a}_3^9, \quad \bar{a}_1 \bar{a}_2^9 a_3^{27},
\end{aligned}
$$

after which there are 17 words before the next complementarity transition. The Watson-Crick road in this system begins with the word $10110^5110^{17}11$. Explicitly, after the first position, the bit 1 occurs exactly in positions $3^{i+1} + i$ and

$3^{i+1} + i + 1$, for all $i \geq 0$. Moreover, the growth function of our system is not $\mathbb{Z}$-rational, [4], which indicates a remarkable generalization of customary $D0L$ systems.

In order to mention some decidability results, we need to consider the following *problem* $\mathbb{Z}_{pos}$: Decide whether or not a negative number appears in a given $\mathbb{Z}$-rational sequence of integers.

The decidability status of $\mathbb{Z}_{pos}$ is open, although the problem is generally believed to be decidable. The input is of course assumed to be given by some effective means such as a linear recurrence with integer coefficients, or a square matrix M with integer entries such that the sequence is read from upper right corners of the powers M^i, $i = 1, 2, 3, \ldots$. Further discussion about the significance of this problem and its different representations can be found in [6].

A Watson-Crick $D0L$ system is called *stable* if its Watson-Crick road consists of only 0's, that is, if the complementarity transition never takes place. The following results were established in [4, 8].

The stability problem is undecidable for Watson-Crick $D0L$ systems with context-sensitive triggers, whereas it is decidable for systems with regular triggers. For standard systems, the stability problem is algorithmically equivalent to the problem $\mathbb{Z}_{pos}$. (In other words, an algorithm for $\mathbb{Z}_{pos}$ can be converted to an algorithm for the stability problem and vice versa.)

The sequence, language, growth and road equivalence problems are all undecidable for Watson-Crick $D0L$ systems with context-sensitive triggers. For standard systems, an algorithm for solving one of the equivalence problems can be converted to an algorithm for solving $\mathbb{Z}_{pos}$. It is an open question whether the conversion works in the other direction for standard systems.

5 Conclusion

We have discussed in this paper only a small fragment of DNA computing. The topics were chosen to illustrate some of the underlying basic principles. Although still young, DNA computing is already a thriving interdisciplinary area of science. The progress in this area can be followed in the Annual Workshop on DNA Based Computers. The Workshop has its internal proceedings that are published later. See [3] for the proceedings of the first workshop. For an introduction to basic microbiology and DNA computing, as well as a survey on language-theoretic models, the reader is referred to [5].

Acknowledgements. We are deeply indebted to Aristid Lindenmayer, not only for what he taught us in biology but also for his vistas in general science. We thank Lucian Ilie for useful discussions and for help in the preparation of the paper.

References

1. L. M. Adleman, Molecular computation of solutions to combinatorial problems, *Science* **226** 1021 – 1024.

2. J. Engelfriet, G. Rozenberg, Fixed point languages, equality languages, and representations of recursively enumerable languages, *J. Assoc. Comput. Mach.* **27** (1980) 499 – 518.

3. R. J. Lipton, E. B. Baum, eds., *DNA Based Computers*, Proc. of the DIMACS Workshop, Princeton, 1995, Amer. Math. Soc., 1996.

4. V. Mihalache, A. Salomaa, Language-theoretic aspects of DNA complementarity, *Theoret. Comput. Sci.*, to appear.

5. Gh. Păun, G. Rozenberg, A. Salomaa, *DNA Computing. New Computing Paradigms*, Springer-Verlag, Berlin, Heidelberg, 1998.

6. G. Rozenberg, A. Salomaa, *The Mathematical Theory of L Systems*, Academic Press, New-York, 1980.

7. A. Salomaa, *Jewels of Formal Language Theory*, Computer Science Press, Rockville, Md., 1981.

8. A. Salomaa, Watson-Crick walks and roads in D0L graphs, *Acta Cybernetica*, to appear.

9. B. A. Trakhtenbrot, A survey of Russian approaches to perebor algorithms, *Ann. Hist. Comput.* **6** (1984) 384 – 400.

10. B. A. Trakhtenbrot, From logic to theoretical computer science, in C. Calude, ed., *People and Ideas in Theoretical Computer Science*, Springer-Verlag, Berlin, 1999, 314 – 341.

Online Data Structures in External Memory

Jeffrey Scott Vitter[1,2][*]

[1] Duke University, Center for Geometric Computing,
Department of Computer Science, Durham, NC 27708–0129, USA
http://www.cs.duke.edu/~jsv/
jsv@cs.duke.edu
[2] I.N.R.I.A. Sophia Antipolis, 2004, route des Lucioles, B. P. 93,
06902 Sophia Antipolis Cedex, France

Abstract. The data sets for many of today's computer applications are too large to fit within the computer's internal memory and must instead be stored on external storage devices such as disks. A major performance bottleneck can be the input/output communication (or I/O) between the external and internal memories. In this paper we discuss a variety of online data structures for external memory, some very old and some very new, such as hashing (for dictionaries), B-trees (for dictionaries and 1-D range search), buffer trees (for batched dynamic problems), interval trees with weight-balanced B-trees (for stabbing queries), priority search trees (for 3-sided 2-D range search), and R-trees and other spatial structures. We also discuss several open problems along the way.

1 Introduction

The *Input/Output* communication (or simply *I/O*) between the fast internal memory and the slow external memory (such as disk) can be a bottleneck in applications that process massive amounts of data [33]. One promising approach is to design algorithms and data structures that bypass the virtual memory system and explicitly manage their own I/O. We refer to such algorithms and data structures as *external memory* (or *EM*) *algorithms and data structures*. (The terms *out-of-core algorithms* and *I/O algorithms* are also sometimes used.) We concentrate in this paper on the design and analysis of online EM memory data structures.

The three primary measures of performance of an algorithm or data structure are *the number of I/O operations performed, the amount of disk space used, and the internal (parallel) computation time*. For reasons of brevity we shall focus in this paper on only the first two measures. Most of the algorithms we mention run in optimal CPU time, at least for the single-processor case.

1.1 Disk Model

We can capture the main properties of magnetic disks and multiple disk systems by the commonly-used *parallel disk model* (PDM) introduced by Vitter and Shriver [69]. Data is transferred in large units of *blocks* of size B so as to amortize the latency of moving the read-write head and waiting for the disk to spin into position. Storage systems such

[*] Supported in part by the Army Research Office through MURI grant DAAH04–96–1–0013 and by the National Science Foundation through research grants CCR–9522047 and EIA–9870734.

as RAID use multiple disks to get more bandwidth [22, 39]. The principal parameters of PDM are the following:

N = problem input data size (items);

Z = problem output data size (items);

M = size of internal memory (items);

B = size of disk block (items);

D = # independent disks,

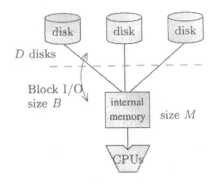

where $M < N$ and $1 \leq DB \leq M$. The first four parameters are all defined in units of items. For notational convenience, we define the corresponding parameters in units of blocks:

$$ n = \frac{N}{B}; \qquad z = \frac{Z}{B}; \qquad m = \frac{M}{B}. $$

For simplicity, we restrict our attention in this paper to the single-disk case $D = 1$, since online data structures that use a single disk can generally be transformed automatically by the technique of disk striping to make optimal use of multiple disks [68].

Programs that perform well in terms of PDM will generally perform well when implemented on real systems [68]. More complex and precise models have been formulated [59, 62, 10]. Hierarchical (multilevel) memory models are discussed in [68] and its references.

1.2 Design Goals for Online Data Structures

Online data structures support the operation of *query* on a collection of data items. The nature of the query depends upon the application at hand. For example, in dictionary data structures, a query consists of finding the item (if any) that has a specified key value. In orthogonal range search, the data items are points in d-dimensional space $\mathbb{R}^d$, for some d, and a query involves finding all the points in a specified query d-dimensional rectangle. Other types of queries include point location, nearest neighbor, finding intersections, etc.

When the data items do not change and the data structure can be preprocessed before any queries are done, the data structure is known as *static*. When the data structure supports insertions and deletions of items, intermixed with the queries, the data structure is called *dynamic*. The primary theoretical challenges in the design and analysis of online EM data structures are three-fold:

1. to answer queries in $O(\log_B N + z)$ I/Os,
2. to use only a linear amount of disk storage space, and
3. to do updates (in the case of dynamic data structures) in $O(\log_B N)$ I/Os.

These criteria correspond to the natural lower bounds for online search in the comparison model. The three criteria are problem-dependent, and for some problems they cannot be met. For dictionary queries, we can do better using hashing, achieving $O(1)$ I/Os per query on the average.

Criterion 1 combines together the I/O cost $O(\log_B N)$ of the search component of queries with the I/O cost $O(\lceil z \rceil)$ for reporting the output, because when one cost is much larger than the other, the query algorithm has the extra freedom to follow a *filtering* paradigm [19], in which both the search component and the output reporting are allowed to use the larger number of I/Os. For example, when the output size Z is large, the search component can afford to be somewhat sloppy as long as it doesn't use more than $O(z)$ I/Os; and when Z is small, the Z output items do not have to reside compactly in only $O(\lceil z \rceil)$ blocks. Filtering is an important design paradigm in online EM data structures.

For many of the online problems we consider, there is a data structure (such as binary search trees) for the internal memory version of the problem that can answer queries in $O(\log N + Z)$ CPU time, but if we use the same data structure naively in an external memory setting (using virtual memory to handle page management), a query may require $\Omega(\log N + Z)$ I/Os, which is excessive.[1] The goal is to build locality directly into the data structure and explicitly manage I/O so that the $\log N$ and Z terms in the I/O bounds of the naive approach are replaced by $\log_B N$ and z, respectively. The relative speedup in I/O performance, namely, $(\log N + Z)/(\log_B N + z)$, is at least $(\log N)/\log_B N = \log B$, which is significant in practice, and it can be as much as $Z/z = B$ for large Z.

1.3 Overview of Paper

In Section 2 we discuss EM hashing methods for dictionary applications. The most popular EM data structure is the B-tree structure, which provides excellent performance for dictionary operations and one-dimensional range searching. We give several variants and applications of B-trees in Section 3. We look at several aspects of multidimensional range search in Section 4. The contents of this paper are modifications of a broader survey by the author [68] with several additions. The reader is also referred to other surveys of online data structures for external memory [4, 27, 32, 56].

2 Hashing for Online Dictionary Search

Dictionary operations consist of insert, delete, and lookup. Given a value x, the lookup operation returns the item(s), if any, in the structure with key value x. The two main types of EM dictionaries are tree-based approaches (which we defer to Section 3) and hashing. The common element of all EM hashing algorithms is a pre-defined hash function $hash : \{\text{all possible keys}\} \rightarrow \{0, 1, 2, \ldots, K - 1\}$ that assigns the N items to K address locations in a uniform manner.

The goals in EM hashing are to achieve an average of $O(1)$ I/Os per insert and delete, $O(\lceil z \rceil)$ I/Os per lookup, and linear disk space. Most traditional hashing methods use a statically allocated table and thus can handle only a fixed range of N. The challenge is to develop dynamic EM structures that adapt smoothly to widely varying values of N.

EM hashing methods fall into one of two categories: *directory* methods and *directoryless* methods. Fagin et al. [29] proposed the following directory scheme, called *extendible hashing*: Let us assume that the size K of the range of the hash function *hash* is sufficiently large. The directory, for $d \geq 0$, consists of a table of 2^d pointers. Each item is assigned to the table location corresponding to the d least significant bits of its hash address. The value of d is set to the smallest value for which each table location has at most B items assigned to it. Each table location contains a pointer to a block where its items are stored. Thus, a lookup takes two I/Os: one to access the

---

[1] We use the notation $\log N$ to denote the binary (base 2) logarithm $\log_2 N$. For bases other than 2, the base will be specified explicitly, as in the base-B logarithm $\log_B N$.

directory and one to access the block storing the item. If the directory fits in internal memory, only one I/O is needed.

Many table locations may few items assigned to them, and for purposes of minimizing storage utilization, they can share the same disk block for storing their items. A table location shares a disk block with all the locations having the same k least significant bits, where k is chosen to be as small as possible so that the pooled items fit into a single disk block. Different table locations may have different values of k.

When a new item is inserted, and its disk block overflows, the items in the block are redistributed so that the invariants on d and k once again hold. Each time d is incremented by 1, the directory doubles in size, which is how extendible hashing adapts to a growing N. The pointers in the new directory are initialized to point to the appropriate disk blocks. The important point is that the disk blocks themselves do not need to be disturbed during doubling, except for the one block that splits.

Extendible hashing can handle deletions in a symmetric way by merging blocks. The combined size of the blocks being merged must be sufficiently less than B to prevent immediate splitting after a subsequent insertion. The directory shrinks by half (and d is decremented by 1) when all the local depths are less than the current value of d.

The expected number of disk blocks required to store the data items is asymptotically $n/\ln 2 \approx n/0.69$; that is, the blocks tend to be about 69% full [54]. At least $\Omega(n/B)$ blocks are needed to store the directory. Flajolet [30] showed on the average that the directory uses $\Theta(N^{1/B}n/B) = \Theta(N^{1+1/B}/B^2)$ blocks, which can be superlinear in N asymptotically! However, in practice the $N^{1/B}$ term is a small constant, typically less than 2.

A disadvantage of directory schemes is that two I/Os rather than one I/O are required when the directory is stored in external memory. Litwin [50] developed a directoryless method called *linear hashing* that expands the number of data blocks in a controlled regular fashion. In contrast to directory schemes, the blocks in directoryless methods are chosen for splitting in a predefined order. Thus the block that splits is usually not the block that has overflowed, so some of the blocks may require auxiliary overflow lists to store items assigned to them. On the other hand, directoryless methods have the advantage that there is no need for access to a directory structure, and thus searches often require only one I/O. A more detailed survey of methods for dynamic hashing is given in [27].

The above hashing schemes and their many variants work very well for dictionary applications in the average case, but have poor worst-case performance. They also do not support sequential search, such as retrieving all the items with key value in a specified range. Some clever work has been done on order-preserving hash functions, in which items with sequential keys are stored in the same block or in adjacent blocks, but the search performance is less robust and tends to deteriorate because of unwanted collisions. (See [32] for a survey.). A much more popular approach is to use multiway trees, which we explore next.

3 Spatial Data Structures

In this section we consider online EM data structures for storing and querying spatial data. A fundamental database primitive in spatial databases and geographic information systems (GIS) is orthogonal range search, which includes dictionary lookup as a special case. A range query, for a given d-dimensional rectangle, returns all the points in the interior of the rectangle. We use range searching in this section as the canonical query on spatial data. Other types of spatial queries include point location queries, ray shooting queries, nearest neighbor queries, and intersection queries, but for brevity we restrict our attention primarily to range searching.

Spatial data structures tend to be of two types: space-driven or data-driven. Quad trees and grid files are space-driven since they are based upon a partitioning of the embedding space, somewhat akin to using order-preserving hash functions, whereas methods like R-trees and kd-trees are organized by partitioning the data items themselves. We shall discuss primarily the latter type in this section.

3.1 B-trees and Variants

Tree-based data structures arise naturally in the online setting, in which the data can be updated and queries must be processed immediately. Binary trees have a host of applications in the RAM model. In order to exploit block transfer, trees in external memory use a block for each node, which can store $\Theta(B)$ pointers and data values. The well-known *B-tree* due to Bayer and McCreight [12, 24, 46], which is probably the most widely used EM nontrivial data structure in practice, is a balanced multiway tree with height roughly $\log_B N$ and with node degree $\Theta(B)$. (The root node is allowed to have smaller degree.) B-trees support dynamic dictionary operations and one-dimensional range search optimally in the comparison model, satisfying the three design criteria of Section 1.2. When a node overflows during an insertion, it splits into two half-full nodes, and if the splitting causes the parent node to overflow, the parent node splits, and so on. Splittings can thus propagate up to the root, which is how the tree grows in height.

In the B^+-*tree* variant, pictured in Figure 1, all the items are stored in the leaves, and the leaves are linked together in symmetric order to facilitate range queries and sequential access. The internal nodes store only key values and pointers and thus can have a higher branching factor. In the most popular variant of B^+-trees, called B^*-*trees*, splitting can usually be postponed when a node overflows, by instead "sharing" the node's data with one of its adjacent siblings. The node needs to be split only if the sibling is also full; when that happens, the node splits into two, and its data and those of its full sibling are evenly redistributed, making each of the three nodes about 2/3 full. This local optimization reduces how often new nodes must be created and thus increases the storage utilization. And since there are fewer nodes in the tree, search I/O costs are lower. When no sharing is done (as in B^+-trees), Yao [71] shows that nodes are roughly $\ln 2 \approx 69\%$ full on the average, assuming random insertions. With sharing (as in B^*-trees), the average storage utilization increases to about $2\ln(3/2) \approx 81\%$ [9, 49]. Storage utilization can be increased further by sharing among several siblings, but insertions and deletions get more complicated.

Persistent versions of B-trees have been developed by Becker et al. [13] and Varman and Verma [65]. Lomet and Salzberg [52] explore mechanisms to add concurrency and recovery to B-trees.

Arge and Vitter [8] give a useful variant of B-trees called *weight-balanced B-trees* with the property that the number of data items in any subtree of height h is $\Theta(a^h)$, for some fixed parameter a of order B. (By contrast, the sizes of subtrees at level h in a regular B-tree can differ by a multiplicative factor that is exponential in h.) When a node on level h gets rebalanced, no further rebalancing is needed until its subtree is updated $\Omega(a^h)$ times. This feature can support applications in which the cost to rebalance a node is $O(w)$, allowing the rebalancing to be done in an amortized (and often worst-case) way with $O(1)$ I/Os. Weight-balanced B-trees were originally conceived as part of an optimal dynamic EM interval tree data structure for answering

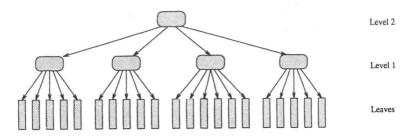

Fig. 1. B$^+$-tree multiway search tree. Each internal and leaf node corresponds to a disk block. All the items are stored in the leaves. The internal nodes store only key values and pointers, $\Theta(B)$ of them per node. Although not indicated here, the leaf blocks are linked together sequentially.

stabbing queries, which we discuss in Section 4.1, but they also have applications to the internal memory RAM model [8, 36]. For example, by setting a to a constant, we get a simple, worst-case implementation of interval trees in internal memory. They also serve as a simpler and worst-case alternative to the data structure in [70] for augmenting one-dimensional data structures with range restriction capabilities.

Weight-balanced B-trees can also be used to maintain parent pointers efficiently in the worst case: When a node splits during overflow, it costs $\Theta(B)$ I/Os to update parent pointers. We can reduce the cost via amortization arguments and global rebuilding to only $\Theta(\log_B N)$ I/Os, since nodes do not split too often. However, this approach will not work if the B-tree needs to support cut and concatenate operations. Agarwal et al. [1] develop an interesting variant of B-trees with parent pointers, called *level-balanced B-trees*, in which the local balancing condition on the degree of nodes is replaced by a global balancing condition on the number of nodes at each level of the tree. Level-balanced B-trees support search and order operations in $O(\log_B N + z)$ I/Os, and the update operations insert, delete, cut, and concatenate can be done in $O\big((1 + (b/B)(\log_m n)\log_b N\big)$ I/Os amortized, for any $2 \leq b \leq B/2$, which is bounded by $O\big((\log_B N)^2\big)$. Agarwal et al. [1] use level-balanced B-trees in a data structure for point location in monotone subdivisions, which supports queries and (amortized) updates in $O\big((\log_B N)^2\big)$ I/Os. They also use it to dynamically maintain planar st-graphs using $O\big((1 + (b/B)(\log_m n)\log_b N\big)$ I/Os (amortized) per update, so that reachability queries can be answered in $O(\log_B N)$ I/Os (worst-case). It is open as to whether these results can be improved. One question is how to deal with non-monotone subdivisions. Another question is whether level-balanced B-trees can be implemented in $O(\log_B N)$ I/Os per update, so as to satisfy all three design criteria. Such an improvement would immediately give an optimal dynamic structure for reachability queries in planar st-graphs.

3.2 Buffer Trees

Many batched problems in computational geometry can be solved by plane sweep techniques. For example, to compute orthogonal segment intersections, we can keep maintain the vertical segments hit by a horizontal sweep line moving from top to bottom. If we use a B-tree to store the active vertical segments, each insertion and query will take $\Omega(\log_B N)$ I/Os, resulting in a huge I/O cost of $\Omega(N \log_B N)$, which can be more than B times larger than the desired bound of $O(n \log_m n)$. One solution suggested in [67] is to use a binary tree in which items are pushed lazily down the tree in blocks of B items at a time. The binary nature of the tree results in a data structure of height $\sim \log n$, yielding a total I/O bound of $O(n \log n)$, which is still nonoptimal by a significant $\log m$ factor.

Arge [5] developed the elegant *buffer tree* data structure to support *batched dynamic* operations such as in the sweep line example, where the queries do not have to be answered right away or in any particular order. The buffer tree is a balanced multiway tree, but with degree $\Theta(m)$, except possibly for the root. Its key distinguishing feature is that each node has a buffer that can store M items (i.e., m blocks of items). Items in a node are not pushed down to the children until the buffer fills. Emptying the buffer requires $O(m)$ I/Os, which amortizes the cost of distributing the M items to the $\Theta(m)$ children. Each item incurs an amortized cost of $O(m/M) = O(1/B)$ I/Os per level. Queries and updates thus take $O((1/B) \log_m n)$ I/Os amortized. Buffer trees can be used as a subroutine in the standard sweep line algorithm in order to get an optimal EM algorithm for orthogonal segment intersection. Arge showed how to extend buffer trees to implement segment trees [15] in external memory in a batched dynamic setting by reducing the node degrees to $\Theta(\sqrt{m})$ and by introducing *multislabs* in each node, which we explain later in a different context.

Buffer trees have an ever-expanding list of applications. They provide, for example, a natural amortized implementation of priority queues for use in applications like discrete event simulation, sweeping, and list ranking. Brodal and Katajainen [17] provide a worst-case optimal priority queue, in the sense that every sequence of B insert and delete-min operations requires only $O(\log_m n)$ I/Os.

3.3 R-trees and Multidimensional Spatial Structures

The *R-tree* of Guttman [37] and its many variants are an elegant multidimensional generalization of the B-tree for storing a variety of geometric objects, such as points, segments, polygons, and polyhedra, using linear storage space. Internal nodes have degree $\Theta(B)$ (except possibly the root), and leaves store $\Theta(B)$ items. Each node in the tree has associated with it a bounding box (or bounding polygon) of all the elements in its subtree. A big difference between R-trees and B-trees is that in R-trees the bounding boxes of sibling nodes are allowed overlap. If an R-tree is being used for point location, for example, a point may lie within the bounding box of several children of the current node in the search. In that case the search must proceed to all such children.

Several heuristics for where to insert new items into an R-tree and how to rebalance it are surveyed in [4, 32, 34]. The methods perform well in many practical cases, especially in low dimensions, but they have poor worst-case bounds. An interesting open problem is whether nontrivial bounds can be proven for the "typical-case" behavior of R-trees for problems such as range searching and point location. Similar questions apply to the methods discussed in the previous section.

The *R*-tree* variant of Beckmann et al. [14] seems to give best overall query performance. Precomputing an R*-tree by repeated insertions, however, is extremely slow. A faster alternative is to use the Hilbert R-tree of Kamel and Faloutsos [41, 42]. Each item is labeled with the position of its center on the Hilbert space-filling curve, and a B-tree is built in a bottom-up manner on the totally ordered labels. Bulk loading a Hilbert R-tree is therefore easy once the center points are presorted, but the quality of the Hilbert R-tree in terms of query performance is not as good as that of an R*-tree, especially for higher-dimensional data [16, 43].

Arge et al. [6] and van den Bercken et al. [64] have independently devised fast bulk loading methods for R*-trees that are based upon buffer trees. Experiments indicate that the former method is especially efficient and can even support dynamic batched updates and queries.

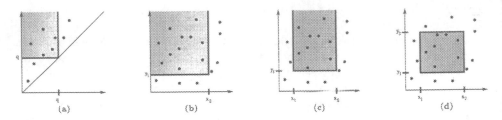

Fig. 2. Different types of 2-D orthogonal range queries: (a) Diagonal corner 2-sided query, (b) 2-sided query, (c) 3-sided query, (d) general 4-sided query.

Related linear-space multidimensional structures, which correspond to multiway versions of well-known internal memory structures like quad trees and kd-trees, include *grid files* [40, 48, 55], *kd-B-trees* [58], *buddy trees* [61], and *hB-trees* [28, 51]. We refer the reader to [4, 32, 56] for a broad survey of these and other interesting methods.

4 Online Multidimensional Range Searching

Multidimensional range search is a fundamental primitive in several online geometric applications, and it provides indexing support for new constraint data models and object-oriented data models. (See [44] for background.) For many types of range searching problems, it is very difficult to develop theoretically optimal algorithms that satisfy the three design criteria of Section 1.2. We have seen some linear-space online data structures in Section 3.3, but their query performance is not optimal. Many open problems remain.

We shall see in Section 4.3 for general 2-D orthogonal queries that it is not possible to satisfy criteria 1 and 2 simultaneously, for a fairly general computational model: At least $\Omega\big(n(\log n)/\log(\log_B N + 1)\big)$ disk blocks of space must be used to achieve a query bound of $O\big((\log_B N)^c + z\big)$ I/Os per query, for any constant c. A natural question is whether criterion 1 can be met if the disk space allowance is increased to $O\big(n(\log n)/\log(\log_B N + 1)\big)$ blocks. And since the lower bound applies only to general rectangular queries, it is natural to ask whether there are data structures that meet criteria 1–3 for interesting special cases of 2-D range searching, such as those pictured in Figure 2. Fortunately, the answers to both questions are "yes!", as we shall explore in the next section.

4.1 Data Structures for 2-D Orthogonal Range Searching

An obvious paradigm for developing an efficient EM data structure is to "externalize" an existing data structure that works well when the problem fits into internal memory. If the internal memory data structure uses a binary tree, then a multiway tree has to be used instead. However, it can be difficult when searching a B-tree to report the outputs in an output-sensitive manner. For example, for certain searching applications, each of the $\Theta(B)$ subtrees of a given node in a B-tree may contribute one item to the query output, which will require each subtree to be explored (costing several I/Os) just to report a single output item. Fortunately, the data structure can sometimes be augmented with a set of filtering substructures, each of which is a data structure for a smaller version of the same problem, in order to achieve output-sensitive reporting. We refer to this approach as the *bootstrapping* paradigm. Each substructure typically needs to store only $O(B^2)$ items and to answer queries in $O(\log_B B^2 + Z'/B) = O(\lceil Z'/B \rceil)$ I/Os, where Z' is the number of items reported. The substructure is allowed to be static if it can be constructed in $O(B)$ I/Os, since we can keep updates in a separate buffer and do a global rebuilding in $O(B)$ I/Os when there are $\Theta(B)$ updates. Such a rebuilding costs $O(1)$ I/Os per update in the amortized sense, but the amortization for the substructures can often be removed and made worst-case by use of weight-balanced B-trees as the underlying B-tree structure.

Arge and Vitter [8] first uncovered the bootstrapping paradigm while designing an optimal dynamic EM data structure for diagonal corner 2-sided 2-D queries (see Figure 2(a)) that meets all three design criteria of Section 1.2. Diagonal corner 2-sided queries are equivalent to stabbing queries: Given a set of one-dimensional intervals, report all the intervals that contain the query value x. (Such intervals are said to be "stabbed" by x.) The global data structure is a multiway version of the well-known interval tree data structure [25, 26], which supports stabbing queries in $O(\log N + Z)$ CPU time and updates in $O(\log N)$ CPU time and uses $O(N)$ space. It is externalized by using a weight-balanced B-tree as the underlying base tree, where the nodes have degree $\Theta(\sqrt{B})$ so that multislabs can be introduced. Each node in the base tree corresponds in a natural way to a one-dimensional range of x-values; its $\Theta(\sqrt{B})$ children correspond to subranges called slabs, and the $\Theta(\sqrt{B}^2) = \Theta(B)$ contiguous sets of slabs are called *multislabs*.

Each inputed interval is stored in the lowest node v in the base tree whose range completely contains the interval. The interval is decomposed by v's slabs into at most three parts: the middle part that completely spans one or more slabs of v, the left end that partially protrudes into a slab w_{left}, and the right end that partially protrudes into a slab w_{right}. The three parts are stored in substructures of v: The middle part is stored in a list associated with the multislab it spans, the left part is stored in a list for w_{left} ordered by left endpoint, and the right part is stored in a list for w_{right} ordered by right endpoint.

Given a query value x, the intervals stabbed by x reside in the substructures of the nodes of the base tree along the search path for x. For each such node v, we consider each of v's multislabs that contains x and report all the intervals in its list. We also walk sequentially through the right-ordered list and left-ordered list for the slab of v that contains x, reporting intervals in an output-sensitive way.

The big problem with this approach is that we have to look at the list for each of v's multislabs that contains x, regardless of how many intervals are in the list. For example, there may be $\Theta(B)$ such multislab lists, but each list may contain only a few stabbed intervals (or worse yet, none at all!). The resulting query performance will be highly nonoptimal. The solution, according to the bootstrapping paradigm, is to use a substructure in each node consisting of an optimal static data structure for a smaller version of the same problem; a good choice is the corner data structure developed by Kanellakis et al. [44]. The corner substructure is used to store all the intervals from the "sparse" multislab lists, namely, those that contain fewer than B intervals, and thus the substructure contains only $O(B^2)$ intervals. When visiting node v, we access only v's non-sparse multislabs lists, each of which contributes $Z' \geq B$ intervals to the output, at an output-sensitive cost of $O(Z'/B)$ I/Os, for some Z'. The remaining Z'' stabbed intervals stored in v can be found by querying v's corner substructure of size $O(B^2)$, at a cost of $O(\lceil Z''/B \rceil)$ I/Os, which is output-sensitive. Since there are $O(\log_B N)$ nodes along the search path, the total collection of Z stabbed intervals are reported in a $O(\log_B N + z)$ I/Os, which is optimal. The use of a weight-balanced B-tree as the underlying base tree permits the rebuilding of the static substructures in worst-case optimal I/O bounds.

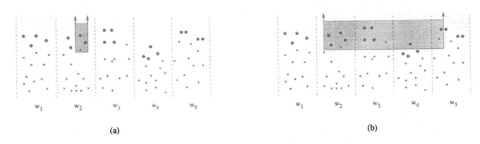

(a)   (b)

Fig. 3. Internal node v of the EM priority search tree, with slabs (children) w_1, w_2, ..., w_5. The Y-sets of each slab, which are stored collectively in v's substructure, are indicated by the bold points. (a) The 3-sided query is completely contained in the x-range of w_2. The relevant (bold) points are reported from v's substructure, and the query is recursively answered in w_2. (b) The 3-sided query spans several slabs. The relevant (bold) points are reported from v's substructure, and the query is recursively answered in w_2, w_3, and w_5. The query is *not* extended to w_4 in this case because not all of its Y-set $Y(w_4)$ (stored in v's substructure) satisfies the query, and as a result none of the points stored in w_4's subtree can satisfy the query.

Stabbing queries are important because, when combined with one-dimensional range queries, they provide a solution to *dynamic interval management*, in which one-dimensional intervals can be inserted and deleted, and intersection queries can be performed. These operations support indexing of one-dimensional constraints in constraint databases. Other applications of stabbing queries arise in graphics and GIS. For example, Chiang and Silva [23] apply the EM interval tree structure to extract at query time the boundary components of the isosurface (or contour) of a surface. A data structure for a related problem, which in addition has optimal output complexity, appears in [3]. The above bootstrapping approach also yields dynamic EM segment trees with optimal query and update bound and $O(n \log_B N)$-block space usage.

Arge et al. [7] provide another example of the bootstrapping paradigm by developing an optimal dynamic EM data structure for 3-sided 2-D range searching (see Figure 2(c)) that meets all three design criteria. The global structure is an externalization of the optimal structure for internal memory—the priority search tree [53]—using a weight-balanced B-tree as the underlying base tree. Each node in the base tree corresponds to a one-dimensional range of x-values, and its $\Theta(B)$ children correspond to subranges consisting of vertical slabs. Each node v contains a small substructure that supports 3-sided queries. Its substructure stores the "Y-set" $Y(w)$ for each of the $\Theta(B)$ slabs (children) w of v. The Y-set $Y(w)$ consists of the highest $\Theta(B)$ points in w's slab that are not already stored in an ancestor of v. Thus, there are a total of $\Theta(B^2)$ points stored in v's substructure.

A 3-sided query of the form $[x_1, x_2] \times [y_1, \infty)$ is answered by visiting a set of nodes in the base tree, starting with the root, and querying the substructure of each node. The following rule is used to determine which children of a visited node v should be visited: We visit v's child w if either

1. w is along the leftmost search path for x_1 or the rightmost search path for x_2 in the base tree, or
2. the entire Y-set $Y(w)$ is reported when v is visited.

(See Figure 3.) Rule 2 provides an effective filtering mechanism to guarantee output-sensitive reporting when Rule 1 is not satisfied: The I/O cost for initially accessing a child node w can be charged to the $\Theta(B)$ points in $Y(w)$ reported from v's substructure; conversely, if not all of $Y(w)$ is reported, then the points stored in w's subtree will be too low to satisfy the query, and there is no need to visit w. (See Figure 3(b).)

Arge et al. [7] also provide an elegant and optimal static data structure for 3-sided range search, which can be used in the EM priority search tree described above to implement the substructures containing $O(B^2)$ points. The static structure is a persistent version of a data structure for one-dimensional range search. When used for $O(B^2)$ points, it occupies $O(B)$ blocks, can be built in $O(B)$ I/Os, and supports 3-sided queries in $O(\lceil Z'/B \rceil)$ I/Os per query, where Z' is the number of points reported. The static structure is so simple that it may be useful in practice on its own.

The dynamic data structure for 3-sided range searching can be generalized using the filtering technique of Chazelle [19] to handle general 4-sided queries with optimal query bound $O(\log_B N)$ and optimal disk space usage $O\big(n(\log n)/\log(\log_B N + 1)\big)$ [7]. The update bound becomes $O\big((\log_B N)(\log n)/\log(\log_B N + 1)\big)$. The outer level of the structure is a $(\log_B N + 1)$-way one-dimensional search tree; each 4-sided query is reduced to two 3-sided queries, a stabbing query, and $\log_B N$ list traversals.

Earlier work on 2-sided and 3-sided queries was done by Ramaswamy and Subramanian [57] using the notion of *path caching*; their structure met criterion 1 but had higher storage overheads and amortized and/or nonoptimal update bounds. Subramanian and Ramaswamy [63] subsequently developed the *p-range tree* data structure for 3-sided queries, with optimal linear disk space and nearly optimal query and amortized update bounds. They got a static data structure for 4-sided range search with the same query bound by applying the filtering technique of Chazelle [19]. The structure can be modified to perform updates, by use of a weight-balanced B-tree as the underlying base tree and the dynamization techniques of [7], but the resulting update bound will be amortized and nonoptimal, as a consequence of the use of their 3-sided data structure.

4.2 Other Range Searching Data Structures

For other types of range searching, such as in higher dimensions and for nonorthogonal queries, different filtering techniques are needed. So far, relatively little work has been done, and many open problems remain.

Vengroff and Vitter [66] develop the first theoretically near-optimal EM data structure for static three-dimensional orthogonal range searching. They create a hierarchical partitioning in which all the points that dominate a query point are densely contained in a set of blocks. Compression techniques are needed to minimize disk storage. With some recent modifications by the author, queries can be done in $O(\log_B N + z)$ I/Os, which is optimal, and the space usage is $O\big(n(\log n)^k/(\log(\log_B N + 1))^k\big)$ disk blocks to support $(3 + k)$-sided 3-D range queries, in which k of the dimensions ($0 \le k \le 3$) have finite ranges. The space bounds are optimal for 3-sided 3-D queries (i.e., $k = 0$) and 4-sided 3-D queries (i.e., $k = 1$). The result also provides optimal $O(\log N + Z)$-time query performance in the RAM model using linear space for answering 3-sided 3-D queries, improving upon the result in [21].

Agarwal et al. [2] consider halfspace range searching, in which a query is specified by a hyperplane and a bit indicating one of its two sides, and the output of the query consists of all the points on that side of the hyperplane. They give various data structures for halfspace range searching in two, three, and higher dimensions, including one that works for simplex (polygon) queries in two dimensions, but with a higher query I/O cost. They have subsequently improved the storage bounds to get an optimal static data structure satisfying criteria 1 and 2 for 2-D halfspace range queries.

The number of I/Os needed to build the data structures for 3-D orthogonal range search and halfspace range search is rather large (more than $\Omega(N)$). Still, the structures shed useful light on the complexity of range searching and may open the way to improved solutions. An open problem is to design efficient construction and update algorithms and to improve upon the constant factors.

Callahan et al. [18] develop dynamic EM data structures for several online problems such as finding an approximately nearest neighbor and maintaining the closest pair of vertices. Numerous other data structures have been developed for range queries and related problems on spatial data. We refer to [4, 32, 56] for a broad survey.

4.3 Lower Bounds for Orthogonal Range Searching

As mentioned above, Subramanian and Ramaswamy [63] prove that no EM data structure for 2-D range searching can achieve criterion 1 using less than $O\big(n(\log n)/\log(\log_B N + 1)\big)$ disk blocks, even if we relax 1 to allow $O\big((\log_B N)^c + z\big)$ I/Os per query, for any constant c. The result holds for an EM version of the pointer machine model, based upon the approach of Chazelle [20] for internal memory.

Hellerstein et al. [38] consider a generalization of the layout-based lower bound argument of Kanellakis et al. [44] for studying the tradeoff between disk space usage and query performance. They develop a model for *indexability*, in which an "efficient" data structure is expected to contain the Z output points to a query compactly within $O(\lceil Z/B \rceil) = O(\lceil z \rceil)$ blocks. One shortcoming of the model is that it considers only data layout and ignores the search component of queries, and thus it rules out the important filtering paradigm discussed earlier in Section 4. For example, it is reasonable for any query algorithm to perform at least $\log_B N$ I/Os, so if the output size Z is at most B, an algorithm may still be able to satisfy criterion 1 even if the output is contained within $O(\log_B N)$ blocks rather than $O(z) = O(1)$ blocks. Arge et al. [7] modify the model to rederive the same nonlinear space lower bound $O\big(n(\log n)/\log(\log_B N + 1)\big)$ of Subramanian and Ramaswamy [63] for 2-D range searching by considering only output sizes Z larger than $(\log_B N)^c B$, for which the number of blocks allowed to hold the outputs is $Z/B = O\big((\log_B N)^c + z\big)$. This approach ignores the complexity of how to find the relevant blocks, but as mentioned in Section 4.1 the authors separately provide an optimal 2-D range search data structure that uses the same amount of disk space and does queries in the optimal $O(\log_B N + z)$ I/Os. Thus, despite its shortcomings, the indexability model is elegant and can provide much insight into the complexity of blocking data in external memory. Further results in this model appear in [47, 60].

One intuition from the indexability model is that less disk space is needed to efficiently answer 2-D queries when the queries have bounded aspect ratio (i.e., when the ratio of the longest side length to the shortest side length of the query rectangle is bounded). An interesting question is whether R-trees and the linear-space structures of Section 3.3 can be shown to perform provably well for such queries. Another interesting scenario is where the queries correspond to snapshots of the continuous movement of a sliding rectangle.

When the data structure is restricted to contain only a single copy of each point, Kanth and Singh [45] show for a restricted class of index-based trees that d-dimensional range queries in the worst case require $\Omega(n^{1-1/d} + z)$ I/Os, and they provide a data structure with a matching bound. Another approach to achieve the same bound is the cross tree data structure of Grossi and Italiano [35], which in addition supports the operations of cut and concatenate.

5 Conclusions

In this paper we have surveyed several useful paradigms and techniques for the design and implementation of efficient online data structures for external memory. For lack of space, we didn't cover several interesting geometric search problems, such as point location, ray shooting queries, nearest neighbor queries, where most EM problems remain open, nor the rich areas of string processing and combinatorial graph problems. We refer the reader to [4, 31, 68] and the references therein.

A variety of interesting challenges remain in range searching, such as methods for high dimensions and nonorthogonal searches as well as the analysis of R-trees and linear-space methods for typical-case scenarios. Another problem is to prove lower bounds without the indivisibility assumption. A continuing goal is to translate theoretical gains into observable improvements in practice. For some of the problems that can be solved optimally up to a constant factor, the constant overhead is too large for the algorithm to be of practical use, and simpler approaches are needed.

Online issue also arise in the analysis of batched EM algorithms: In practice, batched algorithms must adapt in a robust and online way when the memory allocation changes, and online techniques can play an important role. Some initial work has been done on memory-adaptive EM algorithms in a competitive framework [11].

Acknowledgements. The author wishes to thank Lars Arge, Ricardo Baeza-Yates, Vasilis Samoladas, and the members of the Center for Geometric Computing at Duke University for helpful comments and suggestions.

References

1. P. K. Agarwal, L. Arge, G. S. Brodal, and J. S. Vitter. I/O-efficient dynamic point location in monotone planar subdivisions. In *Proceedings of the ACM-SIAM Symposium on Discrete Algorithms*, 11–20, 1999.
2. P. K. Agarwal, L. Arge, J. Erickson, P. G. Franciosa, and J. S. Vitter. Efficient searching with linear constraints. In *Proc. 17th ACM Symposium on Principles of Database Systems*, 169–178, 1998.
3. P. K. Agarwal, L. Arge, T. M. Murali, K. Varadarajan, and J. S. Vitter. I/O-efficient algorithms for contour line extraction and planar graph blocking. In *Proceedings of the ACM-SIAM Symposium on Discrete Algorithms*, 117–126, 1998.
4. P. K. Agarwal and J. Erickson. Geometric range searching and its relatives. In B. Chazelle, J. E. Goodman, and R. Pollack, editors, *Advances in Discrete and Computational Geometry*, volume 23 of *Contemporary Mathematics*, 1–56. AMS Press, Providence, RI, 1999.
5. L. Arge. The buffer tree: A new technique for optimal I/O-algorithms. In *Proceedings of the Workshop on Algorithms and Data Structures*, volume 955 of *Lecture Notes in Computer Science*, 334–345. Springer-Verlag, 1995. A complete version appears as BRICS technical report RS–96–28, University of Aarhus.
6. L. Arge, K. H. Hinrichs, J. Vahrenhold, and J. S. Vitter. Efficient bulk operations on dynamic R-trees. In *Proceedings of the 1st Workshop on Algorithm Engineering and Experimentation*, Baltimore, January 1999.
7. L. Arge, V. Samoladas, and J. S. Vitter. Two-dimensional indexability and optimal range search indexing. In *Proceedings of the ACM Symposium Principles of Database Systems*, Philadelphia, PA, May–June 1999.
8. L. Arge and J. S. Vitter. Optimal dynamic interval management in external memory. In *Proceedings of the IEEE Symposium on Foundations of Computer Science*, 560–569, Burlington, VT, October 1996.
9. R. A. Baeza-Yates. Expected behaviour of B$^+$-trees under random insertions. *Acta Informatica*, 26(5), 439–472, 1989.
10. R. D. Barve, E. A. M. Shriver, P. B. Gibbons, B. K. Hillyer, Y. Matias, and J. S. Vitter. Modeling and optimizing I/O throughput of multiple disks on a bus: the long version. Technical report, Bell Labs, 1997.
11. R. D. Barve and J. S. Vitter. External memory algorithms with dynamically changing memory allocations: Long version. Technical Report CS–1998–09, Duke University, 1998.
12. R. Bayer and E. McCreight. Organization of large ordered indexes. *Acta Inform.*, 1, 173–189, 1972.

13. B. Becker, S. Gschwind, T. Ohler, B. Seeger, and P. Widmayer. An asymptotically optimal multiversion B-tree. *The VLDB Journal*, 5(4), 264–275, December 1996.

14. N. Beckmann, H.-P. Kriegel, R. Schneider, and B. Seeger. The R*-tree: An efficient and robust access method for points and rectangles. In *Proceedings of the SIGMOD International Conference on Management of Data*, 322–331, 1990.

15. J. L. Bentley. Multidimensional divide and conquer. *Communications of the ACM*, 23(6), 214–229, 1980.

16. S. Berchtold, C. Böhm, and H.-P. Kriegel. Improving the query performance of high-dimensional index structures by bulk load operations. In *Proceedings of the International Conference on Extending Database Technology*, 1998.

17. G. S. Brodal and J. Katajainen. Worst-case efficient external-memory priority queues. In *Proceedings of the Scandinavian Workshop on Algorithms Theory*, volume 1432 of *Lecture Notes in Computer Science*, 107–118, Stockholm, Sweden, July 1998. Springer-Verlag.

18. P. Callahan, M. T. Goodrich, and K. Ramaiyer. Topology B-trees and their applications. In *Proceedings of the Workshop on Algorithms and Data Structures*, volume 955 of *Lecture Notes in Computer Science*, 381–392. Springer-Verlag, 1995.

19. B. Chazelle. Filtering search: a new approach to query-answering. *SIAM Journal on Computing*, 15, 703–724, 1986.

20. B. Chazelle. Lower bounds for orthogonal range searching: I. The reporting case. *Journal of the ACM*, 37(2), 200–212, April 1990.

21. B. Chazelle and H. Edelsbrunner. Linear space data structures for two types of range search. *Discrete & Computational Geometry*, 2, 113–126, 1987.

22. P. M. Chen, E. K. Lee, G. A. Gibson, R. H. Katz, and D. A. Patterson. RAID: high-performance, reliable secondary storage. *ACM Computing Surveys*, 26(2), 145–185, June 1994.

23. Y.-J. Chiang and C. T. Silva. External memory techniques for isosurface extraction in scientific visualization. In J. Abello and J. S. Vitter, editors, *External Memory Algorithms and Visualization*, Providence, RI, 1999. AMS Press.

24. D. Comer. The ubiquitous B-tree. *Comput. Surveys*, 11(2), 121–137, 1979.

25. H. Edelsbrunner. A new approach to rectangle intersections, part I. *Int. J. Computer Mathematics*, 13, 209–219, 1983.

26. H. Edelsbrunner. A new approach to rectangle intersections, part II. *Int. J. Computer Mathematics*, 13, 221–229, 1983.

27. R. J. Enbody and H. C. Du. Dynamic hashing schemes. *ACM Computing Surveys*, 20(2), 85–113, June 1988.

28. G. Evangelidis, D. B. Lomet, and B. Salzberg. The hB$^{\Pi}$-tree: A multi-attribute index supporting concurrency, recovery and node consolidation. *VLDB Journal*, 6, 1–25, 1997.

29. R. Fagin, J. Nievergelt, N. Pippinger, and H. R. Strong. Extendible hashing—a fast access method for dynamic files. *ACM Transactions on Database Systems*, 4(3), 315–344, 1979.

30. P. Flajolet. On the performance evaluation of extendible hashing and trie searching. *Acta Informatica*, 20(4), 345–369, 1983.

31. W. Frakes and R. Baeza-Yates, editors. *Information Retrieval: Data Structures and Algorithms*. Prentice-Hall, 1992.

32. V. Gaede and O. Günther. Multidimensional access methods. *Computing Surveys*, 30(2), 170–231, June 1998.

33. G. A. Gibson, J. S. Vitter, and J. Wilkes. Report of the working group on storage I/O issues in large-scale computing. *ACM Computing Surveys*, 28(4), 779–793, December 1996.

34. D. Greene. An implementation and performance analysis of spatial data access methods. In *Proceedings of the IEEE International Conference on Data Engineering*, 606–615, 1989.

35. R. Grossi and G. F. Italiano. Efficient cross-trees for external memory. In J. Abello and J. S. Vitter, editors, *External Memory Algorithms and Visualization*. AMS Press, Providence, RI, 1999.

36. R. Grossi and G. F. Italiano. Efficient splitting and merging algorithms for order decomposable problems. *Information and Computation*, in press. An earlier version appears in *Proceedings of the 24th International Colloquium on Automata, Languages and Programming*, volume 1256 of Lecture Notes in Computer Science, Springer Verlag, 605–615, 1997.

37. A. Guttman. R-trees: A dynamic index structure for spatial searching. In *Proceedings of the ACM SIGMOD Conference on Management of Data*, 47–57, 1985.

38. J. M. Hellerstein, E. Koutsoupias, and C. H. Papadimitriou. On the analysis of indexing schemes. In *Proceedings of the 16th ACM Symposium on Principles of Database Systems*, 249–256, Tucson, AZ, May 1997.

39. L. Hellerstein, G. Gibson, R. M. Karp, R. H. Katz, and D. A. Patterson. Coding techniques for handling failures in large disk arrays. *Algorithmica*, 12(2–3), 182–208, 1994.

40. K. H. Hinrichs. *The grid file system: Implementation and case studies of applications*. PhD thesis, Dept. Information Science, ETH, Zürich, 1985.

41. I. Kamel and C. Faloutsos. On packing R-trees. In *Proceedings of the 2nd International Conference on Information and Knowledge Management*, 490–499, 1993.

42. I. Kamel and C. Faloutsos. Hilbert R-tree: An improved R-tree using fractals. In *Proceedings of the 20th International Conference on Very Large Databases*, 500–509, 1994.

43. I. Kamel, M. Khalil, and V. Kouramajian. Bulk insertion in dynamic R-trees. In *Proceedings of the 4th International Symposium on Spatial Data Handling*, 3B, 31–42, 1996.
44. P. C. Kanellakis, S. Ramaswamy, D. E. Vengroff, and J. S. Vitter. Indexing for data models with constraints and classes. *Journal of Computer and System Science*, 52(3), 589–612, 1996.
45. K. V. R. Kanth and A. K. Singh. Optimal dynamic range searching in non-replicating index structures. In *Proceedings of the 7th International Conference on Database Theory*, Jerusalem, January 1999.
46. D. E. Knuth. *Sorting and Searching*, volume 3 of *The Art of Computer Programming*. Addison-Wesley, Reading MA, second edition, 1998.
47. E. Koutsoupias and D. S. Taylor. Tight bounds for 2-dimensional indexing schemes. In *Proceedings of the 17th ACM Symposium on Principles of Database Systems*, Seattle, WA, June 1998.
48. R. Krishnamurthy and K.-Y. Wang. Multilevel grid files. Tech. report, IBM T. J. Watson Center, Yorktown Heights, NY, November 1985.
49. K. Küspert. Storage utilization in B*-trees with a generalized overflow technique. *Acta Informatica*, 19, 35–55, 1983.
50. W. Litwin. Linear hashing: A new tool for files and tables addressing. In *International Conference On Very Large Data Bases*, 212–223, Montreal, Quebec, Canada, October 1980.
51. D. B. Lomet and B. Salzberg. The hB-tree: a multiattribute indexing method with good guaranteed performance. *ACM Transactions on Database Systems*, 15(4), 625–658, 1990.
52. D. B. Lomet and B. Salzberg. Concurrency and recovery for index trees. *The VLDB Journal*, 6(3), 224–240, 1997.
53. E. M. McCreight. Priority search trees. *SIAM Journal on Computing*, 14(2), 257–276, May 1985.
54. H. Mendelson. Analysis of extendible hashing. *IEEE Transactions on Software Engineering*, SE-8, 611–619, November 1982.
55. J. Nievergelt, H. Hinterberger, and K. C. Sevcik. The grid file: An adaptable, symmetric multikey file structure. *ACM Trans. Database Syst.*, 9, 38–71, 1984.
56. J. Nievergelt and P. Widmayer. Spatial data structures: Concepts and design choices. In M. van Kreveld, J. Nievergelt, T. Roos, and P. Widmayer, editors, *Algorithmic Foundations of GIS*, volume 1340 of *Lecture Notes in Computer Science*. Springer-Verlag, 1997.
57. S. Ramaswamy and S. Subramanian. Path caching: a technique for optimal external searching. *Proceedings of the 13th ACM Conference on Principles of Database Systems*, 1994.
58. J. T. Robinson. The k-d-b-tree: a search structure for large multidimensional dynamic indexes. In *Proc. ACM Conference Principles Database Systems*, 10–18, 1981.
59. C. Ruemmler and J. Wilkes. An introduction to disk drive modeling. *IEEE Computer*, 17–28, March 1994.
60. V. Samoladas and D. Miranker. A lower bound theorem for indexing schemes and its application to multidimensional range queries. In *Proc. 17th ACM Conf. on Princ. of Database Systems*, Seattle, WA, June 1998.
61. B. Seeger and H.-P. Kriegel. The buddy-tree: An efficient and robust access method for spatial data base systems. In *Proc. 16th VLDB Conference*, 590–601, 1990.
62. E. Shriver, A. Merchant, and J. Wilkes. An analytic behavior model for disk drives with readahead caches and request reordering. In *Joint International Conference on Measurement and Modeling of Computer Systems*, June 1998.
63. S. Subramanian and S. Ramaswamy. The P-range tree: a new data structure for range searching in secondary memory. *Proceedings of the ACM-SIAM Symposium on Discrete Algorithms*, 1995.
64. J. van den Bercken, B. Seeger, and P. Widmayer. A generic approach to bulk loading multidimensional index structures. In *Proceedings 23rd VLDB Conference*, 406–415, 1997.
65. P. J. Varman and R. M. Verma. An efficient multiversion access structure. *IEEE Transactions on Knowledge and Data Engineering*, 9(3), 391–409, May/June 1997.
66. D. E. Vengroff and J. S. Vitter. Efficient 3-d range searching in external memory. In *Proceedings of the ACM Symposium on Theory of Computation*, 192–201, Philadelphia, PA, May 1996.
67. J. S. Vitter. Efficient memory access in large-scale computation. In *Proceedings of the 1991 Symposium on Theoretical Aspects of Computer Science*, Lecture Notes in Computer Science. Springer-Verlag, 1991. Invited paper.
68. J. S. Vitter. External memory algorithms and data structures. In J. Abello and J. S. Vitter, editors, *External Memory Algorithms and Visualization*. AMS Press, Providence, RI, 1999. An updated version is available via the author's web page http://www.cs.duke.edu/~jsv/.
69. J. S. Vitter and E. A. M. Shriver. Algorithms for parallel memory I: Two-level memories. *Algorithmica*, 12(2–3), 110–147, 1994.
70. D. Willard and G. Lueker. Adding range restriction capability to dynamic data structures. *Journal of the ACM*, 32(3), 597–617, 1985.
71. A. C. Yao. On random 2-3 trees. *Acta Informatica*, 9, 159–170, 1978.

From Computational Learning Theory to Discovery Science

Osamu Watanabe[1]

Dept. of Mathematical and Computing Sciences, Tokyo Institute of Technology,
Tokyo 152-8552, Japan
watanabe@is.titech.ac.jp

Abstract. Machine learning has been one of the important subjects of AI that is motivated by many real world applications. In theoretical computer science, researchers also have introduced mathematical frameworks for investigating machine learning, and in these frameworks, many interesting results have been obtained. Now we are proceeding to a new stage to study how to apply these fruitful theoretical results to real problems. We point out in this paper that "adaptivity" is one of the important issues when we consider applications of learning techniques, and we propose one learning algorithm with this feature.

1 Introduction

Discovery science[1] is a new area of computer science that aims at (i) developing efficient computational methods which enable automatic discoveries of scientific knowledge and decision making rules and (ii) understanding all the issues concerned with this goal. Of course, discovery science involves many areas, from practical to theoretical, of computer science. For example, *computational learning theory* should play a key role[2] in discovery science by providing various algorithms for knowledge discovery. It is, however, also true that many techniques developed in computational learning theory do not always scale well in a straightforward way and can not just simply be applied to the cases where a huge amount of data need to be handled. In a nutshell, we need to pay more and more attention to "practicality".

There are several issues that we should consider for pursuing the practicality. First of all, as often pointed out, we should consider constant factors seriously when discussing time and space efficiency of algorithms. Note that for some cases, program size of implemented algorithms may also become important. Secondly,

---

[1] This new key word — discovery science — is the name of a project accepted by Japanese government as one of the priority research projects. It is a three-year project on the area described above started from April 1998 (Chair: Prof. Arikawa, Kyushu Univ.). The name "Discovery Science" has been invented by Prof. Arikawa and Prof. Miyano when they were planning this project.

[2] In fact, computational learning theory researchers form the core of the Discovery Science project.

we had better put more emphasis on average-case efficiency than worst-case one. For example, in the PAC learning framework, many concept classes have been proven to be hard to learn efficiently; nevertheless, some of these concept classes may still have learning algorithms that run reasonably fast on average, and this may be enough for some practical applications. On this issue, refer, for example, an average-case learning framework proposed by Zeugmann [17, 11].

In this paper, we point out that "adaptivity" is another important issue for designing practical learning algorithms. Researchers usually design algorithms considering the worst-case, which is in some sense reasonable because algorithms should robustly work under any circumstances. It is, however, often the case that a given situation is much better than the worst one. An *adaptive algorithm* is designed so that it can take advantage of a better situation (if so) to achieve better performance. More precisely, an adaptive algorithm adapts to a given situation (whether it is favorable or not) and change its strategy to get better performance in the current situation. In practice, when using some software, it may be hard to know *a priori* the circumstances where the software is used. Adaptive algorithms work well even in such cases.

The importance of the adaptivity has been mentioned in various fields. In statistics, for example, adaptive methods in statistical tests have been used since the Second World War [16]. In computational learning theory, we have an adaptive boosting algorithm [5]. Shawe-Taylor et al. also proposed the notion of "luckiness" for discussing a way for exploiting simplicity in observed data (see, e.g., [12]). In this paper, we will show one fully adaptive learning algorithm that is constructed based on an adaptive selection technique and an adaptive boosting technique. With this learning algorithm, we would like to demonstrate the meaning and importance of these adaptive techniques.

A *boosting technique* or a *boosting algorithm* is a way to make a "strong" learning algorithm based on a "weak" learning algorithm. The first boosting algorithm was proposed by Schapire [13] for answering *theoretically* to the question of whether a weak learning algorithm can be "boosted" to a strong one [6]. Later Freund [3] gave a simpler and more efficient boosting algorithm that provides much simpler final hypotheses than Schapire's algorithm. From this point, researchers have started considering boosting techniques as practical tools for designing learning algorithms. Then more recently, Freund and Schapire [5] developed an even more simple boosting algorithm — **AdaBoost** — that has several nice features for practical use including adaptivity. Due to these features, **AdaBoost** has been used and experimented for various practical applications (see, e.g., [4, 10, 14]).

A boosting algorithm makes use of a weak learning algorithm (a *weak learner*, in short) that produces a not-so-accurate but simple hypothesis (which we call a *weak hypothesis*). Usually a weak learner is unspecified when discussing boosting algorithms. But if a weak learner is also adaptive, we may be able to obtain a fully adaptive learning algorithm. This is what we will try to do in this paper; that is, we will construct a learning algorithm by combining an adaptive boosting algorithm with an adaptive weak learning algorithm.

In this paper, for the weak learning we consider the simplest learning, *hypothesis selection*. That is, the learning task is simply to select a hypothesis from a given set H of hypotheses that has the best accuracy. Thanks to boosting algorithms, we can now use simple weak hypotheses; hence, the set H of all weak hypotheses could be within reasonable size, and it may still be feasible to search the best hypothesis exhaustively in H. On the other hand, a given dataset X, i.e., a set X of example instances, may be huge, and it is just impossible to check with all instances in X. A standard strategy that we would use in such a case is random sampling. That is, we do the selection on some set S of instances randomly chosen from X. Then, of course, an obtained hypothesis h that performs best on S may not be the best, but intuitively, if S is large enough, then the obtained hypothesis h must be close to the best. In fact, several statistical bounds tell us how big S should be. Here is one problem. In order to calculate the size of S by using any of these statistical bounds, we need to know how well the best hypothesis performs on X, but this is usually hard to know in advance. Fortunately, though, there is an *adaptive* way to do this sampling. Recently, we developed [2] a general method to determine sample size based on the performance of hypotheses on observed examples, and by using this method, we can build an adaptive random sampling algorithm — **AdaSelect** — for hypothesis selection. We use this algorithm for our weak learner.

We cannot simply combine **AdaSelect** with **AdaBoost**. There is one more problem we must solve. The original **AdaBoost** does boosting by subsampling. That is, the algorithm first selects a set S of enough number of examples, and this S is used as a "training set" of its weak learner during the whole boosting process. Therefore, even if we have an adaptive weak learner, the boosting algorithm cannot make use of its adaptivity. This problem does not occur if we use a boosting by filtering algorithm. In this paper, we will propose a modified version of **AdaBoost** — **AdaBoost:F** — that is more appropriate for the boosting by filtering framework. Then we will combine our **AdaSelect** with this **AdaBoost:F**.

In this paper, we will analyze the performance of the proposed learning algorithm. But our analysis is rough and we consider only some simple case. More precise analysis as well as analysis in more general cases is left to our future work.

Basic Notations

We define basic notations used throughout the paper. For any set A, let $\|A\|$ denote the number of elements in A. On the other hand, for any integer x, we use $|x|$ to denote its absolute value. Let $\ln x$ and $\log x$ denote the natural logarithm and the binary logarithm respectively.

For our learning model, we consider the distribution-free PAC learning of Valiant [15], and we discuss about learning Boolean concepts. Throughout this paper, we use X to denote some domain of instances and use F to denote some set of Boolean functions on X from which a target Boolean concept is chosen. On the other hand, we use H to denote a set of weak hypotheses and use symbol h to denote an element of H.

We use $f_* \in F$ to denote a given target. That is, our learning task is to obtain an hypothesis $f: X \to \{0,1\}$ that is close to f_*. More specifically, the "closeness" is defined as the probability that f coincides with f_* on randomly generated $x \in X$ under a given distribution D. That is, the closeness of f to f_* is measured by the following function.

$$\mathrm{cor}_D(f, f_*) \stackrel{\mathrm{def}}{=} \Pr_{x:D} \{ f(x) = f_*(x) \},$$

where we use $\Pr_{x:D}\{\cdots\}$ to denote the probability that $\cdots$ occurs under D. When f_* is clear from the context, we simply write $\mathrm{cor}_D(f, f_*)$ as $\mathrm{cor}_D(f)$. Here we may be able to use an *example generator* $\mathbf{EX}_{D,f_*}$ that generates, at each call, a pair $(x, f_*(x))$ of an instance x and its classification, where x is generated under the distribution D. We use $D(x)$ to denote the probability that x is generated, and in general, by $D(A)$ we mean that the probability that some instance in A is generated.

2 Adaptive Hypothesis Selection

Suppose that we are given a *huge* set X of instances and a large (but still *of manageable size*) set H of hypotheses and that we are asked to select the best (i.e., the closest) or a nearly the best hypothesis from H for some unknown target concept f_* on X. The simplest way is to test each $h \in H$ for all instances of X and select h_* in H that is closest to f_*. Clearly this selection is not feasible since X is huge. Thus, we usually do this selection on some sample set S of instances randomly chosen from X. Then, of course, an obtained hypothesis h that performs best on S may not be the best, but intuitively, if the sample set S is large enough, then the obtained hypothesis h must be close to the best. In fact, several statistical bounds tell us how big S should be. There is, however, one problem. To calculate sufficient sample size by using any of these statistical bounds, we need to know how well the best hypothesis performs on X, but it is usually hard to know in advance. Thus, we would usually use some "safe" lower bound p for this. On the other hand, if the best performance is higher than this lower bound, which may often occurs, then we would do the selection on an unnecessarily large sample set. (Note that smaller p requires larger sample size.)

For solving this problem, researchers have proposed several techniques that are called *sequential analysis* or *adaptive sampling*; see, e.g., [16,9]. An idea common in these techniques is as follows: (i) We do not determine *a priori* sample size. (ii) Instead, we do sampling *on-line* and determine when to stop sampling based on the currently estimated value. This idea often helps us reducing sample size greatly. Our adaptive hypothesis selection — **AdaSelect** — is one of these techniques that fits very well for selecting a nearly the best hypothesis.

Let us specify our problem more clearly. A hypothesis h is considered as the best if $\mathrm{cor}_D(h, f_*)$ is the largest. We use h_* to denote the best hypothesis. Intuitively, the least informative hypothesis is a *random hypothesis* h_{rnd}, a hypothesis that gives 0 or 1 uniformly at random for any instance. Note that

Algorithm AdaSelect
Given: X, H, and $\mathbf{EX}_{D,f_*}$. % Let $N = \|H\|$.
Input: σ, and δ, where $0 < \sigma < 1$ and $0 < \delta < 1$.
begin
   repeat % Initially set $t = 0$ and $S = \emptyset$.
      $t \leftarrow t + 1$;
      $(x, b) \leftarrow \mathbf{EX}_{D,f_*}$;
      $S \leftarrow S \cup \{(x, b)\}$;
      $a_t \leftarrow b\sqrt{\ln(2Nt(t+1)/\delta)/(2t)}$;
   until $\exists h \in H$ [$\mathrm{adv}_S(h) \geq a_t(2/\sigma - 1)$];
   output $h \in H$ with the largest $\mathrm{adv}_S(h)$;
end.
% Where b is some constant that we may consider $b \approx 1$ (see [2]).

Fig. 1. The adaptive hypothesis selection algorithm.

even for this random hypothesis h_{rnd}, we have $\mathrm{cor}_D(h_{\mathrm{rnd}}, f_*) = 1/2$. Hence, intuitively, $\mathrm{cor}_D(h, f_*)$ must be larger than $1/2$ for any reasonable hypothesis h. Thus, it is more natural to measure the performance of a hypothesis h by its *advantage* over the random hypothesis, that is, by using the following function.

$$\mathrm{adv}_D(h, f_*) \overset{\mathrm{def}}{=} \Pr_{x:D}\{h(x) = f_*(x)\} - 1/2.$$

Again when f_* is clear from the context, we simply write $\mathrm{adv}_D(h, f_*)$ as $\mathrm{adv}_D(h)$. Now our problem is stated precisely as follows.

Hypothesis Selection
Given: X, H, and $\mathbf{EX}_{D,f_*}$.
Input: σ and δ, where $0 < \sigma < 1$ and $0 < \delta < 1$.
Goal: With probability $1 - \delta$, find $h \in H$ s.t. $\mathrm{adv}_D(h) \geq (1 - \sigma)\mathrm{adv}_D(h_*)$.

In later discussion, for the simplicity, we will fix σ to $1/2$.

For solving this problem, we propose an algorithm **AdaSelect** described in Figure 1. Here for any set of examples, we use $\mathrm{adv}_S(h)$ to denote the advantage of h on S; that is,

$$\mathrm{adv}_S(h) \overset{\mathrm{def}}{=} \frac{\|\{(x, b) \in S : h(x) = b\}\|}{\|S\|} - \frac{1}{2}.$$

For this algorithm, we can prove the following properties, which are derived immediately from [2, Theorem 3 and Theorem 4].

Theorem 1. *For given inputs σ and δ, with probability $1 - \delta$, **AdaSelect** halts within t_0 steps and yields a hypothesis $h \in H$ such that $\mathrm{adv}_D(h) \geq (1 - \sigma)\mathrm{adv}_D(h_*)$. Letting $\gamma_* = \mathrm{adv}_D(h_*)$ and $N = \|H\|$, the time bound t_0 is estimated as follows.*

$$t_0 = 4\left(\frac{1}{\sigma\gamma_*}\right)^2 \ln\left(\frac{2N}{\sigma\gamma_*\delta}\right).$$

Remark. We measure the running time of the algorithm by regarding one repeat-loop iteration as a basic step of the algorithm.

Intuitive Justification. Here instead of giving a proof of this theorem, we explain the idea behind this algorithm, which gives an intuitive justification to the theorem. In the following, parameters without definition are the same as those in the theorem.

The key ingredient of our algorithm is random sampling. Intuitively, our sample size is justified by the following lemma, which is derived from the Hoeffding bound (see, e.g., [7]).

Lemma 1. *Let S be a set of size t examples obtained by using $\mathbf{EX}_{D,f_*}$ t times. For any ϵ and δ', if $t \geq (1/2\epsilon^2) \ln(N/\delta')$, then the following holds with probability $1 - \delta'$.*

$$\forall h \in H \ [\ cor_S(h) - \epsilon \leq cor_D(h) \leq cor_S(h) + \epsilon \ ].$$

Now let us solve our hypothesis selection problem with this lemma. Here for the simplicity, we let $\sigma = 1/2$, and we assume that δ' is set to some appropriate constant. First we start with $\epsilon_1 = 1/8$ and collect enough number of examples to S. Suppose that h_1 is the best on S and $cor_S(h_1) = 7/8$ (or more). This means by the lemma that $cor_D(h_1) \geq 6/8$, i.e., $adv_D(h_1) \geq 1/4$. On the other hand, since h_1 is the best, we have $cor_S(h_*) \leq 7/8$, which implies again by the lemma that $cor_S(h_*) \leq 1$, i.e., $adv_D(h_*) \leq 1/2$. Hence, $adv_D(h_1) \geq (1/2)adv_D(h_*)$; that is, we can conclude that h_1 has desired advantage. On the other hand, if $cor_S(h) < 7/8$ for all $h \in H$, then we are not sure whether the current best one meets the condition of the problem. In this case we try with $\epsilon_2 = 1/16$. For this ϵ_2, we can conclude that the current best hypothesis h_2 is a desired one if $cor_S(h_2) \geq 11/16$. In this way, we try random sampling while decreasing ϵ (which increases necessary sample size), and as soon as ϵ becomes small enough, we can get a desired hypothesis. Roughly speaking, this is the idea of **AdaSelect**. In **AdaSelect**, the iteration phase is naturally incorporated, and thus, it has better sample complexity. □ *End Justification*

Since the idea of sampling adaptively is natural, various adaptive sampling techniques have been used since the Second World War [16]. However, while there are many techniques proposed for estimating, e.g., cor_D, as far as the author knows, no technique seems applicable for estimating adv_D.

3   Adaptive Boosting

Here we propose a modification of **AdaBoost** that seems more suitable for the boosting by filtering framework.

Let us begin by recalling some basic notions. In the PAC learning model, a learning algorithm can generate examples by using $\mathbf{EX}_{D,f_*}$, and it is expected to obtain some f that is close to f_*. More precisely, an algorithm A is called a *PAC learning algorithm* (in the strong sense) if for any D, and for any input ϵ and δ, $0 < \epsilon, \delta < 1$, by using $\mathbf{EX}_{D,f_*}$, A yields some hypothesis f such that $\mathrm{cor}_D(f, f_*)$ ($\stackrel{\mathrm{def}}{=} \mathrm{Pr}_{x:D}\{ f(x) = f_*(x) \}$) $\geq 1 - \epsilon$ with probability at least $1 - \delta$. On the other hand, an algorithm yielding a hypothesis that is better than the random hypothesis, i.e., the hypothesis predicting 0 or 1 uniformly at random, is called a *weak PAC learning algorithm*. More precisely, for any D and any input δ, $0 < \delta < 1$, a *weak PAC learning algorithm* uses $\mathbf{EX}_{D,f_*}$ and obtains, with probability at least $1 - \delta$, a hypothesis h such that $\mathrm{cor}_D(h, f_*) = 1/2 + \gamma$ for some $\gamma > 0$. This γ is called the *advantage* of h (over the random hypothesis). A hypothesis generated by a weak learning algorithm is called a *weak hypothesis*. Usually, weak hypotheses are much simpler than target functions. We use h to denote a weak hypothesis and H to denote the set of weak hypotheses.

In this paper, for simplifying our discussion, we measure the efficiency of learning algorithms in terms of $1/\epsilon$ and/or $1/\gamma$. That is, we ignore instance size and we assume that δ is fixed to some appropriate constant.

We explain the outline of boosting techniques. Suppose that we are given some weak learning algorithm **WeakLearn**. A boosting algorithm runs this **WeakLearn** several times, say t_0 times, under distributions $D_1, ..., D_{t_0}$ that are slightly modified from the given distribution D and collects weak hypotheses $h_1, ..., h_{t_0}$. A final hypothesis is built by combining these weak hypotheses. Here the key idea is to put more weight, when making a new weak hypothesis, to "problematic instances" for which the previous weak hypotheses perform poorly. That is, at the point when $h_1, ..., h_{t-1}$ have been obtained, the boosting algorithm computes a new distribution D_t that puts more weight on those instances that have been misclassified by most of $h_1, ..., h_{t-1}$. Then a new hypothesis h_t produced by **WeakLearn** on this distribution D_t should be strong on those problematic instances, thereby improving the performance of the combined hypothesis built from $h_1, ..., h_t$.

Boosting techniques are classified into two types depending on the way to execute **WeakLearn** on modified distributions:- boosting by subsampling and boosting by filtering [3]. In the boosting by subsampling framework, a boosting algorithm first obtains, by using $\mathbf{EX}_{D,f_*}$, a set S of enough number of examples as a "training set". Then it runs **WeakLearn** on this S by changing weight of each examples. The goal is to obtain a hypothesis that explains the training set well. On the other hand, in the boosting by filtering framework, a boosting algorithm selects examples from the original domain for each time **WeakLearn** is executed. This selection procedure is regarded as a "filter" between $\mathbf{EX}_{D,f_*}$ and **WeakLearn**. That is, it observes each example generated by $\mathbf{EX}_{D,f_*}$ and either "rejects" it and throws it away or "accepts" it and passes it on to **WeakLearn**; by this process, the boosting algorithm runs **WeakLearn** on modified distributions.

Now we can explain technically the meaning of the "adaptivity" of **AdaBoost**. For using any of the previous boosting algorithms [13, 3], we need to specify a lower bound γ of the advantage of weak hypotheses that one can expect from the weak learner **WeakLearn**. This γ, with other parameters, determines an actual boosting strategy, which works well so long as the weak learner keeps producing weak hypotheses with advantage $\geq \gamma$. But since this boosting strategy is fixed during the whole boosting process, even if some produced weak hypotheses have much better advantage the boosting algorithm cannot exploit such better hypotheses. More specifically, the speed of boosting depends on the advantage of hypotheses and larger advantage results in faster boosting. But since some fixed γ, which should be a "safe" lower bound of the expected advantage, is used throughout the boosting process, the boosting speed is fixed to a certain level that is unnecessarily slow if some of the obtained weak hypotheses have much larger advantage. **AdaBoost** solves this problem! It *adapts* to the accuracies of the obtained weak hypotheses and depending on these accuracies it changes its strategy *on-line*, thereby taking advantage of better hypotheses.

Like the other boosting algorithms, **AdaBoost** can use any weak learning algorithm. Here we would like to use the adaptive selection algorithm **AdaSelect** for the weak learning algorithm of **AdaBoost**, thereby developing a fully adaptive learning algorithm that needs no prior knowledge on the circumstances where it is used. Unfortunately, however, **AdaBoost** is not appropriate for this purpose because it is designed in the boosting by subsampling framework. That is, **AdaBoost** first prepares a set S of examples that is used as a training set of **WeakLearn** during the boosting process; therefore, even if **WeakLearn** is adaptive, its adaptivity cannot be used in **AdaBoost**. This problem does not occur if the algorithm is designed in the boosting by filtering framework.

The original **AdaBoost** does not seem suitable for the boosting by filtering framework, at least in a straightforward way. **AdaBoost** also runs **WeakLearn** several times under modified distributions, but if we use the above mentioned filter for generating examples, then at some step, the probability $\widehat{W}_t^{AD}$ that an example generated by $\mathbf{EX}_{D,f_*}$ is accepted and passed to **WeakLearn** may become so small that a huge number of examples need to be generated by $\mathbf{EX}_{D,f_*}$ for getting one example for **WeakLearn**. Intuitively, this means that the error probability ρ_t of the currently obtained combined hypothesis is small. Unfortunately, however, the probability $\widehat{W}_t^{AD}$ could be very small compared with ρ_t, and hence it may occur that $\widehat{W}_t^{AD}$ becomes very small while the error probability ρ_t is still not sufficiently small. For solving this problem, we propose an alternative way to define distributions.

We define some notations and then describe our algorithm. For any $t \geq 1$, assume that we have already obtained hypotheses $h_1, ..., h_{t-1}$, where each h_i is a weak hypothesis of f_* on some distribution D_i. Let $\varepsilon_1, ..., \varepsilon_{t-1}$ and $\gamma_1, ..., \gamma_{t-1}$ denote the error probability and the advantage of these hypotheses; that is, $\varepsilon_i \stackrel{\text{def}}{=} 1 - \mathrm{cor}_{D_i}(h_i)$ and $\gamma_i \stackrel{\text{def}}{=} \mathrm{adv}_{D_i}(h_i)$ $(= 1/2 - \varepsilon_i)$. We assume that the boosting algorithm somehow can get these γ_i's or their approximations. As in the original **AdaBoost**, we use parameters $\beta_1, ..., \beta_{t-1}$ that are defined as $\beta_i \stackrel{\text{def}}{=} \sqrt{\varepsilon_i/(1 - \varepsilon_i)}$ $(= \sqrt{(1 - 2\gamma_i)/(1 + 2\gamma_i)})$ for each i, $1 \leq i \leq t - 1$. (*Remark.* Here for the simplicity, we define β_i as above, which is the square root of β_i used in [5].) Also a combined hypothesis f_{t-1} of $h_1, ..., h_{t-1}$ is their weighted majority vote that is defined in the same way as **AdaBoost**; that is, f_{t-1} is defined by

Algorithm AdaBoost:F   % ":F" is for *F*iltering
Given: X, $\mathbf{EX}_{D,f_*}$, and **WeakLearn**.
Input: ϵ and δ, where $0 < \epsilon < 1$ and $0 < \delta < 1$.
begin
  repeat   % Initially set $t = 1$.
    call **WeakLearn** where examples are generated by $\mathbf{FiltEX}_{D_t}$;
    if $\mathbf{FiltEX}_{D_t}$ claims "accurate enough" during the above execution **then** exit;
    estimate γ_t; $\beta_t \leftarrow \sqrt{(1 - 2\gamma_t)/(1 + 2\gamma_t)}$;
    $t \leftarrow t + 1$;
  end-repeat;
  output the current weighted majority vote hypothesis f_{t-1};
end.
% For the simplicity, we assume that **WeakLearn** always returns a weak
% hypothesis with desired accuracy.

procedure $\mathbf{FiltEX}_{D_t}$
begin
  repeat
    use $\mathbf{EX}_{D,f_*}$ to generate an example (x, b);

$$p \leftarrow \min\left(\prod_{1 \leq i \leq t-1} \beta_i^{\mathrm{cons}(h_i, x)}, 1 \right);$$

    accept (x, b) with probability p;
  until some accepted example (x, b) is obtained;
  returns (x, b);
  % During the above execution, if $W_{t-1} < \epsilon$ is determined with confidence
  % $1 - \delta$, then terminates the execution by claiming "accurate enough".
end-procedure.

Fig. 2. The adaptive boosting algorithm.

$$f_{t-1}(x) \stackrel{\text{def}}{=} \begin{cases} 1, \text{ if } \displaystyle\prod_{i:h_i(x)=1} \beta_i \geq \prod_{i:h_i(x)=0} \beta_i, \\ 0, \text{ otherwise.} \end{cases}$$

On the other hand, we propose a new weight function. For any hypothesis h and any $x \in X$, define $\mathrm{cons}(h, x) \stackrel{\text{def}}{=} 1$ (resp., -1) if $h(x) = f_*(x)$ (resp., $h(x) \neq f_*(x)$). Then for each instance $x \in X$, its weight $w_{t-1}(x)$ after the $(t-1)$th step is defined as follows.

$$w_{t-1}(x) \stackrel{\text{def}}{=} \begin{cases} D(x) \times \displaystyle\prod_{1 \leq i \leq t-1} \beta_i^{\mathrm{cons}(h_i, x)}, \text{ if } \prod_{1 \leq i \leq t-1} \beta_i^{\mathrm{cons}(h_i, x)} < 1, \text{ and} \\ D(x), \hspace{5.5cm} \text{otherwise.} \end{cases}$$

Let $W_{t-1} \stackrel{\text{def}}{=} \sum_{x \in X} w_{t-1}(x)$. Finally define the next distribution D_t so that $D_t(x) \stackrel{\text{def}}{=} w_{t-1}(x)/W_{t-1}$ for all $x \in X$. Note that D_1 is D.

Our modified version of the adaptive boosting — **AdaBoost:F** — is stated as Figure 2. Note first that $W_{t-1} \overset{\text{def}}{=} \sum_{x \in X} w_{t-1}(x)$ bounds the error probability ρ_{t-1} of the weighted majority vote hypothesis f_{t-1}, that is, the following relation holds.

$$\rho_{t-1} \overset{\text{def}}{=} \Pr_{x:D}\{ f_{t-1}(x) \neq f_*(x) \} \leq W_{t-1}.$$

On the other hand, it is clear from the design of $\textbf{FiltEX}_{D_t}$ that W_{t-1} is the probability that some accepted example is obtained at one repeat-loop iteration in the execution of $\textbf{FiltEX}_{D_t}$. Thus, at some step, if it is hard to get enough number of accepted examples by $\textbf{FiltEX}_{D_t}$, which means that W_{t-1} is small, then $\textbf{FiltEX}_{D_t}$ can stop by claiming that the current f_{t-1} is "accurate enough". (In Figure 2 we omit specifying the way to estimate γ_t and the way to determine $W_{t-1} < \epsilon$; they will be discussed in the next section.)

In the original **AdaBoost**, the above relation does not hold, and this is the reason why we need to modify the way to compute weights. The weight function of **AdaBoost** is $w_{t-1}^{\text{AD}}(x) \overset{\text{def}}{=} D(x) \times \prod_{1 \leq i \leq t-1} \beta_i^{\text{cons}(h_i, x)}$. (*Cf.* $w_{t-1}(x)$ is defined by using the same formula if $D(x) \times \prod_{1 \leq i \leq t-1} \beta_i^{\text{cons}(h_i, x)} \leq D(x)$.) However, by one call of $\textbf{EX}_{D, f_*}$, we cannot generate an example (x, b) with probability larger than $D(x)$; hence, if we want to generate each example (x, b) proportional to $w_{t-1}^{\text{AD}}(x)$, then the probability of generating (x, b) by one call of $\textbf{EX}_{D, f_*}$ should be $\widehat{w}_{t-1}^{\text{AD}}(x) \overset{\text{def}}{=} w_{t-1}^{\text{AD}}(x) \times \prod_{1 \leq i \leq t-1} \beta_i$. Then the probability that some accepted instance is obtained at one repeat-loop iteration of the filter becomes $\widehat{W}_{t-1}^{\text{AD}} \overset{\text{def}}{=} W_{t-1}^{\text{AD}} \times \prod_{1 \leq i \leq t-1} \beta_i$, where W_{t-1}^{AD} is the sum of all $w_{t-1}^{\text{AD}}(x)$. Note that $\widehat{W}_{t-1}^{\text{AD}}$ is much smaller than W_{t-1}^{AD}. Thus, although W_{t-1}^{AD} bounds the error probability ρ_{t-1}, it may occur that $\widehat{W}_{t-1}^{\text{AD}}$ is very small but the error probability ρ_{t-1} is not small enough.

As explained above, we can overcome this problem by our modification. Since the correctness of **AdaBoost:F** is thus clear, what we need to analyze is its efficiency. For this, we discuss how fast W_t decreases. Here we consider the simplest case[3] where the advantage γ_i of each hypothesis h_i is at least γ and $\beta_i = \beta \overset{\text{def}}{=} \sqrt{(1 - 2\gamma)/(1 + 2\gamma)}$.

Theorem 2. *Suppose that the advantage of weak hypotheses provided by* **Weak-Learn** *is always at least γ during the execution of* **AdaBoost:F**. *Then for any ϵ, we have $W_t < \epsilon$ for some $t \leq 1/(2\gamma^2 \epsilon)$.*

Remark. In the following analysis, we approximate $\sqrt{1 - 4\gamma^2}$ by $1 - 2\gamma^2$. (See the proof below for the detail.)

Proof Outline. For any $t \geq 1$, let us consider the situation when the $(t - 1)$th repeat-loop iteration has finished and the tth repeat-loop is about to start in the

---

[3] To tell the truth, I do not know at this moment how to analyze the general case.

main procedure of **AdaBoost:F**, which we simply call "at the tth step". Thus, **WeakLearn** has been called for $t-1$ times, and let $h_1, ..., h_{t-1}$ be the sequence of obtained weak hypotheses. Below we assume that the advantage of the next weak hypothesis h_t is at least γ and discuss how much W_t gets decreased from W_{t-1}.

We introduce some notations. For any instance x, the *advantage* (of correct hypotheses over incorrect ones) on x is the number of correct hypotheses minus that of incorrect hypotheses on x. Throughout the proof, a symbol k is used to denote this advantage. Hence, at the tth step, the value of k ranges from $-(t-1)$ to $t-1$. For any k, let C_k denote the set of instances x with advantage k, and define $\overline{w}_k$ by

$$\overline{w}_k \overset{\text{def}}{=} \begin{cases} D(C_k)\beta^k, & \text{if } k > 0, \text{ and} \\ D(C_k), & \text{otherwise.} \end{cases}$$

Note that $w_{t-1}(x) = D(x)\beta^k$ for all $x \in C_k$ and that $\overline{w}_k$ is the sum of weight $w_{t-1}(x)$ for all $x \in C_k$. Hence, we have $D_{t-1}(C_k) = \overline{w}_k / W_{t-1}$. We also define $W_{t-1}^+ \overset{\text{def}}{=} \sum_{1 \le k \le t-1} \overline{w}_k$ and $W_{t-1}^- \overset{\text{def}}{=} \sum_{-(t-1) \le k \le 0} \overline{w}_k$. That is, W_{t-1}^+ (resp., W_{t-1}^-) is the total weight of instances that are correctly (resp., incorrectly) classified by f_{t-1}. Note that $W_{t-1} = W_{t-1}^+ + W_{t-1}^-$.

Roughly speaking, the weight of instances in $C^- \overset{\text{def}}{=} \cup_{-(t-1) \le k \le 0} C_k$ remains the same and only the weight of instances in $C^+ \overset{\text{def}}{=} \cup_{1 \le k \le t-1} C_k$ gets decreased. But since $W_{t-1}^+ = w_{t-1}(C^+)$ gets decreased, some instances in C^- should move to C^+ because every weak hypothesis has advantage at least γ. Intuitively speaking, the C^+ part works like a pump absorbing instances from the C^- part.

For analyzing this phenomenon, we introduce another weight $\widetilde{w}_k$ for $k \le 0$, which is defined as follows. (A parameter α will be defined later.)

$$\widetilde{w}_k \overset{\text{def}}{=} (|k|\alpha + 1)\overline{w}_k.$$

Define $\widetilde{W}_{t-1}^- \overset{\text{def}}{=} \sum_{-(t-1) \le k \le 0} \widetilde{w}_k$ and $\widetilde{W}_{t-1} \overset{\text{def}}{=} W_{t-1}^+ + \widetilde{W}_{t-1}^-$. It turns out that the analysis becomes much simpler if we analyze $\widetilde{W}_t$ instead of W_t. Notice that this new weight is not used at all in the algorithm, it is used only for our analysis.

For any k, let p_k and q_k denote $\Pr_{x:D_{t-1}}\{h_t(x) = f_*(x) \wedge x \in C_k\}$ and $\Pr_{x:D_{t-1}}\{h_t(x) \ne f_*(x) \wedge x \in C_k\}$ respectively. Also define

$$P^+ \overset{\text{def}}{=} \sum_{1 \le k \le t-1} p_k, \quad P^- \overset{\text{def}}{=} \sum_{-(t-1) \le k \le 0} p_k, \quad P^{+0} \overset{\text{def}}{=} P^+ + p_0,$$

$$Q^+ \overset{\text{def}}{=} \sum_{1 \le k \le t-1} q_k, \quad Q^- \overset{\text{def}}{=} \sum_{-(t-1) \le k \le 0} q_k, \quad P^{-0} \overset{\text{def}}{=} P^- - p_0.$$

Then we have

$$p_k + q_k = D_{t-1}(C_k) = \frac{\overline{w}_k}{W_{t-1}},$$
$$P^+ + P^- = P^{+0} + P^{-0} = \Pr_{x:D_t}\{h_t(x) = f_*(x)\}, \quad \text{and}$$
$$Q^+ + Q^- = \Pr_{x:D_t}\{h_t(x) \ne f_*(x)\}.$$

Furthermore, the following relation holds.

Claim. For any k, we have

$$\Pr_{x:D}\{\, h_t(x) = f_*(x) \wedge x \in C_k \,\} = p_k \cdot W_{t-1} \cdot \beta^{\min(-k,0)}, \quad \text{and}$$
$$\Pr_{x:D}\{\, h_t(x) \neq f_*(x) \wedge x \in C_k \,\} = q_k \cdot W_{t-1} \cdot \beta^{\min(-k,0)}.$$

Now we estimate how $\widetilde{W}_t$ decreases from $\widetilde{W}_{t-1}$. For this, we derive formulas for computing W_t and $\widetilde{W}_t$ inductively. (Below we use, e.g., $\overline{w}_k^{(t)}$ to denote $\overline{w}_k$ just after the tth step. Recall, on the other hand, $\overline{w}_k$ is the value at (the beginning of) the tth step, i.e., just before the tth call of **WeakLearn**.)

For the case $k \geq 1$, we can show the following relation by using Claim 3.

$$\overline{w}_k^{(t)} = W_{t-1}(\beta^{-1} q_{k+1} + \beta p_{k-1}),$$

where $q_t = q_{t+1} = 0$. Summing up $\overline{w}_k^{(t)}$ for $k \geq 1$, we have

$$W_t^+ = W_{t-1} \times \left(\sum_{k=1}^{t} \beta^{-1} q_{k+1} + \beta p_{k-1} \right) = W_{t-1} \times (\beta^{-1}(Q^+ - q_1) + \beta(P^- + p_0)).$$

Note that $W_{t-1}^+ = (P^+ + Q^+) W_{t-1}$. Hence,

$$\Delta_t^+ = W_t^+ - W_{t-1}^+ = W_{t-1} \times \{\, (\beta^{-1} - 1)Q^+ - (1 - \beta)P^+ - \beta^{-1} q_1 + \beta p_0 \,\}.$$

For the case $k \leq 0$, we can prove the following again by using Claim 3.

$$\begin{aligned}
\widetilde{W}_t^- &= \overline{w}_0^{(t)} + (1 + \alpha)\overline{w}_{-1}^{(t)} + (1 + 2\alpha)\overline{w}_{-2}^{(t)} + \cdots + (1 + t\alpha)\overline{w}_{-t}^{(t)} \\
&= W_t \times \{\, (\beta^{-1} q_1 + p_{-1}) + (1 + \alpha)(q_0 + p_{-2}) + (1 + 2\alpha)(q_{-1} + p_{-3}) \\
&\quad + \cdots + (1 + t\alpha)(q_{-(t-1)} + p_{-(t+1)}) \,\},
\end{aligned}$$

where $p_{-t} = p_{-(t+1)} = 0$. On the other hand, by definition we have

$$\begin{aligned}
\widetilde{W}_{t-1}^- &= \overline{w}_0 + (1 + \alpha)\overline{w}_{-1} + (1 + 2\alpha)\overline{w}_{-2} + \cdots + (1 + (t - 1)\alpha)\overline{w}_{-(t-1)} \\
&= W_t \times \{\, (q_0 + p_0) + (1 + \alpha)(q_{-1} + p_{-1}) + (1 + 2\alpha)(q_{-2} + p_{-2}) \\
&\quad + \cdots + (1 + (t - 1)\alpha)(q_{-(t-1)} + p_{-(t-1)}) \,\}.
\end{aligned}$$

Thus,

$$\Delta_t^- = W_t^- - W_{t-1}^- = W_{t-1} \times (\alpha Q^- - \alpha P^{-0} + \beta^{-1} q_1 - p_0).$$

Therefore,

$$\Delta_t = \Delta_t^+ + \Delta_t^- = W_{t-1} \times \{\, (\beta^{-1} - 1)Q^+ + \alpha Q^- - (1 - \beta)P^{+0} - \alpha P^{-0} \,\}.$$

Recall that $Q^+ + Q^- = \Pr_{x:D_t}\{\, h_t(x) \neq f_*(x) \,\}$ and $P^{+0} + P^{-0} = \Pr_{x:D_t}\{\, h_t(x) = f_*(x) \,\}$. Thus, if the advantage of h_t is at least γ, then we have $Q^+ + Q^- \leq 1/2 - \gamma$ and $P^{+0} + P^{-0} \geq 1/2 + \gamma$. Here we may assume that $\beta^{-1} - 1 \geq \alpha \geq$

$1 - \beta$ since $\beta < 1$. (For example, we can set $\alpha = 1 - \beta$.) Then Δ_t is maximized (even though it may be negative) if $Q^+ = 1/2 - \gamma$ and $P^{+0} = 1/2 + \gamma$. That is,

$$\Delta_t \leq W_{t-1} \times ((\beta^{-1} - 1)(1/2 - \gamma) - (1 - \beta)(1/2 + \gamma))$$
$$= W_{t-1} \times \sqrt{1 - 4\gamma^2} - W_{t-1} \approx -2\gamma^2 \cdot W_{t-1}.$$

Now suppose that $W_{t-1} \geq \epsilon$. Then $\widetilde{W}_t$ decreases from $\widetilde{W}_{t-1}$ by at least $2\gamma^2\epsilon$. On the other hand, $\widetilde{W}_0 = W_0 = 1$. Hence, either $W_i < \epsilon$ for some i, $1 \leq i \leq 1/(2\gamma^2\epsilon)$; otherwise, $\widetilde{W}_i < \epsilon$ for some i, $1 \leq i \leq 1/(2\gamma^2\epsilon)$, but $W_i \leq \widetilde{W}_i$, a contradiction. □

The above theorem shows that **AdaBoost:F** needs to call **WeakLearn** $O(1/(\gamma^2\epsilon))$ times. Unfortunately, this is rather big compared with the previous boosting algorithms. For example, the boosting algorithm $\mathbf{B}_{\text{Filt}}$ of [3] needs to call **WeakLearn** $O((1/\gamma^2)\ln(1/\epsilon))$ times. We believe that our analysis is still rough and we may be able to get a better bound. More specifically, we had Δ_t $(= \widetilde{W}_t - \widetilde{W}_{t-1}) \leq W_{t-1}\sqrt{1 - 4\gamma^2} - W_{t-1}$; but if $\widetilde{W}_{t-1} \approx W_{t-1}$, then we could get $\widetilde{W}_t \leq \widetilde{W}_{t-1}\sqrt{1 - 4\gamma^2}$, which gives $O((1/\gamma^2)\ln(1/\epsilon))$ bound. Note that the above bound is obtained by assuming $Q^- = P^- = 0$, in which case we certainly have $\widetilde{W}_{t-1} = W_{t-1}$. Or we may be able to use $\widetilde{w}_{t-1}(x)$ as an actual weight that is used to determine the next distribution. In this case we can also prove that $\widetilde{W}_t \leq \widetilde{W}_{t-1}\sqrt{1 - 4\gamma^2}$.

4 Fully Adaptive Learning

Now that we have obtained an adaptive boosting algorithm using filtering, it is easy to combine it with our adaptive hypothesis selection algorithm. We can simply use **AdaSelect** for **WeakLearn** of **AdaBoost:F**. Then we get a fully adaptive learning algorithm that requires no prior knowledge on the circumstances where it is used.

Let us estimate, though roughly, the efficiency of this learning algorithm. Here again we consider the simplest case. That is, we assume that for a given target function f_*, and for any distribution D' (used in the algorithm) there exists a hypothesis $h \in H$ that has advantage at least γ under D'. We also ignore the size parameter N (i.e., the number of possible weak hypotheses) and the confidence parameter δ (required by both **AdaSelect** and **AdaBoost:F**) since these parameters affect the efficiency only logarithmically. Here we measure running time by counting the number of calls of the generator $\mathbf{EX}_{D,f_*}$. That is, we estimate the number of generator calls executed by our learning algorithm until it obtains an ϵ-close hypothesis for a given target f_*.

First consider each call of **AdaSelect**. Here we simply let $\sigma = 1/2$. Then it follows from Theorem 1 that the number of examples for selecting a nearly the best weak hypothesis is $O((1/\gamma^2)\ln(1/\gamma))$. Note that for getting one example by filtering, we need to generate, on average, $1/W_t$ examples by $\mathbf{EX}_{D,f_*}$; hence, (while $W_t \geq \epsilon$) the number of generator calls is $O(1/\epsilon)$ on average for each example required by **AdaSelect**. Thus, for each call of **AdaSelect**, the generator is called at most $O((1/\epsilon\gamma^2)\ln(1/\gamma))$ times.

The condition $W_{t-1} < \epsilon$ should be tested at some point. For this we can use random sampling. According to the Hoeffding bound, $O(1/\epsilon^2)$ examples is sufficient for this test. Thus, for example, if $1/\gamma^2 > 1/\epsilon$, then the number of generator calls per one call of **AdaSelect**, i.e., $O((1/\epsilon\gamma^2)\ln(1/\gamma))$, is large enough, and this test is achieved during the execution of **AdaSelect**. (We may postpone this test unless W_{t-1} becomes sufficiently small and $\mathbf{FiltEX}_{D_t}$ needs to call $\mathbf{EX}_{D,f_*}$ many times to generate one example.)

Next estimate how many times **AdaSelect** is called in **AdaBoost:F**. Here we consider another point that has been left in the previous section; that is, the estimation of γ_t. Note that a reasonable approximation of the advantage γ_t of an obtained weak hypothesis h_t is available through random sampling. Here again we can use the adaptive sampling, the idea behind our **AdaSelect**. In fact, we can use $\mathrm{adv}_S(h_t)$ computed in **AdaSelect**. It is not hard to show (by using analysis similar to the one in the proof of Theorem 1) that $\mathrm{adv}_S(h_t) \lesssim 3\mathrm{adv}_{D_t}(h_t)/2$. Thus, for γ_t, we may safely use $2\mathrm{adv}_S(h_t)/3$, which is larger than $\mathrm{adv}_{D_t}(h_*)/3 \geq \gamma/3$, where h_* is the optimal hypothesis. Thus, it follows from Theorem 2 that **AdaBoost:F** calls **AdaSelect** at most $O(1/(\epsilon\gamma^2))$ times.

In summary, the total number of generator calls is $O((1/\epsilon\gamma^2) \times \max((1/\epsilon\gamma^2)\ln(1/\gamma), 1/\epsilon^2))$, which is roughly $O((1/\epsilon^2\gamma^4)\ln(1/\gamma))$. Let us compare this number with existing algorithms. For our example, consider here the combination of the boosting algorithm $\mathbf{B}_{\mathrm{Filt}}$ of [3] and the simple batch type random hypothesis selection using the Hoeffding bound. For a given lower bound γ, the simple batch selection needs $O(1/\gamma^2)$ examples, and thus, in total $\mathbf{B}_{\mathrm{Filt}}$ needs to call the generator $\mathbf{EX}_{D,f_*}$ $O((1/\epsilon\gamma^4)\ln(1/\epsilon))$ times. Roughly speaking the additional factors $\ln(1/\gamma)$ and $1/\epsilon$ are what we have to pay for the adaptivity in the hypothesis selection and in the boosting respectively.

Clearly, our obtained bound is not satisfactory. Also we only consider the simplest situation, and for showing the adaptivity of this proposed algorithm, we need to evaluate its efficiency in more general situations where the accuracy of weak hypothesis varies during the boosting. On the other hand, for showing its practical applicability, we need to do some computer experiments on various kinds of datasets. These works are left for the future study.

Acknowledgment

A part of this work, in particular, the adaptive selection part came from a series of joint works [1, 2] with Carlos Domingo and Ricard Gavaldà. I have been enjoying working with these talented researchers, and I particularly thank to them for giving me various useful comments on earlier versions of this manuscript. This work is supported in part by Grant-in-Aid for Scientific Research on Priority Areas (Discovery Science), 1999, the Ministry of Education, Science, Sports and Culture.

References

1. C. Domingo, R. Gavaldà, and O. Watanabe, Practical algorithms for on-line selection, in *Proc. of the First Int'l Conference on Discovery Science, DS'98*, Lecture Notes in Artificial Intelligence 1532:150–161, 1998.
2. C. Domingo, R. Gavaldà, and O. Watanabe, Adaptive sampling methods for scaling up knowledge discovery algorithms, Technical Report C-131, Dept. of Math. and Computing Sciences, Tokyo Institute of Technology, 1999.
3. Y. Freund, Boosting a weak learning algorithm by majority, *Information and Computation*, 121(2):256–285, 1995.
4. Y. Freund and R.E. Schapire, Experiments with a new boosting algorithm, in *Machine Learning: Proc. of the 13th Int'l Conference*, 148–156, 1996.
5. Y. Freund and R.E. Schapire, A decision-theoretic generalization of on-line learning and an application to boosting. *J. Comput. Syst. Sci.*, 55(1):119–139, 1997.
6. M.J. Kearns and L.G. Valiant, Cryptographic limitations on learning boolean formulae and finite automata, *J. Assoc. Comput. Mach.*, 41(1):67–95, 1994.
7. M.J. Kearns and U.V. Vazirani, *An Introduction to Computational Learning Theory*, Cambridge University Press, 1994.
8. Richard J. Lipton and Jeffrey F. Naughton, Query size estimation by adaptive sampling, *Journal of Computer and System Science*, 51:18–25, 1995.
9. R.J. Lipton, J.F. Naughton, D.A. Schneider, and S. Seshadri, Efficient sampling strategies for relational database operations, *Theoretical Computer Science*, 116:195–226, 1993.
10. J.R. Quinlan, Bagging, boosting, and C4.5, in *Proc. of the 13th National Conference on Artificial Intelligence*, 725–730, 1996.
11. R. Reischuk and T. Zeugmann, A complete and tight average-case analysis of learning monomial, in *Proc. 16th Int'l Sympos. on Theoretical Aspects of Computer Science, STACS'99*, 1999, to appear.
12. J. Shawe-Taylor, P.L. Bartlett, R.C. Williamson, and M. Anthony, Structural risk minimization over data-dependent hierarchies, *IEEE Trans. Information Theory*, 44(5):1926–1940, 1998.
13. R.E. Schapire, The strength of weak learnability, *Machine Learning*, 5(2):197–227, 1990.
14. R.E. Schapire, Theoretical views of boosting, in *Computational Learning Theory: Proc. of the 4th European Conference, EuroCOLT'99*, 1999, to appear.
15. L. Valiant, A theory of the learnable, *Communications of the ACM*, 27(11):1134–1142, 1984.
16. A. Wald, *Sequential Analysis*, Wiley Mathematical, Statistics Series, 1947.
17. T. Zeugmann, Lange and Wiehagen's pattern language learning algorithm: an average-case analysis with respect to its total learning time, *Annals of Math. and Artificial Intelligence*, 23(1-2):117–145, 1998.

Bounded Depth Arithmetic Circuits: Counting and Closure

Eric Allender[1], Andris Ambainis[2], David A. Mix Barrington[3], Samir Datta[1], and Huong LêThanh[4]

[1] Department of Computer Science, Rutgers University, Piscataway, {allender, datta}@cs.rutgers.edu. Supported in part by NSF grant CCR-9734918.
[2] Computer Science Division, University of California, Berkeley, ambainis@cs.berkeley.edu. Supported by Berkeley Fellowship for Graduate Studies.
[3] Department of Computer Science, University of Massachusetts, Amherst, barring@cs.umass.edu
[4] Laboratoire de Recherche en Informatique, Université de Paris-Sud, huong@lri.fr

Abstract. Constant-depth arithmetic circuits have been defined and studied in [AAD97,ABL98]; these circuits yield the function classes $\#AC^0$ and $GapAC^0$. These function classes in turn provide new characterizations of the computational power of threshold circuits, and provide a link between the circuit classes AC^0 (where many lower bounds are known) and TC^0 (where essentially no lower bounds are known). In this paper, we resolve several questions regarding the closure properties of $\#AC^0$ and $GapAC^0$ and characterize $\#AC^0$ in terms of counting paths in a family of bounded-width graphs.

1 Introduction

The arithmetic circuit complexity classes $\#AC^0$ and $GapAC^0$ have been the object of intense study [AAD97,ABL98,LêT98,NS98] because:

- they provide new characterizations of the complexity class TC^0 (the problems computable by constant-depth threshold circuits of polynomial size), for which essentially no nontrivial lower bounds have been proved,
- they are closely related to the complexity classes AC^0 and $AC^0[2]$, and thus the well-developed lower-bound techniques for AC^0 and $AC^0[2]$ suffice to show that certain functions are *not* in $\#AC^0$ and $GapAC^0$, and
- they capture a mathematically interesting class of computations lying at the frontier of currently available analysis techniques. We can answer some questions about their structure at this time (possibly giving insight into the structure of related classes such as $\#L$ and $\#P$), while progress on other questions about them is necessary to better understand TC^0 (and hence the power of neural nets).

More background motivating our interest in these classes can be found in [AAD97,ABL98,LêT98] and in the survey article [Al97]. Formal definitions for each are presented in Section 2. Here we report progress on two fronts regarding $\#AC^0$ and $GapAC^0$: closure properties and combinatorial characterizations.

1.1 Closure Properties

A study of the closure properties of #P was initiated by Ogiwara and Hemachandra in [OH93]. It is not known whether #P is closed under such operations as MAX, MIN, division by 2, and decrement. In [OH93] implications and equivalences are established among these closure properties and certain other open questions in complexity theory. In the context of $\#AC^0$ and $GapAC^0$, however, we are able to settle most questions about these and other closure properties. (For instance, they are not closed under MAX or division by 3, but they are closed under decrement; $\#AC^0$ is not closed under division by 2, although $GapAC^0$ is.) In some cases, the answers follow easily from earlier results, but in other cases new analysis is required.

1.2 Combinatorial Characterizations

Although arithmetic classes such as #L and $\#NC^1$ are defined in terms of arithmetic circuits, it is often nice to use equivalent definitions where we count paths in certain families of graphs. For instance, a complete problem for NL is the question of whether a directed acyclic graph has a path from vertex 1 to vertex n, and a complete problem for #L is to count the number of such paths. For any $k \geq 5$, a complete problem for NC^1 is to determine if a width-k directed acyclic graph has a path from vertex 1 to n, but it remains open whether counting the number of such paths is complete for $\#NC^1$. (See [Al97] for a discussion of this problem.) Nonetheless, it was shown in [CMTV96] that a complete problem for the class $GapNC^1$ (the class of all functions that are the difference of two $\#NC^1$ functions) is to compute, in a width-k graph where $k \geq 6$, the number of paths from vertex 1 to n minus the number of paths from vertex 1 to $n - 1$.

The question of whether $\#AC^0$ or $GapAC^0$ possess similar combinatorial characterizations was posed in [AAD97]. It was noted there that certain lemmas and normal forms concerning these classes are fairly complicated to prove, whereas the analogous lemmas for larger classes such as #P, #L, and $\#NC^1$ are much simpler because of those classes' path-based characterizations. The characterization of depth-k AC^0 presented in [BLMS98] in terms of the reachability problem for width-k grid graphs suggests the analogous conjecture that $\#AC^0$ could be characterized by counting the number of paths connecting vertices 1 and n in bounded-width grid graphs.

We disprove this conjecture, showing that – even for width two graphs – this counting problem lies outside $GapAC^0$ and is complete for NC^1 (under ACC^0 reductions). In contrast, we are able to present a particular family of constant-width graphs such that counting paths in these graphs characterizes $\#AC^0$.

2 Preliminaries

This paper studies arithmetic complexity classes. Certainly the best-known arithmetic class is Valiant's class #P [Val79], consisting of functions that map x to the number of accepting computations of an NP-machine on input x. Recently, the class #L (counting accepting computations of an NL-machine) has also received considerable attention [AJ93,Vin91,Tod92a,MV97].

#P and #L can be characterized in terms of uniform arithmetic circuits, as follows: Start with characterizations of NP and NL in terms of uniform Boolean circuits [Ven92]. The classes #P and #L result if we "arithmetize" these Boolean circuits, replacing each OR gate by a + gate, and replacing each AND gate by a × gate, where the input variables $x_1, \ldots, x_n$ now take as values the natural numbers $\{0,1\}$ (instead of the Boolean values $\{0,1\}$), and negated input literals $\overline{x_i}$ now take on the value $1 - x_i$.

The counting classes that result in this way by arithmetizing the Boolean circuit classes SAC^1 and NC^1 were studied in [Vin91,AJMV98,CMTV96]. In this paper, we study $\#AC^0$.

Definition 1. *For any $k > 0$, $\#AC_k^0$ is the class of functions $f : \{0,1\}^* \to \mathbb{N}$ such that, for some polynomial p, for every n there is a depth k circuit C_n of size at most $p(n)$ consisting of unbounded-fan-in $+, \times$-gates (the usual sum and product in $\mathbb{N}$), where inputs to the circuits are from $\{0, 1, x_i, 1 - x_i\}$, and for every $x = x_1 \ldots x_n \in \{0,1\}^n$, $f(x) = C_n(x_1, \ldots, x_n)$. Let $\#AC^0 = \bigcup_{k>0} \#AC_k^0$.*

Definition 2. *$GapAC^0$ is the class of all functions $f : \{0,1\}^* \to \mathbb{Z}$ that can be expressed as the difference of two functions in $\#AC^0$; i.e. $GapAC^0 = \{f : \exists g, h \in \#AC^0 \ f(x) = g(x) - h(x)\}$.*

$\#AC^0$ and $GapAC^0$ were first studied in [AAD97]. Some of the main open questions posed there were subsequently answered in [ABL98], where it was shown that $GapAC^0$ can also be characterized as those functions computed by $\#AC^0$ circuits augmented with -1 as an additional constant.

3   Closure and NonClosure Properties

Following [OH93], let us first consider a very simple closure property: MAX.

Theorem 1. *Neither $\#AC^0$ nor $GapAC^0$ is closed under MAX.*   □

Proof. Let $f(x) = \sum_i x_i$, and let $g(x) = |x|/2$. Let x' denote the result of changing the first 1 in x to a 0 (if such a bit exists). (It is easy to see that x' can be computed from x in Boolean AC^0, and hence this function is also in $\#AC^0$.) Note that the number of 1's in x is less than or equal to $|x|/2$ if and only if the low-order bits of $MAX(f(x), g(x))$ and $MAX(f(x'), g(x'))$ are equal. The low-order bits of any $GapAC^0$ function are computable in $AC^0[2]$, and hence if $MAX(f, g)$ were computable in $GapAC^0$, it would follow that the majority function could be computed in $AC^0[2]$, in contradiction to [Ra87].   □

Corollary 1. *Neither $\#AC^0$ nor $GapAC^0$ is closed under MIN.*   □

Again following [OH93], we next consider the decrement. Given a function f, the decrement operation applied to f is $f \dot{-} 1$ (where the *monus* operation $a \dot{-} b$ is equal to 0 if $b \geq a$, and is equal to $a - b$ otherwise). Not only is $\#AC^0$ closed under decrement, but it is closed under $\dot{-}$ with any $\#AC^0$ function whose growth rate is at most polylogarithmic.

Theorem 2. *If f and g are in $\#AC^0$, and there exists a k such that for all x, $g(x) = O(\log^k |x|)$, then $f \dot{-} g$ is in $\#AC^0$.* $\square$

Note 1. The polylogarithmic bound on g is necessary. To see this, let $f(x) = \sum x_i$, and let $g(x)$ be $|x|/2$ (or any other superpolylogarithmic threshold). Then, $f(x) \dot{-} g(x)$ is nonzero if and only if the number of ones in x exceeds the threshold $g(x)$. If this function were in $\#AC^0$, it would imply the existence of a Boolean AC^0 circuit family computing threshold-g, contradicting [FKPS85,Ha86]. An argument similar to Theorem 1 shows that $f \dot{-} g$ is not even in $GapAC^0$.

Proof. The proof is based on a lemma below whose proof is omitted in this version.

Lemma 1. *If f is a $\#AC^0$ function and g is a function in $\#AC^0$ taking poly-logarithmically bounded values, then the predicates $[f = g]$ and $[f \leq g]$ are computable in AC^0.* $\square$

We build the circuit for $f \dot{-} g$ by induction on the depth of the circuit computing f. The basis, for depth-zero circuits, is trivial. For the inductive step, consider first the case where the output gate is a $+$ gate. Note that

$$(\sum_{i=1}^n f_i) \dot{-} g = \sum_{i=1}^n \left[\sum_{j=1}^{i-1} f_j \leq g < \sum_{j=1}^i f_j \right] \left(f_i \dot{-} (g - \sum_{j=1}^{i-1} f_j) + \sum_{j=i+1}^n f_j \right).$$

It follows from Lemma 1 that $g - \sum_{j=1}^{i-1} f_j$ can be computed in AC^0 (by testing, for small values of a, whether $a + \sum_{j=1}^{i-1} f_j \leq g$). Thus the claim follows by application of Lemma 1 and by closure under sum and product.

Now consider the case where the output gate is $\times$. By Lemma 1, we first check that $\prod_{i=1}^n f_i \geq g$ (if not we output 0). Otherwise there are two cases. In one case, some f_i is greater than g (and the minimum such i can be identified using Lemma 1), in which case $\prod_{i=1}^n f_i \dot{-} g$ is $A_i = f_i \left((\prod_{j \neq i} f_j) - 1 \right) + f_i - g$. Otherwise, all f_i's are less than g, in which case we can find the minimum i such that $\prod_{j=1}^i f_j \geq g$, and the desired monus is

$$B_i = \left(\prod_{j=1}^i f_j \right) \left(\left(\prod_{j=i+1}^n f_j \right) - 1 \right) + \left(\prod_{j=1}^i f_j - g \right).$$

To see that A_i can be computed using $\#AC^0$-circuits, notice that $f_i - g$ can be computed inductively and $\prod_{j \neq i} f_j - 1$ can be written as a telescoping series,

$\sum_{k=1, k \neq i}^{n} (f_k - 1) \prod_{j=k+1}^{n} f_j$, where the $f_k - 1$'s can be computed inductively. As for B_i, notice that $\prod_{j=i+1}^{n} f_j - 1$ can be computed as a telescoping series as for A_i. Now, $f_i \leq g$ and from the minimality of i, $\prod_{j=1}^{i-1} f_j \leq g$. Thus both $\prod_{j=1}^{i} f_j$ and g are polylogarithmic, so their difference can be computed using a $\#AC^0$ circuit. This completes the proof of Theorem 3. □

A similar argument allows us to show the following:

Lemma 2. *If f is any $\#AC^0$ function and g is a function in $\#AC^0$ taking polylogarithmically bounded values, then the function $\lfloor g/f \rfloor$ is in $\#AC^0$.* □

This leads to the question of whether $\lfloor g/f \rfloor$ is in $\#AC^0$ when we do *not* have a polylogarithmic upper bound on g. We give a negative answer by showing the following lower bound.

Theorem 3. *For any integer m that is not a power of 2, the function $\left\lfloor \frac{\sum_i x_i}{m} \right\rfloor$ cannot be computed in GapAC^0.* □

The situation for powers of 2 is more complicated. GapAC^0 is closed under such divisions, but $\#AC^0$ is not.

Theorem 4. *For any integer constant α and any function $F(x) \in \mathrm{GapAC}^0$ the function $\lfloor \frac{F(x)}{2^\alpha} \rfloor$ is computable in GapAC^0.* □

Theorem 5. *The function $\mathrm{EXACTHALF}(x) = \lfloor \frac{x_1 + \cdots + x_n}{2} \rfloor$ cannot be computed in $\#AC^0$.* □

Note 2. We remark that we can actually show that exponential-size circuits are required, using a similar proof.

Proof. We need the following result:

Lemma 3. *[ABFR91] If $p(x_1, \ldots, x_n)$ is a polynomial of degree k with the property that $p(x_1, \ldots, x_n) = \oplus(x_1, \ldots, x_n)$ for all except $\epsilon 2^n$ inputs for $\epsilon < 1/2$, then*

$$k \geq n - O\left(\sqrt{n} \log\left(\frac{1}{\epsilon}\right)\right).$$

Note that

$$\oplus(x_1, \ldots, x_n) = (x_1 + \cdots + x_n) - 2 \cdot \left\lfloor \frac{x_1 + \cdots + x_n}{2} \right\rfloor.$$

Hence, if $\lfloor \frac{x_1 + \cdots + x_n}{2} \rfloor$ could be computed by a polynomial of small degree, $\oplus$ could be computed by a polynomial of small degree as well. Together with Lemma 3, this means that any polynomial p such that $p(x_1, \ldots, x_n) = \lfloor \frac{x_1 + \cdots + x_n}{2} \rfloor$ for all except $\epsilon 2^n$ inputs must have degree at least $n - O\left(\sqrt{n} \log\left(\frac{1}{\epsilon}\right)\right)$.

This result initially seems to have only limited application for proving results about $\#AC^0$, since many functions computed by these arithmetic circuits have linear degree. One of our technical contributions is to show that the effects of large degree are not very great, when the size of the final function is small:

Lemma 4. *Let $c > 0$ be a constant. Let C_n be a depth-D, size-S_n #qAC^0 circuit[1] computing the function f. Suppose that $0 \leq f(x) \leq 2^{\log^c n}$. Let $z_\varepsilon = \left(\log(1/\varepsilon)\log S_n \log^2 n\right)^D$. Then for each ε satisfying[2] $0 < \varepsilon \leq 1/S_n$ there exists a polynomial of degree $O\left(z_\varepsilon \log^{cD} n\right)$ of n variables with the property that $P(x) = f(x)$ for at least $1 - \varepsilon$ fraction of all inputs.* ☐

Suppose that $\left\lfloor \frac{x_1 + \cdots + x_n}{2} \right\rfloor$ could be computed with a #AC^0 circuit of depth D and of size S. We take $c = 1$. By Lemma 4, for each $\varepsilon > 0$ there exists a polynomial P of degree

$$k = O\left(\left(\log(1/\varepsilon)\log S \log^2 n\right)^D \log^D n\right) = polylog(n)$$

such that the number of inputs x where $P(x) \neq \left\lfloor \frac{x_1 + \cdots + x_n}{2} \right\rfloor < 2^{\log n}$ is at most $\varepsilon 2^n$. Let $P'(x) = (x_1 + \ldots + x_n) - 2P(x)$. Then, the number of inputs x where $P'(x) \neq \oplus(x_1, \ldots, x_n)$ is also at most $\varepsilon 2^n$. That leads to a contradiction with corollary 3. This completes the proof of Theorem 5. ☐

In the full paper we show that even if we relax the requirement that we round down accurately when the number of 1's in the input is odd, it is still difficult to compute half the sum of the inputs.

A useful tool for showing non-membership in GapAC^0 was presented by Lu [Lu98]. He defined the following notion of *period*: If $f : \{0,1\}^n \rightarrow \mathbb{N}$ is a symmetric function, consider f as a function from $\{0, 1, \ldots, n\}$ into $\mathbb{N}$. The *period* of f is the least integer $k > 0$ such that $f(x) = f(x+k)$ for $0 \leq x \leq n-k$.

Theorem 6. *[Lu98] A symmetric Boolean function f is in the class qAC^0[2] if and only if it has period $2^{t(n)} = \log^{O(1)} n$ (with possible exceptions at $f(i)$ and $f(n - i)$ for $i = \log^{O(1)} n$).* ☐

Theorem 6 easily yields non-closure results, of which the following corollary is an example.

Corollary 2. *The functions $\left\lfloor \sqrt{\sum_i x_i} \right\rfloor$ and $\left\lfloor \log\left(1 + \sum_i x_i\right) \right\rfloor$ cannot be computed in GapqAC^0. Thus neither #AC^0 nor GapAC^0 are closed under taking of roots or logarithms.* ☐

As a final comment about closure properties, we note that it was shown in [AAD97] that if f is in #AC^0 (or GapAC^0) and $g(x) = O(1)$, then $\binom{f(x)}{g(x)}$ is in #AC^0 (GapAC^0, respectively). It remains an open question if closure holds also if g is allowed to be unbounded, although it is observed in [AAD97] that closure does not hold in general if g is superpolylogarithmic. It is perhaps worth noting that the proof in [AAD97] actually shows that for functions g computable in AC^0, both of the classes #qAC^0 and GapqAC^0 are closed under $\binom{\cdot}{g}$ if and only if g is polylogarithmic. This is related to an open question in [Lu98].

---

[1] qAC^0, qAC^0[2], GapqAC^0, #qAC^0 are counterparts of AC^0, AC^0[2], GapAC^0, #AC^0 when circuits are allowed to have *quasi-polynomial* $(2^{\log^c n})$ size instead of polynomial size.

[2] If $\varepsilon > 1/S_n$, one can use the polynomial for $\varepsilon = 1/S_n$, getting the same result with slightly worse $z_\varepsilon = (\log^2 S_n \log^2 n)^D$.

4 Grid Graphs

The importance of grid graphs to the study of constant-depth circuits was first shown in [BLMS98]. In this paper we use an equivalent notion, that makes it formally easier to present our results.

Definition 3. *A G-graph is a graph that has a planar embedding in which the vertices are grouped in a rectangular array of constant width (the length is a variable) with edges between vertices of adjacent columns only. For any G-graph, let s and t refer respectively to its lower left and upper right vertices. Also, if G_1, G_2 are G-graphs with the same width then $G_1 G_2$ denotes the G-graph formed by merging the rightmost column of G_1 and the leftmost column of G_2. This notation extends naturally to more than two G-graphs.*

G-graphs are important to the study of circuit complexity, since the reachability problem for width-k G-graphs is complete for depth-k AC^0 [BLMS98]. Unfortunately, even for width-2 G-graphs, counting the number of paths from s to t cannot be done in $GapAC^0$. To see this, consider the small G-graph illustrated in Figure 1 which implements the reachability matrix $A = \begin{bmatrix} 2 & 1 \\ 1 & 1 \end{bmatrix}$. That

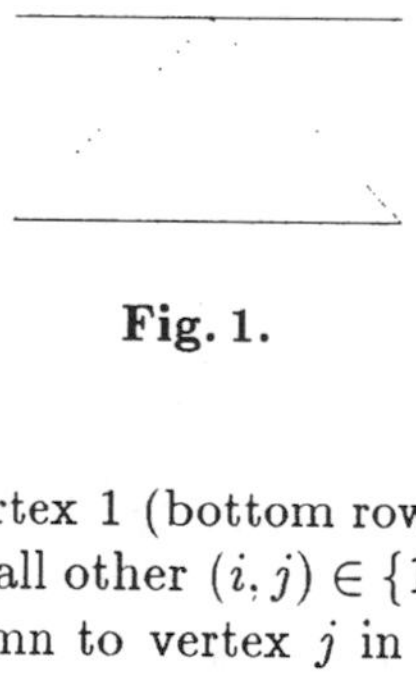

Fig. 1.

is, there are two paths from vertex 1 (bottom row) in the first column to vertex 1 in the third column, and for all other $(i, j) \in \{1, 2\}^2$ there is exactly one path from vertex i in the first column to vertex j in the third column. Recall that all edges are directed from left to right. Note that $A^i = \begin{bmatrix} f_{2i+1} & f_{2i} \\ f_{2i} & f_{2i-1} \end{bmatrix}$ where f_j denotes the j-th Fibonacci number.

Now consider the homomorphism h mapping $\sigma \in \{0, 1\}$ to A^σ. Given a string x, the low-order bit of $h(x)_{1,1}$ will be 0 if and only if the number of 1's in x is equivalent to 1 (mod 3). Since the mod 3 function is not in $AC^0[2]$, it follows that counting the number of paths from s to t is not in $GapAC^0$.

A similar argument shows that this problem is complete for NC^1 under the appropriate reductions.

Theorem 7. *Counting the number of s-t paths in width-two G-graphs is complete for NC^1 under ACC^0 reductions.*

Proof. The group of two-by-two matrices with determinant 1 over the integers mod 5 is non-solvable, and hence multiplication in it is hard for NC^1 by [Ba89].

But given any multiplication in this group, we can construct path-counting problems in a G-graph whose answers modulo 5 are the entries of the product matrix. This is because any two-by-two matrix over $\mathbb{N}$ with determinant 1 can be represented as a product of those two matrices coded for by the columns of Figure 1. (For a proof of this fact, see, e.g., [Gu90, Theorem 3.1].) □

Theorem 8. *Define the σ-depth of a circuit to be the maximum number of $\sum$ gates on any path in the circuit. Arithmetic circuits of σ-depth k can be simulated by counting the number of $s - t$ paths in a G-graph of width $2k + 2$, where the subgraph between any pair of columns is drawn from the family illustrated in Figure 2. Conversely, given a G-graph G, the number of $s - t$ paths in G can be computed by a uniform family of #AC^0 circuits.* □

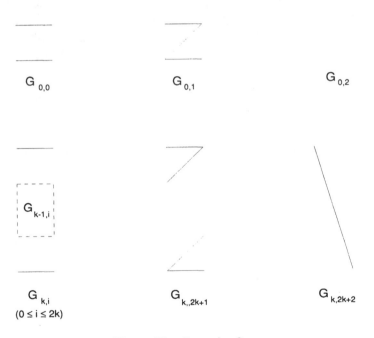

Fig. 2. The G-graphs $G_{i,j}$

Proof. For the forward direction, we construct a function f which associates a graph $f(C)$ with every gate C in a given #AC^0 circuit, such that the number of $s - t$ paths in $f(C)$ is equal to the output of the gate. We assume, without loss of generality, that the circuit is leveled so that we can construct the function f by an induction on its depth. The construction uses the graphs $G_{k,j}$ illustrated in Figure 2.

C is the constant c: $f(C) = G_{k,c}$.
C is the literal l: $f(C) = G_{k,l}$.

C **is a** $\prod$**-gate at** σ**-depth** d **with inputs** $C_1, \dots, C_r$**:**

$$f(C) = f(C_1)G_{k,2d+2}f(C_2)G_{k,2d+2}\dots G_{k,2d+2}f(C_r)$$

C **is a** $\sum$**-gate at** σ**-depth** d **with inputs** $C_1, \dots, C_r$**:**

$$f(C) = G_{k,2d+1}f(C_1)G_{k,2d+1}f(C_2)\dots G_{k,2d+1}f(C_r)G_{k,2d+1}$$

The G-graph for the formula $(x_1 x_2 + \overline{x_3})(\overline{x_2} + x_1 x_4)$ is illustrated in Figure 3.

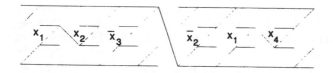

Fig. 3. G-graph for $(x_1 x_2 + \overline{x_3})(\overline{x_2} + x_1 x_4)$

For a G-graph G of width $2k$, let $s_i(G), t_i(G)$ $(1 \le i \le 2k)$ denote the i-th vertex from the bottom on the left boundary and from the top on the right boundary, respectively. Thus with this convention, $s = s_1(G)$ and $t = t_1(G)$. It is straightforward to show by induction that for a gate C at σ-depth d in the circuit, the number of $s_{k-d}(f(C))-t_{k-d}(f(C))$-paths equals the value computed by C.

Conversely, we have a width $2k$ graph $g'_1 \dots g'_n$ (where each g'_i is one of the $G_{k-1,j}$'s illustrated in Figure 2) and we want to compute the number of $s - t$ paths. Due to space limitations, the proof of this direction is omitted here.

$\square$

Acknowledgment

We thank Jin-Yi Cai for pointing us to [Gu90].

References

[Al97]   E. Allender, *Making computation count: Arithmetic circuits in the nineties.* In the Complexity Theory Column, edited by Lane Hemaspaandra, SIGACT NEWS 28, 4:2–15, December 1997.

[AAD97]   M. Agrawal, E. Allender, S. Datta, *On TC^0, AC^0 and arithmetic circuits.* In Proceedings of the 12th Annual IEEE Conference on Computational Complexity, pp:134–148, 1997.

[ABL98]   A. Ambainis, D. M. Barrington, H. LêThanh, *On counting AC^0 circuits with negative constants.* In Proceedings of the 23rd International Symposium on Mathematical Foundations of Computer Science (MFCS), 1998.

[ABFR91] J. Aspnes, R. Beigel, M. Furst, S. Rudich, *The expressive power of voting polynomials.* In Proceedings of the 23th ACM Symposium on Theory of Computing (STOC), pp:402–409, 1991.

[AJ93]   C. Álvarez, B. Jenner, *A very hard logspace counting class.* Theoretical Computer Science, 107:3–30, 1993.

[AJMV98] E. Allender, J. Jiao, M. Mahajan, and V. Vinay, *Non-commutative arithmetic circuits: depth reduction and size lower bounds*, Theoretical Computer Science, 209:47–86, 1998.

[Ba89] D. A. Barrington, *Bounded-Width Polynomial-Size Branching Programs Recognize Exactly Those Languages in NC^1*. Journal of Computer and System Sciences 38(1):150–164, 1989.

[BLMS98] D. M. Barrington, Ch-J Lu, P. B. Miltersen, S. Skyum, *Searching constant width mazes captures the AC^0 Hierarchy*. In Proceedings of the 15th Annual Symposium on Theoretical Aspects of Computer Science, 1998.

[BRS91] R. Beigel, N. Reingold, D. Spielman, *The perceptron strikes back*. In Proceedings of the 6th Annual IEEE Structure in Complexity Theory Conference, 1991.

[CMTV96] H. Caussinus, P. McKenzie, D. Thérien, H. Vollmer, *Nondeterministic NC^1 Computation*. In Proceedings of the 11th Annual IEEE Conference on Computational Complexity, pp:12–21, 1996.

[Gu90] Y. Gurevich. *Matrix decomposition Problem is complete for the average case*. In Proceedings of the 31st Annual IEEE Symposium on Foundations of Computer Science (FOCS), pp:802–811, 1990.

[Ha86] J. Hastad, *Almost optimal lower bounds for small depth circuits*. In Proceedings of the Eighteenth Annual ACM Symposium on Theory of Computing, pp:6–20, 1986.

[FKPS85] R. Fagin, M. Klawe, N. Pippenger, and L. Stockmeyer. *Bounded-depth, polynomial-size circuits for symmetric functions*. Theoretical Computer Science, 36:239–250, 1985.

[LêT98] H. LêThanh, *Circuits Arithmétiques de Profondeur Constante*, Thesis, Université Paris Sud, 1998.

[Lu98] Ch. J. Lu, *An exact characterization of symmetric functions in $qAC^0[2]$*. In Proceedings of the 4th Annual International Computing and Combinatorics Conference (COCOON), 1998.

[MV97] M. Mahajan, V.Vinay, *A combinatorial algorithm for the determinant*. Proceedings of the Eighth Annual ACM-SIAM Symposium on Discrete Algorithms, pp:730–738, 1997.

[NS98] F. Noilhan and M. Santha, *Semantical Counting Circuits*, submitted, 1998.

[OH93] M. Ogiwara, L. Hemachandra, *A complexity theory for feasible closure properties*. Journal of Computer and System Sciences, 46(3):295–325, June 1993.

[Ra87] A. A. Razborov, *Lower bound on size of bounded depth networks over a complete basis with logical addition*. Mathematicheskie Zametki, 41:598–607, 1987. English translation in Mathematical Notes of the Academy of Sciences of the USSR, 41:333–338, 1987.

[Tod92a] S. Toda, *Counting problems computationally equivalent to the determinant*. Manuscript.

[Tod92b] S. Toda, *Classes of arithmetic circuits capturing the complexity of computing the determinant*. IEICE Transactions, Informations and Systems, E75-D:116–124, 1992.

[Val79] L. Valiant, *The complexity of computing the permanent*. Theoretical Computer Science, 8:189–201, 1979.

[Ven92] H. Venkateswaran, *Circuit definitions of non-deterministic complexity classes*. SIAM Journal on Computing, 21:655–670, 1992.

[Vin91] V. Vinay, *Counting auxiliary pushdown automata and semi-unbounded arithmetic circuits*. In Proceedings of the 6th Annual IEEE Structure in Complexity Theory Conference, pp:270–284, 1991.

Parametric Temporal Logic
for "Model Measuring"

Rajeev Alur[*,1,2], Kousha Etessami[2], Salvatore La Torre[1,3], and Doron Peled[2]

[1]University of Pennsylvania [2]Bell Laboratories [3]Università degli Studi di Salerno

Abstract. We extend the standard model checking paradigm of linear temporal logic, LTL, to a "model measuring" paradigm where one can obtain more quantitative information beyond a "Yes/No" answer. For this purpose, we define a *parametric temporal logic*, PLTL, which allows statements such as "a request p is followed in at most x steps by a response q", where x is a free variable. We show how one can, given a formula $\varphi(x_1, \ldots, x_k)$ of PLTL and a system model K, not only determine whether there exists a valuation of $x_1, \ldots, x_k$ under which the system K satisfies the property φ, but if so find valuations which satisfy various optimality criteria. In particular, we present algorithms for finding valuations which minimize (or maximize) the maximum (or minimum) of all parameters. These algorithms exhibit the same PSPACE complexity as LTL model checking. We show that our choice of syntax for PLTL lies at the threshold of decidability for parametric temporal logics, in that several natural extensions have undecidable "model measuring" problems.

1 Introduction

Model checking has become a central methodology for automated verification of reactive systems (cf. [CE81,CK96]). In standard model checking, a system is described by some finite state model K and we use a temporal logic formula φ to define some required property of the behavior of K over time. We wish to check whether or not K indeed satisfies φ. The "yes/no" answer we obtain either reassures us that the system modeled by K behaves correctly, at least with respect to the property φ, or else points out a bug in our system.

Traditional temporal logics such as *linear temporal logic* (LTL) allow only *qualitative* assertions about the temporal ordering of events (for a basic understanding of temporal logic see [Pnu77,MP91,Eme90]). For example, a typical temporal requirement "every request p is followed by a response q," expressed in LTL by the formula $\Box(p \to \Diamond q)$, does not specify any bound on how soon the response should follow the request. In various circumstances, for assessing the efficiency and practicality of the design being modeled, we need additional quantitative guarantees. Consequently, a variety of "real-time" or "quantitative" temporal logics have been proposed (see, for instance, [Koy90,EMSS90,AH93,AFH96]).

---

[*] Supported in part by the NSF CAREER award CCR-9734115 and by the DARPA grant NAG2-1214.

A representative of such logics is *metric temporal logic* (MTL) [Koy90], which permits limiting the scope of temporal operators by subscripting them with natural numbers and a *direction* ("before" ($\leq$) or "after" ($>$)). The quantitative requirement that "every p is followed by q within 5 steps," is expressed by the MTL formula $\Box(p \to \Diamond_{\leq 5}q)$.

Even with quantitative temporal logics, however, model checking still yields only a "yes/no" answer. What if we have no idea whether 5 is the best bound on the response time? We would actually like to *find out* what quantitative bounds can be placed on the eventuality. In this paper, we provide a framework for precisely this kind of "model measuring". We extend linear temporal logic to *parametric temporal logic* (PLTL), in which temporal operators can be subscripted, together with a direction, by a variable ranging over the natural numbers. In particular, $\Diamond_{\leq x}\, p$ will mean "in at most x steps p occurs" and $\Box_{\leq y}\, q$ will mean "for at least y steps q holds." Thus the variables serve to delimit the scope of the temporal operators, but make no *a priori* claim as to what their values should be.

Our response property is thus written in PLTL as $\Box(p \to \Diamond_{\leq x}q)$. The question then becomes: "for what values of x does the formula hold for the system being modeled?" For an operator such as $\Diamond_{\leq x}$, we would like to compute the minimum satisfying value of x, while for an operator such as $\Box_{\leq y}$, we would like to compute the maximum satisfying value of y. In general, a system model K and a formula $\varphi(x_1, \ldots, x_k)$ with multiple parameters, define the set $V(K, \varphi)$ of valuations α of $(x_1, \ldots, x_k)$ under which φ holds for K. We present algorithms to answer various questions:

1. Is there a parameter valuation α for which K satisfies φ?
2. Does K satisfy φ for *any* α?
3. Is the set $V(K, \varphi)$ finite?
4. Find a parameter valuation $\alpha \in V(K, \varphi)$ which minimizes the max (or maximizes the min) parameter value.

The complexity of our algorithms for the above problems is essentially that of ordinary LTL model checking: PSPACE in the formula size and polynomial-time in the size of the model. When all parameterized operators in the formula are of the same polarity, we show how to compute an explicit representation of the set $V(K, \varphi)$ by symbolic constraints on parameter values. The key to our upper-bounds is a novel "pumping lemma" for satisfying models: if a sequence satisfies a formula for large-enough values of the parameters, we can repeat appropriate cycles to obtain a sequence that satisfies the formula for larger parameter values.

We have defined our logic with two restrictions. First, we do not allow equality subscripts (e.g. $\Diamond_{=x}$). Second, the same parameter cannot appear in association with two operators with different polarities (e.g., both $\Diamond_{\leq x}$ and $\Box_{\leq x}$). We show that our logic basically lies at the threshold of decidability for parametric temporal logics, in the sense that removing either of these two restrictions leads to an undecidable "model measuring" problem.

Related work. The need for "parametric" temporal reasoning has been identified by various researchers. For system models with parametric bounds on delays, the reachability problem is known to be undecidable [AHV93,HKPV95]. Algorithms for computing lower and upper bounds on delays between specified events [CY91], or on durations of intervals specified using LTL [CCG96] are known and correspond to special cases of our problem. The model-checking problem for parameterized branching-time logic has been solved [Wan96], but its solution applies only to a CTL-like logic whose path formulas do not admit nesting of temporal modalities.

2 Parametric Temporal Logic

We will first define parametric temporal logic using a full set of parameterized operators, but we will then show, in Lemma 1, that it suffices to consider only two basic parameterized operators in order to capture all of them. We will define our parametric temporal logic so that all formulas are already in positive normal form, where negation may only be applied to atomic propositions. Note that for any number $m \geq 0$, $\Diamond_{\leq m} \varphi$ implies $\Diamond_{\leq m+1} \varphi$, and likewise, $\Diamond_{>m+1} \varphi$ implies $\Diamond_{>m} \varphi$. In other words, these parameterized operators are monotone (either upward or downward). For reasons that will become clear, we wish to separate parameters that subscript upward-monotone operators from those that subscript downward-monotone operators.

A *parametric temporal logic* (PLTL) formula is composed, as in ordinary LTL, of atomic propositions $P = \{p_1, \ldots, p_n\}$ and their negations $\{\neg p_1, \ldots, \neg p_n\}$, the boolean connectives $\wedge$, $\vee$, the ordinary temporal operators *Next* ($\bigcirc$), *Eventually* ($\Diamond$), *Always* ($\square$) and *Until* ($\mathcal{U}$). In addition, we define *parameterized* versions of all temporal operators, using two disjoint sets of parameter variables, $X = \{x_0, x_1, x_2, \ldots\}$ and $Y = \{y_0, y_1, y_2, \ldots\}$, along with constants $\mathbb{N} = \{0, 1, 2, \ldots\}$. For $x \in X \cup \mathbb{N}$ and $y \in Y \cup \mathbb{N}$, the parameterized operators are:

$$\Diamond_{\leq x}, \ \Diamond_{>y}, \ \square_{\leq y}, \ \square_{>x}, \ \mathcal{U}_{\leq x}, \text{ and } \mathcal{U}_{>y}.$$

Formulas are built up in the usual way from these operators and connectives. To give meaning to PLTL formulas, we interpret the variables in X and Y over the natural numbers $\mathbb{N}$. Given an assignment $\alpha : X \cup Y \to \mathbb{N}$ to the variables, along with an ω-word $w = w_0 w_1 w_2 \ldots$ over the alphabet $\Sigma = 2^P$, and a position $i \geq 0$, we inductively define what it means for (w, i, α) to satisfy a formula φ of PLTL, denoted $(w, i, \alpha) \models \varphi$. For convenience of notation, we extend α so that for $m \in \mathbb{N}$, $\alpha(m) = m$. The interpretation of all ordinary temporal operators and connectives is identical to their LTL interpretation. The parameterized operators are interpreted as follows:

1. $(w, i, \alpha) \models \Diamond_{\leq x} \varphi$ iff $\exists j$ such that $(i \leq j \leq i + \alpha(x))$ and $(w, j, \alpha) \models \varphi$
2. $(w, i, \alpha) \models \Diamond_{>y} \varphi$ iff $\exists j$ such that $(j > i + \alpha(y))$ and $(w, j, \alpha) \models \varphi$
3. $(w, i, \alpha) \models \square_{\leq y} \varphi$ iff $\forall j$ such that $(i \leq j \leq i + \alpha(y))$, $(w, j, \alpha) \models \varphi$
4. $(w, i, \alpha) \models \square_{>x} \varphi$ iff $\forall j$ such that $(j > i + \alpha(x))$, $(w, j, \alpha) \models \varphi$
5. $(w, i, \alpha) \models \varphi \, \mathcal{U}_{\leq x} \, \psi$ iff $\exists j$ such that $(i \leq j \leq i + \alpha(x))$ and $(w, j, \alpha) \models \psi$ and $(w, i', \alpha) \models \varphi$ for all i' with $i \leq i' < j$.

6. $(w, i, \alpha) \models \varphi \, \mathcal{U}_{>y} \, \psi$ iff $\exists j$ such that $(j > i + \alpha(y))$ and $(w, j, \alpha) \models \psi$ and $(w, i', \alpha) \models \varphi$ for all i' with $i \le i' < j$.

A parameterized operator Θ_x is *upward-monotone* if for any φ, $\Theta_x \varphi \Rightarrow \Theta_{x+1} \varphi$ and *downward-monotone* if $\Theta_{y+1} \varphi \Rightarrow \Theta_y \varphi$. We now make some basic observations about these operators.

Proposition 1. *Operators parameterized by variables in X are upward-monotone, while those parameterized by variables in Y are downward-monotone.*

The following lemma shows that, without loss of generality, we can confine ourselves to the two parameterized operators $\Diamond_{\le x}$ and $\Box_{\le y}$.

Lemma 1. *The parameterized operators $\Diamond_{\le x}$ and $\Box_{\le y}$, along with ordinary temporal operators, suffice to define all parameterized operators and hence all of PLTL.*

Henceforth, we will implicitly assume the "less than or equal" direction for the subscripts, and write $\Diamond_x$ and $\Box_y$, for $\Diamond_{\le x}$ and $\Box_{\le y}$, respectively. Observe that the logic is closed under negation since the operators $\Diamond_z$ and $\Box_z$ are duals of each other: $\Diamond_z \varphi \Leftrightarrow \neg \Box_z \neg \varphi$.

Let φ be a PLTL formula over P, containing parameter variables $X' \subseteq X$ and $Y' \subseteq Y$, and let $\alpha_{|_{X' \cup Y'}}$ denote the assignment α restricted to those variables. We define $S(\varphi)$ to be the set of assignments to the parameters in φ that make φ satisfiable: $S(\varphi) \doteq \{\alpha_{|_{X' \cup Y'}} \mid \exists w \in (2^P)^\omega \text{ such that } (w, 0, \alpha) \models \varphi\}$. In the rest of the paper, when it is clear, we will not specify the projection and implicitly assume α defines only the variables that are relevant in the given context. Similarly, we define $V(\varphi)$ to be the set of assignments to the parameters in φ that make φ valid: $V(\varphi) \doteq \{\alpha \mid \forall w \in (2^P)^\omega, (w, 0, \alpha) \models \varphi\}$.

A *Kripke structure* $K = (Q, E, L, I)$ over the alphabet 2^P is given by a set of states Q, a transition relation $E \subseteq Q \times Q$, a labeling function $L : Q \mapsto 2^P$ and a set of initial states $I \subseteq Q$. We define a path $\rho \in K$ to be a sequence $q_0 q_1 \ldots$ of states such that $q_0 \in I$ and $E(q_i, q_{i+1})$ for all $i \ge 0$. We extend the definition of L to sequences of states, such that $L(\rho)$ is the ω-word defined by the sequence of labels on the states in ρ. Given a Kripke structure K, define $S(K, \varphi)$ to be those assignments α to the parameters in φ for which there exists a path in K that models φ. In other words, $S(K, \varphi) \doteq \{\alpha \mid \exists \rho \in K \ (L(\rho), 0, \alpha) \models \varphi\}$. Analogously, define $V(K, \varphi) \doteq \{\alpha \mid \forall \rho \in K \ (L(\rho), 0, \alpha) \models \varphi\}$. Note that $S(\varphi)$ is the complement of $V(\neg\varphi)$, and $S(K, \varphi)$ is the complement of $V(K, \neg\varphi)$.

3 Decision Procedures

We begin by considering the fragment with only one parameterized modality, namely, $\Box_y$.

3.1 Parameterized Always

Given a set P of atomic propositions and a set Y of parameters, consider the logic $PLTL_\Box$ whose formulas are generated by the grammar

$$\varphi := p \mid \neg p \mid \varphi \wedge \psi \mid \varphi \vee \psi \mid \bigcirc \varphi \mid \Box \varphi \mid \varphi \mathcal{U} \psi \mid \Box_y \varphi \mid \Box_c \varphi \mid \Diamond_c \varphi$$

where $p \in P$, $y \in Y$ and $c \in \mathbb{N}$. A parameter valuation α for a formula φ of $PLTL_\Box$ assigns values to all the parameters in φ and $\alpha(\varphi)$ denotes the formula of $PLTL_\Box$ obtained by substituting each subscript parameter y in φ by the constant $\alpha(y)$. The formula φ defines the set $S(\varphi)$ of parameter valuations α such that the formula $\alpha(\varphi)$ is satisfiable.

For a formula φ, we use n_φ to denote the number of connectives in φ, k_φ to denote the number of parameter occurrences in φ and c_φ to denote the product of the constants appearing in φ. Given a formula φ of the logic $PLTL_\Box$, the *closure* $cl(\varphi)$ is defined as usual (e.g., $cl(\Box_c \varphi)$ contains all the formulas $\Box_d \varphi$ for $d = 1, \ldots, c$ and $cl(\varphi)$). The size of the closure of a formula φ is proportional to $n_\varphi c_\varphi$ and, thus, can be exponential in the description of φ. We need to consider subsets of the closure that correspond to possible truth assignments to various formulas in the closure. A subset $s \subseteq cl(\varphi)$ of the closure is said to be *consistent*[1] if whenever s contains $\Box_d \psi$, it also contains $\Box_{d'} \psi$ for $0 < d' < d$, and whenever s contains $\Diamond_d \psi$, it also contains $\Diamond_{d'} \psi$ for $d' > d$ with $\Diamond_{d'} \psi \in cl(\varphi)$. The consistency requirement reflects the monotonicity properties of the subscripted temporal operators.

Lemma 2. *For a formula φ of $PLTL_\Box$, the number of consistent subsets of $cl(\varphi)$ is $O(c_\varphi 2^{n_\varphi})$.*

Emptiness. First, observe that by monotonicity property of the operator $\Box_y$, the set $S(\varphi)$ is downwards-closed. That is, if α and β are two valuations such that $\alpha(y) \geq \beta(y)$ for each parameter $y \in Y$ and $\alpha \in S(\varphi)$, then $\beta \in S(\varphi)$. It follows that to test nonemptiness of $S(\varphi)$, it suffices to check satisfiability of the formula obtained by setting each parameter to 0. Second, for a parameter valuation α, the formula $\alpha(\varphi)$ has no parameters and its satisfiability can be checked by algorithms for real-time temporal logics such as MTL [AH93]. Third, since the logic LTL is PSPACE-hard, so is checking emptiness. This leads us to the following theorem:

Theorem 1. *Given a formula φ of $PLTL_\Box$, checking emptiness of $S(\varphi)$ is PSPACE-complete and can be done in time $O(c_\varphi 2^{n_\varphi})$.*

Universality. Given φ, we wish to determine if there is a valuation α such that the resulting formula $\alpha(\varphi)$ is unsatisfiable. For φ, define $N_\varphi = c_\varphi k_\varphi 2^{n_\varphi}$ and let α_N be the valuation that assigns N_φ to each parameter. We will establish that if α_N belongs to the set $S(\varphi)$, then so does every valuation. The next Lemma is the key to our solution.

---

[1] There are many additional standard consistency requirements (e.g. if s contains $\varphi_1 \wedge \varphi_2$, it should also contain both φ_1 and φ_2). These, while important in algorithm implementation, are not required for our counting arguments.

Lemma 3. *Let φ be a formula of $PLTL_\square$, α and β be parameter valuations such that for each parameter y, $\beta(y) \geq \alpha(y) \geq N_\varphi$. Then, if $\alpha \in S(\varphi)$ then $\beta \in S(\varphi)$.*

Proof. First, we can assume that each parameter appears precisely once in φ (if a parameter y appears twice then rename the second occurrence to y' and let $\alpha(y') = \alpha(y)$ and $\beta(y') = \beta(y)$). Suppose there exists a word w such that $(w, 0, \alpha) \models \varphi$. For a parameter z, define α_z such that α_z assigns the value $\alpha(z)+1$ to z and, for the remaining parameters, assigns the same value as α does. Since we can obtain β from α by a sequence of steps, where a step corresponds to incrementing one parameter by one, it suffices to prove that there exists a word w' such that $(w', 0, \alpha_z) \models \varphi$.

For each i, define $\pi_i = \{\psi \in cl(\varphi) \mid (w, i, \alpha) \models \psi\}$ (i.e. π_i consists of those formulas in the closure that are true at position i in w according to valuation α). For each parameter y, the operator $\square_y$ occurs precisely once in φ and let $\square_y \psi_y$ be the corresponding subformula. An index i is said to be y-*critical* if $\square_y \psi_y$ is in π_i, but not in π_{i+1}. It follows that the formula ψ_y holds throughout the interval from position i to $i + \alpha(y)$, but not at position $i + \alpha(y) + 1$. The interval from position $i + 1$ to $i + \alpha(y)$ is said to be a y-*critical interval*. Observe the following properties of such y-critical intervals:

1. The formula $\square_y \psi_y$ is false at all positions in a y-critical interval.
2. If $\square_y \psi_y$ holds at some position j in w, then $\square_y \psi_y$ continues to hold at subsequent positions, unless a y-critical interval is encountered.

The above observations, together with the facts that, for each y, each y-critical interval is at least $N_\varphi = k_\varphi c_\varphi 2^{n_\varphi}$, and there are k_φ parameters, can be used to prove the following lemma.

Lemma 4. *Every z-critical interval I contains a subinterval J of length $c_\varphi 2^{n_\varphi}$ such that for every parameter y, either $\square_y \psi_y$ holds at all positions in J or $\square_y \psi_y$ holds at no position in J.*

Observe that each such π_i is a consistent subset of the closure, and there are at most $c_\varphi 2^{n_\varphi}$ consistent subsets. Hence, every z-critical interval contains two positions i and j such that $\pi_i = \pi_j$ and, for every parameter y, either $\square_y \psi_y \in \pi_l$ for all $i \leq l \leq j$ or $\square_y \psi_y \notin \pi_l$ for all $i \leq l \leq j$. Intuitively, the subsequence from i to j is a cycle in which the truth of all parameterized operators is unchanged. The word w' is obtained by repeating such a cycle in each z-critical interval. For each position l in w', there is a corresponding position $f(l)$ in w. The transformation of w to w', along with the correspondence function f, is illustrated in Figure 1. Since we are pumping inside each z-critical interval and ψ_z holds at all these positions, we can use α_z, instead of α, which increments the value of the parameter z. We prove the following lemma:

Lemma 5. *For each $\psi \in cl(\varphi)$, for each $i \in \mathbb{N}$, if $(w, f(i), \alpha) \models \psi$ then $(w', i, \alpha_z) \models \psi$.*

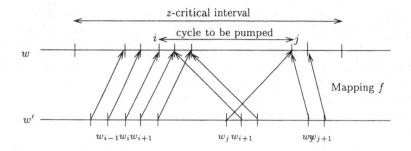

Fig. 1. Transforming w to w' by pumping cycles

The lemma is proved by induction on the structure of ψ. The detailed proof is omitted here. For the cases of temporal operators such as $\bigcirc$, $\square$, $\mathcal{U}$, $\square_c$ and $\diamondsuit_c$, we use the fact that the two end-points of each pumped cycle agree on the truth of all subformulas. For the case of parameterized operator $\square_y\psi_y$, we use the fact that $\square_y\psi_y$ holds either everywhere or nowhere in the pumped cycle. It is worth noting that pumping can make more formulas true (i.e. there may be subformulas ψ and positions i such that $(w, f(i), \alpha) \not\models \psi$ but $(w', i, \alpha_z) \models \psi$).

Thus, checking universality reduces to checking satisfiability of the formula $\alpha_N(\varphi)$. Noting that the product of constants in $\alpha_N(\varphi)$ is $c_\varphi N_\varphi^{k_\varphi}$, we get:

Theorem 2. *Given a formula φ of $PLTL_\square$, checking whether $S(\varphi)$ contains all valuations is PSPACE-complete and can be done in time $O(c_\varphi^{k_\varphi+1} k_\varphi^{k_\varphi} 2^{n_\varphi(k_\varphi+1)})$.*

Finiteness. For $i \in \{1, \ldots, k_\varphi\}$, let α_i be the valuation defined as $y_i = c_\varphi 2^{n_\varphi-k+1}$ and $y_j = 0$ for all $j \neq i$. Observe that, since $\square_0\psi \equiv \psi$, a formula $\alpha_i(\varphi)$ has $n_\varphi - k + 1$ operators. Then, by the downwards-closure of $S(\varphi)$ and Lemma 3, it holds that $S(\varphi)$ is infinite if and only if $\alpha_i(\varphi)$ is satisfiable for some $i \in \{1, \ldots, k_\varphi\}$. This implies the following theorem:

Theorem 3. *Given a formula φ of $PLTL_\square$, checking whether the set $S(\varphi)$ is finite is PSPACE-complete and can be done in time $O(k_\varphi c_\varphi^2 4^{n_\varphi-k+1})$.*

Computing the solution set. By Lemma 3 we know that to compute the solution set $S(\varphi)$ we have to explore a finite space and this can be done through a recursive algorithm computing a description of $S(\varphi)$ which is doubly exponential in number of parameters in φ. It remains open whether one can effectively construct a singly-exponential representation of $S(\varphi)$. In particular, we only know an exponential lower-bound on the number of corner points in the $S(\varphi)$ region, but can not establish a matching upper-bound, from which a singly-exponential representation would follow. It is worth noting that, always by the Lemma 3, if the set $S(\varphi)$ is finite then it is included in the hyper-cube $[0, c_\varphi 2^{n_\varphi-k_\varphi+1} - 1]^{k_\varphi}$ and, then, $S(\varphi)$ can be described by a formula whose size is exponential in number of parameter occurrences in φ.

Optimization. For a formula such $\Box_y p$, we are typically interested in computing the maximum duration for which p holds and, thus, finding the maximum value of y. Given a formula with multiple parameters, we can consider various optimization functions (e.g. sum of all parameters). While all such problems can be solved by computing the explicit representation of the solution set, we present simpler solutions for natural problems, namely, maximizing the minimum and the maximum of all parameters.

Given φ, suppose we wish $\max_{\alpha \in S(\varphi)} \min_{y \in Y} \alpha(y)$, i.e. to maximize the minimum of all parameters. First, due to downwards-closure of $S(\varphi)$, we can assume that the maximizing assignment assigns all parameters the same value. Hence, rename all parameters to a single parameter y. Then, if setting y to N_φ gives a satisfiable formula then all values of y are possible and the answer is ∞. If not, by a binary search over the interval $[0, N_\varphi]$, we can find the maximal value of c such that setting y to c gives a satisfiable formula. Thus, we need $\log N_\varphi$ satisfiability checks, each costing $O(c_\varphi^{k_\varphi+1} k_\varphi^{k_\varphi} 2^{n_\varphi(k_\varphi+1)})$.

Given φ, suppose we wish $\max_{\alpha \in S(\varphi)} \max_{y \in Y} \alpha(y)$, i.e. to maximize the maximum of all parameters. Again, by downwards-closure of $S(\varphi)$, we can assume that the maximizing assignment assigns the value 0 to all parameters but one. Hence, we need to compute $\max_y \{\alpha(y) \mid \alpha \in S(\varphi) \text{ and } \alpha(y') = 0 \text{ for } y' \neq y\}$. So for each parameter y, we can set all others to 0 and maximize y, again by binary search.

Theorem 4. *Given a formula φ of PLTL$_\Box$, maximizing the minimum (resp. the maximum) of parameter values over $S(\varphi)$ is PSPACE-complete and can be done in time $O(c_\varphi^{k_\varphi+1} k_\varphi^{k_\varphi} 2^{n_\varphi(k_\varphi+1)} \log(k_\varphi c_\varphi 2_\varphi^n))$ (resp. $O(c_\varphi^{k_\varphi+1} k_\varphi^{k_\varphi+1} 2^{n_\varphi(k_\varphi+1)})$).*

3.2 The Full Logic PLTL

Before considering the full logic PLTL, we briefly introduce the logic that is the dual of PLTL$_\Box$: the logic PLTL$_\Diamond$ allows parameterized eventualities, but not parameterized always operators. The results for PLTL$_\Diamond$ are analogous to those for PLTL$_\Box$. For instance, the set $S(\varphi)$, for a given PLTL$_\Diamond$ formula φ, is upwards-closed. The analog of Lemma 3 states that if all parameters have values $\geq N_\varphi$ then the value of a parameter can be decremented. This requires the converse of pumping cycles, namely, deletion of appropriate cycles.

Given a formula φ of PLTL, if we instantiate values of the X-parameters (i.e. subscripts of parameterized eventualities), we get a formula of PLTL$_\Box$ and, similarly, if we instantiate values of the Y-parameters, we get a formula of PLTL$_\Diamond$. Furthermore, monotonicity properties continue to hold: if $\alpha \in S(\varphi)$, β is such that $\beta(x) \geq \alpha(x)$ for $x \in X$ and $\beta(y) \leq \alpha(y)$ for $y \in Y$, then $\beta \in S(\varphi)$. With α_Z we denote a parameter valuation for some subset Z of the parameters. Then, the projection $[S(\varphi)]_{\alpha_Z}$ is defined to be the set of valuations $\beta \in S(\varphi)$ such that $\beta(z) = \alpha_Z(z)$ for $z \in Z$. It follows that

1. Checking emptiness and universality of $S(\varphi)$ are both PSPACE.
2. If φ is not a PLTL$_\Box$ formula, the set $S(\varphi)$ is either empty or infinite.

3. Let Z be such that either $X \subseteq Z$ or $Y \subseteq Z$, the projections $[S(\varphi)]_{\alpha z}$ constructed and questions such as emptiness, universality and minimizing/maximizing the minimum/maximum, can be answered in PSPACE.

In general, the set $S(\varphi)$ does not appear tractable, and in particular, as the results in the next section will establish, the question whether $S(\varphi)$ contains a valuation α with $\alpha(x) = \alpha(y)$, is undecidable.

3.3 Model Measuring

Model measuring corresponds to answering questions about $V(K, \varphi)$, the set of parameter valuations for which all the paths in K satisfy φ, As noted earlier, $V(K, \varphi)$ is the complement of $S(K, \neg\varphi)$.

We thus need to convert our results for $S(\varphi)$ to corresponding results about $S(K, \varphi)$. In the same way that, for LTL, model checking and satisfiability are similar problems, our answers for questions about $S(K, \varphi)$ will follow the corresponding answers for $S(\varphi)$. In particular, $S(K, \varphi)$ is downwards-closed, so to check emptiness of $S(K, \varphi)$, we can set all parameters to 0 and check if K satisfies the resulting formula. The pumping lemma 3 also holds with the modification that we have to consider paths in K and identify cycles whose end-points have identical K-states and agree on truth of all subformulas. The corresponding pumping lemma is:

Lemma 6. *Let φ be a formula of PLTL$_\square$, K be a Kripke structure with m states and α and β be parameter valuations such that for each parameter y, $\beta(y) \geq \alpha(y) \geq mN_\varphi$. Then, $\alpha \in S(K, \varphi)$ iff $\beta \in S(K, \varphi)$.*

From this lemma all the analogous results that we obtained for $S(\varphi)$ follow; we simply need to multiply N_φ by the number of states of the model. For instance, given K and φ of PLTL$_\square$, we can compute the maximum of the minimum parameter value over $S(K, \varphi)$ in time $O(m^2 c_\varphi^2 4^{n_\varphi})$. It is worth noting that the complexity of all the problems is polynomial in the size of the model.

4 Stronger Parameterization: Undecidability

The reader might wonder why PLTL was defined as it was. In particular, why did we not allow operators of the form $\lozenge_{=x}$ and why did we not allow the same parameter variable to occur in the same formula in both an upward-monotone and downward-monotone operator? In this section we provide the answer: adding such power would make model measuring undecidable. We begin by considering what happens when you add parameterized equality operators like $\mathcal{U}_{=x}$ to the language. Let us call this language PLTL$^=$.

Theorem 5. *Given any two-counter Turing machine T, there are formulas $\varphi_T(x)$ and $\psi_T(x)$ of PLTL$^=$ such that $S(\varphi_T)$ is non-empty iff T halts and $S(\psi_T)$ is universal iff T halts.*

It follows that for φ in PLTL$^=$, deciding whether $S(\varphi)$ is empty is undecidable, so is deciding whether $V(\varphi)$ is empty. Since there exists a universal Kripke structure that generates all possible ω-words over a given alphabet, the "model measuring" problems (e.g., given K and φ, is $V(K, \varphi)$ is empty) are also undecidable. The fact that introducing an "equality" subscript makes the logic hard is consistent with similar results for real-time temporal logics: for discrete-time logics, such as MTL, introduction of equality causes complexity to jump to EXPSPACE from PSPACE [AH93], while for dense-time logics, such as MITL, introduction of equality causes complexity to jump to undecidable from decidable [AFH96]. Let PLTL$^{\uparrow\downarrow}$ denote the language in which we allow a parameter variable to occur in both upward and downward closed settings inside a formula. The proof of Theorem 5 can be modified to establish:

Corollary 1. *Given a formula φ of PLTL$^{\uparrow\downarrow}$, checking whether $S(\varphi)$ is empty is undecidable, so is checking whether $V(\varphi)$ is empty.*

References

[AFH96] R. Alur, T. Feder, and T.A. Henzinger. The benefits of relaxing punctuality. *Journal of the ACM*, 43(1):116–146, 1996.

[AH93] R. Alur and T.A. Henzinger. Real-time logics: complexity and expressiveness. *Information and Computation*, 104(1):35–77, 1993.

[AHV93] R. Alur, T.A. Henzinger, and M.Y. Vardi. Parametric real-time reasoning. In *Proc. of the 25th ACM STOC*, pp. 592–601, 1993.

[CCG96] S. Campos, E. Clarke, and O. Grumberg. Selective quantitative analysis and interval model checking. In *Proce. Eighth CAV*, LNCS 1102, 1996.

[CE81] E.M. Clarke and E.A. Emerson. Design and synthesis of synchronization skeletons using branching time temporal logic. In *Proc. Workshop on Logic of Programs*, LNCS 131, pp. 52–71, 1981.

[CK96] E.M. Clarke and R.P. Kurshan. Computer-aided verification. *IEEE Spectrum*, 33(6):61–67, 1996.

[CY91] C. Courcoubetis and M. Yannakakis. Minimum and maximum delay problems in real-time systems. In *Proc. Third CAV*, LNCS 575, 1991.

[Eme90] E.A. Emerson. Temporal and modal logic. In *Handbook of Theoretical Computer Science*, vol B, pp. 995–1072. Elsevier Science Publishers, 1990.

[EMSS90] E.A. Emerson, A.K. Mok, A.P. Sistla, and J. Srinivasan. Quantitative temporal reasoning. In *Computer-Aided Verification, 2nd International Conference, CAV'90*, LNCS 531, pp. 136–145, 1990.

[HKPV95] T.A. Henzinger, P. Kopke, A. Puri, and P. Varaiya. What's decidable about hybrid automata. In *Proceedings of the 27th ACM Symposium on Theory of Computing*, pp. 373–382, 1995.

[Koy90] R. Koymans. Specifying real-time properties with metric temporal logic. *Journal of Real-Time Systems*, 2:255–299, 1990.

[MP91] Z. Manna and A. Pnueli. *The temporal logic of reactive and concurrent systems: Specification*. Springer-verlag, 1991.

[Pnu77] A. Pnueli. The temporal logic of programs. In *Proceedings of the 18th IEEE Symposium on Foundations of Computer Science*, pp. 46–77, 1977.

[Wan96] Farn Wang. Parametric timing analysis for real-time systems. *Information and Computation*, 130(2):131–150, 1996.

Communicating Hierarchical State Machines

Rajeev Alur*, Sampath Kannan**, and Mihalis Yannakakis***

Abstract. *Hierarchical state machines* are finite state machines whose states themselves can be other machines. In spite of their popularity in many modeling tools for software design, very little is known concerning their complexity and expressiveness. In this paper, we study these questions for hierarchical state machines as well as for communicating hierarchical state machines, that is, finite state machines extended with both hierarchy and concurrency. We present a comprehensive set of results characterizing (1) the complexity of the reachability, emptiness and universality problems, (2) the complexity of the language inclusion and equivalence problems, and (3) the succinctness relationships between different types of machines.

1 Introduction

Finite state machines (FSMs) are widely used in the modeling of systems in various areas. Descriptions using FSMs are useful to represent the flow of control (as opposed to data manipulation) and are amenable to formal analysis such as model checking [CE81,CK96,Hol97,VW86]. In the simplest setting, an FSM consists of a labeled graph whose vertices correspond to system states and edges correspond to system transitions. In practice, to describe complex systems using FSMs, several extensions are useful such as *communicating FSMs* in which the system is described by a collection of FSMs that operate concurrently and synchronize with one another periodically,

There is a rich body of theoretical results concerning complexity and expressiveness of state machines. By labeling the edges of an FSM with alphabet symbols and by introducing initial and final states, FSMs can be used to define regular languages. Analysis problems of interest include emptiness of the language, model checking with respect to temporal requirements, and inclusion and equivalence of the languages of two machines. For a single FSM, the complexity of some problems depends on whether the machine is deterministic or not. For instance, language equivalence is NL-complete for deterministic machines but PSPACE-complete for nondeterministic ones (cf. [HU79]). Introducing concurrency, that is, considering communicating FSMs, usually costs an

* Department of Computer and Information Science, University of Pennsylvania, and Bell Laboratories, Lucent Technologies. Email: alur@cis.upenn.edu. Supported in part by NSF CAREER award CCR-9734115 and by the DARPA grant NAG2-1214.
** Department of Computer and Information Science, University of Pennsylvania. Email: kannan@cis.upenn.edu.
*** Bell Laboratories, Lucent Technologies. Email: mihalis@research.bell-labs.com.

extra exponential. For instance, simple reachability for communicating FSMs is PSPACE-complete, while trace equivalence is EXPSPACE-complete [HKV97]. Insight into the complexity of analysis problems is also provided by the succinctness afforded by various features. For instance, nondeterministic machines are exponentially more succinct than deterministic ones (cf. [HU79]), concurrent machines are exponentially more succinct than the sequential ones, and concurrent nondeterministic machines are doubly-exponentially more succinct than deterministic FSMs [DH94].

While the impact of features such as nondeterminism and concurrency on complexity and expressiveness of finite-state machines is well understood, there is almost no literature on understanding the impact of introducing *hierarchy* in state machines. In *hierarchical (nested) FSMs*, the states of an FSM can be ordinary states or *superstates* which are FSMs themselves. The notion of hierarchical FSMs was popularized by the introduction of STATECHARTS [Har87], and exists in various object-oriented software development methodologies such as ROOM [SGW94] and the Unified Modeling Language (UML [BJR97]). Hierarchical state machines have two descriptive advantages over ordinary FSMs. First, superstates offer a convenient structuring mechanism that allows us to specify systems by stepwise refinement, and to view it at different levels of granularity. Second, by allowing sharing of component FSMs, we need to specify components only once and then can reuse them in different contexts, leading to modularity and succinct system representations. In a recent paper, it is shown that the succinctness offered by sequential hierarchical state machines comes at no cost: the reachability problem for sequential hierarchical state machines can be solved without constructing the equivalent flattened ordinary FSM, and is P-complete [AY98]. In this paper, we investigate the reachability question for *communicating* hierarchical state machines, language equivalence problems for hierarchical and communicating hierarchical state machines, and succinctness issues.

Our first set of results concern algorithms for reachability in presence of both the concurrency and hierarchy constructs. While reachability of a single hierarchical state machine (HSM) can be solved in linear time [AY98], we show that the product of two HSMs is difficult to analyze and has a PSPACE-complete reachability problem. For *communicating hierarchical state machines* (CHM) that allow arbitrary nesting of the concurrency and hierarchy constructs, we show the reachability problem to be EXPSPACE-complete. This shows that hierarchy, in presence of concurrency, costs an extra exponential. Then, we proceed to identify a restriction on the use of the two constructs that avoids this extra cost. In *well-structured* CHMs, communication among hierarchical components is allowed only at the top level, and for such machines we show that one needs to pay only for concurrency: the reachability problem is PSPACE-complete as in the case of communicating FSMs.

Our second set of results concern checking equivalence of languages of two machines. For a sequential HSM, while language emptiness is P-complete, we show checking universality to be EXPSPACE-complete. It follows that checking language inclusion and equivalence are both EXPSPACE-complete problems. In the case of ordinary FSMs, *deterministic* machines have polynomial-time complexity for universality, inclusion, and equivalence, while the corresponding problems are PSPACE-complete for nondeterministic ones. This motivates us to consider these problems for deterministic HSMs: while universality becomes easy (P-complete), language inclusion is PSPACE-complete, and language equivalence can be solved in PSPACE (a matching lower bound remains an open question). When we consider communicating hierarchical machines, the costs due to concurrency and hierarchy add up: all of universality, language inclusion, and language equivalence are 2EXPSPACE-complete.

Finally, we consider *succinctness* afforded by the hierarchical construct. Starting with deterministic FSMs, we know that nondeterminism can add exponential succinctness. We show that hierarchy can also add exponential succinctness. Furthermore, nondeterministic FSMs and deterministic HSMs are incomparable extensions: both can be exponentially more succinct with respect to each other. Allowing both nondeterminism and hierarchy gives double-exponential succinctness with respect to deterministic FSMs, and curiously enough, this double-exponential gap exists between nondeterministic HSMs and deterministic HSMs also. Allowing nondeterminism, hierarchy, as well as concurrency, gives triple-exponential succinctness with respect to deterministic FSMs (or even deterministic HSMs), and double-exponential succinctness with respect to nondeterministic FSMs (or even nondeterministic HSMs)!

2 Communicating Hierarchical State Machines

There are many variants of definitions of finite-state machines. We choose a definition in which edges are labeled with alphabet symbols. For simplicity, we restrict ourselves to a single initial and a single final state, but generalization to multiple initial and final states poses no technical problems. A *finite-state machine* (FSM) consists of a finite set Q of states, a finite alphabet Σ, an initial state $q^I \in Q$, a final state $q^F \in Q$, a set $\rightarrow \subseteq Q \times \Sigma \times Q$ of transitions. Given a word $\rho = \sigma_0 \sigma_1 \cdots \sigma_n$ over the alphabet Σ, an *accepting run* of the FSM M over ρ is a sequence $q_0 \xrightarrow{\sigma_0} q_1 \xrightarrow{\sigma_1} \cdots \xrightarrow{\sigma_n} q_{n+1}$ such that q_0 equals the initial state q^I, q_{n+1} equals the final state q^F, and for $0 \leq i \leq n$, (q_i, σ_i, q_{i+1}) is a transition of M. The set of words $\rho \in \Sigma^*$ over which M has an accepting run is called *the language of M*, denoted $L(M)$.

Now we proceed to add two features: concurrency and hierarchy. For concurrency, a machine is composed of a set of component machines which synchronize on transitions labeled with common alphabet symbols. For hierarchy, the states of a machine can be other machines. Such states are popularly known as *superstates*. The meaning of such a hierarchical definition is obtained by recursively substituting each superstate by the machine associated with it. Hierarchical definitions allow sharing of patterns. The following formal definition allows arbitrary nesting of the concurrency and hierarchy constructs. A *communicating hierarchical state machine* (CHM) is one of the following three forms:

Base case: An FSM $(Q, \Sigma, q^I, q^F, \rightarrow)$ is a CHM.

Concurrency: If $M_1, M_2, \ldots M_k$ are CHMs then $M_1 \| M_2 \| \cdots \| M_k$ is a CHM.

Hierarchy: If $\mathcal{M}$ is a finite set of CHMs, $N = (Q, \Sigma, q^I, q^F, \rightarrow)$ is an FSM with states Q, and μ is a labeling function $\mu : Q \mapsto \mathcal{M}$ that associates each state $q \in Q$ with a CHM in $\mathcal{M}$, then the triple $(N, \mathcal{M}, \mu)$ is a CHM.

A CHM of the form $M_1 \| M_2 \| \cdots \| M_k$ is called a *product expression*, and each M_i is called a component of the product expression. A CHM of the form $(N, \mathcal{M}, \mu)$ is called a *hierarchical expression*, the FSM N is called the *top-level* of the hierarchical expression, and each CHM in $\mathcal{M}$ is called a component of the hierarchical expression.

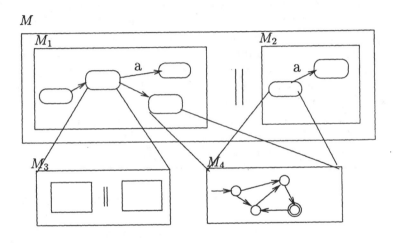

Fig. 1. A schematic sample communicating hierarchical state machine

As an illustration, see Figure 1 that shows a partial CHM. The machine M is product of two hierarchical expressions M_1 and M_2. The states of M_1 and M_2 are mapped to lower-level component machines. For instance, one state of M_1 is mapped to M_3, which in turn is a product of two machines, while another state of M_1 is mapped to the ordinary FSM M_4. Notice the sharing: machine M_4 is associated with states of both M_1 and M_2.

The semantics is defined by mapping each CHM M to an FSM $[\![M]\!]$:

Base case: If M is an FSM, then $[\![M]\!]$ equals M.

Concurrency: If M is the product expression $M_1 \| M_2 \| \cdots \| M_k$, then $[\![M]\!]$ is obtained by taking the product of the FSMs $[\![M_i]\!]$ corresponding to the components. Formally, suppose $[\![M_i]\!] = (Q_i, \Sigma_i, q_i^I, q_i^F, \rightarrow_i)$ for each i. Then,
- The state-space of $[\![M]\!]$ is $Q_1 \times \cdots \times Q_k$.
- The alphabet Σ of $[\![M]\!]$ is $\Sigma_1 \cup \cdots \cup \Sigma_k$.
- The initial state of $[\![M]\!]$ is $\langle q_1^I, \ldots q_k^I \rangle$.

- The final state of $[\![M]\!]$ is $\langle q_1^F, \ldots q_k^F \rangle$.
- For a symbol $\sigma \in \Sigma$, $[\![M]\!]$ has a σ-labeled transition from $\langle q_1, \ldots q_k \rangle$ to $\langle w_1, \ldots w_k \rangle$ iff for every i such that $\sigma \in \Sigma_i$, the FSM $[\![M_i]\!]$ has a transition (q_i, σ, w_i), and for every i such that $\sigma \notin \Sigma_i$, $w_i = q_i$.

Hierarchy: If $M = (N, \mathcal{M}, \mu)$ with top-level FSM $N = (Q, \Sigma, q^I, q^F, \rightarrow)$ then

- A state of $[\![M]\!]$ is of the form (q, w) where $q \in Q$ and w is a state of the FSM $[\![\mu(q)]\!]$ associated with q.
- A symbol σ belongs to the alphabet of $[\![M]\!]$ if σ belongs to the alphabet Σ of the top-level FSM N, or σ belongs to the alphabet of $[\![\mu(q)]\!]$ for some $q \in Q$.
- The initial state of $[\![\mu(q^I)]\!]$ is the initial state of $[\![M]\!]$.
- The final state of $[\![\mu(q^F)]\!]$ is the final state of $[\![M]\!]$.
- $[\![M]\!]$ has two types of transitions
  - For a transition (q, σ, q') of the top-level FSM N, $[\![M]\!]$ has a σ-labeled transition from the final state of $[\![\mu(q)]\!]$ to the initial state of $[\![\mu(q')]\!]$.
  - For $q \in Q$, if (w, σ, w') is a transition of $[\![\mu(q)]\!]$ then $((q, w), \sigma, (q, w'))$ is a transition of $[\![M]\!]$.

Now we can associate a language with each CHM: the language $L(M)$ of a CHM M is the same as the language $L([\![M]\!])$ of the FSM associated with M.

A CHM can be represented by a DAG. A terminal node corresponds to the base case, and has an associated FSM. An internal node may correspond to a product expression or a hierarchical expression. A node for a product expression is labeled with the operator $\|$, and its children are the components of the product. Note that the concurrency operator is associative. Consequently, we assume that the immediate children of a product expression are not themselves product expressions. A node for a hierarchical expression has the top-level FSM associated with it, and the edges connect the states of the top-level FSM with other nodes. When counting the size of the description of a CHM, we consider the size of this DAG representation. For instance, in Figure 1, the size of the FSM M_4 is counted only once, even though it appears multiple times. Two important parameters of this DAG representation are width and depth: width of a CHM M is the maximum number of components in the product nodes, and depth is the length of the longest path in the DAG.

A CHM M is called a *hierarchical state machine* (HSM) if it does not contain any product expression. Thus, HSMs do not involve any concurrency. To illustrate the power of HSMs, we show that HSMs can count with exponential succinctness. The alphabet in this example consists of a single symbol σ. It is easy to construct a sequence of HSMs $M_1, M_2, \ldots M_n$ as follows. M_1 is an FSM with $L(M_1) = \{\sigma\}$, and for $i > 1$, M_i is a hierarchical expression with two superstates, each mapped to M_{i-1} so that $L(M_i) = L(M_{i-1}) \cdot \sigma \cdot L(M_{i-1})$. Thus, the language $L(M_i)$ of the HSM M_i contains precisely the string of length $2^i - 1$.

3 Reachability

The reachability problem for a CHM M is to determine if the final state of $[\![M]\!]$ is reachable from the initial state of $[\![M]\!]$. Alternatively, this can be viewed as checking if the language $L(M)$ is empty. The reachability problem for ordinary FSMs is in NL. Introducing hierarchy in FSMs comes at a minimal cost: the reachability problem for HSMs can be solved in linear time, and is P-complete [AY98]. On the other hand, introducing concurrency in FSMs is expensive: the reachability problem for product of FSMs is PSPACE-complete. Now we want to study the impact of the combination of the two constructs. We begin by considering product of hierarchical state machines.

For ordinary FSMs, the product of two FSMs has a quadratic blow-up. In [AY98], it is shown that the product of an HSM with an FSM can be constructed to yield an HSM with quadratic number of states. As the next result shows, the product of two HSMs cannot be constructed efficiently.

Before we present the result, consider the sequence $P_0, P_1, \ldots P_n$ of HSMs over the alphabet $\{0, 1, \#\}$. P_0 is an FSM with $L(P_0) = \{\#\}$, and for $i > 0$, P_i is a hierarchical expression with two superstates, each mapped to P_{i-1}, so that $L(P_i)$ is the union of $0 \cdot L(P_{i-1}) \cdot 0$ and $1 \cdot L(P_{i-1}) \cdot 1$. Thus, the language accepted by P_n is $\{ w \# w^R \mid w \in \{0, 1\}^n \}$. It is worth noting that the language $\{ w \# w \mid w \in \{0, 1\}^n \}$ cannot be defined succinctly by HSMs (in fact, we can prove that every HSM accepting this language must be of exponential size). Intuitively, an HSM can be viewed as a push-down automaton with bounded stack size.

Recall that for pushdown automata, emptiness of single automaton can be solved in polynomial-time, but emptiness of intersection of two pushdown automata is undecidable. In the case of HSMs, emptiness of a single HSM is linear-time, but emptiness of the intersection of two HSMs is PSPACE-complete.

Proposition 1. *Reachability problem for $M_1 \| M_2$, where M_1 and M_2 are HSMs, is PSPACE-complete.*[1]

In CHMs, the concurrency and hierarchy operators are arbitrarily nested, and the product components can synchronize with each other at different levels of hierarchy. These features make the reachability problem significantly difficult to solve. In fact, to solve the reachability problem for a CHM M, one cannot do better than the obvious solution of constructing the flattened FSM $[\![M]\!]$ (locally), and applying the standard reachability algorithm to it.

Proposition 2. *For a CHM M, the number of states of $[\![M]\!]$ is $O(n^{d^m})$, where each FSM in M has at most n states, M has width $d > 1$ and depth m.*

This implies that reachability problem for a CHM can be solved in time $O(n^{d^m})$, that is, doubly-exponential in the depth in the worst case. The precise complexity class is EXPSPACE.

Theorem 1. *Reachability problem for CHMs is EXPSPACE-complete.*

Since reachability problem for CHMs is EXPSPACE-hard, we wish to identify subclasses with lower complexity. We proceed to define well-structured CHMs

---

[1] A detailed version with proofs can be obtained from the authors.

where arbitrary levels of hierarchy of product components cannot synchronize with each other. A CHM M is said to be *well structured* if for every product expression M' in M, if a proper component M'' of M' is a hierarchical expression, then for every proper component N of M'' and every component N' of M', the alphabet of $[\![N']\!]$ is disjoint from the alphabet of $[\![N]\!]$. Note that the alphabet plays a crucial role in the definition of the concurrency operator since components synchronize on common symbols. The restriction to well structured machines ensures that if two (or more) hierarchical machines are composed together, then they can synchronize only at the top level. For example, in Figure 1, a is a common symbol to the two components M_1 and M_2. Well-structuredness requires that a is used to label transitions of only the top-level FSMs of M_1 and M_2, and cannot appear, for instance, in M_3 or M_4. The reachability problem for well structured CHMs is PSPACE-complete, where the exponential cost is only due to concurrency, but not hierarchy.

Theorem 2. *The reachability problem for a well structured CHM M can be solved in time $O(k \cdot n^d)$, where k is the number of operators in M, each FSM in M has at most n states, and d is its width.*

4   Language Equivalence

In this section, we consider equivalence problem for hierarchical state machines and communicating hierarchical state machines. Each HSM M defines the language $L(M)$. The emptiness problem for HSMs is to determine if $L(M)$ is empty, and can be solved in P using the reachability algorithm. The universality problem for HSMs is to determine if the complement of $L(M)$ is empty. This problem turns out to be much harder:

Theorem 3. *The universality problem for HSMs is ExpSpace-complete.*

Two HSMs M_1 and M_2 are trace equivalent if their languages are identical. This problem, and also the language inclusion problem, have the same complexity as the universality problem:

Theorem 4. *The trace equivalence problem for HSMs is ExpSpace-complete.*

For ordinary FSMs, problems such as universality, inclusion, and equivalence, are much easier if we consider deterministic variants. The results for HSMs show somewhat subtle distinctions between these problems. Recall that an FSM is deterministic if for every state q and every symbol σ, there is at most one σ-labeled transition with source q. An HSM M is deterministic if $[\![M]\!]$ is deterministic. This entails two requirements: each base FSM and each top-level FSM of a hierarchical expression is deterministic, and furthermore, if a state q of a top-level FSM of a hierarchical expression has a σ-labeled outgoing transition, then the final state of the FSM associated with q has no σ-labeled outgoing transition. The latter condition ensures determinism concerning exiting lower-level FSMs.

	Emptiness	Intersection	Universality	Inclusion	Equivalence
FSM	NL	NL	PSPACE	PSPACE	PSPACE
Det FSM	NL	NL	NL	NL	NL
HSM	P	PSPACE	EXPSPACE	EXPSPACE	EXPSPACE
Det HSM	P	PSPACE	P	PSPACE	$\in$ PSPACE
CHM	EXPSPACE	EXPSPACE	2EXPSPACE	2EXPSPACE	2EXPSPACE

Fig. 2. Summary of complexity results

Theorem 5. *For deterministic HSMs, the universality problem is P-complete, and the language inclusion problem is* PSPACE-*complete.*

For deterministic HSMs, trace equivalence can be solved in PSPACE, but its complexity is sandwiched somewhere between that of the P-complete universality problem and the PSPACE-complete language inclusion problem. It remains open to determine its exact complexity.

Finally, we establish that the universality, language inclusion, and language equivalence problems for communicating hierarchical machines are complete for double-exponential space.

Theorem 6. *For CHMs, the universality, language inclusion, and language equivalence problems are* 2EXPSPACE-*complete.*

The results concerning HSMs and CHMs are summarized in Figure 2. The table lists the known complexity bounds for ordinary FSMs also for comparison.

5 Succinctness

In this section we are concerned with the expressive power of the hierarchical construct, both in presence and absence of the concurrency construct. To discuss expressive power, we will look at families of languages $\mathcal{L} = \{L_n | n = 1, 2, \ldots, \}$ and consider the number of states $\#(\mathcal{L}, n)$ needed by a machine that accepts L_n in some particular formalism. Where necessary we adopt the baroque practice of denoting the formalism by a superscript for $\#(\mathcal{L}, n)$. Thus $\#^{FSM}(\mathcal{L}, n)$ denotes the number of states necessary and sufficient for an FSM to recognize L_n. We will say that formalism F_1 can be exponentially more succinct than formalism F_2 if there is a family of languages $\mathcal{L}$ for which $\#^{F_1}(\mathcal{L}, n) = O(\log[\#^{F_2}(\mathcal{L}, n)])$.

While hierarchical state machines define regular languages, they can be much more succinct than ordinary FSMs. Note that there is an exponential translation from HSMs to FSMs, and the translation preserves determinism. Recall that nondeterministic FSMs can be exponentially more succinct than deterministic ones. The following proposition is established by showing that the language $L_n = \{w \# w^R \mid w \in \{0,1\}^n\}$ can be recognized by a deterministic HSM of linear size, while any nondeterministic FSM to recognize L_n must be at least exponential in n.

Proposition 3. *Deterministic HSMs can be exponentially more succinct than nondeterministic FSMs.*

The next result establishes that, while nondeterminism introduces exponential succinctness for ordinary FSM, it introduces doubly-exponential succinctness in presence of hierarchy. The proof uses the language $L_n = \{w \mid w_i = w_{i+2^n}$ for some $i\}$ to establish the gap:

Proposition 4. *Nondeterministic HSMs are doubly-exponentially more succinct than deterministic HSMs.*

Note that the gap between nondeterministic HSMs and nondeterministic FSMs is singly exponential. It is interesting to note that nondeterminism and hierarchy are incomparable extensions, which is established using the language $L_n = \{w \mid w_i = w_{i+n}$ for some $i\}$.

Proposition 5. *Nondeterministic FSMs can be exponentially more succinct than deterministic HSMs.*

Finally, we consider the expressive power added by concurrency and show that this is significant. When unrestricted use of concurrency and hierarchy is allowed, we get double-exponential succinctness compared to both FSMs and HSMs, and triple-exponential succinctness compared to the deterministic variants of FSMs and HSMs. The proof uses the language

$$L_n = \{w_0 \# w_1 \# \cdots \# w_k \mid |w_i| = 2^n \text{ for each } i \text{ and } w_i = w_j \text{ for some } i, j\}.$$

Proposition 6. *Communicating hierarchical machines can be doubly-exponentially more succinct than nondeterministic HSMs (and nondeterministic FSMs), and triply-exponentially more succinct than deterministic HSMs (and deterministic FSMs).*

The various succinctness claims are summarized in Figure 3.

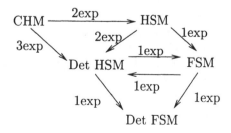

Fig. 3. Summary of succinctness results

6 Conclusions

In this paper, we have answered several questions concerning complexity and succinctness of hierarchical state machines. As the summary figures at the end of each section indicate, the complexity bounds do not change in a uniform way with many peculiarities. In terms of practice, the EXPSPACE-hardness of the reachability problem in presence of unrestricted use of hierarchy and concurrency constructs suggests that modeling languages should enforce well-structured use of the constructs to lower the complexity of the analysis problems. The results concerning the reachability problem should carry over to the more general question of model checking of linear-time requirements. We have presented a comprehensive picture that characterizes the power and complexity of sequential and communicating hierarchical state machines. A few questions concerning subclasses of communicating hierarchical machines, such as the precise complexity of equivalence of deterministic CHMs, remain to be resolved.

References

[AY98]   R. Alur and M. Yannakakis. Model checking of hierarchical state machines. In *Proc. Sixth FSE*, pp. 175–188. 1998.

[BJR97]   G. Booch, I. Jacobson, and J. Rumbaugh. *Unified Modeling Language User Guide*. Addison Wesley, 1997.

[CE81]   E.M. Clarke and E.A. Emerson. Design and synthesis of synchronization skeletons using branching time temporal logic. In *Proc. Workshop on Logic of Programs*, LNCS 131, pp. 52–71. Springer-Verlag, 1981.

[CK96]   E.M. Clarke and R.P. Kurshan. Computer-aided verification. *IEEE Spectrum*, 33(6):61–67, 1996.

[DH94]   D. Drusinsky and D. Harel. On the power of bounded concurrency i: finite automata. *Journal of the ACM*, 41(3), 1994.

[Har87]   D. Harel. Statecharts: A visual formalism for complex systems. *Science of Computer Programming*, 8:231–274, 1987.

[HKV97]   D. Harel, O. Kupferman, and M.Y. Vardi. On the complexity of verifying concurrent transition systems. In *CONCUR*, LNCS 1243, pp. 258–272. 1997.

[Hol97]   G.J. Holzmann. The model checker spin. *IEEE Trans. on Software Engineering*, 23(5):279–295, 1997.

[HU79]   J.E. Hopcroft and J.D. Ullman. *Introduction to Automata Theory, Languages, and Computation*. Addison-Wesley, 1979.

[SGW94]   B. Selic, G. Gullekson, and P.T. Ward. *Real-time object oriented modeling and design*. J. Wiley, 1994.

[VW86]   M.Y. Vardi and P. Wolper. An automata-theoretic approach to automatic program verification. In *Proc. First LICS*, pp. 332–344, 1986.

Small Pseudo-Random Sets Yield Hard Functions: New Tight Explicit Lower Bounds for Branching Programs

(Extended Abstract)

Alexander E. Andreev[1], Juri L. Baskakov[2], Andrea E. F. Clementi[3], José D. P. Rolim[4]

[1] LSI Logic, California,
andreev@lsil.com
[2] Dept. of Mathematics, University of Moscow,
baskakov@matis.math.msu.su
[3] Dept. of Mathematics, University "Tor Vergata" of Rome
clementi@mat.uniroma2.it
[4] Centre Universitaire d'Informatique, University of Geneva, CH,
jose.rolim@cui.unige.ch

Abstract. In several previous works the construction of a computationally hard function with respect to a certain class of algorithms or Boolean circuits has been used to derive small pseudo-random spaces. In this paper, we revert this connection by presenting two new direct relations between the efficient construction of pseudo-random (both two-sided and one-sided) sets for Boolean affine spaces and the explicit construction of Boolean functions having hard *branching program* complexity.

In the case of 1-read branching programs ($1\text{-}Br.Pr.$), we show that the construction of non trivial (i.e. of cardinality $2^{o(n)}$) *discrepancy sets* (i.e. two-sided pseudo-random sets) for Boolean affine spaces of dimension greater than $n/2$ yield a set of explicit Boolean functions having very hard $1\text{-}Br.Pr.$ size. By combining the best known construction of ϵ-biased sample spaces for linear tests and a simple "Reduction" Lemma, we derive the required discrepancy set and obtain a Boolean function in P having $1\text{-}Br.Pr.$ size not smaller than $2^{n-O(\log^2 n)}$ and a Boolean function in $\mathsf{DTIME}(2^{O(\log^2 n)})$ having $1\text{-}Br.Pr.$ size not smaller than $2^{n-O(\log n)}$. The latter bound is optimal and both of them are exponential improvements over the best previously known lower bound that was $2^{n-3n^{1/2}}$ [21].

As for non deterministic syntactic k-read branching programs ($k\text{-}Br.Pr.$), we introduce a new method to derive explicit, exponential lower bounds that involves the construction of *hitting sets* (one-sided pseudo-random sets) for affine spaces of dimension $o(n/2)$. Using an appropriate "orthogonal" representation of small Boolean affine spaces, we efficiently construct these hitting sets thus obtaining an explicit Boolean function in P that has $k\text{-}Br.Pr.$ size not smaller than $2^{n^{1-o(1)}}$ for *any* $k = o\left(\frac{\log n}{\log \log n}\right)$. This improves over the previous best known lower bounds given in [8, 11, 17] for some range of k.

1 Introduction

A *Branching Program* (*Br.Pr.*) is a directed acyclic graph where one of the nodes, called *source*, has fan-in 0 and some other nodes, called *terminals*, have fan-out 0. Each non terminal nodes is labelled by the index of an input Boolean variable and has fan-out 2. The two edges leaving a non terminal node are respectively labelled 0 and 1. A *Br.Pr.* computes a Boolean function $f : \{0,1\}^n \rightarrow \{0,1\}$ on a fixed input as follows. Starting the computation from the source node, if a generic node is reached, the corresponding input variable is tested and the computation chooses the edge corresponding to the actual value of this input variable. The process terminates when a sink node is reached and its label represents the output of f. Clearly, the *Br.Pr.* model can also be made *non deterministic* by allowing the existence of more edges labeled with the same value that leave the same node. The *size* of *Br.Pr.* is the number of its nodes and the *length* is the maximum length of a computation path from the source to a sink.

Theoretical research in *Br.Pr.*'s is extremly active since they represent an important abstraction of several computing models [23, 18]. The size and the length of a given *Br.Pr* provide a measure of, respectively, the space and the time of the corresponding computation. In particular, a super-polynomial lower bound for the *Br.Pr.* size of a function f would imply that f is not computable in non-uniform log-space. However, the best known lower bound for explicit functions in NP is $\Omega(n^2/\log^2 n)$ [15]. Another important aspect of this model lies in the study of time-space trade-offs where finding an explicit function f that requires non-uniform super polynomial size *Br.Pr.*'s of linear length constitutes one of the most important open problems (see [7] for a survey of results and open problems in this field). This result in fact would separate the non-uniform log-space class from the linear-time one (this result is presently available only for uniform computations [9]).

Informally speaking, a linear upper bound on the length of a *Br.Pr.* implies that the average number of times that a fixed variable is tested during the program is only constant. This simple observation has led researchers [8, 11, 19, 20] to investigate the restricted variants of *Br.Pr.*'s that consider this property with the aim to achieve better lower bounds.

A *read-k-times Br.Pr.* is allowed to read each variable at most k times along any valid computation and, in a *syntactic read-k-times Br.Pr.*, this reading restriction holds for any path from the source to any sink. Notice that while a *read-1-time Br.Pr.* is always a syntactic *read-1-time Br.Pr.*, for $k \geq 2$ this does not hold.

To our knowledge, the best known explicit lower bound for *read-1-time-* branching programs (1-*Br.Pr.*'s) is due to Savicky and Zak [20, 21]; they derived a Boolean function in P having, for any sufficiently large n, 1-*Br.Pr.* size not smaller than 2^{n-s}, where $s = O(n^{1/2})$. We also emphasize that for this model there are no known harder explicit functions even in classes larger than P, while a non explicit lower (and optimal) bound of size $\Theta(2^{n-\log n})$ is known.

Concerning non-deterministic syntactic read-k-times *Br.Pr.*'s (*k-Br.Pr.*'s) in the case $k \geq 2$, there are explicit lower bounds of exponential size when

$k = O(\log n)$ [8, 11, 17]. Borodin *et al* [8] showed an explicit family of Boolean functions such that any k-*Br.Pr.* computing it must have a number of labeled edges not smaller than $\exp(\Omega(n)/(4^k * k^3)))$ when $k \leq c \log n$ for a fixed constant $0 < c < 1$. A lower bound of size $\exp(\Omega(\sqrt{n}/k^{2k}))$ has been independently proved by Okolnishnikova [17]. More recently, Jukna studied the Okolnishnikova's function and obtained an exponential gap between the size of any *Br.Pr.* required for such a function and that required for its complement. Finding exponential lower bounds when k grows faster than any logarithmic function or when the branching programs are non syntactic is still an open question.

In several previous works [6, 10, 16, 2] the explicit construction of a computationally hard function with respect to a certain class C of algorithms (or Boolean circuits) has been used to derive small pseudo-random spaces able to de-randomize a somewhat probabilistic version of C. In this paper, we revert this connection by showing how to use the efficient constructions of pseudo-random spaces for *linear tests* [14] to define a set of explicit functions having very hard complexity with respect to *read-1-time-branching programs* and *non deterministic syntactic read-k-times branching programs*.

In the case of 1-*Br.Pr.*'s, we show that the efficient construction of *Discrepancy sets* for Boolean affine spaces can be used to derandomize the two probabilistic constructions of Boolean functions having hard 1-*Br.Pr.* complexity that rely, respectively, on Simon and Szegedy's method [22] (see Theorem 6) and on the concept of *completeness* of *index functions* investigated by Savicky and Zak [20]. Then, since discrepancy sets for Boolean affine spaces can be efficiently derived by ϵ-*biased* sample space w.r.t linear tests [14] (whose efficient constructions have been obtained in [1]), we can prove the following lower bound that exponentially improves that obtained in [20, 21].

Theorem 1. *i). It is possible to construct a family $F^1 = \{F_n^1 : \{0,1\}^n \to \{0,1\}, n > 0\}$ of Boolean functions that belongs to* $\mathsf{DTIME}(2^{O(\log^2 n)}) \cap (\mathsf{P/poly})$ *and such that, for almost every $n > 0$,*

$$L_{1-br}(F_n^1) \geq 2^{n-O(\log n)} .$$

ii). It is possible to construct a family $F^2 = \{F_n^2 : \{0,1\}^n \to \{0,1\}, n > 0\}$ of Boolean functions that belongs to P *and such that, for almost every $n > 0$,*

$$L_{1-br}(F_n^2) \geq 2^{n-O(\log^2 n)} .$$

As for the more general case of k-*Br.Pr.*'s, we introduce a new method to derive explicit, exponential lower bounds Our method relies on the following result. Given any Boolean function $f : \{0,1\}^n \to \{0,1\}$, let $N_f^1 = \{x \in \{0,1\}^n : f(x) = 1\}$ and $L_{k-br}(f)$ be the size of the smallest k-*Br.Pr.* that computes f.

Theorem 2. *Let $t \geq \log^2 n$, $k = o(\log n / \log t)$ and let $f(x_1, \ldots, x_n)$ be a boolean function such that $|N_f^1| \geq 2^{n-1}$ and $L_{k-br}(f) \leq 2^{n^{1-\epsilon}}$ for some constant $0 < \epsilon < 1$. Then, for sufficiently large n, the set N_f^1 contains an affine space of dimension not smaller than $t/4$.*

The proof of this theorem uses some properties of *rectangle* functions introduced by Borodin *et al* in [8].

Theorem 2 implies that the complement of the characteristic function of a family of *hitting sets* (i.e. one-sided random sets) [5, 3, 2] for affine spaces is a good candidate to get hard k-$Br.Pr.$ size. Thus, the goal is to obtain an efficient construction of such hitting sets. In the general definition, given a class $\mathcal{F}$ of Boolean functions of n inputs, a subset $H \subseteq \{0, 1\}^n$ is a *hitting set* for $\mathcal{F}$ if, for any non-zero function $f \in \mathcal{F}$, H contains at least one inputs on which f outputs 1. Let $\mathcal{AFF}(n, s)$ be the set of all n variables linear systems $Ax = b$ (where $A \in \{0, 1\}^{s \times n}$, $x \in \{0, 1\}^n$, and $b \in \{0, 1\}^s$) of at most s linear functions . It turns out that the above mentioned construction of discrepancy sets guarantees a hitting set for $\mathcal{AFF}(n, s)$ only when $s < n/2$, i.e., when the corresponding affine space is large. However, when the affine space is small there is a more efficient way to represent it by using its *orthogonal* space (which is large). Combining this idea with the previous construction of discrepancy sets, we derive an efficient construction of non trivial hitting sets in the case of small affine spaces.

Theorem 3. *For any $n > 0$ and $m \leq n$ it is possible to construct a hitting set $\mathcal{H}(n, m)$ for $\mathcal{AFF}(n, n - m)$ such that $|\mathcal{H}(n, m)| \leq 2^{n - m + m(O(1) \log n)/\sqrt{m}}$. The construction time is polynomial in $|\mathcal{H}(n, m)|$.*

The above construction provides a non trivial hitting set when $m \geq c \log^2 n$ for some constant $c > 0$. This is a strong improvement over the best previously known construction that yields a non trivial hitting set only when $n - m = o(n)$ [3, 13].

We then consider the complement function $F_n^3(x_1 \ldots x_n)$ of the characteristic function of the hitting set $\mathcal{H}(n, m)$ in Theorem 3 (for an appropriate choice of $\log n \leq m < n/2$). By definition of hitting sets, it should be clear that F_n^3 cannot contain any affine subspace of dimension not smaller than m. Hence, Theorem 2 implies the following lower bound that improves over those in [8] and [11] for some range of k.

Theorem 4. *Let $k = o(\frac{\log n}{\log \log n})$. There exists a function $F^3 = \{F_n^3 : \{0, 1\}^n \to \{0, 1\}, n > 0\}$ in P that, for sufficiently large n, $L_{k-br}(F_n^3) \geq 2^{n^{1-o(1)}}$.*

Due to lack of space, we omit the technical proofs of this part (i.e. that concerning k-$Br.Pr.$'s) and we remind the reader to the full version of this paper [4].

2 Pseudo-random sets for affine spaces

Given a subset $W \subseteq \{0, 1\}^n$, its size is denoted by $|W|$, and its probability with respect to the uniform distribution in $\{0, 1\}^n$ is denoted by $\mathbf{Pr}(W)$; Instead, the notation $\mathbf{Pr}_S(W)$ refers to case in which the uniform distribution is defined on the sample space S.

A Boolean function $f : \{0,1\}^N \to \{0,1\}$ is said *linear* if a vector $a = (a_1,..,a_N) \in \{0,1\}^N$ exists such that f can be written as $f(x_1,..,x_N) = a_1x_1 \oplus .. \oplus a_Nx_N$. Given two binary vectors $a = (a_1,\ldots,a_N)$ and $b = (b_1,\ldots,b_N)$ from $\{0,1\}^N$, we define $c = a \oplus b$ as the vector whose the i-th component is given by the xor of the i-th components of a and b. The *inner* product is defined as $<a,b> = a_1b_1 \oplus \ldots \oplus a_Nb_N$. The finite field $GF(2^N)$ will be represented by the standard one-to-one mapping bin : $GF(2^N) \to \{0,1\}^N$ such that $\mathrm{bin}(a+b) = \mathrm{bin}(a) \oplus \mathrm{bin}(b)$ and $\mathrm{bin}(0) = (0,\ldots,0)$.

Furthermore, given any element $a \in GF(2^N)$ and an integer $k > 0$, we will make use of the concatenation of powers $U(a,k) \in \{0,1\}^{kN}$ where $U(a,k) = \mathrm{bin}(a^0)\mathrm{bin}(a^1)\ldots\mathrm{bin}(a^{k-1})$. For the sake of brevity, the notation a^j will replace the term $\mathrm{bin}(a^j)$.

2.1 Discrepancy sets for large affine spaces

In this section, we provide an efficient construction of discrepancy sets for large Boolean affine spaces. Such construction will be then used in Section 3 to derive exponential lower bounds for 1-$Br.Pr.$'s.

Let $\mathcal{AFF}(n,k,s)$ be the set of all n variables linear systems $Ax = b$ (where $A \in \{0,1\}^{s \times n}$, $x \in \{0,1\}^n$, and $b \in \{0,1\}^s$) of at most s linear functions in which at most k variables appear with non-zero coefficients (such variables are said *essential*). The systems in $\mathcal{AFF}(n,k,s)$ will be simply denoted as pairs (A,b).

Definition 1. *Let $\epsilon > 0$. A (multi)set $S \subseteq \{0,1\}^n$ is said to be ϵ-discrepant for $\mathcal{AFF}(n,k,s)$ if, for any feasible system $(A,b) \in \mathcal{AFF}(n,k,s)$ with $\mathrm{rank}(A) = s$, it holds $|\mathbf{Pr}_{x \in S}(Ax = b) - 2^{-s}| \le \epsilon$.*

Note that 2^{-s} equals the probability that x is a solution of (A,b) when x is chosen uniformly at random from $\{0,1\}^n$.

The case in which the linear system has only one equation, i.e. the classes $\mathcal{AFF}(n,k,1)$, has been extensively studied: in particular, Naor and Naor [14] introduced the following definition.

Definition 2. *A subset $S \subseteq \{0,1\}^n$ is ϵ-discrepant for* linear functions *if, for any Boolean linear function $f : \{0,1\}^n \to \{0,1\}$,*

$$|\mathbf{Pr}_S(f(x) = 0) - \mathbf{Pr}_S(f(x) = 1)| \le \epsilon.$$

Further, S is said to be k-wise ϵ-discrepant if the "test" linear functions in the above definition can have at most k non-zero coefficients

According to the definition in [14], a set is an ϵ-*biased* sample space w.r.t linear tests iff it is ϵ-discrepant for linear functions; furthermore, the restriction k on the number of essential variables in the definition of $\mathcal{AFF}(n,k,s)$ is the generalization of the definition of k-wise ϵ-discrepancy set for linear tests given by Naor and Naor.

The main result of [14] is the efficient construction of an ϵ-discrepancy set for linear functions of size $O((n/\epsilon)^{O(1)})$ and a k-wise ϵ-discrepancy set for linear functions of size $O((k \log n)/\epsilon)^{O(1)})$. Three simpler and better (in some parameter ranges) constructions of ϵ-discrepancy sets for linear functions have been introduced by Alon *et al* in [1]. All of them yield sample spaces of size $O((n/\epsilon)^2)$. All such sample spaces can be constructed in time polynomial in n/ϵ. One of these three constructions is called the *powering* construction $\mathcal{L}_{N,z}^* \subseteq \{0,1\}^N$ and is defined as follows.

Definition 3. *[The Powering Sample Space] [1] The generic vector l in the sample space $\mathcal{L}_{N,z}^*$ is specified by two vectors $x, y \in \{0,1\}^z$. The i-th bit of l is the inner product of the i-th power of x and y. Clearly, we have that $|\mathcal{L}_{N,z}^*| = 2^{2z}$.*

Theorem 5. *[1] For any $N > 0$ and $z \leq N$, the set $\mathcal{L}_{N,z}^*$ is $\frac{N}{2^{z+1}}$-discrepant for $\mathcal{AFF}(N,N,1)$.*

So, Alon *et al*'s ϵ-discrepancy set for linear functions is the set $\mathcal{L}_{N,z}^*$ for $z = \log(N/\epsilon)$.

We can now present the following Reduction Lemma (see the full version of this paper in [4] for a proof).

Lemma 1 (The Reduction Lemma). *Let $S \subseteq \{0,1\}^N$. If $\alpha_1, \ldots, \alpha_s$ are linearly independent and $\sigma \in \{0,1\}^s$, then*

$$\left| 2^{-s} - \pi(S, \alpha_1, \ldots, \alpha_s, \sigma_1, \ldots, \sigma_s) \right| \leq \left(2 - \frac{1}{2^{s-1}} \right) \varepsilon(S).$$

Hence if S is ϵ-discrepant w.r.t. $\mathcal{AFF}(N,N,1)$ then it is 2ϵ-discrepant w.r.t. $\mathcal{AFF}(N,N,s)$, for any $s \leq N$.

By applying the Reduction Lemma to Theorem 5 we can easily prove the following

Corollary 1. *If $\alpha_1, \ldots, \alpha_s \in \{0,1\}^N$ are linearly independent and $\sigma \in \{0,1\}^s$, then $\mathcal{L}_{N,z}^*$ is $(N2^{-z})$-discrepant for $\mathcal{AFF}(N,N,N)$.*

The above combination of the Alon *et al*'s powering construction and the Reduction Lemma can be slightly modified in order to obtain a discrepancy set for $\mathcal{AFF}(N,k,s)$ that considers also the number k of essential variables (this construction is described in the full version of the paper [4]).

Corollary 2 (Discrepancy set for $\mathcal{AFF}(N,k,N)$). *For any $N > 0$, and $0 \leq k, z \leq N$, it is possible to construct a set $\mathcal{D}_2(N,k,z)$ which is $(k\lceil \log N \rceil 2^{-z})$-discrepant for $\mathcal{AFF}(N,k,N)$.*

3 Lower bounds for 1-read branching programs

We adopt notations and terminology from [20]. For a *partial* input we mean any element from $\{0, 1, *\}$ where the positions containing 0 or 1 mean that the corresponding input bit is fixed, while the notation $*$ mean that the corresponding input bit is free. We say that a partial input v is defined on the set $I \subseteq \{0, 1\}^n$ if $v_i \in \{0, 1\}$ iff $i \in I$. Partial inputs define subfunctions of a given Boolean functions $f : \{0, 1\}^n \to \{0, 1\}$ in the following natural way. For any set $I \subseteq \{1, 2, ..., n\}$, let $\mathcal{B}(I)$ be the set of all partial inputs defined on I. Given any partial input $v \in \mathcal{B}(I)$, the subfunction $f|_v$ of $f(x_1, \ldots, x_n)$ is obtained by setting $x_i = v_i$ for any $i \in I$. The set of inputs on which $f|_v$ is defined consists of the Boolean rectangle $R(v)$ of dimension $n - |I|$, $R(v) = \{(a_1, \ldots, a_n) : a_i = v(i), i \in I\}$. Given any function $f : \{0, 1\}^n \to \{0, 1\}$ and any subset $I \subseteq \{1, 2, ..., n\}$, let

$$\nu(f, I) = \max_{v \in \mathcal{B}(I)} |\{u \in \mathcal{B}(I) : f|_u = f|_v\}| .$$

3.1 Optimal lower bounds from discrepancy sets of exponential size

In the case of 1-$Br.Pr$.'s, Simon and Szegedy introduced a nice technique to derive explicit lower bounds that enjoys of the following theorem.

Theorem 6. *[22] Let f be a Boolean function of n variables and let $r \leq n$. The size of any 1-$Br.Pr$. computing f is at least $2^{n-r}/(\max\{\nu(f, I) : |I| = n - r\})$.*

Our next goal is to give a suitable interpretation of this theorem for the family of n-inputs Boolean functions $\mathsf{powF}_n = \{f_{n,k}^\alpha : \alpha \in \{0, 1\}^{kn}\}$ where $f_{n,k}^\alpha(x)$ is the inner product between α and the concatenation of the first k powers of x, i.e. $f_{n,k}^\alpha(x) = < \alpha, U(x, k) >$. Let $I \subseteq \{1, 2, ..., n\}$ such that $|I| = n - r$; for any $u, v \in \mathcal{B}(I)$ we consider the *xor* vector $df(u, v) \in \{0, 1\}^n$ where $df(u, v)_i = 1$ iff $i \in I$ and $v_i \neq u_i$. Then the condition (implicitly required by Theorem 6)

$$f_{n,k}^\alpha|_v = f_{n,k}^\alpha|_u . \tag{1}$$

is equivalent to require that for all $x \in R(v)$, $f_{n,k}^\alpha(x) \oplus f_{n,k}^\alpha(x \oplus df(v, u)) = 0$. Therefore, by definition of $f_{n,k}^\alpha$, it is equivalent to require that $\alpha \in \{0, 1\}^{kn}$ is a solution of the following Boolean system of $|R(v)| = 2^r$ linear equations

$$\{< \alpha, (U(x, k) \oplus U(x \oplus df(v, u), k)) >= 0 , \qquad x \in R(v) . \tag{2}$$

So, in order to obtain a lower bound as large as possible, we need to efficiently find an α that does not satisfy the above system for any choice of I and for any $u \neq v$ from $\mathcal{B}(I)$. The first step to this aim is to choose r and k in order to make the equations linearly independent. If indeed we set $r = \lceil \log n \rceil + 1$, and $k = 2^{r+1}$ then, by definitions of $U(x, k)$ and $df(v, u)$, vectors $U(x, k) \oplus U(x \oplus df(v, u), k)$ are linearly independent for any $x \in R(v)$ and for any different $v, u \in \mathcal{B}(I)$. This implies that for any fixed choice of u and v such that $u \neq v$, the number of α satisfying the linear system is $2^{kn}2^{-h}$ where $h = 2^r$.

The key idea is to use the discrepancy set $\mathcal{L}^*_{nk,t}$ (given in Section 2.1) to efficiently de-randomize the probabilistic construction described above. Indeed, let $G(y_1, \ldots, y_{2t})$ (the correct choice of the "price" t is given later) be the Boolean generator of the set $\mathcal{L}^*_{nk,t}$. By applying Corollary 1 with $N = kn$, $s = 2^r$, and $z = t$ we easily have that the system in Eq. (2) for $\alpha = G(\beta)$ is satisfied for not more than $2^{2t}(2^{-2^r} + 2^{r+1}n2^{-t})$ different β's. It follows that the number of β's for which the system is satisfied for some (at least one) I, with $|I| = n - r$, and some (at least one pair) different $v, u \in \mathcal{B}(I)$ is at most

$$2^{2t}(2^{-2^r} + 2^{r+1}n2^{-t}) \binom{n}{r} 2^{2(n-r)}.$$

Now, if we choose $t \geq cn$ for a sufficiently large positive constant c, we have that the above value is bounded by $2^{2t}o(1)$. It follows that an element $\beta_0 \in \{0,1\}^{2t}$ exists such that $\alpha_0 = G(\beta_0)$ does not satisfy System (2) for any I with $|I| = n-r$, and for any $v \neq u$ from $\mathcal{B}(I)$. For any $n > 0$, let $F^0_n = f^{G(\beta)}_{n,k}$ then from the above discussion and from Theorem 6 we can easily obtain the following result.

Theorem 7. *There exists a function $F^0 = \{F^0_n : \{0,1\}^n \to \{0,1\}, n > 0\}$ that is constructable in* DTIME($2^{O(\log^2 n)}$) $\cap$ P/poly *and such that, for almost every $n > 0$, $L_{1-br}(F^0_n) \geq 2^{n-\log(4n)}$.*

3.2 Almost optimal lower bounds from discrepancy sets of almost polynomial size

In [20], Savicky and Zak introduced an nice technique for proving lower bounds for the 1-$Br.Pr.$ model. This technique is based on the analyisis of the complexity of *index* functions defined as

$$X_\phi(a_1, \ldots, a_n) = a_{\phi(a_1, \ldots, a_n)}. \tag{3}$$

where ϕ is any function from $\{0,1\}^n$ to $\{1, \ldots, n\}$. The interest in this kind of functions relies on the following result.

Definition 4. *Let n, s and q be integers and let $\phi : \{0,1\}^n \to \{1, \ldots, n\}$ be a function. We say that ϕ is (s, n, q)-complete if for every $I \subseteq \{1, \ldots, n\}$, $|I| = n - s$, we have:*
i). For every $u \in \mathcal{B}(I)$, the restricted function $\phi|_u$ returns all the values from $\{1, \ldots, n\}$ in its range.
ii). There is at most q different partial inputs u from $\mathcal{B}(I)$ giving different subfunctions $\phi|_u$.

Theorem 8. *[20] Let ϕ be (s, n, q)-complete, then $L_{1-br}(X_\phi) \geq 2^{n-s}/q$.*

From the above Theorem, it should be clear that the goal of proving explicit lower bounds for this model can be achieved by constructing a function ϕ which is (s, n, q)-complete for "small" values of s and q. Savicky and Zak provided a deterministic construction of an (s, n, q)-complete function with $s = O(\sqrt{n})$ and $q = O(n)$ [20], and left the deterministic construction of (s, n, q)-complete functions with $s = o(\sqrt{n})$ and $q = o(2^{\sqrt{n}})$ as an open problem (they gave only a probabilistic construction for $s = O(\log n)$ and $q = 2^{O(\log n)}$. In what follows, we derive, for any sufficiently large n, a deterministic construction of an (s, n, q)-complete function with $s = O(\log n)$ and $q = 2^{O(\log n)}$.

The key-idea is to use the discrepancy set $\mathcal{L}_{N,z}^*$ (with a suitable choice of N and z) in order to construct a Boolean matrix that satisfies the following lemma obtained by Savicky and Zak.

Lemma 2. *[20] Let n and t be two arbitrary positive integer. Let $A \in \{0,1\}^{t \times n}$ be a $(t \times n)$-matrix over $GF(2)$ such that every (t, s)-submatrix has rank at least r. Let $\psi : \{0,1\}^t \to \{1, \ldots, n\}$ be any function such that on every affine subset of $\{0,1\}^t$ of dimension at least r it returns all the values from $\{1, \ldots, n\}$. Then, $\phi(x) = \psi(Ax)$ is $(s, n, 2^t)$-complete.*

Our next goal is thus to provide an explicit construction of this matrix. Given any $(t \times n)$-matrix A, $\mathbf{row}_i(A)$ denotes the i-th row of A, i.e. the vector $(a_{i,1}, \ldots, a_{i,n})$, and $\mathbf{col}_j(A)$ denotes the j-th column of A, i.e. the vector $(a_{1,j}, \ldots, a_{t,j})$. We now consider the discrepancy set $\mathcal{L}_{t,m}^*$ for $\mathcal{AFF}(t, t, t)$ in Corollary 1, and we give the following technical definition. For any pair of positive integers t and m, let

$$\mathcal{L}_{t,m}^2 = \{ z \mid z = x \oplus y, \text{ for some } x, y \in \mathcal{L}_{t,m}^* \} .$$

Definition 5. *A $(t \times n)$-matrix A is (s, r, m)-regular if every (t, s)-submatrix of A has rank at least r and for any $i \neq j$ from $\{1, \ldots, n\}$ it holds*

$$\mathbf{col}_i(A) \oplus \mathbf{col}_j(A) \notin \mathcal{L}_{t,m}^2 . \tag{4}$$

Given any matrix $A \in \{0,1\}^{t \times n}$, we consider the function $\psi_{A,m} : \{0,1\}^t \to \{1, \ldots, n\}$ where $\psi_{A,m}(v)$ returns the first index i such that $v \in (\mathbf{col}_i(A) \oplus \mathcal{L}_{t,m}^*)$ if such index exists, otherwise it returns 1. The functions yielded by (s, r, m)-regular matrices have the following property.

Lemma 3. *If $A \in \{0,1\}^{t \times n}$ is (s, r, m)-regular then for sufficiently large n and for any affine space S of dimension r we have*

$$\psi_{A,m}(S) = \{1, \ldots, n\} .$$

Given any matrix $A \in \{0,1\}^{t \times n}$, let $\phi_{A,m} : \{0,1\}^n \to \{1, \ldots, n\}$ be defined as

$$\phi_{A,m}(a) = \psi_{A,m}(Aa) = (< a, \mathbf{row}_1(A) >, \ldots, < a, \mathbf{row}_t(A) >) ,$$

and consider the function $F_{n,A}^1(x_1, \ldots, x_n) = X_{\phi_{A,m}}(x_1, \ldots, x_n)$. By combining (s, r, m)-regular matrices with Savicky and Zak's technique, we obtain the following result.

Theorem 9. *If* $A \in \{0,1\}^{t \times n}$ *is* (s,r,m)-*regular, then* $L_{1-br}(F_{n,A}^1) \geq 2^{n-s-t}$.

It should be clear that in order to apply the above theorem we need to construct a $(t \times n)$-matrix A which is (s,r,m)-regular for $t, s = O(\log n)$. This construction is achieved by using the generator $G(y_1, \ldots, y_{2k})$ of the discrepancy set $\mathcal{L}_{nt,k}^*$. Indeed, we simply define $A(t,n,G,\beta)$ as the Boolean $(t \times n)$-matrix A whose elements are the output of $G(\beta)$, i.e., $(a_{1,1}, \ldots, a_{1,n}, \ldots, a_{t,1}, \ldots, a_{t,n}) = G(\beta)$.

Lemma 4. *For any* $n \geq 2$, *let*

$$t = 24\lceil \log n \rceil, \quad s = 32\lceil \log n \rceil, \quad r = 10\lceil \log n \rceil, \quad k = t \cdot s + \lceil \log(nt) \rceil, \quad m = 3\lceil \log(nt) \rceil$$

Then, a $\beta \in \{0,1\}^{2k}$ *exists for which the corresponding* $A(t,n,G,\beta)$ *is* (s,r,m)-*regular.*

By combining the above results, we finally obtain the following lower bounds for 1-*Br.Pr.*'s.

Theorem 10. *i*). *There exists a family* $F^1 = \{F_n^1 : \{0,1\}^n \to \{0,1\}, n > 0\}$ *of Boolean functions that belongs to* DTIME($2^{O(\log^2 n)}$) $\cap$ (P/poly) *and such that, for almost every* $n > 0$,

$$L_{1-br}(F_n^1) \geq 2^{n-O(\log n)} .$$

ii). *There exists a family* $F^2 = \{F_n^2 : \{0,1\}^n \to \{0,1\}, n > 0\}$ *of Boolean functions that belongs to* P *and such that, for almost every* $n > 0$,

$$L_{1-br}(F_n^2) \geq 2^{n-O(\log^2 n)} .$$

More Recent Related Works. After the present paper, Kabanets [12] provides a simpler proof of a slightly weaker lower bound for 1-*Br.Pr.*'s using a variant of our method that applies directly the construction of ϵ-biased sample spaces w.r.t. linear tests without using the Reduction Lemma.

Acknowledgements. We would like to thank Oded Goldreich and Luca Trevisan for some crucial comments on the paper. We thank Sasha Razborov and Martin Sauerhoff for helpful pointers. Finally, Andrea Clementi wishes to thank Riccardo Silvestri for his hints in proving Theorem 7. Finally, we thank Petr Savicky for reading carefully the preliminary versions of our paper and for finding out a technical error.

References

1. N. Alon, O. Goldreich, J. Hastad, and R. Peralta (1990), "Simple Constructions of Almost k-wise Independent Random Variables", *Proc. of IEEE-FOCS*, Vol. 2, pp. 544-553.

2. A. Andreev, A. Clementi, and J. Rolim (1997), "Worst-case Hardness Suffices for Derandomization: a New method for Hardness-Randomness Trade-Offs", in Proc. of *ICALP*, LNCS, 1256, pp. 177-187 (to appear also on *TCS*).

3. A. Andreev, A. Clementi, J. Rolim (1997), "Efficient Constructions of Hitting Sets for Systems of Linear Functions", in *ECCC* TR96-029, (Extended Abstract in Proc. of *STACS'97*, LNCS 1200, pp.387-398).

4. A. E. Andreev, J. L. Baskakov, A. E. F. Clementi, J. D. P. Rolim (1997), "Small Random Sets for Affine Spaces and Better Explicit Lower Bounds for Branching Programs", *Electronic Colloquium on Computational Complexity (ECCC)*, 2nd Revision of TR97-053 (http://www.eccc.uni-trier.de/eccc).

5. R. Armoni, M. Saks, A. Wigderson, and S. Zhou (1996), "Discrepancy Sets and Pseudorandom Generators for Combinatorial Rectangles", Proc. of *IEEE-FOCS*, pp. 412-421.

6. Blum M., and Micali S. (1984), "How to generate cryptographically strong sequences of pseudorandom bits", *SIAM J. of Computing*, 13(4), pp. 850-864.

7. A. Borodin (1993), "Time-Space Trade-Offs (getting closer to the barrier?)", Proc. of the *IV ISAAC*, pp. 209-220.

8. A.Borodin, A.Razborov and R.Smolensky (1993), "On lower bounds for read-k times branching programs", *Computational Complexity*, 3, pp. 1–18.

9. L. Fortnow (1997), "Nondeterministic polynomial time versus nondeterministic logarithmic space: Time-space tradeoffs for satisfiability", Proc. of *12-th IEEE Conference on Computational Complexity*, pp. 52-60.

10. R. Impagliazzo, and A. Wigderson (1997), "P= BPP if E requires exponential circuits: Derandomizing the XOR lemma" Proc. of *ACM STOC*, pp. 220-229.

11. S. Jukna (1995), "A Note on Read-k-times Branching programs", *RAIRO Theoretical Informatics and Applications*, 29 (1), pp.75-83. (also in *ECCC*, TR94-027).

12. Valentine Kabanets (1999), "Almost k-Wise Independence and Boolean Functions Hard for Read-Once Branching Programs", *ECCC*, TR99-004.

13. E. Kushilevitz, and Y. Mansour (1993), " Learning Decision Trees Using the Fourier Spectrum", SICOMP 22(6), pp. 1331-1348. Early version: STOC 91.

14. J.Naor, and M.Naor (1990), "Small-bias probability spaces: efficient constructions and aplications", Proc. of *ACM-STOC*, pp. 213-223.

15. E. Neciporuk (1966), "On a Boolean Function", *Soviet. Math. Doklady*, 7, 999-1000.

16. Nisan N., and Wigderson A. (1994), "Hardness vs Randomness", *J. Comput. System Sci.*, 49, pp. 149-167.

17. E.A. Okolnishnikova (1993), "On lower bounds for branching programs", *Siberian Advances in Mathematics*, 3(1), pp. 152-166.

18. A.A. Razbarov (1991), "Lower Bounds for Deterministic and Nondeterministic Branching Programs", *LNCS*, 529, pp. 47-61.

19. M. Sauerhoff (1997), "A Lower Bound for Randomized Read-k-Times Branching Programs", *ECCC*, TR97-019.

20. P. Savicky and S. Zak (1996), "A large lower bound for 1-branching programs", *ECCC*, TR96-036 (Revision 01) (to appear in *Theoretical Computer Science*).

21. P. Savicky and S. Zak (1998), "A read-once lower bound and a (1,+k)-hierarchy for branching programs", (to appear in *Theoretical Computer Science*).

22. J. Simon and M. Szegedy (1993), "A new lower bound theorem for read only once branching programs and its applications", *Advances in Computational Complexity Theory (J.Cai, editor)*, AMS-DIMACS Series, 13, pp.183-193.

23. I. Wegener (1987), *the Complexity of Boolean Functions*, B.G. Teubner, 1 edition.

General Morphisms of Petri Nets
(Extended Abstract)*

Marek A. Bednarczyk and Andrzej M. Borzyszkowski

Institute of Computer Science, Gdańsk Branch, Polish Acad. of Sc.
Abrahama 18, 81-825 Sopot, Poland, http://www.ipipan.gda.pl

Abstract. A new notion of a general morphism of Petri nets is introduced. The new morphisms are shown to properly include the morphisms considered so far. The resulting category of Petri nets is shown to admit products. Potential applications of general morphisms are indicated.

1 Introduction

For mathematically oriented people Petri nets are quite complex objects. The following observation should put the above statement into a proper perspective: it took a quarter of a century from the inception of Petri nets, cf. [12], to the definition of their morphisms, cf. [14, 15].

Winskel's solution to the problem of defining a suitable notion of Petri net morphism was algebraic. He noticed that Petri nets can be viewed as certain 2-sorted algebras. Consequently, Petri net morphisms defined in [14] are homomorphisms of the corresponding algebras.

The dynamic behaviour of a (marked) Petri net N is described by means of its *case graph*. Surely, if the case graph of a net is to be taken as *the* abstract representation of the dynamic behaviour of the net, then Petri net morphisms should give rise to morphisms of transition systems. More formally, the construction of the case graph of a net should be the object part of a functor from *any* category of Petri nets to the category of labelled transition systems described above. Indeed, the notion proposed by Winskel does satisfy the above criterion.

Some years later another class of morphisms was distinguished in an attempt to describe a coreflection between a category of elementary net systems and a category of elementary transition systems, cf. [11]. The morphisms introduced by Nielsen et al., form a subclass of Winskel morphisms (well, not *quite*, this is the price to pay for disallowing isolated places in nets). As such they also satisfy the criterion.

The existence of the case graph functor prompts a natural question. Namely, is it possible to find a converse construction? Such construction should produce a Petri net which *implements* a given transition system. The first results achieved in that direction are due to Ehrenfeucht and Rozenberg, cf. [8], where

---

* Partially supported by LoSSeD workpackage within the CRIT-2 project funded by ESPRIT and INCO programmes, and by the State Committee for Scientific Research grants 8 T11C 018 11 and 8 T11C 037 16.

the so called *synthesis problem* is solved. The problem is to construct a Petri net, the case graph of which is isomorphic to a given transition system, and such that the transitions of the net are the labels of the transition system. The solution proposed in the above seminal paper hinges on the idea of a *region* in a transition system. With this notion one can characterize *elementary* transition systems as those which satisfy two regional separability conditions. Ehrenfeuht and Rozenberg showed that the case graphs of a class of Petri nets are elementary. Conversely, the regions of an elementary transition system taken as places provide a simple synthesis of a net.

This construction was generalized later in various ways. From our point of view it is important that some of these generalizations attempted to make the constructions functorial, cf. [11, 6]. Thus, implicitly, the idea was to synthesize not only Petri nets from transition systems, but also Petri net morphisms from morphisms of the underlying transition systems.

So far, all functors were based on the idea that all regions should become places of the net constructed. The nets synthesized in this way are literally *saturated* with places. The wealth of places to choose from means that even a rather restricted subclass of Winskel's morphisms is sufficient to synthesize all morphisms between elementary transition systems.

Sometimes, though, for instance for readability sake, it is preferable to construct a net with a small number of places. Unfortunately, Winskel morphisms are too demanding to allow synthesis of morphisms even in simple cases.

The general problem: to synthesize a Petri net that realizes a given concurrent behaviour, has already received a good deal of attention, see e.g., [1] for an in depth discussion. But, to the best of our knowledge, functoriality was discussed only for constructions resorting to saturated nets.

The reason seems pretty simple. Within the framework of categories of Petri nets considered until now, constructions other than those returning saturated nets are *not* going to be functorial.

Here, as a remedy, we propose a new class of *general* morphisms and its subclass of *rigid* morphisms. It turns out that Winskel's morphisms are general. The new categories of general Petri nets and their *labelled* counterparts are shown to admit products.

Also, there are enough general morphisms to make the construction of a labelled state machine out of a transition system functorial. This simple observation has important consequences. In a companion paper, see [4], the authors show how the notions and the results presented here can be used to develop a functorial synthesis procedure for a wide class of concurrent behaviours. This procedure works for a class of asynchronous systems, cf. [13, 2], namely those which can be presented as rigid or *mixed* product of (sequential) transition systems, see [7, 16, 10]. In [4] we show that the rigid product of Petri net realizations of a family of transition systems is a realization of the rigid product of the family. Thus, in the light of the results presented here, it is indeed sufficient to provide just *a* functorial realization of sequential systems.

The full version of the paper, cf. [3], contains the proofs of the results presented here as well as more pictures and discussions.

2   Petri Nets

In this paper, for simplicity sake, only finite Petri nets and and finite transition systems are considered. The usual graphical presentation of Petri nets is used throughout. Thus, circles correspond to places, bars to events and arrows describe the flow (multi)-relation. An undecorated arrow has the same meaning as the arrow decorated with number 1. Initial marking is depicted by putting $\hat{M}b$ bullets in a circle corresponding a place b. Given a set X we denote the family of multisets over X by μX.

The dynamic behaviour of a Petri net is described by a *firing relation*. A multiset $A \in \mu E$ of events is called *enabled* at marking M, whenever ${}^{\bullet}A \leq M$. If enabled at M, A can *fire*, and thereby change the marking. The above yields a transition relation $M\,[A\rangle\,M'$ on markings and multisets of actions defined formally as follows

$$M\,[A\rangle\,M' \quad \textit{iff} \quad {}^{\bullet}A \leq M \quad \textit{and} \quad M' = M - {}^{\bullet}A + A^{\bullet}$$

Often, one considers the above relation as defined on reachable markings only. A marking is *reachable* if it can be reached from the initial marking via a finite number of firings. We prefer to consider arbitrary classes of markings closed under firing relation. This leads to a minor generalization of the notion of a Petri net.

Definition 1. *An* augmented *Petri net is a structure* $\mathcal{N} = \langle B, E, F, \hat{M}, \mathcal{M} \rangle$ *where* $\langle B, E, F, \hat{M} \rangle$ *is a Petri net, and where* $\mathcal{M} \subseteq \mu B$ *is a set of markings satisfying the following conditions*

- $\hat{M} \in \mathcal{M}$, *and*
- $M \in \mathcal{M}$ *and* $M\,[e\rangle\,M'$ *implies* $M' \in \mathcal{M}$.

The *case graph* of an augmented Petri net $\mathcal{N}$ is a transition system $\mathcal{C}g(\mathcal{N}) = \langle \mathcal{M}, \hat{M}, E, {}_-\,[\,{}_-\,\rangle\,{}_-\rangle$. This construction, however, provides a very simplistic view of the dynamic behaviour of a Petri net. In particular, all information about the concurrent execution of events is neglected.

An augmented Petri net is *safe*, if all its preconditions, postconditions, all markings in $\mathcal{M}$ and all enabled multisets of events are sets. A *state machine* is a safe Petri net in which all these sets are singletons.

3   Petri Net Morphisms

The new definition of a morphism between the augmented Petri nets follows.

Definition 2. *Let* $\mathcal{N} = \langle B, E, F, \dot{M}, \mathcal{M} \rangle$ *and* $\mathcal{N}' = \langle B', E', F', \dot{M}', \mathcal{M}' \rangle$ *be two augmented Petri nets. A general morphism* $f : \mathcal{N} \to \mathcal{N}'$ *between these nets consists of a partial function* $\eta : E \rightharpoonup E'$ *and a multirelation* $\beta : B \xrightarrow{r} B'$ *which together fulfill the following conditions.*

1. $\beta \dot{M} = \dot{M}'$.
2. $M \in \mathcal{M}$ *implies* $\beta M \in \mathcal{M}'$.
3. $^\bullet(\eta e) \leq \beta(^\bullet e)$.
4. $\beta(e^\bullet) = \beta(^\bullet e) - {}^\bullet(\eta e) + (\eta e)^\bullet$.

In the definition above, ηe is taken to denote the corresponding multiset. In particular $\eta e = \emptyset$ whenever η is undefined on e. If this is the case, condition (4) simplifies to $\beta(e^\bullet) = \beta(^\bullet e)$. General properties of multisets guarantee that in the presence of condition (4) condition (3) is equivalent to $(\eta e)^\bullet \leq \beta(e^\bullet)$.

It is easy to verify that augmented Petri nets and general morphisms form a category.

3.1 The Largest Category of Petri Nets

Conditions (3) and (4) of definition 2 together guarantee that general morphisms map steps in the source net into steps in the target net.

Lemma 1. *Let* $\langle \beta, \eta \rangle : \mathcal{N} \to \mathcal{N}'$ *satisfy conditions (3) and (4) of definition 2. Then* $M_1 [e\rangle M_2$ *in* $Cg(\mathcal{N})$ *implies* $\beta M_1 [\eta e\rangle \beta M_2$ *in* $Cg(\mathcal{N}')$.

The lemma, together with conditions (1) and (2), yields that Petri net morphisms do satisfy the main criterion, i.e., they give rise to morphisms between corresponding case graphs. Another corollary is that the condition (2) follows from the other conditions in case the source net is augmented with reachable markings only.

In fact, the category defined here is the largest category of Petri nets satisfying the main criterion in the sense that the converse to lemma 1 holds.

Theorem 1. *Let* $\mathcal{N}, \mathcal{N}'$ *be two Petri nets. Let* $\beta : B \xrightarrow{r} B'$ *be a multi-relation and* $\eta : E \rightharpoonup E'$ *be a partial function. Assume that the conclusion of lemma 1 holds. Then conditions (3) and (4) of definition 2 are fulfilled.*

Proof. Applying the conclusion of lemma 1 to a special case $^\bullet e [e\rangle e^\bullet$ we obtain $\beta(^\bullet e) [\eta e\rangle \beta(e^\bullet)$. The definition of firing relation yields conditions (3) and (4). $\square$

Assuming the first two conditions we have that $\langle \beta, \eta \rangle$ in the proposition is a Petri net morphism.

3.2 A Comparison with Winskel's Definition

In [14, 15] Winskel proposed another definition. Namely, Petri nets can be seen as 2-sorted algebras. The sort of places comes from the category of multisets and multirelations as morphisms. The sort of events comes from the category of partial functions. Operations are: initial marking, pre- and post-conditions.

With the above in mind, it is only natural to require that the morphisms are homomorphisms of such algebras. In other words, Winskel morphism is a pair $\langle \beta, \eta \rangle$ which satisfies the following conditions.

○ $\beta \hat{M} = \hat{M}'$.
○ $^\bullet(\eta e) = \beta(^\bullet e)$ $\quad and \quad$ $(\eta e)^\bullet = \beta(e^\bullet)$.

It has been shown in [14] that with the above definition the conclusion of lemma 1 holds. In fact, if Winskel's definition is applied to augmented Petri nets the following is immediate.

Proposition 1. *Every Winskel morphism is a general morphism of Petri nets.*

The converse does not hold. It has already been mentioned in the introduction that there is no Winskel morphism between state machines which would give rise to a morphism hiding a transition. Example of a general morphism that does the job is depicted on Fig. 1. In fact, any prospective morphism which would

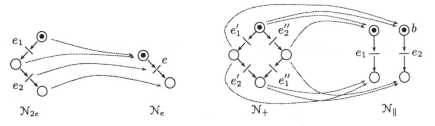

Fig. 1. General, non-Winskel morphism   **Fig. 2.** General morphism from $\mathcal{N}_+$ to $\mathcal{N}_\|$

preserve the initial markings and send e_2 to e would have to look like the general morphism presented there. Unfortunately, since e_1 goes to nothing, it follows from Winskel's definition that, together with e_1, all its preconditions $^\bullet e_1$ and postconditions $e_1^\bullet$ should go to nothing.

Another, more complex example, is presented on Fig. 2. It demonstrates that the need to use general, non-Winskel morphisms does not depend on the partiality of the event part of morphisms. The morphism on Fig. 2 explains how the sequential execution of e_1's and e_2's in $\mathcal{N}_+$ can be simulated by a parallel execution of e_1 and e_2 in $\mathcal{N}_\|$. The multirelation component β of the morphisms is a relation. Clearly, the initial marking is preserved. The singleton initial marking of net $\mathcal{N}_+$ is shared as the precondition of both e_1' and e_2''. In the target net $\mathcal{N}_\|$, the images of e_1' and e_2'' do not have a common precondition. Thus, for example the inequality $^\bullet(\eta e_1') < \beta(^\bullet e_1')$ is strict. In fact, all inequalities are strict in this case. Thus, there is no Winskel morphism from $\mathcal{N}_+$ to $\mathcal{N}_\|$.

3.3   The Case Graph Functor

The case graph functor is not faithful. To see an example consider a somewhat more saturated version $\mathcal{N}_+^{\|}$ of $\mathcal{N}_+$ and the morphism from $\mathcal{N}_+^{\|}$ to $\mathcal{N}_{\|}$, all described on Fig. 3. There is a morphism from $\mathcal{N}_+^{\|}$ to $\mathcal{N}_+$ which simply erases from the

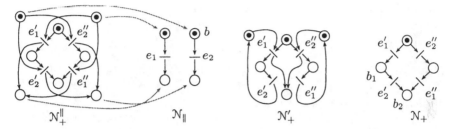

Fig. 3. General morphism from $\mathcal{N}_+^{\|}$ to $\mathcal{N}_{\|}$ **Fig. 4.** Two realizations of $Cg(\mathcal{N}_+)$

source all places that are not present in the target. This morphism is mapped to an isomorphism of the corresponding case graphs. Composing it with the morphism presented on Fig. 2 yields another morphism from $\mathcal{N}_+^{\|}$ to $\mathcal{N}_{\|}$. Although different, both morphisms are glued by the case graph functor.

The case graph functor is not full either. In the example on Fig. 4 both Petri nets have isomorphic case graphs. Yet, no morphism from $\mathcal{N}_+'$ to $\mathcal{N}_+$ realizes the isomorphism between their case graphs.

Indeed, assume there is a morphism $\langle \beta, \eta \rangle : \mathcal{N}_+' \to \mathcal{N}_+$ which maps e_2' in $\mathcal{N}_+'$ to e_2' in $\mathcal{N}_+$. Then this morphism relates the only postcondition of e_2' in $\mathcal{N}_+'$ to place b_2 as the only postcondition of e_2' in $\mathcal{N}_+$ as the following argument shows. Condition (4) of definition 2 implies $\beta(^{\bullet}e_2') + b_2 = \beta(e_2'^{\bullet}) + b_1$. So $\beta(e_2'^{\bullet})b_2 > 0$ follows from $b_1 \neq b_2$. The postcondition constituting $e_2'^{\bullet}$ in $\mathcal{N}_+'$ belongs to the initial marking. Thus, it may only be related to a place in the initial marking of $\mathcal{N}_+$, and we arrive at a contradiction.

Incidently, the isomorphism from $Cg(\mathcal{N}_+)$ to $Cg(\mathcal{N}_+')$ can be realized, cf. Sec. 4, but not as a Winskel morphism.

3.4   The Synthesis of Morphisms on State Machines

The definition of general Petri net morphisms makes it easier to synthesize a net morphism. In case of state machines the task becomes trivial.

Lemma 2. *Let $\mathcal{N}$ and $\mathcal{N}'$ be two state machines. Let $\langle \beta, \eta \rangle : Cg(\mathcal{N}) \to Cg(\mathcal{N}')$ be a morphism of their case graphs. Then, $\langle \beta, \eta \rangle$ is a morphism of Petri nets, $\langle \beta, \eta \rangle : \mathcal{N} \to \mathcal{N}'$.*

If a morphism between case graphs is total on actions, i.e., *synchronous* in Winskel's terminology, then this morphism, qua a Petri net morphism, is a Winskel morphism. And vice versa.

4 Categorical Products

The realization of the rôle of categorical product as a fundamental tool to explain synchronization is due to Winskel, cf. [14, 15]. Here, we investigate useful products formed not in the category of Petri nets with general morphisms, but in a subcategory with *rigid* morphisms.

Definition 3. *Let* $\mathcal{N} = \langle B, E, F, \hat{M}, \mathcal{M} \rangle$ *and* $\mathcal{N}' = \langle B', E', F', \hat{M}', \mathcal{M}' \rangle$ *be two Petri nets such that* $E' \subseteq E$. *A morphism* $\langle \beta, \eta \rangle : \mathcal{N} \to \mathcal{N}'$ *is called* rigid *if* η *is the relation transposed to the inclusion of* E' *into* E.

Let $\mathcal{S} = \langle S, \hat{s}, A, \longrightarrow \rangle$ *and* $\mathcal{S}' = \langle S', \hat{s}', A', \longrightarrow \rangle$ *be two transition systems such that* $A' \subseteq A$. *A morphism* $\langle \sigma, \eta \rangle : \mathcal{S} \to \mathcal{S}'$ *is called* rigid *if* η *is the partial function transposed to the inclusion of* A' *into* A.

Clearly, the case graph functor cuts down to the subcategories with rigid morphisms. Both these subcategories possess products, called *rigid products*, and the case graph functor preserves them. Let us start by recalling the construction of products of transition systems.

Let $\{ \langle S_i, \hat{s}^i, A_i, \longrightarrow \rangle \mid i \in I \}$ be a family of transition systems. Their product in the category of transition systems with rigid morphisms is a transition system $\langle S, \hat{s}, A, \longrightarrow \rangle$ where $S = \prod_{i \in I} S_i$, $(\hat{s})_i = \hat{s}^i$, for all $i \in I$, $A = \bigcup_{i \in I} A_i$, and $s \xrightarrow{a} s'$ iff for all $i \in I$ either $a \in A_i$ and $s_i \xrightarrow{a} s'_i$, or $a \notin A_i$ and $s_i = s'_i$.

The product of Petri nets is defined in a less obvious manner. Essentially, it is the old Winskel construction, cf. [15], except that the synchronization of events is already incorporated into the product (due to the choice of rigid morphisms).

Theorem 2. *Let* $\left\{ \langle B_i, E_i, F_i, \hat{M}^i, \mathcal{M}_i \rangle \mid i \in I \right\}$ *be a family of (augmented) Petri nets. Their rigid product is a Petri net* $\langle B, E, F, \hat{M}, \mathcal{M} \rangle$ *where*

- $B = \biguplus_{i \in I} B_i$, *the disjoint union of places,*
- $E = \bigcup_{i \in I} E_i$, *the union of events, usually sets* E_i *are not disjoint,*
- $F = \Sigma_{i \in I} F_i$
- $\hat{M} = \Sigma_{i \in I} \hat{M}^i$
- $\mathcal{M} = \{ \Sigma_{i \in I} M_i \mid (\forall i \in I) \, M_i \in \mathcal{M}_i \}$

The i*'s projection consists of a relation transposed to the inclusion of* B_i *into* B *and a partial function transposed to the inclusion of* E_i *into* E.

Note that projections are Winskel morphisms. It can be shown that if a cone consists of Winskel morphisms only, the canonical morphism is a Winskel morphism too.

In the rigid product two nets synchronize on shared events. It may be instructive to consider an example of a rigid product and a canonical morphism.

Net $\mathcal{N}'_+$ in Fig. 4 is a rigid product of three state machines—the one with language $(e'_1 e'_2)^\star$, another with $(e''_2 e''_1)^\star$ and yet another with $e'_1 + e''_2$. Here, a synchronization does take place. There are morphisms from $\mathcal{N}_+$ to $\mathcal{N}'_+$ which yield projections on the level of case graphs, their product is a morphism from $\mathcal{N}_+$ to $\mathcal{N}'_+$ yielding identity on case graphs. As we have already mentioned, there is no morphism in the opposite direction.

Proposition 2. *The case graph of a product of a family of (augmented) Petri nets is a product of their case graphs.*

5   Towards Concurrent Realization of Reactive Systems

Net $\mathcal{N}_\|$ on Fig. 2 is a rigid product of its two singleton event components. Here, no synchronization takes place. At first glance it seems that the morphism presented on Fig. 2 is a canonical morphism. But a closer inspection reveals that, composed with a projection on the 1st component, it maps both e'_1 and e''_1 to e_1, and forgets the other events. Thus, it is not rigid.

This brings us to the idea that, in general, *labelled* Petri nets should be used. A labelled (augmented) Petri net is a tuple $\langle B, E, F, \hat{M}, \mathcal{M}, A, \ell \rangle$ where $\langle B, E, F, \hat{M}, \mathcal{M} \rangle$ is an augmented Petri net and $\ell : E \to A$ is a (total) labelling function. The case graph of a labelled Petri net is a transition system $\langle \mathcal{M}, \hat{M}, A, \longrightarrow \rangle$ where $M \overset{a}{\longrightarrow} M'$ iff $M\,[e\rangle\,M'$ and $\ell e = a$ for some $e \in E$. If a transition system $\mathcal{S}$ is (isomorphic to) the case graph of a labelled net $\mathcal{N}$, we may call $\mathcal{N}$ a *concurrent realization* of (the reactive system) $\mathcal{S}$.

Note that the problem of finding a concurrent realization of a reactive system generalizes the *synthesis problem* for Petri nets, cf. [8, 6, 11, 1]. That is, a net can be treated as labelled with an identity labelling. Thus, with a help of the labelling one can find simpler nets as realizations of a given behaviour. For instance, consider a transition system capable of performing twice an action a only. Clearly, no 1-safe net is capable of providing this behaviour. Yet, it is trivial to build a concurrent realization as a labelled state machine.

A *rigid morphism* of two labelled Petri nets $\mathcal{N} = \langle B, E, F, \hat{M}, \mathcal{M}, A, \ell \rangle$ and $\mathcal{N}' = \langle B', E', F', \hat{M}', \mathcal{M}', A', \ell' \rangle$, with $A' \subseteq A$, is a general morphism $\langle \beta, \eta \rangle$ of the underlying Petri nets which preserves the labelling, i.e., $\ell'(\eta e) = \ell e$ iff $\ell e \in A'$. The above means, in particular, that partiality of η is fully controlled by the labelling: ηe is defined iff $\ell e \in A'$.

Now, it is rather obvious that the new case graph construction gives rise to a functor from the category of labelled Petri nets and rigid morphisms to the category of transition system with rigid morphisms. Again, the category of labelled Petri nets with rigid morphisms possesses products, and the case graph functor preserves them. Fig. 2 presents a rather simple example of the product of labelled nets. Net $\mathcal{N}_\|$ is a rigid product of its two simple one-event nets. It remains the rigid product if the net is considered as labelled with the identity labelling. Net $\mathcal{N}_+$ can be treated as a labelled, with labels given implicitly by the morphisms, i.e., $\ell e'_1 = \ell e''_1 = e_1$ and $\ell e'_2 = \ell e''_2 = e_2$. Then, the morphism on Fig. 2 is indeed canonical.

6   Conclusions and Further Research

In this paper we have introduced the notion of general morphism of Petri nets. We have shown that, in a sense, general morphisms yield the largest category of Petri nets. Some properties of the resulting category of nets were also discussed. In particular, it turned out that the category admits products.

Although interesting, the results presented could well be cast aside as a mathematical curiosity — maybe interesting, but not necessarily useful. In the space remaining we hint at a potential area of application.

In lemma 2 we have already shown that the morphisms between case graphs of state machines can be synthesized as general morphisms. Also, there is a simple construction of a labelled state machine which realizes a given transition system: take all states as places, all steps as events with the evident precondition, postcondition and labelling. Take singletons as markings, with the one containing the initial state as the initial marking of the state machine. This construction is functorial in the category of general morphisms. What is more, the resulting labelled state machine is a realization of the transition system.

In the companion paper, see [4], we apply this simple observation together with a result obtained recently by Morin, cf. [10]. He characterized a category of *concrete* asynchronous systems, i.e., those which are (roughly) rigid products of sequential transition systems. In [4] we study labelled 1-safe nets which accept trace languages. Their case graphs are asynchronous systems. The main result reported there says that the case graph of a rigid product of realizations is a realization of the rigid product of the case graphs.

The notion of a Petri net morphism introduced here can be generalized along the lines of [9]. That is, one may consider richer structures on the event part of a Petri net and Petri net morphism. Indeed, definition 2 works fine if one allows mapping an event in a source net to a multiset of events in a target net.

However, as argued in [9], while it is natural to consider Petri nets with monoidal structure on events, in general the monoids need not be free. An example is Milner's synchronization: $\alpha + \bar{\alpha} = 0$. A good candidate could be finitely presentable monoids, i.e. monoids generated by a finite number of events and with a finite number of equalities. Then, a Petri net morphism should preserve these equalities.

Another line of generalization is to consider simulations of transition systems. By a *simulation* between transition systems $S = \langle S, \hat{s}, A, \longrightarrow \rangle$ and $S' = \langle S', \hat{s}', A', \longrightarrow \rangle$ we mean a pair consisting of a relation $\prec \subseteq S \times S'$ and a partial function $\eta : A \rightharpoonup A'$ such that initial states are related and

$$p \xrightarrow{a} q \text{ in } S, \eta a \text{ is defined}, p \prec p' \quad implies \quad p' \xrightarrow{\eta a} q' \text{ in } S' \text{ for some } q', q \prec q'$$

Hence, a morphism of transition systems is a special kind of a simulation.

Brown and Gurr [5] have defined the notion of a simulation of Petri nets in a somewhat restricted way. Their simulation of Petri nets, gives rise to the simulation of their case graphs, as expected. The general simulation of Petri nets would be a pair $\langle \beta, \eta \rangle$ which fulfils conditions (1), (2) and (3) of definition 2 and, additionally, condition

4'. $\beta(e^\bullet) \le \beta({}^\bullet e) - {}^\bullet(\eta e) + (\eta e)^\bullet$.

Again, simulations form a category, in fact, the largest one within the framework. The case graph is a functor—a simulation of the case graphs is a pair $\langle \prec_\beta, \eta \rangle$, where $M \prec_\beta M'$ iff $\beta M \le M'$. Moreover, Winskel definition of products works. However, there is no obvious state machine construction at hand, hence the synthesis problem for transition system simulations requires further research.

References

[1] E. BADOUEL and P. DARONDEAU. Theory of regions, 1998. Manuscript.

[2] M. A. BEDNARCZYK. *Categories of Asynchronous Systems*. Ph.D. thesis, University of Sussex, England, 1988. CST 1-88.

[3] M. A. BEDNARCZYK and A. M. BORZYSZKOWSKI. General morphisms of Petri nets, 1999. IPIPAN Technical Report 874 (24 pp).

[4] M. A. BEDNARCZYK and A. M. BORZYSZKOWSKI. Concurrent realizations of reactive systems, 1999. Submitted.

[5] C. BROWN and D. GURR. Refinement and simulation of nets – a categorical characterization. In K. Jensen, ed., *Proc. Applications and Theory of Petri Nets*, vol. 616 of *LNCS*, pp. 76–92. Springer, 1992.

[6] M. DROSTE and R. M. SCHORTT. Petri nets and automata with concurrency relation – an adjunction. In M. Droste and Y. Gurevich, eds., *Proc. Semantics of Programming Languages and Model Theory*, pp. 69–87, 1993.

[7] C. DUBOC. Mixed products and asynchronous automata. *Theoretical Computer Science*, vol. 48: pp. 183–199, 1986.

[8] A. EHRENFEUCHT and G. ROZENBERG. Partial (set) 2-structures, part I and II. *Acta Informatica*, vol. 27(4): pp. 315–368, 1990.

[9] J. MESEGUER and U. MONTANARI. Petri nets are monoids. *Information and Computation*, vol. 88: pp. 105–155, 1990.

[10] R. MORIN. Decompositions of asynchronous systems. In *Proc. CONCUR'98*, LNCS, pp. 549–564. Springer, 1998.

[11] M. NIELSEN, G. ROZENBERG, and P. S. THIAGARAJAN. Elementary transition systems. *Theoretical Computer Science*, vol. 96: pp. 3–33, 1992.

[12] C. A. PETRI. Fundamentals of a theory of asynchronous information flow. In *Proc. IFIP'62*. North Holland, 1962.

[13] M. SHIELDS. Multitraces, hipertraces and partial order semantics. *Formal Aspects of Computing*, vol. 4: pp. 649–672, 1992.

[14] G. WINSKEL. Petri nets, algebras, morphisms and compositionality. *Information Computation*, 1987.

[15] G. WINSKEL. A category of labelled Petri nets and compositional proof system (extended abstract). In *Proc. Third IEEE Symposium on Logic in Computer Science*, pp. 142–154. IEEE, The Computer Society, Computer Society Press, 1988.

[16] W. ZIELONKA. Notes on finite asynchronous automata. *Theoretical Informatics and Applications*, vol. 21(2): pp. 99–135, 1987.

On Some Tighter Inapproximability Results (Extended Abstract)

Piotr Berman[1] and Marek Karpinski[2]

[1] Dept. of Computer Science, Pennsylvania State University,
University Park, PA 16802
[2] Dept. of Computer Science, University of Bonn,
53117 Bonn

Abstract. We give a number of improved inapproximability results, including the best up to date explicit approximation thresholds for bounded occurence satisfiability problems like MAX-2SAT and E2-LIN-2, and the bounded degree graph problems, like MIS, Node Cover, and MAX CUT. We prove also for the first time inapproximability of the problem of Sorting by Reversals and display an explicit approximation threshold.

Key words: Approximation Algorithms, Approximation Hardness, Bounded Dependency Satisfiability, Breakpoint Graphs, Independent Set, Node Cover, MAX-CUT, Sorting by Reversals.

1 Introduction

The paper studies *explicit* approximation thresholds for bounded dependency, and bounded degree optimization problems. There was a dramatic progress recently in proving tight inapproximability results for a number of NP-hard optimization problems (cf. [H96], [H97], [TSSW96]). In this paper we address bounded instances of the classic NP-hard optimization problems and some related problems. The method uses randomized reductions and applies to a number of problems including Maximum Independent Set in graphs of degree d (d-MIS), bounded degree Minimum Node Cover (d-Node Cover), bounded degree MAX CUT (d-MAX CUT) and bounded occurrence MAX-2SAT (d-OCC-MAX-2SAT), (cf. [PY91], [A94], [BS92], [BF94], [BF95], [AFWZ95]). This yields also the first explicit approximation lower bounds for the small degree graph problems, and the small dependency satisfiability. We apply also this method to prove approximation hardness of the problem of *sorting by reversals*, MIN-SBR, the problem motivated by molecular biology [HP95] (and with a long history of related research, cf., e.g., [GP79], [CB95]), only recently proven to be NP-hard [C97]. Interestingly, its signed version can be computed in polynomial time [HP95], [BH96], [KST97].

The core of the new method is the use of restricted versions of the E2-LIN-2 and E3-LIN-2 problems studied in [H97]. We denote by E2-LIN-2 the problem of maximizing the number of satisfied equations from a given set of linear equations mod 2 with 2 variables per equation. E3-LIN-2 is a similar problem with three variables per equation. E2-LIN-2 can be viewed as a graph problem in the following way: each variable is a node, and an equation $x \oplus y = b$ is an edge $\{x, y\}$ with label b. The special case when all edges have label 1 constitutes MAX CUT problem.

We denote by d-OCC-E2-LIN-2 and d-OCC-E3-LIN-2 the versions of these problems where the number of occurrences of each variable is bounded by d (note that in d-OCC-2-LIN-2 can be also viewed as restricted to graphs of degree d).

The paper proves the following main theorem:

Theorem 1. *For every $\epsilon > 0$, it is NP-hard to approximate*

(1) 3-OCC-E2-LIN-2 and 3-MAX CUT within factor $332/331 - \epsilon$;
(2) 6-OCC-MAX 2SAT within factor $668/667 - \epsilon$;
(3) 3-OCC-MAX 2SAT within factor $2012/2011 - \epsilon$;
(4) 3-OCC-E3-LIN-2 within factor $62/61 - \epsilon$;
(5) 4-MIS within factor $74/73 - \epsilon$ and 4-Node Cover within $79/78 - \epsilon$;
(6) 5-MIS within factor $68/67 - \epsilon$ and 5-Node Cover within $74/73 - \epsilon$;
(7) 3-MIS within factor $140/139 - \epsilon$ and 3-Node Cover within $145/144 - \epsilon$;
(8) MIN-SBR within factor $1237/1236 - \epsilon$.

All these results rely on the reduction to show (1), which forms structures that can be translated into many graph problems with very small and natural gadgets. The complete proofs are to be found in [BK99].

The gaps between the upper and lower approximation bounds are summarized in Table 1. The upper bounds are from [GW94], [BF95], [C98], and [FG95].

2   Sequence of reductions

We start from E2-LIN-2 problem that was most completely analyzed by Håstad [H97] who proved that it is NP-hard to approximate it within a factor $12/11 - \epsilon$. In this paper, we prefer to interpret it as the following graph problem. Given an undirected graph $G = \langle V, E, l \rangle$ where l is a 0/1 edge labeling function. For $S \subset V$, let χ_S be the characteristic function of S. We define $Score(S, \{u, v\}) = \chi_S(u) \oplus \chi_S(v) \oplus l(\{u, v\})$. In turn, $Score(S) = \sum_{e \in E} Score(S, e)$. The objective of E2-LIN-2 is to maximize $Score(S)$.

Our first reduction will have instance transformation τ_1, and will map an instance G of E2-LIN-2 into another instance G' of the same problem that has three properties: G' is a graph of degree 3, its girth (the length of a shortest cycle) is $\Omega(\log n)$, and its set of nodes can be covered with cycles in which all edges are labeled 0. We will use τ_1(E2-LIN-2) to denote this restricted version of E2-LIN-2. The last two properties of τ_1(E2-LIN-2) are important in the subsequent reductions that lead to MIN SBR problem.

To obtain other inapproximability results, we alter the reduction τ_1 in two ways. The first modification results in graphs that have all edges labeled with

Problem	Approx. Upper	Approx. Lower
3-OCC-E2-LIN-2	1.1383	1.0030
3-OCC-E3-LIN-2	2	1.0163
3-MAX CUT	1.1383	1.0030
3-OCC-MAX 2SAT	1.0741	1.0005
6-OCC-MAX-2SAT	1.0741	1.0014
3-MIS	1.2	1.0071
4-MIS	1.4	1.0136
5-MIS	1.6	1.0149
3-Node Cover	1.1666	1.0069
4-Node Cover	1.2857	1.0128
5-Node Cover	1.625	1.0138
MIN-SBR	1.5	1.0008

Table 1. Gaps between known approximation bounds.

1, i.e. it reduces E2-LIN-2 to 3-MAX CUT and allows to complete the proof of (1). The second modification reduces E3-LIN-2 to a very special version of 3-OCC-E3-LIN-2, which we call HYBRID, because a large majority of equations have only two variables. This reduction instantaneously leads to (4).

To show (2), we use an obvious reduction from τ_1(E2-LIN-2): an instance of E2-LIN-2 can be viewed as a set of equivalence statements, and we can replace each equivalence with a pair of implications. On the other hand, we obtain (7) and (5) using reductions from HYBRID.

Although HYBRID problem appears to be very "efficient", we cannot use it in the chain that leads to MIN-SBR. Instead, we use another reduction, with instance translation τ_2, that leads from τ_1(E2-LIN-2) to 4-MIS. This translation replaces each node/variable with a small gadget. The resulting instances of 4-MIS can be transformed into the next problem that we consider, which we call *breakpoint graph decomposition*, BGD. This problem is related to *maximum alternating cycle decomposition*, (e.g. see Caprara, [C97]) but has a different objective function (as with another pair of related problems, Node Cover and MIS, the choice of the objective function affects approximability). An instance of BGD is a so-called breakpoint graph, i.e. an undirected graph $G = \langle V, E, l \rangle$ where l is a 0/1 edge labeling function, which satisfies the following two properties:

(1) for $b \in \{0, 1\}$, each connected component of $\langle V, l^{-1}(b) \rangle$ is a simple path;
(2) for each $v \in V$, the degrees of v in $\langle V, l^{-1}(0) \rangle$ and in $\langle V, l^{-1}(1) \rangle$ are the same.

An alternating cycle C is a subset of E such that $\langle V, C, l|C \rangle$ has the property (ii). A decomposition of G is a partition $\mathcal{C}$ of E into alternating cycles. The objective of BGD is to minimize $cost(\mathcal{C}) = \frac{1}{2}|E| - |\mathcal{C}|$.

By changing the node-replacing gadget of τ_2 and enforcing property (i) by "brute force", we obtain reduction τ_3 that maps τ_1(E2-LIN-2) into BGD. The last reduction, π, converts a breakpoint graph G into a permutation $\pi(G)$, an instance of sorting by reversals, MIN-SBR. We use a standard reduction, i.e. the correspondence between permutations and breakpoints graphs used in the approximation algorithms for MIN-SBR (as done by Bafna and Pevzner, [BP96]). In general, this correspondence is not approximation preserving because of so-called *hurdles* (see [BP96, HP95]). However, the permutations in $\pi(\tau_3(\tau_1$(E2-LIN-2))) do not have hurdles, and consequently for these restricted version of BGD, π is an approximation preserving reducibility with ratio 1.

3   First Reduction

To simplify the first reduction, we will describe how to compute the instance translation using a randomized poly-time algorithm. In this reduction, every node (variable) is replaced with a *wheel*, a random graph that is defined below. The parameter κ used here equals 6.

Definition 2. An *r-wheel* is a graph with $2(\kappa + 1)r$ nodes $W = Contacts \cup Checkers$, that contains $2r$ *contacts* and $2\kappa r$ *checkers*, and two sets of edges, C and M. C is a Hamiltonian cycle in which with consecutive contacts are separated by chains of κ checkers, while M is a random perfect matching for the set of checkers (see Fig. 1 for an example).

Consider an instance G of E2-LIN-2 with n nodes (variables) and m edges (equations). We will transform G into $\tau_1(G)$, an instance of 3-OCC-E2-LIN-2. Let $k = \lceil n/2 \rceil$. A node v of degree d will be replaced with a kd-wheel W_v. All wheel edges are labeled 0 to indicate our preference for such a solution S that either $W_v \subset S$ or $W_v \cap S = \emptyset$. An edge $\{v, u\}$ with label l is replaced with $2k$ edges, each of them has label l and joins a contact of W_v with a contact of W_u. In the entire construction each contact is used exactly once, so the resulting graph is 3-regular.

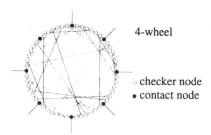

4-wheel

○ checker node
● contact node

Fig. 1. A very small example of a gadget used by τ_1.

We need to elaborate this construction a bit to assure that $\tau_1(G)$ has a large girth. First, we will assure that no short cycle is contained inside a wheel. We can use these properties of an r-wheel W: each cycle different of length lower than $2\kappa r$ must contain at least one edge of the matching M and the expected number of nodes contained in cycles of length $0.2\log_2(\kappa r)$ or less is below $(\kappa r)^{-0.8}$ fraction). Thus we can destroy cycles of length below $0.2\log_2 n$ by deleting matching edges incident to every node on such a cycle and neglect the resulting changes in $Score$.

Later, we must prevent creation of short cycles that include edges between the wheels; this can be done using a construction of Bollobás [B78].

The solution translation is simple. Suppose that we have a solution S for a translated instance. First we normalize S as follows: if the majority of contacts in a wheel W belong to S, we change S into $S \cup W$, otherwise we change S into $S - W$. We convert a normalized solution S into a solution S' of the original problem in an obvious manner: a node belongs to S' iff its wheel is contained in S. We can show that the probability that the normalization decreases the score is very low. Assuming that G has m edges/equations, we have $Score(S) = 2k((3\kappa+2)m + Score(S'))$. Håstad [H97] proved that for E2-LIN-2 instances with $16n$ equations it is NP-hard to distinguish those that have $Score$ above $(12-\epsilon)n$ and those that have $Score$ below $(11+\epsilon)n$, where the positive constant ϵ can be arbitrarily small. By showing that our reduction is correct for $\kappa = 6$ we prove

Theorem 3. *For any $\epsilon \in (0, 1/2)$, it is NP-hard to decide whether an instance of τ_1(E2-LIN-2) $\in$ 3-OCC-E2-LIN-2 with $336n$ edges (equations) has Score above $(332 - \epsilon)n$ or below $(331 + \epsilon)n$.*

4 From HYBRID to k-MIS

We can modify τ_1 to transform E3-LIN-2 rather than E2-LIN-2. Variables (nodes) are still replaced with kd-wheels, and an equation $x \oplus y \oplus z$ is replaced with $2k$ equations, each involving one contact from each of the respective consistency wheels. HYBRID is the resulting set of instances of E3-LIN-2. By analizing this reduction, we can show (4). Furthermore, we can efficiently reduce HYBRID to k-MIS for $k = 3, 4, 5$.

Given an instance S of HYBRID, we will form graph G of degree 4, an instance of 4-MIS. Each variable/node x of S will be replace with a gadget A_x which is an induced subgraph of G. Every gadget contains a *hexagon*, i.e. a cycle of length 6 in which nodes with labels 0 and 1 alternate. Hexagons will have two types: a-hexagons, with 2 chords, and b-hexagons, with 1 chord.

If x and y are connected by an edge (equation with two variables), the hexagons of A_x and A_y will share a pair of adjacent edges; this edge of G corresponds to the equation/edge $x = y$. A checker gadget is simply a hexagon: 3 edges edges of equations connected by three other edges, and one or two diagonals. A contact gadget consists of a hexagon fused with a square; 3 such gadgets are connected by an equation gadget that contains 4 nodes that do not belong to gadgets of nodes/variables. Our best reduction to 5-MIS differs only ib the shape of the contact gadget. Fig. 2 and 3 show these gadgets in detail.

Solution translation is relatively simple. First we show that we can modify each solution S so that each checker and each contact gadget is pure, i.e. it contains only one kind of nodes from S (0-nodes or 1-nodes) and then we perform appropriate accounting. Note that if all gadgets are pure, than the solution translation is obvious: if it contains 0-nodes from S, the respective Boolean variable receives value 0, and similarly for 1.

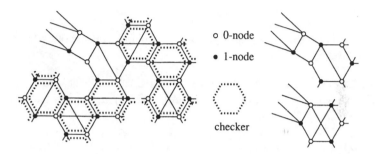

Fig. 2. Consistency wheel for 4-MIS and 5-MIS. The gadget used by 4-MIS to replace a contact node is shown in the upper right corner. The lower right corner is a gadget replacing a contact node in a reduction to 5-MIS.

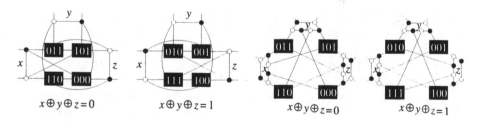

Fig. 3. Equation gadgets for 4-MIS and 5-MIS (left) and the gadgets for 3-MIS (right).

We can describe a similar reduction from HYBRID to 3-MIS. Given a HYBRID system of equations S, we form a graph G of degree 3. Again, each variable x of HYBRID is replaced with a gadget A_x; the gadget of a checker variable is a hexagon, and a gadget of a contact variable is a hexagon augmented with a *trapezoid*, a cycle of 6 nodes that shares one edge with the hexagon. The hexagons used here have no chords. If two variables/nodes x, y are connected by an equation/edge, $x = y$, we connect their hexagons with a pair of edges to form a rectangle in which the edges of the hexagons and the new edges alternate. The rectangle thus formed is a gadget of this equation. If three variables are connected by an equation/hyperedge, say, $x \oplus y \oplus z = 0$, the trapezoids of A_x, A_y and A_z are connected to four special nodes of the gadget of this equation. As a result, the gadget of this equation consists of 3 trapezoid and 4 special nodes, for the total of 22 nodes. The details are shown in Fig 4 and Fig. 3.

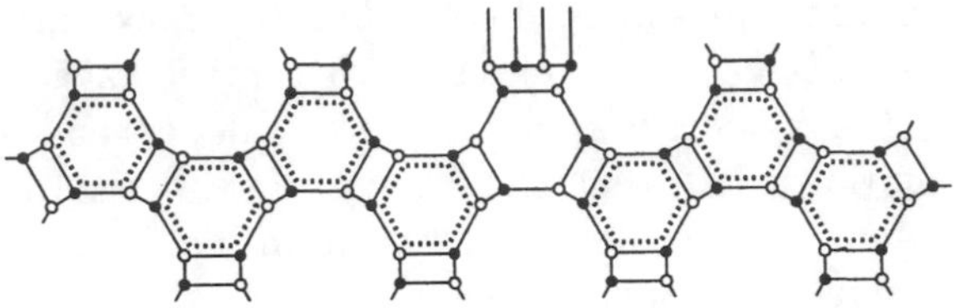

206

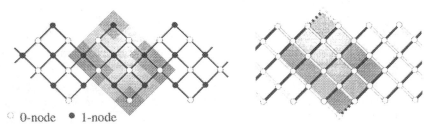

Fig. 4. Consistency wheel for 3-MIS.

The analysis of this reduction (and the two preeceding ones) allows us to prove the following theorem:

Theorem 4. *For any $\epsilon \in (0, 1/2)$, it is NP-hard to decide whether an instance of 4-MIS with 152n nodes has the maximum size of an independent set above $(74 - \epsilon)n$ or below $(73 + \epsilon)n$.*
Further, it is NP-hard to decide if an instance of 4-MIS with 152n nodes has the maximum size of an independent set above $(74 - \epsilon)n$ or below $(73 + \epsilon)n$.
Moreover, it is NP-hard to decide if an instance of 3-MIS with 284n nodes has the maximum size of an independent set above $(140 - \epsilon)n$ or below $(139 + \epsilon)n$.

5   From E2-LIN-2 to 4-MIS, BGD and MIN-SBR

An instance of 4-MIS can be modified to became an instance of BGD in a simple manner: each node can be replace with an alternating cycle of length 4; adjacent nodes will be replaced with a pair such cycles that have an edge (or two) in common. If we are "lucky", after the replacement we indeed obtain a breakpoint graph. Unfortunately, it is not possible to apply such transformation consistently to a graph from Fig. 3. We did not find other gadgets that can replace an equation with three variables and can later be replaced with a fragment of a breakpoint graph. Therefore we will be using a translation from τ_1(E2-LIN-2), shown in Fig 5.

$\circ$ 0-node $\bullet$ 1-node

Fig. 5. A part of 4-MIS instance obtained from τ_1(E2-LIN-2) (left) and its translation within BGD instance (right).

It is easy to see that the size of the resulting 4-MIS graph is $9n$, and that the correspondence between the size of the pure solution and the score in the original τ_1(E2-LIN-2) instance is $i = 3n + s$. The "purifying" normalization proceeds differently than before, for details we refer to [BK99].

The idea of reducing MIS problem to BGD is very simple and natural. Observe that the set E of all edges forms an alternating cycle (AC for short), a disjoint union of ACs is an AC, and a difference of two ACs, one contained in another is also an AC. Thus any disjoint collection of ACs can be extended to a decomposition of AC. Consequently, the goal of BGD is to find a collection of disjoint ACs as close in size to the maximum as possible.

Second observation is that the consequences of *not finding* an AC diminish with the size of AC. Suppose that the input has n breakpoints (edges of one color), and that we neglect to find any AC's with more than k breakpoints. The increase in the cost of the solution is smaller than n/k, while the cost is at least $n/2$. Thus if $k = \Omega(\log n)$, such oversight does not affect the approximation ratio.

The strategy suggested by these observation is to create instances of BGD in which alternating cycles that either have 2 breakpoints, or $\Omega(\log n)$. Then the task of approximating is equivalent to the one of maximizing the size of independent set in the graph $\mathcal{G}$ of all ACs of length 4; we draw an edge between two ACs if they share an edge.

More to the point, we need to find a difficult family of graphs of degree 4 which can be converted into breakpoint graphs by replacing each node with an alternating cycle of size 4. To this end, we can use $\tau_2(\tau_1$(E2-LIN-2)). Fig. 5 shows how this replacement is applied to a cycle of gadget forming a consistency wheel. One of the gadget is shown shaded, and dark gray indicates overlaps with other gadgets; the overlap with a gadget from another wheel consists of two disconnected pieces (note that it exists if this gadget replaces a contact node). The union of ACs used in the replacements is also a disjoint union of 5 ACs (in Fig. 5 these ACs are horizontal zigzags). To apply the reasoning of the previous sections, we need to establish that no cycles of length larger than 4 have to be considered. Here, we omit this reasoning.

At this point the translation is still not correct, as the resulting graphs MUST violated property (i) of BGD: edges of one kind form a collection of cycles: in Fig. 5 such edges form diagonal lines consisting of 5 edges each; such a line crosses to another strip of gadgets and then proceeds without end. However, these cycles induce cycles of gadgets, hence have length $\Omega(\log n)$, moreover, they are disjoint. Therefore we can remove all these cycles by breaking $O(n/\log n)$ contacts between the strips.

Given and instance G of τ_1(E2-LIN-2) with $2n$ nodes and $3n$ edges, this construction creates BGD instance G' with $20n$ breakpoints (edges of one color), and the correspondence between the cost c of a cycle decomposition in G' and s, *Score* of the corresponding solution of G is $c = 20n - 3n - s$. Together with Theorem 3 this implies

Theorem 5. *For any $\epsilon \in (0, 1/2)$, it is NP-hard to decide whether an instance of BGD with 2240n breakpoints has the minimum cost of an alternating cycle decomposition below $(1236 + \epsilon)n$ or above $(1237 - \epsilon)n$.*

Our reduction from BGD to MIN-SBR is straightforward, in particular we can use the procedure GET-PERMUTATION of Caprara [C97, p.77] to obtain permutation $\pi(G)$ from a given breakpoint graph G. The number of reversals needed to sort the resulting permutation is equal to the number of black edges in G, minus the number of cycles in in the optimum cycle cover, plus the number of hurdles, plus 1 if there is a fortress. Therefore the difference between the cost of solution for G differs from that for $\pi(G)$ by the number of hurdles (possibly, plus 1). Now recall that we started from an instance of E2-LIN-2 problem with some n variables and m equations, $n < m$. Our instance of BGD has $\Theta(mn)$ nodes and edges. We can show that the number of hurdles is not larger n, than the number of consistency wheels. In a nutshell, a hurdle is a connected components of the breakpoints in so-called *interleaving graph* that satisfies certain conditions. We can show that breakpoints from each consistency wheel belong to a single connected component. Because n is much smaller than the solution size, we can conclude that Theorem 5 applies also to MIN-SBR.

6   Further Research and Open Problems

It would very interesting to improve still huge gaps between approximation upper and lower bounds for bounded approximation problems of Table 1. The lower bound of 1.0008 for MIN-SBR is the first inapproximability result for this problem. The especially huge gap between 1.5 and 1.0008 for the MIN-SBR problem reflects a great challenge for future improvements.

Acknowledgments

This research was partially supported by NSF grant CCR-9700053, International Computer Science Institute, Berkeley, California, DIMACS, DFG grant 673/4-1, ESPRIT BR grants 7079, 21726 and EC-US 030, and by the Max–Planck Research Prize.
We thank Johan Håstad and Luca Trevisan for stimulating remarks on the preliminary version of this paper.

References

[AFWZ95] N. Alon, U. Feige, A. Wigderson and D. Zuckerman, *Derandomized Graph Products*, Computational Complexity **5** (1995), pp. 60–75.

[A94] S. Arora, *Probabilistic Checking of Proofs and Hardness of Approximation Problems*, Ph. D. Thesis, UC Berkeley, 1994;
available as TR94-476 at ftp://ftp.cs.princeton.edu

[ALMSS92] S. Arora, C. Lund, R. Motwani, M. Sudan and M. Szegedy, *Proof Verification and Hardness of Approximation Problems*, Proc. 33rd IEEE FOCS (1992), pp. 14–23.

[BP96] V. Bafna and P. Pevzner, *Genome rearrangements and sorting by reversals*, SIAM J. on Computing **25** (1996), pp. 272–289.

[BF95] P. Berman and T. Fujito, *Approximating Independent Sets in Degree 3 Graphs*, Proc. 4th Workshop on Algorithms and Data Structures, LNCS Vol. 955, Springer-Verlag, 1995, pp. 449–460.

[BF94] P. Berman and M. Fürer, *Approximating Maximum Independent Set in Bounded Degree Graphs*, Proc. 5th ACM-SIAM SODA (1994), pp. 365–371.

[BH96] P. Berman and S. Hannenhali, *Fast Sorting by Reversals*, Proc. 7th Symp. on Combinatorial Pattern Matching, 1996, pp. 168–185.

[BK99] P. Berman and M. Karpinski, *On Some Tighter Inapproximbility Results*, preliminary version appeared in ECCC TR98-065, the full version available under http://theory.cs.uni-bonn.de/~marek.

[BS92] P. Berman and G. Schnitger, *On the Complexity of Approximating the Independent Set Problem*, Information and Computation **96** (1992), pp. 77–94.

[B78] B. Bollobás, *Extremal Graph Theory*, 1978, Academic Press.

[C97] A. Caprara, *Sorting by reversals is difficult*, Proc. 1st ACM RECOMB (Int. Conf. on Computational Molecular Biology), 1997, pp. 75–83.

[C98] D. A. Christie, *A 3/2-Approximation Algorithm for Sorting by Reversals*, Proc. 9th ACM-SIAM SODA (1998), pp. 244–252.

[CB95] D. Cohen and M. Blum, *Improved Bounds for Sorting Burnt Pancakes*, Discrete Applied Mathematics, Vol. 61, pp. 105-125.

[CK97] P. Crescenzi and V. Kann, *A Compendium of NP Optimization Problems*, Manuscript, 1997;
available at http://www.nada.kth.se/theory/problemlist.html

[FG95] U. Feige and M. Goemans, *Approximating the Value of Two Prover Proof Systems with Applications to MAX-2SAT and MAX-DICUT*, Proc. 3rd Israel Symp. on Theory of Computing and Systems, 1995, pp. 182–189.

[GP79] W. H. Gates, and C. H. Papadimitriou, *Bounds for Sorting by Prefix Reversals*, Discrete Mathematics **27** (1979), pp. 47–57.

[GW94] M. Goemans and D. Williamson, *.878-Approximation Algorithms for MAX CUT and MAX 2SAT*, Proc. 26th ACM STOC (1994), pp. 422–431.

[H96] J. Håstad, *Clique is Hard to Approximate within $n^{1-\epsilon}$*, Proc. 37th IEEE FOCS (1996), pp. 627–636.

[H97] J. Håstad, *Some optimal Inapproximability results*, Proc. 29th ACM STOC, 1997, pp. 1–10.

[HP95] S. Hannenhali and P. Pevzner, *Transforming Cabbage into Turnip (Polynomial time algorithm for sorting by reversals)*, Proc. 27th ACM STOC (1995), pp. 178–187.

[KST97] H. Kaplan, R. Shamir and R.E. Tarjan, *Faster and simpler algorithm for sorting signed permutations by reversals*, Proc. 8th ACM-SIAM SODA, 1997, pp. 344–351.

[PY91] C. Papadimitriou and M. Yannakakis, *Optimization, approximation and complexity classes*, JCSS **43**, 1991, pp. 425–440.

[TSSW96] L. Trevisan, G. Sorkin, M. Sudan and D. Williamson, *Gadgets, Approximation and Linear Programming*, Proc. 37th IEEE FOCS (1996), pp. 617–626.

Decomposition and Composition of Timed Automata

Patricia Bouyer and Antoine Petit

LSV, CNRS UMR 8643, ENS de Cachan, 61 av. du Prés. Wilson,
F-94235 Cachan Cedex, France,
bouyer,petit@lsv.ens-cachan.fr

Abstract. We propose in this paper a decomposition theorem for the timed automata introduced by Alur and Dill [2]. To this purpose, we define a new simple and natural concatenation operation, indexed by the set of clocks to be reset, on timed automata generalizing the classical untimed concatenation.

Then we extend the famous Kleene's and Büchi's theorems on classical untimed automata by simply changing the basic objects to take time into account, keeping the union operation and replacing the concatenation, finite and infinite iterations by the new timed concatenations and their induced iterations.

Thus, and up to our knowledge, our result provides the simplest known algebraic characterization of recognizable timed languages.

1 Introduction

We are interested in this paper in the basic and natural model of so-called timed automata proposed by Alur and Dill [2] to model real-time systems. Since its introduction, this model has been largely studied under several aspects: determinization [3], minimization [1], power of clocks [14], of ε−transitions [11], extensions of the model [4,7] and logical characterization [17] have been considered in particular. Moreover this model has been successfully used for verification and specification of real-time systems [10,18,15].

But there is a lack of algebraic characterizations of timed languages or timed automata. Unlike in the untimed case, there does not exist a notion of timed finite semi-groups and a notion of timed recognizing morphisms. Even the famous Kleene's theorem [16] and its extension to ω−languages by Büchi [13] has only partial counterparts in the framework of timed languages. The most interesting result, due to Asarin, Caspi and Maler [6], proposes such a Kleene theorem for a slightly different notion of timed languages. But the main drawback of their characterization is that it uses in a crucial way the operations of intersection and renaming.

The aim of this paper is to propose, at least up to our knowledge for the first time, a simple Kleene-Büchi theorem for usual timed automata. Precisely, we define a natural concatenation operation on timed automata, indexed by a subset of clocks. We also introduce the finite and infinite iterations corresponding to this composition. Then we prove that any timed automaton is equivalent to a timed automaton built in a modular way from some basic automata using these operations and the classical union operation. Hence our result is very close from Kleene's and Büchi's theorem, we have just changed the basic objects to take time into account, keep the union operation and replace the concatenation, finite and infinite iterations by timed concatenations based naturally on clocks and their induced iterations.

Our proof generalizes one of the proof of Kleene's theorem based on the resolution of equations on set of words, see e.g. [12]. The idea to solve equations on timed languages - in the simple case of automata with a unique clock - was already proposed by Asarin in [5]. Here, we solve equations on multi-clock automata.

For lack of space, this extended draft does not contain all detailed proofs which can be found in the technical report [BP99].

2 Timed automata and constrained generators

In this section, we briefly recall the basic definitions and notations for timed words and finite automata with timing constraints, as well as classical properties of the corresponding families of timed languages. They come mostly from [2].

2.1 Timed words and clocks

Let Z be any set. We write Z^+ (respectively Z^ω) the set of non-empty finite (respectively infinite) sequences of elements in Z, with ε for the empty sequence, and $Z^\infty = Z^+ \cup Z^\omega$ the set of all sequences of elements in Z.

Throughout this paper, we consider a time domain $\mathbb{T}$ which is either the set of non-negative integers $\mathbb{N}$ or the set of non-negative rationals $\mathbb{Q}_+$. A time sequence over $\mathbb{T}$ is a finite or infinite divergent non decreasing sequence $\tau = (t_i)_{i \geq 1}$ of elements in $\mathbb{T}$.

The observable actions of the processes we consider are given by a finite set Σ. A timed word is an element of $(\Sigma \times \mathbb{T})^\infty$, $w = (a_i, t_i)_{i \geq 1}$, also written as a pair $w = (\sigma, \tau)$, where $\sigma = (a_i)_{i \geq 1}$ is a word in Σ^∞ and $\tau = (t_i)_{i \geq 1}$ is a timed sequence in $\mathbb{T}^\infty$ of same length than σ. For instance, $(a, 1.5)(b, 2)(a, 2.5)(b, 3.9)(a, 3.9)$ is a finite timed word, while $((ab)^\omega, (i + 1/i)_{i \geq 1})$ is an infinite timed word.

The concatenation of a finite timed word $u = (a_i, t_i)_{1 \leq i \leq n}$ and of a finite or infinite timed word $v = (a'_i, t'_i)_{1 \leq i}$ is defined only if $t_n \leq t'_1$ and is equal to the timed word $u \cdot v = (a''_i, t''_i)_{1 \leq i}$ with $(a''_i, t''_i) = (a_i, t_i)$ if $1 \leq i \leq n$ and $(a''_i, t''_i) = (a'_{i-n}, t'_{i-n})$ if $n < i$.

Let X be a set of variables with values in $\mathbb{T}$, called clocks. Among X, we distinguish a special clock x_0 which will denote the absolute time.

The guards over X are the formulas defined by the grammar:

$$g ::= \top \mid x \sim c \mid x - y \sim c \mid g \vee g \mid g \wedge g \mid \neg g$$

where x and y are clocks, $c \in \mathbb{T}$ and $\sim$ is a binary operator in $\{<, =, >\}$. The set of all guards over X is denoted by $\mathrm{Guards}(X)$.

A clock valuation $\alpha : X \to \mathbb{T}$ is a mapping that assigns to each clock x a time value $\alpha(x)$. The set of all clock valuations is denoted $\mathbb{T}^X$. We write $\alpha \models g$ when the clock valuation α satisfies the clock constraint g. If Y a subset of X, the valuation $\alpha[Y := 0]$ is defined by, for each clock x in X, $(\alpha[Y := 0])(x) = 0$ if $x \in Y$, $\alpha(x)$ otherwise.

2.2 Timed automata and runs

A Büchi timed automaton over $\Sigma, \mathbb{T}$ and X is a tuple $\mathcal{A} = (Q, T, I, F, R)$, where Q is a finite set of states, $T \subseteq Q \times [\mathrm{Guards}(X) \times \Sigma \times \mathcal{P}(X)] \times Q$ is the set of transitions, $I \subseteq Q$ is the subset of initial states, $F \subseteq Q$ is the subset of final states[1] and $R \subseteq Q$ is a subset of repeated states corresponding to a Büchi condition, as recalled below. Thus, a transition has the form (p, g, a, r, q), where g is a guard, a is an action in Σ and $r \subseteq X$ is the subset of clocks to be reset. We assume that the special clock x_0 is never reset.

The set of all timed automata over the set of actions Σ, the timed domain $\mathbb{T}$ and the set of clocks X is denoted by $\mathrm{TA}(\Sigma, \mathbb{T}, X)$.

In order to define how a timed word is recognized by a timed automaton, we recall the notions of path and of timed run through a path. A path in $\mathcal{A}$ is a non empty finite or infinite sequence of consecutive transitions:

$$P = q_0 \xrightarrow{g_1, a_1, r_1} q_1 \xrightarrow{g_2, a_2, r_2} q_2 \cdots$$

where $(q_{i-1}, g_i, a_i, r_i, q_i) \in T$ for all $i > 0$. The path P is accepting, if it starts in an initial state and either it is finite ending in a final state or it is infinite and a Büchi condition holds: $inf(P) \cap R$ is nonempty, where $inf(P)$ is the set of states which occur infinitely often in P.

A run of the automaton through the path P and from the initial clock valuation $\alpha \in \mathbb{T}^X$ is a triple $R = (\alpha, P, (t_i)_{i>0})$ where $(t_i)_{i>0}$ is a non-decreasing sequence of dates of same length than P; t_i is the time at which transition $q_{i-1} \xrightarrow{g_i, a_i, r_i} q_i$ has been executed. Intuitively, this transition can be performed, only if the guard g_i is satisfied by the current clock valuation and the clocks in r_i are reset at that time. More precisely, the value of clock x at time t is written $x(t)$, so that the clock valuation at time t can be written as the tuple $X(t) = (x(t))_{x \in X}$. Beginning with time $t_0 = \alpha(x_0)$ and clock values $x(t_0) = \alpha(x)$, for all x,[2] the clock valuation at time t is completely determined by the run: for each $i \geq 1$,

$$x(t_i) = \begin{cases} 0 & \text{if } x \in r_i \\ x(t_{i-1}) + t_i - t_{i-1} & \text{otherwise} \end{cases}$$

---

[1] For sake of simplicity, we will always assume that $I \cap F = \emptyset$

[2] In most papers on timed automata, all the clocks, and in particular the absolute time, are initialized to 0. Therefore our definition generalizes the classical one.

and $x(t) = x(t_{i-1}) + t - t_{i-1}$ for $t_{i-1} \leq t < t_i$. Moreover. we require that $X(t_{i-1}) + t_i - t_{i-1} \models g_i$ for all $i \geq 1$.

With every finite (infinite resp.) run we can associate in a natural way a finite (infinite resp.) timed word. designed as the label of R. by

$$\ell(R) = (a_1, t_1)(a_2, t_2) \cdots \in (\Sigma \times \mathbb{T})^{\infty}.$$

If R is finite of length n, we define also the clock valuation $\text{Ends}(R) \in \mathbb{T}^X$ "at the end of R" in the following way:

$$\text{Ends}(R)(x) = \begin{cases} 0 & \text{if } x \in r_n \\ x(t_n) & \text{otherwise} \end{cases}$$

Note that since we have assumed that the clock x_0 is never reset. it holds $\text{Ends}(R)(x_0) = t_n$.

2.3 Timed automata and constrained generators

With our definition. we therefore associate not only one timed language with a timed automaton $\mathcal{A}$ but a family of timed languages indexed by the initial clock valuations. Precisely. for any clock valuation $\alpha \in \mathbb{T}^X$, we define

$$L_{\mathcal{A}}(\alpha) = \{\ell(R) \mid R = (\alpha, P, (t_i)_{i>0}) \text{ for some accepting path } P \text{ in } \mathcal{A}\}$$

For sake of simplicity. we denote $L_{\mathcal{A},+}(\alpha)$ for $L_{\mathcal{A}}(\alpha) \cap (\Sigma \times \mathbb{T})^+$ and $L_{\mathcal{A},\omega}(\alpha)$ for $L_{\mathcal{A}}(\alpha) \cap (\Sigma \times \mathbb{T})^\omega$.

The function Ends on runs allows also to define the set of possible clock valuations after accepting a finite timed word. Precisely. for any timed word $u \in (\Sigma \times \mathbb{T})^+$ and any initial clock valuation $\alpha \in \mathbb{T}^X$, we set

$$\text{Ends}_{\mathcal{A}}(\alpha, u) = \{\text{Ends}(R) \mid R = (\alpha, P, (t_i)_{i>0})$$
$$\text{for some accepting path } P \text{ in } \mathcal{A} \text{ such that } \ell(R) = u\}$$

Note that if $u \notin L_{\mathcal{A},+}(\alpha)$. it holds $\text{Ends}_{\mathcal{A}}(\alpha, u) = \emptyset$. This new function $\text{Ends}_{\mathcal{A}}$ can be viewed as a constraint on the timed words of $L_{\mathcal{A},+}(\alpha)$.

We now define the notion of constrained generator as a generalization of these functions $L_{\mathcal{A}}$ and $\text{Ends}_{\mathcal{A}}$. This notion will be a fundamental tool in the sequel. A constrained generator is a pair $(\mathcal{G}, \Lambda)$ such that

1. $\mathcal{G} : \mathbb{T}^X \longrightarrow \mathcal{P}((\Sigma \times \mathbb{T})^{\infty})$
2. $\Lambda : \mathbb{T}^X \times (\Sigma \times \mathbb{T})^+ \longrightarrow \mathcal{P}(\mathbb{T}^X)$
3. $\forall u \in (\Sigma \times \mathbb{T})^+. u \in \mathcal{G}(\alpha) \Longleftrightarrow \Lambda(\alpha, u) \neq \emptyset$

From the results above. it is clear that for any timed automaton $\mathcal{A}$. the pair $(L_{\mathcal{A}}, \text{Ends}_{\mathcal{A}})$ is a constrained generator. It will be denoted by $\widehat{\mathcal{A}}$ and refered as the constrained generator associated with $\mathcal{A}$.

Two timed automata $\mathcal{A}$ and $\mathcal{B}$ are equivalent. we then denote $\mathcal{A} \equiv \mathcal{B}$ if their associated constrained generators $\widehat{\mathcal{A}}$ and $\widehat{\mathcal{B}}$ are equal. In this case. it holds in particular $L_{\mathcal{A}}(0) = L_{\mathcal{B}}(0)$.

3 Composition of timed automata

3.1 Union

The union of two timed automata $\mathcal{A} = (Q_1, T_1, I_1, F_1, R_1)$ and $\mathcal{B} = (Q_2, T_2, I_2, F_2, R_2)$ with $Q_1 \cap Q_2 = \emptyset$ is simply the timed automaton $\mathcal{A} + \mathcal{B} = (Q_1 \cup Q_2, T_1 \cup T_2, I_1 \cup I_2, F_1 \cup F_2, R_1 \cup R2)$.

3.2 Concatenation

Assume that we want to concatenate two timed automata $\mathcal{A}$ and $\mathcal{B}$. Then, entering in $\mathcal{B}$, the two extreme possibilities are either to reset all the clocks of $\mathcal{A}$ or on the contrary to not reset any clock of $\mathcal{A}$. But on many real examples, none of these two choices is satisfactory. Assume for instance that we want to built a complex product under some global timing constraints and that the construction is made in several parts, each of them having its own timing constraints. Then it is much more natural to allow in the concatenation of timed automata modelizing the subsystems to reset some clocks and to not reset some other clocks.

Following this simple, but powerful, idea, we propose to define the concatenation $\mathcal{A} \underset{c}{\bullet} \mathcal{B}$ of two timed automata $\mathcal{A} = (Q_1, T_1, I_1, F_1, R_1)$ and $\mathcal{B} = (Q_2, T_2, I_2, F_2, R_2)$, depending on a fixed set C of clocks. Intuitively, $\mathcal{A} \underset{c}{\bullet} \mathcal{B}$ is the timed automaton obtained by first performing actions in $\mathcal{A}$, then resetting all the clocks of C and finally performing actions in $\mathcal{B}$. Formally, $\mathcal{A} \underset{c}{\bullet} \mathcal{B}$ is the timed automaton[3] $(Q_1 \cup Q_2 \cup \widetilde{F_1}, T, I_1, F_2, R_1 \cup R_2)$, where $\widetilde{F_1}$ is a copy of F_1, disjoint of $Q_1 \cup Q_2$, with

$$T = T_1 \cup T_2$$
$$\cup \{(q_1, g_1, a_1, r_1 \cup C, \tilde{f_1}) \mid f_1 \in F_1, (q_1, g_1, a_1, r_1, f_1) \in T_1\}$$
$$\cup \{(\tilde{f_1}, g_2, a_2, r_2, q_2) \mid \exists i_2 \in I_2, (i_2, g_2, a_2, r_2, q_2) \in T_2\}$$

3.3 Iterations

We now derive in a natural way two iterations, a finite one and an infinite one, from this composition operator $\underset{c}{\bullet}$. Let $\mathcal{A} = (Q, T, I, F, R)$ be a timed automaton and let C be a subset of clocks. We consider a copy $\tilde{F}$ of F, disjoint from Q. Then the timed automaton $\mathcal{A}^{\overset{+}{c}}$ is defined as follows, $\mathcal{A}^{\overset{+}{c}} = (Q \cup \tilde{F}, T', I, \tilde{F}, R)$ with

$$T' = T \cup \{(q, g, a, r \cup C, \tilde{f}) \mid f \in F, (q, g, a, r, f) \in T\}$$
$$\cup \{(\tilde{f}, g, a, r, q) \mid \exists i \in I, (i, g, a, r, q) \in T\}$$

In a similar way, the infinite iteration of $\mathcal{A}$, denoted $\mathcal{A}^{\overset{\omega}{c}}$ is defined by $\mathcal{A}^{\overset{\omega}{c}} = (Q \cup \tilde{F}, T', I, \emptyset, R \cup \tilde{F})$ where T' is defined as just above.

---

[3] We assume without loss of generality that $Q_1 \cap Q_2 = \emptyset$. Moreover, recall that by hypothesis, $I_1 \cap F_1 = I_2 \cap F_2 = \emptyset$

3.4 Modular constructions of timed automata

For any guard $g \in \text{Guards}(X)$ and any action $a \in \Sigma$, we denote by $\mathcal{A}_{(g,a)}$ the simple timed automaton $(\{q_0, q_1\}, \{(q_0, g, a, \emptyset, q_1)\}, \{q_0\}, \{q_1\}, \emptyset)$. For any clock valuation $\alpha \in \mathbb{T}^X$ and any $t \in \mathbb{T}$, denote by $\alpha + t$ the clock valuation defined by, for any clock x, $(\alpha + t)(x) = \alpha(x) + t$. Then it is immediate to verify that $L_{\mathcal{A}_{(g,a)}}(\alpha)$ is equal to $\{(a, t) \mid \alpha + t \models g\}$. Moreover $\text{Ends}_{\mathcal{A}_{(g,a)}}(\alpha, a) = \{\alpha + t \mid \alpha + t \models g\}$.

From these basic automata and the composition operators define above, we define now a modular family of timed automata as follows.

Definition 1. Let $\text{Mod}(\Sigma, \mathbb{T}, X)$ be the smallest subset of timed automata of $\text{TA}(\Sigma, \mathbb{T}, X)$ generated by the following grammar:

$$\mathcal{A} ::= \mathcal{A}_{(g,a)} \mid \mathcal{A} + \mathcal{A} \mid \mathcal{A}_{\dot{C}} \mathcal{A} \mid \mathcal{A}^{\dot{C}^+} \mid \mathcal{A}^{\overset{\omega}{C}}$$

with $g \in \text{Guards}(X)$ is a guard over X, a an action in Σ and $C \subseteq X$ a subset of clocks such that $x_0 \notin C$.

Note that in this definition the collection of operations is finite (the finite set of clocks X is assumed to be given) but there is an infinite number of generators even if the set of actions Σ is finite.

The main result of this paper is to prove that any timed automaton is equivalent to some timed automaton of $\text{Mod}(\Sigma, \mathbb{T}, X)$. This result can be seen as a Kleene-Büchi theorem for timed automata. Note that contrary to the results of the paper of Asarin, Caspi and Maler [6], we do not need neither intersection nor renaming.

Theorem 2. *Any timed automaton of $TA(\Sigma, \mathbb{T}, X)$ is equivalent to an automaton of $Mod(\Sigma, \mathbb{T}, X)$.*

This theorem will be proved by solving systems of equations on constrained generators. Since we can not assume, a priori, that the solution is always a constraint generator associated with some timed automaton, we need first some technical material on operations on constrained generators.

4 Composition of constrained generators

This section is devoted to the definitions of the composition of constrained generators. Even if these definitions are a bit technical, they are easy to understand keeping in mind that the goal is to obtain definitions such that the following proposition holds.

Proposition 3. *Let $\mathcal{A}$ and $\mathcal{B}$ be two timed automata in $TA(\Sigma, \mathbb{T}, X)$ and $C \subseteq X$ be a subset of clocks. Then it holds:*

1. $\widehat{A+B} = \hat{A} + \hat{B}$
2. $\widehat{A \underset{c}{\bullet} B} = \hat{A} \underset{c}{\bullet} \hat{B}$
3. $A_{\bar{c}}^{\pm} = \hat{A}_{\bar{c}}^{\pm}$
4. $A_{\bar{c}}^{\omega} = \hat{A}_{\bar{c}}^{\omega}$

Throughout this section, $(\mathcal{G}, \Lambda)$ and $(\mathcal{G}', \Lambda')$ are two constrained generators and $C \subseteq X$ is a subset of clocks.

4.1 Union of constrained generators

The union of $(\mathcal{G}, \Lambda)$ and $(\mathcal{G}', \Lambda')$, denoted by $(\mathcal{G}, \Lambda) + (\mathcal{G}', \Lambda')$ is naturally the constrained generator $(\mathcal{G}'', \Lambda'')$ where, for any clock valuation $\alpha \in \mathbb{T}^X$ and any finite timed word $w \in (\Sigma \times \mathbb{T})^+$, $\mathcal{G}''(\alpha) = \mathcal{G}(\alpha) \cup \mathcal{G}'(\alpha)$ and $\Lambda''(\alpha, u) = \Lambda(\alpha, u) \cup \Lambda'(\alpha, u)$.

4.2 Composition of constrained generators

We define the composition $(\mathcal{G}, \Lambda) \underset{c}{\bullet} (\mathcal{G}', \Lambda')$ as the constrained generator $(\mathcal{G}'', \Lambda'')$ where, for any clock valuation $\alpha \in \mathbb{T}^X$ and any finite timed word[4] $w \in (\Sigma \times \mathbb{T})^+$,

$$\mathcal{G}''(\alpha) = \{ u \cdot v \mid u \in \mathcal{G}(\alpha) \cap (\Sigma \times \mathbb{T})^+ \text{ and}$$
$$v \in \mathcal{G}'(\beta[C := 0]) \cap (\Sigma \times \mathbb{T})^\infty \text{ for some } \beta \in \Lambda(\alpha, u) \}$$

and

$$\Lambda''(\alpha, w) = \{ \Lambda'(\beta[C := 0], v) \mid \text{ there exists some } u \in \mathcal{G}(\alpha)$$
$$\text{with } w = u \cdot v \text{ and } \beta \in \Lambda(\alpha, u) \}$$

4.3 Iterations of a constrained generator

We define now inductively, the constrained generator, $(\mathcal{G}, \Lambda)^{\left(\underset{c}{\bullet}\right)^i}$, for $i \geq 1$, by

$$(\mathcal{G}, \Lambda)^{\left(\underset{c}{\bullet}\right)^1} = (\mathcal{G}, \Lambda) \text{ and } (\mathcal{G}, \Lambda)^{\left(\underset{c}{\bullet}\right)^{i+1}} = (\mathcal{G}, \Lambda) \underset{c}{\bullet} (\mathcal{G}, \Lambda)^{\left(\underset{c}{\bullet}\right)^i}$$

and we set $(\mathcal{G}, \Lambda)^{\underset{c}{\overset{+}{\bullet}}} = \Sigma_{i \geq 1} (\mathcal{G}, \Lambda)^{\left(\underset{c}{\bullet}\right)^i}$.

Finally, let $(\mathcal{G}, \Lambda)$ be a constrained generator and let $(\mathcal{G}_1, \Lambda_1) = (\mathcal{G}, \Lambda)^{\underset{c}{\overset{+}{\bullet}}}$. We define $(\mathcal{G}, \Lambda)^{\underset{c}{\overset{\omega}{\bullet}}} = (\mathcal{G}'', \Lambda'')$ by, for any clock valuation $\alpha \in \mathbb{T}^X$ and any finite timed word $w \in (\Sigma \times \mathbb{T})^+$,

$$\mathcal{G}''(\alpha) = (\mathcal{G}_1(\alpha) \cap (\Sigma \times \mathbb{T})^\omega) \cup$$
$$\{ u_0 \cdot u_1 \cdots \mid \text{ there exists a sequence } (\alpha_i)_{i \geq 0} \text{ of clock valuations}$$
$$\text{with } \alpha_0 = \alpha \text{ and for any } i \geq 1, u_{i+1} \in \mathcal{G}(\alpha_i) \cap (\Sigma \times \mathbb{T})^+$$
$$\text{and } \alpha_{i+1} \in \Lambda(\alpha_i, u_i) \}$$

---

[4] Recall that the concatenation of two timed words is a partial operation which has been defined in Section 2.1

and $\Lambda''(\alpha, w) = \emptyset$.

With these definitions, the proof of Proposition 3 is now technical but without major difficulty.

4.4 Basic properties

The following result summarizes the properties of the operators $\overset{\bullet}{c}$ and $\overset{+}{c}$ needed in the following.

Proposition 4. *Let* $(\mathcal{G}, \Lambda)$, $(\mathcal{G}', \Lambda')$ *and* $(\mathcal{G}'', \Lambda'')$ *three constrained generators and let* C, D *two subsets of clocks. Then it holds:*

1. $(\mathcal{G}, \Lambda)\overset{\bullet}{c}((\mathcal{G}', \Lambda') + (\mathcal{G}'', \Lambda'')) = ((\mathcal{G}, \Lambda)\overset{\bullet}{c}(\mathcal{G}', \Lambda')) + ((\mathcal{G}, \Lambda)\overset{\bullet}{c}(\mathcal{G}'', \Lambda''))$
2. $((\mathcal{G}, \Lambda) + (\mathcal{G}', \Lambda'))\overset{\bullet}{c}(\mathcal{G}'', \Lambda'') = ((\mathcal{G}, \Lambda)\overset{\bullet}{c}(\mathcal{G}'', \Lambda'')) + ((\mathcal{G}', \Lambda')\overset{\bullet}{c}(\mathcal{G}'', \Lambda''))$
3. $((\mathcal{G}, \Lambda)\overset{\bullet}{c}(\mathcal{G}', \Lambda'))\overset{\bullet}{D}(\mathcal{G}'', \Lambda'') = (\mathcal{G}, \Lambda)\overset{\bullet}{c}((\mathcal{G}', \Lambda')\overset{\bullet}{D}(\mathcal{G}'', \Lambda''))$
4. $(\mathcal{G}, \Lambda)^{\overset{+}{c}}\overset{\bullet}{c}(\mathcal{G}', \Lambda') = \sum_{i \geq 1}(\mathcal{G}, \Lambda)^{\left(\overset{\bullet}{c}\right)^i}\overset{\bullet}{c}(\mathcal{G}', \Lambda')$

4.5 Equations on constrained generators

We consider two constrained generators $(\mathcal{G}_1, \Lambda_1)$ and $(\mathcal{G}_2, \Lambda_2)$ and a subset C of clocks. The following lemma is the fundamental result allowing to solve systems of equations on constrained generators. It generalizes the result of [5] where, roughly, the case of timed automata with a unique clock is treated.

Lemma 5. *The equation on constrained generators over finite words*

$$(\mathcal{G}, \Lambda) = (\mathcal{G}_1, \Lambda_1)\overset{\bullet}{c}(\mathcal{G}, \Lambda) + (\mathcal{G}_2, \Lambda_2)$$

has for unique solution the constrained generator $(\mathcal{G}_1, \Lambda_1)^{\overset{+}{c}}\overset{\bullet}{c}(\mathcal{G}_2, \Lambda_2) + (\mathcal{G}_2, \Lambda_2)$.

Note that even if the constrained generators $(\mathcal{G}_1, \Lambda_1)$ and $(\mathcal{G}_2, \Lambda_2)$ are associated with some timed automata, we can not assume, a priori, that a solution of the equation, if any, is also associated with a timed automaton. It is the reason why we had to introduce all the technical results on constrained generators.

5 Decomposition of timed automata

We are now ready to prove our main result, Theorem 2. Let $\mathcal{A} = (Q, T, I, F, R)$ be a timed automaton. We assume that for any state q there exists some subset $C_q \subseteq X$ such that for any transition (q', g, a, r, q), it holds $r = C_q$. Note that, changing the set of states Q into the cartesian product $Q \times \mathcal{P}(X)$, it is easy to transform any timed automaton into an equivalent timed automaton verifying this property. We will propose now an algorithm to find a timed automaton $\mathcal{B}$ in $\text{Mod}(\Sigma, \mathbb{T}, X)$ which is equivalent to $\mathcal{A}$.

For any states $i, f \in Q$, we set $A_{i,f} = (Q, T, \{i\}, \{f\}, \emptyset)$ and we consider the constrained generator $\widehat{A_{i,f}}$ associated with $A_{i,f}$. From the definition of run in a timed automaton (see Section 2), it is easy to verify that the following equation holds

$$\widehat{A} = \sum_{i \in I, f \in F} \widehat{A_{i,f}} + \sum_{i \in I, q \in R} \widehat{A_{i,q}} \; \overset{\bullet}{c_q} \; \widehat{A_{q,q}}^{\overset{\omega}{\tilde{c}_q}}$$

which, in terms of timed automata and using Proposition 3, can be rewritten equivalently in

$$A \equiv \sum_{i \in I, f \in F} A_{i,f} + \sum_{i \in I, q \in R} A_{i,q} \; \overset{\bullet}{c_q} \; A_{q,q}^{\overset{\omega}{\tilde{c}_q}} \quad (\dagger)$$

Therefore, in order to prove that A is equivalent to some automaton in $\mathrm{Mod}(\Sigma, \mathbb{T}, X)$, it suffices to prove that for any $q, q' \in Q$, the automaton $A_{q,q'}$ belongs to $\mathrm{Mod}(\Sigma, \mathbb{T}, X)$.

Assume now that $f \in Q$ is fixed, then the family of constrained generators $(\widehat{A_{q,f}})_{q \in Q}$ verifies the system of equations on constrained generators:

$$\begin{cases} \widehat{A_{q,f}} = \varepsilon + \sum_{(q,g,a,C_{q'},q') \in T} \widehat{A_{(g,a)}} \; \overset{\bullet}{c_{q'}} \; \widehat{A_{q',f}} & \text{if } q = f \\ \widehat{A_{q,f}} = \sum_{(q,g,a,C_{q'},q') \in T} \widehat{A_{(g,a)}} \; \overset{\bullet}{c_{q'}} \; \widehat{A_{q',f}} & \text{otherwise} \end{cases}$$

Consider now an arbitrary order $q_1 < q_2 < \ldots < q_n$ on the elements of Q. Then the equation with left member $\widehat{A_{q_n,f}}$ is solved, with $\widehat{A_{q_n,f}}$ as unknown, using the fundamental Lemma 5 - ε has to be added if $q_n = f$:

$$\widehat{A_{q_n,f}} = \left(\sum_{(q_n,g,a,C_{q_n},q_n) \in T} \widehat{A_{(g,a)}} \right)^{\overset{+}{c_{q_n}}} \overset{\bullet}{c_{q_n}} \left(\sum_{(q_n,g,a,C_{q'},q') \in T, q' \neq q_n} \widehat{A_{q',f}} \right)$$

We thus replace $\widehat{A_{q_n,f}}$ by this formula in the $n - 1$ other equations. Step by step, we solve the system using the fundamental Lemma 5. The last step proves that the constrained generator $\widehat{A_{q_1,f}}$ can be expressed using the elementary constrained generators $\widehat{A_{(g,a)}}$ and the composition operators, which is similar to say that the automaton $A_{q_1,f}$ is equivalent to some automaton of $\mathrm{Mod}(\Sigma, \mathbb{T}, X)$. We thus deduce that $A_{q_2,f}$ and then $A_{q_3,f}, \ldots, A_{q_n,f}$ are also equivalent to some automata of $\mathrm{Mod}(\Sigma, \mathbb{T}, X)$.

Finally, for any $q, q' \in Q$, every automaton $A_{q,q'}$ is equivalent to some automaton of $\mathrm{Mod}(\Sigma, \mathbb{T}, X)$ and thus, using the equation $(\dagger)$, A is also equivalent to some automaton of $\mathrm{Mod}(\Sigma, \mathbb{T}, X)$. Theorem 2 is therefore proved.

6 Conclusion

We have proposed in this paper a Kleene-Büchi's theorem for timed languages. We have precisely proved that any timed automaton is equivalent to a timed automaton built on a modular way form basic objects using the operations of union, timed concatenations through subsets of clocks and their induced finite and infinite iterations.

If a timed automaton is given in this modular way, the classical emptiness procedure [2] can also be done in a modular way in parallel with the construction of the automaton, see [8]. Even if the complexity in the worst case is PSPACE (Alur and Dill have shown that the problem is PSPACE-complete), this procedure has given promising much simpler results on some non trivial examples.

References

1. R. Alur, C. Courcoubetis, D.L. Dill, N. Halbwachs, and H. Wong-Toi. Minimization of timed transition systems. In *Proceedings of CONCUR'92*, LNCS 630, 1992.
2. R. Alur and D.L. Dill. A theory of timed automata. *Theoretical Computer Science*, 126:183–235, 1994.
3. R. Alur, L. Fix, and T.A. Henzinger. Event-clock automata: a determinizable class of timed automata. *Theoretical Computer Science*, 211:253–273, 1999.
4. R. Alur and T.A. Henzinger. Back to the future: towards a theory of timed regular languages. In *Proceedings of FOCS'92*, 1992.
5. E. Asarin. Equations on timed languages. In *Proceedings of Hybrid'98*, LNCS, 1998.
6. E. Asarin, P. Caspi and O. Maler. A Kleene theorem for timed automata. In *Proceedings of LICS'97*, 1997.
7. B. Bérard. Untiming timed languages. *Information Processing Letters*, 55:129–135, 1995.
8. P. Bouyer. Automates temporisés et modularité. Rapport de stage de DEA, LSV, ENS de Cachan, 1998.
9. P. Bouyer, and A. Petit. Decomposition and composition of timed automata. Technical report LSV-99-1, LSV, ENS de Cachan, 1999.
10. C. Courcoubetis and M. Yannakakis. Minimum and maximum delay problems in real-time systems. *Formal Methods in System Design*, pages 385–415, 1992.
11. B. Bérard, V. Diekert, P. Gastin, and A. Petit. Characterization of the expressive power of silent transitions in timed automata. *Fundamenta Informaticae*, 36: 145–182, 1998.
12. J.A. Brzozowski. A survey of regular expressions and their applications. In *IRE transactions on Electronic Computers*, EC-11(3): 324–335, 1962.
13. J.R. Büchi. A decision method in restricted arithmetic. In Proc *Int Congr. on Logic, Methodology and Philosophy of Science*, Stanford University, 1960.
14. T.A. Henzinger, P.W. Kopke, and H. Wong-Toi. The expressive power of clocks. In *Proceedings of ICALP'95*, LNCS 944, pages 335–346, 1995.
15. T.A. Henzinger, X. Nicollin, J. Sifakis, and S. Yovine. Symbolic model checking for real-time systems. *Information and Computation*, 111(2):193–244, 1994.
16. S.C. Kleene. Representations of events in nerve and finite automata. *Automata Studies*, Princeton University Press, 3–42, 1956.
17. T. Wilke. Specifying timed state sequences in powerful decidable logics and timed automata. In *Proceedings of Formal Techniques in Real-Time and Fault-Tolerant Systems*, LNCS 863, 1994.
18. H. Wong-Toi and G. Hoffmann. The control of dense real-time discrete event systems. In *Proceedings of the 30th IEEE Conf. on Decision and Control*, pages 1527–1528, 1991.

New Applications of the Incompressibility Method

(*Extended Abstract*)

Harry Buhrman[1], Tao Jiang[2], Ming Li[3], and Paul Vitányi[1]

[1] CWI, Kruislaan 413, 1098 SJ Amsterdam,
The Netherlands, {buhrman,paulv}@cwi.nl
Supported in part via NeuroCOLT II ESPRIT Working Group
[2] Dept of Computing and Software, McMaster University,
Hamilton, Ontario L8S 4K1, Canada, jiang@cas.mcmaster.ca
Supported in part by NSERC and CITO grants
[3] Dept of Computer Science, University of Waterloo,
Waterloo, Ontario N2L 3G1, Canada, mli@math.uwaterloo.ca
Supported in part by NSERC and CITO grants and Steacie Fellowship

Abstract. The incompressibility method is an elementary yet powerful proof technique based on Kolmogorov complexity [13]. We show that it is particularly suited to obtain average-case computational complexity lower bounds. Such lower bounds have been difficult to obtain in the past by other methods. In this paper we present four new results and also give four new proofs of known results to demonstrate the power and elegance of the new method.

1 Introduction

The incompressibility of individual random objects yields a simple but powerful proof technique: *the incompressibility method*. This method is a general purpose tool that can be used to prove lower bounds on computational problems, to obtain combinatorial properties of concrete objects, and to analyze the average complexity of an algorithm. Since the early 1980's, the incompressibility method has been successfully used to solve many well-known questions that had been open for a long time and to supply new simplified proofs for known results. Here we demonstrate how easy the incompressibility method can be used in the particular case of obtaining average-case computational complexity lower bounds. The purpose is to show that our average-case analyses are easy while such analyses using traditional methods are usually more difficult than worst-case analyses.

The Incompressibility Method: A general introduction to the theory and applications of Kolmogorov complexity can be found in [13]. A brief exposition of the basic concepts and notations required in the incompressibility method is also given in [12]. We need the following easy fact (sometimes only implicitly).

Lemma 1. *Let c be a positive integer. For every fixed y, every finite set A contains at least $(1 - 2^{-c})|A| + 1$ elements x with $C(x|A, y) \geq \lfloor \log |A| \rfloor - c$.*

In a typical proof using the incompressibility method, one first chooses an incompressible object (that is, having—almost—maximal Kolmogorov complexity) from the class under discussion. The argument invariably says that if a desired property does not hold for this object, then the object can be compressed. This yields the required contradiction. Furthermore, since most objects are incompressible, the desired property usually holds on average.

Results: We give proofs for new results on: space filling curve fitting lower bounds, multidimensional random walks, communication complexity (average-case[1]) and the number of strings of which the complexity exceeds their length. We give new proofs for known results on: boolean matrix multiplication, majority finding, random walks, and communication complexity (worst case). Our new proofs are much simpler than the old ones.

Related Work: A survey of the use of the incompressibility method is [13] Chapter 6. The most spectacular successes of the method occur in the computational complexity analysis of algorithms. Applications in combinatorics are [14], in random graph theory [5], and a recent average-case analysis of Shellsort is given in [12].

2 Complexity often Exceeds Length

Applications of the incompressibility method sometimes require a large number of totally incompressible strings. Lemma 1 states that there is at least one string of every length n so that $C(x) \geq n$. We show here that this can be strengthened considerably: (i) A positive fraction of all strings of length n have complexity at least n; (ii) There is a fixed constant c such that for every k there is an n with $kc \leq n < (k+1)c$ such that a positive fraction of all strings of length n have complexity exceeding n (here c, k are positive integers). Item (i) can be formulated slightly more general:

Lemma 2. [2] *There is a constant $d > 0$ such that for every n there are at least $\lfloor 2^n/d \rfloor$ strings x of length n with $C(x|n) \geq n$ (respectively, $C(x) \geq n$).*

Proof. It is well-known that there is a constant $c \geq 0$ such that for every n every string x of length n has $C(x|n) \leq n + c$. Hence for every n and every x of length $l(x) \leq n - 2\log(n - l(x)) - c - 1$ we have $C(x|n) \leq C(x|l(x)) + 2\log(n - l(x)) < n$. Consequently, for some constant $c' > 0$ there are at most $2^n - 2^{n-c'}$ programs of length $< n$ available as shortest programs for the strings of length n (there are $2^n - 1$ potential programs and $2^{n-c'} - 1$ thereoff are already taken). Hence there are at least $2^{n-c'}$ strings x of length n with $C(x|n) \geq n$.

In the unconditional case the proof is simpler and for $C(x|l(x)) \leq l(x) + c$ we find that there are at least 2^{n-c} strings x of length n with $C(x) \geq n$. This is

---

[1] As far as we could ascertain there is no written proof of this fact although the result may be known, see Section 7.

[2] A similar result for the *prefix version* $K(\cdot)$ of Kolmogorov complexity (also called *self-delimiting complexity*) is given in [6] using a more complicated argument. Note that neither result implies the other.

because we can dispense with the $2\log(n - l(x))$ term induced by the conditional 'n'. $\square$

Can we prove that the complexity of many strings must *exceed* their lengths? The proof uses an incompressibility argument to show *negative* incompressibility.

Lemma 3. *There are constants $c, d > 0$ such that for every large enough n there are at least $\lfloor 2^n/d \rfloor$ strings x with $n - c \leq l(x) \leq n$ satisfying $C(x|n) > n$ (respectively, $C(x) > n$).*

Proof. **Conditional case:** For every n there are equally many strings of length $\leq n$ to be described and potential programs of length $\leq n$ to describe them. Since some programs do not halt for every large enough n there exists a string x of length at most n such that $n < C(x|n) \leq l(x) + c$.

Let there be $m \geq 1$ such strings. Given m and n we can enumerate all $2^{n+1} - m - 1$ strings x of length $\leq n$ and complexity $C(x|n) \leq n$ by dovetailing the running of all programs of length $\leq n$. The lexicographic first string of length $\leq n$ not in the list, say x, is described by a program p giving m in $\log m$ bits plus an $O(1)$-bit program to do the decoding of x. Therefore, $\log m + O(1) \geq C(x|n) > n$ which proves the theorem for the conditional case.

Unconditional case: This follows similarly by padding the description of x up to length $n + c'$ for a constant c' and adding the description of c' to program p describing x. This way we can first retrieve c' from p and then retrieve n from the length of p. $\square$

So there are lots of strings x that have complexity larger than their lengths. How much larger can this excess get? In the theory of Kolmogorov complexity the laws are invariant with respect to the choice of the particular reference universal Turing machine in the definition of the Kolmogorov complexity, the excess of maximal complexity over the length depends on this choice. Since one can choose a reference universal Turing machine such that $C(x) \leq l(x) + 1$ we cannot generally prove that the excess exceeds 1.

3 Average Time for Boolean Matrix Multiplication

Here is a simple illustration of average-case analysis using the incompressibility method. Consider the well-known problem of multiplying two $n \times n$ boolean matrices $A = (a_{i,j})$ and $B = (b_{i,j})$. Efficient algorithms for this problem have always been a very popular topic in the theoretical computer science literature due to the wide range of applications of boolean matrix multiplication. The best worst-case time complexity obtained so far is $O(n^{2.376})$ due to Coppersmith and Winograd [7]. In 1973, O'Neil and O'Neil devised a simple algorithm described below which runs in $O(n^3)$ time in the worst case but achieves an average time complexity of $O(n^2)$ [19].

Algorithm QuickMultiply(A, B)

1. Let $C = (c_{i,j})$ denote the result of multiplying A and B.
2. For $i := 1$ to n do
3.   Let $j_1 < \cdots < j_m$ be the indices such that $a_{i,j_k} = 1, 1 \leq k \leq m$.
4.   For $j := 1$ to n do
5.   Search the list $b_{j_1,j}, \ldots, b_{j_m,j}$ sequentially for a bit 1.
6.   Set $c_{i,j} = 1$ if a bit 1 is found, or $c_{i,j} = 0$ otherwise.

An analysis of the average-case time complexity of QuickMultiply is given in [19] using probabilitistic arguments. Here we give a simple and elegant proof using incompressibility.

Theorem 1. *Suppose that the elements of A and B are drawn uniformly and independently. Algorithm QuickMultiply runs in $\Theta(n^2)$ time on the average.*

Proof. Let n be a sufficiently large integer. The average time of QuickMultiply is trivially bounded between $\Omega(n^2)$ and $O(n^3)$. By Lemma 1, out of the 2^{2n^2} pairs of $n \times n$ boolean matrices, at least $(n-1)2^{2n^2}/n$ of them are $\log n$-*incompressible* (with Kolmogorov complexities at least $2n^2 - \log n$ bits). Hence, it suffices to consider $\log n$-incompressible boolean matrices.

Take a $\log n$-incompressible binary string x of length $2n^2$, and form two $n \times n$ boolean matrices A and B by having the first half of x correspond to the row-major listing of the elements of A and the second half of x correspond to the row-major listing of the elements of B. We show that QuickMultiply spends $O(n^2)$ time on A and B.

Consider an arbitrary i, where $1 \leq i \leq n$. It suffices to show that the n sequential searches done in Steps 4 – 6 of QuickMultiply take a total of $O(n)$ time. By the statistical results on various blocks in incompressible strings given in Section 2.6 of [13], we know that at least $n/2 - O(\sqrt{n \log n})$ of these searches find a 1 in the first step, at least $n/4 - O(\sqrt{n \log n})$ searches find a 1 in two steps, at least $n/8 - O(\sqrt{n \log n})$ searches find a 1 in three steps, and so on. Moreover, we claim that none of these searches take more than $4 \log n$ steps. To see this, suppose that for some j, $1 \leq j \leq n$, $b_{j_1,j} = \cdots = b_{j_{4 \log n},j} = 0$. Then we can encode x by listing the following items in a self-delimiting manner: (1) A description of the above discussion; (2) The value of i; (3) The value of j; (4) All bits of x except the bits $b_{j_1,j}, \ldots, b_{j_{4 \log n},j}$. This encoding takes at most

$$O(1) + 2\log n + 2n^2 - 4\log n + O(\log \log n) < 2n^2 - \log n$$

bits for sufficiently large n, which contradicts the $\log n$-incompressibility of x.

Hence, the total number of steps required by the n searches is at most

$$\sum_{k=1}^{4 \log n} \left((n/2^k - O(\sqrt{n \log n})) \cdot k \right) + (\log n) \cdot O(\sqrt{n \log n}) \cdot (4 \log n)$$

$$< \sum_{k=1}^{\log n} kn/2^k + O(\log^2 n \sqrt{n \log n})$$

$$= O(n) + O(\log^2 n \sqrt{n \log n}) = O(n). \quad \square$$

4 Space Filling Curves

Niedermeier, Reinhardt and Sanders recently studied the following problem [18]: In an $n \times n$ mesh, consider a computable *curve fitting scheme* that maps the numbers from $\{1, \ldots, n^2\}$ into the mesh, with each number occupying a unique point in the mesh. The goal is to minimize the Euclidean distance between numbers relative to their absolute difference. Many algorithms in parallel computing, computational geometry, and image processing depend on such "locality-preserving" curve fitting schemes for meshes. [18] shows that for any curve fitting scheme, there exists a pair i and j such that $d(i,j) \geq \sqrt{3.5|i-j|} - 1$, where d is Euclidean distance. However, for both theoretical and practical reasons, it would be more interesting to establish distance bounds that hold not only for one pair of i, j's but for "many" pairs. The question of such an "average-case analysis" was open. In fact, many experiments have been performed in the past by researchers in order to determine the average distance between two numbers in a curve fitting scheme [18]. We present the first "average-case" bound here. Our incompressibility argument is in fact simpler than the worst-case analysis in [18].

Theorem 2. *In any computable curve fitting scheme, for each number $1 \leq i \leq n^2$, $d(i,j) \geq \sqrt{0.636|i-j|}$ for $\Omega(n^2)$ different j's. Furthermore, if i is mapped to a corner point, then $d(i,j) \geq \sqrt{2.5|i-j|}$ for $\Omega(n^2)$ different j's.*

Proof. Let $N = n^2$. Consider a computable curve fitting scheme F and let i be a fixed number between 1 and N. Consider incompressible j's satisfying

$$C(j|i, P) \geq \log N, \tag{1}$$

where P is a fixed program to be defined below. It follows from Lemma 2 that there is a constant $c > 0$ such that there are N/c such j's satisfying (1).

Also, we can argue that $|i - j| \leq N/2$ for at least half of the j's. Since if this is not the case, we can change the universal TM in the definition of Kolmogorov complexity by just making the new universal TM print 0 (or 1) whenever the old universal TM prints 1 (or 0, respectively). Then for each j, let $\bar{j}$ be the 1's complement of j, we have either $|i - j| \leq N/2$ or $|i - \bar{j}| \leq N/2$. For all the j's satisfying Inequality (1), if more than half of them do not satisfy $|i - j| \leq N/2$, then we can use the new universal TM such that more than half of the $\bar{j}$'s satisfy $|i - \bar{j}| \leq N/2$. And under the new universal TM, the $\bar{j}$'s satisfy Inequality (1) if the j do so under the old universal TM.

Now given i, an index j can be reconstructed by a fixed program P from a description of at most $\log \pi d(i,j)^2$ bits. [3] [4] Thus, we have

$$\log \pi d(i,j)^2 \geq C(j|i, P) \geq \log N$$

---

[3] Since i and j are placed on the grid points of an $n \times n$ grid the value of $d(i,j)^2$ is an integer. Hence the precise description can be expressed in this claimed number of bits. While it would suffice to describe j by the index of an enumeration of points on the circumference of the disc which would cost $\log 2\pi d(i,j)$ bits this is not possible since $d(i,j)$ is radical.

[4] Here $\pi d(i,j)^2$ is the area of a disc centered on i with radius $d(i,j)$. Since the curve fitting scheme is computable we can enumerate all candidate's for j that are fitted in this circle. The index of j in this enumeration suffices to find j.

for $(N/2c)$-many j's. This implies $d(i,j) \geq \sqrt{N/\pi} \geq \sqrt{2|i-j|/\pi} \approx \sqrt{0.636|i-j|}$ for $(N/2c)$ j's. If F puts i at a corner point, then an index j can in fact be specified by $\log \frac{1}{4}\pi d(i,j)^2$ bits. Carrying out the above calculation, we obtain that

$$d(i,j) \geq \sqrt{4N/\pi} \geq \sqrt{8|i-j|/\pi} \approx \sqrt{2.5|i-j|}$$

for $(N/2c)$-many j's. □

This argument also applies to obtain similar results for other distances (including l_∞ and Manhattan) mentioned in [18].

5 Average Complexity of Finding the Majority

Let $x = x_1 \cdots x_n$ be a binary string. The *majority bit* (or simply, the *majority*) of x is the bit (0 or 1) that occurs more than $\lfloor n/2 \rfloor$ times in x. The majority problem is that, given a binary string x, determine a position i such that x_i is the majority bit of x using only bit comparisons. When x has no majority, we must report so.

The time complexity for finding the majority has been well studied in the literature (see, *e.g.* [1–3, 11, 22]). It is known that, in the worst case, $n - \nu(n)$ bit comparisons are necessary and sufficient [2, 22], where $\nu(n)$ is the number of occurrences of bit 1 in the binary representation of number n. Recently, Alonso, Reingold and Schott [3] studied the average complexity of finding the majority assuming the uniform probability distribution model. Using quite sophisticated arguments based on decision trees, they showed that on the average finding the majority requires at most $2n/3 - \sqrt{8n/9\pi} + O(\log n)$ comparisons and at least $2n/3 - \sqrt{8n/9\pi} + \Theta(1)$ comparisons. Here we present a new simple incompressibility proof establishing an upper bound on the average-case complexity of finding the majority which is precise in the first term. Our proof uses the following standard algorithm.

Algorithm Tournament$(x = x_1 \cdots x_n)$

1. If $n \leq 3$ then find the majority directly.
2. Let $y = \epsilon$.
3. For $i := 1$ to $\lfloor n/2 \rfloor$ do
4.   If $x_{2i-1} = x_{2i}$ then append the bit x_{2i} to y.
5. If n is odd and $\lfloor n/2 \rfloor$ is even then append the bit x_n to y.
6. Call Tournament(y).

Theorem 3. *On the average, algorithm Tournament requires at most $2n/3 + O(\sqrt{n})$ comparisons.*

Proof. Let n be a sufficiently large number. Again, since algorithm Tournament makes at most n comparisons on any string of length n, by Lemma 1, it suffices to consider running time of Tournament on δ-incompressible strings, where $\delta \leq \log n$. Consider an arbitrary $\delta \leq \log n$ and let $x = x_1 \cdots x_n$ be a fixed

δ-incompressible binary string. For any integer $m \leq n$, let $\sigma(m)$ denote the maximum number of comparisons required by algorithm Tournament on any δ-incompressible string of length m.

Among the $\lfloor n/2 \rfloor$ bit pairs $(x_1, x_2), \ldots, (x_{2\lfloor n/2 \rfloor - 1}, x_{2\lfloor n/2 \rfloor})$ that are compared in step 4 of Tournament, there are at least $n/4 - O(\sqrt{n\delta})$ pairs consisting of complementary bits, [13]. Clearly, the new string y obtained at the end of step 4 should satisfy $C(y) \geq l(y) - \delta - O(1)$. Hence, we have the following recurrence relation for $\sigma(m)$:

$$\sigma(m) \leq \lfloor m/2 \rfloor + \sigma(m/4 + O(\sqrt{m\delta}))$$

By straightforward expansion, we obtain that

$$\begin{aligned}
\sigma(n) &\leq \lfloor n/2 \rfloor + \sigma(n/4 + O(\sqrt{n\delta})) \\
&\leq n/2 + \sigma(n/4 + O(\sqrt{n\delta})) \\
&\leq n/2 + (n/8 + O(\sqrt{n\delta})/2) + \sigma(n/16 + O(\sqrt{n\delta})/4 + O(\sqrt{(n\delta)/4})) \\
&= n/2 + (n/8 + O(\sqrt{n\delta})/2) + \sigma(n/16 + (3/4) \cdot O(\sqrt{n\delta})) \\
&\leq \cdots \leq 2n/3 + O(\sqrt{n\delta})
\end{aligned}$$

Using Lemma 1, we can calculate the average complexity of algorithm Tournament as: $\sum_{\delta=1}^{\log n} \frac{1}{2^\delta}(2n/3 + O(\sqrt{n\delta})) + \frac{1}{n}n = 2n/3 + O(\sqrt{n})$ $\square$

6 Multidimensional Random Walks

Consider a random walk in 1 dimension with fixed probability $p = \frac{1}{2}$ of taking a unit step left or right. It is well-known that the maximal distance from the start position in either direction in a random walk of n steps is in the order of $\sqrt{n}$ with high probability. For example, the *Law of the Iterated Logarithm*, [15], says that the limit superior of this distance equals $\sqrt{\frac{1}{2}n \log \log n}$ with probability 1 for n rises unboundedly. In a random walk in $k > 1$ dimensions where each step increases or decreases the distance from the origin by a unit in exactly one dimension in many applications we would like to know the probability of traveling distance d from the origin in any dimension in n steps. Nonetheless, probabilistic analyses of random walks as in [10, 21] apparently are not concerned with flexible tradeoffs between probability (here based on randomness deficiency) [5] and absolute upper or lower bounds on the largest distance traveled from the origin in every dimension as given in the theorem below. These new results may be very useful in applications in the theory of computation.

---

[5] With this approach to random walks we can by varying the complexity of the walk (which implies varying the probability of such a walk in the sense that low complexity has high probability and higher complexity less probability) regulate the possible variation in the distance covered in the walk (high complexity walks have precisely fixed distance while low complexity walks have more uncertainty).

Theorem 4. *Consider a random walk in k dimensions where each step is a unit step in any (but only one at a time) single dimension in positive or negative direction with uniform probability $1/2k$. Let $\delta(\cdot)$ be a monotonic nondecreasing function and let x be a random walk of length n such that $C(x|n) > n - \delta(n)$. If $n \gg k$ then the random walk x has all of the following properties (which therefore hold with probability at least $1 - 1/2^{\delta(n)}$ for a random walk of length n):*

(i) For every dimension, the maximal distance the walk moves away from the starting position in either direction during the walk is $O\left(\sqrt{\frac{n}{k}(\delta(n) + \log\frac{n}{k})}\right)$;

(ii) For every dimension, the maximum distance the walk is away from the starting position in either direction at the end of the walk is $O\left(\sqrt{\delta(n)\frac{n}{k}}\right)$; and

(iii) For every dimension, the minimum distance the walk is away from the starting position in either direction at the end of the walk is $\Omega\left(\sqrt{2^{-\delta(n)}\frac{n}{k}}\right)$.

(iv) For every dimension, the minimum distance the walk is away from the starting position in either direction at the end of an initial m-length segment x' with $x = x'z$ for some z, $C(x'|m) > m - \delta(m)$, and $m \gg k$, is $\Omega\left(\sqrt{2^{-\delta(m)}\frac{m}{k}}\right)$.

Proof. To be given in the full version. $\square$

7 Communication Complexity

Consider the following communication complexity problem (for definitions see the book by Kushilevitz and Nisan [17]). Initially, Alice has a string $x = x_1, \ldots, x_n$ and Bob has a string $y = y_1, \ldots, y_n$ with $x, y \in \{0, 1\}^n$. Alice and Bob use an agreed-upon protocol to compute the inner product of x and y modulo 2

$$f(x, y) = \sum_{i=1}^{n} x_i \cdot y_i \bmod 2$$

with Alice ending up with the result. We are interested in the minimal possible number of bits used in communication between Alice and Bob in such a protocol. Here we prove a lower bound of n, which is tight since the trivial protocol where Bob sends all his n bits to Alice achieves this bound. In [17] the same lower bound is obtained by a different method. We also show an $n - O(1)$ lower bound for the average-case complexity. This lower bound isn't mentioned in [17] and is not implied by the lower bound in in exercise 3.30 in that reference. However, according to [20] exercise 3.30 was proven using a stronger version of our average-case result but the proof may not be written down nor remembered. It seems useful to have a written version as we present below.

Theorem 5. *Assume the discussion above. Every protocol computing the inner product function requires at least n bits of communication.*

Proof. Fix a communication protocol P that computes the inner product. Let A be an algorithm that we describe later. Let z be a string of length $2n$ such that $C(z|A, P, n) \geq 2n$. Let $z = x_1 \ldots x_n y_1 \ldots y_n$ Let Alice's input be $x = x_1 \ldots x_n$

and Bob's input be $y_1 \ldots y_n$. Assume without loss of generality that $f(x, y) = 0$ (the innerproduct of x and y is 0 modulo 2). [6] Run the communication protocol P between Alice and Bob ending in a state where Alice outputs that $f(x, y)$ is 0. Let C be the sequence of bits sent back and forth. Note that P can be viewed as a tree with C a path in this tree [17]. Hence C is self-delimiting. Consider the set S defined by

$$S := \{a : \exists b \text{ such that } P(a, b) = 0 \text{ and induces conversation } C, a, b \in \{0, 1\}^n\}.$$

Given n, P and C, we can compute S. Let the cardinality of S be l. The strings in S form a matrix M over $\mathrm{GF}(2)$ with the ith row of M corresponding to the ith string in S (say in lexicographic ordering). Since for every $a \in S$ it holds that $f(a, y) = 0$ it follows that y is an element of the Null space of M ($y \in \mathrm{Null}(M)$). Application of the Null space Theorem from linear algebra yields:

$$\mathrm{rank}(M) + \dim(\mathrm{Null(M)}) = n. \tag{2}$$

Since the cardinality of S is l and we are working over $\mathrm{GF}(2)$ it follows that the rank of M is at least $\log(l)$ and by (2) it follows that $\dim(\mathrm{Null}(M)) \leq n - \log(l)$. The following is an effective description of z given n and the reconstructive algorithm A explained below:

1. C;
2. the index of $x \in S$ using $\log(l)$ bits; and
3. the index of $y \in \mathrm{Null}(M)$ with $n - \log(l)$ bits.

The three items above can be concatenated without delimiters. Namely, C itself is self-delimiting, while from C one can generate S and hence compute l. From the latter item one can compute the binary length of the index for $x \in S$, and the remaining suffix of the binary description is the index for $y \in \mathrm{Null}(M)$. From the given description and P, n the algorithm A reconstructs x and y and outputs $z = xy$. Consequently, $C(z|A, P, n) \leq l(C) + \log l + (n - \log l)$. Since we have assumed $C(z|A, P, n) \geq 2n$ it follows that $l(C) \geq n$. □

Theorem 6. *The average communication complexity of computing the inner product of two n-bit strings is at least $n - O(1)$ bits.*

8   Acknowledgements

We thank Bill Gasarch for comments, Ian Munro for discussions on related subjects, Rolf Niedermeier for discussions on mesh indexing and their paper [18], and Bill Smyth for introducing us to the paper [3], and Osamu Watanabe for drawing our attention to the random walk problem.

---

[6] If this is not the case, we can simply use a different universal TM U' that does precisely what the current universal TM U does except it flips the first bit of every output. Thus z with first bit flipped would have Kolmogorov complexity $2n$ under U'.

References

1. L. Alexanderson, L.F. Klosinski and L.C. Larson, *The William Lowell Putnam Mathematical Competition, Problems and Solutions: 1965-1984*, Mathematical Association of America, Washington, DC, 1985.
2. L. Alonso, E. Reingold and R. Schott, Determining the majority, *Information Processing Letters* 47, 1993, pp. 253-255.
3. L. Alonso, E. Reingold and R. Schott, The average-case complexity of determining the majority, *SIAM Journal on Computing* 26-1, 1997, pp. 1-14.
4. N. Alon, J.H. Spencer and P. Erdős, *The Probabilistic Method*, Wiley, 1992,
5. H. Buhrman, M. Li, J. Tromp and P.M.B. Vitányi, Kolmogorov Random Graphs and the Incompressibility Method, *SIAM J. Comput*, To appear.
6. G.J. Chaitin, On the number of N-bit strings with maximum complexity, *Applied Mathematics and Computation*, 59(1993), 97–100.
7. D. Coppersmith and S. Winograd. Matrix multiplication via arithmetic progressions. *Proc. of 19th ACM Symp. on Theory of Computing*, 1987, pp. 1-6.
8. C. Domingo, O. Watanabe, T. Yamazaki, A role of constraint in self-organization, *Proc. Workshop on Randomization and Approximation Techniques in Computer Science (RANDOM98)*, LNCS, Springer-Verlag, Heidelberg, 1998, To appear.
9. P. Erdős and J.H. Spencer, *Probabilistic Methods in Combinatorics*, Academic Press, 1974.
10. W. Feller, *An Introduction to Probability Theory and Its Applications, Vols. 1 and 2*, Second Edition, Wiley, 1957.
11. D.H. Greene and D.E. Knuth, *Mathematics for the Analysis of Algorithms*, 3rd ed., Birkhäuser, Boston, MA, 1990.
12. T. Jiang, M. Li, P. Vitányi, Average-Case Complexity of Shellsort, in *these Proceedings*.
13. M. Li and P.M.B. Vitányi, *An Introduction to Kolmogorov Complexity and its Applications*, Springer-Verlag, New York, 2nd Edition, 1997.
14. M. Li and P.M.B. Vitányi, Kolmogorov complexity arguments in combinatorics, *J. Comb. Th., Series A*, 66:2(1994), 226-236. Printing Error, *Ibid.*, 69(1995), 183.
15. A.I. Khinchine, *Fundamenta Mathematicae*, 6(1924), 9–20.
16. A.N. Kolmogorov, Three approaches to the quantitative definition of information. *Problems Inform. Transmission*, 1(1):1-7, 1965.
17. E. Kushilevitz, N. Nisan, *Communication Complexity*, Cambridge Univ. Press, 1997
18. R. Niedermeier, K. Reinhardt, and P. Sanders, Towards optimal locality in Mesh-Indexings. *Proc. FCT'97*, LNCS Vol 1279, Springer-Verlag, 1997, pp. 364-375.
19. P. O'Neil and E. O'Neil. A fast expected time algorithm for boolean matrix multiplication and transitive closure. *Information and Control* 22, 1973, pp. 132-138.
20. N. Nisan, *Personal communication*, 30 Dec. 1998: "I'm not sure where this exercise was proved nor do I remember the details of the proof, but the idea was to take into account the sizes of rectangles when counting the discrepancy on the rectangle."
21. P. Révész, *Random Walk in Random and Non-Random Environments*, World Scientific, Singapore, 1990.
22. M.E. Saks and M. Werman, On computing majority by comparisons, *Combinatorica* 11, 1991, pp. 383-387.

Mobility Types for Mobile Ambients

Luca Cardelli, Giorgio Ghelli, and Andrew D. Gordon

Abstract. An ambient is a named cluster of processes and subambients, which moves as a group. We describe type systems able to guarantee that certain ambients will remain immobile, and that certain ambients will not be dissolved by their environment.

1 Motivation

The ambient calculus [CG98] is a process calculus that focuses primarily on process mobility rather than process communication. An ambient is a named location that may contain processes and subambients, and that can move as a unit inside or outside other ambients. Processes within an ambient may cause their enclosing ambient to move, and may communicate by anonymous asynchronous messages dropped into the local ether. Moreover, processes may open subambients, meaning that they can dissolve an ambient boundary and cause the contents of that ambient to spill into the parent ambient. The ability to move and open ambients is regulated by capabilities that processes must possess by prior knowledge or acquire by communication.

In earlier work [CG99] we studied type systems for the ambient calculus that control the exchange of values during communication. Those type systems are designed to match the communication primitives of the ambient calculus, but are able to express familiar typings for processes and functions. They are therefore successful in showing that the typed ambient calculus is as expressive as typed process and function calculi. Still, those type systems say nothing about process mobility: they guarantee that communication is well-typed wherever it may happen, but do not constrain the movement of ambients.

In this paper we study type systems that control the movement of ambients through other ambients. Our general aim is to discover type systems that can be useful for constraining the mobility behavior of agents and other entities that migrate over networks. Guarantees provided by a type system for mobility could then be used for security purposes, in the sense exemplified by Java bytecode verification [LY97]. The idea of using a type system to constrain dynamic behavior is certainly not new, but this paper makes two main contributions. First, we exhibit type systems that constrain whether or not an ambient is mobile, and whether or not an ambient may be opened. Although previous authors [AP94,RH98,Sew98] use syntactic constraints to determine whether or not a process or location can move, the use of typing to draw this distinction appears to be new. Second, we propose a new mobility primitive as a solution to a problem of unwanted propagation of mobility effects from mobile ambients to those intended to be immobile.

Cardelli and Gordon are at Microsoft Research. Ghelli is at Pisa University.

Section 2 describes our system of mobility and locking annotations. In Section 3 we discuss the mobility primitive mentioned above. Section 4 concludes and surveys related work.

2 Mobility and Locking Annotations

This section explains our basic type system for mobility, which directly extends our previous untyped and typed calculi. Although we assume in this paper some familiarity with the untyped ambient calculus [CG98], we begin by reviewing its main features by example.

The process $a[p[out\ a.in\ b.\langle M\rangle]]\ |\ b[open\ p.(x).Q]$ models the movement of a packet p, which contains a message M, from location a to location b. The process $p[out\ a.in\ b.\langle M\rangle]$ is an ambient named p that contains a single process $out\ a.in\ b.\langle M\rangle$. It is the only subambient of the ambient named a, which itself has a sibling ambient $b[open\ p.(x).Q]$. Terms $out\ a$, $in\ b$, and $open\ p$ are capabilities, which processes exercise to cause ambients to move or to be opened.

In this example, the process $out\ a.in\ b.\langle M\rangle$ exercises the capability $out\ a$, which causes its enclosing ambient, the one named p, to exit its own parent, the one named a, so that $p[in\ b.\langle M\rangle]$ now runs in parallel with the ambients a and b. Next, the process $in\ b.\langle M\rangle$ causes the ambient p to enter b, so that $p[\langle M\rangle]$ becomes a subambient of b. Up to this point, the process $open\ p.(x).Q$ was blocked, but now $open\ p$ can dissolve the boundary p. Finally, the input $(x).Q$ consumes the output $\langle M\rangle$, to leave the residue $a[]\ |\ b[Q\{x\!\leftarrow\!M\}]$, where $Q\{x\!\leftarrow\!M\}$ is the outcome of replacing each occurrence of x in Q with the expression M.

Two additional primitives of our calculus are replication and restriction. Just as in the π-calculus [Mil91], a replication $!P$ behaves the same as an infinite array of replicas of P running in parallel, and a restriction $(\nu n)P$ means: pick a completely fresh name, call it n, then run P.

Operational Semantics We recall the syntax of the typed ambient calculus from [CG99]. This is the same syntax as the original untyped ambient calculus [CG98], except that type annotations are added to the ν and input constructs, and that input and output are polyadic. We explain the types that appear in the syntax in the next section.

Expressions and processes

$M, N ::=$	expressions	$P, Q, R ::=$	processes
n	name	$(\nu n{:}W)P$	restriction
$in\ M$	can enter M	0	inactivity
$out\ M$	can exit M	$P\mid Q$	composition
$open\ M$	can open M	$!P$	replication
ϵ	null M	$M[P]$	ambient
$M.M'$	path	$M.P$	action
		$(x_1{:}W_1,\ldots,x_k{:}W_k).P$	input
		$\langle M_1,\ldots,M_k\rangle$	output

A structural equivalence relation $P \equiv Q$ identifies certain processes P and Q whose behavior ought always to be equivalent:

Structural congruence $(P \equiv Q)$

$$P \mid Q \equiv Q \mid P \qquad\qquad\qquad P \equiv P$$
$$(P \mid Q) \mid R \equiv P \mid (Q \mid R) \qquad Q \equiv P \Rightarrow P \equiv Q$$
$$!P \equiv P \mid !P \qquad\qquad\qquad P \equiv Q, Q \equiv R \Rightarrow P \equiv R$$
$$n \neq m \Rightarrow (\nu n{:}W)(\nu m{:}W')P$$
$$\equiv (\nu m{:}W')(\nu n{:}W)P$$
$$n \notin fn(P) \Rightarrow (\nu n{:}W)(P \mid Q)$$
$$\equiv P \mid (\nu n{:}W)Q \qquad P \equiv Q \Rightarrow (\nu n{:}W)P \equiv (\nu n{:}W)Q$$
$$n \neq m \Rightarrow (\nu n{:}W)m[P] \equiv m[(\nu n{:}W)P] \qquad P \equiv Q \Rightarrow P \mid R \equiv Q \mid R$$
$$P \mid 0 \equiv P \qquad\qquad\qquad P \equiv Q \Rightarrow !P \equiv !Q$$
$$(\nu n{:}Amb^Y[^ZT])0 \equiv 0 \qquad\quad P \equiv Q \Rightarrow M[P] \equiv M[Q]$$
$$!0 \equiv 0 \qquad\qquad\qquad\quad P \equiv Q \Rightarrow M.P \equiv M.Q$$
$$\epsilon.P \equiv P \qquad\qquad\qquad P \equiv Q \Rightarrow (x_1{:}W_1, \ldots, x_k{:}W_k).P$$
$$(M.M').P \equiv M.M'.P \qquad\qquad \equiv (x_1{:}W_1, \ldots, x_k{:}W_k).Q$$

We specify process behavior via a reduction relation, $P \to Q$. The rules on the left describe the effects of, respectively, *in*, *out*, *open*, and communication.

Reduction $(P \to Q)$

$$n[in\ m.P \mid Q] \mid m[R] \to m[n[P \mid Q] \mid R] \qquad P \to Q \Rightarrow P \mid R \to Q \mid R$$
$$m[n[out\ m.P \mid Q] \mid R] \to n[P \mid Q] \mid m[R] \qquad P \to Q \Rightarrow (\nu n{:}W)P \to (\nu n{:}W)Q$$
$$open\ n.P \mid n[Q] \to P \mid Q \qquad\qquad\quad P \to Q \Rightarrow n[P] \to n[Q]$$
$$\langle M_1, \ldots, M_k \rangle \mid (x_1{:}W_1, \ldots, x_k{:}W_k).P \qquad P' \equiv P, P \to Q, Q \equiv Q' \Rightarrow P' \to Q'$$
$$\to P\{x_1 \leftarrow M_1, \ldots, x_k \leftarrow M_k\}$$

The Type System The basic type constructions from [CG99] are the ambient types $Amb[T]$ and the capability types $Cap[T]$. A type of the form $Amb[T]$ describes names that name ambients that allow the exchange of T information within. A type of the form $Cap[T]$ is used to track the opening of ambients: it describes capabilities that may cause the unleashing of T exchanges by means of opening subambients into the current one. An exchange is the interaction of an input and an output operation within the local ether of an ambient. The exchange types, T, can be either *Shh* (no exchange allowed) or a tuple type where each component describes either a name or a capability.

In this paper, we enrich these types with two attributes indicating whether an ambient can move at all, and whether it can be opened. These attributes are intended as two of the simplest properties one can imagine that are connected with mobility. (In another paper [CGG99b] we investigate more expressive and potentially more useful generalizations of these attributes.)

We first describe the locking attributes, Y. An ambient can be declared to be either locked ($\bullet$) or unlocked ($\circ$). Locked ambients can never be opened, while unlocked ambients can be opened via an appropriate capability. The locking attributes are attached to the $Amb[T]$ types, which now acquire the form $Amb^Y[T]$. This means that any ambient whose name has type $Amb^Y[T]$ may (or may not) be opened, and if opened may unleash T exchanges.

We next describe the mobility attributes, Z. In general, a process can produce a number of effects that may be tracked by a type system. Previously we tracked only communication effects, T. We now plan to track both mobility and communication effects by pairs of the form ^ZT, where Z is a flag indicating that a process executes movement operations ($^\frown$) or does not ($^\smile$), and T is as before. A process with effects ^ZT should be allowed to run only within a compatible ambient, whose type will therefore have the form $Amb[^ZT]$. A capability, when used, may now cause communication effects (by open) or mobility effects (by in and out), and its type will have the form $Cap[^ZT]$.

The following table describes the syntax of our types. An ambient type $Amb^Y[^ZT]$ describes the name of an ambient whose locking and mobility attributes are Y and Z, respectively, and which allows T exchanges.

Types

$Y ::=$	locking annotations	$Z ::=$	mobility annotations
$\bullet$	locked	$^\smile$	immobile
$\circ$	unlocked	$^\frown$	mobile
$W ::=$	message types	$T ::=$	exchange types
$Amb^Y[^ZT]$	ambient name	Shh	no exchange
$Cap[^ZT]$	capability	$W_1 \times \cdots \times W_k$	tuple exchange

The type rules are formally described in the next tables. There are three typing judgments: the first constructs well-formed environments, the second tracks the types of messages, and the third tracks the effects of processes. The rules for *in* and *out* introduce mobility effects, and the rule for *open* requires unlocked ambients. The handling of communication effects, T, is exactly as in [CG99].

Good environment $(E \vdash \diamond)$
Good expression of type W $(E \vdash M : W)$
Process with mobility Z **exchanging** T $(E \vdash P : {}^ZT)$

$$\frac{}{\varnothing \vdash \diamond} \qquad \frac{E \vdash \diamond \quad n \notin dom(E)}{E, n{:}W \vdash \diamond} \qquad \frac{E', n{:}W, E'' \vdash \diamond}{E', n{:}W, E'' \vdash n : W}$$

$$\frac{E \vdash \diamond}{E \vdash \epsilon : Cap[^ZT]} \qquad \frac{E \vdash M : Cap[^ZT] \quad E \vdash M' : Cap[^ZT]}{E \vdash M.M' : Cap[^ZT]}$$

$$\frac{E \vdash n : Amb^Y[^ZT]}{E \vdash in\ n : Cap[^\frown T']} \qquad \frac{E \vdash n : Amb^Y[^ZT]}{E \vdash out\ n : Cap[^\frown T']} \qquad \frac{E \vdash n : Amb^\circ[^ZT]}{E \vdash open\ n : Cap[^ZT]}$$

$$\frac{E \vdash M : Cap[^ZT] \quad E \vdash P : {}^ZT}{E \vdash M.P : {}^ZT} \qquad \frac{E \vdash M : Amb^Y[^ZT] \quad E \vdash P : {}^ZT}{E \vdash M[P] : {}^{Z'}T'}$$

$$\frac{E, n{:}Amb^{Y}[^{Z}T] \vdash P : {}^{Z'}T'}{E \vdash (\nu n{:}Amb^{Y}[^{Z}T])P : {}^{Z'}T'} \qquad \frac{E \vdash \diamond}{E \vdash 0 : {}^{Z}T} \qquad \frac{E \vdash P : {}^{Z}T \quad E \vdash Q : {}^{Z}T}{E \vdash P \mid Q : {}^{Z}T}$$

$$\frac{E \vdash P : {}^{Z}T}{E \vdash !P : {}^{Z}T} \qquad \frac{E, n_1{:}W_1, \ldots, n_k{:}W_k \vdash P : {}^{Z}W_1 \times \cdots \times W_k}{E \vdash (n_1{:}W_1, \ldots, n_k{:}W_k).P : {}^{Z}W_1 \times \cdots \times W_k}$$

$$\frac{E \vdash M_1 : W_1 \quad \cdots \quad E \vdash M_k : W_k}{E \vdash \langle M_1, \ldots, M_k \rangle : {}^{Z}W_1 \times \cdots \times W_k}$$

For example, consider the untyped process discussed at the beginning of this section. Suppose that the message M has type W. We can type the process under the assumption that a is a locked, immobile ambient $(Amb^{\bullet}[^{\veebar}Shh])$, that p is an unlocked, mobile ambient $(Amb^{\circ}[^{\frown}W])$, and that b is a locked, mobile ambient $(Amb^{\bullet}[^{\frown}W])$. More formally, under the assumptions $E \vdash a : Amb^{\bullet}[^{\veebar}Shh]$, $E \vdash p : Amb^{\circ}[^{\frown}W]$, $E \vdash b : Amb^{\bullet}[^{\frown}W]$, $E \vdash M : W$, and $E, x{:}W \vdash P : {}^{\frown}W$ we can derive that $E \vdash a[p[out\ a.in\ b.\langle M \rangle]] \mid b[open\ p.(x{:}W).P] : {}^{\veebar}Shh$.

As customary, we can prove a subject reduction theorem asserting the soundness of the typing rules. It can be interpreted as stating that every communication is well-typed, that no locked ambient will ever be opened, and that no in or out will ever act on an immobile ambient. As in earlier work [CG99], the proof is by induction on derivations.

Theorem 1. *If $E \vdash P : {}^{Z}T$ and $P \to Q$ then $E \vdash Q : {}^{Z}T$.*

Remark 1. The type system of [CG99] can be embedded in the current type system by taking $Amb[T] = Amb^{\circ}[^{\frown}T]$ and $Cap[T] = Cap[^{\frown}T]$.

Encoding Channels Communication in the basic ambient calculus happens in the local ether of an ambient. Messages are simply dropped into the ether, without specifying a recipient other than any process that does or will exist in the current ambient. Even within the ambient calculus, though, one often feels the need of additional communication operations, whether primitive or derived.

The familiar mechanism of communication over named channels, used by most process calculi, can be expressed fairly easily in the untyped ambient calculus. We should think, though, of a channel as a new entity that may reside within an ambient. In particular, communications executed on the same channel name but in separate ambients will not interact, at least until those ambients are somehow merged.

The basic idea for representing channels is as follows; see [CG98,CG99] for details. If c is the name of a channel we want to represent, then we use a name c^b to name an ambient that acts as a communication buffer for c. We also use a name c^p to name ambients that act as communication packets directed at c. The buffer ambient opens all the incoming packet ambients and lets their contents interact. So, an output on channel c is represented as a c^p packet that enters c^b (where it is opened up) and that contains an output operation. Similarly, an input on channel c is represented as a c^p packet that enters c^b (where it is opened up) and that contains an input operation; after the input is performed, the rest of the process exits the buffer appropriately to continue execution. The creation of a channel name c is represented as the creation of the two names c^b and c^p. Similarly, the communication of a channel name c is represented as the communication of the two names c^b and c^p.

This encoding of channels can be typed within the type system of [CG99]. Let $Ch[T]$ denote the type of a channel c exchanging messages of type T. This type can be represented as $Amb[T] \times Amb[T]$, which is the type of the pair of names c^b, c^p. Packets named c^p have exchange type T by virtue of performing corresponding inputs and outputs. Buffers named c^p have exchange type T by virtue of opening c^p packets, and unleashing their exchanges.

The natural question now is whether we can type this encoding of channels in the type system given earlier. This can be done trivially by Remark 1, by making all the ambients movable and openable. But this solution is not very satisfactory. In particular, now that we have a type system for mobility, we would like to declare the communication buffers to be both immobile and locked, so that channel communication cannot be disrupted by accidental or malicious activities. Note, for example, that a malicious packet could contain instructions that would cause the buffer to move when the packet is opened. Such a packet should be ruled out as untypable if we made the buffer immobile.

The difficulty with protecting buffers from malicious packets does not arise if we use a systematic translation of a high-level channel abstraction into the lower-level ambient calculus. However, in a situation where code is untrusted (for example, mobile code received from the network), we cannot assume that the ambient-level code interacting with the channel buffers is the image of a high-level abstraction. Thus, we would like to typecheck the untrusted code to make sure that it satisfies the mobility constraints of the trusted environment.

We now encounter a fundamental difficulty that will haunt us for the rest of this section and all of the next. In the type system given earlier, we cannot declare buffers to be immobile, because buffers open packets that are mobile; therefore, buffers are themselves potentially mobile. Packets must, of course, be mobile because they must enter buffers.

We have explored several possible solutions to this problem. In the rest of this section we present a different (more complex) encoding of channels that satisfies several of our wishes. In the next section we add a typed primitive that allows us to use an encoding similar to the original one; this new primitive has other applications as well. In addition, one could investigate more complex type systems that attempt to capture the fact that a well-behaved packet moves once and then becomes immobile, or some suitable generalization of this notion.

The idea for the encoding shown below comes from [CG99], where an alternative encoding of channels is presented. In that encoding there are no buffers; the packets, though, are self-coalescing, so that each packet can act as an exchange buffer for another packet. Here we combine the idea of self-coalescing packets with an immobile buffer that contains them. Since nothing is opened directly within the buffer, the difficulty with constraining the mobility of buffers, described above, disappears. A trace of the difficulty, though, remains in that a process performing an input must be given a mobile type, even when it performs only channel communications.

We formalize our encoding of channels by considering a calculus obtained from the system given earlier by adding operations for creating typed channels $((\nu c{:}Ch[W_1,\dots,W_k])P)$ and for inputs and outputs over them $(c\langle n_1,\dots,n_k\rangle$ and $c(x_1{:}W_1,\dots,x_k{:}W_k).P$, where c is the channel name, and the n_i's are other channel names that are communicated over it). The additional rules for typing channels are as follows:

Channel I/O, where $W = Ch[W_1,\dots,W_k]$

$$\frac{E,n{:}Ch[T] \vdash P : {}^Z T'}{E \vdash (\nu n{:}Ch[T])P : {}^Z T'} \qquad \frac{E \vdash c : W \quad E,x_1{:}W_1,\dots,x_k{:}W_k \vdash P : {}^Z T \quad Z = \frown}{E \vdash c(x_1{:}W_1,\dots,x_k{:}W_k).P : {}^Z T}$$

$$\frac{E \vdash c : W \quad E \vdash M_1 : W_1 \quad \cdots \quad E \vdash_c M_k : W_k}{E \vdash c\langle M_1,\dots,M_k\rangle : {}^Z T}$$

We can translate this extended calculus into the core calculus described earlier. Here, we show the translation of channel types and channel operations; the other types and operations are translated in a straightforward way. We show the complete translation in the full version of this paper [CGG99a].

Expressing channels with ambients

$$\begin{aligned}
[Ch[W_1,\dots,W_k]]^p &= Amb^\circ[\frown [W_1]^b \times [W_1]^p \dots \times [W_k]^b \times [W_k]^p] \\
[Ch[W_1,\dots,W_k]]^b &= Amb^\bullet[\smile Shh] \\
[(\nu c{:}Ch[W_1,\dots,W_k])P] &= (\nu c^b{:}[Ch[W_1,\dots,W_k]]^b) \\
&\quad (\nu c^p{:}[Ch[W_1,\dots,W_k]]^p)(c^b[] \mid [P]) \\
[c\langle n_1,\dots,n_k\rangle] &= c^p[in\ c^b.(!open\ c^p \mid in\ c^p \mid \langle n_1^b,n_1^p,\dots,n_k^b,n_k^p\rangle)] \\
[c(x_1{:}W_1,\dots,x_k{:}W_k).P_{\frown T}] &= (\nu s{:}Amb^\circ[\frown T])(open\ s \mid c^p[in\ c^b.(!open\ c^p \mid in\ c^p \mid \\
&\quad (x_1^b{:}[W_1]^b,x_1^p{:}[W_1]^p,\dots,x_k^b{:}[W_k]^b,x_k^p{:}[W_k]^p). \\
&\quad s[!out\ c^p \mid out\ c^b.[P]])])
\end{aligned}$$

(The translation $[c(x_1{:}W_1,\dots,x_k{:}W_k).P_{\frown T}]$ depends on the type of the process P, which we indicate by the subscript $\frown T$.) Note how a channel named c is encoded by an ambient named c^b whose type is immobile and locked. Therefore, the type system guarantees that the channel cannot be tampered with by rogue processes.

We can show that if $E \vdash P : {}^Z T$ is derivable in the calculus extended with channels then $[E] \vdash [P] : {}^Z [T]$ is derivable in the original calculus, where $[E]$, $[P]$, and $[T]$ are the translations of the environments, processes and exchange types of the extended calculus. Hence, this translation demonstrates a typing of channels in which channels are immobile ambients. However, a feature of this typing is that in an input $c(x_1{:}W_1,\dots,x_k{:}W_k).P$, the process P is obliged to be mobile. The next section provides a type system that removes this obligation.

3 Objective moves

The movement operations of the standard ambient calculus are called "subjective" because they have the flavor of "I (ambient) wish to move there". Other movement operations are called "objective" when they have the flavor of "you (ambient) should move there". Objective moves can be adequately emulated with subjective moves [CG98]: the latter were chosen as primitive on the grounds of expressive power and simplicity.

Certain objective moves, however, can acquire additional interpretations with regard to the typing of mobility. In this section we introduce objective moves, and we distinguish between subjective-mobility annotations (the ones of Section 2) and objective-mobility annotations. It is perhaps not too surprising that the introduction of typing constructs requires the introduction of new primitives. For example, in both the π-calculus and the ambient calculus, the introduction of simple types requires a switch from monadic to polyadic I/O.

We consider an objective move operation that moves to a different location an ambient that has not yet started. It has the form $go\,N.M[P]$ and has the effect of starting the ambient $M[P]$ in the location reached by following, if possible, the path N. Note that P does not become active until after the movement is completed.

Unlike *in* and *out*, this *go* operation does not move the ambient enclosing the operation. Possible interpretations of this operation are to install a piece of code at a given location and then run it, or to move the continuation of a process to a given location.

When assigning a mobility type to the *go* operation, we can now make a subtle distinction. The ambient $M[P]$ is moved, objectively, from one place to another. But after it gets there, maybe the process P never executes subjective moves, and therefore M can be declared subjectively immobile. Moreover, the *go* operation itself does not cause its surrounding ambient to move, so it may also be possible to declare the surrounding ambient subjectively immobile.

Therefore, we can move an ambient from one place to another without noticing any subjective-mobility effects. Still, something got moved, and we would like to be able to track this fact in the type system. For this purpose, we introduce objective-mobility annotations, attached to ambients that may be objectively moved. In particular, an ambient may be objectively mobile, but subjectively immobile.

In conclusion, we achieve the task, impossible in the type system of Section 2, of moving an immobile ambient, once. (More precisely, the possible encodings of the *go* operation in terms of subjective moves are not typable in the type system of Section 2 if we set M to be immobile.) The additional expressive power can be used to give a better typing to communication channels, by causing a communication packet to move into a buffer without requiring the packet to be itself mobile, and therefore without having to require the buffer that opens the packet to be mobile.

To formalize these ideas, we make the following changes to the system of Section 2. Using objective moves we can type an encoding of channels which eliminates the immobility obligation noted at the end of the previous section. Moreover, in the full paper [CGG99a], objective moves are essential for encoding an example language, in which mobile threads migrate between immobile hosts.

Additions to process syntax, structural congruence, and reduction

$P, Q, R ::= go\ N.M[P]$ objective move

    $\cdots$ as in Section 2

$go\ \epsilon.M[P] \equiv M[P]$ $go\ (in\ m.N).n[P] \mid m[Q] \to m[go\ N.n[P] \mid Q]$

$P \equiv Q \Rightarrow$ $m[go\ (out\ m.N).n[P] \mid Q] \to go\ N.n[P] \mid m[Q]$

    $go\ N.M[P] \equiv go\ N.M[Q]$

The types of the system extended with objective moves are the same as the types in Section 2, except that the types of ambient names are $Amb^{Y\,Z'}[^Z T]$, where Y is a locking annotation, T is an exchange type, and Z' and Z are an objective-mobility annotation and a subjective-mobility annotation, respectively.

Modifications and additions to type syntax and typing

$Amb^Y[^Z T]$ becomes $Amb^{Y\,Z''}[^Z T]$ in the syntax of types and in all the rules where it appears. Add the following rule:

$$\frac{E \vdash N : Cap[^{Z'} T'] \quad E \vdash M : Amb^{Y\,Z'}[^Z T] \quad E \vdash P : {}^Z T}{E \vdash go\ N.M[P] : {}^{Z''} T''}$$

Theorem 2. *If $E \vdash P : {}^Z T$ and $P \to Q$ then $E \vdash Q : {}^Z T$.*

4 Conclusions and Related Work

We have argued [CG98,Car99,CG99,GC99] that the idea of an ambient is a useful and general abstraction for expressing and reasoning about mobile computation. In this paper, we qualified the ambient idea by introducing type systems that distinguish between mobile and immobile, and locked and unlocked ambients. Thus qualified, ambients better describe the structure of mobile computations.

The type systems presented in this paper derive from our earlier work on exchange types for ambients [CG99]. That type system tracks the types of messages that may be input or output within each ambient; it is analogous to Milner's sort system for the π-calculus [Mil91], which tracks the types of messages that may be input or output on each channel.

Our mobility annotations govern the ways in which an ambient can be moved. The data movement types of the mobile λ-calculus of Sekiguchi and Yonezawa [SY97] also govern movement, the movement of variables referred to by mobile processes. Their data movement types are checked dynamically, rather than statically. In the setting of the π-calculus, various type systems have been proposed to track the distinction between local and remote references to channels [Ama97,Sew98,SWP98], but none of these systems tracks process mobility.

Our locking annotations allow static checking of a simple security property: that nobody will attempt to open a locked ambient. More complex type systems than ours demonstrate that more sophisticated security properties of concurrent systems can be checked statically: access control [DFPV98,HR98b], allocation of permissions [RH98], and secrecy and integrity properties [Aba97,HR98a,SV98]. Ideas from some of these systems may be applicable to ambients.

References

[Aba97]   M. Abadi. Secrecy by typing in security protocols. In *Proceedings TACS'97*, *LNCS* 1281, pages 611–638. Springer, 1997.

[Ama97]   R. M. Amadio. An asynchronous model of locality, failure, and process mobility. In *Proceedings COORDINATION 97, LNCS* 1282. Springer, 1997.

[AP94]   R. M. Amadio and S. Prasad. Localities and failures. In *Proceedings FST&TCS'94, LNCS* 880, pages 205–216. Springer, 1994.

[Car99]   L. Cardelli. Abstractions for mobile computation. In *Secure Internet Programming, LNCS*. Springer, 1999.

[CG98]   L. Cardelli and A. D. Gordon. Mobile ambients. In *Proceedings FoSSaCS'98*, *LNCS* 1378, pages 140–155. Springer, 1998.

[CG99]   L. Cardelli and A. D. Gordon. Types for mobile ambients. In *Proceedings POPL'99*, pages 79–92. ACM, January 1999.

[CGG99a]   L. Cardelli, G. Ghelli, and A. D. Gordon. Mobility Types for Mobile Ambients. Technical Report, Microsoft Research, 1999 (to appear).

[CGG99b]   L. Cardelli, G. Ghelli, and A. D. Gordon. Ambient groups and mobility types. Unpublished, 1999.

[DFPV98]   R. De Nicola, G. Ferrari, R. Pugliese, and B. Venneri. Types for access control. Submitted for publication, 1998.

[GC99]   A. D. Gordon and L. Cardelli. Equational properties of mobile ambients. In *Proceedings FoSSaCS'99, LNCS* 1578, pages 212–226. Springer, 1999.

[HR98a]   N. Heintz and J. Riecke. The SLam calculus: programming with secrecy and integrity. In *Proceedings POPL'98*, pages 365–377. ACM, 1998.

[HR98b]   M. Hennessy and J. Riely. Resource access control in systems of mobile agents. In *Proceedings HLCL'98, ENTCS* 16(3). Elsevier, 1998.

[LY97]   T. Lindholm and F. Yellin. *The Java Virtual Machine Specification.* Addison-Wesley, 1997.

[Mil91]   R. Milner. The polyadic π-calculus: A tutorial. Technical Report ECS–LFCS–91–180, University of Edinburgh, October 1991.

[RH98]   J. Riely and M. Hennessy. A typed language for distributed mobile processes. In *Proceedings POPL'98*, pages 378–390. ACM, 1998.

[Sew98]   P. Sewell. Global/local subtyping and capability inference for a distributed π-calculus. In *Proceedings ICALP'98, LNCS* 1443, pages 695–706. Springer, 1998.

[SV98]   G. Smith and D. Volpano. Secure information flow in a multi-threaded imperative language. In *Proceedings POPL'98*, pages 355–364. ACM, 1998.

[SWP98]   P. Sewell, P. T. Wojciechowski, and B.C. Pierce. Location independence for mobile agents. In *Workshop on Internet Programming Languages*, 1998.

[SY97]   T. Sekiguchi and A. Yonezawa. A calculus with code mobility. In *Proceedings FMOODS'97*, pages 21–36. IFIP, 1997.

Protein Folding, the Levinthal Paradox and Rapidly Mixing Markov Chains

Peter Clote[*]

Institut für Informatik, Universität München
Oettingenstraße 67, D-80538 München, Germany,
clote@informatik.uni-muenchen.de

Introduction

In [20, 21], A. Šali, E. Shakhnovich and M. Karplus modeled protein folding using a 27-bead heteropolymer on a cubic lattice with normally distributed contact energies; i.e.

$$E = \sum_{1 \leq i < j \leq 27} B_{i,j} \delta(r_{i,j})$$

where $B_{i,j}$ is normally distributed with mean -2 and standard variation 1, $r_{i,j}$ is Euclidean distance between residues i, j, and $\delta(r_{i,j}) = 1$ if $r_{i,j} = 1$ and i, j are not immediate neighbors in the polypeptide chain (i.e. $|i - j| > 1$), else 0.

Using a Monte-Carlo folding algorithm with a local move set between conformations, Šali et al. attempted to answer the Levinthal paradox [13] of how a protein can fold rapidly, i.e. within milliseconds to seconds, despite the magnitude of the conformation space (e.g. approximately $5^{26} \approx 10^{18}$ for the 27-mer). Letting $t_0(P)$ denote the folding time (i.e. *first passage time*) and $\Delta(P)$ denote the energy *gap* between the lowest energy E_{i_0} (native state) and lowest energy E_{i_1} of a misfolded conformation of the protein P with normally distributed contact energy, Šali, Shakhnovich and Karplus observed that $\Delta(P)$ is large exactly when $t_0(P)$ is small.

Using Sinclair's notion of rapid mixing [17] and his modification of the Diaconis-Stroock [6] bound on relative pointwise difference in terms of the subdominant eigenvalue, we provide the first theoretical basis for the principal observation of Šali, Shakhnovich and Karplus. Specifically, we show that the mean first passage time is bounded above by $c_1 \pi_{i_0} \pi_{i_1} + c_2$, where π_{i_0} [resp. π_{i_1}] is the Boltzmann probability of the system being in the native minimum energy state [resp. second minimum]. It follows that this upper bound decreases iff the energy gap $E_{i_1} - E_{i_0}$ increases.[1] From first principles, using the definition of mean first passage time, this is hardly obvious.

---

[*] Research supported by Volkswagen-Stiftung

[1] Our result is somewhat weak, since we prove only that the upper bound for t_0 decreases. As stated in Theorem 1, Sinclair gives both an upper and a lower bound of λ_1 in terms of convergence, hence the upper bound can perhaps be shown to be tight, in which case it would follow that t_0 itself decreases. In any case, our work should be understood as a first mathematical justification for the ŠKK and related observations.

Our result is actually proved for pivot moves (actually, only rotations) with multiple occupancy, rather than local moves, but we are hopeful that our technique can be extended to cover a variant of the model of [20, 21].

1 Markov chains and the second eigenvalue

In this section, we begin with some definitions and well-known results, and state some profound results of Sinclair, relating relative pointwise distance to the second eigenvalue. For undefined concepts, consult Feller [7].

Let P be the transition probability matrix of a (first-order) Markov chain M. M is *irreducible* if for any two states i, j belonging to the state space S of M, there exists n such that $p_{i,j}^{(n)} > 0$. M is *aperiodic* if $d(i) = 1$ for all states $i \in S$, where the period $d(i)$ of state i is the gcd of all $k \geq 1$ such that $p_{i,i}^{(k)} > 0$. If M is irreducible and aperiodic, then there exists n_0 such that P^{n_0} is *positive*, i.e. for all $i, j \in S$, $p_{i,j}^{(n_0)} > 0$. It is well-known that in this case, there exist *stationary* probabilities $p_j^* = \lim_{n \to \infty} p_{i,j}^{(n)}$. In fact, letting

$$d = \max_{\alpha, \beta} \sum_k \max(p_{\alpha,k}^{n_0} - p_{\beta,k}^{n_0}, 0) < 1$$

it can be shown (see [15]) that for all i, $|p_{i,k}^n - p_k^*| \leq d^{n/n_0 - 1}$.

The convergence of an appropriate irreducible, aperiodic Markov chain to stationary probabilities is the basis for the convergence of Monte-Carlo simulations. Namely, define a *neighborhood system* satisfying $i \notin N_i$, $i \in N_j \Leftrightarrow j \in N_i$, $|N_i| = |N_j|$ for all $i, j \in S$. Let $f : S \to \mathbf{R}$ be a function, whose minimum is sought by a Monte-Carlo simulation at temperature T. Define matrix P by setting

$$p_{i,j} = \begin{cases} \frac{\alpha e^{-(f(j)-f(i))/T}}{|N_i|} & \text{if } j \in N_i \text{ and } f(j) > f(i) \\ \frac{\alpha}{|N_i|} & \text{if } j \in N_i \text{ and } f(j) \leq f(i) \\ 0 & \text{if } i \neq j \text{ and } j \notin N_i \\ 1 - \sum_{j \neq i} p_{i,j} & \text{if } i = j. \end{cases}$$

The classic result of Metropolis et al. states that the Markov chain with transition probability matrix P is irreducible and aperiodic, and has the Boltzmann distribution $p_i^* = \frac{e^{-f(i)/T}}{Z}$ as its stationary probability distribution, where the partition function Z satisfies $Z = \sum_{j \in S} e^{-f(j)/T}$. In the sequel, we sometimes denote p_i^* by π_i.

Suppose that $N = P^{n_0}$ is positive, $N^* = \lim_{n \to \infty} N^n$, where P is the transition probability matrix for irreducible, aperiodic Markov chain M.

Let M be a Markov chain with state space S. Following [17], the *relative pointwise distance* is defined as

$$\Delta(t) = \max_{i,j \in S} \frac{|p_{i,j}^{(t)} - p_j^*|}{p_j^*}.$$

Fix a subset $X \subseteq S$ of the state space of Markov chain M. Define *capacity* to be $C_X = \sum_{i \in X} p_i^*$; define the *ergodic flow* out of X to be $F_X = \sum_{i \in X, j \notin X} p_{i,j} p_i^*$. Since $0 < F_X \leq C_X < 1$, the quotient $\Phi_X = F_X / C_X$, may be considered to be the conditional flow out of X, provided the system is in X. The *conductance* $\Phi = \min_{C_X \leq 1/2} \Phi_X$, where the minimum is take over all $X \subseteq S$.

An irreducible, aperiodic Markov chain M with transition probability matrix P is *reversible* if $p_i^* \cdot p_{i,j} = p_j^* \cdot p_{j,i}$ for all $i, j \in S$.

Theorem 1 (A. Sinclair[17]). *Let M be a reversible, irreducible, aperiodic Markov chain, all of whose eigenvalues are non-negative. Then*

$$\Delta(t) \leq \frac{\lambda_1^t}{\min p_i^*}$$

$\lambda_1 < 1$ *is the second largest eigenvalue.[2] Moreover,* $\Delta(t) \leq \frac{(1 - \phi^2/2)^t}{\min \pi_i}$ *and if* $\phi \leq 1/2$ *then* $\Delta(t) \geq (1 - 2\phi)^t$.

With pivot moves (even allowing multiple occupancies), it is clear that the associated Markov chain is reversible. That this is not the case with the chain associated with the local moves of ŠKK, even allowing multiple occupancies, was pointed out by R. Backofen and S. Will (personal communication). It is interesting to note that a modification of approximate bin packing yields a polynomial approximation scheme of the conductance Φ_{CC} when considering subsets of conformations on the compact cube. R. Backofen and S. Will have an even simpler argument for the same result. These points will be covered in the full version of this paper.

2   Relating mean first passage time to energy gap

In this section, we give an application of Sinclair's technique, using his modified form of the Diaconis-Stroock inequality, to provide an upper bound for the subdominant eigenvalue of the transition probability matrix corresponding to a Markov chain for protein folding, using pivot moves with multiple occupancy.

Let S denote the set of all conformations $s = (s_0, \ldots, s_n)$ with multiple, occupancy of the $n + 1$-bead heteropolymer[3] where $s_i \neq s_{i+2}$.[4] It follows that in the case of the 2D [resp. 3D] cubic lattice $|S| = 3^n$ [resp. 5^n]. Assume that $u = (u(0), \ldots, u(n))$, $v = (v(0), \ldots, v(n)) \in S$. Define the *canonical path* $p = (p_1, \ldots, p_m)$ between u, v where all $p_i \in S$, $p_1 = u$, $p_m = v$, $m \leq n$ and for each $i < m$, p_{i+1} is obtained from p_i by performing a *rotation* at the first site j such that $p_i(j) \neq v(j)$. Let P denote the set of all canonical paths between

---

[2] The largest is 1, since $P \cdot (p_1^*, \ldots, p_N^*) = P$, where P is the transition probability matrix for M, and M has N states.

[3] ŠKK consider the 3D cubic lattice. Our analysis is valid for any lattice model - for instance, the 2D cubic or hexagonal, the 3D cubic or face-centered-cubic lattices.

[4] The walk may intersect itself, but may not have consecutive overlapping steps.

ordered pairs (u, v) of distinct conformations. Clearly the length of the longest canonical path is at most n. Given $t = (u, v) \in S \times S$, where v is obtained from u by one move, define $P_t \subseteq P$ to be the set of canonical paths containing edge t. The following lemma illustrates the *injective mapping technique*, introduced by Sinclair [17].

Lemma 1. *With the previous notation, for all $t = (w, w') \in S \times S$, there are at most $|S|$ many paths in P_t.*

PROOF. Suppose that w and w' are identical on sites $0, \ldots, k$ but differ at site $k + 1$. Define $\sigma_k : P_t \times P_t \to S$ by $\sigma_k(u, v) = s$, where

$$s_i = \begin{cases} u_i & 0 \le i \le k \\ s_k + (w_i - w_k) & k + 1 \le i \le n. \end{cases}$$

Then σ_k is injective, since from s, w, w' we can define u, v as follows:

$$u_i = \begin{cases} s_i & 0 \le i \le k \\ s_k + (w_i - w_k) & k + 1 \le i \le n \end{cases}$$

$$v_i = \begin{cases} s_k + (w'_i - w'_k) & 0 \le i \le k \\ s_i & k + 1 \le i \le n. \end{cases}$$

Q.E.D.

Following p. 131 of [17], define

$$b = \max_t \frac{\sum_{p \in P_t} \pi_{p(I)} \cdot \pi_{p(F)}}{\pi_i p_{i,j}}$$

where $t = (i, j)$ and $p(I)$ [resp. $p(F)$] denotes the initial [resp. final] conformation in path p containing edge t. Letting i_0 [resp. i_1] denote the conformation with minimum energy $f(i_0)$ [resp. second lowest energy $f(i_1)$], it is clear that $\pi_{p(I)} \cdot \pi_{p(F)} \le \pi_{i_0} \cdot \pi_{i_1}$. This, together with the previous lemma implies that

$$b \le \frac{|S| \pi_{i_0} \cdot \pi_{i_1}}{c} \tag{1}$$

where $c = \min \pi_i p_{i,j}$, the minimum taken over all pairs (i, j) of conformations, where j is obtained from i by a pivot move.

Modifying work of Diaconis-Stroock [6], Sinclair (cited on p. 131-132 of [17]) proved that $\lambda_1 \le (1 - \frac{1}{b\ell})$ where ℓ is the maximum length of a canonical path. From Theorem 1,

$$\Delta(t) \le \frac{\lambda_1^t}{\min \pi_i}$$

$$\le \frac{(1 - 1/b\ell)^t}{\min \pi_i}$$

$$\le \frac{(1 - c/n|S|\pi_{i_0}\pi_{i_1})^t}{\min \pi_i}.$$

Setting the last inequality to be bounded above by $0 < \epsilon < 1$, and taking logarithms, we find

$$t \ln \left(1 - \frac{c}{n|S|\pi_{i_0}\pi_{i_1}}\right) \leq \ln \epsilon + \ln(\min \pi_i)$$

and so

$$t \leq \frac{\ln \epsilon + \ln(\min \pi_i)}{\ln \left(1 - \frac{c}{n|S|\pi_{i_0}\pi_{i_1}}\right)}.$$

Now

$$\frac{1}{\ln(1-\delta)} = -\frac{1}{\delta} - \frac{1}{2} - \frac{\delta}{12} - \frac{\delta^2}{24} - \frac{19\delta^3}{720} + O(\delta^4).$$

Letting $\delta = \frac{c}{n|S|\pi_{i_0}\pi_{i_1}}$ and dropping higher order terms, we have

$$t \leq (-\ln \epsilon - \ln(\min \pi_i)) \cdot \left(\frac{n|S|\pi_{i_0}\pi_{i_1}}{c} + 1\right). \tag{2}$$

Suppose that $g : S \to \mathbf{R}$ is defined by $g(i) = f(i)$ for $i \neq i_1$ and $g(i_1) > f(i_1)$; i.e. g is identical to f, but the energy gap $\Delta_g = g(i_1) - g(i_0)$ is larger than the energy gap $\Delta_f = f(i_1) - f(i_0)$. Let

$$Z = \sum_{i \in S} e^{-f(i)/T} \qquad\qquad Z' = \sum_{i \in S} e^{-g(i)/T}$$

$$\pi_i = \frac{e^{-f(i)/T}}{Z} \qquad\qquad \pi_i' = \frac{e^{-g(i)/T}}{Z'}$$

$$p_{i,j} = \frac{e^{-(f(j)-f(i))/T}}{N} \qquad\qquad p_{i,j}' = \frac{e^{-(g(j)-g(i))/T}}{N}$$

$$c = \min_{t=(i,j)} \pi_i p_{i,j} \qquad\qquad c' = \min_{t=(i,j)} \pi_i' p_{i,j}'$$

where N is the neighborhood size using pivot moves (for rotation alone, N is 3 in 2D and 5 in 3D).

Lemma 2. *1. $\pi_{i_1} > \pi_{i_1}'$, and for $i \neq i_1$, $\pi_{i_0}' > \pi_{i_0}$.*
2. $\pi_i p_{i,j} < \pi_x p_{x,y} \Leftrightarrow \pi_i' p_{i,j}' < \pi_x' p_{x,y}'$.
3. $\frac{c}{c'} \leq 1$.

The proof is omitted.

Lemma 3. *With the previous notation, if $f(i) = g(i)$ for all $i \in S - \{i_1\}$ and $0 < g(i_1) - f(i_1) < 2\ln\left(\frac{1-\delta}{\delta}\right)$ where $\delta = \frac{e^{-g(i_1)}}{Z'}$, then*

$$\frac{\pi_{i_0}'\pi_{i_1}'}{c'} < \frac{\pi_{i_0}\pi_{i_1}}{c}. \tag{3}$$

Proof of Claim.

$$\frac{\pi'_{i_0}\pi'_{i_1}}{c'} < \frac{\pi_{i_0}\pi_{i_1}}{c} \Leftrightarrow \frac{\pi'_{i_0}}{\pi_{i_0}} \cdot \frac{c}{c'} < \frac{\pi_{i_1}}{\pi'_{i_1}} \Leftrightarrow A \cdot B < C$$

where $A = e^{-(g(i_0)-f(i_0))/T} \cdot \frac{Z}{Z'} = \frac{Z}{Z'}$, since $f(i_0) = g(i_0)$, $B = \frac{c}{c'} \leq 1$, and $C = e^{-(f(i_1)-g(i_1))/T} \cdot \frac{Z'}{Z}$. Letting $a = f(i_1)/T$ and $b = g(i_1)/T$, we have that

$$A \cdot B < C \Leftrightarrow \frac{Z}{Z'} < e^{-a+b} \cdot \frac{Z'}{Z} \Leftrightarrow (Z/Z')^2 < e^{-a+b}.$$

Now $Z = Z' - e^{-b} + e^{-a}$, so

$$(Z/Z')^2 = \left(1 + \frac{e^{-a} - e^{-b}}{Z'}\right)^2 = \left(1 + \frac{e^{-b}(e^{b-a} - 1)}{Z'}\right)^2.$$

Let $x = e^{b-a}$, which is greater than 1 since $b = g(i_1)/T > a = f(i_1)/T$. Letting $\delta = e^{-b}/Z'$, by the quadratic formula it follows that for $1 < x < \left(\frac{1-\delta}{\delta}\right)^2$, we have $(1 - \delta(x-1))^2 < x$, and so in this domain $(Z/Z')^2 < e^{b-a}$. Q.E.D.

It thus follows that for *larger* gap $g(i_1) - g(i_0)$ our upper bound for λ_1 and hence for the relative pointwise distance *decreases*. We now relate relative pointwise distance to mean first passage time.

Following [12], the *fundamental matrix* F is defined by

$$F = (I - (N - N^*))^{-1} = I + \sum_{n=1}^{\infty}(N^n - N^*) = I + \sum_{n=1}^{\infty}(N - N^*)^n.$$

The matrix $\mathcal{M} = (\mu_{i,j})$ of *mean first passage times*, is defined by taking $\mu_{i,j}$ to be the expected number of steps to go from state i to state j. In [12], it is proved that $\mathcal{M} = (I - F + EF_{dg})D$, where I is the identity matrix, E is the matrix, all of whose entries are 1, F_{dg} is obtained from F by setting off-diagonal entries of F to 0, and D is the diagonal matrix with entries $d_{i,i} = 1/p_i^*$. If

$$\Delta(t) = \max_{i \in S} \frac{|p_{i,j}^{(t)} - \pi_j|}{\pi_j} < \epsilon$$

then certainly $|P^t - P^*| < \epsilon \cdot E$, P^t is positive, and $|F| \leq \sum_{i=0}^{\infty}(\epsilon \cdot E)^i$. Suppose that $|S| = N$ so that E is an $N \times N$ matrix, and take $\epsilon < 1/N^2$, so $\epsilon^{1/2} < 1/N$. The following claim is proved by induction.

Claim. For $i \geq 1$, $(\epsilon \cdot E)^i \leq \epsilon^{\frac{n+1}{2}} \cdot E$.

Now, letting $\delta = \epsilon^{1/2}$, it follows that

$$|F| \leq I + \sum_{i=1}^{\infty} \epsilon^{\frac{i+1}{2}} \cdot E = I + E(\frac{1}{1-\delta} - 1 - \delta)$$

and $|I - F| \leq E(\frac{1}{1-\delta} - 1 - \delta)$. Recall that F_{dg} is the diagonal matrix obtained from F by setting off-diagonal values to 0. It follows that $|EF_{dg}| \leq E(\frac{1}{1-\delta} - \delta)$

and so $|I - F + EF_{dg}| \leq |I - F| + |EF_{dg}| \leq E(\frac{2}{1-\delta} - 2\delta - 1)$. Recall that the diagonal matrix D has entries $d_i = 1/p_{i,i}^*$ and 0 off the diagonal. A calculation shows that

$$|(I - F + EF_{dg}) \cdot D| \leq |I - F + EF_{dg}| \cdot |D| \leq \left(\frac{2}{1-\delta} - 2\delta - 1\right) \cdot Q$$

where each row of Q is $(1/p_{1,1}^*, 1/p_{2,2}^*, \ldots, 1/p_{N,N}^*)$. Thus the mean first passage time *after* the t-th step in the Monte-Carlo simulation is bounded by

$$(\frac{2}{1-\delta} - 2\delta - 1) \cdot 1/p_j^*$$

which for $0 < \delta < 1/2$ is at most $2/p_j^*$. Putting things together, we have the following.

Theorem 2. *Let M be a reversible, irreducible, aperiodic Markov chain, all of whose eigenvalues are non-negative and which corresponds to a Monte-Carlo simulation of $n + 1$-bead heteropolymer folding using pivot moves with multiple occupancy. Let N be the size of the state space S of M, $i_0 \in S$ be the native state conformation, and let $c = \min \pi_i p_{i,j}$ where the minimum is taken over all conformations i, j such that j is obtained by a pivot move from i with transition probability $p_{i,j}$. Then the mean first passage time μ_{i,i_0} from random coil conformation i to native state i_0 is bounded above by $c_1 \pi_{i_0} \pi_{i_1} + c_2$, where $c_1 = (nN/c)(2 \ln N - min_{i \in S} \pi_i)$ and $c_2 = (2 \ln N - min_{i \in S} \pi_i) + 2/\pi_{i_0}$.*[5]

PROOF. Given $\epsilon = 1/N^2$, using (2) compute t_0 such that

$$t_0 \leq (-\ln \epsilon - \ln(\min \pi_i)) \cdot \left(\frac{n|S|\pi_{i_0}\pi_{i_1}}{c} + 1\right)$$

and for all larger t, $\Delta(t) \leq \epsilon$. Since $\delta = \epsilon^{1/2} < 1/2$, the expected number of Monte-Carlo steps to visit the native state i_0 from any conformation i at time t_0 is at most $2/\pi_{i_0}$. Finally, $\ln \epsilon < 2 \ln N$. This yields the upper bound with constants c_1, c_2. Finally, by Lemmas 2 and 3, it follows that the energy gap $E_{i_1} - E_{i_0}$ increases iff our upper bound for mean first passage times decreases. This concludes our justification of the ŠKK observation that proteins which fold have a large energy gap between minimum and second minimum energy. Q.E.D.

Note that when the Monte-Carlo temperature is large, the Boltzmann distribution is approximately equal to the uniform distribution, so that $\pi_{i_0} \approx \pi_{i_1} \approx 1/N$. In this case, $p_{i,j} \approx O(\frac{1}{\log N})$ provided there is a pivot transition from conformation i to j, so $c \approx O(\frac{1}{N \log N})$, $c_1 = O(\frac{N \cdot \log^2 N}{N \log N}) = O(\log N)$ and $c_2 = O(N)$. Thus for the uniform distribution, the upper bound $c_1 \pi_{i_0} \pi_{i_1} + c_2$ is $O(\frac{\log N}{N^2} + N) = O(N)$, the Levinthal number. This answers a question of E. Shakhnovich (personal communication).

---

[5] Note that $c_2 \leq 2 \ln N - \pi_{i_0} + 2/\pi_{i_0}$.

Example

The following example may be helpful to understand the mapping $\sigma_k(u, v)$, for a 2D cubic lattice. Consider two heteropolymers u, v with $n = 11$ beads, i.e. a 10-step self-avoiding walks, where u has the form

and v has the form

The following conformations are obtained only by applying rotations, which possibly leads to multiple occupancy conformations. Site 0 is indicated on the figures below. Due to lack of space, we give only the first few moves.

1)

Rotate by π at site 0 to obtain the following.

2)

Rotate by $-\pi/2$ at site 1 to obtain the following.

3)

Rotate by $-\pi/2$ at site 2 to obtain the following.

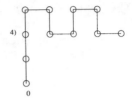

etc. If sites are numbered from $0, \ldots, n = 10$, and $k = 5$, then

$$s_i = \begin{cases} u_i & \text{for } 0 \leq i \leq k = 5 \\ u_k + (v_i - v_k) & \text{for } k + 1 = 6 \leq i \leq n = 11. \end{cases}$$

with figure

One can obtain u, v from s, w, w' by $\sigma_k(u, v) = s$, where

$$u_i = \begin{cases} s_i & \text{for } 0 \leq i \leq k = 5 \\ s_k + (w_i - w_k) & \text{for } k + 1 = 6 \leq i \leq n = 11. \end{cases}$$

and

$$v_i = \begin{cases} s_k + (w'_i - w'_k) & \text{for } 0 \leq i \leq k = 5 \\ s_i & \text{for } k + 1 = 6 \leq i \leq n = 11. \end{cases}$$

Finally, we mention that our simulation results will appear in the final version of this paper.

Acknowledgements

I would like to thank R. Backofen and S. Will, with whom I have discussed over time various aspects of a research program to analyze the runtime for Monte-Carlo simulations of protein folding on lattice models. Though the results of this article were obtained without their collaboration, there are a number of items which we have jointly investigated. I would like to thank E. Bornberg-Bauer and E. Shakhnovich for discussions on various aspects of the HP-model, for copies of their papers and pointers to the literature.

References

1. C.B. Anfinsen. Principles that govern the folding of protein chains. *Science*, 181:223–230, 1973.
2. B. Berger and T. Leighton. *Journal of Computational Biology*.
3. H.S. Chan and K.A. Dill. Compact polymers. *Macromolecules*, 22:4559, 1989.
4. Hue Sun Chan. Kinetics of protein folding. *Nature*, 373:664–665, 23 February 1995. Scientific Correspondence: Criticism to [20].
5. P. Crescenzi, D. Goldman, C. Papadimitriou, A. Piccolboni, and M. Yannakakis. On the complexity of protein folding. *Journal of Computational Biology*, 5(3):523–466, 1998.
6. P. Diaconis and D. Stroock. Geometric bounds for eigenvalues of markov chains. *Annals of Applied Probability*, 1:35–61, 1991.
7. W. Feller. *An introduction to probability theory and its applications*. J. Wiley and Sons, Inc, 1968. Volume 1, Third Edition.
8. W. Hart and S. Istrail. Fast protein folding in the hydrophobic-hydrophobic model within three-eighths of optimal. In *Proceedings of the 27th Annual ACM Symposium on Theory of Computing, Las Vegas*, 1995. 157–168.
9. M. Karplus. Santa Fe, Jan 20–23, 1997.
10. M. Karplus and E. Shakhnovich. Protein folding: theoretical studies of thermodynamics and dynamics. In T.E. Creighton, editor, *Protein Folding*, pages 237–196. iW.H. Freeman and Company, New York, 1992.
11. M. Karplus, A. Šali, and E. Shakhnovich. Kinetics of protein folding. *Nature*, 373:665, 23 February 1995. Scientific Correspondence: Reply to [4].
12. J.G. Kemeny and J.L. Snell. *Finite Markov Chains*. Van Nostrand Company, 1960. 210 pages.
13. C. Levinthal. Are there pathways for protein folding? *J. Chim. Phys.*, 65:44–45, 1968.
14. N. Madras and A.D.Sokol. Nonergodicity of local, length-conserving monte-carlo algorithms for the self-avoiding walk. *J. Stat. Phys.*, 47:573–595, 1987.
15. Y.A. Rozanov. *Probability Theory: A Concise Course*. Dover Publications, Inc., 1977.
16. E. Shakhnovich. Theoretical studies of protein-folding thermodynamics and kinetics. *Current Opinion in Structural Biology*, 7:29–40, 1997.
17. Alistair Sinclair. *Algorithms for random generation and counting: A Markov chain approach*. Birkhäuser, 1993. 146 pages.
18. M. Teeter. An empirical examination of potential energy minimization using the well-determined structure of the protein crambin. *Journal of the American Chemical Society*, 108:7163–7172, 1986.
19. M. Teeter. Water-protein interactions: Theory and experiment. *Annu. Rev. Biophys. Biophys. Chem.*, 20:577–600, 1991.
20. A. Šali, E. Shakhnovich, and M. Karplus. How does a protein fold? *Nature*, 369:248–251, 19 May 1994. Letters to Nature.
21. A. Šali, E. Shakhnovich, and M. Karplus. Kinetics of protein folding: A lattice model study of the requirements for folding to the native state. *J. Molec. Biol.*, 235:1614–1636, 1994.

Decidable Fragments of Simultaneous Rigid Reachability*

Veronique Cortier[1], Harald Ganzinger[2],
Florent Jacquemard[3], and Margus Veanes[2]

[1] École Normale Supérieure de Cachan, dpt Mathématiques
61 Avenue du Président Wilson, 94235 Cachan Cedex, France
`Veronique.Cortier@dptmaths.ens-cachan.fr`
[2] Max-Planck-Institut für Informatik
Im Stadtwald, 66123 Saarbrücken, Germany
`{hg,veanes}@mpi-sb.mpg.de`
[3] LORIA and INRIA, 615 rue du Jardin Botanique,
B.P. 101, 54602 Villers-les-Nancy Cedex, France
`Florent.Jacquemard@loria.fr`

Abstract. In this paper we prove decidability results of restricted fragments of *simultaneous rigid reachability* or *SRR*, that is the nonsymmetrical form of *simultaneous rigid E-unification* or *SREU*. The absence of symmetry enforces us to use different methods, than the ones that have been successful in the context of SREU (for example *word equations*). The methods that we use instead, involve finite (tree) automata techniques, and the decidability proofs provide precise computational complexity bounds. The main results are 1) *monadic SRR with ground rules* is PSPACE-complete, and 2) *balanced SRR with ground rules* is EXPTIME-complete. These upper bounds have been open already for corresponding fragments of SREU, for which only the hardness results have been known. The first result indicates the difference in computational power between fragments of SREU with *ground* rules and *nonground* rules, respectively, due to a straightforward encoding of word equations in monadic SREU (with nonground rules). The second result establishes the decidability and precise complexity of the largest known subfragment of nonmonadic SREU.

1 Introduction

Rigid reachability (RR) is the problem, given a rewrite system R and two terms s and t, whether there exists a substitution θ such that $s\theta$, $t\theta$, and $R\theta$ are ground, and $s\theta$ rewrites in some number of steps via $R\theta$ into $t\theta$. The term "rigid" stems from the fact that for no rule more than one instance can be used in the rewriting process. Simultaneous rigid reachability (SRR) is the problem in which a substitution is sought which simultaneously solves each member of

---
* Full version of this paper is available as: Research Report MPI-I-1999-2-004, Max-Planck-Institut für Informatik.

a system of reachability constraints (R_i, s_i, t_i). A special case of [simultaneous] rigid reachability arises when the R_i are symmetric, containing for each rule $s \rightarrow t$ also its converse $t \rightarrow s$. Such systems arise for example by orienting a set of equations in both directions. The latter problem was introduced by Gallier, Raatz & Snyder [1987] as "simultaneous rigid E-unification" (SREU) in the context of extending tableaux or matrix methods in automated theorem proving to logic with equality. Rigid reachability was initially studied in the context of second-order unification [Farmer 1991, Levy 1998].

Even though the non-simultaneous case of SREU (rigid E-unification) was proved NP-complete by Gallier, Narendran, Plaisted & Snyder [1988], SREU in general was shown by Degtyarev & Voronkov [1995] to be undecidable. Further implications of the latter result are discussed in [Degtyarev, Gurevich & Voronkov 1996]. In a series of papers, SREU has been studied extensively and several sharp boundaries have been laid between its decidable and undecidable fragments. Most recent developments are discussed by Voronkov [1998] and Veanes [1998]. Rigid reachability was shown undecidable by Ganzinger, Jacquemard & Veanes [1998].

The, arguably, most difficult remaining open problem regarding SREU is the decidability of "monadic" SREU, or SREU restricted to signatures where all nonconstant function symbols are unary. The importance of this fragment stems from its close relation to word equations [Degtyarev, Matiyasevich & Voronkov 1996], and to fragments of intuitionistic logic [Degtyarev & Voronkov 1996]. What is known about monadic SREU in general, is that it reduces to a nontrivial extension of word equations [Gurevich & Voronkov 1997]. In the case of ground rules, the decidability of monadic SREU was established in [Gurevich & Voronkov 1997] by reducing it to "word equations with regular constraints". The decidability of the latter problem is an extension of Makanin's [1977] result by Schulz [1990]. Conversely, word equations reduce in polynomial time to monadic SREU [Degtyarev, Matiyasevich & Voronkov 1996]. The first main result of this paper (in Section 3), is that monadic SRR with ground rules is in PSPACE, improving the EXPTIME result in Ganzinger et al. [1998]. Hence, it is unlikely that there is a simple reduction, if any reduction at all, from monadic SREU to monadic SREU with ground rules, or else one would get a considerable simplification of Makanin's [1977] proof. The PSPACE-hardness of monadic SREU with ground rules was shown by Goubault [1994].

To obtain the PSPACE result we use an extension of the intersection nonemptiness problem of a sequence of finite automata that we prove to be in PSPACE. Moreover, using the same proof technique, we can show that simultaneous rigid reachability with ground rules remains in PSPACE, even when just the rules are required to be monadic. Furthermore, in this case PSPACE-hardness holds already for a single constraint with one variable, contrasting the fact that SREU with one variable is solvable in polynomial time [Degtyarev, Gurevich, Narendran, Veanes & Voronkov 1998b].

Our second main result concerns (nonmonadic) SRR with ground rules. In section 4, we show that SRR with ground rules is EXPTIME-complete for "balanced" systems of reachability constraints. Under balanced systems fall for example systems where all occurrences of each variable are at the same depth. It is possible to obtain undecidability of (nonsimultaneous) rigid reachability with ground rules where all but one occurrence of all variables occur at the same depth [Ganzinger et al. 1998]. Moreover, this result generalizes the decidability result by Degtyarev, Gurevich, Narendran, Veanes & Voronkov [1998a] of the largest known decidable fragment of SREU with ground rules and implies EXPTIME-completess of the complexity of this fragment (which is left open in [Degtyarev et al. 1998a]). The key characteristic of solving balanced systems involves finite tree automata techniques over product languages, where it is not necessary to search for solutions encoding a product of a term with its proper subterm. This property is also important in decision procedures for "automata with constraints between brothers" [see, e.g. Comon, Dauchet, Gilleron, Lugiez, Tison & Tommasi 1998].

2   Preliminaries

Rigid Reachability. A *reachability constraint*, or simply a constraint, in a signature Σ, is a triple (R, s, t) where R is a set of rules in Σ, and s and t are Σ-terms. We refer to R, s and t as the *rule set*, the *source term* and the *target term*, respectively, of the constraint. A substitution θ in Σ, *solves* (R, s, t) if θ is grounding for R, s and t, and $s\theta \xrightarrow{*}_{R\theta} t\theta$. The problem of solving constraints is called *rigid reachability*. A system of constraints is *solvable* if there exists a substitution that solves all constraints in that system. *Simultaneous rigid reachability* or *SRR* is the problem of solving systems of constraints. *Monadic* (simultaneous) rigid reachability is (simultaneous) rigid reachability for monadic signatures.

Rigid E-unification is rigid reachability for constraints (E, s, t) with sets of equations E. *Simultaneous Rigid E-unification* or *SREU* is defined accordingly.

Finite tree automata. Finite bottom-up tree automata, or simply, tree automata, from here on, are a generalization of classical automata [Doner 1970, Thatcher & Wright 1968]. Using a rewrite rule based definition [e.g. Coquidé, Dauchet, Gilleron & Vágvölgyi 1994, Dauchet 1993], a *tree automaton* (or *TA*) A is a quadruple (Q, Σ, R, F), where (i) Q is a finite set of constants called *states*, (ii) Σ is a finite *signature* that is disjoint from Q, (iii) R is a system of *rules* of the form $f(q_1, \ldots, q_n) \to q$, where $f \in \Sigma$ has arity $n \geq 0$ and $q, q_1, \ldots, q_n \in Q$, and (iv) $F \subseteq Q$ is the set of *final states*. The *size* of a TA A is $\|A\| = |Q| + |\Sigma| + \|R\|$.

We denote by $L(A, q)$ the set $\{t \in \mathcal{T}_\Sigma \mid t \xrightarrow{*}_R q\}$ of ground terms *accepted* by A in state q. The set of terms *recognized* by the TA A is the set $\bigcup_{q \in F} L(A, q)$. A set of terms is called *recognizable* or *regular* if it is recognized by some TA. A *monadic* TA is a TA with a monadic signature.

Finite string automata. For monadic signatures, we use the traditional, equivalent concepts of alphabets, strings (or words), finite automata, and regular expressions. We will identify an NFA A with alphabet Σ with the set of all rules

$a(q) \to p$, also written as $q \xrightarrow{a}{}_A p$, where there is a transition with label $a \in \Sigma$ from state q to state p in A, and we denote this set of rules also by A. A monadic term $a_1(a_2(\ldots a_n(q)))$ is written, using the *reversed Polish notation*, as the string $q a_n \ldots a_1$.

Then A *accepts a string* $a_1 a_2 \cdots a_n$ if and only if, for some final state q and the initial state q_0 of A, $a_n(\cdots a_2(a_1(q_0))\cdots) \xrightarrow{*}{}_A q$, i.e.,

$$q_0 \xrightarrow{a_1}{}_A q_1 \xrightarrow{a_2}{}_A \cdots \xrightarrow{a_n}{}_A q.$$

The set of all strings accepted by A is denoted by $L(A)$.

Product automata. Let Σ be a signature, m a positive integer, and $\perp$ a new constant. We write $\Sigma_\perp$ for $\Sigma \cup \{\perp\}$ and $\Sigma_\perp^m$ denotes the signature consisting of, for all $f_1, f_2, \ldots, f_m \in \Sigma_\perp$, a unique function symbol $\langle f_1 f_2 \cdots f_m \rangle$ with arity equal to the maximum of the arities of the f_i's.

Let $t_i \in \mathcal{T}_\Sigma \cup \perp$, $t_i = f_i(t_{i1}, \ldots, t_{ik_i})$, where $k_i \geq 0$, for $1 \leq i \leq m$. Let k be the maximum of all the k_i and let $t_{ij} = \perp$ for $k_i < j \leq k$. The *product* $t_1 \otimes \cdots \otimes t_m$ of $t_1, \ldots, t_m$ is defined by recursion on the subterms:

$$t_1 \otimes \cdots \otimes t_m = \langle f_1 f_2 \cdots f_m \rangle (t_{11} \otimes \cdots \otimes t_{1k}, \ldots, t_{m1} \otimes \cdots \otimes t_{mk}) \qquad (1)$$

For example:

$$
\begin{aligned}
f(c, g(c)) \otimes f(g(d), f(c, g(c))) &= \langle f f \rangle (c \otimes g(d), g(c) \otimes f(c, g(c))) \\
&= \langle f f \rangle (\langle cg \rangle (\perp \otimes d), \langle gf \rangle (c \otimes c, \perp \otimes g(c))) \\
&= \langle f f \rangle (\langle cg \rangle (\langle \perp d \rangle), \langle gf \rangle (\langle cc \rangle, \langle \perp g \rangle (\perp \otimes c))) \\
&= \langle f f \rangle (\langle cg \rangle (\langle \perp d \rangle), \langle gf \rangle (\langle cc \rangle, \langle \perp g \rangle (\langle \perp c \rangle)))
\end{aligned}
$$

We write $\mathcal{T}_\Sigma^m$ for the set of all t in $\mathcal{T}_{\Sigma^m}$ such that $t = t_1 \otimes \cdots \otimes t_m$ for some $t_1, \ldots, t_m \in \mathcal{T}_\Sigma \cup \perp$. If $s \in \mathcal{T}_\Sigma^m$ and $t \in \mathcal{T}_\Sigma^n$, where $s = s_1 \otimes \cdots \otimes s_m$ and $t = t_1 \otimes \cdots \otimes t_n$, then $s \otimes t$ denotes the term $s_1 \otimes \cdots \otimes s_m \otimes t_1 \otimes \cdots \otimes t_n$ in $\mathcal{T}_\Sigma^{m+n}$. Given a sequence $t = t_1, \ldots, t_m$ of terms in $\mathcal{T}_\Sigma \cup \perp$, we write $\bigotimes t$ for the product term $t_1 \otimes \cdots \otimes t_m$

Given two automata A_1 and A_2 over $\Sigma_\perp^m$ and $\Sigma_\perp^n$, respectively, the *product* of A_1 and A_2 is an automaton $A_1 \otimes A_2$ over $\Sigma_\perp^{m+n}$ such that

$$L(A_1 \otimes A_2) = L(A_1) \otimes L(A_2) = \{t_1 \otimes t_2 : t_1 \in L(A_1), t_2 \in L(A_2)\}$$

The construction of $A_1 \otimes A_2$ is straightforward, with a state $q_{(q_1, q_2)}$ for all states q_1 in A_1 and q_2 in A_2, [see e.g. Comon et al. 1998]. In general, $\bigotimes_{i=1}^n A_i$ is defined accordingly.

We will use the following construction of Dauchet, Heuillard, Lescanne & Tison [1990] in our proofs.

Lemma 1. *Let R be a ground rewrite system over a signature Σ. There is a TA A such that $L(A) = \{s \otimes t : s, t \in \mathcal{T}_\Sigma, s \xrightarrow{*}{}_R t\}$ that can be constructed in polynomial time from R and Σ.*

3 Monadic SRR

We prove that monadic SRR with ground rules is PSPACE-complete. Our main tool is a decision problem of NFAs, that we define next. In this section we consider only *monadic* signatures.

3.1 Constrained product nonemptiness of NFAs

Given a signature Σ and a positive integer m, we want to select only a certain subset from Σ^m through *selection constraints (bounded by m)*, these are unordered pairs of indices written as $i \approx j$, where $1 \leq i, j \leq m$, $i \neq j$. Given a signature Σ and a set I of selection constraints, we write $\Sigma^m \lfloor I$ for the following subset of Σ^m:

$$\Sigma^m \lfloor I \quad = \quad \{\langle a_1 a_2 \cdots a_m \rangle \in \Sigma^m \quad : \quad (\forall i \approx j \in I)\, a_i = a_j\}$$

For an automaton A, let $A \lfloor I$ denote the reduction of A to the alphabet $\Sigma^m \lfloor I$. We write also $L(A) \lfloor I$ for $L(A \lfloor I)$. The automaton $A \lfloor I$ has the same states as A, and the transitions of $A \lfloor I$ are precisely all the transitions of A with labels from $\Sigma^m \lfloor I$.

We consider the following decision problem, that is closely related to the nonemptiness problem of the intersection of a sequence of NFAs. Consider an alphabet Σ. Let $(A_i)_{1 \leq i \leq n}$, $n \geq 1$, be a sequence of (string product) NFAs over the alphabets $\Sigma_{\perp}^{m_i}$ for $1 \leq i \leq n$, respectively. Let m be the sum of all the m_i and let I be a set of selection constraints. The *constrained product nonemptiness problem of NFAs* is, given $(A_i)_{1 \leq i \leq n}$, and I, to decide if $(\bigotimes_{i=1}^{n} L(A_i)) \lfloor I$ is nonempty. Our key lemma is the following one. Its proof is a straightforward extension of the inclusion part of Kozen's [1977] PSPACE-completess result of the *intersection nonemptiness problem of DFAs*: given a sequence $(A_i)_{1 \leq i \leq n}$ of DFAs, is $\bigcap_{i=1}^{n} L(A_i)$ nonempty?

Lemma 2. *Constrained product nonemptiness of NFAs (or monadic TAs) is in* PSPACE.

The proof of Lemma 2 can be extended in a straightforward manner to finite tree automata. The only difference will be that the algorithm will do "universal choices" when the arity of function symbols (letters) in the component automata is > 1. This leads to *alternating* PSPACE, and thus, by the result of Chandra, Kozen & Stockmeyer [1981], to EXPTIME upper bound for the constrained product nonemptiness problem of TAs.

Although we will not use this fact, it is worth noting that the constrained product nonemptiness problem is also PSPACE-hard, and this so already for DFAs (or monadic DTAs). It is easy to see that $\bigcap_{i=1}^{n} L(A_i)$ is nonempty if and only if $L(\bigotimes_{i=1}^{n} A_i) \lfloor \{i \approx i+1 : 1 \leq i < n\}$ is nonempty.

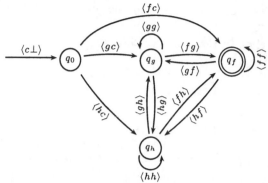

Figure 1: A DFA (or monadic DTA) A that recognizes $\{f(s) \otimes s \ : \ s \in \mathcal{T}_\Sigma\}$, where Σ consists of the unary function symbols f, g, and h, and the constant c. For example A recognizes the string $\langle c\bot\rangle\langle gc\rangle\langle gg\rangle\langle hg\rangle\langle fh\rangle$, i.e., the term $\langle fh\rangle(\langle hg\rangle(\langle gg\rangle(\langle gc\rangle(\langle c\bot\rangle))))$ that is the same as $f(h(g(g(c)))) \otimes h(g(g(c)))$.

3.2 Reduction of monadic SRR with ground rules to constrained product nonemptiness of NFAs

We need the following notion of normal form of a system of reachability constraints. We say that a system S of reachability constraints is *flat*, if each constraint in S is either of the form

- (R, x, t), R is nonempty, x is a variable, and t is a ground term or a variable distinct from x, or of the form
- $(\emptyset, x, f(y))$, where x and y are distinct variables and f is a unary function symbol.

Note that solvability of a reachability constraint with empty rule set is simply unifiability of the source and the target. The following simple lemma is useful.

Lemma 3. *Let S be a system of reachability constraints. There is a flat system that can be obtained in polynomial time from S, that is solvable if and only if S is solvable.*

By using Lemma 2 and Lemma 3 we can now show the following theorem, that is the main result of this section.

Theorem 1. *Monadic SRR with ground rules is PSPACE-complete.*

The crucial step in the proof of Theorem 1 is the construction of an automaton that recognizes the language $\{f(s) \otimes s \ : \ s \in \mathcal{T}_\Sigma\}$. (See Figure 1.) The reason why the proof does *not* generalize to TAs is that the language $\{f(s) \otimes s \ : \ s \in \mathcal{T}_\Sigma\}$ is not regular for nonmonadic signatures. The next example illustrates how the reduction in the proof of Theorem 1 works.

Example 1. Consider a flat system $S = \{\rho_1, \rho_2, \rho_3\}$ with $\rho_1 = (R, y, x)$, $\rho_2 = (\emptyset, y, f(z))$ and $\rho_3 = (\emptyset, z, g(x))$, over a signature $\Sigma = \{f, g, c\}$, where c is a constant. (This system is solvable if and only if the constraint $(R, f(g(x)), x)$ is solvable.)

The construction in the proof of Theorem 1 gives us the monadic TAs A_1, A_2 and A_3 such that

$$L(A_1) = \{s \otimes t : s \xrightarrow[R]{*} t, s, t \in \mathcal{T}_\Sigma\},$$
$$L(A_2) = \{f(s) \otimes s : s \in \mathcal{T}_\Sigma\},$$
$$L(A_3) = \{g(s) \otimes s : s \in \mathcal{T}_\Sigma\},$$

and a set $I = \{1 \approx 3, 5 \approx 4, 6 \approx 2\}$ of selection constraints. So $L(\bigotimes_{i=1}^{3} A_i){\lfloor} I$ is as follows.

$$L(A_1 \otimes A_2 \otimes A_3){\lfloor} I = \{s \otimes t \otimes f(u) \otimes u \otimes g(v) \otimes v :$$
$$s, t, u, v \in \mathcal{T}_\Sigma, \ s \xrightarrow[R]{*} t\}{\lfloor}\{1 \approx 3, 5 \approx 4, 6 \approx 2\}$$
$$= \{s \otimes t \otimes f(u) \otimes u \otimes g(v) \otimes v :$$
$$s, t, u, v \in \mathcal{T}_\Sigma, \ s \xrightarrow[R]{*} t, \ s = f(u), \ g(v) = u, \ v = t\}$$
$$= \{f(g(t)) \otimes t \otimes f(g(t)) \otimes g(t) \otimes g(t) \otimes t :$$
$$t \in \mathcal{T}_\Sigma, \ f(g(t)) \xrightarrow[R]{*} t\}$$

So, solvability of S is equivalent to nonemptiness of $L(A_1 \otimes A_2 \otimes A_3){\lfloor} I$.

3.3 Some decidable extensions of the monadic case

Some restrictions imposed by only allowing monadic function symbols can be relaxed, without losing decidability of SRR for the resulting classes of constraints. One decidable fragment of SRR is obtained by requiring only the rules to be ground and monadic. It can be shown that SRR for this class is still in PSPACE. Furthermore, an easy argument using the intersection nonemptiness problem of DFAs shows that PSPACE-hardness of this fragment holds already for a *single* constraint with *one* variable. This is in contrast with the fact that SREU with one variable and a fixed number of constraints can be solved in polynomial time [Degtyarev et al. 1998*b*].

4 A decidable nonmonadic fragment

In this section, we consider general signatures and give a criteria on the source and target terms of a system of reachability constraints for the decidability of SRR when the rules are ground. Moreover, we prove that SRR is EXPTIME-complete in this case. Our decision algorithm involves essentially tree automata techniques. Let Σ be a signature fixed for the rest of the section.

4.1 Semi-linear sequences of terms

We say that a sequence of terms $(t_1, t_2, \ldots, t_m)$ of (possibly non ground) Σ-terms or $\perp$ is *semi-linear* if one of the following conditions holds for each t_i:

1. t_i is a variable, or
2. t_i is a linear term and no variable in t_i occurs in t_j for $i \neq j$.

Note that if t_i is ground then it satisfies the second condition trivially.

Lemma 4. *Let $(s_1, s_2, \ldots, s_k)$ be a semi-linear sequence of Σ-terms. Then the subset $\{s_1\theta \otimes s_2\theta \otimes \cdots \otimes s_k\theta : \theta$ is a grounding Σ-substitution$\} \subseteq \mathcal{T}_\Sigma^m$ is recognized by a TA the size of which is in $O((\|s_1\| + \|\Sigma\|) \times \ldots \times (\|s_k\| + \|\Sigma\|))$.*

Proof. Let Σ and $s = s_1, s_2, \ldots, s_k$ be given. Let A_i be the TA that recognizes $\{s_i\theta : s_i\theta \in \mathcal{T}_\Sigma\}$ for $1 \leq i \leq k$. The desired TA is $(\bigotimes A_i) \lfloor I$, where I is the set of all selection constraints $i \approx j$ such that s_i and s_j are identical variables. $\boxtimes$

We shall also use the following lemma.

Lemma 5. *Let $A = (\Sigma, Q, R, F)$ be a TA, $s \in \mathcal{T}_\Sigma$, and $p_1, \ldots, p_k$ parallel positions in s. Then there is a TA A', with $\|A'\| \in O(\|A\|^{2k})$, that recognizes the set $\{s_1 \otimes \cdots \otimes s_k : s_1, \ldots, s_k \in \mathcal{T}_\Sigma, s[p_1 \leftarrow s_1, \ldots, p_k \leftarrow s_k] \in L(A)\}$*

4.2 Parallel decomposition of sequences of terms

For technical reasons, we generalize the notion of a product of m terms by allowing *nonground* terms. The resulting term is in an extended signature with $\otimes$ as an additional variadic function symbol. The definition is the same as for ground terms (see (1)), with the additional condition that if one of the t_i's is a variable then

$$t_1 \otimes \cdots \otimes t_m = \otimes(t_1, \ldots, t_m).$$

Consider a sequence $s = s_1, \ldots, s_m$ of terms and let $(\otimes(t_i))_{1 \leq i \leq k}$ be the sequence of all the subterms of the product term $\bigotimes s$ which have head symbol $\otimes$. The *parallel decomposition* of $s = s_1, \ldots, s_m$ or $pd(s)$ is the sequence $(t_i)_{1 \leq i \leq k}$, i.e., we forget the symbol $\otimes$. We need the following technical notion in the proof of Lemma 6: $pdp(s)$ is the sequence $(p_i)_{1 \leq i \leq k}$, where p_i is the position of $\otimes(t_i)$ in $\bigotimes s$.

The following example illustrates these new definitions and lemmas and how they are used.

Example 2. Let $s = f(g(z), g(x))$ and $t = f(y, f(x, y))$ be two Σ-terms, and let R be a ground rewrite system over Σ. We will show how to capture all the solutions of the reachability constraint (R, s, t) as a certain regular set of $\Sigma_\perp^2$-terms. First, construct the product $s \otimes t$.

$$
\begin{aligned}
s \otimes t &= f(g(z), g(x)) \otimes f(y, f(x, y)) \\
&= \langle ff \rangle(g(z) \otimes y, g(x) \otimes f(x, y)) \\
&= \langle ff \rangle(\otimes(g(z), y), \langle gf \rangle(x \otimes x, \perp \otimes y)) \\
&= \langle ff \rangle(\otimes(g(z), y), \langle gf \rangle(\otimes(x, x), \otimes(\perp, y)))
\end{aligned}
$$

The preorder traversal of $s \otimes t$ yields the sequence $\otimes(g(z), y)$, $\otimes(x, x)$, $\otimes(\perp, y)$.

Finally, $pd(s, t)$ is the semi-linear sequence $g(z), y, x, x, \perp, y$. (Note that the sequence $pdp(s, t)$ is 1, 21, 22.) It follows from Lemma 4 that there is a TA A_1 such that $L(A_1) = \{g(z\theta) \otimes y\theta \otimes x\theta \otimes x\theta \otimes \perp \otimes y\theta : \theta \text{ is a grounding } \Sigma\text{-substitution}\}$.

Now, consider a TA A_R that recognizes the product of $\xrightarrow[R]{*}$, see Lemma 1, i.e., $L(A_R) = \{u \otimes v : u \xrightarrow[R]{*} v, \ u, v \in \mathcal{T}_\Sigma\}$. From A_R we can, by using Lemma 5, construct a TA A_2 such that

$$L(A_2) = \{s_1 \otimes s_{21} \otimes s_{22} : s_1, s_{21}, s_{22} \in \mathcal{T}_\Sigma^2, \ \langle ff \rangle(s_1, \langle gf \rangle(s_{21}, s_{22})) \in L(A_R)\}$$

Let A recognize $L(A_1) \cap L(A_2)$. We get that

$$
\begin{aligned}
L(A) &= L(A_1) \cap L(A_2) \\
&= \left\{
\begin{array}{l}
s_1 \otimes s_{21} \otimes s_{22} : (\exists x\theta, y\theta \in \mathcal{T}_\Sigma) \\
\quad s_1 = x\theta \otimes y\theta, \ s_{21} = x\theta \otimes x\theta, \ s_{22} = \perp \otimes y\theta, \\
\quad \langle ff \rangle(s_1, gf(s_{21}, s_{22})) \in L(A_R)
\end{array}
\right. \\
&= \{\theta : \langle ff \rangle(x\theta \otimes y\theta, gf(x\theta \otimes x\theta, \perp \otimes y\theta)) \in L(A_R)\} \\
&= \{\theta : \theta \text{ solves } (R, s, t)\}
\end{aligned}
$$

Hence $L(A) \neq \emptyset$ if and only if (R, s, t) is solvable.

The crucial property that is needed in the example to prove the decidability of the rigid reachability problem is that the parallel decomposition of the sequence consisting of its source and target terms is semi-linear. This observation leads to the following definition.

4.3 Balanced systems with ground rules

A system $((R_1, s_1, t_1), \ldots, (R_n, s_n, t_n))$ of reachability constraints is called *balanced* if the parallel decomposition $pd(s_1, t_1, s_2, t_2, \ldots, s_n, t_n)$ is semi-linear. The proof of Lemma 6 is a generalization of the construction in Example 2.

Lemma 6. *From every balanced system S of reachability constraints with ground rules, we can construct in EXPTIME a TA A such $L(A) \neq \emptyset$ iff S is satisfiable.*

Theorem 2. *Simultaneous rigid reachability is EXPTIME-complete for balanced systems with ground rules.*

Proof. The EXPTIME-hardness follows from [Ganzinger et al. 1998], where we have proved that one can reduce the emptiness decision for intersection of n tree automata to the satisfiability of a rigid reachability constraint $(R, f(x, \ldots, x), f(q_1, \ldots, q_n))$, where R is ground and $q_1, \ldots, q_n$ are constants. $\boxtimes$

The balanced case embeds the case where for each variable x with multiple occurrences in source and target terms, there exists an integer d_x such that x occurs only at positions of length d_x, e.g. with $s_1 = f(x, g(y))$, $t_1 = f(f(y, y), x)$, $s_2 = g(x)$ and $t_2 = g(f(a, z))$. Note that this is a strict subcase of the balanced case, for instance, the system described in example 2, though balanced, does not fulfill this condition.

References

Chandra, A., Kozen, D. & Stockmeyer, L. (1981), 'Alternation', *Journal of the Association for Computing Machinery* **28**(1), 114–133.

Comon, H., Dauchet, M., Gilleron, R., Lugiez, D., Tison, S. & Tommasi, M. (1998), *Tree Automata Techniques and Applications*, unpublished.

Coquidé, J., Dauchet, M., Gilleron, R. & Vágvölgyi, S. (1994), 'Bottom-up tree pushdown automata: classification and connection with rewrite systems', *Theoretical Computer Science* **127**, 69–98.

Dauchet, M. (1993), Rewriting and tree automata, *in* H. Comon & J. Jouannaud, eds, 'Term Rewriting (French Spring School of Theoretical Computer Science)', Vol. 909 of *Lecture Notes in Computer Science*, Springer Verlag, Font Romeux, France, pp. 95–113.

Dauchet, M., Heuillard, T., Lescanne, P. & Tison, S. (1990), 'Decidability of the confluence of finite ground term rewrite systems and of other related term rewrite systems', *Information and Computation* **88**, 187–201.

Degtyarev, A. & Voronkov, A. (1995), Simultaneous rigid *E*-unification is undecidable, UPMAIL Technical Report 105, Uppsala University, Computing Science Department.

Degtyarev, A. & Voronkov, A. (1996), Decidability problems for the prenex fragment of intuitionistic logic, *in* 'Eleventh Annual IEEE Symposium on Logic in Computer Science (LICS'96)', IEEE Computer Society Press, New Brunswick, NJ, pp. 503–512.

Degtyarev, A., Gurevich, Y. & Voronkov, A. (1996), Herbrand's theorem and equational reasoning: Problems and solutions, *in* 'Bulletin of the European Association for Theoretical Computer Science', Vol. 60. The "Logic in Computer Science" column.

Degtyarev, A., Gurevich, Y., Narendran, P., Veanes, M. & Voronkov, A. (1998a), 'Decidability and complexity of simultaneous rigid *E*-unification with one variable and related results', *Theoretical Computer Science*. To appear.

Degtyarev, A., Gurevich, Y., Narendran, P., Veanes, M. & Voronkov, A. (1998b), The decidability of simultaneous rigid *E*-unification with one variable, *in* T. Nipkow, ed., 'Rewriting Techniques and Applications', Vol. 1379 of *Lecture Notes in Computer Science*, Springer Verlag, pp. 181–195.

Degtyarev, A., Matiyasevich, Y. & Voronkov, A. (1996), Simultaneous rigid *E*-unification and related algorithmic problems, *in* 'Eleventh Annual IEEE Symposium on Logic in Computer Science (LICS'96)', IEEE Computer Society Press, New Brunswick, NJ, pp. 494–502.

Doner, J. (1970), 'Tree acceptors and some of their applications', *Journal of Computer and System Sciences* **4**, 406–451.

Farmer, W. (1991), 'Simple second-order languages for which unification is undecidable', *Theoretical Computer Science* **87**, 25–41.

Gallier, J., Narendran, P., Plaisted, D. & Snyder, W. (1988), Rigid *E*-unification is NP-complete, *in* 'Proc. IEEE Conference on Logic in Computer Science (LICS)', IEEE Computer Society Press, pp. 338–346.

Gallier, J., Raatz, S. & Snyder, W. (1987), Theorem proving using rigid *E*-unification: Equational matings, *in* 'Proc. IEEE Conference on Logic in Computer Science (LICS)', IEEE Computer Society Press, pp. 338–346.

Ganzinger, H., Jacquemard, F. & Veanes, M. (1998), Rigid reachability, *in* J. Hsiang & A. Ohori, eds, 'Advances in Computing Science – ASIAN'98, 4th Asian Computing Science Conference, Manila, The Philippines, December 1998, Proceedings', Vol. 1538 of *Lecture Notes in Computer Science*, Springer Verlag, pp. 4–21.

Goubault, J. (1994), Rigid E-unifiability is DEXPTIME-complete, *in* 'Proc. IEEE Conference on Logic in Computer Science (LICS)', IEEE Computer Society Press.

Gurevich, Y. & Voronkov, A. (1997), Monadic simultaneous rigid E-unification and related problems, *in* P. Degano, R. Corrieri & A. Marchetti-Spaccamella, eds, 'Automata, Languages and Programming, 24th International Colloquium, ICALP'97', Vol. 1256 of *Lecture Notes in Computer Science*, Springer Verlag, pp. 154–165.

Kozen, D. (1977), Lower bounds for natural proof systems, *in* 'Proc. 18th IEEE Symposium on Foundations of Computer Science (FOCS)', pp. 254–266.

Levy, J. (1998), Decidable and undecidable second-order unification problems, *in* T. Nipkow, ed., 'Rewriting Techniques and Applications, 9th International Conference, RTA-98, Tsukuba, Japan, March/April 1998, Proceedings', Vol. 1379 of *Lecture Notes in Computer Science*, Springer Verlag, pp. 47–60.

Makanin, G. (1977), 'The problem of solvability of equations in free semigroups', *Mat. Sbornik (in Russian)* **103**(2), 147–236. English Translation in American Mathematical Soc. Translations (2), vol. 117, 1981.

Schulz, K. (1990), Makanin's algorithm: Two improvements and a generalization, *in* K. Schulz, ed., 'Proceedings of the First International Workshop on Word Equations and Related Topics, Tübingen', number 572 *in* 'Lecture Notes in Computer Science'.

Thatcher, J. & Wright, J. (1968), 'Generalized finite automata theory with an application to a decision problem of second-order logic', *Mathematical Systems Theory* **2**(1), 57–81.

Veanes, M. (1998), The relation between second-order unification and simultaneous rigid E-unification, *in* 'Proc. Thirteenth Annual IEEE Symposium on Logic in Computer Science, June 21–24, 1998, Indianapolis, Indiana (LICS'98)', IEEE Computer Society Press, pp. 264–275.

Voronkov, A. (1998), 'Simultaneous rigid E-unification and other decision problems related to Herbrand's theorem', *Theoretical Computer Science*. Article after invited talk at *LFCS'97*.

Text Compression Using Antidictionaries[*]

M. Crochemore[**,1], F. Mignosi[2], A. Restivo[2], and S. Salemi[2]

[1] Institut Gaspard-Monge mac@univ-mlv.fr
[2] Università di Palermo [mignosi,restivo]@altair.math.unipa.it

Abstract. We give a new text compression scheme based on Forbidden Words ("antidictionary"). We prove that our algorithms attain the entropy for balanced binary sources. They run in linear time. Moreover, one of the main advantages of this approach is that it produces very fast decompressors. A second advantage is a synchronization property that is helpful to search compressed data and allows parallel compression. Our algorithms can also be presented as "compilers" that create compressors dedicated to any previously fixed source. The techniques used in this paper are from Information Theory and Finite Automata.
Keywords: data compression, information theory, finite automaton, forbidden word, pattern matching.

1 Introduction

We present a simple text compression method called DCA (Data Compression with Antidictionaries) that uses some "negative" information about the text, which is described in terms of antidictionaries. Contrary to other methods that make use, as a main tool, of dictionaries, *i.e.*, particular sets of words occurring as factors in the text (cf. [7], [15], [17], [19] and [20]), our method takes advantage from words that do not occur as factor in the text, *i.e.*, that are forbidden. Such sets of words are called here antidictionaries.

We describe a static compression scheme that runs in linear time (Sections 2 and 3) including the construction of antidictionaries (Section 5). Variations using statistical or dynamical considerations are discussed in the conclusion (Section 6)

Let w be a text on the binary alphabet $\{0, 1\}$ and let AD be an antidictionary for w. By reading the text w from left to right, if at a certain moment the current prefix v of the text admits as suffix a word u' such that $u = u'x \in AD$ with $x \in \{0, 1\}$, *i.e.*, u is forbidden, then surely the letter following v in the text cannot be x and, since the alphabet is binary, it is the letter $y \neq x$. In other terms, we know in advance the next letter y, that turns out to be redundant or predictable. The main idea of our method is to eliminate redundant letters in order to achieve compression. The decoding algorithm recovers the text w by predicting the letter following the current prefix v of w already decompressed.

The method proposed here presents some analogies with ideas discussed by C. Shannon at the very beginning of Information Theory. In [18] Shannon designed

---

[*] DCA home page at URL http://www-igm.univ-mlv.fr/~mac/DCA.html
[**] Work by this author is supported in part by Programme "Génomes" of C.N.R.S.

psychological experiments in order to evaluate the entropy of English. One of such experiments was about the human ability to reconstruct an english text where some characters were erased. Actually our compression method erases some characters and the decompression reconstruct them.

We prove (Section 4) that the compression rate of our compressor reaches the entropy almost surely, provided that the source is balanced and produced from a finite antidictionary. This type of source approximates a large class of sources, and consequently, a variant of the basic scheme gives an optimal compression for them. The idea of using antidictionaries is founded on the fact that there exists a topological invariant for Dynamical Systems based on forbidden words, invariant that is independent of the entropy [4].

The use of the antidictionary AD in coding and decoding algorithms requires that AD must be structured in order to answer to the following query on a word v: does there exists a word $u = u'x$, $x \in \{0, 1\}$, in AD such that u' is a suffix of v? In the case of positive answer the output should also include the letter y defined by $y \neq x$. One of the main features of our method is that we are able to implement efficiently finite antidictionaries in terms of finite automata. This leads to fast linear-time compression and decompression algorithms that can be realized by sequential transducers (generalized sequential machines). This is especially relevant for fixed sources. It is then comparable to the fastest compression methods because the basic operation at compression and decompression time is just table lookup.

A central notion of the present method is that of minimal forbidden words, which allows to reduce the size of antidictionaries. This notion has also some interesting combinatorial properties. Our compression method includes algorithms to compute antidictionaries, algorithms that are based on the above combinatorial properties and that are described in details in [8] and [9].

The compression method shares also an interesting synchronization property, in the case of finite antidictionaries. It states that the encoding of a block of data does not depend on the left and right contexts except for a limited-size prefix of the encoded block. This is also helpful to search compressed data and the same property allows to design efficient parallel compression algorithms.

2 Basic Algorithms

Let us first introduce the main ideas of our algorithm on its static version. We discuss variations of this first approach in Section 6.

Let w be a finite binary word and let $F(w)$ be the set of factors of w. For instance, if $w = 01001010$ then $F(w) = \{\varepsilon, 0, 1, 00, 01, 10, 001, 010, 100, 101, \ldots\}$ where ε denotes the empty word.

Let us take some words in the complement of $F(w)$, i.e., let us take some words that are not factors of w and that we call *forbidden*. The set of such words AD is called an *antidictionary* for the language $F(w)$. Antidictionaries can be finite as well infinite. For instance, if $w = 01001010$ the words 11, 000, and 10101 are forbidden and the set $\{000, 10101, 11\}$ is an antidictionary for $F(w)$.

The compression algorithm treats the input word in an on-line manner. At a certain step in this process we have read the word v proper prefix of w. If there exists one word $u = u'x$, $x \in \{0, 1\}$, in the antidictionary AD such that u' is a suffix of v, then surely the letter following v cannot be x, i.e., the next letter is y, $y \neq x$. In other words, we know in advance the next letter y that turns out to be "redundant" or predictable. Remark that this argument works only in the case of binary alphabets.

The main idea in the algorithm we describe is to eliminate redundant letters. In what follows we first describe the compression algorithm, ENCODER, and then the decompression algorithm, DECODER. The word to be compressed is noted $w = a_1 \cdots a_n$ and its compressed version is denoted by $\gamma(w)$.

ENCODER (anti-dictionary AD, word $w \in \{0, 1\}^*$)
1. $v \leftarrow \varepsilon$; $\gamma \leftarrow \varepsilon$;
2. **for** $a \leftarrow$ first to last letter of w
3.   **if** for every suffix u' of v, $u'0, u'1 \notin AD$
4. $\gamma \leftarrow \gamma.a$;
5. $v \leftarrow v.a$;
6. **return** $(|v|, \gamma)$;

Remark that the function γ is not injective. In order to have an injective mapping we can consider the function $\gamma'(w) = (|w|, \gamma(w))$. In this case we can reconstruct the original word w from both $\gamma'(w)$ and the antidictionary.

The decoding algorithm works as follow. The compressed word is $\gamma(w) = b_1 \cdots b_h$ and the length of w is n. The algorithm recovers the word w by predicting the letter following the current prefix v of w already decompressed. If there exists one word $u = u'x$, $x \in \{0, 1\}$, in the antidictionary AD such that u' is a suffix of v, then, the output letter is y, $y \neq x$. Otherwise, the next letter is read from the input γ.

DECODER (anti-dictionary AD, word $\gamma \in \{0, 1\}^*$, integer n)
1. $v \leftarrow \varepsilon$;
2. **while** $|v| < n$
3.   **if** for some u' suffix of v and $x \in \{0, 1\}$, $u'x \in AD$
4. $v \leftarrow v \cdot \neg x$;
5.   **else**
6. $b \leftarrow$ next letter of γ;
7. $v \leftarrow v \cdot b$;
8. **return** (v);

The antidictionary AD must be structured in order to answer to the following query on a word v: does there exist one word $u = u'x$, $x \in \{0, 1\}$, in AD such that u' is a suffix of v? In case of a positive answer the output should also include the letter y defined by $y \neq x$. Notice that the letter x considered at line 3 is unique because, at this point, the end of the text w has not been reached so far.

In this approach, where the antidictionary is static and available to both the encoder and the decoder, the encoder must send to the decoder the length of the word $|w|$, in addition to the compressed word $\gamma(w)$, in order to give to the decoder a "stop" criterium. Light variations of previous compression-decompression algorithm can be easily obtained by giving other "stop" criteria. For instance the encoder can send the number of letters that the decoder have to reconstruct after that the last letter of the compressed word $\gamma(w)$ has been read. Or the encoder can let the decoder stop when there is no more letter available in γ (line 6), or when both letters are impossible to be reconstructed according to AD. Doing so, the encoder must send to the decoder the number of letters to erase in order to recover the original message. For such variations antidictionaries can be structured to answer sligthly more complex queries.

In order to get good compression rates (at least in the static approach when the antidictionary has to be sent) we need to minimize in particular the size of the antidictionary. Remark that if there exists a forbidden word $u = u'x$, $x \in \{0, 1\}$ in the antidictionary such that u' is also forbidden then our algorithm will never use this word u in the algorithms. So that we can erase this word from the antidictionary without any loss for the compression of w. This argument leads to consider the notion of *minimal forbidden word* with respect to a factorial language L, and the notion of anti-factorial language, points that are discussed in the next section.

3   Implementation of Finite Antidictionaries

The queries on the antidictionary required by the algorithms of the previous section are realized as follows. We build a deterministic automaton accepting the words having no factor in the antidictionary. Then, while reading the text to encode, if a transition leads to a sink state, the output is the other letter. We denote by $\mathcal{A}(AD)$ the automaton built from the antidictionary AD. An algorithm to build $\mathcal{A}(AD)$ is described in [8] and [9]. The same construction has been discovered by Choffrut *et al.* [6], it is similar to a description given by Aho-Corasick ([1], see [12]), by Diekert *et al.* [13], and it is related to a more general construction given in [5].

The wanted automaton accepts a factorial language L. Recall that a language L is factorial if L satisfies the following property: for any words, u, v, $uv \in L \Rightarrow$ $u \in L$ and $v \in L$. The complement language $L^c = A^* \setminus L$ is a (two-sided) ideal of A^*. Denoting by $MF(L)$ the base of this ideal, we have $L^c = A^* MF(L) A^*$. The set $MF(L)$ is called the set of *minimal forbidden words* for L. A word $v \in A^*$ is forbidden for the factorial language L if $v \notin L$, which is equivalent to say that v occurs in no word of L. In addition, v is minimal if it has no proper factor that is forbidden.

One can note that the set $MF(L)$ uniquely characterizes L, just because $L = A^* \setminus A^* MF(L) A^*$. This set $MF(L)$ is an *anti-factorial language* or a *factor code*, which means that it satisfies: $\forall u, v \in MF(L)$ $u \neq v \Longrightarrow u$ is not a factor of v, property that comes from the minimality of words of $MF(L)$. Indeed, there is a duality between factorial and anti-factorial languages, because we also have the equality: $MF(L) = AL \cap LA \cap (A^* \setminus L)$. After the note made at the end of the previous section, from now on in the paper, we consider only antidictionaries that are anti-factorial languages.

The following theorem is proved in [9]. It is based on an algorithm that has AD as (finite) input, either in the form of a list of words or in the form of a trie $\mathcal{T}$ representing the set. The algorithm can be adapted to test whether $\mathcal{T}$ represents an anti-factorial set, to generate the trie of the anti-factorial language associated with a set of words, or even to built the automaton associated with the anti-factorial language corresponding to any set of words.

Theorem 1. *The construction of* $\mathcal{A}(AD)$ *can be realized in linear time.*

Transducers From the automaton $\mathcal{A}(AD)$ we can easily construct a (finite-state) transducer $\mathcal{B}(AD)$ that realizes the compression algorithm ENCODER. *i.e.*, that computes the function γ. The input part of $\mathcal{B}(AD)$ coincides with $\mathcal{A}(AD)$, with sink states removed, and the output is given as follows: if a state of $\mathcal{A}(AD)$ has two outgoing edges, then the output labels of these edges coincide with their input label; if a state of $\mathcal{A}(AD)$ has only one outgoing edge, then the output label of this edge is the empty word.

Theorem 2. *Algorithm* ENCODER *can be realized by a sequential transducer (generalized sequential machine).*

As to concern the algorithm DECODER, remark (see Section 2) that the function γ is not injective and that we need some additional information, for instance the length of the original uncompressed word, in order to reconstruct it without ambiguity. Therefore, DECODER can be realized by the same transducer as above, by interchanging input and output labels (denote it by $B'(AD)$), with a supplementary instruction to stop the decoding.

The constructions and the results given above on finite antidictionaries and transducers can be generalized also to the case of rational antidictionaries, or, equivalently, when the set of words "produced by the source" is a rational language.

A Synchronization Property In the sequel we prove a synchronization property of automata built from finite antidictionaries, as described above. This property also "characterizes" in some sense finite antidictionaries. This property is a classical one and it is of fundamental importance in practical applications.

Definition 1. *Given a deterministic finite automaton* $\mathcal{A}$, *we say that a word* $w = a_1 \cdots a_k$ *is synchronizing for* $\mathcal{A}$ *if, whenever* w *represents the label of two paths* $(q_1, a_1, q_2) \cdots (q_k, a_k, q_{k+1})$ *and* $(q'_1, a_1, q'_2) \cdots (q'_k, a_k, q'_{k+1})$ *of length* k, *then the two ending states* q_{k+1} *and* q'_{k+1} *are equal.*

If $L(\mathcal{A})$ is factorial, any word that does not belong to $L(\mathcal{A})$ is synchronizing. Clearly in this case synchronizing words in $L(\mathcal{A})$ are much more interesting. Remark also that, since $\mathcal{A}$ is deterministic, if w is synchronizing for $\mathcal{A}$, then any word $w' = wv$ that has w as prefix is also synchronizing for $\mathcal{A}$.

Definition 2. *A deterministic finite automaton A is local if there exists an integer k such that any word of length k is synchronizing. Automaton A is also called k-local.*

Given a finite antifactorial language AD, let $A(AD)$ be the automaton associated with AD as described before that recognizes the language $L(AD)$. Let us eliminate the sink states and edges going to them. Since there is no possibility of misunderstanding, we denote the resulting automaton by $A(AD)$ again.

Theorem 3. *Let AD be a finite antifactorial antidictionary and let k be the length of the longest word in AD. Then automaton $A(AD)$ associated to AD is $(k-1)$-local.*

In other terms, the theorem says that only the last $k-1$ bits matter for determining whether AD is avoided or not. The theorem admits a "converse" that shows that locality characterizes in some sense finite antidictionaries (cf. Propositions 2.8 and 2.14 of [3]).

Theorem 4. *If automaton A is local and $L(A)$ is a factorial language then there exists a finite antifactorial language AD such that $L(A) = L(AD)$.*

Let AD be an antifactorial antidictionary and let k be the length of the longest word in AD. Let also $w = w_1 u v w_2 \in L(AD)$ with $|u| = k - 1$ and let $\gamma(w) = y_1 y_2 y_3$ be the word produced by our encoder of Section 2 with input AD and w. The word y_1 is the word produced by our encoder after processing $w_1 u$, the word y_2 is the word produced by our encoder after processing v and the word y_3 is the word produced by our encoder after processing w_2.

The proof of next theorem is an an easy consequence of previous definitions and of the statement of Theorem 3.

Theorem 5. *The word y_2 depends only on the word uv and it does not depend on the contexts of it, w_1 and w_2.*

The property stated in the theorem has an interesting consequence for the design of pattern matching algorithms on words compressed by the algorithm EN-CODER. It implies that, to search the compressed word for a pattern, it is not necessary to decode the whole word. Just a limited left context of an occurrence of the pattern needs to be processed (cf. [10]). The same property allows the design of highly parallizable compression algorithms. The idea is that the compression can be performed independently and in parallel on any block of data. If the text to be compressed is parsed into blocks of data in such a way that each block overlaps the next block by a length not smaller than the length of the longest word in the antidictionary, then it is possible to run the whole compression process.

4   Efficiency

In this section we evaluate the efficiency of our compression algorithm relatively to a source corresponding to the finite antidictionary AD.

Indeed, the antidictionary AD defines naturally a source $S(AD)$ in the following way. Let $\mathcal{A}(AD)$ be the automaton constructed in the previous section with no sink states and that recognizes the factorial language $L(AD)$ (all states are terminal). To avoid trivial cases we suppose that in this automaton all the states have at least one outgoing edge. Recall that, since our algorithms work on a binary alphabet, all the states have at most two outgoing edges.

For any state of $\mathcal{A}(AD)$ with only one outgoing edge we give to this edge probability 1. For any state of $\mathcal{A}(AD)$ with two outgoing edge we give to these edges probability 1/2. This defines a deterministic (or unifilar, cf. [2]) Markov source, denoted $S(AD)$. Notice also that, by Theorem 3, that $S(AD)$ is a Markov source of finite order or finite memory (cf. [2]). We call a binary Markov source with this probability distribution an *balanced source*.

In what follows we suppose that the graph of the source S, i.e., the graph of automaton $\mathcal{A}(AD)$, is strongly connected. The results that we prove can be extended to the general case by using standard techniques of Markov Chains (cf. [2] and [16]). Recall (cf. Theorem 6.4.2 of [2]) that the entropy $H(S)$ of a deterministic markov source S is $H(S) = -\Sigma_{i,j=1}^{n}\mu_i\gamma_{i,j}\ log_2(\gamma_{i,j})$, where $(\gamma_{i,j})$ is the stochastic matrix of S and $(\mu_1,\cdots,\mu_n)$ is the stationary distribution of S.

Lemma 1. *The entropy of an balanced source S is given by $H(S) = \Sigma_{i\in D}\mu_i$ where D is the set of all states that have two outgoing edges.*

Lemma 2. *Let $w = a_1\cdots a_m$ be a word in $L(AD)$ and let $q_1\cdots q_{m+1}$ be the sequence of states in the path determined by w in $\mathcal{A}(AD)$ starting from the initial state. The length of $\gamma(w)$ is equal to the number of states q_i, $i = 1,\ldots,m$, that belong to D, where D is the set of all states that have two outgoing edges.*

Through a well-known results on "large deviations" (cf. Problem IX.6.7 of [14]), we get a kind of optimality of the compression scheme.

Theorem 6. *The compression rate $\tau(\mathbf{x})$ of an infinite sequence $\mathbf{x}$ emitted by the source $S(AD)$ reaches the entropy $H(S(AD))$ almost surely.*

5   How to build Antidictionaries

In practical applications the antidictionary is not *a priori* given but it must be derived either from the text to be compressed or from a family of texts belonging to the same source to which the text to be compressed is supposed to belong.

There exist several criteria to build efficient antidictionaries that depend on different aspects or parameters that one wishes to optimize in the compression process. Each criterium gives rise to different algorithms and implementations.

All our methods to build antidictionaries are based on data structures to store factors of words, such as, suffix tries, suffix trees, DAWGs, and suffix and factor automata (see for instance Theorem 15 in [9]). In these structures, it is possible to consider a notion of suffix link. This link is essential to design efficient algorithms to build representations of sets of minimal forbidden words in term of tries or trees. This approach leads to construction algorithms that run in linear time according to the length of the text to be compressed.

A rough solution to control the size of antidictionaries is obviously to bound the length of words in the antidictionary. A better solution in the static compression scheme is to prune the trie of the antidictionary with a criterion based on the tradeoff between the space of the trie to be sent and the gain in compression. However, the first solution is enough to get compression rates that reach asymptotically the entropy for balanced sources, even if this is not true for general sources. Both solutions can be designed to run in linear time.

Algorithms for the purpose of this section cannot be described in this extended abstract because of lack of space.

6 Conclusion

In the previous section we presented a static compression scheme in which we need to read twice the text. Starting from the static scheme, several variations and improvements can be proposed. These variations are all based on clever combinations of two elements that can be introduced in our model:

a) statistic considerations,
b) dynamic approaches.

These are classical features that are often included in other data compression methods.

Statistic considerations are used in the construction of antidictionaries. If a forbidden word is responsible of "erasing" few bits of the text in the compression algorithm of Section 2 and its "description" as an element of the antidictionary is "expensive" then the compression rate improves if it is not included in the antidictionary. On the contrary, one can introduce in the antidictionary a word that is not forbidden but that occurs very rarely in the text. In this case, the compression algorithm will produce some "errors" or "mistakes" in predicting the next letter. In order to have a lossless compression, encoder and decoder must be adapted to manage of such "errors". Typical "errors" occur in the case of antidictionaries built for fixed sources as well as in the dynamic approach. Even with "errors", assuming that they are rare with respect to the longest word (length) of the antidictionary, our compression scheme preserves the synchronization property of Theorem 3.

Antidictionaries for fixed sources have also an intrinsic interest. A compressor generator, or compressor compiler can create, starting from words obtained by a source S an antidictionary that can be used to compress all the other words from the same source S, taking into account possible "errors" in predicting the next letter.

In the dynamic approach we construct the antidictionary and we encode the text at the same time. The antidictionary is constructed (also with statistical consideration) by considering the part of text previously read. The antidictionary can change at any step and the algorithmic rules for its construction must be known in advance by both encoder and decoder. They can be derived from the description of a compressor compiler (cf. [11]).

We have realized prototypes of the compression and decompression algorithms. They also implement the dynamic version of the method. They have been tested on the Calgary Corpus (see next table). and experiments show that we get compression ratios equivalent to those of most common compressors (such as pkzip for example).

File	original size (in bytes)	compressed size (in bytes)
bib	111261	35535
book1	768771	295966
book2	610856	214476
geo	102400	79633
news	377109	161004
obj1	21504	13094
obj2	246814	111295
paper1	53161	21058
paper2	382199	2282
pic	513216	70240
progc	39611	15736
progl	71646	20092
progp	49379	13988
trans	93695	22695

We have described DCA, a text compression method that uses some "negative" information about the text, that is described in terms of antidictionaries. The advantages of the scheme are:

- it is fast at decompressing data.
- it produces compressor generators (compressor compilers) for fixed sources.
- it is fast at compressing data for fixed sources.
- it has a synchronization property in the case of finite antidictionaries. property that leads to efficient parallel compression and to search engines on compressed data.

We are considering several generalizations:

- compressor schemes and implementations of antidictionaries on more general alphabets (including, for instance, arithmetic coding).
- use of lossy compression especially to deal with images.
- combination of DCA with other compression schemes; for instance, using both dictionaries and antidictionaries like positive and negative sets of examples as in Learning Theory.
- design of chips dedicated to fixed sources.

Acknowledgements We thanks M.P. Béal. F.M. Dekking and R. Grossi for useful discussions and suggestions.

References

1. A. V. Aho, M. J. Corasick. Efficient string matching: an aid to bibliographic search. *Comm. ACM* 18:6 (1975) 333–340.
2. R. Ash. *Information Theory.* Tracts in mathematics, Interscience Publishers, J. Wiley & Sons, 1985.
3. M. P. Béal. *Codage Symbolique.* Masson, 1993.
4. M.-P. Béal, F. Mignosi, A. Restivo. Minimal Forbidden Words and Symbolic Dynamics. in (*STACS'96*, C. Puech and R. Reischuk, eds., LNCS 1046, Springer, 1996) 555–566.
5. J. Berstel, D. Perrin. Finite and infinite words. in (*Algebraic Combinatorics on Words*, J. Berstel, D. Perrin, eds., Cambridge University Press, to appear) Chapter 1. Available at http://www-igm.univ-mlv.fr/ berstel.
6. C. Choffrut, K. Culik. On Extendibility of Unavoidable Sets. Discrete Appl. Math., 9, 1984, 125-137.
7. T. C. Bell, J. G. Cleary, I. H. Witten. *Text Compression.* Prentice Hall, 1990.
8. M. Crochemore, F. Mignosi, A. Restivo. Minimal Forbidden Words and Factor Automata. in (*MFCS'98*, L. Brim, J. Gruska, J. Slatuška, eds., LNCS 1450, Springer, 1998) 665–673.
9. M. Crochemore, F. Mignosi, A. Restivo. Automata and Forbidden Words. *Information Processing Letters* 67 (1998) 111–117.
10. M. Crochemore, F. Mignosi, A. Restivo, S. Salemi. Search in Compressed Data. in preparation.
11. M. Crochemore, F. Mignosi, A. Restivo, S. Salemi. A Compressor Compiler. in preparation.
12. M. Crochemore, W. Rytter. *Text Algorithms.* Oxford University Press, 1994.
13. V. Diekert, Y. Kobayashi. *Some Identities Related to Automata, Determinants, and Möbius Functions.* Report Nr. 1997/05, Universität Stuttgart, Fakultät Informatik, 1997.
14. R. S. Ellis. *Entropy, Large Deviations, and Statistical Mechanics.* Springer Verlag, 1985.
15. J. Gailly. *Frequently Asked Questions in data compression,* Internet. At the present time available at URL http://www.landfield.com/faqs/compression-faq/
16. J. G. Kemeny, J. L. Snell. *Finite Markov Chains.* Van Nostrand Reinhold, 1960.
17. M. Nelson, J. Gailly. *The Data Compression Book.* M&T Books, New York, NY, 1996. 2nd edition.
18. C. Shannon. Prediction and entropy of printed english. *Bell System Technical J.,* 50-64, January, 1951.
19. J. A. Storer. *Data Compression: Methods and Theory.* Computer Science Press, Rockville, MD, 1988.
20. I. H. Witten, A. Moffat, T. C. Bell. *Managing Gigabytes.* Van Nostrand Reinhold, 1994.

Non-interactive Zero-Knowledge:
A Low-Randomness Characterization of NP

(Extended Abstract)

A. De Santis[1]   G. Di Crescenzo[2]   G. Persiano[1]

[1] Dipartimento di Informatica ed Applicazioni,
Università di Salerno, 84081 Baronissi (SA), Italy
E-mail: {ads,giuper}@dia.unisa.it

[2] Telcordia Technologies, Morristown, NJ, USA
(Work done while visiting Università di Salerno.)
E-mail: giovanni@research.telcordia.com

Abstract. We show that any language L in NP has a non-interactive zero-knowledge proof system which uses $\Theta(\log(1/s) + n^\epsilon)$ random bits, where s is the soundness error, n the length of the input and ϵ can be any constant > 0. In order to achieve this result, we formulate and investigate the problem of randomness-efficient error reduction for non-interactive zero-knowledge proofs, which generalizes the analogue and well-studied problem for BPP computation.

1   Introduction

The class of languages NP is often defined in terms of a proof system between a computationally unbounded prover and a polynomial-time bounded verifier. On input string x, a candidate for membership to a language L, the prover computes a witness w of size polynomial in $|x|$. The verifier, given w, can efficiently verify that $x \in L$. Several variants of such proof systems for NP have been extensively studied in the literature: interactive proofs [20], interactive zero-knowledge proofs [20], non-interactive zero-knowledge proofs [4, 3], probabilistically checkable proofs [13], multi-prover interactive proofs [2] etc.

In non-interactive zero-knowledge proof systems, as for the NP proof system, the proof consists in a single message sent by the prover to the verifier. The additional ingredient is a public random string which helps in computing and verifying the proof; furthermore, the prover convinces the verifier that $x \in L$ with high probability and the verifier does not obtain any additional information he could not compute before. Since randomness is essential in order to achieve the zero-knowledge property (both in the interactive and non-interactive models, see [18, 10]), the non-interactive model for zero-knowledge proofs seems a minimal enough setting for extending the NP proof system in order to achieve the zero-knowledge property. Then the question of how much randomness is essential to this purpose comes out naturally and both lower and upper bounds have appeared in the literature. In this paper we present a non-interactive zero-knowledge proof system for any language in NP which dramatically improves the known upper bounds and gets very close to the known lower bound for some values of the parameters. The main tool in achieving this result consists in formulating and studying the problem of "randomness-efficient error reduction" for non-interactive zero-knowledge (NIZK), that can be seen as a generalization of the analogue problem of pseudo-random generation for BPP computation.

BPP computation and NIZK proofs. The scenario for non-interactive zero-knowledge and the one for BPP computation present some analogies, as we now explain. In the BPP case, the scenario is the following. A random string σ is used by a polynomial-time algorithm A to decide whether an input string x belongs to a certain language L. Here, the algorithm A, on input (σ, x), outputs a bit b such that the probability that $b = \chi_L(x)$ is sufficiently high. In the NIZK case, the scenario is the following. A random string σ is used by an algorithm P to prove whether an input string x belongs to a certain language L. Here, the algorithm P, on input (σ, x), outputs a string π such that the probability that a polynomial-time algorithm V, on input (σ, x, π), verifies that $x \in L$ is sufficiently high. Moreover, the string π does not reveal any knowledge to V other than the fact that $x \in L$.

The problem of randomness-efficient error reduction for BPP computation has been widely studied in the literature (see, e.g., [24]). In this paper we address the problem of randomness-efficient error reduction for the scenario of non-interactive zero-knowledge proofs, as a natural extension from the BPP computation scenario. Namely, given a non-interactive zero-knowledge proof system using a public random string of length, say, r, and achieving soundness error $1/2$, the problem asks to construct a non-interactive zero-knowledge proof system achieving soundness error 2^{-k} (thus giving an error reduction) and using a public random string of length smaller than rk, or, as small as possible (thus giving a randomness-efficient error reduction). We stress that the transformation obtained by directly applying any of the techniques for randomness-efficient error reduction of BPP algorithms does not seem to preserve zero-knowledge.

Our results. We present a non-interactive zero-knowledge proof system for any language in NP using a public random string of length $\Theta(n^\epsilon + \log(1/s))$, for any constant $\epsilon > 0$, where by s we denote the soundness error of the proof system. This performance is optimal (up to a constant) for $s \leq 2^{-n^\epsilon}$ for any $\epsilon > 0$, unless NP=BPP, since it matches the lower bound of $\Omega(\log(1/s) + \log n)$ given in [10]. The zero-knowledge property of our proof system is based on the the intractability of deciding quadratic residuosity modulo composite integers. Previously, non-interactive zero-knowledge proof systems for NP-complete languages have been proposed in [3, 4, 14, 22, 23, 8, 6, 10] and had much larger randomness complexity, the most efficient one using $\Theta(n^\epsilon(p(n) + \log(1/s)))$ random bits, where $p(n)$ is an upper bound on the size of the circuit verifying that $x \in L$.

We consider the problem of randomness-efficient error reduction for non-interactive zero-knowledge both in the computational and in the perfect case (to the best of our knowledge, this problem has never been considered in the literature). In the computational case, assuming the existence of pseudo-random generators only, we present a randomness-efficient procedure that returns a proof system for which the length of the public random string is optimal (up to a constant) with respect to the soundness error. In the perfect case, under no unproven assumption, we present a randomness-efficient procedure which returns proof systems for several languages based on quadratic residuosity which use a shorter public random string than the known protocols in the literature.

Due to lack of space, all formal proofs are omitted.

2 Definitions

We recall definitions for non-interactive zero-knowledge proofs and some background on number-theory, pseudo-random generators and BPP computation.

Non-Interactive Zero-Knowledge. We start by defining non-interactive proof systems, by also parameterizing the completeness and the soundness error.

Definition 1. Let P a probabilistic Turing machine and V a deterministic Turing machine that runs in time polynomial in the length of its second input. We say that (P,V) is a *non-interactive proof system* with parameters (c, s, r) for the language L if the following properties hold:

1. *Completeness.* $\forall x \in L$, it holds that
   $$\text{Prob}\,[\,\sigma \leftarrow \{0,1\}^r; Proof \leftarrow P(\sigma, x): V(\sigma, x, Proof) = 1\,] \geq c.$$
2. *Soundness.* $\forall x \notin L$, for all Turing machines P', it holds that
   $$\text{Prob}\,[\,\sigma \leftarrow \{0,1\}^r; Proof \leftarrow P'(\sigma, x): V(\sigma, x, Proof) = 1\,] \leq s.$$

Define probability space $View(x) = \{\sigma \leftarrow \{0,1\}^r; Proof \leftarrow P(\sigma, x): (\sigma, Proof)\}$. Now we give the definitions of non-interactive computational and perfect zero-knowledge proof systems.

Definition 2. Let (P,V) be a non-interactive proof system with parameters (c, s, r) for the language L. We say that (P,V) is a *non-interactive computational zero-knowledge proof system* with parameters (c, s, r) for the language L if there exists an efficient algorithm S, called the *Simulator*, such that $\forall x \in L$, $|x| = n$, for all efficient non-uniform algorithms D_n, $\forall d > 0$, and all sufficiently large n,
$$|\,\text{Prob}\,[\,s \leftarrow View(x) : D_n(s) = 1\,] - \text{Prob}\,[\,s \leftarrow S(x) : D_n(s) = 1\,]\,| < n^{-d}.$$

Definition 3. Let (P,V) be a non-interactive proof system with parameters (c, s, r) for the language L. We say that (P,V) is a *non-interactive perfect zero-knowledge proof system* with parameters (c, s, r) for the language L if there exists an efficient algorithm S, called the *Simulator*, such that $\forall x \in L$, the probability spaces $S(x)$ and $View(x)$ are equal.

Definition 4. Let (P,V) be a non-interactive proof system (resp., computational zero-knowledge proof system) (resp., perfect zero-knowledge proof system) with parameters (c, s, r) for the language L. We say that (P,V) is a *non-interactive proof system* (resp., *computational zero-knowledge proof system*) (resp., *perfect zero-knowledge proof system*) if it holds that $r = O(n^b)$, for some constant b, and $c = 1 - n^{-\omega(1)}$ and $s = n^{-\omega(1)}$, where n is the length of the common input.

We call the random string σ, input to both P and V, the *reference string*.

Number Theory: Quadratic Residuosity and Blum integers. We say that $y \in Z_x^*$ is a *quadratic residue* modulo x if and only if there is a $w \in Z_x^*$ such that $w^2 \equiv y \bmod x$. If this is not the case, then y is a *quadratic non residue* modulo x. An integer x is a *Blum integer*, in symbols $x \in BL$, if and only if $x = p^{k_1} q^{k_2}$, where p and q are different primes both $= 3 \bmod 4$, and k_1 and k_2 are odd integers. The quadratic residuosity predicate of an integer $y \in Z_x^*$ can be defined as $Q_x(y) = 0$ if y is a quadratic residue modulo x and 1 otherwise. The quadratic residuosity intractability assumption is as follows.

Quadratic Residuosity Assumption (QRA): For each efficient non-uniform algorithm $\{C_n\}_{n \in \mathcal{N}}$, all constants $d > 0$, and all sufficiently large n,

$$\text{Prob}\left[x \leftarrow BL; |x| = n, \ y \leftarrow Z_x^{+1} : C_n(x, y) = Q_x(y) \right] < 1/2 + n^{-d}.$$

We refer to [3, 10] for properties of Blum integers and quadratic residuosity.

Pseudo-random generators. A pseudo-random generator [5] is a very popular cryptographic tool, having several applications also in the construction of protocols, as zero-knowledge proofs. Informally, a pseudo-random generator is a deterministic function that, given as input a short seed of random bits, returns an output polynomially longer than the seed, and such that the output is polynomially indistinguishable from a truly random string of the same length. In the sequel, we will denote as (a, b)-*pseudo-random generator* a pseudo-random generator with domain $\{0, 1\}^a$ and codomain $\{0, 1\}^b$, where $a < b$.

Randomness-efficient error reduction for BPP computation. The problem of constructing randomness-efficient error reductions for BPP algorithms has received a lot of attention in the literature (see [24] for a survey). Informally, solutions to this problem are given by constructions of generators who expand a short truly random string into a longer one, which satisfies a particular pseudo-random property; roughly speaking, the generator outputs many strings of a certain length, and with high probability at least one of such strings belongs to an a-priori fixed set. In this paper we will use a construction for such pseudo-random generators as a black box. Therefore, we consider the following

Definition 5. Let a, b, k be integers. We say that a function $G : \{0, 1\}^a \to \{0, 1\}^{kb}$ is an (a, b, k)-*BPP-pseudo-random generator* if and only if for any set $S \subseteq \{0, 1\}^b$, it holds that $\text{Prob}[s \leftarrow \{0, 1\}^a; (y_1, \dots, y_k) \leftarrow G(s); \exists i \in \{1, \dots, k\}$ such that $y_i \in S] \leq (|S|/2^b)^{k/10}$, where $|y_i| = b$, for $i = 1, \dots, k$.

Many constructions for BPP-pseudo-random generators with particular values of the parameters a, b, k have been given in literature (see [24]). In this paper, we will consider the well-known construction of a BPP-pseudo-random generator based on random walks on expanders, given in [1] (see also [7, 21, 15]). Using this construction, one obtains the following

Theorem 1. [1] *There exists an (a, b, k)-BPP-pseudo-random generator, for* $a = b + \Theta(k)$.

3 Error reduction for NI-computational-ZK

In this section we study the problem of randomness-efficient error reduction for non-interactive *computational* zero-knowledge proof systems. We present a transformation enjoying the following property. Given a proof system using a reference string of a certain length, our transformation returns another proof system for the same language, which uses a reference string whose length is essentially optimal with respect to the soundness error. This transformation should be seen as a first step towards proving the main result of the paper.

A technique in [11, 14]. We recall a technique which was motivated by constructing a non-interactive zero-knowledge proof system for all NP languages which would allow to prove any polynomial number of statements on a fixed size reference string. According to such technique, given the reference string σ, a prover will create a certain NP statement T_σ having the following two properties: 1) if σ is uniformly distributed then with high probability statement T_σ is false; 2) there exists an efficient algorithm that generates a reference string τ which is computationally indistinguishable from a totally random σ and such that T_τ is true. Then, in order to prove the NP statement input '$x \in L$', a prover will prove the statement '$(x \in L) \vee T_\sigma$'. Informally, the resulting protocol is a zero-knowledge proof system since completeness and soundness follow from the above property 1), and computational zero-knowledge follows from the above property 2). Two different implementations of this technique have been given in [11, 14] using cryptographic assumptions. For simplicity, we will use the elegant implementation in [14] to prove Theorem 2.

A transformation for all NP-complete languages. We show a transformation which applies to all NP-complete languages under the assumption of the existence of a pseudo-random generator.

Theorem 2. *Let ϵ be a constant, let s be a function, let H be a $(n^\epsilon, n^\epsilon + \log(1/s) + 1)$-pseudo-random generator and let L be an NP-complete language. If L has a non-interactive computational zero-knowledge proof system (A, B) with parameters $(1, 1/2, r(1/2, n))$ and A runs in time polynomial in n given a polynomial-size witness, then L has a non-interactive computational zero-knowledge proof system (P, V) with parameters $(1, s, r(1/2, p(n)) + \Theta(\log(1/s)))$, for some polynomial p.*

We note that the length of the reference string used by (P, V) can be very small as a function of parameter s, but not necessarily small as a function of n.

Informal description of the transformation. Let L be an NP-complete language and let (A, B) be a non-interactive zero-knowledge proof system with parameters $(1, 1/2, r(1/2, n))$ for L. Now, we construct a new proof system (P, V) for L. First of all the reference string σ is written as $\sigma = \sigma_1 \circ \sigma_2$. The first portion σ_1 is of length $2 \log(1/s)$ and is used to construct a statement T_{σ_1} as in the above recalled technique. The second portion σ_2 of σ is used as a seed for a BPP-pseudo-random generator G. Now, the statement '$(x \in L) \vee T_{\sigma_1}$' is reduced to a statement $z \in L$ using a standard witness-preserving reduction (see [16]).

Now, for $i = 1, \ldots, 10 \log(1/s)$, P proves that $z \in L$ using the original proof system using y_i as a reference string, where $(y_1, \ldots, y_{10\log(1/s)})$ is the output of algorithm G on input σ_2, and by G we denote the generator whose existence is guaranteed by Theorem 1. A formal description of (P,V) follows.

Input to P and V:

1. A NIZK proof system (A,B) for L having parameters $(1, 1/2, r(1/2, n))$;
2. an (a, b, k)-BPP-pseudo-random generator G, where $a = r(1/2, p(n)) + \Theta(\log(1/s))$, $b = r(1/2, p(n))$, and $k = 10 \log(1/s)$;
3. a $(n^\epsilon, n^\epsilon + \log(1/s) + 1)$-pseudo-random generator H, where ϵ is a constant;
4. an n-bit string x and a $(n^\epsilon + \log(1/s) + 1 + a)$-bit reference string $\sigma = \sigma_1 \circ \sigma_2$, where $|\sigma_1| = n^\epsilon + \log(1/s) + 1$ and $|\sigma_2| = r(1/2, p(n)) + \Theta(\log(1/s))$;

Instructions for P and V:

P and V: Let $T_{\sigma_1} = $ '$\exists r_1 \in \{0, 1\}^{\log(1/s)}$ such that $\sigma_1 = H(r_1)$';
             reduce statement '$(x \in L) \vee T_{\sigma_1}$' to statement '$z \in L$';
             set $(y_1, \ldots, y_{10\log(1/s)}) = G(\sigma_2)$.
P: For $i = 1, \ldots, 10 \log(1/s)$, set $\pi_i = A(y_i, z)$ and send π_i to V.
V: For $i = 1, \ldots, 10 \log(1/s)$,
             run algorithm B on input z, π_i and using y_i as a reference string;
             if B rejects then output: REJECT and halt;
        output: ACCEPT and halt.

4 Error reduction for NI-perfect-ZK

In this section we study the problem of randomness-efficient error reduction for non-interactive *perfect* zero-knowledge proof systems. We present a transformation for the language of quadratic non-residuosity modulo Blum integers. Our technique extends to all composed languages over such language, as those given in [9].

The protocol for quadratic non residuosity. We consider the language NQR_x, i.e., the set of integers that are quadratic non-residues modulo a Blum integer x; for a better exposition we make two wlog assumptions (see, e.g., [9]): x has already been proved to be a Blum integer and the reference string is of some efficiently samplable particular form. Recall that a non-interactive perfect zero-knowledge proof system for such language can be obtained as a sequential repetition of a proof system with soundness error $1/2$ [3, 9]. Here, we present a protocol (P,V) that improves this result on the length of the reference string. Formally, we obtain the following

Theorem 3. *(P, V) is a non-interactive perfect zero-knowledge proof system with parameters $(1, s, r)$ for the promised language NQR_x, where $r(s, n) = \Theta(2^{1/s} + n)$, and n denotes the length of the input.*

We note that all previously given non-interactive (computational or perfect) zero-knowledge proof systems use a reference string of length at least $\Omega(n \log(1/s))$. Therefore, our proof system presents an improvement if, say, $s \geq 1/\log n$.

We remark that several attempts of using the ideas in [3,10] to construct a low-randomness protocol end up in a somewhat subtle problem in proving the soundness requirement. Namely, a cheating prover, by observing the reference string, can influence the distribution of the output of the procedure for error reduction that he is using. As an attempt of preventing this, we present a procedure which is particularly sensitive to the case in which the prover is trying to cheat. The procedure forces the prover to use random and independent bits for every choice he makes for partial outputs of the procedure itself. Before we present the formal description of protocol (P,V), we need the following definition. Let x be a Blum integer, let $z \in Z_x^{+1}$, and $b \in \{0,1\}$; then define $\text{sqrt}(x,z,b)$ as the integer $u \in Z_x^{+1}$ such that $u^2 = z \bmod x$, and $u \leq x/2$ if $b = 0$, or $u > x/2$ if $b = 1$. We now formally describe (P,V).

Input to P and V:

1. A Blum integer x and an integer $y \in Z_x^{+1}$.
2. A $(2^k + n)$-bit reference string $\sigma = (z \circ B)$, where $B = \{b(i_1, \ldots, i_k) : i_1, \ldots, i_k \in \{0,1\}\}$, $b(i_1, \ldots, i_k) \in \{0,1\}$, $z \in Z_x^{+1}$ and $k = 1/s$.

Input to P: x's factorization.

Instructions for P and V.

P.1 Set $u_1 = z$, $ind_0 = 0$ and $d(j_1, \ldots, j_k) = b(j_1, \ldots, j_k)$, for all $j_1, \ldots, j_k \in \{0,1\}$.
P.2 For $i = 1, \ldots, k$,
  if $Q_x(u_i) = 0$ then set $l_i = 0$ and $ind_i = 2 \cdot ind_{i-1} + 1$;
  if $Q_x(u_i) = 1$ then set $l_i = 1$ and $ind_i = 2 \cdot ind_{i-1} + 2$;
  let $(i_1, \ldots, i_k)$ be the binary representation of ind_i;
  set $d(i_1, \ldots, i_k) = l_i$; and $r_i = \text{sqrt}(x, u_i \cdot y^{l_i}, b(i_1, \ldots, i_k))$;
  set $u_{i+1} = r_i$ and $D = \{d(j_1, \ldots, j_k) : j_1, \ldots, j_k \in \{0,1\}\}$.
P.3 Send $proof = (u_{k+1}, D, l_1, \ldots, l_k)$ to V.
V.1 Set $ind_0 = 0$ and $ind_i = 2 \cdot ind_{i-1} + 1 + l_i$, for $i = 1, \ldots, k$.
V.2 For $i = k, \ldots, 1$,
  set $r_i = u_{i+1}$ and $ind_i = (ind_{i-1} - 1 - l_i)/2$ and $u_i = r_i^2 \cdot y^{l_i} \bmod x$;
  let $(i_1, \ldots, i_k)$ be the binary representation of ind_i;
  check that $r_i \leq x/2$ if $b(i_1, \ldots, i_k) = 0$ or $r_i > x/2$ if $b(i_1, \ldots, i_k) = 1$.
V.3 Check that $u_1 = z$.
V.4 If all verifications are satisfied then output: ACCEPT else output: REJECT.

Extensions. The technique of previous section allows to obtain soundness error $O(1/\log n)$ when proving a single quadratic residuosity statement by only doubling the length of the reference string needed to obtain soundness error $1/2$ (rather than multiplying it by a factor of $O(\log \log n)$). Using the standard technique of parallel repetition on this protocol, we obtain the following

Theorem 4. *There exists a non-interactive perfect zero-knowledge proof system for language NQR_x with parameters $(1, s, r)$, where $r(s, n) = \Theta(n \log(1/s)/\log \log n)$, where n is the length of the input.*

The above theorem improves over the previous best non-interactive perfect zero-knowledge proof system for NQR_x which achieved $r(s, n) = \Theta(n \log(1/s))$. We remark that our technique also applies to all other non-interactive perfect zero-knowledge proof systems for quadratic residuosity languages in the literature.

e.g., those in [9], including their variants in which many statements are proved using the same reference string [10].

5   Low-randomness NIZK for all NP

In this section we present the main result of the paper. We start with an intermediate result: a non-interactive zero-knowledge proof system for all languages in NP having constant soundness error and using a very short reference string.

Theorem 5. *Let ϵ be a constant > 0 and let L be a language in NP. Under the Quadratic Residuosity Assumption, there exists a non-interactive zero-knowledge proof system for L with parameters $(1, 1/2, r)$, where $r(1/2, n) = n^\epsilon$ and n is the length of the input.*

The proof of Theorem 5 consists in presenting a protocol (P,V) that we first informally describe. First of all, the instance x for L is reduced to a boolean formula ϕ as an instance for 3SAT using a standard witness-preserving reduction. Then, given ϕ and a satisfying assignment t for it, the prover chooses a Blum integer z and a quadratic non-residue y modulo z, and associates an integer $tcom_i \in Z_z^{+1}$ with variable v_i and the integer $y \cdot tcom_i \bmod z$ with $\bar{v}_i$, in such a way that the following property holds: a literal l_i of ϕ is true under assignment t if and only if the integer associated with it is a quadratic non residue modulo z. Then, in order to prove that a 3SAT formula is satisfiable, it is enough for the prover to show: (1) that z and y are correctly constructed, (2) that in each clause there is at least one literal associated with an integer that is a quadratic non residue modulo z. Step (1) is made by proving that $z \in BL$ and $y \in NQR_z$, using a non-interactive perfect zero-knowledge proof system, which we call (A,B). Step (2) could be made by proving for each clause that at least one out of certain three integers is a quadratic non residue. However, it turns out that this would require too much randomness (or soundness would not hold). Instead, for each clause C_i, we prove the statement 'C_i is true' or 'T_σ is true', where T_σ is the statement defined in Section 3. Each of these composed statements is reduced to a membership statement to some NP-complete language (say, 3SAT) and is proved using any known non-interactive zero-knowledge proof system but on *the same* reference string. We drastically reduce the overall size of the reference string for the following two reasons: (a) each of the composed statements has length smaller than n^ϵ, and therefore we can use a not necessarily low-randomness proof system for proving them; (b) since we use the same reference string, we avoid any blowup due to the number of clauses of ϕ. We will denote by (C,D) the mentioned non-interactive zero-knowledge proof system for 3SAT. Although the most efficient reduction is obtained by implementing (A,B) using the protocol in Section 4 and (C,D) using the protocol in [10], choosing any other protocol in the literature for (A,B) and (C,D) would still suffice to prove Theorem 5.

A more formal description of (P,V) follows.

Input to P and V:

1. An n-bit string x, a constant ϵ and constants $c_1, c_2 \geq 1$ such that the reduction in step 3 of (P,V) transforms l-bit instances to l^{c_1}-bit instances and $|T_\sigma| = l^{c_2}$ if $|\sigma| = l$;

2. a NIZK proof system (A,B) for $BL \wedge NQR_z$ having parameters $(1, 1/4, r)$, where $r(1/4, l) = 40l$, on inputs of length l;

3. a NIZK proof system (C,D) for $3SAT$ having parameters $(1, s, r)$, where $r(s, l) = l^{c_3} \log(1/s)$, on inputs of length l, for some constant $c_3 > 1$;

4. a $(n^{\epsilon/2c_1 c_2 c_3}/4, 2n^{\epsilon/2c_1 c_2 c_3}/4)$-pseudo-random generator H;

5. a $O(n^\epsilon)$-bit reference string $\sigma = \sigma_1 \circ \sigma_2 \circ \sigma_3$, where $|\sigma_1| = 10n^{\epsilon/2c_1 c_3}$, $|\sigma_2| = 2n^{\epsilon/2c_1 c_2 c_3}/4$ and $|\sigma_3| = n^{\epsilon/2c_1}(n^{\epsilon/2c_1 c_3} + (3\epsilon/c_1 c_3)\log n + 2)$;

Input to P: A witness w certifying that $x \in L$.
Instructions for P and V.

1. **P and V:** Use a fixed witness-preserving reduction from L to 3SAT on input x, let ϕ be the 3SAT formula thus obtained; let t be its satisfying assignment, let $v_1, \ldots, v_{nv}$ be its variables, and nc be its number of clauses;

2. **P:** Set $l = n^{\epsilon/2c_1 c_3}/4$ and uniformly choose two $(l/2)$-bit primes p, q;
   set $z = pq$ and uniformly choose $y \in NQR_z$;
   for $i = 1, \ldots, nv$, uniformly choose $r_i \in Z_z^{+1}$, set $tcom_i = y^{t(v_i)} \cdot r_i^2 \bmod z$ and $ncom_i = y \cdot tcom_i \bmod z$;
   let $Proof_1 = A(\sigma_1, z, y)$ (where A uses p, q as private input);
   send $((z, y), (tcom_1, ncom_1, \ldots, tcom_{nv}, ncom_{nv}), Proof_1)$ to V;

3. **P and V:** set $com_{i,j} = tcom_h$ if $l_{i,j} = v_h$ or $com_{i,j} = ncom_h$ if $l_{i,j} = \bar{v}_h$, for some $h \in \{1, \ldots, nv\}$, for each literal $l_{i,j}$ of ϕ, and set $S_i = $ "$(com_{i,1} \in NQR_z) \vee (com_{i,2} \in NQR_z) \vee (com_{i,3} \in NQR_z) \vee T_{\sigma_2}$" for each clause $(l_{i,1} \vee l_{i,2} \vee l_{i,3})$ of ϕ;
   use a fixed witness-preserving reduction from L to 3SAT on input S_i, let ψ_i be the 3SAT formula thus obtained, for $i = 1, \ldots, nc$;

4. **P:** Set $Proof_{2i} = C(\sigma_3, \psi_i)$ and send $Proof_{2i}$ to V, for $i = 1, \ldots, nc$;

5. **V:** For $i = 1, \ldots, nv$, check that $ncom_i = y \cdot tcom_i \bmod z$;
   run algorithm B on input (z, y), $Proof_1$, and reference string σ_1;
   run algorithm D on input ψ_i, $Proof_{2i}$, and reference string σ_3, for $i = 1, \ldots, nc$;
   if all verifications are satisfied then output: ACCEPT else output: REJECT.

Now we can finally describe the main result of the paper: a non-interactive zero-knowledge proof system for all languages in NP with arbitrary soundness error and having a very short reference string.

Theorem 6. *Let ϵ be a constant > 0 and let L be a language in NP. Under the Quadratic Residuosity Assumption, there exists a non-interactive zero-knowledge proof system for L with parameters $(1, s, r)$, where $r(s, n) = \Theta(\log(1/s) + n^\epsilon)$, where n is the length of the input.*

We stress that the randomness complexity of our proof system is polynomial in n since the security parameter needed for the zero-knowledge property is chosen as polynomial in n; if it is chosen as polylogarithmic in n then also the randomness complexity of our proof system is polylogarithmic in n (a similar remark applies to Theorem 5). The proof of Theorem 6 directly follows from Theorem 5 and Theorem 2.

References

1. M. Ajtai, J. Komlos, and E. Szemeredi, *Deterministic Simulation in Logspace*, Proc. of STOC 87.
2. M. Ben-Or, S. Goldwasser, J. Kilian and A. Wigderson, *Multi-Prover Interactive Proofs: How to Remove Intractability Assumptions*, Proc. of STOC 88.
3. M. Blum, A. De Santis, S. Micali, and G. Persiano, *Non-Interactive Zero-Knowledge*, SIAM Journal of Computing, vol. 20, no. 6, Dec 1991, pp. 1084–1118.
4. M. Blum, P. Feldman, and S. Micali, *Non-Interactive Zero-Knowledge and Applications*, Proc. of STOC 88.
5. M. Blum and S. Micali, *How to Generate Cryptographically Strong Sequence of Pseudo-Random Bits*, SIAM J. on Computing, vol. 13, no. 4, 1984, pp. 850–864.
6. J. Boyar and R. Peralta, *Short Discreet Proofs*, Proc. of EUROCRYPT 96.
7. A. Cohen and A. Wigderson, *Dispersers, Deterministic Amplification and Weak Random Sources*, Proc. of FOCS 89.
8. I. Damgaard, *Non-interactive circuit-based proofs and non-interactive perfect zero-knowledge with preprocessing*, Proc. of EUROCRYPT 92.
9. A. De Santis, G. Di Crescenzo, and G. Persiano, *The Knowledge Complexity of Quadratic Residuosity Languages*, in Theoretical Computer Science, Vol. 132, pp. 291–317 (1994).
10. A. De Santis, G. Di Crescenzo, and G. Persiano, *Randomness-Efficient Non-Interactive Zero-Knowledge*, Proc. of ICALP 97.
11. A. De Santis and M. Yung, *Cryptographic applications of the meta-proof and the many-prover systems*, Proc. of CRYPTO 90.
12. G. Di Crescenzo, *Recycling Random Bits for Composed Perfect Zero-Knowledge*, Proc. of EUROCRYPT 95.
13. U. Feige, S. Goldwasser, L. Lovasz, S. Safra and M. Szegedy, *Approximating Clique is Almost NP-complete*, Proc. of FOCS 91.
14. U. Feige, D. Lapidot, and A. Shamir, *Multiple Non-Interactive Zero-Knowledge Proofs Based on a Single Random String*, Proc. of STOC 90.
15. Gillman, *A Chernoff Bound for Random Walks on Expanders*, Proc. of STOC 93.
16. M. Garey e D. Johnson, *Computers and Intractability: a Guide to the Theory of NP-Completeness*, W. H. Freeman & Co., New York, 1979.
17. O. Goldreich, S. Micali, and A. Wigderson, *Proofs that Yield Nothing but their Validity or All Languages in NP Have Zero-Knowledge Proof Systems*, Journal of the ACM, vol. 38, n. 1, 1991, pp. 691–729.
18. O. Goldreich and Y. Oren, *Definitions and Properties of Zero-Knowledge Proof Systems*, Journal of Cryptology, vol. 7, 1994, pp. 1–32.
19. S. Goldwasser, and S. Micali, *Probabilistic Encryption*, in Journal of Computer and System Sciences, vol. 28, n. 2, 1984, pp. 270–299.
20. S. Goldwasser, S. Micali, and C. Rackoff, *The Knowledge Complexity of Interactive Proof-Systems*, SIAM J. on Computing, vol. 18, n. 1, 1989.
21. R. Impagliazzo and D. Zuckerman, *How to Recycle Random Bits*, Proc. of FOCS 89.
22. J. Kilian, *On the complexity of bounded-interaction and non-interactive zero-knowledge proofs*, Proc. of FOCS 94.
23. J. Kilian, and E. Petrank, *An efficient zero-knowledge proof system for NP under general assumptions*, Journal of Cryptology, vol. 11, n. 1, pp. 1–28.
24. M. Luby and A. Wigderson, *Pairwise Independence and Derandomization*, ICSI Technical Report TR-95-035.

Timed Alternating Tree Automata:
The Automata-Theoretic Solution to the
TCTL Model Checking Problem

Martin Dickhöfer and Thomas Wilke

[1] Institut für Informatik und Praktische Mathematik
Christian-Albrechts-Universität zu Kiel, 24098 Kiel, Germany
mdi@informatik.uni-kiel.de
[2] Lehrstuhl für Informatik VII, RWTH Aachen, 52056 Aachen, Germany
wilke@informatik.rwth-aachen.de

Abstract. We introduce timed alternating tree automata as a natural extension of timed automata for the purpose of solving the model checking problem for timed computation tree logic (TCTL) following the automata-theoretic approach. This settles a problem posed by Henzinger, Kupferman, and Vardi.

With their pioneering work in the late fifties and early sixties, Büchi, Rabin, Trakhtenbrot and others demonstrated that automata theory is a powerful tool for studying mathematical theories. Since then automata theory has been successfully applied to a variety of problems in mathematical logic and to numerous logic-related problems in computer science. A direction that has been particularly successful is the application of automata theory to model checking problems; for as different specification logics as LTL, CTL, CTL*, and the μ-calculus, model checking algorithms have been obtained using an automata-theoretic approach, see, for instance, [13, 7, 12, 5]. Although the model checking problem for timed computation tree logic (TCTL) has been known to be decidable (to be precise, PSPACE-complete) for almost a decade now, see, for instance, [1, 2], it has withstood a satisfying treatment within an automata-theoretic framework. In fact, as Henzinger, Kupferman, and Vardi point out in the conclusion of [9], an appropriate automata-theoretic framework has not been available. In this paper, we present such a framework for the first time and show how, within this framework, one can derive a model checking algorithm for TCTL. Moreover, the worst-case complexity of the algorithm thus obtained matches the worst-case complexity of previous algorithms.

The automata-theoretic approach to model checking problems can be roughly explained as follows. To check whether or not a given formula φ holds in a system S, one first constructs an automaton A_φ that accepts the unravelings of all systems in which φ holds, then forms an appropriate product automaton $A_\varphi \times S$, and finally solves a certain word problem (or the emptiness problem) for $A_\varphi \times S$. As pointed out in [9], the particular problem that arises in the timed framework is the following. On the one hand, TCTL satisfiability is undecidable; on the other hand, TCTL model checking is decidable, see [2]. So the automaton model to be used in the timed setting would have to have an undecidable emptiness problem (for automata of the form A_φ) but some kind of decidable word problem (for automata of the form $A_\varphi \times S$). This is exactly what happens with the automaton model we suggest in this paper: the "one-node acceptance problem" is the particular word problem that we prove to be decidable, but the emptiness problem is undecidable for our automaton model.

The paper is organized as follows. In Section 1, we introduce our new automaton model. In Section 2, we explain what we understand by the one-node acceptance problem and sketch a proof of its decidability. Section 3 is a reminder of TCTL, and Section 4 finally explains how the TCTL model checking problem can be solved in our framework. Due to space limitations, we cannot give a detailed complexity analysis of the constructions presented. To improve readability of the paper, we use a slightly simplified semantics for TCTL and do not address issues related to non-Zenoness. For details about the general setting, the reader is referred to our technical report [6].

For background on timed automata and the automata-theoretic method, we recommend [4] and [5], respectively.

Acknowledgment. The second author is grateful to Hubert Comon, Laboratoire de Spécification et Vérification, ENS Cachan, for many interesting discussions on the topic of this paper.

Notational Conventions. The set of nonnegative integers is denoted by $\mathbf{N}$. The sets of positive real numbers and nonnegative real numbers are denoted by $\mathbf{P}$ and $\mathbf{R}$, respectively.

1   Timed Alternating Tree Automata

This first technical section introduces our model of timed alternating tree automaton. Traditionally, tree automata are devices that are used to define sets of directed trees, see, for instance, [8] or [11, 10]. But they can as well be used in a slightly more general way to define sets of rooted directed graphs. (What is important is that their runs are directed trees.) We adopt this more general view, as it turns out to be very convenient when dealing with formulas: a tree automaton can then define the set of all models of a given formula (instead of the set of the unravelings of all models).

Timed graphs. A *timed graph (TG)* over an alphabet A is a triple $G = (W, R, \nu)$ where W is a set of *nodes,* $R \subseteq W \times \mathbf{P} \times W$ is a set of *directed timed edges,* and $\nu: W \to A$ is a *labeling.* It is useful to think of an edge (w, d, w') as connecting the nodes w and w' via a direct path of *duration* d. Given a node w, we will write $N(w)$ for $\{(d, w') \mid (w, d, w') \in R\}$, which describes its *neighborhood.*

A *pointed timed graph (PTG)* is a pair (G, w) where G is a timed graph and w a node of G. A very simple but useful PTG, which we will later encounter many times, is the *one-node graph*, denoted $\mathbf{G_1}$. It is defined by

$$\mathbf{G_1} = ((\{\emptyset\}, \{\emptyset\} \times \mathbf{P} \times \{\emptyset\}, \nu), \emptyset) \qquad \text{where } \nu(\emptyset) = \emptyset.$$

So the one-node graph is a PTG with one node, denoted $\emptyset$, which is also labeled by $\emptyset$. And for every positive real number there is a self-loop at $\emptyset$ with that particular duration.

A *path* in a TG $\mathbf{G}$ or a PTG $(\mathbf{G}, w)$ as above is a sequence $w_0, d_0, w_1, d_1, \ldots$ such that $(w_i, d_i, w_{i+1}) \in R$ for all $i \geq 0$. Such a path is said to *start* in w_0. A *maximal* path is a path which is either infinite or finite and cannot be extended.

TATA's—informal description. Timed alternating tree automata (TATA's) are equipped with a finite memory and a finite number of clocks to measure distances in time; their behavior is determined by a complex transition function. The "computation" of a TATA on a PTG proceeds in rounds. At the beginning of every round there are several copies of the TATA on different nodes of the PTG; some nodes might be occupied by many copies, others might not accommodate a single one. During a round, each copy splits up in several new copies, which are sent to neighbored nodes and change their states and clock readings on their way according to the transition function. Initially, there is only one copy residing in the distinguished node of the PTG. Acceptance is defined as usual via path conditions.— A formal description follows.

Clock conditions and assignments. The transition functions of TATA's involve so-called clock conditions, which are as with ordinary timed automata and are defined as follows. Let C be a set whose elements are referred to as *clocks* or *clock variables*. The *clock conditions* over C are generated by the grammar

$$\langle CC \rangle ::= \top \mid \bot \mid c \# n \mid \neg \langle CC \rangle \mid \langle CC \rangle \{ \vee \mid \wedge \} \langle CC \rangle$$
$$\# ::= < \mid \leq \mid > \mid \geq \mid = \mid \neq$$

where c generates the elements of C and n the elements of $\mathbf{N}$. The set of all clock conditions over C is denoted by $CC(C)$.

A *clock assignment* over C is a function $C \to \mathbf{R}$, that is, an element of $\mathbf{R}^C$. In a straightforward way, it is defined what it means for $\alpha \in \mathbf{R}^C$ to satisfy $\gamma \in CC(C)$, denoted $\alpha \models \gamma$. For instance, $\alpha \models c < 5$ if and only if $\alpha(c) < 5$. There are two different kinds of operations on clock assignments that play a role here, one that advances time and another one that resets clocks. Given a clock assignment α and $d \in \mathbf{R}$, $\alpha + d$ denotes the clock assignment α' where $\alpha'(c) = \alpha(c) + d$ for each $c \in C$. Given a clock assignment α and $C' \subseteq C$, $\alpha[C']$ denotes the clock assignment α' where $\alpha'(c) = \alpha(c)$ for $c \notin C'$ and $\alpha'(c) = 0$ for $c \in C'$. By abuse of notation, we use $\mathbf{0}$ to denote the clock assignment that maps every clock to 0 regardless of the underlying set of clocks.

Transition conditions. The values of the transition functions of TATA's are so-called transition conditions, which are defined as follows. Let S be a set whose elements are referred to as *states* and C a set of clocks. The *transition conditions* over S and C are generated by the grammar

$$\langle TC \rangle ::= \top \mid \bot \mid \langle CC \rangle \mid \langle TC \rangle \{ \vee \mid \wedge \} \langle TC \rangle \mid \{ \Box \mid \Diamond \} (\langle CC \rangle, C', s)$$

where s generates the elements of S and C' the subsets of C. The set of all transition conditions over S and C is denoted by $\mathrm{TC}(S, C)$.

Assume we are given a set of states S, a timed graph with set of nodes W, and a set of clocks C. Inductively, we define what it means for $\alpha \in \mathbf{R}^C$, $X \subseteq \mathbf{P} \times W$, and $Y \subseteq W \times \mathbf{R}^C \times S$ to satisfy a transition condition β, denoted $(\alpha, X, Y) \models \beta$. The reader should think of α as a clock assignment assumed by a copy of a TATA in some node of a Kripke structure whose neighborhood is X. The set Y describes what neighbors copies of the TATA are sent to, which state they are in, and what their clock assignment is.

— The boolean constants and connectives are dealt with in the obvious way.
— $(\alpha, X, Y) \models \gamma$ if $\alpha \models \gamma$ (for every clock condition γ).
— $(\alpha, X, Y) \models \Diamond(\gamma, C', s)$ if there exists $(d, w) \in X$ such that $\alpha + d \models \gamma$ and $(w, \alpha + d[C'], s) \in Y$.
— $(\alpha, X, Y) \models \Box(\gamma, C', s)$ if whenever $\alpha + d \models \gamma$ for some $(d, w) \in X$, then $(w, \alpha + d[C'], s) \in Y$.

TATA's—formal definition. We can now give a formal definition of timed alternating tree automata. A *timed alternating tree automaton (TATA)* over an alphabet A is a tuple $\boldsymbol{A} = (S, C, s_I, \tau, F)$ where S is a finite set of *states*, C is a finite set of *clocks*, $s_I \in S$ is an *initial state*, $\tau \colon S \times A \to \mathrm{TC}(S, C)$ is a *transition function*, and F is some *acceptance condition* such as a Büchi condition.

Next, we define runs. Let $\boldsymbol{A}$ be a TATA as above, $\boldsymbol{G} = (W, R, \nu)$ a TG, and assume $\boldsymbol{T} = (V, E, \lambda)$ is a tree with node labels in $W \times \mathbf{R}^C \times S$. Given a node $v \in V$ with $\lambda(v) = (w, \alpha, s)$, we write w_v for w, α_v for α, s_v for s, and L_v for $\{\lambda(v') \mid (v, v') \in E\}$. A node $v \in V$ is *labeled consistently* if $(\alpha_v, N(w_v), L_v) \models \tau(s_v, \nu(w_v))$. Assume u is the root of $\boldsymbol{T}$. Then $\boldsymbol{T}$ is a *run* of $\boldsymbol{A}$ on a PTG $(\boldsymbol{G}, w)$ if $w_u = w$ and every node is labeled consistently. It is said to start with (s_u, α_u).

A *branch* of a run $\boldsymbol{T}$ as above is an infinite path through $\boldsymbol{T}$ starting at the root, i. e., a sequence $v_0, v_1, v_2, \dots$ where v_0 is the root of $\boldsymbol{T}$ and $(v_i, v_{i+1}) \in E$ for all $i \in \mathbf{N}$. Given such a branch, its *state labeling* is the sequence $s_{v_0}, s_{v_1}, s_{v_2}, \dots$

A run is *accepting* if the state labeling of each of its branches is *accepting* with respect to the given acceptance condition F. A run satisfies the *initial condition* if it starts with $(s_I, \mathbf{0})$. It is *successful* when it is accepting and satisfies the initial condition. A PTG $(\boldsymbol{G}, w)$ is *accepted* by a TATA $\boldsymbol{A}$ if there exists a successful run of $\boldsymbol{A}$ on $(\boldsymbol{G}, w)$.

2 The One-Node Acceptance Problem

It is almost folklore that for ordinary finite-state alternating tree automata all standard decision problems such as emptiness, equivalence or containment are decidable. The situation is less satisfactory with timed word automata: emptiness is decidable, but neither equivalence nor containment are, see, for instance, [3]. With timed alternating tree automata, the situation is even less satisfactory: not even emptiness is decidable. But what is decidable is the simplest "word problem" one can imagine, the question whether or not the one-node graph is accepted. This problem is referred to by *one-node acceptance (ONA) problem*.

One-letter alternating ω-automata. To solve the ONA problem (and to determine its complexity), we reduce it to the emptiness problem for "one-letter alternating ω-automata," which has already been solved (and whose complexity has been determined).

We start with a brief review. A *simple transition condition* over a state set S is built up from the elements of S and the boolean constants $\top$ and $\bot$ using $\vee$ and $\wedge$ only. In other words, a simple transition condition of S is a positive boolean combination of elements from $S \cup \{\bot, \top\}$. The set of all these transition conditions is denoted by $\mathrm{STC}(S)$.

A *one-letter alternating ω-automaton (OAOA)* is a tuple $A = (S, s_I, \tau, F)$ where S is a finite set of *states*, s_I is an *initial state*, $\delta : S \to \mathrm{STC}(S)$ is a *transition function*, and F is an *acceptance condition*.

Let A be an OAOA as above and $T = (V, E, \lambda)$ a tree with labels in S. A node v of T is labeled consistently when $L_v \models \tau(\lambda(v))$ where $\models$ is defined in the natural way. The tree T is a run if each of its nodes is labeled consistently; it is accepting if each of its branches is accepting according to the acceptance condition F; it is successful if it is accepting and $\lambda(u) = s_I$ for the root u of T.

Observe that there is no need to refer to an input here, as these automata are one-letter alternating ω-automata, and over a one-letter alphabet there's only one ω-word, and this particular word is implicit in the above definition of a run.

We are interested in whether or not a successful run exists for a given OAOA. The corresponding decision problem is known as the *one-letter emptiness (OLE) problem for OAOA's.* (Of course, for one-letter ω-automata there's only one word problem, as there is only one word, so the word problem and the emptiness problem are essentially the same.) Regardless of the acceptance condition, the OLE problem is decidable for OAOA's; the complexity of this problem does, however, depend on the acceptance condition under consideration.

Regions. In order to reduce the ONA problem to the OLE problem for OAOA's we factorize clock assignments modulo an appropriate equivalence relation, which goes back to the seminal paper by Alur and Dill, [3], on timed automata. We review the key definitions.

Let C be a finite set of clocks and m a natural number. An equivalence relation between clock assignments over C, denoted $\equiv_m$, is defined as follows. Clock assignments $\alpha, \alpha' \in \mathbf{R}^C$ are said to be *equivalent with respect to m*, denoted $\alpha \equiv_m \alpha'$, if the two conditions below are satisfied.

— For every clock c and every natural number $n \leq m$, $\alpha(c) < n$ iff $\alpha'(c) < n$, as well as $\alpha(c) = n$ iff $\alpha'(c) = n$.

— For clocks c, c', if $\alpha(c) \leq m$ and $\alpha(c') \leq m$, then $\mathrm{trc}(\alpha(c)) < \mathrm{trc}(\alpha(c'))$ iff $\mathrm{trc}(\alpha'(c)) < \mathrm{trc}(\alpha'(c'))$. Here, for every $r \in \mathbf{R}$, $\mathrm{trc}(r)$ is the fractional part of r.

For every m, the relation $\equiv_m$ defined in this way is, in fact, an equivalence relation. The set $\mathbf{R}^C/\equiv_m$ will be denoted by R_b, and its elements are called *regions*. The equivalence relation $\equiv_m$ has only a finite number of equivalence classes and enjoys quite a number of important properties. Most importantly, it respects advancing clocks (passage of time), resetting clocks, and the satisfaction relation between clock assignments and clock conditions up to the threshold m. For details, see [4].

Below, we will use the following notation. Given a region $r = \alpha/\equiv_m$ and a set of clocks C', we will write $r[C']$ for $\alpha[C']/\equiv_m$. This is well-defined because of the aforementioned properties of $\equiv_m$. Further, given a region r as above and a clock condition where all clocks are compared only with numbers less than or equal to m, we will write $r \models \gamma$ if and only if $\alpha \models \gamma$. Again, this is well-defined because of the aformentioned properties of $\equiv_m$. The relation $\underset{m}{\to}$ is defined by

$$\underset{m}{\to} = \{(\alpha/\equiv_m, (\alpha + d)/\equiv_m) \mid \alpha \in \mathbf{R}^C, d \in \mathbf{P}\} \ .$$

The reduction. We can now present the reduction we're interested in. Let $A = (S, C, s_I, \tau, F)$ be a TATA over an alphabet A that includes the empty set. We define an OAOA A^ρ—the *discretization* of A—such that A accepts the one-node graph $\mathbf{G_1}$ if and only if A^ρ has a successful run. The bounding parameter m we use is the maximum number the clocks from C are compared to in all transition conditions $\tau(s, a)$ with $s \in S$ and $a \in A$. We set

$$A^\rho = (S \times \mathrm{R}_b, (s_I, \mathbf{0}/\equiv_m), \tau^\rho, F^\rho)$$

and define τ^ρ and F^ρ as follows.

The transition function τ^ρ maps (s, r) to the formula $\tau(s, \emptyset)^r$ where for every transition condition δ, the formula δ^r is obtained from δ by performing the following substitutions in parallel.

— Every subformula $c\#n$ with $r \models c\#n$ is replaced by $\top$.

— Every subformula $c\#n$ with $r \not\models c\#n$ is replaced by $\bot$.

— Every subformula $\Diamond(\gamma, C', s')$ is replaced by $\displaystyle\bigvee_{r \underset{m}{\to} r', r' \models \gamma} (s', r'[C'])$.

— Every subformula $\Box(\gamma, C', s')$ is replaced by $\displaystyle\bigwedge_{r \underset{m}{\to} r', r' \models \gamma} (s', r'[C'])$.

— The acceptance condition F^ρ results from F by an appropriate modification. For instance, if F is a Büchi condition, i.e., F is a subset of S, then $F^\rho = F \times \mathrm{R}_m$.

Theorem 1. *Let A be a TATA. The TATA A accepts the one-node graph $\mathbf{G_1}$ if and only if the OAOA A^ρ has a successful run.*

Since the reduction is computable and the OLE problem for OAOA's is decidable, we immediately get.

Corollary 1. *The ONA problem is decidable.*

To prove the theorem, we turn runs of a TATA A into runs of its discretization A^ρ and vice versa. The constructions needed are more or less straightforward and so are the proofs that they are correct. When non-Zenoness (divergence) is an issue, then the constructions get slightly more complicated while the correctness arguments get involved. For details, see our tech report [6].

3   Timed Computation Tree Logic

In this section, we shortly review syntax and semantics of timed computation tree logic (TCTL). The syntax we use here is from [9]; the semantics is simplified.

Syntax. Let C be a set of clocks and P an arbitrary set whose elements are referred to as *propositions*. The *TCTL formulas* over P and C are generated by the grammar

$$\langle\text{TCTL}\rangle ::= \top \mid \bot \mid p \mid \neg p \mid \langle\text{CC}\rangle \mid c.\langle\text{TCTL}\rangle \mid \langle\text{TCTL}\rangle\{\wedge \mid \vee\}\langle\text{TCTL}\rangle$$
$$\mid \{\text{E} \mid \text{A}\}[\langle\text{TCTL}\rangle\{\text{U} \mid \text{R}\}\langle\text{TCTL}\rangle]$$

where p generates the elements of P and c the elements of C. The letters U and R are supposed to remind of "until" and "release." Formulas starting with E or A are called *path formulas*. Observe that the above grammar is ambiguous; these ambiguities will, however, not cause any difficulties. Clocks should be viewed as variables, and a prefix like "c." should be viewed as a quantifier binding certain occurrences of the clock variable c.

A TCTL formula φ is said to be *closed* if every occurrence of a clock is bound by some clock quantifier. The set of subformulas of a TCTL formula φ (including φ itself) is denoted by $\text{sub}(\varphi)$. The set of subformulas of φ of the shape $\text{A}[\psi\,\text{U}\,\chi]$ is denoted by $\text{AU}(\varphi)$. Accordingly, $\text{EU}(\varphi)$, $\text{AR}(\varphi)$, and $\text{ER}(\varphi)$ are defined. The set of clocks bound in φ is denoted by $C_b(\varphi)$; formally, a clock c belongs to $C_b(\varphi)$ if there is a formula ψ such that $c.\psi \in \text{sub}(\varphi)$. A TCTL formula φ is in *normal form* if whenever $c.\psi \in \text{sub}(\varphi)$ for some ψ, then $c \notin C_b(\psi)$.

For instance, $c.\text{E}[c.\text{E}[\top\,\text{U}\,c=5\wedge p]\,\text{U}\,c=5\wedge p]$ is a closed TCTL formula, but it is not in normal form. This formula is, however, equivalent to $c.\text{E}[c'.\text{E}[\top\,\text{U}\,c'=5\wedge p]\,\text{U}\,c=5\wedge p]$, which is in normal form.

Semantics. TCTL formulas are interpreted in timed Kripke structures, which are timed graphs over alphabets of a special form: a *timed Kripke structure (TKS)* over a set P of *propositional variables* is a timed graph over 2^P, i. e., over the power set of P. A *pointed timed Kripke structure (TPKS)* is a pair $(\boldsymbol{G}, w)$ where $\boldsymbol{G}$ is a timed Kripke structure and w is a node of $\boldsymbol{G}$.

Given a TKS $(\boldsymbol{G}, w)$ over some set P of propositions with $\boldsymbol{G} = (W, R, \nu)$, a clock assignment $\alpha \in \mathbf{R}^C$, and a TCTL formula φ over P and C, we define what it means for φ to hold in $(\boldsymbol{G}, w)$ with respect to α, denoted $(\boldsymbol{G}, w), \alpha \models \varphi$.

— The boolean constants $\top$ and $\bot$ and the boolean connectives $\vee$ and $\wedge$ are dealt with in the obvious way.

— $(\boldsymbol{G}, w), \alpha \models p$ if $p \in \nu(w)$, and $(\boldsymbol{G}, w), \alpha \models \neg p$ if $p \notin \nu(w)$.

— $(\boldsymbol{G}, w), \alpha \models c.\varphi$ if $(\boldsymbol{G}, w), \alpha[\{c\}] \models \varphi$.

— $(\boldsymbol{G}, w), \alpha \models \text{E}[\varphi\,\text{U}\,\psi]$ if there exists a maximal path $w_0, d_0, w_1, d_1, \ldots$ starting in w and $n \geq 0$ such that $(\boldsymbol{G}, w_i), \alpha + d_0 + \cdots + d_{i-1} \models \varphi$ for $i < n$ and $(\boldsymbol{G}, w_n), \alpha + d_0 + \cdots + d_{n-1} \models \psi$.

— $(\boldsymbol{G}, w), \alpha \models \text{A}[\varphi\,\text{U}\,\psi]$ if for every maximal path $w_0, d_0, w_1, d_1, \ldots$ starting in w there exists $n \geq 0$ such that $(\boldsymbol{G}, w_i), \alpha + d_0 + \cdots + d_{i-1} \models \varphi$ for $i < n$ and $(\boldsymbol{G}, w_n), \alpha + d_0 + \cdots + d_{n-1} \models \psi$.

— $(\boldsymbol{G}, w), \alpha \models \text{E}[\varphi\,\text{R}\,\psi]$ if there exists a maximal path $w_0, d_0, w_1, d_1, \ldots$ starting in w such that for every $n \geq 0$, $(\boldsymbol{G}, w_n), \alpha + d_0 + \cdots + d_{n-1} \models \psi$, unless there exists $i < n$ with $(\boldsymbol{G}, w_i), \alpha + d_0 + \cdots + d_{i-1} \models \varphi$.

— $(\boldsymbol{G}, w), \alpha \models \text{A}[\varphi\,\text{R}\,\psi]$ if for every maximal path $w_0, d_0, w_1, d_1, \ldots$ starting in w and for every $n \geq 0$, $(\boldsymbol{G}, w_n), \alpha + d_0 + \cdots + d_{n-1} \models \psi$, unless there exists $i < n$ with $(\boldsymbol{G}, w_i), \alpha + d_0 + \cdots + d_{i-1} \models \varphi$.

It is easy to see that AU and ER are dual to each other just as EU and AR are.

When φ is a closed TCTL formula, then $(G, w), \alpha \models \varphi$ does not depend on α. This is why in these cases we will simply write $(G, w) \models \varphi$ instead of $(G, w), \alpha \models \varphi$ and say that φ holds in (G, w) or that (G, w) is a *model* of φ.

4   The Timed Model Checking Problem

The systems to be model checked are finite-state systems augmented by clocks and clock conditions: a *timed transition system (TTS)* is a tuple (L, C, ν, τ) where L is a finite set of *locations,* C is a finite set of *clocks,* $\nu: L \to 2^P$ is a *propositional valuation,* and $\tau: L \to 2^{\mathrm{CC}(C) \times 2^C \times L}$ is a *transition function.*

With a TTS $S = (L, C, \nu, \tau)$ we associate the TKS $G_S = (L \times \mathbf{R}^C, R, \nu')$ defined as follows. For all $l \in L$, $\alpha \in \mathbf{R}^C$, $d \in \mathbf{P}$, $C' \subseteq C$, $((l, \alpha), d, (l', \alpha + d[C'])) \in R$ if there exists $\gamma \in \mathrm{CC}(C)$ such that $(\gamma, C', l') \in \tau(l)$ and $\alpha + d \models \gamma$. For all $l \in l$ and $\alpha \in \mathbf{R}^C$, $\nu'(l, \alpha) = \nu(l)$. When S is a TTS, l a location of S, and φ a closed TCTL formula, we write $(S, l) \models \varphi$ for $(G_S, (l, 0)) \models \varphi$ and say (S, l) is a *model* of φ.

The *timed model checking problem (TMC problem)* is the task to determine for a given TTS S together with a location l and a closed TCTL formula φ whether or not (S, l) is a model of φ.

4.1   Converting TCTL Formulas to TATA's

The first step in solving the timed model checking problem is constructing a TATA A_φ for every TCTL formula φ which accepts exactly the models of φ.

Let φ be a TCTL formula over P and C in normal form. We define a TATA $A_\varphi = (\mathrm{sub}(\varphi), C, \varphi, \tau, F)$ over 2^P where the transition function is defined inductively as follows. We set $\tau(p, a) = \tau(\neg p, a) = \top$ for $p \in a$, and, symmetrically, $\tau(\neg p, a) = \tau(p, a) = \bot$, for $p \notin a$. Further, we set $\tau(\psi \lor \chi, a) = \tau(\psi, a) \lor \tau(\chi, a)$ and $\tau(\psi \land \chi, a) = \tau(\psi, a) \land \tau(\chi, a)$. Finally, we set:

$$\tau(c.\psi, a) = \tau(\psi, a) ,$$
$$\tau(\gamma, a) = \gamma , \quad \text{for } \gamma \in \mathrm{CC}(C),$$
$$\tau(\mathsf{E}[\psi \, \mathsf{U} \, \chi], a) = \tau(\chi, a) \lor (\tau(\psi, a) \land \Diamond(\mathsf{E}[\psi \, \mathsf{U} \, \chi], \top, C_b(\mathsf{E}[\psi \, \mathsf{U} \, \chi]))) ,$$
$$\tau(\mathsf{A}[\psi \, \mathsf{U} \, \chi], a) = \tau(\chi, a) \lor (\tau(\psi, a) \land \Box(\mathsf{A}[\psi \, \mathsf{U} \, \chi], \top, C_b(\mathsf{A}[\psi \, \mathsf{U} \, \chi]))$$
$$\land \Diamond(\mathsf{A}[\psi \, \mathsf{U} \, \chi], \top, C_b(\mathsf{A}[\psi \, \mathsf{U} \, \chi]))) ,$$
$$\tau(\mathsf{E}[\psi \, \mathsf{R} \, \chi], a) = \tau(\chi, a) \land (\tau(\psi, a) \lor \Diamond(\mathsf{E}[\psi \, \mathsf{R} \, \chi], \top, C_b(\mathsf{E}[\psi \, \mathsf{R} \, \chi]))$$
$$\lor \Box(\mathsf{E}[\psi \, \mathsf{R} \, \chi], \top, C_b(\mathsf{E}[\psi \, \mathsf{R} \, \chi]))) ,$$
$$\tau(\mathsf{A}[\psi \, \mathsf{R} \, \chi], a) = \tau(\chi, a) \land (\tau(\psi, a) \lor \Box(\mathsf{A}[\psi \, \mathsf{R} \, \chi], \top, C_b(\mathsf{A}[\psi \, \mathsf{R} \, \chi]))) .$$

The acceptance condition of A_φ is the Büchi condition given by the set $\mathrm{ER}(\varphi) \cup \mathrm{AR}(\varphi)$.

We prove that the above TATA accepts exactly all models of the given TCTL formula:

Theorem 2. *Let $(\boldsymbol{G}, w)$ be a PTKS and φ a closed TCTL formula in normal form. The PTKS $(\boldsymbol{G}, w)$ is a model of φ if and only if the TATA $\boldsymbol{A}_\varphi$ accepts $(\boldsymbol{G}, w)$.*

The above construction and the proof of the above theorem are similar to the discrete situation as dealt with in [5].

As a consequence of this and the fact that the satisfiability problem for TCTL formulas is undecidable, [2], we note:

Corollary 2. *The emptiness problem for timed alternating tree automata is undecidable.*

4.2   The Product Construction

The second step in solving the timed model checking problem is defining an appropriate product construction that combines a TATA $\boldsymbol{A}$, a TTS $\boldsymbol{S}$, and a location l of $\boldsymbol{S}$ and results in a new TATA which accepts the one-node graph $\mathbf{G_1}$ if and only if $\boldsymbol{A}$ accepts $(\boldsymbol{G_S}, (l, \mathbf{0}))$.

Let $\boldsymbol{A} = (S, C_{\boldsymbol{A}}, s_I, \tau_{\boldsymbol{A}}, F)$ be a TATA, $\boldsymbol{S} = (L, C_{\boldsymbol{S}}, \nu_{\boldsymbol{S}}, \tau_{\boldsymbol{S}})$ a TTS, and l_I a location of $\boldsymbol{S}$. The *product* of $\boldsymbol{A}$ and $(\boldsymbol{S}, l_I)$, simply denoted $\boldsymbol{A} \times (\boldsymbol{S}, l_I)$, is the TATA $(S \times L, C_{\boldsymbol{A}} \cup C_{\boldsymbol{S}}, (s_I, l_I), \tau^*, F^*)$ over $\{\emptyset\}$ where the transition function τ^* maps $((s, l), \emptyset)$ to the formula that is obtained from $\tau_{\boldsymbol{A}}(s, \nu_{\boldsymbol{S}}(l))$ by replacing each occurrence of subformulas of the form $\Diamond(s', \gamma_{\boldsymbol{A}}, C'_{\boldsymbol{A}})$ or $\Box(s', \gamma_{\boldsymbol{A}}, C'_{\boldsymbol{A}})$ by

$$\bigvee_{(\gamma_{\boldsymbol{S}}, C'_{\boldsymbol{S}}, l') \in \tau(s)} \Diamond((s', l'), \gamma_{\boldsymbol{A}} \wedge \gamma_{\boldsymbol{S}}, C'_{\boldsymbol{A}} \cup C'_{\boldsymbol{S}}) \quad \text{and} \quad \bigwedge_{(\gamma_{\boldsymbol{S}}, C'_{\boldsymbol{S}}, l') \in \tau(s)} \Box((s', l'), \gamma_{\boldsymbol{A}} \wedge \gamma_{\boldsymbol{S}}, C'_{\boldsymbol{A}} \cup C'_{\boldsymbol{S}}) ,$$

respectively. The acceptance condition F^* is obtained from F by an appropriate modification. If, for instance, F is a Büchi condition, then $F^* = F \times L$.

We prove:

Theorem 3. *Let $\boldsymbol{A}$ be a restricted TATA, $\boldsymbol{S}$ a TTS, and l a location of $\boldsymbol{S}$. The TATA $\boldsymbol{A}$ accepts $(\boldsymbol{G_S}, l)$ if and only if the TATA $\boldsymbol{A} \times (\boldsymbol{S}, l)$ accepts the one-node graph $\mathbf{G_1}$.*

As a consequence of this theorem and Theorem 2, we obtain:

Corollary 3. *Let $\boldsymbol{S}$ be a TTS, l a location of $\boldsymbol{S}$, and φ a closed TCTL formula in strict normal form. Then $(\boldsymbol{S}, l)$ is a model of φ if and only if $\boldsymbol{A}_\varphi \times (\boldsymbol{S}, l)$ accepts the one-node graph $\mathbf{G_1}$.*

In view of Corollary 1, we can finally state:

Theorem 4. *The timed model checking problem is decidable.*

A closer analysis shows:

Theorem 5. *The timed model checking problem is in PSPACE.*

A use of more complicated and more sophisticated acceptance conditions (hesitant and Libi conditions, see [9]) in the construction of $\boldsymbol{A}_\varphi$ yields the refined complexity bounds from [9]. The details are given in [6].

5 Conclusion

We have provided an automata-theoretic framework for dealing with timed trees (graphs) that allows a satisfying treatment of the model-checking problem for timed computation tree logic. It is conceivable that within this framework one can study timed bisimulation, synthesis of controllers for real-time systems, and model-checking for timed versions of the modal μ-calculus, just as this is known from the theory of discrete systems.

References

1. R. Alur, C. Courcoubetis, and D. L. Dill. Model-checking for real-time systems. In LICS '90, Philadelphia, Pennsylvania, pp. 414–425.
2. R. Alur, C. Courcoubetis, and D. L. Dill. Model-checking in dense real-time. *Inform. and Computation*, 104(1):1–34, 1993.
3. R. Alur and D. L. Dill. Automata for modeling real-time systems. In M. S. Paterson, ed., *ICALP '90*, Warwick, England, Springer, LNCS 443, pp. 322–335.
4. R. Alur and D. L. Dill. A theory of timed automata. *Theoret. Comput. Sci.*, 126(2):183–235, 1994.
5. O. Bernholtz [Kupferman], M. Y. Vardi, and P. Wolper. An automata-theoretic approach to branching-time model checking. In D. L. Dill, ed., *CAV '94*, Stanford, California, Springer, LNCS 818, pp. 142–155.
6. M. Dickhöfer and Th. Wilke. The automata-theoretic method works for TCTL model checking. Techn. Rep. 9811, Inst. f. Informatik u. Prakt. Math., CAU Kiel, 1998. Available as http://www-i7.informatik.rwth-aachen.de/~wilke/publications/Rep9811.html.ps.gz.
7. E. A. Emerson, C. S. Jutla, and A. P. Sistla. On model-checking for fragments of μ-calculus. In C. Courcoubetis, ed., *CAV '93*, Elounda, Greece, Springer, LNCS 697, pp. 385–396.
8. F. Gécseg and M. Steinby. *Tree Automata*. Akadémiai Kiakó, Budapest, 1984.
9. T. A. Henzinger, O. Kupferman, and M. Y. Vardi. A space-efficient on-the-fly algorithm for real-time model checking. In U. Montanari, V. Sassone, eds., *Concur '96*, Pisa, Italy, Springer, LNCS 1119, pp. 514–529.
10. W. Thomas. Languages, automata and logic. In A. Salomaa and G. Rozenberg, eds., *Handbook of Formal Languages*, volume 3. Springer, Berlin, 1997, pp. 389–455.
11. W. Thomas. Automata on infinite objects. In J. v. Leeuwen, ed., *Handbook of Theoretical Computer Science*, vol. B, Elsevier, Amsterdam, 1990, pp. 134–191.
12. M. Y. Vardi. Alternating automata and program verification. In J. v. Leeuwen, ed., *Computer Science Today*, Springer, 1995, LNCS 1000, pp. 471–485.
13. M. Y. Vardi and P. Wolper. An automata-theoretic approach to automatic program verification. In D. Kozen, ed., *LICS 86*, Cambridge, Mass., pp. 322–331.

Space-Time Tradeoffs for Graph Properties

Yevgeniy Dodis[1] and Sanjeev Khanna[2]

[1] Laboratory for Computer Science, MIT, USA. E-mail: `yevgen@theory.lcs.mit.edu`
[2] Department of Fundamental Mathematics Research, Bell Labs, USA. E-mail: `sanjeev@research.bell-labs.com`.

Abstract. We initiate a study of space-time tradeoffs in the cell-probe model under restricted preprocessing power. Classically, space-time tradeoffs have been studied in this model under the assumption that the preprocessing is unrestricted. In this setting, a large gap exists between the best known upper and lower bounds. Augmenting the model with a function family F that characterizes the preprocessing power, makes for a more realistic computational model and allows to obtain much tighter space-time tradeoffs for various natural settings of F. The extreme settings of our model reduce to the classical cell probe and generalized decision tree complexities.

We use graph properties for the purpose of illustrating various aspects of our model across this broad spectrum. In doing so, we develop new lower bound techniques and strengthen some existing results. In particular, we obtain near-optimal space-time tradeoffs for various natural choices of F; strengthen the Rivest-Vuillemin proof of the famous AKR conjecture to show that no non-trivial monotone graph property can be expressed as a polynomial of sub-quadratic degree; and obtain new results on the generalized decision tree complexity w.r.t. various families F.

1 Introduction

It is well known that preprocessing of static data often significantly speeds up the time it takes to answer dynamic queries about it. A data structure with appropriate auxiliary information about the static data can facilitate efficient answering of dynamic queries. Naturally, the more space is available for building such a data structure, the more auxiliary information one can precompute and the faster the queries can be answered. A natural and important question in this context is to characterize the tradeoff between the amount of available preprocessing space and the time it takes to answer the queries.

1.1 The Classical Cell Probe Model

A widely used computational model for studying such tradeoffs is the *cell probe model* introduced by Yao [17]. The *static data structure* problem in the cell probe model is as follows. We are given a function $f : Y \times Q \mapsto \{0, 1\}$, where the first input $y \in Y$ ($|y| = m$) is static, and the second input $q \in Q$ ($|q| = n$) is the dynamic query (typically $n \ll m$, we assume so from now on). We are also given a parameter s which indicates the amount of space available for storing a data structure $D = \{c_1, c_2, \ldots, c_s\}$ containing information about y, where $c_i : Y \mapsto \{0, 1\}$. Each c_i is called a *cell* and the process of generating D given y is called *preprocessing*. It is done only once, after which a given query q is answered by (adaptively) *probing* (the values of the) cells of D, and the time t spent in answering q is the number of probes made in order to compute $f(y, q)$. The objective is to build D so as to be able to compute $f(y, q)$ (for any y and q) by probing as few cells in D as possible, and the goal is to study this optimal worst-case time $t = T_s(f)$ as a function of s, m and n. We emphasize that the time is not the running time of the "probing scheme" but only the *number of accesses* to D. This models the situation when the local computation is cheap/fast but the database access is expensive/slow. Moreover, this measure of time is indicative of a fundamental combinatorial limitation on how fast the queries can be answered for any natural notion of time.

The static data structure problem has been extensively studied in the literature ([1–4, 10–12, 16]). Yet, no explicitly defined function f is known for which $t = \omega(n)$ is proven when space $s = poly(n)$. Moreover, a simple argument demonstrates that showing such a super linear bound for an NP function f would *unconditionally* separate NP from the class of read-twice branching programs [13]; a long-standing question in complexity theory [15]. This situation is to be contrasted with an existential result of Miltersen [10] which states that for a *random* function $f : Y \times Q \mapsto \{0, 1\}$ we have (w.h.p.) $T_s(f) = \Omega(m) \gg n$ even when $s = 2^{n-1}$. In other words, one has to read essentially the whole static input even when exponential preprocessing space is given. The result is not surprising since one cannot hope to "efficiently share" limited information to answer queries about completely unrelated values. Still, constructing an *explicit* function that would close this large gap ($O(n)$ vs. $\Omega(m)$) is a major open question in the cell probe model.

While the strength of the cell probe model lies in the clean framework that it provides for studying space-time tradeoffs, the model is unrealistic in at least two respects. Firstly, the probing scheme is all-powerful: it may compute any arbitrary function with the t bits that it reads. So for example, any (even undecidable) function f can be computed with m probes by storing y directly and reading it completely for any query q (so $s = t = m$). Secondly, the preprocessing stage is allowed to use arbitrarily complex functions c_i in the data structure D. For example, any function f can be computed with exponential space $s = 2^n$ and unit time $t = 1$ by simply storing the answer to every possible query. These two aspects of the model at least partly explain the difficulty in obtaining strong lower bounds in this model.

1.2 Our Model: Cell Probe Model with Restricted Preprocessing Power

The goal of this paper is to study space-time tradeoffs in the cell probe model when the preprocessing power may be restricted, making the model more realistic and fine-tuned (while it is an interesting direction to also limit the power of the probing scheme, we focus on restricting the preprocessing power). We model limited preprocessing power by introducing a new parameter F which is used to denote a (typically infinite) family of (boolean) functions. Given a function family F, we require that the value of each cell c_i in D corresponds to an application of some $g \in$ F to a subset of y's input bits. We call such data structure D F-*restricted*. Thus, while space constraint s limits the *amount* of precomputed information, the function family F limits the *complexity* of precomputed information. The time t in this new parameterized model is denoted by $t = T_{F,s}(f)$, referred to as the *cell probe complexity of f w.r.t.* F. Since the extremal case of unrestricted F is simply the standard static data structure problem, our model is a proper extension of the classical cell probe model.

Another extreme of our model is when the space s is unrestricted but F is restricted. Then, the cell probe complexity of f w.r.t. F is simply the *generalized decision tree complexity* of evaluating f over a worst-case query; we denote this measure by $T_F(f)$. Indeed, unrestricted space implies that we have "precomputed" all possible applications of every $g \in$ F to every appropriate subset of y's input bits. So the question is no longer the one of creating a space-efficient data structure but that of "adaptive expressibility" of a function f on a given query using functions from F. This is precisely the generalized decision tree complexity w.r.t. F. When F consists merely of the identity function (which we call *trivial* F), this is just the (simple) decision tree complexity measure. Unlike the classical data structure problem, it is often possible to tightly characterize the decision tree complexity of a given function (e.g. [5]). Thus, our general model elegantly *unifies the issue of space-efficient data structures with that of adaptive expressibility*, bridging together the cell probe complexity and the generalized decision tree complexity.

1.3 Our Function f: Graph Properties

The objective of our study is to illustrative different aspects of our new model across a broad spectrum of possible settings of F and s (in particular, to illustrate how much tighter space-time tradeoffs can be obtained once we put reasonable restrictions on F, but we do not limit ourselves to this). For this purpose, we use a problem related to verification of graph properties. Aside from combinatorial interest, an important motivation for this choice comes from the fact that graph properties form a rich class of functions having decision tree complexity. In fact, the famous Aandrea-Karp-Rosenberg (AKR) conjecture states that every nontrivial *monotone* graph property P on n-vertex graphs is *evasive*, i.e. its decision tree complexity $D(P) = \binom{n}{2}$[1]. The conjecture is proven up to a constant factor by Rivest and Vuillemin [14], i.e. $D(P) = \Omega(n^2) = \Omega(m)$. As we will see later, this result in fact forms a "base case" in our study (corresponding to trivial F).

Our Setup: Fix a graph property P. Given an n-vertex graph $G = (V, E)$ as a static input, our goal is to preprocess it to answer dynamic queries of the form:

---

[1] As we will see, n will be the size of our query, which is consistent with its usage before. Also, $m = \binom{n}{2}$, i.e. the size of the adjacency matrix of our graph.

"Given $X \subseteq V$, does the subgraph G_X of G induced by X satisfy P?"

We refer to this problem as the *induced subgraph problem*. Thus, $f_P(G, X) = P(G_X)$, $m = \binom{n}{2} = \Theta(n^2)$ and a good lower bound would be of the form $t = \Omega(n^2/polylog(s))$. For notational convenience, we will write $\mathsf{T}_{\mathsf{F},s}(P)$ in place of $\mathsf{T}_{\mathsf{F},s}(f_P)$. Note that every query evaluates the property P on some (sub)graph. The hope is that the distribution of P over induced subgraphs of G is very non-trivial, so that it is hard to reuse space when computing f_P.

2 Overview of Our Results

As we pointed, the induced subgraph problem will be an example problem demonstrating the richness of our model as well as different techniques to show space-time tradeoffs in various settings, ranging from the classical cell probe complexity to the generalized decision tree complexity. In what follows, we describe more precisely some of our results, leaving others out due to space limitations. In particular, we will not talk about oblivious and non-deterministic computation in our model. In the next section we will prove a representative result.

2.1 *Restricted* Space, *Unrestricted* Function Families

We start with the extremal case of unrestricted preprocessing. As remarked by Miltersen *et al.* [13], essentially all known lower bound results for the classical data structure problem can be viewed as applications of the following connection between the cell probe and the communication complexity model [10]. In this model, introduced by Yao [18], Alice is given $y \in Y$, Bob is given $q \in Q$ and they wish to compute $f(y, q)$ by exchanging the minimum number of bits. This number is the deterministic communication complexity of f. We describe the connection of [10] more generally using the notion of *asymmetric communication complexity* introduced in [13]. Here, instead of measuring simply the total number of bits exchanged, we measure the number of bits sent by Alice and Bob *individually*. An $[A, B]$-protocol is a protocol where Alice sends at most A bits and Bob sends at most B bits. A lower bound of $[A, B]$ means that in the worst case, either Alice must send $\Omega(A)$ bits or Bob must send $\Omega(B)$ bits in order to compute f. To obtain the most general result, we consider a variant of the cell probe model where a cell size is an additional parameter b. In other words, rather than storing boolean functions in the data structure, we store b-bit functions $c_i : Y \mapsto \{0, 1\}^b$ and read all b bits per probe.

Lemma 1. [10] *Any cell probe scheme with space s, cell size b and time t for computing f yields a $[tb, t \log s]$-protocol for computing f. Hence, a lower bound of $[A, B]$ implies that $\mathsf{T}_s(f) \geq \Omega(\min(A/b, B/\log s))$.*

Since $B \leq n$ (Bob can always send his entire input), the best possible lower bound obtainable this way is $t = \Omega(\frac{n}{\log s})$ implying that the current proof techniques cannot cross the $\Omega(n/\log s)$ barrier (but they can possibly give this bound for large values of b). We show that such a lower bound can indeed be established for the induced subgraph problem using Lemma 1, for any non-trivial monotone graph property as well as for the property PARITY: "Does G have an odd number of edges?". The first result is shown using the *fooling set method* (see [9]) and the second uses the *richness technique* of [13].

Theorem 1.
- $T_s(P) \geq \Omega(\frac{n}{\log s})$, for any non-trivial monotone property P.
- $T_s(\text{PARITY}) \geq \Omega(\frac{n}{\log s})$ even when the cell size $b = n$.

This is as far as we can get in the classical setting using current techniques.

2.2 *Restricted* Space, *Restricted* Function Families

We now turn our attention to the core of our study where we restrict the pre-processing power by means of a function family F. Our goal here is to develop techniques to beat $\Omega(n/\log s)$ illustrating how restricted preprocessing allows to obtain tighter bounds on query time. In fact, for many natural families F we obtain nearly optimal lower bounds of the form $\Omega(n^2/polylog(s))$. The extreme case where F is trivial (i.e. we are allowed to store just the edges of the graph) reduces to the AKR set-up. An $\Omega(n^2)$ lower bound can thus be obtained for any non-trivial monotone graph property (even on a fixed query set). However, once we allow F to contain more general function families, many evasive properties can now be decided by reading very few cells for any *fixed* query. Yet, as we will show, this efficiency in answering specific queries can provably not be translated into a space-efficient data structure that allows to efficiently answer *all* the queries. As in the classical model, the main difficulty is in efficient sharing of information contained in the cells across different queries. However, unlike the classical model, explicit knowledge about the family F enables us to *reason about the behavior of the precomputed information.*

As an elementary example, consider the following evasive property P: Is G an empty graph? Let F be simply the family of OR functions. Clearly, a single OR can express the property on a given G. In fact, this seems to be a very natural function family for computing P. However, a cell storing an OR of all the edges in the graph is of no use in determining whether an induced subgraph G_X satisfies P. Setting any edge outside of G_X to true fixes this OR to 1 without affecting $P(G_X)$. Intuitively speaking, the cells that are sensitive to "many" edges are useful for answering only very few queries, while "short" cells contain little information forcing us to read many of them to answer a "large" query. Indeed, we prove that if F is restricted to only AND and OR functions, $T_{F,s}(P) = \Omega(n^2/\log^2 s)$ for any evasive property P.

We obtain similar results for more general α-CNF, α-DNF (for constant α) and symmetric function families. We also study the following curious question: What is the time complexity of induced subgraph problem for a property P when the data structure can only contain answers about whether an induced subgraph of the input graph has property P? While any single query can now be answered in one probe, we show $\Omega(n^2/\log^2 s)$ bound for any non-trivial "uniform" monotone property.

Basic Idea: The central technique used for the induced subgraph problem is a probabilistic argument which shows that for any data structuring strategy, there exists an input graph G s.t. (a) it "stabilizes" the value of any cell that is sensitive to many variables (where "many" will depend on space s), and (b) still leaves a large subset X "untouched" such that one can reveal the edges of G_X via an evasive strategy[2]. Since the evasive game on X is now only sensitive to cells with small number of edge variables, we get our desired bounds (same results will apply to monotone graph properties as well by the AKR). We illustarate this "stabilization technique" on α-CNF/α-DNF formulas in Section 3.

2.3   *Unrestricted* Space, *Restricted* Function Families

We now turn our attention to the extreme where the space s is unrestricted and only the family F is restricted. In case of the induced subgraph problem, $T_F(P)$ reduces to the decision tree complexity w.r.t. F of computing P on the *entire vertex set* V. In other words, how many functions from F one needs to evaluate (adaptively in the worst-case) in order to verify if a given graph G satisfies P? When F contains merely the identity function, it is the setting of the AKR and $\Omega(n^2)$ lower bound is known for any non-trivial monotone P [14, 8]. We examine what happens when we allow more powerful functions in F such as AND, OR (more generally, threshold functions), and XOR (more generally, small degree polynomials). Since space is not an issue, even these seemingly simple function families efficiently capture many evasive properties, e.g., $T_{AND}(\text{CLIQUE}) = 1$, $T_{OR}(\text{CONNECTIVITY}) = \Theta(n \log n)$ [5], $T_{XOR}(\text{PARITY}) = 1$. Yet we will show that for large classes of evasive properties, these families are no more powerful than the trivial identity function.

Small Degree Polynomials: We study the family $\mathcal{F}_{\deg \leq k}$ of all multivariate polynomials over $\mathbb{Z}_2$ of degree at most k; the case $k = 1$ gives the XOR family. Let $\deg(f)$ denote the degree of the (unique) multi-linear polynomial q computing a boolean function f over $\mathbb{Z}_2$. Extending the ideas from Rivest and Vuillemin [14], we establish the following theorem:

Theorem 2. *For any non-trivial monotone graph property P, $\deg(P) = \Omega(n^2)$.*

Since $\deg(P) \leq D(P)$ (any decision tree of depth d yields a polynomial of degree at most d), the theorem implies the AKR conjecture (up to a constant factor) and shows that the degree of a monotone graph property over $\mathbb{Z}_2$ essentially matches its decision tree complexity. We note that for a general (even evasive and monotone!) function f, much larger gaps are possible. Moreover, *any* multilinear polynomial over $\mathbb{Z}_2$, invariant under relabeling of vertices, computes some valid graph property (e.g. PARITY has degree 1), but this property can never be monotone unless the degree is large. Using the easy observation that $\deg(P) \leq k T_{\mathcal{F}_{\deg \leq k}}(P)$, we get a tight (e.g., achieved by CLIQUE) general bound:

Corollary 1. *For any non-trivial monotone P, $T_{\mathcal{F}_{deg \leq k}}(P) = \Omega(\frac{n^2}{k})$. In particular, $T_{XOR}(P) = \Omega(n^2)$.*

---

[2] A strategy that forces one to probe all edges of the graph.

This corollary still implies the AKR result as the identity is a trivial XOR function. Thus, having access to 2^m possible XORs is no more powerful than being able to query only an edge at a time!

AND/OR Families: On the other hand, this approach does not work for two most natural extensions of the AKR setup, namely the AND and OR function families, since the degree of these functions can be as large as $\Omega(n^2)$ (in fact, a general bound of $\Omega(n^2)$ does not hold for these families). We develop general techniques for studying these families by essentially reducing their decision tree complexity to a certain measure on simple decision trees. Intuitively, if (simple) decision tree complexity of a property P corresponds to looking at as few edges of G as possible, a good bound on $T_{\text{AND}}(P)$ ($T_{\text{OR}}(P)$) corresponds to looking at as few *missing* (*present*) edges of G as possible. We then develop several techniques to lower bound this measure and obtain $\Omega(n^2)$ bound for many properties. Our techniques are based on examining the combinatorial structure of graph certificates and design of general "edge-revealing" strategies for monotone graph properties. One of the strategies we examined in detail is to answer "no" ("yes") unless forced to say "yes" ("no"). Our study of these strategies might be of independent interest. We remark that our techniques for AND/OR families apply to arbitrary functions and not only to graph properties. We defer the details to the full version.

3 Stabilization Technique

In order to explain the technique, we need two definitions.

Definition 1 (Gadget Graph). An $\langle n, q(n) \rangle$-*gadget graph* $H(V, E)$ is a labeled clique on n vertices such that: (a) each edge is labeled 0 (missing), 1 (present), or $*$ (unspecified), and (b) there exists a subset $Q \subset V$ with $|Q| = q(n)$, such that Q induces a clique where each edge of the clique is labeled $*$. We refer to Q as the *query set* of H.

Definition 2 (Stabilizing Graph). Given an F-restricted data structure D of size s, a graph H is called an $\langle n, q(n), g(s) \rangle$-*stabilizing graph* for D if: (a) H is a $\langle n, q(n) \rangle$-gadget graph, and (b) every cell in D reduces to being a function of at most $g(s)$ edge variables on the partial assignment specified by H.

Now suppose for a function family F we want to show that $T_{F,s}(P) = \Omega(q^2(n)/g(s))$ for every evasive property P. We start by showing existence of a $\langle n, q(n), g(s) \rangle$-stabilizing graph G_D for every F-restricted data structure D. Thus when G_D is presented as the static input, every cell in D reduces to be a function of at most $g(s)$ edge variables. At the same time, we have access to a query set Q whose every edge is unspecified as yet. We present this set Q as the dynamic input to the scheme and play the evasive game for property P on the subgraph induced by Q. Since each cell probe can reveal at most $g(s)$ edge variables, we obtain the desired $\Omega(q^2(n)/g(s))$ lower bound. The following theorem summarizes this argument.

Theorem 3. *If every* F-*restricted data structure of size s has a* $\langle n, q(n), g(s) \rangle$-*stabilizing graph, then for any evasive property* P, $\mathsf{T}_{\mathsf{F},s}(P) = \Omega(q^2(n)/g(s))$.

Thus the heart of our approach is to show the existence of a $\langle n, q(n), g(s) \rangle$-stabilizing graph with suitable parameters. We show existence of such graph using the *probabilistic method*. Typically, we pick a random $\langle n, q(n) \rangle$-gadget graph s.t. for any $h \in \mathsf{F}$, the probability that $h|H$ does not reduce to a function of at most $g(s)$ variables is less than $1/s$. Applying the union bound to the s cells of D, we conclude that $\langle n, q(n), g(s) \rangle$-stabilizing graph exists for *any* D.

As a simple example, let us construct an $\langle n, n/2, \log^2 s \rangle$-stabilizing graph for the family of OR functions, implying that $\mathsf{T}_{\mathsf{OR},s}(P) = \Omega(n^2/\log^2 s)$ for any evasive P. Create H by picking a random subset $Q \subset V$ of size $n/2$ and setting all edges outside Q's induced subgraph to true. Take any OR function $c = e_1 \vee \ldots \vee e_p$ and assume that edges e_i touch k vertices of V. The only way that c is not stabilized to 1 by H, is when all k vertices fall inside Q, i.e. with probability $\binom{n-k}{n/2-k}/\binom{n}{n/2} \leq 1/2^k < 1/s$ if $k > \log s$. So any c that has a reasonable $(> 1/s)$ chance of "surviving" must have $k \leq \log s$, i.e. depends on at most $\log^2 s$ edges.

In the remainder of this section, we construct stabilizing graphs for α-CNF and α-DNF formulas (for constant α), deferring other results to the full version.

Theorem 4. *For any evasive property* P *and constant* α,
$$\mathsf{T}_{\alpha-\mathsf{CNF/DNF},s}(P) = \Omega(n^2/(\log^{\alpha-1} n \log^{2\alpha} s)).$$

First, it suffices to show the claimed lower bound for α-DNF formulas (store any α-CNF by storing its complement α-DNF formula). By Theorem 3, it is enough to show the existence of a $\langle n, n/2, O(\log^{\alpha-1} n \log^{2\alpha} s) \rangle$-stabilizing graph for every α-DNF - restricted data structure D. We will proceed similarly to the case of OR formulas above, but slightly change our random experiment to make the analysis simpler. Let us say that a formula f is *stabilized* by a partial assignment if it fixes the value of f. We will show that, if S is a random subset, constructed by choosing each vertex of V with probability $1/2$, then setting each edge variable in $S \times V$ to $0/1$ uniformly at random (we refer to this experiment as **A**) either stabilizes any α-DNF formula or reduces it to be a function of $O(\log^{\alpha-1} n \log^{2\alpha} s)$ edge variables, with probability $1 - o(1/s)$. Setting then $Q = V \setminus S$, and noticing that $|Q| \geq n/2$ with probability at least $1/2$, we get that the claimed stabilizing graph exists.

The claim is shown by induction on α. The base case of $\alpha = 1$ is just slighly more technical than the case of OR functions. Picking appropriate constants, if 1-DNF formula f has more than $\Omega(log^2 s)$ edges, its edges touch $\Omega(\log s)$ vertices of V, so w.h.p. S contains $\Omega(\log s)$ vertices touched by f. Thus, at least $\Omega(\log s)$ edges will be set to $0/1$ at random in **A**. Since each such setting stabilizes 1-DNF w/pr. $1/2$, w.h.p. f will be stabilized during experiment **A**.

Our inductive step relies on two technical Lemmas, whose proofs we omit due to the space limitations. The first Lemma says that any α-DNF f either has a certain "compact" decomposition into $(\alpha - 1)$-DNF's or it has a "large" number of pairwise disjoint terms. The next Lemma shows that experiment **A** stabilizes α-DNF formulas with large number of pairwise disjoint terms.

Lemma 2. *Let f be an α-DNF formula on N variables and let $0 < r < 1$ be a positive real. Then either*

- *f has a decomposition of the form $l_0 f_0 + l_1 f_1 + \ldots + l_{p-1} f_{p-1}$ where l_i's are literals, f_i's are $(\alpha - 1)$-DNF formulas, and $p \leq \ln(\alpha 2^\alpha N^\alpha)/r$, or*
- *f has at least $(1/2\alpha r)$ pairwise disjoint (i.e. no common variables) terms.*

Lemma 3. *Let f be an α-DNF formula with $\alpha^2 2^{4\alpha+2} \log^2 s$ pairwise disjoint terms. Then experiment **A** stabilizes f with probability at least $1 - 1/s^2$.*

We can now complete the proof. Consider any α-DNF formula f. Let $r = 1/(\alpha^3 2^{4\alpha+3} \log^2 s)$. By Lemma 2, either f has $\alpha^2 2^{4\alpha+2} \log^2 s$ pairwise disjoint terms or it has a representation of the form $l_0 f_0 + l_1 f_1 + \ldots + l_{p-1} f_{p-1}$, where $p \leq p_{\max} = \ln(\alpha n^{2\alpha})/r = O(\log n \log^2 s)$. In case of the first scenario, we know by Lemma 3 that f will be stabilized "almost certainly". Otherwise, we argue that almost certainly f will have no more than $h(\alpha) = O(\log^{\alpha-1} n \log^{2\alpha} s)$ variables. We sketched that $h(1) = O(\log^2 s)$. Using the compact decomposition of f and applying induction to each f_i in the decomposition, we must satisfy the recurrence: $h(\alpha) \leq p_{\max} h(\alpha - 1) + p_{\max} \leq (p_{\max})^{\alpha-1} h(1) + \sum_{i=1}^{\alpha-1} (p_{\max})^i$. Using $h(1) = O(\log^2 s)$, we get $h(\alpha) = O(\log^{\alpha-1} n \log^{2\alpha} s)$.

To analyze the probability of failure, denote by $R(\alpha)$ the probability that a given α-DNF formula does not reduce to a function of at most $h(\alpha)$ distinct variables. Using Lemma 3, we have $R(\alpha) \leq p_{\max} R(\alpha - 1) + \frac{1}{s^2}$. Scaling $h(1)$ by a suitably large constant, it is easy to see that $R(\alpha)$ can be bounded by $o(1/s)$ for any constant α. This completes the proof of Theorem 4.

Remark: The stabilization technique also works for the *randomized complexity*. Using the best known bound of $\Omega(n^{4/3})$ [6] for randomized decision tree complexity of monotone graph properties, we get a bound $\Omega(n^{4/3}/polylog(s))$ for each of the families we considered.

4 Conclusions and Open Problems

We showed that our model provides a uniform framework to study lower bounds across a spectrum of computational models. Using as an example the induced subgraph problem, we showed some techniques for breaking the $\Omega(n/\log s)$ barrier for various natural settings of F. In the process, we also obtained a strengthening of the Rivest-Vuillemin result, showing that monotone graph properties cannot be expressed by polynomials of sub-quadratic degree. Finally, we obtained new results and techniques on the generalized decision tree complexity with respect to some natural families like the AND/OR family.

We introduced a parameterized cell probe model in an effort to examine space-time tradeoffs in computationally realistic preprocessing scenarios. However, for the sake of getting unconditional results and in order to illustrate our new model more cleanly, we only considered *syntactic* restrictions on the preprocessing function family. It is perhaps more interesting to examine *computational* restrictions. For example, to examine the measure T_{poly} (where POLY is the set of polynomial time computable functions), with a hope of obtaining the first super linear lower bound. A complimentary direction is to place some restriction on the power of the probing scheme, that is, to restrict how the information from the data structure is accessed and/or processed. An example of that is *oblivious computation*, where, given a query q, the probing scheme has to decide right away which t cells to access. Again, it is perhaps a feasible intermediate goal to obtain a super linear bound in this setting. Another interesting direction is to examine the effects of randomization, i.e. when the probing scheme might be probabilistic and have a small propbability of error. Finally, it will be extremely interesting to apply our model to some other important problems, like the *nearest neighbor search* problem (see [2, 3]).

References

1. M. Ajtai. A lower bound for finding predecessors in Yao's cell probe model. In *Combinatorica*, 8:235–247, 1988.
2. A. Borodin, R. Ostrovsky, Y. Rabani. Lower Bounds for High Dimensional Nearest Neighbor Search and Related Problems. In *Proc. of STOC*, 1999.
3. A. Chakrabarti, B. Chazelle, B. Gum, A. Lvov. A good neighbor is hard to find. In *Proc. of STOC*, 1999.
4. P. Elias, R.A. Flower. The complexity of some simple retrieval problems. In *J. ACM*, 22:367–379, 1975.
5. A. Hajnal, W. Maass and G. Turan. On the communication complexity of graph properties. In *Proc. of STOC*, pp. 186–191, 1988.
6. P. Hajnal. An $n^{4/3}$ lower bound on the randomized complexity of graph properties. In *Combinatorica*, 11:131–143, 1991.
7. L. Hellerstein, P. Klein, R. Wilber. On the Time-Space Complexity of Reachability Queries for Preprocessed Graphs. In *Information Processing Letters*, 27:261–267, 1990.
8. J. Kahn, M. Saks, D. Sturtevant. A topological approach to evasiveness. In *Proc. of FOCS*, pp. 31–39, 1983.
9. E. Kushilevitz, N. Nisan. Communication Complexity. *Cambridge University Press*, 1997.
10. P. Miltersen. The bit probe complexity measure revisited. In *Proc. of STACS*, pp. 662–671, 1993.
11. P. Miltersen. Lower bounds for union-split-find related problems on random access machines. In *Proc. STOC*, pp. 625–634, 1994.
12. P. Miltersen. On cell probe complexity of polynomial evaluation. In *Theoretical Computer Science*, 143:167–174, 1995.
13. P. Miltersen, N. Nisan, S. Safra, A. Wigderson. On Data Structures and Asymmetric Communication Comlexity. In *Proc. of STOC*, pp. 103–111, 1995.
14. R. Rivest, J. Vuillemin. On recognizing graph properties from adjacency matrices. In *Theoretical Computer Science*, 3:371–384, 1976.
15. I. Wegener. The complexity of Boolean functions. In *Wiley-Teubner series in Computer Science*, 1987.
16. B. Xiao. New bounds in cell probe model. Ph.D. thesis, UC San Diego, 1992.
17. A. Yao. Should tables be sorted. In *J. ACM*, 28:615–628, 1981.
18. A. Yao. Some complexity questions related to distributed computing. In *Proc. of STOC*, pp. 209–213, 1979.

Boundedness of Reset P/T Nets

C. Dufourd[1], P. Jančar[2*], and Ph. Schnoebelen[1]

[1] Lab. Spécification et Vérification, CNRS UMR 5522 & ENS de Cachan, France
[2] Dept. of Computer Science, FEI VŠB-TU, Tech. Univ. Ostrava - Czech Rep.
email: {dufourd,phs}@lsv.ens-cachan.fr, Petr.Jancar@vsb.cz

Abstract. P/T nets with reset and transfer arcs can be seen as counter-machines with some restricted set of operations. Surprisingly, several problems related to boundedness are harder for Reset nets than for the more expressive Transfer nets. Our main result is that boundedness is undecidable for nets with three reset arcs, while it is decidable for nets with two resetable places.

1 Introduction

"Infinite-state transition systems" is a generic name for a large collection of computational models that go beyond finite-state systems but where some decidability results exist. These *infinite systems* (for short) are currently under active study for several reasons. First some applications use models that cannot easily be abstracted into finite-state systems (e.g., hybrid systems). Then, some models only go beyond finite-state in a very specific way (e.g., parameterized systems, lossy channel systems). Finally, verification methods designed for infinite-state systems may help understand where and how to avoid the famous *state explosion problem* in the finite-state framework.

P/T nets are a classical infinite-state model which remains partially analyzable. Many properties (reachability, safety properties, termination, etc.) are decidable and many are not (bisimilarity, language equivalence, etc.). Here we are not concerned with their use in modelling concurrency: we see them as *weak counter machines* that do not have a full-fledged test for zero (i.e., transitions can only test negatively for emptiness of a counter).

Reset nets are P/T nets extended with the possibility of resetting (setting to zero) the content of places. This adds expressive power and makes reachability undecidable [AK77]. *Transfer nets* are even more powerful: they can transfer the whole content of some place to some other one. [DFS98,Duf98] investigate decidability issues in the verification of Reset and Transfer nets : compared to P/T nets, the decidability of reachability is lost but termination, coverability and inevitability remain decidable.

---
* P. Jančar is partially supported by the Grant Agency of the Czech Republic, Grant No. 201/97/0456

The most surprising result in [DFS98] [1] is the undecidability of bounded-ness for Reset nets, knowing it is clearly decidable for Transfer nets [FS98]. Boundedness is a fundamental question: it is to *space* what termination is to *time*. Indeed, termination and boundedness are closely related problems. Bound-edness has been neglected in model-checking of infinite systems because most approaches only refer to the observable behaviour of systems. However, when studying potentially infinite systems, a first question is to check if they really are infinite !

Obviously, boundedness issues for Reset and Transfer nets are difficult ques-tions. [DFS98] uses an involved reduction from Hilbert's 10th problem. [KCK+97] gives a faulty decidability proof for a more general model.

Our contribution. We give a new and simpler proof that boundedness is unde-cidable for Reset nets *even for nets with at most 3 reset arcs* [2].

We prove that this result is tight and that *boundedness is decidable for Reset nets with 2 resetable places*. This threshold value is surprising since 2 reset arcs are enough to simulate strong counter machines quite faithfully (see Theorem 11 in [DFS98]). Exhibiting the exact threshold value is our main result. The proof is based on the possibility of producing a "semilinear" witness of unboundedness. Since we are close to the boundary of this possibility, it is natural that the proof is technically nontrivial. A similar situation appears, e.g., in the case of VASS's: in dimension 2 they are always semilinear, unlike in dimension 3 [HP79].

We also investigate related problems and complete the following table:

	Reset nets	Transfer nets	P/T nets
boundedness	Σ_1-complete	Decidable	Decidable
place-boundedness	Σ_1-complete	Σ_1-complete	Decidable
structural boundedness	Π_2-complete	Π_1-complete	Decidable (PTIME !)
termination	Decidable	Decidable	Decidable
structural termination	Π_1-complete	Π_1-complete	Decidable (PTIME !)

Our results and techniques have applications to models related to Reset net (see below).

Related Works. [AK77] shows that reachability is undecidable when P/T nets are extended with reset arcs. [AL78] shows that coverability is decidable for VASS's with reset arcs. [May98] gives several undecidability results for lossy counter machines with applications to, e.g., Reset and Transfer nets.

Reset and Transfer nets are a subset of Valk's self-modifying nets [Val78]. [LC94,Cia94] consider them from an expressivity perspective.

For many purposes, Reset and Transfer nets are very close to other infinite-state models currently under study. The undecidability of boundedness for Reset

---

[1] Another surprise is that place-boundedness ("is a given place bounded ?") is not de-cidable for Transfer nets while boundedness is. Boundedness and place-boundedness are very similar problems and many papers confuse them.

[2] For lack of space, most proofs are sketched or omitted. They appear in the full version available from the authors.

nets translates into undecidability of boundedness for Lossy VASS's with zero test [BM99]. *Parameterized broadcast protocols* can be encoded into Transfer nets and [EFM99] uses a crucial counter-example inspired from our Figure 1. [BO98] introduces *reconfigurable nets* and shows that boundedness is decidable. These nets can in fact be seen as Transfer nets.

2 Reset and Transfer nets

A P/T net is a tuple $N = \langle P, T, F \rangle$ where $P = \{p_1, ...\}$ and $T = \{t_1, ...\}$ are two disjoint finite sets (of *places*, of *transitions*), and where $F \subseteq P \times T \cup T \times P$ is a set of *arcs*; we denote ${}^\bullet t = \{p \mid (p, t) \in F\}$, and $t^\bullet = \{p \mid (t, p) \in F\}$. We assume the usual graphical presentation.

A *marking* m of N can be identified with a multiset of places; we also say that $m(p)$ denotes the number of *tokens* on place p in m. By $(m < m')$ $m \leq m'$ we denote the (proper) multiset inclusion. A *marked net* is a net with some initial marking m_0.

We write $m \xrightarrow{t} m'$ iff $m \geq {}^\bullet t$ and $m' = m - {}^\bullet t + t^\bullet$ (first the enabling tokens are removed and then the output tokens are added). We use $m \to m'$ when abstracting the transition; similarly we use $m \xrightarrow{u} m'$ (with $u \in T^*$) and $m \xrightarrow{*} m'$.

A *Reset net* is a P/T net with special "reset arcs". Formally, it is a tuple $\langle P, T, F, F_R \rangle$ where $\langle P, T, F \rangle$ is a P/T net and $F_R \subseteq T \times P$ is a set of *reset arcs*. Reset arcs do not change the requirements for enabling a transition. But when $m \xrightarrow{t} m'$, a reset arc (t, p) sets p to zero so that $m'(p) = 0$ ($m'(p) = 1$ if (t, p) is in both F and F_R). We depict reset arcs by crossed edges as in Fig. 1 where $F_R = \{(t_2, p_3), (t_4, p_4)\}$ and $m_0 = (1, 0, 1, 0)$. Observe that $(1, 0, n, 0) \xrightarrow{w(n)} (1, 0, n+1, 0)$ for $w(n) = t_1^n t_2 t_3^n t_4$. Hence the net is unbounded. However no fixed $u, u' \in T^*$ exist s.t. $m_0 \xrightarrow{u} m_1 \xrightarrow{u'} m_2 \xrightarrow{u'} m_3 \cdots$ leads to unboundedness.

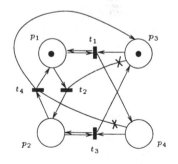

Fig. 1. An unbounded Reset net

A *Transfer net* is a P/T net with special "transfer arcs". Formally, it is a tuple $\langle P, T, F, F_T \rangle$ where $\langle P, T, F \rangle$ is a P/T net and $F_T \subseteq P \times T \times P$ is a set of *transfer arcs* (with the condition that for any p, t there is at most one $(p, t, p') \in F_T$). Transfer arcs do not change the requirements for enabling a transition. But when $m \xrightarrow{t} m'$, m' is obtained by (1) removing the enabling tokens, then (2) transferring all tokens from p to p' when $(p, t, p') \in F_T$, and finally (3) adding the usual output tokens. We omit the tedious formal definitions.

Boundedness and termination problems. A place p is *bounded* in a marked net if there is a bound $k \in \mathbb{N}$ s.t. $m(p) \leq k$ for all m reachable from m_0. A marked net is *bounded* if all its places are. A net is *structurally bounded* if it is bounded for any initial marking (note that the bound k may vary with m_0).

A marked net is *terminating* if it admits no infinite run. A net is *structurally terminating* if it is terminating for any initial marking.

Reset (and Transfer) nets enjoy the monotonicity property: $m_1 \xrightarrow{t} m_2$ and $m_1' > m_1$ imply $m_1' \xrightarrow{t} m_2'$ with $m_2' \geq m_2$ ($m_2' > m_2$ for Transfer nets). Hence

Lemma 1. *A marked Reset net is unbounded iff it has an unbounded nondecreasing run.*

where an *unbounded run* is an infinite sequence of moves $m_0 \xrightarrow{t_1} m_1 \xrightarrow{t_2} m_2 \cdots$ s.t. some place(s) are unbounded along the run (get arbitrarily large values in the m_i's), and where a run is *nondecreasing* if $i < j$ implies $m_i \not\geq m_j$.

Lemma 2. *A marked Transfer net is unbounded iff there exists two sequences $u, u' \in T^*$ s.t. $m_0 \xrightarrow{u} m_1 \xrightarrow{u'} m_2$ and $m_1 < m_2$.*

There exists an effective procedure searching for such u, u', and its termination relies on Dickson's lemma: every infinite sequence of elements of $\mathbb{N}^k$ has an infinite ascending subsequence. The corollary is that boundedness of Transfer nets is decidable.

Transfer nets can simulate Reset nets. If we add a dummy place *dum*, any reset arc (t, p) can be simulated by a transfer arc (p, t, dum). [3] This simulation is quite faithful and preserve almost all behavioural aspects of the nets. That is, except boundedness ! Hence decidability of boundedness for Transfer nets does not entail decidability of boundedness for Reset nets. Figure 1 shows that Lemma 2 does not hold for Reset nets.

Counting reset arcs. If (t, p) is a reset arc, we say p is a *resetable place*. For boundedness issues, there is no need for several reset arcs on the same place.

Lemma 3. *If N is a Reset net with k resetable places, then it is possible to construct a modified N' with k reset arcs s.t. for any initial marking m_0, N with m_0 is bounded iff N' with the corresponding m_0' is.*

3 Undecidability of boundedness for Reset nets

An *m-counter machine* M, with *nonnegative* counters $c_1, c_2, \ldots, c_m$, is a sequence of (labelled) instructions $0 : \text{instr}_0; \ 1 : \text{instr}_1; \ \ldots \ ; \ n : \text{instr}_n$ where $\text{instr}_n = \text{HALT}$ and $\text{instr}_i, \ i = 0, 1, \ldots, n-1$, are of the following two types (assuming $0 \leq k, k_1, k_2 \leq n$ and $c \in \{c_1, c_2, \ldots, c_m\}$)

---

[3] It is believed that Transfer nets are strictly more expressive (in terms of generated languages) than Reset nets but we know of no formal proof for this. Indeed, the example given to that purpose in [Cia94] (his Fig. 14) is flawed and can be encoded into a Reset net.

- $c := c + 1$; goto k
- if $c > 0$ then $(c := c - 1$; goto $k_1)$ else goto k_2

We shall refer to the obvious notion of the (unique) *computation* of M on *given input values* of the counters (the computation is either finite, i.e., halting, or infinite). Note that the order of instructions does not matter when we fix that $0 : \mathtt{instr}_0$ is the initial (starting) instruction.

We say that M is (space-) *bounded for given input values* iff there is $k \in \mathbb{N}$ s.t. the sum $c_1 + \cdots + c_m$ of the counters never exceeds k during the computation on the given input values. Since even 2-counter machines can simulate Turing machines, it is clear that the problem whether a given 2-counter machine is bounded for input values $0, 0$, is undecidable.

Lemma 4. *Given any 2-counter machine M, we can construct a marked Reset net N_M with 3 reset arcs s.t. M is bounded for inputs $0, 0$ iff N_M is bounded.*

Proof. We first transform M into a 3-counter machine M_1 (with a slightly richer set of allowed instructions) as follows: we add a third "capacity" counter K, replace every command (subinstruction) $c := c - 1$ by $(c := c - 1$; $K := K + 1)$, and every $c := c + 1$ by a "controlled incrementation" :

$$(\text{if } K > 0 \text{ then } (K := K - 1; \ c := c + 1) \text{ else goto n+1}).$$

Finally we add 3 instructions

$\quad$ n+1 : if $c_1 > 0$ then $(c_1 := c_1 - 1$; $K := K + 1$; goto n+1) else goto n+2.
$\quad$ n+2 : if $c_2 > 0$ then $(c_2 := c_2 - 1$; $K := K + 1$; goto n+2) else goto n+3.
$\quad$ n+3 : $K := K + 1$; goto 0.

In M_1 only $\mathtt{instr}_{n+3}$ changes (increases by 1) the sum $c_1 + c_2 + K$ of the counters. M is bounded for inputs $0, 0$ iff M_1 is bounded for inputs $0, 0, 0$ (an unbounded run of M yields an unbounded run of M_1: once K is empty, a controlled incrementation has M_1 restarting the computation with one more token in K).

Now we also allow commands (subinstructions) $c := 0$, and introduce the nondeterministic choice operator $[]$. In M_1, we replace every (sub)instruction if $c > 0$ then $\mathtt{comm}_1$ else $\mathtt{comm}_2$ $(c \in \{c_1, c_2, K\})$ by $\mathtt{comm}_1$ $[]$ $(c := 0; \mathtt{comm}_2)$, assuming that any attempt to perform $c := c - 1$ fails when $c = 0$. Thus we get a *nondeterministic* machine M_2. Again only $\mathtt{instr}_{n+3}$ increases the sum of the counters while the other instructions decrease or do not change it.

One can now verify that M_1 is bounded for inputs $0, 0, 0$ iff M_2 is bounded for inputs $0, 0, 0$, i.e., *all* computations of M_2 are bounded. Indeed, any unbounded run of M_2 uses $\mathtt{instr}_{n+3}$ infinitely often as well as $\mathtt{instr}_{n+2}$, $\mathtt{instr}_{n+1}$ and $\mathtt{instr}_0$. After these instructions, the same initial state is reached, possibly with one more token in K. Thus, if there is an unbounded computation, there is one which performs $c := 0$ only when $c = 0$ and this gives an unbounded run of M_1.

Now there only remains to check the easy fact that M_2 can be faithfully simulated by a Reset net N_M, with the place set consisting of "control places" $e_0, e_1, e_2, \ldots, e_{n+3}$ (there is always just one token in one of them, the other being empty) and "counter places" c_1, c_2, K. Since just 3 places are resetable in N_M, we can transform it so that it contains just 3 reset arcs (cf. Lemma 3).

Corollary 1. *Boundedness of Reset nets with three reset arcs is Σ_1-complete.*

Another corollary is that place-boundedness is Σ_1-complete for Reset and Transfer nets (membership in Σ_1 follows from the fact that coverability, "given some m, is there a reachable $m' \geq m$?", is decidable [DFS98]).

We define (an m-counter machine) M to be *totally bounded* iff it is bounded for all inputs.

Lemma 5. *The problem whether a given 2-counters machine is totally bounded is reducible to the structural boundedness problem for Reset nets.*

Lemma 6. *The problem whether a given 2-counters machine does not halt is reducible to the structural boundedness problem for Transfer nets.*

This uses reductions similar to Lemma 4 (see full version). Now, since structural boundedness clearly is in Π_1 for Transfer nets (boundedness being decidable), and in Π_2 for Reset nets (boundedness being in Σ_1), we get

Corollary 2. *Structural boundedness is Π_1-complete for Transfer nets and Π_2-complete for Reset nets.*

This completes the table from the introduction (noting that [May98] shows structural termination is Π_1-hard).

4 Decidability of boundedness for nets with 2 reset arcs

First observe that the boundedness problem is semidecidable: a standard (breadth-first) construction of the reachability set is guaranteed to terminate when this set is finite. Therefore the *semidecidability of unboundedness* is what should be demonstrated. We start with an easy subcase.

Definition 1. *For a marked Reset net, a simple witness is a 4-tuple m_1, m_2, u, p such that m_1 is reachable, $m_1 \xrightarrow{u} m_2$, $m_1 \leq m_2$, $m_1(p) < m_2(p)$, and p is not reset by any transition in the sequence u.*

Repeating u *ad infinitum* (from m_1) yields a run R along which p is unbounded. Hence a simple witness witnesses unboundedness.

Note that a simple witness—if there is any—is surely encountered (and recognized) when constructing the reachability tree. Therefore, unboundedness is semidecidable for nets with simple witnesses. They are characterized by:

Lemma 7. *A marked Reset net admits a simple witness iff it has a run along which either (1) a place is unbounded and reset only finitely many times, or (2) only one place is unbounded (then it can be reset infinitely often).*

easily proven using Dickson's Lemma, the pigeonhole principle, and a bounded-change property: there is $c \in \mathbb{N}$ s.t. $m \xrightarrow{t} m'$ implies $|m(p) - m'(p)| \leq c$ when (p, t) is not a reset arc ($c = 1$ in our case of ordinary arcs).

Thus we further restrict our attention only to the unbounded nets with two reset arcs and without simple witnesses. i.e.. to the unbounded nets with two reset arcs—connected to different places—where along every unbounded run precisely the two resetable places are unbounded and are reset infinitely often. (Recall that Figure 1 shows a relevant example.) We now fix such a marked net N, denoting the resetable places by p_1, p_2 and the transition set by T. First observe that the set $\{m' \mid m \xrightarrow{*}_n m'\}$ is finite for any reachable m and any $n \in \mathbb{N}$, where the subscript n imposes that at most n (occurrences of) reset transitions are used (in the respective transition sequence).

We now also fix an unbounded nondecreasing run R in N and restrict our attention to the markings along R. Such a marking is presented as an (unordered) tuple $(r. p_1 \leftarrow x. p_2 \leftarrow y)$ where r ranges over submarkings on nonresetable places. while x, y are values of the resetable places. The (finite!) range of r is denoted by fcs: it can be viewed as a *finite control states* set. We use $p. p'$ for denoting elements of $\{p_1, p_2\}$: by $\bar{p}$ we mean p_2 (p_1) when $p = p_1$ $(p = p_2)$. Using $(r. p \leftarrow x. -)$ when denoting a marking. we mean that the value for $\bar{p}$ is unimportant ("don't care").

Our decidability proof is based on the fact that R can be supposed to have a "regular" structure. Then a finite amount of information. called a *regular witness*. demonstrates the unboundedness (as was exemplified by the scheme of $w(n)$'s for the net of Figure 1). Now we give the relevant definitions and statements.

Definition 2. *Given a pair* $\langle r. p \leftarrow b_1 \rangle$, $\langle r'. p' \leftarrow b_2 \rangle$. *where* $b_1, b_2 \in \mathbb{N}$ *(and* $p = p'$ *is allowed). by a* path scheme. *of order* n, *we mean a triple* $(w. f. x_0)$, *where* $w : \mathbb{N} \to T^+$, $f : \mathbb{N} \to \mathbb{N}$. $x_0 \in \mathbb{N}$. *such that* $\forall x \geq x_0 : (r. p \leftarrow b_1. \bar{p} \leftarrow$ $x) \xrightarrow{w(x)}_n (r'. p' \leftarrow b_2. \bar{p}' \leftarrow f(x))$ *(note that every* $w(x)$ *contains at most* n *reset transitions). The path scheme has the* maximum property *if for every* $x \geq x_0$ *there is no* $y > f(x)$ *s.t.* $(r. p \leftarrow b_1. \bar{p} \leftarrow x) \xrightarrow{*}_n (r'. p' \leftarrow b_2. \bar{p}' \leftarrow y)$.

Note that if $p = p'$ and $(w. f. x_0)$ has the maximum property then $x_0 \leq x \leq x'$ implies $f(x) \leq f(x')$.

A tuple $\langle r. p \leftarrow b_1 \rangle$ is *sensible* iff for any $m \in \mathbb{N}$ there is $b'_1 \geq b_1$. $m' \geq m$ s.t. $(r. p \leftarrow b'_1. \bar{p} \leftarrow m')$ is reachable. When considering path schemes. we implicitly suppose that $\langle r. p \leftarrow b_1 \rangle$ is sensible. In a straightforward way (putting $f(x) = -1$. etc.) we could handle the case of nonreachability $((r. p \leftarrow b_1. \bar{p} \leftarrow x) \xrightarrow{\,\,}_n (r'. p' \leftarrow b_2. -))$. Then sensibility guarantees the existence of a path scheme with the maximum property – for any order n (and $x_0 = 0$).

By the *composition* of path schemes we mean the natural notion (implicitly assuming some obvious consistency assumptions). We now define regular path schemes – the essence of regular witnesses: it is technically straightforward to show the important fact that *composition of regular path schemes is regular*.

Definition 3. *A function* $g : \mathbb{N} \longrightarrow \mathbb{N}$ *is* $(i. d)$-regular, *where* $0 \leq i < d$. $i. d \in \mathbb{N}$ *iff there are rational constants* ρ_1. ρ_2 *such that: for every* $x \in \mathbb{N}$. $x \mod d = i$ *implies* $g(x) = \rho_1(x) + \rho_2$ $(\in \mathbb{N}$; *note that it imposes* $\rho_1 d \in \mathbb{N})$. *We refer to* ρ_1 (ρ_2) *as the* first (second) coefficient *of* g.

A function $f : \mathbb{N} \longrightarrow \mathbb{N}$ *is* d-regular, *where* $d \in \mathbb{N}$, $0 < d$, *iff there are functions* $f_0, f_1, \ldots, f_{d-1}$ *s.t.* f_i *is* (i, d)-regular $(i = 0, 1, \ldots, d-1)$, *all* f_i's have the same first coefficient ρ *and* $f(x) = f_i(x)$ *for* x mod $d = i$; ρ *is then the coefficient of* f. *We call* f regular *if it is* d-regular *for some* d.

Definition 4. *A path scheme* (w, f, x_0) *is* regular *if* f *is* d-regular *for some* d, *and for each* $i \in \{0, 1, 2, \ldots, d-1\}$ *we have* $m \in \mathbb{N}$, $u_1, v_1, u_2, v_2, \ldots, u_m, v_m, u_{m+1}$ $\in T^*$, *and* (i, d)-regular *functions* $g_1, g_2, \ldots, g_m$ *such that: for every* $x \geq x_0$, x mod $d = i$ *implies* $w(x) = u_1 v_1^{g_1(x)} u_2 v_2^{g_2(x)} \ldots u_m v_m^{g_m(x)} u_{m+1}$.

Definition 5. *A* regular witness *(for the net* N *) is a reachable marking* $(r, p_1 \leftarrow x_0, p_2 \leftarrow 0)$ *together with a regular path scheme* $\langle w, f, x_0 \rangle$ *(of order* n *for some* $n \in \mathbb{N}$ *) which is related to the pair* $\langle r, p_2 \leftarrow 0 \rangle$, $\langle r, p_2 \leftarrow 0 \rangle$ *and has the property* $\forall x \geq x_0 : x < f(x)$.

A regular witness surely witnesses unboundedness. Moreover, such a witness, for convenience accompanied with a sequence demonstrating reachability of $(r, p_1 \leftarrow x_0, p_2 \leftarrow 0)$, can be naturally presented as a string in a fixed alphabet. Whether or not a given string represents a regular witness can be checked by using obvious algorithms. Therefore when a regular witness exists, it can be found by generating and checking all strings. So it remains to show that a regular witness is guaranteed to exist. For this, the next lemma is crucial.

Lemma 8. *For any ("sensible") pair* $\langle r, p \leftarrow b_1 \rangle$, $\langle r', p' \leftarrow b_2 \rangle$, *and* $n \in \mathbb{N}$, *there is a path scheme of order* n *which has the maximum property and is regular.*

Proof. (Sketch.) The key point is the case $n = 0$ (no reset transition used, i.e., we consider $\xrightarrow{*}_0$). Roughly speaking, this handles the segments between two neighbouring resets; that is why the ("sensible") pairs $\langle r, p \leftarrow 0 \rangle$ (p has just been reset), $\langle r', p' \leftarrow - \rangle$ (p' will be reset afterwards) are of interest.

For such a pair, consider a (maybe not regular) path scheme (w, f, x_0) of order 0 which has the maximum property and suppose that $w(x)$ is the shortest possible (among those yielding $f(x)$). Therefore the (finite) run corresponding to $w(x)$ is non-decreasing; it can neither increase (no simple witness exists).

We fix a sufficiently large constant $b \in \mathbb{N}$ (e.g., $b = k!$ where $k = |fcs|$), and imagine now the run $(r, p \leftarrow 0, \bar{p} \leftarrow x) \xrightarrow{w(x)}_0 (r', p' \leftarrow -, \bar{p}' \leftarrow f(x))$ as the corresponding *tour* in the plane – current values of p_1, p_2 give coordinates, current control state is additional (bounded) information. Note that the tour (when long) uses many *cycles* $(r'', p_1 \leftarrow x_1, p_2 \leftarrow y_1) \xrightarrow{*}_0 (r'', p_1 \leftarrow x_2, p_2 \leftarrow y_2)$ – necessarily with $(x_2 - x_1)/(y_2 - y_1) < 0$; a cycle is *elementary* when it contains no shorter cycles (and thus has length k at most). It is also clear that the tour can visit both the initial vertical and initial horizontal belt of breadth b (some of the coordinates being less or equal to b) only boundedly many times (the bound depending on k and b, not on x). When the tour leaves the belts—leaving from either the horizontal or the vertical belt—it can either *return* to the same belt or *zig (zag)* to the other. Now the idea of pumping or deleting elementary cycles helps to realize that lengths of returns are bounded. This idea also implies that a zig (or zag) segment can be supposed to use a "best-rate" elementary cycle – possibly except of a bounded prefix and suffix.

So we have boundedly many possibilities, *patterns*, how to zig-zag and how to arrange the (bounded) segments in between. To each pattern *pat*, there is an associated regular path scheme $\langle w_{pat}, f_{pat}, -\rangle$: the coefficient of the d_{pat}-regular function f_{pat} is determined by the rates of elementary cycles used in zigs and zags, the second coefficients reflecting their bounded prefixes and suffixes as well as the rest of the tour obeying that pattern. For a large x, the (main) coefficient is decisive for the "quality"—the size of $f_{pat}(x)$—of a pattern. If more patterns have the same coefficient, their qualitative order for (large) x depends solely on $x \mod d$ where d is, e.g., the multiple of all d_{pat}'s.

In the general case, when order $n > 0$ is allowed, we have boundedly many patterns how to arrange the resets – and use regular path schemes of order 0 in between. So we can use the same idea as above (using also the fact that composition of regular path schemes is regular).

Now call a pair (r, n), $r \in fcs$, $n \in \mathbb{N}$, *increasing* iff for every $m \in \mathbb{N}$ there are $x_1 < x_2 < \cdots < x_{m+1}$ s.t. $(r, p_1 \leftarrow x_1, p_2 \leftarrow 0) \xrightarrow{*}_n (r, p_1 \leftarrow x_2, p_2 \leftarrow 0) \xrightarrow{*}_n \ldots \xrightarrow{*}_n (r, p_1 \leftarrow x_{m+1}, p_2 \leftarrow 0)$. Note that, since R is nondecreasing, there cannot be more than $k = |fcs|$ resets of p in R without any reset of $\bar{p}$ in between. Using the pigenhole principle (at most k times in succession), we can easily show that there is an increasing pair (r, n) s.t. $(r, p_1 \leftarrow -, p_2 \leftarrow 0)$ appears infinitely often in R. Lemma 8 guarantees a regular path scheme (w, f, x_0) of order n which is related to $\langle r, p_2 \leftarrow 0\rangle$, $\langle r, p_2 \leftarrow 0\rangle$ and has the maximum property. f is d-regular for some d: let ρ be its coefficient and $\rho_0, \rho_1, \ldots \rho_{d-1}$ its second coefficients. The case $\rho < 1$ as well as the case $\rho = 1$ and $\rho_i \leq 0$ for some $i \in \{0, 1, \ldots, d-1\}$ would contradict the choice of r, n (for large x and $m > d$). Thus we have shown

Proposition 1. *For an unbounded marked Reset net with at most two reset arcs and without a simple witness, there is a regular witness.*

5 Conclusion

In this paper we investigated boundedness problems for Reset and Transfer nets, after several surprising results appeared in [DFS98].

We proved that boundedness is undecidable for Reset nets with 3 reset arcs and decidable for Reset nets with 2 resetable places. This is quite surprising since 2 resetable places are enough to recognize any recursive language. The proof technique can be adapted to related problems like structural boundedness and structural termination.

We showed structural boundedness is Π_2-complete for Reset nets, Π_1-complete for Transfer nets. This shows that the paradoxical result "the more powerful Transfer nets have simpler boundedness problems" carries over to structural boundedness and is not just a strange accidental quirk.

Results on Reset and Transfer nets (and similar extensions of the P/T model) have applications to various computational models investigated in the infinite systems community, as we pointed out in the Introduction. E.g., our decidability result hints at interesting questions for stack automata (and extensions), lossy systems, parameterized systems.

References

[AK77]   T. Araki and T. Kasami. Some decision problems related to the reachability problem for Petri nets. *Theor. Comp. Sci.*, 3(1):85–104, 1977.

[AL78]   A. Arnold and M. Latteux. Récursivité et cônes rationnels fermés par intersection. *Calcolo*, XV(IV):381–394, 1978.

[BM99]   A. Bouajjani and R. Mayr. Model checking lossy vector addition systems. In *Proc. 16th Ann. Symp. Theoretical Aspects of Computer Science (STACS'99), Trier, Germany, Mar. 1999*, vol. 1563 of *LNCS*, pp 323–333. Springer, 1999.

[BO98]   E. Badouel and J. Oliver. Reconfigurable nets, a class of high level Petri nets supporting dynamic changes within workflow systems. Research Report 3339, INRIA, January 1998.

[Cia94] G. Ciardo. Petri nets with marking-dependent arc cardinality: Properties and analysis. In *Proc. 15th Int. Conf. Applications & Theory of Petri Nets, Zaragoza, Spain, June 1994*, vol. 815 of *LNCS*, pp 179–198. Springer, 1994.

[DFS98] C. Dufourd, A. Finkel, and Ph. Schnoebelen. Reset nets between decidability and undecidability. In *Proc. 25th Int. Coll. Automata, Languages, and Programming (ICALP'98), Aalborg, Denmark, July 1998*, vol. 1443 of *LNCS*, pp 103–115. Springer, 1998.

[Duf98] C. Dufourd. Réseaux de Petri avec reset/transfert: Décidabilité et indécidabilité. Thèse de Docteur en Sciences de l'École Normale Supérieure de Cachan, October 1998.

[EFM99] J. Esparza, A. Finkel, and R. Mayr. On the verification of broadcast protocols. In *Proc. 14th IEEE Symp. Logic in Computer Science (LICS'99), Trento, Italy, July 1999*, 1999.

[FS98]   A. Finkel and Ph. Schnoebelen. Fundamental structures in well-structured infinite transition systems. In *Proc. 3rd Latin American Theoretical Informatics Symposium (LATIN'98), Campinas, Brazil, Apr. 1998*, vol. 1380 of *LNCS*, pp 102–118. Springer, 1998.

[HP79]   J. Hopcroft and J.-J. Pansiot. On the reachability problem for 5-dimensional vector addition systems. *Theor. Comp. Sci.*, 8(2):135–159, 1979.

[KCK+97] M. Kishinevsky, J. Cortadella, A. Kondratyev, L. Lavagno, A. Taubin, and A. Yakovlev. Coupling asynchrony and interrupts: Place chart nets. In *Proc. 18th Int. Conf. Application & Theory of Petri Nets, Toulouse, France, June 1997*, vol. 1248 of *LNCS*, pp 328–347. Springer, 1997.

[LC94]   C. Lakos and S. Christensen. A general approach to arc extensions for coloured Petri nets. In *Proc. 15th Int. Conf. Applications & Theory of Petri Nets, Zaragoza, Spain, June 1994*, vol. 815 of *LNCS*, pp 338–357. Springer, 1994.

[May98] R. Mayr. Lossy counter machines. Tech. Report TUM-I9830, Institut für Informatik, TUM, Munich, Germany, October 1998.

[Val78] R. Valk. Self-modifying nets, a natural extension of Petri nets. In *Proc. 5th Int. Coll. Automata, Languages, and Programming (ICALP'78), Udine, Italy, Jul. 1978*, vol. 62 of *LNCS*, pp 464–476. Springer, 1978.

Two-Way Finite State Transducers and Monadic Second-Order Logic

Joost Engelfriet and Hendrik Jan Hoogeboom

Leiden University, Institute of Computer Science
P.O. Box 9512, 2300 RA Leiden, The Netherlands

Abstract. Deterministic two-way finite state transductions are exactly the mso definable string transductions. Nondeterministic mso definable string transductions equal compositions of nondeterministic two-way finite state transductions that have the finite visit property. Both families of mso definable string transductions are characterized in terms of Hennie machines.

Introduction

The work of Büchi [2] and Elgot shows how a logical formula may effectively be transformed into a finite state automaton accepting the language specified by the formula. Hence it demonstrates how to relate the specification of a system behaviour (the formula) to a possible implementation (the behaviour of an automaton) – which underlies modern model checking tools. There are many generalizations of the result of Büchi and Elgot, including infinite strings, trees, and traces (a syntactic model for concurrency). We refer to [19] for an overview of the study of formal languages within the framework of mathematical logic.

Here we equate 2DGSM, the family of string transductions realized by (deterministic) two-way finite state transducers (or two-way generalized machines, 2gsm, i.e., finite state automata equipped with a two-way input tape and a one-way output tape) and MSOS, the family obtained by restricting monadic second-order (mso) definable graph transductions to strings. Thus, string transductions that are specified in mso logic can be implemented on 2gsm's, and vice versa.

Graph transductions are defined by specifying the edges of a new (output) graph in terms of logical properties of a given (input) graph [6,8]. This is just a special case of the notion of interpretation of logical structures, well known in mathematical logic [18, Section 6]. The mso definable graph transductions play an important role in the theory of graph rewriting, as the two main families of context-free graph languages can be obtained by applying mso definable graph transductions to regular tree languages.

In Section 2 we extend the model of two-way finite state transducer by allowing the machine to 'jump' to new positions on the tape (not necessarily adjacent to the present position) as specified by an mso formula that is part of the instructions. This 'hybrid' model (in between logic and machine) facilitates the proof of our main result. In Section 3 we recall the definition of mso definable graph transduction, and restrict that general notion to mso definable string transductions by considering their graph representation.

The main result of the paper is presented as Theorem 7 in Section 4. In order to transform a 2gsm into the mso formalism we consider the 'computation space' of a

2gsm on a given input. This is the graph which has a node for each pair consisting of a tape position and a state of the 2gsm. These nodes are connected by edges representing the possible moves of the 2gsm. The construction of this graph, and the reconstruction of the output string from it, are mso definable graph (!) transductions, which can be composed to give the desired result.

In Section 5 we study nondeterminism. This feature can be added to mso definable transductions by introducing 'parameters', i.e., free set variables in the definition of the transduction. The output of the transduction for a given input may then vary for different valuations of these parameters. We show that the two nondeterministic families are incomparable, unlike the deterministic case.

Finite visit machines form the topic of our final section. These machines have a fixed bound on the number of times each of the positions of their input tape may be visited during a computation. We characterize the nondeterministic mso definable string transductions as compositions of (two) nondeterministic 2gsm's with the finite visit property. A more direct characterization can be obtained by considering Hennie transducers, i.e., finite visit 2gsm's that are allowed to rewrite the symbols on their input tape. These machines characterize the mso definable transductions, both in the deterministic case [3] and the nondeterministic case.

1 Preliminaries

By $GR(\Sigma, \Gamma)$ we denote the set of all (finite) directed graphs with node labels in Σ and edge labels in Γ; $*$ denotes the absence of labels. By $MSO(\Sigma, \Gamma)$ we denote monadic second-order (mso) logic over the graphs in $GR(\Sigma, \Gamma)$. The formulas from $MSO(\Sigma, \Gamma)$ are built in the usual way, with both node variables and node-set variables, and with atomic formulas $x = y$, $x \in X$, $\mathrm{lab}_\sigma(x)$ (node x has label σ), $\mathrm{edge}_\gamma(x, y)$ (an edge from x to y with label γ), and $x \preceq y$ (a path from x to y).

There are two ways of representing a string as a graph. First, a string $w \in \Sigma^*$ is represented by the graph nd-gr(w) in $GR(\Sigma, *)$, which is a path where the nodes are labelled by the consecutive symbols of w. Dually, w is represented by the graph ed-gr(w) in $GR(*, \Sigma)$, a path with unlabelled nodes, connected by edges labelled by the symbols of w. Note that ed-gr(λ) consists of one unlabelled node, whereas nd-gr(λ) has no nodes at all. Although nd-gr(w) more directly represents the string w in terms of its positions and their successor relation, the advantage of ed-gr(w) is that it is never empty and thus satisfies all the usual logical laws.

2 Two-Way Machines

A *2-way generalized sequential machine with mso-instructions* (2gsm-mso) is a finite state device equipped with a two-way input tape (read only), and a one-way output tape. Its instructions are given using mso formulas. Special end markers $\vdash$ and $\dashv$ indicate the boundaries of the input. Formally, a 2gsm-mso is a construct $\mathcal{M} = (Q, \Sigma_1, \Sigma_2, \delta, q_{in}, q_f)$, where Q is the finite set of states, Σ_1 and Σ_2 are the input alphabet and output alphabet, q_{in} and q_f are the initial and the final state, and δ is a finite set of *instructions*. Each instruction is of the form $(p, t, \ q, \alpha, \mu)$, where

$p \in Q - \{q_f\}$ is the current state, t is a test to be performed on the input, given as a formula $\varphi(x)$ in $\mathrm{MSO}(\Sigma_1 \cup \{\vdash, \dashv\}, *)$ with one free node variable x, $q \in Q$ is the new state, $\alpha \in \Sigma_2^*$ is the string written on the output tape, and μ describes the move of the reading head on the input tape, given by a formula $\varphi(x, y)$ in $\mathrm{MSO}(\Sigma_1 \cup \{\vdash, \dashv\}, *)$ with two free node variables x and y.

A test $t = \varphi(x)$ is evaluated for the string on the input tape with x valuated as the position taken by the reading head; more precisely, as our logic is defined for graphs, t is true whenever $\mathrm{nd\text{-}gr}(\vdash w \dashv) \models \varphi(u)$, where w is the input, and u is the node corresponding to the position of the reading head.

The 2gsm-mso does not move step-wise on the input tape, but it 'jumps' as specified by the formula $\varphi(x, y)$, as follows: Assuming the machine is in position u, it moves to a position v for which $\mathrm{nd\text{-}gr}(\vdash w \dashv) \models \varphi(u, v)$, where we have identified positions on the input tape with their corresponding nodes of the graph $\mathrm{nd\text{-}gr}(\vdash w \dashv)$. To guarantee that $\varphi(x, y)$ describes a deterministic move of the reading head, we require that it is functional for each input string w, i.e., for every position u there is at most one position v such that $\mathrm{nd\text{-}gr}(\vdash w \dashv) \models \varphi(u, v)$.

The 2gsm-mso $\mathcal{M}$ realizes the transduction $m \subseteq \Sigma_1^* \times \Sigma_2^*$, such that $(w, z) \in m$ whenever there exists a computation with $\vdash w \dashv$ on the input tape, starting in initial state q_{in} with the input head on the symbol $\vdash$, and ending in the accepting state q_f, while z has been written on the output tape.

A 2gsm-mso is *deterministic* (a 2dgsm-mso) if for each state p, each input w, and each input position u, there is at most one instruction (p, t, q, α, μ) that t is satisfied for u.

Restricting ourselves to tests of the form $\mathrm{lab}_\sigma(x)$, $\sigma \in \Sigma_1 \cup \{\vdash, \dashv\}$ (symbol σ under the reading head), and moves of the form $\mathrm{edge}_*(x, y)$, $\mathrm{edge}_*(y, x)$, $x = y$ (right, left, stay), we obtain the well-known 2gsm (and 2dgsm). The families of string transductions realized by 2gsm's and 2gsm-mso's are denoted 2NGSM and 2NGSM^{MSO}, respectively. For deterministic machines, N is replaced by D.

Example 1. Consider the string transduction $m_{ex} =$

$$\{ (a^{i_1} b a^{i_2} b \cdots a^{i_n} b a^{i_{n+1}}, a^{i_1} b^{i_1} a^{i_2} b^{i_2} \cdots a^{i_n} b^{i_n} a^{i_{n+1}}) \mid n \geq 0, i_1, \ldots, i_{n+1} \geq 0 \}$$

It can be realized by a deterministic 2gsm-mso $\mathcal{M}$ as follows. In state 1 it walks along a segment of a's, copying it to the output tape. Then, when the segment is followed by a b, $\mathcal{M}$ jumps back to the first a of the segment for a second pass, in state 2. When the end of the segment is reached for the second time, the machine jumps to the next segment, returning to state 1. At the last a of the input the machine jumps to the right end marker, and switches to the final state 3, cf. Figure 1.

We use the formulas $\mathrm{next}_\Delta(x, y)$ to specify the first position y following x that is labelled by a symbol in Δ, and $\mathrm{fls}_a(x, y)$ denoting the first a in the last segment of a's to the left of x. They can easily be expressed in $\mathrm{MSO}(\Sigma \cup \{\vdash, \dashv\}, *)$.

Let $\Sigma_1 = \Sigma_2 = \{a, b\}$, $Q = \{1, 2, 3\}$, $q_{in} = 2$, $q_f = 3$, and δ consisting of

$$(1, \mathrm{lab}_a(x), 1, a, \mathrm{right}), \quad (1, \mathrm{lab}_b(x), 2, \lambda, \mathrm{fls}_a(x, y)), \quad (1, \mathrm{lab}_\vdash(x), 3, \lambda, \mathrm{stay}),$$
$$(2, \mathrm{lab}_a(x), 2, a, \mathrm{right}), \quad (2, \neg\mathrm{lab}_a(x), 1, \lambda, \mathrm{next}_{\{a, \dashv\}}).$$

Theorem 2. 2DGSM = 2DGSM^{MSO}.

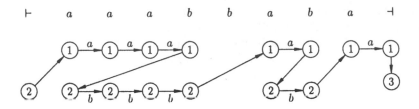

Fig. 1. Computation for (a^3b^2aba, a^3b^3aba) of the 2gsm-mso from Example 1

Proof. A 2dgsm can keep track of the state of another (deterministic) one-way finite state automaton working on the same tape (from left to right or from right to left) [14, 3]. Hence we will assume that a 2dgsm may perform 'regular look-around tests' $t = (R_\ell, \sigma, R_r)$, where $\sigma \in (\Sigma_1 \cup \{\vdash, \dashv\})$, and $R_\ell, R_r \subseteq (\Sigma_1 \cup \{\vdash, \dashv\})^*$ are regular languages. This test t is satisfied if σ is the symbol under the reading head, and the strings to the left and the right of the head belong to R_ℓ and R_r respectively.

Tests: unary node predicates. By Büchi's theorem [2], a test $\varphi(x)$ of a 2dgsm-mso defines a regular language, with one 'marked' symbol, corresponding to the position x. Such a language is a finite union of languages $R_\ell \cdot (\sigma, 1) \cdot R_r$, with regular languages $R_\ell, R_r \subseteq (\Sigma_1 \cup \{\vdash, \dashv\})^*$, and a marked $\sigma \in \Sigma_1 \cup \{\vdash, \dashv\}$. This implies that the test $\varphi(x)$ can be simulated by a finite disjunction of look-around tests.

Moves: binary node predicates. The direction of the move $\varphi(x, y)$ is determined by evaluating the test $(\exists y)(y \prec x \land \varphi(x, y))$ for leftward, and similarly for rightward, and stay. At most one of these tests is true. Assuming a move to the left, consider $y \prec x \land \varphi(x, y)$. It defines a regular language, this time with two marked symbols, corresponding to the positions x and y. Such a language is a finite union of (disjoint) languages $R_\ell \cdot (\tau, 2) \cdot R_m \cdot (\sigma, 1) \cdot R_r$, with regular R_ℓ, R_m, R_r, and marked $\sigma, \tau \in \Sigma_1 \cup \{\vdash, \dashv\}$. The 2dgsm determines which of these languages is applicable by performing the look-around test $(R_\ell \cdot \tau \cdot R_m, \sigma, R_r)$. Then, stepping to the left, it determines position y by simulating (the mirror image of) R_m in the finite state control. Each time the y-x segment belongs to R_m, the machine evaluates the look-around test $(R_\ell, \tau, \Sigma_1^* \dashv)$ to verify the initial segment of the tape. □

3 MSO Definable String Transductions

An *mso definable graph transduction* [4, 5, 9, 18] is a (partial) function $\tau : \mathrm{GR}(\Sigma_1, \Gamma_1) \to \mathrm{GR}(\Sigma_2, \Gamma_2)$ that constructs for a given input graph a new output graph as specified by a number of formulas in $\mathrm{MSO}(\Sigma_1, \Gamma_1)$. For a graph satisfying a given domain formula φ_{dom} we take copies of each of the nodes, one for each element of a finite copy set C. The label of the c-copy of node x ($c \in C$) is determined by a set of formulas $\varphi_\sigma^c(x)$, one for each symbol σ in the output alphabet Σ_2. We keep only those copies of the nodes for which exactly one of these label formulas is true. Edges are defined according to formulas $\varphi_\gamma^{c_1, c_2}(x, y)$: we construct an edge with label $\gamma \in \Gamma_2$ in the output graph from the c_1-copy of x to the c_2-copy of y whenever such a formula holds. The family of mso definable graph transductions is denoted by grMSO. It is closed under composition [6].

We consider mso definable graph transductions as a tool to specify string transductions, representing strings by either nd-gr or ed-gr. The transition from one of

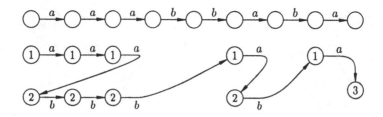

Fig. 2. Edge representation for (a^3b^2aba, a^3b^3aba), cf. Example 3

these representations to the other is (essentially) definable as mso graph transduction, and will be heavily used in the sequel. There is, however, a small technical point: an mso graph transduction maps the empty graph to itself. Hence, using nd-gr, the empty string is mapped to itself. As we do not want to restrict ourselves to this kind of transductions, we choose the string representation ed-gr.

Let $m \subseteq \Sigma_1^* \times \Sigma_2^*$ be a string transduction. By ed-gr(m) we denote its translation to graphs $\{(\text{ed-gr}(w), \text{ed-gr}(z)) \mid (w, z) \in m\}$ in $\text{GR}(*, \Sigma_1) \times \text{GR}(*, \Sigma_2)$. We denote by MSOS the family of all *mso definable string transductions*, i.e., all m such that ed-gr(m) belongs to grMSO.

Example 3. Consider the transduction ed-gr(m_{ex}), where m_{ex} is from Example 1. The formulas for the construction of the output graph have nodes as their reference points, whereas the information (labels) is attached to the edges. Hence we frequently use the formula $\text{out}_\sigma(x) = (\exists y)\text{edge}_\sigma(x, y)$. Similar to Example 1 we have formulas $\text{fps}_a'(x, y)$ denoting the first node in the present segment of a's, and $\text{next}_a'(x, y)$ the next node with outgoing label a.

Choosing the copy set $C = \{1, 2, 3\}$, and the domain formula defining edge representations of strings, the transduction ed-gr(m_{ex}) is defined by the following formulas, cf. Figure 2 (where we have put the copy numbers within the nodes).

$$\varphi_*^1 = \text{out}_a(x), \quad \varphi_*^2 = \text{out}_a(x) \land (\exists y)(x \preceq y \land \text{out}_b(y))$$
$$\varphi_*^3 = \neg\text{out}_a(x) \land \neg\text{out}_b(x), \quad \text{the final node of the string,}$$
$$\varphi_a^{1,1} = \text{edge}_a(x, y), \quad \varphi_a^{1,2} = (\exists z)(\text{edge}_a(x, z) \land \neg\text{out}_a(z)) \land \text{fps}_a'(x, y),$$
$$\varphi_a^{1,3} = \neg(\exists z)(\varphi_a^{1,1}(x, z) \lor \varphi_a^{1,2}(x, z)),$$
$$\varphi_b^{2,2} = \text{edge}_a(x, y), \quad \varphi_b^{2,1} = (\exists z)(\text{edge}_a(x, z) \land \neg\text{out}_a(z)) \land \text{next}_a'(x, y),$$
$$\varphi_b^{2,3} = \neg(\exists z)(\varphi_b^{2,1}(x, z) \lor \varphi_b^{2,2}(x, z)), \quad \varphi_\sigma^{3,j} = \text{false for } j = 1, 2, 3.$$

4 Logic and Machines

In this section we establish our main result, MSOS = 2DGSM. The first steps towards this result were taken already in Section 2 where we have taught the 2dgsm to understand the language of monadic second-order logic. To bridge the final gap between logic and machine, for $m : \Sigma_1^* \to \Sigma_2^*$, we use tape$(m)$ to denote the graph transduction $\{ (\text{nd-gr}(\vdash w \dashv), \text{ed-gr}(z)) \mid (w, z) \in m \}$ from $\text{GR}(\Sigma_1 \cup \{\vdash, \dashv\}, *)$ to $\text{GR}(*, \Sigma_2)$, which is more convenient than ed-gr(m).

Lemma 4. *For $m : \Sigma_1^* \to \Sigma_2^*$, tape$(m) \in$ grMSO iff ed-gr$(m) \in$ grMSO.*

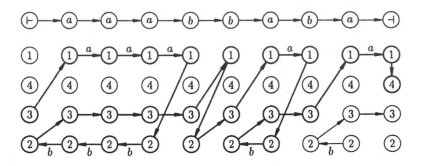

Fig. 3. Mapping nd-gr($\vdash a^3 b^2 aba \dashv$) to $\gamma_{\mathcal{M}}(a^3 b^2 aba)$, cf. proof of Lemma 6.

We can visualize the 'computation space' of a 2dgsm-mso $\mathcal{M}$ on input w by constructing a graph $\gamma_{\mathcal{M}}(w)$ that has as its nodes the pairs $\langle p, u \rangle$, where p is a state of $\mathcal{M}$, and u is a node of nd-gr($\vdash w \dashv$), i.e., one of the positions of the input tape carrying $\vdash w \dashv$. The edges of $\gamma_{\mathcal{M}}(w)$ follow the instructions of $\mathcal{M}$: for each instruction $(p, \varphi, q, \alpha, \psi)$ there is an edge from $\langle p, u \rangle$ to $\langle q, v \rangle$ if $\varphi(u)$ and $\psi(u, v)$ are true. The edge is labelled by the output symbol $\alpha \in \Sigma_2 \cup \{*\}$ (where $*$ represents λ); note that we may indeed assume that α has length at most 1.

As $\mathcal{M}$ is deterministic, every node of $\gamma_{\mathcal{M}}(w)$ has at most one outgoing edge. The output of the computation of $\mathcal{M}$ on w can be read from $\gamma_{\mathcal{M}}(w)$ by starting in node $\langle q_{in}, u \rangle$, representing $\mathcal{M}$ in its initial configuration (with $\mathrm{lab}_\vdash(u)$), and following the path along the outgoing edges. The computation is successful if it ends in a final configuration $\langle q_f, v \rangle$.

Example 5. Consider the 2dgsm with $\Sigma_1 = \Sigma_2 = \{a, b\}$, $Q = \{1, 2, 3, 4\}$, $q_{in} = 3$, $q_f = 4$, and δ consisting of the instructions

$$(1, \mathrm{lab}_a(x), 1, a, \mathrm{right}), \quad (1, \mathrm{lab}_b(x), 2, \lambda, \mathrm{left}), \quad (1, \mathrm{lab}_\dashv(x), 4, \lambda, \mathrm{stay}),$$
$$(2, \mathrm{lab}_a(x), 2, b, \mathrm{left}), \quad (2, \neg\mathrm{lab}_a(x), 3, \lambda, \mathrm{right}),$$
$$(3, \mathrm{lab}_a(x), 3, \lambda, \mathrm{right}), \quad (3, \neg\mathrm{lab}_a(x), 1, \lambda, \mathrm{right}).$$

Like our previous 2dgsm-mso, it realizes the transduction m_{ex}, by copying the segments of a's to the output, once as a's, another time as b's. The computation space $\gamma_{\mathcal{M}}(a^3 b^2 aba)$ is given in Figure 3, lower graph.

Lemma 6. For $m : \Sigma_1^* \to \Sigma_2^*$, $m \in$ 2DGSM^{MSO} iff tape(m) $\in$ grMSO.

Proof. (Only if) We define three mso graph transductions, the composition of which maps nd-gr($\vdash w \dashv$) to ed-gr(z) for each $(w, z) \in m$. As grMSO is closed under composition, this proves the lemma. The first graph transduction τ_1 maps nd-gr($\vdash w \dashv$) to $\gamma_{\mathcal{M}}(w)$; it has copy set $C = Q$, the state set of $\mathcal{M}$. The second graph transduction τ_2 selects the path in $\gamma_{\mathcal{M}}(w)$ corresponding to the successful computation of $\mathcal{M}$ on w (if it exists) by keeping only those nodes that are reachable from the initial configuration and lead to a final configuration (bold in Figure 3). The last graph transduction τ_3 removes unlabelled edges while contracting paths consisting of these edges.

(If) Assume tape(m) is specified by domain formula φ_{dom}, copy set C, node formulas φ_*^c, and edge formulas $\varphi_\sigma^{c_1,c_2}$. We build a 2dgsm-mso $\mathcal{M}$ for m closely following this mso specification. The state set of $\mathcal{M}$ is (in principle) equal to the copy set C: when $\varphi_\sigma^{c_1,c_2}(u,v)$ is true for a pair u,v of nodes, then $\mathcal{M}$, visiting position u of the input tape in state c_1, may move to position v changing to state c_2, while writing σ to the output tape.

In general the formula $\varphi_\sigma^{c_1,c_2}$ is only functional for graphs satisfying the domain formula φ_{dom}, and only when restricted to nodes for which the respective c_1 and c_2 copies are defined. Since our formal definition of 2dgsm-mso demands functional moves, we consider the formulas $\psi_\sigma^{c_1,c_2}(x,y) = \varphi_\sigma^{c_1,c_2}(x,y) \wedge \varphi_*^{c_1}(x) \wedge \varphi_*^{c_2}(y) \wedge \varphi_{\text{dom}}$.

The instructions of $\mathcal{M}$ are all $(c_1, (\exists y)(\psi_\sigma^{c_1,c_2}(x,y)),\ c_2, \sigma, \psi_\sigma^{c_1,c_2}(x,y)\ )$. If no test gives a positive result, this indicates the last position of the output string, and a 'complementary' instruction ends up in the final state q_f. Initially $\mathcal{M}$ has to find the unique node of the output graph without incoming edges. To do this, $\mathcal{M}$ has the new initial state q_{in}, where all possibilities $c_2 \in C$ are tested:
$(q_{in}, (\exists y)[\varphi_*^{c_2}(y) \wedge \neg \text{in}^{c_2}(y)],\ c_2, \lambda, \varphi_*^{c_2}(y) \wedge \neg \text{in}^{c_2}(y)\ )$, where $\text{in}^{c_2}(y)$ abbreviates $(\exists z) \bigvee_{c_1 \in C, \sigma \in \Sigma_2} (\psi_\sigma^{c_1,c_2}(z,y))$. □

We now state our main result, uniting logic and machines.

Theorem 7. MSOS = 2DGSM.

5   Nondeterminism

A nondeterministic variant of mso definable graph transductions was proposed in [4, 5]. All the formulas of the deterministic version may now have additional free node-set variables $X_1, \ldots, X_k$, called 'parameters', the same for each of the formulas. For each valuation of the parameters (by sets of nodes of the input graph) that satisfies the domain formula, the other formulas define the output graph as before. Hence each valuation may lead to a different output graph for the given input graph: nondeterminism. We use grNMSO and NMSOS to denote the nondeterministic counterparts of the families grMSO and MSOS, respectively.

Example 8. Let m_{tw} be the relation $\{ (a^n, w\#w) \mid n \geq 0, w \in \{a,b\}^*, |w| = n \}$. Thus, $m_{\text{tw}} \subseteq \{a\}^* \times \{a, b, \#\}^*$. The relation ed-gr$(m_{\text{tw}})$ belongs to grNMSO. The nodes of the input graph are copied twice, and the parameters determine for each node whether its outgoing edge is copied as a-edge or b-edge.

The copy set C is $\{1, 2\}$, and domain formula $\varphi_{\text{dom}}(X_a, X_b)$ expresses that the input graph is a string representation, while the sets X_a and X_b form a partition of its nodes. All input nodes are copied twice: $\varphi_*^1(x, X_a, X_b) = \varphi_*^2(x, X_a, X_b) = \text{true}$. The edge labels are changed according to X_a and X_b, and the last node of the first copy is connected to the first node of the second copy by an #-edge:

$$\varphi_\sigma^{1,1}(x,y,X_a,X_b) = \varphi_\sigma^{2,2}(x,y,X_a,X_b) = \text{edge}_a(x,y) \wedge x \in X_\sigma, \text{ for } \sigma = a, b,$$
$$\varphi_\#^{1,2}(x,y,X_a,X_b) = \neg(\exists z)\text{edge}_a(x,z) \wedge \neg(\exists z)\text{edge}_a(z,y),$$
$$\varphi_\sigma^{i,j}(x,y,X_a,X_b) = \text{false, for all other combinations } i, j, \sigma.$$

We map aaa to $abb\#abb$ by taking the valuation $\nu(X_a) = \{1\}$, $\nu(X_b) = \{2,3,4\}$.

Unlike the deterministic case, 2NGSM is incomparable to NMSOS. First, because of the constant copy set, the length of the output of a nondeterministic mso transduction is necessarily linear in the length of the input. This is not true for the 2gsm, which can realize the transduction $\{ (a^n, a^{mn}) \mid m, n \geq 1 \}$, by nondeterministically choosing the number m of copies made of the input. Second, the nondeterministic mso transduction m_{tw} of Example 8 is not in 2NGSM. This can be shown using a counting argument: the machine does not have enough configurations to distinguish exponentially many output strings. The relation m_{tw} can be realized as the composition of two 2gsm's, the first nondeterministically mapping a^n to a word $w \in \{a, b\}^*$ with $|w| = n$, the second (deterministically) doubling its input w to $w \# w$. This shows that 2NGSM is not closed under composition [15], as opposed to 2DGSM [3]. In fact, the families 2NGSM^k of compositions of k 2gsm transductions form a strict hierarchy, as proved in [12, 7]. However, the nondeterministic mso transductions in grNMSO and NMSOS are closed under composition [6].

A nondeterministic mso transduction can be 'pre-processed' by a nondeterministic node relabelling of the input graph, by adding to the labels information about the valuation of the parameters. Consider Example 8: the valuation $\nu(X_a) = \{1\}$, $\nu(X_b) = \{2, 3, 4\}$ induces a new label $\langle a, 1, 0 \rangle$ for node 1 and a new label $\langle a, 0, 1 \rangle$ for the other nodes. After this the valuation has become a part of the labelling, and the remaining construction can be performed by a deterministic mso transduction.

By grREL we denote the family of (nondeterministic) node relabellings for graphs. Note that grREL $\subseteq$ grNMSO. We then obtain the following characterization.

Theorem 9. grNMSO = grMSO $\circ$ grREL.

String relabellings can be 'lifted' to graph node relabellings using the representation nd-gr. However, as we are considering the edge representation, we need the family MREL of *marked string relabellings*, that map a string w first to the 'marked version' $\vdash w \dashv$, and then apply a string relabelling. Then we can show that NMSOS = MSOS $\circ$ MREL. Hence, with Theorem 7:

Theorem 10. NMSOS = 2DGSM $\circ$ MREL.

6   Finite Visit Machines

A computation of a 2gsm is called k-*visiting* if each of the positions of the input tape is visited at most k times. The 2gsm M is called *finite visit*, if there exists a constant k such that, for each pair (w, z) in the transduction realized by M, there is a k-visiting computation for (w, z). The family of string transductions realized by finite visit nondeterministic 2gsm is denoted by $2\text{NGSM}_{\text{fin}}$. This is a proper subfamily of 2NGSM because, obviously, every transduction m realized by a finite visit 2gsm is *finitary*, i.e., $m(w)$ is finite for every input w. Note that all transductions in NMSOS are finitary too.

Every deterministic 2gsm is finite visit, as it cannot enter the same input position twice in the same state without entering an infinite loop. A similar argument shows that finitary 2gsm transductions must be realized by finite visit machines: their 'loops' cannot produce output, and thus may be removed from the computation.

Lemma 11. $m \in 2\text{NGSM}_{\text{fin}}$ *iff* $m \in 2\text{NGSM}$ *and* m *is finitary*.

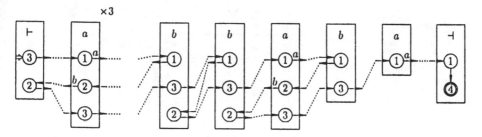

Fig. 4. Track for $\vdash a^3b^2aba\dashv$, Example 5.

It is well known (see, e.g., [1, 3, 10, 11]) that the computation of a finite visit 2gsm on an input tape can be coded as a string of 'visiting sequences'. A visiting sequence stores information concerning the consecutive visits to a position of the input tape. We will use k-*track* as terminology for a string of visiting sequences describing a valid k-visiting computation of a 2gsm. The set of k-tracks of a 2gsm is a regular language, see [10, Lemma 2.2] or [3, Lemma 1]. As an example, consider the 2dgsm from Example 5. Figure 4 depicts a track (for the computation on input a^3b^2aba).

Using standard techniques [3] a finite visit 2gsm (with constant k) can be decomposed into a nondeterministic relabelling of the input tape $\vdash w \dashv$, guessing a string of visiting sequences, followed by a 2dgsm that verifies that it is a k-track, i.e., specifies a valid computation, after which it (deterministically) simulates the k-visiting computation previously guessed. Thus, $2\text{NGSM}_{\text{fin}} \subseteq 2\text{DGSM} \circ \text{MREL} = \text{NMSOS}$. Hence, by Lemma 11, $2\text{NGSM}_{\text{fin}} = 2\text{NGSM} \cap \text{NMSOS}$. And, by Theorem 10 and the closure of NMSOS under composition, we obtain:

Theorem 12. $\text{NMSOS} = 2\text{NGSM}_{\text{fin}} \circ 2\text{NGSM}_{\text{fin}}$.

Our arguments can be extended to obtain the Venn diagram of Figure 5.
The characterization that the transductions in NMSOS are the finitary elements of $\bigcup_{k \geq 1} 2\text{NGSM}^k$, uses a complicated inductive argument that shows that every finitary transduction from 2NGSM^k is in $2\text{DGSM}^k \circ \text{MREL}$. The characterization that the transductions in MSOS are the functional elements of $\bigcup_{k \geq 1} 2\text{NGSM}^k$, follows from [7, Theorem 4.9] and Theorem 7.

Theorem 13. *The Venn diagram of Figure 5 is correct.*

Hennie machines. A 2gsm extended with the power to rewrite the contents of the cell of the input tape, is called a *Hennie machine* if it is finite visit [13, 16, 11]. The families of string transductions realized by nondeterministic and deterministic Hennie machines are denoted by NHM and DHM, respectively. As an example, the transduction m_{tw} from Example 8 is realized by a Hennie machine that first nondeterministically rewrites the input a^n into a string w with $|w| = n$, and then copies w twice to the output tape.

The notion of visiting sequence can be extended to Hennie machines in a straightforward way. Decomposition techniques similar to those discussed above can be used to show $\text{NHM} \subseteq 2\text{DGSM} \circ \text{MREL}$. Again Theorem 10 implies that $\text{NMSOS} = \text{NHM}$.

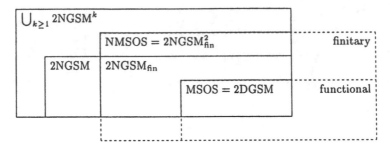

Fig. 5. Relationships between our main families of transductions

For deterministic Hennie machines the decomposition can be improved. Using look-around techniques, the nondeterministic relabelling can be replaced by a 2dgsm. As 2DGSM is closed under composition, we obtain MSOS = DHM.

Theorem 14. MSOS = DHM *and* NMSOS = NHM.

References

1. J.-C. Birget, Two-way automata and length-preserving homomorphisms, *MST* 29 (1996) 191–226.
2. J.R. Büchi, Weak second-order arithmetic and finite automata, *Zeitschrift für Mathematik, Logik und Grundlagen der Mathematik* 6 (1960) 66–92.
3. M.P. Chytil, V. Jákl, Serial composition of 2-way finite-state transducers and simple programs on strings, in: 4th ICALP, *LNCS* vol. 52, Springer Verlag, 1977, pp. 135–147.
4. B. Courcelle, The monadic second-order logic of graphs V: on closing the gap between definability and recognizability, *TCS* 80 (1991) 153–202.
5. B. Courcelle, Monadic second-order definable graph transductions: a survey, *TCS* 126 (1994) 53–75.
6. B. Courcelle, The expression of graph properties and graph transformations in monadic second-order logic, in: *Handbook of graph grammars and computing by graph transformation* vol. 1 (G. Rozenberg, ed.), World Scientific Publishing Co., 1997, pp. 313–400.
7. J. Engelfriet, Three hierarchies of transducers, *MST* 15 (1982) 95–125.
8. J. Engelfriet, Context-free graph grammars, in: [17], pp. 125-213.
9. J. Engelfriet, V. van Oostrom, Logical description of context-free graph-languages, *JCSS* 55 (1997) 489-503.
10. S.A. Greibach, Visits, crosses, and reversals for nondeterministic off-line machines, *Inf. Control* 36 (1978) 174–216.
11. S.A. Greibach, One way finite visit automata, *TCS* 6 (1978) 175–221.
12. S.A. Greibach, Hierarchy theorems for two-way finite state transducers, *Acta Inf.* 11 (1978) 89–101.
13. F.C. Hennie, One-tape, off-line Turing machine computations, *Inf. Control* 8 (1965) 553–578.
14. J.E. Hopcroft, J.D. Ullman, An approach to a unified theory of automata, *The Bell System Technical Journal* 46 (1967) 1793–1829.
15. D. Kiel, Two-way a-transducers and AFL, *JCSS* 10 (1975) 88–109.
16. V. Rajlich, Bounded-crossing transducers, *Inf. Control* 27 (1975) 329–335.
17. G. Rozenberg, A. Salomaa (eds.), *Handbook of Formal Languages*, vol. 3: Beyond Words, Springer Verlag, 1997.
18. D. Seese, Interpretability and tree automata: a simple way to solve algorithmic problems on graphs closely related to trees, in: *Tree Automata and Languages* (M. Nivat, A. Podelski, eds.), Elsevier Science Publishers, 1992, pp. 83–114.
19. W. Thomas, Languages, automata, and logic, in: [17], pp. 389–455.

Partially Ordered Regular Languages
for Graph Queries[*]

Sergio Flesca[1] and Sergio Greco[1]

DEIS, Univ. della Calabria, 87030 Rende, Italy
{flesca,greco}@si.deis.unical.it

Abstract. In this paper we present an extension of regular languages to
support graph queries. The proposed extension is based on the introduction of a partial order on the strings of the languages. We extend regular
expressions, regular grammars and finite state automata by introducing partial orders on strings, production rules and transitions, respectively. The relation among regular expressions, regular grammars and
finite state automata is analyzed. We show how partially ordered languages can be used to define path queries to search graph databases and
present results on their computational complexity. Finally, we present an
application of partially ordered languages for searching the Web.

1 Introduction

Graph data is an emerging model for representing a variety of database contexts ranging from object oriented databases to hypertext data [9, 10, 5, 11]. Also
many of the recursive queries that arise in relational databases are in practice
graph traversals [16]. Recently, several languages and prototypes have been proposed for searching graph-like data such as the Web [1, 12, 3, 13]. All these languages permit to express (declarative) navigational queries, called path queries,
by means of regular expressions denoting paths in the graph [7, 11].

Path queries permit us to express queries of the form "find all objects reachable from a given node by paths whose labels form a word in r" where r is a
regular expression over an alphabet of labels. However, path queries are not satisfactory since the result is the complete set of answers. In practical applications,
where the number of answers can be large, the result should be a (limited) list
of answers ordered with respect to some criteria specified by the user. This is
confirmed by current index servers which enable the user to search documents in
the Web, by defining criteria based on the content of documents [4]. Generally,
the answer of index servers is a list of documents, ordered on the base of the
criteria specified by the user.

Thus, in order to better capture the navigational aspects of graph-like data,
we introduce partially ordered regular languages, an extension of regular languages where strings are partially ordered. Two strings s_1 and s_2 such that
$s_1 > s_2$ denote two paths in the graph with the constraint that the path s_1
should be preferred to the path s_2. Whenever the user wants a limited set of

---

[*] Work partially supported by a MURST grant under the project "Interdata".

answers, the whole graph does not need to be explored and the possibility of expressing a preference between paths should be given to the user. This is a very common situation in searching graph-like data such as the Web, where the number of paths and solutions can be extremely high. Thus, partially ordered languages capture the important aspect of navigational queries such as "search first the paths starting with the edge e_1 and next, in case the solution is not complete, those starting with the edge e_2".

The main contributions of this paper are i) the extension of regular expressions by introducing a partial order between 'alternative' strings; ii) the extension of regular grammars and finite state automata to generate and recognize sets of partially ordered regular strings; iii) results on the complexity of searching a graph by means of partially ordered path queries. A practical contribution is the application of partially ordered languages, in languages for searching graph-like data such as the Web.

2 Preliminaries

We assume familiarity with the basic concepts of regular languages, regular grammars and finite state automata [8] and report only non-standard definitions.

Grammars Given two variables (nonterminal symbols) A and B, we say that A depends on B, written $A \preceq B$ if there is a production $A \rightarrow \alpha B \gamma$ or there exists a variable C such that $A \preceq C$ and $C \preceq B$. A variable A is said to be recursive if $A \preceq A$. Two variables A and B are said to be mutually recursive if $A \preceq B$ and $B \preceq A$. A production $p = A \rightarrow \alpha B \gamma$ is said to be *recursive* if $B \preceq A$. Given a production $p = A \rightarrow \alpha$, we denote with $head(p)$ the head of the rule ($head(p) = A$) and with $body(p)$ the body of the rule ($body(p) = \alpha$).

Transducers A finite (automaton) transducer is 6-tuple $(Q, \Sigma, \Delta, \delta, q_0, F)$ where Δ is a finite output alphabet and δ is a mapping from $Q \times \Sigma$ to $Q \times \Delta$. A nondeterministic transducer is a transducer where the transition function is a mapping from $Q \times \Sigma$ to $2^{Q \times \Delta}$. Moreover, given a symbol $a \in \Sigma$ and a possibly empty string $w \in \Sigma^*$, $\delta(q, aw) = \{(\delta(q', w)[1], s\delta(q', w)[2]) | (q', s) \in \delta(q, a)\}$.

We say that a string w is accepted by a nondeterministic transducer $(Q, \Sigma, \Delta, \delta, q_0, F)$ if $\delta(q_0, w)[1] \cap F \neq \emptyset$. Each string w accepted by M has associated a set of strings in Δ^* defined as follows: $\{s | s \in \delta(q_0, w)[2]\}$. The language accepted by a nondeterministic transducer M is denoted $\mathcal{L}(M)$ whereas the set of strings generated by M is denoted $\mathcal{T}(M)$.

3 Partially ordered languages

3.1 Regular expressions

A partially ordered language over a given alphabet Σ is a pair $\langle L, >_L \rangle$ where L is a (standard) language over Σ (a subset of Σ^*) and $>_L$ is a partial order on the strings of L. Next we extend classical operations defined for standard languages to partially ordered languages. This is carried out by defining, for each operation, the new set of strings and the partial order on this set.

Union. The union of two partially ordered languages $O_1 = \langle L_1, >_{L_1} \rangle$ and $O_2 = \langle L_2, >_{L_2} \rangle$, denoted $O_1 \sqcup O_2$, is equal to $O_3 = \langle L_3, >_{L_3} \rangle$ where $L_3 = L_1 \cup L_2$ and $>_{L_3}$ is defined as follows:

1. if $a >_{L_1} b$ and $a >_{L_2} b$ then $a >_{L_3} b$;
2. if $a >_{L_1} b$ (resp. $a >_{L_2} b$) and $b \notin L_2$ (resp. $b \notin L_1$) then $a >_{L_3} b$.

Observe that the union operator is commutative, i.e. $L_1 \sqcup L_2 = L_2 \sqcup L_2$.

Ordered Union. The ordered union of two languages $O_1 = \langle L_1, >_{L_1} \rangle$ and $O_2 = \langle L_2, >_{L_2} \rangle$, denoted $O_1 \oplus O_2$, is equal to $O_3 = \langle L_3, >_{L_3} \rangle$ where $L_3 = L_1 \cup L_2$ and $>_{L_3}$ is defined as follows:

1. if $a >_{L_1} b$ then $a >_{L_3} b$;
2. if $a >_{L_2} b$ and $b \notin L_1$ then $a >_{L_3} b$;
3. if $a \in L_1$, $b \in L_2$ and $b \notin L_1$ then $a >_{L_3} b$.

Observe that the ordered union operator is not commutative, i.e. $L_1 \oplus L_2 \neq L_2 \oplus L_1$ since, in the ordered union of two languages L_1 and L_2, the strings of L_1 are 'preferred' to the strings of L_2.

Concatenation. The concatenation of two ordered languages $O_1 = \langle L_1, >_{L_1} \rangle$ and $O_2 = \langle L_2, >_{L_2} \rangle$, denoted $O_1 O_2$, is equal to $\langle L_3, >_{L_3} \rangle$ where $L_3 = L_1 L_2$ and $>_{L_3}$ is defined as follows:

$x >_{L_3} y$ if for each $y_1 \in L_1$ and for each $y_2 \in L_2$ such that $y_1 y_2 = y$ there are $x_1 \in L_1$ and $x_2 \in L_2$ such that $x_1 x_2 = x$ and either i) $x_1 >_{L_1} y_1$ or ii) $x_1 = y_1$ and $x_2 >_{L_2} y_2$.

Thus, in the comparison of two strings x and y we search partitions x_1 and x_2 of x and y_1 and y_2 of y and then compare $x_1 x_2$ with $y_1 y_2$. In the comparison of $x_1 x_2$ and $y_1 y_2$ we first compare x_1 and y_1 and then, if $x_1 = y_1$, compare x_2 and y_2.

Closure. The closure (or Kleene star) of an ordered language L, denoted L^*, is defined as usual by using concatenation and union of ordered languages, i.e. $L^* = \bigsqcup_{i=0}^{\infty} L^i$.

The ordered closure (or ordered Kleene star) of an ordered language L, denoted $L^\triangleright$, is defined by using concatenation and ordered union of ordered languages. That is

$$L^\triangleright = \bigoplus_{i=0}^{\infty} L^i$$

Observe that $\oplus$ is not commutative therefore $L^\triangleright$ is equal to $(L^0 \oplus L^1 \oplus L^2 \oplus \ldots \oplus L^i \oplus L^{i+1} \oplus \ldots)$.

For a given language $\langle L, >_L \rangle$, since $>_L$ defines a partial order on the strings of L, from now on we shall omit the subscript L whenever it can be understood from the context.

Example 1. Consider the two partially ordered languages $P = \langle \{a, b\}, \{a > b\} \rangle$ and $Q = \langle \{b, c\}, \{b > c\} \rangle$. Then

1. $P \sqcup Q = \langle \{a, b, c\}, \{b > c\} \rangle$;

2. $P \oplus Q = \langle \{a, b, c\}, \{a > b > c\}\rangle$;
3. $PQ = \langle \{ab, ac, bb, bc\}, \{ab > ac > bb > bc\}\rangle$;
4. $P^0 = \langle \epsilon, \emptyset\rangle$, $P^1 = \langle \{a, b\}, \{a > b\}\rangle$, $P^2 = \langle \{aa, ab, ba, bb\}, \{aa > ab > ba > bb\}\rangle$;
5. $P^0 \sqcup P^1 \sqcup P^2 = \langle \{\epsilon, a, b, aa, ab, ba, bb\}, \{a > b,\ aa > ab > ba > bb\}\rangle$,
6. $P^0 \oplus P^1 \oplus P^2 = \langle \{\epsilon, a, b, aa, ab, ba, bb\}, \{\epsilon > a > b > aa > ab > ba > bb\}\rangle$. $\square$

Definition 1. *Let Σ be an alphabet. The (extended) regular expressions over Σ and the set that they denote are defined recursively as follows:*

1. *$\emptyset$ is a regular expression and denotes the empty language $\langle \emptyset, \emptyset \rangle$;*
2. *ϵ is a regular expression and denotes the language $\langle \{\epsilon\}, \emptyset \rangle$;*
3. *For each $a \in \Sigma$, a is a regular expression and denotes the language $\langle \{a\}, \emptyset \rangle$;*
4. *If r and s are regular expressions denoting the languages R and S, respectively, then a) $r + s$ denotes the language $R \sqcup S$, b) $r > s$ denotes the language $R \oplus S$, c) rs denotes the languages RS, d) r^* denotes the languages R^* and e) $r^\triangleright$ denotes the languages $R^\triangleright$.* $\square$

Observe that an extended regular expression is associated to a partially ordered language where the partial order is implicit.

Example 2. The language associated with the regular expression $(a + b)^*$ consists of all strings over the alphabet $\Sigma = \{a, b\}$. Consider the languages associated with the extended regular expression $(a > b)^*$. As above, the language consists of all strings over $\Sigma = \{a, b\}$ but we now have a partial order between strings which states that the symbol a is preferred to the symbol b. Thus, for every two strings uav and ubw with $u, v, w \in \Sigma^*$ we have $uav > ubw$.

Consider now the language $(a + b)^\triangleright$. In this case we have a partial order on the strings of the language which says that shorter strings are preferred to longer ones. Finally, observe that the language $(a > b)^\triangleright$ has a linear order where strings are ordered following the lexicographic order. $\square$

It is well known that for standard regular languages for a given string w is $(w^*)^* = w^*$ and that $w^* w^* = w^*$. Moreover, for partially ordered languages we have the following equivalence relations:

Proposition 1. *Given an alphabet Σ and letting w be a string on Σ, then*

1. *$(w^\triangleright)^\triangleright = w^\triangleright$, $(w^*)^\triangleright = w^*$, $(w^\triangleright)^* = w^\triangleright$;*
2. *$w^\triangleright w^\triangleright = w^\triangleright$, $w^\triangleright w^* = w^*$, $w^* w^\triangleright = w^*$.* $\square$

3.2 Partially ordered regular grammars

A partially ordered regular grammar is an extension of a regular grammar where the productions are partially ordered.

Definition 2. *A partially ordered regular grammar G^o is a pair $\langle G, >_G \rangle$ where $G = \langle V, T, P, S \rangle$ is a standard grammar whose productions are either of the form $A \rightarrow wA$ or $A \rightarrow w$ such that $w \in (V \cup T)^*$ does not contain variables depending on A and $>_G$ is a partial order on the production of P satisfying the following conditions:*

1. *for each two productions p_1 and p_2 such that $p_1 > p_2$ is $head(p_1) = head(p_2)$;*
2. *there are no two productions p_1 recursive and p_2 not recursive such that $p_1 > p_2$;*
3. *If there is a non recursive production of the form $p_1 = A \to w_1$ and a recursive production $p_2 = A \to w_2 A$ such that $p_1 > p_2$, then for all pairs of productions of the form $p_i = A \to w_i$ and $p_j = A \to w_j A$ must be $p_i > p_j$.* □

Since in the above definition we have considered productions with $n \geq 0$ variables in the body, whereas the standard definition admits at most one variable in the body, in the following we assume that strings are generated by means of leftmost derivations, i.e. by applying the productions to the leftmost variable.

The language generated from an ordered regular grammar $G^o = \langle G, >_G \rangle$, denoted $\mathcal{L}(G^o) = \langle \mathcal{L}(G), >_{\mathcal{L}(G)} \rangle$, is a set of partially ordered strings. Before presenting how the partial order $>_{\mathcal{L}(G)}$ is defined, we introduce the relation $\succ$ between (leftmost) derivations.

Let $p_1 = A \to \beta_1$ and $p_2 = A \to \beta_2$ be two productions in P such that $p_1 > p2$. We say that a derivation d_1 has priority on a derivation d_2 (written $d_1 \succ d_2$), if

1. d_1 and d_2 are, respectively, of the form $\alpha A \gamma \Rightarrow \alpha \beta_1 \gamma \Rightarrow^* w_1$ and $\alpha A \gamma \Rightarrow \alpha \beta_2 \gamma \Rightarrow^* w_2$, or
2. there are three derivations d, d_3 and d_4 such that $d_1 = d d_3$ and $d_2 = d d_4$ and $d_3 \succ d_4$.

Given two strings $w_1, w_2 \in T^*$, we say that $w_1 >_{\mathcal{L}(G)} w_2$ if for each derivation of the form $d_2 = S \Rightarrow^* w_2$ there is a derivation $d_1 = S \Rightarrow^* w_1$ such that $d_1 \succ d_2$.

Example 3. Consider the partially ordered grammar $G^o = \langle (\{a, b, c, d\}, \{S, S_1, S_2\}, \{p_1, p_2, p_3, p_4, p_5, p_6\}, S), \{p_3 > p_4, \ p_5 > p_6\} \rangle$ where the productions are defined as follows

$$p_1 : S \to a S_1 \qquad p_3 : S_1 \to b \qquad p_5 : S_2 \to c$$
$$p_2 : S \to a S_2 \qquad p_4 : S_1 \to c \qquad p_6 : S_2 \to d$$

The strings generated by the grammar are ab, ac and ad and there are four distinct derivations generating these strings:

$$d_1 = S \Rightarrow a S_1 \Rightarrow ab \qquad d_2 = S \Rightarrow a S_1 \Rightarrow ac$$
$$d_3 = S \Rightarrow a S_2 \Rightarrow ac \qquad d_4 = S \Rightarrow a S_2 \Rightarrow ad$$

Since $d_1 \succ d_2$ and $d_3 \succ d_4$ we have only $ac > ad$. □

Two productions $p_1 = A \to \alpha$ and $p_2 = A \to \beta$ with $p_1 > p_2$ are denoted as $A \to \alpha > \beta$ and as $A \to \alpha | \beta$ if p_1 and p_2 are not related. For instance the productions of the grammar of Example 3 can be rewritten as follows: $S \to a((b > c)|(c > d))$ We next present some results on the relation between partially ordered regular grammars and partially ordered regular languages.

Lemma 1. *Let $G^o = \langle G, >_G \rangle$ with $G = \langle V, T, P, S \rangle$ be a partially ordered regular grammar and let $\mathcal{L}(G^o) = \langle \mathcal{L}(G), >_{\mathcal{L}(G)} \rangle$ be the language generated by G^o. Then, $>_{\mathcal{L}(G)}$ is a partial order on $\mathcal{L}(G)$.* □

Theorem 1. *A partially ordered language is regular if and only if it is generated by a partially ordered regular grammar.* □

3.3 Automata for partially ordered regular languages

A partially ordered nondeterministic transducer is a nondeterministic transducer where the input strings recognized are partially ordered.

Definition 3. *A partially ordered nondeterministic transducer is a nondeterministic transducer $M = (Q, \Sigma, \Delta, \delta, q_0, \Gamma)$ where the output alphabet Δ is a set of pairs $(q, d) \in Q \times D$ and D is a partially ordered set. The transition function δ defining a mapping from $Q \times \Sigma$ to $2^{Q \times \Delta}$ must satisfy the following conditions:*

1. *Every element in $\delta(q, a)$ is of the form $(q', (q, p))$ with $p \in D$;*
2. *The graph describing the transition function does not contains cycles with all arcs marked with ϵ.* □

We now introduce a partial order on output strings and next we transfer this order to input strings. Let $e = (q, d) \in \Delta$, then we denote with $e[1]$ the first element of e and with $e[2]$ the second element of e, i.e. $e[1] = q$ and $e[2] = d$. Given a transducer M and an output string os in $\mathcal{T}(M)$, we denote with $first(os)$ and $tail(os)$, respectively, the first element and the tail of os. Given two output strings os_i and os_j, we say that $os_i > os_j$ iff 1) the $first(os_i)[1] = first(os_j)[1]$ and $first(os_i)[2] >_D first(os_j)[2]$, or 2) the $first(os_i) = first(os_j)$ and $tail(os_i) > tail(os_j)$. Given two strings $s_1, s_2 \in \mathcal{L}(M)$, $s_1 > s_2$ iff $\forall os_2 \in \delta(q_0, s_2)[2])$ there is an output string $os_1 \in \delta(q_0, s_1)[2]$ such that $os_1 > os_2$.

A partially ordered nondeterministic transducer M is associated to a partially ordered language $\langle \mathcal{L}(M), >_{\mathcal{L}(M)} \rangle$ where $\mathcal{L}(M)$ is the set of strings accepted by the transducer and $>_{\mathcal{L}(M)}$ is the partial order on $\mathcal{L}(M)$ defined above.

Example 4. Consider language $L = a (b > c) d$. L is accepted by NDFA M whose transition function, with priorities $p_0 > p_1$, is reported in the following table and graphically represented by the following graph.

State	Input	New_State	Output
q_0	a	q_1	q_0, p_0
q_1	b	q_2	q_1, p_0
q_1	c	q_3	q_1, p_1
q_2	d	q_f	q_2, p_0
q_3	d	q_f	q_2, p_0

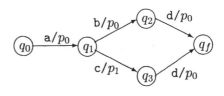

where q_0 is the initial state and q_f is the final state. □

Observe that as for standard finite state automata, the transition function can be represented by means of a graph whose nodes correspond to states but, unlike standard finite state automata, the arcs are labeled with pairs (a, p) denoting the input symbol and the priority. Thus, for each $(q', (q, p)) \in \delta(q, a)$ there is an arc from q to q' labeled with (a, p).

Lemma 2. *Let M be a partially ordered nondeterministic transducer. Then, $>_{\mathcal{L}(M)}$ is a partial order on $\mathcal{L}(M)$.*

Proof (sketch). For each input string there is a finite set of output strings. Since the output strings are partially ordered, from the above definitions, there is also a partial order on the input strings. □

Theorem 2. *A partially ordered language* $\langle L, >_L \rangle$ *is regular only if there is a partially ordered nondeterministic transducer* M *such that* $\langle \mathcal{L}(M), >_{\mathcal{L}(M)} \rangle = \langle L, >_L \rangle$. □

We next present some results on the complexity of comparing two strings.

Lemma 3. *Given an a partially ordered nondeterministic transducer* M, *two input strings* $s_1, s_2 \in \mathcal{L}(M)$ *and an output string* $os_2 \in \delta(q_0, s_2)[2]$. *Checking if an output string* $os_1 \in \delta(q_0, s_1)[2]$ *such that* $os_1 > os_2$ *exists, can be done in time polynomial in the size of* M *and in the length of* s_1. □

Theorem 3. *Given an a partially ordered nondeterministic transducer* M *and two input strings* $s_1, s_2 \in \mathcal{L}(M)$.

1. *The problem of checking if* $s_1 \not> s_2$ *is in* NP;
2. *The problem of checking if* $s_1 > s_2$ *is in* $coNP$.

Proof (sketch)

1. It is sufficient to guess an output string os_2 in $\delta(q_0, s_2)[2]$ and to check that there is no output string $os_1 \in \delta(q_0, s_1)[2]$ such that $os_1 > os_2$. Both guess and check (by lemma 3) can be done in polynomial time.
2. In this case we have to show that for each output string $os_2 \in \delta(q_0, s_2)[2]$ there is an output string $os_1 \in \delta(q_0, s_1)[2]$ such that $os_1 > os_2$. Clearly, this is a $coNP$ problem. □

4 Searching Graph Databases by means of Regular Expressions

Many of the recursive queries that arise in practice in relational databases and, more generally, in graph-like data, are in practice graph transversals. These kind of queries can be formulated by means of regular expressions. A typical query is "find all nodes reachable from a given node by paths whose labels form a word of a regular expression r".

A database graph $G = (N, E, \phi, \Sigma, \lambda)$ is a directed labeled graph, where N is a set of nodes, E is a set of edges, Σ is a finite set of symbols denoting labels associated with arcs, ϕ is an incidence function mapping E to $N \times N$ and λ is an edge labeling function mapping E to Σ. Let $G = (N, E, \phi, \Sigma, \lambda)$ be a database graph and let $p = (v_1, e_1, v_2, e_2, ..., v_n)$ where $v_i \in N$ and $e_j \in E$ be a path in G. The label path of p, denoted $\lambda(p)$, is a subset of Σ^* defined as $\lambda(e_1), ..., \lambda(e_{n-1})$ Given a regular expression R over Σ and a string $w \in \Sigma^*$, we say that w spells a path p in G if $w = \lambda(p)$ and we say that p satisfies R if $\lambda(p) \in \mathcal{L}(R)$.

Given a graph G and a regular expression R over Σ we denote with $LL(G, R)$ the set of strings in $\mathcal{L}(R)$ spelling paths in G, i.e. $LL(G, R) = \{\lambda(p) \mid p \text{ is a path on } G \wedge \lambda(p) \in \mathcal{L}(R)\}$. Moreover, given a node x_0 we denote with $LL(G, R, x_0)$

the set of strings in $\mathcal{L}(R)$ spelling paths in G starting from x_0. A vertex query $Q_N(G, R, x_0)$ on a database graph $G = (N, E, \phi, \Sigma, \lambda)$ is defined as the set of nodes y such that there is a path from x_0 to y in G satisfying R.

Given a database graph G and an extended regular expression R over Σ we denote with $POL(G, R)$ the partially ordered set of strings $\langle LL(G, R), >_{LL(G,R)} \rangle$ where $>_{LL(G,R)}$ is the set of all pairs (x, y) in $>_{\mathcal{L}(R)}$ with both x and y in $LL(G, R)$. Moreover, given a node x_0 we denote with $POL(G, R, x_0)$ the restriction of $POL(G, R)$ to strings spelling paths in G starting from x_0.

Let G be a database graph, x_0 be a node in G and R an extended regular expression. A vertex query $Q_N(G, R, x_0)$ is defined as the partially ordered set of nodes y such that there is a path from x_0 to y in G satisfying R. The partial order on the result S of $Q_N(G, R, x_0)$ is defined as follows: given two nodes x and y in S, $x > y$ iff for each path p_1 from x_0 to y there is a path p_2 from x_0 to x such that $\lambda(p_2) > \lambda(p_1)$.

Example 5. Consider the database graph G shown in Figure 2 and the regular expression $R = (a > b) \, a \, b^*$.

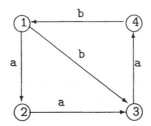

The vertex query $Q_N(G, R, 1)$ gives the following partially ordered set $\langle \{1, 3, 4\}, \{3 > 4, 3 > 1\} \rangle$. Thus, the complete set of answers consists of the sequences of nodes $[3, 4, 1]$ and $[3, 1, 4]$. $\square$

Fact 1 *Let $G = (N, E, \phi, \Sigma, \lambda)$ be a database graph, x, y be two nodes in N and R be a standard regular expression over Σ. Checking if G contains a directed path from x to y satisfying R can be done in polynomial time.* $\square$

Let $Q = Q_N(G, R, x_0)$ be a vertex query and let $\langle S, >_S \rangle$ be the partially ordered set of nodes defined by Q. An answer of Q is any linearly ordered set $X = \langle S, >_X \rangle$ such that $>_X$ satisfies $>_S$. Since Q may have one or more than one answer, we denote with $Ans(Q)$ the complete set of answers.

Theorem 4. *Let $G = (N, E, \phi, \Sigma, \lambda)$ be a database graph, $x_0 \in N$ and R an extended regular expression over Σ.*

1. *Checking if a sequence S is in $Ans(Q_N(G, R, x_0))$ is in NP;*
2. *Computing nondeterministically one answer of $Q_N(G, R, x_0)$ can be done in polynomial time.*

Proof (Sketch) (Part 2.) The database graph G can be seen as a (standard) nondeterministic finite state automaton with initial state x_0. Let M be a partially ordered nondeterministic transducer recognizing $\mathcal{L}(R)$. The transition function of M can be represented by a graph where a label and a priority are associated to each edge. The intersection I of the two graphs gives a partially ordered nondeterministic transducer recognizing the language $LL(G, R, x_0)$. Thus, there is a path in G from x_0 to some node y satisfying R iff there is a path in I from (x_0, q_0) to (y, q_f). An answer is given by computing the nodes y reachable from (x_0, q_0) by visiting the graph I using a depth-first-like algorithm which navigates first the arcs with higher priority.

(Part 1.) Derives from Part 2.

5   Searching the Web

The World Wide Web is a large, distributed, collection of documents connected by hyperlinks. This collection can be represented by means of a directed graph where nodes denote documents and arcs denote hyperlinks. Usually the Web is searched by navigating the graph. Navigational queries are expressed by means of regular expressions denoting paths in the graph. Standard regular expressions can be used to find all documents reached by paths satisfying a regular expression. Since the size of the graph is huge, the number of document accessed can be enormous and not, therefore, useful. Partially ordered regular languages can be used to introduce preferences in searching for documents in the Web.

In this section we show how extended regular expressions can be used to search the Web by means of examples, whereas the formal definition of the language will be presented in the extended version. Since not all documents in the Web are known, documents are searched for by means of path queries starting from a given node (URL specifying a document). We use generalized path queries as defined in [3, 12]. In particular, for labels we use i) the standard "meta-symbols" "%" and "_", used by SQL to denote, respectively, "any character string" and any "character" and ii) the symbols $\Rightarrow$ and $\rightarrow$ to denote, respectively, global (or standard) links and local links. A local link is a standard link connecting two documents stored on the same machine. Thus "a" $\overset{*}{\rightarrow}$ denotes all documents reachable from the document with URL "a" by navigating only local links whereas "a" "$dep\%$" denotes the set of all documents reachable by the document with URL "a" by navigating a local link whose label starts with the string "dep". The following example presents three applications of path queries which use both standard and extended regular expressions.

Example 6. The first query computes all documents reachable from the node with URL "www.unical.it" by navigating first a link with label "departments" or "faculties" and then navigating local links.

FIND ALL Documents d
SUCH THAT "www.unical.it" ("departments" + "faculties") $\overset{*}{\rightarrow}$ d

The next query computes at most 10 documents reachable from the node with URL "www.unical.it" by navigating first a link with label "departments" followed by any number of local links and next, if the solution is not complete, by navigating the link with label "faculties" followed by any number of local links.

FIND 10 Documents d
SUCH THAT "www.unical.it"("departments" > "faculties") $\overset{*}{\rightarrow}$ d

The last query computes at most 10 documents reachable from the node with URL 'www.unical.it" by first navigating local links a and next, if the solution is not complete, by navigating also 'external' links.

FIND 10 Documents d

SUCH THAT "www.unical.it"($\overset{a}{\to}$ > $\overset{e}{\to}$) d   □

Observe that the first query, which uses a standard regular expression, is deterministic whereas the following two queries, which use extended regular expressions, may be nondeterministic. Thus, the first query gives the complete set of documents reachable from "www.unical.it" by means of paths satisfying the regular expression whereas the following queries give a list of at most 10 documents, reached by means of paths satisfying the regular expressions. Moreover, the list of documents computed by the queries also satisfies the partial order defined by the regular expressions.

We conclude by mentioning that a prototype of a language, based on partially ordered path queries to search the Web, is under development at the University of Calabria.

References

1. Abiteboul S. Querying Semi-Structured Data. *Proc. International Conference on Database Theory*, pages 1–18, 1997.
2. Abiteboul S., R. Hull, V. Vianu. *Foundations of Databases*. Addison-Wesley, 1994.
3. Abiteboul S., V. Vianu. Queries and Computation on the Web. *Proc. International Conference on Database Theory*, pages 262–275, 1997.
4. Altavista Help, http://www.altavista.com/av/content/help.htm.
5. Beeri C, Y. Kornatzky, A Logical Query Language for Hypertext Systems. *Proc. European Conference on Hypertexts*, pages 67-80, 1990.
6. Consens M, Mendelzon A., GraphLog: a Visual Formalism for Real Life Recursion. *Proc. Ninth ACM SIGACT-SIGMOD-SIGART Symposium on Principles of Database Systems*, pages 404-416, 1990.
7. Cruz I., Mendelzon A., P. Wood. G^{+}: Recursive Queries Without Recursion. *Proc. 2nd Int. Conf. on Expert Database Systems*, pages 355-368, 1988.
8. Hopcroft J., J. Ullman. *Introduction to Automata Theory, Languages and Computation*. Addison Wesley, 1980.
9. Kifer, M., W. Kim, Y. Sagiv, Querying Object-Oriented Databases, *Proc. ACM-SIGMOD International Conference on Management of Data*, pages 393-402, 1992.
10. Kifer, M., G. Lausen, J. Wu, Logical Foundation of Object-Oriented and Frame Based Languages., *Journal of ACM*, 42(4), pages 741-843, 1995.
11. Mendelzon A., P.T. Wood, Finding Regular Simple Path in Graph Databases, *SIAM Journal on Computing*, 24(6), 1995.
12. Mendelzon A., G. Mihaila, T. Milo, Querying the World Wide Web, *Journal of Digital Libraries*, 1997.
13. Mendelzon A., T. Milo, Formal models of web queries, *Proc. Sixteenth ACM SIGACT-SIGMOD-SIGART Symposium on Principles of Database Systems*, 1997.
14. Minohara T., R. Watanabe. Queries on Structures in Hypertext, *Foundations of Data Organization and Algorithms (FODO)*, pages 394-411, 1993.
15. Tarjan R., Fast Algorithms for Solving Path Problems, *Journal of ACM*, 28, pages 594-614, 1981.
16. Yannakakis M., Graph-theoretic methods in database theory, In *Proc. Ninth ACM SIGACT-SIGMOD-SIGART Symposium on Principles of Database Systems*, pages 230-242, 1990.

Deciding First-Order Properties of Locally Tree-Decomposalbe Graphs

Markus Frick and Martin Grohe

Institut für Mathematische Logik, Eckerstr.1, 79104 Freiburg, Germany
{frick,grohe}@sun2.mathematik.uni-freiburg.de

Abstract. We introduce the concept of a class of graphs being *locally tree-decomposable*. There are numerous examples of locally tree-decomposable classes, among them the class of planar graphs and all classes of bounded valence or of bounded tree-width.

We show that for each locally tree-decomposable class $\mathcal{C}$ of graphs and for each property φ of graphs that is definable in first-order logic, there is a linear time algorithm deciding whether a given graph $G \in \mathcal{C}$ has property φ.

1 Introduction

It is an important task in the theory of algorithms to find feasible instances of otherwise intractable algorithmic problems. A notion that has turned out to be extremely useful in this context is that of *tree-width* of a graph. 3-COLORABILITY, HAMILTONICITY, and many other NP-complete properties of graphs can be decided in linear time when restricted to graphs whose tree-width is bounded by a fixed constant (see [Bod97] for a survey).

Courcelle [Cou90] proved a meta-theorem, which easily implies numerous results of the abovementioned type: *Let $w \geq 1$ and φ be a property of graphs that is definable in monadic second-order logic. Then φ can be decided in linear time on graphs of tree-width at most w.* Although Courcelle's theorem does not give practical algorithms, because the hidden constants are too big, it is still useful since it gives a simple way to recognize a property as being linear time computable on graphs of bounded tree-width. Once this has been done, a more refined analysis using the combinatorics of the particular property may yield a practical algorithm.

Though probably the most successful, bounded tree-width is not the only restriction on graphs that makes algorithmic tasks easier. Other useful restrictions are *planarity* or *bounded valence*, where the *valence* of a graph is the maximal number of neighbors of a vertex. For example, consider the problem k-DOMINATING SET for a fixed k. (Given a graph G, is there a set D of at most k vertices of G such that every vertex of G is either equal or adjacent to a vertex in D?) To solve k-DOMINATING SET in general, we do not know much better than just trying all $O(n^k)$ candidate sets (n always denotes the number of vertices of the input graph). However, on planar graphs k-DOMINATING SET can be solved in time $O(11^k n)$, and on graphs of valence at most λ, it can be solved in time $O((\lambda + 1)^k n)$ [DF99].

Unfortunately, the analogue of Courcelle's theorem does not hold for planar graphs or classes of bounded valence; 3-COLORABILITY is a monadic second-order definable property that remains NP-complete when restricted to the class of planar graphs of valence at most 4 [GJS76]. Instead of monadic second-order, we study the complexity of first-order definable properties.

Seese was the first to give a meta-theorem in the style of Courcelle's theorem for a more general class of graphs; in [See96] he proved that for every $l \geq 1$ and for every first-order property of graphs there is a linear time algorithm that decides whether a given graph of valence at most l has this property.

An observation that has been used for various algorithms on planar graphs (essentially it goes back to Baker [Bak94]) is that there is a bound on the tree-width of a planar graph only depending on its diameter. A different way to see this is that a local neighborhood of a vertex in a planar graph has tree-width bounded by a number only depending on the ratio of this neighborhood. As a matter of fact, given a planar graph G we can compute in linear time a family of subgraphs of bounded tree-width such that a suitably big neighborhood of every vertex of G is completely contained in one of these subgraphs.

We call classes of graphs admitting such a covering algorithm *locally tree-decomposable* (a precise definition is given in Section 4.2). Examples of locally tree-decomposable classes of graphs are all classes of bounded genus, bounded valence, bounded crossing number, and, trivially, bounded tree-width. Eppstein [Epp95] considered a closely related, though slightly weaker concept he called the *diameter-treewidth property* (we call this property *locally bounded tree-width* and refer the reader to Section 4.2 for a discussion of the various concepts). Eppstein proved that the subgraph isomorphism problem for a fixed subgraph H, asking whether a given graph G contains H, is solvable in linear time when restricted to graphs G contained in a class of graphs that is closed under taking minors and satisfies the diameter-treewidth property.

Our main result goes much further:

Theorem 1. *Let C be a class of graphs that is locally tree-decomposable and φ a property definable in first-order logic. Then there is a linear time algorithm deciding whether a given graph $G \in C$ has property φ.*

Examples of first-order definable properties are k-DOMINATING SET and k-INDEPENDENT SET for a fixed k, H-SUBGRAPH ISOMORPHISM (Given G, is $H \subseteq G$) and H-HOMOMORPHISM (Given G, is there a homomorphism $h : H \to G$) for a fixed H, (H, K)-EXTENSION (Given G, is every $H \subseteq G$ contained in some $K \subseteq G$) for fixed $H \subseteq K$.

Thus our theorem generalizes various results solving concrete problems on specific locally tree-decomposable classes such as the class of planar graphs. It also generalizes Seese's [See96] theorem mentioned above, because classes of graphs of bounded valence are locally tree decomposable.

Using the same techniques, we prove another result that applies to the even more general context of classes of graphs of locally bounded tree-width; for such classes we give a quadratic time algorithm for every fixed first-order property.

The complexity of first-order properties of arbitrary graphs, which is also relevant to database theory, has been studied earlier under various aspects. It is long known that every first-order property of graphs can be decided in polynomial time, actually in AC_0 [AU79,Imm82]. A question closer to our theorem is whether deciding first-order properties is *fixed-parameter tractable*, that is, whether there is a fixed c such that every first-order property of arbitrary graphs can be decided in time $O(n^c)$. This question has been brought up by Yannakakis [Yan95]. The theory of fixed-parameter tractability gives some evidence that the answer is no, as has been independently proved by Downey, Fellows, Taylor [DFT96] and Papadimitriou, Yannakakis [PY97] (deciding first-order properties is AW[1]-complete).

The proof of our theorem combines three main ingredients: a refinement of Courcelle's Theorem [Cou90] mentioned above, Gaifman's Theorem [Gai82] stating that first-order properties are local, and algorithmic techniques based on ideas of Baker [Bak94] and Eppstein [Epp95].

2 Preliminaries

In this paper we will confine our attention to properties of *simple undirected graphs*. We consider a graph as a relational structure $G = (V^G, E^G)$, where V^G is a finite set of *vertices* and E^G is a binary relation on V^G. For a subset $U \subseteq V^G$ we let $\langle U \rangle^G$ denote the induced subgraph of G with vertex set U. The union of two graphs G, H is the graph $G \cup H := (V^G \cup V^H, E^G \cup E^H)$.

The distance $d^G(a, b)$ between two vertices $a, b \in V^G$ is the length of the shortest path in G connecting a and b. For $r \geq 1$ and $a \in G$ we define the *r-neighborhood* of a to be $N_r^G(a) := \{b \in V^G \mid d^G(a, b) \leq r\}$. We often omit superscripts ^{G} if G is clear from the context.

The *first-order language* FO of graphs is build up in the usual way from an infinite supply of variables denoted by $x, y, x_1, \ldots$, the relation symbols E and $=$, the connectives $\wedge, \vee, \neg, \rightarrow$, and the quantifiers $\forall, \exists$ ranging over the vertices of the graph in question. For example, the first-order sentence

$$\forall x_1 \forall x_2 \forall x_3 \big((Ex_1x_2 \wedge Ex_1x_3 \wedge Ex_2x_3) \rightarrow \exists y(Ex_1y \wedge Ex_2y \wedge Ex_3y)\big)$$

says that every triangle of a graph is contained in a K_4 (a complete graph on four vertices).

A *free variable* in a first-order formula is a variable x not in the scope of a quantifier $\exists x$ or $\forall x$. A *sentence* is a formula without free variables. The notation $\varphi(x_1, \ldots, x_k)$ indicates that all free variables of the formula φ are among $x_1, \ldots, x_k$; it does not necessarily mean that the variables $x_1, \ldots, x_k$ all appear in φ. For a formula $\varphi(x_1, \ldots, x_k)$, a graph G, and $a_1, \ldots, a_k \in V^G$ we write $G \models \varphi(a_1, \ldots, a_k)$ to say that G satisfies φ if the variables $x_1, \ldots, x_k$

are interpreted by the vertices $a_1, \ldots, a_k$, respectively. For example, letting $\delta_2(x, y) := \left(x = y \vee Exy \vee \exists z (Exz \wedge Ezy)\right)$ we have $G \models \delta_2(a, b)$ if, and only if, $d^G(a, b) \leq 2$. For brevity, we often use notations such as $\varphi(\bar{x})$ instead of $\varphi(x_1, \ldots, x_k)$.

We represent graphs by *adjacency lists*. As our underlying model of computation we use the usual *random access machines* with the logarithmic cost measure (see [AHU74]).

3 Graphs of bounded tree-width

A *tree-decomposition* of a graph G is a pair $(T, (B_t)_{t \in T})$, where T is a tree and $(B_t)_{t \in T}$ a family of subsets of V^G such that $\bigcup_{t \in T} \langle B_t \rangle^G = G$ and for every $a \in G$ the subgraph $\langle \{t \mid a \in B_t\} \rangle^T$ of T is connected. The *width* of $(T, (B_t)_{t \in T})$ is $\max\{|B_t| \mid t \in T\} - 1$. The *tree-width* of G, denoted by $\mathrm{tw}(G)$, is the minimal width of a tree-decomposition of G.

Bodländer [Bod96] proved that for each $w \geq 1$ there is a linear time algorithm that, given a graph G, either computes a tree-decomposition of G of width at most w, or rejects G if $\mathrm{tw}(G) > w$. This result is underlying most of the linear time algorithms on graphs of bounded tree-width.

Recall Courcelle's theorem that we mentioned in the introduction:

Theorem 2 (Courcelle [Cou90]). *Let $w \geq 1$. Then for every sentence φ of monadic second-order logic there is a linear time algorithm that decides whether a given graph G of tree-width at most w satisfies φ.*

Monadic second-order logic is an extension of first-order logic that also allows quantification over sets.

Using known techniques for algorithms on graphs of bounded tree-width, it is not hard to prove the following lemma. We are only going to use the first-order version of the lemma later.

Lemma 1. *Let $w \geq 1$. Then for every formula $\varphi(x)$ of monadic second-order logic there is a linear time algorithm that, given a graph G of tree-width at most w, computes the set $\{a \in V^G \mid G \models \varphi(a)\}$.*

4 Locally tree-decomposable graphs

4.1 Gaifman's Theorem

For every $r \geq 0$ there is a first-order formula $\delta_r(x, y)$ such that for all graphs G and $a, b \in V^G$ we have $G \models \delta_r(a, b) \iff d^G(a, b) \leq r$. In the following, we write $d(x, y) \leq r$ instead of $\delta_r(x, y)$ and $d(x, y) > r$ instead of $\neg \delta_r(x, y)$.

If $\varphi(x)$ is a first-order formula, then $\varphi^{N_r(x)}(x)$ is the formula obtained from $\varphi(x)$ by relativizing all quantifiers to $N_r(x)$, that is, by replacing every subformula of the form $\exists y \psi(x, y, \bar{z})$ by $\exists y (d(x, y) \leq r \wedge \psi(x, y, \bar{z}))$ and every subformula of the form $\forall y \psi(x, y, \bar{z})$ by $\forall y (d(x, y) \leq r \rightarrow \psi(x, y, \bar{z}))$. A formula

$\psi(x)$ of the form $\varphi^{N_r(x)}(x)$, for some $\varphi(x)$, is called r-*local*. The basic property of r-local formulas $\psi(x)$ is that it only depends on the r-neighborhood of x whether they hold at x or not, that is, for all graphs G and $a \in V^G$ we have
$$G \models \psi(a) \iff \langle N_r^G(a) \rangle \models \psi(a).$$

Theorem 3 (Gaifman [Gai82]). *Every first-order sentence is equivalent to a Boolean combination of sentences of the form*
$$\exists x_1 \dots \exists x_k \Big(\bigwedge_{1 \le i < j \le k} d(x_i, x_j) > 2r \wedge \bigwedge_{1 \le i \le k} \psi(x_i) \Big),$$

for suitable $r, k \ge 1$ and an r-local $\psi(x)$.

4.2 Locally tree-decomposable graphs

Definition 1. *(1) Let $r, w, l \ge 1$. An (r, w, l)-tree cover of a graph G is a family $U_1, \dots, U_m$ of subsets of V^G such that*
  (a) For all $a \in V^G$ exists an $i \le m$ such that $N_r^G(a) \subseteq U_i$.
  (b) For $1 \le i \le m$ we have $\mathrm{tw}(\langle U_i \rangle^G) \le w$.
  (c) For $1 \le i \le m$ we have $|\{j \mid 1 \le j \le m, \; U_i \cap U_j \ne \emptyset\}| \le l$.

(2) A class $\mathcal{C}$ of graphs is locally tree-decomposable if for every $r \ge 0$ there exist $w, l \ge 1$ and a linear time algorithm that, given a graph $G \in \mathcal{C}$, computes an (r, w, l)-tree cover of G.

For the purposes of this paper, we could replace (c) in the definition of a tree-cover by the weaker condition
  (c') $\sum_{i=1}^m |U_i| \le l$
(which follows from (c)). However, for some possible extensions of our results, (c) seems to be necessary.

Example 1. Graphs of bounded tree-width. For all $w \ge 1$, the class of all graphs of tree-width at most w is locally tree-decomposable (trivially).

Example 2. Graphs of bounded valence. For all $k \ge 1$, the class of all graphs of valence at most k is locally tree-decomposable. For $r \ge 0$ and a graph G of valence at most k, the family $\{N_r^G(a) \mid a \in V^G\}$ is an $(r, k^r + 1, k^{2r-1} + 1)$-tree cover of G.

Example 3. (Eppstein [Epp95]) *Graphs of bounded genus.* For every surface S, the class of all graphs embeddable in S is locally tree-decomposable (also see Definition 2 and the following discussion).

Example 4. ([Epp95]) *Graphs with no large $K_{3,k}$-minors.* For all $k \ge 1$, the class of all graphs that do not have a $K_{3,k}$-minor is locally tree-decomposable.

Example 5. Graphs of bounded crossing number. For all $k \ge 1$, the class of all graphs of crossing number at most k is locally tree-decomposable (follows from Example 3).

The following definition seems more natural than that of being locally tree-decomposable, but apparently it does not suffice for our linear time algorithm for first-order properties to work.

Definition 2. *A class $\mathcal{C}$ of graphs has* locally bounded tree-width, *if there is a function $\lambda : \mathbb{N} \to \mathbb{N}$ such that for all $r \geq 0$, $G \in \mathcal{C}$, and $a \in V^G$ we have* $\mathrm{tw}(\langle N_r^G(a) \rangle) \leq \lambda(r)$.

Eppstein [Epp95] called (almost) the same property the *diameter-treewidth property*. Implicitly, he used the following:

Lemma 2. *Let $\mathcal{C}$ be a class of graphs that is closed under taking minors and has locally bounded tree-width. Then $\mathcal{C}$ is locally tree-decomposable.*

Proof. Let $\lambda : \mathbb{N} \to \mathbb{N}$ be a function locally bounding the tree-width of the graphs in $\mathcal{C}$.

Let $G \in \mathcal{C}$ and choose an arbitrary vertex $a_0 \in V^G$. For $0 \leq i \leq j \in \mathbb{N}_0$, let $V[i, j] := \{a \in V^G \mid i \leq d^G(a_0, a) \leq j\}$. We claim that $\mathrm{tw}(\langle V[i, j] \rangle) \leq \lambda(j - i + 1)$. This is immediate if $i = 0$ or $i = 1$, because then $V[i, j] \subseteq N_{j+1}(x_0)$. If $i > 1$, we simply contract the connected subgraph $V[0, i - 1]$ to a single vertex b_0. We obtain a minor G' of G, which is also an element of $\mathcal{C}$ by our assumption that $\mathcal{C}$ is closed under taking minors. G' still contains the set $V[i, j]$ as it is, but it is contained in $N_{j-i+1}^{G'}(b_0)$. This proves the claim.

The claim implies that for all $r \geq 0$, the family $(V[i, i + 2r])_{0 \leq i \leq m}$, where $m := \max\{d(a_0, b) \mid b \in V^G\} - 2r$, is an $(r, \lambda(2r + 1), 4r + 1)$-tree cover of G. On input G we can choose an arbitrary a_0 and then compute this tree cover in linear time by breadth-first search.

This shows that $\mathcal{C}$ is locally tree-decomposable. $\qquad\square$

For example, it is not hard to see that the class of all planar graphs has locally bounded tree-width. Since this class is closed under taking minors, it is locally tree-decomposable. A similar argument is used for the other classes in Examples 3 and 4.

4.3 The main algorithm

Recall our main result Theorem 1:

> Let $\mathcal{C}$ be a locally tree decomposable class of graphs. Then for every first-order sentence φ there is a linear time algorithm that decides whether a given graph $G \in \mathcal{C}$ satisfies φ.

Proof. By Gaifman's Theorem 3, without loss of generality we can assume that φ is of the form

$$\exists x_1 \dots \exists x_k \left(\bigwedge_{1 \leq i < j \leq k} d(x_i, x_j) > 2r \wedge \bigwedge_{1 \leq i \leq k} \psi(x_i) \right),$$

for suitably chosen $r, k \geq 1$ and an r-local ψ.

Choose $w, l \geq 1$ with respect to r according to Definition 1(2).

Our algorithm deciding whether a given graph $G \in \mathcal{C}$ satisfies φ proceeds as follows:

I. Compute an (r, w, l)-tree cover $U_1, \ldots, U_m$ of G.

II. Compute a mapping $f : V^G \to \{1, \ldots, m\}$ such that for all $a \in V^G$ we have $N_r^G(a) \subseteq U_{f(a)}$.

III. For $1 \leq i \leq m$, compute the set $R_i := \{a \in U_i \mid \langle U_i \rangle^G \models \psi(a)\}$.

IV. Compute $R := \{a \in V^G \mid a \in R_{f(a)}\}$.

V. Check if there are $a_1, \ldots, a_k \in R$ such that $d(a_i, a_j) > 2r$ for $1 \leq i < j \leq k$. Answer 'yes' if there are such a_i and 'no' otherwise.

To see that the algorithm is correct, note that since $\psi(x)$ is r-local we have $R = \{a \in V^G \mid G \models \psi(a)\}$.

So we shall prove that all five steps can be implemented as linear time algorithms.

I. Can be done in linear time by our choice of w and l.

II. Noting that the number of edges of a graph $G \in \mathcal{C}$ is linear in the number of vertices and remembering that $\sum_{i=1}^m |U_i| \leq ln$, it is not hard to find a linear time algorithm that computes the sets $K_i := \{a \in U_i \mid N_r(a) \subseteq U_i\}$. Then we simply let $f(a) := \min\{i \mid a \in K_i\}$, for $a \in V^G$.

III. For each i, this can be done in time linear in $|U_i|$ by Lemma 1. The total running time is linear, again because $\sum_{i=1}^m |U_i| \leq ln$.

IV. Easy.

V. This is the tricky part. It follows from the following Lemma.

Lemma 3. *Let $\mathcal{C}$ be a class of graphs of locally bounded tree-width and $r, k \geq 1$. Then the following problem can be solved in linear time:*

> *Instance:* A graph $G \in \mathcal{C}$ and a set $R \subseteq V^G$.
> *Question:* Do there exist $a_1, \ldots, a_k \in R$ such that $d(a_i, a_j) > r$ for $1 \leq i < j \leq k$?

Proof. Let $\lambda : \mathbb{N} \to \mathbb{N}$ be a function locally bounding the tree-width of the graphs in $\mathcal{C}$.

Let $G \in \mathcal{C}$ and $R \subseteq V^G$. Our algorithm first checks whether $R = \emptyset$, if this is the case it immediately rejects the input. Otherwise, it proceeds in the following two phases.

Phase 1. The algorithm inductively computes vertices $a_1, \ldots, a_l \in R$, for some $l \leq k$, such that $d^G(a_i, a_j) > r$ for $1 \leq i < j \leq l$ and either $l = k$ or for all $b \in R$ there is an $i \leq l$ such that $b \in N_r(a_i)$. If $l = k$, the algorithm accepts, otherwise it goes into Phase 2.

This task can be performed by a simple induction: For the induction base, pick $a_1 \in R$ arbitrarily and compute $N_r(a_1)$. In the induction step, suppose that we have already produced a list of vertices $a_1, \ldots, a_j$ and computed the sets $N_r(a_i)$, for $1 \leq i \leq j$. If there is a $b \in R$ such that for all $i \leq j$ we have $b \notin N_r(a_i)$, let a_{j+1} be such a b and compute $N_r(a_{j+1})$. Otherwise let $l := j$. The overall time required is linear in n.

Phase 2. The output of Phase 1 are vertices $a_1, \ldots, a_l \in R$ with the properties described above. Consider the graph

$$H := \Big(\{a_1, \ldots, a_l\}, \{(a_i, a_j) \mid d(a_i, a_j) \leq 4r\} \Big)$$

Let $C_1, \ldots, C_m$ be the vertex sets of the connected components of H. Since the diameter of H is at most $(k-1)$, for all $i \leq m$ there is a $j(i) \leq l$ such that $C_i \subseteq N^G_{4r(k-1)}(a_{j(i)})$. For $1 \leq i \leq m$, let $\overline{C}_i := \{a \in V^G \mid \exists b \in C_i \; d(b,a) \leq 2r\}$. Then $\overline{C}_1, \ldots, \overline{C}_m$ are pairwise disjoint and we have $\mathrm{tw}(\langle \overline{C}_i \rangle^G) \leq \mathrm{tw}(\langle N^G_{4rk}(a_{j(i)}) \rangle^G) \leq \lambda(4rk)$.

We let $C := \bigcup_{i=1}^m \overline{C}_i = \bigcup_{i=1}^l N^G_{2r}(a_i)$. Then C is the disjoint union of graphs of tree-width at most $\lambda(4rk)$ and thus $\mathrm{tw}(C) \leq \lambda(4kr)$.

Recall that each $b \in R$ is contained in $N^G_r(a_i)$ for an $i \leq l$. Thus each path of length at most r between two vertices in R is contained in C. So to find out whether there there are $a_1, \ldots, a_k \in R$ such that $d^G(a_i, a_j) > r$ it suffices to find out whether there are $a_1, \ldots, a_k \in R \cap C$ such that $d^{\langle C \rangle}(a_i, a_j) > r$.

Thus we have reduced our problem to a problem on graphs of bounded tree-width. This can be solved in linear time, for example, by Courcelle's Theorem 2, because it is easy to express the problem by a first-order sentence. $\square$

Theorem 4. *Let C be a class of graphs of locally bounded tree-width. Then for every first-order sentence φ there is a quadratic time algorithm that decides whether a given graph $G \in C$ satisfies φ.*

Proof. Again we assume that φ is of the form

$$\exists x_1 \ldots \exists x_k \Big(\bigwedge_{1 \leq i < j \leq k} d(x_i, x_j) > 2r \wedge \bigwedge_{1 \leq i \leq k} \psi(x_i) \Big),$$

for suitably chosen $r, k \geq 1$ and an r-local ψ.

Let $\lambda : \mathbb{N} \to \mathbb{N}$ be a function locally bounding the tree-width of the graphs in C.

Let $G \in C$. For each vertex $a \in V^G$ we let $U_a := N^G_r(a)$, and we have $\mathrm{tw}(\langle U_a \rangle) \leq \lambda(r)$. Note that $\sum_{a \in V^G} |U_a|$ is not necessarily linear in n, but it is at most quadratic.

For each $a \in V^G$ it requires time linear in $|U_a|$ to decide whether $\langle U_a \rangle \models \psi(a)$. Thus the set

$$R := \{a \in V^G \mid G \models \psi(a)\} = \{a \in V^G \mid \langle U_a \rangle \models \psi(a)\}$$

can be computed in time $O(n^2)$.

Now we can apply Lemma 3 and we are done. $\square$

5 Concluding remarks

Arbitrary relational structures. The definitions of locally bounded tree-width and locally tree-decomposable and our algorithms can immediately be extended to arbitrary classes of relational structures.

Uniformity. A closer analysis of our proofs shows that actually for each locally tree-decomposable class C there is a single algorithm that decides, given a formula φ and a graph $G \in C$, whether $G \models \varphi$ in time $O(f(|\varphi|)n)$, where f is some recursive function.

Dependence on the formula size. Our algorithm heavily depends on the size of the formula φ, roughly the hidden multiplicative constant is k-fold exponential in the length of φ, where k is the number of quantifier-alternations in φ.

This makes our algorithm useless for practical applications. Similarly as with Courcelle's Theorem [Cou90], the benefit of our result is to provide a simple way to recognize a property as being linear time computable on certain classes of graphs. Analyzing the combinatorics of the specific property then, one may also find a practical algorithm.

Furthermore, our result gives a unifying framework for numerous other results.

We consider it as one of the main challenges for further research to reduce the dependence on the formula size. For example, is there an algorithm that decides, given a first-order formula φ and a planar graph G (or a tree, or just a word), whether $G \models \varphi$ in time $O(2^{|\varphi|}n^c)$ for some fixed-constant c?

Locally bounded tree-width. The definition of being locally tree-decomposable seems to be quite artificial, it is only justified by the wealth of examples. Locally bounded tree-width, on the other hand, is much more natural. It would be nice if we could improve our Theorem 4 and get a linear time algorithm also for classes of graphs of locally bounded tree-width.

References

[AHU74] A.V. Aho, J.E. Hopcroft, and J.D. Ullman. *The Design and Analysis of Computer Algorithms.* Addison-Wesley, 1974.

[ALS91] S. Arnborg, J. Lagergren, and D. Seese. Easy problems for tree-decomposable graphs. *Journal of Algorithms*, 12:308–340, 1991.

[AU79] A.V. Aho and J.D. Ullman. The universality of data retrieval languages. In *Conference Record of the Sixth Annual ACM Symposium on Principles of Programming Languages*, pages 110–120, 1979.

[Bak94] B.S. Baker. Approximation algorithms for NP-complete problems on planar graphs. *Journal of the ACM*, 41:153–180, 1994.

[Bod96] H.L. Bodlaender. A linear-time algorithm for finding tree-decompositions of small treewidth. *SIAM Journal on Computing*, 25:1305–1317, 1996.

[Bod97] H.L. Bodländer. Treewidth: Algorithmic techniques and results. In I. Privara and P. Ruzicka, editors, *Proceedings 22nd International Symposium on Mathematical Foundations of Computer Science, MFCS'97*, volume 1295 of *Lecture Notes in Computer Science*, pages 29–36. Springer-Verlag, 1997.

[Cou90]   B. Courcelle. Graph rewriting: An algebraic and logic approach. In J. van Leeuwen, editor, *Handbook of Theoretical Computer Science*, volume 2, pages 194–242. Elsevier Science Publishers, 1990.

[DF99]   R.G. Downey and M.R. Fellows. *Parametrized Complexity*. Springer-Verlag, 1999.

[DFT96]   R.G. Downey, M.R. Fellows, and U. Taylor. The parametrized complexity of relational database queries and an improved characterization of $W[1]$. In Bridges, Calude, Gibbons, Reeves, and Witten, editors, *Combinatorics, Complexity, and Logic – Proceedings of DMTCS '96*, pages 194–213. Springer-Verlag, 1996.

[Epp95]   D. Eppstein. Subgraph isomorphism in planar graphs and related problems. In *Proceedings of the Sixth Annual ACM-SIAM Symposium on Discrete Algorithms*, pages 632–640, 1995.

[Gai82]   H. Gaifman. On local and non-local properties. In *Proceedings of the Herbrand Symposium, Logic Colloquium '81*. North Holland, 1982.

[GJS76]   M.R. Garey, D.S. Johnson, and L. Stockmeyer. Some simplified NP-complete graph problems. *Theoretical Computer Science*, 1:237–267, 1976.

[Imm82]   N. Immerman. Upper and lower bounds for first-order expressibility. *Journal of Computer and System Sciences*, 25:76–98, 1982.

[PY97]   C.H. Papadimitriou and M. Yannakakis. On the complexity of database queries. In *Proceedings of the 16th ACM Symposium on Principles of Database Systems*, pages 12–19, 1997.

[See96]   D. Seese. Linear time computable problems and first-order descriptions. *Mathematical Structures in Computer Science*, 6:505–526, 1996.

[Yan95]   M. Yannakakis. Perspectives on database theory. In *Proceedings of the 36th Annual IEEE Symposium on Foundations of Computer Science*, pages 224–246, 1995.

Comparison of Process Algebra Equivalences Using Formats

Vashti Galpin*

Programme for Highly Dependable Systems, Department of Computer Science
University of the Witwatersrand, Private Bag 3, Wits 2050, South Africa
vashti@cs.wits.ac.za, http://www.cs.wits.ac.za/~vashti

Abstract. This research defines a new format called extended *tyft/tyxt*
format. This format is able to express process algebras with structured
or non-atomic labels and their bisimulation-based semantic equivalences.
A general notion of bisimulation is a congruence for this format, under
reasonable technical conditions. The aim of this format is to allow the
comparison of bisimulation-based semantic equivalences and to this end,
this paper defines a number of extensions and gives results showing conditions required to achieve the extensions. This paper also discusses the
process algebras that can be expressed in this format and presents a new
semantic equivalence comparison result for multiprocessor bisimulation
and pomset bisimulation.

1 Introduction

Since the development of CCS [16] and other process algebras, many extensions to these process algebras have been proposed to model different aspects
of concurrent computation. It is important both theoretically and practically to
understand the relationships between these process algebras and between the
semantic equivalences that are defined for them. This paper investigates the
comparison of semantic equivalences based on bisimulation which are defined
for process algebras whose behaviours are described by structured operational
semantics, and expressed as labelled transition systems.

As can be seen by the proliferation of process algebras, it is relatively easy
to design a new process algebra with specific features. This indicates that the
notion of process algebra has wide application and is flexible. A negative aspect
of this proliferation is that it is not immediately obvious how a process algebra
and its semantic equivalences relate to other process algebras and equivalences.

A significant aspect of recent process algebras is the introduction of structured or non-atomic labels; labels that have structure or contain information
beyond what the action is. In CCS, basic actions are viewed as atomic. However,
additional actions are required—to effect communication where the complement
of each action is required, and to represent an internal action or communication where a distinguished action τ is required. So, even in CCS, the actions

---

* This research was supported in part by a Patrick and Margaret Flanagan Scholarship.

are more than simply atomic. In transition systems for process algebras that deal with the dependency between actions, tags or markers appear in the labels (and are stored in the process terms) to keep a record of these dependencies, and these introduce structure in the labels. Examples of these are CCS with locations [5], CCS with local and global causes [14] and CCS with causalities [7]. Other process algebras such as multiprocessor CCS [15] and pomset CCS [6] introduce structure by allowing compound labels.

The aim here is to investigate how comparisons of semantic equivalences can be done, and uses the meta-theory of process algebras, specifically formats to achieve this aim. This research uses many-sorted signatures and algebras as a way of extending the notion of format. Prior work in formats relies on the use of a single-sorted signature and the corresponding term algebra to represent processes, and assumes an atomic set of actions [2, 4, 8, 12, 13]. Moreover, the actions are treated in a different manner to the process terms, since they are treated schematically; namely a rule is understood to represent a number of rules, each with a different action appearing on each transition. This approach is satisfactory for dealing with an atomic action set, but becomes unsatisfactory when dealing with more complex labels, especially in the case where the semantic equivalence does not require an exact match on labels; for example, pomset bisimulation [6] and parameterised location bisimulation [5]. In the new format, both components are dealt with syntactically by using the term algebra of a many-sorted signature, Σ. Process terms have a distinguished sort, and there can be more than one sort for label terms. Allowing label terms to be many-sorted provides a mechanism for comparison. The label terms appear on transitions and can also appear as arguments in process terms. For example, in the case of the original prefix operator of CCS, there is effectively one operator for each action. When expressing this under the new format, there will be a single prefix operator which takes two arguments—an action and a process.

The actual labels of the process algebra are represented as terms in a Σ-algebra. Since there is a unique homomorphism from the term algebra to any Σ-algebra which induces a congruence on the elements of the term algebra, this congruence is then used to match labels in the definition of bisimulation. Moreover, it is possible to work with a congruence over the labels without considering the specific Σ-algebra, and this approach is taken here.

Since the aim of formats is to prove theorems about process algebras based on structural operational semantics in a syntactic manner, the new format is a logical extension to the existing notion of format. Moreover, this syntactic approach permits the comparison of semantic equivalences. This paper only considers extending the *tyft/tyxt* format—negative premises (as in GSOS format [4] and *ntyft/ntyxt* format [13]) and predicates (as in *path* format [2]) are issues for further work.

The paper is structured as follows—Section 2 introduces the new format and presents the congruence result and Section 3 defines extensions and gives the extension results. Section 4 looks at applications of results. Finally Section 5 discusses related work. Due to lack of space, proofs are omitted—they can be found in [11].

2 A new format

First, some standard definitions for many-sorted signatures and algebras. For any set S, an *S-sorted set* A is a family $\{A_s\}_{s \in S}$ of sets indexed by S. A set with a subscript s for $s \in S$ contains only elements of sort s. A *signature* Σ is a pair (S, F) where F is a set of *function symbols* such that F has a mapping $type : F \to S^* \times S$. If $type(f) = (\epsilon, s)$, then f is a *constant symbol*. Write $f : s_1 \ldots s_n \to s$ for $type(f) = (s_1 \ldots s_n, s)$.

Let V be an S-sorted set of variables disjoint from F. *Open* and *closed (ground)* terms are defined in the usual manner. $\mathbf{T}(\Sigma)$ denotes the set of closed terms and $\mathbb{T}(\Sigma)$ the set of open terms. Σ is *sensible* if it admits one ground term for each sort. The set of variables in a term $t \in \mathbb{T}(\Sigma)$, $Var(t)$ is defined in the obvious manner. A *substitution* σ is a mapping in $V \to \mathbb{T}(\Sigma)$ which preserves sorts, and is extended to a mapping $\sigma : \mathbb{T}(\Sigma) \to \mathbb{T}(\Sigma)$ in the standard way.

A Σ-algebra consists of an S-sorted family of non-empty carrier sets $\mathcal{A} = \{A_s\}_{s \in S}$; and a total function $f^{\mathcal{A}} : \mathcal{A}_{s_1} \times \ldots \times \mathcal{A}_{s_n} \to \mathcal{A}_s$ for each $f : s_1 \ldots s_n \to s \in F$. Σ-homomorphisms are defined in the standard way. Both $\mathbb{T}(\Sigma)$ and $\mathbf{T}(\Sigma)$ form Σ-algebras and there is a unique homomorphism denoted $i_{\mathcal{A}}$ from $\mathbf{T}(\Sigma)$ to any Σ-algebra $\mathcal{A}$.

A Σ-*congruence* on $\mathcal{A}$ is an S-sorted equivalence relation $\equiv$ which is compatible with all function symbols, $\equiv = \{\equiv_s\}_{s \in S}$ and for any $f : s_1 \ldots s_n \to s \in F$ and for all $a_i, b_i \in \mathcal{A}_{s_i}$, $a_i \equiv_{s_i} b_i$ $(1 \leqslant i \leqslant n)$ implies $f^{\mathcal{A}}(a_1, \ldots, a_n) \equiv_s f^{\mathcal{A}}(b_1, \ldots, b_n)$. For each Σ-algebra, there exists a congruence over $\mathbf{T}(\Sigma)$, defined as $t \equiv_{\mathcal{A}} t'$ whenever $i_{\mathcal{A}}(t) = i_{\mathcal{A}}(t')$ for $t, t' \in \mathbf{T}(\Sigma)$.

A specific type of sorted set and signature is required to define the format—P is the sort of processes, and only process terms may take other process terms as arguments. S is a set of the sorts of label terms.

Definition 1 (Suitable signature)
A signature $\Sigma = (S \cup \{\mathsf{P}\}, F)$ is called *suitable* if and only if

- S does not contain the distinguished element P and is non-empty,
- for any function symbol $f \in F$ such that $f : s_1 \ldots s_n \to s$, whenever $s \neq \mathsf{P}$ then for all $1 \leqslant i \leqslant n$, $s_i \neq \mathsf{P}$. ∎

Definition 2 (Extended transition system specification and proof)
An *extended transition system specification (eTSS)* is a pair $\mathcal{E} = (\Sigma, R)$ with Σ a suitable signature and R a set of *rules* of the form

$$\frac{\{p_i \xrightarrow{\lambda_i} p_i' \mid i \in I\}}{p \xrightarrow{\lambda} p'}$$

where I is an index set, $p_i, p_i', p, p' \in \mathbb{T}(\Sigma)_\mathsf{P}$, and $\lambda_i, \lambda \in \mathbb{T}(\Sigma)_S$ for $i \in I$.

$p \xrightarrow{\lambda} p'$ is a *transition*; p is the *source*, and p' is the *target* of the transition. The notions of closed, substitution and Var can be extended to transitions in the obvious way. Transitions above the line of a rule are *premises* or *hypotheses* and the transition below the line is the *conclusion* of r. A rule with no premises is an *axiom*.

A *proof* of a transition ψ from $\mathcal{E}$ is a well-founded, upwardly branching tree of which the nodes are labelled by transitions, such that the root is labelled with ψ, and if χ is the label of a node π and $\{\chi_i \mid i \in I\}$ is the set of labels of the nodes directly above π, then there is a rule with premises $\{\phi_i \mid i \in I\}$ and conclusion ϕ in R and a substitution $\sigma : V \to \mathbb{T}(\Sigma)$ such that $\chi = \sigma(\phi)$ and $\chi_i = \sigma(\phi_i)$ for all $i \in I$. If a proof ψ from $\mathcal{E}$ exists, ψ is *provable* from $\mathcal{E}$, notation $\mathcal{E} \vdash \psi$. ∎

The definition of labelled transition system (LTS) can be extended to deal with a sorted set of labels. Let $\mathcal{E} = (\Sigma, R)$ be an eTSS with Σ, a sensible signature. The *LTS* $TS(\mathcal{E})$ specified by $\mathcal{E}$ is given by $TS(\mathcal{E}) = (\mathbf{T}(\Sigma)_\mathsf{P}, \mathbf{T}(\Sigma)_S, \to)$ where $u \xrightarrow{\alpha} u' \iff \mathcal{E} \vdash u \xrightarrow{\alpha} u'$.

It is possible to work with the standard definition of bisimulation, but this would only consider syntactically equal label terms. Assume an S-sorted congruence over label terms. Then only labels with the same sort can be matched—this results in a powerful mechanism for comparison.

Definition 3 (Strong bisimulation with respect to a congruence over a sorted set)
Let $\mathcal{L} = (\mathcal{S}, \mathcal{A}, \to)$ be an LTS, and let $\equiv$ be an S-sorted congruence relation on $\mathcal{A}$. A *strong bisimulation with respect to a congruence relation* $\equiv$ is a symmetric binary relation $\mathcal{R} \subseteq \mathcal{S} \times \mathcal{S}$ such that $(s, t) \in \mathcal{R}$ only if for all $a \in \mathcal{A}$

- whenever $s \xrightarrow{a} s'$, then there exists $t' \in \mathcal{S}$ and $b \in \mathcal{A}$ such that $t \xrightarrow{b} t'$, $a \equiv b$ and $(s', t') \in \mathcal{R}$

Two states, s and t are *strongly bisimilar with respect to* $\equiv$, $s \sim_\equiv t$, if there exists a strong bisimulation $\mathcal{R}$ with respect to $\equiv$ such that $(s, t) \in \mathcal{R}$. Given an LTS $TS(\mathcal{E})$, bisimulation with respect to $\equiv$ over this LTS is denoted $\sim_\equiv^\mathcal{E}$. ∎

The derivation of the new format proceeds in a similar fashion to Groote and Vaandrager [12], but with additional work to deal with the syntactic manner of expressing labels. The format guarantees that bisimulation with respect to a congruence is itself a congruence. This is an important property of process algebra equivalences, since it can be used to show that systems composed of bisimilar components are bisimilar and hence it is reasonable to evaluate a format's effectiveness in terms of whether congruence can be shown. In the rest of this section, let $\Sigma = (S \cup \{\mathsf{P}\}, F)$ be a suitable signature and let $\mathcal{E} = (\Sigma, R)$ be an eTSS.

Definition 4 (Extended *tyft/tyxt* format)
A rule in R is in *extended tyft format* if it has the form

$$\frac{\{p_i \xrightarrow{\lambda_i} y_i \mid i \in I\}}{f(\eta_1, \ldots, \eta_m, x_1, \ldots, x_n) \xrightarrow{\lambda} p}$$

with I an index set, $f : s_1 \ldots s_m \mathsf{P} \ldots \mathsf{P} \to \mathsf{P} \in F$, x_j $(1 \leqslant j \leqslant n)$ and y_i $(i \in I)$ all different variables from V_P, $p \in \mathbb{T}(\Sigma)_\mathsf{P}$, $\lambda \in \mathbb{T}(\Sigma)_S$,

- $\eta_k \in \mathbb{T}(\Sigma)_{s_k}$ such that $\mathrm{Var}_S(\eta_k) \subset V_S - \bigcup_{\substack{1 \leqslant l \leqslant m \\ l \neq k}} \mathrm{Var}_S(\eta_l)$ for $1 \leqslant k \leqslant m$,

- $\lambda_i \in \mathbb{T}(\Sigma)_S$ such that
  $\text{Var}_S(\lambda_i) \subset V_S - (\bigcup_{l \in I, l \neq i} \text{Var}_S(\lambda_l) \cup \bigcup_{1 \leqslant k \leqslant m} \text{Var}_S(\eta_k))$ for all $i \in I$.
- $p_i \in \mathbb{T}(\Sigma)_P$ such that $\text{Var}_S(p_i) \subset V_S - \bigcup_{l \in I} \text{Var}_S(\lambda_l)$ for $i \in I$.

A rule in R is in *extended tyxt format* if it has the form

$$\frac{\{p_i \xrightarrow{\lambda_i} y_i \mid i \in I\}}{x \xrightarrow{\lambda} p}$$

with I an index set, x and y_i ($i \in I$) all different variables from V_P, $p \in \mathbb{T}(\Sigma)_P$, $\lambda \in \mathbb{T}(\Sigma)_S$,

- $\lambda_i \in \mathbb{T}(\Sigma)_S$ such that $\text{Var}_S(\lambda_i) \subset V_S - \bigcup_{l \in I, l \neq i} \text{Var}_S(\lambda_l)$ for all $i \in I$.
- $p_i \in \mathbb{T}(\Sigma)_P$ such that $\text{Var}_S(p_i) \subset V_S - \bigcup_{l \in I} \text{Var}_S(\lambda_l)$ for $i \in I$.

$\mathcal{E}$ is in *extended tyft/tyxt format* if every rule in R is either in extended *tyft* format or extended *tyxt* format. ∎

To summarise, this definition requires that all the x_j's and y_i's are distinct. λ and p can contain any variables; however the λ_i's must have distinct variables from each other and from the p_i's and the η_k's. The η_k's must have distinct variables from each other.

Before the congruence result, here are some technical definitions.

Definition 5 (Compatibility)
Let $\equiv$ be a congruence on $\mathbf{T}(\Sigma)$. It is *compatible* with $r \in R$ if for any $\eta \in \mathbb{T}(\Sigma)_S$ that appears on a transition in a premise of r or as an argument to the function in the source of the conclusion of r, whenever $\sigma(\eta) \equiv \mu$ for $\mu \in \mathbf{T}(\Sigma)_S$, there exists a substitution σ' such that $\mu = \sigma'(\eta)$ and $\sigma(z) \equiv \sigma'(z)$ for all $z \in \text{Var}_S(\eta)$. $\equiv$ is *compatible* with $\mathcal{E}$ if $\equiv$ is compatible with all rules in R. ∎

Note that if $\eta = z$, then the required condition is always fulfilled since one can define $\sigma'(z) = \mu$.

Definition 6 (Well-foundedness)
Let $U = \{p_i \xrightarrow{\lambda_i} p_i' \mid i \in I\}$ be a set of transitions of $\mathcal{E}$. The *dependency graph* of U is a directed (unlabelled) graph with

- Nodes: $\bigcup_{i \in I} \text{Var}_P(p_i \xrightarrow{\lambda_i} p_i')$,
- Edges: $\{\langle x, y \rangle \mid x \in \text{Var}_P(p_i), y \in \text{Var}_P(p_i') \text{ for some } i \in I\}$.

A set of transitions is *well-founded* if any backward chain of edges in the dependency graph is finite. A rule is *well-founded* if the set of its premises is well-founded. An eTSS is *well-founded* if all of its rules are well-founded. ∎

Recently it has been shown that for the *ntyft/ntyxt* format that any rule can be written in a well-founded form [10]. This is an issue for further work for the new format.

Assume an S-sorted congruence over the label terms. The following result states that given process terms that are bisimilar up to the congruence and label terms that are congruent, the two process terms built out of these terms are bisimilar up to the congruence. Hence, bisimulation up to the congruence is a congruence itself.

Theorem 1 (Congruence)

Let Σ be a suitable, sensible signature, let $\mathcal{E}$ be a well-founded eTSS in extended *tyft/tyxt* format and let $\equiv$ be a congruence on $\mathbf{T}(\Sigma)_S$ compatible with $\mathcal{E}$. Then for all $f : s_1 \ldots s_m \mathsf{P} \ldots \mathsf{P} \to \mathsf{P} \in F$, for all terms $\mu_k, \nu_k \in \mathbf{T}(\Sigma)_S$, and for all terms $u_i, v_i \in \mathbf{T}(\Sigma)_\mathsf{P}$,

$$\mu_i \equiv \nu_i \ (1 \leqslant k \leqslant m) \text{ and } u_i \sim_\equiv v_i \ (1 \leqslant i \leqslant n) \Rightarrow$$
$$f(\mu_1, \ldots, \mu_m, u_1, \ldots, u_n) \sim_\equiv f(\nu_1, \ldots, \nu_m, v_1, \ldots v_n). \quad \blacksquare$$

All conditions have been shown to be necessary, except the requirement that the variables in the p_i's be distinct from those in the λ_i's. There is an interaction between this and the use of well-foundedness in the proof. However, if well-foundedness is not required for the proof, it is still open as to whether this condition is necessary.

3   Extension results

These results look at how two eTSSs can be combined and give conditions under which new transitions may be added. This allows comparison of the semantic equivalences defined on the original eTSS and the new combined eTSS.

The notion of the asymmetric sum of two eTSSs is required to define the notion of an extension. The second summand does not necessarily involve a sensible signature, and hence the definitions are asymmetric. Since $\mathcal{E}_0 \oplus\!\!\!\!\!\triangleright \mathcal{E}_1$ is considered as an extension of $\mathcal{E}_0$, there is an inherent lack of symmetry.

Definition 7 (Asymmetric sum of two signatures and two eTSSs)

Let $\Sigma_i = (S_i \cup \{\mathsf{P}\}, F_i)$ for $i = 0, 1$ be two suitable signatures such that $f \in F_0 \cap F_1$ implies that $type_0(f) = type_1(f)$. The *sum* of Σ_0 and Σ_1, $\Sigma_0 \oplus \Sigma_1$ is the signature $\Sigma_0 \oplus \Sigma_1 = (S_0 \cup S_1 \cup \{\mathsf{P}\}, F_0 \cup F_1)$. If Σ_0 is sensible, and $\Sigma_0 \oplus \Sigma_1$ is sensible, then $\Sigma_0 \oplus \Sigma_1$ is *asymmetric* and denoted $\Sigma_0 \oplus\!\!\!\!\!\triangleright \Sigma_1$.

Let $\mathcal{E}_i = (\Sigma_i, R_i)$ for $i = 0, 1$ be two eTSSs with $\Sigma_0 \oplus \Sigma_1$ defined. The *sum* of $\mathcal{E}_0$ and $\mathcal{E}_1$, $\mathcal{E}_0 \oplus \mathcal{E}_1$, is the eTSS $\mathcal{E}_0 \oplus \mathcal{E}_1 = (\Sigma_0 \oplus \Sigma_1, R_0 \cup R_1)$. If $\Sigma_0 \oplus \Sigma_1$ is asymmetric, then $\mathcal{E}_0 \oplus \mathcal{E}_1$ is *asymmetric* and denoted $\mathcal{E}_0 \oplus\!\!\!\!\!\triangleright \mathcal{E}_1$. $\quad \blacksquare$

Let $\Sigma_i = (S_i \cup \{\mathsf{P}\}, F_i)$ for $i = 0, 1$ be two signatures with $\Sigma = \Sigma_0 \oplus\!\!\!\!\!\triangleright \Sigma_1$ defined, and let $\mathcal{E}_i = (\Sigma_i, R_i)$ for $i = 0, 1$ be two eTSSs in extended *tyft/tyxt* format with $\mathcal{E} = \mathcal{E}_0 \oplus\!\!\!\!\!\triangleright \mathcal{E}_1$ defined and let $\mathcal{E} = (\Sigma, R)$. Also, let $\equiv_i$ be congruences over $\mathbf{T}(\Sigma_i)_S$ compatible with $\mathcal{E}_i$ for $i = 0, 1$, and let $\equiv$ be an equivalence over $\mathbf{T}(\Sigma_0 \oplus\!\!\!\!\!\triangleright \Sigma_1)_S$ compatible with $\mathcal{E}$.

An existing definition is that of conservative extension— $\mathcal{E}$ is a *conservative extension of $\mathcal{E}_0$* if no new transitions are added to terms in $\mathbf{T}(\Sigma_0)_\mathsf{P}$ in $TS(\mathcal{E})$ [12]. In [11], the author presents a result which gives conditions under which eTSSs can be conservatively extended. Another existing definition is that of conservative extension up to bisimulation. However, when working with a congruence over the label terms, a more general definition is required—that of a conservative extension up to bisimulation with respect to a congruence, where for all $t_0, u_0 \in \mathbf{T}(\Sigma_0)_\mathsf{P}$, $t_0 \sim^{\mathcal{E}}_{\equiv} u_0$ if and only if $t_0 \sim^{\mathcal{E}_0}_{\equiv_0} u_0$. This can be broken down into the following two definitions which are then used in the comparison of semantic equivalences.

Definition 8 (Refining extension and abstracting extension up to bisimulation with respect to a congruence)

- $\mathcal{E}$ is a *refining extension of $\mathcal{E}_0$ up to bisimulation with respect to* $\equiv$ if for all $t_0, u_0 \in \mathbf{T}(\Sigma_0)_\mathsf{P}$, $t_0 \sim^{\mathcal{E}}_{\equiv} u_0 \Rightarrow t_0 \sim^{\mathcal{E}_0}_{\equiv_0} u_0$.
  $\mathcal{E}$ is an *abstracting extension of $\mathcal{E}_0$ up to bisimulation with respect to* $\equiv$ if for all $t_0, u_0 \in \mathbf{T}(\Sigma_0)_\mathsf{P}$, $t_0 \sim^{\mathcal{E}_0}_{\equiv_0} u_0 \Rightarrow t_0 \sim^{\mathcal{E}}_{\equiv} u_0$. ∎

A notion of free and label-free variable is required. This is followed by definitions of different kinds of rule sets for asymmetric sums of eTSSs.

Definition 9 (Free and label-free variable, pure and label-pure rule)
Let r be a rule. A variable in $\mathrm{Var}_\mathsf{P}(r)$ is *free* if it does not occur in the left hand side of the conclusion or in the right hand side of a premise. A variable in $\mathrm{Var}_S(r)$ is *label-free* if it does not occur in the label of a premise or in the left hand side of the conclusion.

A rule r is *pure* if it is well-founded and contains no free variables from V_P. $\mathcal{E}$ is *pure* if all its rules are pure. A rule r is *label-pure* if it contains no label-free variables from V_S. $\mathcal{E}$ is *label-pure* if all its rules are label-pure. ∎

Definition 10 (Type-1 and type-0 asymmetric sum)
$\mathcal{E}_0 \oplus\!\!\!\!\!\!> \mathcal{E}_1$ is said to be of *type-1* if

- there is no extended *tyft* rule in R_1 containing a function symbol from F_0 in the source of the conclusion that has a conclusion label with a sort from S_0,
- there is no extended *tyxt* rule in R_1 that has a conclusion label of a sort from S_0.

$\mathcal{E}_0 \oplus\!\!\!\!\!\!> \mathcal{E}_1$ is said to be *type-0* if it is type-1 and there is no extended *tyft* rule in R_1 that contains a function symbol from F_0. ∎

Each signature may have its own congruence, so define the following way to combine congruences.

Definition 11 (Sum of two congruences and conservativity)
Let $\equiv_0$ and $\equiv_1$ be two congruences defined on $\mathbf{T}(\Sigma_0)$ and $\mathbf{T}(\Sigma_1)$ respectively. Define the *sum of $\equiv_0$ and $\equiv_1$ ($\equiv_0 \oplus \equiv_1$)* as the smallest congruence over $\mathbf{T}(\Sigma_0 \oplus \Sigma_1)$ containing both $\equiv_0$ and $\equiv_1$. $\equiv_0 \oplus \equiv_1$ is said to be *conservative with respect to $\equiv_i$* if $\equiv_0 \oplus \equiv_1$ on $\mathbf{T}(\Sigma_i)_S$ is the same as $\equiv_i$ on $\mathbf{T}(\Sigma_i)_S$. ∎

Both of the following extension results rely on the fact that the congruence under consideration respects sorts.

Theorem 2 (Refining extension up to bisimulation with respect to a congruence)

Let $\equiv_0 \oplus \equiv_1$ be conservative with respect to $\equiv_0$. If $\mathcal{E}_0$ is pure and label-pure, and $\mathcal{E}_0 \oplus \triangleright \mathcal{E}_1$ is type-1, then $\mathcal{E}_0 \oplus \triangleright \mathcal{E}_1$ is a refining extension. ∎

Different conditions are required to show a similar result for abstracting extensions, namely that the sum is type-0, the second component is well-founded and compatibility holds.

Theorem 3 (Abstracting extension up to bisimulation with respect to a congruence)

Let $\equiv_0 \oplus \equiv_1$ be compatible with $\mathcal{E}_0 \oplus \triangleright \mathcal{E}_1$. If $\mathcal{E}_0$ is pure and label-pure, $\mathcal{E}_1$ is well-founded, and $\mathcal{E}_0 \oplus \triangleright \mathcal{E}_1$ is type-0, then $\mathcal{E}_0 \oplus \triangleright \mathcal{E}_1$ is an abstracting extension. ∎

All conditions have been shown to be necessary except for some of the pureness and label-pureness conditions in the refining extension theorem. It is possible to omit the label-pureness requirement in the previous results by giving a safety condition instead, namely Σ_1 is *safe for* S_0 if no function symbol in $F_1 - F_0$ has a range with a sort from the set S_0. Theorems 2 and 3 can be restated with the removal of label-pureness condition and the addition of the safety condition.

4 Applications

CCS [16], CCS with locations [5], multiprocessor equivalence [15] and pomset bisimulation [6] can be expressed in the extended *tyft/tyxt* format. Applying the extension results, yields a new semantic equivalence result. This involves comparing n-multiprocessor equivalence and pomset bisimulation. Since the rules are not label-pure for these two process algebras (it is the axiom which is not label-pure), it is necessary to use the version of Theorem 2 with safety.

By applying this theorem (and some additional manipulation), the pomset equivalence is shown to be a subset of n multiprocessor equivalence. This is a proper subset since for each n there exist processes which are identified by n multiprocessor equivalence, but not by pomset equivalence. For arbitrary n, consider the following two processes

$$\prod_{k=1}^{n} a_k + \sum_{i=1}^{n} \sum_{\substack{j=1 \ j \neq i}}^{n} a_i.a_j \mid \prod_{\substack{k=1 \ k \neq i \ k \neq j}}^{n} a_k \quad \text{and} \quad \sum_{i=1}^{n} \sum_{\substack{j=1 \ j \neq i}}^{n} a_i.a_j \mid \prod_{\substack{k=1 \ k \neq i \ k \neq j}}^{n} a_k.$$

They are equated by $n - 1$ multiprocessor equivalence since at most $n - 1$ actions can occur simultaneously, but not by the pomset bisimulation since the first process can perform a transition involving all possible actions, namely a transition whose label is mapped by the unique homomorphism $i_{\mathcal{A}_{\text{pomset}}}$ to $a_1 \mid \ldots \mid a_n$, whereas the second process does not have a transition that consists of all n actions since there are at most $n - 1$ parallel components. For more details of these applications, refer to [11].

5 Related work

Verhoef has given a general conservative extension theorem [17] for the *panth* format. By grouping together transitions with the same actions as relations over processes, he uses a similar mechanism to that which is achieved here by using sorts; however he does not use this for the comparison of semantic equivalences.

Astesiano and Reggio [1] define observational structures where process algebras are modelled as many-sorted algebras with predicates, plus a generalisation of bisimulation. This research is not used to compare semantic equivalences.

Ferrari and Montanari [9] propose a format for parameterised structured operational semantics called Algebraic De Simone Format (AdS). They use a two single-sorted signatures, one for processes and one for labels, and use a technique similar to the one used for extended *tyft/tyxt* format for the interpretation of labels. The main differences are that label terms are disjoint from process terms, and the number of label variables which can appear in the term on the transition of the conclusion is equal to the number of premises. A second format is introduced called AdSA (AdS-format with abstractions) where the label signature is modified to be two-sorted, with the second sort having the same operators are the process signature. This permits side conditions over processes in the rules. The focus of the article is on showing congruence for the formats, and developing a parameterised inference system.

Bernstein [3] introduces the *promoted tyft/tyxt* format which uses a single-sorted signature. Terms may appear on transitions, removing the distinction between process and label. The conditions for variables are very different to those of the extended *tyft/tyxt* format. In the conclusion, the same variable may not appear both in the source and label; neither may the same variable appear in the label and target. Furthermore, there must be at most one function symbol in the label of the conclusion, and at least one function symbol in the labels of premises. The focus of the paper is a congruence result and the use of the format for higher-order languages. A detailed comparison of these formats and the extended *tyft/tyxt* format is beyond the scope of this paper.

How does the new format compare to *tyxt/tyft* format? This format involves a single-sorted algebra for the operators of the process algebra and an infinite set of atomic actions which are used in the rules in a schematic manner. The definition implicitly permits operators to be created from actions, such as prefix operators. To translate from *tyft/tyxt* format to the new format, first start with a many-sorted algebra consisting of sorts, P and an action sort A; as well as operators not created from elements of the action set. Next, make all actions constants of sort A and take operators created from elements of the action set, and modify them to take an argument of the action sort. It is simple to replace each different action with a different variable of the sort A; so for example, an axiom such as $a.x \xrightarrow{a} x$ will become $\mathsf{pref}(z_A, x) \xrightarrow{z_A} x$. In the case of matching of actions in a way which contravenes the conditions of label variables, there are two approaches. One involves the use of rule schemata and the other the use of a label algebra with constants to indicate undefined transitions. For further details, see [11].

6 Conclusions

This paper has introduced the extended *tyft/tyxt* format in which labels are treated syntactically. Under certain reasonable technical conditions, bisimulation with respect to a congruence over labels is a congruence for all operators defined in the format. Under somewhat stronger conditions, extension results hold for this format and these results are used to obtain a new semantic equivalence comparison result, relating pomset bisimulation and multiprocessor equivalence.

Acknowledgments I would like to thank Julian Bradfield and anonymous referees for their comments on this paper.

References

1. E. Astesiano and G. Reggio. Observational structures and their logic. *Theoretical Computer Science*, **96**, 249–283, 1992.
2. J.C.M. Baeten and C. Verhoef. A congruence theorem for structured operational semantics with predicates. In E. Best, (ed). *CONCUR '93*, LNCS **715**. Springer-Verlag, 477-492, 1993.
3. K.L. Bernstein. A congruence theorem for structured operational semantics of higher-order languages. In *LICS '98*. IEEE Computer Society, 153-164, 1998.
4. B. Bloom, S. Istrail, and A.R. Meyer. Bisimulation can't be traced. *Journal of the ACM*, **42**, 232–268, 1995.
5. G. Boudol, I. Castellani, M. Hennessy, and A. Kiehn. A theory of processes with localities. *Formal Aspects of Computing*, **6**(2), 165–200, 1994.
6. I. Castellani. Bisimulations for concurrency. Technical Report CST-51-88, PhD Thesis, Department of Computer Science, University of Edinburgh, 1988.
7. P. Darondeau and P. Degano. Causal trees. In G. Ausiello, M. Dezani-Ciancaglini, and S. Ronchi Della Rocca, (eds). *ICALP 88*, LNCS **372**. Springer-Verlag, 234–248, 1989.
8. R. de Simone. Higher-level synchronising devices in MEIJE-SCCS. *Theoretical Computer Science*, **37**, 245–267, 1985.
9. G.L. Ferrari and U. Montanari Parameterized structured operational semantics. *Fundamenta Informaticae*, **34**, 1–31, 1998.
10. W. Fokkink and R. van Glabbeek. Ntyft/ntyxt rules reduce to ntree rules. *Information and Computation*, **126**, 1–10, 1996.
11. V.C. Galpin. Equivalence semantics for concurrency: comparison and application. Technical Report ECS-LFCS-98-397, PhD Thesis, Department of Computer Science, University of Edinburgh, 1998.
12. J.F. Groote and F. Vaandrager. Structured operational semantics and bisimulation as a congruence. *Information and Computation*, **100**, 202–260, 1992.
13. J.F. Groote. Transition systems specifications with negative premises. *Theoretical Computer Science*, **118**, 263–299, 1993.
14. A. Kiehn. Comparing locality and causality based equivalences. *Acta Informatica*, **31**(8), 697–718, 1994.
15. P. Krishnan. Architectural CCS. *Formal Aspects of Computing*, **162**, 162–187, 1996.
16. R. Milner. *Communication and concurrency*. Prentice Hall, 1989.
17. C. Verhoef. A general conservative extension theorem in process algebra. *IFIP Transactions A*, **56**, 149–168, 1994.

Compact Routing Tables for Graphs of Bounded Genus

(Extended Abstract)

Cyril Gavoille[1] and Nicolas Hanusse[1]

LaBRI, Université Bordeaux I,
351, cours de la Libération,33405 Talence Cedex, France
gavoille,hanusse@labri.u-bordeaux.fr

Abstract. For planar graphs on n nodes we show how to construct in
linear time shortest path routing tables that require $8n + o(n)$ bits per
node, and $O(\log^{2+\epsilon} n)$ bit-operations per node to extract the route, with
constant $\epsilon > 0$. We generalize the result for every graph of bounded
crossing-edge number. We also extend our result to any graph of genus
bounded by γ, by building shortest path routing tables of $n \log(\gamma + 1) +
O(n)$ bits per node, and with $O(\log^{2+\epsilon} n)$ bit-operations per node to
extract the route. This result is obtained by the use of dominating sets,
compact coding of non-crossing partitions, and k-page representation of
graphs.

1   Introduction

In point-to-point communication networks or in parallel computers, a routing
function is employed in order to deliver messages between processors. As networks grow in size, it becomes important to reduce the amount of memory kept
in each node for routing purposes. At the same time, it is essential to route messages along paths that are as short as possible. A *universal routing scheme* is an
algorithm which generates a routing function for any given network. One type
of trivial universal routing scheme is based on schemes that keep in each node a
full *routing table* which specifies an output port for every destination. Though
this scheme can guarantee routing along shortest paths, each router has to store
locally $n \log d$ bits of memory, where d is the degree of the router (i.e., the number of output ports) and n is the number of nodes in the network. Therefore,
this scheme is impractical when dealing with large networks.

   In this paper we consider routing table schemes only that generate routing functions that do not change the header of the message along the route,
and depend on the destination only. The underlying topology of the network
is represented by a graph. All the graphs we consider are simple, i.e., without
multi-edges, undirected and connected.

   To avoid the implementation of large routing tables, it is possible to code
in each node the whole map of the network. However, this *centralized approach*
has the following drawback: we need to compute the route with a shortest path

algorithm that takes at least a linear time in the number of nodes. So, the time complexity of this approach is exponential since the length of the input is exponential.

A more practical approach to the routing would store a partial view of the topology of the network, and would compute the route in polynomial time with respect to the size of the input, i.e., in time $\log^{O(1)} n$.

Whereas tight bounds exist for the general case [GP96], no tight bounds exist for the case of planar graphs. Using the centralized approach, $O(n)$ bits are enough, since it is well-known that the number of unlabeled connected planar graphs on n nodes is bounded by c^n, for a constant c such that $3.24 < \log c < 6.25$ (cf. [Tut62,DVW96]). The point is that an enumeration formula of a set of objects does not give an efficient way to compute queries fast on individual objects. The time to extract the route is a priori exponential (at least the cardinality of the set, c^n).

A better solution consists of using efficient and compact encoding of planar graphs. Turán proposed in [Tur84] a coding in $12n$ bits computable in linear time. Jacobson's coding [Jac89] allows adjacency queries scanning $O(\log n)$ bits only, but with a $36n$ bit size encoding. Keeler and Westbrook proposed in [KW95] a more compact encoding in $\log 12$ bits per edge. This leads to a $10.76n$ bit size encoding for dense planar graphs[1], i.e., when $m = 3n - o(n)$. Recently Munro and Raman [MR97] proposed a coding supporting $O(1)$ time adjacency queries (in the standard integer model) with a $14n + o(n)$ bit size encoding. Finally [CGH+98] improved the previous encoding to $4m/3 + 5n + o(n)$ bits, i.e., $9n + o(n)$ bits for dense planar graphs, keeping $O(1)$ time adjacency queries. Note that in the case of planar graphs, shortest paths from one source can be computed in $O(n)$ time [KRRS94] instead of $O(n \log n)$ for Dijkstra's algorithm. In the best case this leads to compact routing tables of size $9n + o(n)$ bits with $O(n)$ time to extract the route, but the time complexity is still exponential.

Finally, no shortest path routing scheme is known for planar graphs that uses less than $n \log d$ bits of space ($n \log n$ in the worst-case) and poly-log time.

1.1 Contribution of this Paper

In this paper we show how to route in poly-log time using tables of size at most $8n + o(n)$ bits per node. The same bound holds for non-planar graphs that are planar after removing $o(n/\log n)$ edges. We push even further the optimization of the table to $9n - 8d + o(n)$ bits for nodes of degree d, for $d > n/8$. Moreover the time to build tables is linear for each node, which is optimal. Note that our space bound is smaller than all the known encodings of planar graphs which support *reasonable* time adjacency queries[2] (cf. [CGH+98]). Hence our approach is not centralized. See Table 1 for a summary.

---

[1] This does not mean that the graph is triangulated. Better encodings have been proposed for this particular case.

[2] One can restrict our attention to encodings which support poly-log time adjacency queries.

Routing table size in bits	Time to extract the route	Comments
$n \log n$	$O(\log n)$	Standard routing tables (in bit-operations)
$6.25n$	$2^{n^{O(1)}}$	Information-theoretic upper bound [Tut62]
$9n + o(n)$	$O(n)$	Compact coding of unlabeled planar graphs with $O(1)$ time adjacency queries [CGH+98] and fast shortest path algorithm [KRRS94]
$8n + o(n)$	$O(\log^{2+\epsilon} n), \epsilon > 0$	Compact routing tables (in bit-operations) [**This paper**]

Table 1. Compact routing tables for planar graphs of n nodes.

The *genus* of a graph G is the smallest integer γ such that G embeds in a surface of genus γ without edge crossings. Planar graphs can be embedded on a sphere, so $\gamma = 0$. We generalize our result to graphs of genus bounded by γ, $\gamma \geqslant 0$, constructing compact routing tables of $n \log (\gamma + 1) + O(n)$ bits with poly-log time to extract the shortest route. In the worst-case, $\gamma = O(n^2)$ and the size becomes the same order as the standard routing tables, i.e., $O(n \log n)$ bits. This new quantification of the routing information clearly shows that embedding and drawing of graph "help" for the routing. We also prove a lower bound $\Omega(n \log k)$ bits for shortest path routing in graphs of pagenumber k. Because of the lack of space, we refer the reader to [GH99] for details and proofs.

2 k-page Embedding and Pagenumber

A k-page embedding of a graph consists of a linear ordering of its nodes drawn in a line and of a partition of its edges into k *pages* so that edges residing on the same page do not intersect (see Figure 1 for an example). Such an embedding is sometimes called *book-embedding*. See [Bil92] for a survey. The *pagenumber* of a graph G is the smallest integer k such that G has a k-page embedding. It is NP-hard to compute the pagenumber for general graphs, but there is a linear time algorithm to compute the pagenumber (and its embedding) of planar graphs. Actually the pagenumber of every planar graph does not exceed 4 (cf. [Yan86]).

We show in [GH99] that $\Omega(kn)$ bits are required in general to code a graph of pagenumber k. This is tight since Jacobson showed in [Jac89] that $9kn$ bits are enough.

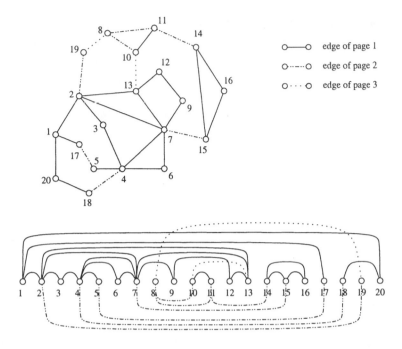

Fig. 1. A planar graph of pagenumber 3 and a 3-page embedding.

3 The Region-Graph and its String Representation

The basic idea of our routing scheme is the following: first we root in each node a minimum spanning tree. Each tree rooted in a node u, say T, represents the routing from u towards all the other nodes in the graph. (Actually our technique works for any tree, not necessary for minimum spanning tree). Roughly speaking, for a given destination v, the routing task in u consists in selecting the unique neighbor of u that is the ancestor of v in T. The destinations having the same ancestor neighbor of u form a *region*. The routing can be implemented by storing in extenso T in u. However, in order to decrease the bit count we store a compact data structure relative to T, called the *region-graph* R_T, that allows to complete our task. In this section we describe how to code such a structure, and in Section 4 we will see how to used it to perform a poly-log time routing algorithm.

3.1 The Region-Graph

Given any graph G, we denote by $V(G)$ its set of nodes, and $E(G)$ its set of edges. Let G be a connected k-page graph with n nodes. We consider a k-page embedding of G. We assume that nodes are labeled with integers taken from $\{1, \ldots, n\}$ linearly ordered by the k-page embedding, and we associate with each edge its unique page p, an integer taken from $\{1, \ldots, k\}$. Let u_0 be a node, let d be the degree of u_0, and let T be an arbitrary spanning tree rooted at u_0. Let us denote by $T - u_0$ the graph obtained from T by removing u_0 and its incident edges. $T - u_0$ is a forest composed of d connected components. Each connected component of $T - u_0$ is a tree called a *region*. We denote by R_i the ith region of $T - u_0$. A region composed of a single node is called an *isolated node*. A region that consists of exactly one edge is called an *isolated edge*. For each tree R_i we choose a root, denoted by $\text{root}(R_i)$, defined as follows: the root of a region R_i which is not an isolated edge is the unique node $r \in V(R_i)$ such that r neighbors u_0. The root of an isolated edge (u, v) is the node $\min\{u, v\}$. We assume that the regions are ordered w.r.t. their root, i.e., $\text{root}(R_1) < \ldots < \text{root}(R_d)$.

Our goal is, given a destination v_0, to find the unique region R_i such that $v_0 \in V(R_i)$. The integer i represents the port of the routing function of u_0. The idea is, starting from v_0, to traverse the region of v_0 (which is a tree) until we reach its roots.

For each page p, $p \in \{1, \ldots, k\}$, let T_p be the subgraph of $T - u_0$ embedded in the pth page of the embedding of G. Formally, $V(T_p) = V \setminus \{u_0\}$, and $E(T_p) = \{(a, b) \mid (a, b) \in E(T - u_0)$ and (a, b) belongs to the page $p\}$. Note that T_{p_0}, for some p_0, may be empty. Let I_i^p be the set of nodes of the ith connected component of T_p. Given a set I_i^p, the *local-root* w.r.t. I_i^p is the closest node to u_0 in T that belongs to I_i^p. Note that the local-root is unique since nodes of I_i^p induce a subtree of T_p, and therefore a connected subtree of T.

The *region-graph* of T, denoted by R_T, is defined as follows: $V(R_T) = V \setminus \{u_0\}$, and $E(R_T) = \cup_p \cup_i \{(a, b) \mid a, b \in I_i^p, a \neq b$, and b is the local-root of $I_i^p\}$. Figure 2 represents a region-graph of a spanning tree T for the example of Figure 1.

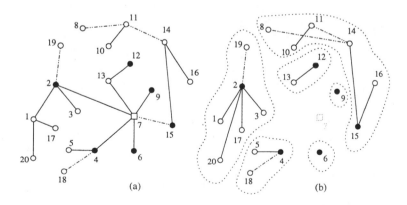

Fig. 2. (a) A spanning tree T rooted in $u_0 = 7$, and (b) its region-graph, R_T. The regions are circled in R_T, and their roots are drawn in black.

Lemma 1. *The region-graph R_T is a forest in which each tree consists of the same set of nodes than the connected component of $T - u_0$.*

According to Lemma 1, and for simplicity, we call each connected component of R_T a *region*.

The main idea in routing along T is to use the region-graph R_T instead of T. The advantage is that to traverse the region of v_0 from v_0 in T we would need an orientation of the edges of the region. That costs n bits of information. As we will see we can recover the father of v_0 in the region-graph without any extra information.

3.2 Coding of the Region-Graph

A partition $P_1 \cup \ldots \cup P_m$ of an ordered set P is a *non-crossing partition* if for all $a, b, c, d \in P$ such that $a < b < c < d$, if $a, c \in P_i$ and $b, d \in P_j$, then $i = j$. Let $\{P_i\}_i$ be a non-crossing partition of P ($\{P_i\}_i$ stands for the set composed of all the P_i's). For each P_i we associate a representative element of P_i, denoted by $\mathrm{cl}(P_i)$. The *representative graph* of $\{P_i\}_i$ w.r.t. the representative function $\mathrm{cl}(\cdot)$ is the graph G_P defined by: $V(G_P) = P$, and $E(G_P) = \cup_i \{(a, b) \mid a, b \in P_i, a \neq b, \text{ and } b = \mathrm{cl}(P_i)\}$. Every representative graph of any non-crossing partition has a straightforward 1-page embedding. We associate with G_P a nested string of parentheses (called a *balanced* string of parentheses), and defined as follows: for each element $u \in P$ (in order and starting from the minimum), and for each edge $(u, v) \in E(G_P)$, we put a symbol (if $u < v$, and a symbol) if $u > v$.

Lemma 2. *For every $p \in \{1, \ldots, k\}$, $\{I_i^p\}_i$ is a non-crossing partition of $V \setminus \{u_0\}$.*

Therefore, the region-graph R_T is the union, over all pages p, of the representative graph of $\{I_i^p\}_i$ with local-root as representative. This gives also an embedding of R_T in at most k pages.

Let S_p be the string of parentheses associated with page p (more precisely, the string of parentheses of the graph representative of $\{I_i^p\}_i$ with local-root as representative). Let $\mathrm{block}_p(u)$, for every node u, be the sub-string of S_p that corresponds to the incident edges of u drawn on page p. Note that $\mathrm{block}_p(u)$ may be empty.

For every node u of R_T distinct from a root (formally, $u \neq \mathrm{root}(R_i)$ for every $i \in \{1, \ldots, d\}$), we define the *parent-page* of u as the integer p such that the edge $(u, v) \in E(R_T)$ is on the page p, where v is the father of u. The parent-page of a root is not defined.

From R_T we associate a string S_T of multiple types of parentheses defined as follows: (1) in every string $\mathrm{block}_p(u)$ rewrite the symbol (by $(_p$, and the symbol) by $)_p$. (2) For each non-isolated node u, let $\mathrm{block}(u)$ be the concatenation of $\mathrm{block}_p(u)$ over all the pages p in an order such that the block of the parent-page of u (if it exists) is located first. (3) For every isolated node u, set $\mathrm{block}(u) = (_p)_p$, with arbitrary p. (4) Finally, S_T consists of the concatenation of $\mathrm{block}(1)\mathrm{block}(2)\ldots\mathrm{block}(u)\ldots\mathrm{block}(n)$, for every $u \in V(R_T)$.

To complete the coding of S_T we add a bitmap P_T which marks the position of the first symbol of each block. Formally, $P_T[i] = 1$ if and only if $S_T[i]$ starts $\mathrm{block}(u)$ for a suitable node u. See the example depicted in Figure 3 corresponding to the region-graph of Figure 2.

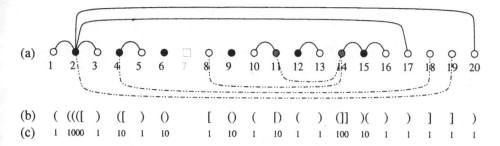

Fig. 3. (a) The 2-page embedding of R_T (local-roots that are not roots are drawn in grey), (b) the string S_T associated with R_T (for simplicity (denotes $(_1$ and [denotes $(_2$, similarly for closing parentheses), and (c) the bitmap P_T.

Lemma 3. S_T and P_T are computable in linear time, and $|S_T| + |P_T| = (n - 1 - d + i)(4 + 2\log k)$, where i is the number of isolated nodes of R_T.

4 Compact Routing in the Region-Graph

4.1 A First Routing Algorithm: Route1

In the following algorithm, $\text{port}(r)$ denotes a function that returns the port number of the root r. Actually, it corresponds to the number of roots r' such that $r' \leqslant r$, since the roots are ordered.

Algorithm $\underline{\text{Route1}}(u_0, v_0)$
  Input: u_0: the sender, v_0: the destination, $v_0 \neq u_0$
  Output: the integer i such that $v_0 \in V(R_i)$

(1) Find the position i of the first symbol of block(v_0) in S_T. Set $u = v_0$.
(2) Find the position j of the matching parentheses of $S_T[i]$.
(3) Find the node u' corresponding to position j.
(4) If $u' = u$, return port(u').
(5) Find the position i' of the first symbol of block(u').
(6) If $i' = j$, let l_u (resp. $l_{u'}$) be the length of the first block of u (resp. u').

   (6a) If $l_u = l_{u'} = 1$, return port($\min\{u, u'\}$)
   (6b) If $l_u > 1$, return port(u), else return port(u')
(7) If $S_T[i']$ and $S_T[j]$ are both in the same page, return port(u').
(8) Set $i = i'$, $u = u'$, and continue at (2).

We consider ω be any function of n not bounded by a constant. So, $n/\omega = o(n)$. W.l.o.g. we assume that $\omega \log n$ is an integer. Let L be the distance between v_0 and the root of its region in R_T.

Lemma 4. Algorithm Route1 runs in $O(L\omega \log n + \omega^2 \log^2 n)$ bit-operations with routing tables of $|S_T| + |P_T| + o(n)$ bits.

The implementation and the correctness of Route1 are given [GH99].

4.2 An $O(\omega \log n)$ steps Routing: Route2

In the time complexity of ROUTE1 (Lemma 4), $L\omega \log n$ becomes the first order term whenever $L > \omega \log n$. Our goal is to bound the number of traversals of the region of v_0, i.e., the number of steps of ROUTE1. For this purpose we select a set of nodes, D_1, satisfying: 1) for every node u at distance greater than $\omega \log n$ from its region's root r in R_T, the path from u to r cuts a node $v \in D_1$ such that the distance[3] between u and v is at most $\omega \log n$ in R_T. 2) D_1 is of size at most $n/(\omega \log n)$.

D_1 can be constructed in linear time using a modified version of Peleg and Upfal's algorithm [PU89] for the construction of $\omega \log n$-dominating sets: for each region R_{i_0} of height h and of root r we divide the nodes other than r into levels $L_1, \ldots, L_h$ according to their height in R_{i_0} (L_i is the set of nodes at distance i, $i \geqslant 1$). We merge these sets into $\omega \log n$ sets $C_1, \ldots, C_{\omega \log n}$ be taking $C_i = \bigcup_{j \geqslant 0} L_{i+j\omega \log n}$. Each C_i is a $\omega \log n$-dominating set for $V(R_{i_0}) \setminus \{r\}$, and satisfies our property 1). Because these sets form a complete disjoint partition of $V(R_{i_0}) \setminus \{r\}$, at least one set C_{i_0} is of size at most $(|V(R_{i_0})| - 1)/(\omega \log n)$. We merge C_{i_0} with D_1. Finally, the total number nodes in D_1 is at most $(n - 1 - d)/(\omega \log n)$, satisfying our property 2).

Now for each node $u \in D_1$ we assign the port of its root. We store this information in a list D_2. It suffices to insert a Step (1.5) between Step (1) and (2) of ROUTE1 to obtain ROUTE2:

$$(1.5) \text{ If there exists } j \text{ such that } u = D_1[j], \text{ return } D_2[j].$$

Clearly, the number of steps for ROUTE2 is bounded by $\omega \log n$.

A *tree-routing family* $\mathcal{F}$ on a graph G is a routing table on G such that for every node the subgraph induced by the set of nodes using the same port is connected. A way to represent a tree-routing family is to use a collection of trees spanning each of these connected subgraphs. So, $\mathcal{F}$ can be seen as a family of spanning trees. So, we can state the main result:

Theorem 1. *Let G be a k-page graph of n nodes, $k \geqslant 1$, and let $\mathcal{F}$ be any tree-routing family on G. $\mathcal{F}$ can be implemented by routing tables of size at most $2n \log k + 4n + o(n)$ bits per node so that the time (per node) to extract the route is $O(\omega^2 \log^2 n)$ bit-operations, where ω is any function as n not bounded by any constant. Moreover, given a k-page embedding of G and given $\mathcal{F}$, the routing tables can be constructed in $O(n)$ time for each node.*

We will see later that for unbounded k the bound of Theorem 1 is tight up to a factor 2.

---

[3] Weights are not taken in account. The distance we are dealing with denotes here the minimum number of edges of a path connecting two nodes.

5 Applications and Extensions of the Main Result

Since the tree-routing family can be chosen arbitrarily, it follows that our result can be extended to any weighted graph (weights are non-negative costs assigned to each edge).

[BK79] shows how to build, for every n, a graph of n nodes, $4n - 9$ edges, genus $\gamma \geqslant (n-3)/3$, and pagenumber $k = 3$. However, Malitz showed in [Mal88] that for every graph $k = O(\sqrt{\gamma})$, which is tight by [HI87].

Therefore, from the main theorem we have, choosing $\omega = O(\log^{\epsilon/2} n)$:

Corollary 1. *Every weighted n-node graph of genus γ, $\gamma \geqslant 0$, has shortest path routing tables of $n\log(\gamma + 1) + O(n)$ bits per node, and with $O(\log^{2+\epsilon} n)$ bit-operations per node to extract the route, for every constant $\epsilon > 0$.*

Corollary 2. *Every weighted n-node planar graph has shortest path routing tables of $8n + o(n)$ bits per node, and with $O(\log^{2+\epsilon} n)$ bit-operations per node to extract the route, for every constant $\epsilon > 0$. Moreover the table can be constructed in time $O(n)$ per node.*

Furthermore, in [GH99], we reduce the size of the tables whenever the degree d of the sender is large: $9n - 8d + o(n)$ where $d > n/8$. We also adapt our technics to graphs of crossing-edge number (the smallest number of edges to remove in order to obtain a planar graph) bounded by $o(n/\log n)$. They support shortest path routing tables of size $8n + o(n)$ as well.

At this point we consider the question of whether the bound of Theorem 1 is tight, i.e., if $\Theta(n\log k)$ bits are necessary to route along any tree-routing family. We show that there are tree-routing families on k-page graphs so that $\Omega(n\log k)$ bits are required. Moreover, this lower bound holds for shortest path routing tables. Let $K_{p,q}$ denote the complete bipartite graph on bipartite size p and q respectively.

Theorem 2. *For every n large enough, and for every k, $2 \leqslant k < n/2$, there exists a shortest path tree-routing family $\mathcal{F}$ on $K_{k,n-k}$, an n-node k-page graph, such that any implementation of $\mathcal{F}$ requires at least $(n - 2k)\log k - O(1)$ bits simultaneously on at least $n\log k/(4 + 2\log k) - o(n)$ nodes.*

Nevertheless, it is still open to find a lower bound that holds for *any* shortest path tree-routing family, or for any shortest path routing table. To our best knowledge, the only lower bound that holds for any shortest path routing tables is the $\sqrt{n}$-lower bound of [EGP98] for n-node trees.

Acknowledgments: We would like to thank Ondreij Sýkora for his bibliographic support, and Mike Robson for his helpful reading.

References

[Bil92]   T. BILSKI, *Embedding graphs in books: A survey*, IEE Proceedings-E, 139 (1992), pp. 134–138.

[BK79]   F. BERNHART AND P. C. KAINEN, *The book thickness of a graph*, Journal of Combinatorial Theory, 27 (1979), pp. 320–331.

[CGH⁺98] R. C.-N. CHUANG, A. GARG, X. HE, M.-Y. KAO, AND H.-I. LU, *Compact encodings of planar graphs via canonical orderings and multiple parentheses*, in 25th International Colloquium on Automata, Languages and Programming (ICALP), K. Guldstrand Larsen, S. Skyum, and G. Winskel, eds., vol. 1443 of Lecture Notes in Computer Science, Springer, July 1998, pp. 1–12.

[DVW96] A. DENISE, M. VASCONCELLOS, AND D. WELSH, *The random planar graph*, Congressus Numerantium, 113 (1996), pp. 61–79.

[EGP98] T. EILAM, C. GAVOILLE, AND D. PELEG, *Compact routing schemes with low stretch factor*, in 17th Annual ACM Symposium on Principles of Distributed Computing (PODC), ACM PRESS, ed., August 1998, pp. 11–20.

[GH99]   C. GAVOILLE AND N. HANUSSE, *Compact routing tables for graphs of bounded genus*, Research Report RR-1213-99, LaBRI, University of Bordeaux, 351, cours de la Libération, 33405 Talence Cedex, France, February 1999. To appear in ICALP '99.

[GP96]   C. GAVOILLE AND S. PÉRENNÈS, *Memory requirement for routing in distributed networks*, in 15th Annual ACM Symposium on Principles of Distributed Computing (PODC), ACM PRESS, ed., May 1996, pp. 125–133.

[HI87]   L. HEATH AND S. ISTRAIL, *The pagenumber of genus g graphs is $O(g)$*, in 19th Annual ACM Symposium on Theory of Computing (STOC), 1987, pp. 388–397.

[Jac89] G. JACOBSON, *Space-efficient static trees and graphs*, in 30th Annual Symposium on Foundations of Computer Science (FOCS), IEEE Computer Society Press, October 1989, pp. 549–554.

[KRRS94] P. KLEIN, S. RAO, M. RAUCH, AND S. SUBRAMANIAN, *Faster shortest-path algorithms for planar graphs*, in 26th Annual ACM Symposium on Theory of Computing (STOC), 1994, pp. 27–37.

[KW95]   K. KEELER AND J. WESTBROOK, *Short encodings of planar graphs and maps*, Discrete Applied Mathematics, 58 (1995), pp. 239–252.

[Mal88] S. M. MALITZ, *Genus g graphs have pagenumber $O(\sqrt{g})$*, in 29th Symposium on Foundations of Computer Science (FOCS), IEEE, ed., October 1988, pp. 458–468.

[MR97]   J. I. MUNRO AND V. RAMAN, *Succint representation of balanced parentheses, static trees and planar graphs*, in 38rd Symposium on Foundations of Computer Science (FOCS), IEEE, ed., October 1997, pp. 118–126.

[PU89]   D. PELEG AND E. UPFAL, *A trade-off between space and efficiency for routing tables*, Journal of the ACM, 36 (1989), pp. 510–530.

[Tur84] G. TURÁN, *Succint representations of graphs*, Discrete Applied Mathematics, 8 (1984), pp. 289–294.

[Tut62] W. T. TUTTE, *A census of planar triangulations*, Canadian Journal of Mathematics, 14 (1962), pp. 21–38.

[Yan86] M. YANNAKAKIS, *Four pages are necessary and sufficient for planar graphs*, in 18th Annual ACM Symposium on Theory of Computing (STOC), 1986, pp. 104–108.

Computing LOGCFL Certificates

Georg Gottlob, Nicola Leone, and Francesco Scarcello

Institut für Informationssysteme,
Technische Universität Wien, Austria
{gottlob,leone,scarcell}@dbai.tuwien.ac.at

Abstract. By results of Ruzzo [13], the complexity class LOGCFL can
be characterized as the class of languages accepted by alternating Turing
Machines (ATMs) which use logarithmic space and have polynomially
sized accepting computation trees. We show that for each such ATM
M recognizing a language A in LOGCFL, it is possible to construct
an L^{LOGCFL} transducer T_M such that T_M on input $w \in A$ outputs an
accepting tree for M on w. It follows that computing single LOGCFL
certificates is feasible in functional AC^1 and is thus highly parallelizable.
Wanke [17] has recently shown that for any fixed k, deciding whether the
treewidth of a graph is at most k is in the complexity-class LOGCFL. As
an application of our general result, it follows that the task of *computing*
a tree-decomposition for a graph of constant treewidth is in functional
LOGCFL, and thus in AC^1. Similar results apply to many other important search problems corresponding to decision problems in LOGCFL.

1 Introduction and Overview of Results

1.1 The main problem studied

The complexity class LOGCFL consists of all languages (or decision problems)
which are logspace reducible to a context free language. It is well-known that
LOGCFL is a very low complexity class containing highly parallelizable problems. In particular, LOGCFL is contained in logspace uniform AC^1 and is thus
a class of highly parallelizable problems.

There is a number of interesting characterizations of LOGCFL (see also Section 2). The following characterization by Ruzzo [13] is of central interest to
this paper: LOGCFL *coincides with the class of all decision problems recognized
by an alternating Turing machine (ATM) using logarithmic space and having
polynomially sized accepting computation trees.*

Here, the logarithmic space refers to the single configurations of the Turing
machine, and an *accepting computation tree* is a tree describing an accepting
computation of the ATM, i.e., a *certificate* that the input belongs to the language
in question (for a more precise definition, see Section 2).

Clearly, a particular positive instance of a LOGCFL problem may be recognized via several, even exponentially many accepting computation trees or certificates.

The main goal of this paper is the study of the following problem: Given a yes-instance w of a LOGCFL problem and an ATM M as above for solving the problem, compute *one* certificate for w w.r.t. M. We refer to this problem shortly as *computing* LOGCFL *certificates*. As seen below, this problem is of high relevance to various applications.

Ruzzo [12] has shown that the *sequential* complexity of parsing strings of context-free languages is not much harder than that of recognizing such strings. Note that parse trees are LOGCFL certificates for the membersip in a CFL. However, it is not at all intuitive that computing a single certificate (out of exponentially many candidates) can be efficiently done in parallel. In fact, problems of this kind are often inherently sequential since computing the i-th bit of a solution may require keeping track of all the previously computed bits.

1.2 Complexity-theoretic Results

Our main result is the following statement:

> **Theorem:** Computing a LOGCFL certificate can be done in (functional) L^{LOGCFL}, and is thus in the parallel class AC^1

Note that the functional class L^{LOGCFL} (often also denoted by FL^{LOGCFL}) can just be considered as the functional version of LOGCFL. First of all, the decision class L^{LOGCFL} is identical to LOGCFL (see [14] and Lemma 1 of this paper). Secondly, by a well-known characterization of Venkateswaran [15], LOGCFL coincides with the class SAC^1 of decision problems solvable by logspace-uniform families of semi-unbounded Boolean circuits of logarithmic depth. It is easily seen that the functional version of SAC^1 exactly coincides with L^{LOGCFL}. Thus functional L^{LOGCFL} has exactly the same parallel complexity as LOGCFL. In particular, functional L^{LOGCFL} is a subclass of functional AC^1 and NC^2.

While it is known that LOGCFL is closed under complementation [4], this property alone is not sufficient to establish our main result (note that, for example, NP is a subset of L^{NP}, the latter class is closed under complementation, but, as said before, computing NP witnesses is most likely not in L^{NP}). In order to prove our main result, we thus establish a number of further useful properties of LOGCFL, that are of independent interest:

- LOGCFL is closed under L^{LOGCFL}-reductions.
- Functional LOGCFL is closed under composition, i.e., the composition of two functions computable by L^{LOGCFL} transducers is itself computable by a L^{LOGCFL} transducer.
- Each logspace ATM M having polynomially sized accepting computation trees can be replaced by a logspace ATM M' such that M and M' recognize the same language, and *all* accepting computation trees of M' are of polynomial size, and correspond (via simple logspace transformations) to the accepting computation trees of M. In other words, we can transform M to an equivalent machine M' where superpolynomial accepting computation trees are cut off. This property is important, because when an ATM M has

accepting computation trees of polynomial size, there may also be undesired additional accepting computation trees of larger size.
- The task of checking whether a given configuration occurs in an accepting computation tree of a given LOGCFL-ATM is itself in LOGCFL.

1.3 Results on Applications

Many relevant decision problems have been shown to be in LOGCFL. Examples are the following:

- Membership of a word in a context-free language specified by a (fixed) CFG. (This is, of course, a trivial example, given the definition of LOGCFL).
- Deciding whether, for a fixed constant k, a graph G has treewidth $\leq k$, i.e., whether a tree-decomposition of width $\leq k$ for G exists [17].
- Deciding whether an acyclic constraint satisfaction problem has a solution [7].

For all these LOGCFL problems (and for many others not mentioned here), there are highly relevant corresponding *search problems*, namely: *compute* a derivation tree for a word w.r.t. a fixed CFG, *compute* a tree decomposition of width $\leq k$ of a graph, and *compute* a solution to a constraint satisfaction problem.

It turns out that for many decision problems in LOGCFL one can devise a natural algorithm on a logspace ATM such that each accepting computation tree corresponds (via a simple logspace transformation) to one solution of the corresponding search problem. Thus, by our main result, not only the decision problem is in LOGCFL, but also the corresponding solution search problem is in L^{LOGCFL}, i.e., in functional LOGCFL.

Wanke [17], for example, has exhibited an alternating logspace procedure which, for fixed k, checks whether a graph has treewidth $\leq k$. If the algorithm accepts, then each accepting computation tree corresponds to a particular tree-decomposition of width $\leq k$ of the input graph. By our main result, it immediately follows that computing k-width tree decompositions for any constant k is in L^{LOGCFL}, and thus in functional LOGCFL.

An important current research area in Computer Science is *Constraint Satisfaction*. In [7] the authors of the present paper have shown that the problem of checking whether an *acyclic constraint satisfaction problem (CSP)* has a solution is LOGCFL-complete. The proof, however, did not use the concept of logspace ATM with polynomial tree-size but instead exploited another characterization of LOGCFL. In the full report [10] we introduce a logspace ATM with polynomially bounded accepting computation trees for checking whether an acyclic CSP has a solution. There is a one-to-one correspondence between the accepting computation trees (if any) of this ATM and the different solutions of the CSP. By our main result, it immediately follows that *computing* a solution to an acyclic CSP is in L^{LOGCFL}.

By combining our results on bounded tree-decompositions and on acyclic constraint satisfaction problems, we can obtain several further complexity results on other concrete problems. In fact, it is well-known that many decision problems on graphs are in LOGCFL if the input graph has bounded treewidth [17, 3, 5]. It is then easy to see that the solution search problems associated to many of these decision problems are in functional LOGCFL. For example, finding a graph m-coloring for a graph of bounded treewidth is in L^{LOGCFL}, i.e., in functional LOGCFL. The *optimization problem* of computing the chromatic number of a graph of bounded treewidth and of computing an optimal coloring are also in functional LOGCFL.

In summary, the following theorem follows from our result and from the mentioned results on decision problems:

Theorem. The following problems are all in functional LOGCFL:

1. Computing – for fixed k – a k tree-decomposition of a graph.
2. Computing a solution to an acyclic constraint satisfaction problem.
3. Computing an m-coloring for a graph of bounded treewidth.
4. Computing the chromatic number of such a graph.
5. Computing an optimal coloring for such a graph.

A proof of this theorem can be found in the full report [10]. Note that our method is applicable to many other search problems related to decision problems in LOGCFL, e.g., to those described by Wanke, see [17], pp. 486-487.

Our work is also connected to interesting recent work of Courcelle, Makowsky, and Rotics [6]. J. Makowsky (personal communication) pointed out to us that from their results it follows that every search problem definable in monadic second order logic can be solved in functional LOGCFL over structures of bounded treewidth admitting tree-decompositions of logarithmic depth.

2 Preliminaries: Previous Characterizations of LOGCFL

In this paper we will use an important characterization of LOGCFL by Alternating Turing Machines. We assume w.l.o.g. that the states of an ATM are partitioned into existential and universal states.

As in [13], we define a *computation tree* of an ATM on a input string w as a tree whose nodes are labeled with configurations of M on w, such that the descendants of any non-leaf labeled by a universal (existential) configuration include all (resp. one) of the successors of that configuration. A computation tree is *accepting* if the root is labeled with the initial configuration, and all the leaves are accepting configurations. Thus, an accepting computation tree yields a certificate that the input is accepted. A complexity measure considered by Ruzzo [13] for the alternating Turing machine is the tree-size, i.e. the minimal size of an accepting computation tree.

Definition 1 ([13]). *A decision problem $\mathcal{P}$ is solved by an alternating Turing machine M within simultaneous tree-size and space bounds $Z(n)$ and $S(n)$ if, for every "yes" instance w of $\mathcal{P}$, there is at least one accepting computation tree for M on w of size (number of nodes) $\leq Z(n)$, each node of which represents a configuration using space $\leq S(n)$, where n is the size of w. (Further, for any "no" instance w of $\mathcal{P}$ there is no accepting computation tree for M.)*

Ruzzo [13] proved the following important characterization of LOGCFL:

Proposition 1 (Ruzzo [13]). LOGCFL *coincides with the class of all decision problems recognized by ATMs operating simultaneously in tree-size* $O(n^{O(1)})$ *and space* $O(\log n)$.

Another important characterization of LOGCFL was found by Venkateswaran [15]. He showed that LOGCFL coincides with the class SAC^1 of problems solvable by logspace-uniform families of semi-unbounded AC^1 Boolean circuits, short SAC^1 circuits.

A *Boolean circuit* G_n with n inputs is a finite dag whose vertices are called *gates* and are labeled as follows. Vertices of indegree zero are called *circuit input gates* and are labeled from the set $\{false, true, z_1, z_2, \ldots, z_n, \neg z_1, \neg z_2, \ldots, \neg z_n\}$. All other vertices, also called *gates*, are labeled either AND or OR. The one vertex with outdegree zero is called *output*. The evaluation of G_n on input of length n is defined in the standard way. A Boolean circuit is thus given as a triple $(V, E, label)$, where V is the set of vertices (gates), E are the edges, and *label* is the labeling of the vertices as described.

A family $\mathcal{G}$ of Boolean circuits is a sequence $\{G_n | n = 0, 1, 2, \ldots\}$, where the nth circuit G_n has n inputs. Such a family is logspace-uniform if there exists a logspace Turing machine which on input 1^n outputs circuit G_n. The language L accepted by a family $\mathcal{G}$ of circuits is defined as follows: $L = \bigcup_{n \geq 0} L_n$, where L_n is the set of input strings accepted by the nth member G_n of the family.

A family $\mathcal{G}$ of Boolean circuits is *semi-unbounded* if there exists a constant c such that each AND gate of any member G_n of $\mathcal{G}$ has its fan-in bounded by c (the OR gates may have unbounded fan-in).

The class SAC^1 consists of all languages accepted by logspace-uniform families $\mathcal{G}$ of semi-unbounded Boolean circuits, where each member circuit G_n has depth $D(G_n) = O(\log n)$ and has size (i.e., number of gates plus inputs) $S(G_n) = O(n^{O(1)})$ (i.e. polynomial). We will refer to such families $\mathcal{G}$ as SAC^1 families of Boolean circuits.

Proposition 2 (Venkateswaran [15]). LOGCFL $= SAC^1$.

Based on the characterization of LOGCFL in Proposition 2, Borodin et al. [4] have shown that LOGCFL is closed under complementation.

3 Useful Lemmas

In this section we prove a number of useful lemmas that will help us to establish our main theorem in the next section. We assume w.l.o.g. that all logspace transducers and all relativized logspace transducers represent total functions and halt in polynomial time on each input. The output of a transducer T on input w is denoted by $T(w)$.

Intuitively, the *composition* $T_1 \circ T_2$ of two L^{LOGCFL} transducers consists of a combination of T_1 and T_2 such that T_2 reads the output of T_1. The input to $T_1 \circ T_2$ is put on the input tape of T_1 and the output of $T_1 \circ T_2$ is written on the output tape of T_2. More formally, the transduction $[T_1 \circ T_2](w)$ of a word w by the composition $T_1 \circ T_2$ is $T_2(T_1(w))$.

L^{LOGCFL} is the class of all problems solvable in deterministic logspace with an oracle in LOGCFL. Denote by $L^{LOGCFL}(LOGCFL)$ the closure of LOGCFL under L^{LOGCFL} reductions, i.e., the class of all problems that are many-one reducible via a deterministic logspace oracle Turing machine (OTM) with oracle in LOGCFL to a problem in LOGCFL. Sudborough [14] remarked (without proof) that LOGCFL = CO-LOGCFL implies that L^{LOGCFL} = LOGCFL. The following lemmas state somewhat stronger results. Their respective proofs use compositions of SAC^1 circuits and can be found in the extended report [10].

Lemma 1. $L^{LOGCFL}(LOGCFL) = L^{LOGCFL} = LOGCFL$.

Proof. (Sketch.) To see that $L^{LOGCFL} = LOGCFL$, note that for a given input w, a logspace machine T can make only polynomially many queries to an oracle. The set of all potential configurations initiating such queries can be computed in logspace and depends only on the length $|w|$ of w. For each such configuration, the decision problem, whether the corresponding query is answered yes is in LOGCFL, thus we can construct (in a uniform manner) a SAC^1 circuit whose output gate is the query result on input w. The work of the base logspace machine T can be simulated by another SAC^1 circuit on the top of all these query-circuits. Altogether, we obtain a SAC^1 circuit simulating the oracle machine. The construction is logspace uniform. The equality $L^{LOGCFL}(LOGCFL) = L^{LOGCFL}$ is proven in a similar way by composing SAC^1 circuits. For details see [10].

Remark. In [8,9] a complexity class C is called *smooth* if $L^C(C) = L^C$. By Lemma 1, LOGCFL is smooth. By results in [8], from the smoothness of LOGCFL and from the fact that LOGCFL is closed under complementation, it follows that every formula of first order logic extended by (possibly nested applications of) generalized quantifiers in LOGCFL is equivalent to a first order formula with a single (and leading) occurrence of an LOGCFL quantifier. A similar result was shown independently in [11].

Lemma 2. *Any function computable by the composition of two L^{LOGCFL} transducers is computable by a single L^{LOGCFL} transducer.*

Proof. (Sketch.) Let T and T' be L^{LOGCFL} transducers. The output size of their composition $T \circ T'$ is bounded by some polynomial. Checking wether some output bit is 1 is in $L^{LOGCFL}(L^{LOGCFL})$ and thus by Lemma 1 in LOGCFL. Computing the entire output can be done by a FOR loop cycling over each (of the polynomially many) potential output positions and is thus in L^{LOGCFL}. For details, see [10].

We denote the set of accepting computation trees of an alternating Turing machine T for word w by $AT(T, w)$.

Note that the definition of ATM with polynomial tree-size does not require that *every* accepting computation tree for each accepted input be of polynomial size, but rather that for each accepted input *there exists at least one* accepting computation tree of polynomial size. Possible additional superpolynomial accepting trees may exist. For technical reasons we wish to get rid of such superfluous superpolynomial accepting computation trees.

One possibility would be to limit ourselves to ATMs where *all* accepting trees are polynomial. For each problem A in LOGCFL, such an ATM must exist. For example, we could easily obtain such an ATM from the specification of a logspace-uniform family of SAC^1 circuits recognizing A (the accepting subtrees of these circuits are all of polynomial size; a suitable SAC^1 family exists by Proposition 2). But this is not really what we want. What we have in mind is to transform an arbitrary given ATM T with tree-size bounded by a polynomial $p(n)$, recognizing a language A into an equivalent ATM T' such that the following conditions are met:

1. the size of all accepting trees of T' is bounded by a polynomial $q(n)$, and
2. each accepting tree t' of T' on input w corresponds to some accepting tree t of T on input w and t is logspace computable from t' by some logspace transducer H,
3. H is "onto", i.e., for each accepting tree t of T on input w whose size is at most $p(|w|)$, there exists an accepting tree $t' \in AT(T', w)$ s.t. $H(t') = t$.

Intuitively, conditions 2 and 3 state that T' basically simulates T and behaves essentially as T, except that all superpolynomial proof trees of T are cut off.

We will obtain T' from T by a method reminiscent of well-known clocking techniques for regular (non alternating) Turing machines. But since it is not a time bound we are after, let us call our technique *tree curbing* rather than clocking.

Lemma 3 (Curbing Lemma). *Let T be a logspace ATM with tree-size bounded by a polynomial p, recognizing a language A. Then there exists a polynomial q and a logspace ATM T' recognizing A such that:*

1. *all accepting trees of T' for input w are of size at most $q(|w|)$, and*
2. *each accepting tree t' of T' on input w corresponds to some accepting tree t of T on input w and t is computable from t' by a DLOGSPACE transducer H,*
3. *H is "onto", i.e., for each accepting tree t of T on input w whose size is at most $p(|w|)$, there exists an accepting tree $t' \in AT(T', w)$ such that $H(t') = t$.*

Proof. (Sketch.) We assume without loss of generality, that every universal non-terminal state of T has exactly two successors. T' is obtained from T by adding some auxiliary (logspace) data structures for keeping track of the tree-size.

In particular, each configuration c of T' has an additional register s able to hold a positive integer up to $p(n)$ (where n is the input-size). Intuitively, the value of s stands for the maximal allowed size of any partial accepting computation tree rooted in configuration c. Note that T' will also maintain further auxiliary data structures to be able to perform a number of logspace computations, which we will not describe in detail.

Thus, for the configuration of T' on input w which simulates the initial configuration of T on input w, s is initialized with $p(|w|)$. To this aim, T' initially computes (in deterministic logspace) the value $p(|w|)$ and stores it in register s. This now reflects the fact that any accepting tree rooted in this configuration should have size at most $p(|w|)$.

T' then continues simulating the behaviour of T on w, except for the following modifications:

- If c is a nonterminal existential configuration of T whose associated register s in the simulation holds value $s(c) > 1$, then all (simulated) successor configurations of c of T are labeled with the value $s = s(c) - 1$ in T'.
- If c is a nonterminal universal configuration of T, whose associated register s in the simulation holds value $s(c) > 2$, and if the successors of c via T are d and e, then T' proceeds to successor configurations simulating d and e, whose corresponding s-values $s(d)$ and $s(e)$ are chosen nondeterministically such that $s(d) + s(e) = s(c) - 1$ and $s(d) \geq 1$ and $s(c) \geq 1$.
- Any configuration of T' corresponding to a nonterminal existential configuration c of T and having an associated s-value $s(c) \leq 1$ becomes a terminal rejecting configuration of T'. (Intuitively, we are in a branch that exceeds its maximum permitted size.)
- Any configuration of T' corresponding to a nonterminal universal configuration c of T and having an associated s-value $s(c) \leq 2$ becomes a terminal rejecting configuration of T'. (Intuitively, we are again in a branch that exceeds its maximum permitted size because we assumed that universal nonterminal configurations of T have at least two successors.)

It is clear that for each accepting proof tree of T for input w, also machine T' will admit at least one corresponding proof tree by making suitable choices of pairs (i, j) at each simulated universal configuration. On the other hand, if T rejects w, then also T' will reject w, because T' simulates T and thus every proof tree of T' corresponds to exactly one proof tree of T. In summary, T' accepts a word w iff T does. All proof trees of T' are clearly of polynomial size (due to the extra-work of the simulating machine T', consisting of some intermediate deterministic logspace computations, they may be larger than the corresponding T proof trees; but in any case they are of polynomial size.)

Clearly, for each proof tree of T' the corresponding proof tree of T can be computed in logspace. A logspace transducer H performing this task essentially just needs to strip off the additional data structures T' maintains, i.e., the register s and all further auxiliary data structures for controlling the simulation, and to delete some irrelevant intermediate configurations.

A consequence of Lemma 3 is that, whenever we consider a logspace ATM T of polynomial tree-size, where we are only interested in the polynomially sized accepting trees (because they represent, e.g. some solutions), we may assume without loss of generality that T has *only* polynomially sized accepting computation trees. Otherwise we can simulate T by a machine T' that behaves like T but cuts off all superpolynomially sized accepting computation trees.

If T is any logspace ATM with only polynomially sized accepting computation trees, then the decision problem $OCCURS_T(w, c)$, where w is an input string to T, and c is a configuration of T on input w, is defined as follows: $OCCURS_T(w, c)$ is true iff the configuration c occurs as a node in at least one accepting computation tree of T on input w.

Lemma 4. $OCCURS_T(w, c)$ *is in* LOGCFL.

Proof. (Sketch.) We construct a machine T' that for each input w simulates T on w and, in addition, checks whether c occurs in some accepting tree. If c is a configuration of T, then $sim(c)$ refers to a corresponding configuration in the simulating machine T'.

Each configuration of T' maintains, in addition to the data structures maintained by T, a Boolean value $flag$. If $flag = 1$ for some specific configuration $sim(d)$ of T', this means that, for any partial *accepting* computation tree t' of T', rooted at $sim(d)$, one of the nodes in t' is $sim(c)$. If there exists any such an accepting tree of T', then there exists a partial accepting computation tree t of T, rooted at configuration d on input w, such that one of the nodes in t is c. The value of the flag is propagated through the alternating computation according to the following rules: (1) The flag is set to 1 at the initial configuration; (2) whenever configuration $sim(c)$ is reached, the flag is set to zero and always remains zero on the entire configuration subtree rooted at $sim(c)$; (3) any existential (nonleaf) configuration transmits the flag value to *all* of its successors; any universal (nonleaf) configuration transmits its flag value to *one* of its successors, while all others get flag value zero; (4) any leaf configuration having flag value one results in a forced reject. By this policy, T' accepts w iff T accepts w via an accepting computation tree one of whose nodes is c.

4 Main Result

Theorem 1. *Let M be a bounded-treesize logspace ATM recognizing a language A. It is possible to construct a L^{LOGCFL} transducer T which for each input $w \in A$ outputs a single (polynomially-sized) accepting tree for M and w.*

Proof. First of all, by Lemma 3, we assume w.l.o.g. that all accepting trees of M are of polynomial size. Moreover, we assume w.l.o.g that M never performs loops on any computation path.

Let T_1 be an L^{LOGCFL} transducer which on input w outputs all configurations c of M on input w that occur in an accepting computation tree of M. T_1 can be implemented by cycling in logspace over all possible configurations of (M, w), querying for each such configuration c the oracle $OCCURS_M(w, c)$, which, by Lemma 4 is in LOGCFL, and outputting those configurations that yield a positive oracle answer. Denote by $G(w)$ the set of configurations output by T_1 on input w.

Let T_2 be a deterministic logspace transducer that reads the output of T_1 and outputs all pairs $\langle c, c' \rangle \in G(w) \times G(w)$ such that c' is an immediate successor configuration of c via M. Let $G_2(w)$ denote the output of T_2. Note that $G_2(w)$ precisely consists of the union of all accepting computation trees for M and w.

It remains to single-out one of these computation-trees.

Let T_3 be a deterministic logspace transducer taking as input the output $G_2(w)$ of T_2 and doing the following. T_3 cuts off all outgoing edges but the first from each node representing an *existential* configuration in $G_2(w)$. The resulting graph is referred-to as $G_3(w)$.

A further L^{NL} (and thus also L^{LOGCFL}) transducer T_4 eliminates all vertices from $G_3(w)$ that are no longer reachable from the root (= the initial configuration). Call the resulting graph $G_4(w)$.

Note that $G_4(w)$ already encodes (as a dag) one particular accepting computation tree t of M on input w. In fact, each path from the root to a terminal node in $G_4(w)$ is an accepting path. Moreover, each existential configuration has only one successor in $G_4(w)$.

The only thing that remains to be done is to deploy the dag $G_4(w)$ in order to obtain the plain tree t. We know that t is of polynomial size, because t is an accepting tree of M on input w, and *all* such accepting trees are of polynomial size. Thus, the deployment can be done by standard logspace techniques by a deterministic logspace transducer T_5.

The composition of the transducers $T_1 \circ T_2 \circ T_3 \circ T_4 \circ T_5$ can, by lemma 2, be simulated by a single LOGCFL transducer T, as desired.

Note that the above procedure actually computes the first (i.e., leftmost) accepting tree for M and w according to the total ordering of computation trees implicitly defined by machine M. If we assume that M proceeds by constructing the witnesses according to some lexicographic order, then our procedure computes the lexicographically first witness.

Finally, let us remark that an alternative proof of our main result can be obtained from the nice results in [1, 2, 16]. However, a closer look reveals that – if done carefully – this is actually more involved than the proof "from first principles" presented here because one has to show that various transformations used in these papers are parsimonious and preserve the information carried by single LOGCFL certificates. Recall that our intent is to compute a LOGCFL certificate of a *specifically given* ATM and not just of *some* equivalent ATM that solves the same decision problem.

Acknowledgements

We are grateful to Janos Makowsky for his useful comments.

This work is partially supported by *FWF (Austrian Science Funds)* under the project Z29-INF and and by *CNR (Italian National Research Council)*, under grant n.203.15.07.

References

1. E. Allender and J. Jiao. Depth reduction for non-commutative arithmetic circuits. In *Proc. 25th Annual Symposium on Theory of Computing*, pp. 515–522, 1993.
2. E. Allender, J. Jiao, M. Mahajan and V Vinay. Non-commutative arithmetic circuits: depth reduction and size lower bounds. *Theoretical Computer Science*, 209(1,2):47–86, 1998.
3. H.L. Bodlaender and T. Hagerup. Parallel Algorithms with Optimal Speedup for Bounded Treewidth. *SIAM J. Computing*, 27(6): 1725-1746, 1998.
4. A. Borodin, S.A. Cook, P.W. Dymond, W.L. Ruzzo, and M. Tompa. Two applications of Inductive Counting for Complementation Problems. *SIAM J. on Computing*, 18:559–578, 1989.
5. B. Courcelle. The Monadic Second-Order Logic of Graphs I: Recognizable Sets of Finite Graphs. *Information and Computation*, 85:12–75, 1990.
6. B. Courcelle, J.A. Makowsky, and U. Rotics. On the Fixed Parameter Complexity of Graph Enumeration Problems Definable in Monadic Second Order Logic. In *Proc. of WG'98*, 1998.
7. G. Gottlob, N. Leone, and F. Scarcello. The Complexity of Acyclic Conjunctive Queries, in *Proc. of the Symposium on Foundations of Computer Science (FOCS'98)*, Palo Alto, CA, pp. 706–715, 1998. A full report (DBAI-TR-98/17) is currently available on the web as: http://www.dbai.tuwien.ac.at/staff/gottlob/acyclic.ps, or by email from the authors.
8. G. Gottlob. Relativized Logspace and Generalized Quantifiers over Ordered Finite Structures. *Journal of Symbolic Logic* Vol. 62:2, June 1997, pp. 545–574. (Short version appeared in LICS'95.)
9. G. Gottlob. Collapsing Oracle-Tape Hierarchies. In *Proceedings of the Eleventh IEEE Conference on Computational Complexity (CCC'96)*. IEEE Computer Science Press, Philadelphia, May 24–27, 1996, pp.33–42.
10. G. Gottlob, N. Leone, and F. Scarcello. Computing LOGCFL Certificates. Technical report DBAI-TR-98/19. Currently available on the web as: http://www.dbai.tuwien.ac.at/staff/gottlob/certificates.ps, or by email from the authors.
11. C. Lautemann,P. McKenzie,T. Schwentick, and H. Vollmer. The Descriptive Complexity Approach to LOGCFL. Proc. 16th Symp. on Theoretical aspects of Computer Science (STACS'99), Springer LNCS vol. 1563, pp. 444-454, 1999.
12. W.L. Ruzzo. On the complexity of general context-free language parsing and recognition. In *Proc. of ICALP'79*, pp.489–487, LNCS, Springer, 1979.
13. W.L. Ruzzo. Tree-Size Bounded Alternation. *Journal of Computer and System Sciences*, 21:218–235, 1980.
14. I.H. Sudborough. Time and Tape Bounded Auxiliary Pushdown Automata. In *Mathematical Foundations of Computer Science 1977*, LNCS 53, Springer-Verlag, pp.493–503, 1977.
15. H. Venkateswaran. Properties that Characterize LOGCFL. *Journal of Computer and System Sciences*, 43:380–404, 1991.
16. V. Vinay. Counting auxiliary pushdown automata and semi-unbounded arithmetic circuits. In *Proc. 6th IEEE Structure in Complexity Theory Conference*, pp.270–284, 1991.
17. E. Wanke. Bounded Tree-Width and LOGCFL. *Journal of Algorithms*, 16:470–491, 1994.

Efficient Techniques for Maintaining Multidimensional Keys in Linked Data Structures

(Extended Abstract)

Roberto Grossi * and Giuseppe F. Italiano **

Abstract. We describe a general paradigm for maintaining multidimensional keys in linked data structures designed for one-dimensional keys. We improve existing bounds and achieve new results in a simple way, without giving up the structural and topological properties of the underlying data structures. This is particularly important, as it allows us to exploit many properties of one-dimensional searching, and makes our approach amenable to practical implementations.

1 Introduction

A vast repertoire of basic searching data structures, such as AVL-trees [1], red-black trees [21], (a, b)-trees [12], weight-balanced BB[α]-trees [18], self-adjusting trees [20], and random search trees [19] (just to name a few) are currently available to researchers and programmers. Many of these data structures exhibit interesting combinatorial properties that make them attractive both from the theoretical and from the practical point of view. They are defined on an ordered set of (one-dimensional) keys, so that searching is driven by comparisons against the keys stored in their nodes: it is usually assumed that any two keys can be compared in $O(1)$ time. In some situations, however, keys can be arbitrarily long (such as strings or multidimensional points, for instance) and are more realistically modeled as k-dimensional keys, for a given positive integer $k > 1$. Similar to one-dimensional keys, k-dimensional keys are subject to lexicographic order and must be suitably stored and efficiently retrieved and maintained. However, comparing two k-dimensional keys can require $O(k)$ time, and can thus produce an undesirable $O(k)$ slowdown as a *multiplicative* factor in the running times of the operations supported by the original data structures.

More efficient *ad hoc* data structures have been designed for k-dimensional keys. A first version of lexicographic or ternary search trees [3] dates back to [6] and is alternative to tries. The dynamic balancing of ternary search trees was investigated with lexicographic D-trees [16], multidimensional B-trees [11], multidimensional AVL-trees [22], lexicographic globally biased trees [2], lexicographic splay trees [20], k-dimensional balanced binary search trees [10], and balanced binary search trees [23] or kBB-trees [24]. Most of these data structures support search, insert, and delete operations in $O(k + \log n)$ time each [2, 10, 22, 23], while some others support also split and concatenate operations in $O(k + \log n)$

---

* Dipartimento di Informatica, Università di Pisa, Italy. Email: `grossi@di.unipi.it`.
** Dipartimento di Informatica, Sistemi e Produzione, Università di Roma "Tor Vergata", Italy. Email: `italiano@info.uniroma2.it`. Partially supported by EU ESPRIT Long Term Research Project ALCOM-IT under contract no. 20244.

time [11, 16, 20, 24]. Moreover, other data structures allow for weighted keys (e.g., dynamic access frequencies) [2, 16, 20, 24].

In all these data structures, rebalancing requires either $\Omega(k)$ rotations or $\Omega(k)$ time per update in the worst case; furthermore, they are mostly *ad hoc* data structures, and do not seem to exploit the vast bulk of existing work on one-dimensional keys. The only exception is perhaps the data structure of [10], which represents the first attempt to store and retrieve k-dimensional keys into regular binary trees. The height of this data structure is $O(\log n)$, while the above data structures have $O(k+\log n)$ height. Unfortunately in [10] each rotation costs $O(k)$ and so the underlying structure has to be based on red-black trees [21], which require $O(1)$ rotations. Other possible drawbacks are that each split requires $O(k \log n)$ time, and that an insertion is rather complicated and must store and traverse several times an entire root-to-leaf path of length $O(\log n)$.

This multitude of *ad hoc* data structures derives from the lack of a general data structural transformation from one-dimensional keys to k-dimensional keys. The goal of this paper is to show that this general transformation is indeed possible: in particular, we present a general technique which is capable of augmenting many kinds of (heterogeneous) linked data structures so that they can operate on k-dimensional keys. When our technique is applicable, the searching cost drops from $O(k \cdot \ell)$ to $O(k + \ell)$ along a search path of ℓ nodes. Our technique exploits many properties of one-dimensional searching, and combines in a variety of novel ways techniques from data structures and string algorithms. It is simple, and therefore amenable to practical implementations.

Using our general framework, we are able to get bounds for several data structures on n keys of dimension k (or n strings of variable length). We first list our contributions when the data structures are rebalanced by rotations. In this case, we obtain new k-dimensional dictionaries based on several underlying data structures, e.g., AVL-trees, red-black trees, random search trees, BB[α]-trees. The height of the new data structure is $O(\log n)$, improved from $O(k + \log n)$. Consequently, the time bounds obtained with our technique are the following: $O(k + \log n)$ for search, insert and delete, and $O(\log n)$ time for split; a concatenate operation takes $O(k + \log n)$ time in general, and $O(\log n)$ time under some conditions (i.e., whenever in concatenating two trees T_1 and T_2 the number of initial characters shared by the largest key in T_1 and the smallest key in T_2 is known). The best bounds for splitting and concatenating in the previous *ad hoc* data structures were $O(k + \log n)$ or more. The space occupied by the new data structure is $O(nk)$ if its nodes store a copy of the keys and $O(n)$ if they only store a pointer to the keys, whereas many of the previous data structures require $O(nk)$ space in the worst case.

An advantage of our technique is that it is *not invasive*, i.e., it preserves many nice topological properties of the data structures. For instance, we can show that an intermixed sequence of m insertions and deletions in a k-dimensional dictionary that is weight-balanced, such as one based on BB[α]-trees, can be supported in $O(m + n)$ time. This improves a factor of $O(k)$ on the previous best bound, $O(k(n + m))$, which could be achieved either with kBB-trees [24] or with k-dimensional balanced search trees [10]. We remark that kBB-trees need $O(k)$ rotations per operation while k-dimensional binary search trees need $O(1)$ rotations, each of which requires $O(k)$ time. Our technique applied on BB[α]-trees involves $O(1)$ rotations per operation, so that each rotation can be implemented in $O(1)$ time. As a byproduct of the fact that rotations take $O(1)$ time with our technique, we can obtain a persistent version [8] of our k-dimensional dictionaries which requires only $O(1)$ additional space per update. The only requirement is that the underlying data structure can be updated in $O(1)$ time instead of $O(k)$ (for example, by using the data structure in [14]). By contrast, the algorithms in [24] use $O(k)$ space per update.

A further example comes from weighted trees, in which the i-th key has a weight (access frequency) w_i. If W is the total weight of the keys, we match the k-dimensional counterpart of the bounds for one-dimensional keys (without the restrictions on deletions of [24]): $O(k + \log W/w_i)$ for search and deletion, $O\big(k + \log(W + w_i)/\min\{w^-, w_i, w^+\}\big)$ for insertion where w^- and w^+ are the weights of the predecessor and successor of the inserted key. We also have $O\big(\log W/(w_i - \delta)\big)$ for demotion (weight decrease by δ) and $O\big(\log(W + \delta)/w_i\big)$ for promotion (weight increase by δ) independently of k.

We now list our contributions when rebalancing is done via splay operations [20]. In this case, we can implement each splay step on k-dimensional keys in $O(1)$ time, thus obtaining a simple k-dimensional version of self-adjusting trees. That is not new, as witnessed by the lexicographic splay trees of [20]. We thus achieve the same bounds, with the notable exception that we can further reduce the depth of the key having weight w_i from $O(k + \log W/w_i)$ to $O(\log W/w_i)$. This has many benefits, including improving to $O(\log W/w_i)$ the cost of splitting when the split node is known. Analogously, we can efficiently implement split, fuse and share operations, and thus achieve k-dimensional 2-3 trees and (a, b)-trees. As a result, we can sort a presorted file of n k-dimensional keys in $O\big(nk + n\log(F/n)\big)$ time, where $0 \leq F \leq n(n-1)/2$ is the number of inversions. This result extends (and reuses) techniques for one-dimensional keys given in [17].

Finally, we can perform finger searching in $O(k + \log d)$ time, where d is the difference between the ranks of two keys searched consecutively [5, 12]. Insertions take $O(1)$ time and deletions $O(\log^* n)$ time by a recent result for one-dimensional keys in [4]. To the best of our knowledge, this was not previously known. One of the applications of this result is the efficient implementation of set operations (union, intersection, etc.) on two sets of m and n keys of dimension k in optimal $\Theta(mk + m\log(n/m))$ time, where $m \leq n$.

We remark that all of these results are obtained with relatively small additional work as they strongly rely on properties of the underlying one-dimensional data structure. Similarly to some *ad hoc* data structures for k-dimensional keys (e.g., ternary search trees [3]), our technique does not inherently need address arithmetic since it can be implemented on a pointer machine [21].

Related Work. The idea of blending data structural techniques and string algorithms is not new and has already produced powerful data structures, such as the suffix array [15] and the string B-tree [9]. We wish to briefly highlight the similarities and the differences between our techniques and these two data structures. Exploiting the relationship between string searching and the lexicographic order of keys is undoubtly a merit of suffix arrays. A major difference is that our search strategy does not assume any peculiar order or topology in the search path, while suffix arrays need to access a compact portion of memory storing the keys in lexicographic order. Moreover, suffix arrays are inherently static while are techniques are dynamic. As for string B-trees, their main feature is to combine the best qualities of a popular dynamic data structure for external memory (the B-tree) and of a space efficient data structure for string search (the suffix array), thus overcoming the computational bottleneck of dealing with keys of unbounded length. When used in main memory as k-dimensional dictionaries, string B-trees get the same search bounds as ours, and they can also be used for performing finger searches. However, their rebalancing time is $\Omega(\log n)$ in the worst case due to the upward replication of the leftmost and rightmost keys in each subtree. It is unclear how to get the sub-logarithmic update bounds that our techniques achieve with self-adjusting, weighted, and finger search trees. Finally, the idea of storing, and efficiently searching for, the suffixes of a string into the nodes of a binary search tree has been employed in the suffix binary search tree [13], but no method for keeping the tree balanced was given.

Some other related work is given by a data structure of Dietz and Sleator [7], which is able to maintain order information in a dynamic list. In order to show the connection, consider the following approach: take an *ad hoc* k-dimensional dictionary D (e.g., a ternary search tree) to keep the k-dimensional keys sorted, and store the sorted sequence of keys as a dynamic list L. Using the data structure of Dietz and Sleator, the list L can be maintained under insertions and deletions in $O(1)$ time, and checking the order between any two elements in the list takes $O(1)$ time. With the help of L, we could thus compare any two k-dimensional keys in $O(1)$ time and apparently circumvent the $O(k)$ multiplicative term: in other terms, we can use any linked data structure *as if* we had constant size keys for comparison purposes. The limit of this approach, however, is given by the bottleneck of accessing and updating the k-dimensional dictionary D, as clearly it cannot be employed as a bootstrapping technique to improve the bounds of the k-dimensional dictionary D itself.

2 The Multidimensional Path Searching Technique

In this section we describe our general technique for maintaining multidimensional keys in linked data structures. Let S be a set of ordered keys where each comparison between two keys has outcome in $[<, =, >]$ and takes constant time. We assume the comparison model for S: thus we cannot hash keys of S nor we can access part of their bits. Following Driscoll et al. [8], we say that a *linked data structure* $\mathcal{D}_S$ storing the keys in set S is a labeled directed graph whose vertices have constant outdegree. $\mathcal{D}_S$ is a finite collection of *nodes*, each of which is able to hold a fixed number of *fields*. Each field is either an *information* field

```
procedure Access(w, v)
    π := {v};
    while  (v ≠ null) and C(v) do
        local computation without comparing w and v;
        if (w = v) then v := neigh_=(v)
            else if (w < v) then v := neigh_<(v)
            else v := neigh_>(v) endif;
        π := insert(π, v);
    endwhile.
```

(storing a key from S, a bit, an integer or a real number) or a *pointer* field to another node, called *neighbor*. As usual, a *null* pointer indicates that no node is pointed to. Without loss of generality, all the nodes are of the same type, i.e., they all have the same fields, and each node stores *at most one key* from S. In the following, as there is no danger of ambiguity, we denote the key stored in a node v by v itself. The size $|\mathcal{D}_S|$ of a data structure $\mathcal{D}_S$ is the total number of the fields contained in all of its nodes.

A linked data structure $\mathcal{D}_S$ is accessed by means of *entry* nodes, which are some special nodes in $\mathcal{D}_S$ that are designed as starting points for the traversal of $\mathcal{D}_S$. A linked data structure supports two types of operations: *access* and *update*. An *access* operation computes an *access set* π containing *accessed nodes*. At the beginning, π contains one of the entry nodes. The access operation consists of *access steps*, each of which keeps record of the fact that a node is visited by inserting it into π. To access a new node, at least one field of an already accessed node (in π) must point to the new node. The size $|\pi|$ of the access set is given by the number of nodes it contains. The cost of an access operation is given by the total number of access steps, and is denoted as $A(n)$, where $n = |S|$ and $A(n) \geq |\pi|$.

A generic access procedure to a linked data structure is described in **procedure** *Access*, where w is the key to be searched and v is an entry node of the linked data structure. At the beginning, the access set π is initialized with an input entry node; next, we continue traversing $\mathcal{D}_S$ as long as a certain condition $C(v)$ is satisfied. This condition $C(v)$ usually involves the information accumulated in the traversal up to the current node (pointed to by variable v) and can also exploit the outcomes in $[<, =, >]$ of the comparisons of w previously determined against the nodes in $\pi - \{v\}$.

The traversal proceeds as follows. Once a node v is reached, we perform some local computation that does not involve a comparison between w and v. After that, we execute this comparison. Based on its outcome, we possibly perform some more local computation and then reach a neighbor of v: we formalize this task by generic functions $neigh_<$, $neigh_=$ and $neigh_>$, which depend on the topology of $\mathcal{D}_S$ and are in charge of performing the local computation after the comparison. Finally, function *insert* updates the access set π. Note that we assume without loss of generality that each node v always stores a key $v \in S$, and that the other fields beside those storing key v can be processed in an arbitrary way. That is, as previously mentioned, we require the comparison model only for the keys in S.

An *update* operation on $\mathcal{D}_S$ is an intermixed sequence of access and update steps, which are responsible for changing the topology of $\mathcal{D}_S$. That change takes places by creating a new node that is added to access set π or by destroying a node in π. New nodes must have all fields initialized, and any field in a node can be changed with the proviso that pointers must be *null* or correctly set. The *total time* of an update operations is the total number of access and update steps executed. The *update time* is the number of update steps only, denoted by $U(n)$, where $n = |S|$. Note that, differently from the case of $A(n)$, we do not necessarily have $U(n)$ lower bounded by the size $|\pi|$ of the access set. The total time of an update operation is indeed bounded by $O(A(n) + U(n))$.

We now present our technique for k-dimensional keys, for a positive integer $k > 1$. Suppose that we wish to operate the same linked data structure on a set V of k-dimensional keys under the lexicographic order $\prec$, rather than on the original set S of keys. Throughout, we assume that $|S| = |V| = n$. By plugging the keys in V into the nodes of linked data structure $\mathcal{D}_S$ we obtain a simple linked data structure for V, denoted by $\mathcal{D}_V$, with the *same* topological properties and the *same* supported operations as those of $\mathcal{D}_S$. Unfortunately, this makes the access time increase to $O(A(n) + |\pi| \cdot k)$ and the update time increase to $O(U(n) \cdot k)$, as each comparison takes now $O(k)$ time. We will show how to improve these bounds.

For any two k-dimensional keys $v, w \in V$, the length of their *longest common prefix*, denoted by $lcp(v, w)$, is the number of initial elements that are pairwise equal. That is, if $v = w$ then $lcp(v, w) = k$; otherwise, $lcp(v, w) = \ell$ if and only if $v[0 \ldots \ell - 1] = w[0 \ldots \ell - 1]$ and $v[\ell] \neq w[\ell]$. We say that elements $v[\ell]$ and $w[\ell]$ are a *mismatch* in the latter case.

Let us now examine $\mathcal{D}_V$ and an access set π that leads to a node v. We define two special nodes in π that are related to v: its *predecessor* π_v^- and its *successor* π_v^+ when π is equivalently seen as a (multi)set of keys. Formally, π_v^- is the greatest key in $\pi - \{v\}$ that is less than v, and π_v^+ is the least key in $\pi - \{v\}$ that is greater than v, in lexicographic order $\prec$. If the predecessor for v does not exist in π or v is an entry node, we set it equal to a special key $-\infty$. Analogously, we use $+\infty$ when the successor for v does not exist or v is an entry node. We use the convention that $lcp(\cdot, \cdot)$ is always zero when at least one of its arguments is $-\infty$ or $+\infty$.

Definition 1. *A linked data structure $\mathcal{D}_S$ over an ordered set S is said to be V-augmentable for a set V of k-dimensional keys under the lexicographic order $\prec$, with $|S| = |V| = n$, if the following conditions hold:*

1. *The set S in $\mathcal{D}_S$ can be replaced by V to obtain an equivalent data structure $\mathcal{D}_V$, so that if a node stores a key that has rank r in S, for $1 \leq r \leq n$, then its key is replaced by the key in V of rank r in $\prec$-order. The supported operations are the same as those in $\mathcal{D}_S$.*

---

procedure k-$Access(w, v)$
    $\pi := \{v\};$ /* initially, $\pi_v^- = -\infty$ and $\pi_v^+ = +\infty$ */
    $\ell := 0;$
    while $(v \neq null)$ **and** $C(v)$ **do**
        local computation without comparing w and v;
        case w **of**   /* compute $lcp = lcp(w, v)$ */
        (a) $w \prec \pi_v^-:$ $lcp := \min\{lcp(w, \pi_v^-), lcp(\pi_v^-, v)\};$
        (b) $w \succ \pi_v^+:$ $lcp := \min\{lcp(w, \pi_v^+), lcp(\pi_v^+, v)\};$
        (c) $\pi_v^- \prec w \prec \pi_v^+:$
            choose $x \in \{\pi_v^-, \pi_v^+\}$ such that $lcp(x, w) = \max\{lcp(\pi_v^-, w), lcp(w, \pi_v^+)\};$
            $lcp := lcp(x, v);$
            if $(\ell \leq lcp)$ **then** $\ell := lcp := \ell + lcp(v[\ell \ldots k-1], w[\ell \ldots k-1]);$
        endcase;
        /* compare w and v by using lcp */
        if $(lcp = k)$ **then** $v := neigh_=(v)$
            else if $(w[lcp] < v[lcp])$ **then** $v := neigh_<(v)$
            else $v := neigh_>(v)$ **endif**;
        $\pi := insert(\pi, v);$
    endwhile.

---

2. Each node $v \in \mathcal{D}_V$ can be augmented with a pair of pointers to its predecessor π_v^- and its successor π_v^+ for any access path π leading to v, along with two integers $lcp(\pi_v^-, v)$ and $lcp(\pi_v^+, v)$ denoting the lengths of their lcps.

3. The size $|\mathcal{D}_V|$ of the augmented data structure is still $O(|\mathcal{D}_S|)$ plus the space required by V.

4. If the update time for $\mathcal{D}_S$ is $U(n)$, the information described in condition 2 can be maintained in $\mathcal{D}_V$ in $O(U(n))$ time.

Theorem 1. Let $\mathcal{D}_S$ be a linked data structure with access time $A(n)$ and update time $U(n)$, where $n = |S|$. If $\mathcal{D}_S$ is V-augmentable for a set V of k-dimensional keys, $|V| = |S|$, the resulting data structure $\mathcal{D}_V$ has access time $O(A(n) + k)$ and update time $O(U(n))$. The space required $|\mathcal{D}_V|$ is either $O(|\mathcal{D}_S|)$ when the nodes can store pointers to the keys or $O(|\mathcal{D}_S| + nk)$ when nodes need to store explicitly the keys in V.

As the update and space bounds of Theorem 1 follow directly from Definition 1, we show the bound for the access time in the rest of this section. We postpone the discussion of the update operations to the next section, where we relate them to the topology of the data structures at hand.

To prove that the access time is $O(A(n) + k)$, we extend the general procedure Access to **procedure** k-Access, so as to deal with the k-dimensional keys in V. The rationale behind this procedure can be summarized as follows. First, the local computation not involving a comparison between w and v is performed under the hypothesis that all comparisons of w against the keys in $\pi - \{v\}$ have been correctly carried out in the previous iterations of the **while** loop. By using a careful bookkeeping based upon a Dietz-Sleator list (mentioned in Section 1), we can maintain a list order on the keys in π in $O(1)$ time. It suffices to insert

v into the list for $\pi - \{v\}$, in its correct position by using its predecessor π_v^- and its successor π_v^+. We analogously keep a list order on $\pi - \{v\} \cup \{w\}$ as we know the predecessor and the successor of w in $\pi - \{v\}$ by induction. As a result, when visiting node v, we can compare any two keys in $\pi \cup \{w\}$ in $O(1)$ time, except v and w themselves. Second, the **case** statement is in charge of computing $lcp = lcp(w, v)$ under the assumption that the elements $w[0 \ldots \ell - 1]$ have been examined in the previous iterations. Third, the nested **if** statements after the **case** statement rely on the value of lcp to infer the outcome of the comparison between w and v as follows: (1) $w = v$ if and only if $lcp = k$; (2) $w \prec v$ if and only if $lcp < k$ and $w[lcp] < v[lcp]$; (3) $w \succ v$ if and only if $lcp < k$ and $w[lcp] > v[lcp]$.

Intuitively, the efficiency of our technique derives from the property that at most one pairwise comparison of elements in w and v is performed, except for the **if** statement in case (c). But in the latter case, we compare "fresh" elements in $w[\ell \ldots k - 1]$. The crux of the method is therefore the computation of lcp in the **case** statement the procedure. Toward this end, we exploit the following properties of lcp's among generic k-dimensional keys x, y and z. We say that the keys are *ordered* if either $x \prec y \prec z$ or $x \succ y \succ z$. Otherwise, they are unordered.

Property 1. Let x, y and z be three k-dimensional keys: (1) [Triangle Inequality] If the keys are unordered, $lcp(x, z) \geq \min\{lcp(x, y), lcp(y, z)\}$. (2) [Triangle Equality] If the keys are ordered, $lcp(x, z) = \min\{lcp(x, y), lcp(y, z)\}$. (3) [Maximal Locality] If the keys are ordered, $lcp(x, y) \geq lcp(x, z)$.

Note that Property 1.2 allows us to compute one lcp from other two lcp's in some cases. In the other cases, we can use Property 1.1 to infer at least a lower bound on the former lcp in terms of the latter two lcp's. Finally, Property 1.3 states that, the closer the keys are in (increasing or decreasing) $\prec$-order, the longer their lcp's are.

These tools suffice to prove by induction that $lcp(w, v)$ is indeed correctly computed by the pseudocode of the procedure. The inductive hypothesis that holds *before* visiting v consists of two parts:

1. The key w to be searched has been compared against all keys $x \in \pi - \{v\}$ in $\prec$-order and the outcomes of the comparisons along with their $lcp(x, w)$ are known, for every such x.
2. For a positive integer ℓ, the elements in $w[0 \ldots \ell - 1]$ have been compared successfully in $\pi - \{v\}$, where $\ell = \max_{x \in \pi - \{v\}} lcp(x, w)$. That is, no accessed node shares more than ℓ initial elements with w.

Lemma 1. *The* **case** *statement in the pseudocode of the access operation in procedure k-Access correctly computes $lcp = lcp(w, v)$.*

As far as time complexity is concerned, the outcome of comparisons of w against the predecessor and successor of v, along with their lcp's, are available in node v by condition 2 of Definition 1 and by induction. It therefore takes constant time to select one of cases (a)–(c) by recording the values of lcp and the outcome of the comparison in each accessed node. When we stop the traversal and the access operation terminates, $O(A(n))$ time has been spent plus the overhead for handling k-dimensional keys. This overhead amounts to a total of $O(|\pi| + k)$, as at each accessed node we either execute $O(1)$ constant-time instructions and comparisons or we increase ℓ by some non-negative value Δ_ℓ in $O(1 + \Delta_\ell)$ time. The sum of all such values is $O(k)$ and so the total increase time is $O(|\pi| + k)$. Putting all pieces together, we need $O(A(n) + k)$ time as $A(n) \geq |\pi|$. This completes the sketch of the proof of the main result in this section, namely Theorem 1.

3 Classical Data Structures Revisited

We can apply the general technique presented in the previous section to several data structures. For lack of space, we cannot cover any details of the method, and refer the reader to the full version of this paper. In classical balanced binary search trees, searching costs $O(k + \log n)$ as the access time is $A(n) = O(\log n)$ in Theorem 1. As for updates in T, we can show that (single and double) rotations can be supported in $O(1)$ time. Split and concatenate rely on rotations and thus can be dealt with analogously to rotations.

Theorem 2. *Any balanced binary search tree can be searched in $O(k + \log n)$ time and can be restructured via rotations, insertions, deletions, splits and concatenates in $O(k + \log n)$ time. Splits and deletes require $O(\log n)$ time if the target node is known.*

We note that Theorem 2 can be applied to other data structures, such as AVL-trees, red-black trees, random search trees, and BB[α]-trees, producing the bounds listed in the Introduction. When rebalancing is done via splay operations [20], we can implement each splay step by at most two single rotations in $O(1)$ time, thus obtaining a simple k-dimensional version of self-adjusting splay trees which have $O(\log n)$ height (instead of $O(k + \log n)$).

Theorem 3. *The amortized cost of an operation supported by a k-dimensional splay trees with n nodes is $O(k + \log n)$. If the node on which a delete or split operation is performed is known, these two operations take $O(\log n)$ time.*

The weighted version of the bounds in Theorem 3 are those in [20, Section 2] plus an $O(k)$ additive term. Finally, data structures that store the keys in their leaves and are maintained under split, fuse and share steps, such as 2-3-trees, B-trees and (a, b)-trees, offer an interesting example in which *more* than one feasible access set can lead to the *same* node. We can prove that only $O(1)$ distinguishable access sets lead to any node, and so each node requires only $O(1)$ *lcp* values maintained in constant time under split, fuse and share operations [12]. We can use a recent result on finger search trees [4] to obtain the theorem below.

Theorem 4. *There exists a k-dimensional finger search trees for a set of n keys that supports arbitrary finger searches in $O(k + \log d)$ time, and neighbor insertions in $O(1)$ time and deletions in $O(\log^* n)$ time in the worst case. If an insertion of a key is not preceded by a search of the key, then it costs $O(k)$ time.*

References

1. G. M. Adel'son-Vel'skii and E. M. Landis. An algorithm for the organization of information. *Soviet Mathematics Doklady*, 3 (1962), 1259–1263.
2. Samuel W. Bent, Daniel D. Sleator and Robert E. Tarjan. Biased search trees. *SIAM Journal on Computing* 14 (1985), 545–568.
3. Jon L. Bentley and Robert Sedgewick. Fast algorithms for sorting and searching strings. In *Proc. 8th ACM-SIAM Symp. on Discrete Algorithms* (1997), 360–369.
4. Gerth Stølting Brodal. Finger search trees with constant insertion time. In *Proc. 9th ACM-SIAM Symp. on Discrete Algorithms* (1998), 540–549.
5. Mark R. Brown and Robert E. Tarjan. Design and analysis of a data structure for representing sorted lists. *SIAM Journal on Computing* 9 (1980), 594–614.
6. Henry A. Clampett. Randomized binary searching with the tree structures. *Communications of ACM* 7 (1964), 163–165.
7. Paul F. Dietz and Daniel D. Sleator. Two algorithms for maintaining order in a list. In *Proc. 19th ACM Symp. on Theory of Computing* (1987), 365–372.
8. James R. Driscoll, Neil Sarnak, Daniel D. Sleator, and Robert E. Tarjan. Making data structures persistent. *J. of Computer and System Sciences* 38 (1989), 86–124.
9. Paolo Ferragina and Roberto Grossi. The String B-Tree: A new data structure for string search in external memory and its applications. *Journal of ACM*, to appear. Preliminary version in *Proc. 27th ACM Symp. on Theory of Comp.* (1995) 693–702.
10. Teofilo F. Gonzalez. The on-line d-dimensional dictionary problem. In *Proc. 3rd ACM-SIAM Symp. on Discrete Algorithms* (1992), 376–385.
11. Ralf H. Gueting and Hans-Peter Kriegel. Multidimensional B-tree: An efficient dynamic file structure for exact match queries. In *Proc. 10th GI Conference*, Informatik-Fachberichte, Springer, 33 (1980), 375–388.
12. Scott Huddleston and Kurt Mehlhorn. A new data structure for representing sorted lists. *Acta Informatica* 17 (1982), 157–184.
13. Robert W. Irving. Suffix binary search trees. Research Report, Department of Computer Science, University of Glasgow, April 1997.
14. Christos Levcopoulos and Mark H. Overmars. A balanced search tree with $O(1)$ worst-case update time. *Acta Informatica* 26 (1988), 269–277.
15. Udi Manber and Eugene W. Myers. Suffix arrays: A new method for on-line string searches. *SIAM Journal on Computing* 22 (1993), 935–948.
16. Kurt Mehlhorn. Dynamic binary search. *SIAM J. on Computing* 8 (1979), 175–198.
17. Kurt Mehlhorn. *Data structures and algorithms: 1. Searching and sorting*, Springer, (1984).
18. Jürg Nievergelt and Edward M. Reingold. Binary search trees of bounded balance. *SIAM Journal on Computing* 2 (1973), 33–43.
19. Raimund Seidel and Cecilia R. Aragon. Randomized search trees. *Algorithmica* 16 (1996), 464–497.
20. Daniel D. Sleator and Robert E. Tarjan. Self-adjusting binary search trees. *Journal of ACM* 32 (1985), 652–686.
21. Robert E. Tarjan. *Data structures and network algorithms*, CBMS-NSF Reg. Conf. Ser. Appl. Math. 44, SIAM (1983).
22. Vijay K. Vaishnavi. Multidimensional height-balanced trees. *IEEE Transactions on Computers* C-33 (1984), 334–343.
23. Vijay K. Vaishnavi. Multidimensional balanced binary trees. *IEEE Transactions on Computers* C-38 (1989), 968–985.
24. Vijay K. Vaishnavi. On k-dimensional balanced binary trees. *Journal of Computer and System Sciences* 52 (1996), 328–348.

On the Complements of Partial k-Trees [*]

Arvind Gupta, Damon Kaller, and Thomas Shermer

Simon Fraser University, Burnaby, BC, V5A 1S6, Canada,
{arvind,kaller,shermer}@cs.sfu.ca

Abstract. We introduce new techniques for studying the structure of partial k-trees. In particular, we show that the complements of partial k-trees provide an intuitively-appealing characterization of partial k-tree obstructions. We use this characterization to obtain a lower bound of $2^{\Omega(k \log k)}$ on the number of obstructions, significantly improving the previously best-known bound of $2^{\Omega(\sqrt{k})}$. Our techniques have the added advantage of being considerably simpler than those of previous authors.

1 Introduction

Robertson and Seymour's [RS] seminal work on graph minors yields a low-order polynomial-time recognition algorithm for any family of graphs closed under minors. They show that any minor-closed graph family has a finite *obstruction* set, the set of minimal graphs *not* in the family. Since an input graph belongs to any minor-closed family exactly when no minor of the graph is an obstruction, polynomial-time recognition is possible for many fundamental graph families, including, the family of graphs embeddable on any fixed surface, and even some families for which the recognition problem was not previously known to be decidable [FL88]. Unfortunately, there does not seem to be a general technique for actually generating the obstructions of a minor-closed graph family.

The partial k-trees (graphs of bounded treewidth) are a minor-closed family have received considerable attention because they subsume such important graph classes as trees, series-parallel graphs, outerplanar graphs and Halin graphs. Many $\mathcal{NP}$-hard graph problems can be solved in polynomial (often linear) time over partial k-trees using dynamic-programming. Such algorithms rely on the input graph being parsed into a *width-k tree decomposition*, which is then processed in order from its leaves to its root.

Although the Robertson-Seymour proof established the existence of an $O(n^2)$ recognition algorithm for partial k-trees, the proof was non-constructive. Arnborg et al. [ACP87] were the first to find an explicit polynomial-time algorithm; however, its $O(n^{k+2})$ running time made it infeasible in practice. After a long series of papers on this problem, Bodlaender finally settled the question with a linear-time algorithm [Bod96]; however it also had an exponential in a polynomial in k. A different approach was taken by Sanders [San95] who restricted

---

[*] Funded by the Natural Sciences and Engineering Research Council of Canada.

his attention to partial 4-trees and developed a fast algorithm by applying a powerful set of reductions. As part of the proof, Sanders notes that these reductions can be used to generate obstructions; the number of reductions required seems intimately related to the number of obstructions. In general, knowing the structure of obstructions helps in developing more powerful reduction techniques which can then be used to devise more efficient recognition algorithms.

Computing obstructions for partial k-trees seems difficult and few papers have been written on this topic. Fellows and Langston [FL89] showed that it is possible to find obstructions given a finite congruence for the family and a bound on the treewidth of the obstruction, but their proof gives no upper bounds on the numbers of obstructions. Gupta and Impagliazzo [GI97] show how obstructions can be found for the union of two minor closed planar graph families, given the obstructions of the original families. Lagergren [Lag91] showed a doubly-exponential upper bound on the size of an obstruction for partial k-trees.

Partial 1-trees, and partial 2-trees have just one obstruction. Arnborg et al. [APC90] found the four obstructions for partial 3-trees. Takahashi et al. [TUK94] characterized all the acyclic obstructions for partial k-paths (a subclass of partial k-trees), and showed that there are $\Omega(k!^2)$ of them. However, obstructions for partial k-paths are not always obstructions for partial k-trees, so this result does not directly yield information about k-tree obstructions. Ramachandramurthi [Ram97] showed that the total number of obstructions of partial k-trees of size $k + 3$ is $2^{\Omega(\sqrt{k})}$. His proof is quite technical, involving a detailed analysis of the structure of the obstructions, and triple sums over number partitions.

In this paper we develop a new technique for investigating the structure of obstructions for partial k-trees. We introduce the *cowidth* of a graph: the cowidth of an n-vertex graph is $n - k$. In particular, we study the complements of graphs with cowidth at most 4. Although at first blush this may seem to be equivalent to directly studying partial k-trees, there is an inherent advantage to looking at the complement. Whereas a partial k-tree is constructed by starting with a k-tree and deleting edges, the complement involves adding edges so the underlying structure is never lost. This allows us to look for basic structures that must exist in the complement of any graph with some fixed cowidth. Our techniques yield a very simple proof of Ramachandramurthi's result. We obtain a closed-form simple expression counting all obstructions of size $k + 3$ for a partial k-tree. We then find obstructions of size $k + 4$ and show that there are $2^{\Omega(k \log k)}$ such obstructions. This significantly improves the bounds of Ramachandramurthi.

2 Preliminaries

Our graphs are finite, simple, loop-free and undirected. A *nonedge* of a graph $G = (V, E)$ is a pair of vertices in V that are not the endpoints of any edge in E. The *complement* of G is the graph $G^c = (V, \overline{E})$, where $\overline{E}$ is the set of non-edges of G. For emphasis, when we deal with G and its complement, we will call G the *primal* graph. We also use the symbol H for a graph, when we are primarily considering H as the complement of some primal graph. If G' is isomorphic to a subgraph of G, we will sometimes write that G *contains* G'.

G is a *k-tree* if it is K_{k+1} or if it is obtained from a k-tree G' by adding a new vertex v that is adjacent to all the vertices of a K_k in G'. A *partial k-tree* is a subgraph of a k-tree. There are several equivalent definitions of partial k-trees, the best-known based on elimination orderings or tree decompositions. In connection with the latter, partial k-trees are also known as the graphs of *treewidth* at most k. The *tree cowidth* of G, denoted q, is the number of vertices of G minus its treewidth, ($q = n - k$). Henceforth we refer to this as *cowidth*. Notice that G has cowidth at least q if and only if it has treewidth at most $n - q$ (i.e. it is a partial $(n - q)$-tree). We study graphs with tree cowidth at most 4.

The graph obtained by deleting a vertex v from G is denoted $G - v$. Similarly, deleting an edge $e = uv$ from G yields $G - e$ or $G - uv$. Adding an isolated vertex v yields $G + v$, and adding edge $e = uv$ yields $G + e$ or $G + uv$. A *contraction* of an edge uv is the graph $G\langle uv \rangle$ formed by deleting u and v, and replacing them with a new vertex $\langle uv \rangle$ with edges to those vertices of G that were connected to either u or v. A *minor* of G is any graph obtainable from G by applying a sequence of the operations: delete an isolated vertex; delete an edge; and contract an edge.

A class $\mathcal{C}$ of graphs is *minor-closed* if every minor of a graph in $\rfloor$ is also in $\mathcal{C}$. Examples of minor-cllosed classes include planar graphs and partial k-trees for fixed k. For a minor-closed graph class $\mathcal{C}$, any graph not in $\mathcal{C}$ is *forbidden*; no graph of $\mathcal{C}$ can have a forbidden minor. A graph O is an *obstruction* for $\mathcal{C}$ if O is forbidden and no minor of O is forbidden. Our focus is on partial k-trees, so we use *k-obstruction* to mean an obstruction for the class of partial k-trees.

Tree decompositions. A *tree decomposition* $\mathcal{T}$ of a graph G is pair $(T, \mathcal{X})$ such that $T = (V_T, E_T)$ is a tree, $\mathcal{X} = \{X_a\}_{a \in V_T}$, where $X_a \subseteq V$ is called the *bag* corresponding to $a \in V_T$, and satisfies: every vertex of G is in some $X_a \in \mathcal{X}$; every edge of G has both endpoints in some $X_a \in \mathcal{X}$; and if $a, b, c \in V_T$ with b on the path between a and c, then $X_a \cap X_c \subseteq X_b$.

The *width* of the tree decomposition is one less than the size of the largest bag. The *cowidth* of the tree decomposition is the number of vertices in the graph minus the width of the tree decomposition; the cowidth of the graph is the maximum cowidth over all of its tree decompositions. A tree decomposition is *smooth* if each bag contains $k + 1$ vertices, and adjacent bags differ by exactly one vertex. Bodlaender [Bod96] showed that a tree decomposition can be converted to a smooth tree decomposition with the same width. Therefore the number of vertices in the tree of a smooth tree decomposition is $q = n - k$, the cowidth of the decomposition. We assume that all tree decompositions are smooth.

For a cowidth-q tree decomposition of G, there are two vertices in the symmetric difference of two bags at adjacent nodes of the tree. A vertex not in every bag is a differing vertices across some edge of the tree. Since there are $q - 1$ edges in the tree, there are $r \leq 2q - 2$ vertices $v_1, v_2, \ldots, v_r$ of G not in every bag.

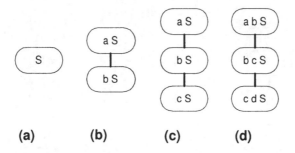

Fig. 1. Tree decompositions for $1 \leq q \leq 3$.

Let S be the vertices of G that are in every bag. We may record a cowidth-q tree decomposition of G as a tree where each vertex is labeled with a bag that is simply S union a subset of $\{v_1, v_2, \ldots, v_r\}$. Two tree decompositions are equivalent if the vertex names $v_1, v_2, \ldots, v_r$ of one decomposition can be permuted so that there is a label-preserving isomorphism between the tree decompositions. This view of tree decompositions has several noteworthy attributes. Two graphs have equivalent tree decompositions only if they have the same cowidth, two graphs with a different number of vertices *can* have equivalent tree decompositions and the number of nonequivalent tree decompositions for cowidth q is easily seen to be finite and a function of q.

Figure 1 shows all the nonequivalent tree decompositions for cowidth 1, 2, and 3; in each case there is only one possible tree (a path), and for cowidth 1 or 2 there is only one decomposition (parts (a) and (b) of the figure, respectively). For cowidth 3 there are two tree decompositions, (parts (c) and (d) of the figure). Figure 2 shows all of the nonequivalent tree decompositions for cowidth 4.

Witnesses. A graph $G = (V, E)$ of cowidth at least 2 has the tree decomposition of Figure 1b. Since a is not in any bag with b, ab must be a nonedge of E. If any graph G has any nonedge ab, then it has the tree decomposition of Figure 1b, and thus has cowidth at least 2. We can summarize this as:

Lemma 1. *A graph has cowidth at least two iff its complement contains an edge.*

The graph consisting of two vertices and one edge (i.e., K_2) is the *2-witness*. The presence of a 2-witness (as a subgraph) in the complement of a graph G bears witness to the fact that G has cowidth at least two (G is a partial $n - 2$ tree). This method works in general: For $\mathcal{T}$ a cowidth-q tree decomposition, let V^* be the set of vertices $v_1, v_2, \ldots v_r$ in some, but not all, the bags of $\mathcal{T}$. Form a graph $W = (V^*, E^*)$ where $v_i v_j \in E^*$ iff there is no bag of the tree decomposition that contains both v_i and v_j. If some graph G has this tree decomposition, then no edge of E^* is in G, or equivalently, W is a subgraph of the complement of G. Conversely, any graph that has W as a subgraph of its complement will have the tree decomposition $\mathcal{T}$. We call W the *witness for* $\mathcal{T}$, and as $\mathcal{T}$ had cowidth q, we also call W a *q-witness*. Since there are a finite number of tree decompositions of cowidth q, there are a finite number of q-witnesses.

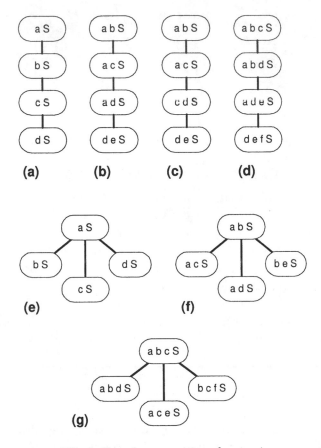

Fig. 2. Tree decompositions for $q = 4$.

Theorem 1. *G has cowidth $\geq q$ iff its complement contains a q-witness.*

Figure 3a and Figure 3b shows the 3-witnesses for the tree decompositions of Figure 1c, and Figure 1d. The 4-witnesses are shown in Figure 4; each subfigure is the witness of the corresponding tree decomposition in Figure 2. Notice that nonequivalent tree decompositions have isomorphic witnesses, (parts (a) and (e), and parts (b) and (f)). A graph whose complement contains such a witness can have either tree decomposition. Isomorphic witnesses are not considered distinct in the class of q-witnesses; thus there are 5 4-witnesses, not 7.

Obstruction complements. A contraction viewed in the complement is a *complement contraction*, or *c-contraction*. Formally, a *c-contraction* of a nonedge uv in H is the graph $H[uv]$ formed by replacing u and v in H by a new vertex $[uv]$ connected to those vertices of H that were connected to *both* u and v. In the complement H of G, the three minor operations on G are: Delete a universal vertex; add an edge to H, and C-Contract an edge of H. The structure of graphs H that is a *k-obstruction complement* is characterized in the next lemma.

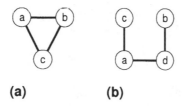

Fig. 3. The two 3-witnesses

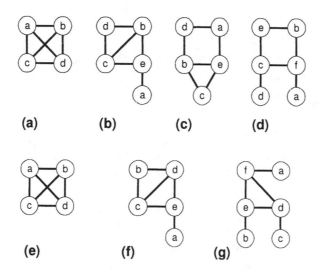

Fig. 4. The 4-witnesses

Lemma 2. *H is a $(n - q)$-obstruction complement iff the following hold:*

(OC1) *H contains no universal vertex.*

(OC2) *H contains no q-witness.*

(OC3) *For every nonedge uv in H, H + uv contains a q-witness.*

(OC4) *For every nonedge uv in H, H[uv] contains a $(q - 1)$-witness.*

There are no n-vertex obstructions for partial $(n - 1)$-trees or for partial $(n-2)$-trees; the only obstruction is the complete graph. The structure of $(n-q)$-obstruction complements for $q \geq 3$ are not so trivial and we focus on $(n - 3)$-obstructions and $(n - 4)$-obstructions for the remainder of the paper.

3 A Characterization of $(k + 3)$-Obstructions

We use our techniques to improve the results of Ramachandramurthi, characterizing and counting the obstructions for partial k-trees of size $k+3$. These are the n vertex minimal graphs with treewidth greater than $n - 3$; hence, their cowidth is 2. We begin by characterizing the graphs with cowidth at most 2 (they do not contain the two 3-witnesses, K_3 and P_3). Recall that a *star* on $n \geq 1$ vertices is the complete bipartite graph $K_{1,n-1}$ (i.e. a tree of diameter at most two). A *star forest* is a forest in which each tree is a star.

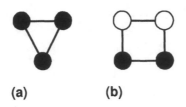

Fig. 5. The 4-witness schemes

Lemma 3. *G is not a partial $(n-3)$-tree iff its complement is a star forest.*

Let $p(n)$ be the number of partitions of the integer n. We can count the number of nonisomorphic graphs on n vertices that are not partial $(n-3)$-trees.

Lemma 4. *There are $p(n)$ nonisomorphic graphs that are not partial $(n-3)$-trees.*

We next consider $(n-3)$-obstructions.

Theorem 2. *A graph H is an $(n-3)$-obstruction complement iff it is a star forest with at least three components and no isolated vertices.*

Ramachandramurthi obtained a direct, but very complicated, characterization of the obstruction primal from which he derived a count of the number of these obstructions, (this involved a triple summation of integer partitions). By counting the complements, we obtain a simple closed-form expression for the number of obstructions, also in terms of integer partitions. ¿From our expression, we can easily derive a slightly better lower bound.

Theorem 3. *The number of obstructions for partial k-trees with $n = k + 3$ vertices is $p(n) - p(n-1) - \lfloor \frac{n}{2} \rfloor$.*

By examining the number of partitions of n that have at most one odd addend, of which there are at least $p(\lfloor \frac{n}{2} \rfloor)$, we can show:

Corollary 3.3a. *For $n \geq 10$, the number of obstructions for partial k-trees on $n = k + 3$ vertices is $\geq p(\lfloor \frac{n}{2} \rfloor)$.*

4 $(k + 4)$-Obstructions

In dealing with complements and witnesses for cowidth 4, it is useful to define *low-degree* as degree 2 or less, and *high-degree* as degree 3 or more.

Working directly with 4-witnesses yields cumbersome case analyses. However, the structure of these witnesses allows us to represent them with the two vertex-colored graphs of Figure 5; we call these the *4-witness schemes*. Each scheme W represents several graphs; W represents graph G if G is a minimal graph containing W such that each black vertex of W has degree 3 in G. For example, the witness scheme of Figure 5a represents the witnesses of Figure 4a,b,g; Figure 5b represents Figure 4a-d. We say that a graph H contains a witness scheme if any of the graphs represented by the scheme is a subgraph of H.

Lemma 5. *Graph H is the complement of a partial $(n-4)$-tree iff it contains a high-degree C_3, or it contains a C_4 with an edge between two high-degree vertices.*

The *girth* of a graph G is the length of the shortest cycle in G.

Corollary 4.3b. *A graph H with girth ≥ 5 is the complement of a graph that is not a partial $(n-4)$-tree.*

Let $H_{\geq 3}$ be the subgraph of H induced by the high-degree vertices.

Corollary 4.3c. *If H is an $(n-4)$-obstruction complement, then $H_{\geq 3}$ has girth at least 5.*

We now check condition (OC3). We assume that H contains no universal vertex and no 4-witness. In H, we call a vertex v *ripe* if it has degree two, and either v forms a triangle with two high-degree vertices, or v is adjacent to a high-degree vertex w and vw is an edge in a 4-cycle of H. (OC3) is satisfied for any edge addition involving a ripe vertex.

Lemma 6. *If H is an $(n-4)$-obstruction complement, then the distance between any two non-ripe vertices in H is at most three.*

Corollary 4.3d. *If H is an $(n-4)$-obstruction complement, then the distance between any two high-degree vertices in H is at most three.*

We consider the $(n-4)$-obstruction complements with no low-degree vertices.

Theorem 4. *For H having minimum degree $\delta \geq 3$, H is an $(n-4)$-obstruction complement iff H has girth at least 5 and diameter at most 3.*

We now consider $(n-4)$-obstruction complements that contain low-degree vertices; in this extended abstract, we make several statements without proof. It is straightforward to show that these obstruction complements contain no degree-zero or degree-one vertices; the low-degree vertices must therefore have degree two. The degree-two vertices of a graph naturally form chains and (isolated) cycles; in $(n-4)$-obstruction complements, isolated cycles cannot exist. Thus, the degree-two vertices form chains. Our analysis of these obstruction complements is based on the length of the longest such chain.

We introduce *angels* a class of graphs that are $(n-4)$-obstruction complements; Figure 6 shows an angel. An angel consists of: a 5-cycle $B = abxyz$, a nonempty set $C = \{c_i\}$ of vertices adjacent to a, a nonempty set $D = \{d_i\}$ of vertices adjacent to b, a set T of degree-two vertices, each adjacent to either a and some c_i, or b and some d_i, and a set U of degree-two vertices, each adjacent to some c_i and some d_j. Furthermore B, C, D, T, and U are pairwise disjoint, every c_i and d_j is adjacent to an element of $T \cup U$, and for every pair (c_i, d_j), the number of common neighbors of c_i and d_j in U is not 1. In Figure 6, the high-degree vertices are shown in black, and ripe vertices in gray.

A *connector* for c_i and d_j is a set of (at least two) common neighbors of c_i and d_j in U, and their incident edges. Although the figure is planar, in general, the graph of connectors between C and D is an arbitrary bipartite graph.

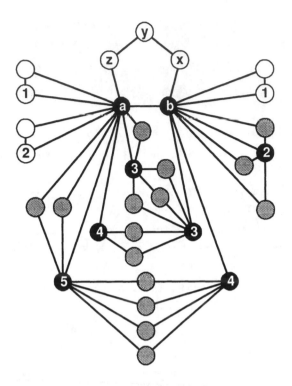

Fig. 6. A sample angel.

Theorem 5. *Let H be a graph containing a path of at least three degree-two vertices. Then H is an $(n-4)$-obstruction complement iff H is an angel.*

Lemma 7. *There are at least n^n nonisomorphic angels having $6n+6$ vertices.*

Theorem 6. *There are $2^{\Omega(k \log k)}$ obstructions for partial k-trees.*

5 Conclusions

In this paper we detailed a new technique for tackling the problem of computing obstructions on partial k-trees, a class that is important both in the graph minors theorem and form an algorithmic point of view. We showed that the complements of partial k-trees have a very rich structure; a complement of size $k+q$ must contain *as a subgraph* one of a finite number of *witness* graphs. For $q=4$, we introduced *witness schemes* that more succinctly describes the witnesses.

We presented a simple proof of a result of Ramachandramurthi [Ram97] that the number of partial k-tree obstructions with $k+3$ vertices is at least $2^{\Omega(\sqrt{k})}$. We obtained a better lower-bound of $2^{\Omega(k \log k)}$ for the number of these obstructions; in terms of integer partitions, we derived a closed-form expression for this number, whereas Ramachandramurthi's expression involved triple summations of integer partitions. We also considered partial k-tree obstructions with $k + 4$ vertices, and used the $q = 4$ witness schemes to show that the number of such obstructions is at least exponential in $k \log k$. More importantly, we gave a simple characterization of the obstructions with $k + q$ vertices, for $q \leq 4$.

We have developed a general procedure for determining witness schemes for any cowidth. The problem is to translate the scheme into obstructions; although witnesses give a method of determining forbidden graphs (i.e., graphs that are not partial k-trees) it is much more difficult to find all the obstructions corresponding to a witness scheme. On the other hand, our schemes seem to exhibit a recursive structure from which obstructions might be obtained.

Finally, we point out that if would be infeasible to actually check for an exponential number of obstructions in practice. However, we believe that it may be possible to, for example, check whether a graph is "one operation" away from containing a witness scheme and thereby perform membership tests quickly.

References

[ACP87] S. Arnborg, D. Corneil, and A. Proskurowski. Complexity of finding embeddings in a k-tree. *SIAM J. of Algebraic and Discrete Methods*, 8:277–284, 1987.

[APC90] S. Arnborg, A. Proskurowski, and D. Corneil. Forbidden minors characterization of partial 3-trees. *Discrete Math*, 80:1–19, 1990.

[Bod96] H.L. Bodlaender. A linear time algorithm for finding tree-decompositions of small treewidth. *SICOMP*, 25:1305–1317, 1996.

[FL88] M. Fellows and M. Langston. Nonconstructive tools for proving polynomial-time decidability. *JACM*, 35(3):727–739, July 1988.

[FL89] M. Fellows and M. Langston. An analogue of the myhill-nerode theorem and its use in computing finite-basis characterizations. In 30th *FOCS*, 802–811, 1989.

[GI97] A. Gupta and R. Impagliazzo. Bounding the size of planar intertwines. *SIAM J. on Discrete Mathematics*, 10(3):337–358, 1997.

[Lag91] J. Lagergren. An upper bound on the size of an obstructions. In N. Robertson and P. Seymour, editors, *Contemporary Mathematics*, volume 147, pages 601–621. American Mathematical Society, 1991.

[Ram97] S. Ramachandramurti. The structure and number of obstructions to treewidth. *Siam J. on Discrete Mathematics*, 10(1):146–157, 1997.

[RS] N. Robertson and P. Seymour. Graph Minors XVI. Wagner's conjecture. submitted.

[San95] D. Sanders. On linear recognition of tree-width at most four. *Siam J. on Discrete Mathematics*, 9(1):101–117, 1995.

[TUK94] A. Takahashi, S. Ueno, and Y. Kajitani. Minimal acyclic forbidden minors for the family of graphs with bounded path-width. *Discrete Mathematics*, 127:293–304, 1994.

Approximation Results for Kinetic Variants of TSP

Mikael Hammar and Bengt J. Nilsson

Department of Computer Science, Lund University,
Box 118, S-221 00 Lund, Sweden
e-mail: {mikael, bengt}@cs.lth.se

Abstract. We study the approximation complexity of certain kinetic variants of the Traveling Salesman Problem where we consider instances in which each point moves with a fixed constant speed in a fixed direction. We prove the following results.

1. If the points all move with the same velocity, then there is a PTAS for the Kinetic TSP.
2. The Kinetic TSP cannot be approximated better than by a factor of two by a polynomial time algorithm unless P=NP, even if there are only two moving points in the instance.
3. The Kinetic TSP cannot be approximated better than by a factor of $2^{\Omega(\sqrt{n})}$ by a polynomial time algorithm unless P=NP, even if the maximum velocity is bounded. The n denotes the size of the input instance.

Especially the last result is surprising in the light of existing polynomial time approximation schemes for the static version of the problem.

1 Introduction

Consider a cat in a field with an ample supply of mice. The cat's objective is to catch all the mice while exerting the minimum amount of energy. The cat therefore wishes to use the shortest possible path to chase the mice. A major difficulty is the fact that the mice are moving. This problem is an instance of the *Kinetic Traveling Salesman Problem*.

The *Traveling Salesman Problem*, TSP for short, is probably the best known intractable problem. It asks for the shortest closed tour that visits the nodes in a given weighted complete graph exactly once. This deceptively simple problem lies at the heart of combinatorial optimization and it has spawned a wealth of research in complexity theory and operations research; see Lawler et al. [7].

In the kinetic traveling salesman problem, we look at TSP for moving points in the Euclidean plane. We consider instances in which each point moves with a fixed velocity. This is a natural and both theoretically and practically important generalization of TSP (e.g. several scheduling problems can be reduced to solving variants of kinetic TSP). The complexity status of the problem, especially with respect to approximation, is a paradigmatic question. Helvig, Robins and Zelikovsky [6] give a polynomial time algorithm to solve the problem when the moving points are restricted to lie on the real line. They also give a $2 + \epsilon$-approximation algorithm for the Kinetic TSP if the number of points with non-zero speed is small. We prove the following results.

1. If the points all move with the same speed and in the same direction, then there is a PTAS for the Kinetic TSP. This generalizes the result of Chalasani et al. [3, 4].
2. The Kinetic TSP cannot be approximated better than by a factor of two by a polynomial time algorithm unless P=NP, even if there are only two moving points in the instance.
3. The Kinetic TSP cannot be approximated better than by a factor of $2^{\Omega(\sqrt{n})}$ by a polynomial time algorithm unless P=NP, even if the maximum speed is bounded. The n denotes the size of the input instance.

Especially the last result is surprising in the light of existing polynomial time approximation schemes [1, 2, 8, 9] for the static version of the problem.

In the next section, we state definitions and give preliminary results concerning Kinetic TSP. Specifically, we give an overview of the original reduction of Garey et al. [5] proving the NP-hardness of the Euclidean TSP, since it plays an important role in our later reductions. In Section 3, we prove the existence of a PTAS for the case when all points move with the same speed in the same direction. In Sections 4 and 5, we prove the stated inapproximability results and we conclude the presentation with a discussion of open problems.

2   Preliminaries and Notation

In the *Euclidean Traveling Salesman Problem* we are given a set of points $S = \{s_1, s_2, \ldots, s_n\}$ in the Euclidean plane. The objective is to compute the shortest tour that visits all points. The Euclidean *Minimum Hamiltonian path Problem*, MHP, is the problem of finding a shortest path that visits all points of S, starting at s_1 and ending at s_n.

As Chalasani et al. [4] we distinguish between *space-points* and *moving points*. A space-point is a point in a coordinate system, whereas a moving point is a point-object in space, the Euclidean plane in our case, that travels with a given velocity. The coordinates of a moving point s can be described by the function $s(t) = (x + tv\cos\alpha, y + tv\sin\alpha)$, where $v \geq 0$ is the point's speed and α is its direction. If $v = 0$ we say that the point is static. The *traveling salesman* is described by a special point that can move with variable speed and direction. The initial position s_0 of the salesman is assumed to be $(0, 0)$ and its maximal speed is assumed to be 1. The path taken by the salesman is denoted P and $P(t)$ is the position of the salesman at time t. If $P(t) = s(t)$ then we say that the salesman *visits* s at time t. P is called a *salesman path* of S if all points in S have been visited by the salesman. If the salesman also returns to its initial position, then we call the resulting tour a *salesman tour*.

We can now define the kinetic traveling salesman problem for moving points in the plane.

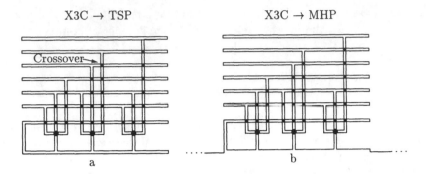

Fig. 1. Typical instances produced by the X3C reduction.

Definition 1. *A set of moving points* $S(t) = \{s_1(t), s_2(t), \ldots, s_n(t)\}$ *in the plane with the Euclidean metric is given. A point* $s_i(t)$ *in* $S(t)$ *moves with the speed* $v_i < 1$. *The objective of the* Kinetic *Traveling Salesman Problem (KTSP) is to compute a salesman tour, starting and ending at the initial point* $s_0 = (0,0)$, *that minimizes the traveling time. The* Translational *Traveling Salesman Problem (TTSP) is a restricted version of KTSP, where all points of* S *have the same speed and direction.*

The following lemma provides an important fact concerning the speed of the salesman.

Lemma 1. *An optimal salesman moves with maximal speed.*

From now on we assume that the salesman travels with maximal speed and since the maximal speed is 1, there is no difference between the distance travelled and the traveling time.

Generally, we use OPT to denote a shortest tour or path, unless more specific notation is needed. Given a tour or a path P in the Euclidean plane, we let $\mathcal{C}(P)$ denote the length of P.

Garey et al. [5] prove that the Euclidean traveling salesman problem is NP-hard by a reduction from the problem *exact cover by 3-sets*, X3C:

Given a family $\mathcal{F} = \{F_1, F_2, \ldots, F_r\}$ of 3-element subsets of a set U of $3k$ elements, does there exist a subfamily $\mathcal{F}' \subseteq \mathcal{F}$ of pairwise disjoint sets such that $\bigcup_{F \in \mathcal{F}'} F = U$?

If there exists such a subfamily for $\mathcal{F}$ then we say that $\mathcal{F} \in X3C$, otherwise we say that $\mathcal{F} \notin X3C$.

Let S be an instance of TSP produced by Garey et al.'s reduction, such that $|S| = n$. The points of S lie on a unit grid G of size less that $n \times n$ and a naive tour visiting all points of S has length $l < 2n$. These results follow directly from Garey et al.'s construction. Figure 1a is a schematic overview of a TSP-instance produced by the reduction. Each line segment in the figure represents a set of points on a line such that the distance between a point and its successor is one unit.

Garey et al. prove that the length of OPT is less or equal to some specific value L^* if and only if an exact cover exists for the X3C-instance. Their construction also makes sure that an optimal tour has integral length. Thus, if there is no exact cover, then OPT has at least the length $L^* + 1$. Out of this fact the following lemma follows directly.

Lemma 2. *There is no polynomial time approximation algorithm for TSP producing a tour APX such that $C(APX) < C(OPT) + 1$ unless $P = NP$.*

The lemma holds also for the minimum Hamiltonian path problem, since the reduction of Garey et al. also works for that problem. In this case, the reduction from X3C results in instances of the type in Figure 1b, where we have opened the bottom tube. Observe that the length of the minimum Hamiltonian path in Figure 1b is equal to the length of the corresponding minimum traveling salesman tour in Figure 1a. Instances produced by the X3C reduction will from now on be called *GGJ-instances*.

3   A PTAS for TTSP

Let us start this section by analyzing the translational MHP. A set $S(t) = \{s_1(t), \ldots, s_n(t)\}$ of moving points is given together with a starting point $s_0 = (0,0)$. All points move in the same direction α and with the same speed v. We can assume, w. l. o. g., that $\alpha = \frac{\pi}{2}$. Thus a point $s_i(t)$ is defined as

$$s_i(t) = (x + tv \cos \frac{\pi}{2}, y + tv \sin \frac{\pi}{2}) = (x, y + tv).$$

The traveling distance c_{ij} between two points $s_i(t)$ and $s_j(t)$ is the time needed by a salesman, moving with speed 1, to travel from s_i to s_j, i.e.

$$c_{ij} = \frac{v}{1-v^2}(y_j - y_i) + \sqrt{\frac{(x_j - x_i)^2}{1-v^2} + \frac{(y_j - y_i)^2}{(1-v^2)^2}}$$

Note that the traveling distance is independent of time and that the cost function c_{ij} is asymmetric. Consider the function

$$d(s_i, s_j) = \frac{c_{ij} + c_{ji}}{2} = \sqrt{\frac{(x_j - x_i)^2}{1-v^2} + \frac{(y_j - y_i)^2}{(1-v^2)^2}}$$

and the bijective mapping $f_v(s)$ from a moving point $s = (x, y)$ to a static point in the Euclidean plane:

$$f_v(s) = \left(\frac{x}{\sqrt{1-v^2}}, \frac{y}{1-v^2} \right)$$

Let $P = (s_{i_1}, \ldots, s_{i_n})$ be a path in the translational instance, then $C(P) = \sum_{k=1}^{n-1} c_{i_k, i_{k+1}} = \frac{v(y_{i_n} - y_{i_1})}{1-v^2} + \sum_{k=1}^{n-1} d(s_{i_k}, s_{i_{k+1}})$ by simple calculations. With this it is easy to prove the following result.

Lemma 3. *Let S_T be an instance of the translational MHP with specified starting and endpoint, and let S_E be the corresponding Euclidean instance after the transformation using f_v. A salesman path in S_T is optimal if and only if the corresponding Euclidean Hamiltonian path in S_E is optimal.*

Proof. Let $P = (s_{i_1}, \ldots, s_{i_n})$ denote a salesman path in S_T and let P' denote the corresponding Hamiltonian path in S_E. Observe that $\mathcal{C}(P') = \sum_{j=1}^{n-1} d(s_{i_j}, s_{i_{j+1}})$. Therefore, $\mathcal{C}(P) = \mathcal{C}(P') + \frac{v(y_{i_n} - y_{i_1})}{1 - v^2}$. Note that the last term is fixed since both the starting point and the endpoint were given. It follows that P is optimal if and only if P' is optimal. $\qquad\square$

Consider an arbitrary instance of the translational MHP with specified starting point s_0 and ending point s_n. We can transform this instance into an instance of the Euclidean MHP using the bijective mapping f_v. Given this new instance, we compute a Hamiltonian path APX_E such that $\mathcal{C}(APX_E) \leq (1+\epsilon)\mathcal{C}(OPT_E)$, using a PTAS for the Euclidean MHP problem. Such schemes can be constructed by modifying any PTAS for the Euclidean TSP [1, 2, 8, 9]. Here OPT_E denotes a minimal Hamiltonian path in the Euclidean instance. Let APX_T and OPT_T denote the corresponding paths in the translational MHP-instance. Observe that OPT_T is an optimal salesman path by Lemma 3. We have

$$\mathcal{C}(APX_T) = \frac{v(y_n - y_1)}{1 - v^2} + \mathcal{C}(APX_E) \tag{1}$$

$$\leq \frac{v(y_n - y_1)}{1 - v^2} + (1 + \epsilon)\mathcal{C}(OPT_E) \tag{2}$$

$$= \mathcal{C}(OPT_T) + \epsilon\mathcal{C}(OPT_E) \tag{3}$$

$$\leq (1 + \frac{\epsilon}{1 - v})\mathcal{C}(OPT_T).$$

The last inequality holds since OPT_T is at least as long as the shortest path between s_1 and s_n, i.e. $\mathcal{C}(OPT_T) \geq \frac{|y_n - y_1|}{1 + v}$. Hence,

$$\mathcal{C}(OPT_E) = \mathcal{C}(OPT_T) - \frac{v(y_n - y_1)}{1 - v^2} \leq \mathcal{C}(OPT_T) + \frac{v|y_n - y_1|}{(1 - v)(1 + v)}$$

$$\leq \mathcal{C}(OPT_T) + \frac{v\mathcal{C}(OPT_T)}{1 - v} = \frac{\mathcal{C}(OPT_T)}{1 - v}.$$

It follows that APX_T is a $(1 + \frac{\epsilon}{1-v})$-approximation of the optimal path. Thus, we have a PTAS for the translational MHP.

With this approximation scheme we can now give a PTAS for the translational TSP. We use the same approach as Chalasani et al. [3, 4]. The difficulty of the translational TSP is that the initial point s_0, is not moving, which creates an asymmetry that we must be able to handle. Assume that $P = (s_0, s_1(t), \ldots, s_n(t), s_0)$ is an optimal salesman tour. It follows easily that the optimal salesman path starting from s_0 and ending at $s_n(t)$ is a part of that tour. For each possible such ending point $s_i(t)$, $i \geq 1$, we compute a $(1 + \frac{\epsilon}{2(1-v)})$-approximate salesman path. This gives us n paths that can easily be turned into salesman tours. The algorithm returns the shortest of these tours.

Theorem 1. *The algorithm described above is a PTAS for the translational TSP.*

Proof. Let OPT_H denote the length of the optimal salesman path, starting from s_0 and ending at $s_i(t)$. The length of the optimal salesman tour P is $C(P) = OPT_H + l$, assuming s_i is the last moving point visited by the tour P and l is the length of the last segment in the tour (between the points $s_i(t)$ and s_0). There is a tour P' among the tours our algorithm computes, that also has $s_i(t)$ as the last unvisited point. The length of P' is $C(P') = (1 + \frac{\epsilon}{2(1-v)})OPT_H + l'$, where l' is the length between $s_i(t)$ and s_0. A salesman that travels along P' visits $s_i(t)$ at time $t = (1 + \frac{\epsilon}{2(1-v)})OPT_H$, whereas the optimal salesman visits $s_i(t)$ at time $t = OPT_H$. The time difference is $\frac{\epsilon}{2(1-v)}OPT_H$ and in that time period, $s_i(t)$ moves the length $\frac{v\epsilon}{2(1-v)}OPT_H$. The triangle inequality assures us that l' does not exceed $l + \frac{v\epsilon}{2(1-v)}OPT_H$. The cost of our approximate tour is thus $C(P') \leq (1 + \frac{\epsilon}{2(1-v)})OPT_H + l + \frac{v\epsilon}{2(1-v)}OPT_H = (1 + \frac{(1+v)\epsilon}{2(1-v)})OPT_H + l < (1 + \frac{\epsilon}{1-v})OPT_H + l$. The last inequality holds since the speed does not exceed 1. The ratio between the costs of P and P' becomes

$$\frac{C(P')}{C(P)} < \frac{(1 + \frac{\epsilon}{1-v})OPT_H + l}{OPT_H + l} \leq (1 + \frac{\epsilon}{1-v}).$$

The proof is completed, since the cost of the returned salesman tour does not exceed that of P'. □

Observe that our technique differs from that of Chalasani et al. [4] only in the bijective mapping f_v with which the transformation was performed. Thanks to this mapping we were able to generalize their result. If the speeds are bounded by a constant, then the algorithm is a true PTAS.

4 Two Reductions for KTSP

The kinetic traveling salesman problem is in general not as easily approximated as the translational TSP. Helvig, Robins and Zelikovsky [6] give a $2 + \epsilon$-approximation algorithm for kinetic TSP-instances with n points of which $O(\frac{\log n}{\log \log n})$ are moving. The simple construction described in Figure 2 shows that their algorithm is close to optimal.

The figure contains a GGJ-instance, chosen as Type a in Figure 1, at distance D from the origin and two moving points p_1 and p_2, both with speed $v < 1$. We assume that the salesman starts at the origin at time $t = 0$. The point p_1 moves horizontally and lies at the same altitude as the bottom line of the GGJ-instance and intersects the line l at time D. Point p_2 moves parallel to p_1 and reaches the origin at time $2D + L^*$. Recall that a GGJ-instance is constructed so that if $\mathcal{F} \in X3C$, then an optimal salesman tour is at most L^* long. Otherwise the length is at least $L^* + 1$.

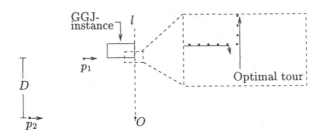

Fig. 2. Kinetic TSP-instance with two moving points.

Because of the large speed of the moving points, it follows that the first point to be visited is p_1 and that p_2 is visited before that point reaches the origin. Otherwise, the tour has unbounded length.

If $\mathcal{F} \in X3C$, then an optimal salesman can catch p_1, continue along the GGJ-instance's optimal salesman tour and still has time to catch p_2 before it reaches the origin.

If $\mathcal{F} \notin X3C$, then an optimal salesman does not have time to catch all the points in the GGJ-instance before he has to turn back and catch p_2. This means that he must traverse the distance D at least four times. From this we get:

Theorem 2. *It is NP-Hard to get an approximation ratio less than 2 for the kinetic TSP, even if there are only two moving points in the instance.*

In Theorem 2 we assume that the speed v can be arbitrarily close to 1. With more moving points we can restrict the speed to $v = 1/2$ and still get a lower bound of 2 on the approximation ratio. We claim the following theorem.

Theorem 3. *It is NP-Hard to get an approximation ratio less than 2 for the kinetic TSP, even if the speed of the moving points is restricted to $v = 1/2$.*

5 Exponential Inapproximation of KTSP

In this section, we present a gap producing reduction from X3C to the kinetic TSP. First, we give a description of the KTSP-instance that we use in the reduction. The KTSP-instance is a uniformly expanding instance. A uniformly expanding instance contains moving points of the form $s_i(t) = (v_i t \cos \alpha, v_i t \sin \alpha)$. This implies that at time $t = 0$ all points are located at the origin and that the relative distances within the instance do not change over time. To make the construction work, we assume that the salesman begins his pursuit at time $t_0 > 0$ (if he starts at time $t = 0$, he visits all points at once, without moving). Observe that salesman tours in uniformly expanding TSP-instances are in a sense symmetric. Consider namely a salesman tour P. If we reverse the order in which the points are visited, the length of the new tour is equal to the length of P.

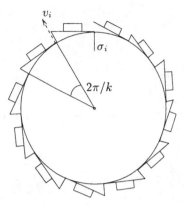

Fig. 3. One circle of the inapproximable KTSP-instance.

The KTSP-instance consists of l circles $C_1, \ldots, C_l$, with radii $r_1, r_2, \ldots, r_l$. Each circle consists of $k = \lceil 9\pi l \rceil$ small expanding identical GGJ-instances produced by the X3C-reduction of Garey et al. The GGJ-instances are placed on the circles as shown in Figure 3. A sequence of evenly distributed points is placed along the line segment between the rightmost point and the leftmost point of the previous GGJ-instance. The spacing of these points equals the spacing of the points along the bottom line segment of the GGJ-instance. At the topmost GGJ-instance's rightmost point we let the sequence of points point towards the origin. Let σ_i denote this special sequence on circle C_i; see Figure 3.

Each GGJ-instance initially contains m points but we have extended the bottom line of the GGJ-instances with $5m$ points on each side; see Figure 4. Thus, each GGJ-instance consists of $11m$ moving points. We let $l = (11m)^a$, for some $a > 1$. The number of points between consecutive GGJ-instances is less than m, if $k > 35$. On the special sequences σ_i we place $5m$ points for technical reasons. The total number of points in the instance, denoted n, is therefore between $12mkl$ and $14mkl$, for large k and l. The rightmost point of a GGJ-instance is placed on the circle and the bottom line of the GGJ-instance follows the circle's tangent line at that point. Each circle C_i is expanding with a speed v_i, i.e. the rightmost point of each GGJ-instance on C_i has a speed v_i, directed away from the center and the radius of C_i is $r_i = v_i t$.

We let $v_1 = \frac{1}{2e}$ and $v_i = (1 + \frac{9\pi}{k})v_{i-1}$. This implies that the largest circle's speed, v_l, is bounded by $v_l = (1 + \frac{9\pi}{k})^l v_1 = (1 + \frac{1}{l})^l v_1 < ev_1 = \frac{1}{2}$. Hence, $r_1 \leq r_2 \leq \ldots \leq r_l$. Observe that the GGJ-instances are uniformly expanding, i.e. the distance between two points s_i and s_j is $d(s_i, s_j) = d_{ij}t$, where d_{ij} is constant. The expansion rate is such that the distance between the leftmost and the rightmost point is $tv_i \tan \frac{2\pi}{k}$. Therefore, we let $u_i = v_i \tan \frac{2\pi}{k}$ define the expansion rate; see Figure 4. The fastest point of a GGJ-instance is the leftmost point and this point has the speed $\sqrt{v_i^2 + (v_i \tan \frac{2\pi}{k})^2} \leq v_i(1 + \frac{2\pi}{k})$. Thus, no

Fig. 4. A small expanding GGJ-instance.

point belonging to circle C_i has a speed exceeding $v_i(1 + \frac{2\pi}{k})$, which implies that the maximal speed is bounded.

From now on we simply denote our newly constructed instance the *KTSP-instance*.

Theorem 4. *For every $\gamma > 0$, there exists no polynomial-time algorithm that achieves an approximation ratio of $2^{\Omega(n^{1/2-\gamma})}$ for the kinetic traveling salesman problem.*

Proof. (Sketch) Given the detailed description of the KTSP-instance, we can prove that any optimal salesman visits the GGJ-instances circlewise, one at a time. Furthermore, the time it takes to go from any moving point s_i to any other moving point s_j in the KTSP-instance, depends linearly on the starting time, i.e. assuming that a salesman starts at s_i at time t, it would take him time $\kappa_{ij}t$ to go to s_j, where κ_{ij} is constant. The implication of this is that if a salesman starts at the rightmost point of a GGJ-instance at time t, then it would take him time Kt to visit all points in the instance and move to the rightmost point of the next GGJ-instance in the KTSP-instance. Observe that K is independent of t. From this we can draw the conclusion that the optimal tour in a small expanding GGJ-instance is independent on the starting time. Since we know that an optimal salesman visits the points in the KTSP-instance circlewise, one at a time, it is not too difficult to see that it would take him time $CK^{kl}t_0$ to visit all points in the KTSP-instance, assuming that he begins at the origin at time t_0. Here C is a constant that comes from the salesmans leaps between circles.

We can show that if $\mathcal{F} \in X3C$, then $K \leq L$ for some L and if $\mathcal{F} \notin X3C$, then $K > (1 + \frac{1}{11km})L$.

Since the expanding GGJ-instances are identical, the inapproximability ratio becomes

$$\frac{CL^{kl}(1 + \frac{1}{11km})^{kl}}{CL^{kl}} \in 2^{\Omega(n^{1/2-\gamma})}$$

$\square$

6 Conclusions

We have investigated kinetic variants of TSP. Our major result proves an exponential lower bound on the approximation factor for such problems unless P=NP even when the velocities are bounded. Even so, we feel that the bound is coarse and can probably be improved. Also, the question of good upper bounds on the approximation ratio comes to mind.

The use of the mapping f_v described in Section 3 is actually a generic method that can be used to solve a large class of tour problems when instances perform constant translational movement in time.

The translational TSP PTAS that we present can be used in an $O(1)$-approximation algorithm for KTSP, assuming that the number of different velocities of the instances is bounded by a constant and that the maximum velocity of the instances considered is bounded.

References

1. S. Arora. Polynomial time approximation schemes for Euclidean TSP and other geometric problems. In *Proc. 37th Annual Symposium on Foundations of Computer Science (FOCS)*, pages 2–11, 1996.
2. S. Arora. Polynomial time approximation schemes for Euclidean TSP and other geometric problems. Manuscript, 1997.
3. P. Chalasani and R. Motwani. Approximating capacitated routing and delivery problems. Technical Report STAN-CS-TN-95-24, Department of Computer Science, Stanford University, 1995.
4. P. Chalasani, R. Motwani, and A. Rao. Approximation algorithms for robot grasp and delivery. In *Proceedings of the 2nd International Workshop on Algorithmic Foundations of Robotics*, pages 347–362, 1996.
5. M. R. Garey, R. L. Graham, and D. S. Johnson. Some NP-complete geometric problems. In *Proc. 8th Annual ACM Symposium on Theory of Computing*, pages 10–21, 1976.
6. C. S. Helvig, G. Robins, and A. Zelikovsky. Moving-target TSP and related problems. In *Proc. 6th Annual European Symposium on Algorithms (ESA)*, 1998.
7. E. L. Lawler, J. K. Lenstra, A. H. G. Rinnooy Kan, and D. B. Shmoys. *The TRAVELING SALESMAN PROBLEM, A Guided Tour of Combinatorial Optimization.* John Wiley & Sons Ltd., 1985.
8. J. S. B. Mitchell. Guillotine subdivisions approximate polygonal subdivisions: Part II – a simple polynomial-time approximation scheme for geometric TSP, k-MST, and related problems. To appear in SIAM J. Computing.
9. S. B. Rao and W. D. Smith. Approximating geometrical graphs via "spanners" and "banyans". In *STOC*, pages 540–550, 1998.

Distributed Probabilistic Polling
and Applications to Proportionate Agreement

Yehuda Hassin and David Peleg*

Department of Applied Mathematics and Computer Science, The Weizmann Institute of Science, Rehovot, 76100 Israel. {hassin,peleg}@wisdom.weizmann.ac.il.

Abstract. This paper considers a probabilistic local polling process, examines its properties and proposes its use in the context of distributed network protocols for achieving consensus. The resulting consensus algorithm is very simple and light-weight, yet it enjoys some desirable properties, such as proportionate agreement (namely, reaching a consensus value of one with probability proportional to the number of ones in the inputs), resilience against dynamic link failures and recoveries, and (weak) self-stabilization.

1 Introduction

1.1 Motivation

Distributed algorithms can be loosely classified into two categories whose formal definition turns out to be rather elusive, but whose behavior has distinctly different characteristics. For lack of a better name, let us refer to those classes as *light-weight* (or *fuzzy*) vs. *heavy-weight* (or *structured*) algorithms.

The first category contains complex algorithms based on involved procedures, which must be performed in some precise and nontrivial order. Their correct execution depends on intricate interrelationships between the individual actions taken by many remote processors. This category includes a variety of algorithms for tree constructions, leader election, consensus, resource allocations and more.

The opposite category of "light-weight" fuzzy algorithms consists of algorithms based on a small number of simple local operations, which are performed periodically and in the same way at all processors. The success of the algorithm thus relies only on the (possibly slow) convergence of the global process induced by these local actions.

While light-weight processes are less "focused" and slower to converge to their desired output, they have certain significant advantages. The main two advantages, which seem to be surprisingly hard to capture formally or quantify, can be described as *ease of use* and *inherent resilience*.

By "inherent resilience" we attempt to capture the following key element: in a very large system, complex algorithms which heavily rely on each processor

---

* Supported in part by a grant from the Israel Science Foundation and by a grant from the Israel Ministry of Science and Art.

performing its task precisely and in tight coordination with its colleagues, are doomed to fail, whereas a global convergence process based on simple repetitive actions of the processors has better failure resilience. Indeed observe that many natural (be it physical, chemical or biological) processes operate in this light-weight and fuzzy manner, which seems to make them less sensitive to "noise" or transient local failures.

This paper focuses on the study of a light-weight repetitive *probabilistic polling* process on networks. The process can be described as follows. Consider a weighted graph G, whose vertices are initially colored black or white. The process proceeds in synchronous rounds. In each round, each vertex recolors itself synchronously according to the colors of its neighbors. There are many different possible rules for the recoloring, such as majority, averaging and so on. Here we concentrate on a *probabilistic* rule, by which each vertex chooses at random one neighbor (with probability dependent on the edge weights) and adopts its color. This process seems to be natural and very basic, and we are interested in its behavior, fundamental properties, and performance guarantees.

Our interest in this process is twofold. From a graph-theoretical point of view, this process is relevant to the problem of estimating the potential influence of small coalitions of vertices in graphs. Specifically, the paper addresses the question of the probability to end up in the all-white state, for any given graph and initial coloring.

The second reason for our interest in the polling process stems from our interest in exploring the possibility of exploiting such a process as a light-weight alternative to various heavy-weight and structured *consensus* protocols (cf. [L95,AW98]), especially under benign fault models.

The consensus problem [LSM82] involves helping a group of processors starting with different views to converge to a common opinion. In a simplified model where an opinion comprises a single bit, this goal can be rephrased as follows: starting with an arbitrary assignment of 0/1 bits to the vertices, ensure that the vertices converge into an identical output bit. Identifying 0/1 bits with W/B colors, the above polling process can be interpreted as a consensus algorithm, whose appropriateness depends to some extent on its convergence properties.

Consensus protocols are typically required to function correctly under various fault models, including malicious ones, where some processors are assumed to be corrupt and deliberately play against the rules of the protocol. The probabilistic polling process seems to be too weak to handle such "byzantine" behavior. Nevertheless, we show that it is sufficiently robust to function well in the setting of a *dynamic network*, in which links may disconnect and revive from time to time (cf. [AAG87]). This model subsumes also some benign node-fault models, such as the "omission" and "fail-stop" models.

There are marked differences between the polling process and other approaches to reaching consensus. On the negative side, the process is much slower to converge than other (structured) consensus algorithms. Another notable weakness of the polling process is the lack of termination detection.

On the positive side, the probabilistic polling process is in fact suitable for solving a "repetitive" variant of the consensus problem, in which the variables are occasionally changed by failures or other external forces, and the process must repeatedly bring the system back to a monochromatic view. Put another way, this process is "self-stabilizing" in a weak sense, i.e., assuming an adversary is allowed to arbitrarily change the colors of some of the nodes, the process will eventually converge back to a monochromatic state, albeit not necessarily to the original one.

Another advantage of the probabilistic polling process is what may be called *proportionate agreement*. Since consensus protocols are geared at leading the vertices from disagreement to a common opinion, there are many natural situations in which it may be desirable that the final common opinion faithfully represents the initial opinions of the participants. This property is indeed reflected, under a rather liberal interpretation, in the formal statement of the consensus problem. This is done by including the so-called "non-triviality" or "validity" property, which requires that if the initial input bit of *all* vertices is zero (respectively, one), then the final decision must be the same. However, this is an extremely weak form of reflecting the initial opinions. *Proportionate agreement* is fairly stronger property, requiring that the final consensus value is zero or one with probability based on their proportion in the initial inputs.

In fact, we formulate and use a slightly stronger variant of this property, which applies in a model where different processors have different *reliability* levels. Each processor is assigned a weight representing its reliability level, which yields a node-weighted version of proportionate agreement, in which the output should reflect the opinions of different processors in proportion to their reliability level. It turns out that a proper selection of the parameters of the probabilistic polling protocol will ensure proportionate agreement.

Finally, note that the probabilistic polling process does not require the use of processor Ids or any data structures (although certain global knowledge is needed, in particular, an upper bound on the degree-to-reliability ratio of the nodes), hence it can be operated in an anonymous network setting, in which some algorithms for the standard consensus problem fail to operate.

Now, it should be made clear that some of those desirable properties can be achieved also by a standard structured protocol, using techniques such as BFS tree construction and broadcast and convergecast operations on trees (enabling proportionate agreement via direct counting), coupled with compilers designed to transform static network protocols into ones designed for dynamic networks [AAG87], or non-self-stabilizing protocols into self-stabilizing ones [AD97,KP97]. However, as explained earlier, the outcome of a design based on a combination of these formidable techniques would very likely be a cumbersome algorithm which will be hard to program and maintain, as well as resource-expensive. Hence our interest in light-weight methods is well-justified even assuming that heavy-weight algorithms with identical properties can be constructed.

1.2 Previous Work

Processes of similar nature to our probabilistic polling can model the influence and flow of information in a variety of different environments, such as societies, genetic processes and distributed multiprocessor systems. In all of those cases, it is interesting to understand how the local rules used by the individual participants affect the global behavior of the system. Indeed, discrete influence systems of this type were studied in areas such as social influence [H59,F56,D74] and neural networks [GO80,GFP85,PS83]. In biological and physical systems the prevailing interpretation is that nature operates on the basis of micro rules which cause the macro behavior observed from outside the system.

Some combinatorial questions were studied as well in some of the models, concerning the power of small sets. Much of the research in this area concentrated on the deterministic model with the majority rule (i.e., where each node of the graph recolors itself in each round by the color currently appearing at the majority of its neighbors), and in fact, on the special case of the static (single round) process [LPRS93,BBPP96]. A survey of this subject can be found in [P96]. The dynamic, synchronous, deterministic majority-based version of the process was studied in [GO80,PS83,P96a,GFP85].

Some related results concern a probabilistic asynchronous model called the *voter model*, introduced by [HL75]. This is a continuous time Markov process with a state space consisting of all the 2-colorings of V. The process evolves according to the following mechanism. Attached to each vertex is a clock which rings at an exponentially distributed (unit) rate independently of all other clocks. When its clock rings, the vertex chooses a neighbor at random and adopts its color. This process was extensively studied in infinite grid graphs [HL75], and the model for arbitrary finite connected graphs is studied in [DW83].

1.3 Our Results

In Section 2 we introduce the model formally, analyze the underlying Markov chain and prove our main theorem, establishing that the probability of the process ending in the all-white state is proportional to the sum of the edge weights of the initially colored white nodes. In the special unweighted case, this probability is $\sum_{i \in W} \frac{d_i}{2m}$, where m is the number of edges, W is the set of nodes initially colored white and d_i is the degree of node i. The theorem is generalized also to processes on graphs with multiple colors (instead of two).

Then, Section 3 deals with applying the polling process in the context of distributed computing. We use the main theorem to construct an algorithm for a variant of the consensus problem, in the dynamic network model, with the additional property of proportionate agreement.

2 Convergence probabilities of the polling process

This section introduces the model formally, and states the main theorem concerning the probability of ending up in the all-white state. The probabilistic model is just a finite Markov chain, where the probability to move to another state is the product of the probabilities of each node transition (since choosing a neighbor at random is done independently of the choices made by other nodes). A useful property of the model is that the chain always ends in a monochromatic fixed point, and the main theorem calculates the probability to end up in the all-white fixed point.

2.1 Definition of the Model

Every node in a connected non-bipartite undirected graph $G = (V, E)$ is initially colored white or black, or assigned value '1' or '0' respectively. The set of neighbors of node i, denoted $\Gamma(i)$, consists of all nodes j such that $(i, j) \in E$. For simplicity it is assumed (at this stage) that the graph contains no self loops. The sizes of the sets V, E and $\Gamma(i)$ are denoted n, m and d_i respectively. The system has an associated weight matrix $H = (h_{ij})$, labeling each edge $e = (i, j)$ by a directional weight $h_{ij} > 0$, such that $\sum_{j \in \Gamma(i)} h_{ij} = 1$ (i.e., H is stochastic).

Our work focuses on the discrete time synchronous model, i.e., it is assumed that there exists a global clock providing the processors in the system with discrete points in time, $0, 1, 2, \ldots$. Processors act simultaneously at time t, and the state of each processor v at time $t + 1$ is determined on the basis of the actions of the processors in v's neighborhood (including v itself) at time t. In particular, in each round t, every node i chooses randomly a neighbor, with the probability of choosing j set to the weight h_{ij}, and recolors itself with j's color.

Our coloring process can be formally described as follows. For integer $t \geq 0$, let $S_t = (S_t^1, \ldots, S_t^n)$ be an n-bit random variable representing the global state of the process at time t, where S_t^i, the ith bit of S_t, is defined as

$$S_t^i = \begin{cases} 1, \text{ if node } i \text{ has value 1 at time } t, \\ 0, \text{ if node } i \text{ has value 0 at time } t, \end{cases}$$

(We use S to denote a random variable, representing the state of the process, and lower-case s, a, b, to denote an actual state in the state space S. Specifically, we always denote the initial coloring/state by s. We focus our attention on two special states, namely, the all-ones state denoted **1** and the all-zeros state denoted **0**.) The transition from S_t to the next state, S_{t+1}, is thus performed by setting S_{t+1}^i to be S_t^j with probability h_{ij}, for every i. This transition occurs simultaneously at all nodes, i.e., the process is synchronous.

The process defined by the weight matrix H is in fact a Markov chain which we denote by $\mathcal{M}_H = \mathcal{M}_H(G)$. Every state of the chain is of the form $a = (a^1, \ldots, a^n)$, where $a^i \in \{0, 1\}$ is the value/color of node i. The set of nodes colored white (resp. black) in the state a is denoted W_a (resp. B_a).

Recall (cf. [MR95] p.129-133) that for a connected, non-bipartite G and such a stochastic matrix H there is a unique stationary distribution π_H, meaning that $\sum_{i=1}^n \pi_H(i) = 1$ and $\pi_H \cdot H = \pi_H$. For the process state $S_t \in \{0, 1\}^n$, we define the random variable $\pi_H(S_t) = \sum_{i=1}^n \pi_H(i) \cdot S_t^i$. For any random variable Z define $\mathbb{E}_s(Z)$ to be $\mathbb{E}(Z \mid S_0 = s)$.

2.2 Absorption probability to the all-white state

In this section we prove the main theorem, concerning the probability $\rho_{s1}(G)$ of the process $\mathcal{M}_H(G)$ reaching the all-white state when starting with initial coloring s.[1]

The first lemma classifies the state space of $\mathcal{M}_H$. (Proofs are deferred to the full paper.)

Lemma 1. *In the chain $\mathcal{M}_H$, there are only two absorbing states $\{1,0\}$; All other states are transient.*

Note that if the graph is bipartite, then there is another absorbing state.

Our analysis is based on the following idea. Whenever a Markov chain on states $\{0, \ldots, n\}$ has exactly two absorbing states, 0 and n, the expectation of the process state is easy to compute. Since all other states are transient, the expectation as time goes to infinity is just $pn + (1 - p)0 = np$, where p is the probability of being absorbed to n. But sometimes the expectation of a random variable associated with a Markov chain can be calculated directly. This happens, in particular, if the variable is a *Martingale* (see [F66] p. 399), whose expectation stays constant throughout the process.

Lemma 2. $\lim_{t \to \infty} \mathbb{E}_s(\pi_H(S_t)) = \rho_{s1}$.

Next, let us prove that the random variable $\pi_H(S_t)$ is a martingale.

Lemma 3. *For every $t \geq 0$, $\mathbb{E}_s(\pi_H(S_t)) = \sum_{i \in W_s} \pi_H(i)$.*

Our main theorem, concerning the probability $\rho_{s1}(G)$, follows immediately from Lemma 2 and Lemma 3.

Theorem 1. *For a connected non-bipartite graph, where $h_{ij} > 0$ for every $(i,j) \in E$, in the process $\mathcal{M}_H$ the probability to be absorbed into the all-white state is $\rho_{s1} = \sum_{i \in W_s} \pi_H(i)$.*

As a special case we can deduce ρ_{s1} for the uniform case, i.e., when choosing each neighbor with the same probability $1/d_i$. It is known that the stationary distribution of a uniform random walk is $\pi(i) = d_i/2m$, hence we conclude

Corollary 1. *For a connected non-bipartite graph, in the uniform process, the probability to be absorbed into the all-white state is $\rho_{s1} = \sum_{i \in W_s} \frac{d_i}{2m}$.*

Remark 1: One can always add self loops hence converting the graph into a non-bipartite one.

Remark 2: The process can be generalized to k colors. For each color c, the probability to end up in this color will be as if c is white and all others are colored black.

---

[1] We omit the parameter G when it is clear from the context.

2.3   Time bounds

The expected time of absorption can be bounded whenever H represents a reversible markov chain, i.e. $\pi_H(i)h_{ij} = \pi_H(j)h_{ji}$. A known technique is to look at the reversed process. At time t we can ask, for a vertex i, from which vertex did i get its current color, or in other words, which neighbor it picked at random. Continuing to ask this question backwards in time, we can track the current coloring from the initial coloring. Considering a random walk starting from each node, one can see that if two such walks meet, then they continue together from that point on. When this happens we say that the two walks have *collapsed*.

The crucial observation is that if all the walks collapse to a single walk in the backward process, then this certainly implies a monochromatic color in our (forward) process. We use results on the simultaneous meeting time of two uniform random walks on a connected non-bipartite graph G, in order to bound the meeting time of n walks. As mentioned in [TW93], in the uniform case, this meeting time is bounded by $O(n^3 \log n)$. (This follows from the fact that the meeting time of two walks is bounded by $O(n^3)$.)

In the full paper we give a complete analysis of the expected convergence time of the weighted process. Let $M_{ij}(G)$ be the meeting time for two random walks which started at i and j in a graph G, and define M as

$$M = \max_{G,i,j}\{\mathbb{E}(M_{ij}(G))\} .$$

Theorem 2. *The expected time it takes to reach a monochromatic color in the weighted process, where H represents a reversible Markov chain, is bounded by $O(M \log n)$.*

3   Application to Consensus

3.1   The consensus problem

In this section we explore the possibility of using the probabilistic polling process as a tool in designing consensus-type algorithms in distributed networks. Consider n processors connected by a synchronous communication network $G(V, E)$. Each processor i has an input bit $s^i \in \{0,1\}$, and it is required to decide on an output bit $y^i \in \{0,1\}$. A *consensus algorithm* is required to guarantee the following properties:

- *Agreement*: $y^i = y^j$ for every i and j.
- *Validity*: For $a \in \{0,1\}$, if $s^i = a$ $\forall i$ then $y^i = a$ $\forall$ processor i.
- *Stopping*: All processors decide on some value after finite time.

In this section we utilize a variant of the polling process as an algorithmic tool for solving the following variant of the consensus problem, named the *proportionate agreement* problem. Suppose that every processor in the network has an associated *reliability factor* $0 \le R_i \le 1$, representing its resilience against failures, such that $\sum_i R_i = 1$. Intuitively, a high value of R_i indicates that processor i is more reliable, and hence its opinion should be assigned higher weight in making the decision. Therefore, the probability with which the final decision is 1 should reflect the combined reliability of the processors i with input $s^i = 1$. Thus a *proportionate agreement algorithm* is required to guarantee the following properties:

- *Convergence to Agreement*: With probability 1, $y^i = y^j$ for every i and j after a finite number of steps.
- *Proportionality*: If W_s is the set of nodes with input 1 then the probability to end in the all-1 state is $\sum_{i \in W_s} R_i$.

As mentioned earlier, the probabilistic polling process is too weak to handle *malicious* (e.g., Byzantine) failures. In this section we first describe and analyze our agreement algorithm in a fault-free environment, and then extend our treatment to the dynamic setting.

3.2 Consensus by Proportion

In this section we present Algorithm **PropCon** for the *proportionate agreement* problem. The algorithm is based on applying the process $\mathcal{M}_H$ to the network with some suitably chosen weight matrix H. As proved in Section 2, the process $\mathcal{M}_H$ ends up in one of the initial values of the processors. Moreover, by assigning appropriate values to the weight matrix H it is possible to ensure the desired property that if the initial proportion of the white nodes' reliability is α, then the probability to end up in the all-white state is α as well. In order to define such a matrix H we need an upper bound on the degree-to-reliability ratio of the nodes. For concreteness, define $k = \max_{i \in V} \lceil \frac{d_i}{R_i} \rceil$. This choice guarantees that $k R_i \geq d_i$ for all i. Now normalize the reliability factor by setting $\tilde{R}_i = k R_i$ (hence $\sum_{i \in V} \tilde{R}_i = k$). Now the matrix H can be defined as

$$
H_{ij} = \begin{cases} \frac{1}{\tilde{R}_i}, & \text{if } (i,j) \in E \\ 1 - \frac{d_i}{\tilde{R}_i}, & \text{if } i = j \\ 0, & \text{otherwise.} \end{cases}
$$

Theorem 3. *Algorithm **PropCon** solves the proportionate agreement problem.*

In the full paper we show the following time bound, relying on Thm. 2.

Theorem 4. *The expected convergence time of algorithm **PropCon** is bounded by $O(kn \log n)$.*

3.3 Dynamic Networks

In this section we show that algorithm **PropCon** has certain resilience properties against communication failures. We consider the *dynamic network* model (cf. [AAG87]) in which link failures might occur at any moment. A failed link is disconnected and does not transfer any messages. After a while, a failed link may recover and resume its normal functioning state. A potential outcome of the type of failures dealt with here is the disconnection of the network, i.e., the network might be decomposed into a number of connected components. Nonetheless, it is assumed that eventually the network stabilizes on some connected topology. Our goal is to ensure convergence to the **1** state (either during the dynamic stage or after the network quiets down) with probability ρ_{s1} controlled by our algorithm's parameters.

Formally, we define a *stabilizing dynamic network*, denoted by $DynNet(G, T_0, \tilde{E})$, as follows. The underlying graph of the network is G. At any time t, the actual topology of the network is represented by an edge set E_t, which is some arbitrary subgraph of G. However, from some step T_0, there are no more disconnections or faults until the process ends in a monochromatic state, i.e., $E_t = \tilde{E}$ for every $t > T_0$, where $\tilde{E}$ represents an edge set of a connected undirected graph for the final topology of the network.

The perhaps surprising result of this section is that our algorithm is rather robust, in the sense that even in the face of a continually changing network topology, the topology of the operating portion of the network before each round does not affect ρ_{s1} at all.

The only delicate point about applying algorithm **PropCon** in the dynamic setting involves the random selection of a neighbor in a changing environment (in which the node's degree and set of neighbors constantly change). In the dynamic variant of algorithm **PropCon**, this is done as follows. Node i chooses randomly according to the weight matrix H a neighbor (or itself if $h_{ii} > 0$). If j was chosen, a request is send to j asking for its value. However, if no answer is received, due to a link failure, then i remains with its color. This way of choosing neighbors at random defines a weight matrix H_t, which depends on the topology of the network at time t. If some communication links have failed at time t then the probability that node i chooses itself increases. Defining $C_i^t = \{j \mid (i,j) \in E \setminus E_t\}$, the set of edges which are disconnected at time t, we have

$$
H_{ij}^t = \begin{cases} h_{ij}, & \text{if } (i,j) \in E_t \\ 0, & \text{if } (i,j) \in E \setminus E_t \\ h_{ii} + \sum_{k \in C_i^t} h_{ik}, & \text{if } i = j. \end{cases}
$$

We denote this process by $\mathcal{M}_{pc}$.

Applying Algorithm **PropCon** as just explained, the probability to end up in the all-white state remains proportional to the fraction of nodes *initially* colored white. The reason why the probability ρ_{s1} does not change is that the process $\mathcal{M}_{pc}$ is still a martingale.

Theorem 5. *For any initial coloring s and $DynNet(G, T_0, \tilde{E})$, the probability to end in the all-white state, when applying the process $\mathcal{M}_{pc}$ is $\rho_{s1} = \sum_{i \in W_s} R_i$.*

Acknowledgments

We are grateful to Uri Feige for helpful discussions and suggestions, and particularly for suggesting the approach taken in order to prove Thm. 2.

References

[AAG87] Y. Afek, B. Awerbuch and E. Gafni. Applying static network protocols to dynamic networks. In *Proc. 28th IEEE Symp. on Foundations of Computer Science,* October 1987. 358-370.

[AD97] Y. Afek and S. Dolev. Local stabilizer. In *Proc. 5th ISTCS,* IEEE Computer Soc. Press, 1997.

[AW98] H. Attiya and J. Welch. Distributed Computing: Fundamentals, Simulations and Advanced Topics. McGraw-Hill, England, 1998.

[BBPP96] J-C. Bermond, J. Bond, D. Peleg and S. Pereness. Tight bounds on the size of 2-monopolies. In *Proc. 3rd SIROCCO,* 1996.

[D74] M.H. Degroot, Reaching a consensus. *Journal of the American Statistical Association,* March 1974, Volume 69, Number 345, 118-121.

[DW83] P. Donnely and D. Welsh. Finite particle systems and infection models. In *Proc. Camb. Phil. Soc.* (1983), 94, 167-182.

[F56] J.R.P. French. A formal theory of social power. *Psych. Review* 63 (1956) 181-194.

[F66] W. Feller. *An Introduction to Probability Theory and Its Applications,* Volume 1. Wiley, New York, 1966.

[GO80] E. Goles and J. Olivos. Periodic behavior of generalized threshold functions. *Discrete Mathematics,* 30:187-189, 1980.

[GFP85] E. Goles, F. Fogelman-Soulie and D. Pellegrin. Decreasing energy functions as a tool for studying threshold networks. *Discrete Applied Mathematics* 12 (1985) 261-277.

[H59] F. Harary. A criterion for unanimity in French's theory of social power. In D. Cartwright, ed., *Studies in Social power,* (Inst. Soc. Res., Ann Arbor, MI, 1959) 168-182.

[HL75] R. Holley and T.M. Ligget. Ergodic theorems for weakly interacting infinite systems and the voter model. *Ann. Probab.* 3 643-663 1975.

[KP97] S. Kutten and B. Patt-Shamir. Sphere packing and local majorities in graphs. In *Proc. 2nd ISTCS,* pages 141-149. IEEE Computer Soc. Press, June 1993.

[LSM82] L. Lamport, R. Shostak and M. pease. The Byzentine generals problem. *ACM Transactions on Programming Language and Systems,* 4(3):382-401, July 1982.

[LPRS93] N. Linial, D. Peleg, Y. Rabinovich and M. Saks. Sphere packing and local majorities in graphs. In *Proc. 2nd ISTCS,* pages 141-149. IEEE Computer Soc. Press, June 1993.

[L95] N. Lynch. Distributed Algorithms. Morgan Kaufmann, San Mateo, California, 1995.

[MR95] R. Motwani and P. Raghavan. *Randomized Algorithms.* 1995.

[P96] D. Peleg. Local majority voting, small coalitions and controlling monopolies in graphs: a review. In *Proc. 3rd SIROCCO,* 1996.

[P96a] D. Peleg. Size bounds for dynamic monopolies. In *Proc. 4th SIROCCO,* 1997.

[PS83] S. Poljak and M. Sura. On periodical behavior in societies with symmetric influences. *Combinatorica,* 3:119-121, 1983.

[TW93] P. Tetali and P. Winkler. Simultaneous reversible markov chains. *Combinatorics Paul Erdós is Eighty (Volume 1),* 1993, pp. 433-451.

Bisimulation Equivanlence Is Decidable for Normed Process Algebra (Extended Abstract)

Yoram Hirshfeld[1,*] and Mark Jerrum[2,**]

[1] School of Mathematical Sciences, The Raymond and Beverly Sackler Faculty of
Exact Sciences, Tel Aviv University, Ramat Aviv, Tel Aviv 69978, Israel.
[2] Department of Computer Science, University of Edinburgh, The King's Buildings,
Edinburgh EH9 3JZ, United Kingdom.

Abstract. We present a procedure for deciding whether two normed
PA terms are bisimilar. The procedure is "elementary," having doubly
exponential non-deterministic time complexity.

1 Discussion

Let Atom be a finite set of *atomic processes* or *atoms*, Act a finite set of *actions*,
and Π a collection of *productions* of the form $X \xrightarrow{a} Y$, where $X, Y \in$ Atom
and $a \in$ Act. Regarding the atoms as states of a system, we can think of the
production $X \xrightarrow{a} Y$ as specifying a possible evolution, or *derivation* of the system
from state X to Y via action a. What we have is nothing more than a finite state
automaton, familiar from formal language theory.

We can generalise this situation somewhat by allowing both the states and
the right hand sides of productions to be terms constructed from atoms using
an associative, non-commutative operator "$\cdot$" that we think of as "sequential
composition." The productions specify the derivations available to atoms, and
hence, by extension, to terms: the derivations available to a general term $P =
X_1 \cdot \cdots \cdot X_n$ are precisely those of the form

$$P \xrightarrow{a} X_1' \cdot X_2 \cdot \cdots \cdot X_n,$$

where $X_1 \xrightarrow{a} X_1'$ is a derivation of the atom X_1. (Note that X_1' is not in general an atom, and may be ε, the empty term.) The non-commutativity of the
sequential composition operator is reflected in the restriction that productions
can be applied only to the leftmost atom.

By way of example, if Atom $= \{X\}$, Act $= \{a, b\}$, and the available pro-
ductions are $X \xrightarrow{a} X \cdot X$ and $X \xrightarrow{b} \varepsilon$, then the states reachable (by some sequence of derivations) from X are ε, X, $X \cdot X$, $X \cdot X \cdot X$, $\ldots$, and the available

---

* The first author was supported in part by EPSRC Visiting Research Fellowships
GR/K83243 and GR/M06468.
** The second author is supported in part by Esprit Working Group No. 21726,
"RAND2."

action-sequences from state X to itself are ε, ab, $abab$, $aabb$, $ababab$, ..., i.e., all "balanced parenthesis sequences."

In the field of concurrency theory, systems defined by sets of productions of the form just described are known as "context-free" or "Basic Process Algebra" (BPA) processes. (What we have been terming "states" are commonly referred to as *processes* in concurrency theory.) In language-theoretic terms, a BPA process is equivalent to a pushdown automaton with one state. However, concurrency theory is distinguished from formal language theory in having a different set of concerns: given two BPA processes P and Q we are interested not in whether the action-sequences available to the P and Q are equal as sets (a static notion), but in whether P and Q are "behaviourally equivalent" in a dynamical sense.

What is the "correct" notion of behavioural equivalence for concurrent processes? A popular and mathematically fruitful answer is the relation of bisimilarity: two processes are *bisimilar*, or *bisimulation equivalent*, if, roughly, they may evolve together in such a way that whenever the first process performs a certain action, the second process is able to respond by performing the same action, and *vice versa*. (Precise definitions of this and other terms appearing in this section will be given in §2.) The notion of bisimulation equivalence was introduced by Park [14] around 1980, and has been intensively studied since. Bisimilarity plays an important role in algebraic theories of concurrency, such as that based on Milner's CCS [12].

As we have already seen, a BPA process may have infinitely many states, so it is by no means clear, a priori, that there is an effective procedure for deciding whether two BPA processes P and Q are bisimilar. The first such procedure was presented by Christensen, Hüttel and Stirling [7], though no upper bound on complexity could be offered at the time. Subsequently, Burkart, Caucal and Steffen showed the decision problem to be "elementary," i.e., to have time-complexity bounded by some constant-height tower of exponentials [3].

With an eye to modelling concurrent systems, we may introduce an associative, commutative operator "$|$" representing "parallel composition." *Basic Parallel Processes* (BPP) are terms constructed from atoms using just this parallel composition operator. Derivations on atoms may be defined, as in BPA, by a finite set of productions, and then extended to terms in the natural way. The commutativity of the parallel composition operator expresses itself in the ability of a process $P \mid Q \mid R$, say, to evolve through any of P, Q or R undergoing a derivation. Bisimilarity of pairs of BPPs was shown to be decidable by Christensen, Hirshfeld and Moller [6], but is not known to be elementary.

It is natural to consider processes built from atoms using both sequential and parallel composition operators. As before, derivations on atoms may be defined by a grammar, the productions of which have atoms on the left hand side, and arbitrary terms on the right. The derivation relation extends to terms in the natural way, respecting the commutativity of parallel composition; so that, for example, if $U, X, Y, Z \in$ Atom and $U \xrightarrow{a} U'$, $X \xrightarrow{a} X'$, $Y \xrightarrow{a} Y'$ and $Z \xrightarrow{a} Z'$ are possible derivations, then (adopting the convention that "$\cdot$" binds more tightly than "$\mid$"), the process $(U \mid X) \cdot Y \mid Z$ has all of

$$(U' \mid X) \cdot Y \mid Z, \quad (U \mid X') \cdot Y \mid Z \quad \text{and} \quad (U \mid X) \cdot Y \mid Z'$$

as possible derivatives (via action a), but not $(U \mid X) \cdot Y' \mid Z$. This set-up can be viewed as a fragment of the process algebra ACP, the *Algebra of Communicating Processes* of Bergstra and Klop [2]; we refer to this fragment as *PA*. As a model for concurrent systems, PA still lacks the important element of synchronisation (the "C" in "ACP"), but at least it represents a step towards the kind of expressivity that would be required to describe realistic concurrent systems. The absence of synchronisation severely limits the expressive power of PA, but at the same time opens the door to decidability results. Note that bisimilarity of pairs of general ACP terms is undecidable; indeed, merely adding synchronisation to BPP already destroys decidability, as was shown by Christensen [4, §8.2].

An open problem of some years' standing is whether bisimilarity of PA processes is decidable and, if so, how great is its computational complexity. We are not able to provide a complete answer to this question. However, we are able to present a decision procedure for the subclass of "normed" PA processes. The property of being normed applies to processes generally, independently of how they are described (in BPA, BPP, PA, or whatever). A process P is said to be *normed* if, for all P^* that can be reached from P via some sequence of derivations, there is a further sequence of derivations that reduces P^* to ε. For processes described in BPA, BPP or PA, a sufficient condition for being normed is that all atoms $X \in \text{Atom}$ can be reduced to ε via some derivation sequence. Our decidability result is the first that applies to syntactically unrestricted PA terms, though a number of partial results had already been obtained by restricting the form of terms. E.g., Kučera [11], demonstrates decidability in the case that parallel composition occurs only at the top level.

The assumption of normedness seems innocuous; nevertheless, experience suggests that normed processes are easier to cope with than arbitrary ones. For both BPA and BPP, bisimilarity was shown to be decidable first for normed processes: in the case of BPA by Baeten, Bergstra and Klop [1], and in the case of BPP by Christensen, Hirshfeld and Moller [5]. Furthermore, Hirshfeld, Jerrum and Moller have presented polynomial-time algorithms for deciding bisimilarity both for normed BPA [9] and normed BPP [10]. The same phenomenon now reappears in the context of PA.

At the core of the problem of deciding bisimilarity of PA processes lies the surprising complexity of interactions that can occur between sequential and parallel composition. In particular, there are situations in which the sequential composition of two processes $P_1 \cdot P_2$ may be equivalent to a parallel composition $Q_1 \mid Q_2$ of two other processes. A trivial example is given by $\text{Atom} = \{X\}$, $\text{Act} = \{a, b\}$ and productions $X \xrightarrow{a} X \mid X$ and $X \xrightarrow{b} \varepsilon$, a system which is equivalent to the example using sequential composition given earlier. But this is just the simplest case, and the equivalence $P_1 \cdot P_2 \sim Q_1 \mid Q_2$ in fact has an infinite set of solutions of apparently unbounded complexity.

The key to our approach is to develop a structure theory for PA that completely classifies the situations in which a sequential composition of two processes can be bisimilar to a parallel composition. Fortunately, the infinite collection of examples mentioned earlier can be covered using a small number of patterns (applied recursively). As a consequence of the classification we obtain a decision procedure for bisimilarity in normed PA. The full proof of decidability is long and technically involved, so we are able to offer in this extended abstract only a rough indication of its main features. For full details, refer to the technical report [8].

Unfortunately, the structure theory we develop relies crucially on unique decomposition of processes into sequential and parallel prime components, which in turn relies on normedness, so there seems little hope of a direct extension to the general (un-normed) case. It is a chastening thought that we have absolutely no information concerning the complexity of deciding bisimilarity for general (un-normed) PA: the two extremes—that bisimilarity is in the class P, or that it is undecidable—are perfectly consistent with our current lack of knowledge.

2 Notation and basic facts about PA

Recall that Atom is a finite set of *atomic processes* or *atoms*, and Act a finite set of *actions*. We let U, X, Y, Z stand for generic atoms, and a, b, c for generic actions; other naming conventions will be introduced as and when convenient. The set Proc of *processes* contains all terms in the free algebra over Atom generated by the non-commutative associative operator " $\cdot$ " of *sequential composition*, and the commutative associative operator " $|$ " of *parallel composition*.

A PA process is defined by a finite set Π of *productions*, each of the form

$$X \xrightarrow{a} P, \tag{1}$$

where $X \in$ Atom, $a \in$ Act and $P \in$ Proc. A production such as (1) specifies a *derivation* available to X: atomic process X undergoes action a to become process P. The notion of derivation may be extended to arbitrary processes $P \in$ Proc in the natural way:

– if $P \xrightarrow{a} P'$ then $P \cdot Q \xrightarrow{a} P' \cdot Q$;
– if $P \xrightarrow{a} P'$ then $P \mid Q \xrightarrow{a} P' \mid Q$;
– if $Q \xrightarrow{a} Q'$ then $P \mid Q \xrightarrow{a} P \mid Q'$.

(The last rule adds nothing new, but is included to emphasise the commutative nature of parallel composition.) If $P \xrightarrow{a} Q$ for some action a we say that Q is an *immediate derivative* of P. We drop the label a from the derivation $P \xrightarrow{a} Q$ in cases where the associated action a is unimportant.

We write $P \rightsquigarrow P^*$—and say that P^* is a *derivative* of P—if there is some sequence of processes $P_0, P_1, \ldots, P_l$ such that

$$P = P_0 \rightarrow P_1 \rightarrow \cdots \rightarrow P_{l-1} \rightarrow P_l = P^*;$$

the number l is the *length* of the derivation sequence. Note that an immediate derivative corresponds to the special case $l = 1$. The collection of all derivations defines a structure known as a *labelled transition system*: formally, this is just a labelled directed multigraph on vertex set Proc, in which there is an edge labelled a from P to P' precisely when $P \overset{a}{\to} P'$. Note that the finite set of productions Π may define an infinite labelled transition system.

When writing PA processes we adopt a couple of conventions: sequential composition binds more tightly than parallel composition, and exponentiation is used to denote a parallel composition of several copies of a process, thus

$$P^k = \underbrace{P \mid \ldots \mid P}_{k \text{ copies}}.$$

The norm $\|P\|$ of a process $P \in$ Proc is the length of a shortest derivation sequence $P \rightsquigarrow \varepsilon$ if such a sequence exists, and ∞ otherwise. A process P is said to be *normed* if every derivative P^* of P has finite norm. Note that if all atoms $X \in$ Act have finite norm, than all processes $P \in$ Proc will be normed.

Observation 1. *If P and Q have finite norm, then $\|P \cdot Q\| = \|P \mid Q\| = \|P\| + \|Q\|$.*

A binary relation $\mathcal{R}$ on Proc is a *bisimulation* if the following conditions are satisfied:

- for all $P, Q, P' \in$ Proc and $a \in$ Act such that $P \mathcal{R} Q$ and $P \overset{a}{\to} P'$, there exists $Q' \in$ Proc such that $Q \overset{a}{\to} Q'$ and $P' \mathcal{R} Q'$; and
- for all $P, Q, Q' \in$ Proc and $a \in$ Act such that $P \mathcal{R} Q$ and $Q \overset{a}{\to} Q'$, there exists $P' \in$ Proc such that $P \overset{a}{\to} P'$ and $P' \mathcal{R} Q'$.

The property of being a bisimulation is closed under union, so there is a unique maximal bisimulation that we shall denote by " $\sim$ ". Two processes P, Q such that $P \sim Q$ are said to be *bisimilar* or *bisimulation equivalent*. Note that bisimilarity is well defined for PA, being invariant under rearrangement of terms, using associativity of sequential composition and associativity and commutativity of parallel composition.

By way of example, suppose Atom $= \{H, K, X\}$, Act $= \{a, b, c\}$, and Π is the set of productions

$$X \overset{a}{\to} X^2, \; X \overset{b}{\to} \varepsilon, \; K \overset{c}{\to} X, \; K \overset{c}{\to} K \mid X, \; H \overset{c}{\to} K \mid X^2 \text{ and } H \overset{c}{\to} H \mid X.$$

Then

$$H \cdot X \sim K \cdot X \mid K \cdot X, \tag{2}$$

as can be verified by explicit construction of a bisimulation R containing the pair $\langle H \cdot X, K \cdot X \mid K \cdot X \rangle$.

This relatively simple example hints at the technical difficulties that lie at the heart of the problem of deciding bisimilarity of PA processes: observe that an equation such as (2) may hold even though the l.h.s. is formally a sequential composition and the r.h.s. a parallel composition, and even though both sides are infinite state (i.e., the set of processes reachable from either side is infinite).

The bisimulation relation on PA processes possesses algebraic structure which is crucial to our decision procedure.

Observation 2. *Bisimulation equivalence is a congruence under sequential and parallel composition. That is, $P \cdot R \sim Q \cdot R$, $R \cdot P \sim R \cdot Q$ and $P \mid R \sim Q \mid R$, for all P, Q, R satisfying $P \sim Q$.*

For normed processes the situation is even better. We say that a normed process P is a *sequential prime* (respectively a *parallel prime*) if it is not bisimilar to any process of the form $P_1 \cdot P_2$ (respectively $P_1 \mid P_2$) with $\|P_1\|, \|P_2\| > 0$. The use of the term "prime" here is justified by the following facts.

Proposition 1. *Suppose $P_1 \cdot P_2 \cdots \cdots P_n \sim Q_1 \cdot Q_2 \cdots \cdots Q_m$, where the processes P_i and Q_j are sequential primes of finite non-zero norm. Then $n = m$, and $P_i \sim Q_i$, for all $1 \leq i \leq n$.*

Proof. See, for example, Hirshfeld et al. [9].

Proposition 2. *Suppose $P_1 \mid P_2 \mid \ldots \mid P_n \sim Q_1 \mid Q_2 \mid \ldots \mid Q_m$, where the processes P_i and Q_j are parallel primes of finite non-zero norm. Then $n = m$, and there exists a permutation π of the integers $\{1, 2, \ldots, n\}$ such that $P_i \sim Q_{\pi(i)}$, for all $1 \leq i \leq n$.*

Proof. See, for example, Christensen et al. [5].

(The phenomenon of unique decomposability of processes was first noted by Milner and Moller [13].) Note that Propositions 1 and 2 require the component processes to have finite norm. It is because we make extensive use of unique decomposition that our decision procedure is restricted to normed processes.

Note also that Propositions 1 and 2 imply a converse to Observation 2, which allows cancellation of like components. Thus, if P, Q, R are normed and $P \cdot R \sim Q \cdot R$, then $P \sim Q$. In fact, the cancelled processes do not need to be equal, merely bisimilar. Similar cancellation rules can be formulated for the other two cases in Observation 2. Cancellation fails for general (possibly infinite norm) processes.

3 Outline of the decidability proof

To motivate our approach, let us attempt to build a (non-deterministic) decision procedure directly from the definition of bisimilarity. Given a pair of processes $\langle P, Q \rangle$, we wish to decide whether $P \sim Q$. We try all derivations $P \xrightarrow{a} P'$ (note that there are finitely many) and for each one guess a matching derivation $Q \xrightarrow{a} Q'$. (By "matching" derivation we mean one for which $P' \sim Q'$.) Symmetrically, for each derivation $Q \xrightarrow{a} Q'$ we guess a matching derivation $P \xrightarrow{a} P'$. Let us call the process of generating all pairs $\langle P', Q' \rangle$ derived from $\langle P, Q \rangle$ an "expansion step." If there exists a derivation $P \xrightarrow{a} P'$ that is not matched by any derivation $Q \xrightarrow{a} Q'$ (i.e., Q is incapable of performing action a), we say the expansion step fails; in this case, we immediately halt and reject.

Otherwise we consider all the derived pairs of processes $\langle P', Q' \rangle$ and apply the expansion step to *them* to build a second level of derived processes, and then a third, and so on. If $P \sim Q$ then the nondeterministic choices can be made so that no expansion step fails. Conversely, if $P \not\sim Q$ then, eventually, some expansion step must fail, whatever nondeterministic choices are made.

The main (and only) objection to the above approach is that the derived processes can grow without limit, so that the procedure will not in general terminate in the case $P \sim Q$. We counter this objection by combining the expansion step with a complementary simplification step that cuts in when the norm of P and Q becomes larger than the norm of any atom. In this situation, P and Q must either be sequential or parallel compositions. If P and Q are of the same kind—both sequential or both parallel—the simplification step is straightforward. For example, if $P = P_1 \cdot P_2$ and $Q = Q_1 \cdot Q_2$ with $||P_1|| \geq ||Q_1||$, then we guess a process R with norm $||R|| = ||P_1|| - ||Q_1||$; then we replace the pair $\langle P, Q \rangle$ by the two smaller pairs $\langle P_1, Q_1 \cdot R \rangle$ and $\langle R \cdot P_2, Q_2 \rangle$. This is an appropriate action, since, by unique factorisation,

$$ P \sim Q \iff \exists R \left[P_1 \sim Q_1 \cdot R \wedge R \cdot P_2 \sim Q_2 \right]. $$

A similar simplification step is available when P and Q are both parallel compositions.

The difficult case for simplification is when (say) P is a sequential composition, and Q a parallel composition, leading to a so-called "mixed equation." For this case we develop a structure theory that classifies the situations when $P \sim Q$. The range of possible mixed equations is remarkably rich, and it is this fact that leads to the technical complexities of the proof. Nevertheless, the classification can be described with sufficient precision to allow the simplification step described above to be extended to mixed equations.

4 Structure theory for mixed equations

A *mixed equation* is an equivalence of the form

$$ F \cdot G \sim P_1 \mid \cdots \mid P_n, \tag{3} $$

where $P_1, \ldots, P_n$ are parallel primes, and $n \geq 2$. We assume that F is chosen to have minimum possible norm, so that F is not itself a sequential composition. An overview of the taxonomy of mixed equations is presented in Figure 1.

A *unit* is an atom of norm one. We typically use X, Y and Z to denote units. We say that an atom Y is *monomorphic* if $Y \to Y'$ entails $Y' \sim Y$ or $Y' \sim \varepsilon$. The first distinction we draw is between mixed equations for which $G \sim X^m$ for some unit X, and the remainder. The remainder is easy to deal with: it transpires that F must be a monomorphic atom, in which case (3) is said to

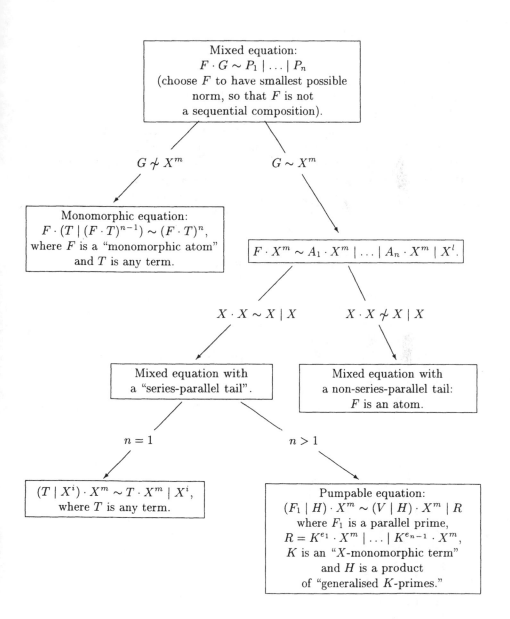

Fig. 1. Taxonomy of mixed equations

be a *monomorphic equation*. The class of monomorphic equations has a simple enough structure that we do not need to subdivide it further.

The case $G \sim X^m$ is much more problematic. We show that in this case the mixed equation (3) has the general form

$$F \cdot X^m \sim A_1 \cdot X^m \mid \cdots \mid A_n \cdot X^m \mid X^l. \tag{4}$$

At this point we make a further distinction between the situation $X \cdot X \sim X \mid X$ (of a mixed equation with a "series-parallel tail") and the remainder. Again, the remainder is the easier to deal with, as the possibilities are more restricted; specifically, it is possible to show that F must be an atom.

Finally we are left with the mixed equations with a series-parallel tail. If $n = 1$, i.e., there is only one non-trivial parallel component on the r.h.s., then the general form of such equations is easy to describe. The main technical difficulty in the proof lies in characterising equations with $n > 1$, a class we term the *pumpable equations*. Equation (2) is an example of a pumpable equation, but a simple one; pumpable equations can be much more complex! However, even this simple example will suffice to indicate the origin of the term "pumpable." In a pumpable equation, there is a parallel component on the r.h.s., unique up to bisimilarity, that can be "pumped" arbitrarily many times by injecting processes from a class we term "generalised K-primes." In this instance we obtain by pumping the infinite sequence of equations

$$H \cdot X \sim K \cdot X \mid K \cdot X$$
$$(H \mid K) \cdot X \sim (K \mid K) \cdot X \mid K \cdot X = K^2 \cdot X \mid K \cdot X$$
$$(H \mid K^2) \cdot X \sim (K \mid K^2) \cdot X \mid K \cdot X = K^3 \cdot X \mid K \cdot X$$
$$\vdots$$
$$(H \mid K^i) \cdot X \sim (K \mid K^{i-1}) \cdot X \mid K \cdot X = K^i \cdot X \mid K \cdot X$$
$$\vdots$$

We say that a term K is X-*monomorphic* if $K \to K'$ entails $K' \sim K \mid X^i$ or $K' \sim X^i$, for some integer i, possibly zero. Note that in our example, K is indeed X-monomorphic. In general, a generalised K-prime is built from an X-monomorphic term K by a certain inductive construction.

The following "metatheorem" summarises numerous actual theorems in the full version of the paper. By providing a complete characterisation of mixed equations, it enables us to construct a decision procedure for bisimulation equivalence along the lines suggested in §3.

Metatheorem 1. *There are effective characterisations of the following classes of mixed equations:*

- *monomorphic equations;*
- *mixed equations with a non-series-parallel tail;*
- *mixed equations with a series-parallel tail and only one non-trivial parallel component on the r.h.s.;*
- *pumpable equations.*

Acknowledgement

The authors thank Colin Stirling for useful discussions on the structure of mixed equations.

References

1. J. C. M. BAETEN, J. A. BERGSTRA and J. W. KLOP, Decidability of bisimulation equivalence for processes generating context-free languages, *Journal of the ACM* **40** (1993), 653–682.
2. J. A. BERGSTRA and J. W. KLOP, Algebra of communicating processes with abstraction. *Theoretical Computer Science* **37** (1985), 77–121.
3. Olaf BURKART, Didier CAUCAL and Bernhard STEFFEN, An elementary bisimulation decision procedure for arbitrary context-free processes. Proceedings of MFCS '95: 20th International Symposium on Mathematical Foundations of Computer Science, *Lecture Notes in Computer Science* **969**, Springer-Verlag, 1995, 423–433.
4. Søren CHRISTENSEN, *Decidability and Decomposition in Process Algebras* (PhD. Thesis). Internal Report ECS-LFCS-93-278, Laboratory for Foundations of Computer Science, University of Edinburgh, September 1993.
5. Søren CHRISTENSEN, Yoram HIRSHFELD, and Faron MOLLER, Decomposability, decidability and axiomatisability for bisimulation equivalence on basic parallel processes. *Proceedings of the Eighth Annual IEEE Symposium on Logic in Computer Science* (LICS 93), IEEE Computer Society Press, 1993, 386-396.
6. Søren CHRISTENSEN, Yoram HIRSHFELD, and Faron MOLLER, Bisimulation equivalence is decidable for basic parallel processes. Proceedings of CONCUR 93: Fourth International Conference on Concurrency Theory, *Lecture Notes in Computer Science* **715**, Springer-Verlag, 1993, 143–157.
7. Søren CHRISTENSEN, Hans HÜTTEL and Colin STIRLING, Bisimulation equivalence is decidable for all context-free processes, *Information and Computation* **121** (1995), 143–148.
8. Yoram HIRSHFELD and Mark JERRUM, Bisimulation equivalence is decidable for normed Process Algebra, *Internal Report ECS-LFCS-98-386*, Laboratory for Foundations of Computer Science, University of Edinburgh, May 1998. URL: http://www.dcs.ed.ac.uk/lfcsreps/EXPORT/98/ECS-LFCS-98-386/index.html.
9. Yoram HIRSHFELD, Mark JERRUM and Faron MOLLER, A polynomial algorithm for deciding bisimilarity of normed context-free processes, *Theoretical Computer Science* **158** (1996), 143–159.
10. Yoram HIRSHFELD, Mark JERRUM and Faron MOLLER, A polynomial algorithm for deciding bisimulation equivalence of normed Basic Parallel Processes, *Mathematical Structures in Computer Science* **6** (1996), 251–259.
11. Antonín KUČERA, How to parallelize sequential processes. Proceedings of CONCUR 97: Eighth International Conference on Concurrency Theory, *Lecture Notes in Computer Science* **1243**, Springer-Verlag, 1997, 302–316.
12. Robin MILNER, *Communication and Concurrency*, Prentice Hall, 1989.
13. Robin MILNER and Faron MOLLER, Unique decomposition of processes, *Theoretical Computer Science* **107** (1993), 357–363.
14. D. M. R. PARK, Concurrency and Automata on Infinite Sequences. Theoretical Computer Science: Fifth GI-Conference, *Lecture Notes in Computer Science* **104**, Springer-Verlag, 1981, 167–183.

A Framework for Decidable Metrical Logics

Yoram Hirshfeld and Alexander Rabinovich

Tel Aviv University
{yoram, rabino}@math.tau.ac.il

Abstract. We propose a framework for defining decidable temporal logics. It is strong enough to define in it all the decidable temporal logics that we found in the literature. We use as semantics the standard model of the positive real line and we use robust logical notions and techniques.

1 Introduction

Obviously the main model for the progression of time is the real line with its natural order and possibly some arithmetical operations. We shall use here the model R^+ of the non negative real numbers that has 0 as its starting moment. The main model for the evolving of a system in time is a function f from R^+ to a finite set of propositions (about the system) where $f(t)$ is the set of propositions that hold at the moment t. This is called a *signal*. Alternatively we may think of every proposition as a one place predicate $P(t)$ which holds or not at time t.

The main tool in Mathematical Logic that deals with signals is the well developed branch of the *Monadic Logic of Order (MLO)*. It is of course possible to code up signals in alternative ways like *Timed Sequences* (provided the signal does not vary to often); it may also be of some advantage to use MLO in some syntactically sugared ways like the different temporal logics; but when doing so one should keep eye contact with the central model and its main tools and be able to justify the deviation. Indeed the classical treatment of pure temporal logics in [5] does it within MLO.

In recent years much effort was put into building formalisms that extend temporal logics to deal with the length of intervals of time (see [3, 17] for surveys). These efforts were not fruitless but we feel that they suffer from the use of mutant models and from ignoring (except for [17, 6]) Monadic Logic. Many formalisms were suggested. Though they are called logics most of them employ ad hoc programming language and automata theory constructs and not robust logical notions, syntax and semantics.

We offer here a novel treatment that does everything within the standard model of real signals, and with standard monadic logic. We propose a logical framework for defining decidable temporal logics. The framework is an expressive decidable monadic logic. It is strong enough to define in it all the decidable temporal logics that we found in the literature. For example the connective $(X\ then Y)_1$ - "X and then Y will occur within one time unit" is straightforwardly formulated in this logic.

The framework has the additional benefit that the discussion applies uniformly to all signals and not only to signals with *finite variability*, i.e - signals that change only finitely often in any bounded interval of time. We benefit from the theory of Mathematical Logic and all the expressiveness and decidability proofs use Ehrenfeucht's equivalences for MLO.

The work continues [7] where the basic framework to discuss metric extensions of MLO in the standard model was developed.

In Section 2, we shall define and discuss the following sequence of logics:

$$MLO \subseteq MLO_{timer} \subseteq L_1 \subseteq L_2 \subseteq MLO_1$$

MLO is the Monadic Logic of Order, MLO_1 is the Monadic Logic of Order with the $+1$ function. L_1 is a fragment of MLO_1 that uses the $+1$ function only in a naturally restricted way as defined in Section 2.2. L_1 is decidable by [7]. MLO_{timer} is a fragment of L_1 in which the use of the $+1$ is even more systematically restricted (the formulas in first-order timer normal form of Section 2.3). L_2 is introduced here for the first time (see Definition 2). L_2 is much more expressive as exemplified by example 5.1, but it is still decidable.

In Section 3 we recall the general notion of one dimensional temporal logic. In Section 4 we present the main technical theorems for defining decidable temporal logics. Section 5 provides a collection of examples.

It is not easy to compare our work to the extensive efforts made in the field as the models vary from each other. All the previous papers use as a model some kind of an ω-sequence. Such a sequence cannot faithfully represent the real line. Clearly signals with infinite variability cannot be modeled by a sequence. The popular logic $MITL$ of [2] is equivalent to our logic L_1 for finite variability models. A more detailed comparison can be found in [7].

2 Monadic Logic of Order and its Metrical Extensions

2.1 Monadic Logic of Order (MLO)

The syntax of MLO has in its vocabulary *individual (first order) variables* $t_0, t_1, \ldots,$ *unary predicate names* $X_0, X_1, \ldots,$ and one binary relation $<$ (the order). *Atomic formulas* are of the form $X(t)$, $t_1 < t_2$ and $t_1 = t_2$. *MLO formulas* are obtained from atomic formulas using the Boolean connectives $\neg, \vee, \wedge, \rightarrow, \leftrightarrow$ and the (first order) quantifiers $\exists t$ and $\forall t$. We will occasionally refer to *Second order* MLO formulas where the unary predicate names are considered as variables and second order quantifiers $\exists X$ and $\forall X$ are allowed. As usual if φ is a formula we may write $\varphi(t_1, \ldots, t_k; X_1, \ldots, X_m)$ to indicate that the free variables in φ are among $t_1, \ldots, t_k$ and $X_1, \ldots, X_m$.

A *(canonical real time) model* is the non negative real line R^+ with its natural order and some unary predicates. We shall not repeat the inductive definition saying when is a formula satisfied. Recall that in order to check if the formula $\varphi(t_1, \ldots t_k; X_1, \ldots, X_m)$ is true we need to specify what are the elements $\tau_1, \ldots, \tau_k$ in R^+ and the predicates (subsets) $P_1, \ldots, P_m$ over R^+ which are assigned to the variables $t_1, \ldots, t_k, X_1, \ldots, X_m$. Hence the notation will usually be

$$\langle R^+, \tau_1, \ldots, \tau_k; P_1, \ldots, P_m \rangle \models_{MLO} \varphi(t_1, \ldots, t_k; X_1, \ldots, X_m)$$

which we also abbreviate to $R^+ \models \varphi[\tau_1, \ldots, \tau_k; P_1, \ldots, P_m]$ or even to $R^+ \models \varphi[\bar{\tau}, \bar{P}]$ where the bar denotes a tuple of appropriate length. When we define the semantics of a second order formula or when we deal with validity and satisfiability of a first order formula it is necessary to specify over which predicates should the variables X range. In *full MLO* they range over all unary predicates (i.e. – subsets). A requirement that is often imposed in the literature is that in every bounded time interval a system can change its state only finitely many times. This requirement is called *finite variability* (or *non-Zeno*) requirement. We consider also finite variability interpretations of first-order and second-order MLO. Under these interpretations monadic predicates range over predicates with finite variability.

2.2 Monadic Logic with a +1 Function - MLO_1

The syntax of MLO_1 extends the syntax of MLO by a one place function $t+1$. Its atomic formulas are those of MLO and formulas $t_i = t_j + 1$. Other formulas are constructed from the atomic formulas exactly as for MLO. The function $t + 1$ is interpreted over the reals in the standard way.

We use the standard notation 0 for the minimal element, n for $0 + 1 + \cdots + 1$ (n times) and $t - 1$ for 0 when $t < 1$ and for the unique t_1 such that $t_1 + 1 = t$ when $t \geq 1$.

MLO_1 is is too strong and the satisfiability problem can be easily shown to be undecidable (see e.g. [2, 7]). We shall, therefore, identify two decidable fragments of MLO_1.

These fragment will use the function $t + 1$ only in a very restricted form. We introduce some syntactical sugar to MLO_1 – the "bounded quantifiers" $(\exists t)_{>t_0}^{<t_0+1}$ and $(\exists t)_{>t_0-1}^{<t_0}$ as follows: if φ is a formula of MLO_1 then we use the shorthand:

$$(\exists t)_{>t_0}^{<t_0+1}\varphi \equiv \exists t(t_0 < t < t_0 + 1 \wedge \varphi)$$

$$(\exists t)_{>t_0-1}^{<t_0}\varphi \equiv \exists t(t_0 - 1 < t < t_0 \wedge \varphi)$$

More general bounded quantifiers $(\exists t)_{>t_0+m}^{<t_0+n}$ for integers n and m are defined similarly: $(\exists t)_{>t_0+m}^{<t_0+n}\varphi \equiv \exists t(t_0 + m < t < t_0 + n \wedge \varphi)$. The quantifiers with weak inequality replacing the strict inequality in one or both ends of the interval with integers $m < n$ are defined similarly.

Definition 1 (The fragment L_1) L_1 *is the fragment of MLO_1 which is built from the atomic formulas $t_1 < t_2, t_1 = t_2, X(t)$ using Boolean connectives, first order quantifiers and the following rule:*

*if $\varphi(t)$ is a formula of L_1 with t its only first order free variable,
m and n integers, and $m < n$, then the formulas*
$(\exists t)_{>t_0+m}^{<t_0+n}\varphi$, $(\exists t)_{\geq t_0+m}^{<t_0+n}\varphi$, $(\exists t)_{\geq t_0+m}^{\leq t_0+n}\varphi$, $(\exists t)_{>t_0+m}^{\leq t_0+n}\varphi$ *are in L_1.*

Definition 2 (The fragment L_2) L_2 *is the fragment of MLO_1 which is built from the atomic formulas $t_1 < t_2, t_1 = t_2, X(t)$ using Boolean connectives, first order quantifiers and the following rule:*

*if $\varphi(t_0, t)$ is a formula of L_2 with t_0, t its only first order free variables,
m and n integers, and $m < n$ then the formulas*
$(\exists t)_{>t_0+m}^{<t_0+n}\varphi$, $(\exists t)_{\geq t_0+m}^{<t_0+n}\varphi$, $(\exists t)_{\geq t_0+m}^{\leq t_0+n}\varphi$, $(\exists t)_{>t_0+m}^{\leq t_0+n}\varphi$ *are in L_2.*

Note that the only difference between L_2 and L_1 is that after a bounded quantifier in L_1 only a formula with one free variable may appear, whereas in L_2 it can contain two variables one of which must appear in the bounds of the quantifier. L_2 is much more expressive than L_1. Note that if we allow another free variable t_1 in $(\exists t)_{>t_0}^{<t_0+1}\varphi(t_0, t, t_1)$ then $t_1 = t_0 + 1$ is expressible and we obtain the full power of MLO_1

2.3 Decidability

Notation. For every n we define the formula:

$$\text{Timer}_n(X_1, \ldots X_n, Y_1, \ldots, Y_n) \equiv \bigwedge_i \forall t(Y_i(t) \longleftrightarrow (\forall t_1)^{\leq t}_{>t-1} X_i(t_1))$$

i.e. each Y_i is a timer that measures if X_i persisted for at least one unit of time.

A formula is said to be in first (second) order **timer normal form** if it has the form

$$\exists \bar{Z}. \text{Timer}_n(X_1, \ldots, X_n, Y_1, \ldots, Y_n) \wedge \phi,$$

where ϕ is a first (second) order monadic formula and $\bar{Z}$ is a list of monadic variables that may contain $X_1, \ldots, X_n, Y_1, \ldots, Y_n$; all these monadic variables may occur in ϕ.

Theorem 3. *[7]*

1. *The satisfiability of the formulas in first-order timer normal form is decidable.*
2. *The satisfiability of the formulas in the second-order timed normal form under the finite variability semantics is decidable.*

Note: Unless explicitly otherwise stated as in Theorem 3(2) all the decidability and expressiveness results in this paper, like Theorem 3(1), hold both for the unrestricted canonical semantics and for finite variability canonical semantics. This is so since the property "X has finite variability" is expressible in pure first-order monadic logic [10], and because the transformations used in the analysis of the expressiveness apply uniformly to both semantics.

We will show (see Section 4)

Theorem 4. *The satisfiability and validity problems for L_2 formulas are decidable.*

This Theorem extends the result of [7], where we have proved that L_1 is decidable.

3 Temporal Logic (TL) and its Metric Extensions

The syntax of Temporal Logic (TL) has in its vocabulary *Predicate variables* $X_1, X_2, \ldots$ and some *(modal) connective names* with prescribed arity $O_1^{(k_1)} \ldots O_n^{(k_n)}$ (the arity notation is usually omitted). For example the "sometime in the future" connective $\Diamond$ has arity 1. The "_until_" connective has arity 2.

Atomic formulas are just variables X_i and *temporal formulas* are obtained from the atoms using Boolean connectives and applying the modal connectives: if $\varphi_1, \ldots, \varphi_{k_i}$ are temporal formulas then so is $O^{(k_i)}(\varphi_1, \ldots, \varphi_{k_i})$. As usual we write φ *until* ψ instead of *until* (φ, ψ).

Every connective $O^{(k)}$ is interpreted in R^+ as an operator $O_M^{(k)} : [P(R^+)]^k \to P(R^+)$ which assigns "the set of points where $O[P_1, \ldots, P_k]$ holds" to the k-tuple $\langle P_1, \ldots, P_k \rangle$. In the usual way an operator $O P_\varphi$ is assigned to every temporal formula φ by structural induction. Satisfaction relation $\models$ is defined as usual

$$(R^+, P_1, \ldots, P_n, \tau) \models \varphi \text{ iff } \tau \in O P_\varphi(P_1, \ldots, P_n)$$

Let φ be a formula of some logic L. Assume that $\varphi(Y, X_1, \ldots, X_n)$ has the property that for every $P_1, \ldots, P_n$ there is a unique Q such that $R^+ \models \varphi(Q, P_1, \ldots, P_n)$; then the connective O is defined by φ if $Q = O_M(P_1, \ldots, P_n) \Longleftrightarrow R^+ \models \varphi(Q, P_1, \ldots, P_n)$.

Assume that for every connective $O^{(k)}$ there is a formula $\overline{O}(t_0, X_1, \ldots, X_k)$ of some logic L such that:

$$O_M^{(k)}(P_1, \ldots, P_k) = \{\tau \mid R^+ \models \overline{O}[\tau; P_1, \ldots, P_k]\} \ .$$

This formula is called a *truth table* of $O^{(k)}$. For example the connective $\Diamond X$, "X has happened before" is defined by the truth table $\varphi(t_0, X) \equiv \exists t < t_0 . X(t)$.

It is clear that if $\varphi(t_0, X)$ is a truth table of an operator O then O is defined by the formula $\forall t . Y(t) \leftrightarrow \varphi(t, X)$.

Definition 5 *We say that a temporal logic T is expressively complete with respect to a fragment L of first order logic iff (1) every formula of T has a truth table in L and (2) every formula of L with one free variable is a truth table for a formula of T.*

3.1 Propositional Temporal Logic (PTL)

Propositional temporal logics are temporal logics with connectives defined in MLO. There are such logics which are expressively complete with respect to MLO. In particular we shall denote by PTL (Propositional Temporal Logic) the temporal logic that was proven expressively complete in [8], with the two connectives X *until* Y and X *since* Y.

– The modality X *until* Y has a truth table
  $\psi(t_0, X, Y) \equiv \exists t_1(t_0 < t_1 \wedge Y(t_1) \wedge \forall t(t_0 < t < t_1 \rightarrow X(t)))$.
– The modality X *since* Y has a truth table
  $\psi(t_0, X, Y) \equiv \exists t_1(t_0 > t_1 \wedge Y(t_1) \wedge \forall t(t_1 < t < t_0 \rightarrow X(t)))$.

3.2 Quantitative Temporal Logic (QTL)

We identified in [7] a temporal logic which is expressively complete for the Monadic Logic L_1: QTL is the temporal logic constructed from an expressively complete set of modalities for MLO *and* two new modalities $\Diamond_1 X$ - "X will happen within one unit of time" and $\Diamond_1 X$ - "X happened during the previous unit of time" defined by the tables (in t_0): $\Diamond_1 X$: $(\exists t)_{>t_0}^{\leq t_0+1} X(t)$ and $\Diamond_1 X$: $(\exists t)_{>t_0-1}^{\leq t_0} X(t)$.

Proposition 6 *[7] QTL is expressively complete for the Monadic Logic L_1 and is decidable.*

It is clear that $\Diamond_1 X$ and $\Diamond_1 X$ are the most basic metrical modalities. They are expressible in all formalisms for reasoning about real time, in particular in the popular MITL [2]. MITL was interpreted on timed state sequences and trace interval sequences and was shown to be decidable in these models [2]. Trace interval sequences encode finite variability predicates and from the decidability of MITL on trace interval sequences it is easy to derive the decidability of QTL and MITL under finite variability interpretation. On the other hand MITL modalities are expressible in L_1 [7]. Therefore from the decidability of L_1 under arbitrary canonical interpretation it follows that MITL is also decidable under arbitrary canonical interpretation.

3.3 Stronger Decidable Temporal Logics

Stronger decidable temporal logics maybe obtained by adding to QTL some more temporal connectives which are defined in the Monadic Logic L_2. Some examples will be discussed in Section 5 but none seems to be as natural as the $\Diamond_1$ connective. We also conjecture that the Logic L_2 has no finite base, i.e there is no finite set of connectives defined in L_2 which is expressively complete, but this is the subject of future work.

Definition 7 *A formula* $(\exists t)^{\prec t_0+n}_{\succ t_0+m} \phi$ *of* L_2 *is called* unnested *if the formula* ϕ *is in pure MLO,* $m < n$ *and* $\prec \in \{\leq, <\}$ *and* $\succ \in \{\geq, >\}$.

Definition 8 *A logic* T' *is* effectively more expressive *than a logic* T *if for every formula* p *of* T *one can effectively construct a formula* p' *of* T' *such that* p *is equivalent to* p'.

Proposition 9 *Let* T *be a temporal logic. Assume that every connective has a table definable in* L_2. *Then there is an effectively more expressive temporal logic* T' *such that every connective of* T' *has a table definable by an unnested* L_2 *formula.*

Proposition 10 *Let* L *be a temporal logic. Assume that every connective has an operator that is defined by a formula in first-order (second-order) timer normal form. Then the operator of every* L *formula is effectively definable by a formula in first-order (respectively second-order) timer normal form.*

Note that Proposition 10 does not hold if we write everywhere "defined by a truth table" instead of "defined by a formula". This is the reason why we generalized the notion of truth table to that of a defining formula.

4 Main Technical Results

Theorem 11. *1. Let* $\varphi(t_0, t)$ *be a formula of first-order MLO and* $m < n$ *be integers. The operator with truth table* $(\exists t)^{\leq t_0+n}_{\leq t_0+m} \varphi(t_0, t)$ *is definable by a formula in first-order timer normal form, which is effectively constructed from* φ. *Similarly for the tables with one or two weak inequalities replacing the strict ones.*

   2. Let $\varphi(t_0, t)$ *be a formula of second-order MLO and* $m < n$ *be integers. The operator with truth table* $(\exists t)^{\leq t_0+n}_{\leq t_0+m} \varphi(t_0, t)$ *is definable by a formula* ψ *in second-order timer normal form, moreover,* ψ *is effectively constructed from* φ. *Similarly for the tables with one or two weak inequalities replacing the strict ones.*

   3. Let $\varphi(t_0, t)$ *be a formula of second-order MLO and* $m < n$ *be integers. For the semantics of finite variability predicates the operator with truth table* $(\exists t)^{\leq t_0+n}_{>t_0+m} \varphi(t_0, t)$ *is definable by a formula* ψ *in second-order timer normal form, moreover,* ψ *is effectively constructed from* φ. *Similarly for the tables with one or two weak inequalities replacing the strict ones.*

About the proof: Given an interval I and monadic predicates on I we denote by $Th^n(I)$ the set of all sentences with quantifier depth n that are true in I with these predicates. The key observation for (1) is that Th^n of a lexicographical sum of two intervals is definable from the Th^n theory of the summands [4]. For (2) and (3) we use a similar theorem for monadic second order logic [14].

Theorem 12. *1. Assume that every connective of a temporal logic* T *has a truth table of the form* $(\exists t)^{\leq t_0+n}_{>t_0+m} \varphi(t_0, t)$, *where* $\varphi(t_0, t)$ *is a formula of first-order MLO and* $m < n$ *are integers. Then* T *is decidable. Similarly for the tables with one or two weak inequalities replacing the strict ones.*

   2. Assume that every connective of a temporal logic T *has a a truth table definable in* L_2. *Then* T *is decidable.*

3. *Assume that every connective of a temporal logic T has a truth table of the form $(\exists t)^{\leq t_0+n}_{\leq t_0+m}\varphi(t_0, t)$, where $\varphi(t_0, t)$ is a formula of second-order MLO and $m < n$ are integers. Then T is decidable under finite variability semantics. Similarly for the tables with one or two weak inequalities replacing the strict ones.*

Proof. (Sketch) (1) and (3) follows from Theorem 11, Proposition 10 and Theorem 3. (2) follows from (1) and Proposition 9.

Observe that satisfiability of L_2 formulas is effectively reducible to the satisfiability of L_2 formulas with one free variable. This observation together with Theorem 12 implies Theorem 4 (Section 2) that states that L_2 is decidable.

5 Decidable Extension of QTL

5.1 Example

We add to QTL a new temporal connective $(\Diamond X_1, \Diamond X_2)_1$: "$X_1$ and then X_2 will both happen within one unit of time". The table for this connective is given by the MLO_1 formula $\exists t_1 t_2. (t_0 < t_1 < t_2 < t_0 + 1 \wedge X_1(t_1) \wedge X_2(t_2))$. This can be easily reformulated as a L_2 formula: $(\exists t)^{\leq t_0+1}_{> t_0}.\exists t_1 t_2(t_0 < t_1 < t_2 < t \wedge X_1(t_1) \wedge X_2(t_2))$. Therefore the extended logic is decidable by Theorem 12. The following proposition shows that this is a *proper* extension of QTL

Proposition 13 *The connective $(\Diamond X_1, \Diamond X_2)$ is not expressible in QTL (or equivalently in $MITL$).*

Proof. (Sketch) Let $X(t)$ be a predicate that is true exactly at the points $n \times \frac{2}{3}$ for all natural numbers n. It can be shown by structural induction that every QTL formula concerning X is equivalent from some point t_0 on to either X or to $\neg X$ or to *true* or to *false*. On the other hand the formula $(\Diamond X, \Diamond X)_1$ does not have this property.

Similarly we can obtain a proper increasing hierarchy of connectives $(\Diamond X_1, \ldots, \Diamond X_n)_1$ which are all definable in L_2 by formulas

$$(\exists t)^{\leq t_0+1}_{> t_0}.\exists t_1 t_2 \ldots t_n(t_0 < t_1 < \ldots < t_n < t \wedge \bigwedge_i X_i(t_i)).$$

In contrast one can show

Proposition 14 *TL extended by the connective which states that the interval (t_0, t_0+1) can be partitioned into three subintervals such that X_1 holds on the first subinterval, X_2 holds on the second and X_3 holds on the third is undecidable.*

In the next subsection we provide some definitions about finite variability signals and thereafter define a variety of decidable connectives to illustrate the expressive power of L_2.

5.2 Finite Variability Signals and their Traces

A string $l_0 l_1 \ldots l_n$ is **stuttering free** iff it is non empty and no two adjacent symbols in it are equal.

Recall that a function η from a bounded subinterval (a, b) of the reals into a finite set Σ has *finite variability* if there exists a finite increasing sequence $a = a_0 < a_1 \ldots < a_n = b$ such that η is constant on every interval (a_i, a_{i+1}).

A function f from R^+ to Σ has finite variability if for every bounded interval I the restriction of f to I has finite variability.

The following lemma is straightforward.

Lemma 15 *Suppose that $\eta : (a, b) \to \Sigma$ has finite variability, then there exists a unique increasing sequence $a = a_0 < a_1 < a_2 \ldots < a_n = b$ such that*

1. *η is almost constant on every interval (a_i, a_{i+1}), i.e., for every i there is $l_i \in \Sigma$ such that the set $\{x \in (a_i, a_{i+1}) : \eta(x) \neq l_i\}$ is finite.*
2. *For every $i < n - 1$, the value of η on (a_i, a_{i+1}) differs from the value of η on (a_{i+1}, a_{i+2}).*

Definition 16 *(Trace of a finite variability function.) Let η be a finite variability function over (a, b) and let $a_0, \ldots, a_n$ be as in Lemma 15. For $i < n$ let l_i be the values of η on (a_i, a_{i+1}). The trace of η (denoted by $\mathrm{trace}(\eta)$) is the stuttering free string $l_0 l_1 \ldots l_{n-1}$.*

Trace of a tuple: Let $\langle \eta_1, \ldots, \eta_n \rangle$ be an n-tuple of finite variability functions from (a, b) into $\{0, 1\}$. With this n-tuple we associate a function η from (a, b) into $\{0, 1, \ldots, 2^n - 1\}$ defined as $\eta(t) = i$ if $\langle \eta_1(t), \ldots, \eta_n(t) \rangle$ is the binary representation of i. The above mapping defines a one-to-one correspondence between the set of n-tuple of finite variability functions from (a, b) into $\{0, 1\}$ and finite variability functions from (a, b) into $\{0, \ldots, 2^n - 1\}$. The trace of an n-tuple (denoted by $\mathrm{trace}(\eta_1, \ldots, \eta_n)$) is defined as the trace of the corresponding function.

5.3 Automata Modality

Let R be a regular expression over the alphabet $\{0, 1\}^n$ and let $k < m$ be integers. Define the n-ary connective $R_{k,m}$ as follows: $R_{k,m}(X_1, \ldots, X_n)$ holds at t_0 if there is $t' \in (t_0 + k, t_0 + m)$ such that $\mathrm{trace}(Y_1, \ldots, Y_n) \in R$, where Y_i is the restriction of X_i to (t_0, t').

Proposition 17 *The extension of QTL by the connectives $R_{k,m}$ is decidable for finite variability semantics.*

Proof. (Sketch) It is straightforward to show that for every regular expression R there is a formula $\phi_R(t_0, t, \bar{X})$ in pure monadic second order logic such that $\phi_R(t_0, t, \bar{X})$ holds iff $\mathrm{trace}(Y_1, \ldots, Y_n) \in R$, where Y_i is the restriction of X_i to (t_0, t). Hence, by Theorem 12, the logic is decidable.

5.4 Decidable Modalities about a Whole Interval

Let s be a stuttering free string over the alphabet $\{0, 1\}^n$ and let $k < m$ be integers.

Define an n-ary connective s_m as follows: $s_m(X_1, \ldots, X_n)$ holds at t_0 if $\mathrm{trace}(Y_1, \ldots, Y_n) = s$, where Y_i is the restriction of X_i to $(t_0, t_0 + m)$.

Proposition 18 *The extension of QTL by the connectives s_m is decidable.*

Proof. (Sketch) We will show that the connective s_m is definable in L_2 and therefore, the extension is decidable. It is easy to write a a first order monadic formula $\phi_1(\bar{X}, t_0, t)$ which says that the trace of $\overline{X}$ on the interval (t_0, t) is s; it is also easy to write a first order monadic formula $\phi_2(\bar{X}, t_0, t)$ which says that the trace of $\overline{X}$ on the interval (t_0, t) has length greater than the length of s. The desirable formula is:

$$(\exists t)^{\leq t_0+n}_{>t_0} \phi_1 \wedge \neg(\exists t)^{\leq t_0+n}_{>t_0} \phi_2.$$

Observe that the s_1 connective specifies what will happen on the entire interval of length one and it is still decidable unlike the connectives discussed in Proposition 14.

5.5 Duration Calculus Connectives

The Duration Calculus (DC for brevity) [16] is a formalism for the specification of real time systems. The Duration Calculus is based on interval logic and uses real numbers to model time. DC has been successfully applied in case studies of software embedded systems, e.g., a gas burner [13], a railway crossing [15] and has been used to define the real time semantics of other languages.

DC formulas specify properties of intervals. For the lack of space we will not define the syntax and the semantics of DC. Let us note here that the basic semantical relation is whether a formula D holds on an interval I.

It was shown in [12, 11] that the propositional fragment of DC is a fragment of first-order monadic logic of order. Hence for every formula D of Propositional Duration Calculus and integers $k < m$ the following connectives are definable in L_2:

1. $D_{k,m}$ holds at t_0 iff there is $t \in (t_0 + k, \ t_0 + m)$ such that D holds on the interval (t_0, t).
2. D_k holds at t_0 iff there is $t \in (t_0, \ t_0 + k)$ such that D holds on the interval (t_0, t).
3. D_k^{sub} holds at t_0 iff there is a subinterval I of $(t_0, \ t_0 + k)$ such that D holds on I.

5.6 More Connectives

Note that all connectives mentioned above specify only non metrical properties of subintervals of $(t_0, \ t_0 + k)$. Connectives that specify metrical properties can be also easily formulated in L_2. For example, it is straightforward to say in L_2 that interval $(t_0, \ t_0 + 5)$ contains a subinterval of length at least one where X holds and a subinterval of length at least three where Y is dense.

A formula $\varphi(t_0, t)$ is fictious outside $(t_0, \ t)$ if it depends only on the values of X inside $(t_0, \ t)$. All connectives defined above used only such formulas inside bounded quantifiers. It is conceivable that interesting connectives may rise from the use of a formula $\varphi(t_0, t)$ which is not fictious outside $(t_0, \ t)$.

6 Conclusion

We developed a logical framework for defining decidable temporal logics. It is strong enough to define in it all the decidable temporal logics that we found in the literature. We use as semantics the standard model of the positive real line with all the signals or with finite variability signals.

In the survey [3] sixteen models for real time logics are provided (see Section 2.2 there). The canonical model and the finite variability canonical model are not among these models; the sixteen models are all ω-sequences either of points on the time line ("state sequences") or of time intervals ("interval trace sequences"). These models do not faithfully reflect the real line. They were probably chosen in order to prove decidability by reduction to Alur-Dill timed automata [1] which in turn are reduced to ω-automata. Our proof of decidability is automata free and works for general predicates as well as finite variability predicates. A more detailed comparison of the canonical model to sequence models and of QTL to the other formalisms can be found in [7].

For finite variability models the complexity of the satisfiability problem for pure first-order monadic logic is non-elementary while it is PSPACE complete for pure TL. In [7] we described a polynomial reduction of QTL to pure temporal logic (as far as satisfiability is concerned). The proof uses pure logical equivalences which are valid in all canonical models. By a simple analysis of the complexity of the translation of

$MITL$ into QTL we obtain easily the complexity results about $MITL$ [2] without tailoring special automata as in the previous proofs. The analysis of the complexity of the temporal logics with L_2 definable modalities is left as future endeavor.

It is easy to modify the theory to deal with more general time lines. For the rational line Rabin [9] proved that pure *second order* monadic logic is decidable and we obtain a stronger version of Theorem 12. For more general orders that do not have a natural $+1$ function the function should be replaced by a binary relation $R(t_1, t_2)$ satisfying some simple axioms that can be interpreted as expressing a notion of "t_2 is not too far ahead of t_1". A closer analysis will be needed to find out under what conditions on the order do we have Theorem 12.

Wilke [17] uses monadic logic to obtain stronger decidable logics. His main recipe for defining decidable connectives is like Proposition 17 but for the state sequence model. His work very much influenced ours both conceptually and technically.

Acknowledgments

We thank the anonymous referees for their valuable remarks that helped to improve the paper.

References

1. R. Alur, D. Dill A theory of timed Automata. Theoretical Computer Science 126 (1994), 183-235.
2. R. Alur, T. Feder, T.A. Henzinger. The Benefits of Relaxing Punctuality. Journal of the ACM 43 (1996) 116-146.
3. R. Alur, T.A. Henzinger. Logics and Models of Real Time: a survey. In Real Time: Theory and Practice. Editors de Bakker et al. LNCS 600 (1992) 74-106.
4. A. Ehrenfeucht. An application of games to the completeness problem for formalized theories. Fundamenta mathematicae 49,129-141,1961.
5. D.M. Gabbay, I. Hodkinson, M. Reynolds. Temporal Logics volume 1. Clarendon Press, Oxford (1994).
6. T.A. Henzinger, J.F. Raskin, P.Y. Schobbens. The Regular Real Time Languages. 25th ICALP (1998).
7. Y. Hirshfeld and A. Rabinovich Quantitative Temporal Logic. Submitted, 1998.
8. H. Kamp. Tense Logic and the Theory of Linear Order. Ph.D. thesis, University of California L.A. (1968).
9. M. O. Rabin, Decidability of second order theories and automata on infinite trees. In *Trans. Amer. Math. Soc.*,141,pp 1-35, 1969.
10. A. Rabinovich. On the Decidability of Continuous Time Specification Formalisms. Journal of Logic and Computation vol.8 No5, (1998) pp 669-678.
11. A. Rabinovich. On Expressive Completeness of Duration and Mean Value Calculi. Proceedings of Express 97. In the Electronic Notes of Theoretical Computer Science vol 7, 1997.
12. A. Rabinovich. Expressive Completeness of Duration Calculus. To appear in Journal of Information and Computation.
13. A. Ravn, H. Rischel and K. Hansen. Specifying and verifying requirement of real time systems. *IEEE Transaction on Software Eng.*, 1993.
14. S. Shelah. The monadic theory of order. *Ann. of Math.*, 102, pp 349-419, 1975.
15. J. Skakkæbak, A. Ravn, H. Rischel, Zhou Chaochen. Specification of Embedded Real time Systems. In Proc. of 1992 Euromicro workshop on Real Time Systems. IEEE Computer Society Press.

16. Zhou Chaochen, C.A.R. Hoare and A. Ravn. A calculus of Duration. *Information processing Letters*, 40(5):269-279, 1991.
17. T. Wilke. Specifying Time State Sequences in Powerful Decidable Logics and Time Automata. In Formal Techniques in Real Time and Fault Tolerance Systems. LNCS 863 (1994), 694-715.

On the Power of Las Vegas II.
Two-Way Finite Automata[*]

Juraj Hromkovič[1], and Georg Schnitger[2]

[1] Lehrstuhl für Informatik I, RWTH Aachen,
Ahornstraße 55, 52074 Aachen, Germany
[2] Fachbereich Informatik, Johann Wolfgang Goethe Universität Frankfurt,
Robert Mayer Straße 11-15, 60054 Frankfurt am Main, Germany

Abstract. The investigation of the computational power of randomized computations is one of the central tasks of complexity and algorithm theory. This paper continues in the comparison of the computational power of Las Vegas computations with the computational power of deterministic and nondeterministic ones. While for one-way finite automata the power of different computational modes was successfully determined one does not have any nontrivial result relating the power of determinism, Las Vegas and nondeterminism for two-way finite automata. The three main results of this paper are the following ones.

(i) If, for a regular language L, there exist small two-way nondeterministic finite automata for both L and $L^{\complement}$, then there exists a small two-way Las Vegas finite automaton for L.

(ii) There is a quadratic gap between nondeterminism and Las Vegas for two-way finite automata.

(iii) For every $k \in \mathbb{N}$, there is a regular language S_k such that S_k can be accepted by two-way Las Vegas finite automaton with $O(k)$ states, but every two-way deterministic finite automaton recognizing S_k has at least $\Omega(k^2 / \log_2 k)$ states.

1 Introductions and Definitions

The comparative study of the computational power of deterministic, randomized and nondeterministic computations is one of the central tasks of complexity and algorithm theory. This is not surprising because the current view on the specification of the class of tractable problems is that the computing problems are tractable (practically solvable) if there exist randomized polynomial-time algorithms for them. In this paper we focus on the power of Las Vegas computations.[1] The central questions P versus ZPP and ZPP versus NP are unresolved. But for restricted models some progress has been achieved. A linear relation between determinism and Las Vegas was established for the time complexity of

---

[*] The work on this paper has been supported by DFG-Project HR 14/3-2.
[1] The term "Las Vegas" was introduced by Babai [Ba79] to distinguish probabilistic algorithms that reply correctly when they reply at all from those that occasionally (with some bounded probability) make a mistake.

CREW PRAMs [DKR94] and one-way communication complexity [DHRS97]. A polynomial relation between determinism and Las Vegas is known for the combinational complexity of non-uniform circuits (see, for instance, [We87]), two-way communication complexity [MS82], the size of one-way finite automata [DHRS97] and the size of OBDDs [DHRS97]. The last result is in contrast to the exponential gap between Las Vegas and determinism for one-time-only branching programs [Sa99] that are a generalization of OBDDs. An exponential gap between Las Vegas and nondeterminism is known for one-way finite automata [DHRS97], two-way and one-way communication complexity (see, for instance, [AHY83], [Hr97], [KN97], [PS84], [Ya79]) and OBDDs [Sa97][2].

In this paper we concentrate on two-way finite automata. In contrast to the well-developed theory of one-way finite automata we do not know to answer basic questions (like whether there is a polynomial relation between determinism and nondeterminism) for two-way automata. Only when restricting this model to so-called two-way sweeping finite automata, Sipser [Si80] has proved an exponential gap between determinism and nondeterminism. Whether an exponential gap exists in the general case is a famous old open problem [Be80], [Mi81], [SS78], [Si79], [Si80]. Two-way Las Vegas finite automata have not been considered up till now.

In this paper we consider four finite automata models: two-way deterministic finite automaton (2DFA), two-way Las Vegas finite automaton (2LFA), two-way self-verifying nondeterministic finite automaton (2SVNFA) and two-way nondeterministic finite automaton (2NFA). For 2DFAs and 2NFAs we consider the standard definition used in the literature [HU79], [Si80]. The states of these automata are considered to be divided into three disjoint sets of working, accepting and rejecting states. No action is possible from any rejecting or accepting state. For convenience we assume that the nondeterministic choice of 2NFAs is bounded by 2. For every automaton A, $L(A)$ denotes the language accepted by A. A configuration of an finite automaton A is a pair (p, i_1), where p is a state of the automaton A and i_1 is the position of the head on the input tape.

For 2LVFAs and 2SVNFAs we consider the standard definitions as introduced in [DHRS97]. A 2SVNFA M can be viewed as a 2NFA with four types of states: working, accepting, rejecting and neutral ("I do not know") states. There is no possible move from accepting, rejecting and neutral states. M is not allowed to make mistakes: If there is a computation of M on an input x finishing in an accepting (rejecting) state, then x must be in $L(M)$ (x may not be in $L(M)$, i.e. $x \in (L(M))^c$). For every input y there is at least one computation of M that finishes either in an accepting state (if $y \in L(M)$) or in an rejecting state (if $y \notin L(M)$).

A 2LVFA A may be viewed as a 2SVNFA with probabilities assigned to every nondeterministic branching. The probability of a computation of A is defined through the transition probabilities of A. We require for every $y \in L(A)$

[2] There are several further results for Monte Carlo randomized (one-sided error and two-sided error) computations but we do not deal with this form of randomization here.

$(y \notin L(A))$ that A reaches an accepting (rejecting) state with a probability of at least $1/2$.

For any regular language L we define $s(L)$, $ns(L)$, $svns(L)$ and $lvs(L)$ respectively as the size (the number of states) of a minimal one-way deterministic, nondeterministic, self-verifying nondeterministic and Las Vegas finite automaton for L. Analogously, we define $s_2(L)$, $ns_2(L)$, $svns_2(L)$ and $lvs_2(L)$ for two-way versions of these automata. In [DHRS97] it is proved that $lvs(L) \geq \sqrt{s(L)}$ for every regular language L and the optimality of this lower bound is proved by constructing a language L' with $s(L') = \Omega((lvs(L'))^2)$. Moreover, exponential gaps between $svns(L)$ and $lvs(L)$, and between $svns(L)$ and $ns(L)$ are established in [DHRS97].

The proofs of these results are based on the following fact that $s(L)$ is exactly the number of messages of the best uniform one-way communication protocol for L. For every mode of computation the number of messages of the best one-way protocol is a lower bound on the number of states of the corresponding finite automata model. Since we know the relations between determinism, Las Vegas and nondeterminism for two-way communication protocols and the number of messages of the best two-way deterministic (Las Vegas, nondeterministic) protocols for L is a trivial lower bound on $s_2(L)$ ($lvs_2(L)$, $ns_2(L)$), the first idea could be to investigate the relations between $s_2(L)$, $lvs_2(L)$, $svns_2(L)$ and $ns_2(L)$ in the same way as in the one-way case. But in the two-way case this approach does not work because there is an exponential gap between $s_2(L)$ and the numbers of messages of the optimal two-way protocol[3].

We focus on the relation between $lvs_2(L)$ on one side and the other measures on the other side. Our main results are as follows:

1. For every regular language L,

$$lvs_2(L) \leq 4 \cdot svns_2(L) + 3.$$

2. There is a sequence of regular languages $\{M_k\}_{k=1}^{\infty}$ such that
   (i) $ns_2(M_k) \leq 2k + O(1)$,
   (ii) $lvs_2(M_k) \geq k^2 - 2$.
3. There is a sequence of regular languages $\{S_k\}_{k=1}^{\infty}$ such that
   (i) $lvs_2(S_k) = O(k)$,
   (ii) $s_2(S_k) = \Omega(k^2/\log k)$ and
   (iii) $lvs(S_k) = 2^{\Omega(k)}$.
4. There is a sequence of regular languages $\{L_k\}_{k=1}^{\infty}$ such that
   (i) $ns(L_k) = O(k^3)$ and $ns_2(L_k) = O(k)$,
   (ii) $ns((L_k)^C) \geq 2^k$ and so $s(L_k) \geq lvs(L_k) \geq 2^k$,
   (iii) $lvs_2(L_k) = O(k)$.

By the first result, small two-way nondeterministic finite automata for L and L^C imply a small 2LVFA for L. The second result shows a quadratic gap between nondeterminism and Las Vegas. The third result shows an almost quadratic gap

---

[3] This contrasts to the one-way case where the complexities measures are even equal

between determinism and Las Vegas for two-way finite automata. The last result shows that two-way Las Vegas can be essentially better than one-way nondeterminism. A consequence is an exponential gap between one-way Las Vegas finite automata and two-way ones. Moreover, the language L_k is a candidate for an exponential gap between two-way Las Vegas and two-way determinism.

The paper is organized as follows. Section 2 verifies the first two results that compare nondeterminism and Las Vegas. In section 3 the last two results focusing on the comparison of Las Vegas and determinism are presented. The last section 5 is devoted to a discussion and the formulation of some open problems.

2 Las Vegas versus Nondeterminism

In this section we show that in some sense the power of 2LVFAs is not too far from 2SVNFAs. First we present a simple claim.

Claim. For any language L:

$$\max\left\{ns_2(L), ns_2(L^\complement)\right\} \leq svns_2(L) \leq ns_2(L) + ns_2(L^\complement) + 1.$$

Proof. Every 2SNFA A can be transformed into a 2NFA B by adding the neutral states of A to the set of rejecting states of A. Obviously $L(A) = L(B)$ and $s(A) = s(B)$. If one takes the rejecting states of A as the accepting ones of an 2NFA C, and the accepting and the neutral states of A as the rejecting ones of C, then $L(C) = (L(A))^\complement$ and $s(C) = s(A)$. Thus, $svns(L) \geq \max\left\{ns(L), ns(L^\complement)\right\}$.

Let E and F be two 2NFAs such that $L(E) = (L(F))^\complement$. A 2SNFA D recognizing $L(E)$ can be constructed as follows. D connects a new initial state via ε-moves to the initial states of E and F. The set of accepting sets of D is exactly the set of accepting states of E, and the set of rejecting states of D is exactly the set of accepting of F. All remaining non-working states of E and F are neutral states of D. □

We first establish a linear relation between $svns_2(L)$ and $lvs_2(L)$ for every regular language L, i.e. small nondeterministic finite automata for L and $L^\complement$ imply the existence of a small two-way Las Vegas finite automaton for L.

Theorem 1. *For every regular language L,*

$$svns_2(L) \leq lvs_2(L) \leq 4 \cdot svns_2(L) + 3.$$

Proof. We give a proof idea only. $svns_2(L) \leq lvs_2(L)$ is obvious because every 2LVNFA can be viewed as a 2SVNFA. To simulate an 2SVNFA by a 2LVFA it is sufficient to modify the method of Macarie and Seiferas [MS97] used to simulate two-way nondeterministic k-head finite automata by two-way one-sided error probabilistic k-head finite automata for $k \geq 2$. □

Now, we show that nondeterminism can be more powerful than Las Vegas for two-way automata. Towards this goal we consider the following languages

$$M_k = \{w \in \{0,1\}^* \mid \text{if } w = w_1 w_2 ... w_m, \ w_i \in \{0,1\}, \text{ for } i = 1, ..., m,$$
$$\text{then there exists } r \in \mathbb{N} \text{ such that } w_{r(k^2-1)} = 1\}$$

for any $k \in \mathbb{N}$.

Theorem 2. *For any positive integer k:*

(i) $ns_2(M_k) = 2k + O(1)$,
(ii) $lvs_2(M_k) \geq k^2 - 2$.

Proof. (i) We first describe a 2NFA A_k that accepts M_k. A_k moves $r \cdot (k+1)$ steps to the right for some nondeterministically guessed $r \in \mathbb{N}$, and checks whether $w_{r \cdot (k+1)} = 1$. Then A_k moves $l \cdot (k-1)$ steps to the left for some $l \in \mathbb{N}$. If after these $l \cdot (k-1)$ steps to the left A_k reaches the left endmarker, then $r \cdot (k+1) = l \cdot (k-1)$, i.e. the index of the right most visited position is divisible by $(k^2 - 1) = (k+1) \cdot (k-1)$.

(ii) Following Claim 2 it is sufficient to prove $ns_2(M_k^{\complement}) \geq k^2 - 2$. We prove it by contradiction.

Let B_k be a 2NFA accepting $M_k^{\complement}$ and $s(B_k) < k^2 - 2$. We consider the word $1^{k^2-2}0$ which does not belong to M_k, i.e. $1^{k^2-2}0 \in M_k^{\complement}$. Using standard pumping argument we show that B_k must accept $1^{k^2-2+k^2!}0$. Let D be an accepting computation of B_k on $1^{k^2-2}0$. We can write D as $C_1, C_2, ..., C_m$ for some $m \in \mathbb{N}$, where

1. for $\forall i \in \{0, 1, ..., \lceil m/4 \rceil - 1\}$, C_{1+4i} is a part of the computation D in which only the symbols of the input part $\notcent 1^{k^2-2}$ were read and the last action in C_{1+4i} was the movement to the right after reading $\notcent$.
2. for every $i \in \{1, 2, ..., \lfloor m/2 \rfloor\}$, C_{2i} is a part of the computation D in which every 1 has been read at least once by M_k, no symbol different from 1 was read, and in the last step of C_{2j} the reading head was moved to a symbol different from 1.
3. for $\forall i \in \{0, 1, ..., L(m-3)/4\}$, C_{3+4i} is a part of the computation D in which only the symbols of the input part $1^{k^2-2}0\$ were read, and the last action in C_{3+4i} was the movement to the left after reading 0.

The computation parts of the kind 2. are called **exhaustive walks** (on 1^{k^2-2}), and the other parts (of the kind 1. and 3.) are called **local walks** (on 1^{k^2-2}). As one can see at Figure 1 the reading head crosses the whole subword 1^{k^2-2} from one side to the other side in any exhaustive walk (parts C_2, C_4 and C_6 at Figure 1).

Intuitively, in any local walk the number of 1's in the input cannot be measured. Since every exhaustive walk C_{2j} consists of at least $k^2 - 2$ steps, and $s(B_k) < k^2 - 2$, a state p_j has appeared at least twice in C_{2j}. Moreover, we

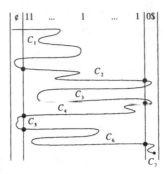

Fig. 1. A partition of a computation an the input $1^{k^2-2}0$.

may assume that B_k is in the state p_j in different configurations $\langle p_j, i_{j,1}\rangle$, and $\langle p_j, i_{j,2}\rangle$, $i_{j,1} < i_{j,2}$. So, C_{2j} may be written as

$$C_{2j} = C_{2j,1}, \langle p_j, i_{j,1}\rangle, C_{2j,2}, \langle p_j, i_{j,2}\rangle, C_{2j,3}.$$

Now, we consider the word $1^{k^2-2+k^2!}0$ that is obviously in M_k and so not in M_k^C. We construct an accepting computation H of B_k on $1^{k^2-2+k^2!}$.
Let, for any configuration C, $\tilde{C}$ denote the state of C. Analogously, for any computation $F = F_1, ..., F_m$, $\tilde{F} = \tilde{F}_1, ..., \tilde{F}_m$ is the sequence of states of F. So, the computation H on $1^{k^2-2+k^2!}$ can be determined by $\tilde{H}$ as follows:

$$\tilde{H} = \tilde{C}_1, \tilde{C}_{2,1}, \left(p_1, \tilde{C}_{2,2}\right)^{k^2!/(i_{1,2}-i_{1,1})} p_1, \tilde{C}_{2,3},$$

$$\tilde{C}_3, \tilde{C}_{4,1}, \left(p_2, \tilde{C}_{4,2}\right)^{k^2!/(i_{2,2}-i_{2,1})} p_2, \tilde{C}_{4,3},$$

$$\tilde{C}_5, ..., \tilde{C}_m.$$

This construction works because $0 < i_{j,2}, -i_{j,1} \leq k^2 - 2$ for every i, and so $i_{j,2} - i_{j,1}$ divides $k^2!$ for every j.

$\square$

3　Las Vegas versus Determinism

The goal of this section is to find a family of languages $S_1, S_2, S_3, ...$, such that S_k can be recognized with $O(k)$ states by 2LVFAs but not within a linear number of states by 2DFAs. Following the result of section 2 we see that we have to search for languages S_k such that both S_k and S_k^C are easy for two-way nondeterministic finite automata but not for the deterministic ones. To achieve this goal we shall consider languages whose words define directed, acyclic graphs embedded in the two-dimensional grid. The idea is to define the membership of a word in S_k in such a way that one requires (for the acceptance) the existence of a directed path leading from the upper boundary to the lower boundary of the layout of the corresponding graph. Usually, to find a path nondeterministically is easy. But the main point is that we restrict the class of graphs considered (and their layouts, too) in such a way that it is also easy to nondeterministically verify the non-existence of such paths. On the other hand the class of graphs considered is sufficiently complicated for a superlinear lower bound on the number of states of 2DFAs.

In what follows, we consider the alphabet $\Sigma = \{\#, a_1, a_2, a_3, ..., a_{10}\}$, where the a_i's have the geometrical interpretations as depicted at Figure 2. Each a_i represents a square of the layout of a graph in the two-dimensional grid. Each such square contains either four or five vertices. Each of the four boundaries of the square contains exactly one vertex. The fifth vertex, if any, lies in the middle of the square (see the interpretation of symbols a_7, a_8, a_9, a_{10}). Some directed edges between the vertices of the squares are allowed. Following Figure 2, we see that the edges lead only from the left to the right or downwards. Note, that this is a crucial fact in our construction. If we would allow edges in other directions, then we would not be able to find any simple 2LVFA for the language constructed. On the other hand if one would take still a harder restriction like the prohibition of the use of $a_6{}^4$, then we would not be able to prove any superlinear lower bound on the size of two-way deterministic finite automata.

In what follows, we consider that only words from

$$U = \bigcup_{i=1}^{\infty} U_i, \ U_i = \#^{i+1} \left(\# \Sigma^i \#\right)^* \#^{i+1},$$

have geometrical representations. Figure 3 shows the geometrical interpretations for two words x and y from U_4. The symbol $\#$ defines the boundary of the layout and every subword from $\#\Sigma^i\#$ correspond to one row of the picture. So, the words from U_i correspond to layouts with i columns and an arbitrary number of rows. For any $x \in L$, we denote by $G(x)$ the directed, acyclic graph determined by x, and $Pic(x)$ denotes the layout of $G(x)$ in the grid as depicted at Figure 3. In what follows we will speak about rows and columns of pictures (graph layout). The rows are ordered in the order of their occurrence in the input word. For instance $a_5a_4a_2a_7$ is the first row of $Pic(x)$. The columns are ordered from the left to the right. For instance, the second column of $Pic(y)$ correspond to $a_4a_8a_2$. For any row R of a $Pic(z)$ for a $z \in U_i$, we distinguish three classes of vertices of $G(x)$:

---

[4] This corresponds to the requirement for the planarity of the layout.

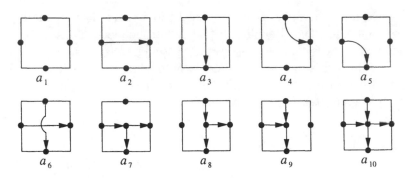

Fig. 2. The geometrical interpretation of the symbols of Σ.

- the *upper vertices* of R (exactly i vertices),
- the *middle vertices* of R (j vertices with $i + 1 \leq j \leq 2i + 1$),
- the *lower vertices* of R (exactly i vertices)

with the obvious meaning. So, the lower vertices of the m-th row R_m are the upper vertices of the $(m + 1)$-th row R_{m+1}. The only own vertices of every row are its middle vertices. Similarly, we speak about *left*, *middle* and *right* vertices for every column of a picture. The upper vertices of the first row of a picture $Pic(z)$, $z \in U$, are called the *sources of the graph* $G(z)$. The lower vertices of the last row of a picture $Pic(z)$, $z \in U$, are called the *destinations of the graph* $G(z)$. For every $i \in \mathbb{N}$ and every $z \in U_i$, $s_1(z)$, $s_2(z)$, ..., $s_i(z)$ ($d_1(z)$, $d_2(z)$, ..., $d_i(z)$) denote of the sources (the destinations) of $G(z)$. Note, that $s_i(z)$ and $d_i(z)$ are the middle vertices of the i-th column of $Pic(z)$.

Before defining some special languages we give an obvious claim about U_i's.

Claim. For every $i \in \mathbb{N}$, the language U_i can be accepted by a one-way deterministic finite automaton with $3 \cdot (i + 2)$ states.

Observe, that one can interpret a two-way finite automaton A as moving within $Pic(x)$ instead on x. Obviously, each horizontal movement in the picture corresponds to one step on A on x. To realize a vertical movement A needs to move $k + 2$ steps using $k + 2$ special states.

To get a quadratic gap between 2LVFAs and 2DFAs we consider very special graph layouts. Let, for every even $k \in \mathbb{N}$,

$$
\begin{aligned}
S_k = \{ &x \in U_k \mid x = \#^{k+1} \# x_1 \# x_2 \# ... \# x_{k/2+4} \# \#^{k+1}, \\
&|x_i| = k \text{ for } i = 1, ..., k/2 + 4, \\
&x_1, x_{k/2+4} \in a_1^* a_3 a_1^*, x_2 = (a_3 a_1)^{k/2}, x_{k/2+3} = (a_1 a_3)^{k/2}, \\
&\text{for } i = 3, 4, ..., k/2 + 2, x_i \in (a_0 a_3)^{i-3} a_4 b (a_6 b)^*, b \in \{a_6, a_{10}\}, \\
&G(x) \text{ contains a directed path from a source to a destination} \}.
\end{aligned}
$$

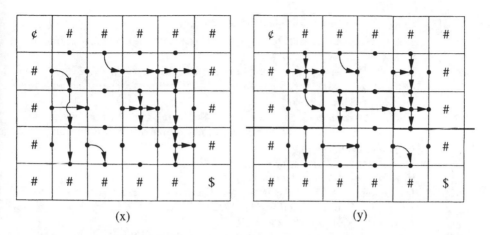

Fig. 3. The geometrical interpretation of the input words
$x = \#^6 a_5 a_4 a_2 a_7 \# \# a_6 a_1 a_{10} a_3 \# \# a_3 a_5 a_1 a_8 \#^6$ and
$y = \#^6 a_{10} a_4 a_1 a_9 \# \# a_4 a_8 a_2 a_{10} \# \# a_3 a_2 a_1 a_5 \#^6$.

Observe, that for every $x \in S_k$, $G(x)$ contains exactly one path from a source to a destination, because there is only one source with outdegree 1 (given by x_1) and only one destination with indegree 1 (given by $x_{k/2+4}$). The middle part $x_2 \# x_3 \# ... \# x_{k/2+3}$ of x enables to connect any upper vertex of the second row laying in an odd column $2j - 1$ ($j = 1, ..., k/2$) with any lower vertex of the $(k/2 + 3)$-rd row that lies in one of the columns $2j, 2j + 2, ..., k$. The proof of the next theorem is omitted in this extended abstract.

Theorem 3. *For any positive, even integer k,*

(i) $svns(S_k) = O(k^3)$ and $svns_2(S_k) = O(k)$,
(ii) $lvs_2(S_k) = O(k)$,
(iii) $s_2(S_k) = \Omega(k^2/\log k)$,
(iv) $s(S_k) \geq 2^{k/2}$ and $lvs(S_k) \geq 2^{k/4}$.

Sakoda and Sipser [SS78] proved an exponential gap between 2DFAs and NFAs by presenting a language B_n with $s_2(B_n) = O(n^2)$ and $ns(B_n) \geq 2^n$. The next theorem improves this gap (if 2DFAs are exchanged by 2LVFAs) by giving a language L_n with $ns(L_n^C) = 2^{\Omega(lvs_2(L_n))}$.

Theorem 4. *For every $k \in \mathbb{N}$, there is a regular language L_k with*

(i) $ns_2(L_k) = O(k)$ and $ns(L_k) = O(k^2)$,
(ii) $ns((L_k)^C) \geq 2^k$ and so $s(L_k) \geq lvs(L_k) \geq 2^k$, and
(iii) $lvs_2(L_k) = O(k)$.

References

[AHY83] Aho, A.V., Hopcroft, J.E., Yannakakis, M.: On notions of information transfer in VLSI circuits. In: Proc. *15th Annual ACM STOCS*, ACM 1983, pp. 133–139.

[Ba79]   Babai, L.: Monte Carlo algorithms in graph isomorphism techniques. Re-
          search Report no. 79-10, Département de mathématiques et statistique, Uni-
          versité de Montréal 1979.

[Be80]   Berman, P.: A note on sweeping automata. In Proc. of *7th ICALP '80* (J.W.
          de Bakker and Jan van Leeuwen, editors), *Lecture Notes in Computer Sci-
          ence 85*, 1980, pp. 91–97.

[DHRS97] Ďuriš, P., Hromkovič, J., Rolim, J.D.P., Schnitger, G.: Las Vegas versus
          determinism for one-way communication complexity, finite automata and
          polynomial-time computations. In: Proc. *STACS '97, Lecture Notes in Com-
          puter Science* 1200, Springer 1997, pp. 117–128 (extended version submitted
          to Information and Computation).

[DKR94]   Dietzelfelbinger, M., Kutylowski, M., Reischuk, R.: Exact lower bounds for
          computing Boolean functions on CREW PRAMs. *J. Computer System Sci-
          ences* 48 (1994), pp. 231-254.

[Gi77]   Gill, J.: Computational complexity of probabilistic Turing machines. *SIAM
          J. Comput.* 6 (1977), pp. 675–695.

[Hr97]   Hromkovič, J.: *Communication Complexity and Parallel Computing.*
          Springer-Verlag 1997.

[HU79]   Hopcroft, J.E., Ullman, J.D.: *Introduction to Automata Theory, Languages
          and Computations.* Addison-Wesley, 1979.

[KN97]   Kushilevitz, E., Nisan, N.: *Communication Complexity*, Cambridge Univer-
          sity Press 1997.

[Mi81]   Micali, S.: Two-way deterministic finite automata are exponentially more
          succinct than sweeping automata. *Information Processing Letters*, 12(2),
          1981, pp. 103–105

[MS82]   Mehlhorn, K., Schmidt, E.: Las Vegas is better than determinism in VLSI
          and distributed computing. In: Proc. *14th ACM STOC'82*, ACM 1982, pp.
          330–337.

[MS97]   Macarie, I.I., Seiferas, J.I.: Strong equivalence of nondeterministic and ran-
          domized space-bounded computations. Manuscript.

[PS84]   Papadimitrou, Ch., Sipser, M.: Communication complexity. *J. Computer
          System Sciences* 28, pp. 260–269

[Sa97]   Sauerhoff, M.: On nondeterminism versus randomness for read-once branch-
          ing programs. *Electronic Colloquium on Computational Complexity*, TR 97
          - 030.

[Sa99]   Sauerhoff, M.: On the size of randomized OBDDs and read-once branch-
          ing programs for *k*-stable functions. In: Proc. *STACS '99, Lecture Notes in
          Computer Science*, 1563, Springer 1999, pp. 488–499.

[Si79]   Sipser, M.: Lower bounds on the size of sweeping automata. In: Proc. *11th
          ACM STOC*, 1979, pp. 360–364.

[Si80]   Sipser, M.: Lower bounds on the size of sweeping automata. *J. of Computer
          and System Sciences* 21 (1980), pp. 195–202.

[SS78]   Sakoda, W. J., Sipser, M.: Nondeterminism and the size of two way finite
          automata. In: *Proc. of 10th ACM STOC*, ACM 1978, pp. 275–286.

[We87]   Wegener, I.: *The Complexity of Boolean Functions.* Wiley-Teubner Series in
          Computer Science, John Wiley and Sons Ltd., and Teubner, B.G., Stuttgart
          1987.

[Ya79]   Yao, A.C.: Some complexity questions related to distributed computing. In:
          Proc. *11th ACM STOC*, ACM 1979, pp. 209–213.

Stable Marriage with Incomplete Lists and Ties

Kazuo Iwama[1]*, David Manlove[2]**, Shuichi Miyazaki[1] and Yasufumi Morita[1]

[1] School of Informatics, Kyoto University, Kyoto 606-8501, Japan
{iwama, shuichi, ymorita}@kuis.kyoto-u.ac.jp
[2] Dept. of Computing Science, University of Glasgow, Glasgow G12 8QQ, Scotland
davidm@dcs.gla.ac.uk

Abstract. The original stable marriage problem requires all men and women to submit a complete and strictly ordered preference list. This is obviously often unrealistic in practice, and several relaxations have been proposed, including the following two common ones: one is to allow an incomplete list, i.e., a man is permitted to accept only a subset of the women and vice versa. The other is to allow a preference list including ties. Fortunately, it is known that both relaxed problems can still be solved in polynomial time. In this paper, we show that the situation changes substantially if we allow both relaxations (incomplete lists and ties) *at the same time*: the problem not only becomes NP-hard, but also the optimal cost version has no approximation algorithm achieving the approximation ratio of $N^{1-\epsilon}$, where N is the instance size, unless P=NP.

1 Introduction

An instance of the *stable marriage problem* [4] consists of N men and N women. Each person has his/her *strictly* ordered preference list containing *all* the members of the opposite sex. A matching M is a one-one correspondence between *all* the men and *all* the women. If a man m and a woman w are matched in M, we say m and w are *partners* in M, and we write $M(m) = w$ and $M(w) = m$. A man m and a woman w form a *blocking pair* for a matching M if m and w are not partners in M, but m prefers w to $M(m)$ and w prefers m to $M(w)$. If there is no blocking pair for M, then M is called *stable*. The stable marriage problem was first studied by Gale and Shapley [1]. They showed that there always exists at least one stable matching in any instance and gave an $O(N^2)$-time algorithm, the so-called Gale-Shapley algorithm, to find one.

Since then, this problem has been constantly one of the most popular combinatorial problems from both theoretical and practical view points [e.g., 4]. Considering practical applications, however, the above restrictions for preference lists, namely total order and completeness, appear to be too strict on many occasions, and therefore some extensions of this problem have been proposed. The popular ones are (i) the stable marriage problem with unacceptable partners [4], and (ii) the stable marriage problem with indifference [4, 6]. In the first extension, each person is allowed to declare one or more unacceptable partners. Thus each person's preference list may be incomplete. Gale and Sotomayor [2]

---

* Supported in part by Scientific Research Grant, Ministry of Japan, 10558044, 09480055 and 10205215.
** Supported by Engineering and Physical Sciences Research Council grant number GR/M13329.

studied this extension and showed that there is a polynomial-time algorithm which determines whether there exists a stable matching and finds one if one exists (see also [4]). Thus the problem does not become essentially harder. (In this paper, the term "matching" when incomplete lists are allowed refers to a one-one correspondence between *all* the men and *all* the women, as is the definition for complete lists.)

In the second extension, each person is allowed to have a preference list with ties. m and w form a blocking pair if m and w are not partners in M, but m *strictly* prefers w to $M(m)$ (i.e., w and $M(m)$ are not tied in m's list) and w *strictly* prefers m to $M(w)$. A matching containing no such blocking pair is called *weakly stable*. (Henceforth, usage of the term "a stable matching" when ties are allowed in the lists refers to weak stability.) However, this extension also does not make the problem significantly difficult; it is known that there always exists a stable matching (and a polynomial-time algorithm finds one) [4].

Now arises the natural question, i.e., whether or not the situation changes if we apply both extensions at the same time, which was open since [6]. Our main purpose of this paper is to show that the situation does change, i.e., the problem is now NP-complete if we allow both incomplete lists and ties. The problem is also intractable for *complete* lists if the question is not the existence of stable matchings but obtaining *optimal cost* stable matchings. We furthermore show that it is probably not possible to obtain good approximation algorithms for the optimal cost problem: unless P=NP, any approximation algorithm cannot achieve $N^{1-\epsilon}$ for any $\epsilon > 0$ as its approximation ratio.

The general perception for the stable marriage problem has been that it is basically not hard [1, 4, 6]. Our results could alter this common perception. (In the case of non-bipartite setting, i.e., for the so-called hospitals/residents problem and the stable roommates problem, some intractable results have been reported [8], but none previously for the bipartite setting.)

2 Stable Marriage Problems

Recall that the original stable matching problem requires each person's preference list to be *complete* (i.e., all the members of the opposite sex must be included) and to be *totally ordered*. We focus on the three possible relaxations concerning these two restrictions. All these problems (including the original one) ask if there exists a stable matching. The first three problems are known to be in P [2, 4]. Our main result is the NP-completeness of the last one, shown in Sec.3.

SMP-CLTO: the stable marriage problem with complete list and total order.
SMP-ILTO: the stable marriage problem with incomplete list and total order.
SMP-CLT: the stable marriage problem with complete list and ties.
SMP-ILT: the stable marriage problem with incomplete list and ties.

If we consider the *cost* of a matching, we can introduce an optimization version of the stable marriage problem. Suppose that, under a stable matching M, a man m is matched with a woman w who is at the ith position in m's list. Then it is defined that the cost of the position of woman w in m's list is i and the cost of the matching M for man m is also i. The cost for a woman w is similarly defined. If there are ties in the list, then the cost of positions are determined as usual: for example, if m's list is $w_3, (w_2, w_4, w_5), w_1$, where w_2, w_4 and w_5 are tied in the list, then the cost of the positions for w_3, w_2, w_4, w_5 and w_1 are 1, 2, 2, 2 and 5, respectively. The cost of the matching M is the sum of the costs of M for all $2N$ people. (The stable matching that minimizes this cost is called the *egalitarian stable matching* [4].) Here we consider the following two problems whose preference lists are always complete:

MIN-SMP: Preference lists must be a total order.
MIN-SMP-TIES: Preference lists may contain ties.

Both problems ask to find a stable matching whose cost is as small as possible. It is known that an optimal solution for MIN-SMP may be obtained in polynomial time [4]. We shall show the NP-hardness and inapproximability of MIN-SMP-TIES in Sec.4.

3 Intractability Results

Now we prove the NP-completeness of SMP-ILT. Note that this proof is further extended to show the inapproximability of MIN-SMP-TIES in the next section.
Theorem 1. SMP-ILT is NP-complete.
Proof. It is easy to see that SMP-ILT is in NP: given a matching M, one can check, for each man m and woman w, whether m and w form a blocking pair. This can be done in polynomial time. To show the NP-hardness, let us consider the problem ONE-IN-THREE 3SAT: given a 3CNF formula, it asks if there exists a truth assignment such that exactly one literal in each clause is true.

It is known that ONE-IN-THREE 3SAT remains NP-complete even if a 3CNF formula does not include negative literals [3]. So, we translate this restricted problem into SMP-ILT. Given f, which is an instance of ONE-IN-THREE 3SAT, we construct an instance $T(f)$ of SMP-ILT consisting of (1) a set of men and the same number of women, (2) each man's preference list, and (3) each woman's preference list. Let n and l be the numbers of variables and clauses of $f = C_1 \cdot C_2 \cdots C_l$, respectively. Let t_i be the number of appearances of the variable x_i and let $t = \max\{t_1, t_2, \cdots, t_n\}$.

3.1 The set of Men and Women

$T(f)$ consists of $9l + 3n + t + 3$ men and the same number of women. We first introduce the following set of men, who are divided into the following groups:

Group (A): $t + 3$ men $m_{A,1}, \cdots, m_{A,t+3}$. Necessary for a technical reason.
Group (B): $3l$ men $m_{B,i,j}$ for $1 \le i \le l$ and $1 \le j \le 3$. The three men $m_{B,i,1}$, $m_{B,i,2}$ and $m_{B,i,3}$ correspond to the clause C_i.
Group (C): n men $m_{C,1}, \cdots, m_{C,n}$. $m_{C,i}$ is associated with the variable x_i.
Group (D): $2n$ men $m_{D,1}^+, m_{D,1}^-, \cdots, m_{D,n}^+, m_{D,n}^-$. $m_{D,i}^+$ and $m_{D,i}^-$ are associated with the variable x_i. (Note that these $+$ and $-$ signs do not relate to the polarity or the true/false value of x_i.)
Group (E): $6l$ men $m_{E,i,j}^+, m_{E,i,j}^-$. For each $1 \le i \le n$ and $1 \le j \le l$, $m_{E,i,j}^+$ and $m_{E,i,j}^-$ exist if and only if the literal x_i appears in the clause C_j. (Recall that $\overline{x_i}$ never appears in f.) Since there are $3l$ literals, $6l$ men will be introduced.

The same number ($9l + 3n + t + 3$) of women are also divided into the following five groups:

Group (a): $t + 3$ women $w_{a,1}, \cdots, w_{a,t+3}$ as Group (A) of the men.
Group (b): $2n$ women $w_{b,i}^0$ and $w_{b,i}^1$ ($1 \le i \le n$). Two women $w_{b,i}^0$ and $w_{b,i}^1$ are associated with the variable x_i.

Group (c): n women $w_{c,i}$ $(1 \leq i \leq n)$. $w_{c,i}$ is associated with the variable x_i.

Group (d): $6l$ women $w_{d,i,j}^0$ and $w_{d,i,j}^1$. For $1 \leq i \leq n$ and $1 \leq j \leq l$, two women $w_{d,i,j}^0$ and $w_{d,i,j}^1$ exist if and only if the literal x_i appears in the clause C_j.

Group (e): $3l$ women $w_{e,i,j}$. Similarly as Group-(d) women, a woman $w_{e,i,j}$ exists if and only if the literal x_i appears in the clause C_j.

3.2 Men's Preference Lists

We then construct each man's preference list (obviously in polynomial time). For better exposition, we use an example of f, i.e., $f_0 = (x_1 + x_2 + x_3)(x_1 + x_3 + x_4)$, for which the men's preference lists will turn out to be as illustrated in Table 2. As for each Group-(A) man $m_{A,i}$, his list only includes the single woman $w_{a,i}$.

Recall that the three men $m_{B,i,1}$, $m_{B,i,2}$ and $m_{B,i,3}$ in Group (B) are associated with the clause C_i. We show how to construct preference lists of men $m_{B,2,1}$, $m_{B,2,2}$ and $m_{B,2,3}$ who are associated with $C_2 = (x_1 + x_3 + x_4)$ of f_0. Since literals x_1, x_3 and x_4 appear in C_2, six women $w_{d,1,2}^0$, $w_{d,1,2}^1$ (associated with x_1 in C_2), $w_{d,3,2}^0$, $w_{d,3,2}^1$ (associated with x_3 in C_2), and $w_{d,4,2}^0$, $w_{d,4,2}^1$ (associated with x_4 in C_2) have been introduced. $m_{B,2,1}$ writes $w_{d,1,2}^1$, $w_{d,3,2}^1$ and $w_{d,4,2}^1$ at the first position. (These three women are tied in the list.) Both $m_{B,2,2}$ and $m_{B,2,3}$ write $w_{d,1,2}^0$, $w_{d,3,2}^0$ and $w_{d,4,2}^0$ at the first position. Intuitively speaking, the man $m_{B,i,1}$ will be matched with the woman who corresponds to the literal having the value 1, and men $m_{B,i,2}$ and $m_{B,i,3}$ will be matched with the women who correspond to literals having the value 0.

Each man in Group (C) selects $t + 5$ women at the 1st through $(t+5)$th positions of the preference lists. The women at the 1st through $(t+3)$th positions are $w_{a,1}$ through $w_{a,t+3}$, in this order. $m_{C,i}$ writes the woman $w_{b,i}^0$ at the $(t+4)$th position and the woman $w_{b,i}^1$ at the $(t + 5)$th position. Intuitively speaking, assigning a man $m_{C,i}$ to the woman $w_{b,i}^0$ (respectively $w_{b,i}^1$) means assigning 0 (respectively 1) to the variable x_i.

Then we construct preference lists of Group-(D) men. We show how to construct preference lists using men $m_{D,1}^+$ and $m_{D,1}^-$ for f_0. (Again, see Table 2.) Recall that these two men are associated with the variable x_1. The man $m_{D,1}^+$ writes the woman $w_{c,1}$ at the 2nd position. (The 2nd position is always determined without depending on f.) Then, $m_{D,1}^+$ writes the woman $w_{b,1}^0$ at the $t + 3(= 5)$th position. Since x_1 appears in clauses C_1 and C_2, two women $w_{d,1,1}^1$ and $w_{d,1,2}^1$ have been introduced. $m_{D,1}^+$ writes $w_{d,1,1}^1$ and $w_{d,1,2}^1$ at the 3rd and 4th positions, respectively. The other positions are filled with (some of) $w_{a,1}$ through $w_{a,5}$; $m_{D,1}^+$ writes $w_{a,i}$ at the ith position if the ith position is blank. Generally speaking, there are t_i women of the form $w_{d,i,j}^1$ corresponding to the variable x_i. (Recall that t_i is the number of appearances of the literal x_i.) $m_{D,i}^+$ writes these women at 3rd through $(t_i + 2)$th positions. Since $t_i \leq t$, these women's positions never go to the $(t + 3)$th position which is already occupied by $w_{b,i}^0$.

$m_{D,1}^-$'s list is similarly constructed. $m_{D,1}^-$ writes the woman $w_{c,1}$ at the 1st position and writes the woman $w_{b,1}^1$ at the $t + 3(= 5)$th position. There are two women $w_{d,1,1}^0$ and $w_{d,1,2}^0$ associated with the variable x_1 since x_1 appears in C_1

and C_2. $m_{D,1}^-$ writes $w_{d,1,1}^0$ and $w_{d,1,2}^0$ at the 3rd and 4th positions, respectively. Blanks are filled as above.

Now we move to Group-(E) men: the man $m_{E,1,2}^+$, associated with x_1 in C_2, writes the woman $w_{e,1,2}$ at the 2nd position and writes $w_{d,1,2}^1$ at the same position as $m_{D,1}^+$ (associated with x_1) wrote it. $m_{E,1,2}^-$ writes $w_{e,1,2}$ at the 1st position and writes $w_{d,1,2}^0$ at the same position as $m_{D,1}^-$ wrote it. Blanks are filled with women $w_{a,1}$ through $w_{a,5}$ similarly as the Group-(D) men did. Now the men's lists are completed. Table 2 shows the whole lists of men of $T(f_0)$.

3.3 Women's Preference Lists

Finally, we construct the women's preference lists. We construct the women's preference lists automatically from the men's preference lists. First, we determine the total order of all men; the position of each man in the order is called his *rank*. The rank of each man of our current example $T(f_0)$ is shown in Table 2, e.g., $m_{A,1}$ is the highest and $m_{E,4,2}^-$ is the lowest. Generally speaking, the men are lexicographically ordered, where the significance of the indices of $m_{\alpha,\beta,\gamma}^\delta$ is in the order of α, β, γ and δ, e.g., α is the most significant index and δ is the least significant index. For α, the priority is given to A, B, C, D and E in this order. For β and γ, the smaller number precedes the larger number. For δ, $+$ precedes $-$.

Women's lists are constructed based on this order. First of all, the preference list of a woman w does not include a man m if w does not appear on m's preference list. Consider two men m_i and m_j included in w's list. w strictly prefers m_i to m_j if and only if (1) the rank of m_i is higher than that of m_j, and (2) the position of w in m_i's list is higher than or equal to the position of w in m_j's list. One might think that a woman's list can contain a partial order in this construction. However, in our translation, each woman's list contains only ties.

It helps much to know that, by our construction of the women's preference lists, we can determine whether a matching includes a blocking pair or not from only the men's preference lists. Consider two men m_i and m_j who are matched with w_i and w_j, respectively. Then, (m_i, w_j) is a blocking pair if and only if (i) m_i strictly prefers w_j to w_i, (ii) m_i's rank is higher than m_j's rank, and (iii) the position of w_j in m_i's list is higher than or equal to the position of w_j in m_j's list. Observe that the combination of conditions (ii) and (iii) means that w_j strictly prefers m_i to m_j.

3.4 Useful Lemmas

Now the translation is completed. Next, we show a series of lemmas which summarize several conditions for a matching M for $T(f)$ to be a solution. Proofs are not so difficult and are omitted. Recall that we write $M(m) = w$ if a man m and a woman w are matched in M.

Lemma 1. If a matching M for $T(f)$ is a solution, then $M(m_{A,i}) = w_{a,i}$ $(1 \leq i \leq t+3)$. Namely, each man in Group (A) is matched with the woman at the first position on his list.

Lemma 2. If a matching M for $T(f)$ is a solution, then for each i $(1 \leq i \leq n)$, $M(m_{C,i}) = w_{b,i}^0$ or $M(m_{C,i}) = w_{b,i}^1$.

Lemma 3. Suppose that a matching M for $T(f)$ is a solution. Then for all $1 \leq i \leq n$, (i) if $M(m_{C,i}) = w_{b,i}^0$ then $M(m_{D,i}^+) = w_{c,i}$ and $M(m_{D,i}^-) = w_{b,i}^1$. (ii) Otherwise, i.e., if $M(m_{C,i}) = w_{b,i}^1$, then $M(m_{D,i}^+) = w_{b,i}^0$ and $M(m_{D,i}^-) = w_{c,i}$.

Lemma 4. Suppose that a matching M for $T(f)$ is a solution. Then the following statements (i) and (ii) are true for all i $(1 \leq i \leq n)$. (i) If $M(m_{C,i}) = w^0_{b,i}$ then $M(m^+_{E,i,j}) = w^1_{d,i,j}$ and $M(m^-_{E,i,j}) = w_{e,i,j}$ for all j. (ii) If $M(m_{C,i}) = w^1_{b,i}$ then $M(m^+_{E,i,j}) = w_{e,i,j}$ and $M(m^-_{E,i,j}) = w^0_{d,i,j}$ for all j.

Then we go back to Group-(B) men. Let $C_j = (x_{j_1} + x_{j_2} + x_{j_3})$ be the jth clause in f. Then recall that there are three men $m_{B,j,1}$, $m_{B,j,2}$ and $m_{B,j,3}$, and six women $w^0_{d,j_1,j}$, $w^1_{d,j_1,j}$, $w^0_{d,j_2,j}$, $w^1_{d,j_2,j}$, $w^0_{d,j_3,j}$ and $w^1_{d,j_3,j}$ (see Table 1).

$m_{B,j,1}$	$w^1_{d,j_1,j}$	$w^1_{d,j_2,j}$	$w^1_{d,j_3,j}$
$m_{B,j,2}$	$w^0_{d,j_1,j}$	$w^0_{d,j_2,j}$	$w^0_{d,j_3,j}$
$m_{B,j,3}$	$w^0_{d,j_1,j}$	$w^0_{d,j_2,j}$	$w^0_{d,j_3,j}$

Table 1. Preference lists of men associated to C_j

Lemma 5. Suppose that a matching M for $T(f)$ is a solution. Then, for any $i \in \{j_1, j_2, j_3\}$, if $w^1_{d,i,j}$ is matched with $m_{B,j,1}$, then $w^0_{d,i,j}$ is *not* matched with any of $m_{B,j,2}$ and $m_{B,j,3}$. Namely, for any i and j, one of $w^0_{d,i,j}$ and $w^1_{d,i,j}$ is matched with a man in Group (B) and the other is matched with a man not in Group (B).

Lemma 6. Suppose that a matching M for $T(f)$ is a solution. Then, for each i and j, the following statements (i), (ii) and (iii) are true: (i) If $M(m_{B,j,1}) = w^1_{d,i,j}$ then $M(m_{C,i}) = w^1_{b,i}$. (ii) If $M(m_{B,j,2}) = w^0_{d,i,j}$ then $M(m_{C,i}) = w^0_{b,i}$. (iii) If $M(m_{B,j,3}) = w^0_{d,i,j}$ then $M(m_{C,i}) = w^0_{b,i}$.

3.5 Correctness of the Reduction

Now we are ready to show the correctness of the reduction. To make the argument clear, we denote the *literal* x_i in the clause C_j by x^j_i and regard x^j_i as a different object from the *variable* x_i. Let us consider the following *association rule* between an assignment for variables (and literals) of f and a matching M for $T(f)$: (i) assign 1 to the *variable* x_i if and only if the man $m_{C,i}$ and the woman $w^1_{b,i}$ are matched in M, and assign 0 to the *variable* x_i if and only if the man $m_{C,i}$ and the woman $w^0_{b,i}$ are matched in M. (ii) Assign 1 to the *literal* x^j_i if and only if the woman $w^1_{d,i,j}$ is matched with the man $m_{B,j,1}$ in M, and assign 0 to the *literal* x^j_i if and only if the woman $w^0_{d,i,j}$ is matched with the man $m_{B,j,2}$ or $m_{B,j,3}$.

Lemma 7. The association rule is consistent, namely, if M is a solution for $T(f)$, then the following two statements hold: (i) if $x_i = 1$ then $x^j_i = 1$ for all j. (ii) If $x_i = 0$ then $x^j_i = 0$ for all j. (Proof is omitted.)

Now suppose that there exists a solution M^* for $T(f)$. Then we can show that there exists a solution for f by the following four steps: (1) first, we determine the value of each variable of f. By Lemma 2, either $M^*(m_{C,i}) = w^0_{b,i}$ or $M^*(m_{C,i}) = w^1_{b,i}$ for all i. Due to this, we determine the assignment using the association rule: if $M^*(m_{C,i}) = w^0_{b,i}$ then $x_i = 0$, otherwise, i.e., if $M^*(m_{C,i}) = w^1_{b,i}$, then $x_i = 1$. (2) Again we use the association rule to determine the value of literals: if $M^*(w^1_{d,i,j}) = m_{B,j,1}$, then $x^j_i = 1$. If $M^*(w^0_{d,i,j}) = m_{B,j,2}$ or $M^*(w^0_{d,i,j}) = m_{B,j,3}$, then $x^j_i = 0$. It should be noted, by Lemma 5, that only one value is assigned to each literal x_i^j. (3) Let, for $1 \leq j \leq l$, the jth clause of f be $C_j = (x_{j_1} + x_{j_2} + x_{j_3})$. Then the preference lists of the three men associated to C_j are the ones described in Table 1. Since M^* is a solution, these men must be matched in the way described in Lemma 5. There are six different possibilities. Suppose that $M^*(m_{B,j,1}) = w_{d,j_1,j}^1$, $M^*(m_{B,j,2}) = w_{d,j_2,j}^0$ and $M^*(m_{B,j,3}) = w_{d,j_3,j}^0$. Then, by the assignment determined in (2) above, we have $x_{j_1}^j = 1$, $x_{j_2}^j = 0$ and $x_{j_3}^j = 0$, namely, exactly one literal in C_j is true. It is not hard to see that, in the other five cases also, exactly one literal in C_j is true. (4) By Lemma 7, this assignment is actually a solution of f.

Conversely, suppose that there exists a solution for f of ONE-IN-THREE 3SAT. Then, again using the association rule, we determine partners for the men in Groups (B) and (C). Partners for the men in Groups (A), (D) and (E) are automatically determined using Lemmas 1, 3 and 4. The fact that this matching is a solution for $T(f)$ can be easily seen from Lemmas 1 through 5. □

3.6 An Alternative Proof of Theorem 1

An alternative, shorter proof of the NP-completeness of SMP-ILT may be obtained by transforming from the problem EXACT MAXIMAL MATCHING, which takes a graph G and an integer K as input, and asks whether G has a maximal matching M with $|M| = K$. EXACT MAXIMAL MATCHING is NP-complete, even for bipartite graphs – this follows from the NP-completeness of the minimization version, MINIMUM MAXIMAL MATCHING, for the same class of graphs [9].

Proof. Membership of SMP-ILT in NP was established in Theorem 1. To show the NP-hardness of SMP-ILT, we transform from EXACT MAXIMAL MATCHING for bipartite graphs; let $G = (V, E)$ and K be an instance of this problem. Then G has a bipartition $\langle U, W \rangle$. Without loss of generality we may assume that $|U| = |W| = n$, and that $K \leq n$. Let $U = \{m_1, m_2, \ldots, m_n\}$ and $W = \{w_1, w_2, \ldots, w_n\}$. We construct an instance I of SMP-ILT as follows: let $U \cup X$ be the set of men, and let $W \cup Y$ be the set of women, where $X = \{x_1, x_2, \ldots, x_{n-K}\}$ and $Y = \{y_1, y_2, \ldots, y_{n-K}\}$. For any m_i $(1 \leq i \leq n)$, let M_i contain the women w_j such that $\{m_i, w_j\} \in E$. For any w_j $(1 \leq j \leq n)$, let W_j contain the men m_i such that $\{m_i, w_j\} \in E$. Create preference lists for each person as follows:

$$
\begin{aligned}
m_i &: \text{(members of } M_i\text{)} \ (y_1 \ldots y_{n-K}) & (1 \leq i \leq n) \\
x_i &: \hspace{3.2cm} (w_1 \ldots w_n) & (1 \leq i \leq n - K) \\
w_j &: \text{(members of } W_j\text{)} \ (x_1 \ldots x_{n-K}) & (1 \leq j \leq n) \\
y_j &: \hspace{3.2cm} (m_1 \ldots m_n) & (1 \leq j \leq n - K)
\end{aligned}
$$

In a preference list, persons within parentheses are tied. We claim that G has a maximal matching of size exactly K if and only if I has a stable matching.

For, suppose that G has a maximal matching M where $|M| = K$. We construct a matching M' in I as follows. For each edge $\{m_i, w_j\}$ in M, we let w_j be the partner of m_i in M'. The $n - K$ remaining unmatched men in U are given a partner from Y, and likewise, the $n - K$ remaining unmatched women in W are given a partner from X. Clearly M' is a matching in I, and it is straightforward to verify that M is stable.

Conversely suppose that M' is a stable matching in I. Then each of the $n - K$ women in Y is matched with a man in U. Thus in M', exactly K men of the form m_i is matched with a woman of the form w_j; let M contain the corresponding

$\{m_i, w_j\}$ edges in G. Clearly M is a matching in G of size K, and the stability of M' implies that M is maximal. $\square$

The above transformation can be modified to show that SMP-ILT remains NP-complete even if the ties occur in the preference lists of one sex only, any tie occurs at the tail of some person's preference list, and a tie is of length 2 (details are omitted). This restriction arises naturally in practice: for example, in the applicants-hospitals matching problem, although applicants might be able to rank hospitals in strict order, a large hospital may wish to rank only a subset of its applicants in strict order, expressing indifference among the remainder.

4 Optimization Problems and Inapproximability

Once the NP-completeness of a problem is proved, our next step is to try to find approximation algorithms for its optimization version. A goodness measure of an approximation algorithm T of a *minimization* problem P is defined as usual: let x be an instance of the problem P of size N. Also, let $opt(x)$ and $T(x)$ be the costs of an optimal solution and a solution obtained by the algorithm T, respectively. T is said to be an $r(N)$-*approximation algorithm* if, for every x, $T(x)/opt(x) \leq r(N)$. If there exists a polynomial-time bounded $r(N)$-approximation algorithm for P, then we say that P is approximable within $r(N)$.

There are several optimization problems that have only poor approximation algorithms. Among others, MAX-CLIQUE has received much attention recently because of its novel use of PCP. The latest result [5] says that this problem is not approximable within $N^{1-\epsilon}$ for any $\epsilon > 0$ assuming NP$\neq$coRP, where N denotes the number of vertices in a given graph. MIN-UN-3SAT is also hard, which requires, given a 3CNF formula, to find a truth assignment that minimizes the number of unsatisfied clauses. So MIN-UN-3SAT is basically the same problem as MAX-3SAT; only the cost function differs. It is shown that MIN-UN-3SAT is not approximable within $N^{1-\epsilon}$ for any $\epsilon > 0$, where N is the number of clauses in a given formula [7]. This result is obtained using a reduction from 3SAT, its NP-complete counterpart. The reduction makes many "copies" of an instance for 3SAT, which amplifies the gap of the cost between yes-instances and no-instances. We exploit this technique to show the inapproximability result for MIN-SMP-TIES. In doing so, a crucial point is how to "amplify" the gap, or how to "copy" the original instance so that the cost of solution will increase in a very different rate depending on the answer (yes/no) of the original instance. In the case of 3SAT, this is almost trivial since if the original formula is satisfiable then the number of unsatisfiable clauses is still zero for arbitrarily many copies. Our present case is not that easy.

Theorem 2. If P$\neq$NP, then MIN-SMP-TIES is not approximable within $N^{1-\epsilon}$ for any $\epsilon > 0$.

Proof. Let I be an instance of SMP-ILT obtained in the proof of Theorem 1. Let $K = 9l + 3n + t + 3$, which is the number of men and also the number of women in I. We translate I into an instance of MIN-SMP-TIES. Our target instance has $2K^c$ men and the same number of women, where c is some constant. First of all, we introduce the set M_U of K^c men $m_{0,1}, m_{0,2}, \cdots, m_{0,K^c}$ and W_U of K^c women $w_{0,1}, w_{0,2}, \cdots, w_{0,K^c}$. Next, we introduce another K^{c-1} sets $M_1, M_2, \cdots, M_{K^{c-1}}$ of men, each of which contains exactly K men. Similarly, we introduce K^{c-1} sets $W_1, W_2, \cdots, W_{K^{c-1}}$ of women, each of which contains K women. $M_1, M_2, \cdots, M_{K^{c-1}}$ can be considered to be "copies" of the set of men in I, namely, we associate each man in M_i with each man in I, and each woman in W_i with each woman in I, by one-to-one correspondence. Now we have $2K^c$ men and $2K^c$ women in total.

Then we generate each person's preference list. Each man $m_{0,i}$ in M_U writes the woman $w_{0,i}$ in W_U at the top of his preference list, and then writes the other $2K^c - 1$ women arbitrarily. Each woman $w_{0,i}$ in W_U writes the man $m_{0,i}$ in M_U at the top of her preference list, and then writes the other $2K^c - 1$ men arbitrarily. It should be noted that in any stable matching, $m_{0,i}$ must be matched with $w_{0,i}$ since they write each other at the top of their preference lists.

Recall that, the men in M_i play the same role as the men in I and also the women in W_i play the same role as the women in I. The list of a man m (in M_i) is just the same as the list of the man m' in I who corresponds to m (but, of course, the women in the list are not the ones in I but the corresponding women in W_i). We call these women, i.e., the ones who now exist in m's list, *proper* for m. Note that m's list is not yet complete, so we have to make it complete. First, we add K^c women in W_U to the list arbitrarily but in total order right after the proper women, and then finally we add the remaining women to the list arbitrarily and in total order. The women's lists are similar; namely, a list of each woman w in W_i is the same as the list of w' in I. We also call these men in the list *proper* for w. Then we add K^c men in M_U and we add the remaining men arbitrarily as before. Now we have an instance, J, of MIN-SMP-TIES. As shown in [4], there is always a stable matching for J if we do not care its cost.

Thus the list of m in M_i includes proper women at the beginning, and then the long sequence of $w_{0,j}$ in W_U, and finally improper women. Hence, if m is not matched with a proper woman, he has to "jump" the long sequence of $w_{0,j}$'s and has to be matched with some improper woman. Formally, we can claim that the optimal cost for J is at most K^{c+1} when there is a stable matching for I and is greater than $2K^{2c-1}$ otherwise. Hence if there were a polynomial-time approximation algorithm with approximation ratio as good as $(2K^{2c-1})/K^{c+1} = 2K^{c-2}$, then it could determine whether there is a stable matching for I in polynomial time (recall that c is a constant). Note that the size, N, of J is $2K^c$ and it follows that $2K^{c-2} = \frac{2}{2^{1-\frac{2}{c}}} N^{1-\frac{2}{c}} > N^{1-\frac{2}{c}}$, which completes the proof. $\square$

References

1. D. Gale and L. S. Shapley, "College admissions and the stability of marriage," *Amer. Math. Monthly*, Vol.69, pp.9-15, 1962.
2. D. Gale and M. Sotomayor, "Some remarks on the stable matching problem," *Discrete Applied Mathematics*, Vol.11, pp.223-232, 1985.
3. M. R. Garey and D. S. Johnson, "Computers and Intractability, A Guide to The Theory of NP-Completeness," Freeman, San Francisco, 1979.
4. D. Gusfield and R. W. Irving, "The Stable Marriage Problem: Structure and Algorithms," MIT Press, Boston, MA, 1989.
5. J. Håstad, "Clique is hard to approximate within $n^{1-\epsilon}$," *Proc. FOCS96*, pp.627–636, 1996.
6. R. W. Irving, "Stable marriage and indifference," *Discrete Applied Mathematics*, Vol.48, pp.261-272, 1994.
7. T. Ohguro, "On the hardness of approximating minimization problems: in comparison with maximization classes," *Technical Report of IEICE*, COMP94-112 pp.89-96, 1995.
8. E. Ronn, "NP-complete stable matching problems," *J. Algorithms*, Vol.11, pp.285-304, 1990.
9. M. Yannakakis and F. Gavril, "Edge dominating sets in graphs," *SIAM J. Applied Mathematics*, Vol.18, No.1, pp.364–372, 1980.

$m_{A,1}$	$w_{a,1}$						
$m_{A,2}$	$w_{a,2}$						
$m_{A,3}$	$w_{a,3}$						
$m_{A,4}$	$w_{a,4}$						
$m_{A,5}$	$w_{a,5}$						
$m_{B,1,1}$	$w^1_{d,1,1}$	$w^1_{d,2,1}$	$w^1_{d,3,1}$				
$m_{B,1,2}$	$w^0_{d,1,1}$	$w^0_{d,2,1}$	$w^0_{d,3,1}$				
$m_{B,1,3}$	$w^0_{d,1,1}$	$w^0_{d,2,1}$	$w^0_{d,3,1}$				
$m_{B,2,1}$	$w^1_{d,1,2}$	$w^1_{d,3,2}$	$w^1_{d,4,2}$				
$m_{B,2,2}$	$w^0_{d,1,2}$	$w^0_{d,3,2}$	$w^0_{d,4,2}$				
$m_{B,2,3}$	$w^0_{d,1,2}$	$w^0_{d,3,2}$	$w^0_{d,4,2}$				
$m_{C,1}$	$w_{a,1}$	$w_{a,2}$	$w_{a,3}$	$w_{a,4}$	$w_{a,5}$	$w^0_{b,1}$	$w^1_{b,1}$
$m_{C,2}$	$w_{a,1}$	$w_{a,2}$	$w_{a,3}$	$w_{a,4}$	$w_{a,5}$	$w^0_{b,2}$	$w^1_{b,2}$
$m_{C,3}$	$w_{a,1}$	$w_{a,2}$	$w_{a,3}$	$w_{a,4}$	$w_{a,5}$	$w^0_{b,3}$	$w^1_{b,3}$
$m_{C,4}$	$w_{a,1}$	$w_{a,2}$	$w_{a,3}$	$w_{a,4}$	$w_{a,5}$	$w^0_{b,4}$	$w^1_{b,4}$
$m^+_{D,1}$	$w_{a,1}$	$w_{c,1}$	$w^1_{d,1,1}$	$w^1_{d,1,2}$	$w^0_{b,1}$		
$m^-_{D,1}$	$w_{c,1}$	$w_{a,2}$	$w^0_{d,1,1}$	$w^0_{d,1,2}$	$w^1_{b,1}$		
$m^+_{D,2}$	$w_{a,1}$	$w_{c,2}$	$w^1_{d,2,1}$	$w_{a,4}$	$w^0_{b,2}$		
$m^-_{D,2}$	$w_{c,2}$	$w_{a,2}$	$w^0_{d,2,1}$	$w_{a,4}$	$w^1_{b,2}$		
$m^+_{D,3}$	$w_{a,1}$	$w_{c,3}$	$w^1_{d,3,1}$	$w^1_{d,3,2}$	$w^0_{b,3}$		
$m^-_{D,3}$	$w_{c,3}$	$w_{a,2}$	$w^0_{d,3,1}$	$w^0_{d,3,2}$	$w^1_{b,3}$		
$m^+_{D,4}$	$w_{a,1}$	$w_{c,4}$	$w^1_{d,4,2}$	$w_{a,4}$	$w^0_{b,4}$		
$m^-_{D,4}$	$w_{c,4}$	$w_{a,2}$	$w^0_{d,4,2}$	$w_{a,4}$	$w^1_{b,4}$		
$m^+_{E,1,1}$	$w_{a,1}$	$w_{e,1,1}$	$w^1_{d,1,1}$				
$m^-_{E,1,1}$	$w_{e,1,1}$	$w_{a,2}$	$w^0_{d,1,1}$				
$m^+_{E,1,2}$	$w_{a,1}$	$w_{e,1,2}$	$w_{a,3}$	$w^1_{d,1,2}$			
$m^-_{E,1,2}$	$w_{e,1,2}$	$w_{a,2}$	$w_{a,3}$	$w^0_{d,1,2}$			
$m^+_{E,2,1}$	$w_{a,1}$	$w_{e,2,1}$	$w^1_{d,2,1}$				
$m^-_{E,2,1}$	$w_{e,2,1}$	$w_{a,2}$	$w^0_{d,2,1}$				
$m^+_{E,3,1}$	$w_{a,1}$	$w_{e,3,1}$	$w^1_{d,3,1}$				
$m^-_{E,3,1}$	$w_{e,3,1}$	$w_{a,2}$	$w^0_{d,3,1}$				
$m^+_{E,3,2}$	$w_{a,1}$	$w_{e,3,2}$	$w_{a,3}$	$w^1_{d,3,2}$			
$m^-_{E,3,2}$	$w_{e,3,2}$	$w_{a,2}$	$w_{a,3}$	$w^0_{d,3,2}$			
$m^+_{E,4,2}$	$w_{a,1}$	$w_{e,4,2}$	$w^1_{d,4,2}$				
$m^-_{E,4,2}$	$w_{e,4,2}$	$w_{a,2}$	$w^0_{d,4,2}$				

Table 2. Preference lists of men of $T(f_0)$

Average-Case Complexity of Shellsort

(*Preliminary Version*)

Tao Jiang[1], Ming Li[2], and Paul Vitányi[3]

[1] Dept of Computing and Software, McMaster University,
Hamilton, Ontario L8S 4K1, Canada, jiang@cas.mcmaster.ca
Supported in part by NSERC and CITO grants
[2] Dept of Computer Science, University of Waterloo,
Waterloo, Ontario N2L 3G1, Canada, mli@math.uwaterloo.ca
Supported in part by NSERC and CITO grants and Steacie Fellowship
[3] CWI, Kruislaan 413, 1098 SJ Amsterdam,
The Netherlands, paulv@cwi.nl
Supported in part via NeuroCOLT II ESPRIT Working Group

Abstract. We prove a general lower bound on the average-case complexity of Shellsort: the average number of data-movements (and comparisons) made by a p-pass Shellsort for any incremental sequence is $\Omega(pn^{1+1/p})$ for every p. The proof method is an incompressibility argument based on Kolmogorov complexity. Using similar techniques, the average-case complexity of several other sorting algorithms is analyzed.

1 Introduction

The question of a nontrivial general lower bound (or upper bound) on the average complexity of Shellsort (due to D.L. Shell [15]) has been open for about four decades [7, 14]. We present such a lower bound for p-pass Shellsort for every p.

Shellsort sorts a list of n elements in p passes using a sequence of increments $h_1, \ldots, h_p$. In the kth pass the main list is divided in h_k separate sublists of length $\lceil n/h_k \rceil$, where the ith sublist consists of the elements at positions j, where $j \bmod h_k = i - 1$, of the main list ($i = 1, \ldots, h_k$). Every sublist is sorted using a straightforward insertion sort. The efficiency of the method is governed by the number of passes p and the selected increment sequence $h_1, \ldots, h_p$ with $h_p = 1$ to ensure sortedness of the final list. The original $\log n$-pass [1] increment sequence $\lfloor n/2 \rfloor, \lfloor n/4 \rfloor, \ldots, 1$ of Shell [15] uses worst case $\Theta(n^2)$ time, but Papernov and Stasevitch [10] showed that another related sequence uses $O(n^{3/2})$ and Pratt [12] extended this to a class of all nearly geometric increment sequences and proved this bound was tight. The currently best asymptotic method was found by Pratt [12]. It uses all $\log^2 n$ increments of the form $2^i 3^j < \lfloor n/2 \rfloor$ to obtain time $O(n \log^2 n)$ in the worst case. Moreover, since every pass takes at least n steps, the average complexity using Pratt's increment sequence is $\Theta(n \log^2 n)$. Incerpi and Sedgewick [2] constructed a family of increment sequences for which

---

[1] "log" denotes the binary logarithm and "ln" denotes the natural logarithm.

Shellsort runs in $O(n^{1+\epsilon/\sqrt{\log n}})$ time using $(8/\epsilon^2)\log n$ passes, for every $\epsilon > 0$. B. Chazelle (attribution in [13]) obtained the same result by generalizing Pratt's method: instead of using 2 and 3 to construct the increment sequence use a and $(a+1)$ for fixed a which yields a worst-case running time of $n\log^2 n(a^2/\ln^2 a)$ which is $O(n^{1+\epsilon/\sqrt{\log n}})$ for $\ln^2 a = O(\log n)$. Plaxton, Poonen and Suel [11] proved an $\Omega(n^{1+\epsilon/\sqrt{p}})$ lower bound for p passes of Shellsort using any increment sequence, for some $\epsilon > 0$; taking $p = \Omega(\log n)$ shows that the Incerpi-Sedgewick / Chazelle bounds are optimal for small p and taking p slightly larger shows a $\Theta(n\log^2 n/(\log\log n)^2)$ lower bound on the worst case complexity of Shellsort. Since every pass takes at least n steps this shows an $\Omega(n\log^2 n/(\log\log n)^2)$ lower bound on the worst-case of every Shellsort increment sequence. For the *average-case* running time Knuth [7] showed $\Theta(n^{5/3})$ for the best choice of increments in $p = 2$ passes; Yao [17] analyzed the average case for $p = 3$ but did not obtain a simple analytic form; Yao's analysis was improved by Janson and Knuth [3] who showed $O(n^{23/15})$ average-case running time for a particular choice of increments in $p = 3$ passes. Apart from this no nontrivial results are known for the average case; see [7, 13, 14].

Results: We show a general $\Omega(pn^{1+1/p})$ lower bound on the average-case running time of p-pass Shellsort under uniform distribution of input permutations for every p. [2] This is the first advance on the problem of determining general nontrivial bounds on the *average-case* running time of Shellsort [12, 7, 17, 2, 11, 13, 14]. Using the same simple method, we also obtain results on the average number of stacks or queues (sequential or parallel) required for sorting under the uniform distribution on input permutations. These problems have been studied before by Knuth [7] and Tarjan [16] for the worst case.

Kolmogorov complexity and the Incompressibility Method: The technical tool to obtain our results is the incompressibility method. This method is especially suited for the average case analysis of algorithms and machine models, whereas average-case analysis is usually more difficult than worst-case analysis using more traditional methods. A survey of the use of the incompressibility method is [8] Chapter 6, and recent work is [1]. The most spectacular successes of the method occur in the computational complexity analysis of algorithms.

Informally, the Kolmogorov complexity $C(x)$ of a binary string x is the length of the shortest binary program (for a fixed reference universal machine) that prints x as its only output and then halts [6]. A string x is *incompressible* if $C(x)$ is at least $|x|$, the approximate length of a program that simply includes all of x literally. Similarly, the *conditional* Kolmogorov complexity of x with respect to y, denoted by $C(x|y)$, is the length of the shortest program that, *with* extra information y, prints x. A string x is incompressible *relative* to y if $C(x|y)$ is large in the appropriate sense. For details see [8]. Here we use that, both absolutely and relative to any fixed string y, there are incompressible strings of

---

[2] The trivial lower bound is $\Omega(pn)$ comparisons since every element needs to be compared at least once in every pass.

every length, and that *most* strings are nearly incompressible, by *any* standard.
[3] Another easy one is that significantly long subwords of an incompressible string are themselves nearly incompressible by *any* standard, even relative to the rest of the string. In the sequel we use the following easy facts (sometimes only implicitly).

Lemma 1. *Let c be a positive integer. For every fixed y, every finite set A contains at least $(1 - 2^{-c})|A| + 1$ elements x with $C(x|A, y) \geq \lfloor \log |A| \rfloor - c$.*

Lemma 2. *If A is a set, then for every y every element $x \in A$ has complexity $C(x|A, y) \leq \log |A| + O(1)$.*

The first lemma is proved by simple counting. The second lemma holds since x can be described by first describing A in $O(1)$ bits and then giving the index of x in the enumeration order of A.

2 Shellsort

A Shellsort computation consists of a sequence comparison and inversion (swapping) operations. In this analysis of the average-case lower bound we count just the total number of data movements (here inversions) executed. The same bound holds for number of comparisons automatically. The average is taken over the uniform distribution of all lists of n items.

The proof is based on the following intuitive idea: There are $n!$ different permutations. Given the sorting process (the insertion paths in the right order) one can recover the correct permutation from the sorted list. Hence one requires $n!$ pairwise different sorting processes. This gives a lower bound on the minimum of the maximal length of a process. We formulate the proof in the crisp format of incompressibility.

Theorem 1. *The average number of inversions in p-pass Shellsort on lists of n keys is at least $\Omega\left(pn^{1+1/p}\right)$ for every increment sequence.*

Proof. Let the list to be sorted consist of a permutation π of the elements $1, \ldots, n$. Consider a $(h_1, \ldots, h_p)$ Shellsort algorithm A where h_k is the increment in the kth pass and $h_p = 1$. For any $1 \leq i \leq n$ and $1 \leq k \leq p$, let $m_{i,k}$ be the number of elements in the h_k-*chain* containing element i that are to the left of i at the beginning of pass k and are larger than i. Observe that $\sum_{i=1}^{n} m_{i,k}$ is the number of inversions in the initial permutation of pass k, and that the

---

[3] By a simple counting argument one can show that whereas some strings can be enormously compressed, like strings of the form $11 \ldots 1$, the majority of strings can hardly be compressed at all. For every n there are 2^n binary strings of length n, but only $\sum_{i=0}^{n-1} 2^i = 2^n - 1$ possible shorter descriptions. Therefore, there is at least one binary string x of length n such that $C(x) \geq n$. Similarly, for every length n and any binary string y, there is a binary string x of length n such that $C(x|y) \geq n$.

insertion sort in pass k requires precisely $\sum_{i=1}^{n}(m_{i,k}+1)$ comparisons. Let M denote the total number of inversions:

$$M := \sum_{k=1}^{p} \sum_{i=1}^{n} m_{i,k}. \tag{1}$$

Claim. Given all the $m_{i,k}$'s in an appropriate fixed order, we can reconstruct the original permutation π.

Proof. The $m_{i,p}$'s trivially specify the initial permutation of pass p. In general, given the $m_{i,k}$'s and the final permutation of pass k, we can easily reconstruct the initial permutation of pass k. □

Let M as in (1) be a fixed number. Let permutation π be an incompressible permutation having Kolmogorov complexity

$$C(\pi|n, A, P) \geq \log n! - \log n. \tag{2}$$

where P is the encoding program in the following discussion. The description in Claim 2 is effective and therefore its minimum length must exceed the complexity of π:

$$C(m_{1,1}, \ldots, m_{n,p}|n, A, P) \geq C(\pi|n, A, P). \tag{3}$$

Any M as defined by (1) such that every division of M in $m_{i,k}$'s contradicts (3) would be a lower bound on the number of inversions performed. There are

$$D(M) := \sum_{i=1}^{np-1} \binom{M}{np-i} = \binom{M+np-1}{np-1} \tag{4}$$

possible divisions of M into np nonnegative integral summands $m_{i,k}$'s. Every division can be indicated by its index j in an enumeration of these divisions. Therefore, a self-delimiting description of M followed by a description of j effectively describes the $m_{i,k}$'s. The length of this description must by definition exceed its Kolmogorov complexity. That is,

$$\log D(M) + \log M + 2 \log \log M \geq C(m_{1,1}, \ldots, m_{n,p}|n, A, P) + O(1).$$

We know that $M \leq pn^2$ since every $m_{i,k} \leq n$. We can assume[4] $p < n$. Together with (2) and (3), we have

$$\log D(M) \geq \log n! - 4 \log n + O(1). \tag{5}$$

By (4) $\log D(M)$ is bounded above by [5]

$$\log \binom{M+np-1}{np-1} = (np-1) \log \frac{M+np-1}{np-1} + M \log \frac{M+np-1}{M}$$

---

[4] Otherwise we require at least n^2 comparisons.

[5] Use the following formula ([8], p. 10),

$$\log \binom{a}{b} = b \log \frac{a}{b} + (a-b) \log \frac{a}{a-b} + \frac{1}{2} \log \frac{a}{b(a-b)} + O(1).$$

$$+\frac{1}{2}\log\frac{M+np-1}{(np-1)M}+O(1).$$

By (5) we have $M \to \infty$ for $n \to \infty$. Therefore, the second term in the right-hand side equals

$$\log\left(1+\frac{np-1}{M}\right)^{M} \to \log e^{np-1}$$

for $n \to \infty$. Since $0 < p < n$ and $n \le M \le pn^2$,

$$\frac{1}{2(np-1)}\log\frac{M+np-1}{(np-1)M} \to 0$$

for $n \to \infty$. Therefore, the total right-hand side goes to

$$(np-1)\left(\log\left(\frac{M}{np-1}+1\right)+\log e\right)$$

for $n \to \infty$. Together with (5) this yields

$$M = \Omega(pn^{1+1/p}).$$

Therefore, the running time of the algorithm is as stated in the theorem for every permutation π satisfying (2). By lemma 1 at least a $(1-1/n)$-fraction of all permutations π require that high complexity. Therefore, the following is a lower bound on the expected number of inversions of the sorting procedure:

$$(1-\frac{1}{n})\Omega(pn^{1+1/p})+\frac{1}{n}\Omega(0) = \Omega(pn^{1+1/p})$$

This gives us the theorem. $\square$

Compare our lower bound on the average-case with the Plaxton-Poonen-Suel $\Omega(n^{1+\epsilon/\sqrt{p}})$ worst case lower bound [11]. Some special cases of the lower bound on the average-case complexity are:

1. When $p = 1$, this gives asymptotically tight bound for the average number of inversions for Insertion Sort.
2. When $p = 2$, Shellsort requires $\Omega(n^{3/2})$ inversions (the tight bound is known to be $\Theta(n^{5/3})$ [7]);
3. When $p = 3$, Shellsort requires $\Omega(n^{4/3})$ inversions (the best known upper bound is $O(n^{23/15})$ in [3]);
4. When $p = \log n/\log\log n$, Shellsort requires $\Omega(n\log^2 n/\log\log n)$ inversions;
5. When $p = \log n$, Shellsort requires $\Omega(n\log n)$ inversions. When we consider comparisons, this is of course the lower bound of average number of comparisons for every sorting algorithm.
6. In general, when $p = p(n) > \log n$, Shellsort requires $\Omega(n \cdot p(n))$ inversions (it requires that many comparisons anyway since every pass trivially makes n comparisons).

In [14] it is mentioned that the existence of an increment sequence yielding an average $O(n\log n)$ Shellsort has been open for 30 years. The above lower bound on the average shows that the number p of passes of such an increment sequence (if it exists) is precisely $p = \Theta(\log n)$; all the other possibilities are ruled out.

3 Sorting with Queues and Stacks

Knuth [7] and Tarjan [16] have studied the problem of sorting using a network of queues or stacks. In particular, the main variants of the problem are: assuming the stacks or queues are arranged sequentially or in parallel, how many stacks or queues are needed to sort n numbers. Here, the input sequence is scanned from left to right. We will concentrate on the average-case analyses of the above two main variants, although our technique in general apply to arbitrary acyclic networks of stacks and queues as studied in [16].

3.1 Sorting with Sequential Stacks

The sequential stack sorting problem is in [7] exercise 5.2.4-20. We have k stacks numbered $S_0, \ldots, S_{k-1}$ arranged sequentially from right to left. The input is a permutation π of the elements $1, \ldots, n$. Initially we feed the elements of π to S_0 at most one at a time in the order in which they appear in π. At every step we can pop a stack (the popped elements will move to the left) or push an incoming element on a stack. The question is how many stack are needed for sorting π. It is known that $k = \log n$ stacks suffice, and $\frac{1}{2} \log n$ stacks are necessary in the worst-case [7, 16]. Here we prove that the same lower bound also holds on the average with a very simple incompressibility argument.

Theorem 2. *On the average, at least $\frac{1}{2} \log n$ stacks are needed for sequential stack sort.*

Proof. Fix an incompressible permutation π such that

$$C(\pi|n, P) \leq \log n! - \log = n \log n - O(\log n),$$

where P is an encoding program to be specified in the following.

Assume that k stacks is sufficient to sort π. We now encode such a sorting process. For every stack, exactly n elements pass through it. Hence we need perform precisely n pushes and n pops on every stack. Encode a push as 0 and a pop as 1. It is easy to prove that different permutations must have different push/pop sequences on at least one stack. Thus with $2kn$ bits, we can completely specify the input permutation π. [6] Then, as before,

$$2kn \geq \log n! - \log n = n \log n - O(\log n).$$

Hence, approximately $k \geq \frac{1}{2} \log n$ for incompressible permutations π.

Since most (a $(1 - 1/n)$th fraction) permutations are incompressible, we can calculate the average-case lower bound as:

$$\frac{1}{2} \log n \cdot \frac{n-1}{n} + 1 \cdot \frac{1}{n} \approx \frac{1}{2} \log n.$$

$\square$

---

[6] In fact since each stack corresponds to precisely n pushes and n pops where the pushes and pops form a "balanced" string, the Kolmogorov complexity of such a sequence is at most $g(n) := 2n - \frac{3}{2} \log n + O(1)$ bits. So $2kg(n)$ bits would suffice to specifiy the input permutation. But this does not yield a nontrivial improvement.

3.2 Sorting with Parallel Stacks

Clearly, the input sequence $2, 3, 4, \ldots, n, 1$ requires $n - 1$ parallel stacks to sort. Hence the worst-case complexity of sorting with parallel stacks is $n - 1$. However, most sequences do not need these many stacks to sort in the parallel arrangement. The next two theorems show that on the average, $\Theta(\sqrt{n})$ stacks are both necessary and sufficient. Observe that the result is actually implied by the connection between sorting with parallel stacks and *longest increasing subsequences* given in [16] and the bounds on the length of longest increasing subsequences of random permutations given in, [5, 9, 4]. However, the proofs in [5, 9, 4] use deep results from probability theory (such as Kingman's ergodic theorem) and are quite sophisticated. Here we give simple proofs using incompressibility arguments.

Theorem 3. *On the average, the number of parallel stacks needed to sort n elements is $O(\sqrt{n})$.*

Proof. Consider an incompressible permutation π satisfying

$$C(\pi|n) \geq \log n! - \log n. \tag{6}$$

We use the following trivial algorithm (which is described in [16]) to sort π with stacks in the parallel arrangement . Assume that the stacks are named $S_0, S_1, \ldots$ and the input sequence is denoted as $x_1, \ldots, x_n$.

Algorithm Parallel-Stack-Sort

1. For $i = 1$ to n do
   Scan the stacks from left to right, and push x_i on the the first stack S_j whose top element is larger than x_i. If such a stack doesn't exist, put x_i on the first empty stack.
2. Pop the stacks in the ascending order of their top elements.

We claim that algorithm Parallel-Stack-Sort uses $O(\sqrt{n})$ stacks on the permutation π. First, we observe that if the algorithm uses m stacks on π then we can identify an increasing subsequence of π of length m as in [16]. This can be done by a trivial backtracing starting from the top element of the last stack. Then we argue that π cannot have an increasing subsequence of length longer than $e\sqrt{n}$, where e is the natural constant, since it is compressible by at most $\log n$ bits.

Suppose that σ is a longest increasing subsequence of π and $m = |\sigma|$ is the length of σ. Then we can encode π by specifying:

1. a description of this encoding scheme in $O(1)$ bits;
2. the number m in $\log m$ bits;
3. the combination σ in $\log \binom{n}{m}$ bits;
4. the locations of the elements of σ in π in at most $\log \binom{n}{m}$ bits; and
5. the remaining π with the elements of σ deleted in $\log(n - m)!$ bits.

This takes a total of

$$\log(n - m)! + 2\log\frac{n!}{m!(n - m)!} + \log m + O(1) + 2\log\log m$$

bits. Using Stirling approximation and the fact that $\sqrt{n} \leq m = o(n)$, we the above expression is upper bounded by:

$$\log n! + \log\frac{(n/e)^n}{(m/e)^{2m}((n - m)/e)^{n-m}} + O(\log n)$$

$$\approx \log n! + m\log\frac{n}{m^2} + (n - m)\log\frac{n}{n - m} + m\log e + O(\log n)$$

$$\approx \log n! + m\log\frac{n}{m^2} + 2m\log e + O(\log n)$$

This description length must exceed the complexity of the permutation which is lower-bounded in (6). This requires that (approximately) $m \leq e\sqrt{n} = O(\sqrt{n})$. This yields an average complexity of Parallel-Stack-Sort of:

$$O(\sqrt{n}) \cdot \frac{n - 1}{n} + n \cdot \frac{1}{n} = O(\sqrt{n}).$$

□

Theorem 4. *On the average, the number of parallel stacks required to sort a permutation is $\Omega(\sqrt{n})$.*

Proof. Let A be any sorting algorithm using parallel stacks. Fix an incompressible permutation π with $C(\pi|n, P) \geq \log n! - \log n$, where P is the program to do the encoding discussed in the following. Suppose that A uses T parallel stacks to sort π. This sorting process involves a sequence of moves, and we can encode this sequence of moves as a sequence of the following items: "push to stack i" and "pop stack j", where the element to be pushed is the next unprocessed element from the input sequence and the popped element is written as the next output element. Each of these term requires $\log T$ bits. In total, we use $2n$ terms precisely since every element has to be pushed once and popped once. Such a sequence is unique for every permutation.

Thus we have a description of an input sequence with length $2n\log T$ bits, which must exceed $C(\pi|n, P) \geq n\log n - O(\log n)$. It follows that $T \geq \sqrt{n} = \Omega(\sqrt{n})$. This yields the average-case complexity of A:

$$\Omega(\sqrt{n}) \cdot \frac{n - 1}{n} + 1 \cdot \frac{1}{n} = \Omega(\sqrt{n}).$$

□

3.3 Sorting with Parallel Queues

It is easy to see that sorting cannot be done with a sequence of queues. So we consider the complexity of sorting with parallel queues. It turns out that all the result in the previous subsection also hold for queues.

As noticed in [16], the worst-case complexity of sorting with parallel queues is n since the input sequence $n, n - 1, \ldots, 1$ requires n queues to sort. We show in the next two theorems that on the average, $\Theta(\sqrt{n})$ queues are both necessary and sufficient. Again, the result is implied by the connection between sorting with parallel queues and longest *decreasing* subsequences given in [16] and the bounds in [5, 9, 4] (with sophisticated proofs). Our proofs are almost trivial given the proofs in the previous subsection.

Theorem 5. *On the average, the number of parallel queues needed to sort n elements is upper bounded by $O(\sqrt{n})$.*

Proof. The proof is very similar to the proof of Theorem 3. We use a slightly modified greedy algorithm as described in [16]:

Algorithm Parallel-Queue-Sort

1. For $i = 1$ to n do
   Scan the queues from left to right, and append x_i on the the first queue whose rear element is smaller than x_i. If such a queue doesn't exist, put x_i on the first empty queue.
2. Delete the front elements of the queues in the ascending order.

Again, we can claim that algorithm Parallel-Queue-Sort uses $O(\sqrt{n})$ queues on any permutation π that cannot be compressed by more than $\log n$ bits. We first observe that if the algorithm uses m queues on π then a decreasing subsequence of π of length m can be identified, and we then argue that π cannot have a decreasing subsequence of length longer than $e\sqrt{n}$, in a way analogous to the argument in the proof of Theorem 3. □

Theorem 6. *On the average, the number of parallel queues required to sort a permutation is $\Omega(\sqrt{n})$.*

Proof. The proof is the same as the one for Theorem 4 except that we should replace "push" with "enqueue" and "pop" with "dequeue". □

4 Conclusion

The incompressibility method is a good tool to analyzing the average-case complexity of sorting algorithms. Simplicity has been our goal. Examples of such average-case analyses of some other algorithms are given in [1]. This methodology and applications can be easily taught to undergraduate students.

The average-case performance of Shellsort has been one of the most fundamental and interesting open problems in the area of algorithm analysis. The simple average-case analysis of Insertion Sort (1-pass Shellsort), stack-sort and queue-sort are further examples to demonstrate the generality and simplicity of our technique in analyzing sorting algorithms in general. Some open questions are:

1. Tighten the average-case lower bound for Shellsort. Our bound is not tight for $p = 2$ passes.
2. For sorting with sequential stacks, can we close the gap between $\log n$ upper bound and the $\frac{1}{2} \log n$ lower bound?

5 Acknowledgements

We thank Don Knuth, Ian Munro, and Vaughan Pratt for discussions and references on Shellsort.

References

1. H. Buhrman, T. Jiang, M. Li, and P. Vitányi, New applications of the incompressibility method, in *the Proceedings of ICALP'99*.
2. J. Incerpi and R. Sedgewick, Improved upper bounds on Shellsort, *Journal of Computer and System Sciences*, 31(1985), 210–224.
3. S. Janson and D.E. Knuth, Shellsort with three increments, *Random Struct. Alg.*, 10(1997), 125-142.
4. S.V. Kerov and A.M. Versik, Asymptotics of the Plancherel measure on symmetric group and the limiting form of the Young tableaux, *Soviet Math. Dokl.* 18 (1977), 527-531.
5. J.F.C. Kingman, The ergodic theory of subadditive stochastic processes, *Ann. Probab.* 1 (1973), 883-909.
6. A.N. Kolmogorov, Three approaches to the quantitative definition of information. *Problems Inform. Transmission*, 1:1(1965), 1–7.
7. D.E. Knuth, *The Art of Computer Programming, Vol.3: Sorting and Searching*, Addison-Wesley, 1973 (1st Edition), 1998 (2nd Edition).
8. M. Li and P.M.B. Vitányi, *An Introduction to Kolmogorov Complexity and its Applications*, Springer-Verlag, New York, 2nd Edition, 1997.
9. B.F. Logan and L.A. Shepp, A variational problem for random Young tableaux, *Advances in Math.* 26 (1977), 206-222.
10. A. Papernov and G. Stasevich, A method for information sorting in computer memories, *Problems Inform. Transmission*, 1:3(1965), 63–75.
11. C.G. Plaxton, B. Poonen and T. Suel, Improved lower bounds for Shellsort, *Proc. 33rd IEEE Symp. Foundat. Comput. Sci.*, pp. 226–235, 1992.
12. V.R. Pratt, *Shellsort and Sorting Networks*, Ph.D. Thesis, Stanford Univ., 1972.
13. R. Sedgewick, Analysis of Shellsort and related algorithms, presented at the *Fourth Annual European Symposium on Algorithms*, Barcelona, September, 1996.
14. R. Sedgewick, Open problems in the analysis of sorting and searching algorithms, Presented at *Workshop on Prob. Analysis of Algorithms*, Princeton, 1997.
15. D.L. Shell, A high-speed sorting procedure, *Commun. ACM*, 2:7(1959), 30–32.
16. R.E. Tarjan, Sorting using networks of queues and stacks, *Journal of the ACM*, 19(1972), 341–346.
17. A.C.C. Yao, An analysis of $(h, k, 1)$-Shellsort, *J. of Algorithms*, 1(1980), 14–50.

Linear-Time Construction of Two-Dimensional Suffix Trees *

(Extended Abstract)

Dong Kyue Kim   Kunsoo Park

Department of Computer Engineering
Seoul National University, Seoul 151-742, Korea
{dkkim,kpark}@theory.snu.ac.kr

Abstract. The suffix tree of a string S is a compacted trie that represents all suffixes of S. Linear-time algorithms for constructing the suffix tree have been known for quite a while. In two dimensions, however, linear-time construction of two-dimensional suffix trees has been an open problem. We present the first linear-time algorithm for constructing two-dimensional suffix trees.

1 Introduction

The suffix tree T_S of a string S is a compacted trie that represents all suffixes of S. It was designed as a space-efficient alternative [16] to Weiner's position tree [21]. The suffix tree has been a fundamental data structure in the area of string processing algorithms [3, 4]. When the alphabet Σ of the given string S is of constant size, linear-time algorithms for constructing the suffix tree have been known for quite a while [16, 20]. In a more general case of integer alphabets, i.e., input symbols are integers in the range $[0, n^c]$ where n is the length of S and c is a constant, Farach [5] recently gave a linear-time construction algorithm.

In two dimensions, Gonnet [11] first introduced a notion of suffix tree for a matrix, called the *PAT-tree*. Giancarlo [7] proposed the Lsuffix tree that is a generalization of the suffix tree to square matrices, and gave an $O(n^2 \log n)$-time construction algorithm for an $n \times n$ matrix. Giancarlo and Grossi [8] proposed CRCW PRAM algorithms for the construction of Lsuffix trees. Giancarlo and Grossi [9, 10] introduced the general framework of two-dimensional suffix tree families and gave an expected linear-time construction algorithm. Two-dimensional suffix arrays (extension of Manber and Myers's suffix arrays [15]) are also constructed in $O(n^2 \log n)$ time [7, 14]. Even in the case of constant-size alphabets, linear-time construction of two-dimensional suffix trees has been an open problem.

We present the first linear-time algorithm for constructing two-dimensional suffix trees in the case of integer alphabets (and thus in the case of constant-size alphabets as well). To do that, we propose the Isuffix tree that is similar to the Lsuffix tree in its definition, but that is essential in linear-time construction. As a corollary of our linear-time construction of two-dimensional suffix trees, two-dimensional suffix arrays can be constructed in linear time.

---

* This work is supported by S.N.U. Research Fund 99-11-1-063.

Giancarlo's $O(n^2 \log n)$-time construction of Lsuffix trees has mainly two bottlenecks that incur $O(\log n)$ factors. One is that suffix links are not defined from internal nodes to internal nodes and thus dynamic trees [19] are needed to follow suffix links. The other is that it traverses the suffix tree from top to bottom and each branching from a node to its child requires $O(\log n)$ time in the case of integer alphabets or in two dimensions.

A new approach in constructing suffix trees in recent sequential and parallel algorithms [5, 6, 13, 17] consists of the following three steps.

1. Recursively construct suffix trees for some subsets of positions (e.g., the set of odd positions in one dimension).
2. Construct a suffix tree for the remaining positions (e.g., the set of even positions in one dimension) from the suffix trees in step 1. The suffix trees in steps 1 and 2 are called partial suffix trees.
3. Merge the partial suffix trees into the final suffix tree.

We take this approach, and eliminate the two bottlenecks as follows. Our contribution in the linear-time construction is twofold.

- We give an appropriate *definition of suffix links in two dimensions*, which eliminates the need of dynamic trees and allows us to handle the third step (merging) in linear time.
- The first and second steps of the new approach are easy in one dimension, but there is no obvious way to extend them to two dimensions. We design a new way of constructing suffix trees from top to bottom using a technique called *bucket partitioning* (instead of branching), which is used in both the first and second steps of our construction.

To use an Isuffix tree for pattern matching purposes, we need to construct the *refined Isuffix tree* as in [7]. The refinement in each internal node of an Isuffix tree is essentially the same as conversion from suffix arrays to suffix trees, which can be done in linear time. Hence, the overall construction takes linear $O(n^2)$ time up to the refined Isuffix tree. When we search for an $m \times m$ pattern matrix, we need to use branching, so pattern matching takes $O(m^2 \log |\Sigma|)$ time as in [7].

2 Preliminaries

Linear representation of square matrices. Given an $n \times n$ matrix A, we denote by $A[i : k, j : l]$ the submatrix of A with corners (i, j), (k, j), (i, l), and (k, l). When $i = k$ or $j = l$, we omit one of the repeated indices. An entry of matrix A is an integer in the range $[0, n^c]$ for some constant c. The integers in A can be mapped into integers in the range $[1, n^2]$ by linear-time sorting. Hence we assume that $\Sigma = \{1, 2, \ldots, n^2\}$.

Let $I\Sigma = \bigcup_{i=1}^{\infty} \Sigma^i$, where the letter I represents linear shapes (see Fig. 1). We refer to the elements of $I\Sigma$ as *Icharacters*. Two Icharacters are *equal* if and only if they are equal as strings. Given two Icharacters Iw and Iu of equal length, $Iw \prec Iu$ if and only if Iw as a string is lexicographically smaller than Iu as a string.

We describe a linearization method for a square matrix $A[1 : n, 1 : n]$ [2, 7, 14]. When we cut a matrix along the main diagonal, it is divided into an upper right half and a lower left half. Let $a(i) = A[i+1, 1 : i]$ and $b(i) = A[1 : i+1, i+1]$

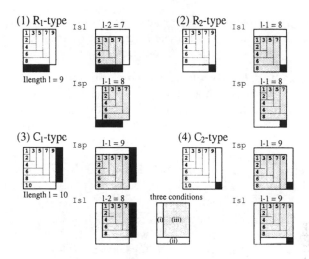

Fig. 1. Four types of internal nodes. (A black area has a mismatch.)

for $1 \leq i < n$, i.e., $a(i)$ is a row of the lower left half and $b(i)$ is a column of the upper right half. Then $a(i)$'s and $b(i)$'s can be regarded as Icharacters.

The linearized string IA of matrix $A[1:n, 1:n]$, called the *Istring of matrix A*, is the concatenation of Icharacters $IA[1], \ldots, IA[2n-1]$ that are defined as follows: (i) $IA[1] = A[1,1]$; (ii) $IA[2i] = a(i)$, $1 \leq i < n$; (iii) $IA[2i + 1] = b(i)$, $1 \leq i < n$. For each Icharacter $IA[l]$, $1 < l \leq 2n-1$, $tail(IA[l])$ is the last symbol of $IA[l]$ and $body(IA[l])$ is the maximal proper prefix of $IA[l]$. The *Ilength*, *Isubstring*, and *Iprefix* of an Istring IA can be defined as in one-dimensional strings if we regard Icharacters of IA as atomic elements.

Isuffix trees. For $1 \leq i, j \leq n$, the *suffix S_{ij} of matrix A* is the largest square submatrix of A that starts at position (i, j) in A. That is, $S_{ij} = A[i : i + k, j : j + k]$ where $k = n - \max(i, j)$. If we add special symbols to A as in [14], we can make all suffixes of A distinct. Consider a suffix S_{ij}, $1 \leq i, j \leq n$, of matrix A. The Istring of S_{ij} is called an *Isuffix* of A and denoted by IS_{ij}. The position (i, j) is called the *index of Isuffix IS_{ij}*. Note that the number of all Isuffixes of A is n^2.

The *Isuffix tree $IST(A)$* of matrix A is a compacted trie that represents all Isuffixes of A. Each edge (u, v) of $IST(A)$ is labeled with $label(u, v)$ that is a nonempty Isubstring of an Isuffix of A. For each node v, let $L(v)$ denote the Istring obtained by concatenating the labels on the path from the root to v. The leaf corresponding to Isuffix IS_{ij} will be denoted by l_{ij}. The *level* of a node v in an Isuffix tree is $|L(v)|$.

We define an *order $\prec_I$* on positions of matrix A: $(a, b) \prec_I (i, j)$ if and only if $A[a, b]$ appears before $A[i, j]$ in Istring IA when IA is regarded as a one-dimensional string. For each internal node u of Isuffix tree $IST(A)$, we define the *min-index* of u to be the minimum position (i, j) in $\prec_I$ such that l_{ij} is a descendant of u.

The *least common ancestor* of two nodes v and w in a tree is denoted by $\mathtt{lca}(v, w)$. By the results of [12, 18] the computation of $\mathtt{lca}$ of two nodes can be done in constant time after linear-time preprocessing on a tree. The Ilength of the *longest common Iprefix* of two Istrings $I\alpha$ and $I\beta$ is denoted by $\texttt{Ilcp}(I\alpha, I\beta)$. For all nodes u, v in Isuffix tree $IST(A)$, the following property is satisfied between $\texttt{Ilcp}$ and $\texttt{lca}$: $\texttt{Ilcp}(L(u), L(v)) = |L(\texttt{lca}(u, v))|$.

Isuffix links and Isuffix pointers. For an internal node u in Isuffix tree $IST(A)$, let $v_1, \ldots, v_r$ be the children of u and $I\sigma_1, \ldots, I\sigma_r$ be the first Icharacters of $label(u, v_1), \ldots, label(u, v_r)$, respectively. If $body(I\sigma_1) = \cdots = body(I\sigma_r)$ then u is called *singular*. We define the *locus* of an Istring $I\alpha$ to be the node u such that $L(u) = I\alpha$ in $IST(A)$. The *extended* locus of $I\alpha$ is the locus of the shortest Istring that has $I\alpha$ as its Iprefix.

We categorize internal nodes u and define the *Isuffix link* and the *Isuffix pointer* of u, denoted by $\texttt{Isl}(u)$ and $\texttt{Isp}(u)$, respectively. Let $L(u) = IS_{ab}[1..l]$ for some Isuffix IS_{ab} such that $l = |L(u)| \geq 3$. (See Fig. 1.)

- R_1*-type* if l is odd and u is not singular: Since the locus v of $IS_{a+1,b}[1..l-2]$ (the shaded area) exists in $IST(A)$, we define the Isuffix link $\texttt{Isl}(u) = v$. The locus of $IS_{a,b+1}[1..l-1]$ does not always exist. Thus, we define the Isuffix pointer $\texttt{Isp}(u)$ that points to the extended locus of $IS_{a,b+1}[1..l-1]$.
- R_2*-type* if l is odd and u is singular: Since the locus v of $IS_{a+1,b}[1..l-1]$ exists in $IST(A)$, we define the Isuffix link $\texttt{Isl}(u) = v$. Note that $|L(v)| = l-1$ because u is singular. As in the R_1-type, $\texttt{Isp}(u)$ points to the extended locus of $IS_{a,b+1}[1..l-1]$ in $IST(A)$. Both of the R_1-type and the R_2-type will be called the R-type.
- C_1*-type* if l is even and u is not singular: When l is even, we consider $IS_{a,b+1}$ (rather than $IS_{a+1,b}$) to define the Isuffix link $\texttt{Isl}(u)$. $\texttt{Isl}(u)$ and $\texttt{Isp}(u)$ point to the locus of $IS_{a,b+1}[1..l-2]$ and the extended locus of $IS_{a+1,b}[1..l-1]$, respectively.
- C_2*-type* if l is even and u is singular: $\texttt{Isl}(u)$ and $\texttt{Isp}(u)$ point to the locus of $IS_{a,b+1}[1..l-1]$ and the extended locus of $IS_{a+1,b}[1..l-1]$, respectively. Both of the C_1-type and the C_2-type will be called the C-type.

If u is the R-type, we say that the *row-link* of u is the Isuffix link $\texttt{Isl}(u)$ and the *column-link* of u is the Isuffix pointer $\texttt{Isp}(u)$. If u is the C-type, we say that the *row-link* of u is $\texttt{Isp}(u)$ and the *column-link* of u is $\texttt{Isl}(u)$.

The Isuffix links of all internal nodes in $IST(A)$ form a tree, called the Isl-tree, rooted at the root of $IST(A)$. We define the depth $D(u)$ of each internal node u in the Isl-tree as follows. For each Isuffix link $\texttt{Isl}(u) = v$, $D(u) = D(v)+1$ if u is singular; otherwise, $D(u) = D(v)+2$. Then, we have $|L(u)| = D(u)$ by definition of Isuffix links.

3 Constructing Isuffix trees

3.1 Algorithm outline

We divide all Isuffixes IS_{ij} of matrix A into four types. An Isuffix IS_{ij} is *type-1* if both of i and j are odd; *type-2* if i is even and j is odd; *type-3* if i is odd and j is even; *type-4* if both of i and j are even. Let $IST(A_r)$, $1 \leq r \leq 4$, be the Isuffix tree for all type-r Isuffixes of A. $IST(A_1), \ldots, IST(A_4)$ are called *partial* Isuffix trees.

The construction algorithm for the Isuffix tree $IST(A)$ consists of the following five steps.

Step 1. *Construct T_{rows} and T_{cols} of matrix A.* We will compare two Icharacters using a similar method to the one used in [7]. Let *rows* (resp. *cols*) be the string obtained by concatenating the rows (resp. columns) of A in row (resp. column) major order. We construct one-dimensional suffix trees T_{rows} and T_{cols} for strings *rows* and *cols*, respectively, by Farach's algorithm [5] such that all leaves in T_{rows} and T_{cols} are in lexicographic order of corresponding suffixes. Now we can perform a comparison of Icharacters in constant time using lca operations. This technique was also used in [2].

Step 2. *Recursively compute $IST(B_r)$, $1 \leq r \leq 3$.* We define three *encoded* matrices B_1, B_2 and B_3. For all start positions $(2i - 1, 2j - 1)$, $1 \leq i, j \leq n/2$, of type-1 Isuffixes of A, we make 4-tuples $\langle A[2i - 1, 2j - 1], A[2i, 2j - 1], A[2i - 1, 2j], A[2i, 2j]\rangle$. Radix-sort all the tuples in linear time, and map each tuple into an integer in the range $[1, n^2]$. We assign the integer of each tuple $\langle A[2i - 1, 2j - 1], A[2i, 2j - 1], A[2i - 1, 2j], A[2i, 2j]\rangle$ to $B_1[i, j]$ in the encoded matrix B_1. Let $A_2 = A[2 : n, 1 : n]$ and $A_3 = A[1 : n, 2 : n]$. Then type-2 (resp. type-3) Isuffixes of A are type-1 Isuffixes of matrices A_2 (resp. A_3). We perform the same procedure on A_2 and A_3 to make the encoded matrices B_2 and B_3, respectively. The Isuffix trees $IST(B_r)$ of B_r, $1 \leq r \leq 3$, are constructed recursively.

Step 3. *Compute $IST(A_r)$ from $IST(B_r)$, $1 \leq r \leq 3$.* We construct $IST(A_r)$, $1 \leq r \leq 3$, by decoding the encoded Isuffix tree $IST(B_r)$ in linear time. Since two encoded Icharacters in B_r corresponds to four Icharacters in A, two levels of $IST(B_r)$ are converted to four levels of $IST(A_r)$. A difficulty is that the lexicographic order of Isuffixes of A_r may not be that of corresponding Isuffixes of B_r because four Icharacters of A_r do not appear in the right order in the encoded two Icharacters of B_r. We solve this difficulty by bucket partitioning as in Step 4. The details are omitted.

Step 4. *Construct $IST(A_4)$ by using $IST(A_r)$, $1 \leq r \leq 3$.* In Section 3.2 we will describe the construction algorithm of $IST(A_4)$ that is a new way of constructing suffix trees using bucket partitioning.

Step 5. *Merge the four partial Isuffix trees into $IST(A)$.* In Section 3.3 we will describe a generic merge procedure and show how to merge four partial Isuffix trees by using Isuffix links and Isuffix pointers.

3.2 Construction of $IST(A_4)$

We construct the Isuffix tree $IST(A_4)$ directly (i.e., without recursion) from $IST(A_r)$, $1 \leq r \leq 3$, in linear time. For a type-1 (resp. type-4) Isuffix IS_{ij}, we define $Ihead_{ij}$ to be the longest Iprefix of IS_{ij} which is also an Iprefix of a type-1 (resp. type-4) Isuffix IS_{ab} for some $(a, b) \prec_I (i, j)$. Let $minh(i, j)$ denote the min-index of the locus of $Ihead_{ij}$.

Lemma 1. *For a type-1 Isuffix $IS_{2i-1,2j-1}$, let $Ihead_{2i-1,2j-1} = IS_{2a-1,2b-1}[1..l]$ for $l \geq 3$ and some index $(2a - 1, 2b - 1)$. Then $IS_{2a,2b}[1..l - 2]$ is an Iprefix of $Ihead_{2i,2j}$.*

Our construction algorithm of $IST(A_4)$ consists of three stages. In the first stage we preprocess $IST(A_1)$ and obtain from $IST(A_1)$ some information on matching Iprefixes of type-4 Isuffixes by Lemma 1. The second stage constructs a tree IST that is the same as $IST(A_4)$ except that children of each node of IST are unordered. Here we use a technique called bucket partitioning to traverse tree

IST from top to bottom without branching. In order to get $IST(A_4)$, the third stage sorts the children of all internal nodes in IST.

Stage 1. The preprocessing consists of three steps.

1. We first sort the characters of A using buckets. Let $C_4(\sigma)$ be the bucket that has all positions $(2i, 2j)$ such that $A[2i, 2j] = \sigma$.

2. Preprocess the Isuffix tree $IST(A_1)$.

- For each internal node u of $IST(A_1)$, find the min-index of u.
- For each type-1 Isuffix $IS_{2i-1,2j-1}$, find the locus of $head_{2i-1,2j-1}$.

Both of two substeps above can be computed in $O(n^2)$ time by a postorder traversal of $IST(A_1)$. Let $v_1, \ldots, v_r$ be the children of an internal node u in $IST(A_1)$ and let $(i_1, j_1), \ldots, (i_r, j_r)$ be the min-indices of $v_1, \ldots, v_r$, respectively. Then the min-index of u is the minimum in $\prec_I$ (say (i_{min}, j_{min})) of all (i_k, j_k), $1 \leq k \leq r$. Moreover, node u is the locus of $head_{i_k j_k}$ for all (i_k, j_k) except (i_{min}, j_{min}). The locus of $head_{i_{min}, j_{min}}$ will be computed in an ascendant of u.

3. Construct a multiple queue that contains information on matching Iprefixes of type-4 Isuffixes. Let $Q[k]$, $1 \leq k \leq 2n-1$, be an array of queues. Each element of a queue $Q[k]$ is a pair of indices of type-4 Isuffixes. For each type-1 Isuffix $IS_{2i-1,2j-1}$, let u be the locus of $head_{2i-1,2j-1}$ in $IST(A_1)$ and let $k = |L(u)| - 2$.

- If $k \geq 1$, let $(2a-1, 2b-1) = minh(2i-1, 2j-1)$. Since $|head_{2i-1,2j-1}| \geq 3$, Isuffixes $IS_{2i,2j}$ and $IS_{2a,2b}$ have a matching Iprefix of length at least k by Lemma 1. Insert a pair $\langle (2i, 2j), (2a, 2b) \rangle$ into queue $Q[k]$.
- If $k < 1$, we cannot get a matching Iprefix of $IS_{2i,2j}$ from $IS_{2i-1,2j-1}$. However, from the bucket $C_4(A[2i, 2j])$ we know which Isuffixes have the same first symbol as $IS_{2i,2j}$. Insert $\langle (2i, 2j), (2a, 2b) \rangle$ into queue $Q[1]$, where $(2a, 2b)$ is the smallest element of bucket $C_4(A[2i, 2j])$. (If $(2i, 2j)$ itself is the smallest, we do nothing.)

Stage 2. Construct tree IST from top to bottom in at most $2n - 1$ iterations.

In the kth iteration we construct level k of IST. Let (u, v) be an edge in the Isuffix tree $IST(A_4)$ such that $|L(u)| < k \leq |L(v)|$ for some k. At the beginning of the kth iteration, (u, v) is called an *open* edge, denoted by $(u, I\sigma)$ where $I\sigma$ is the first Icharacter of $label(u, v)$. For every open edge $e = (u, I\sigma)$, we will maintain $Slist_e$ that contains some type-4 indices $(2i, 2j)$ such that the leaf $l_{2i,2j}$ will be a descendant of u in $IST(A_4)$. For the kth iteration, we maintain $Elist_k$ that contains all open edges e such that $Slist_e$ contains at least two elements and all Isuffixes whose indices are in $Slist_e$ have a common Iprefix of length k.

We construct tree IST by partitioning Isuffixes until all type-4 Isuffixes are separated and the multiple queue becomes empty. Initially, make the root r of the tree IST. Recall that the first Icharacter of an Istring is a single symbol. For each bucket $C_4(\sigma)$, let (i_σ, j_σ) be the smallest index in $C_4(\sigma)$. Make an open edge $e = (r, \sigma)$ and insert (i_σ, j_σ) into $Slist_e$. The kth iteration for $k \geq 1$ is as follows.

1. Extract all pairs $\langle (2i, 2j), (2a, 2b) \rangle$ from queue $Q[k]$. For each pair $\langle (2i, 2j), (2a, 2b) \rangle$, find the open edge e that has $(2a, 2b)$ in $Slist_e$, and insert $(2i, 2j)$ into $Slist_e$. By this, $Slist_e$ contains at least two elements. If $Slist_e$ has exactly two elements (i.e., previously e was not in $Elist_k$), insert e into $Elist_k$.

2. Extract all open edges from $Elist_k$. For each extracted open edge $e = (u, I\sigma)$, let $(i_1, j_1), \ldots, (i_r, j_r)$ be the type-4 indices in $Slist_e$. Isuffixes $IS_{i_1 j_1}, \ldots, IS_{i_r j_r}$ have a common Iprefix of length k. Let $Ib_l, 1 \leq l \leq r$, be the $(k+1)$-st Icharacter of the Isuffix whose index is (i_l, j_l) (i.e., $Ib_l = IS_{i_l j_l}[k+1]$). We partition the indices $(i_1, j_1), \ldots, (i_r, j_r)$ by Icharacters $Ib_1, \ldots, Ib_r$. If $Ib_1, \ldots, Ib_r$ are single symbols, we may use the method of partitioning r elements using buckets (with two-way pointers) in $O(r)$ time [1]. However, because $Ib_1, \ldots, Ib_r$ are Icharacters, we cannot use buckets based on single symbols. The main idea of our partitioning is to use some internal nodes in Isuffix tree $IST(A_3)$ or $IST(A_2)$ as buckets. After partitioning the indices, there are two cases.

- If all indices are in the same bucket, insert e into $Elist_{k+1}$ and keep all indices $(i_1, j_1), \ldots, (i_r, j_r)$ in $Slist_e$.
- If the indices are in s different buckets with Icharacters $I\sigma_1, \ldots, I\sigma_s$, create a new node v (i.e., $|L(v)| = k$) and an edge $e = (u, v)$. Create new open edges $e_l = (v, I\sigma_l), 1 \leq l \leq s$. Insert indices in the same bucket into $Slist_{e_l}$ for every e_l. If $Slist_{e_l}$ contains at least two elements, insert e_l into $Elist_{k+1}$.

Bucket partitioning. We describe how to partition indices $(i_1, j_1), \ldots, (i_r, j_r)$ in $O(r)$ time. Recall that $IS_{i_1 j_1}[1..k] = \cdots = IS_{i_r j_r}[1..k]$ and we are partitioning with the $(k+1)$-st Icharacters $Ib_1, \ldots, Ib_r$. If some $(k+1)$-st Icharacters are different, there must exist an internal node w in $IST(A_3)$ (resp. $IST(A_2)$) such that $L(w)$ is an Iprefix of IS_{i_l+1, j_l} (resp. IS_{i_l, j_l+1}) of Ilength $k-2$ or $k-1$ for every $1 \leq l \leq r$, when k is odd (resp. even). We will use some children $v_1, \ldots, v_s$ of w as buckets for partitioning.

Assume that k is odd (the other case is similar). For every adjacent indices (i_c, j_c) and (i_d, j_d) (i.e., $d = c + 1$), do the following. Find the node $w' = \text{lca}(l_{i_c+1, j_c}, l_{i_d+1, j_d})$ in $IST(A_3)$. Let v_c and v_d be the children of w such that l_{i_c+1, j_c} and l_{i_d+1, j_d} are descendants of v_c and v_d, respectively.

1. If $|L(w')| = k - 2$ or $k - 1$, then $w' = w$ and Icharacters Ib_c and Ib_d are different. Insert (i_c, j_c) and (i_d, j_d) to buckets v_c and v_d, respectively.
2. If $|L(w')| \geq k$, then w' is a proper descendant of w and $Ib_c = Ib_d$. Indices (i_c, j_c) and (i_d, j_d) will be inserted into the same bucket. The name of the bucket (i.e., a child of w) will be determined when an index of this bucket falls into case 1 with another index. (If all $Ib_1, \ldots, Ib_r$ are the same, all indices are in one bucket and w may not exist.)

Stage 3. Sort the children of all internal nodes simultaneously. This can be done in $O(n^2)$ time by using leaves of T_{rows} and T_{cols} as buckets. The details are omitted.

3.3 Merging partial Isuffix trees

We describe how to merge four partial Isuffix trees $IST(A_r), 1 \leq r \leq 4$, into the final Isuffix tree $IST(A)$ in $O(n^2)$ time. We first merge $IST(A_1)$ and $IST(A_2)$ into $IST(A_{12})$, and merge $IST(A_3)$ and $IST(A_4)$ into $IST(A_{34})$, simultaneously. Then, we merge $IST(A_{12})$ and $IST(A_{34})$ into $IST(A)$.

A generic merge procedure. We describe a generic procedure to merge two Isuffix trees IST_1 and IST_2 into IST_{12}, which is a coupled-breadth-first version of Farach's coupled-depth-first search algorithm [5]. We will construct a *structurally merged tree* (*SM*-tree) of IST_1 and IST_2 that is structurally isomorphic to the merged tree IST_{12}, and then compute IST_{12}.

The generic procedure basically follows a coupled-breadth-first search of Isuffix trees IST_1 and IST_2 by levels. To visit all nodes u by ascending order of levels, we maintain a multiple queue. Let $Q[k]$, $1 \leq k \leq 2n - 1$, be an array of queues. Each queue $Q[k]$ has *to-be-merged pairs*, which are defined below, as its elements. Let u be a merged node of IST_1 and IST_2. Let v and w be children of u such that v is in IST_1, w is in IST_2, and $label(u, v)$ and $label(u, w)$ begin with the same Icharacter. Then (u, v) and (u, w) are called a *to-be-merged* pair. A to-be-merged pair (u, v) and (u, w) will be denoted by a tuple $\langle u, v, w \rangle$.

Suppose that two internal nodes u_1 in IST_1 and u_2 in IST_2 are merged into a node u in IST_{12}. Let v_i, $1 \leq i \leq I$, be the ith child of u_1 and w_j, $1 \leq j \leq J$, be the jth child of u_2, where I and J are the numbers of children of u_1 and u_2, respectively. Let Ia_i and Ib_j be the first Icharacter of $label(u_1, v_i)$ and $label(u_2, w_j)$, respectively. When u is created in IST_{12}, we need to find to-be-merged pairs among the edges (u_1, v_i)'s and (u_2, w_j)'s. The procedure $Pair(u_1, u_2)$ finds all to-be-merged pairs $\langle u, v_i, w_j \rangle$ such that $Ia_i = Ib_j$ and inserts $\langle u, v_i, w_j \rangle$ into queue $Q[k]$ where $k = \min\{|L(v_i)|, |L(w_j)|\}$. This can be done in $O(I + J)$ time because the children of u_1 (resp. u_2) are sorted lexicographically by the first Icharacters of $label(u_1, v_i)$ (resp. $label(u_2, w_j)$).

We now describe our coupled-BFS algorithm. The output of a coupled-BFS algorithm is a structurally merged tree (SM-tree). Initially, we perform $Pair(r_1, r_2)$ where r_1 and r_2 are the root nodes of IST_1 and IST_2. At the beginning of stage k of our coupled-BFS algorithm, $Q[k]$ has every to-be-merged pair $\langle u, v, w \rangle$ such that $k = \min\{|L(v)|, |L(w)|\}$. In stage k, we extract a to-be-merged pair $\langle u, v, w \rangle$ from $Q[k]$ and do the following procedure until no elements are left in $Q[k]$. Assume without loss of generality that $k = |L(v)| \leq |L(w)|$. Here we wish to solve the *prefix decision problem*: Given a to-be-merged pair $\langle u, v, w \rangle$, decide whether $L(v)$ is an Iprefix of $L(w)$. (How to solve this problem will be described later.)

There are two cases depending on whether or not $L(v)$ is an Iprefix of $L(w)$.

- $L(v)$ *is not an Iprefix of* $L(w)$. Since $\langle u, v, w \rangle$ is a to-be-merged pair and $L(u)$ is not an Iprefix of $L(w)$, the longest common Iprefix $I\alpha$ of $L(v)$ and $L(w)$ satisfies $|L(u)| + 1 \leq |I\alpha| < k$. We make a new node u' (called a *refinement* node) and new edges (u', v) and (u', w). Since there are no more to-be-merged pairs in two subtrees rooted at v and w, we insert no tuples into queues. Notice that we do not know the Ilength of $label(u, u')$ nor the order of $label(u', v)$ and $label(u', w)$ since the prefix decision problem simply returns 'No' in this case.

- $L(v)$ *is an Iprefix of* $L(w)$. If $L(v) = L(w)$ then there can be new to-be-merged pairs between children of v and children of w. Thus we perform $Pair(v, w)$. Otherwise (i.e., $|L(v)| < |L(w)|$), create a new node w' (called an *extra* node) between u and w such that $label(u, w') = label(u, v)$ and $label(w', w) = label(u, w) - label(u, v)$. Perform $Pair(v, w')$ in which there is at most one to-be-merged pair.

We now construct IST_{12} from the SM-tree that is structurally isomorphic to IST_{12}. We need to compute $|L(t)|$ for every refinement node t (which has two children). We first construct the Isl-tree of the SM-tree, and then compute the depths of all internal nodes in the Isl-tree by traversing the Isl-tree [5]. By definition of Isl-trees, we get $|L(u)|$ for every internal node u in the SM-tree. The lexicographic order of two children c_1 and c_2 of a refinement node t is the order of the first Icharacters of $label(t, c_1)$ and $label(t, c_2)$. This ordering can be done in constant time by using T_{rows} or T_{cols}.

The merging algorithm. When we merge $IST(A_1)$ and $IST(A_2)$ and merge $IST(A_3)$ and $IST(A_4)$ by the generic merge procedure, we will perform the kth stage of the coupled-BFS simultaneously. What remains in the merge procedure is to solve the prefix decision problem, which we do by using Isuffix links and Isuffix pointers (i.e., row-links and column-links). In Section 2 we defined row-links and column-links in the final Isuffix tree $IST(A)$. However, since all Isuffixes of A are divided into four partial Isuffix trees, row-links and column-links of a partial Isuffix tree are in different partial Isuffix trees. For example, let $L(u) = IS_{ab}[1..l]$ for some type-1 Isuffix IS_{ab} in $IST(A_1)$. The row-link of u is v such that $L(v)$ is an Iprefix of type-2 Isuffix $IS_{a+1,b}$. Hence v is in $IST(A_2)$. Similarly, the column-link of u is in $IST(A_3)$. The following table shows the places of the row-link and the column-link of a node u.

u in	row-link	column-link	u in	row-link	column-link
$IST(A_1)$	$IST(A_2)$	$IST(A_3)$	$IST(A_3)$	$IST(A_4)$	$IST(A_1)$
$IST(A_2)$	$IST(A_1)$	$IST(A_4)$	$IST(A_4)$	$IST(A_3)$	$IST(A_2)$

We compute all row-links and column-links for four partial Isuffix trees in $O(n^2)$ time as follows. For each internal node u in $IST(A_r)$, $1 \leq r \leq 4$, let (a, b) and (i, j) be the min-indices of (arbitrarily selected) two children of u. Since $u = \mathtt{lca}(l_{ab}, l_{ij})$, the row-link of u is $\mathtt{lca}(l_{a+1,b}, l_{i+1,j})$ and the column-link of u is $\mathtt{lca}(l_{a,b+1}, l_{i,j+1})$, which can be computed in constant time using $\mathtt{lca}$ operations.

Prefix decision. Consider a to-be-merged pair $\langle u, v, w \rangle$ where v is in $IST(A_1)$ and w is in $IST(A_2)$. Let $L(v) = IS_{ab}[1..k]$ and $L(w) = IS_{ij}[1..l]$ for some Isuffixes IS_{ab} and IS_{ij}. Assume that $k \leq l$. We solve the prefix decision problem in constant time as follows. Consider the case that v is the C_1-type. (The other cases are similar.) Since v is the C_1-type, $\mathtt{Isl}(v)$ is the column-link of v in $IST(A_3)$. Let w' be the column-link of w in $IST(A_4)$. Since $L(v) = IS_{ab}[1..k] = A[a : a + r, b : b + r - 1]$ where $r = k/2$, $L(v)$ is an Iprefix of $L(w)$ if and only if the following three conditions hold: (i) $A[a : a + r - 1, b] = A[i : i + r - 1, j]$; (ii) $A[a + r, b : b + r - 1] = A[i + r, j : j + r - 1]$; (iii) $A[a : a + r - 1, b + 1 : b + r - 1] = A[i : i + r - 1, j + 1 : j + r - 1]$. (See Fig. 1.)

The conditions (i) and (ii) can be checked in constant time by using T_{rows} and T_{cols}. The condition (iii) can be checked as follows. Since $A[a : a + r - 1, b + 1 : b + r - 1] = L(\mathtt{Isl}(v))$ and $A[i : i + r - 1, j + 1 : j + r - 1]$ is an Iprefix of $L(w')$, we will check whether $L(\mathtt{Isl}(v))$ is an Iprefix of $L(w')$. Since $|L(\mathtt{Isl}(v))| = k - 2$, $\mathtt{Isl}(v)$ has been processed in the coupled-BFS that merges $IST(A_3)$ and $IST(A_4)$. There are two cases depending on whether $\mathtt{Isl}(v)$ was merged with a node of $IST(A_4)$.

• $\mathtt{Isl}(v)$ *was not merged with a node of* $IST(A_4)$. It means that there exists no node y in $IST(A_4)$ such that $\mathtt{Ilcp}(L(\mathtt{Isl}(v)), L(y)) \geq k - 2$. Hence, $L(\mathtt{Isl}(v))$ cannot be an Iprefix of $L(w')$.

• $\mathtt{Isl}(v)$ *was merged with a node x of* $IST(A_1)$. Since node x may be an extra node, let z be the nearest descendant of x that is a node in the original $IST(A_4)$ (z is unique because an extra node has only one child). Since we are at stage k, the path length between x and z is $O(1)$. Since both z and w' are nodes in $IST(A_4)$, we can use an $\mathtt{lca}$ operation on z and w' in the original $IST(A_4)$. $L(\mathtt{Isl}(v))$ is an Iprefix of $L(w')$ if and only if $|L(\mathtt{lca}(z, w'))| \geq k - 2$.

Finally, we merge two Isuffix trees $IST(A_{12})$ and $IST(A_{34})$. The merging process is similar except that row-links of $IST(A_{12})$ or $IST(A_{34})$ are in the same Isuffix tree and column-links are in the other Isuffix tree.

Acknowledgement. We are grateful to Martin Farach, Raffaele Giancarlo and Roberto Grossi for their valuable comments and suggestions.

References

1. A.V. Aho, J.E. Hopcroft and J.D. Ullman, The Design and Analysis of Computer Algorithms, *Addison-Wesley*, 1974.
2. A. Amir and M. Farach, Two-dimensional dictionary matching, *Inform. Processing Letters* 21 (1992), 233–239.
3. A. Apostolico, The myriad virtues of subword trees, *Combinatorial Algorithms on Words*, Springer-Verlag, (1985), 85-95
4. M. Crochemore and W. Rytter, Text Algorithms, *Oxford University Press*, 1994.
5. M. Farach, Optimal suffix tree construction with large alphabets, *IEEE Symp. Found. Computer Science* (1997), 137–143.
6. M. Farach and S. Muthukrishnan, Optimal logarithmic time randomized suffix tree construction, *Int. Colloq. Automata Languages and Programming* (1996), 550–561.
7. R. Giancarlo, A generalization of the suffix tree to square matrices with application, *SIAM J. Comput.* 24, (1995), 520–562.
8. R. Giancarlo and R. Grossi, Parallel construction and query of suffix trees for two-dimensional matrices, *ACM Symposium on Parallel Algorithms and Architectures* (1993), 86–97.
9. R. Giancarlo and R. Grossi, On the construction of classes of suffix trees for square matrices: algorithms and applications, *Information and Computation* 130 (1996), 151–182.
10. R. Giancarlo and R. Grossi, Suffix Tree Data Structures for Matrices. Chap. 11 in Pattern Matching Algorithms, A. Apostolico and Z. Galil eds, *Oxford University Press*, (1997), 293–340.
11. G.H. Gonnet, Efficient searching of text and pictures, *Technical report, Univ. of Waterloo* OED-88-02, (1988).
12. D. Harel and R.E. Tarjan. Fast algorithms for finding nearest common ancestors, *SIAM J. Comput.* 13 (1984), 338–355.
13. R. Hariharan, Optimal parallel suffix tree construction, *IEEE Symp. Found. Computer Science* (1994), 290–299.
14. D.K. Kim, Y.A. Kim, and K. Park, Constructing suffix arrays for multi-dimensional matrices, *Symp. Combinatorial Pattern Matching* (1998), 249–260.
15. U. Manber and G. Myers, Suffix arrays: A new method for on-line string searches, *SIAM J. Comput.* 22, (1993), 935–938.
16. E.M. McCreight, A space-economical suffix tree construction algorithms, *J. Assoc. Comput. Mach.* 23 (1976), 262–272.
17. S.C. Sahinalp and U. Vishkin, Symmetry breaking for suffix tree construction, *IEEE Symp. Found. Computer Science* (1994), 300–309.
18. B. Schieber and U. Vishkin, On finding lowest common ancestors: simplification and parallelization, *SIAM J. Comput.* 17, (1988), 1253–1262.
19. D.D. Sleater and R.E. Tarjan, A data structure for dynamic trees, *J. Comput. System Sci.* 26, (1983), 362–391.
20. E. Ukkonen, On-line construction of suffix trees, *Algorithmica* 14 (1995), 249–260.
21. P. Weiner, Linear pattern matching algorithms, *Proc. 14th IEEE Symp. Switching and Automata Theory* (1973), 1–11.

A Connection between the Star Problem and the Finite Power Property in Trace Monoids* (Extended Abstract)**

Daniel Kirsten

Dresden University of Technology, Department of Computer Science,
Institute of Software Engineering I, D-01062 Dresden, Germany
dk11@inf.tu-dresden.de, http://www.inf.tu-dresden.de/~dk11

Abstract. This paper deals with a connection between the star problem and the finite power problem in trace monoids. Both problems are decidable in trace monoids without C4 submonoid [21] but remain open in all other trace monoids.

We show a connection between these problems. Assume two disjoint trace monoids $\mathbb{M}(\Gamma, I_\Gamma)$ and $\mathbb{M}(\Delta, I_\Delta)$. Assume further a recognizable language $L \subseteq \mathbb{M}(\Gamma, I_\Gamma) \times \mathbb{M}(\Delta, I_\Delta)$ such that every trace in L contains at least one letter in Γ and at least one letter in Δ. Our main theorem asserts that L^* is recognizable iff L has the finite power property.

1 Overview

1.1 Trace Monoids and Recognizable Trace Languages

CARTIER and FOATA introduced trace monoids in 1969 [2]. Since MAZURKIEWICZ proposed them as a potential model for concurrent processes in 1977 [14], they are systematically examined, see e.g., the recent surveys [4, 5].

Assume an alphabet Σ and an irreflexive and symmetric relation I which we call *independence*. We call the pair (Σ, I) an *independence alphabet*. We denote by $\approx_I$ the congruence on Σ^* which is induced by $ab \approx_I ba$ for any $a, b \in \Sigma$ with aIb. We call the factorization of the free monoid Σ^* under $\approx_I$ the *trace monoid* $\mathbb{M}(\Sigma, I)$, its elements, i.e., the congruence classes of $\approx_I$ *traces*, and its subsets *trace languages*. The words in a trace only differ in the order of their letters. Hence, we can define the length $|t|$ for some trace $t \in \mathbb{M}(\Sigma, I)$ as the length of any word in the congruence class t. If I is the biggest irreflexive relation over Σ, then $\mathbb{M}(\Sigma, I)$ is the free commutative monoid over Σ. If $I = \emptyset$, then $\mathbb{M}(\Sigma, I)$ is the free monoid Σ^*.

We call some trace $t \in \mathbb{M}(\Sigma, I)$ *non-connected* iff there are two non-empty traces $t_1, t_2 \in \mathbb{M}(\Sigma, I)$ with $t = t_1 t_2$ such that we have aIb for every letter a

---

* This work has been supported by the postgraduate program "Specification of discrete processes and systems of processes by operational models and logics" of the German Research Community (Deutsche Forschungsgemeinschaft).

** See orchid.inf.tu-dresden.de/gdp/publikation.html for full papers [12, 13].

in t_1 and every letter b in t_2. Otherwise, we call t *connected*. We call a trace language *connected* iff it contains only connected traces.

For any $\Gamma \subseteq \Sigma$, we denote by $\mathbb{M}(\Gamma, I)$ the trace monoid over Γ and $I \cap \Gamma \times \Gamma$. If we can split Σ into two non-empty disjoint subsets Γ and Δ such that aIb for every $a \in \Gamma$ and every $b \in \Delta$, then we call the independence alphabet *non-connected*. In this case, $\mathbb{M}(\Sigma, I)$ is naturally isomorphic to $\mathbb{M}(\Gamma, I) \times \mathbb{M}(\Delta, I)$ with componentwise concatenation. Otherwise, $\mathbb{M}(\Sigma, I)$ is not isomorphic to a Cartesian Product of trace monoids and we call (Σ, I) connected.

Two particular trace monoids play a crucial role: the so-called P3 and C4 which are up to isomorphism defined by $\{a, c\}^* \times \{b\}^*$ and $\{a, c\}^* \times \{b, d\}^*$, respectively. We denote the elements of a Cartesian Product by, e.g., $\binom{aacac}{bb}$. Some trace $\binom{u}{v}$ in P3 or C4 is connected iff u or v is the empty word λ.

A central topic in trace theory is the concept of recognizable trace languages, which can be considered as a generalization of regular languages in free monoids. For an introduction to the concept of recognizability, I recommend [1]. See [4, 17] for a survey on recognizable trace languages.

We call a language $L \subseteq \mathbb{M}(\Sigma, I)$ *recognizable* iff there is a finite monoid Q, a homomorphism $h : \mathbb{M}(\Sigma, I) \to Q$, and a set $F \subseteq Q$, such that $L = h^{-1}(F)$. We call $[Q, h, F]$ an *automaton*, Q the *states*, and F the *accepting states*. Like recognizable sets in any monoid, recognizable trace languages are closed under union, intersection, and complement, and the empty set and the complete monoid are recognizable languages. Moreover, every finite trace language is recognizable, and due to FLIESS [6, 17], we know that the concatenation of two recognizable trace languages yields a recognizable trace language.

1.2 The Star Problem and the Finite Power Property

Opposed to recognizable languages in free monoids, recognizable trace languages are not closed under iteration (KLEENE-*). This fact raises the so called *star problem*: Given a recognizable trace language L, is L^* recognizable?

The *finite power problem* is related to the star problem: Given a recognizable language L, has L the finite power property, shortly FPP, i.e., is there an $n \geq 0$ such that $L^* = L^0 \cup L^1 \ldots \cup L^n$? We abbreviate the union $L^0 \cup L^1 \ldots \cup L^n$ by $L^{0,\ldots,n}$. If some recognizable trace language L has the FPP, then L^* is recognizable by the closureship of recognizable trace languages under concatenation and union.

Although during the recent 15 years many papers have dealt with these two problems, only partial results have been achieved. The star problem in the free monoid is trivial due to KLEENE's Theorem from 1956, and it is decidable in free commutative monoids due to GINSBURG and SPANIER [8, 9]. BRZOZOWSKI raised the finite power problem in the free monoid in 1966, and it took more than 10 years till SIMON and HASHIGUCHI independently showed its decidability [23, 11]. In 1984, OCHMAŃSKI examined recognizable trace languages in his PhD thesis [18] and stated the star problem. During the eighties, OCHMAŃSKI [18], CLERBOUT and LATTEUX [3], and MÉTIVIER [15] independently proved that the iteration of a connected recognizable trace language yields a recognizable trace language. In 1990, OCHMAŃSKI showed the decidability of the star problem in C4 for finite trace languages containing at most one non-connected trace [19]. He used the decidability of the FPP in free monoids which marks the beginning of the examination of connections between the FPP and the star problem.

In 1992, SAKAROVITCH showed (as a conclusion of a more general result) that the star problem is decidable in trace monoids which do not contain a P3-submonoid [22]. Just in the same year, GASTIN, OCHMAŃSKI, PETIT, and ROZOY showed the decidability of the star problem in P3 [7]. Decidability of the FPP in free monoids plays a crucial role in their proof.

MÉTIVIER and RICHOMME further developed these ideas. They showed decidability of the FPP for connected recognizable trace languages and decidability of the star problem for trace languages containing at most four traces and for finite languages containing at most two connected traces [16].

The subsequent years were designated by stagnation. One did not achieve new results and one ceased the research on the star problem and the FPP.

1.3 An Inductive Approach

Provided that the star problem and the FPP are decidable, a probably promising approach to show their decidability is to establish an induction on independence alphabets. We have strong results due to RICHOMME for trace monoids over connected independence alphabets (Σ, I): If the star problem (resp. the FPP) is decidable in $\mathbb{M}(\Gamma, I)$ for any strict subset $\Gamma \subset \Sigma$, then the star problem (resp. the FPP) is decidable in $\mathbb{M}(\Sigma, I)$ [13, 21].

In trace monoids over non-connected independence alphabets the situation is more difficult. We have partial results due to MÉTIVIER and RICHOMME for trace monoids of the form $\mathbb{M}(\Gamma, I) \times \{b\}^*$ for some independence alphabet (Γ, I) and some letter $b \notin \Gamma$. If the star problem is decidable in $\mathbb{M}(\Gamma, I) \times \{b\}^*$, then the FPP is decidable in $\mathbb{M}(\Gamma, I)$ [16]. Consequently, if the star problem is decidable in every trace monoid, then so is the FPP [16]. If both the star problem and the FPP are decidable in $\mathbb{M}(\Gamma, I)$, then both problems are decidable in $\mathbb{M}(\Gamma, I) \times \{b\}^*$ [21]. Using the latter induction step and the step for connected independence alphabets, RICHOMME proved that both the star problem and the FPP are decidable in every trace monoid without a C4 submonoid [21].

An induction step for trace monoids $\mathbb{M}(\Sigma, I)$ of the form $\mathbb{M}(\Gamma, I) \times \mathbb{M}(\Delta, I)$ for arbitrary trace monoids $\mathbb{M}(\Gamma, I)$ and $\mathbb{M}(\Delta, I)$ remains open. Assume that both the star problem and the FPP are decidable in both $\mathbb{M}(\Gamma, I)$ and $\mathbb{M}(\Delta, I)$. In [13, 20], we reduced the decidability of the star problem in $\mathbb{M}(\Gamma, I) \times \mathbb{M}(\Delta, I)$ to the question whether the star problem is decidable for recognizable languages $L \subseteq \mathbb{M}(\Gamma, I) \times \mathbb{M}(\Delta, I)$ such that every trace in L contains at least one letter in Γ and at least one letter in Δ. Moreover, we showed exactly the same reduction for the FPP [13, 20].

Consequently, the two central questions concerning the star problem and the FPP are the decidability of the star problem and the decidability of the FPP for recognizable languages L in trace monoids of the form $\mathbb{M}(\Gamma, I) \times \mathbb{M}(\Delta, I)$ such that every trace in L contains at least one letter in Γ and at least one letter in Δ.

1.4 Main Results

In 1994, RICHOMME conjectured a crucial connection between these two questions [20]. The main result of the present paper is a proof for his conjecture:

Theorem 1. Assume some trace monoid $\mathbb{M}(\Sigma, I)$ which is isomorphic to a Cartesian Product $\mathbb{M}(\Gamma, I) \times \mathbb{M}(\Delta, I)$. Assume further a recognizable language $L \subseteq \mathbb{M}(\Gamma, I) \times \mathbb{M}(\Delta, I)$ such that every trace in L contains at least one letter in Γ and at least one letter in Δ.
Then, the language L^* is recognizable iff L has the FPP. □

As already mentioned, for every recognizable trace language L, L^* is recognizable if L has the FPP, i.e., one direction of Theorem 1 is obviously true even in a more general way. We prove the other direction as a corollary of Theorem 2, below. We need the notion of *generators*. Assume a trace monoid $\mathbb{M}(\Sigma, I)$ and some language $T \subseteq \mathbb{M}(\Sigma, I)$ with $\lambda \notin T$. Assume further that T is *concatenation closed*, i.e., $T^2 \subseteq T$. Then, T is a semigroup. The *generators* of T are the traces in T which cannot be factorized into traces in T, i.e., $\text{Gen}(T) = T \setminus T^2$. We have $\text{Gen}(T)^+ = T$ and moreover, for every language $L \subseteq \mathbb{M}(\Sigma, I)$ with $L^+ = T$, we have $\text{Gen}(T) \subseteq L$. See [12, 13] for details.

Theorem 2. Assume some trace monoid $\mathbb{M}(\Sigma, I)$ which is isomorphic to a Cartesian Product $\mathbb{M}(\Gamma, I) \times \mathbb{M}(\Delta, I)$. Assume a recognizable, concatenation closed language $T \subseteq \mathbb{M}(\Gamma, I) \times \mathbb{M}(\Delta, I)$ such that every $t \in T$ contains at least one letter in Γ and least one letter in Δ. Then, $\text{Gen}(T)$ has the FPP. □

Example 1. We consider the recognizable, concatenation closed language $T = \binom{a^+}{b^+}$. The generators of T are $\text{Gen}(T) = \binom{a}{b+} \cup \binom{a^+}{b}$. We can easily verify that $\text{Gen}(T)$ has the FPP. Assume some integers $n, m > 0$ and consider $t = \binom{a^n}{b^m}$. If $m = 1$ or $n = 1$, then t is a generator. Otherwise, we can factorize t into two generators of T by $t = \binom{a}{b^{m-1}}\binom{a^{n-1}}{b}$. Thus, we have $\text{Gen}(T)^+ = \text{Gen}(T) \cup \text{Gen}(T)^2$, i.e., $\text{Gen}(T)$ has the FPP. Further, for every language $L \subseteq \{a\}^* \times \{b\}^*$ with $L^+ = T$, we have $\text{Gen}(T) \subseteq L$, and thus, $L \cup L^2 = T$, i.e., $L^* = L^{0,\ldots,2}$. □

We close this section by deriving Theorem 1 from Theorem 2.

Proof of Theorem 1: Assume some language L as in Theorem 1. If L has the FPP, then L^* is recognizable because of the closure properties of recognizable trace languages. Conversely, assume that L^* is recognizable. Then, so is L^+. By Theorem 2, $\text{Gen}(L^+)$ has the FPP. We have $\text{Gen}(L^+) \subseteq L$. Thus, there is an $l > 0$ with $L^* = \text{Gen}(L^+)^* = \text{Gen}(L^+)^{0,\ldots,l} \subseteq L^{0,\ldots,l} \subseteq L^*$, i.e., $L^* = L^{0,\ldots,l}$. □

After we discussed some conclusions of Theorem 1 in Part 1.5, we prove Theorem 2. In Section 2, we deal with algebraic tools and in Section 3, we use them to prove Theorem 2.

1.5 Conclusions and Future Steps

Already in 1994, RICHOMME conjectured that the trace monoids with a decidable star problem are exactly the trace monoids with a decidable FPP. In [20], he showed that the decidability equivalence of the star problem and the FPP can be obtained as a conclusion of Theorem 1. However, up to now, it remained open to prove Theorem 1.

In [13], we give a proof for the decidability equivalence of the star problem and the FPP. It is based on induction steps on independence alphabets.

The unsolved cases of the star problem and the FPP lead us to one and the same question: Assume two trace monoids and a recognizable language L as in Theorem 1. Can we decide whether L^* is recognizable, i.e., whether L has the FPP, provided that both the star problem and the FPP are decidable in both $\mathbb{IM}(\Gamma, I)$ and $\mathbb{IM}(\Delta, I)$?

2 Algebraic Tools

2.1 Semigroups and Ideals

Ideal theory originates from GREEN and other pioneers in semigroup theory. We deal with some notions and results from ideal theory. For more detailed information, I recommend teaching books on semigroups, e.g. [10].

Assume a non-empty semigroup Q. We call a set $H \subseteq Q$ a *subsemigroup* of Q iff $HH \subseteq H$. We call a set $U \subseteq Q$ a *left ideal* of Q iff $QU \subseteq U$. We call a subset $J \subseteq Q$ an *ideal* of Q iff $JQ \subseteq J$ and $QJ \subseteq J$. Every semigroup has itself and the empty set as ideals. We call a left ideal $U \subseteq Q$ (ideal $J \subseteq Q$) *proper* iff U (resp. J) is non-empty and different from Q.

I developed the following classification for the proof of Theorem 1. It is based on classic results and ideas from ideal theory. See [12, 13] for a proof.

Proposition 1. *Every non-empty finite semigroup Q satisfies one of the following assertions:*

(A) *Q has not any proper left ideal.*
(B) *Q has proper left ideals U, V such that $U \cup V = Q$ and $U \cap V$ is an ideal of Q.*
(C) *Q has an ideal J such that $Q \setminus J$ yields a singleton $\{r\}$ with $r^2 \in J$.*
(D) *Q has a proper ideal J and a subsemigroup H such that $J \cap H = \emptyset$ and $J \cup H = Q$.* □

A non-empty finite semigroup which satisfies assertion (A) cannot satisfy one of the other assertions. However, assertions (B), (C), and (D) are not exclusive. We need a lemma for non-empty finite semigroups without proper left ideals.

Lemma 1. *Assume a non-empty finite semigroup Q which has not any proper left ideal. Then, for every $p, p', q \in Q$, the equality $pq = p'q$ implies $p = p'$.* □

Proof: Just assume three elements $p, p', q \in Q$ such that $pq = p'q$ and $p \neq p'$. We have $QQ \subseteq Q$, and thus, $QQq \subseteq Qq$ such that Qq is a left ideal. Further, the product Qq yields a proper subset of Q, because the result of the product pq "occurs twice", such that at least one element of Q cannot occur in Qq. Consequently, the set Qq is a proper left ideal of Q. □

2.2 Product Automata

We introduce a special kind of automata called product automata. Def. 1 and Lemma 2 are based on MEZEI's Theorem and its proof (cf. Theorem 1.5 in [1]).

Whenever we deal with a Cartesian Product of some semigroups S_1 and S_2, we denote the canonical projections by $\Pi_1 : (S_1 \times S_2) \to S_1$ and $\Pi_2 : (S_1 \times S_2) \to S_2$.

Definition 1. *Assume two disjoint trace monoids $\mathbb{M}_1$ and $\mathbb{M}_2$. A product automaton $\mathcal{A}$ over $\mathbb{M}_1 \times \mathbb{M}_2$ is a quintuple $[P, R, g, h, F]$, where*

- *P and R are non-empty finite semigroups,*
- *g and h are surjective homomorphisms $g : \mathbb{M}_1 \to P$, $h : \mathbb{M}_2 \to R$,*
- *F is a subset of $P \times R$.* □

We define the surjective homomorphism $\binom{g}{h} : (\mathbb{M}_1 \times \mathbb{M}_2) \to (P \times R)$ componentwise from g and h. A product automaton $\mathcal{A}$ defines a recognizable language by $L(\mathcal{A}) = \binom{g}{h}^{-1}(F)$. A trace $t \in \mathbb{M}_1 \times \mathbb{M}_2$ belongs $L(\mathcal{A})$ iff we obtain a pair in F if we apply g and h on the first and second compound of t, respectively. See [12, 13] for a proof of the following lemma:

Lemma 2. *Assume two disjoint trace monoids $\mathbb{M}_1$ and $\mathbb{M}_2$, and a recognizable language $T \subseteq \mathbb{M}_1 \times \mathbb{M}_2$. There is a product automaton for T.* □

We examine connections between product automata and ideal theory. Assume a concatenation closed recognizable language $T \subseteq \mathbb{M}_1 \times \mathbb{M}_2$. Assume further a product automaton $[P, R, g, h, F]$ for T. Then, F is a subsemigroup of $P \times R$. Let us denote $\Pi_2(F)$ by Q. Then, $Q = h \circ \Pi_2(T) = \Pi_2 \circ \binom{g}{h}(T)$ is a subsemigroup of R. Assume a subset $W \subseteq Q$. We define $T_W \subseteq T$ by

$$T_W = \{\, t \in T \mid h \circ \Pi_2(t) \in W \,\}$$

Proposition 2. *Assume a non-empty, concatenation closed set $T \subseteq \mathbb{M}_1 \times \mathbb{M}_2$. Assume a product automaton $\mathcal{A} = [P, R, g, h, F]$ for T. Let Q denote $\Pi_2(F)$. For every subset $W \subseteq Q$, the product automaton $\mathcal{A}_W = [P, R, g, h, F \cap (P \times W)]$ defines T_W. If W is a nonempty subset (subsemigroup, left ideal, ideal) of Q, then T_W is a nonempty subset (subsemigroup, left ideal, ideal) of T.* □

Proof: The quintuple $\mathcal{A}_W$ is a product automaton. For $t \in T_W$, we have $\binom{g}{h}(t) \in F$ and $\binom{g}{h}(t) \in P \times W$. Thus, we have $\binom{g}{h}(t) \in F \cap (P \times W)$. Hence, $T_W \subseteq L(\mathcal{A}_W)$.

Conversely, let $t \in L(\mathcal{A}_W)$. Then, we have $\binom{g}{h}(t) \in F$ and $\binom{g}{h}(t) \in (P \times W)$. Hence, $t \in T$ and $h \circ \Pi_2(t) \in W$, i.e., $t \in T_W$. Thus, $L(\mathcal{A}_W) \subseteq T_W$.

Let $f : T \to Q$ be the restriction of $h \circ \Pi_2$ to T. Then, f is a surjection from T to Q and $T_W = f^{-1}(W)$. If W is nonempty subset (subsemigroup, left ideal, ideal) of Q, so is its preimage T_W under f. □

3 Proof of Theorem 2

In this section, we prove Theorem 2. We assume two disjoint trace monoids $\mathbb{M}_1$ and $\mathbb{M}_2$ and abbreviate $\mathbb{M}_1 \setminus \{\lambda\}$ and $\mathbb{M}_2 \setminus \{\lambda\}$ by $\mathbb{M}_1^+$ and $\mathbb{M}_2^+$, respectively, such that the traces in $\mathbb{M}_1^+ \times \mathbb{M}_2^+$ are the traces in $\mathbb{M}_1 \times \mathbb{M}_2$ which contain at least one letter in $\mathbb{M}_1$ and at least one letter in $\mathbb{M}_2$.

Theorem 2 Assume two disjoint trace monoids $\mathbb{M}_1$ and $\mathbb{M}_2$. Assume some concatenation closed, recognizable language $T \subseteq (\mathbb{M}_1^+ \times \mathbb{M}_2^+)$.
Then, the set of generators of T has the FPP. $\qquad\qquad\qquad\qquad\square$

Theorem 2 is obviously true if $T = \emptyset$ such that we can assume $T \neq \emptyset$ in the rest of the proof. The general structure is the following: Just assume a non-empty language T as in Theorem 2. By Lemma 2, there is a product automaton $\mathcal{A} = [P, R, g, h, F]$ for T. Because T is non-empty, $\Pi_2(F)$ is non-empty. We use Proposition 1 on $\Pi_2(F)$. At first, we deal with the case that $\Pi_2(F)$ satisfies assertion (A) in Proposition 1.

After that, we deal with the cases that $\Pi_2(F)$ satisfies one of the assertions (B), (C), or (D). We will do this by an induction on the cardinal of $\Pi_2(F)$.

3.1 Q does not have proper left ideals

In this subsection, we prove the following special case of Theorem 2.

Proposition 3. *Assume a non-empty, concatenation closed set $T \subseteq \mathbb{M}_1^+ \times \mathbb{M}_2^+$ which is recognized by a product automaton $[P, R, g, h, F]$, such that the semi-group $\Pi_2(F)$ does not have proper left ideals.*
Then, $\mathrm{Gen}(T)$ has the FPP. Moreover, we have $T = \mathrm{Gen}(T)^{1,\dots,|\Pi_2(F)|+1}$. $\quad\square$

We introduce some notions. We assume a language T as in Proposition 3.

Definition 2. *Assume some traces $t, t_1, s_1 \in T$. We call the pair (t_1, s_1) a most oblique cut of t iff $t = t_1 s_1$ and for $t_1', s_1' \in T$ with $t = t_1' s_1'$ we have either*

- $|\Pi_1(t_1')| > |\Pi_1(t_1)|$ *or*
- $|\Pi_1(t_1')| = |\Pi_1(t_1)|$ *and* $|\Pi_2(t_1')| \leq |\Pi_2(t_1)|$. $\qquad\qquad\square$

This definition is based on very similar techniques by RICHOMME [20]. We try to factorize t in T into traces $t_1, s_1 \in T$ such that the first component of t_1 is small, but, the second compound of t_1 is big. There is a most oblique cut of t iff $t \notin \mathrm{Gen}(T)$.

Lemma 3. *Assume some traces $t, t_1, s_1 \in T$ such that (t_1, s_1) is a most oblique cut of t. Then, the trace t_1 is a generator of T.* $\qquad\qquad\qquad\qquad\square$

Proof: Assume that t_1 is not a generator of T. We factorize t_1 into $t_{1a}, t_{1b} \in T$. We have $t = t_{1a} t_{1b} s_1$ and $t_{1a}, t_{1b} s_1 \in T$. Further, we have $|\Pi_1(t_{1a})| < |\Pi_1(t_1)|$, since $\Pi_i(t_{1b}) \neq \lambda$. This contradicts that (t_1, s_1) is a most oblique cut. $\qquad\square$

Proof of Proposition 3: We denote by Q the semigroup $\Pi_2(F)$. Assume some trace $t \in T$. We factorize t into generators of T by successive most oblique cuts. We factorize t into a generator t_1 and a trace s_1 in T. Then, we factorize s_1 and so on, until a most oblique cut yields two generators. We obtain an $n > 0$ and generators $t_1, \dots, t_n$ of T such that $t_1 \dots t_n = t$. For $i \in \{1, \dots, n-1\}$, the pair $(t_i, t_{i+1} \dots t_n)$ is a most oblique cut of $t_i \dots t_n$.

We introduce two notions for lucidity. For $i \in \{1, \ldots, n\}$, we define $u_i = \Pi_1(t_i)$ and $v_i = \Pi_2(t_i)$. For $i \in \{1, \ldots, n\}$, we have $h(v_i) \in Q$, because $t_i \in T$.

We show by a contradiction that $n \leq |Q| + 1$. We assume $n > |Q| + 1$. By $h(v_{i+1} \ldots v_n) = h(v_{i+1}) \ldots h(v_n) \in Q$ for $1 \leq i < n$ and $n-1 > |Q|$, we get the existence of $1 \leq i < j < n$ such that $h(v_{i+1} \ldots v_n) = h(v_{j+1} \ldots v_n)$.

Then, $h(v_i) \cdot h(v_{i+1} \ldots v_n) = h(v_i \ldots v_n) = h(v_i \ldots v_j) \cdot h(v_{j+1} \ldots v_n)$. Since Q does not have proper left ideals, we apply Lemma 1 and get $h(v_i) = h(v_i \ldots v_j)$.

By $t_i \in T$, we have $\binom{g}{h}\binom{u_i}{v_i} \in F$. Because $h(v_i) = h(v_i \ldots v_j)$, we obtain $\binom{g}{h}\binom{u_i}{v_i \ldots v_j} \in F$, and thus, we have $\binom{u_i}{v_i \ldots v_j} \in T$. Similarly, $t_{i+1} \ldots t_n \in T$ implies $\binom{g}{h}\binom{u_{i+1} \ldots u_n}{v_{i+1} \ldots v_n} \in F$. By $h(v_{i+1} \ldots v_n) = h(v_{j+1} \ldots v_n)$, we have $\binom{g}{h}\binom{u_{i+1} \ldots u_n}{v_{j+1} \ldots v_n} \in F$, and therefore, $\binom{u_{i+1} \ldots u_n}{v_{j+1} \ldots v_n} \in T$. Thus, $\binom{u_i}{v_i \ldots v_j} \cdot \binom{u_{i+1} \ldots u_n}{v_{j+1} \ldots v_n} \in T$ form a factorization of $t_i \ldots t_n$ and contradict that $(t_i, t_{i+1} \ldots t_n)$ is not a most oblique cut of $t_i \ldots t_n$.

Finally, our assumption $n > |Q| + 1$ lead us to a contradiction. Therefore, $t \in \mathrm{Gen}(T)^{1, \ldots, |Q|+1}$, i.e., $T = \mathrm{Gen}(T)^{1, \ldots, |Q|+1}$. □

Example 2. This method fails for the language $T = \{\binom{a}{b}\} \cup \{\binom{a^n}{b^m} \mid n, m \geq 2\}$. In any product automaton $[P, R, g, h, F]$ for T the semigroup $\Pi_2(F)$ has a proper left ideal. For every $n > 0$, the factorization of $\binom{a^n}{b^n}$ by most oblique cuts yields n times the factor $\binom{a}{b}$, i.e., the number of factors is unlimited.

3.2 Q fulfills assertion (B), (C), or (D)

We prove the remaining cases of Theorem 2 by an induction on the cardinal of Q. In the case that Q is a singleton, we already know by Proposition 3 that Theorem 2 is true for T, because the singleton semigroup does not have proper left ideals. We show the following induction step:

Proposition 4. *Let $n > 1$. Assume that Theorem 2 holds for every non-empty, concatenation closed language T' in $\mathrm{I\!M}_1^+ \times \mathrm{I\!M}_2^+$ which is recognized by a product automaton $[P', R', g', h', F']$ with $|\Pi_2(F')| < n$. Let $[P, R, g, h, F]$ be a product automaton for a language T such that*

- *T is a non-empty, concatenation closed language in $\mathrm{I\!M}_1^+ \times \mathrm{I\!M}_2^+$,*
- *$|\Pi_2(F)| = n$, and,*
- *$\Pi_2(F)$ satisfies one of the assertions (B),(C), or (D) in Proposition 1.*

Then, $\mathrm{Gen}(T)$ has the FPP. □

Proof: We denote by Q the semigroup $\Pi_2(F)$. We deal with the case that Q satisfies assertion (D) in Proposition 1. See [12] for the other cases.

There are a proper ideal J and a subsemigroup H such that $J \cap H = \emptyset$ and $J \cup H = Q$. We examine T_J and T_H by Proposition 2. They are non-empty disjoint subsets of T. Their union yields T. Both T_J and T_H are concatenation closed. Further, T_J is an ideal of T. Moreover, T_J is recognized by the product automaton $[P, R, g, h, F \cap (R \times J)]$. We have $\Pi_2(F \cap (R \times J)) = J \subset Q$, i.e.,

$|\Pi_2(F \cap (R \times J))| < |Q| = n$. By the inductive hypothesis, Theorem 2 is true for T_J. There is an integer l_J such that $T_J = \text{Gen}(T_J)^{1,\ldots,l_J}$. Accordingly, there is an integer l_H such that $T_H = \text{Gen}(T_H)^{1,\ldots,l_H}$.

We show $T = \text{Gen}(T)^{1,\ldots,2l_H l_J + l_J}$. Assume some $t \in T$.

Case 1: t is a generator of T_H.

Assume $t_1, t_2 \in T$ with $t_1 t_2 = t$. If t_1 or t_2 belongs to the ideal T_J, then $t \in T_J$. If $t_1, t_2 \in T_H$, then $t \notin \text{Gen}(T_H)$. Thus, t cannot be factorized, i.e., $t \in \text{Gen}(T)$.

Case 2: t is a trace of T_H.

We can factorize t into l_H or less generators of T_H. By case 1, such a factorization is a factorization of t into generators of T. Thus, $t \in \text{Gen}(T)^{1,\ldots,l_H}$.

Case 3: t is a generator of T_J.

The trace t is not necessarily a generator of T. There are $t_1, t_2, t_3 \in T$ with
$$t_1 t_2 t_3 = t, \quad t_1 \in T_H \cup \{\lambda\}, \quad t_2 \in T_J, \quad \text{and} \quad t_3 \in T_H \cup \{\lambda\}.$$
There exist desired t_1, t_2, t_3, e.g., $t_1 = \lambda$, $t_2 = t$, $t_3 = \lambda$. We choose a triple t_1, t_2, t_3 such that $|t_2|$ is minimal. We examine t_2. By a contradiction, we show $t_2 \in \text{Gen}(T)$. Assume $t_2', t_2'' \in T$ with $t_2' t_2'' = t_2$, i.e., $t = t_1 t_2' t_2'' t_3$.

We distinguish four cases: If $t_2', t_2'' \in T_J$, then $t_1 t_2', t_2'' t_3 \in T_J$, because T_J is an ideal. Thus, $t_1 t_2'$ and $t_2'' t_3$ form a factorization of t into traces in T_J such that $t \notin \text{Gen}(T_J)$ which is a contradiction. If $t_2', t_2'' \in T_H$, then $t_2 = t_2' t_2'' \in T_H$, because T_H is subsemigroup. This is also a contradiction. If $t_2' \in T_H$ and $t_2'' \in T_J$, then $t_1 t_2', t_2'', t_3$ contradict the choice of t_1, t_2, t_3, because $|t_2''| < |t_2|$. If $t_2' \in T_J$ and $t_2'' \in T_H$, then we obtain a contradiction in a similar way.

Thus, t_2 is a generator of T. By case 2, we can factorize each of t_1 and t_3 into l_H or less generators of T. Therefore, $t \in \text{Gen}(T)^{1,\ldots,2l_H + 1}$.

Case 4: t is a trace in T_J.

We can factorize t into l_J or less generators of T_J and apply case 3 on each of them. Hence, $t \in \text{Gen}(T)^{1,\ldots,2l_H l_J + l_J}$. □

3.3 Completion of the Proof

Proof of Theorem 2: The theorem is obviously true if $T = \emptyset$. By Proposition 3, it is true for every non-empty, concatenation closed language $T \subseteq \mathbb{M}_1^+ \times \mathbb{M}_2^+$ of some product automaton $[P, R, g, h, F]$ with $|\Pi_2(F)| = 1$.

Assume some $n > 1$. Assume that Theorem 2 is true for every concatenation closed language $T' \subseteq \mathbb{M}_1^+ \times \mathbb{M}_2^+$ of some product automaton $[P', R', g', h', F']$ with $|\Pi_2(F')| < n$. Then, Theorem 2 is true for every concatenation closed language $T \subseteq \mathbb{M}_1^+ \times \mathbb{M}_2^+$ of a product automaton $[P, R, g, h, F]$ with $|\Pi_2(F)| = n$, because $\Pi_2(F)$ satisfies one of the assertions (A), (B), (C), (D) in Proposition 1 such that we can apply Proposition 3 or 4. □

4 Acknowledgments

I acknowledge M. DROSTE's lecture "Algebraic Theory of Automata" in which I came in touch with ideal theory and [10]. I thank to D. KUSKE, G. RICHOMME, and anonymous referees for reading a preliminary version and giving useful hints.

482

References

1. J. Berstel. *Transductions and Context-Free Languages*. B.G.Teubner, Stuttg., 1979.
2. P. Cartier and D. Foata. *Problèmes combinatoires de commutation et réarrangements*, volume 85 of *LNCS*. Springer-Verlag, Berlin, 1969.
3. M. Clerbout and M. Latteux. Semi-commutations. *Inf. and Comp.*, 73:59–74, 1987.
4. V. Diekert and Y. Métivier. Partial commutation and traces. In G. Rozenberg and A. Salomaa, editors, *Handbook of Formal Languages, Vol. 3, Beyond Words*, pages 457–534. Springer-Verlag, Berlin, 1997.
5. V. Diekert and G. Rozenberg, eds., *The Book of Traces*. World Scientific, 1995.
6. M. Fliess. Matrices de Hankel. *J. Math. Pures et Appl.*, 53:197–224, 1974.
7. P. Gastin, E. Ochmański, A. Petit, and B. Rozoy. Decidability of the star problem in $A^* \times \{b\}^*$. *Information Processing Letters*, 44(2):65–71, 1992.
8. S. Ginsburg and E. Spanier. Bounded regular sets. In *Proceedings of the AMS*, volume 17:5, pages 1043–1049, 1966.
9. S. Ginsburg and E. Spanier. Semigroups, Presburger formulas, and languages. *Pacific Journal of Mathematics*, 16:285–296, 1966.
10. P. A. Grillet. *Semigroups: An Introduction to the Structure Theory*, volume 193 of *Monographs and Textbooks in Pure and Applied Mathematics*. Marcel Dekker, Inc., New York, 1995.
11. K. Hashiguchi. A decision procedure for the order of regular events. *Theoretical Computer Science*, 8:69–72, 1979.
12. D. Kirsten. A connection between the star problem and the finite power property in trace monoids. Technical Report ISSN 1430-211X, TUD/FI98/09, Department of Computer Science, Dresden University of Technology, October 1998.
13. D. Kirsten and G. Richomme. Decidability equivalence between the star problem and the finite power problem in trace monoids. Technical Report ISSN 1430-211X, TUD/FI99/?, Department of Computer Science, Dresden University of Technology and Technical Report at LaRIA, Université de Picardie Jules Verne, Amiens, April 1999 (submitted).
14. A. Mazurkiewicz. Concurrent program schemes and their interpretations. DAIMI Rep. PB 78, Aarhus University, 1977.
15. Y. Métivier. Une condition suffisante de reconnaissabilité dans un monoïde partiellement commutatif. *R.A.I.R.O. - Inform. Théorique et Appl.*, 20:121–127, 1986.
16. Y. Métivier and G. Richomme. New results on the star problem in trace monoids. *Information and Computation*, 119(2):240–251, 1995.
17. E. Ochmański. Recognizable trace languages. Chapter 6 in [5], pages 167-204.
18. E. Ochmański. *Regular Trace Languages (in Polish)*. PhD thesis, Warszawa, 1984.
19. E. Ochmański. Notes on a star mystery. *Bulletin of the EATCS*, 40:252–257, 1990.
20. G. Richomme. Decidability equivalence between the star problem and the finite power property problem in trace monoids. Internal report 835-94, LaBRI - Université Bordeaux I, 1994.
21. G. Richomme. Some trace monoids where both the star problem and the finite power property problem are decidable. In I. Privara et al., editors, *MFCS'94 Proceedings*, volume 841 of *LNCS*, pages 577–586. Springer-Verlag, Berlin, 1994.
22. J. Sakarovitch. The "last" decision problem for rational trace languages. In I. Simon, editor, *LATIN'92 Proceedings*, volume 583 of *LNCS*, pages 460–473. Springer-Verlag, Berlin, 1992.
23. I. Simon. Limited subsets of a free monoid. In *Proceedings of the 19th IEEE Annual Symposium on Foundations of Computer Science*, pages 143–150. North Carolina Press, 1978.

Two Techniques in the Area of the Star Problem

Daniel Kirsten[1*] and Jerzy Marcinkowski[2**]

[1] Department of Computer Science, Dresden University of Technology,
D-01062 Dresden, Germany, dk11@inf.tu-dresden.de
[2] Institute of Computer Science, University of Wrocław, Przesmyckiego 20, 51151
Wrocław, Poland, jma@tcs.uni.wroc.pl

Abstract. Decidability of the Star Problem, the problem whether the language $\mathbb{P}^*$ is recognizable for a recognizable language $\mathbb{P}$, remains open. We slightly generalize the problem and show that then its decidability status depends strongly on the assumptions considering the trace monoid and finiteness of $\mathbb{P}$. More precisely, we show that for finite set $\mathbb{P} \subset \{A, B\}^* \times \{C\}^*$ and recognizable $\mathbb{R}$ it is decidable whether $\mathbb{P}^* \cap \mathbb{R}$ is recognizable, but the problem becomes undecidable if we consider recognizable (infinite) $\mathbb{P}$ or finite $\mathbb{P} \subset \{A, B\}^* \times \{C, D\}^*$.

1 Introduction

Free partially commutative monoids, also called trace monoids, were introduced in 1969 [2]. Since Mazurkiewicz proposed them as a potential model for concurrent processes in 1977 [10], they are systematically examined, see e.g., [4,5].

Here, we only deal with trace monoids of the form $\Sigma^* \times \Gamma^*$ for two disjoint alphabets Σ and Γ. In particular, we consider the set P3 $= \{A, B\}^* \times \{C\}^*$ and C4 $= \{A, B\}^* \times \{C, D\}^*$, for some symbols A, B, C, D. The elements of the set $\Sigma^* \times \Gamma^*$ are called *traces* and its subsets are called *trace languages* or *languages*.

A central topic in trace theory is the study of recognizable languages which can be considered as a natural generalization of regularity. A word $w \in (\Sigma \cup \Gamma)^*$ represents a trace $[u, v] \in \Sigma^* \times \Gamma^*$ if and only if we obtain u and v by restricting w to the letters in Σ and Γ, respectively. For instance, in P3, each of the words $CCAABCB$, $AABBCCC$, and $ACABCCB$ (among others) represents the trace $[AABB, CCC]$. A trace language $L \subseteq \Sigma^* \times \Gamma^*$ is called *recognizable* if and only if the set of all(!) words in $(\Sigma \cup \Gamma)^*$ which represent some trace in L yields a language which is regular, in the standard sense. See [4] or Chapter 6 in [5] for a recent survey. Recognizable trace languages are closed under union, intersection, and complement. The empty set and the complete monoid are recognizable (cf. [1]). Further, recognizable trace languages are closed under concatenation [6], and finite trace languages are recognizable. But unlike regular languages, recognizable trace languages are not closed under Kleene closure.

* Supported by the postgraduate program "Specification of discrete processes and systems of processes by operational models and logics" of the German Research Community (Deutsche Forschungsgemeinschaft).
** Supported by Polish KBN grant 8T11C02913.

Consider for example the finite recognizable language $L = \{AC, BC\} \subseteq P3$. The words which represent traces in L^* are $\{w \in \mathcal{A}^* : |w|_A + |w|_B = |w|_C\}$ where $|w|_S$ is the number of occurrences of the symbol S in w. Clearly, this is not a recognizable language. On the other hand, it is not very hard to see that if $L_7 = \{AC, A^7, C^7\}$ then L_7^* is recognizable.

1.1 The Star Problem

One of the most famous and beautiful open problems in trace theory, known as the **Star Problem**, is if the recognizability of the Kleene closure $\mathbb{P}^*$ is a decidable property of a given recognizable set $\mathbb{P}$. The problem was stated for the first time in [14] and then in many papers including [4]. But despite of the effort of many researchers (e.g. [3, 11, 16, 12, 13]) not much is known about its decidability status. It is known that for so called *connected* recognizable languages $\mathbb{P}$, the language $\mathbb{P}^*$ is recognizable [3, 11, 14]. The Star Problem is decidable in trace monoids without the P3 submonoid [16], in P3 [7], and further in all trace monoids without the C4 submonoid [15]. This is the strongest known positive result. Even for finite languages $\mathbb{P}$, only some decidable subcases are known [13].

On the other hand, the first author of this paper has shown that it is undecidable whether for recognizable $\mathbb{R}, \mathbb{P} \subseteq C4$ the intersection $\mathbb{R} \cap \mathbb{P}^*$ is recognizable [9]. He mentioned that the same problem is decidable in trace monoids without P3 submonoid (like in [16]), and he asked for its decidability in P3 and for finite $\mathbb{P}$.[1] Here we answer these questions.

1.2 Our Contribution

We give a classification of the decidability status of the recognizability of the language $\mathbb{R} \cap \mathbb{P}^*$ for most of the assumptions which were considered before (like level of complication of the monoid and finiteness of the language).

First (in Section 2), we use Hashiguchi's distance automata to show how to decide recognizability of $\mathbb{R} \cap \mathbb{P}^*$ for recognizable $\mathbb{R}$ and finite $\mathbb{P}$ in P3. Then, (in Section 3) we introduce a new simple technique to show that this positive result can neither be improved to recognizable infinite $\mathbb{P}$ nor to the monoid C4.

| | Recognizability of $\mathbb{P}^*$ | | Recognizability of $\mathbb{P}^* \cap \mathbb{R}$ | |
	Finite $\mathbb{P}$	Recogn. $\mathbb{P}$	Finite $\mathbb{P}$	Recogn. $\mathbb{P}$
$P3 = \{A, B\}^* \times \{C\}^*$	decidable [7]	decidable [7]	decidable [This paper]	undecidable [This paper]
$C4 = \{A, B\}^* \times \{C, D\}^*$	OPEN	OPEN	undecidable [This paper]	undecidable [9]

---

[1] If $\mathbb{R}$ is finite, then obviously $\mathbb{R} \cap \mathbb{P}^*$ is finite and hence recognizable.

2 The Positive Result

The main result of this Section is:

Theorem 1. *Let* $\mathbb{R}, \mathbb{P} \subseteq \Sigma^* \times \{c\}^*$ *be recognizable languages. Assume that* $\mathbb{P}$ *is finite. We can decide whether the intersection* $\mathbb{R} \cap \mathbb{P}^*$ *is recognizable.*

The theorem will follow from Lemma 7 and 8, below.

2.1 The Tools

The following result is a special case of Mezei's Theorem (cf. [1]):

Theorem 2. *Consider alphabets* Σ *and* Γ. *A set* T *is recognizable in* $\Sigma^* \times \Gamma^*$ *if and only if there exist an integer* n, *regular languages* $K_1, \ldots, K_n \subseteq \Sigma^*$ *and regular languages* $L_1, \ldots, L_n \subseteq \Gamma^*$ *such that* $T = K_1 \times L_1 \cup \ldots \cup K_n \times L_n$. $\square$

The notion of distance automata and Theorem 4 are due to Hashiguchi [8].

Definition 3 *A* distance automaton *is a five-tuple* $\mathcal{A} = [Q, E, s, F, \delta]$ *where*

- Q *is a finite set called* states, $s \in Q$ *is called* initial state, *and* $F \subseteq Q$ *are the* accepting states,
- $E \subseteq Q \times \Sigma \times Q$ *is a finite set of* edges,
- $\delta : E \to \{0, 1\}$ *is a function called* distance function.

A distance automaton accepts a regular language $L(\mathcal{A}) \subseteq \Sigma^*$ as usual. To every run of the automaton we assign an integer called its distance, which is simply the sum of the distances of each edge in the run. The distance of a word $w \in L(\mathcal{A})$, denoted by $\delta(w)$, is the least integer n such that $\mathcal{A}$ accepts w by a run with a distance n. We call a distance automaton $\mathcal{A}$ *limited in distance* if and only if there is some integer d such that for $w \in L(\mathcal{A})$ we have $\delta(w) \leq d$. We use the following result from [8]:

Theorem 4. *It is decidable whether a distance automaton is limited in distance.*

The next observation holds because of closure properties of recognizable sets.

Observation 5 *Let* $\mathbb{R}, \mathbb{P} \subseteq \Sigma^* \times \Gamma^*$ *be recognizable sets, and let* $\mathbb{R}_1, \ldots, \mathbb{R}_n$ *be a partition of* $\mathbb{R}$ *into recognizable sets. Then,* $\mathbb{R} \cap \mathbb{P}^*$ *is recognizable if and only if for* $i \in \{1, \ldots, n\}$ *the intersection* $\mathbb{R}_i \cap \mathbb{P}^*$ *is recognizable.* $\square$

For a language T and $n \geq 0$, we denote by $T^{0,\ldots,n}$ the union $T^0 \cup T^1 \ldots \cup T^n$, where T^n is concatenation of n copies of the set T.

Lemma 6 *Let* $\mathbb{R}, \mathbb{P} \subseteq \Sigma^* \times \Gamma^*$ *be recognizable sets with* $\mathbb{R} \subseteq (\Sigma^* \times \Gamma^{0,\ldots,n})$ *for some integer* n. *Then the intersection* $\mathbb{R} \cap \mathbb{P}^*$ *is recognizable.* $\square$

Proof: Let $\mathbb{R}_w = \mathbb{R} \cap [\Sigma^* \times \{w\}]$, for $|w| \leq n$. Then $\mathbb{R}_w \cap \mathbb{P}^*$ is recognizable for each w and so $\mathbb{R} \cap \mathbb{P}^*$ is a union of a finite set of recognizable sets. $\square$

2.2 The Easier Case

Lemma 7 *Consider recognizable sets* $\mathbb{R}, \mathbb{P} \subseteq \Sigma^* \times \Gamma^*$. *We can decide whether* $\mathbb{R} \cap \mathbb{P}^*$ *is recognizable if* $\mathbb{P}$ *is a finite subset of* $(\Sigma^+ \times \Gamma^*)$.

Notice that we do not require here that Γ is a singleton.
Proof: Let $[Q, h, q_0, F]$ be an automaton for $\mathbb{R}$, where Q is the set of states, $q_0 \in Q$ is the initial state, h is the transition function and $F \subset Q$ is the set of accepting states.

We split $\mathbb{P}$ into two languages $\mathbb{P}_\lambda = \mathbb{P} \cap (\Sigma^+ \times \lambda)$ and $\mathbb{P}_+ = \mathbb{P} \cap (\Sigma^+ \times \Gamma^+)$. We show that the following three assertions are equivalent:

(1) The set $\mathbb{R} \cap \mathbb{P}^*$ is recognizable.
(2) There is an integer n_c' such that $(\mathbb{R} \cap \mathbb{P}^*) \subseteq (\Sigma^* \times \Gamma^{0,\ldots,n_c'})$.
(3) The intersection $\mathbb{R} \cap ((\mathbb{P}_\lambda^* \mathbb{P}_+ \mathbb{P}_\lambda^*)^{|Q|+1} \cup \ldots \cup (\mathbb{P}_\lambda^* \mathbb{P}_+ \mathbb{P}_\lambda^*)^{2|Q|+1})$ is empty.

The implication (2)→(1) follows from Lemma 6. We show (1)→(2). Assume that $\mathbb{R} \cap \mathbb{P}^*$ is recognizable, but nevertheless, an integer n_c' in (2) does not exist. By Theorem 2, there is some $w \in \Sigma^*$ and some infinite language $L \subseteq \Gamma^*$ such that $\{w\} \times L \subseteq \mathbb{R} \cap \mathbb{P}^* \subseteq \mathbb{P}^*$. Since every trace in $\mathbb{P}$ contains at least one letter in Σ and at most n_c occurrences of letters from Γ, the length of the words in L cannot exceed $n_c |w|$. This contradicts the assumption that L is infinite.

(2)→(3). We assume that the intersection in (3) is not empty. So there is an integer l with $|Q| + 1 \le l \le 2|Q| + 1$ and traces $t_1, \ldots, t_l \in \mathbb{P}_\lambda^* \mathbb{P}_+ \mathbb{P}_\lambda^* \subseteq \mathbb{P}^*$ such that $t_1 \ldots t_l \in \mathbb{R}$. Because $|Q| < l$, there are two integers i, j with $0 < i < j \le l$ such that $h(q_0, t_1 \ldots t_i) = h(q_0, t_1 \ldots t_j)$. Obviously, we have $h(q_0, t_1 \ldots t_j) = h(h(q_0, t_1 \ldots t_i), t_{i+1} \ldots t_j)$. We can "pump $t_{i+1} \ldots t_j$": For $k \in \mathcal{N}$, we have

$$h(q_0, t_1 \ldots t_i) = h(q_0, t_1 \ldots t_i(t_{i+1} \ldots t_j)^k) \qquad \text{and}$$
$$h(q_0, t_1 \ldots t_l) = h(q_0, t_1 \ldots t_i(t_{i+1} \ldots t_j)^k t_{j+1} \ldots t_l).$$

The last value belongs to F so we have $(t_1 \ldots t_i)(t_{i+1} \ldots t_j)^*(t_{j+1} \ldots t_l) \subseteq \mathbb{R}$. We also have $(t_1 \ldots t_i)(t_{i+1} \ldots t_j)^*(t_{j+1} \ldots t_l) \subseteq \mathbb{P}^*$, since $t_1, \ldots, t_l \in \mathbb{P}^*$. The traces $t_{i+1}, \ldots, t_j$ contain at least one subtrace in $\mathbb{P}_+$, i.e., they contain one letter from Γ. Hence, by pumping $t_{i+1} \ldots t_j$, we see that an integer n_c' as in assertion (2) cannot exist.

(3)→(2) Similar pumping argument like above works here.

Finally, we can decide by standard techniques of automata theory whether intersection in (3) yields the empty set. □

2.3 The Harder Case

Lemma 8 *Let* $\mathbb{R}, \mathbb{P} \subseteq \Sigma^* \times \{c\}^*$ *be recognizable languages. Assume that* $\mathbb{P}$ *is finite and contains some trace in* $\{\lambda\} \times \{c\}^+$. *We can decide whether the intersection* $\mathbb{R} \cap \mathbb{P}^*$ *is recognizable.*

Proof: By Theorem 2, we can split $\mathbb{R}$ into finitely many Cartesian Products and apply Observation 5. Consequently, it suffices to consider the case that $\mathbb{R} = K \times L$ for recognizable languages $K \subseteq \Sigma^*$ and $L \subseteq \{c\}^*$. If L is finite then $\mathbb{R} \cap \mathbb{P}^*$ is recognizable by Lemma 6. Hence, it suffices to consider infinite languages L in the rest of the proof. If L is infinite, we can split L into a finite language and finitely many languages of the form $\{c^{m+iz} \mid i \in \mathcal{N}\}$ for some integers $m, z > 0$. By splitting L, we can split $\mathbb{R}$ to use Observation 5, again. Hence, it suffices to consider languages L of the form $\{c^{m+iz} \mid i \in \mathcal{N}\}$ for some integers $m, z > 0$.

We show that it suffices to consider languages L of the form $\{c^{m+iz} \mid i \in \mathcal{N}\}$ such that additionally $[\lambda, c^z] \in \mathbb{P}^*$. Consider some $n > 0$ such that $[\lambda, c^n] \in \mathbb{P}$. We can split L into n languages: for $j \in \{0, \dots, n-1\}$, we define a language $\{c^{(m+jz)+i(nz)} \mid i \in \mathcal{N}\}$. Then, $[\lambda, c^{nz}] \in \mathbb{P}^*$. As above, we can split $\mathbb{R}$ by splitting L and use Observation 5.

Let $P_0, P_1, \dots$ be the unique family of recognizable languages such that

$$\mathbb{R} \cap \mathbb{P}^* = (P_0 \times c^m) \cup (P_1 \times c^{m+z}) \cup (P_2 \times c^{m+2z}) \dots$$

For every $[u, v] \in (\mathbb{R} \cap \mathbb{P}^*)$, we also have $[u, v][\lambda, c^z] \in (\mathbb{R} \cap \mathbb{P}^*)$. Consequently, we have $P_0 \subseteq P_1 \subseteq P_2 \dots$ By Theorem 2, we easily obtain that $\mathbb{R} \cap \mathbb{P}^*$ is recognizable iff there is some integer l such that for $i \geq l$ we have $P_l = P_i$.

We will show how to use Theorem 4 to decide whether the integer l does exist. First notice that the Hashiguchi theorem remains true if we allow E to be a finite subset of $Q \times \Sigma^* \times Q$.

Now, consider a finite automaton for K. Let Q be its set of states, δ its transition function, q_0 its initial state and $F \subseteq Q$ the set of accepting states.

We define a distance automaton $\mathcal{A} = [\bar{Q}, \bar{E}, \bar{s}, \bar{F}, \bar{\delta}]$ as follows:

$\bar{Q} = \{(q, j) \mid q \in Q, 0 \leq j \leq m + z\}$

For every $(q, j) \in \bar{Q}$ and $(w, c^i) \in \mathbb{P}$ we define an edge $[(q, j), w, (\delta(q, w), k)]$, where k is $i + j$ if it is smaller than $m + z$, or $m \leq k < m + z$ and $k = i + j$ (mod z), otherwise. The distance $\bar{\delta}$ of such an edge is 0 if $i = 0$ or 1, otherwise.

The initial state $\bar{s}$ of $\mathcal{A}$ is $(q_0, 0)$ and $\bar{F} = \{(q, m) \mid q \in F\}$. Now, it is straight-forward to show that (2) holds iff $\mathcal{A}$ is limited in distance. $\qquad \square$

Remarkably, Lemma 8 remains true for infinite recognizable languages $\mathbb{P}$. The proof is technically more involved and will be given in the full paper.

3 Negative Results

In this part of the paper we prove the two negative results mentioned in the introduction. In Subsection 3.1, we present the undecidable problem later used for the reductions. Then, in Subsections 3.2-3.4 we prove:

Theorem 9. *Let $\mathbb{R}$ be a recognizable language over the monoid $\{A, B\}^* \times \{C, D\}^*$, and $\mathbb{P}$ a finite language over the same monoid. The problem if the language $\mathbb{P}^* \cap \mathbb{R}$ is recognizable is undecidable.*

Then, in subsection 3.5 we show how to modify the argument to get:

Theorem 10. *Let $\mathbb{R}$ and $\mathbb{P}$ be recognizable languages over the monoid $\{A, B\}^* \times \{C\}^*$. The problem if the language $\mathbb{P}^* \cap \mathbb{R}$ is recognizable is undecidable.*

Notice that we can treat blocks of A and B, of some fixed length as single symbols. So instead of $\{A, B\}$ we can consider any finite alphabet. The same holds for $\{C, D\}$.

3.1 The Tool

Consider an alphabet $\{v, u\} \cup W$ for some finite set W such that $u, v \notin W$ and $b \in W$. Let $\Pi \subset W \times (W \cup \{v\})$ and $\Psi \subset W \times (W \cup \{v\})$ be any two relations. We say that a word x encodes a $\Pi\Psi$-computation if it is of the form: $vw_n^1 w_n^2 \ldots w_n^n vw_{n-1}^1 w_{n-1}^2 \ldots w_{n-1}^{n-1} v \ldots vw_2^1 w_2^2 vbu$ for some $n \geq 2$ and $\Pi(w_i^j, w_{i+1}^j)$ and $\Psi(w_i^j, w_i^{j+1})$ hold for each $1 \leq j \leq i \leq n$, where w_i^{i+1} is understood to be v. The proof of the following theorem is left as an exercise.

Theorem 11. *The problem, if for given Π, Ψ there exist only finitely many words encoding a $\Pi\Psi$-computation, is undecidable.* □

3.2 First easy idea: how to propagate the information

In this section we show how to use a (unary, non-increasing) counter to propagate information along some, possibly long, word.

Consider a nondeterministic finite automaton $\mathcal{A}$ with two tapes, with one head over each tape. The heads are only allowed to move in one direction, from left to right. The alphabet of the first tape is $\{v, u\} \cup W$ for some finite set W with $b \in W$ and the alphabet of the second tape is $\{s\}$. We assume that all the words given as an input to our automaton have the form $[(vW^*)^* vbu, ss^*]$. Notice that the last is a regular expression, and so the language of the words under consideration is recognizable. Call this language $\mathbb{R}_0$. One almost can think that this is the $\mathbb{R}$ from Theorem 9.

Definition 12 *A word $[x, y]$ is called* fair *if it is of the form*
$$[vW^n vW^{n-1} v \ldots vW^3 vW^2 vbu, s^{n+1}]$$

$\mathcal{A}$ will be constructed to accept exactly the words which are not fair. It has four states: *normal*, which is the initial state, *counting*, *checking*, and *error*.

Definition 13 *The following are the instructions of $\mathcal{A}$:*
  (i) $[normal, w, \lambda, normal]$ *for each $w \in W$*
  (ii) $[normal, v, s, normal]$
  (iii) $[normal, v, s, counting]$
  (iv) $[counting, w, s, counting]$ *for each $w \in W$*
  (v) $[counting, v, s, error]$ *and* $[counting, u, s, error]$
  (vi) $[error, w, \lambda, error]$ *for each $w \in W \cup \{v\}$*
  (vii) $[error, \lambda, s, error]$
  (viii) $[error, u, \lambda, normal]$
  (ix) $[counting, w, \lambda, checking]$ *for each $w \in W$*
  (x) $[checking, w, \lambda, checking]$ *for each $w \in W \cup \{v\}$*
  (xi) $[checking, u, \lambda, normal]$

To make the meaning of the instructions clear for the reader let us explain that the first instruction allows (if $\mathcal{A}$ is in the *normal* state) to move the first head one cell right, but only if there is some $w \in W$ in this cell. The second head does not move then. The state remains *normal*.

The third instruction, to continue the example, can be executed if the state is *normal*. If the symbol to be read on the first tape is v and there is an s to be read on the second tape it moves both the heads one cell right, and changes the state to *counting*.

We say that the automaton $\mathcal{A}$ accepts if it has a run reading the complete input (this means, both the words, to the end) and then halting in the state *normal*. Notice that the last executed instruction in an accepting run must be either (viii) or (xi) (this is the only way to read u).

Lemma 14 *Let $[x,y] \in \mathbb{R}_0$. An accepting run of $\mathcal{A}$ exists for an input $[x,y]$ if an only if $[x,y]$ is not fair.*

Proof: Suppose $[x,y]$ is fair. Because of the u in the end of x the only way to accept the word $[x,y]$ is to change the state to *counting* while reading one of the v symbols and then, after some steps, change the state to *checking* or *error*. We will use the following lemma which can be proved by easy induction:

Lemma 15 *If $\mathcal{A}$ reads a fair input, the current state is normal and no other state was entered so far, then the number of symbols s to be read is equal to the length of the currently read W-block (by W-block we mean a maximal subword of x which does not contain any v or u).* $\square$

Now, imagine that the automaton changes the state into *counting* while reading some v. Then, according to the last Lemma it still has some k symbols s to read on the second tape and a W-block of length k followed by v on the first tape. If it continues making k steps according to the rule (iv) then, when seeing the next v it has no more symbols s and cannot continue reading. If it decides to use the rule (ix) changing the state into *checking* after less then k steps then it can use the rules (x) and (xi) to read all the symbols on the first tape, but some s remain unread on the second tape.

Suppose $[x,y]$ is not fair. Then $\mathcal{A}$ can make some moves in the *normal* state and reach a configuration in which $v w_1, w_2 \ldots w_m v$ is prefix of the word to be read on the first tape, there are exactly $k+1$ symbols s on the second tape and $m \neq k$. We will show how $\mathcal{A}$ can accept this configuration.

First suppose $m < k$. In this case the automaton can first execute the instruction (iii), changing the state into *counting*. Then m times the instruction (iv) is executed. In this moment there is still at least one s on the second tape, and the symbol to be read on the first tape is v. The automaton executes (v) and changes the state to *error*. Then it executes (vii) a number of times to get rid of all the symbols s on the second tape, and (vi) followed by (viii) to read all the input on the first tape.

Now suppose that $m > k$. In this case execute the instruction (iii), changing the state into *counting* and k times the instruction (iv). Then there are are no more symbols s and the symbol to be read on the first tape is some $w \in W$. The automaton can change the state into *checking* (by (ix)) and complete an accepting run by using (x) some number of times and then (xi). □

3.3 Second easy idea: how to remember the state

The most obvious problem one encounters while trying to translate the idea of the previous section into a negative solution of a version of the Star Problem is *how to remember the state of the automaton*. To do this we treat the symbols w, v, u, s as strings of "smaller" symbols. More precisely we define:

$v = \bar{v}cccc, u = \bar{u}cccc, w = \bar{w}cccc$ for $w \in W$ and $s = \bar{s}kkkk$

Notice that the definition of $\mathbb{R}_0$ from the previous subsection does not require any change. But the rules of $\mathcal{A}$ will be modified:

(i) $[\bar{w}cccc, \lambda]$ for each $w \in W$

(ii) $[\bar{v}cccc, \bar{s}kkkk]$

(iii) $[\bar{v}c, \bar{s}k]$

(iv) $[ccc\bar{w}c, kkk\bar{s}k]$ for each $w \in W$

(v) $[ccc\bar{v}cc, kkk\bar{s}kk]$ and $[ccc\bar{u}cc, kkkskk]$

(vi) $[cc\bar{w}cc, \lambda]$ for each $w \in W \cup \{v\}$

(vii) $[\lambda, kk\bar{s}kk]$

(viii) $[cc\bar{u}ccccc, kk]$

(ix) $[ccc\bar{w}cccc, kk]$ for each $w \in W$

(x) $[cc\bar{w}cc, \lambda]$ for each $w \in W \cup \{v\}$

(xi) $[cc\bar{u}ccccc, kk]$

Call the last set of rules $\mathbb{P}$. Notice that $\mathbb{P}$ is a finite language. By induction one can prove:

Lemma 16 *1. Suppose $[x, y] \in \mathbb{R}_0$. Then $[x, y] \in \mathbb{P}^*$ if and only if there is a run of $\mathcal{A}$ accepting $[x, y]$.*

2. $\mathbb{P}^* \cap \mathbb{R}_0$ is the set of all words in $\mathbb{R}_0$ which are not fair. □

3.4 Encoding a $\Pi\Psi$ computation

Once we know how to encode the states of the finite automaton we can come back to our automaton from Section 3.2. We will add some new states and instructions to it, so it not only will be able to accept unfair words but also the words which are fair but are not an encoding a valid computation.

Let Π, Ψ be relations, like in subsection 3.1.

Definition 17 *We say that a trace $[x, y]$ encodes a $\Pi\Psi$-computation if $[x, y]$ is fair, and the word x encodes a $\Pi\Psi$-computation.*

The automaton $\mathcal{A}_{\Pi\Psi}$ will be like $\mathcal{A}$ but with some new states and instructions. Its set of legal inputs will be $\mathbb{R}$ defined as the set of such words $[x, y] \in \mathbb{R}_0$ that if $w_1 \in W$ and $w_2 \in W \cup \{v\}$ are such that $w_1 w_2$ is a subword of x then $\Psi(w_1, w_2)$ holds. Clearly, $\mathbb{R}$ is a recognizable language.

Definition 18 *All the states of $\mathcal{A}$ are states of $\mathcal{A}_{\Pi\Psi}$. Also, counting$_w$ is a state of $\mathcal{A}_{\Pi\Psi}$ for each $w \in W$. The instructions of $\mathcal{A}_{\Pi\Psi}$ are all the instructions of $\mathcal{A}$ and, additionally:*

(vii) $[normal, w, \lambda, counting_w]$ for each $w \in W$

(viii) $[counting_w, w', s, counting_w]$ for each $w \in W$ and each $w' \in W \cup \{v\}$

(ix) $[counting_w, w', s, checking]$ for each w, w' such that $\Pi(w, w')$ does not hold

Now, let $\mathbb{P}_{\Pi\Psi}$ be the recognizable set built out of the instructions of automaton $\mathcal{A}_{\Pi\Psi}$ in the same way as $\mathbb{P}$ was built, in Section 3.3 from the instructions of the automaton $\mathcal{A}$. Clearly, this cannot be done using quadruples of c symbols. Instead we use blocks of length greater than the cardinality of W.

Lemma 19 *1. An accepting run of $\mathcal{A}_{\Pi\Psi}$ exists for an input $[x, y]$ if an only if $[x, y]$ does not encode a $\Pi\Psi$-computation.*

2. Suppose $[x, y] \in \mathbb{R}$. Then $[x, y] \in \mathbb{P}^*_{\Pi\Psi}$ if and only if there is a run of $\mathcal{A}_{\Pi\Psi}$ accepting $[x, y]$.

3. $\mathbb{P}^*_{\Pi\Psi} \cap \mathbb{R}$ is the set of all the traces in $\mathbb{R}$ which do not encode a $\Pi\Psi$-computation.

Proof: Repeat the proofs of Lemma 14 and Lemma 16. □

Theorem 9 will now follow from the last lemma, from Lemma 11 and from the following lemma, which is not very hard to prove:

Lemma 20 $\mathbb{P}^*_{\Pi\Psi} \cap \mathbb{R}$ *is a recognizable language if and only if there exist only finitely many words encoding a $\Pi\Psi$-computation.* □

3.5 The monoid $\{A, B\}^* \times \{C\}^*$

Now we show that the technique already presented in this Section can also be used for the proof of Theorem 10.

Again, we treat blocks of A and B, of some fixed length as single symbols. So, like before, instead of $\{A, B\}$ we can consider any finite alphabet. This is however not the case with $\{C\}$. This is why we cannot use exactly the same method as in subsection 3.3 to remember the state of the automaton $\mathcal{A}$ (this requires an additional symbol k). On the other hand, it is not possible to say:

Convention 21 *Let us just use only c to remember the state, forget about the k (so we have simply $[cccwc, s]$ in the line (iv) of the description of $\mathbb{P}$, instead of $[cccwc, kkksk]$).*

The only reason why we cannot do that is the instruction (vii) of the automaton $\mathcal{A}$: it allows reading on the second tape without reading on the first tape. To overcome the problem we define:

Definition 22 $\mathcal{B}$ *is an automaton, similar to $\mathcal{A}$, with the only difference that the instructions (v),(vi),(vii) and (viii) of $\mathcal{A}$ are removed and replaced by the new instruction   (xii) $[counting, v(W + \{v\})^* u, ss^*, normal]$*

The state error is also removed from $\mathcal{B}$ as redundant.

It is very easy to notice that $\mathcal{B}$ accepts exactly the same words as $\mathcal{A}$ does. Now we can repeat for $\mathcal{B}$ the definition of $\mathbb{P}$ given in Section 3.3, but obeying Convention 21. Notice that the $\mathbb{P}$ constructed in this way is a recognizable language over $\{A, B\}^* \times \{C\}^*$, but no longer a finite language. This is due to the use of $*$ in the instruction (xii). To finish the proof of Theorem 10 just repeat the argument of subsections 3.3 - 3.4 with the obvious changes.

References

1. J. Berstel. *Transductions and Context-Free Languages*. B. G. Teubner, 1979.
2. P. Cartier, D. Foata. *Problèmes combinatoires de commutation et réarrangements*, volume 85 of *LNCS*. Springer-Verlag, Berlin, 1969.
3. M. Clerbout, M. Latteux. Semi-commutations. *Information and Computation*, 73:59–74, 1987.
4. V. Diekert, Y. Métivier. Partial commutation and traces. In G. Rozenberg and A. Salomaa, editors, *Handbook of Formal Languages, Vol. 3, Beyond Words*, pages 457–534. Springer-Verlag, Berlin, 1997.
5. V. Diekert, G. Rozenberg, editors. *The Book of Traces*. World Scientific, 1995.
6. M. Fliess. Matrices de hankel. *J. Math. Pures et Appl.*, 53:197–224, 1974.
7. P. Gastin, E. Ochmański, A. Petit, B. Rozoy. Decidability of the star problem in $A^* \times \{b\}^*$. *Information Processing Letters*, 44(2):65–71, 1992.
8. K. Hashiguchi. Limitedness theorem on finite automata with distance functions. *Journal of Computer and System Sciences*, 24:233–244, 1982.
9. D. Kirsten. Some undecidability results related to the star problem in trace monoids. In C. Meinel and S. Tison, editors, *STACS'99 Proceedings*, volume 1563 of *LNCS*, pages 227–236. Springer-Verlag, Berlin, 1999.
10. A. Mazurkiewicz. Concurrent program schemes and their interpretations. DAIMI Rep. PB 78, Aarhus University, 1977.
11. Y. Métivier. Une condition suffisante de reconnaissabilité dans un monoïde partiellement commutatif. *R.A.I.R.O. - Informatique Théorique et Applications*, 20:121–127, 1986.
12. Y. Métivier, G. Richomme. On the star operation and the finite power property in free partially commutative monoids. Proceedings of STACS 94, volume 775 of LNCS, pages 341–352. Springer-Verlag, Berlin, 1994.
13. Y. Métivier, G. Richomme. New results on the star problem in trace monoids. *Information and Computation*, 119(2):240–251, 1995.
14. E. Ochmański. *Regular Trace Languages (in Polish)*. PhD thesis, Warszawa, 1984.
15. G. Richomme. Some trace monoids where both the star problem and the finite power property problem are decidable. In I. Privara et al., editors, *MFCS'94 Proceedings*, volume 841 of *LNCS*, pages 577–586. Springer-Verlag, Berlin, 1994.
16. J. Sakarovitch. The "last" decision problem for rational trace languages. In I. Simon, editor, *LATIN'92 Proceedings*, LNCS 583, pages 460–473. Springer, 1992.

Approximations by OBDDs and the Variable Ordering Problem

Matthias Krause[1], Petr Savický[2] and Ingo Wegener[3]

[1] Theoretische Informatik, Univ. Mannheim, 68131 Mannheim, Germany
  e-mail: krause@informatik.uni-mannheim.de
[2] Institute of Computer Science, Academy of Sciences of Czech Republic
  Pod vodárenskou věží 2, 182 07 Praha 8, Czech Republic
  e-mail: savicky@uivt.cas.cz
[3] FB Informatik, LS 2, Univ. Dortmund, 44221 Dortmund, Germany
  e-mail: wegener@ls2.cs.uni-dortmund.de

Abstract. Ordered binary decision diagrams (OBDDs) and their variants are motivated by the need to represent Boolean functions in applications. Research concerning these applications leads also to problems and results interesting from a theoretical point of view. In this paper, methods from communication complexity and information theory are combined to prove that the direct storage access function and the inner product function have the following property. They have linear π-OBDD size for some variable ordering π and, for most variable orderings π', all functions which approximate them on considerably more than half of the inputs, need exponential π'-OBDD size. These results have implications for the use of OBDDs in experiments with genetic programming.

1 Introduction

Branching programs (BPs) or binary decision diagrams (BDDs), which is just another name, are representations of Boolean functions $f \in B_n$, i.e., $f \colon \{0,1\}^n \to \{0,1\}$. They are compact but not useful for manipulations of Boolean functions, since operations like satisfiability test, equivalence test or minimization lead to hard problems. Bryant [5] has introduced π-OBDDs (ordered BDDs), since they can be manipulated efficiently (see [6] and [17] for surveys on the areas of application).

Definition 1. A permutation π on $\{1, \ldots, n\}$ describes the variable ordering $x_{\pi(1)}, \ldots, x_{\pi(n)}$. A π-OBDD is a directed acyclic graph $G = (V, E)$ with one source. Each sink is labelled by a Boolean constant and each inner node by a Boolean variable. Inner nodes have two outgoing edges one labelled by 0 and the

[1] Supported by DFG grant Kr 1521/3-1.
[2] The research was partially supported by GA of the Czech Republic, Grant No. 201/98/0717.
[3] Supported by DFG grant We 1066/8-1 and by the DFG as part of the Collaborative Research Center "Computational Intelligence" (531).

other by 1. If an edge leads from an x_i-node to an x_j-node, then $\pi^{-1}(i)$ has to be smaller than $\pi^{-1}(j)$, i.e., the edges have to respect the variable ordering. The π-OBDD represents a Boolean function $f \in B_n$ defined in the following way. The input a activates, for x_i-nodes, the outgoing a_i-edge. Then $f(a)$ is equal to the label of the sink reached by the unique activated path starting at the source. The size of G is measured by the number of its nodes. An OBDD is a π-OBDD for an arbitrary π.

One-way communication complexity (see e.g. [10], [13]) leads to lower bounds for OBDDs. This method is almost the same as counting the number of subfunctions of f if the first variables according to the variable ordering are replaced by constants. There are functions, for which the OBDD size is very sensitive to the chosen variable ordering. Moreover, given a π-OBDD for a function f, it is NP-hard to find an optimal variable ordering for f, see [4], or even to approximate the optimal variable ordering, see [15].

Definition 2. i) For $n = 2^k$, the direct storage access function (or multiplexer) on $k+n$ variables is the function $\text{DSA}_n(a_0, \ldots, a_{k-1}, x_0, \ldots, x_{n-1}) = x_{\|a\|}$, where $\|a\|$ is the number whose binary representation is $(a_0, \ldots, a_{k-1})$.
ii) For any even n, the inner product function on n variables is the function $\text{IP}_n(x_1, \ldots, x_n) = x_1 x_2 \oplus x_3 x_4 \oplus \ldots \oplus x_{n-1} x_n$.

Clearly, these two functions have π-OBDD size $O(n)$ for the ordering of the variables used in the definition of the functions. On the other hand, they need exponential π-OBDD size for most of the variable orderings (a fraction of $1 - n^{-\varepsilon}$ for DSA_n and even a fraction of $1 - 2^{-\varepsilon n}$ for IP_n, see [18]). In this paper, we investigate the influence of the variable ordering for approximate representations of functions. If not stated otherwise, by a random input $\tilde{x}$ we mean an input $\tilde{x}$ chosen from the uniform distribution on $\{0, 1\}^n$.

Definition 3. A function $g \in B_n$ is a c-approximation of $f \in B_n$ if $Pr(f(\tilde{x}) = g(\tilde{x})) \geq c$ for a random input $\tilde{x}$ chosen from the uniform distribution on $\{0, 1\}^n$.

One of the two constant functions 0 and 1 always is a $1/2$-approximation. Hence, we consider c-approximations for $c > 1/2$.

We prove the following strengthenings of the previously mentioned lower bounds on the π-OBDD complexity of DSA_n and IP_n for a random ordering. For most of the orderings π, every function that is a $(1/2 + \varepsilon)$-approximation of DSA_n or IP_n, where ε, $0 < \varepsilon < 1/2$ is any constant, requires a π-OBDD of exponential size.

The problem of approximation is motivated by experiments in genetic programming using OBDDs, where one searches for a good approximation of an unknown function given by examples. Our results have consequences for the situation that the unknown function has a small OBDD for some ordering, but this ordering is not known. For more details see Section 4.

2 The Direct Storage Access Function

First, we state the result informally. There are only a few variable orderings π which allow an approximation g_n of DSA_n which is essentially better than the trivial approximations by the constants 0 and 1 (which are $1/2$-approximations) and which, moreover, has a π-OBDD size growing not exponential.

Theorem 1. *Let $0 < \delta < \varepsilon$. For every large enough n, the following property holds for a fraction of at least $1 - n^{-2\varepsilon^2/\ln 2}$ of the variable orderings π for DSA_n. Each function which is a $(\frac{1}{2} + \varepsilon + n^{-(\varepsilon-\delta)/2})$-approximation of DSA_n has a π-OBDD size which is bounded below by e^{n^δ}.*

The complete proof of this theorem is contained in [11]. Here, the most important arguments are presented. The proof is split into Lemmas 1 and 2. Recall that an ordering π for DSA_n is a permutation of $n + k$ variables, where $k = \log n$. In order to simplify the terminology, we assume that the first $n' =_{\mathrm{def}} \lfloor (1 - 2\varepsilon)n \rfloor$ variables according to π are given to Alice and the other ones to Bob. First, we derive a property of random variable orderings π.

Lemma 1. *With probability at least $1 - n^{-2\varepsilon^2/\ln 2}$, Alice obtains at most $(1-\varepsilon)k$ address variables, i.e., a-variables.*

The proof relies on Chernoff's bound and may be found in [11]. In the following, we fix a variable ordering π where Alice gets at most $(1 - \varepsilon)k$ address variables. She also gets at least $(1 - 2\varepsilon)n - k$ data variables. If Alice's address variables are fixed, there are at least n^ε data variables left which may describe the output. On the average, at least $(1 - 2\varepsilon)n^\varepsilon - o(1)$ of these variables are given to Alice. In order to enable Bob to compute the output exactly, Alice has to send him the value of her address variables and those data variables which can describe the output. If the information given from Alice is much smaller than this, Bob can compute the value of DSA_n only with probability close to $1/2$. The information given from Alice to Bob is measured by the logarithm of the size of a π-OBDD computing the function DSA_n.

For a rigorous argument, let π be an ordering and let A (resp. B) be the set of address variables given in π to Alice (resp. Bob) and let X (resp. Y) be the set of data variables given in π to Alice (resp. Bob). Clearly, $|A \cup X| = n'$ and every computation in any π-OBDD reads first (some of) the variables in $A \cup X$ and then (some of) the variables in $B \cup Y$. Let g be a function represented by a π-OBDD G of size s. Because of the definition of c-approximations, we consider random inputs $(\tilde{a}, \tilde{b}, \tilde{x}, \tilde{y})$ where $\tilde{a}$ is a random setting of variables in A, etc. In this situation, the following holds.

Lemma 2. $\Pr(\mathrm{DSA}_n(\tilde{a}, \tilde{b}, \tilde{x}, \tilde{y}) = g(\tilde{a}, \tilde{b}, \tilde{x}, \tilde{y})) \leq 1 - \frac{|X|}{2n} + \frac{1}{2n}\left(2 \cdot 2^{|A|}|X| \ln s\right)^{1/2}.$

It is easy to show how Lemma 2 implies Theorem 1.

Proof of Theorem 1. Recall that $k = \log n$ and let $s < e^{n^\delta}$. For every ordering π, we have $(1 - 2\varepsilon)n - k - 1 \leq |X| \leq n$. Moreover, Lemma 1 implies that with probability at least $1 - n^{-2\varepsilon^2}$, we have $|A| \leq (1-\varepsilon)k$. By substituting these estimates into the bound from Lemma 2, we obtain that the probability that DSA_n and g have the same value is at most $\frac{1}{2} + \varepsilon + \frac{1}{\sqrt{2}}n^{-(\varepsilon-\delta)/2} + \frac{\log n}{2n} < \frac{1}{2} + \varepsilon + n^{-(\varepsilon-\delta)/2}$. This implies the theorem. $\square$

Let $H(U)$ be the entropy of a random variable U and $H(U \mid E)$ resp. $H(U \mid V)$ the entropy of U given an event E or a random variable V resp. Moreover, let $H^*(x) = -x \log x - (1-x) \log(1-x)$ for $x \in (0,1)$.

For each (a, b, y), let

$$q(a, b, y) = \Pr(\mathrm{DSA}_n(a, b, \tilde{x}, y) = g(a, b, \tilde{x}, y))$$

for random assignments $\tilde{x}$ to the variables in X. The probability, we are interested in, is the average of all $q(a, b, y)$. Let $q(a, b)$ denote the average of $q(a, b, y)$ over all possible y and, similarly, let $q(a)$ denote the average of $q(a, b, y)$ over all possible b and y. Moreover, for each partial input a, let I_a be the set of partial inputs b such that the variable $x_{\|(a,b)\|}$ or $x_{a,b}$, for simplicity, is given to Alice. Note that $H^*(x)$ is maximal for $x = 1/2$ and the maximum is equal to 1. Hence, if $|I_a| \gg \log s$, Lemma 3 implies that for most of $b \in I_a$, $q(a, b)$ is close to $1/2$. Moreover, the average of $|I_a|$ over all possible a is exactly $|X|/2^{|A|}$. Using this in the situation given by the assumption of the theorem, we can guarantee that $|I_a| \gg \log s$ in average over all possible a and derive that the average of $q(a, b, x, y)$ is close to $1/2$. The proof of Lemma 2 formalizes this using convexity in several steps and may be found in [11].

Lemma 3. *For every a, we have*

$$\sum_{b \in I_a} H^*(q(a,b)) \geq |I_a| - \log s.$$

Proof. Consider the π-OBDD computing the function g described before Lemma 2. For any settings a, x, let $h(a, x)$ be the first node, where the computation for a, x reaches a node testing a variable in $B \cup Y$ or a sink. Note that a computation for a, b, x, y depends on a, x only via $h(a, x)$. This means, there is a function $\Phi_{b,y}$ such that $g(a, b, x, y) = \Phi_{b,y}(h(a, x))$. Note that the size of the range of h is at most s.

Claim ([11]). Let U and V be random variables taking values in $\{0, 1\}$. Then $H^*(\Pr(U = V)) \geq H(U \mid V)$.

If (a, b, y) is fixed and $b \in I_a$, DSA_n outputs $x_{a,b}$. Using the claim and the fact that $H(U \mid f(V)) \geq H(U \mid V)$ for each function f, we conclude

$$H^*(q(a, b, y)) = H^*(\Pr(\tilde{x}_{a,b} = \Phi_{b,y}(h(a, \tilde{x}))))$$

$$\geq H(\tilde{x}_{a,b} \mid \Phi_{b,y}(h(a, \tilde{x}))) \geq H(\tilde{x}_{a,b} \mid h(a, \tilde{x})).$$

Now we use the fact $H(U_1 \mid V) + \ldots + H(U_r \mid V) \geq H((U_1, \ldots, U_r) \mid V)$ for $\tilde{x}_{a,b}$, $b \in I_a$, and the vector $\tilde{x}_a$ of these random variables. This implies

$$\sum_{b \in I_a} H(\tilde{x}_{a,b} \mid h(a, \tilde{x})) \geq H(\tilde{x}_a \mid h(a, \tilde{x})).$$

In the next step we apply the equalities $H(U \mid V) = H(U, V) - H(V)$ and $H(U, f(U)) = H(U)$ to obtain

$$H(\tilde{x}_a \mid h(a, \tilde{x})) = H(\tilde{x}_a, h(a, \tilde{x})) - H(h(a, \tilde{x})) = H(\tilde{x}_a) - H(h(a, \tilde{x})).$$

We have $H(h(a, \tilde{x})) \leq \log s$, since there are only s different possibilities for $h(a, \tilde{x})$. The random variables $\tilde{x}_{a,b}$, $b \in I_a$, are independent and take values in $\{0, 1\}$, i.e., $\tilde{x}_a$ is uniformly distributed over $\{0, 1\}^{|I_a|}$ and $H(\tilde{x}_a) = |I_a|$. This implies

$$H(\tilde{x}_a \mid h(a, \tilde{x})) \geq |I_a| - \log s.$$

Putting all our considerations together, we obtain

$$\sum_{b \in I_a} H^*(q(a, b, y)) \geq |I_a| - \log s.$$

The function H^* is concave. Hence, this inequality implies Lemma 3. $\square$

3 The Inner Product Function

In this section, we prove results on the inner product function which are of the same flavor as the results on the direct storage access function in Section 2. The difference is that we can prove stronger bounds on the quality of approximation even for a larger fraction of variable orderings and larger OBDDs.

Theorem 2. *Let* $0 < \delta < 1/9$. *The following property holds for a fraction of at least* $1 - e^{-4\delta^2 n}$ *of the variable orderings* π *for* IP_n. *Each function which is at least a* $(\frac{1}{2} + 2^{-\frac{1}{16}(1-9\delta)n-\frac{1}{2}})$-*approximation of* IP_n *has a* π-*OBDD size which is bounded below by* $2^{\delta n}$.

Proof. First, we derive a property of random variable orderings π. It is convenient to rename the variables such that $IP_n(x, y) = x_1 y_1 \oplus \ldots \oplus x_{n/2} y_{n/2}$. We give the first $n/2$ variables according to π to Alice and the other ones to Bob. An index i is called a singleton if x_i is given to Alice and y_i to Bob or vice versa.

Lemma 4 ([11]). *With probability at least* $1 - e^{-4\delta^2 n}$, *a random variable ordering leads to at least* $(1 - \delta)n/8$ *singletons.*

We estimate the probability that $IP_n(\tilde{x}) = g(\tilde{x})$ on a random input $\tilde{x} = (\tilde{x}_1, \ldots, \tilde{x}_{n/2}, \tilde{y}_1, \ldots, \tilde{y}_{n/2})$, where g is a function represented by a π-OBDD of size s, assuming, we know the number of singletons determined by the ordering π.

Lemma 5. *Let π be a variable ordering, such that Alice gets among her $n/2$ variables at least t singletons. Let g be a function represented by a π-OBDD G of size s. Then, $\Pr(\mathrm{IP}_n(\tilde{x}) = g(\tilde{x})) \leq \frac{1}{2} + s^{1/2}2^{-t/2-1/2}$.*

First we show how this claim implies the theorem. Let $t = \frac{1}{8}(1 - \delta)n$. Assuming $s < 2^{\delta n}$, we obtain

$$s^{1/2}2^{-t/2} < 2^{\delta n/2} \cdot 2^{-(1-\delta)n/16} = 2^{-\frac{1}{16}(1-9\delta)n}$$

and the theorem follows from Lemmas 4 and 5. $\square$

Proof of Lemma 5. We consider the communication matrix for IP_n with respect to the partition of the variables between Alice and Bob, i.e., we have $2^{n/2}$ rows corresponding to the different input vectors for the variables of Alice and similarly $2^{n/2}$ columns. Each matrix entry is the value of IP_n on the input of the row input and the column input. If we fix all variables x_j and y_j where j is not a singleton, we obtain IP_{2t} or its negation as subfunction. Hence, the communication matrix can be partitioned to $2^t \times 2^t$-submatrices which are communication matrices for IP_{2t} or its negation. For each of these submatrices $M = (M_{ij})$, w.l.o.g. Alice is the owner of all x-variables and Bob the owner of all y-variables.

It follows by an averaging argument that there is an assignment to the variables x_j and y_j where j is not a singleton such that $\Pr(\mathrm{IP}_n^*(\tilde{x}) = g^*(\tilde{x})) \geq \Pr(\mathrm{IP}_n(\tilde{x}) = g(\tilde{x}))$ for the resulting subfunctions IP_n^* and g^* of IP_n and g resp. By the above arguments, we can assume w.l.o.g. that $\mathrm{IP}_n^* = \mathrm{IP}_{2t}$. In order to prove the lemma, it is sufficient to prove

$$\Pr(\mathrm{IP}_n^*(\tilde{x}) = g^*(\tilde{x})) \leq \frac{1}{2} + s^{1/2}2^{-t/2-1/2}.$$

Let M^* be the communication matrix of g^* and let $\rho(M, M^*)$ denote the number of entries, where M and M^* do not agree. Then

$$\Pr(\mathrm{IP}_n^*(\tilde{x}) = g^*(\tilde{x})) = 1 - \rho(M, M^*)/2^{2t}.$$

We will prove that

$$\rho(M, M^*) \geq \frac{1}{2}2^{2t} - s^{1/2}2^{3t/2-1/2}$$

which implies the lemma.

Since g^* can be represented by a π-OBDD whose size is bounded by s, it follows from the well-known relations between one-way communication complexity and π-OBDD size that the communication matrix of g^* has at most s different rows. Let $r_1, \ldots, r_s$ contain the different rows of M^*. We partition M^* to a small number of constant submatrices which intuitively implies that M and M^* are quite different. We permute the rows (i.e., renumber the input vectors of Alice) such that we have at first a_1 rows equal to r_1, then a_2 rows equal to r_2 and so on. The block of a_k equal rows can be partitioned for some b_k to an

$a_k \times b_k$-matrix consisting of zeros only and an $a_k \times (2^t - b_k)$-matrix consisting of ones only. Altogether we have partitioned M^* to at most $2s$ constant submatrices whose sizes are $a_k \times b_k$ and $a_k \times (2^t - b_k)$, $1 \le k \le s$.

Now we consider the corresponding submatrices of M. It is known from Lindsey's Lemma (see, e.g., Babai, Frankl, and Simon (1986)) that for each subset A of a rows of M and each subset B of b columns of M it holds that

$$\left| \sum_{i \in A, \ j \in B} (-1)^{M_{ij}} \right| \le (2^t ab)^{1/2}$$

i.e., each not too small submatrix is not constant. It follows that we have to negate at least $\frac{1}{2}(ab - (2^t ab)^{1/2})$ entries of an $a \times b$ submatrix of M to obtain a constant submatrix.

By the conclusion from Lindsey's Lemma, it follows that

$$\rho(M, M^*) \ge \sum_{1 \le k \le s} \frac{1}{2}(a_k b_k - (2^t a_k b_k)^{1/2} + a_k(2^t - b_k) - (2^t a_k(2^t - b_k))^{1/2})$$

Hence,

$$\rho(M, M^*) \ge \sum_{1 \le k \le s} \frac{1}{2}(2^t a_k - (2^t a_k)^{1/2}(b_k^{1/2} + (2^t - b_k)^{1/2})).$$

The sum of all a_k is equal to 2^t and $b_k^{1/2} + (2^t - b_k)^{1/2} \le 2^{(t+1)/2}$. Hence,

$$\rho(M, M^*) \ge \frac{1}{2}2^{2t} - \sum_{1 \le k \le s} 2^{t-1/2} a_k^{1/2}.$$

Since $x^{1/2}$ is concave, we obtain the minimum value of the right hand side for $a_k = 2^t/s$ for all $k = 1, 2, \ldots, s$. By a routine calculation, we can derive the proposed bound on $\rho(M, M^*)$ and hence also the theorem. $\square$

4 The Motivation from and Conclusion for Genetic Programming

Genetic programming has been introduced by Koza [12] as a heuristic approach to construct a program which computes a function which agrees with a list of inputs and corresponding outputs. In the case of Boolean functions, OBDDs seem to be a good "programming language". The reasons for the choice of OBDDs are explained in more detail in [11] and we refer to [7],[8],[9], [14] and [19] for experiments for genetic programming with OBDDs.

Here we are faced with the problem that we are given a list $(x, f(x)), x \epsilon S \subseteq \{0,1\}^n$, of *training examples* of the unknown concept $f : \{0,1\}^n \to \{0,1\}$. The aim is to find a function $g : \{0,1\}^n \to \{0,1\}$ which agrees with f on the examples from S and, moreover, yields a justifiable approximation of f. For this reason we assume that the examples x are drawn independently and randomly. Then, algorithmic learning theory and, in particular, Occam's razor theorem ([2],[3]) implies that OBDDs of size s which represent a function g and agree with f on the $m = |S|$ examples are likely to be a good approximation of f, if S is small enough compared to m (for precise results see [11]). In this situation the OBDD represents all training examples using much less space than the list of examples, i.e., the OBDD is a *compression* of the set of training examples.

The results of the previous sections imply that DSA_n and IP_n are hard to approximate by any π-OBDD for a random π. In the next theorem, we prove, moreover, that any function f that is hard to approximate in this sense has also the following property. If we have a set of training examples for function f^π, which is obtained from the function f by an unknown permutation π of the variables, then a reasonable compression of the examples requires also to optimize the ordering of variables used to represent g. More exactly, if we choose an ordering of the variables for solving the minimization problem at random before we start the minimization process and the ordering is not modified during the process, then, with high probability, almost no compression is possible.

Theorem 3. *Let f, s, γ, ε and a distribution D on $\{0,1\}^n$ be such that the following is true: if an ordering π is chosen from the uniform distribution on all orderings, then with probability at least $1 - \gamma$, every π-OBDD h of size at most s satisfies $\Pr(f(\tilde{x}) = h(\tilde{x})) \leq \frac{1}{2} + \varepsilon$, where $\tilde{x}$ is chosen from the distribution D. Let $\tilde{S}$ be a set of m independent random examples chosen from D and let π be a random ordering. Then, with probability $1 - \gamma - (es)^s \left(\frac{1}{2} + \varepsilon\right)^m$, there is no π-OBDD g of size at most s that agrees with f on all training examples in $\tilde{S}$.*

Proof. Let us call an ordering bad, if it has the property mentioned in the theorem. A random ordering is bad with probability at least $1 - \gamma$. Since the examples are chosen independently on the ordering, the distribution of the examples does not change, if we condition according to the ordering. Let us estimate the conditional probability that the m examples may be expressed using a function g of π-OBDD size at most s under the condition that the ordering π is bad. Every π-OBDD of size at most s matches all the examples with probability at most $\left(\frac{1}{2} + \varepsilon\right)^m$. Multiplying this by $(es)^s$, which is an upper bound to the number of π-OBDDs of size at most s, see [11], yields an upper bound on the required conditional probability. Hence, the conditional probability that the examples may not be expressed in complexity at most s is at least $1 - (es)^s \left(\frac{1}{2} + \varepsilon\right)^m$. It follows that the probability that the ordering is bad and, moreover, the examples may not be expressed in size at most s is at least $(1 - \gamma) \left(1 - (es)^s \left(\frac{1}{2} + \varepsilon\right)^m\right)$. This implies the theorem. $\square$

This general result may be combined with the results of Sections 2 and 3 to obtain the following.

Corollary 1. *For every large enough n, if we take $m = n^{\Theta(1)}$ examples for DSA_n from the uniform distribution and choose a random ordering π of the* *variables, then with probability at least* $1 - n^{-1/2}$, *there is no* π-*OBDD of size* $\frac{1}{10}m/\log m$ *matching the given* m *training examples.*

Proof. Let $\varepsilon, \varepsilon'$ be such that $\sqrt{\ln 2}/2 < \varepsilon < \varepsilon' < 1/2^{1/10} - 1/2$. Moreover, let $\delta < \varepsilon$ be any small positive number and let $s = \frac{1}{10}m/\log m$. Using Theorem 1, we obtain for every large enough n that a random ordering π satisfies the following. With probability at least $1 - n^{-2\varepsilon^2/\ln 2}$, there is no $(\frac{1}{2} + \varepsilon')$-approximation among the functions of π-OBDD complexity at most $s \leq e^{n^\delta}$. Note that in our situation, $(es)^s \leq 2^{m/10}$. Using also Theorem 3, with probability at least $1 - n^{-2\varepsilon^2/\ln 2} - 2^{m/10}\left(\frac{1}{2} + \varepsilon'\right)^m \geq 1 - n^{-1/2}$, there is no π-OBDD of size at most s matching the given m training examples for DSA_n. $\square$

Corollary 2. *Let* $0 < \alpha < 1$ *be a constant. For every large enough* n, *if we take* $m = n^{O(1)}$, $m \geq n$, *examples for* IP_n *from the uniform distribution and choose a random ordering* π *of the variables, then with probability at least* $1 - e^{-\Omega(n)}$, *there is no* π-*OBDD of size at most* $(1 - \alpha)m/\log m$ *matching the given* m *training examples.*

Proof. Let δ and ε be positive numbers such that $\delta < \frac{1}{9}$ and $\frac{1}{2} + \varepsilon < \left(\frac{1}{2}\right)^{1-\alpha}$. Moreover, let $s = (1 - \alpha)m/\log m$. By Theorem 2, for every large enough n, a random ordering π satisfies the following. With probability at least $1 - e^{-4\delta^2 n}$, there is no $(\frac{1}{2} + \varepsilon)$-approximation of IP_n among the functions of π-OBDD complexity at most $s \leq 2^{\delta n}$. Note that $(es)^s \leq 2^{(1-\alpha)m}$. Together with Theorem 3, we obtain that with probability at least $1 - e^{-4\delta^2 n} - 2^{(1-\alpha)m}\left(\frac{1}{2} + \varepsilon\right)^m = 1 - e^{-\Omega(n)}$, there is no π-OBDD of size at most s matching the given m random training examples for IP_n. $\square$

On the other hand, for the functions DSA_n and IP_n, there are orderings, for which a good compression is possible. This suggests that including the optimization of the variable ordering into the minimization procedure often is necessary to get a good quality of the computed generalization.

References

1. L. Babai, P. Frankl and J. Simon. Complexity classes in communication complexity theory. 27. FOCS, pp. 337–347, 1986.
2. A. Blumer, A. Ehrenfeucht, D. Haussler and M. Warmuth. Occam's Razor. Information Processing Letters, 24, pp. 377–380, 1987.
3. A. Blumer, A. Ehrenfeucht, D. Haussler and M. Warmuth. Learnability and the Vapnik-Chervonenkis Dimension. Journal of the ACM, 36, pp. 929–965, 1989.
4. B. Bollig and I. Wegener. Improving the variable ordering of OBDDs is NP-complete. IEEE Trans. on Computers 45, pp. 993–1002, 1996.
5. R. E. Bryant. Graph-based algorithms for Boolean function manipulation. IEEE Trans. on Computers 35, pp. 677–691, 1986.

6. R. E. Bryant. Symbolic manipulation with ordered binary decision diagrams. ACM Computing Surveys 24, pp. 293–318, 1992.
7. S. Droste. Efficient genetic programming for finding good generalizing Boolean functions. Genetic Programming'97, pp. 82–87, 1997.
8. S. Droste. Genetic programming with guaranteed quality. Genetic Programming'98, pp. 54–59, 1998.
9. S. Droste and D. Wiesmann. On representation and genetic operators in evolutionary algorithms. Submitted to IEEE Trans. on Evolution Computation, 1998.
10. J. Hromkovič. *Communication Complexity and Parallel Computing.* Springer, 1997.
11. M. Krause, P. Savický and I. Wegener. Approximations by OBDDs and the variable ordering problem. ECCC, TR99-011, www.eccc.uni-trier.de/eccc, 1999.
12. J. Koza. *Genetic Programming: On the Programming of Computers by Means of Natural Selection.* Cambridge, MA: The MIT Press, 1992.
13. E. Kushilevitz and N. Nisan. *Communication Complexity.* Cambridge University Press, 1997.
14. H. Sakanashi, T. Higuchi, H. Iba and K. Kakazu. An approach for genetic synthesizer of binary decision diagram. IEEE Int. Conf. on Evolutionary Computation, ICEC'96, pp. 559–564, 1996.
15. D. Sieling, On the existence of polynomial time approximation schemes for OBDD minimization. STACS'98, LNCS 1373, pp. 205–215, 1998.
16. I. Wegener. *The Complexity of Boolean functions.* Wiley-Teubner series in computer science, 1987.
17. I. Wegener. Efficient data structures for Boolean functions. Discrete Mathematics 136, pp. 347–372, 1994.
18. I. Wegener. *Branching Programs and Binary Decision Diagrams – Theory and Applications.* To appear: SIAM Monographs on Discrete Mathematics and Applications, 1999.
19. M. Yanagiya. Efficient genetic programming based on binary decision diagrams. IEEE Int. Conf. on Evolutionary Computation ICEC'95, pp. 234–239, 1995.

Simulation Preorder on Simple Process Algebras

Antonín Kučera[*1] and Richard Mayr[2]

[1] Faculty of Informatics MU, Botanická 68a, 60200 Brno, Czech Repubic, tony@fi.muni.cz
[2] Institut für Informatik TUM, Arcisstr. 21, 80290 München, Germany, mayrri@in.tum.de

Abstract. We consider the problem of simulation preorder/equivalence between infinite-state processes and finite-state ones. We prove that simulation preorder (in both directions) and simulation equivalence are *intractable* between all major classes of infinite-state systems and finite-state ones. This result is obtained by showing that the problem whether a BPA (or BPP) process simulates a finite-state one is $PSPACE$-hard, and the other direction is co-$\mathcal{NP}$-hard; consequently, simulation equivalence between BPA (or BPP) and finite-state processes is also co-$\mathcal{NP}$-hard.

The *decidability border* for the mentioned problem is also established. Simulation preorder (in both directions) and simulation equivalence are decidable in $EXPTIME$ between pushdown processes and finite-state ones. On the other hand, simulation preorder is undecidable between PA and finite-state processes in both directions. The obtained results also hold for those PA and finite-state processes which are deterministic and normed, and thus immediately extend to trace preorder. Regularity (finiteness) w.r.t. simulation and trace equivalence is also shown to be undecidable for PA.

Finally, we describe a way how to utilize decidability of bisimulation problems to solve certain instances of undecidable simulation problems. We apply this method to BPP processes.

1 Introduction

We study the decidability and complexity of checking simulation preorder and equivalence between certain infinite-state systems and finite-state ones. The motivation is that the intended behavior of a process can often be easily specified by a finite-state system, while the actual implementation may contain components which are infinite-state (e.g. counters, buffers). The task of formal verification is to prove that the specification and the implementation are equivalent.

The same problem has been studied recently for strong and weak bisimilarity [11, 14], and it has been shown that these equivalences are not only *decidable*, but also *tractable* between certain infinite-state processes and finite-state ones. Those issues (namely the complexity ones) are dramatically different from the 'symmetric' case when we compare two infinite-state processes. Here we consider (and answer) analogous questions for simulation, giving a complete overview (see Fig. 1).

---

[*] Supported by a Research Fellowship granted by the Alexander von Humboldt Foundation and by a Post-Doc grant GA ČR No. 201/98/P046.

The state of the art: Simulation preorder/equivalence is known to be undecidable for BPA [7] and BPP [9] processes. An interesting positive result is that simulation preorder (and hence also equivalence) is decidable for Petri nets with at most one unbounded place [1]. In [12] it is shown that simulation preorder between Petri nets and finite-state processes is *decidable* in both directions. Moreover, a related problem of *regularity* (finiteness) of Petri nets w.r.t. simulation equivalence is proved to be undecidable.

Our contribution: In Section 3 we concentrate on the complexity issues for simulation preorder and equivalence with finite-state processes. We prove that the problem whether a BPA (or BPP) process simulates a finite-state one is $PSPACE$-hard, and the other direction is co-$\mathcal{NP}$-hard. Consequently, simulation equivalence between BPA (or BPP) and finite-state processes is also co-$\mathcal{NP}$-hard. Hence, the main message of this section is that simulation with finite-state systems is unfortunately *intractable* for any studied class of infinite-state systems (assuming $\mathcal{P} \neq \mathcal{NP}$)—see Fig. 1. It contrasts sharply with the complexity issues for strong and weak bisimilarity; for example, weak bisimilarity between BPA and finite-state processes, and between normed BPP and finite-state processes is in $\mathcal{P}$ [14].

In Section 4 we establish the decidability border of Fig. 1. First we prove that simulation preorder between PDA processes and finite-state ones is *decidable* in $EXPTIME$ in both directions. Consequently, simulation equivalence is also in $EXPTIME$. Then we show that simulation preorder between PA and finite-state processes is *undecidable* in both directions. It is rather interesting that the undecidability results hold even for those PA and finite-state processes which are *deterministic* and *normed*. Simulation *equivalence* between such processes is decidable (it coincides with bisimilarity [11]); however, as soon as we allow just one nondeterministic state in PA processes, simulation equivalence becomes undecidable. We also show that all the obtained undecidability results can be formulated in a 'stronger' form—it is possible to *fix* a PA or a finite-state process in each of the mentioned undecidable problems. Then we demonstrate that regularity of (normed) PA processes w.r.t. simulation equivalence is also undecidable. Again, it contrasts with regularity w.r.t. bisimilarity for normed PA processes, which is decidable in polynomial time [13]. All the obtained undecidability results also hold for trace preorder and trace equivalence, and therefore they might be also interesting from a point of view of 'classical' automata theory (see the last section for further comments).

Finally, in Section 5 we study the relationship between bisimilarity and simulation equivalence. Our effort is motivated by a general trend that problems for bisimilarity (equivalence, regularity) are often decidable, but the corresponding problems for simulation equivalence are not. We propose a way how to use existing algorithms for 'bisimulation' problems to solve certain instances of the corresponding (and possibly undecidable) 'simulation' ones. Such techniques are interesting from a practical point of view, as only small instances of undecidable problems can be solved in an ad-hoc fashion, and some kind of computer support is absolutely necessary for problems of 'real' size.

In the last section we give a summary of existing results in the area of comparing infinite-state systems with finite-state ones and discuss language-theoretic aspects of the obtained results.

The missing proofs can be found in the full version of the paper [15].

2 Definitions

Let $Act = \{a, b, c, \ldots\}$ and $Const = \{X, Y, Z, \ldots\}$ be disjoint countably infinite sets of *actions* and *process constants*, respectively. The class of *general process expressions* G is defined by $E ::= \epsilon \mid X \mid E\|E \mid E.E$, where $X \in Const$ and ϵ is a special constant that denotes the empty expression. Intuitively, '.' is a sequential composition and '$\|$' is a parallel composition. We do not distinguish between expressions related by *structural congruence* which is given by the following laws: '.' and '$\|$' are associative, '$\|$' is commutative, and 'ϵ' is a unit for '.' and '$\|$'.

A *process rewrite system* [16] is specified by a finite set Δ of *rules* which have the form $E \xrightarrow{a} F$, where $E, F \in G$ and $a \in Act$. $Const(\Delta)$ and $Act(\Delta)$ denote the sets of process constants and actions which are used in the rules of Δ, respectively (note that these sets are finite). Each process rewrite system Δ defines a unique transition system where states are process expressions over $Const(\Delta)$, $Act(\Delta)$ is the set of labels, and transitions are determined by Δ and the following inference rules (remember that '$\|$' is commutative):

$$\frac{(E \xrightarrow{a} F) \in \Delta}{E \xrightarrow{a} F} \qquad \frac{E \xrightarrow{a} E'}{E.F \xrightarrow{a} E'.F} \qquad \frac{E \xrightarrow{a} E'}{E\|F \xrightarrow{a} E'\|F}$$

We extend the notation $E \xrightarrow{a} F$ to elements of Act^* in a standard way. Moreover, we say that F is *reachable* from E if $E \xrightarrow{w} F$ for some $w \in Act^*$.

Various subclasses of process rewrite systems can be obtained by imposing certain restrictions on the form of rules. To specify those restrictions, we first define the classes S and P of *sequential* and *parallel* expressions, composed of all process expressions which do not contain the '$\|$' and the '.' operator, respectively. We also use 1 to denote the set of process constants. The hierarchy of process rewrite systems is presented in Fig. 1; the restrictions are specified by a pair (A, B), where A and B are the classes of expressions which can appear on the left-hand and the right-hand side of rules, respectively. This hierarchy contains almost all classes of infinite state systems which have been studied so far; BPA, BPP, and PA processes are well-known [2], PDA correspond to pushdown processes (as proved by Caucal in [4]), PN correspond

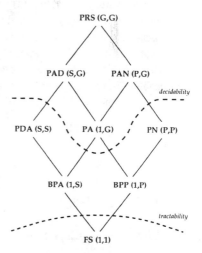

Fig. 1. A hierarchy of PRS

to Petri nets, etc. In Fig. 1 we also indicated the decidability/tractability border for simulation preorder and equivalence with finite-state systems which is established in the following sections.

Processes are considered as states in transition systems generated by process rewrite systems. We also assume that for each system Δ there is some distinguished process expression which is considered as the *initial state* of Δ. In what follows, we often identify process rewrite systems with their initial states. A process P is said to be *deterministic* iff each reachable state of P has at most one a-successor for every $a \in Act$. A PA process Δ is *normed* iff $X \rightarrow^* \epsilon$ for every $X \in Const(\Delta)$.

In this paper we compare infinite-state processes with finite-state ones w.r.t. certain 'behavioral' preorders and equivalences.

Definition 1. *We say that* $w \in Act^*$ *is a* trace *of a process* E *iff* $E \xrightarrow{w} E'$ *for some* E'. *Let* $Tr(E)$ *be the set of all traces of* E. *We write* $E \sqsubseteq_t F$ *iff* $Tr(E) \subseteq Tr(F)$. *Moreover, we say that* E *and* F *are* trace equivalent, *written* $A =_t B$, *iff* $Tr(E) = Tr(F)$.

Trace preorder and equivalence are very similar to language inclusion and equivalence of 'classical' automata theory. In concurrency theory, trace equivalence is usually considered as being too coarse. A plethora of finer 'behavioral' equivalences have been proposed [19]. It seems that *simulation* and *bisimulation* equivalence are of special importance, as their accompanying theory has been developed very intensively.

Definition 2. *A* binary relation R *over process expressions is a* simulation *if whenever* $(E, F) \in R$ *then for each* $a \in Act$: *if* $E \xrightarrow{a} E'$ *then* $F \xrightarrow{a} F'$ *for some* F' *s.t.* $(E', F') \in R$. *A symmetric simulation is called* bisimulation. *A process* E *is* simulated *by a process* F, *written* $E \sqsubseteq_s F$, *if there is a simulation* R *s.t.* $(E, F) \in R$. *We say that* E *and* F *are* simulation equivalent, *written* $E =_s F$, *iff* $E \sqsubseteq_s F$ *and* $F \sqsubseteq_s E$. *Similarly, we say that* E *and* F *are* bisimilar *(or* bisimulation equivalent*), written* $E \sim F$, *iff there is a bisimulation relating them.*

Another natural (and studied) problem is decidability of *regularity* (i.e. 'semantical finiteness') of processes w.r.t. certain behavioral equivalences. A process E is *regular* w.r.t. bisimulation (or simulation, trace) equivalence iff there is a finite-state process F such that $E \sim F$ (or $E =_s F$, $E =_t F$, respectively).

Almost all undecidability results in this paper are obtained by reduction of the halting problem for Minsky counter machines (the halting problem is undecidable even for Minsky machines with two counters initialized to zero [17]).

Definition 3. *A* counter machine M *with nonnegative counters* $c_1, c_2, \cdots, c_m$ *is a sequence of instructions* $1: INS_1, \cdots, k: INS_k$ *where* $k \in \mathbb{N}$, $INS_k = \mathtt{halt}$, *and every* INS_i $(1 \leq i < k)$ *is in one of the following forms (where* $1 \leq l, l', l'' \leq k$, $1 \leq j \leq m$).

$- c_j := c_j + 1; \quad \mathtt{goto}\ l$
$- \mathtt{if}\ c_j = 0\ \mathtt{then\ goto}\ l'\ \mathtt{else}\ (c_j := c_j - 1; \quad \mathtt{goto}\ l'')$

3 The Tractability Border

In this section we show that the problem whether a BPA (or BPP) process simulates a finite-state one is *PSPACE*-hard. The other preorder is shown to be co-$\mathcal{NP}$-hard. Consequently, we also obtain co-$\mathcal{NP}$-hardness of simulation equivalence between BPA (or BPP) and finite-state processes. As simulation preorder and equivalence are easily decidable for finite-state processes in polynomial time, the tractability border for simulation preorder/equivalence with finite-state systems of Fig. 1 is established.

Theorem 1. *Let* P *be a BPA (or BPP) process,* F *a finite-state process. The problem whether* $F \sqsubseteq_s P$ *is PSPACE-hard.*

Theorem 2. *Let P be a BPA (or BPP) process, F a finite-state process. The problem whether $P \sqsubseteq_s F$ is co-$\mathcal{N}\mathcal{P}$-hard.*

Theorem 3. *The problems of simulation equivalence between BPA and finite-state processes, and between BPP and finite-state processes are co-$\mathcal{N}\mathcal{P}$-hard.*

4 The Decidability Border

In this section we establish the decidability border of Fig. 1. We show that simulation preorder (in both directions) and simulation equivalence with finite-state processes are decidable for PDA processes in $EXPTIME$. It is possible to reduce each of the mentioned problems to the model-checking problem for an (almost) fixed formula φ of the alternation-free modal μ-calculus (we would like to thank Javier Esparza who observed the idea of our proof).

Then we turn our attention to PA processes. We prove that simulation preorder is *undecidable* between PA processes and finite-state ones in both directions. It is somewhat surprising, as for the subclasses BPP and BPA we have positive decidability results. Moreover, simulation preorder is undecidable even if we consider those PA and finite-state processes which are *deterministic* and *normed*. Thus, our undecidability results immediately extend to trace preorder (which coincides with simulation preorder on deterministic processes). It is worth noting that simulation *equivalence* between deterministic PA and deterministic finite-state processes is decidable, as it coincides with bisimilarity which is known to be decidable [11]. However, as soon as we allow just one nondeterministic state in PA processes, simulation equivalence with finite-state processes becomes undecidable (there is even a fixed normed deterministic finite-state process F such that simulation equivalence with F is undecidable for PA processes). The same applies to trace equivalence.

Finally, we also prove that regularity (finiteness) of PA processes w.r.t. simulation and trace equivalence is undecidable, even for the normed subclass of PA. Again, the role of nondeterminism is very special as regularity of normed deterministic PA processes w.r.t. simulation and trace equivalence coincides with regularity w.r.t. bisimilarity, which is easily decidable in polynomial time [13]. However, just one nondeterministic state in the PA process makes the undecidability proof possible.

Theorem 4. *Simulation preorder is decidable between PDA processes and finite-state ones in $EXPTIME$ (in both directions).*

Corollary 1. *Simulation equivalence between PDA and finite-state processes is decidable in $EXPTIME$.*

Theorem 5. *Let P be a deterministic PA process and F a deterministic finite-state process. It is undecidable whether $P \sqsubseteq_s F$.*

Proof. Let $\mathcal{M}$ be an arbitrary two-counter machine with counters initialized to m_1, m_2. We construct a deterministic PA process $P(\mathcal{M})$ and a deterministic finite-state process $F(\mathcal{M})$ s.t. $P(\mathcal{M}) \sqsubseteq_s F(\mathcal{M})$ iff the machine $\mathcal{M}$ does not halt. Let $Act :=$

$\{zero_1, inc_1, dec_1, zero_2, inc_2, dec_2\}$. The PA process $P(\mathcal{M})$ is defined by the following rules:

$$Z_1 \xrightarrow{zero_1} Z_1 \quad Z_1 \xrightarrow{inc_1} C_1.Z_1 \quad C_1 \xrightarrow{inc_1} C_1.C_1 \quad C_1 \xrightarrow{dec_1} \epsilon$$
$$Z_2 \xrightarrow{zero_2} Z_2 \quad Z_2 \xrightarrow{inc_2} C_2.Z_2 \quad C_2 \xrightarrow{inc_2} C_2.C_2 \quad C_2 \xrightarrow{dec_2} \epsilon$$

The initial state is $(C_1^{m_1}.Z_1) \parallel (C_2^{m_2}.Z_2)$.

The process $F(\mathcal{M})$ corresponds to the finite control of $\mathcal{M}$. For every instruction of the form $n : c_i := c_i + 1$; goto n' we have an arc $n \xrightarrow{inc_i} n'$. For every instruction of the form $n :$ if $c_i = 0$ then goto n' else $c_i := c_i - 1$; goto n'' fi we have arcs $n \xrightarrow{zero_i} n'$ and $n \xrightarrow{dec_i} n''$. Then we add a new state all and arcs $all \xrightarrow{a} all$ for every $a \in Act$. Finally, we complete the process $F(\mathcal{M})$ in the following way: for every node n, except for the one which corresponds to the final state $halt$ of $\mathcal{M}$, and every $a \in Act$, if there is no arc $n \xrightarrow{a} n'$ for any n', then add an arc $n \xrightarrow{a} all$. The initial state of $F(\mathcal{M})$ corresponds to the initial state of $\mathcal{M}$.

The state of $P(\mathcal{M})$ corresponds to the contents of the counters of $\mathcal{M}$ and the state of $F(\mathcal{M})$ corresponds to the state of the finite control of $\mathcal{M}$. A round in the simulation game corresponds to a computational step of $\mathcal{M}$.

The only problem is that $P(\mathcal{M})$ may do steps that do not correspond to steps of the counter machine, e.g. $P(\mathcal{M})$ does a step dec_1 when the current state in $F(\mathcal{M})$ expects inc_1. In all these cases the construction of $F(\mathcal{M})$ ensures that $F(\mathcal{M})$ can (and must) respond by a step that ends in the state all. After such a step $F(\mathcal{M})$ can simulate anything. It is easy to see that $P(\mathcal{M}) \not\sqsubseteq_s F(\mathcal{M})$ iff $P(\mathcal{M})$ can force $F(\mathcal{M})$ to enter the state $halt$ via a sequence of moves which correspond to the correct simulation of $\mathcal{M}$. Thus, $P(\mathcal{M}) \sqsubseteq_s F(\mathcal{M})$ iff the machine $\mathcal{M}$ does not halt. $\qquad\square$

Remark 1. Theorem 7 still holds under an additional condition that both the PA process and the finite-state one are normed. We can make the PA process normed by adding the following rules: $Z_1 \xrightarrow{x_1} \epsilon, C_1 \xrightarrow{x_1} \epsilon, Z_2 \xrightarrow{x_2} \epsilon, C_2 \xrightarrow{x_2} \epsilon$. Observe that the resulting process is still deterministic. To make sure that $F(\mathcal{M})$ can simulate the actions x_1, x_2, we add the rules $n \xrightarrow{x_1} all$ and $n \xrightarrow{x_2} all$ for every state n of $F(\mathcal{M})$ (this also includes the rules $all \xrightarrow{x_1} all$ and $all \xrightarrow{x_2} all$). The process $F(\mathcal{M})$ is made normed by introducing a new state *terminated* where no action is enabled, and a rule $all \xrightarrow{x} terminated$. It is easy to see that these new systems $P'(\mathcal{M})$ and $F'(\mathcal{M})$ are deterministic and normed, and still satisfy the property that $P'(\mathcal{M}) \sqsubseteq_s F'(\mathcal{M})$ iff the machine $\mathcal{M}$ does not halt.

The halting problem is undecidable even for two-counter machines with counters initialized to zero. The construction of $P(\mathcal{M})$ is then independent of $\mathcal{M}$. Furthermore, there exists a universal Minsky machine $\mathcal{M}'$; the halting problem for $\mathcal{M}'$ (with given input values) is undecidable, and the construction of $F(\mathcal{M}')$ is independent of those input values. Hence, we can conclude the following:

Theorem 6. *There is a normed deterministic PA process $\overline{P}$ and a normed deterministic finite-state process $\overline{F}$ such that*

- *the problem whether $\overline{P} \sqsubseteq_s F$ for a given (normed and deterministic) finite-state process F is undecidable,*

- *the problem whether $P \sqsubseteq_s \overline{F}$ for a given (normed and deterministic) PA process P is undecidable.*

Theorem 7. *Let P be a deterministic PA process and F a deterministic finite-state process. It is undecidable whether $F \sqsubseteq_s P$.*

Proof. Let $\mathcal{M}$ be an arbitrary two-counter machine with counters initialized to m_1, m_2. We construct a deterministic PA process $P(\mathcal{M})$ and a deterministic finite-state system $F(\mathcal{M})$ s.t. $F(\mathcal{M}) \sqsubseteq_s P(\mathcal{M})$ iff the machine $\mathcal{M}$ does not halt.

Let $Act := \{zero_1, inc_1, dec_1, zero_2, inc_2, dec_2, \tau\}$. For the construction of $P(\mathcal{M})$ we start with the same PA process as in Theorem 5 and extend it by the following rules, which handle all the behaviors that are 'illegal' in a given state of $P(\mathcal{M})$ w.r.t. the counter values it represents.

$$Z_1 \xrightarrow{dec_1} A_1 \qquad C_1 \xrightarrow{zero_1} A_1 \qquad A_1 \xrightarrow{a} A_1 \text{ for every } a \in \{zero_1, inc_1, dec_1, \tau\}$$
$$Z_2 \xrightarrow{dec_2} A_2 \qquad C_2 \xrightarrow{zero_2} A_2 \qquad A_2 \xrightarrow{a} A_2 \text{ for every } a \in \{zero_2, inc_2, dec_2, \tau\}$$

The intuition is that an illegal step that concerns the counter i (with $i \in \{1, 2\}$) always introduces the symbol A_i, and from then on everything can be simulated. The initial state is $(C_1^{m_1}.Z_1) \parallel (C_2^{m_2}.Z_2)$. Note that $P(\mathcal{M})$ is deterministic; a term that contains both A_1 and A_2 can do the action τ in two different ways, but the result is always the same.

The system $F(\mathcal{M})$ corresponds to the finite control of $\mathcal{M}$. For every instruction of the form $n : c_i := c_i + 1; \text{goto } n'$ we have an arc $n \xrightarrow{inc_i} n'$. For every instruction of the form $n : \text{if } c_i = 0 \text{ then goto } n' \text{ else } c_i := c_i - 1; \text{goto } n'' \text{ fi}$ we have arcs $n \xrightarrow{zero_i} n'$ and $n \xrightarrow{dec_i} n''$. For the unique final state $halt$ of the finite control of $\mathcal{M}$ we add the rule $halt \xrightarrow{\tau} halt$. Note that a reachable state of $P(\mathcal{M})$ cannot do τ, unless it contains A_1 or A_2. Every step in the simulation game corresponds to a computational step of $\mathcal{M}$. It follows that $F(\mathcal{M}) \not\sqsubseteq_s P(\mathcal{M})$ iff $F(\mathcal{M})$ can reach the state $halt$ via a sequence of legal steps that correspond to steps of the counter machine (and do not introduce the symbol A_1 or A_2 in $P(\mathcal{M})$). Thus, $F(\mathcal{M}) \sqsubseteq_s P(\mathcal{M})$ iff the machine $\mathcal{M}$ does not halt. $\square$

Remark 2. Theorem 7 still holds under an additional condition that both the PA process and the finite-state one are normed. The system $F(\mathcal{M})$ is made normed as follows: We introduce a new state *terminated* where no action is enabled, and rules $n \xrightarrow{x} terminated$ for every other state n of $F(\mathcal{M})$. To assure that $P(\mathcal{M})$ can always simulate the action x, we add the rules $Z_1 \xrightarrow{x} \epsilon, C_1 \xrightarrow{x} \epsilon, A_1 \xrightarrow{x} \epsilon$. To make $P(\mathcal{M})$ normed, it now suffices to add the following: $Z_2 \xrightarrow{y} \epsilon, C_2 \xrightarrow{y} \epsilon, A_2 \xrightarrow{y} \epsilon$. It is easy to see that these new processes $P'(\mathcal{M})$ and $F'(\mathcal{M})$ are deterministic and normed, and still satisfy the property that $F'(\mathcal{M}) \sqsubseteq_s P'(\mathcal{M})$ iff the machine $\mathcal{M}$ does not halt.

A proof of the following theorem is the same as of Theorem 6:

Theorem 8. *There is a normed deterministic PA process $\overline{P}$ and a normed deterministic finite-state process $\overline{F}$ such that*

- *the problem whether $F \sqsubseteq_s \overline{P}$ for a given (normed and deterministic) finite-state process F is undecidable,*

– *the problem whether* $\overline{F} \sqsubseteq_s P$ *for a given (normed and deterministic) PA process* P
  is undecidable.

We have seen that simulation preorder is undecidable between deterministic PA processes and deterministic finite-state ones in both directions. However, simulation *equivalence* (as well as any other equivalence of the linear time/branching time spectrum of [19]) is *decidable* for such a pair of processes, because it coincides with bisimilarity which is known to be decidable [11]. Hence, it is interesting that simulation equivalence becomes *undecidable* as soon as we consider PA processes with just one nondeterministic state; this is proved in the following theorem:

Theorem 9. *There is a fixed normed deterministic finite-state process* F *s.t. the problem whether* $P =_s F$ *for a given normed PA process* P *is undecidable.*

Proof. We reduce the second undecidable problem of Theorem 6 to the problem if $P =_s F$. Let P' be a normed deterministic PA process, $\overline{F}$ be the fixed deterministic normed finite-state system derived from the finite control of the universal counter machine as in Theorem 6. We construct a normed PA process P and a fixed deterministic normed finite-state process F such that $P' \sqsubseteq_s \overline{F}$ iff $P =_s F$. It suffices to define F by $F \xrightarrow{a} \overline{F}$, and P by $P \xrightarrow{a} P'$, $P \xrightarrow{a} \overline{F}$. It follows immediately that $P =_s F$ iff $P' \sqsubseteq_s \overline{F}$. Note that P is not deterministic; however, it contains only one state (the initial state) where an action can be done in two different ways. □

On the other hand, simulation equivalence remains decidable between deterministic PA and *arbitrary* (possibly nondeterministic) finite-state systems. This is a consequence of a more general result—see the next section.

Remark 3. All undecidability results which have been proved in this section immediately extend to trace preorder and trace equivalence, because trace preorder and trace equivalence coincide with simulation preorder and simulation equivalence in the class of deterministic processes, respectively.

Now we prove that regularity w.r.t. simulation and trace equivalence is undecidable for normed PA processes with at least one nondeterministic state. It is interesting that regularity of normed deterministic PA processes w.r.t. any equivalence of the linear time/branching time spectrum of [19] is easily decidable in polynomial time, as it coincides with regularity w.r.t. bisimilarity which is known to have this property [13].

Theorem 10. *Regularity w.r.t. simulation equivalence and trace equivalence is undecidable for normed PA processes.*

5 The Relationship between Simulation and Bisimulation

In this section we concentrate on the relationship between simulation and bisimulation equivalence. It is a general trend that decidability results for bisimulation equivalence are positive, while the 'same' problems for simulation equivalence are undecidable. Major examples of that phenomenon come from the areas of equivalence-checking and regularity-testing (cf. the decidability issues for BPP and BPA processes which are summarized in the last section).

Theorem 11. *For every finitely branching transition systems T_1, T_2 there are finitely branching transition systems $\mathcal{B}(T_1), \mathcal{B}(T_2)$ such that $T_1 =_s \mathcal{B}(T_1)$, $T_2 =_s \mathcal{B}(T_2)$, and $\mathcal{B}(T_1), \mathcal{B}(T_2)$ are simulation equivalent iff they are bisimilar, i.e. $\mathcal{B}(T_1) =_s \mathcal{B}(T_2) \Leftrightarrow \mathcal{B}(T_1) \sim \mathcal{B}(T_2)$.*

Theorem 11 can be used as follows: if we are to decide simulation equivalence between T_1, T_2, we can try to construct $\mathcal{B}(T_1), \mathcal{B}(T_2)$ and decide bisimilarity between them. Similarly, regularity of T w.r.t. $=_s$ can be tested by constructing $\mathcal{B}(T)$ and checking its regularity w.r.t. $\sim$ (the construction of $\mathcal{B}(T)$ is not effective in general, of course).

As simulation preorder between finite-state processes is decidable, the system $\mathcal{B}(T)$ can be effectively constructed for any finite-state system T. Moreover, if T is deterministic then $\mathcal{B}(T) = T$. Thus, as a consequence of Theorem 11 we obtain:

Theorem 12. *Simulation equivalence is decidable between deterministic PA processes and (arbitrary) finite-state ones.*

Theorem 11 can also be applied in a nontrivial way. In a full version of our paper [15] we provide a little 'case-study'. We design a rich subclass of BPP processes where $\mathcal{B}(T)$ is effectively constructible; consequently, simulation equivalence as well as regularity w.r.t. simulation equivalence are decidable in this subclass.

6 Summary and Conclusions

The known decidability results in the area of equivalence/preorder checking between infinite-state processes and finite-state ones are summarized in the table below. The results which have been obtained in this paper are in boldface. In the case of trace preorder/equivalence/regularity we distinguish between deterministic infinite-state processes (left column) and general ones (right column); finite-state systems can be considered as deterministic here, because the subset construction [8] preserves trace equivalence.

	BPA		BPP		PA		PDA		PN	
$\sim$ FS	yes [6]		yes [5]		yes [11]		yes [18]		yes [12]	
reg. $\sim$	yes [3]		yes [10]		?		?		yes [10]	
$\sqsubseteq_s$ FS	**YES**		yes [12]		**NO**		**YES**		yes [12]	
FS $\sqsubseteq_s$	**YES**		yes [12]		**NO**		**YES**		yes [12]	
$=_s$ FS	**YES**		yes [12]		**NO**		**YES**		yes [12]	
reg. $=_s$	?		?		**NO**		?		no [12]	
$\sqsubseteq_t$ FS	yes	yes	yes [12]	yes [12]	**NO**	**NO**	yes	yes	yes [12]	yes [12]
FS $\sqsubseteq_t$	yes	no	yes [12]	yes [12]	**NO**	no	yes	no	yes [12]	yes [12]
$=_t$ FS	yes	no	yes [12]	yes [12]	yes [11]	no	yes	no	yes [12]	yes [12]
reg. $=_t$	yes	no	yes [10]	?	?	no	yes	no	yes [10]	no [12]

The results for trace preorder/equivalence might be also interesting from a point of view of automata theory (trace preorder and equivalence are closely related to language inclusion and equivalence, respectively). All 'trace' results for BPA and PDA are immediate consequences of the 'classical' ones for language equivalence (see [8]). It is interesting to compare those decidability issues with the ones for PA, especially in the deterministic subcase. Trace preorder with finite-state systems tends to be decidable for deterministic processes; the class PA is the only exception. At the same time, trace *equivalence* with finite-state systems is *decidable* for deterministic PA. The PA processes we used in our undecidability proofs are parallel compositions of two deterministic and normed BPA processes (which can be seen as deterministic CF grammars). The parallel composition corresponds to the *shuffle* operator on languages [8]. Thus, our results bring some new insight into the power of shuffle on (deterministic) CF languages.

Interesting open questions are left in the area of regularity-testing. We can conclude that all the '?' problems are at least semidecidable, as it is possible to enumerate all finite-state systems and decide equivalence with them.

References

1. P.A. Abdulla and K. Čerāns. Simulation is decidable for one-counter nets. In *Proceedings of CONCUR'98*, volume 1466 of *LNCS*, pages 253–268. Springer-Verlag, 1998.
2. J.C.M. Baeten and W.P. Weijland. *Process Algebra*. Number 18 in Cambridge Tracts in Theoretical Computer Science. Cambridge University Press, 1990.
3. O. Burkart, D. Caucal, and B. Steffen. Bisimulation collapse and the process taxonomy. In *Proceedings of CONCUR'96*, volume 1119 of *LNCS*, pages 247–262. Springer-Verlag, 1996.
4. D. Caucal. On the regular structure of prefix rewriting. *Theoretical Computer Science*, 106:61–86, 1992.
5. S. Christensen, Y. Hirshfeld, and F. Moller. Bisimulation is decidable for all basic parallel processes. In *Proceedings of CONCUR'93*, volume 715 of *LNCS*, pages 143–157. Springer-Verlag, 1993.
6. S. Christensen, H. Hüttel, and C. Stirling. Bisimulation equivalence is decidable for all context-free processes. *Information and Computation*, 121:143–148, 1995.
7. J.F. Groote and H. Hüttel. Undecidable equivalences for basic process algebra. *Information and Computation*, 115(2):353–371, 1994.
8. J.E. Hopcroft and J.D. Ullman. *Introduction to Automata Theory, Languages, and Computation*. Addison-Wesley, 1979.
9. H. Hüttel. Undecidable equivalences for basic parallel processes. In *Proceedings of TACS'94*, volume 789 of *LNCS*, pages 454–464. Springer-Verlag, 1994.
10. P. Jančar and J. Esparza. Deciding finiteness of Petri nets up to bisimilarity. In *Proceedings of ICALP'96*, volume 1099 of *LNCS*, pages 478–489. Springer-Verlag, 1996.
11. P. Jančar, A. Kučera, and R. Mayr. Deciding bisimulation-like equivalences with finite-state processes. In *Proceedings of ICALP'98*, volume 1443 of *LNCS*, pages 200–211. Springer-Verlag, 1998.
12. P. Jančar and F. Moller. Checking regular properties of Petri nets. In *Proceedings of CONCUR'95*, volume 962 of *LNCS*, pages 348–362. Springer-Verlag, 1995.
13. A. Kučera. Regularity is decidable for normed PA processes in polynomial time. In *Proceedings of FST&TCS'96*, volume 1180 of *LNCS*, pages 111–122. Springer-Verlag, 1996.
14. A. Kučera and R. Mayr. Weak bisimilarity with infinite-state systems can be decided in polynomial time. Technical report TUM-I9830, Institut für Informatik, TU-München, 1998.
15. A. Kučera and R. Mayr. Simulation preorder on simple process algebras. Technical report TUM-I9902, Institut für Informatik, TU-München, 1999.
16. R. Mayr. Process rewrite systems. *Information and Computation*. To appear.
17. M.L. Minsky. *Computation: Finite and Infinite Machines*. Prentice-Hall, 1967.
18. D.E. Muller and P.E. Schupp. The theory of ends, pushdown automata, and second order logic. *Theoretical Computer Science*, 37(1):51–75, 1985.
19. R.J. van Glabbeek. The linear time—branching time spectrum. In *Proceedings of CONCUR'90*, volume 458 of *LNCS*, pages 278–297. Springer-Verlag, 1990.

Solos in Concert

Cosimo Laneve[1] and Björn Victor[2]

[1] Dept. of Computer Science, University of Bologna, Italy.
[2] Dept. of Computer Systems, Uppsala University, Sweden.

Abstract. We present a calculus of mobile processes without prefix or summation, and using two different encodings we show that it can express both action prefix and guarded summation. One encoding gives a strong correspondence but uses a match operator; the other yields a slightly weaker correspondence but uses no additional operators.

1 Introduction

The fusion calculus was introduced by Parrow and Victor [15, 20, 16] as a simplification and extension of the π-calculus [6]. The simplification is easy to see: there is only one binding operator where π has two; input and output are completely symmetric which they are not in π; and it has only one sensible bisimulation congruence where π has three. The extension is that the effects of communication need not be local to the recipient process. Furthermore the fusion calculus contains the π-calculus as a proper subcalculus and thus inherits all its expressive power.

In recent years the *asynchronous* π-calculus [3, 5] has gained interest; here the asymmetry between input and output is further increased by dropping continuations from output prefixes. The resulting calculus has significant expressive power, and is also motivated by practical implementation in distributed systems.

In the fusion calculus it would be unfortunate to break the symmetry between input and output in order to develop an asynchronous subcalculus. Indeed, in this paper we show that continuations may be removed both from inputs and outputs – hereafter called *solos* – without loss of expressive power. More precisely, the *fusion calculus of solos*, where prefixes are replaced by solos and summation is removed, is expressive enough to encode prefixes and guarded summation.

We give two different encodings. One preserves strong barbed bisimulation but uses a match operator; the other yields weak barbed bisimulation but uses no additional operators. Both preserve divergence.

A key of our encodings in this paper is the use of *catalyst agents* of the type $(z)u\,zz$, which inputs the same name twice. If some agent in parallel composition with $(z)u\,zz$ sends any two names on u, they will be fused and made indistinguishable everywhere. In one of our encodings such a fusion effect enables an agent guarded by a match construction testing two names for equality; in the other it removes the restriction of a private communication channel, thereby enabling the communication. The fusion effect performed by the reduction relation of the fusion calculus plays a crucial role in these encodings – the same machinery cannot be used in the π-calculus.

Another important factor is that the calculus is polyadic: an input or output can carry arbitrarily many objects. In the strictly monadic calculus we strongly conjecture that the expressiveness of prefixes is strictly greater than that of solos.

Related work: Parrow shows in [13] that in the π-calculus without match, any agent can be encoded as a *concert of trios*, i.e., a parallel composition of possibly replicated prefixes $\alpha_1 . \alpha_2 . \alpha_3$ up to weak open equivalence [18]. He also shows that *duos*, i.e., prefixes nested to depth 2, are not sufficient. In this paper we show that for the fusion calculus, it suffices with *solos*, i.e., we do not need prefixes at all.

Nestmann and Pierce show in [10] that input-guarded choice $\sum_i u_i(\widetilde{x}_i) . P_i$ can be encoded in the asynchronous π-calculus without choice, up to coupled bisimulation [14], and in [9] Nestmann gives encodings of separate and mixed guarded choice. While these encodings involve increasingly complex communication protocols, our encodings of separate choice are simpler and work up to stronger equivalences.

In [11] Palamidessi shows that there can not exist an encoding of mixed choice into the asynchronous π-calculus which is *uniform* and preserves a *reasonable* semantics. A *uniform* encoding is compositional, meaning that $[\![P \mid Q]\!] = [\![P]\!] \mid [\![Q]\!]$, and respects injective renaming of free names. A *reasonable* semantics distinguishes two processes P and Q if the actions in some computation of P are different from those in any computation of Q; in particular it is sensitive to divergence. Nestmann [9] argues that these criteria are too strong for practical purposes, and that by allowing a top-level context (but keeping the inner encoding compositional), or relaxing reasonableness, many practically motivated encodings turn out to be "good". Indeed even more theoretically motivated encodings often use top-level contexts, including our second encoding in this paper; our first encoding does not need this, but is in fact uniform and reasonable in Palamidessi's sense.

Yoshida in [21] presents separation results between subcalculi of the asynchronous π-calculus (without match and choice) by means of concurrent combinators, and shows the non-existence of encodings between such subcalculi. Here a concept of *standard encoding* is used, which means that the encoding is homomorphic, respects injective substitutions, and preserves weak observations and reductions. In addition to this the encodings are required to be *message-preserving*, i.e., $[\![\overline{u}\,x]\!] \approx \overline{u}\,x$. While our first encoding is standard by this definition, neither one is message-preserving. Yoshida works with monadic calculi, where the requirement may be quite sensible, but in a polyadic setting this requirement seems very strong, especially when only considering encoded contexts. Yoshida also proves that the *reflexive π-calculus*, a variant of the π-calculus similar to the monadic fusion calculus of solos, does not contain a synchronizer agent such as $a(x) . b(y) . \overline{c}\,y$, and is therefore less expressive than the monadic asynchronous π-calculus. In this paper we show that in the polyadic fusion calculus of solos such an agent can indeed be encoded, although our encodings are not message-preserving, but rather adds a "protocol header" to the data being sent and received.

Acknowledgement: We thank Uwe Nestmann and Joachim Parrow for valuable comments and remarks.

2 The Fusion Calculus of Solos

In this section we first present a subcalculus of the fusion calculus where we use *solos* of the form $u\,\widetilde{x}$ in place of general prefixes of the form $u\,\widetilde{x}\,.\,P$, and leave out summation. We present the syntax and semantics, review the barbed equivalences and congruences, and introduce a barbed expansion preorder.

2.1 Syntax and Semantics

We assume an infinite set $\mathcal{N}$ of *names* ranged over by $u, v, \ldots, z$. Names represent communication channels, which are also the values transmitted. We write $\widetilde{x}$ for a (possibly empty) finite sequence $x_1 \cdots x_n$ of names.

Definition 1. *The* solos, *ranged over by* α, *and the* agents, *ranged over by* $P, Q, \ldots$, *are defined by*

$$
\begin{array}{llcll}
\alpha ::= u\,\widetilde{x} & \text{(Input)} & \qquad P ::= \mathbf{0} & \text{(Inaction)} \\
 \overline{u}\,\widetilde{x} & \text{(Output)} & \qquad \alpha & \text{(Solo)} \\
& & \qquad Q \mid R & \text{(Composition)} \\
& & \qquad (x)Q & \text{(Scope)} \\
& & \qquad [x = y]Q & \text{(Match)}
\end{array}
$$

In solos, the names $\widetilde{x}$ are the *objects* of the solo, and the name u is the *subject*. We write a to stand for either u or $\overline{u}$, thus $a\widetilde{x}$ is the general form of a solo.

A Composition allows two solos to interact. The Scope $(x)Q$ limits the scope of x to Q; the name x is said to be *bound* in $(x)P$. We write $(\widetilde{x})P$ for $(x_1) \cdots (x_n)P$, $n \geq 0$. The *free names* in P, denoted fn(P), are the names in P with a non-bound occurrence. As usual we will not distinguish between alpha-variants of agents, i.e., agents differing only in the choice of bound names.

A Match $[x = y]Q$ acts like Q if x and y are the same name. We use M, N to stand for a match operator, and write "match sequence" for a sequence of match operators, ranged over by $\widetilde{M}, \widetilde{N}$. We also write $\widetilde{M} \Leftrightarrow \widetilde{N}$ if the conjunction of all matches in $\widetilde{M}$ logically implies all elements in $\widetilde{N}$ and vice versa. We write n(M) for the names occurring in M.

2.2 Semantics

In the style of the Chemical Abstract Machine [1], we now define a structural congruence which equates all agents we will never want to distinguish for any semantic reason, and then use this when giving the operational semantics.

Definition 2. *The structural congruence,* $\equiv$, *between agents is the least congruence satisfying the abelian monoid laws for Composition (associativity, commutativity and* $\mathbf{0}$ *as identity), and the scope laws*

$$(x)0 \equiv 0, \quad (x)(y)P \equiv (y)(x)P, \quad [x = x]P \equiv P$$
$$(x)MP \equiv M(x)P, \quad \text{if } x \notin \mathrm{n}(M)$$
$$P \mid (z)Q \equiv (z)(P \mid Q), \quad \text{if } z \notin \mathrm{fn}(P)$$

We write $\{\widetilde{x} = \widetilde{y}\}$ for the smallest total equivalence relation on $\mathcal{N}$ relating each x_i with y_i, and say that a substitution σ *agrees with* the equivalence φ if $\forall x, y : x \varphi y \Leftrightarrow \sigma(x) = \sigma(y)$.

The reduction relation of the fusion calculus is the least relation satisfying the rules in Table 1, where structurally equivalent agents are considered the same. Here and in the following we use $\mathrm{dom}(\sigma) = \{u : \sigma(u) \neq u\}$ and $\mathrm{ran}(\sigma) = \{\sigma(u) : \sigma(u) \neq u\}$.

$$(\widetilde{z})\left(\widetilde{M u\,\widetilde{x}} \mid \widetilde{N \bar{u}\,\widetilde{y}} \mid R \right) \longrightarrow R\sigma$$

$$\text{if } |\widetilde{x}| = |\widetilde{y}|, \widetilde{M} \Leftrightarrow \widetilde{N} \Leftrightarrow \text{true},$$
$$\sigma \text{ agrees with } \{\widetilde{x} = \widetilde{y}\}, \mathrm{ran}(\sigma) \cap \widetilde{z} = \emptyset,$$
$$\text{and } \mathrm{dom}(\sigma) = \widetilde{z}$$

$$\frac{P \longrightarrow P'}{P \mid Q \longrightarrow P' \mid Q} \qquad \frac{P \longrightarrow P'}{(x)P \longrightarrow (x)P'}$$

$$\frac{P \equiv Q \quad Q \longrightarrow Q' \quad Q' \equiv P'}{P \longrightarrow P'}$$

Table 1. Reduction rules for the fusion calculus of solos.

For examples and motivations we refer the reader to [15, 20, 16].

2.3 Equivalence and Preorder

We will use the standard idea of *barbed bisimulation* developed by Milner and Sangiorgi [7] in the setting of CCS, further investigated in a π-calculus setting by Sangiorgi [17], and later used in many other calculi as an intuitive observational equivalence. The idea is that two agents are considered equivalent if their reductions match and they are indistinguishable under global observations.

Definition 3. *The observation relation is the least relation satisfying the rules below.*

$$x\,\widetilde{y} \downarrow x \qquad\qquad [x = x]P \downarrow y \text{ if } P \downarrow y$$
$$\bar{x}\,\widetilde{y} \downarrow x \qquad\qquad (P \mid Q) \downarrow x \quad \text{if } P \downarrow x \text{ or } Q \downarrow x$$
$$\qquad\qquad\qquad (x)P \downarrow y \quad\; \text{if } P \downarrow y \text{ and } x \neq y$$

Definition 4. *A strong barbed bisimulation is a symmetric binary relation S between agents such that $P\,S\,Q$ implies:*

1. *If $P \longrightarrow P'$ then $Q \longrightarrow Q'$ and $P'\,S\,Q'$.*
2. *If $P \downarrow x$ for some x, then $Q \downarrow x$.*

P is strong barbed bisimilar to Q, written $P \overset{.}{\sim} Q$, if $P \, S \, Q$ for some strong barbed bisimulation S.

To define the weak barbed bisimulation and congruence, we change $Q \longrightarrow Q'$ to $Q \longrightarrow^* Q'$ and $Q \downarrow x$ to $Q \longrightarrow^* \downarrow x$ (written $Q \Downarrow x$) in Definition 4.

Definition 5. *A weak barbed bisimulation is a symmetric binary relation S between agents such that $P \, S \, Q$ implies:*

1. *If $P \longrightarrow P'$ then $Q \longrightarrow^* Q'$ and $P' \, S \, Q'$.*
2. *If $P \downarrow x$ for some x, then $Q \Downarrow x$.*

P is weak barbed bisimilar to Q, written $P \overset{.}{\approx} Q$, if $P \, S \, Q$ for some weak barbed bisimulation S.

We will also make use of an expansion relation [8], an asymmetric form of weak barbed bisimulation where $P \lesssim Q$ means that $P \overset{.}{\approx} Q$ in a way such that P does no more reductions than Q. In the following we write $P \overset{\frown}{\longrightarrow} P'$ if $P \longrightarrow P'$ or $P \equiv P'$.

Definition 6. *A weak barbed expansion is a binary relation S between agents such that $P \, S \, Q$ implies:*

1. *If $P \longrightarrow P'$ then $Q \longrightarrow^+ Q'$ and $P' \, S \, Q'$.*
2. *If $Q \longrightarrow Q'$ then $P \overset{\frown}{\longrightarrow} P'$ and $P' \, S \, Q'$.*
3. *If $P \downarrow x$ for some x then $Q \Downarrow x$.*
4. *If $Q \downarrow x$ for some x then $P \downarrow x$.*

Q expands P, written $P \lesssim Q$, if $P \, S \, Q$ for some weak barbed expansion S. We often write $Q \gtrsim P$ instead of $P \lesssim Q$.

3   Encodings of Prefixes

In this section and the following we display the expressiveness of the fusion calculus of solos by means of encodings. We first encode the general prefix operator of the fusion calculus using solos. Two such encodings are presented: one using match operators, resulting in a strong operational correspondence with the encoded terms; and one using only solos, scope and parallel composition, yielding a weaker correspondence.

We now add the prefix operator to the calculus by allowing processes of the form $\alpha . P$. We add two observation rules:

$$x\,\widetilde{y}.P \downarrow x \qquad\qquad \overline{x}\,\widetilde{y}.P \downarrow x$$

and the following reduction rule:

$$(\widetilde{z})\big(\widetilde{M}u\,\widetilde{x}.P \mid \widetilde{N}\overline{u}\,\widetilde{y}.Q \mid R\big) \longrightarrow (P \mid Q \mid R)\sigma$$

if $|\widetilde{x}| = |\widetilde{y}|$, $\widetilde{M} \Leftrightarrow \widetilde{N} \Leftrightarrow \mathsf{true}$, σ agrees with $\{\widetilde{x} = \widetilde{y}\}$, $\mathrm{ran}(\sigma) \cap \widetilde{z} = \emptyset$ and $\mathrm{dom}(\sigma) = \widetilde{z}$. We call the resulting calculus the *fusion calculus with prefix*, f_{pre}. In this calculus we regard a solo $a\widetilde{x}$ as shorthand for the prefix $a\widetilde{x} . 0$.

$$[\![u\,\widetilde{x}\,.\,P]\!] \stackrel{def}{=} (zw)(u\,\widetilde{x}zww \mid [z=w][\![P]\!])$$

$$[\![\overline{u}\,\widetilde{x}\,.\,P]\!] \stackrel{def}{=} (zw)(\overline{u}\,\widetilde{x}wwz \mid [z=w][\![P]\!])$$

$$[\![[x=y]P]\!] \stackrel{def}{=} [x=y][\![P]\!]$$

$$[\![P \mid Q]\!] \stackrel{def}{=} [\![P]\!] \mid [\![Q]\!]$$

$$[\![(x)P]\!] \stackrel{def}{=} (x)[\![P]\!]$$

Table 2. Encoding of prefixes using match. z and w are fresh.

3.1 Encoding using Match

The encoding of prefixes using match, shown in Table 2, utilizes the fusion power of two interacting solos. The encoding of an input prefix $u\,\widetilde{x}\,.\,P$ creates two fresh names z and w. The continuation P of the prefix is guarded by a match operator checking for equality between z and w; being fresh, these are initially different from each other, so P cannot reduce. The input prefix action $u\,\widetilde{x}$ is encoded by a solo with the same subject and polarity, but with three additional objects zww appended to $\widetilde{x}$. An output prefix $\overline{u}\,\widetilde{y}\,.\,Q$ is encoded symmetrically, but with the order of the additional objects changed to wwz. When such input and output solos interact, the result is a fusion of the names z and w on each side of the interaction, thus triggering the continuations P and Q. Increasing polyadicity of names to encode the temporal ordering of prefixes was also used by Parrow in [12].

To get acquainted with the encoding of Table 2 we detail the interactions of the encoding of two parallel agents:

$$
\begin{aligned}
&[\![(x)(u\,x\,.\,P \mid \overline{u}\,y\,.\,Q)]\!] \\
&\stackrel{def}{=} (x)(\ (zw)(u\,xzww \mid [z=w][\![P]\!]) \\
&\qquad\qquad \mid (zw)(\overline{u}\,ywwz \mid [z=w][\![Q]\!])) \\
&\equiv (xz_1z_2w_1w_2)(\ u\,xz_1w_1w_1 \mid [z_1=w_1][\![P]\!] \\
&\qquad\qquad\qquad \mid \overline{u}\,yw_2w_2z_2 \mid [z_2=w_2][\![Q]\!]) \\
&\longrightarrow (z_1)(([z_1=w_1][\![P]\!] \mid [z_2=w_2][\![Q]\!])\{y/x, z_1/w_1, z_1/w_2, z_1/z_2\}) \\
&\equiv ([\![P \mid Q]\!])\{y/x\} \\
&= [\![(P \mid Q)\{y/x\}]\!]
\end{aligned}
$$

which corresponds exactly to the result of the encoded prefix agents interacting.

This operational correspondence is formalized in the following lemmas:

Lemma 7. *For P an agent of f_{pre},*

1. *if $P \equiv P'$ then $[\![P]\!] \equiv [\![P']\!]$;*
2. *if $P \longrightarrow P'$ then $[\![P]\!] \longrightarrow [\![P']\!]$;*
3. *if $P \downarrow x$ then $[\![P]\!] \downarrow x$.*

Lemma 8. *For P an agent of f_{pre},*

1. *if $[\![P]\!] \longrightarrow Q$, then $P \longrightarrow P'$ such that $Q \equiv [\![P']\!]$;*

2. *if $[\![P]\!] \downarrow x$ for some x, then $P \downarrow x$.*

We have full abstraction up to barbed bisimulation:

Theorem 9. *For P, Q two agents of f_{pre}, $P \stackrel{.}{\sim} Q$ iff $[\![P]\!] \stackrel{.}{\sim} [\![Q]\!]$.*

Proof. By Lemmas 7 and 8, showing that $\{([\![P]\!], [\![Q]\!]) : P \stackrel{.}{\sim} Q\}$ and $\{(P, Q) : [\![P]\!] \stackrel{.}{\sim} [\![Q]\!]\}$ are barbed bisimulations.

3.2 Encoding without Match

While the encoding above has very pleasant properties, it may for reasons of minimality be desirable to cope without the match operator. A new encoding is presented in Table 3.

$$
\begin{aligned}
U_v &\equiv (z)v\,zzv \\
[\![u\,\widetilde{x}\,.\,P]\!]_v &\stackrel{def}{=} (wv')(w\,\widetilde{x}vv' \mid [\![P]\!]_{v'} \mid (y)(\overline{v}\,uwy \mid U_y)) \\
[\![\overline{u}\,\widetilde{x}\,.\,P]\!]_v &\stackrel{def}{=} (wv')(\overline{w}\,\widetilde{x}v'v \mid [\![P]\!]_{v'} \mid (y)(\overline{v}\,uwy \mid U_y)) \\
[\![[x = y]P]\!]_v &\stackrel{def}{=} [x = y][\![P]\!]_v \\
[\![(x)P]\!]_v &\stackrel{def}{=} (x)[\![P]\!]_v \\
[\![P \mid Q]\!]_v &\stackrel{def}{=} [\![P]\!]_v \mid [\![Q]\!]_v \\[4pt]
(\![P]\!) &\stackrel{def}{=} (v)([\![P]\!]_v \mid U_v)
\end{aligned}
$$

Table 3. Encoding of prefixes without using match. v, w and v' are fresh.

In Table 2 the subject of a prefix is encoded through a solo with the same subject. In Table 3 the subject of a prefix is instead encoded by a fresh scoped name w. Consequently it has no reactions. Instead the whole encoding has a parameter v, and an interaction over this parameter can fuse the fresh name to the original subject, removing the scope of w and eventually enabling a reaction. In order to achieve this we introduce *catalyst agents* $U_v \equiv (z)v\,zzv$ and we add an initial catalyst in the top level encoding $(\![\cdot]\!)$.

An example illustrating the encoding follows:

$$(\![(x)(u\,x\,.\,P \mid \overline{u}\,y\,.\,Q)]\!)$$

$$\stackrel{def}{=} (vx)\big(\ (wv')(w\,xvv' \mid [\![P]\!]_{v'} \mid (y)(\overline{v}\,uwy \mid U_y)) \tag{1}$$
$$\mid (wv')(\overline{w}\,yv'v \mid [\![Q]\!]_{v'} \mid (y)(\overline{v}\,uwy \mid U_y))$$
$$\mid (z)v\,zzv\big)$$

$$\longrightarrow (vxwv_1'v_2')\big(\ u\,xvv_1' \mid [\![P]\!]_{v_1'} \mid (z)v\,zzv \tag{2}$$
$$\mid \overline{w}\,yv_2'v \mid [\![Q]\!]_{v_2'} \mid (y)(\overline{v}\,uwy \mid U_y)\big)$$

$$\longrightarrow (vxv_1'v_2')(u\,xvv_1' \mid [\![P]\!]_{v_1'} \mid \overline{u}\,yv_2'v \mid [\![Q]\!]_{v_2'} \mid U_v) \tag{3}$$

$$\longrightarrow (v)([\![P]\!]_v \mid [\![Q]\!]_v \mid U_v)\{y/x\}$$

$$\stackrel{def}{=} (v)(\llbracket P \mid Q \rrbracket_v \{y/x\} \mid U_v)$$
$$= \llbracket (P \mid Q)\{y/x\} \rrbracket \tag{4}$$

Initially the solos corresponding to the prefix actions can not interact, since their subjects are locally scoped. Expanding the definitions we can see at (1) that the catalyst $(z)v\,zzv$ can interact with one of the terms $\overline{v}\,uwy$, thereby changing the subject of the prefix solo, removing the scope. The initial catalyst is consumed when it interacts with the term $\overline{v}\,uwy$, but this interaction also changes the subterm U_y into a new catalyst U_v. This can be used at (2) to remove the scope of the other prefix solo, enabling the interaction between the two prefixes at (3) and producing another new catalyst. Observe that as a side effect of this latter interaction, the continuations $\llbracket P \rrbracket_{v_1'}$ and $\llbracket Q \rrbracket_{v_2'}$ are now enabled since v_1' and v_2' are fused with v. We end up with the desired result (4).

The operational and observational correspondences of the encoding are expressed by the following lemmas.

Lemma 10. *For P an agent of f_{pre},*

1. *$P \equiv Q$ implies $\llbracket P \rrbracket \equiv \llbracket Q \rrbracket$;*
2. *$P \longrightarrow Q$ implies $\llbracket P \rrbracket \longrightarrow^+ \llbracket Q \rrbracket$;*
3. *$P \downarrow x$ implies $\llbracket P \rrbracket \Downarrow x$.*

Lemma 11. *For P an agent of f_{pre},*

1. *if $\llbracket P \rrbracket \longrightarrow Q$, then $P \stackrel{\frown}{\longrightarrow} P'$ such that $Q \gtrsim \llbracket P' \rrbracket$;*
2. *if $\llbracket P \rrbracket \longrightarrow^* Q$, then $P \longrightarrow^* P'$ such that $Q \gtrsim \llbracket P' \rrbracket$;*
3. *if $\llbracket P \rrbracket \stackrel{\frown}{\longrightarrow} \downarrow x$ for some x, then $P \downarrow x$;*
4. *if $\llbracket P \rrbracket \Downarrow x$ for some x, then $P \Downarrow x$.*

Proof. 1. By induction on the depth of the derivation.
2. By induction on the number of reductions in the left hand side, using (1).
3. By induction on the depth of the derivation.
4. By induction on the number of reductions in the left hand side, using (3).

The results of the previous encoding are weakened because of the weaker form of operational correspondence.

Theorem 12. *For P, Q two agents of f_{pre}, $P \stackrel{\cdot}{\approx} Q$ iff $\llbracket P \rrbracket \stackrel{\cdot}{\approx} \llbracket Q \rrbracket$.*

Proof. Using the fact that $\{(P, Q) : P \gtrsim \stackrel{\cdot}{\approx} \lesssim Q\}$ and $\{(P, Q) : P \lesssim \stackrel{\cdot}{\approx} \gtrsim Q\}$ are both weak barbed bisimulations, it is easy to show that $\{(\llbracket P \rrbracket, \llbracket Q \rrbracket) : P \stackrel{\cdot}{\approx} Q\}$ and $\{(P, Q) : \llbracket P \rrbracket \stackrel{\cdot}{\approx} \llbracket Q \rrbracket\}$ are weak barbed bisimulations. We then use Lemmas 10 and 11 to complete the proof.

3.3 Replication and Recursion

We can add replication to the f_{pre} calculus by the structural law $!P \equiv P \mid !P$. Extending our first encoding using match (Table 2) with $[\![!P]\!] = ![\![P]\!]$, Lemmas 7, 8 and Theorem 9 still hold. We can further strengthen these results by proving preservation of divergence properties.

Theorem 13. *For P an agent of f_{pre} with replication, P diverges iff $[\![P]\!]$ diverges.*

Extending the second encoding (Table 3) in the same way does not preserve divergence, since $[\![!u\,.\,\mathbf{0}]\!]$ could reduce indefinitely even though the original term can not reduce. However, if we replace replication with guarded recursion, introduced by the structural law $A(\widetilde{y}) \equiv P\{\widetilde{y}/\widetilde{x}\}$ if $A(\widetilde{x}) \stackrel{def}{=} P$ and $|\widetilde{x}| = |\widetilde{y}|$, and the requirement that process variables only occur under a prefix, then Lemmas 10 and 11 and Theorem 12 still hold, and furthermore:

Theorem 14. *For P an agent of f_{pre} with guarded recursion, P diverges iff $(\!(P)\!)$ diverges.*

3.4 Other translations

There is a simpler translation which requires that channels carry just one message more instead of two, with the added cost of a further book-keeping interaction for every original interaction. We only show the translation rules for prefixes since the others are the same:

$$[\![u\,\widetilde{x}\,.\,P]\!]_v \stackrel{def}{=} (wz)(w\,\widetilde{x}z \mid (v')(z\,v'v \mid [\![P]\!]_{v'}) \mid (y)(\overline{v}\,uwy \mid U_y))$$
$$[\![\overline{u}\,\widetilde{x}\,.\,P]\!]_v \stackrel{def}{=} (wz)(\overline{w}\,\widetilde{x}z \mid (v')(\overline{z}\,vv' \mid [\![P]\!]_{v'}) \mid (y)(\overline{v}\,uwy \mid U_y))$$

Once replication has been added, we can also get rid of the catalyst agents inside the encodings of prefixes of $[\![\,\cdot\,]\!]_v$. Instead we use a replicated catalyst at top level. Catalysts now need only two objects:

$$[\![u\,\widetilde{x}\,.\,P]\!]_v \stackrel{def}{=} (wv')(w\,\widetilde{x}vv' \mid [\![P]\!]_{v'} \mid \overline{v}\,uw)$$
$$[\![\overline{u}\,\widetilde{x}\,.\,P]\!]_v \stackrel{def}{=} (wv')(\overline{w}\,\widetilde{x}v'v \mid [\![P]\!]_{v'} \mid \overline{v}\,uw)$$
$$(\!(P)\!) \stackrel{def}{=} (v)([\![P]\!]_v \mid !\,(z)v\,zz)$$

We can also get rid of the initial book-keeping reductions that enable unguarded prefixes in the encoding of Table 3, as well as the initial catalyst agent of $(\!(\cdot)\!)$, by considering the following auxiliary function (again we only illustrate the rules for prefixes):

$$(\!(u\,\widetilde{x}\,.\,P)\!) \stackrel{def}{=} (z)(u\,\widetilde{x}z \mid (vv')(z\,vv' \mid [\![P]\!]_{v'} \mid v\,zzv))$$
$$(\!(\overline{u}\,\widetilde{x}\,.\,P)\!) \stackrel{def}{=} (z)(\overline{u}\,\widetilde{x}z \mid (v)(\overline{z}\,vv \mid [\![P]\!]_v))$$

4 Encoding Choice

In this section we present encodings of the choice operator; $P + Q$ allows P or Q to take part in reduction, and discards the other branch when doing so. Here we add the mismatch operator $[x \neq y]P$, which can act like P if x and y are different. We extend the ranges of $M, N, \widetilde{M}$ and $\widetilde{N}$ and the definition of $\widetilde{M} \Leftrightarrow \widetilde{N}$ appropriately, add the reduction rule

$$\frac{P \longrightarrow P', \; x \neq y}{[x \neq y]P \longrightarrow P'}$$

and the observation rule $[x \neq z]P \downarrow y$ if $P \downarrow y$ and $x \neq z$. We also extend our previous encodings homomorphically for the mismatch operator.

Restricting the general choice operator $P + Q$ to guarded choice, $\sum_I \alpha_i . P_i$, and further requiring that all α_i in a guarded choice have the same polarity (all inputs or all outputs), we can extend the encoding of Table 2 by replacing the encoding of prefixes by the following, where z and w are fresh:

$$\left[\!\!\left[\sum_I u_i \, \tilde{x}_i . P_i \right]\!\!\right] \stackrel{def}{=} (zw) \prod_I [z \neq w](u_i \, \tilde{x}_i zww \mid [z = w][\![P_i]\!])$$

$$\left[\!\!\left[\sum_I \overline{u_i} \, \tilde{x}_i . P_i \right]\!\!\right] \stackrel{def}{=} (zw) \prod_I [z \neq w](\overline{u_i} \, \tilde{x}_i wwz \mid [z = w][\![P_i]\!])$$

The mismatch operator is used in a "test-and-set" construction which tests two names z and w for inequality, and if they are not equal, atomically makes them so. Only one branch of the choice can succeed in doing this. The interaction between an input and an output prefix now not only enables the continuations of the prefixes, but also *disables* the other branches of the choice.

Lemmas 7, 8 and Theorems 9 and 13 still hold for this extended encoding (Lemma 7(2) and 8(1) respectively weakened from $\longrightarrow$ and $\equiv$ to $\longrightarrow \dot{\sim}$ and $\dot{\sim}$ in their consequences).

The encoding of Table 3 can also be extended in a similar way, replacing the encodings of prefixes (v and v' are fresh):

$$\left[\!\!\left[\sum_I u_i \, \tilde{x}_i . P_i \right]\!\!\right]_v \stackrel{def}{=} (v') \prod_I [v \neq v'](w)(w \, \tilde{x}_i vv' \mid [\![P_i]\!]_{v'} \mid (y)(\overline{v} \, u_i wy \mid U_y))$$

$$\left[\!\!\left[\sum_I \overline{u_i} \, \tilde{x}_i . P_i \right]\!\!\right]_v \stackrel{def}{=} (v') \prod_I [v \neq v'](w)(\overline{w} \, \tilde{x}_i v'v \mid [\![P_i]\!]_{v'} \mid (y)(\overline{v} \, u_i wy \mid U_y))$$

Lemmas 10 and 11 and Theorem 12 as well as Theorem 14 hold also for this encoding (Lemma 10(2) weakened from $\longrightarrow$ to $\longrightarrow \dot{\approx}$ in the consequence).

References

[1] G. Berry and G. Boudol. The chemical abstract machine. *Theoretical Computer Science*, 96:217–248, 1992.

[2] M. Boreale. On the expressiveness of internal mobility in name-passing calculi. *Theoretical Computer Science*, 195(2):205–226, 1998.

[3] G. Boudol. Asynchrony and the π-calculus (note). Rapport de Recherche 1702, INRIA Sophia-Antipolis, May 1992.

[4] R. Cleaveland, editor. *Proc. of CONCUR '92*, volume 630 of *LNCS*. Springer, 1992.

[5] K. Honda and M. Tokoro. On asynchronous communication semantics. In M. Tokoro, O. Nierstrasz, and P. Wegner, editors, *Object-Based Concurrent Computing 1991*, volume 612 of *LNCS*, pages 21–51. Springer, 1992.

[6] R. Milner, J. Parrow, and D. Walker. A calculus of mobile processes, part I/II. *Journal of Information and Computation*, 100:1–77, Sept. 1992.

[7] R. Milner and D. Sangiorgi. Barbed bisimulation. In W. Kuich, editor, *Proc. of ICALP '92*, volume 623 of *LNCS*, pages 685–695. Springer, 1992.

[8] R. Milner and D. Sangiorgi. The problem of "weak bisimulation up-to". In Cleaveland [4].

[9] U. Nestmann. What is a 'good' encoding of guarded choice? In C. Palamidessi and J. Parrow, editors, *Proc. of EXPRESS '97*, volume 7 of *ENTCS*. Elsevier Science Publishers, 1997. Revised version accepted (1998) for *Journal of Information and Computation*.

[10] U. Nestmann and B. C. Pierce. Decoding choice encodings. In U. Montanari and V. Sassone, editors, *Proc. of CONCUR '96*, volume 1119 of *LNCS*, pages 179–194. Springer, 1996.

[11] C. Palamidessi. Comparing the expressive power of the synchronous and the asynchronous π-calculus. In *Proc. of POPL '97*, pages 256–265. ACM, Jan. 1997.

[12] J. Parrow. Interaction diagrams. *Nordic Journal of Computing*, 2:407–443, 1995.

[13] J. Parrow. Trios in concert. In G. Plotkin, C. Stirling, and M. Tofte, editors, *Proof, Language and Interaction: Essays in Honour of Robin Milner*, 1998. To appear.

[14] J. Parrow and P. Sjödin. Multiway synchronization verified with coupled bisimulation. In Cleaveland [4], pages 518–533.

[15] J. Parrow and B. Victor. The fusion calculus: Expressiveness and symmetry in mobile processes. In *Proc. of LICS '98*, 1998.

[16] J. Parrow and B. Victor. The tau-laws of fusion. In Sangiorgi and de Simone [19], pages 99–114.

[17] D. Sangiorgi. *Expressing Mobility in Process Algebras: First-Order and Higher-Order Paradigms*. PhD thesis, LFCS, University of Edinburgh, 1993.

[18] D. Sangiorgi. A theory of bisimulation for the π-calculus. *Acta Informatica*, 33:69–97, 1996.

[19] D. Sangiorgi and R. de Simone, editors. *Proc. of CONCUR '98*, volume 1466 of *LNCS*. Springer, Sept. 1998.

[20] B. Victor and J. Parrow. Concurrent constraints in the fusion calculus. In K. G. Larsen, S. Skyum, and G. Winskel, editors, *Proc. of ICALP '98*, volume 1443 of *LNCS*, pages 455–469. Springer, July 1998.

[21] N. Yoshida. Minimality and separation results on asynchronous mobile processes: Representability theorem by concurrent combinators. Technical Report 5/98, School of Cognitive and Computing Sciences, University of Sussex, UK, Sept. 1998. An extended abstract appeared in *Proc. of CONCUR'98*, LNCS 1466.

Shortest Anisotropic Paths on Terrains *

Mark Lanthier, Anil Maheshwari,
Jörg-Rüdiger Sack

School of Computer Science, Carleton University,
Ottawa, Ontario K1S5B6, Canada

Abstract. We discuss the problem of computing shortest an-isotropic paths on terrains. Anisotropic path costs take into account the length of the path traveled, possibly weighted, and the direction of travel along the faces of the terrain. Considering faces to be weighted has added realism to the study of (pure) Euclidean shortest paths. Parameters such as the varied nature of the terrain, friction, or slope of each face, can be captured via face weights. Anisotropic paths add further realism by taking into consideration the direction of travel on each face thereby e.g., eliminating paths that are too steep for vehicles to travel and preventing the vehicles from turning over. Prior to this work an $O(n^n)$ time algorithm had been presented for computing anisotropic paths. Here we present the first polynomial time approximation algorithm for computing shortest anisotropic paths. Our algorithm is simple to implement and allows for the computation of shortest anisotropic paths within a desired accuracy. Our result addresses the corresponding problem posed in [12].
Keywords: *computational geometry, shortest path, approximation, aniosotropic paths.*

1   Introduction

1.1   Motivation

Shortest path problems arise in many application areas like geographical information systems[5] and robotics. They are among the fundamental problems in computational geometry and other areas such as graph algorithms. In these areas objects are often modeled via terrains. A *terrain* is a set of points and edges (connecting them) whose projection onto the xy-plane forms a triangulation.

A large body of work has centered around the computation of Euclidean shortest paths (we refer the reader to the survey in [9]). For terrains, Sharir and Schorr presented an algorithm for computing Euclidean shortest paths [11] and now we know of a number of different algorithms (see cf. [2, 6, 9]). *Weighted shortest paths* (introduced by [8]) provide more realism in that they can incorporate terrain attributes such as variable costs for different regions. This allows one to take into consideration e.g. that the cost of traveling through water, sand, or on

---

* Research supported in part by NSERC. Proofs will be provided in full version.
[5] We encountered several shortest path related problems in our R&D on GIS (see [13])

a highway is typically different. The NP-hardness and the large time complexities of 3-d shortest paths algorithms even for special problem instances have motivated the search for approximate solutions to the shortest path problem. For weighted shortest path approximations on planar subdivisions or polyhedra, more recently, several algorithms have been proposed [1, 2, 6, 7].

In the model introduced by [8], the direction of travel along a face is not captured. The direction of travel plays an important role in determining the physical effects incurred on a vehicle (e.g., car, truck, robot, or even person) traveling along a terrain surface. Through *anisotropism*, we can identify certain directions of travel that represent inclines that are too steep to ascend or unsafe to travel due to possible dangers such as overturning, sliding or wheel slippage. It is for these reasons that we investigate *anisotropic* paths, i.e., paths that take into account the direction of travel as well as length and other physical properties. The model was introduced by Rowe and Ross [10] and it subsumes all previously published criteria for traversal for isotropic weighted region terrain. They present an algorithm which runs in $O(n^n)$ time in the worst case for an n-vertex terrain. The high time complexity of this algorithm motivates the study of approximation algorithms for anisotropic shortest path problems. Refer to [9, 10] for applications, further pointers and discussion on regular grid based heuristics for these problems.

The quality of an approximate solution is assessed in comparison to the correct solution. One particular class of approximation algorithms produces ϵ-approximations of the shortest path. Since mostly the geographic models are approximations of reality anyway and high-quality paths are favored over optimal paths that are "hard" to compute, approximation algorithms are suitable and necessary. In ϵ-approximation algorithms accuracy, arbitrarily high, can be traded off against run-time. Such algorithms are appealing and are thus well studied, in particular, from a theoretical view-point. In this paper we address the problem of computing an ϵ-approximation $\Pi'(s,t)$ to a shortest anisotropic path $\Pi(s,t)$ for a point vehicle between two points, s and t, on a terrain $\mathcal{P}$ with n faces, where $\frac{\|\Pi'(s,t)\|}{\|\Pi(s,t)\|} < 1 + \epsilon$, for any given $\epsilon > 0$.

1.2 Preliminaries

Our algorithm is designed for the model developed by Rowe and Ross [10]. The model allows two main forces to act against the propulsion of the vehicle, namely friction and gravity. The model assumes no net acceleration over the path from s to t and a cost of zero for turning. Let P be composed of n triangular faces, each face $f_j, 1 \leq j \leq n$ having a cost μ_j pertaining to the coefficient of kinetic friction for that face w.r.t. the moving vehicle. Let mg be the weight of the vehicle, where m is the vehicle's mass and g is the force of gravity. Denote by θ the minimum angle between any two adjacent edges of any face on $\mathcal{P}$. Now consider a segment s_i of the shortest path which crosses a face f_j of $\mathcal{P}$. Let ϕ_j be the inclination angle (gradient) of f_j and let φ_i be the inclination angle of s_i w.r.t. to the XY plane (see Figure 1a)). Using this model, the cost of travel for

s_i is: $mg(\mu_j \cos \phi_j + \sin \varphi_i) \cdot |s_i|$. We assume that mg is constant for the problem instance and is set to one in our analysis. The cost due to the force of friction is represented by $\mu_j \cos \phi_j \cdot |s_i|$. Therefore, it is convenient to define $w_j = \mu_j \cos \phi_j$ to be the weight of face f_j. Let W (resp. w) be the maximum (resp. minimum) of all $w_j, 1 \le j \le n$.

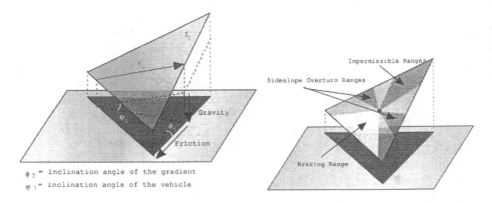

Fig. 1. a) The forces of friction and gravity that act against the propulsion of the vehicle. b) The up to three ranges representing impermissible travel and the braking range of a single face.

The cost due to gravity is represented by $|s_i| \sin \varphi_i$ which is the change in elevation of the path segment. Hence the work expended against gravity is equal to the difference in height between s and t which is independent of the path taken. In the case where the cost formula is positive, we will assign a cost of $w_j |s_i|$ to s_i passing through face f_j. For certain inclination angles, the cost formula could become negative (i.e., $\varphi_i < -\arcsin(\mu_j \cos \phi_j)$) violating the above assumption that there is no net acceleration. We denote the angle $\varphi_i = -\arcsin(\mu_j \cos \phi_j)$ in which this sign change occurs as a *critical braking angle*. To compensate, the cost formula is adjusted so that the energy gained going downhill is exactly compensated by the energy required to brake. So, vehicles neither accelerate nor do they gain or lose energy when traveling in a braking range. To do this, we replace the $\mu_j \cos \phi_j$ friction factor of the cost formula by $-\sin \varphi_i$ which causes the gravity force to be cancelled out resulting in zero cost travel. Notice that the negative gravity force has already been extracted from the metric leaving a cost of $-\sin \varphi_i |s_i|$ for segment s_i. Such a segment is called a *braking* segment and it can be shown that $-\sin \varphi_i \ge w_j$.

The model assumes that each face has up to three ranges of angles that define directions on a face that are impermissible for traveling. Together, with the braking range, there are up to four important angular ranges per face as shown in Figure 1b). The boundary angles of the impermissible ranges are called *critical impermissibility angles*. The boundary angles of the braking range are called *critical braking angles*. For the regular angular ranges (i.e., neither impermissible nor braking), the range is bounded by critical impermissibility or braking angles. We will also think of these as the critical angles for the regular range. A path is said to be *valid* if and only if it does not travel in any of the impermissible directions. If any of the impermissible ranges overlap, they are combined to create a single impermissible range. In some cases, the ranges may cover all possible angles and that represents an *isotropic obstacle*.

Let φ_c be a critical impermissibility angle for one of the critical impermissibility ranges of a face f_j of $\mathcal{P}$. Let u and v be the two unit vectors representing the directions on the boundaries of the range. Thus, the angle that u and v make with the horizontal plane is φ_c. Let α_c be the angle between these two vectors when placed end-to-end. Let α_j be the minimum of all α_c for the impermissible ranges and let α be the minimum of all $\alpha_j, 1 \leq j \leq n$. Let λ to be the minimum angle of all braking and regular range angles.

Rowe and Ross [10] show that this model allows for three types of segments which we denote as *direction types*. We say a segment of a path is *braking* if it travels in a braking heading, otherwise it is a *regular* segment. A path is said to be a *switchback path* if it zig-zags (possibly an infinite number of times) along a matched pair of critical impermissibility directions. In our algorithm, we will treat and report switchback paths (denoted as z_i) as a single segment, say s_i, and assign a weight to it which incorporates the length of the switchback path itself. It can be shown that a switchback path between two points a and b on a face f_j which uses directions defined by u and v has length at most $\frac{|\overline{ab}|}{\sin(\alpha_j/2)}$. Our algorithm is able to detect whether or not a valid path exists. The analysis will assume the existence.

Let v be a vertex of $\mathcal{P}$. Define h_v to be the minimum distance from v to the boundary of the union of its incident faces. Define a polygonal cap C_v, called a *sphere*, around v, as follows. Let $r_v = \epsilon h_v$ for some $0 < \epsilon$. Let r be the minimum r_v over all v. Let vuw be a triangulated face incident to v. Let u' (w') be at the distance of r_v from v on vu (vw). This defines a triangular sub-face $vu'w'$ of vuw. The spherical cap (sphere) C_v around v consists of all such sub-faces incident at v.

1.3 Overview of Our Approach

Our approach is to discretize the polyhedral terrain in a natural way, by placing Steiner points along the edges of the polyhedron (as in our earlier subdivision approach [2, 6] but with substantial differences as illustrated below). We construct a graph G containing Steiner points as vertices and edges as those interconnections between Steiner points that correspond to segments which lie completely in triangular faces of the polyhedron. The geometric shortest path problem on polyhedra is thus stated as a graph problem so that the existing efficient algorithms (and their implementations) for shortest paths in graphs can be used. The main difference to [6, 2] and to other related work (e.g., [3–5]) lies in the placement of Steiner points, due to the directional restrictions imposed on the path segments in this case.

We introduce a logarithmic number of Steiner points along each edge of $\mathcal{P}$, and these points are placed in a geometric progression along an edge. They are chosen w.r.t. (i) the vertex joining two edges of a face such that the distance between any two adjacent points on an edge is at most ϵ times the shortest possible path segment that can cross that face between those two points (ii) eight direction ranges (three impermissible, one braking and four regular) such that the approximation segment is of the same type as that of the shortest path segment.

A problem arises when placing these Steiner points near vertices of the face since the shortest possible segment becomes infinitesimal in length. A similar issue was encountered by [1, 2, 5, 4]. The problem arises since the distance between adjacent Steiner points, in the near vicinity of a vertex, would have to be infinitesimal requiring an infinite number of Steiner points. We address this problem by constructing spheres centered around each vertex of the polyhedron. Here lies a further difference to our earlier approach. While the algorithms in [1, 2] never add Steiner points within the spheres for anisotropic paths we do.

We show that there exist a path in the graph G with cost that is within $(1+f(\epsilon))$ times the shortest path costs, where $f(\epsilon)$ is a function of ϵ and geometric parameters of the terrain. The running time of our algorithm is the cost for computing the graph G plus that of running a shortest path algorithm in G.

2 Our Approximation Scheme

2.1 Computing the Graph

We begin by constructing a graph G_j for each face f_j of $\mathcal{P}$ by adding Steiner points along edges of f_j in three stages. In the *first stage*, we add enough Steiner points to ensure that the distance between adjacent Steiner points on an edge is at most $f(\epsilon)$ times the length of a shortest path segment which passes through it, for some function $f(\epsilon)$ which is independent of n. This is done using the algorithm of [2]. The *second stage* of Steiner points are required to ensure that there exists an approximation segment with the same direction type as a shortest path segment which passes between the same Steiner points. Recall that our model of computation allows for eight direction ranges per face. Second stage adds a set of Steiner points to f_j corresponding to the braking range and (up to four) regular ranges. We give here a description of how to add the Steiner points corresponding to the braking range; the Steiner point sets for the regular ranges are constructed in a similar manner. In the *third stage*, we expand G_j by placing additional vertices within at least one of the spheres around a vertex of f_j.

Stage 1: For each vertex v of face f_j we do the following: Let e_q and e_p be the edges of f_j incident to v. First, place Steiner points on edges e_q and e_p at distance r_v from v; call them q_1 and p_1, respectively. By definition, $|\overline{vq_1}| = |\overline{vp_1}| = r_v$. Define $\delta = (1 + \epsilon \sin \theta_v)$ if $\theta_v < \frac{\pi}{2}$, otherwise $\delta = (1 + \epsilon)$. We now add Steiner points $q_2, q_3, ..., q_{\iota_q-1}$ along e_q such that $|\overline{vq_j}| = r_v \delta^{j-1}$ where $\iota_q = \log_\delta(|e_q|/r_v)$. Similarly, add Steiner points $p_2, p_3, ..., p_{\iota_p-1}$ along e_p, where $\iota_p = \log_\delta(|e_p|/r_v)$.

Stage 2: (see Figure 2) Let u and v be the critical angle directions for the range on the plane of f_j. Consider now each vertex v of f_j and apply the following algorithm twice (once as is and then again where u and v are swapped):

$q \leftarrow v$.
WHILE (q does not lie within C_{v_i} of f_j, where $v_i \neq v$) DO {
    $x_q \leftarrow$ the ray from q in direction u.
    IF (x_q intersects an edge e of f_j) THEN {
        $p \leftarrow$ intersection point of x_q and e.
        Add Steiner point p on e.
        $x_p \leftarrow$ the ray from p in direction $-v$.
        IF (x_p does not intersect an edge e of f_j) THEN STOP
        ELSE {
            $q \leftarrow$ intersection of x_p with e.
            Add Steiner point q on e.} } }

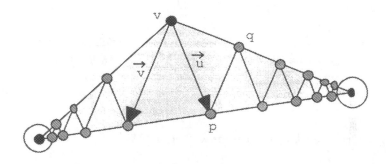

Fig. 2. Adding Steiner points to a face corresponding to a braking range.

Note that when applying this stage to the adjacent faces of f_j, additional Steiner points will be added to the edges of f_j. When creating the graph for an adjacent face f_{j+1}, each edge of f_j may also gain a set of Steiner points due to this second stage construction. Hence, each edge may have two such sets of Steiner points.//

Stage 3: For each Steiner point p of face f generated in stages 1 and 2, extend a ray from p in each critical angle direction u defined for f as well as the negative critical direction $-u$. Consider the spheres C_1, C_2 and C_3 around the vertices of f. If this ray intersects an edge e_p of f at some point x within C_i, $1 \leq i \leq 3$ then add a Steiner point at x. Let q_a and q_{a+1} be two adjacent Steiner points added on an edge within a sphere C_v as just mentioned. If $|\overline{q_a q_{a+1}}| > r_v(\delta - 1)$ then we add additional evenly spaced Steiner points between q_a and q_{a+1}. We add only enough Steiner points to ensure that the distance between two adjacent points is at most $r_v(\delta - 1)$.

    The Steiner points generated in all 3 stages along with the vertices of f_j become vertices of G_j. Connect a pair of vertices in G_j by two oppositely directed edges if and only if 1) they represent Steiner points lying on different edges of f_j or 2) they represent adjacent Steiner points lying on the same edge of f_j. In addition, for each vertex of G_j which corresponds to a vertex, say v, of f_j, connect it with two oppositely directed edges to 1) all vertices of G_j that represent Steiner points lying on the edge opposite to v, and 2) the two vertices of G_j corresponding to the two closest Steiner points that lie on the two incident edges of v.

Keep in mind that although we just described the addition of these Steiner points w.r.t. the two critical directions u and v for the braking range, we must also add similar sets of Steiner points for the regular ranges. Having added vertices and edges to G_j we must now assign appropriate weights to the edges. For each edge $\vec{ab}$ of G_j, we set its weight as follows: If $\vec{ab}$ is regular then its weight is set to $w_j|\vec{ab}|$. If $\vec{ab}$ is braking then its weight is set to $-\sin\theta_i|\vec{ab}|$ where θ_i is the declination angle of $\vec{ab}$. Note that this weight is positive since $\sin\theta_i$ is negative for downward angles. If $\vec{ab}$ is switchback then its weight is set to $\frac{w_j}{\sin\frac{\alpha}{2}}|\vec{ab}|$. This completes the construction of G_j. The graph G is defined to be the union $G_1 \cup G_2 \cup ... \cup G_n$.

Claim 2.11. *$G = (V, E)$ is connected and has $V = O(n\log_\delta(|L|/r)+n\log_{\mathcal{F}}(r/|L|))$ vertices and $E = O(n(\log_\delta(|L|/r) + \log_{\mathcal{F}}(r/|L|))^2)$ edges, where $\mathcal{F} = \frac{1+\cos(\theta+\lambda)}{1+\cos(\theta-\lambda)}$, θ is the minimum angle between any two adjacent edges of any face on $\mathcal{P}$, $\delta = 1 + \epsilon\sin\theta$ and λ is the minimum of all braking and regular range angles.*

2.2   Constructing the Approximated Path

We describe here the construction of a path $\Pi'(s, t)$ in G. In the section to follow, we will bound the cost of this path. Note however that Dijkstra's algorithm may produce a better path than the one constructed here. Recall that a switchback path z_i of $\Pi(s, t)$ within face f_j is represented with a single segment (i.e. s_i) of $\Pi(s, t)$ whose weight encapsulates the distance of the switchback path. Each s_i, must be of one of the following types:

i) $s_i \cap C_v = \emptyset$,

ii) $s_i \cap C_v = $ subsegment of s_i, or

iii) $s_i \cap C_v = s_i$.

Let $C_{\sigma_1}, C_{\sigma_2}, ..., C_{\sigma_\kappa}$ be a sequence of spheres (listed in order from s to t) intersected by type ii) segments of $\Pi(s, t)$ such that $C_{\sigma_a} \neq C_{\sigma_{a+1}}$. Now define subpaths of $\Pi(s, t)$ as being one of two kinds:

Definition 1. Between-sphere subpath: *A path consisting of a type ii) segment followed by zero or more consecutive type i) segments followed by a type ii) segment. These subpaths will be denoted as $\Pi(\sigma_a, \sigma_{a+1})$ whose first and last segments intersect C_{σ_a} and $C_{\sigma_{a+1}}$, respectively. We will also consider paths that begin or/and end at a vertex to be a degenerate case of this type of path containing only type i) segments.*

Definition 2. Inside-sphere subpath: *A path consisting of one or more consecutive type iii) segments all lying within the same C_{σ_a}; these are denoted as $\Pi(\sigma_a)$. (Note that inside-sphere subpaths of $\Pi(s,t)$ always lie between two between-sphere subpaths. That is, $\Pi(\sigma_a)$ lies between $\Pi(\sigma_{a-1},\sigma_a)$ and $\Pi(\sigma_a,\sigma_{a+1})$).*

Let x and y be the endpoints of s_i and let x (respectively y) lie on edge e_q (respectively e_p) of f_j. Let q_a and q_b (respectively p_a and p_b) be the Steiner points on e_q (respectively e_p) between which x (respectively y) lies.

Claim 2.21. *At least one of $\overrightarrow{q_a p_b}$ or $\overrightarrow{q_b p_a}$ is of the same direction type as s_i.*

We begin our path construction by choosing a segment s_i' in G_j which approximates a segment s_i crossing face f_j. If s_i is a type i) or type ii) segment, then choose s_i' to be one of $\overrightarrow{q_a p_a}$, $\overrightarrow{q_a p_b}$, $\overrightarrow{q_b p_a}$ and $\overrightarrow{q_b p_b}$ such that s_i' is of the same direction type as s_i and $\|s_i'\|$ is minimized. Claim 2.21 ensures that at least one of these segments is of the same type as s_i. For the sake of analysis, we will assume that s_i' is chosen so as to have the same direction type as s_i and we will bound s_i' accordingly. In practice however, we may choose a segment with less cost, since we are choosing the minimum of these four. Note that this choice also pertains to the special case in which $e_q = e_p$. Note also that if s_i is of type ii), then one of q_a, q_b, p_a or p_b may degenerate to a vertex of f_j. In the case where s_i is a type iii) segment, there is no corresponding segment s_i' in $\Pi'(s,t)$.

At this point, we have approximations for all type i) and type ii) segments but they are disconnected and therefore do not form a path joining s and t. We will now add edges joining consecutive type i) or type ii) segments of $\Pi(s,t)$. Let s_i and s_{i+1} be two consecutive segments of $\Pi(s,t)$ that are type i) or type ii) with corresponding approximation segments s_i' of G_j and s_{i+1}' of G_{j+1}, respectively. Let e be the edge of $\mathcal{P}$ joining faces f_j and f_{j+1}. Let q be the endpoint of s_i' lying on e and let p be the endpoint of s_{i+1}' lying on e. It is easily seen that either $q = p$ or q and p are adjacent Steiner points on e. If $q = p$, then s_i' and s_{i+1}' are already connected. If $q \neq p$ then let s_i'' be the edge in G_j from q to p.

The addition of these segments (i.e. all s_i'') ensures that all segments of between-sphere subpaths are connected to form subpaths. We now need to interconnect the between-sphere subpaths so that $\Pi'(s,t)$ is connected.

Consider two consecutive between-sphere subpaths of $\Pi'(s,t)$, say $\Pi'(\sigma_{a-1},\sigma_a)$ and $\Pi'(\sigma_a,\sigma_{a+1})$. They are disjoint from one another, however, the first path ends at a Steiner point within sphere C_{σ_a} and the second path starts at a Steiner point within C_{σ_a}. Join the end of $\Pi'(\sigma_{a-1},\sigma_a)$ and the start of $\Pi'(\sigma_a,\sigma_{a+1})$ to vertex v_{σ_a} by two segments (which are edges of G created in Stage 3). These two segments together will form an inside-sphere subpath and will be denoted as $\Pi'(\sigma_a)$. This step is repeated for each consecutive pair of between-sphere subpaths so that all subpaths are joined to form $\Pi'(s,t)$. Constructing a path in this manner results in a connected path that lies on the surface of $\mathcal{P}$.

2.3 Bounding the Approximation

We give a bound $\|\Pi'(s,t)\|$ on the cost of $\Pi'(s,t)$. To begin, a bound is shown for each of the between-sphere path segments. The claims to follow bound the approximation segments of the type i) and type ii) face crossing segments of $\Pi(s,t)$. Assume therefore that s_i' is a type i) or type ii) face-crossing segment. The claims give bounds for the three possible direction types of s_i'. That is, we bound the weighted cost of s_i' for the cases in which s_i' (and hence s_i) is regular, braking and switchback, respectively. For the following claims, we will assume that $s_i' = \overline{q_a p_h}$; similar proofs hold when $s_i' = \overline{q_b p_a}$.

Claim 2.31. *Let s_i and s_i' be two segments as discussed above, passing through a face f_j which has weight w_j. Then*
i) if s_i and s_i' are regular then $\|s_i'\| \leq (1 + 2\epsilon)\|s_i\|$
ii) if s_i and s_i' are braking then $\|s_i'\| \leq \left(1 + \frac{2\epsilon}{w_j}\right)\|s_i\|$.

iii) if s_i and s_i' are switchback then $\|s_i'\| \leq \left(1 + \frac{2\epsilon}{\sin\frac{\alpha}{2}}\right)\|s_i\|$
iv) $\|s_i''\| \leq \frac{\epsilon}{\sin\frac{\alpha}{2}}\|s_i\|$.

Lemma 1. *If $\Pi'(\sigma_{a-1}, \sigma_a)$ is a between-sphere subpath of $\Pi'(s,t)$ corresponding to an approximation of $\Pi(\sigma_{a-1}, \sigma_a)$ then $\|\Pi'(\sigma_{a-1}, \sigma_a)\| \leq (1 + \max(\frac{1}{\sin\frac{\alpha}{2}} + \frac{2}{w}, \frac{3}{\sin\frac{\alpha}{2}})\epsilon)\|\Pi(\sigma_{a-1}, \sigma_a)\|$, where w is the minimum weight of the faces of $\mathcal{P}$.*

Claim 2.32. *Let $\Pi'(\sigma_{a-1}, \sigma_a)$ be a between-sphere subpath of $\Pi'(s,t)$ corresponding to an approximation of $\Pi(\sigma_{a-1}, \sigma_a)$ then*
$$\|\Pi'(\sigma_a)\| \leq \left(\frac{2W\epsilon}{w(1-2\epsilon)\sin\frac{\alpha}{2}}\right)\|\Pi(\sigma_{a-1}, \sigma_a)\|, \text{ where } 0 < \epsilon < \tfrac{1}{2}.$$

Using the results of Claim 2.32 and Lemma 1, it can be shown that:

Lemma 2. *If $\Pi(s,p)$ is a shortest anisotropic path in $\mathcal{P}$, where s is a vertex of $\mathcal{P}$ and p is a vertex of G then there exists an approximated path $\Pi'(s,p) \in G$ such that $\|\Pi'(s,p)\| \leq (1 + f(\epsilon))\|\Pi(s,p)\|$ where $0 < \epsilon < \tfrac{1}{2}$ and*
$$f(\epsilon) = \epsilon\left(\frac{2W\epsilon}{w(1-2\epsilon)\sin\frac{\alpha}{2}} + \max\left(\frac{1}{\sin\frac{\alpha}{2}} + \frac{2}{w}, \frac{3}{\sin\frac{\alpha}{2}}\right)\right).$$

Theorem 1. *Let $\mathcal{P}$ be a polyhedral surface with maximum and minimum face weights W and w, respectively such that $W \geq \sin\frac{\alpha}{2}$, where α is the minimum angle defined by any pair of matched critical impermissible and braking angles. Let $\Pi(s,t)$ be a shortest weighted path on $\mathcal{P}$, where s and t are vertices of $\mathcal{P}$ then there exists an approximated path $\Pi'(s,t) \in G$ such that $\|\Pi'(s,t)\| \leq (1 + f(\epsilon))\|\Pi(s,t)\|$, where $f(\epsilon) = \left(\frac{3W\epsilon}{w\sin\frac{\alpha}{2}}\right)$. Moreover, $\|\Pi'(s,t)\|$ can be computed by running Dijkstra's shortest path algorithm on the graph $G = (V,E)$ computed in Claim 2.11 in time $O(V \log V + E)$.*

3 Conclusion

We presented an algorithm for computing an ϵ-approximation to a shortest anisotropic path on the terrain. A similar, but simplified methodology allows for the computation of an approximation to within an additive factor of the shortest anisotropic path. Both algorithms expand on and generalize edge subdivision schemes we had introduced earlier [1, 2] (we have recently generalized this work to 3D). Thus one general technique gives rise to Euclidean, weighted and anisotropic path algorithms. The differences are not as significant for the implementation as they are for the analysis. All graph construction schemes are easy to implement and they require only running a shortest path algorithm in a graph. We believe that the approximations within an additive factor will be of special interest for practitioners. The ϵ-approximations are also of theoretical interest as they require new ideas (as also discussed here).

Acknowledgments: The authors would like to thank Lyudmil Aleksandrov for helpful discussion on Claim 2.11.

References

1. L. Aleksandrov, M. Lanthier, A. Maheshwari and J.-R. Sack, "An ϵ-Approximation Algorithm for Weighted Shortest Path Queries on Polyhedral Surfaces", *14th European Workshop on Computational Geometry*, Barcelona, Spain, 1998.
2. L. Aleksandrov, M. Lanthier, A. Maheshwari and J.-R. Sack, "An ϵ-Approximation Algorithm for Weighted Shortest Paths on Polyhedral Surfaces", *SWAT '98*, LNCS 1432, Stockholm, Sweden, 1998, pp. 11-22.
3. J. Choi, J. Sellen and C.K. Yap, "Approximate Euclidean Shortest Path in 3-Space", *Proc. 10th Annual Symp. on Computational Geometry*, 1994, pp. 41-48.
4. G. Das and G. Narasimhan, "Short Cuts in Higher Dimensional Space", *Proceedings of the 7th Annual Canadian Conference on Computational Geometry*, Québec City, Québec, 1995, pp. 103-108.
5. C. Kenyon and R. Kenyon, "How To Take Short Cuts", *Discrete and Computational Geometry*, Vol. 8, No. 3, 1992, pp. 251-264.
6. M. Lanthier, A. Maheshwari and J.-R. Sack, "Approximating Weighted Shortest Paths on Polyhedral Surfaces", *Proceedings of the 13th Annual ACM Symposium on Computational Geometry*, 1997, pp. 274-283.
7. C. Mata and J. Mitchell, "A New Algorithm for Computing Shortest Paths in Weighted Planar Subdivisions", *Proceedings of the 13th Annual ACM Symposium on Computational Geometry*, 1997, pp. 264-273.
8. J.S.B. Mitchell and C.H. Papadimitriou, "The Weighted Region Problem: Finding Shortest Paths Through a Weighted Planar Subdivision", *Journal of the ACM*, **38**, January 1991, pp. 18-73.
9. J.S.B. Mitchell, "Geometric Shortest Paths and Network Optimization", in J.-R. Sack and J. Urrutia Eds.,*Handbook on Computational Geometry*, Elsevier Science B.V., to appear 1999.
10. N.C. Rowe, and R.S. Ross, "Optimal Grid-Free Path Planning Across Arbitrarily Contoured Terrain with Anisotropic Friction and Gravity Effects", IEEE Transactions on Robotics and Automation, Vol. 6, No. 5, October 1990, pp. 540-553.
11. M. Sharir and A. Schorr, "On Shortest Paths in Polyhedral Spaces", *SIAM Journal of Computing*, **15**, 1986, pp. 193-215.
12. R. Tamassia et al., "Strategic Directions in Computational Geometry", ACM Computing Surveys, Vol. 28, No. 4, December 1996.
13. Paradigm Group Webpage, School of Computer Science, Carleton University, http://www.scs.carleton.ca/~ gis.

Relations between Local and Global Periodicity of Words (Extended Abstract)

A. Lepistö

Turku Centre for Computer Science
and
Department of Mathematics, University of Turku,
20014 Turku, Finland

Abstract. Mignosi, Restivo and Salemi [MRS] proved a remarkable result giving an optimal bound for the order of a repetition (of words) such that if all long enough prefixes of an infinite word possess such a repetition then the word is ultimately periodic. We consider the same problem with respect to two parameters: the order $\rho \in \mathbb{R}$ and length $p \in \mathbb{N}$ of a word repeated at the ends of prefixes of an infinite words. We compute, for each p, the optimal value of ρ, which turns out to define a step function. Our results can be interpreted to define optimal borderline between a predictable and chaotic behaviour.

1 Introduction

One of the fundamental topics in mathematical research is to search for connections between local and global regularities. We consider such a problem in connection with infinite words. The regularity is specified as a periodicity.

The research behind this paper is motivated by a remarkable result of Mignosi, Restivo and Salemi (cf. [MRS]) where they characterized one-way infinite ultimately periodic words by the means of local periods. In this characterization the golden ratio, or actually its square, is in a special role. An infinite word w is ultimately periodic if and only if all except finite number of prefixes of w contains as a suffix a repetition of order φ^2, i.e. a suffix of the form v^k , $v \neq 1$, k rational and $k > \varphi^2$ with φ being the golden ratio $(1 + \sqrt{5})/2$. Moreover, they showed that the bound φ^2 is optimal meaning that it cannot be replaced by any smaller number without destroying the equivalence.

In the paper by Karhumäki, Lepistö and Plandowski (cf. [KLP]) there was introduced a new aspect of that result. In that aspect we ask how it affects to the order of repetition if we restrict the lengths of the periods in these repetitions to be bounded from above. We say that an infinite word w over a finite alphabet is (ρ, p)-*repetitive*, where $\rho > 1$ is a real number and p is a positive integer, if all except finitely many prefixes of w contain as a suffix a repetition of order ρ of a word of length at most p, i.e. a word of the form $v^{\rho'}$ with $\rho' \geq \rho$ and $|v| \leq p$.

Our goal here is to establish an answer to one of the open questions mentioned in [KLP]. As in the work of Mignosi, Restivo and Salemi, the famous Fibonacci word works as an example here. Now, if we let a "local regularity" mean that an infinite word contains almost everywhere, that is to the left from any except finitely many positions, a certain repetition, and let the "global regularity" mean that the word is ultimately periodic, we have a nontrivial connections between the local and the global regularities.

Let $\mathcal{LO}(\rho, p)$ be the set of nonultimately periodic (ρ, p)-repetitive words and $\mathcal{BO}(p)$ be the "limes superior" of those values of ρ for which the set $\mathcal{LO}(\rho, p)$ is not empty. With the above notions we determine the values of the function $\mathcal{BO}$ and, we show that this function is a "step function", i.e. this function is constant in some intervals. The values giving bounds for these intervals are basically the Fibonacci numbers. There are some exceptions which are 4, 8 and 12. At the same time, we also show that the infinite Fibonacci word is in a central position when determining the values of $\mathcal{BO}(p)$ for $p > 13$.

The paper is organized as follows. In Section 2 we fix our notation and introduce necessary notions. We also recall a reduction result from [KLP] allowing us to restrict only on binary alphabets. Section 3 is divided into two subsections in which we determine the values of $\mathcal{BO}(p)$ for $1 \leq p \leq 13$. Section 4 is devoted to provide the maximal order or repetitions greater than 2, with bounded length or periods, occurring in the infinite Fibonacci word. In Section 5 we present our main result and, finally, in Section 6 we introduce a spectral intepretation of the previous result.

The proofs of the results of this paper are often very long and can be found in [Le].

2   Preliminaries

In this section we define formally our basic notions as well as fix the terminology, if necessary cf. [Lo] and [CK].

We consider *finite* and *one-way infinite words* over a finite alphabet A. The sets of such words are denoted by A^* and A^ω, respectively. A *factor* of a word is any consecutive sequence of its symbols. By $\mathrm{Pref}_k(w)$ ($\mathrm{Suff}_k(w)$) we mean a prefix (suffix, respectively) of w of length k. For a rational number $k \geq 1$, we say that a word w is a *kth power* if there exists a word v such that $w = v^k$, where v^k denotes the word $v'v''$ with $v' = v^{\lfloor k \rfloor}$ and $v'' = \mathrm{Pref}_{|w|(k-\lfloor k \rfloor)} v$. Next we say that w contains a *repetition of order $\rho \geq 1$* if it contains as a factor a kth power with $k \geq \rho$. Note that here ρ is allowed to be any real number ≥ 1.

Next we define our central notions. Let $\rho \geq 1$ be a real number and $p \geq 1$ an integer. We say that a finite word w' is *(ρ, p)-legal* if u ends with a repetition of order ρ of a word of length at most p. Formally, the above means that, there exists a $k \geq \rho$, k rational and words u and v, with $|v| \leq p$, such that

$$w' = uv^k.$$

By saying that a finite word w' is *(ρ^+, p)-legal* we mean that we require a repetition of order strictly greater than ρ. Furthermore, we say that an infinite word w is *(ρ, p)-repetitive* if there exists an integer n_0 such that each prefix of w of length at least n_0 is (ρ, p)-legal. Formally, the above means that, for each $n \geq n_0$, there exists a $k \geq \rho$ and words u and v, with $|v| \leq p$, such that

$$\mathrm{Pref}_n(w) = uv^k.$$

As for legality, we also define the notion (ρ^+, p)-repetitive. An infinite word w is (ρ^+, p)-repetitive if we require instead of a repetition of order ρ a repetition of order strictly greater than ρ. In the previous definition.

Note that the above definition can be extended to the case where $p = \infty$. Our goal is to look for connections between (ρ, p)-repetitive and *ultimately periodic* words, i.e. words which are of the form uv^ω for some finite words u and v. If $w = uv^\omega$ we say that $|u|$ is a *threshold* and $|v|$ a *period* of w, and that v is a *word period* of w.

As another important notion we need that of the *Fibonacci morphism* τ. It is a morphism from $A^* = \{a, b\}^*$ into itself defined by

$$\tau : \begin{array}{l} a \mapsto ab \\ b \mapsto a. \end{array}$$

Recall that the *Fibonacci word*

$$(1) \qquad \alpha_F = \lim_{n \to \infty} \tau^n(a)$$

is the only fixed point (in A^ω) of τ.

We also introduce the Fibonacci blocks. Fibonacci blocks are word "b" and its images obtained by applying the Fibonacci morphism in a repetitive fashion. More formally, we will denote them by $\mathcal{F}_i$ such that for positive i's the ith Fibonacci block is

$$\mathcal{F}_i = \tau(b)^i, \text{ for } i > 0.$$

We also define the Fibonacci function in the following way:

$$F(i) = |\mathcal{F}_i|.$$

Finally we define the following three languages and one function:

$$\mathcal{UL}(n) = \{w \in A^\omega | w = uv^\omega, u, v \in A^+\};$$

$$\mathcal{LR}(\rho, p) = \{w \in A^\omega | w \text{ is a } (\rho, p)\text{-repetitive word}\};$$

$$\mathcal{LO}(\rho, p) = \{w \in A^\omega | w \in \mathcal{LO}(\rho, p) \text{ and } w \text{ is a nonultimatelu periodic word}\};$$

and

$$\mathcal{BO}(p) = \limsup\{\rho | \mathcal{LO}(\rho, p) \neq \emptyset\}.$$

In our terminology a remarkable result of Mignosi, Restivo and Salemi, cf. [MRS], can be stated as

Theorem 1 *An infinite word is ultimately periodic if and only if it is (φ^2, ∞)-repetitive, where $\varphi = (1 + \sqrt{5})/2$.* $\qquad\square$

As also shown in [MRS] the number φ, i.e. the number of *golden ratio*, plays an important role here. Indeed, Theorem 1 is optimal:

Theorem 2 *The infinite Fibonacci word (1) is (k, ∞)-repetitive for any $k < \varphi^2$, but not ultimately periodic.* □

Next we recall a reduction result. This result allows us to restrict our considerations into a binary alphabet when looking values for the function $\mathcal{BO}(n)$. A detailed proof for this theorem can be found in [KLP].

Theorem 3 *If there exists a nonultimately periodic (ρ, p)-repetitive word over a finite alphabet then there is also such a word over a binary alphabet.* □

The importance of the above theorem is that now we can consider, without loss of generality, only words over a binary alphabet, say $A = \{a, b\}$. Indeed, for a fixed value of ρ or p, if there exist at all nonultimately periodic (ρ, p)-repetitive words, then there exists such a word over A. Consequently, to determine the smallest p for a fixed ρ, or the largest ρ for a fixed p, such that the (ρ, p)-repetitiveness does not require the word to be ultimately periodic, it is enough to study only binary words.

3 Optimal bounds for n less than 14

By Theorem 3, we can assume that A is a binary alphabet, say $A = \{a, b\}$, without loss of generality when we are searching values for $\mathcal{BO}(n)$. Clearly, the language of $(1, n)$-repetitive infinite words over the alphabet A contains all infinite words over A, including some nonultimately periodic infinite words. Then, by the definition of function $\mathcal{BO}$, we can determine that $\mathcal{BO}(n) \geq 1$, for all $n \geq 1$, and

$$\mathcal{BO}(m) \leq \mathcal{BO}(n), \text{ for } m < n.$$

When searching value for $\mathcal{BO}(n)$ there are two separate things to be considered. The first one is that there actually exists a $(\mathcal{BO}(n), n)$-repetitive nonultimately periodic word. The other one is that such words are optimal, i.e. that there are only ultimately periodic $(\mathcal{BO}(n)^+, n)$-repetitive words. In order to do these checks, we consider two cases depending whether or not $\mathcal{BO}(n)$ is greater than 2. And, as we will see, the smallest value of n obtaining $\mathcal{BO}(n) > 2$ is 12.

3.1 Optimal bounds for n from 1 to 3

We start by studying $(1^+, 1)$- and $(1^+, 2)$-repetitive words. Because a repetition of order greater than 1 with period 1 is actually a repetition of order greater or equal than 2, any $(1^+, 1)$-repetitive word is also $(2, 1)$-repetitive. Similarly, any $(1^+, 2)$-repetitive word is actually $(3/2, 2)$-repetitive. This follows from the facts that a repetition of order greater than 1 with period 1 is a repetition of order greater than or equal to 2 and a repetition of order greater than 1 with period 2 is a repetition of order greater than or equal to 3/2.

From the above we can determine the following result.

Theorem 4
$$\mathcal{BO}(1) = 1 = \mathcal{BO}(2).$$

Proof Let us first find the value for $\mathcal{BO}(1)$. By the definition of (ρ, p)-repetition word we conclude that any $(2, 1)$-repetitive word has a suffix in which there exists a square of a letter of A at every position. And, that implies that such a word is of the form uc^ω, where $u \in A^*$ and $c \in A$, i.e. that word is ultimately periodic. Then, because $\mathcal{BO}(1) \geq 1$, we obtain $\mathcal{BO}(1) = 1$.

Next we consider the value of $\mathcal{BO}(2)$. A $(3/2, 2)$-legal word having a suffix of the form cc, $c \in A$, can be continued only by c if we want to preserve the $(3/2, 2)$-legality. Similarly, a $(3/2, 2)$-legal word having a suffix of the form cd, $c, d \in A$, $c \neq d$ can be continued only by c if we want to preserve the $(3/2, 2)$-legality. Thus, a $(3/2, 2)$-repetitive word has a suffix of the form c^ω or $(cd)^\omega$, where $c, d \in A$, $c \neq d$. In other words, all $(3/2, 2)$-repetitive words, as well as $(1^+, 2)$-repetitive words, are ultimately periodic. □

Next we are going to find the optimal bound for $n = 3$. Basically we can divide all $(5/3, 3)$-legal binary words into six distinct sets depending on the form of the suffix. Let x, y be different letters in A. Then, these cases can be denoted as the following: $xyxy$, $xyxx$, $xyyxy$, $xyxxy$, $xxyy$ and xxx. Let us note that those words having a suffix of the form $xxxy$, $xxxyx$ or $xxyyx$ are not $(5/3, 3)$-legal. Together these nine different forms for suffixes covers all words, i.e. any given finite word has a suffix which fits to one of these nine forms.

Now, by observing how a $(5/3, 3)$-legal word can be continued by one letter while preserving $(5/3, 3)$-legality, we can construct a graph which shows how a $(5/3, 3)$-legal binary word can be continued while preserving $(5/3, 3)$-legality. Because we do not have much space to use for proofs we only mention here that from this graph we can determine finally the following characterization for binary $(5/3, 3)$-repetitive words. By G_a and G_b we denote the words bab and aba, respectively.

Theorem 5 *Let $A = \{a, b\}$ be a binary alphabet and $w \in A^\omega$. Then the following conditions are equivalent:*

- *$w \in \mathcal{LO}(5/3, 3)$;*
- *w is of the form uv, where $u \in A^+$ is $(5/3, 3)$-legal, v is of the form $(aG_a^* bG_b^*)^\omega$ such that sequence of labels i corresponding G_i and letters a, b is nonultimately periodic.* □

It is worth mentioning that the infinite Fibonacci word is an example of nonultimately periodic $(5/3, 3)$-repetitive word. We have now shown that there are nonultimately periodic $(5/3, 3)$-repetitive words, i.e. $\mathcal{BO}(3) \geq 5/3$.

From Theorem 5 it follows that in any $(5/3, 3)$-repetitive binary word over A factor $ababba$ or $babaab$ occurs infinitely many times. And, a prefix of ending to one of these factors is not $((5/3)^+, 3)$-legal word. Thus, any $(5/3, 3)$-repetitive binary word cannot be $((5/3)^+, 3)$-repetitive. By Theorem 3, we obtain the following result.

Theorem 6

$$\mathcal{BO}(3) = 1 \, ^2/_3. \qquad \qquad \square$$

3.2 Optimal bounds for n from 4 to 13

Next we are going to find values of $\mathcal{BO}(n)$ for values of n from 4 to 13. Basically, the cases $n = 4$ and $n = 5$ are similar to the case $n = 3$. In these cases, the corresponding graphs obtained by considering how $(7/4, 4)$-, $((7/4)^+, 4)$-, $(2, 5)$- and $(2^+, 5)$-legal words can be continued are only larger. Again, we will not present the proofs of the following result here.

Theorem 7

$$\mathcal{BO}(4) = 1 \, ^3/_4, \quad \mathcal{BO}(5) = 2. \qquad \qquad \square$$

For the latter equality in the theorem, a proof can be found from [KLP]. As we see, the optimal bounds obtained above are less than or equal to 2. From Theorem 7 it follows that

$$\mathcal{BO}(n) \geq 2, \text{ for } n \geq 5,$$

because the function $\mathcal{BO}$ is increasing. In our search for nonultimately periodic $(2^+, p)$-repetitive words, we can use a more effective way to find them. This way deals with a certain block division of infinite words.

Note that, by the definition of function $\mathcal{LO}$, we obtain $\mathcal{LO}(r, k) \subset \mathcal{LO}(r, m)$, for $k \leq m, r \geq 1$, which implies

$$A^\omega \cap \mathcal{LO}(2, n) \neq \emptyset,$$

for $5 < n < 12$. Therefore, it is sufficient to show that

$$A^\omega \cap \mathcal{LO}(2^+, p) = \emptyset, p > 5m,$$

in order to prove that

$$\mathcal{BO}(n) = 2, \text{ for } 5 < n \leq p.$$

Finally, by doing some quite time consuming search we can conclude the following:

Theorem 8

$$\mathcal{BO}(11) = 2, \quad \mathcal{BO}(12) = 2 \, ^1/_{12}, \quad \mathcal{BO}(12) = 2 \, ^2/_{13}. \qquad \qquad \square$$

As we observed earlier, this result implies that

$$\mathcal{BO}(n) = 2, \text{ for } 5 < n \leq 11.$$

4   Fibonacci blocks and repetitions

In this section we present some results about the maximal value of order of repetitions which can be achieved when considering consecutive Fibonacci blocks. In particular, we consider mainly right repetitions, i.e. repetitions starting from some position, not ending to some position as left repetitions. From our point of view this information for right repetitions can be applied also for left repetitions as we will see.

Because of lack of space we only present here some results without proofs. Let us mention here that some of the elementary results used in complete proofs are already known (cf. [MP] and [MRS]). There are also some other sources were those results can be found. The following lemma is essential when we are searching for lengths of periods of possible repetitions in Fibonacci-blocks (cf. [MP]).

Lemma 9 *Let $u, v, w \in A^*$ be words such that $w = \tau^2(u) = \tau(v)$. Then, if w contains a repetition rxr, where $r \in A^+$, $x \in A$ and $|rx| \geq 3$, also v contains a repetition sys, where $s \in A^+$, $y \in A$, such that*

$$\tau(sy) \in \{rx, xr\}.$$

Moreover, if w contains a repetition $xrxrx$, where $r \in A^+$, $x \in A$, also v contains a square ss, where $s \in A^+$, such that

$$\tau(s) \in \{rx, xr\}. \qquad \square$$

Important part of the previous lemma is the fact that if there is an "almost" square, i.e. a word of the form rxr, with $r \in A^*$ and $x \in A$, factor in w then there is also an "almost" square factor in v. Also the relation between the lengths of periods in these repetitions is important. In matter of fact it gives us a way to study about repetitions in Fibonacci-blocks.

Before we continue, we shall introduce *M-functions M_n*. The definition of a M-function for $n \geq 1$ is the following:

$$M_n(i) = \max\{k | u \in A, u^k \text{ is a factor of } \mathcal{F}_n\mathcal{F}_{n-1}\mathcal{F}_n\mathcal{F}_{n-1}, \text{starting from}$$

$$\text{position } i, |u| \leq F(n)\}, \text{ for } 1 \leq i \leq F(n+1).$$

For $n = -1$ and $n = 0$ we set $M_{-1}(1) = 1$ and $M_0(1) = 1$. We also define a minimality function

$$N(n) = \min_{1 \leq i \leq F(n+1)} M_n(i).$$

For small values of n functions M_n are quite easy to calculate by looking for repetitions. The values of functions M_1, M_2, M_3 and M_4 are presented in the following table.

$$\mathbf{M_1} : i \quad\quad 1 \quad 2$$
$$M_1(i) \quad 1 \quad 1$$

$$\mathbf{M_2} : i \quad\quad 1 \quad 2 \quad 3$$
$$M_2(i) \quad {}^3/_2 \quad 1 \quad 2$$

$$\mathbf{M_3} : i \quad\quad 1 \quad 2 \quad 3 \quad 4 \quad 5$$
$$M_3(i) \quad 2 \quad {}^5/_3 \quad 2 \quad {}^5/_2 \quad 2$$

$$\mathbf{M_4} : i \quad\quad 1 \quad 2 \quad 3 \quad 4 \quad 5 \quad 6 \quad 7 \quad 8$$
$$M_4(i) \quad {}^6/_5 \quad 2 \quad 2 \quad {}^5/_2 \quad 2 \quad 3 \quad {}^8/_3 \quad {}^7/_3$$

Table 1 Functions M_1, M_2, M_3 and M_4

By studying more carefully about order of repetitions in infinite words constructed from Fibonacci blocks, we obtain the following result.

Theorem 10 *Let $n \geq 3$ be integer. Then*

$$N(2n - 1) = \frac{F(n + 1) - 1}{F(n - 1)} \;\; and \;\; N(2n) = \frac{F(2n + 2) - F(n + 1) - 1}{F(2n)}. \quad \Box$$

In Table 2 below we present some approximations for the values of the function N.

k	$F(k)$	$N(k)$	k	$F(k)$	$N(k)$
1	1	1	11	144	$2\,^1/_2$
2	2	1	12	233	$2\,^{122}/_{233}$
3	3	$1\,^2/_3$	13	377	$2\,^7/_{13}$
4	5	2	14	610	$2\,^{171}/_{305}$
5	8	2	15	987	$2\,^4/_7$
6	13	$2\,^2/_{13}$	16	1597	$2\,^{931}/_{1597}$
7	21	$2\,^1/_3$	17	2584	$2\,^{10}/_{17}$
8	34	$2\,^6/_{17}$	18	4181	$2\,^{2494}/_{4181}$
9	55	$2\,^2/_5$	19	6765	$2\,^3/_5$
10	89	$2\,^{41}/_{89}$	20	10946	$2\,^{3310}/_{5473}$

Table 2 Values of function $N(n)$ for small n

We have studied right repetitions in Fibonacci blocks. But how this is connected to the left repetitions in the infinite Fibonacci word. That is why we need to consider how reversed Fibonacci blocks occur in the infinite Fibonacci word. And, the following result will tell it to us. In the same time, it also shows that these values for the function N in the case of right-handed repetitions gives us the maximal order of repetition for period less than or equal to corresponding

Fibonacci number found as a factor in the infinite Fibonacci word. Here, for an finite word w, the notation w^r means the reverse of w, i.e. the word obtained by reading letters from w in reverse order.

Lemma 11 *The infinite Fibonacci word can be expressed as*

$$\alpha_F = \mathcal{F}_1^r \mathcal{F}_2^r \mathcal{F}_3^r \mathcal{F}_4^r \ldots . \qquad \square$$

In the following section we are going to consider the relation between maximal order of repetition required "almost" everywhere and ultimate periodicity.

5 Optimal bound for n greater than 13

The final piece of information needed to prove the last step in our work is essentially the following fact. For those $(\rho^+, p+1)$-repetitive words which yields the optimal value of $\mathcal{BO}(p+1)$, where ρ can be written in the form

$$\rho = 2 + {}^m/_n$$

such that $\gcd(m, n) = 1$ and $2 \le m < n$, we can obtain a procedure which is based on those (ρ, p)-repetitive words which yields the optimal value for $\mathcal{BO}(p)$. The proof for this procedure is quite long and it requires that we understand (ρ, p)-repetitive and -legal words in a specific way. By this procedure we can eventually prove the following result.

Theorem 12 *Let $n \ge 6$ be an integer. Then*

$$\mathcal{BO}(F(n)) = N(n).$$

Moreover, the function $\mathcal{BO}$ is constant between the Fibonacci numbers greater than 13. $\qquad \square$

This result shows that the Fibonacci morphism has quite crucial role when considering those words which gives the optimal values for the function $\mathcal{BO}$.

6 Spectrum of occurrences of letters

Let us think that an infinite word is a dynamical process which extends finite words symbol by symbol. Then if the process is controlled by the assumption that the $(\mathcal{BO}(n)^+, n)$-repetitiveness is preserved, then the process is completely predictable. On the other hand, if the assumption is made, as little as possible, weaker, i.e. we consider $(\mathcal{BO}(n), n)$-repetitive words, then the process becomes completely unpredictable, that is chaotic.

In the following we use the term spectrum to indicate all possible values for the quotient

$$\lim_{n \to \infty} \frac{|\mathrm{Pref}_n(w_\tau)|_a}{|\mathrm{Pref}_n(w_\tau)|_b}$$

in the interval $[0, \infty]$. Formally, denoting by $|w|_a$ the number of a's in the word w, this can be stated as follows:

Theorem 13 *Let w be a $(\mathcal{BO}(n)^+, n)$-repetitive word then the set of all possible values for*

$$\lim_{n \to \infty} \frac{|\mathrm{Pref}_n(w_\tau)|_a}{|\mathrm{Pref}_n(w_\tau)|_b}$$

is finite. i.e. the spectrum of $(\mathcal{BO}(n)^+, n)$-repetitive words is dicrete.

On the other hand, for $(\mathcal{BO}(n), n)$-repetitive words that spectrum has both distinct values and some intervals. □

Note that, for any given value τ in these intervals in that spectrum there is a $(\mathcal{BO}(n), n)$-repetitive word such that

$$\lim_{n \to \infty} \frac{|\mathrm{Pref}_n(w_\tau)|_a}{|\mathrm{Pref}_n(w_\tau)|_b} = \tau$$

The above is a simple example of an exact borderline between a predictable and chaotic behaviour. As an example we present in the following figure the spectrum for $n = 6$.

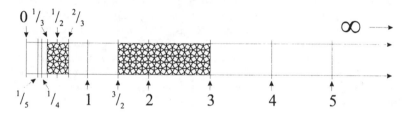

Fig. 1 Spectrum for $n = 6$

Acknowlegment

I want to thank Prof. Juhani Karhumäki, who is my supervisor, for useful and valuable advices.

References

[CK]   C. Choffrut and J. Karhumäki, *Combinatorics of Words*, in: G. Rozenberg and A. Salomaa (eds.), *Handbook of Formal Languages*, Vol. 1, Springer, 329–438, 1997.

[KLP]   J. Karhumäki, A. Lepistö and W. Plandowski, Locally Periodic Infinite Words and a Chaotic Behaviour, (to appear).

[Le]   A. Lepistö, On Relations Between Local and Global Periodicity and Chaotic Behaviour, PhD. Thesis, University of Turku, (to appear).

[Lo]   M. Lothaire, *Combinatorics on Words*, Addison-Wesley, 1983.

[MP]   F. Mignosi and G. Pirillo, Repetitions in the Fibonacci infinite word, *RAIRO Theor. Inform. Appl.* **26**, 199–204, 1992.

[MRS]   F. Mignosi, A. Restivo and S. Salemi, A periodicity theorem on words and applications, *in MFCS'95*, Springer LNCS **969**, 337–348, 1995.

Efficient Merging, Construction, and Maintenance of Evolutionary Trees

Andrzej Lingas, Hans Olsson, and Anna Östlin

Department of Computer Science, Lund University, Box 118, S-221 00 Lund, Sweden,
e-mail: {Andrzej.Lingas, Hans.Olsson, Anna.Ostlin}@dna.lth.se.

Abstract. We present new techniques of *efficiently merging and up-dating partial evolutionary trees* in the so called experiment model. We show that two partial evolutionary trees for disjoint sets of species can be merged using experiments in time $O(dn)$, where n is the size of the resulting evolutionary tree and d is its maximum degree. We prove our upper time bound for merging evolutionary trees to be asymptotically optimal. We show also that after $O(n \log n)$-time preprocessing, a partial evolutionary tree can be maintained under a sequence of m species insertions or deletions in time $O(dm \log(n + m))$. By applying our algorithm for merging evolutionary trees, or alternatively, our algorithm for updating evolutionary trees, we obtain an $O(dn \log n)$-time bound on the problem of constructing an evolutionary tree of size n and maximum degree d from experiments. The classic $O(n \log n)$-time bound on sorting in the comparison model can be seen as a very special case of this upper bound.

1 Introduction

Consider the problem of constructing an unknown tree using some partial information on the tree topology available at some cost. More precisely, the partial information is in the form of the topological subtree induced by a subset of the leaves and the cost corresponds to the time taken by the construction of the subtree in a given model. We introduce techniques of efficiently merging and updating such partial subtrees and apply them to the efficient construction and maintenance of evolutionary trees in the experiment model.

The problem of constructing evolutionary trees is basic in computational biology. It has been studied extensively in several papers [1–7]. An *evolutionary tree* is a tree where the leaves represent species and internal nodes represent their common ancestors, see Fig. 1. There are many different approaches to the problem of constructing an evolutionary tree reflecting, among other things, different kinds of available data.

A well known approach to the problem of constructing an evolutionary tree is based on experiments. An *experiment* determines how three species are related in the evolutionary tree, i.e., returns the topological subtree (without weights on the edges) for the three species. For example, the experimental technique of Ahlquist and Sibley [8] may be used to perform such an experiment. Fig. 1 shows an example of a tree and the outcome of experiments. Note that there are two different types of trees one can get from an experiment.

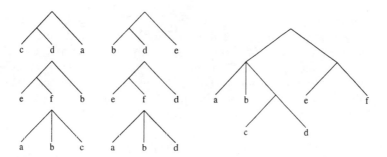

Fig. 1. An example of experiment results and the corresponding evolutionary tree.

Interestingly, the problem of sorting distinct numbers a_1, a_2,... ,a_n in the comparison model can be modeled as a special case of the problem of constructing an evolutionary tree from experiments as follows. The binary tree to construct is like a caterpillar. It is composed of a single rooted path on n nodes and a set of n leaves, each pending from a unique node of the path and labeled uniquely by one of the input numbers, so the labels of the leaves along the path form, say, an increasing sequence. The outcome of the experiment for a triple a_{i_1}, a_{i_2}, a_{i_3} gives the maximum of the numbers in the triple. Thus, it can be obtained by two comparisons. In case the minimum in the triple is known, such an experiment is equivalent to a single comparison.

The problem of constructing evolutionary trees using experiments have been studied by Kannan, Lawler, and Warnow [6]. In [6], they present several algorithms for evolutionary trees. The fastest of them applies to binary evolutionary trees. It runs in time $O(n \log n)$ and performs at most $4n\log_2 n$ experiments. Experiments are expensive and hence it is important to minimize their number. The algorithm for binary trees that performs the smallest number of experiments presented in [6] runs in time $O(n^2)$ and requires at most $n \log_2 n$ experiments. For trees not restricted to be binary Kannan *et al.* present an $O(n^2)$-time algorithm which requires $O(dn \log n)$ experiments, where d is the maximum degree in the tree [6]. For the unrestricted degree case Kannan *et al.* present an $O(n^2)$-time algorithm using $O(n^2)$ experiments [6]. Recently, Kao *et al.*, by using the so called randomized tree splitting [7], have shown that an evolutionary tree for n species can be determined from experiments in expected time $O(dn \log n \log \log n)$. In [7], there has also been given an $\Omega(n(\log n + d))$ bound on the number of experiments required to construct an evolutionary tree of maximum degree d for n species.

In this paper, we introduce new techniques of merging evolutionary trees and updating them for the purpose of their efficient construction and dynamic maintenance in the experiment model. We are not aware of any prior methods for the important issues of efficiently merging and updating evolutionary trees.

Our first main result is an algorithm for merging two evolutionary trees for disjoint sets of species running in time $O(dn)$, where n is the size of the resulting evolutionary tree and d is its maximum degree. Our merging algorithm yields a deterministic algorithm for constructing an evolutionary tree for n species from experiments running in time $O(dn \log n)$. This is a substantial improvement over the corresponding deterministic $O(n^2)$-time bound from [6], and the corresponding randomized $O(dn \log n \log \log n)$-time bound from [7]. Our second main result is a lower bound on the number of experiments necessary to perform in order to merge two evolutionary trees. It asymptotically matches the upper time provided by our merging algorithm proving its asymptotic optimality. Our third main result is an efficient algorithm for updating evolutionary trees in the experiment model. After $O(n \log n)$-time preprocessing, it can maintain a partial evolutionary tree under a sequence of m species insertions or deletions in time $O(dm \log(n + m))$. Observe that this dynamic algorithm yields an alternative proof of our $O(dn \log n)$-time bound on evolutionary tree construction.

In the literature, another variant of the experiment model based on quartets of species is often considered [2]. In this variant, the input to the experiment consists of four different species, say a, b, c and d, and the output is an undirected tree on four leaves labeled with a, b, c and d respectively, revealing the topology of the subtree of the evolutionary tree induced by the quartet. Note that if we fix some species as the root of the evolutionary tree then all the experiments on quartets including this particular species are equivalent to triple experiments for the other three species. By this simple observation, all upper bounds established in the triple variant of the experiment model immediately carry over to the quartet variant. As for lower bounds, note that the output of an experiment on a, b, c and d returning a directed tree on four leaves labeled with a, b, c, d can easily be deduced from the output of $O(1)$ experiments on triples in $\{a, b, c, d\}$. Since such a directed tree on a, b, c, d immediately yields the topology of an undirected one on a, b, c, d, also the lower bounds valid in the triple variant of the experiment model carry over up to constants to the (undirected) quartet variant.

Section 2 presents our efficient method of merging partial evolutionary trees with disjoint sets of leaves. Section 3 presents our lower bound on the number of experiments necessary to merge two evolutionary trees. Our method of efficiently updating evolutionary trees in the experiment model is given in Section 4.

2 Efficiently merging partial evolutionary trees

Throughout the paper, we shall denote by T an arbitrary fixed rooted evolutionary tree for a set of n species. We shall identify the leaves of T with the unique species labeling them. By the *degree* of a node v in a rooted tree, $deg(v)$ for short, we shall mean the number of children of v in the tree.

Given a subset S of leaves of T, the *partial evolutionary tree* induced by S, denoted by $T \parallel S$, is the minimum size tree that has S as the set of its leaves and is homeomorphic to the subtree of T composed of paths in T joining each pair of leaves in S. The node of $T \parallel S$ corresponding to the root of the subtree of T is the root of $T \parallel S$. For a partial evolutionary tree U, the set of its leaves will be denoted by S_U.

The problem of *merging two partial evolutionary trees* L and R consists in constructing the partial evolutionary tree $T \parallel (S_L \cup S_R)$, denoted by $L \cup R$, on the basis of L, R and experiments on triples in $(S_L \cup S_R)^3$.

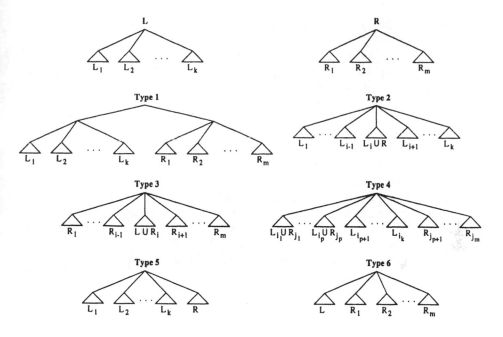

Fig. 2. The six different types of the tree $L \cup R$.

Theorem 1. *Let L, R be two partial evolutionary trees with disjoint sets of leaves. The merging of L and R into $L \cup R$ can be done in time $O(\sum_{v \in L \cup R} \deg^2(v))$ using at most $\sum_{v \in L \cup R} \deg^2(v)$ experiments.*

Proof. Let $L_1, ..., L_k$ denote the complete subtrees of L respectively rooted at the children of the root of L, and let the subtrees $R_1, ..., R_m$ of R be defined symmetrically.

We can distinguish six different types of the tree $L \cup R$, see Fig. 2.

1. The roots of L and R are exactly the children of the root of $L \cup R$.
2. The sequence of the complete subtrees rooted at the children of the root of $L \cup R$ has the form $L_1, ..., L_{i-1}, L_i \cup R, L_{i+1}, ..., L_k$, where $1 \leq i \leq k$.
3. The sequence of the complete subtrees rooted at the children of the root of $L \cup R$ has the form $R_1, ..., R_{i-1}, R_i \cup L, R_{i+1}, ..., R_m$, where $1 \leq i \leq m$.
4. The sequence of the complete subtrees rooted at the children of the root of $L \cup R$ has the form $L_{i_1} \cup R_{j_1}, L_{i_2} \cup R_{j_2}, ..., L_{i_p} \cup R_{j_p}, L_{i_{p+1}}, ..., L_{i_k}, R_{j_{p+1}}, ..., R_{j_m}$.
5. The roots of $L_1, ..., L_k$ and R are exactly the children of the root of $L \cup R$.
6. The roots of $R_1, ..., R_m$ and L are exactly the children of the root of $L \cup R$.

To see that $L \cup R$ is always of one of the six types note that otherwise one of the complete subtrees rooted at the children of the root of $L \cup R$ would exactly include some proper and non-empty subset of S_{L_i} or S_{R_j} for some $1 \leq i \leq k$ or some $1 \leq j \leq m$. Then, the root of L_i or R_j would overlap with that of $L \cup R$ which would contradict the topology of L or R.

For $i = 1, ..., k$, let l_i be a fixed leaf in S_{L_i}. Similarly, for $j = 1, ..., m$, let r_j be a fixed leaf in S_{R_j}.

The time complexity of the following multi-case merging method will depend only on the squares of the degrees in $L \cup R$ and not on the product of the degrees in L and R. The method starts from performing the experiment on the triple l_1, l_2, r_1. Then, it branches depending on the outcome of the experiment. To describe the possible outcomes we shall denote the fact that the lowest common ancestor of leaves a, b is below that of leaves a and c in T by $((a, b), c)$. If the lowest common ancestors for all pairs from $\{a, b, c\}$ overlap, we just write (a, b, c).

Case $((l_1, r_1), l_2)$. $L \cup R$ cannot be of type 1, 5 or 6 here. If it is of type 2 then one of the complete subtrees rooted at the children of the root of $L \cup R$ is $L_1 \cup R$. If it is of type 3 then one of the complete subtrees rooted at the children of the root of $L \cup R$ is $L \cup R_1$. Finally, if it is of type 4 then one of the complete subtrees rooted at the children of the root of $L \cup R$ is $L_1 \cup R_1$.

To determine $L \cup R$, we perform the experiment on the triple l_1, r_2, l_2. There are four possible outcomes:

$((l_1, r_2), l_2)$, then $L \cup R$ is of type 2 and it remains to construct $L_1 \cup R$ in order to determine $L \cup R$.

$((l_1, l_2), r_2)$, then $L \cup R$ is of type 3 and symmetrically it remains to construct $L \cup R_1$ in order to determine $L \cup R$.

$((l_2, r_2), l_1)$, then $L \cup R$ is of type 4 and two of the complete subtrees rooted at the children of the root of $L \cup R$ are $L_1 \cup R_1$ and $L_2 \cup R_2$, respectively. To determine the remaining subtrees $L_{i_q} \cup R_{j_q}$ we perform the experiments on the triples l_1, l_i, r_j for all i, j satisfying $2 < i \le k$ and $2 < j \le m$. Whenever the outcome is $((l_i, r_j), l_1)$, $L_i \cup R_j$ must be one of the complete subtrees rooted at the children of the root of $L \cup R$.

(l_1, l_2, r_2), then $L \cup R$ is also of type 4 and similarly it is sufficient to perform the experiments on all the triples l_1, l_i, r_j where $2 \le i \le k$ and $2 \le j \le m$.

Case $((l_2, r_1), l_1)$. This case reduces to the previous one by swapping L_1 and L_2.

Case (l_1, l_2, r_1). Similarly as in the two previous cases, $L \cup R$ cannot be of type 1 or 6 here and if it is of type type 3 then one of the complete subtrees rooted at the children of the root of $L \cup R$ is $L \cup R_1$.

To determine $L \cup R$, we perform the experiment on the triple r_1, r_2, l_1. If its outcome is:

$((r_1, r_2), l_1)$ then $L \cup R$ is of type 2 or 5. In this subcase if there is an index i such that $L_i \cup R$ is one of the complete subtrees rooted at a child of the root of $L \cup R$ then $L \cup R$ is of type 2. We can easily verify whether or not such an index exists, and if so, find it, e.g., by performing the experiments on the triples r_1, l_i, l_{i+1} for all i satisfying $1 \le i < k$.

$((l_1, r_1), r_2)$ then $L \cup R$ is of type 3 and $L \cup R_1$ is one of the complete subtrees rooted at the children of the root of $L \cup R$.

(l_1, r_1, r_2) or $((l_1, r_2), r_1)$ then $L \cup R$ is of type 4. By performing the experiments on all the triples l_i, r_j, r_{j+1} where $1 \le i \le k$ and $1 \le j \le m - 1$, we can easily determine all the subtrees $L_{i_q} \cup R_{j_q}$ where $1 \le q \le k$.

Case $((l_1, l_2), r_1)$. $L \cup R$ can be only of type 1, 3 or 6 here. To determine $L \cup R$, we perform the experiment on the triple l_1, r_1, r_2. If its outcome is:

$((\mathbf{r_1},\mathbf{r_2}),\mathbf{l_1})$, we are done since $L \cup R$ is simply of type 1.

$(\mathbf{l_1},\mathbf{r_1},\mathbf{r_2})$, $L \cup R$ is of type 3 or 6. In this subcase, if there is an index j such that $L \cup R_j$ is one of the complete subtrees rooted at a child of the root of $L \cup R$ then $L \cup R$ is of type 3, otherwise it is of type 6. We can easily verify whether or not such an index exists, and if so, find it, by performing the experiments on all the triples l_1, r_j, r_{j+1}, where $1 \leq j \leq m - 1$.

$((\mathbf{l_1},\mathbf{r_1}),\mathbf{r_2})$ (or $((\mathbf{l_1},\mathbf{r_2}),\mathbf{r_1})$, respectively) then $L \cup R$ is of type 3 and $L \cup R_1$ (or $L \cup R_2$, respectively) is one of the complete subtrees rooted at the children of the root of $L \cup R$.

Complexity analysis. Let w be the root of $L \cup R$. Observe that if $L \cup R$ is respectively of type 1, 2, 3, 4, 5, or 6 then $deg(w) = 2$, $deg(w) = k$, $deg(w) = m$, $deg(w) \geq \max\{k,m\}$, $deg(w) = k+1$, or $deg(w) = m+1$ respectively. Also, we have k, $m \geq 2$. Hence, by straightforward examination of all the cases, we infer that for any type of the resulting $L \cup R$, we use at most $deg(w)^2$ experiments apart from the experiments used to merge respective subtrees on subsequent recursion levels. The upper bound on the number of experiments easily follows by induction. To complete the proof it is sufficient to observe that our method requires a number of steps proportional to the number of experiments. □

By Theorem 1 and the sparsity of trees, we obtain the following corollary.

Corollary 1. *Two evolutionary trees with disjoint sets of leaves can be merged in time $O(dn)$ using at most dn experiments, where n is the size of the resulting tree and d is its maximum degree.*

Theorem 2. *An evolutionary tree of maximum degree d for n species can be built using experiments in time $O(dn \log n)$.*

Proof. We split the set of species (i.e., leaves) into two parts, of size $\lceil \frac{n}{2} \rceil$ and $\lfloor \frac{n}{2} \rfloor$, respectively. Next, we recursively construct the partial evolutionary tree for each of the parts, and merge the two resulting trees. Now, Corollary 1 together with the logarithmic recursion depth yield the theorem thesis.

If the maximum degree d in the tree is known in advance it is possible to improve the time upper bound in Theorem 2. Simply, we can limit the recursion depth to $\lceil \log_2(n/d) \rceil$, and use the quadratic time algorithm by Kannan et al. for the $O(n/d)$ subtrees of size at most d to reduce the upper bound to $O(nd + dn \log(n/d))$.

3   The lower bound

Theorem 3. *The merging of two evolutionary trees with disjoint sets of leaves requires in the worst case $\Omega(dn)$ experiments where n is the size of the resulting tree and d is its maximum degree.*

Proof. For the sake of exposition, we shall give a simplified proof which works for an infinite subsequence of the possible sizes n of the resulting tree, in this extended abstract. Technical details of its extension to include all possible sizes

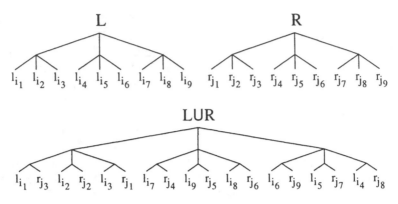

Fig. 3. An example of $L \cup R$.

and its combinatorial refinements leading to better constants are provided in the full version of the paper.

Consider two isomorphic complete d-ary rooted trees L and R (i.e., each non-leaf node in L or R has exactly d children) with disjoint sets of leaves, see Fig. 3. Next, consider an algorithm, say A, for merging evolutionary trees. We shall act as an adversary constructing in a top-down fashion the tree $L \cup R$ of type 4 (see the proof of Theorem 1) all the way down, forcing A to perform $\Omega(dn)$ experiments. The tree $L \cup R$ after removing its leaves will be isomorphic to L and R. All its nodes adjacent to leaves will have degree exactly 2. All its remaining non-leaf nodes will have degree d.

Let $L_1, ..., L_d$ denote the complete subtrees of L respectively rooted at the children of the root of L, and let the subtrees $R_1, ..., R_d$ of R be defined symmetrically. It follows that the complete subtrees rooted at the children of the root have the form $L_{i_1} \cup R_{j_1}, ..., L_{i_d} \cup R_{j_d}$. We claim that the algorithm A in order to determine the pairs $L_{i_1}, R_{j_1}, ..., L_{i_d}, R_{j_d}$ forming the aforementioned subtrees has to perform in the worst case so many experiments on triples l_i, r_j, x, where l_i is any leaf in L_i and r_i is any leaf in R_j, $1 \le i, j \le d$, that the number of different pairs (l_i, r_j) of leaves induced by the triples is at least $\binom{d}{2}$.

To prove the claim we play the following game with A as long as the following condition holds: *There are still at least two perfect pairings (matchings) of the L_i's with R_j's so the respective pairs could be merged without contradicting experiments performed so far and our current intentions.* To model the game we use an originally complete, bipartite graph G on $\{L_1, ..., L_d\} \cup \{R_1, ..., R_d\}$. Whenever A performs an experiment on a triple l_i, r_j, x, where x is a leaf outside L_i and R_j, we set the outcome of the experiment to be (l_i, r_j, x). Note that such an outcome excludes the possibility that the pairs of subtrees corresponding to the pairs of leaves are the subject of merging. Therefore, we remove the edge (if not already removed) connecting L_i with R_i from the bipartite graph G. Also, depending on whether x is a leaf of some $L_{i'}$ or some $R_{j'}$, we remove the edge connecting $L_{i'}$ with R_j or L_i with $R_{j'}$, respectively. Similarly, if A performs an experiment on a triple l_i, r_j, x, where x is a leaf of L_i or R_j, we set the outcome to $((l_i, x), r_j)$ if x is a leaf of L_i and to $((r_j, x), l_i)$ if x is a leaf of R_j. Here our setting is rather neutral as oppose to (l_i, r_j, x) which would witness that L_i is merged with R_j. The neutrality of the setting follows from the lack of the form of the outcome which would contradicts the possibility of merging L_i with R_j. However, our intention in this case is clear, we won't merge L_i with R_j. Therefore, also in this case we remove the edge (if not already removed) connecting L_i with R_j from G. The question is what is the minimum number of aforementioned pairs of leaves induced by the experiments performed by A necessary to finish the game. This minimum number is clearly at least the minimum number of edges necessary to delete from G, originally isomorphic to $K_{d,d}$, so there is left a unique perfect matching. The latter number is in turn at least the number of pairs of edges in the perfect matching, i.e., $\binom{d}{2}$, since for each such a pair, say (L_{i_1}, R_{j_1}), (L_{i_2}, R_{j_2}), at least one of the two cross edges (L_{i_1}, R_{j_2}), (L_{i_2}, R_{j_1}) has to be deleted.

Importantly, no pair (l_q, r_q), where $l_q \in L_q, r_q \in R_q$ and $L_{i_q} \cup R_{j_q}$ is a subtree of $L \cup R$, is accounted for in the at least $\binom{d}{2}$ aforementioned pairs of leaves. For this reason, we can apply the same lower bound argument recursively to each of the subtrees $L_{i_q} \cup R_{j_q}$ of $L \cup R$ obtaining d pairwise disjoint sets of pairs of leaves, each containing at least $\binom{d}{2}$ elements different from the aforementioned ones, and then proceed analogously with the subtrees of the subtrees *etc.*

By induction on the depth of $L \cup R$, we conclude that the algorithm A has to yield at least $\binom{d}{2}$ times the number of nodes in $L \cup R$ of degree d distinct pairs of leaves. Since the number of nodes of degree d in $L \cup R$ is $\Omega(\frac{n}{d})$, where n is the number of nodes in $L \cup R$, we obtain an $\Omega(dn)$ bound on the number of distinct pairs of leaves yielded by A. Now it is sufficient to observe that each experiment can generate at most two distinct pairs of leaves.

4 Dynamic Construction of Evolutionary Trees

In this section, we present an efficient dynamic algorithm for maintaining an evolutionary tree under a sequence of leaf (species) insertions and deletions in the experiment model. Our algorithm relies on the following fact.

Fact 1 (see [6]) *Let v be an internal node of the evolutionary tree for a set U of species. Let $W \subseteq U$, and let $W_1, ..., W_q$ be the splitting of W into non-empty components induced by v. For any $u \in U \setminus W$, we can determine whether u belongs to any of the components of U induced by v that is a superset of one of the components $W_1, ..., W_q$, and if so, also the index of the component, in time $O(q)$ by performing $\lceil \frac{q}{2} \rceil$ experiments.*

The basic data structure used by our dynamic algorithm is a *tree of leaf separators with threshold b* for the current evolutionary tree T of maximum degree d and $0 < b < 1$. The root of the tree of leaf separators is a vertex of T whose removal disconnects T into subtrees of leaf size non-exceeding b times that for T. Importantly, only the original leaves of T are accounted for in the leaf size of its subtrees. The children of the root are in turn the roots of the trees of leaf separators for the aforementioned subtrees. Each edge of the tree of leaf separators is labeled by the number of leaves in the subtree of T for which its lower endpoint is the root of the (sub)tree of leaf separators.

The following lemma can be easily proved using the standard idea for finding vertex separators in rooted trees (e.g., see Lemma 3 in [6]).

Lemma 2. *The tree of leaf separators with threshold $\frac{1}{2}$ for T can be constructed in time $O(l \log n)$, where l is the number of vertices in T, and n is the number of leaves in T.*

Proof. If the root of T satisfies the requirements for the root for the tree of leaf separators with threshold $\frac{1}{2}$, we recursively construct the (sub)trees of leaf separators for the subtrees of T respectively rooted at its children. Then, it remains to append the roots of the (sub)trees of leaf separators to the root. Otherwise, we iterate the aforementioned test for the child of the root for which the subtree rooted at it has more than half of the leaves of T, and so on until a vertex passing the test is found. Then we proceed analogously with the subtrees of T resulting from removing the vertex. Importantly, the father of the vertex in T is treated as the root of the subtree of T resulting from removing the vertex and all the subtrees of T rooted at its children. Since each vertex of T is involved in $O(\log n)$ tests, the total time complexity is $O(l \log n)$. □

Given a tree S of leaf separators, with the initial threshold $\frac{1}{2}$ and the maintained threshold $\frac{2}{3}$ for T, our dynamic algorithm is simple. In case of leaf insertion, we start from the root of S. By Fact 1, we can determine whether the leaf to insert should extend one of the leaf subsets induced by the root or form a new separate one by performing $O(d)$ experiments. In the former case, we go to the child of the root in S corresponding to the leaf subset and proceed recursively. Otherwise, it is sufficient to hang the new leaf at the root. Note that the depth of S is $O(\log n)$, where n is the number of leaves in T. Hence, the total time, including experiments, taken by the insertion is $O(d \log n)$. After an insertion of a new single leaf w in T, S is not necessarily a tree of leaf separators for the updated T. For this reason, we increase each number labeling an edge on the path in S tracing the insertion of w by one provided that the augmented number does not exceed the threshold $\frac{2}{3}$ on the leaf size of the corresponding subtree of T. Otherwise, we simply compute from scratch a (sub)tree of leaf separators with threshold $\frac{1}{2}$ for the whole subtree T' of T (extended by w) for which the upper endpoint of the edge is the root of the (sub)tree of leaf separators. Consequently, we replace the complete subtree of S rooted at the upper endpoint with the (sub)tree computed from scratch by substituting the root of the latter for the upper endpoint. Since initially the replaced (sub)tree of leaf separators had threshold $\frac{1}{2}$ we can charge at least $\frac{1}{6}$ times the number of leaves in T' leaf insertions with this costly operation. It follows from Lemma 2 that this additional cost of maintaining the tree of leaf separators for T under leaf insertions is at most proportional to the number of leaf insertions times the logarithm of the number of species.

Leaf deletions can be handled similarly. First, we trace the leaf to delete using the tree of leaf separators, then we delete the leaf and update the tree of leaf separators similarly.

Theorem 4. *After $O(n \log n)$-time preprocessing, we can maintain the evolutionary tree for n species under a sequence of m species insertions and deletions in time $O(dm \log(n + m))$.*

Note that as an immediate corollary of Theorem 4, we obtain the $O(dn \log n)$-time bound on the construction of an evolutionary tree of maximum degree d for n species derived in Section 2. This gives an alternative proof of Theorem 2.

5 Final Remarks

The merging and updating techniques for evolutionary trees presented in this paper should be useful in finding efficient algorithms for several other problems involving construction and maintenance of unknown or partially unknown trees (both within computational biology as well as outside it, e.g., in distributed computing).

In Introduction we have observed that the problem of sorting distinct numbers in the comparison model can be expressed as a special case of the problem of constructing an evolutionary tree from experiments. Our observation immediately yields an $\Omega(n \log n)$ bound on the number of experiments that have to be performed in the worst case in order to construct an evolutionary tree for n species, confirming the information-theoretic $\Omega(n \log n)$ bound from [6]. Our $\Omega(dn)$ bound on the number of experiments that have to be performed in the worst case in order to merge two evolutionary trees into one of size n and maximum degree d clearly yields the corresponding $\Omega(dn)$ bound for the problem of constructing an evolutionary tree. This confirms the $\Omega(dn)$ bound for the evolutionary tree construction problem from [7]. It is an intriguing open problem whether one could establish a lower bound on the number of experiments for the evolutionary tree construction problem that would be superlinear in nd for $d = O(n/\log n)$.

References

1. A. Amir and D. Keselman. Maximum agreement subtree in a set of evolutionary trees: Metrics and efficient algorithms. *SIAM Journal on Computing*, 26:1656–1669, 1997.
2. D. Bryant and M. Steel. Fast algorithms for constructing optimal trees from quartets. In *Proceedings of the 10th Annual ACM-SIAM Symposium on Discrete Algorithms*, pages 147–155, 1999.
3. J. C. Culbertson and P. Rudnicki. A fast algorithm for constructing trees from distance matrices. *Information Processing Letters*, 30(4):215–220, 1989.
4. M. Farach and M. Thorup. Fast comparison of evolutionary trees (extended abstract). In *Proceedings of the 5th Annual ACM-SIAM Symposium on Discrete Algorithms*, pages 481–488, 1994.
5. M. R. Henzinger, V. King, and T. J. Warnow. Constructing a tree from homeomorphic subtrees, with applications to computational biology. In *Proceedings of the 7th Annual ACM-SIAM Symposium on Discrete Algorithms*, pages 333–340, 1996.
6. S. K. Kannan, E. L. Lawler, and T. J. Warnow. Determining the evolutionary tree using experiments. *Journal of Algorithms*, 21:26–50, 1996.
7. M. Y. Kao, A. Lingas, and A. Östlin. Balanced randomized tree splitting with applications to evolutionary tree constructions. In *Proceedings of the 16th Annual Symposium on Theoretical Aspects of Computer Science*, pages 184–196, 1999.
8. C.G. Sibley and J.E. Ahlquist. Phylogeny and classification of birds based on the data of dna-dna-hybridization. *Current Ornithology*, 1:245–292, 1983.

Formalizing a Lazy Substitution Proof System for μ-calculus in the Calculus of Inductive Constructions

Marino Miculan[*]

Dipartimento di Matematica e Informatica, Università di Udine
Via delle Scienze, 206, I-33100, Udine, Italy. `miculan@dimi.uniud.it`

Abstract. We present a Natural Deduction proof system for the propositional modal μ-calculus, and its formalization in the Calculus of Inductive Constructions. We address several problematic issues, such as the use of *higher-order abstract syntax* in inductive sets in presence of recursive constructors, the encoding of modal (sequent-style) rules and of context sensitive grammars. The formalization can be used in the system Coq, providing an experimental computer-aided proof environment for the interactive development of error-free proofs in the μ-calculus. The techniques we adopt can be readily ported to other languages and proof systems featuring similar problematic issues.

Introduction

The μ-calculus, often referred to as μK, is a temporal logic which subsumes many modal and temporal logics, such as PDL, CTL, CTL^*, $ECTL$. Despite its expressive power, μK enjoys nice properties such as decidability, axiomatizability and the finite model property. Therefore, the μ-calculus is an ideal candidate as a logic for the verification of processes. Nevertheless, like any formal systems, its applicability to non trivial cases is limited by long, difficult, error-prone proofs.

This drawback can be (partially) overcome by supplying the user with a *computer-aided proof environment*, that is, a system in which he can represent (*encode, formalize*) the formal system, more or less abstractly: its syntax, axioms, rules and inference mechanisms. After having supplied the proof environment with a representation of the formal system, the user should be able to correctly manipulate (the representations of) the proofs.

Clearly, the implementation of a proof environment for a specific formal system is a complex, time-consuming, and daunting task. An alternative, and promising solution is to develop a general theory of logical systems, that is, a *Logical Framework*. A Logical Framework is a metalogical formalism for the specification of both the *syntactic* and the *deductive* notions of a wide range of formal systems. Logical Frameworks provide suitable means for representing and deal with, in the metalogical formalism, the *proofs* and *derivations* of the object system. Much of the implementation effort can be expended once and for all; hence, the implementation of a Logical Framework yields a *logic-independent proof development environment*. Such an environment is able to check validity of deductions in any formal system, after it has been provided by the specification of the system in the formalism of the Logical Framework.

In recent years, several different frameworks have been proposed, implemented and applied to many formal systems. *Type theories* have emerged as

---

[*] Work partially supported by Italian MURST-97 grant *Tecniche formali...*

leading candidates for Logical Frameworks. Simple typed λ-calculus and minimal intuitionistic propositional logic are connected by the well-known *proposition-as-types* paradigm [3]. Stronger type theories, such as the *Edinburgh Logical Framework*, the *Calculus of Inductive Constructions* and *Martin-Löf's type theory*, were especially designed, or can be fruitfully used, as a logical framework [7, 2, 15]. In these frameworks, we can represent faithfully and uniformly all the relevant concepts of the inference process in a logical system: syntactic categories, terms, assertions, axiom schemata, rule schemata, tactics, etc. via the *judgments-as-types, proofs-as-λ-terms* paradigm [7]. The key concept is that of *hypothetico-general* judgment [11], which is rendered as a type of the dependent typed λ-calculus of the Logical Framework. With this interpretation, a judgment is viewed as a type whose inhabitants correspond to proof of this judgment.

It is worthwhile noticing that Logical Frameworks based on type theory directly give rise to proof systems in *Natural Deduction style* [6]. This follows from the fact that the typing systems of the underlying λ-calculi are in Natural Deduction style, and rules and proofs are represented by λ-terms. As it is well-known, Natural Deduction style systems are more suited to the practical usage, since they allow for developing proofs the way mathematicians normally reason.

These type theories have been implemented in logic-independent systems such as Coq, LEGO and ALF [2, 9, 10]. These systems can be readily turned into interactive proof development environments for a specific logic: we need only to provide the specification of the formal system (the *signature*), i.e. a declaration of typed constants corresponding to the syntactic categories, term constructors, judgments, and rule schemata of the logic. It is possible to prove, informally but rigorously, that a formal system is *adequately* represented by its specification. This proof usually exhibit bijective maps between objects of the formal system (terms, formulæ, proofs) and the corresponding λ-terms of the encoding.

In this paper, we investigate the applicability of this approach to the propositional μ-calculus. Due to its expressive power, we adopt the Calculus of Inductive Constructions (CIC), implemented in the system Coq. Beside its expressive power and importance in the theory and verification of processes, the μ-calculus is interesting also for its syntactic and proof theoretic peculiarities. These idiosyncrasies are mainly due to the negative arity of "μ" (i.e., the bound variable x ranges over the same syntactic class of $\mu x \varphi$); a context-sensitive grammar due the condition on $\mu x \varphi$; rules with complex side conditions (sequent-style "proof" rules). These anomalies escape the "standard" representation paradigm of CIC; hence, we need to accommodate special techniques for enforcing these peculiarities. Moreover, since generated editors allow the user to reason "under assumptions", the designer of a proof editor for a given logic is urged to look for a Natural Deduction formulation of the system. Hence, we introduce a new proof system in Natural Deduction style for μK, the *lazy substitution* system $\mathbf{N}^{ls}_{\mu K}$. This system should more natural to use than traditional Hilbert-style systems; moreover, it takes best advantage of the possibility of manipulating assumptions offered by CIC in order to implement the problematic substitution of formulæ for variables. In fact, substitutions are delayed as much as possible, and are kept in the derivation context by means of assumptions. This mechanism fits perfectly the stack discipline of assumptions of Natural Deduction, and it is neatly formalized in CIC.

Due to lack of space, full proofs and the complete Coq signature will be omitted; see [12] for an extended version of this paper.

1 Syntax, semantics and consequence relation of μK

The language of μK is an extension of the syntax of propositional dynamic logic. Let Act be a set of *actions* (ranged over by a, b, c), and Var a set of propositional variables (ranged over by x, y, z); then, the syntax of the μ-calculus on Act is:

$$\Phi: \quad \varphi, \psi ::= f\!f \mid \neg\varphi \mid \varphi \supset \psi \mid [a]\varphi \mid x \mid \mu x\varphi$$

where the formation of $\mu x\varphi$ is subject to the *positivity condition:* every occurrence of x in φ has to appear inside an even number of negations (In the following we will spell out this condition more in detail). We call *preformulæ* the language obtained by dropping the positivity condition. The variable x is *bound* in $\mu x\varphi$; the usual conventions about α-equivalence apply. Given a set $X \subseteq Var$ of variables, we denote by $\Phi_X \overset{\text{def}}{=} \{\varphi \in \Phi \mid FV(\varphi) \subseteq X\}$ the set of formulæ with free variables in X. Capture-avoiding substitutions are the usual maps $\Phi \to \Phi$, written as lists of the form $\{\varphi_1/x_1, \ldots, \varphi_n/x_n\}$; they are ranged over by σ, τ. We denote by $\varphi\sigma$ the formula obtained by applying the substitution σ to φ.

The interpretation of μ-calculus comes from Modal Logic. A model for the μ-calculus is a transition system, that is, a pair $\mathcal{M} = \langle S, [\![\cdot]\!]\rangle$ where S is a (generic) nonempty set of *(abstract) states*, ranged over by s, t, r, and $[\![\cdot]\!]$ is the interpretation of command symbols: for all a, we have $[\![a]\!] : S \to \mathcal{P}(S)$.

Formulæ of μ-calculus may have free propositional variables; therefore, we need to introduce *environments*, which are functions assigning sets of states to propositional variables: $Env \overset{\text{def}}{=} Var \to \mathcal{P}(S)$. Given a model $\mathcal{M} = \langle S, [\![\cdot]\!]\rangle$ and an environment ρ, the semantics of a formula is the set of states in which it holds, and it is defined by extending $[\![\cdot]\!]$ compositionally:

$$[\![f\!f]\!]\rho \overset{\text{def}}{=} \emptyset \qquad [\![\varphi \supset \psi]\!]\rho \overset{\text{def}}{=} (S \setminus [\![\varphi]\!]\rho) \cup [\![\psi]\!]\rho$$

$$[\![x]\!]\rho \overset{\text{def}}{=} \rho(x) \qquad [\![[a]\varphi]\!]\rho \overset{\text{def}}{=} \{s \in S \mid \forall r \in [\![a]\!]s : r \in [\![\varphi]\!]\rho\}$$

$$[\![\neg\varphi]\!]\rho \overset{\text{def}}{=} S \setminus [\![\varphi]\!]\rho \qquad [\![\mu x\varphi]\!]\rho \overset{\text{def}}{=} \bigcap\{T \subseteq S \mid [\![\varphi]\!]\rho[x \mapsto T] \subseteq T\}$$

It is customary to view a formula φ with a free variable x as defining a function $\varphi_x^\rho : \mathcal{P}(S) \to \mathcal{P}(S)$, such that for all $U \subseteq S: \varphi_x^\rho(U) = [\![\varphi]\!]\rho[x \mapsto U]$. The intuitive interpretation of $\mu x\varphi$ is then the *least fixed point* of φ_x^ρ. The syntactic condition on the formation of $\mu x\varphi$ ensures the monotonicity of φ_x^ρ, and hence, by Knaster-Tarski's theorem, the existence of the lfp as well [8]. This does not hold if we drop the condition on the formation of $\mu x\varphi$; e.g., the formula $\neg x$ identifies the function $(\neg x)_x^\rho(T) = S \setminus T$, which is not monotone and has no (least) fixed point.

In order to have a semantical counterpart of the syntactic notion of "deduction", we introduce a consequence relation for the μ-calculus:

Definition 1. *Let $\mathcal{M} = \langle S, [\![\cdot]\!]\rangle$ be a model for μK. The* consequence relation *for μK with respect to $\mathcal{M}$ is a relation $\models_{\mathcal{M}} \subseteq \mathcal{P}_{<\omega}(\Phi) \times \Phi$, defined as follows (where $[\![\Gamma]\!]\rho \overset{\text{def}}{=} \bigcap_{\varphi \in \Gamma} [\![\varphi]\!]\rho$): $\Gamma \models_{\mathcal{M}} \varphi \iff \forall\rho.[\![\Gamma]\!]\rho \subseteq [\![\varphi]\!]\rho$.* The (absolute) consequence relation *for μK is: $\Gamma \models \varphi \iff \forall\mathcal{M}.\Gamma \models_{\mathcal{M}} \varphi$.*

$$\frac{}{posin(x,f\!f)} \qquad \frac{y \in Var}{posin(x,y)} \qquad \frac{negin(x,\varphi)}{posin(x,\neg\varphi)}$$

$$\frac{negin(x,\varphi) \quad posin(x,\psi)}{posin(x,\varphi \supset \psi)} \qquad \frac{posin(x,\varphi)}{posin(x,[a]\,\varphi)}$$

$$\frac{\text{for } z \neq x : posin(x,\varphi[z/y])}{posin(x,\mu y\varphi)}$$

$$\frac{}{negin(x,f\!f)} \qquad \frac{y \neq x}{negin(x,y)} \qquad \frac{posin(x,\varphi)}{negin(x,\neg\varphi)}$$

$$\frac{posin(x,\varphi) \quad negin(x,\psi)}{negin(x,\varphi \supset \psi)} \qquad \frac{negin(x,\varphi)}{negin(x,[a]\,\varphi)}$$

$$\frac{\text{for } z \neq x : negin(x,\varphi[z/y])}{negin(x,\mu y\varphi)}$$

Fig. 1. The positivity proof system.

2 A proof system for the positivity condition

Since we aim to encode the μ-calculus in some logical framework, we need to enforce the context-sensitive condition on the formation of formulæ of the form $\mu x\varphi$. That is, we ought to specify in detail the condition of "occurring positive in a formula" for a variable. This notion can be represented by two new judgments on formulæ and variables, *posin* and *negin*, which are derived by means of the rules in Figure 1. Roughly, $posin(x,\varphi)$ holds iff all occurrences of x in φ are positively; dually, $negin(x,\varphi)$ holds iff all occurrences of x in φ are negative. Notice that if x does not occur in φ, then it occurs both positively and negatively. More formally, the notions these auxiliary judgments capture are the following:

Definition 2 ((Anti)Monotonicity). *For $\varphi \in \Phi$, $x \in Var$, we say that φ is monotone on x (written $Mon_x(\varphi)$) iff $\forall \mathcal{M}, \forall \rho, \forall U, V \subseteq S : U \subseteq V \implies \varphi_x^\rho(U) \subseteq \varphi_x^\rho(V)$. We say that φ is antimonotone on x (written $AntiMon_x(\varphi)$) iff $\forall \mathcal{M}, \forall \rho, \forall U, V \subseteq S : U \subseteq V \implies \varphi_x^\rho(U) \supseteq \varphi_x^\rho(V)$.*

These notions refer directly to the semantic structures in which formulæ take meaning. In fact, the syntactic conditions of positivity/negativity are sound wrt the semantic condition of monotonicity/antimonotonicity:

Proposition 1. $\vdash posin(x,\varphi) \Rightarrow Mon_x(\varphi)$ *and* $\vdash negin(x,\varphi) \Rightarrow AntiMon_x(\varphi)$.

The converse of Proposition 1 does not hold. Consider e.g. $\varphi \stackrel{\text{def}}{=} (x \supset x)$: clearly, $[\![\varphi]\!]\rho = S$ always, and hence $(x \supset x)_x^\rho$ is both monotone and antimonotone. However, x does not occur only positively nor only negatively in φ. Hence, we cannot derive $\vdash posin(x,(x \supset x))$ nor $\vdash negin(x,(x \supset x))$. This is generalized in the following result, which can be proved by induction on the syntax of φ:

Proposition 2. *If $x \in FV(\varphi)$ occurs both positively and negatively in φ then neither $posin(x,\varphi)$ nor $negin(x,\varphi)$ are derivable.*

We can restrict ourselves to only positive formulæ without loss of generality: by Lyndon Theorem [4], every monotone formula is equivalent to a positive one.

3 The proof system $\mathbf{N}_{\mu K}^{ls}$

Usually, systems for μ-calculus are given in Hilbert style [8]. Here we present $\mathbf{N}_{\mu K}^{ls}$ (Figure 2), a *lazy substitution* proof system in Natural Deduction style for μK. This system is called "lazy" after that substitutions of formulæ for variables are delayed as much as possible—and may be not performed at all.

$$\neg\text{-I} \; \frac{\substack{(\varphi)\\\vdots\\ \textit{ff}}}{\neg\varphi} \qquad \supset\text{-I} \; \frac{\substack{(\varphi)\\\vdots\\ \psi}}{\varphi\supset\psi} \qquad \text{RAA} \; \frac{\substack{(\neg\varphi)\\\vdots\\ \textit{ff}}}{\varphi} \qquad \text{Sc} \; \frac{[a]\Gamma \quad \psi}{[a]\psi}^{\;[\Gamma]}$$

$$\neg\text{-E} \; \frac{\varphi \quad \neg\varphi}{\textit{ff}} \qquad \supset\text{-E} \; \frac{\varphi\supset\psi \quad \varphi}{\psi} \qquad\qquad \text{CNGR} \; \frac{\varphi\equiv\psi \quad \varphi}{\psi}$$

$$\mu\text{-I} \; \frac{\varphi\{z/x\}}{\mu x\varphi}^{\;(z\mapsto \mu x\varphi)}\; z \text{ fresh} \qquad\qquad \mu\text{-E} \; \frac{\mu x\varphi \quad \substack{(z\mapsto\psi),[\varphi\{z/x\}]\\\vdots\\ \psi}}{\psi}\; z \text{ fresh}$$

$$\frac{x\mapsto\varphi}{x\equiv\varphi} \qquad \frac{\varphi\equiv\psi \quad \psi\equiv\xi}{\varphi\equiv\xi} \qquad \frac{}{\varphi\equiv\varphi} \qquad \frac{\varphi\equiv\psi}{\psi\equiv\varphi}$$

$$\frac{\varphi\equiv\psi}{\neg\varphi\equiv\neg\psi} \qquad \frac{\varphi_1\equiv\psi_1 \quad \varphi_2\equiv\psi_2}{(\varphi_1\supset\varphi_2)\equiv(\psi_1\supset\psi_2)} \qquad \frac{\varphi\equiv\psi}{[a]\varphi\equiv[a]\psi} \qquad \frac{\varphi\{z/x\}\equiv\psi\{z/x\}}{\mu x\varphi\equiv\mu x\psi}\; z \text{ fresh}$$

Fig. 2. The lazy substitution, Natural Deduction-style proof system $\mathbf{N}^{ls}_{\mu K}$ for μ-calculus: logical system (top), and congruence system (bottom).

$\mathbf{N}^{ls}_{\mu K}$ is composed by two derivation systems, the *logical* one and the *congruence* one. Roughly, the logical system allows for deriving formulæ from formulæ (*assumptions*) and *bindings*, which are judgments of the form $x \mapsto \varphi$, where $x \in \text{Var}$ and $\varphi \in \varPhi$. The congruence system allows for deriving judgments of the form $\varphi \equiv \psi$, from a list of bindings. More precisely, we introduce the following

Definition 3. *A set of assumptions (denoted by Γ) is any finite set of formulæ; a binding list (denoted by Δ) is a list $\langle x_1 \mapsto \varphi_1, \ldots, x_n \mapsto \varphi_n\rangle$ such that for all $i \neq j$: $x_i \neq x_j$, and for all $i \leq j$: $x_i \notin \text{FV}(\varphi_j)$.*

A derivation of φ from assumptions Γ and bindings Δ is denoted by $\Delta; \Gamma \vdash \varphi$; a derivation of $\varphi \equiv \psi$ from Δ is denoted by $\Delta \vdash \varphi \equiv \psi$.

The logical system is composed by a standard set of rules for classical propositional logic, extended by Scott's rule Sc for minimal modal logic, the congruence rule CNGR, and the intro/elimination rules μ-I, μ-E. The rules for μ have a direct semantic interpretation: the introduction rule states that (the meaning of) $\mu x\varphi$ is a prefixed point of φ^ρ_x; the elimination rule states that (the meaning of) $\mu x\varphi$ implies, and then "is less than", any prefixed point of φ^ρ_x. Therefore, these rules state that (the meaning of) $\mu x\varphi$ is the least fixed point, of φ^ρ_x.

In rule Sc, the square brackets surrounding Γ mean that ψ may depend only on the discharged assumption Γ. Similarly, in rule μ-E, the formula $\varphi\{z/x\}$ is the only assumption that the subderivation of ψ may depend on. These "modal" side conditions can be explicated clearly by a Gentzen-like presentation:

$$\text{Sc} \; \frac{\Delta; \Gamma \vdash \psi}{\Delta; [a]\Gamma \vdash [a]\psi} \qquad\qquad \mu\text{-E} \; \frac{\Delta; \Gamma \vdash \mu x\varphi \quad \Delta, z \mapsto \psi; \varphi\{z/x\} \vdash \psi}{\Delta; \Gamma \vdash \psi}\; z \text{ fresh}$$

No logical rule requires a binding as a premise; bindings are only discharged, in rules requiring a substitution (i.e., rules μ-I, μ-E). In these rules, variables are not textually replaced by the corresponding formula, but only by an α-equivalent ("fresh") variable. The discharged hypothesis keeps in the derivation context the binding between the substituted variable and the corresponding formula. These hypotheses form a binding list which is used by the congruence system: roughly, we can prove $\Delta \vdash \varphi \equiv \psi$ iff φ and ψ are the same formula, "up to Δ". More precisely, a binding list Δ corresponds to a particular form of substitution, which can be defined by induction on Δ as $\sigma_{\langle\rangle} \stackrel{\text{def}}{=} \{\}$, $\sigma_{\Delta, x \mapsto \varphi} \stackrel{\text{def}}{=} \sigma_\Delta \circ \{\varphi/x\}$. Then, $\equiv$ is the smallest congruence which contains σ_Δ:

Proposition 3. *For all Δ, for all $\varphi, \psi \in \Phi$: $\Delta \vdash \varphi \equiv \psi \iff \varphi\sigma_\Delta = \psi\sigma_\Delta$*

The resulting system is then sound and complete:

Theorem 1. *For all Δ, for all Γ finite and $\varphi \in \Phi$: $\Delta; \Gamma \vdash \varphi \iff \Gamma\sigma_\Delta \models \varphi\sigma_\Delta$*

Proof. (Sketch) Soundness ($\Rightarrow$) is proved by showing that each rule is sound. Completeness ($\Leftarrow$) can be proved by proving that axioms and rules of a complete Hilbert-style system (e.g., Kozen's one [17]) are derivable in $\mathbf{N}^{ls}_{\mu K}$. $\qquad\square$

Corollary 1. *For Γ finite set of formulæ, φ formula: $\emptyset; \Gamma \vdash \varphi \iff \Gamma \models \varphi$.*

4 Encoding the language of μ-calculus

The encoding of the language of μ-calculus is quite elaborate. The customary approach, is to define an inductive type, $\mathtt{o:Set}$, whose constructors correspond to those of the language of μK. In order to take full advantage of α-conversion and substitution machinery provided by the metalanguage, we adopt the *higher order abstract syntax* [5, 7]. In this approach, binding constructors (like μ) are rendered by higher-order term constructors; that is, they take a *function*. The naïve representation of μ would be $\mathtt{mu:(o\text{->}o)\text{->}o}$; however, this solution does not work inside an inductive definition of CIC, because it leads to a non-well-founded definition [2, 5].

The second problem is the presence of a context-sensitive condition on the applicability of μ: in order to construct a formula of the form $\mu x \varphi$, we have to make sure that x occurs positively in φ. Inductive types do not support this kind of restriction, since they define only context-free languages [13].

In order to overcome the first problems, we adopt the *bookkeeping* technique [13]. We introduce a separate type, $\mathtt{var}$, for the identifiers. These variables act as "placeholders" for formulæ: they will be bound to formulæ in the application of μ-I and μ-E rules, by means of an auxiliary judgment. There are no constructors for type $\mathtt{var}$: we only assume that there are infinitely many variables.

```
Parameter var : Set.
Axiom var_nat : (Ex [srj:var->nat](n:nat)(Ex [x:var](srj x)=n)).
```

Then, we define the set of preformulæ of μ-calculus, also those not well formed:

```
Parameter Act : Set.
Inductive o   : Set := ff : o | Not : o -> o | Imp : o -> o -> o
       | Box : Act -> o -> o | Var : var -> o | mu : (var->o) -> o.
```

Notice that, the argument of $\mathtt{mu}$ is a function of type $\mathtt{var\text{->}o}$. In general, this may arise *exotic terms*, i.e. terms which do not correspond to any preformula of the μ-calculus [5, 13]. These terms are built by using the $\mathtt{Case}$ term constructor of inductive type theory, over the type of variables. This cannot be achieved in our approach since var is not declared as an inductive set. Of course, the price we pay is that equality between variables is not decidable [13, Section 11.2].

Now, we have to rule out all the non-well-formed formulæ. At the moment, the only way for enforcing in CIC context-sensitive conditions over languages is to define a subtype by means of Σ-types. As a first step, we formalize the system for positivity/negativity presented in Figure 1, introducing two judgments posin, negin of type var->o->Prop. A careful analysis of the proof system (Figure 1) points out that the derivation of these judgments is completely syntax driven. It is therefore natural to define these judgments as *recursively defined functions*, instead of inductively defined propositions. This is indeed feasible, but the rules for the binding operators introduce an implicit quantification over the set of variables *different from the one we are looking for*. This is rendered by assuming a new variable (y) and that it is different from the variable x (see last cases):

```
Fixpoint posin [x:var;A:o] : Prop :=
 <Prop>Cases A of  ff => True | (Not B) => (negin x B)
 | (Imp A1 A2) => (negin x A1)/\(posin x A2) | (Box a B) => (posin x B)
 | (Var y) => True | (mu F)  => (y:var)~(x=y)->(posin x (F y))
 end
with negin [x:var;A:o] : Prop :=
 <Prop>Cases A of  ff => True | (Not B) => (posin x B)
 | (Imp A1 A2) => (posin x A1)/\(negin x A2) | (Box a B) => (negin x B)
 | (Var y) => ~(x=y) | (mu F)  => (y:var)~(x=y)->(negin x (F y))
 end.
```

Therefore, in general a goal (posin x A) can be Simplified (i.e., by applying the Simpl tactic, in Coq) to a conjunction of only three forms of propositions: True, negations of equalities or implications from negations of equalities to another conjunction of the same form. These three forms are dealt with simply in Coq, hence proving this kind of goals is a simple and straightforward task.

Similarly, a preformula is well formed when every application of μ satisfies the positivity condition:

```
Fixpoint iswf [A:o] : Prop :=
 <Prop>Cases A of  ff => True | (Var y) => True | (Not B) => (iswf B)
 | (Imp A1 A2) => (iswf A1)/\(iswf A2) | (Box a B) => (iswf B)
 | (mu F)  => (x:var)(iswf (F x))/\((notin x (mu F)) -> (posin x (F x)))
 end.
```

In the case of μ, we locally assume the fact that the x we introduce does not appear in the formula, i.e. it is *fresh*. Although this is automatically achieved by the metalanguage, we may need this information for proving (posin x (F x)). This is achieved by the hypothesis (notin z (mu F)). The judgment notin and the dual isin (see [12]) are auxiliary judgments for occur-checking. Roughly, (notin x A) holds iff x does not occur free in A; dually for isin.

Finally, each formula of the μ-calculus is therefore represented by a pair preformula-proof of its well-formedness:

```
Record wfo: Set := mkwfo {prp : o; cnd : (iswf prp)}.
```

In order to estabilish that our encoding is faithful, we introduce the following notation: for $X = \{x_1, \ldots, x_n\} \subset Var$, let $\Xi_X \stackrel{\text{def}}{=} x_1 : \text{var}, \ldots, x_n : \text{var}, \circ_X \stackrel{\text{def}}{=}$

$\{ \mathtt{t} \mid \varXi_X \vdash \mathtt{t} : \mathtt{o}, \mathtt{t} \text{ canonical} \}$ and $\mathtt{wfo}_X \overset{\text{def}}{=} \{ \mathtt{t} \in \mathtt{o}_X \mid \exists \mathtt{d}. \varXi_X \vdash \mathtt{d} : (\mathtt{iswf\ t}) \}$.
We can then define the *encoding map* $\varepsilon_X : \varPhi_X \to \mathtt{o}_X$, as follows:

$$\varepsilon_X(x) = \mathtt{x} \qquad \varepsilon_X(\varphi \supset \psi) = (\mathtt{Imp}\ \varepsilon_X(\varphi)\ \varepsilon_X(\psi))$$
$$\varepsilon_X(\neg\varphi) = (\mathtt{Not}\ \varepsilon_X(\varphi)) \qquad \varepsilon_X([a]\varphi) = (\mathtt{Box\ a}\ \varepsilon_X(\varphi))$$
$$\varepsilon_X(\mathit{ff}) = \mathtt{ff} \qquad \varepsilon_X(\mu x \varphi) = (\mathtt{mu}\ [\mathtt{x:var}]\varepsilon_{X,x}(\varphi))$$

Theorem 2. *The map ε_X is a compositional bijection between $\varPhi_X$ and $\mathtt{wfo}_X$.*

Proof. (Sketch) Long inductions. First, one proves that $\mathtt{posin}, \mathtt{negin}$ adequately represent the positivity/negativity proof system. Then, a preformula φ is a formula iff each application of μ is valid, iff for each application of μ there exists a (unique) witness of $\mathtt{posin}$, iff there exists an inhabitant of $(\mathtt{iswf}\ \varepsilon_X(\varphi))$. $\qquad\square$

5 Encoding the proof system $\mathbf{N}^{ls}_{\mu K}$

In the encoding paradigm of Logical Frameworks, a proof system is usually represented by introducing a *proving judgment* over the set of formulæ, like $\mathtt{T:o}$ $\mathtt{-> Prop}$. A type $(\mathtt{T\ phi})$ should be intended, therefore, as "φ is true;" any term which inhabits $(\mathtt{T\ phi})$ is a witness (a proof) that φ is true. Each rule is then represented by a type constructor of $\mathtt{T}$. Moreover, substitution schemata for binding operators need not to be implemented "by hand", because they are inherited from the metalanguage. This is the case, for instance, of "$\forall$" in First Order Logic; for further examples and discussion, we refer to [5, 7].

However, in representing the proof system $\mathbf{N}^{ls}_{\mu K}$, two difficult issues arise: the encoding of proof rules, like SC and μ-E, and the substitution of formulæ for variables in rules μ-I and μ-E. Moreover, Scott's rule is parametric in the number of assumptions which have to be "boxed". These issues escape the standard encoding paradigm, so we have to accommodate some special technique.

Actually, in the underlying theory of CIC there is no direct way for enforcing on a premise the condition that it is a theorem (i.e. that it depends on no assumptions) or, more generally, that a formula depends only on a given set of assumptions. This is because the typing rules of PTS's are strictly in Natural Deduction style. Therefore, in presence of sequent-style rules like SC and μ-E, one could encode a complete sequent calculus introducing the type $\mathtt{olist}$ of lists of formulæ, the sequent judgment $\mathtt{Seq:olist->o->Prop}$, and all the machinery of Gentzen's original system [6]. This would lead to an unusable proof system: even if our rules have a Natural Deduction flavour, all the goals would be crammed with the list of hypotheses, and we should deal with supplementary structural rules for manipulating the list of assumptions.

Instead, we represent more efficiently the assumption set by means of the proof context provided by CIC, i.e., by taking advantage of the possibility of reasoning "under assumptions" [1]. First, we represent $\mapsto$ and $\equiv$ by means of two judgments $\mathtt{bind:var->o->Prop}$ and $\mathtt{cngr:o->o->Prop}$, respectively. The former has no constructor (it declared as a $\mathtt{Parameter}$), while the latter is rendered as an inductive predicate, as expected. In particular, the congruence rule for μ is rendered by means of a locally quantified variable (see [12] for the whole listing):

```
Parameter bind : var -> o -> Prop.
Inductive cngr : o -> o -> Prop :=
```

```
cngr_bind : (x:var)(A:o)(bind x A) -> (cngr (Var x) A)
(... other rules ...)
| cngr_mu :(A,B:var->o)((x:var)(cngr (A x) (B x)))->(cngr (mu A) (mu B)).
```

Then, we introduce the basic proving judgment, T:U->o->Prop, where U a set with *no* constructors. Elements of U will be called *worlds* for suggestive reasons. Each pure rule (i.e., with no side condition), is parameterized over a generic world, like the following:

```
Axiom Imp_E : (w:U)(A,B:o)(T w (Imp A B)) -> (T w A) -> (T w B).
```

Therefore, in a given world all the classical rules apply as usual. It should be noticed, however, that we require a locally introduced formula to be well formed. This is the case of ⊃-I:

```
Axiom Imp_I : (w:U)(A,B:o)(iswf A)->((T w A)->(T w B))->(T w (Imp A B)).
```

Indeed, it can be shown that if we allow for non-well formed formulæ in these "negative positions," we get easily an inconsistent derivation.

Proof rules, on the other hand, are distinguished by *local* quantifications of the world parameter, in order to make explicit the dependency between a conclusion and its premises. The rule μ-E is encoded as follows:

```
Axiom mu_E   : (F:var->o)(iswf A) ->
  ((z:var)(notin z (mu F)) -> (bind z A) -> (w':U)(T w' (F z))->(T w' A))
  -> (w:U)(T w (mu F)) -> (T w A).
```

The idea behind the use of the extra parameter is that in making an assumption, we are forced to assume the existence of a world, say w, and to instantiate the judgment T also on w. This judgment then appears as an hypothesis on w. Hence, deriving as premise a judgment, which is universally quantified with respect to U, amounts to establishing the judgment for the generic world w' on which only the given assumptions are made, i.e. on the given assumptions.

This idea can be suitably generalized to take care of an unlimited number of assumptions. In fact, a generic sequent $\varphi_1, \ldots, \varphi_n \vdash \varphi$ is faithfully represented by the type (w:U)(T w A_1)->...->(T w A_n)->(T w A) where $A_i = \varepsilon_X(\varphi_i)$ and $A = \varepsilon_X(\varphi)$. The locally quantified world w forces any proof of (T w A) to depend only on the given assumptions. The problem is capturing the parametric flavour expressed by the "...". At this end, we introduce lists of formulæ and the auxiliary function Sequent:U->o->olist->Prop:

```
Inductive olist : Set := nil : olist | cons : o -> olist -> olist.
Fixpoint Sequent [w:U;B:o;l:olist] : Prop :=
    Cases l of
        nil => (T w B)    | (cons A t) => (T w A)->(Sequent w B t)
    end.
```

Therefore, the aforementioned representation of $\varphi_1, \ldots, \varphi_n \vdash \varphi$ is denoted by (w:U)(Sequent w B G) where G is the list composed by $A_1, \ldots, A_n$. In fact, (Sequent w B G) is exactly $\beta\iota\delta$-equivalent (it can be reduced) to (T w A_1)-> ...->(T w A_n) -> (T w B). We can therefore represent Scott's rule as follows:

```
Fixpoint Boxlist [a:Act; l:olist] : olist :=
Cases l of nil => nil | (cons B t) => (cons (Box a B) (Boxlist a t)) end.
Axiom Sc  : (G:olist)(B:o)(a:Act) ((w':U)(Sequent w' B G)) ->
            (w:U)(Sequent w (Box a B) (Boxlist a G)).
```

where the map `Boxlist:Act->olist->olist` represents exactly the "$[a]\Gamma$" notation of rule SC. Hence, we can use the conversion tactics provided by Coq for automatically converting applications of `Sequent` to the right proposition.

The encoding of μ-E (and μ-I) uses also the auxiliary judgment `bind`. Following the idea of $\mathbf{N}^{ls}_{\mu K}$, the context $\varphi(\cdot)$ of $\mu x \varphi(x)$ is filled by a fresh (i.e., locally quantified) variable z. The binding between z and the corresponding formula is kept in the derivation environment by the hypothesis (`bind z A`). This hypothesis can be used in the derivation of congruence judgments, for replacing formulæ only when it is needed. For an example, see [12].

The discharged hypothesis (`notin z (mu F)`) in rule `mu_E` reflects at the logical level, the fact that z is fresh. Although freshness of z obviously holds, it cannot be inferred *in* the system because it belongs to the metalevel of the system. Hence, we reify it by means of the discharged hypothesis, which may be needed in the rest of derivation for inferring well-formedness of discharged formulæ in rules RAA, ⊃-I, ¬-I.

In order to state the adequacy of our formalization w.r.t. $\mathbf{N}^{ls}_{\mu K}$, we introduce the following notation. Let $X \subset Var$ be finite, and $\varphi_1, \ldots, \varphi_n, \varphi \in \Phi_X$; then, for $x_1, \ldots, x_n \in X$, we denote by $\delta_X(x_1 \mapsto \varphi_1, \ldots, x_n \mapsto \varphi_n)$ the context $b_1: (\text{bind } x_1 \ \varepsilon_X(\varphi_1)), \ldots b_n: (\text{bind } x_n \ \varepsilon_X(\varphi_n))$, and, for $\mathbf{w}:U$, we denote by $\gamma_{X,\mathbf{w}}(\varphi_1, \ldots, \varphi_n)$ the context $h_1: (\text{T } \mathbf{w} \ \varepsilon_X(\varphi_1)), \ldots, h_n: (\text{T } \mathbf{w} \ \varepsilon_X(\varphi_n))$.

Theorem 3. *Let $X \subset Var$ be finite, Δ a binding list such that $\mathrm{FV}(\Delta) \subseteq X$, and $\Gamma \subset \Phi_X$ finite. Then, for all $\varphi_1, \varphi_2 \in \Phi_X$:*

1. $\Delta \vdash \varphi_1 \equiv \varphi_2$ *iff there is* t *such that* $\Xi_X, \delta_X(\Delta) \vdash t : (\text{cngr } \varepsilon_X(\varphi_1) \ \varepsilon_X(\varphi_2))$
2. $\Delta; \Gamma \vdash \varphi_1$ *iff there is* t *such that* $\Xi_X, \delta_X(\Delta), \mathbf{w}:U, \gamma_{X,\mathbf{w}}(\Gamma) \vdash t : (\text{T } \mathbf{w} \ \varepsilon_X(\varphi_1))$.

Proof. (Sketch) Directions ⇒ are proved by induction on the proofs of $\Delta \vdash \varphi_1 \equiv \varphi_2$ and $\Delta; \Gamma \vdash \varphi_1$. Directions ⇐ are proved by induction on the syntax of t: each constructor of (`cngr A B`) and (`T w A`) corresponds to a rule of $\mathbf{N}^{ls}_{\mu K}$. □

6 Conclusions

In this paper we have introduced an original proof system $\mathbf{N}^{ls}_{\mu K}$ for the propositional modal μ-calculus, and its formalization in the Calculus of Inductive Constructions. Beside the formalization, $\mathbf{N}^{ls}_{\mu K}$ is interesting on its own for several reasons: it is in Natural Deduction style, it has been proved complete with respect to logical consequences (while traditional Hilbert-style proof systems are complete with respect to theorems), and its usage should be easier than axiomatic proof systems. Moreover, in $\mathbf{N}^{ls}_{\mu K}$ substitutions of formulæ for variables are not always performed, but they may be delayed until actually needed.

In the encoding, we have addressed several problematic issues. First, the use of the higher order abstract syntax frees us from a tedious encoding of the mechanisms involved in the handling of α-conversion, because it is automatically inherited from the metalevel. Secondly, substitution is represented by a congruence proof system, whose proofs are syntax-driven and can be highly automatized in the Coq environment. Thirdly, we have faithfully represented the context-sensitive language of μ-calculus by formalizing the notion of "well-formed formula." Finally, the modal nature of impure rules of μ-calculus (SC and μ-E) has been effectively rendered, although Logical Frameworks do not support directly modal rules. The techniques we have adopted can be readily ported to other formalisms featuring similar problematic issues.

From a proof-theoretical point of view, rule Sc is not satisfactory, since it breaks the typical introduction/elimination pattern of Natural Deduction systems. Whether there is a truly Natural Deduction formulation of the system remains an open question.

The implementation of substitution by means of an environment of bindings has been previously investigated in the context of logic programming by Miller [14], and in that of model checking by Stirling and Walker [16]. This latter fact deserves further investigation. For instance, $\mathbf{N}^{ls}_{\mu K}$ could be integrated with a model checker in a simple and efficient way; moreover, the model checker could be implemented in Coq, and its correctness formally verified.

Acknowledgements. The author is grateful to Furio Honsell and an anonymous referee for many useful remarks.

References

1. A. Avron, F. Honsell, M. Miculan, and C. Paravano. Encoding modal logics in Logical Frameworks. *Studia Logica*, 60(1):161–208, Jan. 1998.
2. *The Coq Proof Assistant Reference Manual - Version 6.2*. INRIA, Rocquencourt, May 1998. Available at ftp://ftp.inria.fr/INRIA/coq/V6.2/doc.
3. A. Church. A formulation of the simple theory of types. *JSL*, 5:56–68, 1940.
4. G. D'Agostino, M. Hollenberg. Logical questions concerning the μ-calculus: interpolation, Lyndon, and Łoś-Tarski. To be published in the *JSL*, 1999.
5. J. Despeyroux, A. Felty, and A. Hirschowitz. Higher-order syntax in Coq. In *Proc. of TLCA'95*. LNCS 902, Springer-Verlag, 1995.
6. G. Gentzen. Investigations into logical deduction. In M. Szabo, ed., *The collected papers of Gerhard Gentzen*, pages 68–131. North Holland, 1969.
7. R. Harper, F. Honsell, and G. Plotkin. A framework for defining logics. *J. ACM*, 40(1):143–184, Jan. 1993.
8. D. Kozen. Results on the propositional μ-calculus. *TCS*, 27:333–354, 1983.
9. Z. Luo, R. Pollack, *et al. The LEGO proof assistant*. Department of Computer Science, University of Edinburgh. http://www.dcs.ed.ac.uk/home/lego
10. L. Magnusson and B. Nordström. The ALF proof editor and its proof engine. In *Proc. of TYPES'93*, LNCS 806, pages 213–237. Springer-Verlag, 1994.
11. P. Martin-Löf. On the meaning of the logical constants and the justifications of the logic laws. TR 2, Dip. di Matematica, Università di Siena, 1985.
12. M. Miculan. Encoding the μ-calculus in Coq. Available at http://www.dimi.uniud.it/~miculan/mucalculus
13. M. Miculan. *Encoding Logical Theories of Programs*. PhD thesis, Dipartimento di Informatica, Università di Pisa, Italy, Mar. 1997.
14. D. Miller. Unification of Simply Typed Lambda-Terms as Logic Programming. In *Proc. of Eighth Intl. Conf. on Logic Programming*. MIT, 1991.
15. B. Nordström, K. Petersson, and J. M. Smith. Martin-Löf's type theory. In *Handbook of Logic in Computer Science*. Oxford University Press, 1992.
16. C. Stirling, and D. Walker. Local model checking in the modal μ-calculus. *Theoretical Computer Science*, 89:161–177, 1983.
17. I. Walukiewicz. Completeness of Kozen's axiomatisation. In D. Kozen, editor, *Proc. 10th LICS*, pages 14–24, June 1995. IEEE.

Leader Election by d Dimensional Cellular Automata

Codrin Nichitiu[1] and Eric Rémila[1,2]

[1] LIP, ENS-Lyon, CNRS UMR 5668,
46 Allée d'Italie, 69364 Lyon Cedex 07, France.
[2] Grima, IUT Roanne, Université J. Monnet St-Etienne
20 avenue de Paris, 42334 Roanne Cedex, France.
{codrin,Eric.Remila}@ens-lyon.fr

Abstract. We present a cellular algorithm in $O(w^2)$ for the leader election problem on a finite connected subset F of $\mathbb{Z}^d$ of excentricity w, for any fixed d. The problem consists in finding an algorithm such that when setting the elements of F to a special state, and all the others to a state #, the cellular automaton iterates a finite number of steps and eventually sets only one precise element of F to a special state called leader state, and all the others to a different state. We describe the algorithm in detail, outline its proof and complexity, and discuss the possible extensions on more general Cayley graphs.

1 Introduction

The leader election problem, or queen bee problem, has been introduced in 1971, in dimension two by [3]. This problem can be informally seen as a reverse firing squad synchronization problem, because here we have all the cells in the same state at initialization, and we want a unique cell to be in a special state at the end of the computation (assimilated to "general" state), while all the others have to be in another state, sort of "soldier" state.

In dimension two, several authors have proposed different solutions, and among the last and the best ones we have to cite [1] and [4] for two dimensions. Their idea is to follow the perimeter of the figure, using a compass. This way the time complexity is linear in the perimeter, thus in the number of cells.

In arbitrary dimensions, the problem is much more difficult, and the best solution we knew of before this paper was the one of [2]. He proposed the use of search algorithms in finite labyrinths. However, the time complexity is $O(n^5)$, where n is the number of cells.

We present here another solution, using a new approach. We make use of a spanning lattice, similar to the spanning tree introduced by [6]. This lattice is constructed through signals starting from points susceptible to be elected as global leaders. We actually have several lattices growing at the same time, so when they hit each other they compete for survival, only one wins, and at the end, the best makes its leader the global leader.

2 Definitions

We consider cellular automata over $\mathbb{Z}^d$, where $d \in \mathbb{N}$, $d > 1$. $\mathbb{Z}^d$ is ordered by the lexicographic order $<_L$.

2.1 General definitions

Definition 1. *Let Σ be a finite set called alphabet, Q be a finite set called set of states, and δ be a function $\delta : Q \times \Sigma \to Q$, called the transition function. Let also $s \in Q$ and $F \subset Q$ be respectively the start state and the final states. Then a finite state automaton (FSA) is a 5-uple $(\Sigma, Q, s, F, \delta)$.*

Definition 2. *Let $x \in \mathbb{Z}^d$, $x = (x_1, x_2, \ldots, x_n)$, and let $e_i = (0, \ldots, 0, 1, 0, \ldots, 0)$ the point with 1 as the i-th coordinate. We call neighbor of x any element of the set $N_x = \{x - e_i, x + e_i \mid 1 \le i \le d\}$. We see that we can order the elements of N_x according to the sign: $x - e_i$ before $x + e_i$ and thereafter according to i, writing, for example, $x - (1, 0, 0, \ldots, 0) <_N x + (0, 1, 0, \ldots, 0)$.*

Definition 3. *A cellular automaton over $\mathbb{Z}^d$ is a triple (Q, δ, π) as defined, where $\Sigma = Q^{2d}$. A configuration is a function $c : \mathbb{Z}^d \to Q$. Given two configurations c_1 and c_2, we note $c_1 = \delta(c_2)$ if $c_2(x) = \delta(c_1(x), c_1(\pi_x^1), \ldots, c_1(\pi_x^{2d}))$, where π_x^i gives the i-th neighbor of x.*

2.2 Leader election

The problem of leader election is defined as follows: Find a cellular automaton on $\mathbb{Z}^d$ such that given a finite connected subset $S \subset \mathbb{Z}^d$, the cellular automaton starts with all the cells members of S in a certain state, exactly the same all over, and with the cells outside S marked with a special symbol #, and after t steps, with t finite, only one cell of S is in a special state, called global leader state, and all the others are in another state, meaning that they cannot be the leader. We also impose that the cells marked with # never change this state, thus confining the computation to the set S.

3 Algorithm

3.1 Idea

We present the algorithm through examples in the integer plane, i.e. in two dimensions. However, the general rules and the proofs are extended to $\mathbb{Z}^d$. Our CA will have the π function defined according to the order of N_x from Definition 2.

We call a cell a *local leader* when the only neighbors it has in the figure are on the positive senses of the coordinate axis, and this is a property of the cell independent of the algorithm.

Each cell which is a local leader (here, any with no neighbors south or west), becomes the root of a spanning lattice, constructed through signals issued from it and propagated across the surface occupied with cells. This lattice expands in pulses until it hits another similar lattice or until it fills the whole region. In the first case, one of the two lattices dies off, and in the second one, it makes the leader the unique global one. The lexicographic ordering $<_L$ of the two local leaders generating the lattices, decides, making the smaller win as global leader.

3.2 Examples

Consider a rectangle: only one local leader, the south-western corner. From this cell a lattice starts growing, until reaching the borders. The local leader sends a lattice expansion signal to its northern and eastern neighbors, propagated farther. Each cell receiving a signal from a direction sends it in the other three. When a cell receives several signals, it considers them all as fathers, and sends further the signal to the others left, named sons, "building" the lattice.

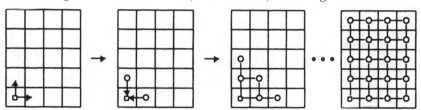

Fig. 1: initial phase   expansion steps   region filled

We said the growth is pulsed ; this means after one expansion step we have a report step, when the lattice border cells may send back a "report" signal, each cell to its fathers, and these propagate them back to the root of the lattice. We need this in case of conflict, in order to make the conflicts be synchronously solved, as we explain farther in the paper.

For this example, we only need to consider the termination of the algorithm. During the expansion step, if a cell has no neighbor to send further the expansion signal, then it switches to a "dead-end" state, otherwise it sends or it carries over, towards the root, a "border signal". On the other hand, when a father has only dead-end sons, it switches also to dead-end state. Thus, when the root has only dead-end sons, it knows that it is the global leader.

This algorithm also works for any figure with only one local leader. How about several local leaders ? At "mid-way" at some point of the expansions, there is a conflict between the two lattices. Therefore we have to identify and order the lattices in a certain way. Since we can have an unbounded number of local leaders and we want a finite number of states, we cannot decide to have different states for different lattices (we wouldn't even know how to assign them locally).

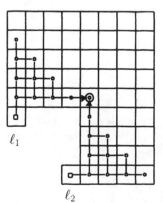

Fig. 2: conflict in two-concentric-circle cell

However, we can borrow an idea from [4], briefly shown in figure 2, which originally consists in measuring the coordinate difference between the emitter of a signal and its receiver using the time difference between a reference signal and a coordinate signal, retarded (resp. accelerated) when changing the sense to the negative (resp. positive) one along the coordinate axis.

3.3 Solving the conflicts

We consider some "grown" lattices of the same maximum length (from each root to the respective border), and we study only the expansion step leading to their touching, thus to a conflict.

Measuring the coordinate difference using signals We borrow an idea from [4], based on signals. A signal can informally be seen as special (sub)state s "propagating" from a cell c to another cell c', along a specific path $(c, c_1, \ldots, c_p = c')$ of length p.

For each coordinate, (here for x and y), the local leader sends a signal, at variable speed, to all its children. When the coordinate signals go along the positive sense of the coordinate axis, they go fast, that is, if the cell receives the signal at time t, then at time $t + 1$ the neighbor receives it, and the signal is said to travel at speed 1 (maximal). If the coordinate signals go along the negative sense, the reverse happens : they are received at time t and received by the neighbor at time $t + 3$, traveling at speed $1/3$. And, when a coordinate signal travels along a different axis, it goes at a speed in between, which is $1/2$. Thus, the acceleration and deceleration are with respect to the "reference" speed $1/2$.

These signals serve the double purpose of expanding the lattice and measuring the coordinate difference.

The former is done by memorizing the neighboring source cells (as fathers) when receiving a coordinate signal. Actually, the (possibly) fastest coordinate signals "open" the path, followed by the subsequent coordinate signals. We will see this in detail in the next section.

The latter is done as follows: suppose we have an emitter cell $c_0 = (x_0, y_0, \ldots)$ and a receiver cell $c = (x_c, y_c, \ldots)$. The x-coordinate signal is sent at time 0, it arrives at the cell c time t_c, and it travels a path of length l (i.e. it crosses l edges to get there). Then the simple law of speed and distance tells us that

$$x_c - x_0 = 2l - t_c \qquad (1)$$

The figure 3 shows the path of the x and y coordinate signals from ℓ_1 to the cell marked with two concentric circles in the figure 2. We call this a *beam* of coordinate signals.

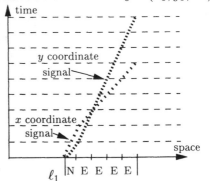

Fig. 3 : coord. measure signals

Conflicts Suppose now we have two synchronous emitter cells $\ell_1 = (x_1, y_1, \ldots)$ and $\ell_2 = (x_2, y_2, \ldots)$, as in figure 2. Let c be the "conflict cell" (the one with two concentric circles on the figure 2). It happens that the length l of the path from the emitters to it is the same. We have from the equality (1)

$$x_c - x_1 = 2l - t_1 \text{ and } x_c - x_2 = 2l - t_2$$

where t_1 (respectively t_2) denotes the arrival time of the x coordinate signal from ℓ_1 (resp. ℓ_2) in c.

Then,

$$x_1 < x_2 \iff t_1 < t_2 \tag{2}$$

Therefore, the cell c is able to find the minimun in sense of the lexicographic order $<_L$ (see figure 6). One method is to store the order of arrival for each coordinate signal, and at the end, to make the right choice.

We actually see that it is enough to know which signal arrived first from which of the beams, all this for each coordinate. We explain the implementation of this in the section 3.4, paragraph Conflict.

However, we need that the emitters be synchronous and that they be at equal distances from the conflict cell. All this is actually possible because

– at the beginning all the local leaders are synchronized (initialization)
– the lattices expand "uniformly"
– we ensure the further synchronization (next paragraph).

Synchronization We set up a second signal, called a sweep signal, going slower than any coordinate signal (at speed $1/3$), but along the same paths.

Thus, a cell "takes" the decision when all sweep signals have arrived (simultaneosly, or at exactly three time units difference), sending it back to the local leaders through other signals: border signal to the winner, destroy signal to the losers. On the other hand, with the sweep signal system we make sure that all the border cells send back their report at the same time.

If we consider the figure 3, and show the space-time diagram of the sweep and x (East-West) coordinate signals issued from the two local leaders ℓ_1 and ℓ_2 on the path containing the conflicting cell, we get the figure 4.

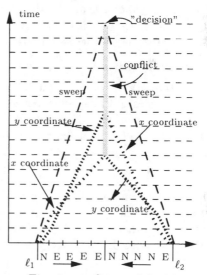

Fig. 4 : conflict and decision; the arrows give the edge label orientation

3.4 Memory structure

The states of each cell are elements of a cartesian product: action to be taken, signal information, conflict information. By abuse of language, we call states the first components, depicted in figure 5.

Fig 5: FSA schematic diagram

Signals We associate with each cell a signal transmission vector SV, composed of $d + 4$ counters for each signal (d coordinates, reference, sweep, destroy and border). The counter $SV[i]$ encodes how long the signal i has been held in the cell. A value of 0 in $SV[i]$ means the signal i (coordinate, sweep, destroy or border) is not in the cell, a value of 1 means the signal just arrived, and so on, with values no greater than 3.

Neighborhood Each cell has also an array NV of $2d$ elements ordered as in def. 2) with values from $\{?, S, F, FW, FL\}$ meaning no information, son, father, father winner, father loser. FW and FL serve to communicate to its fathers the decision taken by a conflict cell.

Conflict We also need a $d \times 2d$ boolean matrix CM such that $CM[i,j] = 1$ means the neighbor j (in the same order as above) is among the very first to have sent the i-coordinate signal to the conflict cell, and otherwise, $CM[i,j] = k$ means the neighbor j is among the ones having sent the i-coordinate signal one time unit *after* the j' with $CM[i,j'] = k - 1$. Here, k is 1, 2 or 3. Otherwise, $CM[i,j] = 0$. The two decision cases are discussed farther.

3.5 Transition rules

Initialization At starting time, all cells are in start state. When a cell is in start state, if it is a local leader, it switches to potential global leader state, otherwise, it switches to inactive state.

The cells bordering the figure (outside it) are all marked with a special symbol #, and the arrays of all the figure cells are all set to zero.

Expansion The cell being in potential global leader state sends the coordinate signals to its neighbors. When a cell being in inactive state receives one coordinate signal, it changes the NV to note the source of the signal as father, and waits for the other coordinate signals and for the sweep signal. It also switches immediately to conflict state (it can switch to conflict state also according to Odd case, explained farther). If it receives several coordinate signals from different sources, it notes them all as its fathers in the NV array.

When a cell being in lattice state receives some coordinate signals, it propagates them farther, according to the delay rules to its children.

Dead-end and stop If, all the unknown neighbors (i.e. marked with ?) of a cell are actually in state #, and all its children are in dead-end state, the cell switches to dead-end state. If the cell being in potential global leader state sees all its children in dead-end state, then it switches to global leader state.

Conflict and decision. Even case When a cell switched to conflict state from inactive state, it waits to receive all the coordinate and the sweep signals. Whenever it receives a coordinate signal, say for coordinate i, the first time, it writes 1 to $CM[i,j]$ where j runs through the neighbors which sent it this signal the first. This way, only these neighbors are noted as potential winners, and, at the end, the cell takes a decision, according to the lexicographic order of the coordinates, switching to decision state, and setting the NV appropriately: if the i-th neighbor is a winning father, it puts $NV[i]$ to FW, and for all j which denote the losing fathers, it puts $NV[j]$ to FL. Thus, when a cell is in lattice state and sees some of its children switching to conflict state and then to decision state, it looks in their NV arrays at the right elements, to "learn" the outcome of the conflict. If at least one of its children tells it that it is FL, then it propagates the destroy signal back to its fathers, thus back towards its potential global leader, otherwise, it propagates the border signal.

Odd case This happens when two local leaders are separated by a path of odd length. Then two cells enter the conflict state being also neighbors, each one belonging to a lattice and only one. When this happens, the cell "ignore" each other and behave as said before. However, at the next expansion they might receive some coordinate signals from the established fathers *and also* from unknown neighbors (of S, not yet fathers or children). The reasoning would be the same as the one described in section 3.3, but there is a difference : the length l is no longer the same, it is l from the "known" part ℓ_1 and $l+1$ from the "unknown" part (ℓ_2). Thus the relation (2) becomes

$$x_1 < x_2 \iff l_1 < t_2 + 2 \qquad (3)$$

This is why the values in CM go from 1 to 3. Therefore, we add the case of switching to conflict state from lattice state: if a cell being in lattice state and still having unknown neighbors in S receives a coordinate signal, then it switches to conflict state. It also starts filling the CM matrix with values from 1 to 3, and at the end decides again about the order, this way:

1. if the signals with 1 arrived at least from some unknown neighbors, then these neighbors win and only them
2. else if the signals with 2 arrived at least from some unknown neighbors, then the same happens
3. else if the signals with 3 arrived at least from some unknown neighbors, then they win, but *also with* the known (fathers) neighbors which sent signals arriving first (CM value 1).
4. else only the known father neighbors which sent signals first win (CM value 1)

See as an example the figure 5, a slight modification of figure 2.

Decision transmission The decisions are taken when the last sweep arrives.

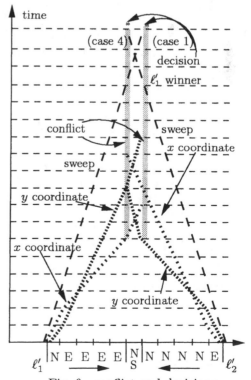

Fig. 6 : conflict and decisions

In all cases, the signals arrive (also) from some unknown neighbors, and the decisions are notified only to these unknown neighbors, because in case of signal crossing (that is even length), each of the conflict cell takes care of the other's fathers. Also, the FW values of NV are switched thereafter to F, and all the others (F or FL) to ?.

Report When a cell is in lattice state and it receives from its children a border or destroy signal, it propagates it up to its fathers.

Destruction When a cell being in potential global leader state receives at least one destroy signal from one of its children, then it sends the destroy signal to all its children and it switches to inactive state. When a cell being in lattice state or dead-end state receives a destroy signal from one of its fathers, then it propagates it to all its children, and it switches to inactive state.

Updating and iteration When a cell being in potential global leader state receives from all its children only border signals, it starts a new expansion period, sending again the coordinate signals.

4 Analysis

4.1 Definitions

We have been talking about lattices and about constructed and expanded lattices. We now outline the proof of the correctness of the algorithm.

Definition 4. *The distance of two cells is defined as the length of the shortest path through S from one to the other. By constructed lattice of radius h of a local leader ℓ we mean a ball $B(\ell, h)$ of S (i.e. the set of cells of S at most at distance h from ℓ on paths only within S), centered in a local leader, in which all the cells are in special states : potential global leader state, lattice state or dead-end state, and have the NV appropriately set. The cell being in the local leader state (that is the potential global leader) has no father and is (transitively) the father of all the other members of the constructed lattice. The relations father-son are oriented outwards from the leader to the borders and the cells which have to be in dead-end state (because all their children are in dead-end state or are marked with #) are in this state.*

4.2 Proofs

If we look at the evolution of the algorithm, we can remark a certain periodicity. The start of the h-th period is the moment when the potential global leaders "know what to do", i.e. at the beginning to start the expansion, and afterwards to continue or to destroy themselves. We denote by this the time coordinates $m_h = m_{h-1} + 4h$, where $m_1 = 1$.

Proposition 1. *Let $h < w$. At the start of the h-th period the constructed lattices are of radius h, with h being the maximum distance between a cell and the future global leader.*
   The main loop gives the main steps of the h-th period:

1. *at (relative) time coordinate 0, the potential global leaders have decided either to expand or to destroy, and are about to send the appropriate signals. Their constructed lattices of radius h are disjoint, with no signals being held for transmission, and the rest of the cells are in the inactive state.*
2. *at time h, the constructed lattices which had to be destroyed are indeed destroyed, and all their cells switched to inactive state, having no more signals held to be transmitted to neighbors and clearing the neighbor array NV.*
3. *between time h+1 and time 3h+3 the expansion of the surviving constructed lattices is completed, and conflicts detected by the new border cells.*
4. *at time 3h + 3 the sweep signals have reached the borders, and the conflicts are solved.*
5. *at time 4h+4 the decisions are reported to the local leaders, and a new period starts.*

Proof. Straightforward, by induction, and by the construction of the algorithm. We can emphasize that there is no interference between the expansion and the destruction of two neighboring constructed lattices, because the destroy signal travels as fast as the fastest coordinate signal, but has a one-cell-shorter path to go to a same cell, element of the current border.

Also, since the report signals only travel within each constructed lattice, there is no interference either, and they "safely" get back to the local leaders, informing them about the possibility of expansion or necessity to destroy themselves.

We also insist on the synchronization of the process, all lattices starting the expansion at the same moment, and solving the conflicts, sending back the decisions and restarting the loop again at the same moment. This is ensured by the sweep signals traveling at a constant speed, along the same distance, the radius h, from the local leaders to the borders, and the report signals, traveling again at a constant speed, along the same maximal distance, and by the fact that the local leaders wait for all the report signals to come before restarting the period. □

Proposition 2. *The constructed lattice rooted in the local leader which should be elected according to the lexicographic order of the coordinates never looses any conflict.*

Proof. By the construction of the algorithm, from the way the conflicts are handled. The beam of coordinate signals from the future global leader will arrive "earlier" than any other coordinate signals (that is with the appropriate mark), thus making the border cell take the right decision each time. □

Proposition 3. *If there is only one potential global leader at the beginning of a time period (at a m_i moment), then the algorithm finishes electing it as the global one.*

Proof. The dead-end states start propagating themselves towards the root once the border cells are reached by the sweep signal, and by the construction of the algorithm, the potential global leader becomes global. □

Theorem 1. *The algorithm finishes in $2(w^2 + w)$ time steps, where w is the length of the longest among the shortest paths starting from the global leader and going to the border of the figure.*

Proof. From the way the conflicts are handled, we see that after each conflict at least one constructed lattice will dissapear. Since between the conflicts the constructed lattices only grow, if at the beginning there are several ones, during the evolution their number decreases strictly monotonically. We arrive in the case of the previous proposition and thus the algorithm stops.

On the other hand, we can only look at the evolution of the constructed lattice of the future global leader. This constructed lattice keeps expanding itself, without delay, and without being destroyed (previous propositions), and

$$m_w = 4\sum_{k=1}^{w} k = 4\frac{w(w + 1)}{2}. \qquad \square$$

5 Discussion

Compared to [1] and to [4], this solution can be slower, since it is quadratic in the excentricity, while the previous ones are linear in the surface, which can be linear in the excentricity, but has the advantage of extending the algorithm to any dimensions.

We can think of extending this algorithm to other types of graphs. We can do this on labeled trees and we can hope to do it on some special Cayley graphs, under specific conditions. More work has to be done to relax as much as possible of these conditions, or to classify the graphs and find necessary conditions for the leader election problem to be solvable.

References

1. A. Beckers and T. Worsch. A perimeter-time CA for the queen bee problem. In *Cellular Automata: Research towards Industry. (Proceedings of ACRI'98)*. Springer Verlag London, 1998.
2. A. Hemmerling. Concentration of multidimensional tape-bounded systems of turing automata and cellular spaces. In *Proceedings of FCT 1979*, 1979.
3. A. R. Smith III. Two-dimensional formal languages and pattern recognition by cellular automata. In *IEEE Conference Record of 12th Annual Symposium on Switching and Automaa Theory*, 1971.
4. J. Mazoyer, C. Nichitiu, and E. Remila. Compass permits leader election. In *Proceedings of SODA 1999*. SIAM, 1999.
5. P. Rosenstiehl, J. R. Fiksel, and A. Holliger. Intelligent graphs: Networks of finite automata capable of solving graph problems. In *Graph Theory and Computing*, pages 210–265. R.C. Reed (editor), Academic Press, New York, 1973.
6. A. Wu and A. Rosenfeld. Cellular graph automata. I. Basic concepts, graph property measurement, closure properties. *Information and Control*, 42:305–329, 1979.

New Upper Bounds for MaxSat

Rolf Niedermeier[1*] and Peter Rossmanith[2]

[1] Wilhelm-Schickard-Institut für Informatik, Universität Tübingen
Sand 13, D-72076 Tübingen, Fed. Rep. of Germany
niedermr@informatik.uni-tuebingen.de
[2] Institut für Informatik, Technische Universität München
Arcisstr. 21, D-80290 München, Fed. Rep. of Germany
rossmani@in.tum.de

Abstract. Given a boolean formula F in conjunctive normal form and an integer k, is there a truth assignment satisfying at least k clauses? This is the decision version of the Maximum Satisfiability (MaxSat) problem we study in this paper. We improve upper bounds on the worst case running time for MaxSat. First, Cai and Chen showed that MaxSat can be solved in time $|F|2^{O(k)}$ when the clause size is bounded by a constant. Imposing no restrictions on clause size, Mahajan and Raman and, independently, Dantsin et al. improved this to $O(|F|\phi^k)$, where $\phi \approx 1.6181$ is the golden ratio. We present an algorithm running in time $O(|F|1.3995^k)$. The result extends to finding an optimal assignment and has several applications, in particular, for parameterized complexity and approximation algorithms. Moreover, if F has K clauses, we can find an optimal assignment in $O(|F|1.3972^K)$ steps and in $O(1.1279^{|F|})$ steps, respectively. These are the fastest algorithm in the number of clauses and the length of the formula, respectively.

1 Introduction

Despite being NP-hard, many problems have to be solved in practice. Besides approximation or heuristic algorithms, it is often important to have exact algorithms with proven performance bounds. Thus, there are big efforts to develop efficient exponential time algorithms as recent publications show [5, 2, 10, 12–14, 19, 22]. In particular, it becomes more and more clear that there are tight connections between improving the worst-case upper bound and and developing heuristics that are used in practical algorithms [10, 17].

There are two problems from logic playing a major role in computational complexity theory—Satisfiability (Sat) and Maximum Satisfiability (MaxSat). Research on nontrivial upper bounds for Sat was initiated by Monien and Speckenmeyer [15, 16] and subsequently has seen several improvements. We refer to Pudlák [23] for a recent survey, omitting any details here. Let us only emphasize

* Supported by a Feodor Lynen fellowship of the Alexander von Humboldt-Stiftung, Bonn, and the Center for Discrete Mathematics, Theoretical Computer Science and Applications (DIMATIA), Prague.

that in this field even small or seemingly tiny improvements in the bases of the exponential terms can mean significant progress. For instance, for the Satisfiability of a propositional formula consisting of K clauses, Hirsch [12] improved the upper bound of order 1.25993^K of Monien and Speckenmeyer [15] to 1.23883^K (omitting polynomial terms). With respect to the length $|F|$ of the given formula, he improved Kullmann and Luckhardt's [13] upper bound from $1.08006^{|F|}$ to $1.07578^{|F|}$.

So far, with respect to developing good upper bounds researchers have paid a bit less attention to MAXSAT. However, it is a problem of central importance in computer science: It plays a major role in the theory of computational complexity and approximation algorithms [1, 20, 21], it is an important problem in parameterized complexity theory [6, 9, 10], and it has numerous applications, see, e.g., [3, 4, 11]. We refer to Crescenzi and Kann [7] for a survey on approximation results for MAXSAT. Here, let us only mention that there does not exist a polynomial time approximation algorithm with an approximation factor arbitrarily close to 1 unless $P = NP$ [1]. Dantsin et al. show how to move the approximation factor arbitrarily close to 1 using an exponential time algorithm [8]. As to parameterized complexity, the following is known: The natural parameterized version of MAXSAT is to determine whether at least k clauses of a CNF formula F with K clauses can be satisfied. Cai and Chen [6] proved that for constant q parameterized MAXqSAT is *fixed parameter tractable,* implying that every problem in the optimization class *MaxSNP* is also fixed parameter tractable. More precisely, Cai and Chen showed that it can be solved in time $O(|F|2^{O(k)})$. Without any restriction on clause size, Mahajan and Raman [14] improved the running time to $O(|F|1.6181^k)$. The same running time was achieved independently by Dantsin et al. [8] who use it as a basis for developing an exponential time approximation algorithm. Note that the time bound of $O(|F|1.6181^k)$ transfers easily into the time bound $O(|F| + k^2 1.6181^k)$ using a standard technique of parameterized complexity theory called reduction to problem kernel [14]. This technique also applies to our algorithms, giving analogous results. By more refined techniques the polynomial factor before the exponential term can be made even smaller.

Our main results are as follows. We present an $O(|F|1.3995^k)$ time algorithm for MAXSAT, where $|F|$ is the length of the formula in conjunctive normal form. Surprisingly, if we want to determine the maximum number of satisfiable clauses, we get the time bound $O(|F|1.3972^K)$, where K is the number of clauses in F. We also prove the time bound $O(1.1279^{|F|})$ for the same problem, which implies a bound of $O(1.2722^K)$ steps for MAX2SAT, since then $|F| \leq 2K$. This also implies improvements to results of Mahajan and Raman [14] concerning the MAXCUT problem and a "different parameterization" of MAXSAT. For example, in the case of MAXCUT, where we are given an undirected graph on n vertices and m edges and a positive integer k and ask for the existence of a cut of size at least k. We improve Mahajan and Raman's time bound of $O(m + n + k4^k)$ to $O(m + n + k^2 2.6196^k)$. Finally, we can improve the approximation algorithm of Dantsin et al. [8] by simply replacing their exponential time algorithm by our faster one. A technical report contains all proofs that are omitted here [18].

2 Basic definitions

We assume familiarity with basic notions of logic and use a similar notation as in [12]. We represent the boolean values true and false by 1 and 0, respectively. A *truth assignment* I can be defined as a set of literals that contains no complementary pairs. For a variable x we have $I(x) = 1$ iff $x \in I$ and $I(x) = 0$ iff $\bar{x} \in I$. We only deal with propositional formulas in conjunctive normal form. These are often represented in *clause form*, i.e., as a set of clauses, where a clause itself is a set of literals. We will represent formulas as *multisets* of sets, since a formula might contain several identical clauses. For the satisfiability problem multiple clauses can be eliminated, but this is of course no longer true if we are interested in the *number* of satisfiable clauses. The formula $(x \vee y \vee \bar{z}) \wedge (x \vee y \vee \bar{z}) \wedge (\bar{x} \vee z) \wedge (\bar{y} \vee z)$ will be represented as $\{\{x, y, \bar{z}\}, \{x, y, \bar{z}\}, \{\bar{x}, z\}, \{\bar{y}, z\}\}$.

Note that the outer curly brackets denote a multiset and the inner curly brackets denote sets of literals. A subformula, i.e., a subset of clauses, is called *closed* if it is a minimal subset of clauses such that no variable in this subset occurs also outside of this subset in the rest of the formula. A clause that contains the same variable positively and negatively, e.g., $\{x, \bar{x}, y, \bar{z}\}$, is satisfied by every assignment. We will not consider such clauses, but we assume that such clauses are always replaced by a special clause $\top$, which denotes a clause that is always satisfied. We call a clause containing r literals simply an *r-clause*. A formula in *2CNF* is one consisting of 1- and 2-clauses. The *length of a clause* is its cardinality and the *length of a formula* is the sum of the lengths of its clauses. Let l be a literal occurring in a formula F. We call it an (i, j)-*literal* if l occurs exactly i times positively and exactly j times negatively in F. In analogy, we get (i^+, j)-, (i, j^+)-, and (i^+, j^+)-*literals* by replacing "exactly" by "at least" at the appropriate positions and get (i^-, j)-, (i, j^-)- and (i^-, j^-)-*literals* by replacing "exactly" by "at most."

For a literal l and a formula F, let $F[l]$ be the formula originating from F by replacing all clauses containing l by $\top$ and removing $\bar{l}$ from all clauses. To estimate the time complexity of our algorithms, the following notion is useful: $S(F)$ denotes the number of $\top$-clauses in F, $maxsat(F)$ denotes the maximum number of simultaneously satisfiable clauses in F. We say two formulas F and G are *equisatisfiable*, if $maxsat(F) = maxsat(G)$. A formula that contains only $\top$-clauses is called *final*. Among equisatisfiable ones there is exactly one final formula.

Definition 1 A formula is called *nearly monotone* if negative literals occur only in 1-clauses. It is called a *simple formula* if it is nearly monotone and each pair of variables occurs together in at most one clause.

For a variable x, we say $\tilde{x}$ occurs in a clause C if $x \in C$ or $\bar{x} \in C$.

For example, $\tilde{x}$ occurs in $\{\bar{x}, y, z\}$ and in $\{x, y, z\}$, but x occurs only in $\{x, y, z\}$ and $\bar{x}$ occurs only in $\{\bar{x}, y, z\}$. As a rule, we will use x, y, z to denote variables and l to denote a literal. To simplify presentation, we usually assume w.l.o.g. that a variable occurs at least as often positively as it occurs negatively in the formula.

3 The algorithm

In the following, we present algorithms that solve MAXSAT by mapping a formula to the unique, equisatisfiable, final formula. We distinguish two possibilities: If a formula is replaced by one other formula, we speak of a *transformation rule*; if one formula is replaced by several other formulas, we speak of a *splitting rule*. The resulting formula or formulas are then solved recursively, a technique that goes back to the DAVIS–PUTNAM-procedure. In what follows, we provide a quite extensive list of transformation and splitting rules, which form the key to our improved algorithm (see Subsection 3.3).

3.1 Transformation rules

A transformation rule $\frac{F}{F'}$ replaces F by F', where F' and F are equisatisfiable, but F' is simpler. We will use the following transformation rules, whose correctness is easy to check.

Pure literal rule. $\dfrac{F}{F[x]}$ if x is a $(1^+, 0)$-literal.

Complementary 1-clause rule. $\dfrac{F}{\{\top\} \cup G}$ if $F = \{\{\bar{x}\}, \{x\}\} \cup G$.

Dominating 1-clause rule. $\dfrac{F}{F[l]}$ if $\bar{l}$ occurs i times in F, and l occurs at least i times in a 1-clause.

Resolution rule. $\dfrac{\{\{\bar{x}\} \cup K_1, \{x\} \cup K_2\} \cup G}{\{\top, K_1 \cup K_2\} \cup G}$ if G does not contain $\tilde{x}$.

Small subformula rule. Let $F = \{\{x', y', \dots\}, \{x'', y'', \dots\}, \{x''', y''', \dots\}\} \cup G$, where G contains neither $\tilde{x}$ nor $\tilde{y}$ and $x', x'', x''' \in \{x, \bar{x}\}$ and $y', y'', y''' \in \{y, \bar{y}\}$. Then $\dfrac{F}{\{\top, \top, \top\} \cup G}$, since there is always an assignment to x and y only that already satisfies $\{\{x', y', \dots\}, \{x'', y'', \dots\}, \{x''', y''', \dots\}\}$.

Star rule. A formula $\{\{\bar{x}_1\}, \{\bar{x}_2\}, \dots, \{\bar{x}_r\}, \{x_1, x_2, \dots, x_r\}, \{x_1, x_2, \dots, x_r\}\}$ is an r-star. Let F be an r-star, then $\dfrac{F}{\{\top, \dots, \top\}}$, where the "$\top$-multiset" contains $r + 1$ many $\top$'s.

Definition 2 A formula is *reduced* if no transformation rule is applicable, each literal occurs at least as often positively as negatively, and it contains no empty clauses. Using the above transformation rules, $Reduce(F)$ denotes the corresponding reduced, equisatisfiable formula.

Observe that in the rest of the paper many arguments will rely on the fact that we are dealing with a reduced formula.

3.2 Splitting rules

A splitting rule replaces a formula F by several formulas F_i such that F and at least one F_i are equisatisfiable. The *branching vector* of a rule $\frac{F}{F_1,\dots,F_r}$ is $(b_1,\dots,b_r)$ if $S(F) + b_i \leq S(Reduce(F_i))$ for all $1 \leq i \leq r$ and all F for which the rule is applicable. The branching vectors will be used to determine the time complexity of the algorithm using these rules. Determining the values of the branching vectors often involves some further case distinction. The full paper contains the proof that always one of the subsequent transformation rules is applicable to a reduced formula [18].

Some variable occurs exactly three times. In the following, we present seven splitting rules **T1–T7** and an analysis with respect to $S(F)$. These rules are applicable if F is reduced and all literals in F are w.l.o.g. $(2,1)$, $(3,1)$, or $(2,2)$-literals. Moreover, there must be at least one $(2,1)$-literal x.

The branching vectors are: **T1:** $(3,2)$ or $(4,1)$, **T2:** $(3,3)$, **T3:** $(3,2)$, **T4:** $(4,2)$, **T5:** $(4,1)$, **T6:** $(2,3)$ or $(3,2)$ or $(4,1)$, **T7:** $(4,1)$ or $(3,2)$.

We prove here only representatively **T3** (see below): Two clauses contain x, hence $S(F)+2 \leq S(F[x])$. In $F[x]$, however, y is a $(1,1)$-literal and the resolution rule is applicable leading to $S(F) + 3 \leq S(Reduce(F[x]))$. In $F[\bar{x}]$, y is a $(1,1)$-literal, too. So, $S(F)+2 \leq S(Reduce(F[\bar{x}]))$. Together, we obtain the branching vector $(3,2)$.

T1 $\quad\dfrac{F}{F[y'],\,F[\bar{y'}]}\quad$ if $F = \{\{\bar{x},y',\dots\},\{x,\dots\},\{x,\dots\},\{y'',\dots\},\{y''',\dots\},\dots\}$
and $y',y'',y''' \in \{y,\bar{y}\}$.

T2 $\quad\dfrac{F}{F[l],\,F[\bar{l}]}\quad$ if $F = \{\{\bar{x},\bar{l},\dots\},\{x,l,\dots\},\{x,\dots\},\{l,\dots\},\dots\}$.

T3 $\quad\dfrac{F}{F[x],\,F[\bar{x}]}\quad$ if $F = \{\{\bar{x},y,\dots\},\{x,y,\dots\},\{x,\dots\},\{\bar{y},\dots\},\dots\}$
and y is a $(2,1)$-literal.

T4 $\quad\dfrac{F}{F[y],\,F[\bar{y}]}\quad$ if $F = \{\{\bar{x},y,\dots\},\{x,\bar{y},\dots\},\{x,\dots\},\{y,\dots\},\dots\}$
and y is a $(2,1)$-literal.

T5 $\quad\dfrac{F}{F[x],\,F[\bar{x}]}\quad$ if $F = \{\{\bar{x}\},\{x,y,\dots\},\{x,z,\dots\},\{y,\dots\},\{\bar{y}\},\{\bar{z}\},\dots\}$
and y and z are $(2,1)$-literals.

T6 $\quad\dfrac{F}{F[l],\,F[\bar{l}]}\quad$ if $F = \{\{\bar{x},\dots\},\{x,l,\dots\},\{x,\dots\},\dots\}$ and l is a $(3,1)$- or
$(2,2)$-literal and $\bar{l}$ occurs with $\tilde{x}$ in exactly one clause.

T7 $\quad\dfrac{F}{F[l],\,F[\bar{l}]}\quad$ if $F = \{\{\bar{x},y,\dots\},\{x,y,\dots\},\{x,y,\dots\},\{\bar{y},\dots\},\dots\}$,
there is a literal l that occurs in a clause with $\tilde{y}$,
and $\bar{l}$ occurs also in a clause with no $\tilde{y}$.

All variables occur exactly four times. Here, we assume that F is reduced, contains no closed subformulas, and each variable occurs exactly four times. The following branching vectors can be proved: **D1:** $(4, 1)$, **D2:** $(3, 3)$, **D3:** $(4, 1)$, **D4:** $(2, 2)$, **D5:** $(3, 4, 5)$, **D6:** $(1, 4, 11)$.

D1 $\dfrac{F}{F[l], F[\bar{l}]}$ if $F = \{\{\bar{x}, l, \ldots\}, \{x, \ldots\}, \{x, \ldots\}, \{x, \ldots\}, \ldots\}$.

D2 $\dfrac{F}{F[x], F[\bar{x}, y]}$ if $F = \{\{\bar{x}\}, \{x, y\}, \{x, \ldots\}, \{x, \ldots\}, \ldots\}$.

D3 $\dfrac{F}{F[x], F[\bar{x}]}$ if $F = \{\{\bar{x}\}, \{x, l, \ldots\}, \{x, \ldots\}, \{x, \ldots\}, \ldots\}$
and $\tilde{l}$ occurs in 1 or 2 clauses that do not contain $\tilde{x}$.

D4 $\dfrac{F}{F[x], F[\bar{x}]}$ if $F = \{\{\bar{x}, \ldots\}, \{\bar{x}, \ldots\}, \{x, \ldots\}, \{x, \ldots\}, \ldots\}$.

D5 $\dfrac{F}{F[y], F[\bar{y}, z], F[\bar{y}, \bar{z}]}$ if $F = \{\{\bar{x}\}, \{x, y, z\}, \{x, \ldots\}, \{x, \ldots\}, \{\bar{y}\}, \{y, \ldots\}, \{y, \ldots\}, \{\bar{z}\}, \{z, \ldots\}, \{z, \ldots\}, \ldots\}$.

D6 $\dfrac{F}{F[\bar{x}], F[x, \bar{y}], F[x, y, \bar{z}_1, \bar{z}_2, \ldots, \bar{z}_6]}$
if $F = \{\{\bar{x}\}, \{x, y, \ldots\}, \{x, \ldots\}, \{x, \ldots\}, \{y, z_1, z_2, z_3, \ldots\}, \{y, z_4, z_5, z_6, \ldots\}, \{\bar{y}\}, \ldots\}$ and F is simple and each positive clause has size at least 4.

One interesting point in **D2** is that $F[\bar{x}, \bar{y}]$ is missing, which is possible since if there is an optimal assignment with $x = y = 0$, then there is also an optimal assignment with $x = 1$. **D5** and **D6** are similar.

There is a literal that occurs at least five times. Let F be reduced.

F1 $\dfrac{F}{F[x], F[\bar{x}]}$ if $\tilde{x}$ occurs at least five times in F.
We get $S(F[x]) \geq S(F) + a$ and $S(F[\bar{x}]) \geq S(F) + b$ with $a, b \geq 1$ and $a + b = 5$.

3.3 Details and analysis of the algorithm

The correctness of Algorithm B in Fig. 1 to compute the maximum number of satisfiable clauses follows from the correctness of all transformation and splitting rules and the fact that at least one rule is always applicable. A good data structure to represent formulas in conjunctive normal form is important. For the high-level description of transformation and splitting rules, we used the representation as a multiset of sets of literals. The actual implementation of the algorithm will use a refinement of this representation. We represent literals as natural numbers. A positive literal x_i is represented as the number i and the negative literal $\bar{x}_i$ by $-i$. A clause is represented as a list of literals and a formula as a list of clauses. Moreover, for each variable there is additionally a list of pointers that point to each occurrence of the variable in the formula. It is easy to see that finding an applicable rule and applying it takes only polynomial time in the length of the formula. With more care, it can be done in linear time.

Algorithm B (Fig. 1) constructs an equisatisfiable formula $\{\top, \dots, \top\}$ from a formula F by using transformation and splitting rules. It can be easily converted to answer our decision version of MAXSAT and to compute also an optimal assignment.

Input: A formula F in clause form
Output: An equisatisfiable formula $B(F) = \{\top, \dots, \top\}$
Method:
$F \leftarrow Reduce(F)$;
if F is final **then return** F
else if $F = F_1 \oplus F_2 \oplus \cdots \oplus F_m$ **then return** $B(F_1) \cup B(F_2) \cup \cdots \cup B(F_m)$
else if F has less than 6 unresolved clauses **then return** $A(F)$
else
    choose an applicable splitting rule $\dfrac{F}{F_1, \dots, F_r} \in \{\textbf{T1–T7}, \textbf{D1–D6}, \textbf{F1}\}$;
    return $\max\{B(F_1), \dots, B(F_r)\}$
fi

Fig. 1. Algorithm B. Note that $F_1 \oplus F_2 \oplus \cdots \oplus F_m$ denotes the decomposition of F into closed subformulas and $\max\{B(F_1), \dots, B(F_r)\}$ is the multiset with the maximum number of $\top$'s. **D4** is chosen only if no other rule is applicable. For small formulas the result is computed as $A(F)$ by some naive exponential time algorithm A.

We follow Kullmann and Luckhardt [13] (also cf. [12]) in the analysis of the running time. Algorithm B generates a *branching tree* whose nodes are labeled by formulas that are recursively processed. The children of an inner node F are computed by a transformation rule (one child) or a splitting rule (more than one child). The *value* of a node F is $S(F)$. The values of all children of F are bigger than $S(F)$. If the children of F were computed according to a rule $\frac{F}{F_1, F_2, \dots, F_r}$ then $(S(Reduce(F_1)) - S(F), \dots, S(Reduce(F_r)) - S(F))$ is the *branching vector* of this node. The *branching number* of a branching vector $(k_1, \dots, k_r)$ is $1/\xi$, where ξ is the unique zero in the unit interval of the (reflected) characteristic polynomial $1 - \sum_{i=1}^{r} z^{k_i}$. If $\alpha_{\max}$ is the maximal branching number in the whole branching tree, then the tree contains $O(\alpha_{\max}^V)$ nodes, where V is the maximum value of a node in the tree [13]. Here, the number of clauses K is an upper bound on the value $S(F)$. Hence, the size of the branching tree is $O(\alpha_{\max}^K)$. Here $\alpha_{\max} = \sqrt{2}$ is the branching number of **D4**, but it cannot occur in all nodes, so the result is slightly better than $\sqrt{2}^K$. (See the full paper for details.)

Theorem 3 *For a formula F in conjunctive normal form, $maxsat(F)$ can be computed in $O(|F| \cdot 1.3995^k)$ steps or $O(|F| \cdot 1.3972^K)$ steps, where $|F|$ is the length of the given formula F, k is the number of satisfiable clauses in F, and K is the number of clauses in F.*

From the parameterized complexity point of view, assuming a parameter value $k < K$, the following corollary is of interest.

Corollary 4 *To determine an assignment satisfying at least k clauses of a boolean function F in CNF takes $O(k^2 \cdot 1.3995^k + |F|)$ steps.*

Proof. Using *reduction to problem kernel*, Mahajan and Raman show that an algorithm that solves MAXSAT in $O(|F| \cdot \gamma^k)$ steps can be transformed into an algorithm that solves the above problem in $O(k^2\gamma^k + |F|)$ steps [14].

Corollary 4 improves Theorem 7 of Mahajan and Raman [14] by decreasing the exponential term from $\phi^k \approx 1.6181^k$ to 1.3995^k. Analogously, the running time for MAXqSAT is improved to $O(qk \cdot 1.3995^k + |F|)$. In addition, Mahajan and Raman also introduced a "more suitable parameterization" of MAXSAT, asking whether at least $\lceil K/2 \rceil + k$ clauses are satisfiable. Recall that, K being the total number of clauses in F, *every* formula has an assignment that fulfills at least half of its clauses. Mahajan and Raman reduce this variant to the original problem we study here. They obtain a time complexity of $O(|F| + k^2\phi^{6k}) = O(|F| + k^2 17.9443^k)$ [14]. Plugging in our better bound, we automatically get $O(|F| + k^2 1.3995^{6k}) = O(|F| + k^2 7.5135^k)$.

4   A bound with respect to the length of a formula

In this section, we analyze the running time of MAXSAT algorithms with respect to the length of a formula. In the previous section, the value of a node F' in the branching tree was $S(F')$. In this section, it will be $|F| - |F'|$, i.e., the reduction in length relative to the root F. For the analysis of Algorithm B in terms of the reduction in length, note that applying the resolution rule reduces the length by 2.

Owing to the dominating 1-clause rule, we can often assume that a satisfied clause is not a 1-clause. In these cases, the length is reduced at least by 2. If x is an (a, b)-literal in a reduced formula F, then x occurs at most $b - 1$ times in a 1-clause. Hence, $|F| - |F[x]| \geq 2a + 1$. For example, look at **F1** (Subsection 3.2). If x is a $(4, 1)$-literal, the length reduction for $F[x]$ is at least 9; for a $(3, 2)$-literal it is at least 7. This proves that the branching vector with respect to length reduction of **F1** is at least $(7, 5)$.

We introduce a new splitting rule:

D4' $\dfrac{F}{F[l_2], F[\bar{l}_2]}$ if $F = \{\{l_1, \dots\}, \{l_1, l_2, \dots\}, \{\bar{l}_1, \dots\}, \{\bar{l}_1\}\}$, l_1 is a $(2, 2)$-literal, and l_2 is a $(3, 1)$- or $(2, 2)$-literal

Here, $|F| - |Reduce(F[l_2])| \geq 8$ and $|F| - |F[\bar{l}_2]| \geq 4$, so the branching vector is $(8, 4)$.

We modify the algorithm such that **D4′** is applied whenever possible and **D4** is applied for a $(2, 2)$-literal x only if $\tilde{x}$ does not occur in a 1-clause. The branching vector for **D4** is then $(6, 6)$. Altogether, the branching vectors are: **T1:** $(9, 4)$ or $(8, 5)$, **T2:** $(7, 7)$, **T3:** $(7, 6)$, **T4:** $(8, 6)$, **T5:** $(10, 3)$ or $(9, 7)$, **T6:** $(8, 4)$ or $(7, 5)$, **T7:** $(10, 3)$, **D1:** $(8, 4)$, **D2:** $(7, 8)$, **D3:** $(8, 4)$, **D4:** $(6, 6)$, **D4′:** $(8, 5)$, **D5:** $(8, 11, 14)$, **D6:** $(4, 16, 32)$, **F1:** $(9, 5)$ or $(7, 5)$.

Theorem 5 *We can solve* MAXSAT *in* $O(1.1279^{|F|})$ *steps.*

Proof. Take Algorithm B with preference of **D4′** over **D4**. The above analysis shows that the size of the branching tree is smaller than $1.1279^{|F|}$. Each node of the tree is processed in linear time.

Theorem 5 should be compared to the best known result for the "simpler" Satisfiability problem obtained by Hirsch [12]. He proves the time bound $O(1.0757^{|F|})$. Moreover, Theorem 5 implies an upper bound of $O(1.2722^K)$ for the MAX2SAT problem, using $|F| \leq 2K$, where K denotes the number of clauses in F. Mahajan and Raman also studied the Maximum Cut problem (MAXCUT) for undirected graphs: Given a graph $G = (V, E)$ on n vertices and m edges and an integer k, is there a set $S \subset V$ such that at least k edges of G have one endpoint in V and one endpoint in $V - S$? They prove that MAXCUT can be solved in time $O(m+n+k4^k)$ [14]. Using a reduction to MAX2SAT (also see "Method 2" in [14]), MAXCUT can be solved in $O(m + n + k^2 1.2722^{4k}) = O(m+n+k^2 2.6196^k)$ steps, thus basically decreasing the base of the exponential function from 4 to 2.6196.

5 Conclusion

Using refined techniques of Davis–Putnam character, we improved previous results on the worst case complexity of MAXSAT, one of the fundamental optimization problems.

To improve the upper time bounds further is an interesting open problem. In particular, can MAX2SAT, MAX3SAT, or, generally, MAXqSAT be solved faster than the general problem? A completely different question is to investigate the performance of our algorithms in practice and whether they may also serve as a basis for efficient heuristic algorithms.

References

1. S. Arora, C. Lund, R. Motwani, M. Sudan, and M. Szegedy. Proof verification and hardness of approximation problems. In *Proc. of 33d FOCS*, pages 14–23, 1992.
2. R. Balasubramanian, M. R. Fellows, and V. Raman. An improved fixed parameter algorithm for vertex cover. *Information Processing Letters*, 65(3):163–168, 1998.
3. R. Battiti and M. Protasi. Reactive Search, a history-base heuristic for MAX-SAT. *ACM Journal of Experimental Algorithmics*, 2:Article 2, 1997.
4. R. Battiti and M. Protasi. Approximate algorithms and heuristics for MAX-SAT. In D.-Z. Du and P. M. Pardalos, editors, *Handbook of Combinatorial Optimization*, volume 1, pages 77–148. Kluwer Academic Publishers, 1998.

5. R. Beigel and D. Eppstein. 3-Coloring in time $o(1.3446^n)$: A no MIS algorithm. In *Proc. of 36th FOCS*, pages 444–452, 1995.
6. L. Cai and J. Chen. On fixed-parameter tractability and approximability of NP optimization problems. *J. Comput. Syst. Sci.*, 54:465–474, 1997.
7. P. Crescenzi and V. Kann. A compendium of NP optimization problems. Available at http://www.nada.kth.se/theory/problemlist.html, Apr. 1997.
8. E. Dantsin, M. Gavrilovich, E. A. Hirsch, and B. Konev. Approximation algorithms for Max SAT: A better performance ratio at the cost of a longer running time. Technical Report PDMI preprint 14/1998, Steklov Institute of Mathematics at St. Petersburg, 1998.
9. R. G. Downey and M. R. Fellows. *Parameterized Complexity*. Springer-Verlag, 1999.
10. R. G. Downey, M. R. Fellows, and U. Stege. Parameterized complexity: A framework for systematically confronting computational intractability. In F. Roberts, J. Kratochvíl, and J. Nešetřil, editors, *Proc. of 1st DIMATIA Symposium*, AMS-DIMACS Proceedings Series, 1997. To appear.
11. P. Hansen and B. Jaumard. Algorithms for the maximum satisfiability problem. *Computing*, 44:279–303, 1990.
12. E. A. Hirsch. Two new upper bounds for SAT. In *Proc. of 9th SODA*, pages 521–530, 1998.
13. O. Kullmann and H. Luckhardt. Deciding propositional tautologies: Algorithms and their complexity. 1997. Submitted to *Information and Computation*.
14. M. Mahajan and V. Raman. Parametrizing above guaranteed values: MaxSat and MaxCut. Technical Report TR97-033, ECCC Trier, 1997. To appear in *Journal of Algorithms*.
15. B. Monien and E. Speckenmeyer. Upper bounds for covering problems. Technical Report Reihe Theoretische Informatik, Bericht Nr. 7/1980, Universität Gesamthochschule Paderborn, 1980.
16. B. Monien and E. Speckenmeyer. Solving satisfiability in less than 2^n steps. *Discrete Applied Mathematics*, 10:287–295, 1985.
17. R. Niedermeier. Some prospects for efficent fixed parameter algorithms (invited paper). In B. Rovan, editor, *Proceedings of the 25th Conference on Current Trends in Theory and Practice of Informatics (SOFSEM)*, number 1521 in Lecture Notes in Computer Science, pages 168–185. Springer-Verlag, 1998.
18. R. Niedermeier and P. Rossmanith. New upper bounds for MaxSat. Technical Report KAM-DIMATIA Series 98-401, Faculty of Mathematics and Physics, Charles University, Prague, July 1998.
19. R. Niedermeier and P. Rossmanith. Upper bounds for Vertex Cover further improved. In C. Meinel and S. Tison, editors, *Proceedings of the 16th Symposium on Theoretical Aspects of Computer Science*, number 1563 in Lecture Notes in Computer Science, pages 561–570. Springer-Verlag, 1999.
20. C. H. Papadimitriou. *Computational Complexity*. Addison-Wesley, 1994.
21. C. H. Papadimitriou and M. Yannakakis. Optimization, approximation, and complexity classes. *J. Comput. Syst. Sci.*, 43:425–440, 1991.
22. R. Paturi, P. Pudlák, M. Saks, and F. Zane. An improved exponential-time algorithm for k-SAT. In *Proc. of 39th FOCS*, pages 628–637, 1998.
23. P. Pudlák. Satisfiability—algorithms and logic (invited paper). In *Proceedings of the 23d Conference on Mathematical Foundations of Computer Science*, number 1450 in Lecture Notes in Computer Science, pages 129–141, Brno, Czech Republic, Aug. 1998. Springer-Verlag.

Polynomial and Rational Evaluation and Interpolation (with Structured Matrices)*

Vadim Olshevsky

Dept. of Math. & Comp. Sci.
Georgia State University,
Atlanta, GA 30303
volshevsky@cs.gsu.edu

Victor Y. Pan

Dept. of Math. & Comp. Sci.
Lehman College, CUNY,
Bronx, NY 10468
vpan@alpha.lehman.cuny.edu

Summary: Polynomial and rational interpolation and multipoint evaluation are classical subjects, which remain central for the theory and practice of algebraic and numerical computing and have extensive applications to sciences, engineering and signal and image processing. In spite of long and intensive study of these subjects, several major problems remained open. We achieve substantial progress, based on our new matrix representations of the problems with the use of node polynomials. In particular:

1. We show strong correlation between rational and polynomial problems as well as between evaluation and interpolation, which enables our unified algorithmic treatment of all these subjects.

2. In applications of real polynomial evaluation and interpolation to sciences, engineering, and signal and image processing, most important is the case where input/output is represented in Chebyshev bases. In this case we rely on fast cosine/sine transforms (FCT/FST) to decrease the arithmetic cost of the known solutions from order of n to $O(\log^2 n)$ per node point.

3. In the general complex case, we devise new effective approximation algorithms for polynomial and rational evaluation and interpolation, for all input polynomials of degree $n - 1$ and all sets of n nodes. The algorithms support the arithmetic complexity bounds of $O(\log n)$ per node point for approximate solution of these classical problems within the output error bound $\epsilon = 2^{-b}$, $\log b = O(\log n)$, taken relative to the specified input parameters. This substantially improved the known estimate of $O(\log^2 n)$ per point.

Our algorithms supporting the cited complexity bounds allow their NC and work optimal parallelization. Our results also include new exact solution algorithms with arithmetic cost $O(\log^2 n)$ per node point for a) Trummer's problem of rational evaluation, which (unlike Gerasoulis algorithm) is interpolation-free, and b) rational interpolation with unknown poles, which exploits the matrix structure instead of the customary reduction to Euclidean algorithm. Technically, we exploit correlation among various problems of polynomial and rational interpolation, their matrix representations and transformations (mappings) into each other of both problems and the associated structured matrices.

* This work was supported by NSF grants CCR 973235, CCR 9625344, CCR 9732206, GSU ORSP Award, and PSC CUNY Award 669363

1   Introduction

Our subjects are polynomial and rational interpolation and multipoint evaluation, to which we will refer hereafter as *p.i.*, *r.i.*, *p.e.* and *r.e.*, respectively. Our main results are stated in the summary as well as in our Theorems 3.1, 5.2, 6.1 and Corollaries 5.1, 5.2, and 6.1. This includes nontrivial matrix equations (5.2) and (5.3), which extend a result of [BKO,a] and serve as the basic tools for our transformations of problems of p.i., p.e., r.i. and r.e. Our techniques involved in particular in the derivation of these equations and the cited transformations may be of independent interest. Our present study of r.i. has no overlap with [OP98] because, unlike [OP98], we assume neither the so called passivity conditions nor any boundary conditions.

In the next sections we will state the problems formally, give some background, including motivation and known difficulties, specify our contribution stated in the summary and recall the known results for comparison. Our complexity estimates are given in terms of the number of arithmetic operations and comparisons involved, to all of which we will refer as *ops*. (We will assume the customary arithmetic models of RAM (PRAM) or circuits [AHU74], [KR90], [G86]. The computations of sections 2-6 can be assumed over any field, except that we rely on the cost bound $O(n \log n)$ for polynomial multiplication modulo x^n, ignoring the extra factor $\log \log n$, required over abstract fields (cf. [BP94], pp. 12, 13, 56).) Since the basic blocks of our algorithms are FFT, FCT, FST, and linear operations with vectors, parallel versions of our algorithms can be also implemented efficiently under some more realistic models such as the hypercube and butterfly network models [Le92].

2   Classical polynomial evaluation and interpolation

We first define a vector $\mathbf{x} = (x_i)_{i=0}^{n-1}$ of n distinct nodes, a polynomial $c(x) = \sum_{j=0}^{n-1} c_j x^j$, the vectors $\mathbf{c} = (c_j)_{j=0}^{n-1}$ of its coefficients and $\mathbf{v} = (v_i)_{i=0}^{n-1}$, $v_i = c(x_i)$, of its values at the nodes x_i, as well as the *node polynomial* $h_{\mathbf{x}}(x) = \prod_{i=0}^{n-1}(x - x_j)$ (having the coefficient vector $\mathbf{h_x}$) and its derivative $h'_{\mathbf{x}}(x) = \frac{dh_{\mathbf{x}}(x)}{dx} = \sum_{j=0}^{n-1} \prod_{j \neq i}(x - x_j)$. Having these definitions, we state the problems of (multipoint) polynomial evaluation (p.e.) and interpolation (p.i.).

Problem 2.1, *p.e.*

Input: two vectors $\mathbf{c}$ and $\mathbf{x}$ and the coefficient vector $\mathbf{h_x}$ of the node polynomial $h_{\mathbf{x}}(x)$.

Output: the vector $\mathbf{v}$.

Problem 2.2, *p.i.*

Input: two vectors $\mathbf{x}$ and $\mathbf{v}$ and the vector $\mathbf{h_x}$.

Output: the vector $\mathbf{c}$.

Problems 2.1 and 2.2 reverse each other. P.e. and its solution can be trivially extended to the evaluation at n points of polynomials of degree $m - 1 \neq n - 1$.

Given $\mathbf{x}$, one may compute the vector $\mathbf{h_x}$ by a fan-out algorithm in $O(\log^2 n)$ ops per node point [AHU74], [BM75], [BP94], p.25.

Remark 2.1. We assume $\mathbf{h_x}$ being a part of the input (and similarly with $\mathbf{h_y}$ for Problem 3.1 of section 3) for in many practical computations $\mathbf{x}$ is fixed while $\mathbf{c}$ and $\mathbf{v}$ vary. We will use such assumptions only in section 7, where we decrease the complexity estimates below the level of $\log^2 n$ per node.

The classical numerically stable algorithms solve Problems 2.1 and 2.2 by using order of n ops per node [CdB80]. More recent algorithms solve both problems by using order of $\log^2 n$ ops per node [AHU74], [BM75], [BP94], page 25, which is within factor $\log n$ from a lower bound of [Str73]. Recursive application of polynomial division, however, makes these algorithms *numerically unstable*, that is, their output may be easily contaminated completely by small input or roundoff errors (cf. [PZHY97]). This motivates the search for numerically stable algorithms for p.e./p.i. that use $o(n)$ ops per node point, which will be one of our subjects in section 7.

3   Problems of rational evaluation and interpolation

In rational evaluation (r.e.) and interpolation (r.i.) the input/output polynomial $c(x)$ of p.e./p.i. is replaced by a ratio

$$r(x) = u(x)/v(x), \ u(x) = \sum_{j=0}^{n-1} u_j x^j, \ v(x) = x^n + \sum_{i=0}^{n-1} v_i x^i. \tag{3.1}$$

If the poles of $r(x)$ are simple and available, it is convenient to state the problems of r.e./r.i. based on the following customary decomposition:

$$r(x) = \sum_{j=0}^{n-1} \frac{s_j}{x - y_j}. \tag{3.2}$$

Problem 3.1, *polarized r.e.* (*Trummer's problem*).
  Input: a *node vector* $\mathbf{x} = (x_i)_{i=0}^{n-1}$ and a *pole vector* $\mathbf{y} = (y_j)_{j=0}^{n-1}$, with $2n$ distinct entries; the vector $\mathbf{h_y}$ and a vector $\mathbf{s} = (s_j)_{j=0}^{n-1}$.
  Output: the vector $\mathbf{t} = (t_i)_{i=0}^{n-1}$, where $t_i = r(x_i) = \sum_{j=0}^{n-1} s_j/(x_i - y_j)$, $i = 0, \ldots, n-1$.
  Problem 3.2, *polarized r.i.*
  Input: two vectors $\mathbf{x}$ and $\mathbf{y}$ (as in Problem 3.1) and a vector $\mathbf{t} = (t_i)_{i=0}^{n-1}$.
  Output: the vector $\mathbf{s} = (s_j)_{j=0}^{n-1}$ satisfying $t_i = r(x_i) = \sum_{j=0}^{n-1} s_j/(x_i - y_j)$, $i = 0, \ldots, n-1$.
  Problems 3.1 and 3.2 represent approximation of complex and real functions by rational functions and allow fast and numerically stable solution of r.e./r.i. problems as well as their natural and widely used matrix generalizations and extensions. Problems 3.1 and 3.2 are also most customary forms for

representation of r.e./r.i. used in the study of particle simulation, the n-body problem of celestial mechanics, integral equations, evaluation of Riemann's zeta function and conformal maps (see some bibliography in [PACLS98]).

Numerically stable solution of each of Problems 3.1 and 3.2 requires $2n-1$ ops per node. Order of $\log^2 n$ ops per node can be achieved at the expense of losing numerical stability [BP94], pp. 129-131.

In the rest of this section, we will study r.e. and r.i. based on (3.1).

Problem 3.3, $r.e.$

Input: three vectors, $\mathbf{u} = (u_j)_{j=0}^{n-1}$, $\mathbf{v} = (v_j)_{j=0}^{n-1}$ and $\overline{\mathbf{x}} = (x_i)_{i=0}^{2n-1}$.

Output: the vector $\mathbf{t} = (t_i)_{i=0}^{2n-1}$, where $t_i = r(x_i)$, $i = 0, \ldots, 2n-1$, for $r(x)$ of (3.1).

Problem 3.4, $r.i.$

Input: two vectors, $\mathbf{t}$ and $\overline{\mathbf{x}}$.

Output: the vectors $\mathbf{u}$ and $\mathbf{v}$ such that $t_i = r(x_i)$, $i = 0, \ldots, 2n-1$, for $r(x)$ of (3.1).

We evaluate $u(x_0)$, $v(x_0)$, ..., $u(x_{2n-1})$, $v(x_{2n-1})$ (cf. Problem 2.1) to obtain the next result.

Theorem 3.1. *Problem 3.3 can be solved in $O(\log^2 n)$ ops per node.*

The next simple algorithm uses $O(\log^2 n)$ ops per node to reduce Problem 3.1 to Problem 3.3 (w.l.o.g. assume that $n = 2^h$).

Algorithm 3.1,

Input: two vectors $\mathbf{s}$ and $\mathbf{y}$.

Output: the vectors $\mathbf{u}$ and $\mathbf{v}$ such that (3.1) and (3.2) define the same rational function $r(x)$.

Computations:

Initialization: write $u_j^{(0)}(x) = s_j$, $v_j^{(0)}(x) = x - y_j$, $r_j^{(0)}(x) = u_j^{(0)}(x)/v_j^{(0)}(x)$, $j = 0, \ldots, n-1$.

Stage g, g=1, ..., h: compute the coefficients of the polynomials $u_j^{(g)}(x)$, $v_j^{(g)}(x)$, whose ratios $r_j^{(g)}(x) = u_j^{(g)}(x)/v_j^{(g)}(x)$ satisfy the equations $r_j^{(g)}(x) = r_{2j-1}^{(g-1)}(x) + r_{2j}^{(g-1)}(x)$, $j = 0, 1, \ldots, n/2^g$. Finally, write $r(x) = r_0^{(h)}(x) = u(x)/v(x)$, where the polynomials $u(x)$ and $v(x)$ satisfy (3.1) and (3.2), and output the vectors $\mathbf{u}$ and $\mathbf{v}$ of their coefficients.

For the converse transition from Problem 3.3 to Problem 3.1, we need to have the vector $\mathbf{y}$ of n distinct roots of the polynomial $v(x)$ of (3.1). The computational cost of the known best polynomial rootfinders is a little higher than one for r.e./r.i. [P95a], [P96], but, as mentioned, in many applications of r.e./r.i., the vector $\mathbf{y}$ is given. In this case the transition is simply via p.e. because $s_j = u(y_j)/v'(y_j)$, $j = 0, \ldots, n-1$. (Indeed, multiply by $v(x)$ both sides of the equation $\sum_j \frac{s_j}{x - y_j} = \frac{u(x)}{v(x)}$, to cancel the denominators, substitute $x = y_j$ into the resulting equation, and observe that $v(y_i)/(y_i - y_j)$ equals 0 for $i \neq j$ and $v'(y_j)$ for $i = j$.)

4 Modified problems of polynomial evaluation and interpolation

The format of Problems 2.1 and 2.2 for p.e. and p.i. is appropriate for computations over finite fields (polynomial factorization, coding and decoding) and where the vector $\mathbf{x}$ is formed by the (scaled) roots of 1, which turns Problems 1.1 and 1.2 into forward and inverse discrete Fourier transforms, effectively solved by FFT in $O(n \log n)$ ops, that is, in $O(\log n)$ ops per node point (see [BP94], pp. 9-10, on the cost estimates, and pp. 252-256, on the numerical stability of FFT). In many practical computations, however, one needs p.e./p.i. with real node vectors $\mathbf{x}$, and then the problems (in particular, p.i.) immediately become severely ill-conditioned. To overcome this difficulty, the customary recipe is to generalize Problems 2.1 and 2.2 by writing

$$c(x) = c_{\mathbf{P}}(x) = \sum_{j=0}^{n-1} c_j P_j(x) \tag{4.1}$$

where the n components $P_0(x), \ldots, P_{n-1}(x)$ of the *bases vector* $\mathbf{P} = (P_j(x))_{j=0}^{n-1}$ form a bases in the linear space of polynomials of degree at most $n - 1$ such as ones made of Chebyshev polynomials of the first or the second kind,

$$P_j(x) = T_j = T_j(x) = 2^{-j} \cos(j \arccos x), \tag{4.2}$$

$$P_j(x) = U_j = U_j(x) = \sin((j + 1) \arccos x) / \sin(\arccos x). \tag{4.3}$$

(4.2), (4.3) are the most customary choices for p.e./p.i. on real intervals where the real functions $\sum_{j=0}^{\infty} c_j P_j(x)$ are most effectively approximated by partial sums (4.1) under these choices of $P_j(x)$ [SB80], [Ri90].

Fast cosine/sine transforms (hereafter, referred to as *FCT/FST*) replace FFT wherever bases (4.2) and (4.3) replace the monomial bases, and this is reflected by rapid growth of the current library of algorithms based on FCT/FST [Po96], [SN96]. Generalized p.e./p.i. problems cover bases (4.2) and (4.3) as well as the monomial bases $\{P_j(x) = x^j\}$.

Problem 4.1, *generalized p.e.*

Input: vectors $\mathbf{P} = (P_j(x))_{j=0}^{n-1}, \mathbf{x}$, and $\mathbf{c_P} = (c_j)_{j=0}^{n-1}$.

Output: the vector $\mathbf{v} = (v_i)_{j=0}^{n-1}$, where $v_i = c_{\mathbf{P}}(x_i) = \sum_{j=0}^{n-1} c_j P_j(x_i)$, $i = 0, \ldots, n - 1$.

Problem 4.2, *generalized p.i.*

Input: vectors $\mathbf{x}, \mathbf{P}$, and $\mathbf{v} = (v_i)_{i=0}^{n-1}$.

Output: the vector $\mathbf{c_P} = (c_j)_{j=0}^{n-1}$ such that $c_{\mathbf{P}}(x_i) = \sum_{j=0}^{n-1} c_j P_j(x_i) = v_i$, $i = 0, \ldots, n - 1$.

5 Matrix versions of the problems and the mappings of the matrices and the problems

Hereafter, diag $(m_i)_{i=0}^{n-1}$ denotes the $n \times n$ diagonal matrix with diagonal entries $m_0, \ldots, m_{n-1}$. $V(\mathbf{x}) = (x_i^j)_{i,j=0}^{n-1}$, $V_{\mathbf{P}}(\mathbf{x}) = (P_j(x_i))_{i,j=0}^{n-1}$ and $C(\mathbf{x}, \mathbf{y}) =$

$(\frac{1}{x_i - y_j})_{i,j=0}^{n-1}$ denote the $n \times n$ *Vandermonde, polynomial Vandermonde* and *Cauchy matrices*, respectively, defined by vectors $\mathbf{P}, \mathbf{x}$ and $\mathbf{y}$. Problems 2.1, 2.2, 3.1, 3.2, 4.1 and 4.2 amount to computation of the vectors $\mathbf{v} = V(\mathbf{x})\mathbf{c}$, $\mathbf{c} = V^{-1}(\mathbf{x})\mathbf{v}$, $\mathbf{v} = V_{\mathbf{P}}(\mathbf{x})\mathbf{c_P}$, $\mathbf{c_P} = V_{\mathbf{P}}^{-1}(\mathbf{x})\mathbf{v}$, $\mathbf{t} = C(\mathbf{x}, \mathbf{y})\mathbf{s}$ and $\mathbf{s} = C^{-1}(\mathbf{x}, \mathbf{y})\mathbf{t}$, respectively.

Matrix representation facilitates both solution and analysis of the cited problems. Our main tool will be the mappings of structured matrices, which is a recipe first proposed for p.e. and p.i. in [PLST93], [PZHY97] as an extension of the general approach of [P90] to the unification and improvement of algorithms for various classes of structured matrices by means of mapping such classes of matrices into each other. We will rely on the next formula, due to [BKO,a] (earlier known for the special case of $\mathbf{P} = (x^j)_{j=0}^{n-1}$ [FHR93], [BP94], p.131):

Theorem 5.1. *Under the previous notation, let two vectors $\mathbf{x}$ and $\mathbf{y}$, each of dimension n, have $2n$ distinct components and let $h_{\mathbf{y}}(x) = \prod_{j=0}^{n-1}(x - y_j), h'_{\mathbf{y}}(x) = dh_{\mathbf{y}}(x)/dx = \sum_{i=0}^{n-1} \prod_{j \neq i}(x - y_j)$. Then*

$$V_{\mathbf{P}}(\mathbf{x}) = \{\text{diag}(h_{\mathbf{y}}(x_i))_{i=0}^{n-1}\} C(\mathbf{x}, \mathbf{y})\{\text{diag}(1/h'_{\mathbf{y}}(y_j))_{j=0}^{n-1}\} V_{\mathbf{P}}(\mathbf{y}). \quad (5.1)$$

The next corollaries are due to [PACLS98], [PACPS98]:

Corollary 5.1 *Under the assumptions of Theorem 5.1, we have*

$$V_{\mathbf{P}}^{-1}(\mathbf{x}) = V_{\mathbf{P}}^{-1}(\mathbf{y})\{\text{diag}(h_{\mathbf{x}}(y_i))_{i=0}^{n-1}\} C(\mathbf{y}, \mathbf{x})\{\text{diag}(1/h'_{\mathbf{x}}(x_j))_{j=0}^{n-1}\}. \quad (5.2)$$

Corollary 5.2 *Let $\mathbf{x}, \mathbf{y}, \mathbf{z}$ be three vectors of dimension n having $3n$ distinct components. Then*

$$C(\mathbf{x}, \mathbf{y}) = \{\text{diag}(\frac{h_{\mathbf{z}}(x_i)}{h_{\mathbf{y}}(x_i)})_{i=0}^{n-1}\} C(\mathbf{x}, \mathbf{z})\{\text{diag}(\frac{h_{\mathbf{y}}(z_j)}{h'_{\mathbf{z}}(z_j)})_{j=0}^{n-1}\} C(\mathbf{z}, \mathbf{y}). \quad (5.3)$$

Corollaries 5.1 and 5.2 enable various reductions of Problems 2.1, 2.2, 3.1-3.4, 4.1 and 4.2 to each other. In section 7, we will show some promising extensions of the known solution algorithms for p.e./p.i. based on such reductions. Next, we will use a matrix version of Problem 3.4, where $V(\overline{\mathbf{x}}) = (x_i^j)_{i=0,j=0}^{2n-1,n-1}$, $V(\overline{\mathbf{x}}, \mathbf{t}) = (V(\overline{\mathbf{x}}), \{\text{diag}(t_i)_{i=0}^{2n-1}\} V(\overline{\mathbf{x}}))$, $V(\overline{\mathbf{x}}, \mathbf{t})$ is a $2n \times 2n$ matrix.

Theorem 5.2. *Problem 3.4 can be written as a linear system of equations $V(\overline{\mathbf{x}}, \mathbf{t})(\begin{smallmatrix} \mathbf{u} \\ -\mathbf{v} \end{smallmatrix}) = (t_i x_i^n)_{i=0}^{2n-1}$. $O(n \log^2 n)$ ops suffice to test whether the matrix $V(\overline{\mathbf{x}}, \mathbf{t})$ is nonsingular and, if so, to compute the solution $\mathbf{u}, \mathbf{v}$.*

Proof. The vector equation is verified by inspection. Now, observe that the matrix $V(\overline{\mathbf{x}}, \mathbf{t})$ is Vandermonde-like, having F-rank at most 2, according to the definitions of [BP94]. Apply the algorithms of [P90], [P99] to test if the matrix $V(\overline{\mathbf{x}}, \mathbf{t})$ is nonsingular and, if so, to solve the above linear system in $\mathbf{u}, \mathbf{v}$. Q.E.D.

6 Effective choices of the node vectors and the fast exact solution algorithms for generalized p.e. and p.i.

Let $\mathbf{P} = (\mathbf{x}^j)_{j=0}^{n-1}$ be the monomial bases, fix a proper scalar a, and let $\mathbf{y}$ be a scaled vector of the n-th roots of 1, $\mathbf{y} = a\mathbf{w}$, $\mathbf{w} = (w^j)_{j=0}^{n-1}$, $w = w(n) = exp(2\pi\sqrt{-1}/n)$. In this case, $h_{\mathbf{y}}(x) = x^n - a^n$, $h'_{\mathbf{y}}(x) = nx^{n-1}$, and the values $h_{\mathbf{y}}(x_i) = x_i^n - a^n$ and $h'_{\mathbf{y}}(y_j) = ny_j^{n-1}$ can be immediately computed for all i and j in $O(n \log n)$ ops, $V_{\mathbf{P}}(\mathbf{y})$ and $V_{\mathbf{P}}^{-1}(\mathbf{y})$ are the matrices of the scaled forward and inverse discrete Fourier transform (DFT), which can be multiplied by a vector in $O(n \log n)$ ops (cf. [BP94], pp. 9-10).

Dealing with Chebyshev bases (4.2), (4.3), we choose node vectors $\mathbf{y}$ such that $V_{\mathbf{P}}(\mathbf{y})$ turns into one of the matrices of DCT or DST (see [Po96], [SN96], [KO96]). Such a matrix can be multiplied by a vector in $O(n \log n)$ ops. As an immediate application, we improve the known complexity bounds for Problems 4.1, 4.2 from order of n [Ri90], [SB80] to $O(\log^2 n)$ per node.

Theorem 6.1 *[OP99]. Under (4.2), (4.3), Problems 4.1 and 4.2 can be solved by using $O(n \log^2 n)$ ops, that is, $O(\log^2 n)$ per node point.*

Proof By Theorem 5.1 and Corollary 5.1, each of Problems 4.1 and 4.2 can be reduced to multiplication of the matrices $V_{\mathbf{P}}(\mathbf{y})$, $V_{\mathbf{P}}^{-1}(\mathbf{y})$, $C(\mathbf{x}, \mathbf{y})$ and/or $C(\mathbf{y}, \mathbf{x})$ by a vector and to two Problems 2.1. By choosing $\mathbf{y}$ from a table of [KO96] (up to scaling), we reduce the multiplications of $V_{\mathbf{P}}(\mathbf{y})$ and $V_{\mathbf{P}}^{-1}(\mathbf{y})$ by vectors to DCTs/DSTs and perform them in $O(n \log n)$ ops. The scaling of vector $\mathbf{y}$ keeps its components distinct from ones of $\mathbf{x}$, so that the matrix $C(\mathbf{x}, \mathbf{y})$ is well-defined. The known algorithms (cf. sections 2 and 3) use $O(n \log^2 n)$ ops to support the other steps of the computation. *Q.E.D.*

Corollary 6.1 *Given a polynomial $c(x)$ in monomial bases, its representations in the bases of (4.2) or (4.3) can be computed in $O(n \log^2 n)$ ops (or $O(\log^2 n)$ per node); $O(n \log^2 n)$ ops also suffice for the converse transition.*

Proof. Fix any node vector $\mathbf{x}$ and evaluate $c(x)$ on $\mathbf{x}$ by using the representation of $c(x)$ in the given bases. Then interpolate to $c(x)$ expressed in the new bases. Apply Theorem 6.1 and the known fast algorithms for p.e./p.i. in the monomial bases (cf. [BP94], section 1.4). *Q.E.D.*

7 Approximation algorithms for the evaluation and interpolation

Some approximation algorithms for Problems 2.1, 2.2, and 3.1 working under certain restrictions on the input decrease the computational cost estimates versus the exact solution algorithms. [R88] uses $O(u^3)$ ops per node to approximate the output vector $\mathbf{v}$ of Problem 2.1 with the error bound $2^{-u} \sum_{i=0}^{n-1} |c_i|$.

[P95] yields the cost bound $O(\log^2 u + \min (u, \log n))$. Both algorithms assume the node set on a fixed real interval, rely on the real approximation theorems, and extend neither to p.e. with nonreal input nodes nor to p.i.

The state of the art of the problem of approximate p.e. is reflected in [W98], where *p.e. on a set of points on a fixed circle* is viewed as an extension of DFT. Even in this simplest case further restrictions on the input are required to improve the known cost bound of $O(\log^2 n)$ ops per node.

Let us relax such restrictions by projecting the variable x onto the real line to yield a fast approximation algorithm. We assume Problem 2.1 of p.e. where all input nodes x_i lie on the unit circle, that is, $|x_i| = 1$ for all i, and where, w.l.o.g., the input coefficient vector $\mathbf{c}$ is real. Express the complex variable x as $x = y + \sqrt{y^2 - 1}$. As x ranges on the unit circle, $x = e^{2\pi i \phi}, i = \sqrt{-1}$, we have real $y = \operatorname{Re} x = \cos \phi$, ranging between -1 and 1. As x ranges among the k-th roots of 1, y ranges among the Chebyshev real nodes lying in the interval from -1 to 1. We also have

$$c(x) = c_0(y) + c_1(y)\sqrt{y^2 - 1}, \tag{7.1}$$

where $c_0(y)$ and $c_1(y)$ are two polynomials of degrees at most $n - 1$; $c_0(y) = \operatorname{Re} c(y), c_1(y) = \operatorname{Im} c(y)/|\sqrt{y^2 - 1}|$, for $-1 \le y \le 1$. Now, for $k \ge n$, evaluate $c(x)$ at the k-th roots of 1 (DFT). By (7.1), this defines $c_0(y)$ and $c_1(y)$ on the Chebyshev nodes. By interpolation, recover $c_0(x)$ and $c_1(x)$. The entire computation costs $O(k \log k)$ ops. Then apply the approximation algorithms of [R88] or [P95] to evaluate $c_0(y)$ and $c_1(y)$ on the set $\{y_i\} = \{\operatorname{Re} x_i\}$ Finally, apply (7.1) to evaluate $c(x)$ on the input set $\{x_i\}$.

Let us next follow [PZHY97] to solve both Problems 2.1 and 2.2 of p.e./p.i. approximately (for an arbitrary complex node vector $\mathbf{x}$), by means of the reduction to Trummer's problem based on (5.1) and (5.2). Choose $\mathbf{y} = a\mathbf{w}$, for a scalar a and the vector $\mathbf{w}$ of the n-th roots of 1, which turns $V(\mathbf{y})$ of (5.1) and $V^{-1}(\mathbf{y})$ of (5.2) into the matrices of scaled forward and inverse DFT, respectively. Now, the values $h_{\mathbf{y}}(x_i)$ and $h'_{\mathbf{y}}(y_j)$ can be computed in $O(n \log n)$ ops for all i and j, and, clearly, n ops suffice to multiply a diagonal matrix by a vector. Therefore, the overall cost is $O(n \log n)$ ops, that is, $O(\log n)$ ops per point (in terms of n).

We choose the scalar a to separate the components of $\mathbf{y}$ from ones of $\mathbf{x}$. Application of the above algorithm to Problem 2.2 (cf. (5.2)) involves Problem 2.1, at the stage where one computes $h'_{\mathbf{x}}(x_j)$, for $j = 0, \ldots, n - 1$.

Instead of the vector $\mathbf{y} = a\mathbf{w}$, which represents a scaled set of the n-th roots of 1, one may choose $\mathbf{y}$ ranging in a scaled Chebyshev set. In this case only real values are involved into the computations when the input is real.

The proposed transformations reduce p.e./p.i. essentially to Trummer's problem. Fast and numerically stable Multipole algorithms [GR87], [CGR88] give its approximate solution. The initial results of numerical experiments in [PZHY97] show that this approach is indeed effective in the case of p.e.

8 Discussion

The proposed techniques of matrix transformations for polynomial and rational evaluation and interpolation promise several further effective extensions, such as the extension of Theorem 6.1 to Problem 3.2 based on an appropriate matrix equation easily deduced from (5.1) in [OP99].

Among the important problems closely related to p.e./p.i., the multiplication of the transpose of a Vandermonde matrix and the inverse of such a transpose by a vector can be easily treated by extending our techniques.

As an example of possible modifications of our algorithms, one may exploit the next alternative to (5.2) free of $h'_\mathbf{x}(x_i)$:

$$V_\mathbf{P}^{-1}(\mathbf{x}) = V_\mathbf{P}^{-1}(\mathbf{y})\{\mathrm{diag}(\frac{h'_\mathbf{y}(y_i)h_\mathbf{y}(x_i)}{h'_\mathbf{x}(y_i)})_{i=0}^{n-1}\}C(\mathbf{y},\mathbf{x})\{\mathrm{diag}(\frac{h_\mathbf{x}(y_j)}{h_\mathbf{y}(x_j)h'_\mathbf{y}(x_j)})_{j=0}^{n-1}\}.$$

References

[AHU74] A. V. Aho, J. E. Hopcroft, J. D. Ullman, *The Design and Analysis of Computer Algorithms*, Addison-Wesley, Reading, Mass, 1974.

[BKO,a] T. Boros, T. Kailath, V. Olshevsky, Pivoting and Backward Stabillity of Fast Algorithms for Solving Cauchy Linear Systems (submitted).

[BM75] A. Borodin, I. Munro, *The Computational Complexity of Algebraic and Numeric Problems*, American Elsevier, New York, 1975.

[BP94] D. Bini, V. Y. Pan, *Polynomial and Matrix Computations, Volume 1: Fundamental Algorithms*, Birkhäuser, Boston, 1994.

[CdB80] C.D. Conte, C. de Boor, *Elementary Numerical Analysis: an Algorithmic Approach*, McGraw-Hill, New York, 1980.

[CGR88] J. Carier, L. Greengard, V. Rokhlin, A Fast Adaptive Multipole Algorithm for Particle Simulation, *SIAM J. Sci. Stat. Comput.*, **9**, 669–686, 1988.

[FHR93] T. Fink, G. Heinig, K. Rost, An Inversion Formula and Fast Algorithms for Cauchy-Vandermonde Matrices, *Linear Algebra Appl.*, **183**, 179–191, 1993.

[G86] J. von zur Gathen, Parallel Arithmetic Computations: a Survey, *Lecture Notes in Computer Science*, **233**, 93-112, Springer, Berlin, 1986.

[GR87] L. Greengard, V. Rokhlin, A Fast Algorithm for Particle Simulation, *J. of Comput. Physics*, **73**, 325-348, 1987.

[KO96] T. Kailath, V. Olshevsky, Displacement Structure Approach to Discrete-Trigonometric-Transform Based Preconditioners of G. Strang and of T. Chan, *Calcolo*, **33**, 191-208, 1996.

[KR90] R. Karp, V. Ramachandran, A Survey of Parallel Algorithms for Shared Memory Machines, *Handbook for Theoretical Computer Science* (J. van Leeuwen editor), 869–941, North Holland, Amsterdam, 1990.

[Le92] F. T. Leighton, Introduction to Parallel Algorithms and Architectures: Arrays, Trees & Hypercubes, *Morgan Kaufmann*, San Mateo, CA 1992.

[OP98]   V. Olshevsky, V. Y. Pan, A Unified Superfast Algorithm for Boundary Rational Tangential Interpolation Problem, *Proc. 39th Ann. IEEE Symp. Foundations of Comp. Sci.*, 192-201, IEEE Comp. Soc. Press, 1998.

[OP99]   V. Olshevsky, V. Y. Pan, Polynomial and Rational Interpolation and Multipoint Evaluation with Application of Structured Matrices, preprint, 1999 (submitted).

[P90]   V. Y. Pan, Computations with Dense Structured Matrices, *Math. of Computation*, **55**, **191**, 179–190, 1990.

[P95]   V. Y. Pan, An Algebraic Approach to Approximate Evaluation of a Polynomial on a Set of Real Points, *Advances in Computational Mathematics*, **3**, 41–58, 1995.

[P95a]   V. Y. Pan, Optimal (up to Polylog Factors) Sequential and Parallel Algorithms for Approximating Complex Polynomial Zeros, *Proc. 27th Ann. ACM Symposium on Theory of Computing*, 741–750, ACM Press, New York, 1995.

[P96]   V. Y. Pan, Optimal and Nearly Optimal Algorithms for Approximating Polynomial Zeros, *Computers & Math. (with Applications)*, **31**, **12**, 97–138, 1996.

[P99]   V. Y. Pan, Superfast Divide-and-Conquer Algorithm for Structured Matrices, preprint, 1999 (submitted).

[PACLS98] V. Y. Pan, M. AbuTabanjeh, Z. Chen, E. Landowne, A. Sadikou, New Transformations of Cauchy Matrices and Trummer's Problem, *Computer and Math. (with Applics.)*, **35**, **12**, 1-5, 1998.

[PACPS98] V. Y. Pan, M. AbuTabanjeh, Z. Chen, S. Providence, A. Sadikou, Transformations of Cauchy Matrices for Trummer's Problem and a Cauchy-like Linear Solver, *Proc. of 5th Annual International Symposium on Solving Irregularly Structured Problems in Parallel, (Irregular98)*, (A. Ferreira, J. Rolim, H. Simon, S.-H. Teng Editors), *Lecture Notes in Computer Science*, **1457**, 274-284, Springer, 1998.

[PLST93] V. Y. Pan, E. Landowne, A. Sadikou, O. Tiga, A New Approach to Fast Polynomial Interpolation and Multipoint Evaluation, *Computers & Math. (with Applications)*, **25**, **9**, 25–30, 1993.

[Po96]   B. Porat, *A Course in Digital Signal Processing*, Wiley, New York, 1996.

[PZHY97] V. Y. Pan, A. Zheng, X. Huang, Y. Yu, Fast Multipoint Polynomial Evaluation and Interpolation via Computations with Structured Matrices, *Annals of Numerical Math.*, **4**, 483–510, January 1997.

[R88]   V. Rokhlin, A Fast Algorithm for the Discrete Laplace Transformation, *J. of Complexity*, **4**, 12-32, 1988.

[Ri90]   T. Rivlin, *Chebyshev Polynomials*, Wiley, New York, 1990.

[SB80]   J. Stoer, R. Bulirsch, *Introduction to Numerical Analysis*, Springer, New York, 1980.

[SN96]   G. Strang, T. Nguyen, *Wavelet and Filterbanks*, Wellesley-Cambridge Press, Cambridge, Mass., 1996.

[Str73]   V. Strassen, Die Berechnungskomplexetät von elementarysymmetrischen Funktionen und von Interpolationskoeffizienten, *Numerische Mathematik*, **20**, **3**, 238-251.

[W98]   A. F. Ware, Fast Approximate Fourier Transforms for Irregularly Spaced Data, *SIAM Review*, **40, 4**, 838-856, 1998.

Low Redundancy in Static Dictionaries with O(1) Worst Case Lookup Time

Rasmus Pagh[*]

BRICS[**], Department of Computer Science, University of Aarhus,
8000 Aarhus C, Denmark
Email: pagh@brics.dk

Abstract. A *static dictionary* is a data structure for storing subsets of a finite universe U, so that membership queries can be answered efficiently. We study this problem in a unit cost RAM model with word size $\Omega(\log |U|)$, and show that for n-element subsets, constant worst case query time can be obtained using $B + O(\log \log |U|) + o(n)$ bits of storage, where $B = \lceil \log_2 \binom{|U|}{n} \rceil$ is the minimum number of bits needed to represent all such subsets. For $|U| = n \log^{O(1)} n$ the dictionary supports constant time rank queries.

1 Introduction

Consider the problem of storing a subset S of a finite set U, such that membership queries, "$u \in S$?", can be answered in worst-case constant time on a unit cost RAM. Since we are interested only in membership queries, we assume that $U = \{0, \ldots, m - 1\}$. We restrict the attention to the case where elements of U can be represented within a constant number of machine words. In particular it is assumed that the usual RAM operations (including multiplication) on numbers of size $m^{O(1)}$ can be done in constant time.

Our goal will be to solve this data structure problem using little memory, measured in consecutive bits (A part of the last word may be unused, and the query algorithm must work regardless of the contents of this part). We express the complexity in terms of $m = |U|$ and $n = |S|$, and often consider the asymptotics when n is a function of m. Since the queries can distinguish any two subsets of U, we need at least $\binom{m}{n}$ different memory configurations, that is, at least $B = \lceil \log \binom{m}{n} \rceil$ bits (log is base 2 throughout this paper). Using Stirling's approximation to the factorial function, one can get (see [3]):

$$B = n \log \frac{m}{n} + (m - n) \log \frac{m}{m - n} - O\left(\log \frac{n(m - n)}{m}\right) \ . \tag{1}$$

[*] Supported in part by the ESPRIT Long Term Research Programme of the EU under project number 20244 (ALCOM-IT)

[**] Basic Research in Computer Science,
Centre of the Danish National Research Foundation.

For $n = o(m)$ the dominant term is $n \log \frac{m}{n}$, since $(m - n) \log \frac{m}{m-n} = \Theta(n)$ (see Lemma 8). It should be noted that using space very close to B is only possible if elements of S are stored *implicitly*, since explicitly representing all elements requires $n \log m = B + \Omega(n \log n)$ bits.

Previous Work

The (static) dictionary is a very fundamental data structure, and it has been heavily studied. We will focus on the development in space consumption for worst case constant time lookup schemes. A bit vector is the simplest possible solution to the problem, but the space complexity of m bits is poor compared to B unless $n \approx m/2$. During the 70's, schemes were suggested which obtain a space complexity of $O(n)$ words, that is $O(n \log m)$ bits, for restricted cases (e.g. "dense" or very sparse sets). It was not until the early 80's that Fredman, Komlós and Szemerédi (FKS) [5] found a hashing scheme using $O(n)$ words in the general case. A refined solution in their paper uses $B + O(n \log n + \log \log m)$ bits. Brodnik and Munro [3] construct a static dictionary using $O(B)$ bits for any m and n. In the journal version of this paper [2], they achieve $B + O(\frac{B}{\log \log \log m})$ bits, and raise the question whether a more powerful model of computation is needed to further tighten the gap to the information theoretic minimum.

No lower bound better than the trivial B bits is known without restrictions on the data structure or the query algorithm (see [4], [8] and [11]).

This Paper

The result of Brodnik and Munro is strengthened, bringing the additional term of the space complexity, which we shall call the *redundancy*, down to $o(n) + O(\log \log m)$ bits. The exact order of the bound, compared with a lower bound on the redundancy of the solution in [2], is given in the table below[1].

Range	Brodnik & Munro	This paper
$n < m/\log \log m$	$\min(n \log \log m, \frac{m}{(\log \log m)^{O(\log \log \log m)}})$	$n \frac{\log^2 \log n}{\log n} + \log \log m$
$n \geq m/\log \log m$		$m \frac{\log \log m}{\log m}$

We also show how to associate information from some domain to each element of S (solving the *partial function* problem), with the same redundancy as above in the sparse case, and $O(n)$ bits in the dense case.

The main observation is that one can save space by "compressing" the hash table part of data structures based on (perfect) hashing, storing in each cell not the element itself, but only a *quotient* — information that distinguishes it from the part of U that hashes to this cell. This technique, referred to as *quotienting*, is described in Sect. 2, where a $B + O(n + \log \log m)$ bit scheme is presented.

---

[1] The bounds given are asymmetric in the sense that if S is replaced by $U \backslash S$ we get another bound although the problems obviously have the same difficulty. However, for simplicity we focus on $n \leq m/2$ and leave the symmetry implications to the reader.

For dense subsets another technique is used, building upon the ideas of range reduction and a "table of small ranges" (both used in [2]). This results in a dictionary, treated in Sect. 3, that supports rank queries. The rank query capability is subsequently used in an improved solution for the non-dense case, described in Sect. 4.

2   First solution

This section presents a static dictionary with a space consumption of $B + O(n + \log \log m)$ bits. As mentioned in the overview, the compact representation achieved stems from the observation that each bucket j of a hash table may be resolved with respect to the part of the universe hashing to bucket j, which we denote by A_j. We phrase this in terms of injective functions on the A_j. Consider the lookup procedure of a dictionary using a perfect hash function h, and a table T:

```
proc lookup(x)
   return (T[h(x)]=x);
end
```

If q is a function which is 1-1 on each A_j (we call this a *quotient function*), and we let T'[j]:=q(T[j]), then the following program is equivalent:

```
proc lookup'(x)
   return (T'[h(x)]=q(x));
end
```

Thus, given a description of q, it suffices to use the hash table T'. The gain is that q may have a range significantly smaller than U (ideally q would enumerate the elements of each A_j), and thus fewer bits are needed to store the elements of T'.

The FKS perfect hashing scheme [5] has a quotient function which is evaluable in constant time, and costs no extra space in that its parameters k, p and a are part of the data structure already:

$$q_{k,p} : u \mapsto (u \operatorname{div} p) \cdot \lceil p/a \rceil + (k \cdot u \operatorname{mod} p) \operatorname{div} a \ . \tag{2}$$

Intuitively, this function gives the information that is thrown away by the modulo applications of the scheme's top-level hash function:

$$h_{k,p} : u \mapsto (k \cdot u \operatorname{mod} p) \operatorname{mod} a \tag{3}$$

where p is prime and k, a positive integers. (So in fact $q_{k,p}$ is 1-1 even on the elements hashing to each bucket in the top level hash table). Since $p = O(m)$ and $a = n$ in the FKS scheme, the range of $q_{k,p}$ has size $O(m/n)$, so $\log \frac{m}{n} + O(1)$ bits suffice to store each hash table element. We prove that $q_{k,p}$ is indeed a quotient function for $h_{k,p}$:

Lemma 1. *Let $A_j(k,p) = \{u \in U \mid h_{k,p}(u) = j\}$ be the subset of U hashing to j. For any j, $q_{k,p}$ is 1-1 on $A_j(k,p)$. Furthermore, $q_{k,p}[U] \subseteq \{0,\ldots,r-1\}$, where $r = \lceil m/p \rceil \cdot \lceil p/a \rceil$.*

Proof. Let $u_1, u_2 \in A_j(k,p)$. If $q_{k,p}(u_1) = q_{k,p}(u_2)$ then u_1 div $p = u_2$ div p and $(k \cdot u_1 \bmod p)$ div $a = (k \cdot u_2 \bmod p)$ div a. By the latter equation and since $h_{k,p}(u_1) = h_{k,p}(u_2)$, we have $k \cdot u_1 \bmod p - k \cdot u_2 \bmod p$. Since p is prime and $k \neq 0$ this implies $u_1 \bmod p = u_2 \bmod p$. Since also u_1 div $p = u_2$ div p it must be the case that $u_1 = u_2$, so $q_{k,p}$ is indeed 1-1 on $A_j(k,p)$. The bound on the range of $q_{k,p}$ is straightforward. $\quad\square$

Schmidt and Siegel [9] show how to simulate the FKS hashing scheme in a "minimal" version (i.e. the hash table has size n), using $O(n + \log\log m)$ bits of storage for the hash function, still with constant lookup time. Their top-level hash function is not (3), but the composition of two functions of this kind, h^1 and h^2 (with quotient functions q^1 and q^2). A corresponding quotient function is $u \mapsto (q^1(u), q^2(h^1(u)))$, which has a range of size $O(m/n)$. One can thus get a space usage of $n \log \frac{m}{n} + O(n)$ bits for the hash table elements, and $O(n + \log\log m)$ bits for the hash function, so using (1) we have:

Proposition 2. *The static dictionary problem with worst case constant lookup time can be solved using $B + O(n + \log\log m)$ bits of storage.*

3 Improvement for Dense Subsets

In this section we describe data structures which are more space efficient for dense subsets than that of the previous section. They will support queries on the ranks of elements (where the rank of u is defined as $\mathrm{rank}(u) = |\{v \in S | v \leq u\}|$). Using rank queries it is possible to do membership queries; therefore we will call the data structures presented *static rank dictionaries*.

Two solutions will be given. The first one has redundancy dependent on m, namely $O(\frac{m \log\log m}{\log m})$ bits. The second solution achieves redundancy $O(\frac{n \log^2 \log n}{\log n})$ bits, for $m = \log^{O(1)} n$.

3.1 Block Compression

The initial idea is to split the universe into blocks $U_i = \{b \cdot i, \ldots, b \cdot (i+1) - 1\}$ of size $b = \lceil \frac{1}{2} \log m \rceil$, and store each block in a compressed form. If a block contains i elements from S, the compressed representation is the number i followed by a number in $\{1, \ldots, \binom{b}{i}\}$ corresponding to the particular subset with i elements. Extraction of information from a compressed block is easy, since any function of the block representations can be computed by table lookup (the crucial thing being that since representations have size at most $\frac{1}{2} \log m + \log\log m$ bits, the number of entries in such a table makes its space consumption negligible compared to $\frac{m \log\log m}{\log m}$ bits). Alternatively, assume that the RAM has instructions to extract the desired information. Let $n_i = |S \cap U_i|$ and $B_i = \lceil \log \binom{b}{n_i} \rceil$. The overall space consumption of the above encoding is $\sum_i B_i + O(\frac{m \log \log m}{\log m})$. Let s denote the number of blocks, $s = O(m/\log m)$. A lemma from [3] bounds the above sum:

Lemma 3. *The following inequality holds:* $\sum_{i=0}^{s-1} B_i < B + s$.

Proof. We have $\sum_{i=0}^{s-1} B_i < \sum_{i=0}^{s-1} \log \binom{b}{n_i} + s \leq B + s$. The latter inequality follows from the fact that $\prod_{i=0}^{s-1} \binom{b}{n_i}$ is the number of sets having n_i elements in block i, which is a subset of all n-subsets in U. $\square$

We need an efficient mechanism for extracting rank information from the compressed representation. The following result contained in [10] is used:

Proposition 4. *A sequence of integers* $z_1, \ldots, z_k$ *where* $|z_i| = n^{O(1)}$ *and* $|z_{i+1} - z_i| = \log^{O(1)} n$ *can be stored in a data structure allowing constant time access, and using* $O(k \log \log n)$ *bits of memory.*

Proof. Every $\log n$th integer is stored "verbatim", using a total of $O(k)$ bits. All other integers are stored as offsets of size $\log^{O(1)} n$ relative to the previous of these values, using $O(k \log \log n)$ bits in total. $\square$

A sequence of pointers to the compressed blocks can be stored in this way, using $O(\frac{m \log \log m}{\log m})$ bits. Also, the rank of the first element in each block can be stored like this. Ranks of elements within a block can be found by table lookup, as sketched above. So we have:

Proposition 5. *A static rank dictionary with worst case constant query time can be represented using* $B + O(\frac{m \log \log m}{\log m})$ *bits.*

3.2 Interval Compression

Our first solution to the static rank dictionary problem has the drawback that the number of compressed blocks (and hence the redundancy) grows almost linearly with m. The number of compressed units can be reduced to $O(\frac{n \log \log n}{\log n})$, for $m = n \log^{O(1)} n$, by clustering suitable adjacent blocks together into *intervals* of varying length (bounded by $\log^{O(1)} m$). This will reduce the space needed to store the pointers to compressed units and the rank of the first element in each unit to $O(\frac{n \log^2 \log n}{\log n})$ bits. Since the lengths of intervals are not fixed, we store the starting positions of the intervals, using $O(\frac{n \log^2 \log n}{\log n})$ bits. Observing that Lemma 3 is independent of the sizes of the compressed units, this will show:

Theorem 6. *For* $m = n \log^{O(1)} n$, *a static rank dictionary with worst case constant query time can be represented using* $B + O(\frac{n \log^2 \log n}{\log n})$ *bits.*

Let $c \geq 1$ be a constant such that $m \leq \frac{n \log^c n}{2c}$. We show how to partition U into "small blocks" U_i satisfying $|S \cap U_i| < \frac{\log n}{2c \log \log n}$. These blocks will be the building stones of the intervals to be compressed. The main tool is the rank dictionary of Prop. 5, which is used to locate areas with a high concentration of elements from S. More specifically, split U into $n \log \log n$ blocks and store the positions of the blocks which are *not* small, i.e. contain at least $\frac{\log n}{2c \log \log n}$ elements from S. Since at most $\frac{2cn \log \log n}{\log n}$ blocks are not small, the memory for this data structure is $O(\frac{n \log^2 \log n}{\log n})$. The part of the universe corresponding to the non-small blocks has size at most $\frac{n \log^{c-1} n}{2c}$. The splitting into $n \log \log n$ blocks is repeated for this sub-universe, and so on for $c - 1$ steps, until the entire sub-universe has size at most $\frac{n \log n}{2c}$, and hence all $n \log \log n$ blocks must be small. This defines our partition of U into small blocks. Given $u \in U$ it takes time $O(c)$ to use the rank dictionaries to find the associated block number (blocks are numbered "from left to right", i.e. according to the elements they contain).

Note that every small block has size at most $\log^c n / \log \log n$. We are interested in intervals (of consecutive small blocks) which are *compressible*, that is, can be stored using $\frac{1}{2} \log n + O(\log \log n)$ bits. Intervals of at most $\log n$ consecutive small blocks, containing at most $\frac{\log n}{2c \log \log n}$ elements of S, have this property by (1). The "greedy" way of choosing such compressible intervals from left to right results in $O(\frac{n \log \log n}{\log n})$ intervals (note that for $m = n \log^{\Omega(1)} n$ this is optimal since the entire compressed representation has size $\Omega(n \log \log n)$). To map block numbers into interval numbers we use Prop. 5, and the space usage is once again $O(\frac{n \log^2 \log n}{\log n})$ bits. Having found the intervals to compress, the construction proceeds as that leading to Prop. 5.

4 Improvement for Non-dense Subsets

Section 2 gave a solution to the static dictionary problem with space usage $B + O(n + \log \log m)$. To achieve redundancy sub-linear in n, we cannot use the hash functions of [9], since the representation is $\Omega(n)$ bit redundant (and it is far from clear whether a minimal, perfect hash function can have $o(n)$ bit redundancy *and* be evaluable in constant time). Also, it must be taken care of that $o(1)$ bit is wasted in each hash table cell, that is, nearly all bit patterns in all cells must be possible independently.

To use less space for storing the hash function, we will not require it to be perfect, but only to be perfect on some sufficiently large subset of S, which we handle first. The rest of S may then be handled by a dictionary that wastes more bits per element.

We will use the hash function (3). The family is indexed by k, p — the range a will depend only on m and n. Parameter p, where $p > a$, will be chosen later. The following result from [5] shows that it is possible to choose k such that $h_{k,p}$ is "almost 1-1 on S" when hashing to a super-linear size table:

Lemma 7. *If the map $u \mapsto u \bmod p$ is 1-1 on S, there exists k, $0 < k < p$, such that $h_{k,p}$ is 1-1 on a set $S_1 \subseteq S$, where $|S_1| \geq (1 - O(\frac{n}{a}))|S|$.*

Without loss of generality, we will assume S_1 to be maximal, that is, $h_{k,p}[S_1] = h_{k,p}[S]$.

The idea will be to build two dictionaries: One for S_1 of Lemma 7, and one for $S_2 = S \backslash S_1$. Lookup may then be accomplished by querying both dictionaries. The dictionary for S_1 consists of the function $h_{k,p}$ given by Lemma 7, together with an a-element "virtual" hash table ($a = n \log^{O(1)} n$ to be determined). The virtual table contains $n_1 = |S_1|$ non-empty cells; to map their positions into n_1 consecutive memory locations, we need a partial function defined on $h_{k,p}[S]$, mapping bijectively to $\{1, \ldots, n_1\}$. The static rank dictionary of Theorem 6 is used for this (two rank queries are used in order to determine if a cell is empty). For a good estimate of the memory used, we show:

Lemma 8. $B = n \log \frac{m}{n} + \frac{n}{\ln 2} - \Theta(n^2/m) - O(\log n)$.

Proof. By (1), it suffices to show the following:

$$(m - n) \log \frac{m}{m - n} = \frac{n}{\ln 2} - \Theta(n^2/m) . \tag{4}$$

We can assume $n = o(m)$. The Taylor series $\ln(1 - x) = -\sum_{i>0} x^i/i$ shows $\ln(1 - 1/x) = -1/x - 1/2x^2 - O(x^{-3})$. Writing $(m - n) \log \frac{m}{m-n} = \frac{n-m}{\ln 2} \ln(1 - n/m)$ and plugging in the above with $x = m/n$ gives the result. $\square$

Thus, the memory for the rank dictionary is $n_1 \log \frac{a}{n_1} + \frac{n_1}{\ln 2} + O(\frac{n \log^2 \log n}{\log n}) = n_1 \log \frac{a}{n} + \frac{n_1}{\ln 2} + O(\frac{n \log^2 \log n}{\log n} + n^2/a)$ bits.

We next show that the memory used for the hash table elements in the S_1 dictionary, $n_1 \lceil \log r \rceil$ bits, where r is the number defined in Lemma 1, can be made close to $n_1 \log \frac{m}{a}$ by suitable choice of p and a.

Lemma 9. *For any A with $3n \le A = O(n \log n)$, there exists a prime p, $3A \le p = O(n^2 \ln m)$, and a value of a, $A/3 \le a \le A$, such that:*

1. *The map $u \mapsto u \bmod p$ is 1-1 on S.*
2. *$n_1 \lceil \log r \rceil = n_1 \log \frac{m}{a} + O(na/m + n^{12/21})$.*

Proof. We first show how to make $\lceil \log r \rceil$ close to $\log r$ by suitable choice of a:

Sublemma 10. *For any $x, y \in \mathbf{R}_+$ and $z \in \mathbf{N}$, with $x/z \ge 3$, there exists $z' \in \{z + 1, \ldots, 3z\}$, such that $\lceil \log \lceil x/z' \rceil + y \rceil \le \log(x/z') + y + O(z/x + 1/z)$.*

Proof. Since $x/z \ge 3$, it follows that $\log \lceil \frac{x}{z} \rceil + y$ and $\log \lceil \frac{x}{3z} \rceil + y$, have different integer parts. So there exists z', $z < z' \le 3z$, such that $\lceil \log \lceil \frac{x}{z'} \rceil + y \rceil \le \log \lceil \frac{x}{z'-1} \rceil + y$. A simple calculation gives $\log \lceil \frac{x}{z'-1} \rceil + y = \log \frac{x}{z'-1} + y + O(z/x) = \log \frac{x}{z'} + \log \frac{z'}{z'-1} + y + O(z/x) = \log \frac{x}{z'} + y + O(z/x + 1/z)$, and the conclusion follows. $\square$

Since $\log r = \log \lceil p/a \rceil + \log \lceil m/p \rceil$ and $p/A \ge 3$, the sublemma gives (for any p) an a in the correct range such that $\lceil \log r \rceil = \log r + O(a/p + 1/a)$.

Parameter $p = O(n^2 \ln n)$ is chosen such that $u \mapsto u \bmod p$ is 1-1 on S, and such that r is not much larger than m/a.

Sublemma 11. *In both of the following ranges, there exists a prime p, such that $u \mapsto u \bmod p$ is 1-1 on S:*

1. $n^2 \ln m \leq p \leq 3n^2 \ln m$.
2. $m < p < m + m^{12/21}$.

Proof. The existence of a suitable prime between $n^2 \ln m$ and $3n^2 \ln m$ is guaranteed by the prime number theorem (in fact, at least half of the primes in the interval will work). See [5, Lemma 2] for details. By [7] the number of primes between m and $m + m^\theta$ is $\Omega(m^\theta / \log m)$ for any $\theta > 11/20$. Take $\theta = 12/21$ and let p be such a prime; naturally the map is then 1-1. □

A prime in the first range will be our choice when $m > n^2 A$, otherwise we choose a prime in the second range. For an estimate of $\log r$ in terms of m, n and a, we look at the two cases:

1. $\log r \leq \log(\frac{m}{a}(1 + \frac{a}{p} + \frac{p}{m})) = \log(m/a) + O(a/p + p/m) = \log(m/a) + O(1/n)$.
2. $\log r = \log\lceil p/a \rceil \leq \log\lceil \frac{m+m^{12/21}}{a} \rceil \leq \log(\frac{m}{a}(1 + \frac{a}{m} + m^{-9/21})) = \log(m/a) + O(a/m + m^{-9/21})$.

This, together with $\lceil \log r \rceil = \log r + O(a/p + 1/a)$, shows that the n_1 hash table entries use $n_1 \log(m/a) + O(na/m + n^{12/21})$ bits. □

For the choices of k, p and a given by Lemmas 7 and 9, we can now compute the total space consumption for the S_1 dictionary:

- $O(\log n + \log \log m)$ bits for the k, p and a parameters, and for various pointers (the whole data structure has size $< n \log m$ bits).
- $n_1 \log \frac{a}{n} + \frac{n_1}{\ln 2} + O(\frac{n \log^2 \log n}{\log n} + n^2/a)$ bits for the "virtual table" mapping.
- $n_1 \log \frac{m}{a} + O(\frac{na}{m} + n^{12/21})$ bits for the hash table contents.

This adds up to $n_1 \log \frac{m}{n} + \frac{n_1}{\ln 2} + O(\frac{n^2}{a} + \frac{na}{m} + \frac{n \log^2 \log n}{\log n} + \log \log m)$ bits.

The S_2 dictionary is implemented using the refined FKS dictionary [5] with a space consumption of $n_2 \log \frac{m}{n_2} + O(n_2 \log n + \log \log m) = n_2 \log \frac{m}{n} + O(\frac{n^2 \log n}{a} + \log \log m)$ bits. Thus, the total space usage of our scheme is:

$$n \log \frac{m}{n} + \frac{n}{\ln 2} + O\left(\frac{n^2 \log n}{a} + \frac{na}{m} + \frac{n \log^2 \log n}{\log n} + \log \log m\right) \text{ bits.} \quad (5)$$

By Lemma 8 this is

$$B + O\left(\frac{n^2 \log n}{a} + \frac{na}{m} + \frac{n \log^2 \log n}{\log n} + \log \log m\right) \text{ bits.} \quad (6)$$

We now get the main theorem:

Theorem 12. *The static dictionary problem with worst case constant lookup time can be solved with storage:*

1. $B + O(n \log^2 \log n / \log n + \log \log m)$ *bits, for* $n < m / \log \log m$.
2. $B + O(m \frac{\log \log m}{\log m})$ *bits, for* $n \geq m / \log \log m$.

Proof. In case 1 use the rank dictionary of Theorem 6 when $m \leq n \log^3 n$, and choose $A = \Theta(n \log^2 n)$ in the above construction when $m > n \log^3 n$. In case 2 use the rank dictionary of Prop. 5. □

We have not associated any information with the elements of our set. The technique presented in this section extends to storing a partial function defined on S, mapping into a finite set V (whose elements are representable within $O(1)$ words). The information theoretical minimum is then $B^V = \lceil \log \binom{m}{n} + n \log |V| \rceil$, and for $m = \Omega(n \log^3 n)$ we get the exact same redundancy as in Theorem 12. The data structure is a simple modification of that described in this section; the size a of the virtual hash table is chosen such that the information packed in a hash table cell (quotient and function value) comes from a domain of size close to a power of 2. In the dense range, the rank dictionary can be used to index into a table of function values, but in general $\Omega(n)$ bits will be wasted in the table since $|V|$ need not be a power of 2.

Theorem 13. *The static partial function problem with worst case constant lookup time can be solved with storage:*

1. $B^V + O(n \log^2 \log n / \log n + \log \log m)$ *bits, for* $n < m / \log^3 m$.
2. $B^V + O(n)$ *bits, for* $n \geq m / \log^3 m$.

By using the dictionary of Prop. 2 to store S_2 and choosing a smaller in the data structure of described in this section, it is possible to achieve redundancy $o(n)$ when $n = o(m)$.

5 Conclusion and Final Remarks

We have seen that for the static dictionary problem it is possible to come very close to using storage at the information theoretic minimum, while retaining constant lookup time. From a data compression point of view this means that a sequence of bits can be coded in a number of bits close to the first-order entropy, in a way which allows efficient random access to the original bits.

The important ingredient in the solution is the concept of quotienting. Thus, the existence of an efficiently evaluable corresponding quotient function is a good property of a hash function. It is also crucial for the solution that the hash function used hashes U quite evenly to the buckets.

Quotienting works equally well in a dynamic setting, where it can be used directly to obtain an $O(B)$ bit scheme. However, lower bounds on the time for maintaining ranks under insertions and deletions (see [6]) show that our constructions involving the rank dictionary will not dynamize well.

It has not been described how to build the dictionary. It is, however, relatively straightforward to design a randomised algorithm which uses expected $O(n + p(n,m))$ time, where $p(n,m)$ is the expected time required for finding a prime in the range specified by Sublemma 11. By [1] we have that $p(n,m) = (\log n + \log \log m)^{O(1)}$.

It would be interesting to determine the exact redundancy necessary to allow constant time lookup. In particular, it is remarkable that no lower bound is known in a *cell probe* model (where only the number of memory cells accessed is considered). As for upper bounds, a less redundant way of mapping the elements of the virtual table to consecutive memory locations would immediately improve the asymptotic redundancy of our scheme. The idea of finding a replacement for the $h_{k,p}$ hash function, which can hash to a smaller "virtual table" or be 1-1 on a larger subset of S will not bring any improvement, because of a very sharp rise in the memory needed to store a function which performs better than $h_{k,p}$.

Acknowledgements: I would like to thank my supervisor, Peter Bro Miltersen, for encouragement and advice. Thanks also to Jakob Pagter and Theis Rauhe for their help on improving the presentation.

References

[1] L. Adleman and M. Huang. Recognizing primes in random polynomial time. In Alfred Aho, editor, *Proceedings of the 19th Annual ACM Symposium on Theory of Computing*, pages 462–469, New York City, NY, May 1987. ACM Press.

[2] A. Brodnik and J. I. Munro. Membership in constant time and almost minimum space. *To appear in SIAM Journal on Computing.*

[3] A. Brodnik and J. I. Munro. Membership in constant time and minimum space. *Lecture Notes in Computer Science*, 855:72–81, 1994.

[4] Faith Fich and Peter Bro Miltersen. Tables should be sorted (on random access machines). In *Algorithms and data structures (Kingston, ON, 1995)*, pages 482–493. Springer, Berlin, 1995.

[5] Michael L. Fredman, János Komlós, and Endre Szemerédi. Storing a sparse table with $O(1)$ worst case access time. *J. Assoc. Comput. Mach.*, 31(3):538–544, 1984.

[6] Michael L. Fredman and Michael E. Saks. The cell probe complexity of dynamic data structures. In *Proceedings of the Twenty First Annual ACM Symposium on Theory of Computing*, pages 345–354, Seattle, Washington, 15–17 May 1989.

[7] D. R. Heath-Brown and H. Iwaniec. On the difference between consecutive primes. *Invent. Math.*, 55(1):49–69, 1979.

[8] Peter Bro Miltersen. Lower bounds for static dictionaries on RAMs with bit operations but no multiplication. In *Automata, languages and programming (Paderborn, 1996)*, pages 442–453. Springer, Berlin, 1996.

[9] Jeanette P. Schmidt and Alan Siegel. The spatial complexity of oblivious k-probe hash functions. *SIAM J. Comput.*, 19(5):775–786, 1990.

[10] Robert Endre Tarjan and Andrew Chi Chih Yao. Storing a sparse table. *Communications of the ACM*, 22(11):606–611, November 1979.

[11] Andrew Chi Chih Yao. Should tables be sorted? *J. Assoc. Comput. Mach.*, 28(3):615–628, 1981.

Finite Automata with Generalized Acceptance Criteria

Timo Peichl and Heribert Vollmer

Theoretische Informatik, Universität Würzburg,
Am Exerzierplatz 3, D-97072 Würzburg, GERMANY

Abstract. We examine the power of nondeterministic finite automata with acceptance of an input word defined by a so called *leaf language*, i. e., a condition on the sequence of leaves in the automaton's computation tree. We study leaf languages either taken from one of the classes of the Chomsky hierarchy, or taken from a time- or space-bounded complexity class. We contrast the obtained results with those known for leaf languages for Turing machines and Boolean circuits.

1 Introduction

Let M be a nondeterministic finite automaton and w be an input word. Usually w is said to be accepted by M if and only if there is at least one possible computation path of M which accepts w. In this paper we look at the tree $T_M(w)$ of all computations that automaton M on input w can possibly perform. An node v in this tree corresponds to a configuration C of M at a certain point during its computation on input w, where such a configuration is given by the state of M and the portion of the input which is still unscanned. The children of v in the computation tree are all successor configurations of C, i. e., if the transition function of M has several entries for this particular C, then each of these will lead to a successor configuration and a child of v in the computation tree. The leaves in the tree correspond to those configurations that M reaches when all input symbols are consumed.

Now the acceptance criterion of nondeterministic automata can be rephrased as follows: An input word w is accepted by M if and only if in the computation tree of M on x, there is at least one leaf corresponding to an accepting state.

Using the concept of computation trees, we will study modified acceptance criteria in this paper. Consider for example the following question: If we say that a word is accepted by M if and only if the number of accepting leaves in the computation tree is divisible by a fixed prime number p, can non-regular languages be recognized in this way? The acceptance here is thus given by a more complicated condition on the cardinality of the set of accepting paths in the computation tree. (For the definition of the class REG we just require that this cardinality is non-zero.) But we do not only consider such cardinality conditions in the present paper.

If we attach certain symbols to the leaves in $T_M(w)$, e. g., the symbol 1 to an accepting leaf and 0 to a non-accepting leaf, then the computation tree of M

on input w defines a word, which we get by concatenating the symbols attached to the leaves, read from left to right (in a natural order of the paths of $T_M(w)$ we define below). We call this string the *leaf word* of M on w. Observe that the length of the leaf word can be exponential in the length of w. Generally, an acceptance criterion is nothing else than the set of those leaf words that make M accept its input; that is, such a criterion is defined by a so called *leaf language* L over the alphabet of the leaf symbols. By definition a word is accepted by M if and only if the leaf word of M on input w is in L. In the example above we used the set of all binary words with a number of 1's divisible by p as leaf language.

We now ask what class of languages such automata can accept given a particular class of leaf languages. E. g., what if we allow all regular languages as acceptance criteria, can non-regular languages be recognized? The main result of this paper is a negative answer to this question. As another example, if the criterion is given by a context-free language, then we see that non-regular, even non context-free languages can be recognized. To mention a final example, if we allow leaf languages from the circuit class NC^1 (a class whose power is captured in a sense by the regular languages, since there are regular languages complete for NC^1 under uniform projections, a very strict reducibility [2]), then we obtain that even PSPACE-complete languages can be accepted by such finite automata.

In this paper we study in a systematic way the power of acceptance criteria given by leaf languages which are (1) taken from a (complexity) class defined via space or time restrictions for Turing machines, or (2) taken from a (formal language) class of the Chomsky hierarchy.

The power of *nondeterministic Turing machines* whose acceptance is given by a leaf language is well-studied, see, e. g., [4, 14, 10, 12]; recently the model has also been applied to Boolean circuits [6]. However, in the context of the probably most basic type of computation device, the finite automaton, leaf languages have not been considered so far. The present paper closes this gap. As had to be expected, our results differ quite a lot from those obtained in the above cited papers. However, in the context of leaf languages taken from a complexity class we will see that interestingly finite automata as underlying model are essentially as powerful as polynomial-time Turing machines.

Due to lack of space, most proofs in this abstract have to remain sketchy or are even omitted.

2 Preliminaries

We assume the reader is familiar with basic automata and machine models from formal language theory and complexity theory, see, e. g., [11, 1, 3].

Our Turing machines are standard multi-tape machines, see [11]. For the definition of sublinear time classes we use *indexing machines*. These machines cannot directly access their input tape, but instead have to write down a number in binary on a so called index tape. When they enter a specified read state with $bin(i)$ on the index tape, they are supplied with the ith input symbol. We use the so called *standard* (or, *proviso U*) *model* which does not delete its index tape after a read operation, see [5, 13].

In our main proof we make use of a generalized model of automata, known as alternating finite automata (AFA). These were introduced by Chandra, Kozen, and Stockmeyer in [7] and work similar to the better known alternating Turing machines. Although the model at first sight seems to be more powerful than deterministic automata, it was shown the class of languages they accept is REG [7]. The following exposition is basically from [15].

Let $B = \{0, 1\}$ and Q be a set. Then B^Q is the set of all mappings of Q into B. Note that $u \in B^Q$ can be considered as a $|Q|$-dimensional vector with entries in B.

An *alternating finite automaton (AFA)* is a quintuple $A = (Q, \Sigma, g, s, F)$ where Q is the finite set of states, Σ is the input alphabet, $s \in Q$ is the starting state, $F \subseteq Q$ is the set of final states and g is a function from Q into the set of all functions from $\Sigma \times B^Q$ into B. Note that $g(q)$, for $q \in Q$, is a function from $\Sigma \times B^Q$ into B in the following denoted by g_q.

How does an AFA work? Inductively, we define the language accepted by a state $q \in Q$ as follows: A state $q \in Q$ accepts the empty word λ if and only if $q \in F$. Having a nontrivial input $x = ay$, $a \in \Sigma$, $y \in \Sigma^*$, q reads the first letter a and calls all states to work on the rest y of the input in parallel. The states working on y will accept or reject and those results can be described by a vector $u \in B^Q$. Now the value $g_q(a, u) \in B$ shows whether q accepts or rejects. An AFA A accepts an input when the initial state s accepts it.

One form to represent an alternating finite automaton $A = (Q, \Sigma, g, s, F)$ is to give a system of equations, for all $q \in Q$:

$$X_q = \sum_{a \in \Sigma} a \cdot g_q(a, X) + \epsilon_q, \quad q \in Q.$$

X_q represents the state $q \in Q$ and X is the vector of all variables X_q. If $\epsilon_q = \lambda$ then q is an accepting state, i. e., for all $q \in Q$:

$$\epsilon_q = \begin{cases} \lambda & \text{if } q \in F \text{ and} \\ 0 & \text{otherwise.} \end{cases}$$

The equation $X_q = a \cdot X_r + b \cdot (X_r \wedge \overline{X_s}) + c \cdot 0$, for example, shows that q is not an accepting state. In this state there is a deterministic transition into r when reading an a and it definitely rejects when reading a c. If a b is read then q will accept if and only if r accepts the rest of the input and s rejects it.

It is clear that one obtains a nondeterministic automaton with a system of equations in which only the $\vee$ function occurs. A more detailed elaboration of this topic and a proof of the following statement is given in [7, 15].

Proposition 1. *The class of languages accepted by alternating finite automata is* REG.

3 Leaf Automata

The basic model we use is that of nondeterministic finite automata. On an input word w such a device defines a tree of possible computations. We want to consider this tree with an order on the leaves. Therefore we make the following definition:

A *finite leaf automaton* is a tuple $M = (Q, \Sigma, \delta, s, \Gamma, v)$, where Σ is an alphabet, the *input alphabet*; Q is the finite set of *states*; $\delta \colon Q \times \Sigma \to Q^+$ is the *transition function*; $s \in Q$ is the *initial state*; Γ is an alphabet, the *leaf alphabet*; and $v \colon Q \to \Gamma$ is a function that associates with a state q its *value* $v(q)$.

If we contrast this with the definition of nondeterministic finite automata, where we have that $\delta(q, a)$ is a *set* of states, we here additionally fix an ordering on the possible successor states by arranging them in a string from Q^+.

Let M be as above. The computation tree $T_M(w)$ of M on input w is a labeled, directed, rooted tree defined as follows:

1) The root of $T_M(w)$ is labeled (s, w).
2) Let v be a node in $T_M(w)$ labeled by (q, x), where $x \neq \lambda$, $x = ay$ for $a \in \Sigma$, $y \in \Sigma^*$. Let $\delta(q, a) = q_1 q_2 \cdots q_k$. Then v has k children in $T_M(w)$, and these are labeled by $(q_1, y), (q_2, y), \ldots, (q_k, y)$ in this order.

We now consider an extension $\delta^* \colon Q \times \Sigma^* \to Q^+$ of the transition function δ as follows:

1) $\delta^*(q, x) = q$ for all $q \in Q$, if x is the empty word.
2) $\delta^*(q, x) = \delta^*(q_1, y)\delta^*(q_2, y) \cdots \delta^*(q_k, y)$, if $q \in Q$, $x = ay$ for $a \in \Sigma$, $y \in \Sigma^*$, and $\delta(q, a) = q_1 q_2 \cdots q_k$.

Let $\hat{v} \colon Q^+ \to \Gamma^+$ be the homomorphic extension of v. If now $w \in \Sigma^*$, then leafstring$^M(w) =_{\text{def}} \hat{v}(\delta^*(s, w))$ is the *leaf string* of M on input w.

If we look at the tree $T_M(w)$ and attach the symbol $v(q)$ to a leaf in this tree with label (q, ε), then leafstring$^M(w)$ is the string of symbols attached to the leaves, read from left to right in the order induced by δ.

As an example, suppose $M = (Q, \Sigma, \delta, s, F)$ is a usual non-deterministic finite automaton, where $F \subseteq Q$ is the set of accepting states. Define a leaf automaton $M' = (Q, \Sigma, \delta', s, \Gamma, v)$, where $\Gamma = \{0, 1\}$, $v(q) = 1$ if $q \in F$ and $v(q) = 0$ else, and $\delta'(q, a)$ is the set $\delta(q, a)$ ordered arbitrarily. Then obviously, M accepts input w if and only if leafstring$^{M'}(w)$ contains at least one letter 1, i.e., leafstring$^{M'}(w) \in 0^*1(0 + 1)^*$. Conversely, every leaf automaton with $\Gamma = \{0, 1\}$ may be thought of as a non-deterministic finite automaton.

In the above example we used the language $0^*1(0 + 1)^*$ as acceptance criterion. We want to use arbitrary languages below. Therefore we define: Let $M = (Q, \Sigma, \delta, s, \Gamma, v)$ be a leaf automaton, and let $A \subseteq \Gamma^*$. The language $\mathsf{Leaf}^M(A) = \{ w \in \Sigma^* \mid \text{leafstring}^M(w) \in A \}$ is the language accepted by M with acceptance criterion A. The class $\mathsf{Leaf}^{\text{FA}}(A)$ consists of all languages $B \subseteq \Sigma^*$, for which there is a leaf automaton M with input alphabet Σ and leaf alphabet Γ such that $B = \mathsf{Leaf}^M(A)$. If $\mathcal{C}$ is a class of languages then $\mathsf{Leaf}^{\text{FA}}(\mathcal{C}) =_{\text{def}} \bigcup_{A \in \mathcal{C}} \mathsf{Leaf}^{\text{FA}}(A)$.

Our example above shows that $\mathsf{Leaf}^{\mathrm{FA}}(0^*1(0+1)^*) = \mathrm{REG}$. It will be our aim in the upcoming section to identify $\mathsf{Leaf}^{\mathrm{FA}}(\mathcal{C})$ for different classes $\mathcal{C}$.

We will also consider a more restricted form of leaf automata, defined as follows: Let $M = (Q, \Sigma, \delta, s, \Gamma, v)$ be such that $|\delta(q,a)| \leq 2$ for all $q \in Q$ and $a \in \Sigma$; that is, at every step, M has at most two possible successor states. In terms of the computation tree $T_M(x)$ this means that leaves trivially have no successors and inner nodes have either one or two successors. Observe that all paths have length exactly n. Thus a path is given by a word $p \in \{\mathrm{L}, \mathrm{R}\}^n$, describing how one has to move from the root to the leaf (L stands for left, R for right). Since there may be inner nodes in $T_M(x)$ with only one successor, there may be words $q \in \{\mathrm{L}, \mathrm{R}\}^n$ with no corresponding path. In this case we say that *path q is missing*. We say that the computation tree $T_M(x)$ is *balanced*, if the following holds: There is a path $p \in \{\mathrm{L}, \mathrm{R}\}^n$ in $T_M(x)$ such that to the left of p no path is missing, and to the right of p all paths are missing. Thus p is the rightmost path in $T_M(x)$, and $T_M(x)$ informally is a complete binary tree with a missing subpart in the right.

For $A \subseteq \Gamma^*$, the class $\mathsf{BLeaf}^{\mathrm{FA}}(A)$ consists of all languages $B \subseteq \Sigma^*$, for which there is a leaf automaton M with input alphabet Σ and leaf alphabet Γ such that for all input words $w \in \Sigma^*$, the computation tree $T_M(w)$ is balanced, and $B = \mathsf{Leaf}^M(A)$.

We will compare the classes $\mathsf{Leaf}^{\mathrm{FA}}(\mathcal{C})$ with $\mathsf{Leaf}^{\mathrm{P}}(\mathcal{C})$, $\mathsf{Leaf}^{\mathrm{L}}(\mathcal{C})$, $\mathsf{Leaf}^{\mathrm{LOGT}}(\mathcal{C})$ (the class of languages definable with leaf languages taken from $\mathcal{C}$ as acceptance criterion for nondeterministic Turing machines operating respectively in polynomial time, logarithmic space, and logarithmic time), and $\mathsf{Leaf}^{\mathrm{NC^1}}(\mathcal{C})$ (languages definable with leaf languages taken from $\mathcal{C}$ as acceptance criterion for so called programs over automata, a model which corresponds to the circuit class NC^1 [2]; our $\mathsf{Leaf}^{\mathrm{FA}}$-model can be obtained from this latter $\mathsf{Leaf}^{\mathrm{NC^1}}$-model by omitting the programs but taking only finite automata). Due to space restrictions, we cannot give precise definitions here, but refer the reader to [10, 12, 6].

4 Acceptance Criteria Given by a Complexity Class

We first turn to leaf languages defined by time- or space-bounded Turing machines.

Theorem 2. *Let $t(n) \geq \log n$. Then $\mathsf{BLeaf}^{\mathrm{FA}}(\mathrm{ATIME}(t(n))) = \mathrm{ATIME}(t(2^n))$.*

Proof (sketch). ($\supseteq$): Let $A \subseteq \Sigma^*$, $A \in \mathrm{ATIME}(t(2^n))$ via Turing machine M. Define the leaf automaton $N = (\Sigma, Q, \delta, s, \Sigma, v)$, where $Q = \{s\} \cup \{q_a \mid a \in \Sigma\}$, $v(q_a) = a$ for all $a \in \Sigma$, and δ is given as follows (cf. also [6]):

$$\delta(s, a) = s q_a \quad \text{for all } a \in \Sigma, \quad \text{and}$$
$$\delta(q_b, a) = q_b q_b \quad \text{for all } a, b \in \Sigma.$$

The reader may check that given input $x = x_1 \cdots x_n$, the automaton N produces the leaf word

$$v(s) x_n \, x_{n-1}^2 \, x_{n-2}^4 \, x_{n-3}^8 \cdots x_1^{2^{n-1}};$$

hence the ith symbol of x is equal to the 2^{n+1-i}th symbol in leafstring$^N(x)$. It is clear that the computation tree of N is always balanced.

Now define the indexing machine M' operating essentially as M, but when M reads its ith input symbol then M' reads its 2^{n+1-i}th input symbol. To simulate M's read operations, M' on input of length 2^m (corresponding to input $x_1 \cdots x_m$ of machine M) first initializes its index tape with the string 10^m. Now head movements of M can easily be simulated by adjusting the index tape (movements to the right correspond to deleting a 0, movements to the left to adding a 0). M' thus accepts the language pad$^N(A) = \{$leafstring$^N(x) \mid x \in A\}$ in time $t(2^m)$ with respect to input length $n = 2^m$, hence $A \in \mathsf{BLeaf}^{\mathrm{FA}}(\mathrm{ATIME}(t(n)))$.

($\subseteq$): Let $A \in \mathsf{BLeaf}^{\mathrm{FA}}(\mathrm{ATIME}(t(n)))$; let N be the corresponding leaf automaton, and let M be the Turing machine accepting the leaf language in time t. Define M' as follows: M' works as M, but when M reads its ith input symbol, M' guesses the input symbol and then branches universally. On one of these branches the simulation of M is continued, on the other branch M' simulates N on its ith path and halts accepting iff the output symbol in this simulation coincides with the previously guessed symbol. This is possible, since the computation tree of N is balanced. □

At this point, two remarks are in order. First, observe that, for the left-to-right inclusion, to obtain the time bound $t(2^n)$ for machine M' we make essential use of its ability to branch existentially and universally; hence this works only for alternating machines. Second, for the above simulation it is necessary that the computation tree produced by N is balanced. Both requirements are no longer needed as soon as t is at least linear, as we state next.

Theorem 3. *Let* $t(n) \geq n$. *Then* $\mathsf{BLeaf}^{\mathrm{FA}}(\mathrm{DTIME}(t(n))) = \mathrm{DTIME}(t(2^n))$ *and* $\mathsf{Leaf}^{\mathrm{FA}}(\mathrm{DTIME}(t(n))) = \mathrm{DTIME}(t(2^{O(n)}))$.

The above result can be generalized to any reasonable complexity measure. Let Φ be one of DTIME, NTIME, DSPACE, NSPACE, Σ_kTIME, $\bigoplus$TIME, $\ldots$. Let $t(n) \geq n$ in case of a time-restriction, and $t(n) \geq \log n$ in case of a space-restriction. Then $\mathsf{Leaf}^{\mathrm{FA}}(\Phi(t(n))) = \Phi(t(2^{O(n)}))$. In fact, using Hertrampf's locally definable acceptance types [8, 9], we obtain $\mathsf{Leaf}^{\mathrm{FA}}((\mathcal{F})\mathrm{TIME}(t)) = (\mathcal{F})\mathrm{TIME}(t(2^{O(n)}))$ for any locally definable acceptance type $\mathcal{F}$.

This yields in particular:

Corollary 4. *1)* $\mathsf{BLeaf}^{\mathrm{FA}}(\mathrm{NC}^1) = \mathrm{ALINTIME}$.
2) $\mathsf{BLeaf}^{\mathrm{FA}}(\mathrm{L}) = \mathsf{Leaf}^{\mathrm{FA}}(\mathrm{L}) = \mathrm{LIN}$.
3) $\mathsf{BLeaf}^{\mathrm{FA}}(\mathrm{NL}) = \mathsf{Leaf}^{\mathrm{FA}}(\mathrm{NL}) = \mathrm{NLIN}$.
4) $\mathsf{BLeaf}^{\mathrm{FA}}(\mathrm{POLYLOGSPACE}) = \mathsf{Leaf}^{\mathrm{FA}}(\mathrm{POLYLOGSPACE}) = \mathrm{PSPACE}$.
5) $\mathsf{BLeaf}^{\mathrm{FA}}(\mathrm{P}) = \mathsf{Leaf}^{\mathrm{FA}}(\mathrm{P}) = \mathrm{E}$.
6) $\mathsf{BLeaf}^{\mathrm{FA}}(\mathrm{NP}) = \mathsf{Leaf}^{\mathrm{FA}}(\mathrm{NP}) = \mathrm{NE}$.

The above proof makes use of fairly standard padding techniques. The main point is the definition of automaton N which pads a word of length n into a word of length 2^n (or $2^{O(n)}$ in the unbalanced case). Turing machines and Boolean circuits can pad up to length $2^{n^{O(1)}}$, therefore similar proofs show that, e. g., the classes $\mathsf{Leaf}^P(\mathrm{NC}^1)$, $\mathsf{Leaf}^L(\mathrm{NC}^1)$, $\mathsf{Leaf}^{\mathrm{NC}^1}(\mathrm{NC}^1)$, $\mathsf{Leaf}^P(\mathrm{POLYLOGSPACE})$, $\mathsf{Leaf}^L(\mathrm{POLYLOGSPACE})$, and $\mathsf{Leaf}^{\mathrm{NC}^1}(\mathrm{POLYLOGSPACE})$ all coincide with $\mathrm{ATIME}(n^{O(1)}) = \mathrm{PSPACE}$ [10, 12, 6]. Hence we see that here in the context of complexity classes as leaf languages, the ability to pad is the central point, and Turing machines, Boolean circuits, and finite automata behave quite similar.

5 Acceptance Criteria Given by a Formal Language Class

We now consider in turn the different classes that make up the Chomsky hierarchy of formal languages.

5.1 Regular Languages

Here we state and prove our main result.

Theorem 5. $\mathsf{BLeaf}^{\mathrm{FA}}(\mathrm{REG}) = \mathsf{Leaf}^{\mathrm{FA}}(\mathrm{REG}) = \mathrm{REG}$.

Proof. The inclusion $\mathsf{BLeaf}^{\mathrm{FA}}(\mathrm{REG}) \subseteq \mathsf{Leaf}^{\mathrm{FA}}(\mathrm{REG})$ is trivial. To show $\mathrm{REG} \subseteq \mathsf{BLeaf}^{\mathrm{FA}}(\mathrm{REG})$ we define the leaf language $B = \{1\} \in \mathrm{REG}$ over $\mathcal{B} = \{0, 1\}$. Let $A \in \mathrm{REG}$ be given. Then there exists a DFA N which accepts A. We use N as the leaf automaton producing the leaf string 1 or 0 when accepting or rejecting. Thus we have: $x \in A \Leftrightarrow \mathrm{leafstring}^N(x) = 1 \Leftrightarrow \mathrm{leafstring}^N(x) \in B$. Of course, the computation tree of N is always balanced.

Finally we have to show $\mathsf{Leaf}^{\mathrm{FA}}(\mathrm{REG}) \subseteq \mathrm{REG}$. Let $A \in \mathsf{Leaf}^{\mathrm{FA}}(\mathrm{REG})$ be a language over the alphabet Σ. Then there exist a DFA M and a leaf automaton N with the following property: $x \in A \Leftrightarrow M$ accepts $\mathrm{leafstring}^N(x)$. Let the automata N and M be given by $N = (Q_N, \Sigma, \delta_N, s_N, \Gamma, v)$ and $M = (Q_M, \Gamma, \delta_M, s_M, F_M)$. For $q \in Q_N$ and $a \in \Sigma$ we denote the branching degree by $r(q, a) = |\delta_N(q, a)|$ and write $\delta_N(q, a) = \delta_{N,1}(q, a) \dots \delta_{N,r(q,a)}(q, a)$.

We construct an AFA $L = (Q_L, \Sigma, g, s_L, F_L)$ which accepts A. The set of states is defined by $Q_L = \{s_L\} \cup (Q_M \times Q_M \times Q_N)$. In the sequel we will denote a state $q_L \in Q_L \setminus \{s_L\}$ by a triple, e. g., $q_L = (q_0, q_e, q_N)$, with the following intuition: When starting in q_L, L will accept if and only if the leaf string produced by the leaf automaton N starting in q_N leads M from q_0 to q_e. L follows the computation of N, while it guesses an accepting sequence of states of M. At the end L checks whether this sequence coincides with the sequence of states one gets when following M working on the leaf string. This will be done by using the principle of "divide and conquer."

We define the function g as well as the set of final states F_L by systems of equations as described in Sect. 2:

$$s_L = \sum_{x \in \Sigma} x \cdot g_{s_L, x} + \varepsilon_{s_L} \quad \text{with} \quad \varepsilon_{s_L} = \begin{cases} \lambda & \text{if } \delta_M\Big(s_M, v(s_N)\Big) \in F_M, \\ 0 & \text{otherwise,} \end{cases}$$

$$g_{s_L,x} = \bigvee_{q_1,\ldots,q_{r-1}\in Q_M,\, q_r\in F_M} \left[\bigwedge_{i=1}^{r} \Big(q_{i-1}, q_i, \delta_{N,i}(s_N, x) \Big) \right],$$

$$q_0 = s_M, \text{ and } r = r(s_N, x).$$

Note that the branching degree r depends on the state and the letter of the input, so the value of r might differ for different x in $g_{s_L,x}$. Remember that $s_L \in F_L \Leftrightarrow \epsilon_{s_L} = \lambda$. For $q_L = (q_0, q_e, q_N) \in Q_L$ we define:

$$q_L = \sum_{x\in \Sigma} x \cdot g_{q_L,x} + \epsilon_{q_L} \text{ with } \epsilon_{q_L} = \begin{cases} \lambda & \text{if } \delta_M\Big(q_0, v(q_N)\Big) = q_e, \\ 0 & \text{otherwise,} \end{cases}$$

$$g_{q_L,x} = \bigvee_{q_1,\ldots,q_{r-1}\in Q_M} \left[\bigwedge_{i=1}^{r-1} \Big(q_{i-1}, q_i, \delta_{N,i}(q_N, x) \Big) \wedge \Big(q_{r-1}, q_e, \delta_{N,r}(q_N, x) \Big) \right],$$

$$\text{and } r = r(q_N, x).$$

Again, r depends on q_N and x, and we have $q_L \in F_L \Leftrightarrow \epsilon_{q_L} = \lambda$.

Now we must show that the alternating automaton L accepts the language A. The state $q_L = (q_0, q_e, q_N) \in Q_L$ has the following intuitive meaning: Starting NFA N in state q_N on the input y we obtain a leaf string w. Starting L in q_L, the input y will be accepted if and only if this leaf string leads M from state q_0 to q_e, i. e., in the notation of [11], if $\hat{\delta}_M(q_0, w) = q_e$. We prove this by induction on y:

$|y| = 0$: For $y = \lambda$ the leaf string is the letter $v(q_N)$. Starting in $q_L = (q_0, q_e, q_N)$, $y = \lambda$ will be accepted if and only if $\epsilon_{q_L} = \lambda$. This is true for $\delta_M\Big(q_0, v(q_N)\Big) = q_e$, i. e., the leaf string $v(q_N)$ leads M from q_0 to q_e.

Assuming this to be correct for all $y \in \Sigma^*$, $|y| < n$, we now consider the case $|y| = n$: Let $q_L = (q_0, q_e, q_N)$ be the current state of L and $y = y_1 \cdots y_n$. In state q_N, N branches into $r = r(q_N, y_1) = |\delta_N(q_N, y_1)|$ subtrees when it reads y_1. According to the equation for g_{q_L,y_1}, L in state q_L accepts y if and only if there exists a sequence of states $q_1, \ldots, q_{r-1} \in Q_M$ with the following property: In each subtree i (r resp.), $i = 1, \ldots, r-1$, the word $y_2 \cdots y_n$ will be accepted when starting respectively in state $\Big(q_{i-1}, q_i, \delta_{N,i}(q_N, y_1) \Big)$ or $\Big(q_{r-1}, q_e, \delta_{N,r}(q_N, y_1) \Big)$. Following our induction assumption this is true if and only if in each subtree, M is transduced from q_{i-1} to q_i (from q_{r-1} to q_e resp.) by the corresponding leaf string. Thus L accepts y starting in q_L if and only if M is lead from q_0 to q_e by the whole leaf string.

Analogously, L accepts the input y, $|y| > 0$, starting from s_L if there is additionally to the states $q_i \in Q_M$ an accepting state $q_r \in F_M$ such that $\delta_M^*(s_M, \text{leafstring}^N(y)) = q_r$. If $y = \lambda$ then N produces the single letter leaf string $v(s_N)$, and we have: $\lambda \in A \Leftrightarrow M$ accepts $v(s_N) \Leftrightarrow \delta_M\Big(s_M, v(s_N)\Big) \in F_M \Leftrightarrow \epsilon_{s_L} = \lambda \Leftrightarrow L$ accepts $y = \lambda$.

Thus we have $L(L) = A$. $\qquad\square$

The just given result is much different from corresponding results for other models: It is known that $\mathsf{Leaf}^P(\mathrm{REG}) = \mathrm{PSPACE}$ and $\mathsf{Leaf}^L(\mathrm{REG}) = \mathrm{P}$.

5.2 Contextfree Languages

Theorem 6. $\text{CFL} \subsetneqq \text{BLeaf}^{\text{FA}}(\text{CFL}) \subseteq \text{Leaf}^{\text{FA}}(\text{CFL}) \subseteq \text{DSPACE}(n^2) \cap \text{E}.$

Proof (sketch). The $\subsetneqq$ follows from the fact that we can show $\text{BLeaf}^{\text{FA}}(\text{CFL})$ is closed under "weak intersection," a property not shared by CFL. The first $\subseteq$ is immediate; the second $\subseteq$ follows from $\text{CFL} \subseteq \text{DSPACE}(\log^2(n)) \cap \text{P}$ and the results given in Sect. 4. □

5.3 Contextsensitive and Recursively Enumerable Languages

Finally we obtain the following (statement 2 of course follows directly from the equality CSL = NLIN and the results given in Sect. 4):

Theorem 7. *1)* $\text{BLeaf}^{\text{FA}}(\text{RE}) = \text{Leaf}^{\text{FA}}(\text{RE}) = \text{RE}.$
2) $\text{BLeaf}^{\text{FA}}(\text{CSL}) = \text{NSPACE}(2^n)$ *and* $\text{Leaf}^{\text{FA}}(\text{CSL}) = \text{DSPACE}(2^{O(n)}).$

6 Conclusion

We examined the acceptance power of nondeterministic finite automata with different kinds of leaf languages. Comparing our results with those known for nondeterministic Turing machines with leaf language acceptance, we saw that if the leaf language class is a formal language class then we obtain a huge difference in computational power, but in the case of a resource-bounded leaf language class the difference between finite automata, Boolean circuits, and Turing machines (almost) disappears. This is due to the fact that in all three cases only the power of the devices to pad out their given input to a long leaf string is the central point.

It is known that the operator $\text{Leaf}^{\text{LOGT}}(\cdot)$ is a *closure operator*: $\text{Leaf}^{\text{LOGT}}(\mathcal{C})$ coincides with the closure of $\mathcal{C}$ under DLOGTIME reductions [12]. In the beginning the authors had the hope to be able to show that also the operator $\text{Leaf}^{\text{FA}}(\cdot)$ is some form of closure operator. However, the results from Sect. 4 prove that this is not the case. If $\mathcal{C}$ is a reasonable, large enough complexity class, then $\text{Leaf}^{\text{FA}}(\mathcal{C}) \subsetneqq \text{Leaf}^{\text{FA}}(\text{Leaf}^{\text{FA}}(\mathcal{C}))$, hence the operator $\text{Leaf}^{\text{FA}}(\cdot)$ lacks the property of being closed. In this sense, the Leaf^{FA}-model is even more complicated than the $\text{Leaf}^{\text{LOGT}}$-model.

The main remaining open question of course is if the upper and lower bounds obtained in Theorem 6 for $\text{Leaf}^{\text{FA}}(\text{CFL})$ can be strengthened. Our results here leave a lot of room for improvement, and certainly one would expect to be able to give stronger bounds. Nevertheless, we have been unable so far to do so. An idea would be to follow the proof of Theorem 5. For each language $A \in \text{Leaf}^{\text{FA}}(\text{CFL})$ one can construct an alternating pushdown automaton which accepts A. But unfortunately this yields not more than $\text{Leaf}^{\text{FA}}(\text{CFL}) \subseteq \text{E}$, because in [7] Chandra, Kozen, and Stockmeyer showed that the set ALT-PDA of all languages accepted by such automata equals E. One might hope that the lower bound $\text{PSPACE} = \text{Leaf}^{\text{NC}^1}(\text{CFL})$ could be transfered to our context – after all, there is a very strong connection between the class NC^1 and finite automata, since there are regular languages complete for NC^1 under very strict reductions such as uniform projections, see [2]. However our Theorem 6 shows that this hope is not justified; we have $PSPACE \not\subseteq Leaf^{FA}(CFL)$.

Acknowledgment. We are grateful to K. W. WAGNER–Würzburg for helpful hints and discussions.

References

[1] J. L. Balcázar, J. Díaz, and J. Gabarró. *Structural Complexity I*. Texts in Theoretical Computer Science. Springer Verlag, Berlin Heidelberg, 2nd edition, 1995.

[2] D. A. Mix Barrington, N. Immerman, and H. Straubing. On uniformity within NC^1. *Journal of Computer and System Sciences*, 41:274–306, 1990.

[3] D. P. Bovet and P. Crescenzi. *Introduction to the Theory of Complexity*. International Series in Computer Science. Prentice Hall, London, 1994.

[4] D. P. Bovet, P. Crescenzi, and R. Silvestri. A uniform approach to define complexity classes. *Theoretical Computer Science*, 104:263–283, 1992.

[5] L. Cai and J. Chen. On input read-modes of alternating Turing machines. *Theoretical Computer Science*, 148:33–55, 1995.

[6] H. Caussinus, P. McKenzie, D. Thérien, and H. Vollmer. Nondeterministic NC^1 computation. *Journal of Computer and System Sciences*, 57:200–212, 1998.

[7] A. K. Chandra, D. Kozen, and L. J. Stockmeyer. Alternation. *Journal of the Association for Computing Machinery*, 28:114–133, 1981.

[8] U. Hertrampf. Locally definable acceptance types for polynomial time machines. In *Proceedings 9th Symposium on Theoretical Aspects of Computer Science*, volume 577 of *Lecture Notes in Computer Science*, pages 199–207. Springer Verlag, 1992.

[9] U. Hertrampf. Complexity classes defined via k-valued functions. In *Proceedings 9th Structure in Complexity Theory*, pages 224–234. IEEE Computer Society Press, 1994.

[10] U. Hertrampf, C. Lautemann, T. Schwentick, H. Vollmer, and K. W. Wagner. On the power of polynomial time bit-reductions. In *Proceedings 8th Structure in Complexity Theory*, pages 200–207, 1993.

[11] J. E. Hopcroft and J. D. Ullman. *Introduction to Automata Theory, Languages, and Computation*. Addison-Wesley Series in Computer Science. Addison-Wesley, Reading, MA, 1979.

[12] B. Jenner, P. McKenzie, and D. Thérien. Logspace and logtime leaf languages. *Information & Computation*, 129:21–33, 1996.

[13] K. Regan and H. Vollmer. Gap-languages and log-time complexity classes. *Theoretical Computer Science*, 188:101–116, 1997.

[14] N. K. Vereshchagin. Relativizable and non-relativizable theorems in the polynomial theory of algorithms. *Izvestija Rossijskoj Akademii Nauk*, 57:51–90, 1993. In Russian.

[15] S. Yu. Regular languages. In R. Rozenberg and A. Salomaa, editors, *Handbook of Formal Languages*, volume I, chapter 2, pages 41–110. Springer Verlag, Berlin Heidelberg, 1997.

A Variant of the Arrow Distributed Directory with Low Average Complexity

(Extended abstract)

David Peleg* and Eilon Reshef

Department of Computer Science and Applied Mathematics,
The Weizmann Institute, Rehovot 76100, Israel.
E-mail: {peleg,eilon}@wisdom.weizmann.ac.il.

Abstract. This paper considers an enhancement to the *arrow distributed directory protocol*, introduced in [8]. The arrow protocol implements a directory service, allowing nodes to locate mobile objects in a distributed system, while ensuring mutual exclusion in the presence of concurrent requests. The arrow protocol makes use of a *minimum spanning tree* (MST) T_m of the network, selected during system initialization, resulting in a worst-case overhead ratio of $(1 + stretch(T_m))/2$. However, we observe that the arrow protocol is correct communicating over any spanning tree T of G.

We show that the *worst-case* overhead ratio is minimized by the *minimum stretch spanning tree* (MSST), and that the problem cannot be approximated within a factor better than $(1 + \sqrt{5})/2$, unless $\mathcal{P} = \mathcal{NP}$. In contrast, other trees may be more suitable if one is interested in the *average-case* behavior of the network. We show that in the case where the distribution of the requests is fixed and known in advance, the expected communication is minimized using the *minimum communication cost spanning tree* (MCT). It is shown that the resulting MCT problem is a restricted case for which one can find a tree T over which the expected communication cost of the arrow protocol is at most 1.5 times the expected communication cost of an optimal protocol.

We also show that even if the distribution of the requests is not fixed, or not known to the algorithm in advance, then if the adversary is oblivious, one may use probabilistic approximation of metric spaces [2, 3] to ensure an expected overhead ratio of $O(\log n \log \log n)$ in general, and an expected overhead ratio of $O(\log n)$ in the case of constant dimension Euclidean graphs.

1 Introduction

Many distributed systems support some concept of *mobile objects*. A mobile object can be a file, a process, or any other data structure. Such an object lives on one node at a time, and moves from one node to another in response to requests

---

* Supported in part by grants from the Israel Science Foundation and from the Israel Ministry of Science and Art.

by *clients*. A *directory service* allows nodes to locate mobile objects (*navigation*) and ensures mutual exclusion in the presence of concurrent requests (*synchronization*). In such a system, a *directory service* allows nodes to locate such objects, while ensuring mutual exclusion in the presence of concurrent requests.

The *arrow distributed directory protocol* [8] is a simple and elegant protocol for implementing such a directory service. To formally analyze the behavior of the arrow distributed directory protocol, we model the distributed system as a weighted graph $G = (V, E, \omega)$, where each vertex represents a node in the system, and each edge represents a bi-directional communication link. The cost of sending a message along an edge e is the weight of the edge $\omega(e)$.

The arrow distributed directory protocol implements a directory that tracks the location of a single object by a *spanning tree* T of G that serves as the communication backbone of the directory service. Whereas the original presentation of the algorithm in [8] refers to a minimum-weight spanning tree (MST), we observe that the arrow protocol is correct communicating over any spanning tree T of G, and thus, one may consider using trees other than an MST as the communication backbone of the protocol.

The protocol operates as follows. Each node v holds a single pointer, denoted $link(v)$, which may point to any of its neighbors in the tree T. If $link(v)$ is not `null`, the mobile object is expected to be in the tree component containing $link(v)$. When a node r requests the object, it sends a *find* message to $link(r)$ and clears $link(r)$. When a node u receives a *find* message from some node v, it first examines $link(u)$. If $link(u)$ is w, then u forwards the message to w. Otherwise, the object is in u or is expected to arrive to u, and thus u buffers the request until it receives the object and has completed using it. Finally, it sets $link(u)$ to point to v. When the object is ready to be sent, u sends the object to the requester r along the shortest path in the graph G between u and r. The directory tree is initialized so that following the links from any node leads to the node where the object resides. Despite the protocol's simplicity, it is shown in [8] that the algorithm ensures mutually exclusive access to the object and ensures that every node that sends a *find* request eventually receives the object.

To analyze the overhead imposed by the arrow protocol $\mathcal{A}$, the communication cost of the protocol is compared against an *optimal* directory $\mathcal{OPT}$ in which synchronization and navigation are "free". The optimal directory accepts only serial requests and delivers each request directly. Consider a sequence S of requests issued by the nodes $v_{k_1}, \ldots, v_{k_\ell}$. To deliver the object from v_{k_i} to $v_{k_{i+1}}$, the arrow directory routes a *find* message from $v_{k_{i+1}}$ to v_{k_i} along the unique path in the spanning tree T, paying $d_T(v_{k_{i+1}}, v_{k_i})$, where $d_T(v_i, v_j)$ is the weight of the path in T between v_i and v_j, and routes the object back from v_{k_i} to $v_{k_{i+1}}$ along the shortest path in the graph, paying another $d_G(v_{k_i}, v_{k_{i+1}})$, where $d_G(v_i, v_j)$ is the weight of the shortest path in G between v_i and v_j. In contrast, the optimal directory routes both the request and the object along the shortest path, paying $2d_G(v_{k_i}, v_{k_{i+1}})$.

Denote

$$c(T) \triangleq \sum_{i=1}^{\ell-1} d_T(v_{k_i}, v_{k_{i+1}}), \qquad c(G) \triangleq \sum_{i=1}^{\ell-1} d_G(v_{k_i}, v_{k_{i+1}}).$$

The overall communication of the arrow protocol serving the sequence S over the tree T is

$$c(\mathcal{A}) = c(T) + c(G),$$

whereas the overall communication cost of the optimal directory is $c(\mathcal{OPT}) = 2c_G(S)$.

Thus, the overhead ratio ρ imposed by the arrow protocol on a sequence of requests S is

$$\rho \triangleq \frac{c(\mathcal{A})}{c(\mathcal{OPT})} = \left(1 + \frac{c(T)}{c(G)}\right)/2.$$

We discuss two measures of the overhead ratio, namely, the *worst-case* overhead and the *average-case* overhead. The worst-case overhead is the maximal value of ρ, taken over all possible serial executions $v_{k_1}, \ldots, v_{k_\ell}$, i.e.,

$$OH \triangleq \max_S \{\rho(S)\}.$$

To minimize OH, one is required to find a tree T that minimizes the overhead of a single request, i.e., minimizes

$$stretch(T) \triangleq \max_{i,j} \left\{ \frac{d_T(v_i, v_j)}{d_G(v_i, v_j)} \right\}.$$

This problem, called *minimum stretch spanning tree*, is known to be $\mathcal{NP}$-hard [5], and it is shown in Section 2 that the problem cannot be approximated better than $(1 + \sqrt{5})/2$, unless $\mathcal{P} = \mathcal{NP}$. It is thus reasonable to develop algorithms for optimizing the *average-case* behavior of the protocol.

In analyzing the average-case behavior, we are interested in the *expected* communication cost $\mathbb{E}[c(\mathcal{A})]$, where the expectation is taken over all possible serial executions of length ℓ and over the possible coin tosses of the algorithm $\mathcal{A}$. In addition we may look at the *expected overhead*, which is the expected value of ρ,

$$\overline{OH} \triangleq \mathbb{E}[\rho(S)].$$

In these cases, we show that trees other than the minimum stretch spanning tree may ensure lower communication cost.

We consider two different models of the network behavior. In Section 3, we discuss the *independent* (IND) model. In this model, a probability p_i is associated with each node v_i, and requests to the mobile object are generated independently according to the probability distribution $\bar{P} = (p_1, \ldots, p_n)$, i.e., the probability that the next request is generated by v_i is p_i, independently of previous requests. We show that in the IND model, the optimal tree is the solution for a special instance of the *minimum communication spanning tree (MCT)* problem defined next, based on the probability distribution $\bar{P}$.

The MCT problem was introduced in [10], and can be formalized as follows. An instance of the problem is a complete undirected graph $G = (V, E)$, where every pair of vertices $\{v_i, v_j\}$ in V is assigned a nonnegative weight $\omega(v_i, v_j)$ and a nonnegative communication requirement $r(v_i, v_j)$. We are asked to find a spanning tree T of G, for which the total *communication cost*, i.e.,

$$c_{MCT}(T) \triangleq \sum_{i,j} [r(v_i, v_j) \cdot d_T(v_i, v_j)],$$

is minimized. MCT is known to be $\mathcal{NP}$-hard even in the *uniform* case, in which all requirements are equal, i.e., $r(v_i, v_j) = 1$ for every i and j [11].

We show that the MCT problem that corresponds to the IND probabilistic model of the network behavior is a restricted case in which the requirement matrix is a product of the vector $\bar{P}$ and its transpose, i.e., $R = \bar{P}^T \cdot \bar{P}$, hence $r(v_i, v_j) = p_i \cdot p_j$. We refer to this special case of the MCT problem as the *independent-requirements (IR)* MCT problem. Furthermore, we show that in this special case one can find in polynomial time a spanning tree T whose communication cost is at most twice the communication cost in the original graph G. This implies that the expected communication cost of the arrow protcol over T is at most 1.5 times the expected communication cost of the optimal directory protocol, i.e., $\mathbb{E}[c(\mathcal{A})] \leq 1.5 \cdot \mathbb{E}[c(\mathcal{OPT})]$. We show that this bound is tight.

In Section 4, we consider the *oblivious* (OBLIV) model, in which the distribution of the requests is not fixed, or not known to the algorithm in advance. In this case, we show that if the adversary is oblivious [4], in the sense that it does not see the coin tosses of the tree construction algorithm, or it specifies the series of requests $v_{k_1}, \ldots, v_{k_\ell}$ in advance, one may use a randomized tree construction algorithm, based on probabilistic approximation of metric spaces [2, 3]. This construction ensures an expected overhead ratio of $\overline{OH} = O(\log n \log \log n)$ in general, and an expected overhead ratio of $\overline{OH} = O(\log n)$ in the case of constant dimension Euclidean graphs (relying on [14, 7]).

In the rest of the discussion, we assume that the graph at hand is complete and metric, i.e., the weights obey the triangle inequality. Note that if this is not the case, one may complete the graph into a complete metric graph by adding "virtual" links, physically implemented by the corresponding shortest paths, without affecting the results.

2 Minimum Stretch Spanning Tree

Given a spanning tree T over a weighted graph $G = (V, E, \omega)$, let $stretch(T)$ denote the maximum stretch over all pairs of vertices in the tree T, i.e.,

$$stretch(T) \triangleq \max_{i,j} \{stretch_T(v_i, v_j)\}.$$

The *minimum stretch spanning tree* (MSST) problem is to find the spanning tree T that minimizes $stretch(T)$. The problem was shown to be $\mathcal{NP}$-hard in [5].

It is interesting to note that although there are algorithms that ensure an *average* stretch of $O(\log n \log \log n)$ [3], no simple upper bound holds in the case of the *worst-case* stretch. For example, any spanning tree of the n-vertex ring has an average stretch slightly less than 2, but a worst-case stretch of $n - 1$. Further, in the case of the 2-dimensional n-vertex grid, the results of [1] imply the existence of a spanning tree with an average stretch of $O(\log n)$, but also that any spanning tree has an edge whose stretch is $\Omega(\sqrt{n})$.

The following lemma provides an alternative, and sometimes more convenient, characterization of $stretch(T)$.

Lemma 1. $stretch(T) = \max_{(v_i, v_j) \in E} \{ stretch_T(v_i, v_j) \}$.

Proof. Let $s = \max_{(v_i, v_j) \in E} \{ stretch_T(v_i, v_j) \}$. Clearly $s \leq stretch(T)$. For the converse, consider any two vertices v_i and v_j, and let $\langle v_i = v_{l_0}, v_{l_1}, \ldots, v_{l_k} = v_j \rangle$ be some shortest path between them. Then,

$$d_T(v_i, v_j) \leq \sum_{i=1}^{k} d_T(v_{l_{i-1}}, v_{l_i}) \leq s \cdot \sum_{i=1}^{k} d_G(v_{l_{i-1}}, v_{l_i}) = s \cdot d_G(v_i, v_j). \quad \blacksquare$$

Note that the same argument shows that one can also ignore pairs (v_i, v_j) for which $\omega(v_i, v_j) > d_G(v_i, v_j)$.

In the remainder of this section we show that MSST cannot be approximated within any ratio $\rho < (1 + \sqrt{5})/2$. We give a reduction from the 3SAT problem defined as follows. An instance I of 3SAT is a set of variables $x_1, \ldots, x_n$ and a set of disjunctive clauses $c_1, \ldots, c_m$, each containing exactly three literals, where a literal is either a variable x_i or its negation. The satisfiability problem is to decide whether there exists an assignment to the variables x_i such that all the clauses are satisfied.

Given an instance I of SAT, we construct an instance $G_I = (V_I, E_I)$ of MSST with a *gap* of $(1 + \sqrt{5})/2 - \epsilon$, namely: if a satisfying assignment exists, then the graph contains a spanning tree T whose stretch is at most t, for some t. Otherwise, every spanning tree T of G_I has a stretch of $((1 + \sqrt{5})/2 - \epsilon) \cdot t$ or more.

Theorem 2. *For every $\epsilon > 0$, no polynomial time algorithm can approximate the minimum stretch spanning tree within a factor of $(1 + \sqrt{5})/2 - \epsilon$, unless $\mathcal{P} = \mathcal{NP}$.*

Proof Sketch. The proof is along the lines of [5]. Construct an instance $G = (V_I, E_I)$ of MSST as follows.

The vertex set V_I contains a vertex for each clause c_j, a vertex for each literal x_i or $\bar{x}_i$, and an additional vertex z. The edge set E_I contains a path between each clause c_j and each literal x_i or $\bar{x}_i$ it contains, a path between each literal x_i and its negation $\bar{x}_i$, and an edge between z and each literal x_i or $\bar{x}_i$.

Throughout the discussion below real numbers are used; rounding may be needed to convert the numbers into rationals. The construction uses a value

t which is assumed to be large enough to accommodate for the rounding. In particular, we assume $t \geq 1000/\epsilon$.

The following gadget is used to force an edge $e = (v_i, v_j) \in E_I$ to be included in any candidate spanning tree T: replace the edge e with a path of $2t$ edges, $e'_1, \ldots, e'_{2t}$ each of weight $\omega(e)/2t$. Clearly, if all the edges e'_i are included in a spanning tree T, their stretch is 1. Otherwise, if an edge $e'_i = (u, v)$ is removed from the graph, $d_T(u, v) \geq \omega(e) \geq 2t \cdot d_G(u, v)$, and hence its stretch is at least $2t$. Edges replaced by the above gadget are called *protected*.

Following are the exact details of the construction. The path connecting z and a literal vertex x_i or $\bar{x}_i$ consists of exactly one edge with weight $l_1 = 1$. The path connecting x_i and $\bar{x}_i$ consists of a protected edge of length $l_2 = t - 1$. The path connecting a clause c_j and a contained literal x_i or $\bar{x}_i$ is composed of edges of weight $1 + 2\alpha + \epsilon$, with a total path length of $l_3 = \alpha t$. The optimal value of α follows from the proof, and is set to be $(\sqrt{5} - 1)/4$.

A spanning tree T induces a truth assignment φ such that x_i is assigned "true" (resp. "false") if the edge (z, x_i) (resp. $(z, \bar{x}_i)$) is in T. To complete the proof of the theorem, we prove the following two complementary observations (details are deferred to the full paper). If an instance $I \in$ SAT has a satisfying assignment, then there exists a spanning tree T_I such that $stretch(T_I) \leq t$. On the other hand, if an instance $I \in$ SAT does not have a satisfying assignment, then $stretch(T) \geq ((1 + \sqrt{5})/2 - \epsilon)t$ for every spanning tree T of G_I. ∎

3 Known Distribution

In this section we discuss the average-case behavior of the arrow protocol in the IND model. This model assumes an underlying distribution based on a probability vector $\bar{P} = (p_1, \ldots, p_n)$, i.e., the probability that the next request is generated by v_i is p_i, independent of previous requests.

It turns out that in this model, the communication cost is minimized when the communication backbone of the protocol is exactly the minimum communication cost spanning tree (MCT) for the independent-requirements case based on $\bar{P}$.

Theorem 3. *In the IND model, the expected communication cost of the arrow protocol is minimized using a tree T which is the minimum communication cost spanning tree for a network G with independent requirements $r(v_i, v_j) = p_i \cdot p_j$.*

Proof. Consider a sequence of requests $S = \langle v_{k_1}, \ldots, v_{k_\ell} \rangle$ served over a spanning tree T. By linearity of expectation, the expected communication cost of the protocol over T is

$$\mathbb{E}[c(\mathcal{A})] = \sum_{1 \leq i < l} \mathbb{E}[d_T(v_{k_i}, v_{k_{i+1}}) + d_G(v_{k_i}, v_{k_{i+1}})].$$

Under the distribution $\bar{P}$, and since the requests are independent, the probability that in the m-th request the object is delivered from node v_i to node v_j

is exactly $p_i \cdot p_j$. Thus, the expected communication of any single request is fully determined by the probability distribution $\bar{P}$. Denote the cost of a single request

$$c_R(T) \triangleq \mathbb{E}[d_T(v_k, v_{k+1})] = \sum_{i,j} p_i p_j d_T(v_i, v_j),$$

and

$$c_R(G) \triangleq \mathbb{E}[d_G(v_k, v_{k+1})] = \sum_{i,j} p_i p_j d_G(v_i, v_j).$$

Using this notation, $\mathbb{E}[c(T)] = (\ell - 1) \cdot c_R(T)$, $\mathbb{E}[c(G)] = (\ell - 1) \cdot c_R(G)$, and $\mathbb{E}[c(\mathcal{A})] = (\ell - 1) \cdot (c_R(T) + c_R(G))$.

Since $c_R(G)$ is independent of T, the communication cost is minimized using a tree that minimizes $c_R(T)$ (independent of the sequence S), i.e., minimizes $\sum_{i,j} p_i p_j d_T(v_j, v_i)$. The problem of finding such a tree is precisely the IR instance of MCT defined for $\bar{P}$. ∎

Next we present a 2-approximation algorithm IR-MCT for the independent-requirements MCT problem defined above.

Algorithm IR-MCT Let T_i denote a shortest-path tree from v_i, i.e., a tree for which $d_{T_i}(v_i, v_j) = d_G(v_i, v_j)$ for every j. If there is more than one such tree, select one arbitrarily.

Algorithm IR-MCT examines the trees T_i for all i, $1 \leq i \leq n$, and selects the best shortest-path tree, namely, the tree T_i for which the communication cost $c_R(T_i)$ is minimized.

Analysis The following lemma asserts that the cost of the best tree is at most twice the communication cost in the original graph, namely $c_R(T) \leq 2 \cdot c_R(G)$. In particular, this is a 2-approximation algorithm, i.e., $c_R(T) \leq OPT_{MCT}(G)$, where $OPT_{MCT}(G)$ is the communication cost of the best spanning tree.

Lemma 4. *There exists a vertex v_i such that $c_R(T_i) \leq 2 \cdot c_R(G)$.*

Proof. Select a tree T randomly from $\{T_1, \ldots, T_n\}$, picking T_i with probability p_i. The expectation of the cost of T is

$$\mathbb{E}[c_R(T)] = \sum_i p_i \cdot c_R(T_i) = \sum_i p_i \cdot \left(\sum_{j,k} p_j p_k d_{T_i}(v_j, v_k) \right)$$

$$\leq \sum_{i=1}^{n} p_i \cdot \left(\sum_{j,k} p_j p_k (d_{T_i}(v_j, v_i) + d_{T_i}(v_i, v_k)) \right).$$

Since T_i is a shortest-path tree from v_i, $d_{T_i}(v_i, v_j) = d_G(v_i, v_j)$ for every j, and thus

$$\mathbb{E}[c_R(T)] \leq \sum_{i=1}^{n} p_i \cdot \left(\sum_{j,k} p_j p_k (d_G(v_j, v_i) + d_G(v_i, v_k)) \right)$$

$$= \sum_{i=1}^{n} p_i \cdot \left(2 \cdot \sum_{j=1}^{n} p_j d_G(v_j, v_i) \right) = 2 \cdot c_R(G).$$

Therefore, at least one of the trees T_i satisfies $c_R(T_i) \leq 2 \cdot c_R(G) \leq 2 \cdot OPT_{MCT}(G)$. ∎

Corollary 5. *In the IND model, one can find in polynomial time a tree T for which the expected communication cost satisfies $\mathbb{E}[c(T)] \leq 1.5 \cdot \mathbb{E}[c(\mathcal{OPT})]$.*

Proof. Run algorithm IR-MCT to find a 2-approximation for the independent-requirements MCT problem. The algorithm ensures that the MCT communication cost satisfies $c_R(T) \leq 2c_R(G)$. Therefore, $\mathbb{E}[c(\mathcal{A})] \leq 3(\ell - 1)c_R(G)$.

On the other hand, the optimal directory would still need to communicate back and forth along the shortest path, so the optimal communication is

$$\mathbb{E}[c(\mathcal{OPT})] = 2 \cdot \mathbb{E}[c(G)] = 2(\ell - 1) \cdot c_R(G).$$

Thus, $\mathbb{E}[c(\mathcal{A})] \leq 1.5 \cdot \mathbb{E}[c(\mathcal{OPT})]$. ∎

Note that in the n-vertex clique G_n with $p_i = 1$ for every i, $c_R(G_n) = n(n-1)$, but in every spanning tree T of G_n, $d_T(v_i, v_j) \geq 2$ for every $(v_i, v_j) \notin T$, and thus $c_R(T) \geq (n - 1) \cdot 1 + (n - 1)^2 \cdot 2 \approx 2c_R(G)$. Thus, the above result is essentially tight. Specifically, the algorithm of [15] can be generalized to provide a polynomial time approximation scheme (PTAS) for the restricted case of MCT where the requirement matrix is a product of a vector and its transpose, but the communication cost therein does not compare directly to $c_R(G)$, and hence this technique cannot be used to provide a provably better ratio.

Further, the above construction suggests that even if the behavior of the network is unknown in advance, a heuristic that randomly selects a shortest-path tree may provide better performance in practice than the minimum-weight spanning tree heuristic used in [8]. In particular, if the graph G is unweighted, the shortest-path heuristic provides a non-trivial result, whereas all spanning trees T of G have the same weight.

4 Oblivious Adversary

In this section we consider the expected average-case behavior of the arrow protocol in the OBLIV model, in which the distribution of the requests is not fixed, or not known to the algorithm in advance. Rather, we assume that the adversary is oblivious [4], so it does not see the coin tosses of the tree construction algorithm, or specifies the series of requests $v_{k_1}, \ldots, v_{k_\ell}$ in advance.

We use the following definition, due to [2]:

Definition 6. [2] A complete metric graph G is α-probabilistically approximated by a probability distribution $\mathcal{D}_G$ of (spanning) trees of G if for every pair of vertices v_i, v_j,

$$\mathbb{E}_{\mathcal{D}_G} \left[\frac{d_T(v_i, v_j)}{d_G(v_i, v_j)} \right] \leq \alpha.$$

The following results realize the above definition:

Proposition 7. **[3]** *Every complete metric graph G can be $O(\log n \log \log n)$-approximated by a probability distribution $\mathcal{D}_G$ of spanning trees of G. Furthermore, the distribution $\mathcal{D}_G$ is realizable by a probabilistic polynomial-time algorithm $\tilde{A}$ (i.e, for every spanning tree T, $\mathbb{P}[\tilde{A}(G) = T] = \mathbb{P}_{\mathcal{D}_G}[T]$).*

Proposition 8. **[14, 7]** *Every Euclidean graph G embedded in $\mathbb{R}^d$ can be $O(d \log n)$-approximated by a probability distribution $\mathcal{D}_G$ of spanning trees of G. Furthermore, the distribution $\mathcal{D}_G$ is realizable by a probabilistic polynomial-time algorithm $\tilde{A}$.*

Now, given a probability distribution $\mathcal{D}_G$ of spanning trees of G, one may randomly pick a tree according to $\mathcal{D}_G$, and use it as the communication backbone of the arrow distributed directory protocol.

Theorem 9. *If a graph G is α-probabilistically approximated by a probability distribution $\mathcal{D}_G$ of spanning trees, then the expected overhead ratio of the arrow protocol over a spanning tree T drawn randomly according to $\mathcal{D}_G$ satisfies $\overline{OH} \leq (\alpha + 1)/2$.*

Proof. The expected overhead ratio of the arrow protocol over a sequence of requests $S = \langle v_{k_1}, \ldots, v_{k_\ell} \rangle$ is

$$\overline{OH} = \mathbb{E}\left[\frac{c(\mathcal{A})}{c(\mathcal{OPT})}\right] = \left(1 + \mathbb{E}\left[\frac{c(T)}{c(G)}\right]\right)/2.$$

However, $c(G)$ is independent of the selection of the tree T, and since T is drawn randomly according to $\mathcal{D}_G$,

$$\mathbb{E}[c(T)] = \mathbb{E}[\sum_{1 \leq i < l} d_T(v_i, v_{i+1})] = \sum_{1 \leq i < l} \mathbb{E}[d_T(v_i, v_{i+1})]$$
$$\leq \sum_{1 \leq i < l} \alpha \cdot d_G(v_i, v_{i+1}) \leq \alpha \cdot c(G).$$

Hence,

$$\mathbb{E}\left[\frac{c(\mathcal{A})}{c(\mathcal{OPT})}\right] \leq (1 + \alpha)/2. \quad \blacksquare$$

Corollary 10. *Using a spanning tree drawn randomly as in Proposition 7, the expected overhead ratio of the arrow distributed directory protocol satisfies $\overline{OH} = O(\log n \log \log n)$.* $\quad \blacksquare$

Corollary 11. *In constant dimension Euclidean networks, using a spanning tree drawn randomly as in Proposition 8, the expected overhead ratio of the arrow distributed directory protocol satisfies $\overline{OH} = O(\log n)$.* $\quad \blacksquare$

References

1. N. Alon, R.M. Karp, D. Peleg, and D. West. A graph-theoretic game and its application to the k-server problem. *SIAM J. on Computing*, pages 78–100, 1995.
2. Y. Bartal. Probabilistic approximation of metric spaces and its algorithmic applications. In *Proc. 37th IEEE Symp. on Foundations of Computer Science*, pages 184–193, 1996.
3. Y. Bartal. On approximating arbitrary metrics by tree metrics. In *Proc. 30th Annual ACM Symp. on Theory of Computer Science*, 1998.
4. S. Ben-David, A. Borodin, R.M. Karp, G. Tardos, A. Wigderson. On the Power of Randomization in Online Algorithms In *Proc. 22nd Annual ACM Symp. on Theory of Computer Science*, pages 379–386, May 1990.
5. L. Cai, D.G. Corneil. Tree Spanners. *SIAM J. Disc. Math.*, 8:359–387, 1995.
6. M. Charikar, C. Chekuri, A. Goel, and S. Guha. Rounding via trees: deterministic approximation algorithms for group steiner trees and k-median. In *Proc. 39th Annual ACM Symp. on Theory of Computer Science*, 1998.
7. M. Charikar, C. Chekuri, A. Goel, S. Guha, and S. Plotkin. Approximating a Finite Metric by a Small Number of Tree Metrics. In *Proc. 39th IEEE Symp. on Foundations of Computer Science*, November 1998.
8. Michael J. Demmer, Maurice P. Herlihy. The Arrow Distributed Directory Protocol. In *Proc. 17th ACM Symp. on Principles of Distributed Computing*, August 1998.
9. M.R. Garey and D.S. Johnson. *Computers and Intractability: a Guide to the Theory of NP-Completeness*. W. H. Freeman and Co., San Francisco, CA, 1979.
10. T.C. Hu. Optimum communication spanning trees. *SIAM J. on Computing*, pages 188–195, 1974.
11. D.S. Johnson, J.K. Lenstra, and A.H.G. Rinnooy-Kan. The complexity of the network design problem. *Networks*, 8:275–285, 1978.
12. A. Kershenbaum. *Telecommunications network design algorithms*. McGraw-Hill Book Co., 1993.
13. M.S. Manasse, L.A. McGeoch, D.D. Sleator. Competitive Algorithms for On-Line Problems. In *Proc. 20th Annual ACM Symp. on Theory of Computer Science*, pages 322–330, May 1988.
14. D. Peleg, E. Reshef. Deterministic Polylog Approximation for Minimum Communication Spanning Trees. In *Proc. 25th International Colloquium on Automata, Languages, and Programming*, pages 670–681, July 1998.
15. B.Y. Wu, G. Lancia, Y. Bafna, K.M. Chao, R. Ravi, and C.Y. Tang. A polynomial time approximation scheme for minimum routing cost spanning trees. In *Proc. 9th ACM-SIAM Symp. on Discrete Algorithms*, pages 21–32, January 1998.
16. R. Wong Worst case Analysis of Network Design Problem Heuristics. In *SIAM J. Algebraic Discr. Meth.*, 1:51–63, 1980.

Closed Freyd- and κ-categories

John Power[1]* and Hayo Thielecke[2]**

1 University of Edinburgh, Edinburgh EH9 3JZ, Scotland.
2 QMW, University of London, London E1 4NS, UK.

Abstract. We give two classes of sound and complete models for the computational λ-calculus, or λ_c-calculus. For the first, we generalise the notion of cartesian closed category to that of closed Freyd-category. For the second, we generalise simple indexed categories. The former gives a direct semantics for the computational λ-calculus. The latter corresponds to an idealisation of stack-based intermediate languages used in some approaches to compiling.

1 Introduction

The computational λ-calculus, or λ_c-calculus, is a natural fragment of a call-by-value programming language such as ML. Its models were defined to be λ_c-models, which consist of a small category $\mathcal{C}$ with finite products, and a strong monad $\mathcal{T}$ on $\mathcal{C}$, such that $\mathcal{T}$ has Kleisli exponentials. The class of λ_c-models is sound and complete for the calculus, but it does not provide direct models in that a term of type X in context Γ is not modelled by an arrow in $\mathcal{C}$ from the semantics of Γ to the semantics of X, but by a derived construction in terms of the monad.

In this paper, we give two different equivalent formulations of λ_c-models, one generalising the notion of cartesian closed category, the other given by an indexed category with structure. We investigate natural languages for these structures, and we prove the various equivalences. This builds upon our work in [11], in which we proved an equivalence between premonoidal categories with extra structure (now called *Freyd*-categories) and indexed categories with added structure, which we called κ-categories. We include an appendix recalling the definitions and relationship.

Although these two new formulations are equivalent to λ_c-models, they are not the same as them. That is, the primitives in each are different. We explore this point by formulating languages motivated by each of the two models. One of the languages emphasises the role of structural rules of weakening and contraction, while the other emphasises the sequencing of intermediate values (inherent in the `let` of λ_c) by keeping an explicit stack.

A Freyd-category consists of a symmetric premonoidal category $\mathcal{K}$ together with a category with finite products $\mathcal{C}$ and an identity on objects strict symmetric

---
* This work is supported by EPSRC grant GR/J84205: Frameworks for programming language semantics and logic.
** Supported by EPSRC grant GR/L54639.

premonoidal functor $J: \mathcal{C} \longrightarrow \mathcal{K}$, where a premonoidal category is essentially a monoidal category except that the tensor need only be a functor in two variables separately, and not necessarily a bifunctor: given maps $f: A \to A'$ and $g: B \to B'$, the evident two maps from $A \otimes B$ to $A' \otimes B'$ may differ. Such structures arise naturally in the presence of computational effects, where the difference between these two maps is a result of sensitivity to evaluation order. A program phrase in environment Γ is modelled by a morphism in the premonoidal category with domain $[\![\Gamma]\!]$. The semantics here suggests a multiplicative approach to sequents.

In a κ-category, a program phrase in environment Γ is modelled by an element $1 \longrightarrow [\![B]\!]$ in a category that implicitly depends on Γ, i.e., by an arrow from 1 to $[\![B]\!]$ in the fibre of the indexed category over $[\![\Gamma]\!]$. A κ-category has a weak first-order notion of binding, given by the assertion that reindexing along projections has a left adjoint. In programming terms, that corresponds to a special form that binds an identifier but is not reifying in the sense that it does not produce a *first-class* function. In Hasegawa's original account, the κ-calculus was motivated purely by categorical considerations. However, such a first-order binder was independently devised by Douence and Fradet to give a high-level account of stack operations in compiling [1].

In [11], we gave an equivalence between Freyd-categories and κ-categories. Here, we extend that equivalence to model higher-order structure. It is not as simple as asking for a routine extension of the notion of closedness from that for a cartesian category to a premonoidal category, as one usually considers λ-terms as values, and we distinguish between values and computations. This leads us to a notion of closedness for a Freyd-category [9]. To give a closed Freyd-category is equivalent to giving a strong monad with Kleisli exponentials on a cartesian category. But to give a strong monad on a cartesian category is to give an ordinary monad on the associated κ-category, where the cartesian category is regarded as a degenerate symmetric premonoidal category. So we examine the relationships between all four notions: a closed Freyd-category, a strong monad with Kleisli exponentials on a cartesian category, a monad on a simple fibration, and a closed κ-category.

The paper is organised as follows. We extend our equivalence between Freyd-categories and κ-categories to one incorporating higher-order structure in Section 2. In Section 3, we consider two calculi designed to fit the primitives of these two categorical settings: one a slight variant of λ_c, the other an extension of Hasegawa's κ-calculus. Section 4 concludes.

2 Closed Freyd-categories, closed κ-categories, and λ_c-models

In previous work [11], recalled in Appendix A, we considered two ways of modelling environments. In this section, we extend that to model higher-order structure, allowing us two ways to model the λ_c-calculus [7]. We define and relate closed Freyd-categories and closed κ-categories with λ_c-models.

Definition 1. *A strong monad T on a cartesian category C has* Kleisli *exponentials if for every object A, the functor $J(A \times -): C \longrightarrow$* **Kleisli**$(T)$ *has a right adjoint.*

Observe that if a cartesian category C is closed, then every strong monad on it has Kleisli exponentials. The converse is almost but not quite true.

Definition 2. *A Freyd-category $J: C \longrightarrow K$ is* closed *if for every object A, the functor $J(A \otimes -): C \longrightarrow K$ has a right adjoint.*

Observe that it follows that the functor $J: C \longrightarrow K$ has a right adjoint, and so K is the Kleisli category for a monad on C. A variant of one of the main theorems of [9] is

Theorem 1. *To give a closed Freyd-category is to give a cartesian category together with a strong monad on it for which Kleisli exponentials exist.*

That is as good a result as one can imagine to relate closed Freyd-categories with strong monads. So now we turn to κ-categories.

Definition 3. *A κ-category $H: C^{\mathrm{op}} \longrightarrow Cat$ is* closed *if for every object A of C, every object has a generic map from A into it, i.e., for every object B of C, there is an object $[A \to B]$ and a map* apply$: A \longrightarrow B$ *in $H_{[A \to B]}$ such that for every object C and every map $f: A \longrightarrow B$ in H_C, there exists a unique map $\Lambda f: C \longrightarrow [A \to B]$ in C such that $H_{\Lambda f}(\mathsf{apply}) = f$.*

$$C \xrightarrow{\ \Lambda f\ } [A \to B]$$

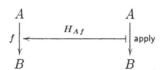

Using the notation of Appendix A, we have

Proposition 1. *For any closed Freyd-category J, the κ-category $\mathsf{s}(J)$ is closed, and for any closed κ-category H, there is a Freyd-category J unique up to coherent isomorphism such that $\mathsf{s}(J)$ is isomorphic to H.*

Proof. Most of this follows from Theorem 4 in the appendix. Close inspection of the construction of $\mathsf{s}(J)$ yields the rest: the assertion of the existence of a generic map from any object C into any object A is routinely equivalent to the assertion that the corresponding Freyd-category is closed.

Relating this to monads, it was remarked by Plotkin and shown in [8] that

Proposition 2. *To give a strong monad with Kleisli exponentials on a cartesian category C is to give an indexed monad on the indexed category $\mathsf{s}(C)$.*

Finally, just as one can build the Kleisli construction from a monad on an ordinary category, one can build the Kleisli construction from a monad on an indexed category, in particular on a κ-category; and there is an equivalence between monads and identity on objects indexed functors that have indexed right adjoints. Thus we have

Proposition 3. *To give a monad on* $\mathsf{s}(C)$ *for a cartesian category C is to give a κ-category H such that* $\mathrm{inc}: \mathsf{s}(C) \longrightarrow H$ *has an indexed right adjoint.*

Putting this together, we have

Theorem 2. *Given a cartesian category C, the following are equivalent:*

1. *to give a strong monad with Kleisli exponentials on C*
2. *to give a closed Freyd-category $J: C \longrightarrow K$*
3. *to give a monad on $\mathsf{s}(C)$ subject to a closedness condition*
4. *to give a κ-category $H: C^{op} \longrightarrow Cat$ such that* $\mathrm{inc}: \mathsf{s}(C) \longrightarrow H$ *has an indexed right adjoint.*

The key result about the λ_c-calculus in [7] is that it has a sound and complete class of models given by the λ_c-models. But in Theorem 2, we have characterised λ_c-models. So one has

Theorem 3. *Both closed Freyd-categories and closed κ-categories form sound and complete classes of models for the computational λ-calculus.*

3 λ- and κ-calculi

Because of the categorical equivalence results in Section 2, we know that we can model the computational λ-calculus in closed Freyd-categories and closed κ-categories. Our aim here is not to study completeness of calculi; that is routine, given our analysis in the last section and the previous analysis by Moggi. Rather, we want to formulate languages that correspond more directly to our models in an effort to expose their different character. Furthermore, at least one of these languages appears to have independent interest [1]. Following our categorical equivalence result, we connect them by a stack-passing transformation.

3.1 Computational λ-calculus and Freyd-categories

In this section, we sketch how closed Freyd-categories give semantics for the λ_c-calculus. We already know, by Theorem 2, that the λ_c-calculus has a sound and complete class of models given by closed Freyd-categories, but the point here is to see how the primitives of the calculus as we will express it correspond to the primitives of the definition of closed Freyd-category.

Raw terms are given by the following grammar:

$$V ::= x \mid () \mid (V, V) \mid \lambda x.M$$
$$p ::= x \mid () \mid (x, x)$$
$$M ::= V \mid \mathtt{let}\, p = M \,\mathtt{in}\, M \mid VV$$

Though this is not strictly necessary, we chose here a calculus in which a pair (M, N) would have to be explicitly sequenced, as it were, by writing

$$\texttt{let } x = M \texttt{ in let } y = N \texttt{ in } (x, y)$$

(or, if one wants right-to-left evaluation order, $\texttt{let } y = N \texttt{ in let } x = M \texttt{ in } (x, y)$). This is meant to emphasize that, in a *premonoidal* setting, we need to take a little more care than in a monoidal one.

We first consider a first order fragment of the λ_c-calculus. Like monoidal categories, premonoidal categories naturally correspond to calculi with multiplicative contexts.

$$\frac{\Gamma \vdash N : A \quad \Delta, x : A \vdash M : B}{\Gamma, \Delta \vdash \texttt{let } x = N \texttt{ in } M : B} \qquad \frac{\Gamma \vdash N : \texttt{unit} \quad \Delta \vdash M : B}{\Gamma, \Delta \vdash \texttt{let } () = N \texttt{ in } M : B}$$

$$\frac{\Gamma \vdash N : A_1 * A_2 \quad \Delta, x_1 : A_1, x_2 : A_2 \vdash M : B}{\Gamma, \Delta \vdash \texttt{let } (x_1, x_2) = N \texttt{ in } M : B}$$

The $\texttt{let}$-construct of the computational λ-calculus is interpreted by sequential composition (together with the premonoidal tensor for concatenation of contexts).

In a *symmetric* premonoidal category [10], we can permute variables in the sequents:

$$\frac{\Gamma, x : A, y : B, \Delta \vdash M : C}{\Gamma, y : B, x : A, \Delta \vdash M : C}$$

Semantically, this rule is interpreted by precomposition with $[\![\Gamma]\!] \otimes c \otimes [\![\Delta]\!]$, where c is the symmetry isomorphism $[\![B]\!] \otimes [\![A]\!] \cong [\![A]\!] \otimes [\![B]\!]$.

Furthermore, for a Freyd-category $J : \mathcal{C} \longrightarrow \mathcal{K}$ (Definition 4), we can add weakening and contraction in sequents

$$\frac{\Gamma \vdash M : B}{\Gamma, x : A \vdash M : B} \qquad \frac{\Gamma, x : A, y : A \vdash M : C}{\Gamma, x : A \vdash M[y := x] : C}$$

Weakening and contraction are interpreted by the counit $[\![\Gamma]\!] \otimes [\![A]\!] \longrightarrow [\![\Gamma]\!]$ and comultiplication $[\![\Gamma]\!] \otimes [\![A]\!] \longrightarrow [\![\Gamma]\!] \otimes [\![A]\!] \otimes [\![A]\!]$ of the comonad as described in Definition 5.

And as we have finite products in $\mathcal{C}$, we have additive sequents for first-order values:

$$\frac{}{x_1 : B_1, \ldots, x_n : B_n \vdash x_i : B_i} \qquad \frac{}{\Gamma \vdash () : \texttt{unit}} \qquad \frac{\Gamma \vdash V_1 : B_1 \quad \Gamma \vdash V_2 : B_2}{\Gamma \vdash (V_1, V_2) : B_1 * B_2}$$

Finally, if we have a *closed* Freyd-category (Definition 2), we can interpret λ-terms (giving them a call-by-value semantics). We add multiplicative sequents for λ-abstraction and application:

$$\frac{\Gamma, x : A \vdash M : B}{\Gamma \vdash \lambda x.M : A \to B} \qquad \frac{\Gamma \vdash V : A \to B \quad \Delta \vdash W : A}{\Gamma, \Delta \vdash VW : B}$$

The adjunction giving the closed structure codifies two principles of the call-by-value λ-calculus: λ-abstractions are values; and only values may be substituted for arguments.

The calculus, upon the addition of the predicates and rules due to Moggi, is equivalent to the λ_c-calculus [7]: we do not have types TX as they are equivalent to certain exponentials, while Moggi's constructors [_] and μ may be taken to be given by certain λ-terms and applications respectively. One can avoid π-terms by use of pattern matching.

3.2 κ-calculus and closed κ-categories

In Hasegawa's account [2], higher-order structure was added to the κ-calculus by a binder dual to the κ-binder. This does not seem to generalize to call-by-value. Instead, we add a thunking construct to the κ-calculus that corresponds to the closed structure on a κ-category.

Hasegawa originally compared his first-order function abstraction $\kappa x.M$ to lambda in early Lisp (i.e. lacking first-class functions). More recently, such a first-order binder has been found useful in compiling [1,5]; it was called λ_s in [1]. Roughly speaking the reason is that a curried function $\lambda x_1. \ldots. \lambda x_n.M$ would need to build n intermediate closures, an unnecessary expense if the function is immediately applied to n arguments. An uncurried n-ary function would avoid building closures, but not heap-allocation, as an n-tuple would have to be constructed before the function could be applied. By contrast, $\kappa x_1. \ldots. \kappa x_n.M$ would simply consume n arguments by popping them from the stack. To turn this into a first-class function, a separate operation is needed (which we call mkthunk).

To adapt the κ-calculus to call-by-value, we introduce two kinds of judgements for values and computations, respectively. As usual, a value judgement is of the form $x_1:C_1,\ldots,x_n:C_n \vdash V:B$. A computation judgement of κ-calculus is of the form

$$x_1:C_1,\ldots,x_n:C_n \mid A_1,\ldots,A_m \mapsto M:B_1,\ldots,B_k$$

where A_i and B_j are types. Intuitively, $A_1,\ldots,A_m$ is the type of the stack *before* M is run, and $B_1,\ldots,B_k$ the type of the stack *after* M has run. (Douence and Fradet [1] also proposed a type system for their calculus, but typing failed to be preserved by the associativity law for sequential composition, essentially because their types do not keep track of the whole stack.) Our version of κ-calculus is a combination of [1] and [2]:

$$\frac{\Gamma \mid S \mapsto M:S' \quad \Gamma \mid S' \mapsto N:S''}{\Gamma \mid S \mapsto M;N:S''} \qquad \overline{\Gamma,x:A,\Gamma' \vdash x:A}$$

$$\frac{\Gamma \vdash V:C}{\Gamma \mid S \mapsto \text{push}\,V:C,S} \qquad \frac{\Gamma,x:C \mid S \mapsto M:S'}{\Gamma \mid C,S \mapsto \kappa x.M:S'}$$

$$\frac{\Gamma \mid S \mapsto M:S'}{\Gamma \vdash \text{mkthunk}\,M:[S \to S']} \qquad \overline{\Gamma \mid [S \to S'],S,S'' \mapsto \text{apply}:S',S''}$$

A computation judgement denotes a morphism from $A_1 \times \cdots \times A_m$ to $B_1 \times \cdots \times B_k$ in the fibre over $C_1 \times \cdots \times C_n$. A value judgement denotes a morphism in the base in the usual fashion. Most of the categorical semantics is fairly evident from the syntax and follows Hasegawa [2]; for instance ";" is interpreted by composition (in diagrammatic order) in the fibre over $\llbracket \Gamma \rrbracket$. The κ-binder is interpreted by the κ-adjunction (Definition 6). The denotation of $\mathtt{push}\, V$ is given by reindexing $\kappa^{-1} \mathrm{id}_{C \times S}$ along the denotation of V. The higher-order structure in terms of $\mathtt{mkthunk}$ is given by the adjunction making a κ-category closed (Definition 3). (A similar decomposition of λ into binding and thunking underlies Levy's call-by-push-value paradigm [6].)

The intended meaning of the κ-calculus is that the most recently pushed value is popped by κ, and that $\mathtt{apply}$ forces a thunk (made by $\mathtt{mkthunk}$) from the top of the stack:

$$(\mathtt{push}\, V); (\kappa x.M) = M[x{:} = V]$$
$$(L; M); N = L; (M; N)$$
$$\mathtt{push}\, (\mathtt{mkthunk}\, M); \mathtt{apply} = M$$

3.3 Syntactic translations

Because of the categorical equivalence results, we know that the languages in this section are in some sense equivalent. Here we give syntactic translations motivated by that equivalence.

In one direction, Douence and Fradet [1] remark that the $\mathtt{let}$ of the computational λ-calculus can be translated into the κ-binder. The translation of λ-calculus into κ-calculus is then essentially the same as their compilation in Figure 4 of [1]:

$$(\mathtt{let}\, x = M \,\mathtt{in}\, N)^\dagger = M^\dagger; \kappa x.N^\dagger$$
$$x^\dagger = \mathtt{push}\, x$$
$$(\lambda x.M)^\dagger = \mathtt{push}\, (\mathtt{mkthunk}\, (\kappa x.M^\dagger))$$
$$VW^\dagger = W^\dagger; V^\dagger; \mathtt{apply}$$

The translation of $\mathtt{let}$ explains the naming and sequencing of λ_c in terms of the pushing and popping of κ-calculus. For example, we read the right hand side of the equation as: evaluate M, leaving a value on the top of the stack; then pop that value and call it x in N.

It is slightly less obvious if κ-calculus can be translated into computational λ-calculus. After all, there is no stack for the κ-binder to pop. A solution is to provide a variable that acts as a stack. A κ-term M is translated into a λ-term M^* with a distinguished free variable s as follows:

$$(\kappa x.M)^* = \mathtt{let}\, (x, s) = s \,\mathtt{in}\, M^*$$
$$(M; N)^* = \mathtt{let}\, s = M^* \,\mathtt{in}\, N^*$$
$$x^* = x$$

$$(\text{push}\,V)^* = (V^*, s)$$
$$(\text{mkthunk}\,M)^* = \lambda s.M^*$$
$$\text{apply}^* = \text{let}\,(f, x) = s\,\text{in}\,fx$$

The rule for apply is somewhat awkward, as it only preserves typing if the remainder of the stack is empty. For the general case, one would need to reformat the stack before and after the function is applied, in effect by defining coherence isomorphisms.

4   Conclusions and directions for further work

Because of the equivalence of closed Freyd-categories and closed κ-categories to a strong monad with Kleisli exponentials, the known soundness and completeness results for the traditional interpretation of computational λ-calculus carry over in a routine fashion. (Soundness and completeness of a graphical notation similar to our variant of computational λ-calculus was shown by Jeffrey [3].)

We believe our equivalence expresses, at an abstract level, a semantic link between computational λ-calculus and stack-based intermediate languages used in compiling. It seems encouraging in this regard that the decomposition of λ into a first-order binder (which we called κ) and the creation of a first-class function (an operation we called thunking) arose both in compiling and from the notion of closed structure on a κ-category. Though much more remains to be done to flesh out this connection, it seems that relatively low-level constructs can have clean categorical semantics.

Acknowledgements   Thanks to Peter O'Hearn and Paul Levy for discussions.

References

1. R. Douence and P. Fradet. A Taxonomy of Functional Language Implementations Part I : Call-by-Value , INRIA Research Report No 2783, 1995.
2. M. Hasegawa. Decomposing typed lambda calculus into a couple of categorical programming languages, *Proc. CTCS*, Lect. Notes in Computer Science 953 (1995).
3. A. Jeffrey. Premonoidal categories and a graphical view of programs. http://www.cogs.susx.ac.uk/users/alanje/premon/paper-title.html .
4. G.M. Kelly. *The basic concepts of enriched categories.* CUP (1982).
5. X. Leroy. The ZINC experiment : an economical implementation of the ML language. Technical Report RT-0117, INRIA, Institut National de Recherche en Informatique et en Automatique, 1990.
6. P. B. Levy. Call-by-push-value: a subsuming paradigm (extended abstract). In J.-Y Girard, editor, *Typed Lambda-Calculi and Applications*, Lecture Notes in Computer Science, April 1999.
7. E. Moggi. Computational Lambda calculus and Monads, *Proc. LICS 89*, IEEE Press (1989) 14-23.
8. E. Moggi. Notions of computation and monads, Information and Computation 93 (1991) 55-92.

9. A.J. Power. Premonoidal categories as categories with algebraic structure (submitted).
10. A.J. Power and E.P. Robinson. Premonoidal categories and notions of computation, *Proc. LDPL '96*, Math Structures in Computer Science.
11. A.J. Power and H. Thielecke. Environments, Continuation Semantics and Indexed Categories, Proc. Theoretical Aspects of Computer Science, Lecture Notes in Computer Science (1997) 391-414.

A   Freyd-categories and κ-categories

We refer the reader to [10] for the definition of symmetric premonoidal category and associated structures.

Definition 4. *A* Freyd-category *consists of a category C with finite products, a symmetric premonoidal category $\mathcal{K}$, and an identity on objects strict symmetric premonoidal functor $J: C \longrightarrow \mathcal{K}$.*

We will sometimes write $\mathcal{K}$ for a Freyd-category, as the rest of the structure is usually implicit.

Definition 5. *A* comonoid *in a premonoidal category $\mathcal{K}$ consists of an object $\mathbf{C}$ of $\mathcal{K}$, and central maps $\delta: \mathbf{C} \longrightarrow \mathbf{C} \otimes \mathbf{C}$ and $\nu: \mathbf{C} \longrightarrow I$ making the usual associativity and unit diagrams commute. A comonoid map from $\mathbf{C}$ to $\mathbf{D}$ in a premonoidal category $\mathcal{K}$ is a central map $f: \mathbf{C} \longrightarrow \mathbf{D}$ that commutes with the comultiplications and counits of the comonoids.*

Given a premonoidal category $\mathcal{K}$, comonoids and comonoid maps in $\mathcal{K}$ form a category $\mathbf{Comon}(\mathcal{K})$ with composition given by that of $\mathcal{K}$. Moreover, any strict premonoidal functor $H: \mathcal{K} \longrightarrow \mathcal{L}$ lifts to a functor $\mathbf{Comon}(H): \mathbf{Comon}(\mathcal{K}) \longrightarrow \mathbf{Comon}(\mathcal{L})$. Trivially, any comonoid $\mathbf{C}$ yields a comonad $- \otimes \mathbf{C}$, and any comonoid map $f: \mathbf{C} \longrightarrow \mathbf{D}$ yields a functor from $\mathbf{Kleisli}(- \otimes \mathbf{D})$, the Kleisli category of the comonad $- \otimes \mathbf{D}$, to $\mathbf{Kleisli}(- \otimes \mathbf{C})$, that is the identity on objects. So we have a functor $\mathsf{s}(\mathcal{K}): \mathbf{Comon}(\mathcal{K})^{\mathrm{op}} \longrightarrow \mathcal{C}at$. Given a category C with finite products, every object A of C has a unique comonoid structure, given by the diagonal and the unique map to the terminal object. So $\mathbf{Comon}(C)$ is isomorphic to C. Thus, given a Freyd-category $J: C \longrightarrow \mathcal{K}$, we have a functor $\kappa(J): C^{\mathrm{op}} \longrightarrow \mathcal{C}at$ given by $\mathsf{s}(\mathcal{K})$ composed with the functor induced by J from $C \cong \mathbf{Comon}(C)$ to $\mathbf{Comon}(\mathcal{K})$.

Definition 6. *A κ-category consists of a small category C with finite products, together with an indexed category $H: C^{\mathrm{op}} \longrightarrow \mathcal{C}at$ such that*

- *for each object A of C, $\mathbf{Ob}\, H_A = \mathbf{Ob}\, C$, and for each arrow $f: A \longrightarrow B$ in C, the functor $H_f: H_B \longrightarrow H_A$ is the identity on objects*
- *for each projection $\pi: B \times A \longrightarrow B$ in C, the functor H_π has a left adjoint L_B given on objects by $- \times A$*

– (the Beck-Chevalley condition) *for every arrow* $f: B \longrightarrow B'$ *in* C, *the natural transformation from* $L_B \circ H_{f \times \mathrm{id}_A}$ *to* $H_f \circ L_{B'}$ *induced by the adjointness is the identity.*

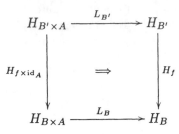

Proposition 4. *Given a κ-category $H: C^{\mathrm{op}} \longrightarrow Cat$, there is an indexed functor* $\mathrm{inc}: s(C) \longrightarrow H$ *as follows: for each A in C, we have a functor from $s(C_A)$ to H_A. On objects, it is the identity. To define inc_1 on arrows, given $f: A \longrightarrow B$ in C, consider the arrow $\iota_B: 1 \longrightarrow B$ in H_B corresponding under the adjunction to id_B in H_1. Applying H_f to it gives a map $H_f(\iota_B): 1 \longrightarrow B$ in H_A, or equivalently, under the adjunction, a map from A to B in H_1. Define $\mathrm{inc}_1(f)$ to be that map.*

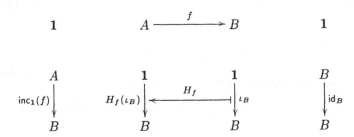

This plus naturality determines the rest of the structure.

Theorem 4. *Let C be a small category with finite products. Given a κ-category $H: C^{\mathrm{op}} \longrightarrow Cat$, there is a small Freyd-category $J: C \longrightarrow K$, unique up to isomorphism, for which H is isomorphic to $\kappa(J)$. The correspondence extends to an equivalence between the 2-category of small Freyd-categories and that of κ-categories.*

Typed Exceptions and Continuations
Cannot Macro-Express Each Other

Jon G. Riecke[1] and Hayo Thielecke[2]

[1] Bell Laboratories, Lucent Technologies
700 Mountain Avenue, Murray Hill, NJ 07974 USA
riecke@bell-labs.com
[2] Queen Mary and Westfield College, University of London, London E1 4NS, UK
ht@dcs.qmw.ac.uk

Abstract. The most powerful control constructs in modern programming languages are continuations and exceptions. Although they can be used interchangeably in some cases, they are fundamentally different semantically. We consider two simply-typed functional languages with exceptions and continuations, respectively. We give two theorems, one that holds in the language with exceptions and one that holds in the language with continuations. A fortiori, these theorems imply that exception constructs cannot be used to macro-express continuation constructs, and that continuation constructs cannot be used to macro-express exception constructs.

1 Introduction

Nearly all programming languages contain constructs for manipulating the control flow by "jumping". The most powerful of these control constructs are exceptions as in Standard ML [14], CAML [10], or Java [5] on the one hand, and continuations as in Standard ML of New Jersey or Scheme [7] on the other. Unlike crude `goto`, they allow jumps into and out of procedures, and they carry values along with the jump.

There are two crucial differences between exceptions and continuations. One difference lies in the fact that when an exception is raised, control is transferred to the *dynamically* enclosing exception handler, whereas continuations return control to a single point. The other difference lies in the indefinite extent of continuations: a procedure may invoke a continuation that was created at its point of definition, even if the procedure containing that definition has already returned. Such "upward" continuations have no counterpart with exceptions. On the other hand, the dynamic nature of handlers is also a source of additional expressive power.

One consequence of these differences is that exceptions can be stack-allocated, while continuations with their indefinite extent need to be heap-allocated in general. Although illuminating, this does not constitute a firm distinction: one could conceive a (very inefficient) implementation of continuations with a stack that is never popped (compare [22] in light of [19]). Hence we need a more absolute criterion for comparing expressiveness. Two such criteria are pertinent here: Turing completeness, and the ability to break contextual equivalences [4].

Lillibridge [11, 12] compares continuations and exceptions in terms of Turing completeness. First, Lillibridge shows that all expressions in the simply-typed language with continuations terminate. Second, he shows that property does *not* hold for exceptions. Even though this argument sheds some light on the distinctions between continuations and exceptions, it is only a partial answer, as Lillibridge states [12]. The main problem is that the argument is not robust. For instance, if we add recursion to the core language, then the language of continuations becomes Turing complete as well. In fact, the argument thus relies on the special typing of exceptions, and not on the operations themselves. For instance, one can write an infinite loop in Standard ML by

```
exception Foo of (exn -> int)
fun loop x = case x of Foo g => g x
```

and writing the expression `loop (Foo loop)`.

A notion of expressiveness more generally applicable than Turing completeness was used by Landin [4, 8, 9]:

It is impossible to introduce assignment into pure LISP merely by a definition. The proof of this is that no mere definition can interfere with the interchangeability of "*x*" and "**cons**(**car**(*x*),**cdr**(*x*))". So there is a firm distinction between having and not having assignment.

To paraphrase Landin, the expressive power of assignment is evidenced by the fact that it can break the η-law for products, namely $(\pi_1 M, \pi_2 M) = M$.

Another law for product, sometimes called copyability, is the equation

$$(\lambda x.(x,x)) M = (M,M).$$

It was used by the second author to argue for the expressive power of `callcc` [21]. Our first main result continues that work by showing that an equivalence related to the copyability equivalence *cannot* be broken by exceptions, so that continuations cannot be encoded using exceptions. Conversely, our second main result is that two terms that can quite easily be distinguished with exceptions cannot be distinguished by continuations. The proof is technically the most novel of this paper and relies on the "answer type" of continuations being polymorphic and hence in some sense inaccessible.

2 Languages

We begin with precise descriptions of the three languages, a call-by-value, slightly simplified version of PCF [18] (VPCF for short), the enhanced version with continuations (VPCF+C), and the enhanced version with exceptions (VPCF+E).

2.1 VPCF

The core language is given by following grammar, where *op* abbreviates either the `succ` or the `pred` operations.

$$s ::= \mathtt{int} \mid (s \to s)$$
$$V ::= x \mid n \mid (\lambda x : s. M)$$
$$M ::= V \mid (M\, M) \mid \Omega \mid (\mathtt{rec}\, f(x : s).\, M) \mid (op\, M) \mid (\mathtt{if0}\, M \mathtt{\, then\,} M \mathtt{\, else\,} M)$$

Table 1. Typing rules for VPCF.

[Var]	$\Gamma \vdash x : \Gamma(x), \ x \in dom(\Gamma)$	[Int]	$\Gamma \vdash n : \texttt{int}$

$$[Op] \quad \frac{\Gamma \vdash M : \texttt{int}}{\Gamma \vdash (op\,M) : \texttt{int}} \qquad\qquad [If] \quad \frac{\Gamma \vdash M : \texttt{int} \quad \Gamma \vdash N_i : t}{\Gamma \vdash (\texttt{if0}\ M \ \texttt{then}\ N_1 \ \texttt{else}\ N_2) : t}$$

$$[Lam] \quad \frac{\Gamma, x : s_1 \vdash M : s_2}{\Gamma \vdash (\lambda x : s_1.\,M) : (s_1 \to s_2)} \qquad\qquad [App] \quad \frac{\Gamma \vdash M : (s_1 \to s_2) \quad \Gamma \vdash N : s_1}{\Gamma \vdash (M\,N) : s_2}$$

$$[Omega] \quad \Gamma \vdash \Omega : s \qquad\qquad [Rec] \quad \frac{\Gamma, f : (s_1 \to s_2), x : s_1 \vdash M : s_2}{\Gamma \vdash (\texttt{rec}\ f(x : s_1).\,M) : (s_1 \to s_2)}$$

The syntactic category s ranges over simple types; the category V over values; and the category M over terms. A recursive function f with argument x is defined using the construct $(\texttt{rec}\ f(x : s).\,M)$, where M is the body of the recursive definition. VPCF includes a divergent term Ω, even though it is definable from recursion, to simplify certain proofs. Following standard conventions, we identify terms up to renaming of bound variables and use the notation $M[x := N]$ for the capture-free substitution of N for x in M [1]. Finally, we often omit types when they can be reconstructed.

Typing rules for VPCF appear in Table 1. In the judgement $\Gamma \vdash M : s$, a typing context Γ is a finite, partial function from variables to types with domain $dom(\Gamma)$.

The operational semantics of VPCF is given using evaluation contexts [3]. The evaluation contexts are defined by the grammar

$$E ::= [\cdot] \mid (E\,M) \mid (V\,E) \mid (\texttt{succ}\ E) \mid (\texttt{pred}\ E) \mid (\texttt{if0}\ E \ \texttt{then}\ M \ \texttt{else}\ M)$$

These contexts define a left-to-right, call-by-value evaluation strategy, and specify the location of the next subterm to be reduced. In other words, any closed, well-typed term can be parsed into an evaluation context and a redex in the hole of the context. The operational rules are

$$
\begin{aligned}
E[(\lambda x.\,P)\,V] \quad &\to\ E[P[x := V]] \\
E[\texttt{succ}\ n] \quad &\to\ E[n+1] \\
E[\texttt{pred}\ 0] \quad &\to\ E[0] \\
E[\texttt{pred}\ (n+1)] \quad &\to\ E[n] \\
E[\texttt{if0}\ 0 \ \texttt{then}\ M \ \texttt{else}\ N] \quad &\to\ E[M] \\
E[\texttt{if0}\ (n+1) \ \texttt{then}\ M \ \texttt{else}\ N] \quad &\to\ E[N] \\
E[\texttt{rec}\ f(x : s_1).\,M] \quad &\to\ E[M[f := (\lambda x : s_1.\,(\texttt{rec}\ f(x : s_1).\,M)\,x)]]
\end{aligned}
$$

For VPCF and its extensions, we use $\to^*$ for the reflexive, transitive closure of $\to$. Finally, we use a notion of contextual equivalence due to Morris [16]:

Definition 1. *Suppose M, N are VPCF terms such that $\Gamma \vdash M : s$ and $\Gamma \vdash N : s$. Then M and N are contextually equivalent, written $M \equiv_{VPCF} N$, if for any VPCF context $C[\cdot]$ (a term with zero or more holes) such that $\emptyset \vdash C[M] : \texttt{int}$ and $\emptyset \vdash C[N] : \texttt{int}$, $C[M] \to^* n$ iff $C[N] \to^* n$.*

This relation, appropriately subscripted, will also be used in the extensions of VPCF.

2.2 VPCF+Exceptions

The enhanced language with exceptions, called VPCF+E, is obtained by making the following additions to the grammar of VPCF:

$$s ::= \ldots \mid (s\ \text{exn})$$
$$V ::= \ldots \mid e_s$$
$$M ::= \ldots \mid (\text{raise}\ M\ M) \mid (\text{handle}\ M\ M\ M)$$

The symbol e_s ranges over an infinite set of typed exception constants. In the handle construct, the first expression is the exception to be handled, the second is the handler, and the third is the expression that might raise the exception to be handled. The typing rules for VPCF+E are those for VPCF and

$$[\textit{Exception}]\ \Gamma \vdash e_s : (s\ \text{exn}) \qquad [\textit{Raise}]\ \frac{\Gamma \vdash M : (s\ \text{exn}) \qquad \Gamma \vdash N : s}{\Gamma \vdash (\text{raise}\ M\ N) : t}$$

$$[\textit{Handle}]\ \frac{\Gamma \vdash M : (s\ \text{exn}) \qquad \Gamma \vdash N : (s \to t) \qquad \Gamma \vdash P : t}{\Gamma \vdash (\text{handle}\ M\ N\ P) : t}$$

The operational semantics is also an extension of that for VPCF. The grammar of evaluation contexts becomes

$$E ::= \ldots \mid (\text{raise}\ E\ M) \mid (\text{raise}\ V\ E)$$
$$\mid (\text{handle}\ E\ M\ M) \mid (\text{handle}\ V\ E\ M) \mid (\text{handle}\ V\ V\ E)$$

Let E_e denote the set of evaluation contexts that do not contain a handler for e along the spine. The operational rules are those for VPCF and

$$E[\text{handle}\ e\ V\ V'] \qquad\qquad \to E[V']$$
$$E[\text{handle}\ e\ V\ E_e[\text{raise}\ e\ V']] \to E[V\ V']$$

2.3 VPCF+Continuations

The language with continuations, called VPCF+C, is obtained by adding the following constructs to the syntax of types and terms:

$$s ::= \ldots \mid (s\ \text{cont})$$
$$M ::= \ldots \mid (\text{callcc}\ M) \mid (\text{throw}\ M\ M)$$

The additional typing rules for the new constructs are the following:

$$[\textit{Callcc}]\ \frac{\Gamma \vdash M : (s\ \text{cont} \to s)}{\Gamma \vdash (\text{callcc}\ M) : s} \qquad [\textit{Throw}]\ \frac{\Gamma \vdash M : (s\ \text{cont}) \qquad \Gamma \vdash N : s}{\Gamma \vdash (\text{throw}\ M\ N) : t}$$

The operational semantics requires a new class of values for continuations and additions to the grammar of evaluation contexts:

$$V ::= \ldots \mid (\gamma x : s.\ E[x])$$
$$E ::= \ldots \mid (\text{callcc}\ E) \mid (\text{throw}\ E\ M) \mid (\text{throw}\ V\ E)$$

These continuation values are not a part of VPCF+C; in particular, they cannot be used in contexts for $\equiv_{VPCF+C}$. The operational rules are those for VPCF and

$$E[\texttt{callcc}\,(\lambda x.\,P)] \qquad \to E[P[x := (\gamma x : s.\,E[x])]]$$
$$E[\texttt{throw}\,(\gamma x : s.\,E'[x])\,V] \to E'[V]$$

3 Exceptions cannot encode continuations

One difference between exceptions and continuations can be explained on an intuitive level: once an exception is raised, a program cannot return to the site where the exception was raised. Continuations, however, can be "upward escaping" in the sense that they may be stored inside lambda abstractions and invoked multiple times. For instance, the following expression (see also [21])

$$argfc = \texttt{callcc}\,(\lambda k.\,\texttt{throw}\,k\,(\lambda x.\,\texttt{throw}\,k\,(\lambda y.\,x)))$$

grabs a continuation and immediately throws a functional value to that continuation. The continuation is, however, reinvoked whenever the function is called.

This argument, as stated in the introduction, does not yield a formal difference; we need something more concrete to show the expressiveness of allowing "upward" continuations. The following proposition establishes that difference:

Proposition 1. *Let M be a VPCF+E term such that* $\emptyset \vdash M : (\texttt{int} \to \texttt{int})$. *Let*

$$S = (\lambda x : (\texttt{int} \to \texttt{int}).\,\lambda p.\,p\,x\,x)$$
$$D = (\lambda x : (\texttt{int} \to \texttt{int}).\,\lambda y : (\texttt{int} \to \texttt{int}).\,\lambda p.\,p\,x\,y)$$

Then $(S\,M) \equiv_{VPCF+E} (D\,M\,M)$, *but there is an M such that* $(S\,M) \not\equiv_{VPCF+C} (D\,M\,M)$.

The proposition can be used to deduce that exceptions cannot express `callcc` and `throw`. Suppose, for instance, we could define closed VPCF+E terms having the same operational behavior as `callcc` and `throw`. Then the *argfc* function could be transliterated into VPCF+E, yielding a counterexample to the proposition.

To see the $(S\,M) \not\equiv_{VPCF+C} (D\,M\,M)$ part, pick M to be *argfc*. Let

$$P = \lambda x.\,\lambda y.\,((x\,1);(y\,2))$$

where $(Q;N)$ is an abbreviation for $((\lambda d.\,N)\,Q)$ with d a fresh variable. Then one may show $((S\,M)\,P) \to^* 1$ and $((D\,M\,M)\,P) \to^* 2$. (This example can be easily tested in Standard ML of New Jersey.)

We are left only with proving $(S\,M) \equiv_{VPCF+E} (D\,M\,M)$. To carry out the proof, we define a way of relating terms containing occurrences of $(S\,M)$ and $(D\,M\,M)$. Define a substitution to be a map from variables to terms. The necessary relation, called $\sim$, is defined by induction:

- $N \sim N$;
- If $N \sim N'$ and $P \sim P'$ and $Q \sim Q'$, then $(N\,P) \sim (N'\,P')$, $(\lambda x.\,N) \sim (\lambda x.\,N')$, $(op\,M) \sim (op\,M)$, $(\texttt{if0}\,N\,\texttt{then}\,P\,\texttt{else}\,Q) \sim (\texttt{if0}\,N'\,\texttt{then}\,P'\,\texttt{else}\,Q')$, and similarly for `rec`, `handle`, and `raise`;

Table 2. Natural Semantics of VPCF+E

$$V \Downarrow V$$

$$\frac{N \Downarrow n}{(\text{succ } N) \Downarrow (n+1)}$$

$$\frac{N \Downarrow 0}{(\text{pred } N) \Downarrow 0}$$

$$\frac{N \Downarrow (n+1)}{(\text{pred } N) \Downarrow n}$$

$$\frac{N \Downarrow 0 \quad P_1 \Downarrow R}{(\text{if0 } N \text{ then } P_1 \text{ else } P_2) \Downarrow R}$$

$$\frac{N \Downarrow (n+1) \quad P_2 \Downarrow R}{(\text{if0 } N \text{ then } P_1 \text{ else } P_2) \Downarrow R}$$

$$\frac{P \Downarrow (\lambda x. P_1) \quad Q \Downarrow V \quad P_1[x := V] \Downarrow R}{(P Q) \Downarrow R}$$

$$\frac{N \Downarrow e \quad P \Downarrow V}{(\text{raise } N P) \Downarrow (\text{raise } e V)}$$

$$\frac{N \Downarrow V \quad P \Downarrow V' \quad Q \Downarrow V''}{(\text{handle } N P Q) \Downarrow V''}$$

$$\frac{N \Downarrow e \quad P \Downarrow V \quad Q \Downarrow (\text{raise } e V') \quad (V V') \Downarrow R}{(\text{handle } N P Q) \Downarrow R}$$

$$\frac{N \Downarrow (\text{raise } e V)}{(op N) \Downarrow (\text{raise } e V)}$$

$$\frac{N \Downarrow (\text{raise } e V)}{(\text{if0 } N \text{ then } P_1 \text{ else } P_2) \Downarrow (\text{raise } e V)}$$

$$\frac{P \Downarrow (\text{raise } e V)}{(P Q) \Downarrow (\text{raise } e V)}$$

$$\frac{P \Downarrow V \quad Q \Downarrow (\text{raise } e V')}{(P Q) \Downarrow (\text{raise } e V')}$$

$$\frac{N \Downarrow (\text{raise } e V)}{(\text{raise } N P) \Downarrow (\text{raise } e V)}$$

$$\frac{N \Downarrow V \quad P \Downarrow (\text{raise } e V')}{(\text{raise } N P) \Downarrow (\text{raise } e V')}$$

$$\frac{N \Downarrow (\text{raise } e' V)}{(\text{handle } N P Q) \Downarrow (\text{raise } e' V)}$$

$$\frac{N \Downarrow V \quad P \Downarrow (\text{raise } e' V')}{(\text{handle } N P Q) \Downarrow (\text{raise } e' V')}$$

$$\frac{N \Downarrow e \quad P \Downarrow V' \quad Q \Downarrow (\text{raise } e' V'') \quad e \neq e'}{(\text{handle } N P Q) \Downarrow (\text{raise } e' V'')} \qquad (\text{rec } f(x:s). P) \Downarrow (\lambda x : s. P[f := (\text{rec } f(x:s). P)])$$

– If $\sigma \sim \sigma'$, then

$$(S \, \sigma(M)) \sim (D \, \sigma'(M) \, \sigma'(M)),$$

where $\sigma \sim \sigma'$ if the substitutions have the same domain, and for any variable x in the domain, $\sigma(x) \sim \sigma'(x)$.

To prove the proposition more easily, we also use a natural semantics [6]; this form of semantics rewrites a term M into a final answer in one step via a relation $\Downarrow$. Let R range over results, which in this case are either values V or uncaught exceptions ($\text{raise } e V$). Then define the relation $\Downarrow$ by the rules in Table 2. It is not hard to show that the natural semantics is just a reformulation of the original operational semantics:

Lemma 1. *Suppose $\emptyset \vdash P : s$. Then $P \to^* V$ iff $P \Downarrow V$, and $P \to^* E_e[\text{raise } e V]$ iff $P \Downarrow (\text{raise } e V)$.*

Finally, we need a lemma stating the connection between terms related by $\sim$.

Lemma 2. *Suppose $P \sim Q$.*

– *If $P \Downarrow V$, then there is a V' such that $Q \Downarrow V'$ and $V \sim V'$.*

– *If $Q \Downarrow V'$, then there is a V such that $P \Downarrow V$ and $V \sim V'$.*

These lemmas give us enough machinery to prove the $(S\,M) \equiv_{VPCF+E} (D\,M\,M)$ part of the proposition. Suppose M is a VPCF+E term such that $\emptyset \vdash M : (\texttt{int} \to \texttt{int})$, and let S, D be as above. Suppose $C[\cdot]$ is a VPCF+E context such that $\emptyset \vdash C[S\,M] : \texttt{int}$ and $\emptyset \vdash C[D\,M\,M] : \texttt{int}$. Note that $C[S\,M] \sim C[D\,M\,M]$. Thus, by Lemma 2, $C[S\,M] \Downarrow n$ iff $C[D\,M\,M] \Downarrow n$. By Lemma 1, $C[S\,M] \to^* n$ iff $C[D\,M\,M] \to^* n$.

4   Continuations cannot encode exceptions

Continuations have a static flavor: if a continuation is reified and escapes, throwing to that continuation returns control to the point the continuation was reified. Exceptions, on the other hand, have a dynamic nature: raising an exception returns control to a handler that is determined dynamically. This turns out to give additional expressive power, in that a procedure may dynamically handle exceptions raised inside its arguments. To give evidence of this expressive power, we prove the following

Proposition 2. *Suppose F, G are closed VPCF+C lambda abstractions with $\emptyset \vdash F :$ $(\texttt{int} \to \texttt{int}) \to \texttt{int}$ and $\emptyset \vdash G : \texttt{int} \to \texttt{int}$. For $i = 1, 2$, define*

$$P_i = (F\ (\lambda d.\ G\ 0; \Omega)); (F\ (\lambda d.\ i))$$

Then $P_1 \equiv_{VPCF+C} P_2$, but there are lambda abstractions F, G in VPCF+E such that $P_1 \not\equiv_{VPCF+E} P_2$.

To see $P_1 \not\equiv_{VPCF+E} P_2$, define

$$F = (\lambda h.\ \texttt{handle}\ e\ (\lambda d.\ 0)\ (h\ 0)) \qquad G = (\lambda d.\ \texttt{raise}\ e\ 0)$$

Then $P_1 \to^* 1$ and $P_2 \to^* 2$.

The equivalence in VPCF+C can be explained intuitively. Essentially, there are just two cases: either F ignores its functional argument, in which case both P_i and P_j must return the same result, or F calls its argument. In that case, control must either escape (if G performs a `callcc` and a `throw`), or it must get stuck evaluating Ω.

A direct formalization of this intuition, using the techniques of the last section, proves elusive. Instead, the proof goes by applying a cps transform to VPCF+C. The target language is VPCF+α, formed by enhancing the grammar of types with a new base type α. The type α has no additional term constructors for it, intuitively representing the abstractness of the answer type of continuations [13]. The abstractness of the answer type has not, to our knowledge, been exploited in quite the way the proof does here.

The cps transform divides into a translation on types and on terms. For types, let

$$\begin{aligned} \texttt{int}^* &= \texttt{int} & (s \to t)^* &= (s^* \to \bar{t}) \\ (s\ \texttt{cont})^* &= (s^* \to \alpha) & \bar{s} &= (s^* \to \alpha) \to \alpha \end{aligned}$$

where s^* represents the "values" of type s, and $\bar{s}$ represents the computations of type s; these notions are derived from Moggi's account of side effects using the computational lambda calculus [15]. The cps transform on terms, given in Table 3, takes a derivation of the judgement $\Gamma \vdash M : s$ to a derivation of the judgement $\Gamma^* \vdash \bar{M} : \bar{s}$, where Γ^* has the same domain as Γ, and $\Gamma^*(x) = (\Gamma(x))^*$. It is not hard to prove

Table 3. Cps transform from VPCF+C to VPCF+α.

[Var]	$\Gamma^* \vdash (\lambda\kappa : s^* \to \alpha.\ \kappa\,x) : \overline{\Gamma(x)}$
[Int]	$\Gamma^* \vdash (\lambda\kappa : \mathtt{int} \to \alpha.\ \kappa\,n) : \overline{\mathtt{int}}$
[Omega]	$\Gamma^* \vdash (\lambda\kappa : s^* \to \alpha.\ \Omega) : \overline{s}$

$$[Op] \qquad \frac{\Gamma^* \vdash \overline{M} : \overline{\mathtt{int}}}{\Gamma^* \vdash (\lambda\kappa : \mathtt{int} \to \alpha.\ \overline{M}\,(\lambda m : \mathtt{int}.\ \kappa\,(op\,m))) : \overline{\mathtt{int}}} \quad m, \kappa \text{ fresh}$$

$$[\mathit{If}] \qquad \frac{\Gamma^* \vdash \overline{M} : \overline{\mathtt{int}} \qquad \Gamma^* \vdash \overline{N_i} : \overline{s}}{\Gamma^* \vdash (\lambda\kappa : \mathtt{int} \to \alpha.\ \overline{M}\,(\lambda m : \mathtt{int}.\ \mathtt{if0}\ m\ \mathtt{then}\ (\overline{N_1}\ \kappa)\ \mathtt{else}\ (\overline{N_2}\ \kappa))) : \overline{s}} \quad m, \kappa \text{ fresh}$$

$$[Lam] \qquad \frac{\Gamma^*, x : s^* \vdash \overline{M} : \overline{t}}{\Gamma^* \vdash (\lambda\kappa : (s \to t)^* \to \alpha.\ \kappa\,(\lambda x : s^*.\ \overline{M})) : \overline{(s \to t)}} \quad \kappa \text{ fresh}$$

$$[App] \qquad \frac{\Gamma^* \vdash \overline{M} : \overline{(s \to t)} \qquad \Gamma^* \vdash \overline{N} : \overline{s}}{\Gamma^* \vdash (\lambda\kappa : t^* \to \alpha.\ \overline{M}\,(\lambda m : (s \to t)^*.\ \overline{N}\,(\lambda n : s^*.\ m\,n\,\kappa))) : \overline{t}} \quad m, n, \kappa \text{ fresh}$$

$$[Rec] \qquad \frac{\Gamma^*, f : (s_1 \to s_2)^*, x : s_1^* \vdash \overline{M} : \overline{s_2}}{\Gamma^* \vdash (\lambda\kappa : (s_1 \to s_2)^* \to \alpha.\ \kappa\,(\mathtt{rec}\,f(x : s_1^*).\ \overline{M})) : \overline{(s_1 \to s_2)}} \quad \kappa \text{ fresh}$$

$$[Callcc] \qquad \frac{\Gamma^* \vdash \overline{M} : \overline{(s\ \mathtt{cont} \to s)}}{\Gamma^* \vdash (\lambda\kappa : s^* \to \alpha.\ \overline{M}\,(\lambda m : (s\ \mathtt{cont} \to s)^*.\ m\,\kappa\,\kappa)) : \overline{s}} \quad m, \kappa \text{ fresh}$$

$$[Throw] \qquad \frac{\Gamma^* \vdash \overline{M} : \overline{(s\ \mathtt{cont})} \qquad \Gamma^* \vdash \overline{N} : \overline{s}}{\Gamma^* \vdash (\lambda\kappa : t^* \to \alpha.\ \overline{M}\,(\lambda m : (s\ \mathtt{cont})^*.\ \overline{N}\,(\lambda n : s^*.\ m\,n))) : \overline{t}} \quad m, n, \kappa \text{ fresh}$$

Proposition 3. *If $\Gamma \vdash M : s$ is derivable, then $\overline{\Gamma} \vdash \overline{M} : \overline{s}$ is derivable.*

The proof goes by induction on the structure of the typing derivation. We can also prove, using techniques of Plotkin [17], that the translation is adequate:

Theorem 1 (Adequacy). *Consider any closed VPCF+C term M such that $\emptyset \vdash M : \mathtt{int}$. Let κ_0 be a variable of type $(\mathtt{int} \to \alpha)$. Then $M \to^* n$ iff $(\overline{M}\ \kappa_0) \to^* \kappa_0\,n$.*

The key lemma in proving the proposition is the following:

Lemma 3. *Suppose F, G are closed, recursion-free lambda abstractions in VPCF+C such that $\emptyset \vdash F : (\mathtt{int} \to \mathtt{int}) \to \mathtt{int}$ and $\emptyset \vdash G : (\mathtt{int} \to \mathtt{int})$. Let*

$$P_i = (F\ (\lambda d.\ G\,0;\Omega));(F\ (\lambda d.\ i))$$

Then $\overline{P_i} \equiv_{VPCF+\alpha} \overline{P_j}$ for any numerals i, j.

Proof. Because F, G are lambda abstractions, simple β reduction shows that

$$\overline{P_i} \equiv_{VPCF+\alpha} \lambda\kappa.\ F^*\ (\lambda d.\ \lambda\kappa.\ G^*\ 0\ (\lambda m.\ \Omega))\ (\lambda m.\ F^*\ (\lambda d.\ \lambda\kappa.\ \kappa\,i)\ \kappa)$$

Let $s = (\texttt{int} \to \texttt{int})^*$. Using a series of lemmas, we can show that F^* is equivalent, in the sense of $\equiv_{VPCF+\alpha}$, to one of the following forms:

$$\Omega \qquad\qquad (\lambda x : s.\, \Omega)$$
$$(\lambda x : s.\, x\, S) \qquad\qquad (\lambda x : s.\, \lambda y : \texttt{int} \to \alpha.\, \Omega)$$
$$(\lambda x : s.\, \lambda y : \texttt{int} \to \alpha.\, y\, n) \qquad (\lambda x : s.\, \lambda y : \texttt{int} \to \alpha.\, y\, \Omega)$$
$$(\lambda x : s.\, \lambda y : \texttt{int} \to \alpha.\, x\, S_1\, S_2)$$

The first, second, and fourth cases imply that for all i, $\overline{P_i} \equiv_{VPCF+\alpha} (\lambda \kappa.\, \Omega)$. The third and last cases imply that for all i, $\overline{P_i} \equiv_{VPCF+\alpha} (\lambda \kappa.\, G^*\, 0\, (\lambda m.\, \Omega))$. The fifth case implies that for all i, $\overline{P_i} \equiv_{VPCF+\alpha} (\lambda \kappa.\, \kappa\, n)$. Finally, the sixth case implies that for all i, $\overline{P_i} \equiv_{VPCF+\alpha} (\lambda \kappa.\, \kappa\, \Omega)$. In all cases, $\overline{P_i}$ is equivalent to a term that does not depend on i. Thus, for any numerals i, j, $\overline{P_i} \equiv_{VPCF+\alpha} \overline{P_j}$. By adequacy, $P_i \equiv_{VPCF+C} P_j$.

The proof of Proposition 2 now follows straightforwardly.

5 Conclusions and directions for further work

For the typed languages we have given, we have shown that neither continuations nor exceptions can encode the other. While this may be expected by some, we know of no formal proof; in fact we were surprised by the subtlety of the proof and the failure of our initial brute-force attempts.

In addition to showing the impossibility of macro-encodings of one in terms of the other, we believe that the examples shed light on the nature of the difference between static and dynamic control. In particular, in the inequivalence for exceptions there are two functions which *statically* have no knowledge of each other in that they do not pass arguments or results to each other, and yet they can communicate via an exception. This may be seen as a failure of modular reasoning.

Sitaram and Felleisen used an equivalence similar to the one in Section 4 as an argument for the additional expressive power of the "prompt", or control delimiter [20]. We can regard this as evidence of the essentially dynamic nature of the prompt; compare `dynamic-wind` in Scheme [7]. They gave an informal argument for the validity of this equivalence for continuations alone, but no hint of a formal proof.

The results here leave open a few issues. First, are there ways of showing that the various forms of exceptions cannot macro-express each other? The examples here concern only one form, closest in spirit to that of CAML; Standard ML has local exceptions, which seems more powerful, and LISP has no handlers, which seems less powerful. Second, do the results carry over to untyped languages? In fact, the proof that exceptions cannot encode continuations does work for the untyped versions of VPCF+E and VPCF+C; it seems less clear how to adapt the other proof to the untyped setting.

The proof methods developed here are probably applicable elsewhere. For instance, one can show for the typed cps transform above that all recursion-free terms of cps type are representable as the target of recursion-free VPCF+C terms. This gives a kind of representation theorem, much along the lines given by Danvy and Lawall [2], except in the typed setting. An interesting consequence is that "prompts" are not in the target of the cps transform, and that fact may lead to a full abstraction theorem for VPCF+C.

References

1. H. P. Barendregt. *The Lambda Calculus: Its Syntax and Semantics*, volume 103 of *Studies in Logic*. North-Holland, 1981. Revised Edition, 1984.
2. O. Danvy and J. L. Lawall. Back to direct style II: First-class continuations. In *Proceedings, 1992 ACM Conference on Lisp and Functional Programming*, pages 299–310. ACM, 1992.
3. M. Felleisen. The theory and practice of first-class prompts. In *Conference Record of the Fifteenth Annual ACM Symposium on Principles of Programming Languages*, pages 180–190. ACM, 1988.
4. M. Felleisen. On the expressive power of programming languages. *Science of Computer Programming*, 17:35–75, 1991.
5. J. Gosling, B. Joy, and G. Steele. *The Java(tm) Language Specification*. Addison Wesley, 1996.
6. G. Kahn. Natural semantics. In *Proceedings Symposium on Theoretical Aspects of Computer Science*, volume 247 of *Lect. Notes in Computer Sci.*, New York, 1987. Springer-Verlag.
7. R. Kelsey, W. Clinger, and J. Rees, editors. Revised^5 report on the algorithmic language Scheme. *Higher-Order and Symbolic Computation*, 11(3):7–105, 1998.
8. P. J. Landin. A generalization of jumps and labels. Report, UNIVAC Systems Programming Research, August 1965.
9. P. J. Landin. A generalization of jumps and labels. *Higher-Order and Symbolic Computation*, 11(2), 1998.
10. X. Leroy and P. Weis. *Manual de reference du language Caml*. InterEditions, Paris, 1998.
11. M. Lillibridge. Exceptions are strictly more powerful than call/cc. Technical Report CMS-CS-95-178, School of Computer Science, Carnegie Mellon University, 1995.
12. M. Lillibridge. Uncaught exceptions can be strictly more powerful than call/cc. *Higher-Order and Symbolic Computation*, 12(1):275–307, 1999.
13. A. R. Meyer and M. Wand. Continuation semantics in typed lambda-calculi (summary). In R. Parikh, editor, *Proceedings of the Conference on Logics of Programs, 1985, Lecture Notes in Computer Science 193*, pages 219–224. Springer-Verlag, 1985.
14. R. Milner, M. Tofte, R. Harper, and D. MacQueen. *The Definition of Standard ML (Revised)*. MIT Press, 1997.
15. E. Moggi. Notions of computation and monads. *Information and Control*, 93:55–92, 1991.
16. J. H. Morris. Lambda-calculus models of programming languages. Technical Report MAC-TR-57, M.I.T. Lab. for Computer Science, 1968.
17. G. D. Plotkin. Call-by-name, call-by-value and the λ-calculus. *Theoretical Computer Sci.*, 1:125–159, 1975.
18. Plotkin, G. D. LCF considered as a programming language. *Theoretical Computer Sci.*, 5:223–257, 1977.
19. J. C. Reynolds. The discoveries of continuations. *Lisp and Symbolic Computation*, 6(3/4):233–247, November 1993.
20. D. Sitaram and M. Felleisen. Reasoning with continuations II: Full abstraction for models of control. In *Proceedings of the 1990 ACM Conference on Lisp and Functional Programming*, pages 161–175. ACM, 1990.
21. H. Thielecke. Using a continuation twice and its implications for the expressive power of call/cc. *Higher-Order and Symbolic Computation*, 12(1), 1999.
22. A. van Wijngaarden. Recursive definition of syntax and semantics. In T. B. Steel, Jr, editor, *Formal Language Description Languages for Computer Programming, Proceedings of an IFIP Working Conference*, pages 13–24, 1964.

Automata, Power Series, and Coinduction:
Taking Input Derivatives Seriously
(Extended Abstract)

J.J.M.M. Rutten

CWI, P.O. Box 94079, 1090 GB Amsterdam
janr@cwi.nl, http://www.cwi.nl/~janr

Formal power series are functions $\sigma : A^* \to k$ from the set of words over some alphabet A to some semiring k. Examples include formal languages ($k = \{0,1\}$) and power series in classical analysis ($k = \mathbb{R}$, viewing the elements of A as variables). Because of their relevance to many different scientific areas, both in mathematics and computer science, a large body of literature on power series exists. Most approaches to the subject are essentially algebraic. The aim of this paper is to show that it is worthwhile to view power series from a dual perspective, called coalgebra (see [Rut96] for a general account). In summary, this amounts to supplying the set of all power series with a deterministic automaton structure, which has the universal property of being final. Finality then forms the basis for both definitions and proofs by *coinduction*, which is the coalgebraic counterpart of induction.

Coinductive *definitions* of operators on formal power series take the shape of what we have called *behavioural differential equations*, since they are formulated in terms of (a generalization of) Brzozowski's [Brz64] notion of input *derivative*: the input derivative σ_a of a series σ can intuitively be understood as the specification of the *behaviour* of σ after the input a has been accepted. For instance, the following behavioural differential equation defines the input derivative $(\sigma \parallel \tau)_a$ of the so-called shuffle product of σ and τ in terms of the input derivatives of σ and τ: $(\sigma \parallel \tau)_a = (\sigma_a \parallel \tau) + (\sigma \parallel \tau_a)$. It will be shown that these equations (one for each $a \in A$), together with an *initial condition*, determine a unique solution, which is taken as the formal definition of the shuffle product. Coinductive definitions allow easy proofs by the coinduction *proof* principle, which says that two series are equal whenever they are related by a bisimulation relation (which is the coalgebraic counterpart of a congruence relation). For coinductively defined operators, the construction of such bisimulations often is immediate from the defining differential equations.

The reader familiar with formal power series will know how to give a more elementary definition (cf. [BR88, p.20]) of the shuffle product mentioned as an example above, and therefore would call the differential equation a *property*. Our motivation for taking this and similar such differential equations as a *definition*, is three-fold: Firstly, the form of such equations will allow easy proofs by coinduction of many properties of the operators they define. In Section 4, a number of laws for the familiar operators on formal power series, will be shown to have easy proofs by coinduction. For instance, it takes a two-line proof to show that $\langle \sigma \parallel (\tau \parallel \rho), (\sigma \parallel \tau) \parallel \rho \rangle$ is contained in a bisimulation relation, implying that $\parallel$ is associative. Secondly, the approach can be easily generalized to define new operators. This will be illustrated, in Section 5, by the definition of a new operator σ_{-1}, called shuffle inverse, because it satisfies $\sigma \parallel \sigma_{-1} = 1$ (to be proved by coinduction). It is unclear to us how this operator could be defined without the use of coinduction. Furthermore, many classical differential equations for analytic functions on $\mathbb{R}$ appear as particular instances of behavioural equations. Thirdly, we shall show, in Section 8, how from behavioural differential equations defining operators on power series, nondeterministic automata (with multiplicities in k) can be derived that implement these operators. The construction of these automata is again dictated by the shape of the differential equations, and is syntactic in the sense that their state space consists of expressions. The automata thus obtained are finite for rational power series (giving a new proof of the well-known fact that rational implies recognizable), and, in fact, generally very small. To give a flavour of this, the following two state automaton derives from the defining differential equation of the inverse operator σ^{-1} (with $\sigma \times \sigma^{-1} = 1$) on power series:

$$\text{computes} \quad (2 + 3X + 7X^2)^{-1} = \frac{1}{2} - \frac{3}{4}X - \frac{5}{8}X^2 + \cdots$$

And so we see the following general scheme emerging: (a) (rational) behaviour is *specified* by differential equations, which often can be solved in a canonical way, giving rise to (b) (finite) nondeterministic automata that (efficiently) *implement* the specified behaviour. We see (a) and (b) as the two main contributions of our work.

Related work: The perspective of the present paper is essentially coalgebraic, and generalizes [Rut98], which deals with languages and regular expressions. The notion of input derivative of formal power series, generalizes Brzozowski's original definition for regular expressions [Brz64, Con71]. Its relation with *function derivatives* f' of functions f on $\mathbb{R}$ will be explained by invoking an example from [PE98], where a coinductive treatment of analytic functions in terms of their Taylor expansions is given. Our present theory generalizes the settings of [Rut98]: $k = \mathbb{B}$ and A is arbitrary, and [PE98]: $k = \mathbb{R}$ and $A = \{X\}$, since we are dealing with formal power series in many non-commutative variables (A is arbitrary) over any semiring (k is arbitrary). Although it is well known that rational series can be finitely represented (see [BR88], which has been our main reference on formal power series), also the syntactic construction of k-nondeterministic automata from their defining differential equations is to the best of our knowledge new.

Acknowledgements: I am grateful to Maurice Nivat, who offered me the opportunity to present a preliminary version of this paper at the Univ. of Paris VII.
Note: For a slightly more 'extended' abstract of the present ideas, amongst others containing some examples we had to leave out here, see: Technical Report SEN-R9901, CWI, 1999, which is available via `ftp.cwi.nl` or `www.cwi.nl`.

1 Preliminaries

We briefly recall the definitions of semiring and formal power series, and give a coalgebraic presentation of the notion of deterministic automaton.

Semirings: A semiring is something like a ring without subtraction. More formally, a semiring $k = \langle k, +, \times, 0, 1 \rangle$ consists of a set k together with two binary operations $+$ and $\times$ (sum and product) and two constants 0 and 1, such that $(k, +, 0)$ is a commutative monoid with 0 as identity; $(k, \times, 1)$ is a monoid with 1 as identity; product is distributive with respect to sum; and $0x = x0 = 0$, all $x \in k$ (writing xy for $x \times y$). The following semirings will occur in examples in the paper: the Boolean semiring $\mathbb{B} = (\{0, 1\}, \vee, \wedge, 0, 1)$, the reals $\mathbb{R} = (\mathbb{R}, +, \times, 0, 1)$, and the max-plus semiring $\mathbb{R}_{\max} = ([-\infty, \infty), \max, +, -\infty, 0)$. Note that both $\mathbb{B}$ and $\mathbb{R}_{\max}$ are *idempotent* semirings in that they satisfy $x + x = x$.

Words: Let A be a possibly infinite set and let A^* be the set of all finite words over A. Prefixing a word w in A^* with a letter a in A is denoted by aw. Concatenation of words w and w' is denoted by ww'. Let ε denote the empty word.

Formal power series: A *formal power series* is a function $\sigma : A^* \to k$. The set of all series is denoted by $k\langle\langle A \rangle\rangle$. A series σ assigns to each finite word $w \in A^*$ a *coefficient* $\sigma(w)$ in k, which may be interpreted as the *multiplicity* with which the word w occurs in σ. These multiplicities may have different interpretations, depending on the semiring k. If $k = \mathbb{B}$ then $\sigma(w)$ is either 1 or 0, indicating whether or not w belongs to σ, which in this case simply is a set of words. In other cases, the elements of A are best viewed as (formal non-commutative) *variables*. A basic but important example is $A = \{X\}$ and $k = \mathbb{R}$, when one gets the usual power series. As usual, k and A can be considered as subsets of $k\langle\langle A \rangle\rangle$, by taking $x \in k$ as the function $x : A^* \to k$ with $x(\varepsilon) = x$, and 0 everywhere else; similarly, $a \in A$ is identified with $a : A^* \to k$, defined by $a(a) = 1$, and 0 otherwise.

Deterministic automata: Let A be a possibly infinite set and let k be a semiring. A *deterministic automaton* (or Moore machine) with inputs in A and outputs in k is a pair $S = (S, \langle o_S, t_S \rangle)$ consisting of a set S of *states*, and a pair of functions: an *output function* $o_S : S \to k$, and a *transition function* $t_S : S \to S^A$. Here S^A is the set of all functions from A to S. The transition function t_S assigns to a state s a function $t_S(s) : A \to S$, which specifies the state $t_S(s)(a)$ that is reached after an input symbol a has been consumed. We shall sometimes write $s \xrightarrow{x}$ for $o_S(s) = x$ and $s \xrightarrow{a} s'$ for $t_S(s)(a) = s'$. Also we shall simply write o and t whenever the automaton S is clear from the context. A *homomorphism* between automata $S = (S, \langle o, t \rangle)$ and $S' = (S', \langle o', t' \rangle)$ is any function $f : S \to S'$ such that for all s in S, $o(s) = o'(f(s))$ and, for all a in A, $f(t(s)(a)) = t'(f(s))(a)$. A subset $i : S' \subseteq S$ of an automaton S is a *subautomaton* if i is a homomorphism. For a state s in S, $\langle s \rangle$ denotes the subautomaton *generated* by s. Homomorphisms map subautomata to subautomata. A relation $R \subseteq S \times S'$ is a *bisimulation* between two automata S and S' if, for all s in S, s' in S', and a in A: if $s \, R \, s'$ then $o(s) = o'(s')$ and $t(s)(a) \, R \, t'(s')(a)$. If there exists a bisimulation (between S and itself) containing $s, s' \in S$, then we write

$s \sim s'$ (s and s' are *bisimilar*). Bisimilarity itself is a bisimulation relation and an equivalence relation.

2 The automaton of formal power series

The set $k\langle\langle A\rangle\rangle$ of formal power series is turned into a deterministic automaton with inputs in A and outputs in k, having the universal property of being *final* and satisfying a principle of *coinduction*.

For an input a in A, the *input derivative* σ_a (or $\partial\sigma/\partial a$ or $a^{-1}\sigma$) of a series $\sigma : A^* \to k$ is defined by $\sigma_a(w) = \sigma(aw)$, for $w \in A^*$. The *constant part* (or output) of a series σ is defined by $\sigma(\varepsilon)$. These notions determine an automaton structure $k\langle\langle A\rangle\rangle = (k\langle\langle A\rangle\rangle, \langle o_k, t_k\rangle)$, defined, for $\sigma \in k\langle\langle A\rangle\rangle$ and $a \in A$, by $o_k(\sigma) = \sigma(\varepsilon)$ and $t_k(\sigma)(a) = \sigma_a$.

Theorem 1. *The automaton* $k\langle\langle A\rangle\rangle$ *satisfies the principle of (1) coinduction: for all series* σ *and* τ *in* $k\langle\langle A\rangle\rangle$, *if* $\sigma \sim \tau$ *then* $\sigma = \tau$. *Moreover,* $k\langle\langle A\rangle\rangle$ *is (2) final: for any automaton* S *there exists a unique homomorphism* $l : S \to k\langle\langle A\rangle\rangle$; *it satisfies: for* $s, s' \in S$, $s \sim s'$ *iff* $l(s) = l(s')$.

The series $l(s)$ is called the *behaviour* of the state s of the automaton S, and is defined as the function that assigns to any word w in A^* the output of the state that is reached from s after reading w; that is, for $w = a_0 \cdots a_{n-1}$,

$$l(s)(a_0 \cdots a_{n-1}) = o(s_n), \quad \text{where} \quad s = s_0 \xrightarrow{a_0} s_1 \xrightarrow{a_1} \cdots \xrightarrow{a_{n-1}} s_n.$$

We say that s *represents* the series $l(s)$, and also that $l(s)$ is the series *accepted* by the state s. Since it is easily shown that l is a homomorphism, this proves the existence half of Part (2). Uniqueness follows from Part (1), which is easily proved by induction on the length of words $w \in A^*$. The proof of this theorem also follows from general coalgebraic reasoning (see, e.g., [Rut96]). Note that it does not depend on the semiring structure of k.

Coinduction serves as a *proof* principle: in order to show $\sigma = \tau$, it is sufficient to establish the existence of a bisimulation relation R with $\sigma \, R \, \tau$. The proof principle will be illustrated in some detail in Section 4. Finality will be used as a *coinductive definition* principle (for instance, in Section 3).

The relation between derivatives f' of functions f on $\mathbb{R}$, and input derivatives σ_a of formal power series σ is explained by the following example on analytic functions, taken from [PE98]. Let $k = \mathbb{R}$ and $A = \{X\}$. Thus $\mathbb{R}\langle\langle X\rangle\rangle = \mathbb{R}^{\{X\}^*} \cong \mathbb{R}^\omega$, where $\omega = \{0, 1, \ldots\}$ is the set of natural numbers. In other words, formal power series are now infinite sequences, also called streams, of real numbers. Consider the set $\mathcal{A}$ of functions that are analytic in 0. For analytic functions, the n-th derivative $f^{(n)}(0)$ exists, for all $n \geq 0$. Following [PE98], $\mathcal{A}$ can be turned into an automaton by defining $o_\mathcal{A} : \mathcal{A} \to \mathbb{R}$ and $t_\mathcal{A} : \mathcal{A} \to \mathcal{A}$ (identifying $\mathcal{A}^{\{X\}} \cong \mathcal{A}$) by $o_\mathcal{A}(f) = f(0)$ and $t_\mathcal{A}(f) = f'$. Because $\mathbb{R}\langle\langle X\rangle\rangle$ is a final automaton, there exists a unique homomorphism $l : \mathcal{A} \to \mathbb{R}\langle\langle X\rangle\rangle$, which maps a function f to the series of its *Taylor* coefficients: $l(f) = (f(0), f'(0), f''(0), \ldots)$. Because l is a homomorphism, $l(f)_X = l(f')$. In words, the input derivative of the Taylor series of f is equal to the Taylor series of the derivative of f.

3 Behavioural differential equations

A number of operators on formal power series will be defined by *coinduction*. Similar to the way one can define, for instance, a function of exponentiation $exp : \mathbb{R} \to \mathbb{R}$ by specifying a differential equation and initial condition: $exp' = exp$ and $exp(0) = 1$, coinductive definitions of (elements of and) operators on $k\langle\langle A \rangle\rangle$ amount to the specification of *behavioural differential equations*. It will be a consequence of the finality of the automaton $k\langle\langle A \rangle\rangle$ that the systems of differential equations we shall use, have unique solutions.

Plunging into the matter, the aim of this section is to prove the following theorem.

Theorem 2. *There are unique functions* $+$, $\times$, $(-)^*$, $\|$, *and* $(-)^{-1}$, *called* sum, product, star, shuffle product, *and* inverse, *satisfying the following behavioural differential equations: For all* $\sigma, \tau \in k\langle\langle A \rangle\rangle$ *and* $a \in A$,

differential equation	initial condition
$(\sigma + \tau)_a = \sigma_a + \tau_a$	$(\sigma + \tau)(\varepsilon) = \sigma(\varepsilon) + \tau(\varepsilon)$
$(\sigma\tau)_a = \sigma_a\,\tau + \sigma(\varepsilon)\tau_a$	$(\sigma\tau)(\varepsilon) = \sigma(\varepsilon)\tau(\varepsilon)$
$(\sigma^*)_a = \sigma_a\,\sigma^*$	$(\sigma^*)(\varepsilon) = 1$
$(\sigma \parallel \tau)_a = (\sigma_a \parallel \tau) + (\sigma \parallel \tau_a)$	$(\sigma \parallel \tau)(\varepsilon) = \sigma(\varepsilon)\tau(\varepsilon)$
$(\sigma^{-1})_a = -\sigma(\varepsilon)^{-1}\sigma_a\,\sigma^*$	$(\sigma^{-1})(\varepsilon) = \sigma(\varepsilon)^{-1}$

Note that we have written $\sigma\tau$ for $\sigma \times \tau$, and that we use the same symbols for sum and product on $k\langle\langle A \rangle\rangle$ as for sum and product on k, respectively. Also note that in the expression $\sigma(\varepsilon)\tau_a = \sigma(\varepsilon) \times \tau_a$ above, we are interpreting $\sigma(\varepsilon)$, which is an element of k, as an element of $k\langle\langle A \rangle\rangle$, following the convention described in Section 1. Observe that in the definition of the initial conditions, the operators of the semiring structure of k are used. Finally note that the latter equation assumes k to be a *ring* rather than a semiring, since it uses subtraction. It is moreover *partial* since it only applies to such σ for which $\sigma(\varepsilon)$ is invertible in k. Whenever we shall write $-\sigma(\varepsilon)^{-1}$, both conditions will silently be assumed to apply. If either of these conditions does not hold then we put $(\sigma^{-1})_a = 0$ and $(\sigma^{-1})(\varepsilon) = 0$ (simply in order to keep all functions total).

Proof of Theorem 2: Let the set $\mathcal{E}$ of *expressions* be given by the following syntax: $E ::= \underline{\sigma} \mid E + F \mid EF \mid E^* \mid (E \parallel F) \mid E^{-1}$, where we write EF rather than $E \times F$, and where for every series σ in $k\langle\langle A \rangle\rangle$ a *symbol* $\underline{\sigma}$ is included in $\mathcal{E}$. The set $\mathcal{E}$ is next supplied with an automaton structure $(\mathcal{E}, \langle o_{\mathcal{E}}, t_{\mathcal{E}} \rangle)$. The functions $o_{\mathcal{E}} : \mathcal{E} \to k$ and $t_{\mathcal{E}} : \mathcal{E} \to \mathcal{E}^A$ are defined by induction on the structure of expressions, using the automaton structure of $k\langle\langle A \rangle\rangle$ for the symbols $\underline{\sigma}$, and following the structure of the differential equations in Theorem 2 for the operators: $o_{\mathcal{E}}(\underline{\sigma}) = \sigma(\varepsilon)$, $o_{\mathcal{E}}(E + F) = o_{\mathcal{E}}(E) + o_{\mathcal{E}}(F)$, $o_{\mathcal{E}}(EF) = o_{\mathcal{E}}(E \parallel F) = o_{\mathcal{E}}(E)o_{\mathcal{E}}(F)$, $o_{\mathcal{E}}(E^*) = 1$, $o_{\mathcal{E}}(E^{-1}) = o_{\mathcal{E}}(E)^{-1}$. (The latter expression should be interpreted as 0 if the inverse in k does not exist.) Writing E_a for $t_{\mathcal{E}}(E)(a)$, the function $t_{\mathcal{E}} : \mathcal{E} \to \mathcal{E}^A$ is given by the following clauses: $(\underline{\sigma})_a = \underline{\sigma_a}$, $(E + F)_a = E_a + F_a$, $(EF)_a = E_a\,F + o_{\mathcal{E}}(E)F_a$, $(E^*)_a = E_a\,E^*$, $(E \parallel F)_a = (E_a \parallel F) + (E \parallel F_a)$, $(E^{-1})_a = -o_{\mathcal{E}}(E)^{-1}E_a\,E^*$. (Read $\underline{0}$ for the last expression whenever $-o_{\mathcal{E}}(E)^{-1}$

is undefined.) Because $\mathcal{E}$ now has been turned into an automaton $(\mathcal{E}, \langle o_\mathcal{E}, t_\mathcal{E} \rangle)$, and because $k\langle\langle A \rangle\rangle$ is a final automaton, there exists, by Theorem 1, a unique homomorphism $l : \mathcal{E} \to k\langle\langle A \rangle\rangle$, which assigns to each expression E the formal power series $l(E)$ it represents. It can be used to define the operators on $k\langle\langle A \rangle\rangle$ that we are looking for: $\sigma + \tau = l(\underline{\sigma} + \underline{\tau})$, $\sigma\tau = l(\underline{\sigma}\,\underline{\tau})$, $\sigma^* = l(\underline{\sigma}^*)$, $\sigma \parallel \tau = l(\underline{\sigma} \parallel \underline{\tau})$, $\sigma^{-1} = l(\underline{\sigma}^{-1})$. (Note that the symbols for the operators on $k\langle\langle A \rangle\rangle$ are the same as the syntactic operators. The type will always be clear from the context.) One can show that $l(\underline{\sigma}) = \sigma$ and that l is compositional, e.g., $l(EF) = l(E)l(F)$, using the principle of coinduction (Theorem 1) and the fact that bisimilarity on $\mathcal{E}$ is a congruence relation (e.g., if $E \sim E'$ and $F \sim F'$ then $EF \sim E'F'$). For instance, the first statement follows by coinduction from the fact that $\{\langle l(\underline{\sigma}), \sigma \rangle \mid \sigma \in k\langle\langle A \rangle\rangle\}$ is a bisimulation relation on $k\langle\langle A \rangle\rangle$. One can now readily prove that the operators we have defined are solutions of their defining differential equations, using the fact that l is a compositional homomorphism. Uniqueness of these solutions follows from the uniqueness of l. $\quad\square$

Either by coinduction or, alternatively, using the uniqueness part of Theorem 2, one can prove that the above coinductive definitions of the operators on $k\langle\langle A \rangle\rangle$ coincide with the usual ones. For instance, $(\sigma^*)(w) = \sum_{n\geq 0} \sigma^n(w)$, if $\sigma(\varepsilon) = 0$.

Given the correspondence between derivative and input derivative, mentioned at the end of Section 2, one can easily show that the Taylor series of the *product* of analytic functions equals the *shuffle* product of their corresponding Taylor series: $l(fg) = l(f) \parallel l(g)$, where $(fg)(x) = f(x)g(x)$, as usual. (A proof by coinduction is easy, using the fact that $(fg)' = f'g + fg'$, which is of the same shape as the defining differential equation for $\parallel$.) This fact will be used in the definition of the shuffle inverse in Section 5. The correspondence between derivative and input derivative also shows that many classical differential equations, such as the example of *exp* mentioned at the beginning of this section, have a unique corresponding behavioural differential equation. For *exp*, this is the equation $(e)_X = e$ (with initial condition $e(\varepsilon) = 1$), which determines a unique series $e = (1, 1, 1, \ldots)$ in $\mathbb{R}\langle\langle X \rangle\rangle$, that is, the Taylor series of *exp*.

4 Proofs by coinduction

The use of coinduction is illustrated by proving some of the following familiar laws:

(1) $1 + \sigma\sigma^* = \sigma^*$, if $\sigma(\varepsilon) = 0$	(6) $\sigma = \sigma(\varepsilon) + \sum_{a \in A} a\sigma_a$
(2) $\sigma = \tau\sigma + \rho \Rightarrow \sigma = \tau^*\rho$, if $\tau(\varepsilon) = 0$	(7) $\sigma \parallel (\tau + \rho) = (\sigma \parallel \tau) + (\sigma \parallel \rho)$
(3) $(\sigma + \tau)^* = \sigma^*(\tau\sigma^*)^*$, if $\tau(\varepsilon) = 0$	(8) $\sigma \parallel (\tau \parallel \rho) = (\sigma \parallel \tau) \parallel \rho$
(4) $(\sigma + \tau)^* = (\sigma^*\tau)^*\sigma^*$, if $\tau(\varepsilon) = 0$	(9) $\sigma\sigma^{-1} = 1$
(5) $\sigma^* = (1 + \sigma)^*$	(10) $\sigma^{-1}\sigma = 1$

Coinductive proofs of equalities such as $\sigma_0 = \tau_0$ always proceed in the same way, by defining, in stages, a bisimulation relation R containing $\langle \sigma_0, \tau_0 \rangle$. The first pair to be included in R is $\langle \sigma_0, \tau_0 \rangle$. Next the following step is repeated until it does not yield any new pairs: the a-derivatives of the pairs $\langle \sigma, \tau \rangle$ already in

R are computed—for the operators, these are precisely given by the defining differential equations—and the resulting pairs $\langle \sigma_a, \tau_a \rangle$ are added to R. When adding a pair $\langle \sigma, \tau \rangle$ to R, at any stage of its construction, we should check that the constant parts are equal: $\sigma(\varepsilon) = \tau(\varepsilon)$. If this does not hold, the procedure aborts, and we conclude $\sigma \neq \tau$. Otherwise, the relation R that is thus obtained is by construction a bisimulation, and $\sigma_0 = \tau_0$ follows by coinduction. For instance, (1) follows by coinduction from the fact that

$$R_1 = \{ \langle 1 + \sigma\sigma^*, \sigma^* \rangle \mid \sigma \in k\langle\langle A \rangle\rangle, \ \sigma(\varepsilon) = 0 \} \cup \{ \langle \sigma, \sigma \rangle \mid \sigma \in k\langle\langle A \rangle\rangle \}$$

is a bisimulation relation on $k\langle\langle A \rangle\rangle$: if $\sigma(\varepsilon) = 0$ then $(1 + \sigma\sigma^*)(\varepsilon) = 1 = \sigma^*(\varepsilon)$; moreover, $\langle (1 + \sigma\sigma^*)_a, (\sigma^*)_a \rangle = \langle 0 + \sigma_a\sigma^* + 0\sigma_a\sigma^*, \sigma_a\sigma^* \rangle = \langle \sigma_a\sigma^*, \sigma_a\sigma^* \rangle$, which is in R_1 again. Similarly,

$$R_2 = \{ \langle \alpha\sigma + \beta, \alpha\tau^*\rho + \beta \rangle \mid \alpha, \beta \in k\langle\langle A \rangle\rangle \}$$

is a bisimulation relation, for σ, τ, ρ with $\sigma = \tau\sigma + \rho$ and $\tau(\varepsilon) = 0$, implying (2) by coinduction. All the other laws are proved similarly. To mention one last example, let R_8 be the smallest relation on $k\langle\langle A \rangle\rangle$ such that $\langle \sigma \parallel (\tau \parallel \rho), (\sigma \parallel \tau) \parallel \rho \rangle \in R_8$, for all $\sigma, \tau, \rho \in k\langle\langle A \rangle\rangle$, and such that $\langle \sigma_1, \tau_1 \rangle, \langle \sigma_2, \tau_2 \rangle \in R_8$ implies $\langle \sigma_1 + \sigma_2, \tau_1 + \tau_2 \rangle \in R_8$. It is straightforward to prove that R_8 is a bisimulation (using (7)), whence (8) by coinduction. Note that for none of the proofs above, additional structure had to be introduced. Notably, there is no need of turning $k\langle\langle A \rangle\rangle$ into a topological semiring, which is what is usually done (see, for instance, [BR88, Lm 4.1, p.5]).

5   Shuffle inverse

The correspondence between the product of two functions on the reals and the *shuffle* product of their corresponding Taylor series (mentioned at the end of Section 3), suggests the following definition of an operator that acts as a quotient with respect to the shuffle product. Recalling the familiar quotient law for derivatives: $(f^{-1})' = -f'(1/f^2) = -f'(ff)^{-1}$, consider the following behavioural differential equation: $(\sigma_{-1})_a = -\sigma_a \parallel (\sigma \parallel \sigma)_{-1}$ with initial condition $(\sigma_{-1})(\varepsilon) = \sigma(\varepsilon)^{-1}$. Note that we write σ_{-1} rather than σ^{-1}, since the latter notation is used, in Section 3, for the inverse with respect to multiplication. Further note that k is assumed to be a ring and that the above equation only applies to such σ for which $\sigma(\varepsilon)$ is invertible in k. The above equation has a unique solution, which can be proved along the same lines as Theorem 2. Assuming that k is a ring, the following equalities hold for all $\sigma \in k\langle\langle A \rangle\rangle$ for which $\sigma(\varepsilon)$ is invertible in k, showing that the shuffle inverse behaves as intended: $\sigma \parallel \sigma_{-1} = 1$ and $(\sigma_{-1})_{-1} = \sigma$. This can be readily proved by coinduction. It is not immediately obvious how this operator could be defined without coinduction. For now, we are satisfied with the fact that it has been possible to define it at all. Its use for the theory of power series is to be studied further.

6 Rational series

We recall the notion of rational series, and illustrate the need of nondeterministic automata with multiplicities in k in order to obtain finite representations for them. Let the set $\mathcal{R}$ of *regular expressions* be given by the following syntax: $E ::= x \in k \mid a \in A \mid F + F \mid EF \mid E^*$. Note that, for convenience, we write x and a rather than $\underline{x}$ and $\underline{a}$ and that, under the embedding of k and A in $k\langle\langle A \rangle\rangle$, $\mathcal{R}$ is a subset of the set of expressions $\mathcal{E}$, introduced in (the proof of) Theorem 2. A series σ is called *rational* if there exists a regular expression E with $\sigma = l(E)$, where $l : \mathcal{E} \to k\langle\langle A \rangle\rangle$ is the unique homomorphism of Theorem 2. Because l is compositional, a series is rational iff it is contained in the smallest subset of $k\langle\langle A \rangle\rangle$ that contains k and A (viewed as subsets of $k\langle\langle A \rangle\rangle$) and that is closed under the operators of sum, product, and star. In order to see whether a series σ is rational or not, it is sufficient to look at the subautomaton $\langle \sigma \rangle$ of $k\langle\langle A \rangle\rangle$ that it generates. This subautomaton is generally infinite: for instance, $\langle (xa)^* \rangle = \{x^n(xa)^* \mid n \geq 0\}$. This example is typical in the sense that the generated subautomaton of a rational series is characterized by the property that it is *finitely generated*. We shall not prove this in the present paper, but in Section 8, we shall see another, truly finitary characterization of rational power series (from which this property easily follows). There it will be shown that a rational series is recognized by a finite *nondeterministic* automaton with multiplicities in the semiring k.

7 Nondeterministic automata

In order to give a truly finite representation of rational series, this section introduces (a coalgebraic formulation of) nondeterministic automata and gives a coinductive definition of their behaviour. In Section 8, *finite* nondeterministic automata for rational series will be constructed.

A *k-nondeterministic automaton* (*nd-automaton* for short, also called k-transducer) with inputs in A and outputs in k is a pair $S = (S, \langle o, t \rangle)$ consisting of a set S of *states*, and a pair of functions: an *output function* $o : S \to k$, and a *nondeterministic transition function* $t : S \to k(S)^A$. Here $k(S)^A$ is the set of all functions from A to $k(S)$, which at its turn is defined by

$$k(S) = \{\phi : S \to k \mid supp\,(\phi) \text{ is finite }\}$$

where $supp\,(\phi) = \{s \in S \mid \phi(s) \neq 0\}$ is the *support* of ϕ. The observation function o assigns to each state s in S a multiplicity $o(s)$ in k. The transition function t assigns to a state s in S a function $t(s) : A \to k(S)$, which specifies for any a in A a function $t(s)(a) \in k(S)$. Such a function can be viewed as a kind of nondeterministic or distributed state, and specifies for any state s' in S a multiplicity $t(s)(a)(s')$ in k with which the a-transition from s to s' occurs. We shall sometimes write $s \xrightarrow{a|x} s'$ for $t(s)(a)(s') = x$ and $s \xrightarrow{x}$ for $o(s) = x$.

The *behaviour* of a state in a nd-automaton, which is again a formal power series, is defined coinductively. To this end, we shall first associate with every nondeterministic automaton $\langle o, t \rangle : S \to k \times k(S)^A$ a corresponding *deterministic* automaton. The set of states of the new automaton is given by the set $k(S)$ (of distributed states) mentioned above. Next the set $k(S)$ is turned into a determin-istic automaton $(k(S), \langle \hat{o}, \hat{t} \rangle)$, by defining an observation function $\hat{o} : k(S) \to k$ and a deterministic transition function $\hat{t} : k(S) \to k(S)^A$, as follows:

$$\hat{o}(\phi) = \sum_{s \in S} o(s)\phi(s), \quad \hat{t}(\phi)(a)(s) = \sum_{s' \in S} \phi(s')\,(t(s')(a)(s))$$

Note that both these sums exist because ϕ in $k(S)$ has finite support. The behaviour of a nd-automaton S can now be defined in terms of the, by Theorem 1, unique homomorphism $\lambda : k(S) \to k\langle\langle A \rangle\rangle$, which assigns to each configuration ϕ in $k(S)$ the formal power series $\lambda(\phi)$ it represents. Because of the existence of the obvious inclusion $\{\cdot\} : S \to k(S)$, with $\{s\}(s') = 1$ if $s = s'$, and $= 0$ otherwise, we have obtained a function $\lambda \circ \{\cdot\} : S \to k\langle\langle A \rangle\rangle$, which is the coinductive definition of the behaviour of $(S, \langle o, t \rangle)$ that we were after.

The term 'multiplicity' used above may have many different interpretations, depending on the semiring k. If $k = \mathbb{B}$ then $\mathbb{B}$-nondeterministic automata are precisely the classical nondeterministic automata, with $o : S \to \mathbb{B}$ specifying which states are terminal (accepting), and where for a state $s \in S$ and input letter $a \in A$, $t(s)(a) \in \mathbb{B}(S) \cong \mathcal{P}_f(S)$ gives the (finite) set of possible next states. The construction of a deterministic automaton above amounts in this case exactly to the familiar power set construction.

8   Recognizability

A formal power series $\sigma \in k\langle\langle A \rangle\rangle$ is *recognizable* if there exists a *finite* nd-automaton S and a state $s \in S$ such that $\lambda(\{s\}) = \sigma$ (with λ as defined in Section 7). The pair (S, s) is then called a *finite representation* of σ. In this section, we construct a finite representation for any *rational* series $l(E)$, with E a regular expression, thus giving a new proof of the well-known fact that any rational series is recognizable (cf. [BR88]). The representation is *syntactic* in the sense that its state space consists of (regular) expressions.

To this end, the entire set $\mathcal{R}$ of regular expressions is turned into an (infi-nite) nondeterministic automaton $(\mathcal{R}, \langle o_\mathcal{R}, t_\mathcal{R} \rangle)$, such that the behaviour of E is precisely given by $l(E)$. As we shall see, the subautomaton $\mathcal{R}_E \subseteq \mathcal{R}$ generated by E is finite, giving a finite representation $(\mathcal{R}_E, E)$ of $l(E)$.

The observation function $o_\mathcal{R} : \mathcal{R} \to k$ is defined by $o_\mathcal{R}(E) = o_\mathcal{E}(E)$, where $o_\mathcal{E}$ is the observation function for expressions, defined in Section 3. The nonde-terministic transition function $t_\mathcal{R} : \mathcal{R} \to k(\mathcal{R})^A$ is defined by induction on the structure of regular expressions, following the shape of the behavioural differen-tial equations of Theorem 2. We mention a few typical cases:

$$t_\mathcal{R}(E + F)(a)(G) = t_\mathcal{R}(E)(a)(G) + t_\mathcal{R}(F)(a)(G)$$

$$t_\mathcal{R}(EF)(a)(G) = \begin{cases} t_\mathcal{R}(E)(a)(E') + o_\mathcal{R}(E)\,t_\mathcal{R}(F)(a)(G) & \text{if } G = E'F \\ o_\mathcal{R}(E)\,t_\mathcal{R}(F)(a)(G) & \text{otherwise} \end{cases}$$

Applying now the definitions from Section 7, we can prove by coinduction that $\lambda(\{E\}) = l(E)$, for any regular expression $E \in \mathcal{R}$. Because the subautomaton $\mathcal{R}_E$ of $\mathcal{R}$ generated by E is finite, we have:

Theorem 3. *For a regular expression E in $\mathcal{R}$, $(\mathcal{R}_E, E)$ is a finite representation of $l(E)$ (hence any rational series is recognizable).* $\qquad\square$

Finite representations for the shuffle product and the inverse (with respect to multiplication) of rational expressions can be obtained in a similar fashion, by extending the above approach, leading to nd-automata such as the two state automaton depicted in the introduction.

9 Discussion

We briefly mention some of the work that remains to be done: (1) General formats for behavioural differential equations, ensuring the existence of a unique solution, should be determined. (2) The effectiveness of the coinduction proof principle is to be further investigated, as well as the minimization of finite representations, to which it is closely related (cf. [Rut98]). (3) The example of the shuffle inverse should be further investigated. (4) Many more examples of specifications by behavioural differential equations and the corresponding implementations are to be studied, amongst others involving tropical and idempotent semirings as described in [Gun98]. (5) Applying the universal coalgebraic definition of bisimulation directly to nd-automata (and not only to deterministic automata as we have done here) will yield notions of equivalence that have an interest in their own right. For instance, taking $k = \mathbb{R}$ gives a notion of bisimulation that is (under conditions) probabilistic bisimulation. (6) The use of nd-automata for the representation of Taylor series of analytic functions, such as the trigonometric functions, yields surprising results and deserves further study.

References

[BR88]   J. Berstel and C. Reutenauer. *Rational series and their languages*, volume 12 of *EATCS Monographs on Theoretical Computer Science*. Springer, 1988.

[Brz64]   J.A. Brzozowski. Derivatives of regular expressions. *Journal of the ACM*, 11(4):481–494, 1964.

[Con71]   J.H. Conway. *Regular algebra and finite machines*. Chapman and Hall, 1971.

[Gun98]   J. Gunawardena. *Idempotency*. Pub. of the Newton Institute. CUP, 1998.

[PE98]   D. Pavlović and M. Escardó. Calculus in coinductive form. In LICS'98.

[Rut96]   J.J.M.M. Rutten. Universal coalgebra: a theory of systems. Report CS-R9652, CWI, 1996. To appear in Theoretical Computer Science.

[Rut98]   J.J.M.M. Rutten. Automata and coinduction (an exercise in coalgebra). Report SEN-R9803, CWI, 1998. Also in the proceedings of CONCUR '98, LNCS 1466, 1998, pp. 194-218.

Accessing Multiple Sequences
Through Set Associative Caches

Peter Sanders

Max-Planck-Institut für Informatik,
Im Stadtwald, 66123 Saarbrücken, Germany.
E-mail: sanders@mpi-sb.mpg.de
WWW: http://www.mpi-sb.mpg.de/~sanders

Abstract. The cache hierarchy prevalent in todays high performance processors has to be taken into account in order to design algorithms which perform well in practice. We start from the empirical observation that external memory algorithms often turn out to be good algorithms for cached memory. This is not self evident since caches have a fixed and quite restrictive algorithm choosing the content of the cache. We investigate the impact of this restriction for the frequently occurring case of access to multiple sequences. We show that any access pattern to $k = \Theta(M/B^{1+1/a})$ sequential data streams can be efficiently supported on an a-way set associative cache with capacity M and line size B. The bounds are tight up to lower order terms.

Keywords: Set associative cache, external memory algorithm, memory hierarchy, multi merge.

1 Introduction

The mainstream model of computation used by algorithm designers in the last half century [13] assumes a single processor with unit memory access cost. However, the mainstream computers sitting on our desktops have increasingly deviated from this model in the last decade [7–9, 12, 19]. Even without taking disks and tapes into account the memory hierarchy usually has four levels: registers, first-level cache, second-level cache and main memory. We concentrate on the relation between one cache level and the main memory since registers can only be used in a restricted way and multiple cache levels would complicate the analysis. Alos, in many applications, the traffic between two levels forms the main bottleneck. Including all overheads for cache miss, memory latency and translation from logical over virtual to physical memory addresses, a main memory access can be two orders of magnitude slower than a first-level cache hit while the main memory is three to five orders of magnitude larger. Most machines have separate caches for data and code so that we can disregard instruction reads as long as the programs remain reasonably short. A cache of size M can store M/B *cache lines* of size B (we use the size of the data elements of the underlying application as unit). All accesses to the next lower level of memory are done in units of cache lines. An *a-way set associative cache* consists of $M/(aB)$ *cache sets* each of which can store a cache lines. A cache line starting at memory address xB can only be stored in set number $x \bmod M/(aB)$. Caches usually use the following fixed replacement strategy: On a cache miss, the least recently used (LRU) line in the set of x is replaced by the new line. In order to get fast, compact caches with acceptable power dissipation, a is a small constant between one (*direct mapped cache*) and eight.

Although the technological details are likely to change in the future, physical principles imply that fast memories must be small and are likely to be more expensive than slower memories so that we will have to live with memory hierarchies when talking about sequential algorithms for large inputs.

The general approach of this paper is to model one cache level and the main memory by the single disk single processor variant of the external memory model by Vitter and Shriver [22] where M is the size of the internal memory, B is the block transfer size, i.e., we use the word pairs "cache line" and "memory block", "cache" and "internal memory", "main memory" and "external memory" and "I/O" and "cache fault" as synonyms if the context does not indicate otherwise. We include set associative caches into this model by disallowing explicit access to the internal memory, i.e., the cache replacement strategy decides which external memory references can be satisfied from the internal memory. We call this model *cached memory*.

An almost ubiquitous principle behind efficient external memory algorithms is to read or write $k = \mathcal{O}(M/B)$ sequential streams of data [21]. For example, k-way merge sort is based on reading and radix sort, buffer trees [1] or external memory list ranking [18] are based on writing k sequences. Empirically, many of these algorithms also perform well on cached memory. For example, in a study by LaMarca and Ladner [11], k-way merging performs best among algorithms tried and even Sibeyn's quite involved external memory list ranking algorithm [18] performs better than a simple pointer chasing although the latter executes only a fraction of the instructions. We have designed an external memory priority queue based on k-way merging which performs $\mathcal{O}((I/B) \log_{M/B} I/M)$ I/Os for any sequence of operations with I insertions [17]. This algorithm is similar to previous algorithms with the same asymptotic performance [1, 3, 5, 4] yet performs at least a factor of three fewer I/Os. Running in the cache hierarchy of a workstation the algorithm is several times faster than an optimized binary heap implementation which is empirically the best algorithm for small queues [17]. Similarly, an external memory version of a simple parallel algorithm for generating random permutations turns out to be several times faster on a cached memory than the conventional sequential algorithm which executes only half as many instructions [16]. This algorithm is based on writing k sequences to memory.

Unfortunately, most of these algorithms can fail miserably on set associative caches because an adversary can schedule the accesses in such a way that all recent accesses use the same cache set. In Section 2 we show that it is sufficient to randomize the starting addresses of the data streams and to reduce k by a factor $\mathcal{O}(B^{1/a})$ in order to ensure that the expected number of cache misses after N accesses is only a small fraction larger than the N/B first reference misses which have to occur when streaming through N elements. We give upper and lower bounds on the expected number of cache faults which are tight up to lower order terms for the range of inputs which allow efficient operations.

Related Work

Caches are intensively studied in computer architecture and compiler design (e.g. [7]). Evaluations are usually based on simulations. This yields useful quantitative results if traces of meaningful benchmarks are simulated. Simulations also have the advantage that interactions between many complicated features for mitigating cache faults like victim caches, write buffers or out-of-order execution can be modeled. However, each simulation only yields results for one particular combination of architecture, algorithm, implementation, compiler and input. This is undesirable for algorithm designers who would like to estimate the performance of a family of algorithms for many systems and all possible inputs before starting to implement. Simulations are unacceptable for theoreticians who would like to quantify the relative power of different machine models. Furthermore, the external memory algorithms we have in mind, produce so many irregular memory references and data dependencies that the additional architectural optimizations mentioned above cannot completely hide the general structure of the cache defined by the parameters M, B and a.

Simple analytical cache models have long been known [15, 10]. However, in these *independent reference models* the cache lines are assumed to be accessed in random order according to some fixed probability distribution. This assumption is not warranted for accessing sequences and we will see that it can lead to wrong predictions about the impact of the associativity a.

Fricker and Robert [6] have proposed a model for accessing sequences. However, it is limited to one particular access schedule while we allow an adversary to schedule the accesses. Furthermore, their model can only be evaluated numerically for a particular set of parameters and needs at least quadratic time in the number of memory accesses whereas our analysis yields closed form formulas.

On the application side, cache optimizations play an important role in high performance numerical computations but the data access patterns occurring there are often quite regular or at least predictable. Therefore, the basic techniques used in numerical computations are of little help in optimizing irregular and unpredictable access patterns.

External memory algorithms are a well established branch of algorithmics [21, 20]. Our approach to randomize the starting addresses of sequences is similar to the approach used by Barve et al. [2] in order to efficiently use parallel disks for k-way merging. However, we do not want to bound the maximum contention but the fraction of overloaded cache sets. Furthermore, for k-way merging, a clever prefetching algorithm is available whereas we have to live with a fixed replacement strategy. Correspondingly, the analysis techniques are different.

Overview

After defining the problem in Section 2 we derive an upper bound on the number of cache misses due to sequence accesses in Section 3. In Section 4 this bound is refined to take interferences between sequence data and work areas with arbitrary access patterns into account. Section 5 complements this with a lower bound. Finally, Section 5 summarizes the results and compares the bounds numerically for a particular example.

2   Multiple Data Streams

Consider k sequences stored in arrays. These elements are read (or written) sequentially. An adversary is allowed to schedule the accesses to these sequences, i.e, it is allowed to choose N and $s_1, \ldots, s_N \in \{1, \ldots, k\}$ in the following code:

for $t := 1$ **to** N **do**
    work on the current element of sequence s_t
    advance sequence s_t to the next element

The analysis is done for starting addresses x_j of the arrays with the property that the values $x_j \bmod M$ are uniformly distributed independent random variables. If the actual code does not use randomization, the analysis will yield average case bounds. The code can also actively randomize the starting addresses. For example, when allocating memory for a sequence of length l, the algorithm can choose a random offset $0 \leq X < M$, allocate a memory block of length $l + X$ and put the sequence at the end of this block. Note that in a system with virtual memory, this wastes only one page of physical memory since the beginning of the block is never accessed. If the lengths of all sequences are known in advance (e.g., for k-way merge sort), it should be possible to waste even less memory since we additionally have the choice in which order to allocate the sequences. This may be important for large k and large second level caches in order to avoid running out of virtual address space.

3   An Upper Bound

We start with the simplifying assumption that all memory accesses are sequence accesses. In Section 4, we will see that this is often a good approximation.

Theorem 1. *Given an a-way set associative cache with capacity M and cache line size $B < M/a$. Any schedule of N sequential accesses to $k < M\alpha(a)/B$ sequences with randomized starting address[1] causes at most*

$$\mathbf{E}[X_a] \leq N \left(\frac{1}{B} + \left(\frac{kB}{M\alpha(a)} \right)^a + \mathcal{O}\left(\frac{k}{M\alpha(a) - kB} \right) \right) + k \tag{1}$$

cache misses, where $\alpha(a) = \sqrt[a]{a!}/a$.

---

[1] Closer inspection of the proof shows that it is sufficient if the starting addresses are $(a + 1)$-wise independent.

We analyze the different types of cache misses seperately. Whenever a cache line is accessed for the first time we have a *first reference miss* (also called *compulsory miss*).

Lemma 1. *There are at most N/B first reference cache misses.* ∎

Conflict misses arise when more than a cache lines are mapped to the same cache set. We first look at the case that frequent accesses to one sequence fill up multiple entries of a cache set:

Lemma 2. *There are at most $N(k-1)/(M-B+1) \approx Nk/M$ conflict misses with one sequence occupying at least two entries of a cache set.*

Proof. Consider the accesses for a particular sequence b. Let N_b denote the length of sequence b. An access to b can only cause a conflict miss with a sequence b' occupying at least two entries of the accessed cache set, if b' has made at least $M-B+1$ accesses after the last access to b (due to LRU replacement). Since there are at most $N - N_b$ accesses by other sequences overall, sequence b can suffer at most $\lfloor (N - N_b)/(M - B + 1) \rfloor$ of the conflict misses under consideration. Summing over all sequences yields the claimed bound. ∎

The most interesting cache misses are those conflict misses where different sequences access the same cache set.

Lemma 3. *Any schedule of N sequential accesses to k sequences with randomized starting address causes at most*

$$\mathbf{E}[X_a] \leq N\frac{B-1}{B}\left(\left(\frac{(k-1)(B-1)}{M\alpha(a)}\right)^a + \frac{k-1}{M\alpha(a) - (k-1)(B-1)}\right) + k \quad (2)$$

cache misses due to conflicts between different sequences, where $\alpha(a) = \sqrt[a]{a!}/a$.

Proof. Let c_{bj} denote the probability that the cache set addressed by sequence b in its j-th access has been accessed by at least a other sequences since the last access of sequence b. By linearity of expectation the expected number of this type of conflict misses can be bounded by

$$\mathbf{E}[X_a] \leq k + \frac{B-1}{B}\sum_{b}\sum_{j=1}^{N_b} c_{bj}$$

where N_b denotes the total number of accesses to sequence b. The factor $(B-1)/B$ stems from the fact that the first access to each cache line cannot cause a conflict miss since it causes a first reference miss.

Now we focus on a particular sequence (we therefore drop the b indices for now). Let

$$\bar{B} := \{1, \ldots, k\} \setminus \{b\} \ .$$

Let z_{ij} denote the number of accesses made to sequence $i \in \bar{B}$ between the $(j-1)$-th and j-th access by sequence b and let

$$z_j := \sum_{i \in \bar{B}} z_{ij}$$

denote the total number of possibly conflicting accesses. The probability that sequence i uses the same cache set between these two accesses is

$$p_{ij} = \min\left(1, (z_{ij} + B - 1)\frac{a}{M}\right)$$

if $z_{ij} > 0$ and 0 otherwise. We have

$$c_{bj} \leq \min\left(1, \sum_{I \subseteq \bar{B}, |I|=a} \prod_{i \in I} p_{ij}\right)$$

since the sequences are shifted independently. We now relax the integrality requirement on z_{ij} and also ignore that p_{ij} is truncated to zero for $z_{ij} = 0$ and solve a constrained maximization problem for the function $\sum_j p_j$ where

$$p_j := \min\left(1, \sum_{I \subseteq \bar{B}, |I|=a} \prod_{i \in I} \frac{a}{M}(z_{ij} + B - 1)\right) .$$

First, observe that for fixed z_j, p_j is maximized by choosing all coefficients identical, i.e.,

$$p_j \leq \min\left(1, \binom{k-1}{a}\left(\left(\frac{z_j}{k-1} + B - 1\right)\frac{a}{M}\right)^a\right) .$$

A global maximum for this bound is achieved by setting as many of the z_j as possible to a value just large enough to achieve an estimate $p_j = 1$. Since $\binom{k-1}{a} \leq \frac{(k-1)^a}{a!}$ we get

$$p_j \leq \frac{(k-1)^a}{a!}\left(\frac{\frac{z_j}{k-1} + B - 1}{M}\right)^a = \left(\frac{z_j + (k-1)(B-1)}{M\alpha(a)}\right)^a$$

so $z_j \geq M\alpha(a) - (k-1)(B-1)$ is needed for estimating $p_j = 1$. There are at most $(N - N_b)/(M\alpha(a) - (k-1)(B-1))$ of these terms each contributing 1 to $\sum_j c_{bj}$. The remaining z_j have to be set to 0 now so that we get a contribution of at most

$$N_b\binom{k-1}{a}\left(\frac{(B-1)a}{M}\right)^a \leq N_b\left(\frac{(k-1)(B-1)}{M\alpha(a)}\right)^a$$

for these small terms of $\sum_j p_j$.[2] Summing over all sequences b we get

$$\sum_{b=1}^{k}\sum_{j=1}^{N_b} c_{bj} \leq N\left(\frac{k-1}{M\alpha(a) - (k-1)(B-1)} + \left(\frac{(k-1)(B-1)}{M\alpha(a)}\right)^a\right) .$$

∎

Theorem 1 is an immediate consequence of lemmata 1, 2 and 3.

---

[2] Note that this way of estimation is only for technical convenience and gives no hint on actual worst case access schedules: The zero z_j only have a contribution because we ignore the truncation of p_{ij} to zero and the nonzero z_j are counted twice.

4 A Notion of Working Set

Theorem 1 accounts for the most important source of conflict misses. However, in practice our application will have additional frequently accessed data which comes into conflict with the sequence data. In particular, we usually need k sequence pointers and additional data structures of size $\mathcal{O}(k)$ for deciding which sequence is accessed next. We formalize this concept by defining a *working set* of size w to be data touching w/B cache lines such that no two of them are mapped to the same cache set. In particular, this is the case if the working set consists of w words of contiguous aligned memory.

Lemma 4. *Let Y_a denote the number of conflict misses predicted by lemmata 2 and 3 for an a-way associative cache. With a working set of size $w \leq M/a$, the expected number of conflict misses involving both the working set and the k sequences can be bounded by $2\mathbf{E}[Y_{a-1}]wa/M$.*

Proof. An access to stream b conflicts with the working set with probability wa/M. This can lead to a conflict miss if before the last access of stream b, one sequence has made at least $M - B + 1$ accesses or if $a - 1$ other cache lines have accessed this cache set. The number of these events can be bounded using lemmata 2 and 3 respectively. The factor two is a conservative estimate to account for the cases when working set data is evicted from the cache and has to be reloaded later. ∎

Substituting the previously derived bounds we can conclude that Theorem 1 extends to the case where the working set is taken into account.

Corollary 1. *Given an a-way set associative cache with capacity M and cache line size $B < M/a$. For any schedule of N sequential accesses to k sequences with randomized starting address and any number of accesses to a working set of size $\mathcal{O}(k) \leq M/a$, Relation (1) bounds the number of cache faults.*

Only for a working set of size $\Omega(Bk)$, conflict misses involving the working set begin to dominate.

5 A Lower Bound

The bound from Theorem 1 and Corollary 1 on the expected number of cache misses is asymptotically tight. Indeed for the most interesting case of $k = o(M/B)$, when conflict misses are rare, the bound is tight up to lower order terms:

Theorem 2. *There are access schedules to $k < M/(aB)$ sequences such that any strategy to choose the starting addresses of the sequences incurs*

$$\mathbf{E}[X_a] \geq N\left(\frac{1}{B} + \frac{B-1}{B}\left(\frac{(k-a)B}{M\alpha(a)}\right)^a \max\left\{\left(1 - \frac{kaB}{M}\right), \frac{1}{e}\right\}\right) - \mathcal{O}(kM)$$

$$(3)$$

cache faults on the average, where $\alpha(a) = \sqrt[a]{a!}/a$.

Proof. Suppose that the adversary first "randomly forwinds" the sequences, i.e., it accesses the first X_i elements of sequence i where the X_i are random variables choosen uniformly and independently from $\{1, M\}$.

Even disregarding the conflict misses during forwinding, we have

$$\mathbf{E}[X_a] \geq N/B + P_{\text{miss}}(N - kM)(B-1)/B \geq N/B + P_{\text{miss}}N(B-1)/B - kM$$

where N/B is the number of first reference misses and where P_{miss} is the probability of a conflict miss after forwinding when one of the last $B-1$ elements of a cache line are accessed.

After forwinding, the cache sets currently accessed by the sequences are independent and uniformly distributed over the entire possible range regardless which starting addresses have been used. If the adversary subsequently accesses the sequences in a round robin fashion then an access to a sequence implies a cache miss if the $k-1$ previous accesses to the other sequences have accessed the same cache set at least a times. The probability for this event is

$$P_{\text{miss}} := \sum_{i \geq a} \binom{k-1}{i} \left(\frac{aB}{M}\right)^i \left(1 - \frac{aB}{M}\right)^{k-i-1} \tag{4}$$

For the purpose of numerical evaluation this is already all we need since the above tail of a binomial distribution can be efficiently evaluated using a continued fraction development of the incomplete beta function [14, Section 6.4]. For an easy to interpret closed form formula it suffices to work with the first summand:

$$P_{\text{miss}} > \binom{k-1}{a} \left(\frac{aB}{M}\right)^a \left(1 - \frac{aB}{M}\right)^{k-a-1}$$

$$> \frac{(k-a)^a}{a!} \left(\frac{aB}{M}\right)^a \left(1 - \frac{aB}{M}\right)^k \quad = \left(\frac{(k-a)B}{M\alpha(a)}\right)^a \left(1 - \frac{aB}{M}\right)^k$$

$$\geq \left(\frac{(k-a)B}{M\alpha(a)}\right)^a \max\left\{\left(1 - \frac{kaB}{M}\right), \frac{1}{e}\right\}$$

The latter estimation uses the relations $(1 - aB/M)^k \geq 1/e$ for $k < M/(aB)$ and $(1 - aB/M)^k \geq (1 - kaB/M)$. ∎

6   Discussion

If we set the number of sequences k to $cM/B^{1+1/a}$ for some constant c, we can see from Theorem 1 and Corollary 1 that the probability of a conflict miss is $c^a a^a/(Ba!)$+"lower order terms", i.e., it is of the same order as the fraction of first reference misses. For larger k we get a considerable performance degradation.

Perhaps the most interesting qualitative conclusion is that for large cache lines, the associativity can have a remarkably high impact on cache efficiency. This stands in contrast to the results one would get by blindly applying the independent refenrence model, namely that associativity is of little help. The independent reference model must fail because k long sequences access all cache lines about equally frequently but nevertheless exhibit significant locality if k is not too large.

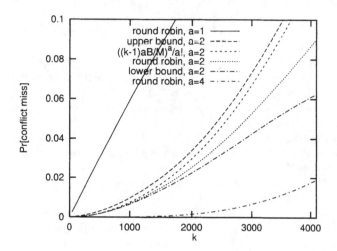

Fig. 1. Conflict miss probabilities for $B = 64$, $M = 2^{20}$. Exact values are computed for the difficult random round robin schedule from Section 5. For $a = 2$ the worst case upper bound from Theorem 1, a simple approximation and the simple lower bound from Corollary 1 are also shown.

We can also draw quantitative conclusions, since for $k = \mathcal{O}(M/B^{1+1/a})$ the derived bounds are tight up to lower order terms. At least for large B this also works out in practice. For example, consider the conflict miss probabilities shown in Fig. 1. The parameters used there represent a possible configuration of the 2-way associative second level cache of the MIPS R10000 processor [12]. Namely, 4 Mbytes divided into cache lines of 256 bytes each. We assume a unit of 4 bytes so that $M = 2^{20}$ and $B = 64$. In this situation, a conflict miss probability of $1/B \approx 1.5\%$ should not be exceeded to match the number of first reference misses. For the range k around 1000 fulfilling this condition, both upper and lower bounds are quite accurate. Even for larger k they clearly separate the behavior of the 2-way associative cache from direct mapped and 4-way associative alternatives. While a direct mapped cache can only support a few hundred sequences efficiently, a 4-way associative version still works quite well for $k = 4000$. Still, a fully associative cache could support 2^{14} sequences without conflict misses.

References

1. L. Arge. The buffer tree: A new technique for optimal I/O-algorithms. In *4th Workshop on Algorithms and Data Structures*, number 955 in LNCS, pages 334–345. Springer, 1995.

2. R. D. Barve, E. F. Grove, and J. S. Vitter. Simple randomized mergesort on parallel disks. *Parallel Computing*, 23(4):601–631, 1997.

3. Gerth Stølting Brodal and Jyrki Katajainen. Worst-case efficient external-memory priority queues. In *6th Scandinavian Workshop on Algorithm Theory*, number 1432 in LNCS, pages 107–118. Springer Verlag, Berlin, 1998.

4. A. Crauser, P. Ferragina, and U. Meyer. Efficient priority queues in external memory. working paper, October 1997.

5. R. Fadel, K. V. Jakobsen, J. Katajainen, and J. Teuhola. External heaps combined with effective buffering. In *4th Australasian Theory Symposium*, volume 19-2 of *Australian Computer Science Communications*, pages 72–78. Springer, 1997.

6. C. Fricker and P. Robert. An analytical cache model. Technical Report 1496, INRIA, Le Chesnay, 1991.

7. J. L. Hennessy and D. A. Patterson. *Computer Architecture a Quantitative Approach*. Morgan Kaufmann, 1996.

8. Intel Corporation, P.O. Box 5937, Denver, CO, 80217-9808, http://www.intel.com. *Intel Archtecture Software Developer's Manual. Volume I: Basic Architecture*, 1997. Ordering Number 243190.

9. J. Keller. The 21264: A superscalar alpha processor with out-of-order execution. In *Microprocessor Forum*, October 1996.

10. A. LaMarca and R. E. Ladner. The influence of caches on the performance of heaps. *ACM Journal of Experimental Algorithmics*, 1(4), 1996.

11. A. LaMarca and R. E. Ladner. The influence of caches on the performance of sorting. In *8th ACM-SIAM Symposium on Discrete Algorithm*, pages 370–379, 1997.

12. MIPS Technologies, Inc. *R10000 Microprocessor User's Manual*, 2.0 edition, 1998. http://www.mips.com.

13. J. von Neumann. First draft of a report on the EDVAC. Technical report, University of Pennsylvania, 1945.

14. W. H. Press, S.A. Teukolsky, W. T. Vetterling, and B. P. Flannery. *Numerical Recipes in C*. Cambridge University Press, 2nd edition, 1992.

15. G. Rao. Performance analysis of cache memories. *Journal of the ACM*, 25(3):378–395, 1978.

16. P. Sanders. Random permutations on distributed, external and hierarchical memory. *Information Processing Letters*, 67(6):305–310, 1998.

17. Peter Sanders. Fast priority queues for cached memory. In *ALENEX '99, Workshop on Algorithm Engineering and Experimentation*, LNCS. Springer, 1999.

18. J. Sibeyn. From parallel to external list ranking. Technical Report MPI-I-97-1-021, Max-Planck Institut für Informatik, 1997.

19. Sun Microsystems. *UltraSPARC-IIi User's Manual*, 1997.

20. D. E. Vengroff. *TPIE User Manual and Reference*, 1995. http://www.cs.duke.edu/~dev/tpie_home_page.html.

21. J. S. Vitter. External memory algorithms. In *6th European Symposium on Algorithms*, number 1461 in LNCS, pages 1–25. Springer, 1998.

22. J. S. Vitter and E. A. M. Shriver. Algorithms for parallel memory I: Two level memories. *Algorithmica*, 12(2–3):110–147, 1994.

T(A) = T(B)?

Géraud Sénizergues

LaBRI et Université de Bordeaux I, 351, Cours de la Libération 33405 Talence, France [**]

Abstract. The equivalence problem for deterministic pushdown transducers with inputs in a free monoid X^* and outputs in a linear group $H = \mathrm{GL}_n(\mathbb{Q})$, is shown to be *decidable*.

Keywords: deterministic pushdown transducers; rational series; finite dimensional vector spaces; matrix semi-groups; test-sets; complete formal systems.

1 Introduction

We show here that, given two deterministic pushdown *transducers* (dpdt's for short) A, B from a free monoid X^* into a *linear group* $H = \mathrm{GL}_n(\mathbb{Q})$, one can decide whether $\mathrm{S}(A) = \mathrm{S}(B)$ or not (i.e. whether A, B compute the same function $f : X^* \to H$).

This main result generalizes the decidability of the equivalence problem for deterministic pushdown *automata* ([Sén97],[Sén98b]). It immediately implies that the same problem is decidable for any group (or monoid) H, as soon as H is embeddable in a linear group $\mathrm{GL}_n(\mathbb{Q})$. Hence we obtain as a corollary the decidability of the equivalence problem for dpdt's A, B from a free monoid X^* into a *free group* $H = \mathrm{F}(Y)$, or a *free monoid* $H = Y^*$.

Our main result generalizes several other known results about transducers:

- the case where $H = Y^*$ had been adressed in previous works [IR81,CK86b,TS89] and was known to be decidable in the case where A is a *strict-real-time* dpdt while B is a general dpdt [TS89].

- the case where H is an *abelian* group was known to be decidable by ([Sén98b, section 11], [Sén98a]).

Our solution leans on a combination of the methods developed in ([Sén97], [Sén98b]) for the equivalence problem for dpda's, with the methods developped in ([Gub85], [CK86a]) for Ehrenfeucht's conjecture (about the existence and computability of test-sets).

The full proofs corresponding to this extended abstract can be found in [Sén99]. More general information about equivalence problems for transducers can be found in [Cul90],[Lis96].

[**] email:ges@labri.u-bordeaux.fr
   fax: 05-56-84-66-69
   URL: http://www.labri.u-bordeaux.fr/~ges

2 Preliminaries

2.1 Formal power series

The reader is refered to [BR88] for formal power series. Let us just review some vocabulary. Let $(B, +, \cdot, 0, 1)$ where $B = \{0, 1\}$ denote the semi-ring of "booleans". Let M be some monoid. By $(B\langle\langle\ M\ \rangle\rangle, +, \cdot, \emptyset, 1_M)$ we denote the semi-ring of *boolean series* over M: the set $B\langle\langle\ M\ \rangle\rangle$ is defined as B^M; the sum and product are defined as usual; $B\langle\langle\ M\ \rangle\rangle$ is isomorphic with $(\mathcal{P}(M), \cup, \cdot, \emptyset, \{1_M\})$. The usual ordering $\leq$ on B extends to $B\langle\langle\ M\ \rangle\rangle$ by: $S \leq S'$ iff $\forall w \in M, S_w \leq S'_w$. We focus here on monoids of the form $M = K \times W^*$ (the direct product of the group K by the free monoid W^*) and $M = K * W^*$ (the free product of K by W^*, see [LS77, p.174-178] for more information on free products). Let $M = K * W^*$ and M' be another monoid containing K. A map $\psi : B\langle\langle\ M\ \rangle\rangle \to B\langle\langle\ M'\ \rangle\rangle$ is called a *substitution* iff it is a semi-ring homomorphism which is σ-additive and which induces the identity map on K (i.e. $\forall k \in K, \psi(k) = k$).

2.2 Finite K-automata

K-automata Let $(K, \cdot)$ be some group. We call a finite K-automaton over the finite alphabet W any 7-tuple $\mathcal{M} =< K, W, Q, \delta, k_0, q_0, Q' >$ such that Q is the finite set of states, δ, the set of transitions, is a finite subset of $Q \times W \times K \times Q$, $k_0 \in K$, $q_0 \in Q$ and $Q' \subseteq Q$. The series recognized by $\mathcal{M}$, $S(\mathcal{M})$, is the element of $B\langle\langle\ K * W^*\ \rangle\rangle$ defined by: $S(\mathcal{M}) = k_0 \cdot A \cdot B^* \cdot C$, where $A \in B_{1,Q}\langle\langle\ K * W^*\ \rangle\rangle, B \in B_{Q,Q}\langle\langle\ K * W^*\ \rangle\rangle$, and $C \in B_{Q,1}\langle\langle\ K * W^*\ \rangle\rangle$ are given by: $A_{1,q} = \emptyset(\text{ if } q \neq q_0)$, $A_{1,q_0} = \epsilon$, $B_{q,q'} = \sum_{(q,v,k,q')\in\delta} v \cdot k$, $C_{q,1} = \emptyset \ (\text{ if } q \notin Q'), C_{q,1} = \epsilon \ (\text{ if } q \in Q')$. $\mathcal{M}$ is said W-*deterministic* iff,

$$\forall r \in Q, \forall v \in W, \text{Card}(\{(k, r') \in K \times Q \mid (r, v, k, r') \in \delta\}) \leq 1. \tag{1}$$

2.3 Pushdown H-automata

Let $(H, \cdot)$ be some group. We call a *pushdown H-automaton* over the finite alphabet X any 7-tuple

$$\mathcal{M} =< H, X, Z, Q, \delta, q_0, z_0 >$$

where Z is the finite stack-alphabet, Q is the finite set of states, $q_0 \in Q$ is the initial state, z_0 is the initial stack-symbol and $\delta : QZ \times (X \cup \{\epsilon\}) \to \mathcal{P}_f(H \times QZ^*)$, is the transition mapping. Let $q, q' \in Q, \omega, \omega' \in Z^*, z \in Z, h \in H, w \in X^*$ and $a \in X \cup \{\epsilon\}$; we note $(qz\omega, h, aw) \longmapsto_{\mathcal{M}} (q'\omega'\omega, h \cdot h', w)$ if $(h', q'\omega') \in \delta(qz, a)$. $\longmapsto^*_{\mathcal{M}}$ is the reflexive and transitive closure of $\longmapsto_{\mathcal{M}}$. For every $q\omega, q'\omega' \in QZ^*$ and $h \in H, w \in X^*$, we note $q\omega \xrightarrow{(h,w)}_{\mathcal{M}} q'\omega'$ iff $(q\omega, 1_H, w) \longmapsto^*_{\mathcal{M}} (q'\omega', h, \epsilon)$. $\mathcal{M}$ is said *deterministic* iff it fulfills the following disjunction:

$$\text{either Card}(\delta(qz, \epsilon)) = 1 \text{ and for every } x \in X, \text{Card}(\delta(qz, x)) = 0, \tag{2}$$

$$\text{or } \mathrm{Card}(\delta(qz, \epsilon)) = 0 \text{ and for every } x \in X, \mathrm{Card}(\delta(qz, x)) \leq 1. \qquad (3)$$

We call *mode* every element of $QZ \cup \{\epsilon\}$. For every $q \in Q, z \in Z$, qz is said ϵ-*bound* (respectively ϵ-*free*) iff condition (2) (resp. condition (3)) in the above definition of deterministic H-automata is realized. The mode ϵ is said ϵ-free. A H-dpda $\mathcal{M}$ is said *normalized* iff, for every $qz \in QZ, x \in X$:

$$q'\omega' \in \delta_2(qz, x) \Rightarrow |\omega'| \leq 2, \text{ and } q'\omega' \in \delta_2(qz, \epsilon) \Rightarrow |\omega'| = 0, \qquad (4)$$

where $\delta_2 : QZ \times (X \cup \{\epsilon\}) \to \mathcal{P}_f(QZ^*)$, is the second component of the map δ. Given some deterministic pushdown H-automaton $\mathcal{M}$ and a finite set $F \subseteq QZ^*$ of configurations, the *series* (in $\mathrm{B}\langle\langle\ H \times X^*\ \rangle\rangle$) *recognized by $\mathcal{M}$ with final configurations F* is defined by

$$S(\mathcal{M}, F) = \sum_{c \in F} \sum_{q_0 z_0 \xrightarrow{(h,w)} \mathcal{M} c} (h, w).$$

For every pair (h, w) having a coefficient 1 in the series $S(\mathcal{M}, F)$, h can be seen as the "output" of the automaton $\mathcal{M}$ on the "input" w. $\mathcal{M}$ can then be named a deterministic pushdown *transducer* from X^* to H.
We suppose that Z contains a special symbol e subject to the property:

$$\forall q \in Q, \delta(qe, \epsilon) = \{(1_H, q)\} \text{ and } \mathrm{im}(\delta_2) \subseteq \mathcal{P}_f(Q(Z - \{e\})^*). \qquad (5)$$

2.4 Monoids acting on semi-rings

Actions of monoids The general notions of right-action and σ-right-action of a monoid over a semi-ring is the same as in [Sén97, §2.3.2].

M acting on $\mathrm{B}\langle\langle\ M\ \rangle\rangle$ (residuals action) We recall the following classical σ-right-action $\bullet$ of the monoid M over the semi-ring $\mathrm{B}\langle\langle\ M\ \rangle\rangle$: for all $S, S' \in \mathrm{B}\langle\langle\ M\ \rangle\rangle, u \in M$

$$S \bullet u = S' \Leftrightarrow \forall w \in M, \ S'_w = S_{u \cdot w}. \qquad (6)$$

(i.e. $S \bullet u$ is the *left-quotient* of S by u , or the *residual* of S by u). For every $S \in \mathrm{B}\langle\langle\ M\ \rangle\rangle$ we denote by $\mathrm{Q}(S)$ the set of residuals of S: $\mathrm{Q}(S) = \{S \bullet u \mid u \in M\}$. Let us denote by $\mathrm{B}_{n,m}\langle\langle\ M\ \rangle\rangle$ the set of matrices of dimension n, m with entries in $\mathrm{B}\langle\langle\ M\ \rangle\rangle$. The right-action $\bullet$ on $\mathrm{B}\langle\langle\ M\ \rangle\rangle$ is extended componentwise to $\mathrm{B}_{n,m}\langle\langle\ M\ \rangle\rangle$: for every $S = (s_{i,j}), u \in M$, the matrix $T = S \bullet u$ is defined by $t_{i,j} = s_{i,j} \bullet u$. The notation $\mathrm{Q}(S) = \{S \bullet u \mid u \in M\}$, is extended to matrices as well. Given $n \geq 1, m \geq 1$, and $S \in \mathrm{B}_{n,m}\langle\langle\ M\ \rangle\rangle$ we denote by $\mathrm{Q}_r(S)$ the set of *row-residuals* of S:

$$\mathrm{Q}_r(S) = \bigcup_{1 \leq i \leq n} \mathrm{Q}(S_{i,*}).$$

The ordering $\leq$ on B is extended componentwise to $\mathrm{B}_{n,m}\langle\langle\ M\ \rangle\rangle$.

$K \times X^*$ **acting on** $\mathsf{B}\langle\!\langle\ K * V^*\ \rangle\!\rangle$ **(automaton action)** Let us fix now a deterministic (normalized) H-dpda $\mathcal{M}$ and a group K containing H.

H-grammar The *variable* alphabet $V_\mathcal{M}$ associated with $\mathcal{M}$ is defined as: $V_\mathcal{M} = \{[p, z, q] \mid p, q \in Q, z \in Z\}$. The context-free H-grammar associated with $\mathcal{M}$ is then $G_\mathcal{M} = < H, X, V_\mathcal{M}, P_\mathcal{M} >$ where $P_\mathcal{M} \subseteq V_\mathcal{M} \times (H * (X \cup V_\mathcal{M})^*)$ is the set of all the pairs of one of the following forms:

$$([p, z, q], x \cdot h \cdot [p', z_1, p''][p'', z_2, q]) \text{ or } ([p, z, q], x \cdot h \cdot [p', z', q]) \text{ or } ([p, z, q], a \cdot h) \quad (7)$$

where $p, q, p', p'' \in Q, x \in X, a \in X \cup \{\epsilon\}, (h, p'z_1z_2) \in \delta(pz, x), (h, p'z') \in \delta(pz, x), (h, q) \in \delta(pz, a)$.

Action $\otimes$ As long as the automaton $\mathcal{M}$ is fixed, we can safely skip the indexes in $V_\mathcal{M}, P_\mathcal{M}$. We define a σ-right-action $\otimes$ of the monoid $K \times (X \cup \{e\})^*$ over the semi-ring $\mathsf{B}\langle\!\langle\ K * V^*\ \rangle\!\rangle$ by: for every $p, q \in Q, z \in Z, x \in X, h \in H, k \in K$:

$$[p, z, q] \otimes x = \sum_{([p,z,q],m)\in P} m \bullet (1_H, x), \quad (8)$$

$$[p, z, q] \otimes e = h \text{ iff } ([p, z, q], h) \in P, \quad (9)$$

$$[p, z, q] \otimes e = \emptyset \text{ iff } (\{[p, z, q]\} \times H) \cap P = \emptyset, \quad (10)$$

$$k \otimes x = \emptyset, \quad k \otimes e = \emptyset. \quad (11)$$

The action is extended by: for every $k \in K, \beta \in K * V^*, y \in X \cup \{e\}, S \in \mathsf{B}\langle\!\langle\ K * V^*\ \rangle\!\rangle, k \in K$,

$$(k \cdot [p, z, q] \cdot \beta) \otimes y = k \cdot ([p, z, q] \otimes y) \cdot \beta, \quad S \otimes k = k^{-1} \cdot S. \quad (12)$$

Action $\odot$ We define the map $\rho_\epsilon : \mathsf{B}\langle\!\langle\ K * V^*\ \rangle\!\rangle \rightarrow \mathsf{B}\langle\!\langle\ K * V^*\ \rangle\!\rangle$ as the unique σ-additive map such that,

$$\rho_\epsilon(\emptyset) = \emptyset, \quad \rho_\epsilon(\epsilon) = \epsilon,$$

for every $k \in K, S \in \mathsf{B}\langle\!\langle\ K * V^*\ \rangle\!\rangle$,

$$\rho_\epsilon(k \cdot S) = k \cdot \rho_\epsilon(S),$$

and for every $p \in Q, z \in Z, q \in Q, \beta \in K * V^*$,

$$\rho_\epsilon([p, z, q] \cdot \beta) = \rho_\epsilon(([p, z, q] \otimes e) \cdot \beta) \text{ if } pz \text{ is } \epsilon - \text{bound and,}$$

$$\rho_\epsilon([p, z, q] \cdot \beta) = [p, z, q] \cdot \beta \text{ if } pz \text{ is } \epsilon - \text{free.}$$

We call ρ_ϵ the ϵ-reduction map. We then define $\odot$ as the unique right-action of the monoid $K \times X^*$ over the semi-ring $\mathsf{B}\langle\!\langle\ K * V^*\ \rangle\!\rangle$ such that: for every $S \in \mathsf{B}\langle\!\langle\ K * V^*\ \rangle\!\rangle, k \in K, x \in X$,

$$S \odot (k, x) = \rho_\epsilon(\rho_\epsilon(S) \otimes (k, x)).$$

Let us consider the unique substitution $\varphi : \mathsf{B}\langle\langle\ K * V^*\ \rangle\rangle \rightarrow \mathsf{B}\langle\langle\ K \times X^*\ \rangle\rangle$ fulfilling: for every $v \in V$,

$$\varphi(v) = \sum_{\substack{k \in K, u \in X^* \\ v \odot (k,u) = \epsilon}} (k, u)$$

(in other words, φ maps every subset $L \subseteq K * V^*$ on the set generated by the grammar G from the set of axioms L).

Lemma 21 *For every* $S \in \mathsf{B}\langle\langle\ K * V^*\ \rangle\rangle, k \in K, u \in X^*$,

1. $\varphi(\rho_\epsilon(S)) = \varphi(S)$
2. $\varphi(S \odot (k,u)) = \varphi(S) \bullet (k,u)$, *i.e.* φ *is a morphism of right-actions.*

We denote by $\equiv$ the kernel of φ i.e.: for every $S, T \in \mathsf{B}\langle\langle\ K * V^*\ \rangle\rangle$,

$$S \equiv T \Leftrightarrow \varphi(S) = \varphi(T).$$

3 Effective test-sets for morphic sets

3.1 Morphic sets

Let $(M, \cdot, 1_M)$ be a monoid.

Definition 31 *A subset* $L \subseteq M$ *is said morphic iff there exists an element* $u \in M$, *a finite sequence* $\psi_1, \psi_2, \ldots, \psi_m (m \geq 1)$ *of homomorphisms* $\psi_i : M \rightarrow M$ *and a rational subset* $\mathcal{R}$ *of* $\{\psi_1, \psi_2, \ldots, \psi_m\}^*$ *such that:*

$$L = \{\psi(u) \mid \psi \in \mathcal{R}\}.$$

Remark 32 *In the particular case where* M *is a finitely generated free monoid* X^*, *and* $\mathcal{R} = \{\psi_1, \psi_2, \ldots, \psi_m\}^*$ *the notion of "morphic subset" coincides with the classical notion of "DT0L language" ([RS80]).*

3.2 Test-sets

Definition 33 *Let* $(M, \cdot, 1_M), (N, \cdot, 1_N)$ *be two monoids and* $L \subseteq M$. *A subset* $F \subseteq L$ *is called a test-set for* L *with respect to* N *iff,* F *is finite and, for every pair of homorphisms* $\eta, \eta' : M \rightarrow N$, *if* η *agrees with* η' *on* F, *then it also agrees on* L:

$$[\forall x \in F, \eta(x) = \eta'(x)] \Rightarrow [\forall x \in L, \eta(x) = \eta'(x)].$$

Theorem 34 *Let* $(M, \cdot, 1_M)$ *be a finitely generated monoid,* L *be a morphic subset of* M, n *a non-negative integer and* $H = \mathrm{M}_{n,n}(\mathbb{Q})$ *(the monoid of square* n *by* n *matrices with entries in* $\mathbb{Q}$). *Then* L *admits a test-set* F *with respect to* H *and such a test-set can be computed from any* $(m+2)$-*tuple* $u, \psi_1, \ldots, \psi_m, \mathcal{R}$ *defining* L.

We use here the arguments of [CK86a, p.79], combined with the main idea of [Gub85] for establishing the *existence* of a test-set. We then use the algorithm of [Buc85, p.11-13] to *construct* such a test-set.

4 Series and matrices

4.1 Deterministic series and matrices

Let us fix a group $(K, \cdot)$ and a structured alphabet $(W, \smile)$.(We recall it just means that $\smile$ is an equivalence relation over the set W).

Definition 41 Let $n, m \in \mathbb{N}, S, T \in B_{n,m}\langle\langle\ K * W^* \ \rangle\rangle$. S, T are said proportional and we note $S \approx T$, if and only if, there exists $k \in K$ such that $S = k \cdot T$.

Definition 42 Let $m \in \mathbb{N}, S \in B_{1,m}\langle\langle\ K * W^* \ \rangle\rangle : S = (S_1, \cdots, S_m)$. S is said left-deterministic iff either
(1) $\forall i \in [1, m], S_i = \emptyset$ or
(2) $\exists i_0 \in [1, m], S_{i_0} \approx \epsilon$ and $\forall i \neq i_0, S_i = \emptyset$ or
(3) $\exists i_0 \in [1, m], S_{i_0} \not\approx \emptyset$ and $S_{i_0} \not\approx \epsilon$ and $\forall i, j \in [1, m], \forall k \in K, A \in W, \beta, \gamma \in K * W^*, [k \cdot A \cdot \beta \leq S_i, \gamma \leq S_j] \Rightarrow \exists A' \in W, \beta' \in K * W^*, A \smile A'$ and $\gamma = k \cdot A' \cdot \beta'$.

Definition 43 Let $m \geq 1, S \in B_{1,m}\langle\langle\ K * W^* \ \rangle\rangle$. S is said deterministic iff, for every $u \in K * W^*$, $S \bullet u$ is left-deterministic.

Definition 44 Let $S \in B_{n,m}\langle\langle\ K * W^* \ \rangle\rangle$. S is said deterministic iff, for every $i \in [1, n], S_{i,*}$ is a deterministic row-vector.

We denote by $\mathsf{DB}_{n,m}\langle\langle\ K * W^* \ \rangle\rangle$ the subset of deterministic matrices of dimension (n, m) over $\mathsf{B}\langle\langle\ K * W^* \ \rangle\rangle$.

Lemma 45 For every $S \in \mathsf{DB}_{n,m}\langle\langle\ K * W^* \ \rangle\rangle, T \in \mathsf{DB}_{m,s}\langle\langle\ K * W^* \ \rangle\rangle$, $S \cdot T \in \mathsf{DB}_{n,s}\langle\langle\ K * W^* \ \rangle\rangle$.

Let us call a matrix $S \in B_{n,m}\langle\langle\ K * W^* \ \rangle\rangle$ rational iff every component $S_{i,j}$ for $i \in [1, n], j \in [1, m]$ is rational.

Proposition 46 Let $m \geq 1$, $S \in \mathsf{DB}_{1,m}\langle\langle\ K * W^* \ \rangle\rangle$. Then S is rational if and only if $Q(S)/ \approx$ is finite

Norm Proposition 46 suggests the following notion of norm. For every $S \in \mathsf{DB}_{n,m}\langle\langle\ K * W^* \ \rangle\rangle$, the norm of S is defined by:

$$\|S\| = \mathrm{Card}(\mathsf{Q}_r(S)/ \approx) \in \mathbb{N} \cup \{\infty\}.$$

It follows from proposition 46 that a deterministic matrix $S \in \mathsf{DB}_{n,m}\langle\langle\ K * W^* \ \rangle\rangle$ is rational iff it has a finite norm. As well, a special notion of deterministic "finite m-K-automata" can be devised, such that these automata recognize exactly the deterministic rational $(1, m)$-row-vectors (see [Sén99, definition 4.11]).

Lemma 47 Let $S \in \mathsf{DB}_{n,m}\langle\langle\ K * W^* \ \rangle\rangle, T \in \mathsf{DB}_{m,s}\langle\langle\ K * W^* \ \rangle\rangle$. Then $\|S \cdot T\| \leq \|S\| + \|T\|$.

4.2 Algebraic properties

Let $(W, \smile)$ be the structured alphabet $(V, \smile)$ associated with the H-dpda $\mathcal{M}$ and let K be a group containing H. The notion of *linear combination* of series is defined as in [Sén97, §3.2.1]. The subsequent notions of *space* of series and *linear independence* of series can be easily adapted to $\mathrm{DRB}\langle\langle K * W^* \rangle\rangle$.(We recall this last notion originated in [Mei89, lemma 11 p.589 [1]]).

5 Deduction systems

5.1 General systems

We use here a notion of *deduction system* which was inspired by [Cou83]. The reader is referred to [Sén97, section 4] for a precise definition of this notion and of the related notion of *strategy*.

5.2 Systems $\mathcal{K}_0, \mathcal{H}_0$

Let $H = \mathrm{GL}_n(\mathbb{Q})$. We define here a particular deduction system $\mathcal{H}_0$ "Taylored for the equivalence problem for H-dpda's" and also an auxiliary more general deduction system $\mathcal{K}_0$.

Given a fixed H-dpda $\mathcal{M}$ over the terminal alphabet X, we consider the variable alphabet V associated to $\mathcal{M}$ (see §2.4), a denumerable alphabet U (we call it the alphabet of *parameters*), the group $K = \mathrm{F}(U) * H$ [2] and the set $\mathrm{DRB}\langle\langle K * V^* \rangle\rangle$ (the set of Deterministic Rational Boolean series over $K * V^*$).

The set of assertions is defined by :

$$\mathcal{A} = \mathbb{N} \times \mathrm{DRB}\langle\langle K * V^* \rangle\rangle \times \mathrm{DRB}\langle\langle K * V^* \rangle\rangle$$

i.e. an assertion is here a *weighted equation* over $\mathrm{DRB}\langle\langle K * V^* \rangle\rangle$. The "cost-function" $J : \mathcal{A} \to \mathbb{N} \cup \{\infty\}$ is defined by :

$$J(n, S, S') = n + 2 \cdot \mathrm{Div}(S, S'),$$

where $\mathrm{Div}(S, S')$, the divergence between S and S', is defined by:
$\mathrm{Div}(S, S') = \inf\{|u|, u \in X^*, \exists k \in K, (k, u) \leq \varphi(S) \Leftrightarrow (k, u)) \nleq \varphi(S')\}$.
(Notice that: $J(n, S, S') = \infty \Longleftrightarrow S \equiv S'$).

---

[1] numbering of the english version
[2] these values of H, K are fixed, up to corollary 63

We define a binary relation $|\!|\!\!-\ \subset \mathcal{P}_f(\mathcal{A}) \times \mathcal{A}$, the *elementary deduction relation*, as the set of all the pairs having one of the following forms:

$(K0)$ $\{(p, S, T)\}$ $|\!|\!\!-\ (p+1, S, T)$

$(K1)$ $\{(p, S, T)\}$ $|\!|\!\!-\ (p, T, S)$

$(K2)$ $\{(p, S, S'), (p, S', S'')\}$ $|\!|\!\!-\ (p, S, S'')$

$(K3)$ $\emptyset$ $|\!|\!\!-\ (0, S, S)$

$(K'3)$ $\emptyset$ $|\!|\!\!-\ (0, S, T)$ for $T \in \{\emptyset, \epsilon\}, S \equiv T$

$(K4)$ $\{(p+1, S \odot x, T \odot x) \mid x \in X\}$ $|\!|\!\!-\ (p, S, T)$
where $(\forall k \in K, S \not\equiv k \wedge T \not\equiv k)$

$(K5)$ $\{(p, S, S')\}$ $|\!|\!\!-\ (p+2, S \odot x, S' \odot x)$
for $x \in X$

$(K6)$ $\{(p, S_1 \cdot T + S_2, T)\}$ $|\!|\!\!-\ (p, S_1^* \cdot S_2, T)$
where $(\forall k \in K, S_1 \not\equiv k)$

$(K7)$ $\{(p, S_1, T_1), (p, S_2, T_2)\}$ $|\!|\!\!-\ (p, S_1 + S_2, T_1 + T_2)$

$(K8)$ $\{(p, S, S')\}$ $|\!|\!\!-\ (p, S \cdot T, S' \cdot T)$

$(K9)$ $\{(p, T, T')\}$ $|\!|\!\!-\ (p, S \cdot T, S \cdot T')$

$(K10)$ $\emptyset$ $|\!|\!\!-\ (0, S, \rho_\epsilon(S))$

$(K11)$ $\emptyset$ $|\!|\!\!-\ (0, S, \rho_e(S))$,

where $p \in \mathbb{N}, S, S', T, T' \in \mathrm{DRB}\langle\!\langle\ K * V^*\ \rangle\!\rangle, (S_1, S_2), (T_1, T_2) \in \mathrm{DRB}_{1,2}\langle\!\langle\ K * V^*\ \rangle\!\rangle$. The map ρ_ϵ involved in rule $(K10)$ was defined in §2.4 and we define the new map ρ_e involved in rule $(K11)$ as the unique substitution $\mathrm{B}\langle\!\langle\ K * V^*\ \rangle\!\rangle \to \mathrm{B}\langle\!\langle\ K * V^*\ \rangle\!\rangle$ such that, for every $p, q \in Q, z \in Z$,

$$\rho_e([p, e, q] = \emptyset(\ \text{if } p \neq q), \quad \rho_e([p, e, q] = \epsilon(\ \text{if } p = q), \quad \rho_e([p, z, q] = [p, z, q](\ \text{if } z \neq e),$$

where e is the "dummy" symbol introduced in (5). ρ_e maps every $S \in \mathrm{DRB}\langle\!\langle\ K * V^*\ \rangle\!\rangle$ into an image $\rho_e(S) \in \mathrm{DRB}\langle\!\langle\ K * V^*\ \rangle\!\rangle$.

Let us define $|\!\!-\ $ by : for every $P \in \mathcal{P}_f(\mathcal{A}), A \in \mathcal{A}$,

$$P |\!\!-\ A \Longleftrightarrow P \ \overset{<*>}{|\!|\!\!-}\ \circ |\!|\!\!-\overset{[1]}{}_{0,3,4,10,11} \circ\ \overset{<*>}{|\!|\!\!-}\ \{A\},$$

where $|\!|\!\!-\ _{0,3,4,10,11}$ is the relation defined by $K0, K3, K'3, K4, K10, K11$ only. We let $\mathcal{K}_0 = <\mathcal{A}, J, |\!\!-\ >$. We define $\mathcal{H}_0$ as the system obtained by replacing K by H in the above definitions.

Lemma 51 : $\mathcal{K}_0, \mathcal{H}_0$ *are deduction systems.*

By $\mathrm{Hom}_H(K, K)$ we denote the set of homomorphisms $\psi : K \to K$ which leave H pointwise invariant. $\mathcal{K}_0$ is "compatible with homomorphisms" in the following sense

Lemma 52 *For every* $P \in \mathcal{P}(\mathcal{A})$ *and every homomorphism* $\psi \in \mathrm{Hom}_H(K, K)$, *if* P *is a* $\mathcal{K}_0$-*proof then* $\psi(P)$ *is a* $\mathcal{K}_0$-*proof too.*

For every integer $t \in \mathbb{N}$, we denote by $\tau_t : \mathcal{A} \to \mathcal{A}$ the translation on the weights: $\forall p \in \mathbb{N}, S, T \in \mathrm{DRB}\langle\!\langle\ K * V^*\ \rangle\!\rangle, \tau_t(p, S, T) = (p+t, S, T)$.

5.3 Regular proofs

Let us use the notation $\text{Par}(S) \subseteq U$ for the set of parameters occuring in a given series S. (The notation is extended to assertions and sets of assertions in a natural way).

Definition 53 (germs) *We call a H-germ any 9-tuple $G = (n, \alpha, \beta, \gamma, (P_i)_{0 \leq i \leq n}, (A_i)_{0 \leq i \leq n}, (B_{i,j})_{0 \leq i \leq n, 0 \leq j \leq \alpha(i)}, (C_{i,k})_{0 \leq i \leq n, 0 \leq k \leq \beta(i)}, (\psi_{i,j})_{0 \leq i \leq n, 0 \leq j \leq \alpha(i)})$ such that*

1. *n is a non-negative integer,*
2. *α, β are two integer mappings: $[0, n] \to \mathbb{N}$,*
3. *γ is a mapping: $\{(i, j) \in \mathbb{N} \times \mathbb{N} \mid 0 \leq i \leq n, 0 \leq j \leq \alpha(n)\} \to [0, n]$,*
4. *every P_i is a finite subset of $\mathcal{A}$,*
5. *$A_i, B_{i,j}, C_{i,k}$ are assertions belonging to P_i ,*
6. *let $U_i = \text{Par}(A_i)$, $U_G = \cup_{0 \leq i \leq n} U_i, K_G = \text{F}(U_G) * H$; $U_0 = \emptyset$ and every assertion of P_i belongs to $\mathbb{N} \times \text{DRB}\langle\!\langle\, K_i * V^* \,\rangle\!\rangle \times \text{DRB}\langle\!\langle\, K_i * V^* \,\rangle\!\rangle$*
7. *every assertion $C_{i,k}$ has the form: $C_{i,k} = (\pi_{i,k}, S_{i,k}, T_{i,k})$ where $S_{i,k} \in K, T_{i,k} \in K$,*
8. *$A_i \notin \{B_{i,j} \mid 0 \leq j \leq \alpha(i)\} \cup \{C_{i,k} \mid 0 \leq k \leq \beta(i)\}$,*
9. *P_i is a proof relative to the set of hypotheses $\{B_{i,j} \mid 0 \leq j \leq \alpha(i)\} \cup \{C_{i,k} \mid 0 \leq k \leq \beta(i)\}$,*
10. *$\psi_{i,j} \in \text{Hom}_H(K_{\gamma(i,j)}, K_i)$ and there exists some non-negative integer $t \in \mathbb{N}$ such that $\tau_t(\psi_{i,j}(A_{\gamma(i,j)})) = B_{i,j}$.*

Definition 54 (rational sets of homomorphisms) *Let G be a H-germ defined as in definition 53. We define rational subsets $(\mathcal{R}_i)_{0 \leq i \leq n}$ of $\text{Hom}_H(K, K)$ by $\mathcal{R}_i = \{\psi_{i_0, j_0} \circ \psi_{i_1, j_1} \cdots \circ \psi_{i_\ell, j_\ell} \mid i_0 = 0, \ell \geq 0, \forall k \in [0, \ell], 0 \leq j_k \leq \alpha(i_k), \forall k \in [0, \ell - 1] i_{k+1} = \gamma(i_k, j_k)$ and $i = \gamma(i_\ell, j_\ell)\}$.*

Definition 55 *Let G be a H-germ. We define the* set *of assertions* associated *with G, as the set: $\text{P}(G) = \bigcup_{\substack{\psi_i \in \mathcal{R}_i \\ 0 \leq i \leq n}} \psi_i(P_i)$.*

Definition 56 (germs of proofs) *Let G be a H-germ. G is called a germ of proof iff, for every $i \in [0, n], k \in [0, \beta(i)], \psi_i \in \mathcal{R}_i, \psi_i(S_{i,k}) = \psi_i(T_{i,k})$.*

Definition 57 (regular proofs) *Let $P \subseteq \mathbb{N} \times \text{DRB}\langle\!\langle\, H * V^* \,\rangle\!\rangle \times \text{DRB}\langle\!\langle\, H * V^* \,\rangle\!\rangle$. P is called a regular proof iff there exists some germ of proof G such that $P = \text{P}(G)$.*

(One can check that, due to lemma 52, "regular proofs" are indeed $\mathcal{H}_0$-proofs).

Theorem 58 *The set of all germs of proof is recursively enumerable.*

The proof of theorem 58 leans essentially on theorem 34 applied on the monoid $M = K_G$ (see point (6) of definition 53).

6 Completeness of $\mathcal{H}_0$

Theorem 61 *Let $A_0 \in \mathbb{N} \times \text{DRB}\langle\langle\ H * V^*\ \rangle\rangle \times \text{DRB}\langle\langle\ H * V^*\ \rangle\rangle$. If A_0 is true (i.e. $J(A_0) = \infty$) then A_0 has some regular $\mathcal{H}_0$-proof.*

Which might be rephrased as: the system $\mathcal{H}_0$ is "regularly"-complete. Let us sketch the main ideas of the proof ([Sén99, section 10]). There exists a constant $D_2 \in \mathbb{N}$ such that $\|\ A_0\ \| \leq D_2$ and

- with the help of §4.2, we can devise a *strategy* $\mathcal{S}$, producing from every assertion A, with $\|\ A\ \| \leq D_2$, a finite $\mathcal{K}_0$-proof P, whose hypotheses still have a norm $\leq D_2$;

- we consider the set $\mathcal{F}(D_2)$ of all assertions $A' = (p', S', T')$ with a norm $\leq D_2$ and where S', T' are *generic* (this notion is close to that of *transducer schema* defined in [CK86a]); this set is finite: $\mathcal{F}(D_2) = \{A_i \mid 1 \leq i \leq n\}$;

- the $(n+1)$-tuple $(P_i)_{0 \leq i \leq n}$ of proofs produced by $\mathcal{S}$ from all the $A_i, 0 \leq i \leq n$, can be extended into a H-germ $G = (n, *, *, *, (P_i)_{0 \leq i \leq n}, (A_i)_{0 \leq i \leq n}, *, *, *)$ and $\mathsf{P}(G)$ is a regular proof of A_0.

Theorem 62 *Let $H = \text{GL}_n(\mathbb{Q})$ for some $n \in \mathbb{N}$. The equivalence problem for deterministic H-pushdown automata is decidable.*

Corollary 63 *Let H be a finitely generated free group or free monoid. The equivalence problem for deterministic H-pushdown automata is decidable.*

Proof: It suffices to notice that $Y^* \hookrightarrow F(Y) \hookrightarrow \text{GL}_2(\mathbb{Q})$ (see [LS77, prop.12.3 p.167]) and to apply theorem 62.

References

[BR88]   J. Berstel and C. Reutenauer. *Rational Series and their Languages.* Springer, 1988.

[Buc85] B. Buchberger. Basic features and development of the critical-pair/completion algorithm. In *Proceedings 1st RTA*, pages 1–45. LNCS 202, 1985.

[CK86a] K. CulikII and J. Karhumäki. The equivalence of finite-valued transducers (on HDT0L languages) is decidable. *Theoretical Computer Science*, pages 71–84, 1986.

[CK86b] K. CulikII and J. Karhumäki. Synchronizable deterministic pushdown automata and the decidability of their equivalence. *Acta Informatica 23*, pages 597–605, 1986.

[Cou83] B. Courcelle. An axiomatic approach to the Korenjac-Hopcroft algorithms. *Math. Systems theory*, pages 191–231, 1983.

[Cul90] K. CulikII. New techniques for proving the decidability of equivalence problems. *Theoretical Computer Science*, pages 29–45, 1990.

[Gub85] V.S. Guba. A solution of Ehrenfeucht's conjecture. *unpublished note*, 1985.

[IR81]   O.H. Ibarra and L. Rosier. On the decidability of equivalence problem for deterministic pushdown transducers. *Information Processing Letters 13*, pages 89–93, 1981.

[Lis96] L.P. Lisovik. Hard sets methods and semilinear reservoir method with applications. In *Proceedings 23rd ICALP*, pages 229–231. Springer, LNCS 1099, 1996.

[LS77]   R.C. Lyndon and P.E. Schupp. *Combinatorial Group Theory*. Springer Verlag, 1977.

[Mei89] Y.V. Meitus. The equivalence problem for real-time strict deterministic pushdown automata. *Kibernetika 5 (in russian, english translation in Cybernetics and Systems analysis)*, pages 14–25, 1989.

[RS80]   G. Rozenberg and A. Salomaa. *The Mathematical Theory of L-systems*. Academic Press, New-York, 1980.

[Sén97] G. Sénizergues.   L(A) = L(B)?   In *Proceedings INFINITY 97*, pages 1–26. Electronic Notes in Theoretical Computer Science 9, URL: http://www.elsevier.nl/locate/entcs/volume9.html, 1997.

[Sén98a] G. Sénizergues. The equivalence problem for deterministic pushdown transducers into abelian groups. In *Proceedings MFCS'98*, pages 305–315. Springer, LNCS 1450, 1998.

[Sén98b] G. Sénizergues. L(A) = L(B)? Technical report, LaBRI, Université Bordeaux I, 1998. Improved version of report 1161-97, submitted to TCS, accessible at URL, http://www.labri.u-bordeaux.fr/~ges, pages 1-166, april 1998.

[Sén99] G. Sénizergues. T(A) = T(B)? Technical report, nr 1209-99, LaBRI, 1999. Pages 1-61. Can be accessed at URL,http://www.labri.u-bordeaux.fr/~ges.

[TS89]   E. Tomita and K. Seino. A direct branching algorithm for checking the equivalence of two deterministic pushdown transducers, one of which is real-time strict. *Theoretical Computer Science*, pages 39–53, 1989.

Many-Valued Logics and Holographic Proofs

Mario Szegedy

AT&T Shannon Labs, Florham Park NJ 07932, USA,
ms@research.att.com,
WWW home page: http://www.research.att.com/info/ms

Abstract. We reformulate the subject of holographic proof checking in terms of three-valued logic. In this reformulation the recursive proof checking idea of Arora and Safra gets an especially elegant form. Our approach gives a more concise and accurate treatment of the holographic proof theory, and yields easy to check proofs about holographic proofs. A consequence of our results is that for any $\epsilon > 0$ MAX3SAT instances cannot be approximated in $TIME(2^{n^{1-\epsilon}})$ within a factor which tends to 1 when n tends to infinity, unless 3SAT can be solved in $TIME(2^{n^{1-\epsilon}})$ for some $\epsilon > 0$.

1 Introduction

The Theory of the Holographic (or Probabilistically Checkable) Proofs, widely known for its in-approximability consequences, is one with the deepest mathematical structures in the area of computer science. Unfortunately, its language still reflects its origin, which lies in the cryptographic part of computer science. Being as appealing and intuitive as it is, this language gives an almost free license to hand-waving arguments. Several examples can be brought for claims that first appeared intuitively obvious and their proof was neglected, but it required years to prove them. A notable example is the parallel repetition theorem eventually proven by Ran Raz [11]. In this article we make an effort to restate claims and proofs of the theory in a framework that provides a greater precision.

Formally, a holographic verifier V is a randomized non-deterministic machine that computes an NP predicate $f(x) = (\exists w)\ S(x, w)$ in the following sense: if $f(x) = 1$ then $(\exists w')$ such that V accepts (x, w') with probability 1; if $f(x) = 0$ then $(\forall w')$ V rejects (x, w') with probability 0.5. x is often called the theorem candidate, and w' the holographic proof candidate for x.

Babai et. al. (BFLS) in [5] require that the verifier works in poly-logarithmic time. Since most individual bits of input x are checked with very small probability by a randomized sub-linear time verifier, only functions indifferent to small input changes can be verified this way. Babai et. al. therefore replace the original function f with another function g such that for every input x: $g(E(x)) = f(x)$, where E is an encoding function. Clearly, g suffers from some combinatorial restrictions, and it is undefined for those strings that are not of the form $E(x)$. In section 6 we generalize BFLS type theorems for any function g with small $NRAM[\epsilon]$ complexity (a measure we introduce in Section 5.2).

Fig. 1. The circuit interpretation of a PCP theorem. (An approximate AND function outputs 1 if all inputs are 1, and it outputs 0 if at least half of the inputs are 0. The output is undefined otherwise.)

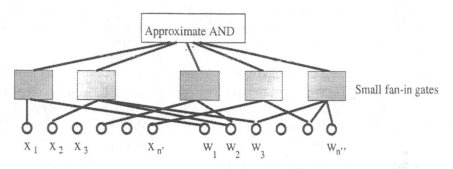

Arora and Safra in [3] observed that verifiers can be composed in the following sense. For a fixed random choice r of a (non-adaptive) verifier V there is a fixed set of bits $b_1 \ldots b_l$ which it reads, and there is a fixed function $h_r(b_1 \ldots b_l)$ it computes. One can hope that adding a holographic proof w_r' for every r will allow a composed verifier to first randomly choose r and then act as a verifier V_r for h_r. The idea can be implemented only if V_r is a BFLS type verifier. But BFLS type verifiers read only encoded inputs, and $b_1 \ldots b_l$ is not encoded! At least, early proof systems did not have this property. In [3] and [2] a technique called *proof segmentation* was developed to ensure that the verifier reads encoded pieces of input, but this introduces extra complications into the holographic proof theory.

The technical difficulties that arose with the *proof composition* lead us to the development of a framework in which proof composition becomes just a composition of functions. An arbitrary composition of functions over some logic is called a *circuit*, and in our new framework we will represent verifiers with circuits. A holographic verifier can be thought of as a circuit with an approximate-AND gate on the top and small fan-in gates at the bottom as shown in Figure 1. The output of this circuit may be undefined for certain (x, w') pairs. We treat this uncertainty by introducing an "indeterminate" logical value following the lead of Lukasiewicz, Kleene and others. All elements of the circuits we construct will compute functions over a *three-valued logic*. Our main reasons to give a logical value to the uncertain outcome are to ensure that all gates do meaningful computation for all inputs, and that functions we construct compose.

We reformulate statements of the PCP theory as replacement rules for non-deterministic circuits over a three-valued logic. Although our reformulation mostly concerns the high level structure of the proofs of the theory, we find it important to mention that the changes we propose are not solely a matter of form. We generalize proof checking results to functions with small NRAM[ϵ] complexity. This in turn makes proof compositions simpler, for we have a greater freedom in choosing the outer verifier. By unnecessitating some details of the usual proof compositions we can simplify holographic proofs and reduce their proof size.

The space limits of this abstract allow us to reformulate only the theorems of Babai, Fortnow, Levin and Szegedy [5], of Arora, Lund, Motwani, Sudan and Szegedy [2] and of Polischuk and Spielman [10], but we shall treat the entire PCP theory in a survey paper that will appear in the fifth volume of the Handbook of Combinatorial Optimization, edited by D.-Z. Du and P.M. Pardalos.

With our approach we were able to reveal imprecisions in [10], and correct them in an elegant manner. As a benefit of our tight analysis of [10] we obtain that MAX3SAT instances can be transformed into approximate MAX3SAT instances in $TIME(n^{1+\epsilon})$ for any $\epsilon > 0$ implying that MAX3SAT cannot be approximated in $TIME(2^{n^{1-\epsilon}})$ unless it can be solved exactly in $TIME(2^{n^{1-\epsilon'}})$ for any $\epsilon' < \epsilon$. As a bonus, our framework naturally supports those constructions where the verifier has a "weak acceptance condition" and a "strong acceptance condition."

A change we make compared to previous approaches is that we stop talking about "families of functions" and "polynomial time." We take a combinatorialist-finitist view, and all objects we deal with will be of fixed size. We believe this also helps being more accurate. Obviously, we will still need some notion of computational complexity, which we will discuss in Sections 5 and 5.2. The paper is readable without prior knowledge of the PCP theory.

2 Many-Valued Logics, LK Functions

We denote the set of the usual Boolean truth values by $B = \{0, 1\}$. We introduce the indeterminate truth value $\frac{0}{1}$, and we denote the extended set of truth values by $LK = \{0, 1, \frac{0}{1}\}$ (echoing the initials of Lukasiewitz and Kleene). Note that in the literature the indeterminate truth value is often denoted by $\frac{1}{2}$. We would like to view LK as $2^B \setminus \{\emptyset\}$, where $0 \leftrightarrow \{0\}$, $1 \leftrightarrow \{1\}$, and $\frac{0}{1} \leftrightarrow \{0, 1\}$, but we would also like to have $B \subseteq LK$. To resolve this conflict we introduce a commutative binary operation $\uplus : LK \times LK \to LK$ defined by: $0 \uplus 0 = 0$, $0 \uplus 1 = \frac{0}{1}$, $1 \uplus 1 = 1$, $\frac{0}{1} \uplus x = \frac{0}{1}$ for $x \in LK$, and a (reflexive) partial order $\sqsubseteq$ on LK: $0 \sqsubseteq \frac{0}{1}$, $1 \sqsubseteq \frac{0}{1}$ and 0 and 1 are incomparable.

For every $x \in LK^n$ we can assign a sub-cube $Q_x \subseteq B^n$ which is the product set obtained by taking one or two different choices for every coordinate of x depending on whether the coordinate in question is determinate or indeterminate. Thus e.g. $Q_{\frac{0}{1}0\frac{0}{1}1} = \{0001, 1001, 0011, 1011\}$.

Definition 1. *Let $f : B^n \to LK$ be a function. We call f an LK function. We define $f^{ext} : LK^n \to LK$ by $f^{ext}(x) = \uplus_{z \in Q_x} f(z)$.*

Our extension effects the $\wedge$, $\vee$ and $\neg$ operators in the following standard way:

$\wedge$	0	1	$\frac{0}{1}$
0	0	0	0
1	0	1	$\frac{0}{1}$
$\frac{0}{1}$	0	$\frac{0}{1}$	$\frac{0}{1}$

$\vee$	0	1	$\frac{0}{1}$
0	0	1	$\frac{0}{1}$
1	1	1	1
$\frac{0}{1}$	$\frac{0}{1}$	1	$\frac{0}{1}$

x	$\neg x$
0	1
1	0
$\frac{0}{1}$	$\frac{0}{1}$

3 LK Circuits

Every circuit is a scheme which describes a way of composing functions. Functions that participate in the composition are called gates. Let C be a circuit made of LK functions (in particular its gates may compute Boolean functions). To reconcile the input and output type differences of the gates we need to extend each gate to LK valued inputs. If we do this extension via Definition 1 then C becomes an *LK circuit*.

We shall use LK circuits to compute LK functions as in Definition 3. Note that LK circuits are realistic devices. In example 1 we describe the *Overwhelming Majority Gate*, which is our chief example to an LK gate.

Example 1. The *overwhelming majority gate*, $MAJ_n(p, q)$ (for $p \geq q$) has n input wires and one output wire and its output is 1 if at least pn input wires are set to 1, and 0 if less than qn input wires are set to 1. In all other cases the output is $\frac{0}{1}$. ($MAJ_n(0.5, 0.5)$ is the majority gate in the usual sense, and $MAJ_n(1, 1 - \epsilon)$ for any $\epsilon > 0$ is called the approximate-AND function.)

Remark 1. Let us denote by EXT_n the set of functions $LK^n \to LK$ that can be written as f^{ext} for some $f : B^n \to LK$, and let $EXT = \cup_n EXT_n$. One can show that any composition of functions in EXT remains in EXT. All LK valued functions that occur in our discussion belong to EXT, therefore the values they take on their Boolean inputs already define them.

4 Nondeterministic LK Circuits

The notion of non-determinism in the LK world is given by the definition below:

Definition 2 (Non-deterministic LK circuits). *Let $C(x, y)$ be an LK circuit. For $x \in B^n$ we define:*

$$C^N(x) = \begin{cases} 0 \text{ if } & (\forall y) \ C(x, y) = 0 \\ 1 \text{ if } & (\exists y) \ C(x, y) = 1 \\ \frac{0}{1} \text{ otherwise} \end{cases} \tag{1}$$

For a non-deterministic LK circuit C we define $ND(C) = |y|$, the number of its non-deterministic input bits. In the classical framework this parameter corresponds to the proof size.

5 Complexity Measures for LK Functions and Circuits

5.1 Deterministic and Non-Deterministic RAM Complexities

Definition 3. *A computational device M (either a RAM operating on Boolean values, or an LK circuit) is said to compute an LK function $f : B^n \to LK$ if for every $x \in B^n$: $M(x) \sqsubseteq f(x)$. We also say that an LK function $f_1 : B^n \to LK$ is more restrictive than an LK function $f_2 : B^n \to LK$ if for every $x \in B^n$: $f_1(x) \sqsubseteq f_2(x)$.*

Definition 4. *The RAM (NRAM) complexity of an LK function $f : LK^n \to LK$ is any pair (m, a) of positive integers such that there is a deterministic (non-deterministic) Random Access Machine with program length at most a which can compute f (in the sense of Definition 3) in time at most m.*

Note, that there may not be a unique (m, a) pair where both m and a are the smallest, but we will call any pair satisfying Definition 4 "the" RAM complexity. This will never lead us to a confusion. The RAM model we use in Definition 4 is a fixed universal RAM model. Its central processing unit can add, multiply, shift, and compare to 0 in unit time. The only restriction we make is that the absolute value of the largest integer that may occur in any register during the computation must be upper bounded by the running time.

5.2   The RAM[ϵ] (NRAM[ϵ]) Complexity

Definition 5 (ϵ-separation). *Let $A, B \subseteq B^n$. We say that A and B are ϵ-separated if for every $x \in A$, $x' \in B$ the Hamming distance of x and x' is at least ϵn.*

Definition 6. *The RAM[ϵ] (NRAM[ϵ]) complexity of an LK function $f : LK^n \to LK$ is any pair (m, a) of positive integers such that there is a deterministic (non-deterministic) Random Access Machine M with program length at most a which computes f (in the sense of Definition 3) in time at most m, moreover $\{x \mid M(x) = 1\}$ and $\{x \mid f(x) = 0\}$ are ϵ-separated.*

The above definition is meaningful iff $\{x \mid f(x) = 0\}$ and $\{x \mid f(x) = 1\}$ are ϵ-separated. Otherwise a machine M satisfying the definition cannot be found. The notion of NRAM[ϵ] complexity is central in our discussion. It gives a concise way to talk about functions that are both "encoded" *and* have bounded NRAM complexity.

5.3   Complexity Measures for Sets of Gates of LK Circuits

Definition 7 (Total and Maximum Complexity). *Let C be an LK circuit, and $\{g_1, \ldots, g_k\}$ be a subset of its gates. Let the NRAM complexity of g_i be (m_i, a_i). Then we define the* total *complexity of $\{g_1, \ldots, g_k\}$ as $\sum_{i=1}^{k} m_i$, and the corresponding* maximum *complexity of $\{g_1, \ldots, g_k\}$ as the pair $(\max_{1 \leq i = 1 \leq k} m_i, \max_{1 \leq i \leq k} a_i)$. The notions extend to the RAM[ϵ] and NRAM[ϵ] complexities, for any fixed ϵ.*

6   Proof Checking Theorems

What BFLS and akin proof checking theorems roughly assert is that for every function $f : B^n \to B$ with NRAM complexity at most (m, a) there is a non-deterministic LK circuit C with structure as in Figure 1 which computes an encoded version of f such that the parameters of C are small in terms of m and

a. In this section we generalize these proof checking theorems to LK functions with a bound on their NRAM[ϵ] complexity. (Lemma 1 of the next section asserts that the usual form of proof checking theorems are implied by our theorems.) In this section all majority gates are weighted as in Definition 12.

Theorem 1 (Babai, Fortnow, Levin and Szegedy [5]). *For every $\delta > 0$, $\epsilon > 0$ there is a constant $c_{\delta,\epsilon}$ such that for every LK function $f : B^n \to LK$ with NRAM[ϵ] complexity (m, a) there is a non-deterministic LK circuit $C = MAJ(1, 1/2)(g_1, \ldots, g_{m'})$ computing f such that:*

1. *$ND(C) \leq c_{\delta,\epsilon} m^{1+\delta}$ (recall that $ND(C)$ is the number of non-deterministic variables for C).*
2. *the maximum complexity of $\{g_1, \ldots, g_{m'}\}$ is at most $(c_{\delta,\epsilon} \log^{\frac{1}{\delta}} m, c_{\delta,\epsilon} a)$.*

Theorem 2 (Arora, Lund, Motwani, Sudan and Szegedy [2]). *For every $\epsilon > 0$ there is a constant c_ϵ such that for any LK function $f : B^n \to LK$ with NRAM[ϵ] complexity (m, a) there is a a non-deterministic LK circuit $C = MAJ(1, 1/2)(g_1, \ldots, g_{m'})$ computing f such that:*

1. *The total complexity of $\{g_1, \ldots, g_{m'}\}$ is at most $c_\epsilon m^3$,*
2. *The corresponding maximum complexity of $\{g_1, \ldots, g_{m'}\}$ is $(c_\epsilon a, c_\epsilon a)$.*

Theorem 3 (Polischuk and Spielman [10]). *For every $\delta > 0$, $\epsilon > 0$ there is a constant $c_{\delta,\epsilon}$ such that for any LK function $f : B^n \to LK$ with NRAM[ϵ] complexity (m, a) there is a non-deterministic LK circuit $C = MAJ(1, 1 - 1/c_{\delta,\epsilon})(g_1, \ldots, g_{m'})$ computing f such that:*

1. *The total complexity of $\{g_1, \ldots, g_{m'}\}$ is $c_{\delta,\epsilon} m^{1+\delta}$,*
2. *The corresponding maximum complexity of $\{g_1, \ldots, g_{m'}\}$ is $(c_{\delta,\epsilon}, c_{\delta,\epsilon})$.*

Theorems 1 and 2 are just slightly more general than their original form, while Theorem 3 bounds an extra parameter compared to its counterpart in [10]. Theorem 3 is a common generalization of Theorem 1 and Theorem 2. We could have added to each theorem that the circuits in them can be very efficiently constructed, but the intention of this write-up is to strictly adhere to the finitist view. We shall however provide exact information in the complete version. For now we only point out that all our proofs are constructive in a very strong sense.

7 An Approximation Theoretic Consequence

Theorem 4. *For every $\delta > 0$ there is a constant c_δ and an algorithm $A \in DTIME(n^{1+\delta})$ which inputs a 3SAT instance φ and outputs a 3SAT instance $A(\varphi)$ such that*

1. *The size of $A(\varphi)$ is at most $c_\delta |\varphi|^{1+\delta}$*
2. *If φ is satisfiable then $A(\varphi)$ is also satisfiable.*
3. *If φ is not satisfiable then at least $\frac{1}{c_\delta}$ fraction of the clauses of $A(\varphi)$ is not satisfiable.*

Corollary 1. *If for some* $\delta > 0$ *it is possible to approximate the number of satisfiable clauses of 3CNF formuli in* $DTIME(O(2^{n^{1-\delta}}))$ *within a factor arbitrarily close to 1 (as n grows to infinity), then 3SAT is in* $DTIME(O(2^{n^{1-\delta'}}))$ *for any* $\delta' < \delta$.

Remark 2. If we care only about NP completeness of a problem, instance size changes during NP hardness reductions have no relevance. However, C. Schnorr has noticed that in spite of new results that show the non-approximability of the length of the shortest vector in a lattice there are very good practical approximation algorithms for lattices whose dimension is in the thousands. To explain this phenomenon he pointed out that instance sizes blow up by a very large factor when 3SAT instances get mapped to SVP instances during NP hardness reductions.

Proof (of Theorem 4). The next definition gives our version of input-encoding:

Definition 8. *An encoding scheme E with parameters* (ϵ, c_0, c_1) *is a sequence* $\{E_n\}_{n=1}^{\infty}$ *of codes such that:*

1. *For every* $n > 0$ *the code* E_n *has dimension n and length* $c_0 n$.
2. E_n *is quickly computable: it has NRAM complexity* $(c_1 n \log^2 n, c_1)$.
3. *For* $x \neq y$, $|x| = |y| = n$, $dist(E(x), E(y)) > \epsilon c_0 n$, *where dist is the Hamming distance.*

Definition 9. *Let* $f : B^n \to LK$ *and E be an encoding scheme with parameters* (ϵ, c_0, c_1). *We define* $F_{f,E} : B^{c_0 n} \to LK$, *called the encoding of f using scheme E by:*

$$F_{f,E}(z) = \begin{cases} 0 \text{ if } & (\exists x) \ (z = E(x) \ \wedge \ f(x) = 0) \\ 1 \text{ if } & (\exists x) \ (z = E(x) \ \wedge \ f(x) = 1) \\ \frac{0}{1} \text{ otherwise} \end{cases} \tag{2}$$

Lemma 1. *Let the NRAM complexity of f be* (m, a) *and let E be an encoding scheme with parameters* (ϵ, c_0, c_1). *Then the* $NRAM[\epsilon]$ *complexity of* $F_{f,E}$ *is at most* $(m + c_1 n \log^2 n, a + c_1)$.

We are now ready to proceed with the proof of Theorem 4. Recall that a 3CNF formula is an expression of the form $\bigvee_{i=1}^{l}(x_{i_1} \wedge x_{i_2} \wedge x_{i_3})$. If we encode this expression with a string of length $n = 3l \log l$ in the natural way (i.e. as a sequence of l triplets of integers), then there is a non-deterministic RAM machine M working in time $O(n \log n)$ that outputs 1 iff the encoded expression is satisfiable. Let us fix n and denote by $3SAT_n$ the function that M computes on inputs of size n. By the above remark $3SAT_n$ has NRAM complexity $(cn \log n, c)$, where c is an upper bound on the program length of M and on the constant occurring in the $O(n \log n)$ expression. Let E be an encoding scheme with parameters $(1/4, c_0, c_1)$ (one can show that for some constants c_0, c_1 such scheme exists). Let $F_{3SAT_n, E}$ be the encoding of $3SAT_n$ using scheme E (see definition 9). By Lemma 1 the NRAM[1/4] complexity of $F_{3SAT_n,E}$ is at most $(2cc_1 n \log^2 n, c + c_1)$. We apply Theorem 3 with $\epsilon \to 1/4$, $\delta \to \delta/2$ and $f \to F_{3SAT_n,E}$, and obtain that there is a constant c_3 and a non-deterministic circuit $C = MAJ(1, 1 - 1/c_3)(g_1, \ldots, g_{m'})$ such that C computes $F_{3SAT_n,E}$ and:

1. The total complexity of $\{g_1, \ldots, g_{m'}\}$ is at most $c_3(2cc_1 n \log^2 n)^{1+\delta/2}$, and hence $m' \leq c_3(2cc_1 n \log^2 n)^{1+\delta/2}$.
2. The maximum complexity of $\{g_1, \ldots, g_{m'}\}$ is upper bounded by (c_3, c_3).

Let ψ_i be the 3CNF form of g_i for $1 \leq i \leq m'$ (without loss of generality we can assume that each g_i is Boolean). Since the size of ψ_i $(1 \leq i \leq m')$ depends only on c_3, the number of clauses of ψ_i $(1 \leq i \leq m')$ is at most c_4 for some constant c_4. C is non-deterministic, and hence the formula $\Psi = \wedge_{1 \leq i \leq m'} \psi_i$ takes two different sets of input variables: a set associated with the original input bits of $F_{3SAT_n,E}$, and a set w', which corresponds to the non-deterministic variables of C. Now if $\varphi = \bigvee_{i=1}^{l}(x_{i_1} \wedge x_{i_2} \wedge x_{i_3})$ is an arbitrary 3CNF formula that can be represented with a string of length n in the natural way, we can construct a 3CNF formula Ψ_φ by letting $\Psi_\varphi(w') = \Psi(E(\varphi), w')$. Since Ψ is created from the g_is of C, and C has a $MAJ(1, 1 - 1/c_3)$ gate on the top, and since each ψ_i has size at most c_4, we have:

1. If φ is satisfiable then $\Psi_\varphi(w')$ is also satisfiable.
2. There is a constant $\epsilon_1 > 0$ which depends only on δ such that if φ is not satisfiable then for every w' at least ϵ_1 fraction of the clauses of Ψ_φ are not satisfied.

The size of Ψ_φ is at most $c_4 c_3(2cc_1 n \log^2 n)^{1+\delta/2} \leq c_4 c_3(12cc_1 l \log^3 l)^{1+\delta/2} \leq O(l^{1+\delta})$. One can also show that the construction time of Ψ_φ is nearly linear in l. ∎

8 General Replacement Rules for Deterministic and Nondeterministic LK Circuits

In general, we say that in an LK circuit C we can replace a gate g with another gate g' if the resulting new circuit C' computes the same or a more restrictive function than C. Our goal is to describe the high level structure of the PCP theorems as a sequence of gate or sub-circuit replacements in non-deterministic LK circuits. In the sequel we shall describe rules that govern the replacebility of gates of LK circuits. The easiest of all rules is the following:

Lemma 2 (Deterministic Replacement). *We can replace a gate g (or a sub-circuit S) of a deterministic or non-deterministic LK circuit C with a deterministic gate g' (or a sub-circuit S') as long as g' (or S') computes the same or a more restrictive function than g (or S).*

8.1 Replacement and Non-determinism

Let $C(x, y)$ be a non-deterministic Boolean circuit with a gate g. Assume that g' is a non-deterministic gate using non-deterministic variables y' that computes exactly the same function as deterministic gate g (in formula: $(\forall z)[g(z) = (\exists y')g'(z, y')]$). Can we replace g by g' such that we join the original and the new non-deterministic resources y and y'?

Not always. Assume that C is simply $\neg g$. Then the new non deterministic circuit computes $(\exists y')\neg g'(z, y')$, which is not the same as $\neg(\exists y')g'(z, y')$. We shall resolve this problem by introducing the notion of *positive position* for a gate of a circuit, and stating that the above oddity does not occur for gates in a positive position.

Definition 10 (Monotone LK Functions). *Let us define an ordering relation on LK by:* $0 < \frac{0}{1} < 1$. *An LK problem P is monotone non-decreasing if whenever x_1 is coordinate-wise less or equal than x_2, $P(x_1) \leq P(x_2)$ follows.*

Definition 11 (Positive Position). *Let $C(x, y)$ be a non-deterministic LK circuit. A gate g of C is in a positive position if all gates above g compute monotone non-decreasing LK functions.*

Below we give a sufficient condition for replacing gates with non-deterministic gates in non-deterministic LK circuits:

Lemma 3 (Non-deterministic Replacement). *We can replace a gate g (or a sub-circuit S') in a non-deterministic LK circuit C with a non-deterministic gate g' (or a non-deterministic sub-circuit S') as long as g' (or S') computes the same or a more restrictive function than g (or S), and g (or the topmost gate of S) is in a positive position in C. The non-deterministic variables of g' (or S') should be added to those of C.*

9 Theorems for Replacements

9.1 Replacements Involving the Majority Gate

Lemma 4. *Let C be a two-level circuit of nm inputs with a $MAJ_n(p_1, q_1)$ on top and $MAJ_m(p_2, q_2)$ gates on the first level. Then C can be replaced with a single $MAJ_{nm}(p_1 p_2, 1 - (1 - q_1)(1 - q_2))$ gate.*

Proof. Consider an input which sets the output of C_1 to 1. This requires for the top level gate to receive at least np_1 1s from the first level. Each first level gate outputting 1 must have at least mp_2 of its inputs set to 1. Altogether there must be at least mnp_1p_2 ones in the entire input. But under this condition $MAJ_{nm}(p_1p_2, 1 - (1 - q_1)(1 - q_2))$ outputs 1 as well. It can be similarly shown that when C_1 outputs 0, $MAJ_{nm}(p_1p_2, 1 - (1 - q_1)(1 - q_2))$ also outputs 0. $\blacksquare$

Definition 12. *Let $w = (w_1, \ldots, w_n)$ be a non-negative valued weight vector. We define $MAJ_w(p, q)$ as the function which outputs 1 if $\sum_{i=1}^n x_i w_i \geq p \sum_{i=1}^n w_i$, outputs 0 if $\sum_{i=1}^n x_i w_i < q \sum_{i=1}^n w_i$, and outputs $\frac{0}{1}$ otherwise.*

Theorem 5 (Merging Lemma). *Let C be an arbitrary two-level circuit with $MAJ_w(p_1, q_1)$ on top and $MAJ_{w'}(p_2, q_2)$ gates on the first level, and assume that all weights are rational. Then C can be replaced with a single $MAJ_{w'}(p_1 p_2, 1 - (1 - q_1)(1 - q_2))$ gate for some appropriate w' with rational weights.*

Proof. The theorem follows from Lemma 4. ∎

9.2 The Polischuk-Spielman Replacement

Theorem 6. *For every $\epsilon > 0$ there is a constant c_ϵ such that for every LK function $f : B^n \to LK$ with $NRAM[\epsilon]$ complexity (m, a) there is a non-deterministic LK circuit $C = MAJ(1, 1 - 1/c_\epsilon)(g_1, \ldots, g_{m'})$ computing f such that:*

1. *The total $NRAM[1/c_\epsilon]$ complexity of $\{g_1, \ldots, g_{m'}\}$ is $(c_\epsilon m \log^4 m)$*
2. *The corresponding maximum $NRAM[1/c_\epsilon]$ complexity of $\{g_1, \ldots, g_{m'}\}$ is $(c_\epsilon \sqrt{m} \log^4 m, c_\epsilon a)$*

The proof is omitted from this abstract.

10 Proof Composition Without Segmentation

Proof of Theorem 3: Let $\delta > 0$, $\epsilon > 0$ and let $f : B^n \to LK$ be an LK function with $NRAM[\epsilon]$ complexity (m, a). By Theorem 6 there is a constant c_ϵ and a non-deterministic LK circuit $C = MAJ(1, 1 - 1/c_\epsilon)(g_1, \ldots, g_{m'})$ computing f such that the $NRAM[1/c_\epsilon]$ complexity of g_i is (m_i, a_i) for $1 \leq i \leq m'$ and $\sum_{i=1}^{m'} m_i \leq c_\epsilon m \log^4 m$, $\max_{1 \leq i \leq m'} m_i \leq c_\epsilon \sqrt{m} \log^4 m$, and $\max_{1 \leq i \leq m'} a_i \leq c_\epsilon a$.

We are going to replace each g_i again using Theorem 6. To be careful, notice that g_i $(1 \leq i \leq m')$ is in a positive position. Let $\epsilon_1 = 1/c_\epsilon$. The circuit $C_i = MAJ(1, 1 - 1/c_{\epsilon_1})(g_1^i, \ldots, g_{m_i'}^i)$ that replaces g_i is a two level circuit such that its first level gates have maximum complexity $(c_{\epsilon_1} \sqrt{m_i} \log^4 m_i, c_{\epsilon_1} c_\epsilon a)$ and total complexity $c_{\epsilon_1} m_i \log^4 m_i$. After all the replacements we have a three level circuit C'. The bottom level gates of C' are $g_1^1, \ldots, g_{m_1'}^1, \ldots, g_1^{m'}, \ldots, g_{m_{m'}'}^{m'}$ with total complexity $\sum_{i=1}^{m'} c_{\epsilon_1} m_i \log^4 m_i \leq c_{\epsilon_1} \log^4 m \sum_{i=1}^{m'} m_i \leq c_{\epsilon_1} c_\epsilon m \log^8 m$, and maximum complexity at most $(c_{\epsilon_1} \max_{1 \leq i \leq m'} \sqrt{m_i} \log^4 m_i, c_{\epsilon_1} c_\epsilon a)$, which is at most $(c_{\epsilon_1} \sqrt{c_\epsilon} m^{1/4} \log^6 m, c_{\epsilon_1} c_\epsilon a)$.

In the next step we replace the **MAJ** gates on the top two levels of C' with a single majority gate using the Merging Lemma. This way we obtain a circuit $C^2 = MAJ(1, 1 - 1/c_\epsilon c_{\epsilon_1})(g_1^1, \ldots, g_{m_1'}^1, \ldots, g_1^{m'}, \ldots, g_{m_{m'}'}^{m'})$ with bounds on the total and maximum complexities of the gates on the first level as above. We now proceed inductively in fashion similar to above (in each round replacing all bottom level gates by Theorem 6 and then merging the top two levels of the resulting circuit) to construct two-level circuits $C^3, C^4, \ldots, C^{\lceil \log(9/\delta) \rceil}$ such that there are constants $c_2, c_3, \ldots, c_{\lceil \log(9/\delta) \rceil}$ dependent only on ϵ that for $1 \leq i \leq \lceil \log(9/\delta) \rceil$:

1. The top gate of C^i is a $MAJ(1, 1 - 1/c_i)$ gate.
2. The total NRAM$[1/c_i]$ complexity of the bottom level gates of C^i is at most $c_i m \log^{4i} m$.
3. The corresponding maximum NRAM$[1/c_i]$ complexity of the bottom level gates is at most $(c_i m^{1/2^i} \log^{4i} m, c_i a)$.

Assume that the bottom level gates of $C^{\lceil \log(9/\delta) \rceil}$ are $h_1, \ldots, h_{m''}$. They have maximum NRAM$[1/c_{\lceil \log(9/\delta) \rceil}]$ complexity at most $cm^{2\delta/9}$ for some constant c.

We apply Theorem 2 to replace each h_i with a circuit D_i of total complexity $c'c^3 m^{2\delta/3}$ and maximum complexity (c', c') for some constant c'. The total complexity of the bottom level gates of the newly obtained three-level circuit, C'', is at most $c'' m^{1+\delta}$, and their maximum complexity is (c'', c'') for some constant c''. We merge the top two levels of C'' using the Merging Lemma. The resulting circuit has the claimed parameters. ∎

References

1. S. Arora and C. Lund, Hardness of approximations. In *Approximation Algorithms for NP-hard problems*, D. Hochbaum, ed. PWS Publishing, 1996.
2. S. Arora, C. Lund, R. Motwani, M. Sudan, and M. Szegedy, Proof verification and the intractability of approximation problems. Proceedings of the 33rd *Symposium on Foundations of Computer Science*, IEEE 1992.
3. S. Arora and S. Safra. Probabilistic checking of proofs: a new characterization of NP. To appear *Journal of the ACM*. Preliminary version in *Proceedings of the Thirty Third Annual Symposium on the Foundations of Computer Science*, IEEE, 1992.
4. L. Babai, L. Fortnow, and C. Lund, Non-deterministic exponential time has two-prover interactive protocols. *Computational Complexity*, 1:3-40, 1991.
5. L. Babai, L. Fortnow, L. Levin, and M. Szegedy, Checking computations in polylogarithmic time. *Proceedings of the Twenty Third Annual Symposium on the Theory of Computing*, ACM, 1991.
6. L. Babai and K. Friedl, On slightly superlinear transparent proofs. *Univ. Chicago Tech. Report*, CS-93-13, 1993.
7. U. Feige, S. Goldwasser, L. Lovász, S. Safra, and M. Szegedy, Interactive proofs and the hardness of approximating cliques. *Journal of the ACM*, 43(2):268-292, March 1996.
8. L. Fortnow, J. Rompel, and M. Sipser, On the power of multi-prover interactive protocols. *Theoretical Computer Science*, 134(2):545-557, November 1994.
9. S. Goldwasser, S. Micali, and C. Rackoff, The knowledge complexity of interactive proof-systems. *SIAM J. on Computing*, 18(1):186-208, February 1989.
10. A. Polishchuk and D. Spielman, Nearly Linear Sized Holographic Proofs. *Proceedings of the Twenty Sixth Annual Symposium on the Theory of Computing*, ACM, 1994.
11. R. Raz, A parallel repetition theorem. *Proceedings of the Twenty Seventh Annual Symposium on the Theory of Computing*, ACM, 1995.
12. M. Sudan, *Efficient Checking of Polynomials and Proofs and the Hardness of Approximation Problems*. Ph.D. Thesis, U.C. Berkeley, 1992. Also appears as ACM Distinguished Theses, Lecture Notes in Computer Science, no. 1001, Springer, 1996.

On the Complexity and Inapproximability of Shortest Implicant Problems

Christopher Umans*

Computer Science Division
U.C. Berkeley
Berkeley, CA 94720-1776
umans@cs.berkeley.edu

Abstract. We investigate the complexity and approximability of a basic optimization problem in the second level of the Polynomial Hierarchy, that of finding shortest implicants. We show that the DNF variant of this problem is complete for a complexity class in the second level of the hierarchy utilizing $\log^2 n$-limited nondeterminism. We obtain inapproximability results for the DNF and formula variants of the shortest implicant problem that show that trivial approximation algorithms are optimal for these problems, up to lower order terms. It is hoped that these results will be useful in studying the complexity and approximability of circuit minimization problems, which have close connections to implicant problems.

1 Introduction

Circuit minimization problems have been extensively studied since the 1950's as important practical problems in logic synthesis, and, since the early 1970's, as natural problems in the second level of the Polynomial Hierarchy. These problems are widely believed to be Σ_2^p-complete; however, they have defied precise complexity classification until very recently, when the Minimum Equivalent DNF problem was shown to be Σ_2^p-complete [11], verifying a conjecture of Stockmeyer [9]. Still, very little has been proved about the complexity of the other major circuit minimization problems: the only non-trivial hardness result known for the Minimum Equivalent Expression problem is $P_{||}^{NP}$-hardness [5], and nothing better than trivial coNP-hardness is know for the Minimum Equivalent Circuit problem. The precise complexity is also unknown for many other variants of these problems, such as the "Π_2^p" versions ("Is C a minimal circuit?"). And, despite the continuing importance of these problems in logic synthesis and the significant effort spent designing heuristic and approximate solutions, no formal results (positive or negative) on the approximability of circuit minimization problems are known. This is partly attributable to the dearth of other well-studied optimization problems in the second level of the hierarchy.

---

* Supported in part by an NSF Graduate Research Fellowship and NSF grant CCR-9626361

As a first step towards improving the current state of knowledge with respect to the complexity and approximability of circuit minimization problems, and in order to expand the available "tools" with which to work in the second level of the hierarchy, we focus in this paper on a basic optimization problem that is closely connected to circuit minimization, namely, *finding shortest implicants*.

The connection between implicant finding and circuit minimization is not surprising; since the introduction of the now-classic Quine-McCluskey algorithm [8, 6], most heuristic and exact methods for DNF minimization have been based on explicitly or implicitly generating the prime implicants of the input function (see [2, 10]), and manipulating implicants also plays an important role in other circuit minimization problems [3]. Implicant problems have already proven their usefulness in the context of complexity results for circuit minimization — in [11], a variant of the shortest implicant problem is a critical intermediate step in the reduction showing that the Minimum Equivalent DNF problem is Σ_2^p-complete.

Our results. In this paper, we settle the complexity of the DNF variant of the shortest implicant problem, proving it complete for a class in the second level of the hierarchy utilizing limited non-determinism. Previous work [11] placed the problem in a similar (larger) class but did not establish the hardness result. We also note that the complement of this problem, properly interpreted, is a "robust" version of CNF SAT, and that other "log-robust" variants of NP-complete problems are complete for this class.

We also obtain optimal inapproximability results for the DNF and formula variants of the shortest implicant problem. For the formula version, this improves the inapproximability factor from $n^{1/2-\epsilon}$ (in [11]) to $n^{1-\epsilon}$. The main technical aspect of the proof involves the fairly delicate construction of formulae whose shortest implicants and implicates are almost as large as the formula itself. These results indicate that the best approximation algorithms for these problems are trivial ones – for the DNF variant, the algorithm returns the shortest term of the input DNF; for the formula variant, the algorithm returns any satisfying assignment. In other words, no non-trivial exploitation of the special structure of formulae or DNF formulae aids in the approximation of the shortest implicant problem.

Practical significance of complexity results in the second level of the hierarchy. In the more common case of NP-complete problems, a completeness result removes the likelihood of an efficient exact solution and justifies a concentration of effort on approximate or heuristic solutions. It might be argued that for circuit minimization and shortest implicant problems, for which coNP-hardness can be trivially proved, more precise complexity characterizations are of little more than academic interest to practitioners. However, one quickly realizes that most reasonable methods for approximately or heuristically solving these problems requires the exact solution of TAUTOLOGY as a "subroutine." Indeed, at least one major software suite for logic minimization (ESPRESSO) utilizes just such a TAUTOLOGY subroutine [3], which of course has been tuned to work reasonably quickly on most real-world instances. In this context an "efficient" algorithm is an algorithm in P^{NP}, and a hardness result requires placing the problem in a complexity class above NP or coNP. It is therefore appropriate to investigate the complexity of these problems *relative to an NP oracle*, which requires precisely the sort of characterizations in the second level of the hierarchy that we provide in this paper.

2 Preliminaries

Let f be a Boolean function. An *implicant* of f is a conjunction that implies f; an *implicate* of f is a disjunction that is implied by f. For each implicant C, there is a natural associated partial assignment that sets the variable x_i to 1 if the literal x_i appears in conjunction C and to 0 if the literal $\overline{x_i}$ appears in C. When this partial assignment is applied to f, we get a function f' that is a tautology; in this way, we can think of an implicant of f as a partial assignment that forces f to one. Similarly, an implicate of f can be thought of as a partial assignment that forces f to zero.

If C is an implicant (resp. implicate) of f, then by vars(C) we mean the set of variables appearing in conjunction (resp. disjunction) C. The *length* of C is simply $|\text{vars}(C)|$. We adopt the following shorthand: $SI(f)$ denotes the length of the shortest implicant of f; $SC(f)$ denotes the length of the shortest implicate (sometimes called clause) of f; $S(f)$ is defined to be $\min\{SI(f), SC(f)\}$. In other words, $SI(f)$ is the smallest number of variables that must be fixed in order to force f to one; $SC(f)$ is the smallest number of variables that must be fixed to force f to zero, and $S(f)$ is the smallest number of variables that must be fixed to force f to a constant.

If ϕ is a formula, then $|\phi|$ is the *size* of ϕ, defined to be the number of occurrences of literals in ϕ, and $L(f)$ denotes the formula complexity of Boolean function f, i.e. the size of the smallest formula that computes f.

The two variants of the shortest implicant problem that we deal with in this paper are:

SHORTEST IMPLICANT[DNF]. Given a DNF formula ϕ and an integer k, is there an implicant of ϕ that contains k or fewer literals?

SHORTEST IMPLICANT[FORMULA]. Given a $(\wedge, \vee, \neg)$-formula ϕ and an integer k, is there an implicant of ϕ that contains k or fewer literals?

A technique used throughout this paper involves substituting formulae for individual variables. This can be thought of as "weighting" the variables. The following lemma (proof omitted) describes how these substitutions affect the length of the shortest implicants and implicates of a formula:

Lemma 1. *Let g and $f(x_1, x_2, \ldots, x_n)$ be Boolean functions, let $V \subseteq \{x_1, x_2, \ldots, x_n\}$ and let $f' = f(\phi_1, \phi_2, \ldots \phi_n)$, where ϕ_i is an independent copy of g if $x_i \in V$ and ϕ_i is just x_i otherwise. Then the following hold:*

1. *$SI(f') \geq \min_C \{|\text{vars}(C) \setminus V| + S(g)|\text{vars}(C) \cap V|\}$, where C ranges over all implicants of f.*

2. *if C is an implicant of f and vars(C) ∩ V = ∅ then C is an implicant of f'.*

By symmetry, the lemma also holds if "implicant" is replaced by "implicate" and "$SI(f')$" is replaced by "$SC(f')$."

3 Complexity of finding shortest implicants of a DNF

We first restate a positive result from [11]:

Lemma 2 ([11]). *Let $\phi = t_1 \vee t_2 \vee \ldots \vee t_n$ be a DNF formula. Then any shortest implicant C of ϕ may be obtained from some term t_i with at most $\log n$ additions of literals and at most $\log n$ deletions of literals (C is "$\log n$-close" to t_i).*

The class required to capture the complexity of SHORTEST IMPLICANT[DNF] we call $GC(\log^2 n, \text{coNP})$, after the "guess then check" framework of Cai and Chen [1] (however they are predominantly concerned with classes in this framework with far weaker verifiers). The class $GC(\log^2 n, \text{coNP})$ can be described as all languages L expressible as:

$$L = \{I : \exists X \text{ such that } R(I, X)\},$$

where $|X| \leq O(\log^2 |I|)$ and R is a coNP predicate. Notice that the usual logical characterization of Σ_2^p is identical except that $|X|$ is bounded only by some polynomial in $|I|$.

Theorem 1. SHORTEST IMPLICANT[DNF] *is $GC(\log^2 n, \text{coNP})$-complete.*

Proof. Membership in the class follows from Lemma 2. Hardness is via a generic reduction. Let L be a language in $GC(\log^2 n, \text{coNP})$, and let I be an instance. Let ϕ be a 3-DNF obtained from $R(I, X)$ via a Cook reduction. Formula ϕ consists of Boolean variables $x_1, x_2 \ldots x_k$ that constitute X (with $k = c \log^2 |I|$ for some constant c), and additional Boolean variables $y_1, y_2, \ldots y_m$. Using standard methods, we can ensure that no term of ϕ contains more than one x variable. Instance I is in L if and only if there exists an implicant of ϕ consisting of exactly the variables $x_1, x_2, \ldots x_k$.

We think of the variables $x_1, x_2 \ldots x_k$ as being grouped into $r = \log |I|$ blocks of $s = k/r$ variables each. We group the terms of ϕ similarly, with ϕ_i containing the disjunction of exactly those terms of ϕ in which some variable in the ith group appears (i.e. ϕ_1 contains those terms of ϕ that include one of $x_1, x_2, \ldots x_s$; ϕ_2 contains terms that include one of $x_{s+1}, x_{s+2}, \ldots x_{2s}$; etc...). Some terms in ϕ include no x variables at all, and we let ϕ_0 contain the disjunction of these terms. Because no term of ϕ contains more than one x variable, $\phi_0, \phi_1, \phi_2, \ldots, \phi_r$ partition the terms of ϕ, and of course $\phi \equiv \phi_0 \vee \phi_1 \vee \phi_2 \vee \cdots \vee \phi_r$.

Within each group of x variables, there are $t = 2^s = |I|^c$ possible partial assignments to those x variables. Denote by ϕ_{ij} the formula ϕ_i in which the jth partial assignment is applied to the x variables in the formula, for $1 \leq i \leq r$ and $1 \leq j \leq t$.

Finally, we define the following DNF formula f involving new variables a_{ij} and z_i:

$$
\begin{array}{rcccccc}
f = & a_{11}\overline{z_1} & \vee & a_{12}\overline{z_1} & \vee \ldots \vee & a_{1t}\overline{z_1} \\
\vee & z_1 a_{21}\overline{z_2} & \vee & z_1 a_{22}\overline{z_2} & \vee \ldots \vee & z_1 a_{2t}\overline{z_2} \\
& \vdots & & \vdots & \vdots & \vdots \\
\vee & z_{r-2}a_{(r-1)1}\overline{z_{r-1}} & \vee & z_{r-2}a_{(r-1)2}\overline{z_{r-1}} & \vee \ldots \vee & z_{r-2}a_{(r-1)t}\overline{z_{r-1}} \\
\vee & z_{r-1}a_{r1} & \vee & z_{r-1}a_{r2} & \vee \ldots \vee & z_{r-1}a_{rt}
\end{array}
$$

It is straightforward to verify that every implicant of f that consists of *only* the a variables must include at least one a_{ij} variable for each $i \in \{1 \ldots r\}$, and that every such conjunction is an implicant of f.

We are now one step away from the final formula. First we define ϕ' as follows:

$$
\phi' = f \wedge \left(\phi_0 \vee \bigvee_{i=1}^{r} \bigvee_{j=1}^{t} (a_{ij} \wedge \phi_{ij}) \right)
$$

When multiplied out into DNF, ϕ' is a 7-DNF. Finally, define ϕ'' to be ϕ' in which all variables except for the a variables have been substituted for by parity on $r+1$ variables. Notice that the resulting formula is still only polynomially large when multiplied out into DNF, because the DNF representations of the parity formulas each have $2^{r+1}/2 = |I|$ terms, and there are a constant number (at most 7) of substitutions per term of ϕ'.

We claim that ϕ'' has an implicant of length at most r if and only if $I \in L$.

($\Leftarrow$) If $I \in L$, then there exists an implicant of ϕ consisting of exactly the x variables. Let A be the corresponding partial assignment. By Lemma 1 it is sufficient to exhibit an implicant of ϕ' of length at most r consisting of only the a variables. The implicant of ϕ' consists of a_{ij} for each $1 \le i \le r$, where the partial assignment A when restricted to the ith group of x variables is the jth possible partial assignment. This is an implicant of f by our previous claim, and it is an implicant of the second half of ϕ' because its corresponding partial assignment preserves at least those terms in ϕ_A.

($\Rightarrow$) If there exists an implicant of ϕ'' of length at most r, then there must exist an implicant C of ϕ' of length at most r that consists of only the a variables. If not, then $SI(\phi'') > r$ by Lemma 1, a contradiction. Implicant C must be an implicant of f and so by our previous claim it must include at least one a_{ij} for each $i \in \{1 \ldots r\}$. Therefore, it includes *exactly* one a_{ij} for each such i, which implies that there is a partial assignment to ϕ consisting of exactly the x variables: for each $i \in \{1 \ldots r\}$, the ith group of x variables takes on the jth possible value, where a_{ij} is the single variable from among $\{a_{i1}, a_{i2}, \ldots a_{it}\}$ that appears in C. $\square$

More on the class GC($\log^2 n$, coNP). The complement of GC($\log^2 n$, coNP) also contains some interesting natural problems, notably:

ROBUST CNF-SAT Given a CNF formula ϕ and an integer k, is ϕ_ρ satisfiable for all restrictions ρ that set at most k variables to constants?

which is simply the complement of the CNF version of SHORTEST IMPLICANT[DNF] (which asks for the shortest implic*ate* of a CNF formula). By the previous theorem, it is complete for the complement of $GC(\log^2 n, \text{coNP})$. The "robust" versions of some other NP-complete problems are also complete for this class, although the $\log n$ restriction appears explicitly in the problem statement. For example, one can show that LOG-ROBUST DOMINATING SET (the problem of determining whether a graph has a small dominating set even after the deletion of at most $\log n$ edges) is complete for the complement of $GC(\log^2 n, \text{coNP})$.

The class $GC(\log^2 n, \text{coNP})$ appears to be only slightly larger than coNP. It is unlikely to include P^{NP} or even NP itself; intuitively, it does not possess enough "existential nondeterminism" to contain NP. This contrasts with the class $NP[\log^2 n]^{NP}$ [1] which *does* contain P^{NP}, and was the previous best upper bound on the complexity of SHORTEST IMPLICANT[DNF] [11]. Clarifying the relationship between $GC(\log^2 n, \text{coNP})$ is an interesting open quesion.

4 Inapproximability of shortest implicant problems

In this section we consider the approximability of SHORTEST IMPLICANT[DNF]and SHORTEST IMPLICANT[FORMULA].

SHORTEST IMPLICANT[DNF]. By the positive result in section 3, the algorithm that returns the shortest term in the input DNF formula is an approximation algorithm that is guaranteed to return an implicant that is within a $\log m$ *additive* factor of optimal, where m is the number of terms in the input formula. In the next theorem we show that this algorithm is essentially optimal (up to a small constant factor):

Theorem 2. SHORTEST IMPLICANT[DNF] *is coNP-hard to approximate to within an* $(1/4 - \epsilon) \log m$ *additive factor, where* m *is the number of terms in the input formula, for any constant* $\epsilon > 0$.

Proof. Let ϕ be an instance of 3-DNF TAUTOLOGY. We obtain ϕ' by "weighting" each variable by substituting parity on $\log m$ variables (via Lemma 1). The new formula has $O(m^4)$ terms.

If ϕ is a positive instance (i.e. it has an implicant of length zero), then ϕ' has a shortest implicant of length zero. The largest implicant returned by a $(1/4 - \epsilon) \log m$ additive approximation algorithm has length at most $(1/4 - \epsilon) \log m^4$. Otherwise, the shortest implicant of ϕ has length at least one, and so the shortest implicant of ϕ' has length at least $\log m$.

Clearly, for any $\epsilon > 0$, $(1/4 - \epsilon) \log m^4 = (1 - 4\epsilon) \log m < \log m$, and so the largest answer the approximation algorithm might give on a positive instance is strictly smaller than the smallest answer it might give on a negative instance. $\square$

---

[1] The class $NP[\log^2 n]$ is a subclass of NP in which the usual NDTM is permitted only $O(\log^2 n)$ nondeterministic steps. It is studied in [4, 7].

SHORTEST IMPLICANT[FORMULA]. We now give an optimal inapproximability result for SHORTEST IMPLICANT[FORMULA] (up to lower order terms), which implies that the best approximation algorithm simply returns a single satisfying assignment if there is one (achieving a factor n approximation). In [11] the following theorem is proved; we sketch the relevant aspects of the proof:

Theorem 3 ([11]). SHORTEST IMPLICANT[FORMULA] *is Σ_2^p-hard to approximate to within an $n^{1/2-\epsilon}$ factor, for any constant $\epsilon > 0$.*

Proof. (sketch) We begin with an instance of QSAT$_2$ given by $\exists X_1 \forall X_2 \phi$, where $X_1 = \{x_1, x_2, \ldots x_m\}$ and X_2 are the sets of existential and universal variables, respectively, and ϕ is a DNF formula involving the variables in X_1 and X_2. We define the formula ϕ' using additional variables $w_1, w_2, \ldots w_m$ as follows:

$$\phi' = \phi \wedge \bigwedge_{i=1}^{m} (x_i \overline{w_i} \vee \overline{x_i} w_i).$$

It is easy to show that if the instance of QSAT$_2$ is a positive instance, then ϕ' has an implicant of length $2m$ consisting of exactly the x and w variables; if the instance of QSAT$_2$ is a negative instance, then all implicants of ϕ' have length at least $2m+1$, and include all of the x and w variables and at least one variable from X_2.

We define ϕ'' to be ϕ' in which each variable in X_2 has been weighted by a parity formula on N^c variables (as described in Lemma 1), where $N = |\phi'|$ and c is a constant to be determined later. Then the largest answer an $n^{1/2-\epsilon}$-approximate algorithm might give on input ϕ'' if the instance of QSAT$_2$ is a positive instance is $2m \cdot O(N^{(2c+1)(1/2-\epsilon)})$ (since in this case there exists an implicant of ϕ'' of length $2m$, and $|\phi''| \leq O(N^{(2c+1)})$ because each substituted parity formula has quadratic size). The smallest answer an $n^{1/2-\epsilon}$ algorithm might give on input ϕ'' if the instance of QSAT$_2$ is a negative instance is $2m+N^c$, by Lemma 1 and our above observation about the structure of the implicants of ϕ'' in this case.

Finally, for sufficiently large N and $c \geq (3/4)\epsilon^{-1}$, we have

$$2m \cdot O(N^{(2c+1)(1/2-\epsilon)}) < 2m + N^c,$$

and hence an $n^{1/2-\epsilon}$-approximate algorithm for SHORTEST IMPLICANT[FORMULA] can distinguish between positive and negative instances of QSAT$_2$. $\square$

Notice that the $1/2$ in the approximation factor comes from the fact that the parity formulae have quadratic size. By Krapchenko's lower bound (cf. [12]), smaller parity formulae are not possible. However, there may exist smaller formulae that retain the critical property of the parity formulae used in the proof: namely, they have no "short" implicants or implicates. To make this formal, we need a definition: if f is a Boolean formula, let $R(f) = \log L(f)/\log S(f)$. Notice that $R(\text{parity}) = 2$, and that $R(f) \geq 1$ for any formula f.

If there exists an efficiently constructible formula family $F = (f_i)$ for which $R(f_i) < 2$ for all i, then we can use that family in place of the parity formulae in the above proof to obtain improved inapproximability to within an $n^{1/R(F)-\epsilon}$ factor. By the next lemma, it suffices to find a individual formula f instead of a family. The proof follows easily from Lemma 1.

Lemma 3 (Composition Lemma). *Let $f(x_1, x_2, \ldots, x_n)$ be a Boolean formula, and let $f' = f(f_1, f_2, \ldots, f_n)$, where $f_1, f_2, \ldots, f_n$ are independent copies of f. Then $R(f') \leq R(f)$.*

The following theorem is proved in the appendix:

Theorem 4. *There exists a formula f for which $R(f) \leq 1 + \delta$ for any $\delta > 0$.*

From this we have the following inapproximability result for SHORTEST IMPLICANT[FORMULA]:

Theorem 5. SHORTEST IMPLICANT[FORMULA] *is Σ_2^p-hard to approximate to within an $n^{1-\epsilon}$ factor, for any constant $\epsilon > 0$.*

Proof. Initially, the reduction exhaustively searches for the smallest formula f for which $R(f) \leq 1 + \delta$ (where δ depends on ϵ). The time required for the search is just a constant overhead in this context. Once such an f is located (its existence is guaranteed by Theorem 4) we compose it with itself repeatedly to obtain a formula whose shortest implicants and implicates are at least the desired length, and substitute it as we did with the parity formula in the proof of Theorem 3. $\square$

5 Conclusions and open problems

As noted in the introduction, natural optimization problems that are complete for the second level of the Polynomial Hierarchy are quite rare. In this paper we have not only added SHORTEST IMPLICANT[FORMULA] to this category, but also have established optimal inapproximability results for it. We have also given perhaps the first example of a natural problem that is complete for a class of limited non-determinism in the second level of the hierarchy, demonstrating the usefulness of limited non-determinism for classifying problems even at this level of hardness. Together with the results in [11], the complexity and inapproximability of shortest implicant problems are now well-understood, and it is hoped that their close relation to circuit minimization problems can now be exploited to prove completeness and formal approximability results for these important real-world problems.

In addition to the major open problems concerning circuit minimization problems, there are several smaller questions raised by this paper: (1) are there other natural complete problems for $GC(\log^2 n, \text{coNP})$ or its complement, preferably ones that do not include an explicit mention of $\log n$ in their definition? (2) what is the relation of $GC(\log^2 n, \text{coNP})$ to surrounding complexity classes (conditional on reasonable complexity-theoretic assumptions)? (3) are there other applications (perhaps in formula complexity) of the "restriction-resistant" formulae constructed in the appendix?

References

[1] Liming Cai and Jianer Chen. On the amount of nondeterminism and the power of verifying. *SIAM Journal on Computing*, 26(3):733–750, 1997.

[2] Olivier Coudert. Two-level logic minimization: an overview. *Integration, the VLSI journal*, 17(2):97–140, 1994.

[3] Srinivas Devadas, Adhijit Ghosh, and Kurt Keutzer. *Logic Synthesis*. McGraw-Hill, Inc., 1994.

[4] Josep Diaz and Jacobo Toran. Classes of bounded nondeterminism. *Mathematical Systems Theory*, 23(1):21–32, 1990.

[5] Edith Hemaspaandra and Gerd Wechsung. The minimization problem for boolean formulas. In *Proceedings of the 38th Annual Symposium on Foundations of Computer Science (FOCS '97)*, pages 575–84, 1997.

[6] E. J. McCluskey. Minimization of boolean functions. *Bell Systems Technical Journal*, 35(5):1417–44, 1956.

[7] Christos H. Papadimitriou and Mihalis Yannakakis. On limited nondeterminism and the complexity of the V–C dimension. *Journal of Computer and System Sciences*, 53(2):161–70, 1996.

[8] W. V. Quine. The problem of simplifying truth functions. *American Mathematics Monthly*, 59(8):521–531, 1952.

[9] L. J. Stockmeyer. The polynomial-time hierarchy. *Theoretical Computer Science*, 3(1):1–22, 1976.

[10] Tadeusz Strzemecki. Polynomial-time algorithms for generation of prime implicants. *Journal of Complexity*, 8(1):37–63, 1992.

[11] Christopher Umans. The minimum equivalent DNF problem and shortest implicants. In *Proceedings of the 39th Annual Symposium on Foundations of Computer Science (FOCS '98)*, pages 556–563, 1998.

[12] Ingo Wegener. *The complexity of Boolean functions*. Teubner, 1987.

A   Appendix: Existence of a formula f with $R(f) \leq 1 + \epsilon$

In this appendix we prove Theorem 4. We first note that relatively simple formulae will not suffice:

Theorem 6. *Let f be a monotone or read-once formula. Then $R(f) \geq 2$.*

Proof. (sketch) We show that the product $SI(f)SC(f)$ is a formal complexity measure (cf. [12]), and hence a lower bound for $L(f)$, by a simple induction on the size of the formula. Then $S(f) = \min\{SI(f), SC(f)\} \leq (SI(f)SC(f))^{1/2} \leq L(f)^{1/2}$, so $R(f) \geq 2$. □

We now proceed with the proof of Theorem 4. The following is the key lemma:

Lemma 4. *If there exists a formula g with $R(g) = c$ then there exists a formula g' with $R(g') \leq 2 - 1/c + \epsilon$ for any $\epsilon > 0$.*

Proof. First, we use the Composition Lemma to obtain a sequence of formulae $g_1, g_2, g_3, \ldots$ for which $R(g_i) \leq c$ for all i: let g_1 be g composed with itself so that $a = S(g_1)$ is sufficiently large (this requirement will be made more precise below), and define g_n for $n > 1$ to be g_1 composed with itself $n - 1$ times, so $S(g_n) \geq a^n$. Let m be the smallest even integer such that $m \geq a^c$.

Next, define recursively a sequence of formula $f_0, f_1, f_2, \ldots$ built from $g_1, g_2, \ldots$. In the following, superscripts identify multiple independent copies of each formula, and "maj" is a formula that is true if at least $m/2$ of its m arguments are true, where m is even.

$$f_0 = x \qquad f_n = \bigwedge_{i=1}^{m} \left(g_n^{(i)} \neg \mathrm{maj}(g_n^{(1)}, \ldots g_n^{(m)}) \vee f_{n-1}^{(i)} \right)$$

For $n > 0$, f_n is true iff for at least $(m/2 + 1)$ distinct values of i, $g_n^{(i)}$ is zero and $f_{n-1}^{(i)}$ is one, and for all other values of i, either $g_n^{(i)}$ is one or $f_{n-1}^{(i)}$ is one. We now determine bounds on $SC(f_n)$, $SI(f_n)$ and $L(f_n)$:

- For $SC(f_n)$: an implicate of f_n ($n > 0$) must either (1) force $g_n^{(i)}$ to zero and $f_{n-1}^{(i)}$ to zero for some i, or (2) for at least $m/2$ values of i force $g_n^{(i)}$ to one or $f_{n-1}^{(i)}$ to zero. In the first case, the implicate has length at least $a^n + SC(f_{n-1})$; in the second, the implicate has length at least $(m/2) \min\{a^n, SC(f_{n-1})\}$. We know that $SC(f_0) = 1$, and by induction, $SC(f_n) \geq a^n$; here we use the fact that we can select a large enough so that $m/2 \geq a$.
- For $SI(f_n)$: an implicant of f_n ($n > 0$) must force at least $m/2 + 1$ of the f_{n-1} to one. Again by induction we have that $SI(f_n) \geq (m/2 + 1)^n \geq (m/2)^n$. As an upper bound, notice that forcing all of the f_{n-1} to one forces the whole formula to one, so for $n > 0$, $SI(f_n) \leq mSI(f_{n-1})$. We know that $SI(f_0) = 1$, so by induction, $SI(f_n) \leq m^n$.
- For $L(f_n)$: we have the following recurrence: $L(f_0) = 1$ and $L(f_n) \leq p(m)a^{cn} + mL(f_{n-1}) \leq p(m)m^n + mL(f_{n-1})$, where $p(m) \leq O(m^d)$ is a fixed polynomial in m accounting for all of the occurrences of copies of g_n. It is easy to verify the upper bound $L(f_n) \leq m^n + p(m)nm^n \leq O(nm^{n+d})$.

Now, we take g_n' to be the disjunction of $k = \lceil SI(f_n)/SC(f_n) \rceil$ independent copies of f_n. This has the effect of multiplying the length of the shortest implicate by k, so that $S(g_n') = SI(f_n)$. We have:

$$R(g_n') \leq \frac{\log\left(O(nm^{n+d})\lceil \frac{m^n}{a^n} \rceil\right)}{\log((m/2)^n)} \leq \frac{\log\left(O(nm^d(m^2/a)^n)\right)}{\log((m/2)^n)}$$

As n approaches infinity, this last expression approaches $\log(m^2/a)/\log(m/2)$. By choosing a sufficiently large initially, this value can be made arbitrarily close to $2 - 1/c$. Then taking n sufficiently large yields a formula $g' = g_n'$ with $R(g') \leq 2 - 1/c + \epsilon$ for any $\epsilon > 0$.

One detail remains: the final step in the construction makes sense only if $SI(f_n) \geq SC(f_n)$; if this inequality does not hold, then we observe that f_n itself satisfies the lemma. $\square$

Now we apply this lemma repeatedly, starting with parity (for which $c = 2$), to show that for any $\delta > 0$, there exists an f with $R(f) \leq 1 + \delta$, thus proving Theorem 4.

The Wave Propagator Is Turing Computable

Klaus Weihrauch, Ning Zhong

Theoretische Informatik
FernUniversität Hagen
58084 Hagen, Germany

Abstract. Pour-El/Richards [PER89] and Pour-El/Zhong [PEZ97] have shown that there is a computable initial condition f for the three dimensional wave equation $u_{tt} = \Delta u$, $u(0,x) = f(x)$, $u_t(0,x) = 0$, $t \in \mathbb{R}$, $x \in \mathbb{R}^3$, such that the unique solution is not computable. This very remarkable result might indicate that the physical process of wave propagation is not computable and possibly disprove Turing's thesis. In this paper computability of wave propagation is studied in detail. Concepts from TTE, Type-2 theory of effectivity, are used to define adequate computability concepts on the spaces under consideration. It is shown that the solution operator of the Cauchy problem is computable on continuously differentiable initial conditions, where one order of differentiability is lost. The solution operator is also computable on Sobolev spaces. Finally the results are interpreted in a simple physical model.

1 Introduction

By Turing's Thesis a numerical function is computable by a physical device, if and only if it is computable by a Turing machine. The "if"-part is plausible, since every Turing machine can be simulated by a computer program which operates correctly as long as sufficient time and storage are available and no errors occur. On the other hand every program for a modern digital computer can be simulated by a Turing machine. What is more, most physicists believe that for processes which can be described by well-established theories (finitely many point masses interacting gravitationally, electromagnetic waves, quantum systems etc.) the future behavior can be computed with arbitrary precision at least in principle from sufficiently precisely given initial conditions, where the computations can be performed on digital computers, hence on Turing machines. Nevertheless, there might exist physical processes which are not Turing computable in this way.

Is Turing's computability concept sufficiently powerful to model all kind of physical processes? If the answer is yes, then perhaps Turing's Thesis could be derivable from the laws of physics or it should even be considered as fundamental law of physics itself. Otherwise, possibly Turing's Thesis had to be corrected. In the following we shall concentrate on a special type of physical processes, namely on scalar waves in Euclidean Space. We start from remarkable results by Pour-El/Richards [PER89] and Pour-El/Zhong [PEZ97], who constructed computable initial conditions f for the three dimensional wave equation

$$(**) \quad \begin{cases} u_{tt} = \Delta u, \\ u(0, x) = f(x), u_t(0, x) = 0, t \in \mathbb{R}, x \in \mathbb{R}^3 \end{cases}$$

such that the unique solutions are not computable. These examples have considerably confused logicians and computer scientists as well as physicists most of which accept Turing's Thesis or at least believe that wave propagation can be predicted (arbitrarily precisely) by means of digital computers. Various interpretations of the examples have been proposed and the discussions are still going on. Do these examples mean that the behavior of some physical devices cannot be described by Turing machines? If so, there might be a numerical function which is computable on a physical machine but not on a Turing machine and Turing's Thesis were false.

While for discrete sets there is a generally accepted computability theory, for real functions and other functions from analysis several non-equivalent computability concepts have been proposed, none of which, however, has been accepted by the majority of mathematicians or computer scientists. In this paper we use a computability concept, which is based on A.Turing's definition of computable real numbers [Tur36] and A.Grzegorczyk's definition of computable real functions [Grz55]. Among the various extensions which are consistent to each other (e.g., [PER89,Ko91,KW84,Eda95]) we use the representation approach, "Type-2 theory of effectivity" (TTE), which seems to be the most appropriate one for our purpose.

In the next section we in summarize some definitions from TTE and introduce computability concepts on the spaces we shall use later. In Section 3 we study wave propagation on spaces of continuously differentiable functions. We prove that on appropriate computation spaces the solution operator is computable and hence (as is well-known) continuous where one order of differentiability may be lost. However, the solution operator has computational irregularities for instances in which it is not continuous. This includes the Pour-El/Richards counter-example. In Section 4 we consider waves from Sobolev spaces and prove that also in this very natural setting the solution operator for the Cauchy problem of the wave equation is computable. Finally, in Section 5 we discuss the relation of our results to physics.

2   Computability on Second Countable Spaces

This section summarizes some basic concepts from Type-2 theory of effectivity (TTE) and introduces the computability concepts on the spaces we need for studying wave propagation. More details about TTE can be found in [KW85] [Wei87,Wei97,Wei]. In TTE, Turing machines are not only used to transform finite sequences $w \in \Sigma^*$ but also infinite sequences $p \in \Sigma^\omega$ of symbols. Every computable function is continuous w.r.t. the discrete topology on Σ^* and Cantor topology on Σ^ω. Finite or infinite sequences of symbols can be used as codes or names of objects from "abstract" sets M. This way Turing machines can used to compute functions on sets like the rational numbers $\mathbb{Q}$ or the real numbers $\mathbb{R}$.

A notation (representation) of a set M is a possibly partial surjective function $\nu :\subseteq \Sigma^* \to M$ ($\delta :\subseteq \Sigma^\omega \to M$). Let (M, δ) and (M', δ') be represented sets. An element $x \in M$ is δ-computable. iff it has a computable δ-name $p \in \Sigma^\omega$ (i.e., $\delta(p) = x$). A function $g :\subseteq \Sigma^\omega \to \Sigma^\omega$ is a (δ, δ')-realization of a function $f :\subseteq M \to M'$, iff $f \circ \delta(p) = \delta' \circ g(p)$ for all $p \in \mathrm{dom}(f \circ \delta)$. The function f is called (δ, δ')-computable (-continuous). iff it has a computable (continuous) (δ, δ')-realization. An extension to functions with several arguments is straightforward. The representation δ is reducible (t-reducible) to δ'. $\delta \leq \delta'$ ($\delta \leq_t \delta'$). iff the identical embedding is (δ, δ')-computable (-continuous). Equivalence (t-equivalence) is defined by $\delta \equiv \delta' : \Longleftrightarrow \delta \leq \delta'$ and $\delta' \leq \delta$ ($\delta \equiv_t \delta' : \Longleftrightarrow \delta \leq_t \delta'$ and $\delta' \leq_t \delta$). Two representations of a set M induce the same computability (continuity) on M. iff they are equivalent (t-equivalent). An extension to notations is straightforward.

There is an "effective" representation $\eta : \Sigma^\omega \to F^{\omega\omega}$ (where $F^{\omega\omega}$ is a set of continuos functions $f :\subseteq \Sigma^\omega \to \Sigma^\omega$ containing an extension of every continuous partial function $g :\subseteq \Sigma^\omega \to \Sigma^\omega$) which satisfies the utm-theorem (universal Turing machine theorem) and the smn-theorem. A natural representation $[\delta \to \delta']$ of the (δ, δ')-continuous functions $f : M \to M'$ is defined by $[\delta \to \delta'](p) = f$. iff $\eta(p)$ is a (δ, δ')-realization of f. It has the remarkable property that for any representation γ of a set of continuous functions $f : M \to M'$. the evaluation function $(f, x) \mapsto f(x)$ is $(\gamma, \delta, \delta')$-computable iff $\gamma \leq [\delta \to \delta']$.

Among the numerous representations of a set the "admissible representations" are of particular interest. For an admissible representation a name of an element $x \in M$ is a sequence $p = (w_0, w_1, w_2, \ldots)$ of words. where each $w_i \in \Sigma'$ encodes a "property" $A_i \subseteq M$ of x (x has the property A_i iff $x \in A_i$). For defining a computability concept on M it suffices to specify a countable supply $\sigma \subseteq 2^M$ of "atomic properties" and a notation $\nu :\subseteq \Sigma^* \to \sigma$ of this set σ.

Definition 1. *A computation space is a triple* $\mathbf{S} = (M, \sigma, \nu)$, *where* M *is a set,* $\sigma \subseteq 2^M$ *is a countable set such that* $\{A \in \sigma \mid x \in A\} = \{A \in \sigma \mid y \in A\}$ *implies* $x = y$ *for all* $x, y \in M$, *and* $\nu :\subseteq \Sigma^* \to \sigma$ *is a notation of the set* σ *(with* $\mathrm{dom}(\nu) \subseteq \Sigma'$*) such that* $\{(u, v) \mid \nu(u) = \nu(v)\}$ *is recursively enumerable.*

We shall call the elements of σ "atomic properties". Each element of M can be identified by its atomic properties and ν has a r.e. domain. The induced representation and topology are:

Definition 2. *Let* $\mathbf{S} = (M, \sigma, \nu)$ *be a computation space. Let* $\tau_\mathbf{S}$ *be the topology on* M *generated by* σ *as a subbase. Define the standard representation* $\delta_\mathbf{S} :\subseteq \Sigma^\omega \to M$ *by* $\delta_\mathbf{S}(p) = x$ *iff* $p = (w_0, w_1, w_2, \ldots)$ *with* $\{w \in \mathrm{dom}(\nu) \mid x \in \nu(w)\} = \{w_0, w_1, w_2, \ldots\}$.

Therefore, a $\delta_\mathbf{S}$-name of x is a list of (all ν-names of) all atomic properties of x in arbitrary order. For computation spaces $\mathbf{S} = (M, \sigma, \nu)$ and $\mathbf{S}' = (M', \sigma', \nu')$. a function $f :\subseteq M \to M'$ is $(\delta_\mathbf{S}, \delta_{\mathbf{S}'})$-computable. iff there is some Type-2 machine which for any $x \in \text{dom}(f)$ maps any list of all atomic properties of x to a list of all atomic properties of $f(x)$.

For functions between computation spaces $\mathbf{S} = (M, \sigma, \nu)$ and $\mathbf{S}' = (M', \sigma', \nu')$ continuity has a very elementary interpretation in terms of atomic properties. By definition, a function $f :\subseteq M \to M'$ is continuous at $x \in \text{dom}(f)$ iff for all $A' \in \sigma'$ with $f(x) \in A'$ there are $A_1, A_2, \ldots, A_k \in \sigma$ such that $x \in A_1 \cap A_2 \cap \ldots \cap A_k$ and $f[A_1 \cap A_2 \cap \ldots \cap A_k] \subseteq A'$. Informally this means that every atomic property A' of $f(x)$ follows already from *finitely many* atomic properties $A_1, A_2, \ldots, A_k$ of x. The following continuity theorem is fundamental.

Theorem 3. *A function is $(\delta_{\mathbf{S}}, \delta_{\mathbf{S}'})$-continuous iff it is $(\tau_{\mathbf{S}}, \tau_{\mathbf{S}'})$-continuous. Every $(\delta_{\mathbf{S}}, \delta_{\mathbf{S}'})$-computable function is $(\tau_{\mathbf{S}}, \tau_{\mathbf{S}'})$-continuous.*

The above computability definition is applicable to most of the spaces considered in analysis and in particular in physics. For fixing a computability concept on M choose a countable set σ of "atomic properties" (which selects a concept of "approximation" on M) and a notation ν of σ (which selects a concept of computation). Although for a set M the set σ and a notation ν of σ can be chosen almost arbitrarily, in most applications the set σ of atomic properties (and therefore the topology $\tau_{\mathbf{S}}$) as well as the notation ν of it are determined by the available properties like results of better and better measurements, of a preceeding computation or of throwing the dice. In the following we introduce some concrete computation spaces which we shall use later.

Euclidean Space $\mathbb{R}^n$:
Let $\sigma := \{B(x, r) \mid x \in \mathbb{Q}^n, r \in \mathbb{Q}, r > 0\}$ be the set of open balls with rational center and radius and let ν be some standard notation of σ. Let $\rho_n := \delta_{\mathbf{S}} :\subseteq \Sigma^\omega \to \mathbb{R}^n$ be the associated representation ($\rho := \rho_1$). Obviously, $\tau_{\mathbf{S}}$ is the standard topology $\tau_{\mathbb{R}^n}$ on $\mathbb{R}^n$. Then a function $f : \mathbb{R}^n \to \mathbb{R}$ is (ρ_n, ρ)-computable iff it is computable in the sense of Grzegorczyk [Grz55,PER89], G-computable for short.

$C(\mathbb{R}^n) := \{f : \mathbb{R}^n \to \mathbb{R} \mid f \text{ is continuous}\}$:
Let $\sigma_n := \{R_{arcd} \mid a \in \mathbb{Q}^n, r, c, d \in \mathbb{Q}, r > 0, c < d\}$ be the set of atomic properties where $R_{arcd} := \{f \in C(\mathbb{R}^n) \mid f[\overline{B}(a, r)] \subseteq (c, d)\}$, and let ν_n be some standard notation of σ_n. Let $\delta_n := \delta_{\mathbf{S}}$ be the associated representation of $C(\mathbb{R}^n)$. The associated topology $\tau_n := \tau_{\mathbf{S}}$ is known as the compact open or strong topology on $C(\mathbb{R}^n)$. One can show $\delta_n \equiv [\rho_n \mapsto \rho]$. Consequently, $f, x \mapsto f(x)$ is (δ, ρ_n, ρ)-computable $\iff$ $\delta \leq \delta_n$ for all representations δ of $C(\mathbb{R}^n)$, i.e., δ_n is $\leq$-complete in the set of all representations δ of $C(\mathbb{R}^n)$ for which the evaluation function is computable. Therefore, the representation δ_n is tailor-made for computing function values [Wei87,Wei95,Wei97].

$C^1(\mathbb{R}^n) := \{f \in C(\mathbb{R}^n) \mid \partial_{x_i} f \in C(\mathbb{R}^n) (1 \leq i \leq n)\}$:
Let $\sigma_n^1 := \{R_{arcd}^i \mid 0 \leq i \leq n, a \in \mathbb{Q}^n, r, c, d \in \mathbb{Q}, r > 0, c < d\}$ with $R_{arcd}^0 := R_{arcd} \cap C^1(\mathbb{R}^n)$ and $R_{arcd}^i := \{f \in C^1(\mathbb{R}^n) \mid \partial_{x_i} f \in R_{arcd}\}$ be the set of atomic properties and let ν_n^1 be a standard notation of σ_n^1. Then $\tau_n^1 := \tau_{\mathbf{S}}$ is the smallest topology τ on $C^1(\mathbb{R}^n)$ such that the functions $f \mapsto f$ and $f \mapsto \partial_{x_i} f$ ($1 \leq i \leq n$) are (τ, τ_n)-continuous. Furthermore, the representation $\delta_n^1 := \delta_{\mathbf{S}}$ is

$\leq$-complete in the set of all representations δ of $C^1(\mathbb{R}^n)$ for which the functions $f \mapsto f$ and $f \mapsto \partial_{x_i} f$ $(1 \leq i \leq n)$ are (δ, δ_n)-computable. Roughly speaking, a δ_n^1-name of f is a combination of δ_n-names of f, $\partial_{x_1} f$, $\partial_{x_2} f$, ... and $\partial_{x_n} f$. The representation δ_n^1 is tailor-made for computing function values as well as first partial derivatives.

$C^k(\mathbb{R}^n)$ of k-times continuously differentiable functions $f : \mathbb{R}^n \to \mathbb{R}$:
Generalize the case of $C^1(\mathbb{R}^n)$ straightforwardly. A δ_n^k-name of a function $f \in C^k(\mathbb{R}^n)$ is a combination of δ_n-names of all partial derivatives $\partial^\alpha f$ with $|\alpha| \leq k$.

$L^2(\mathbb{R}^n)$:
For $x_i, y_i \in \mathbb{R}$ define $(x_1, \ldots, x_n) < (y_1, \ldots, y_n)$. iff $x_i < y_i$ for $i = 1, \ldots, n$. For $a, b \in \mathbb{R}^n$ with $a < b$ define $\mathbb{I}_{ab}(x) := (1,$ if $a < x < b$, 0 otherwise). Let $M_0 := \{\sum_{i=1}^k c_i \cdot \mathbb{I}_{a,b_i} \mid k \in \mathbb{N}, c_i$ rational complex, $a_i, b_i \in \mathbb{Q}^n, a_i < b_i\}$ be the countable set of rational complex valued finite step functions. The set M_0 is dense in the metric space $(L^2(\mathbb{R}^n), d)$, where $d(f,g) := (\int_{\mathbb{R}^n} |f(x)-g(x)|^2 dx)^{1/2}$. Let $\sigma := \{B(f, 2^{-n}) \mid f \in M_0, n \in \mathbb{N}\}$ (a set of open balls) be the set of atomic properties of a computation space $\mathbf{S} = (L^2(\mathbb{R}^n), \sigma, \nu)$. where ν is a canonical notation of σ. Then $\tau_\mathbf{S}$ is the canonical topology on $L^2(\mathbb{R}^n)$. Define $\delta_L := \delta_\mathbf{S}$.

By definition. for a computation space $\mathbf{S} = (M, \sigma, \nu)$ a standard name of $x \in M$ is a list of *all* names of *all* atomic properties $A \in \sigma$ with $x \in A$. In all practical cases there are equivalent representations (defining the same computability concept on M) which are much simpler and therefore more useful for concrete computations.

3 Continuously Differentiable Initial Conditions

We consider the Cauchy problem of the three dimensional wave equation

$$(*) \quad \begin{cases} u_{tt} = \Delta u, \\ u(0, x) = f(x), u_t(0, x) = g(x), t \in \mathbb{R}, x \in \mathbb{R}^3. \end{cases}$$

Classically it is known that if the Cauchy data satisfy $f \in C^k(\mathbb{R}^3)$ and $g \in C^{k-1}(\mathbb{R}^3)$, then the initial value problem $(*)$ has a unique solution given by

$$u(t, x) = \frac{1}{4\pi t} \int_{|y-x|=t} g(y) d\sigma(y) + \frac{\partial}{\partial t} \left(\frac{1}{4\pi t} \int_{|y-x|=t} f(y) d\sigma(y) \right)$$

$$= \int_{S^2} [tg(x+tn) + f(x+tn) + t \nabla f(x+tn) \cdot n] d\sigma(n)$$

$$(3.1)$$

where $u \in C^{k-1}(\mathbb{R}^4)$. First we prove that the solution operator mapping f and g to u is computable. We prepare the proof by two lemmas.

Lemma 4. *For ρ-computable $a, b \in \mathbb{R}$ the function $f \mapsto \int_a^b f(x) dx$ is (δ_1, ρ)-computable on $C(\mathbb{R})$.*

It is well known and proved easily that there is a Type-2 machine, which for any δ_1-name of some $f \in C(\mathbb{R})$ computes a ρ-name of its integral from a to b.

Lemma 5. *The function $f \mapsto \int_{S^2} f(n)\, d\sigma(n)$ is (δ_3, ρ)-computable.*

Theorem 6. *For $k \geq 1$ the solution operator $S : (f, g) \mapsto u$ of the Cauchy problem $(*)$ mapping $f \in C^k(\mathbb{R}^3)$ and $g \in C^{k-1}(\mathbb{R}^3)$ to the solution $u \in C^{k-1}(\mathbb{R}^4)$ is $(\delta_3^k, \delta_3^{k-1}, \delta_4^{k-1})$-computable.*

Corollary 7. *Consider $k \geq 1$.*

1. *The solution operator*

$$S' : (f, g, t) \mapsto u(t, \cdot)$$

of the Cauchy problem $(*)$ mapping $f \in C^k(\mathbb{R}^3)$, $g \in C^{k-1}(\mathbb{R}^3)$ and $t \in \mathbb{R}$ to the solution $u(t, \cdot) \in C^{k-1}(\mathbb{R}^3)$ is $(\delta_3^k, \delta_3^{k-1}, \rho, \delta_3^{k-1})$-computable.
2. *For each $t \in \mathbb{R}$ (computable $t \in \mathbb{R}$) the solution operator*

$$S''(t)(f, g) \mapsto u(t, \cdot)$$

of the Cauchy problem $(*)$ mapping $f \in C^k(\mathbb{R}^3)$ and $g \in C^{k-1}(\mathbb{R}^3)$ to the solution $u(t, \cdot) \in C^{k-1}(\mathbb{R}^3)$ at time t is $(\delta_3^k, \delta_3^{k-1}, \delta_3^{k-1})$-continuous (-computable).

Remember that "δ-computable" implies "δ-continuous" and by Theorem 3 for standard representations of computation spaces "δ-continuous" is equivalent to "continuous". Remember also that computable operators map computable elements to computable ones.

Theorem 6 and Corollary 7 indicate that the solution u of the wave equation can be less regular than the initial data. There is a possible loss of one order of differentiability: $u(0, \cdot) = f \in C^k(\mathbb{R}^3)$ and $u_t(0, \cdot) = g \in C^{k-1}(\mathbb{R}^3)$ guarantee only $u \in C^{k-1}(\mathbb{R}^4)$, $u(t, \cdot) \in C^{k-1}(\mathbb{R}^3)$ and $u_t(t, \cdot) \in C^{k-2}(\mathbb{R}^3)$. For concrete counter-examples see [WZ98].

By Corollary 7, on $C^1(\mathbb{R}^3)$ the special solution operator $f \mapsto S'(f, 0, 1)$ is (δ_3^1, δ_3)-computable, hence (τ_3^1, τ_3)-continuous by Theorem 3. We show, however, that it is not (τ_3, τ_3)-continuous, hence not (δ_3, δ_3)-computable, on $C^1(\mathbb{R}^3)$. (Remember that a linear operator is continuous everywhere or nowhere.)

Theorem 8. *For any $t \in \mathbb{R} \setminus \{0\}$, the wave propagator $S_t : f \mapsto S'(f, 0, t)$, which sends the initial Cauchy data $f \in C^1(\mathbb{R}^3)$ and $g \equiv 0$ to the solution at time t, is not (τ_3, τ_3)-continuous.*

By this theorem no finite set of atomic properties listed by a δ_3-name of $f \in C^1(\mathbb{R}^3)$ suffices to guarantee a "narrow" atomic property for a δ_3-name of the solution. In other words, the topology τ_3 associated with the representation δ_3 on the domain $C^1(\mathbb{R}^3)$ of the solution operator is not sufficiently fine for determining a δ_3-name of the continuous solution.

In summary, for $t \neq 0$ the solution operator S_t does not necessarily map $C(\mathbb{R}^3)$ into itself, does not necessarily map $C^1(\mathbb{R}^3)$ into itself, maps $C^1(\mathbb{R}^3)$ to $C(\mathbb{R}^3)$ and is (τ_3^1, τ_3)-continuous but not (τ_3, τ_3)-continuous on $C^1(\mathbb{R}^3)$.

Parallel to these topological irregularities of the solution operator there are computational ones. Myhill gave an example [Myh71] of a δ_1-computable differentiable function $f \in C^1(\mathbb{R})$ such that the derivative $f' \in C(\mathbb{R})$ is not δ_1-computable. (Notice that the differentiation operator D on $C^1(\mathbb{R})$ is *not* (τ_1, τ_1)-continuous.) A more general situation where noncontinuity causes noncomputability is the "First Main Theorem" by Pour-El and Richards [PER89]. As an important application they show:

Theorem 9. *(Pour-El/Richards) There is a δ_3-computable function $f \in C^1(\mathbb{R}^3)$ (i.e., continuously differentiable function) such that the solution of the Cauchy problem $(**)$ at time $t = 1$, $u(1, \cdot)$, is not δ_3-computable.*

This result has been strengthened by Pour-El and Zhong [PEZ97]. According to a general theorem by Brattka [Bra97] any function of sufficiently high degree of discontinuity with some weak computability properties maps some computable elements to noncomputable ones.

4   The Wave Propagator on Sobolev Spaces

While the wave propagator does not preserve $C^k \times C^{k-1}$ regularity. for any real number s it preserves $H^s \times H^{s-1}$ regularity. where H^s is the Sobolev space of order s. In this section we show that the wave propagator is even computable when operating on initial data from Sobolev spaces.

Definition 10.   *For any $s \in \mathbb{R}$, the Sobolev space $H^s(\mathbb{R}^d)$ is the set of all generalized functions u such that $(1 + |\xi|^2)^{s/2}\hat{u}(\xi) \in L^2(\mathbb{R}^d)$, where $\hat{u}(\xi)$ is the Fourier transform of u. $H^s(\mathbb{R}^d)$ is a separable Hilbert space with the norm*

$$\|u\|_s = \|u\|_{H^s(\mathbb{R}^d)} = \left(\int_{\mathbb{R}^d} (1 + |\xi|^2)^s |\hat{u}(\xi)|^2 d\xi \right)^{1/2}.$$

L^2-computability induces a natural computability concept on $H^s(\mathbb{R}^d)$. In the following let δ_L be the representation of $L^2(\mathbb{R}^3)$ from Section 2.

Definition 11.   *For any $s \in \mathbb{R}$ define a representation δ^s of $H^s(\mathbb{R}^3)$ by*

$$\delta^s(p) = f :\iff \delta_L(p) = (1 + |\xi|^2)^{s/2}\hat{f}.$$

Sobolev spaces are suitable for analyzing the wave equation computationally as well: The solution operator of $(*)$ propagates Sobolev computability. As our main theorem of this section we prove that the operator $(f, g, t) \mapsto S_W(t)(f, g)$ is a computable operator which for any t sends every initial Cauchy data $(f, g) \in H^s(\mathbb{R}^3) \times H^{s-1}(\mathbb{R}^3)$ to the Cauchy data $(f_t, g_t) \in H^s(\mathbb{R}^3) \times H^{s-1}(\mathbb{R}^3)$ at time t. In other words. there is a Type-2 Turing machine which computes a name for the corresponding solution when fed with a name of the time t and names of the initial data.

We prepare the proof by computational versions of the facts that $f + f' \in L^2$ and $f(x)g(x) \in L^2$. if $f, f' \in L^2$ and g is continuous and bounded.

Lemma 12.

1. *Addition* $(f, f') \mapsto f + f'$ *on* L^2 *is* $(\delta_L, \delta_L, \delta_L)$-*computable.*
2. *Multiplication*

$$\mathrm{Mul} : (f, g, N) \mapsto fg \ \text{where} \ fg(x) := f(x)g(x)$$

for $f \in L^2(\mathbb{R}^3), g \in C(\mathbb{R}^3)$ *and* $N \in \mathbb{R}$ *with* $\forall x\, |g(x)| < N$ *is* $(\delta_L, \delta_3, \rho, \delta_L)$-*computable.*

Corollary 13. *Let* $h : \mathbb{R} \times \mathbb{R}^3 \to \mathbb{R}$ *be* (ρ, ρ_3, ρ)-*computable and* $b : \mathbb{R} \to \mathbb{R}$ *be* (ρ, ρ)-*computable such that* $|h(t, x)| \le b(t)$ *for all* $x \in \mathbb{R}^3$ *and* $t \in \mathbb{R}$. *Then* $(f, t) \mapsto fh(t, \cdot) \in L^2$ *for* $f \in L^2$ *and* $t \in \mathbb{R}$ *is* $(\delta_L, \rho, \delta_L)$-*computable.*

For the precise statement of the theorem we use the product $[\delta, \delta']$ of two representations δ and δ' canonically defined by $[\delta, \delta']\langle p, p'\rangle := (\delta(p), \delta'(p'))$.

Theorem 14. *Let* $s \in \mathbb{R}$ *be an arbitrary real number. Then the wave propagator*

$$S'_W : H^s(\mathbb{R}^3) \times H^{s-1}(\mathbb{R}^3) \times \mathbb{R} \to H^s(\mathbb{R}^3) \times H^{s-1}(\mathbb{R}^3)$$

mapping initial data in $H^s(\mathbb{R}^3) \times H^{s-1}(\mathbb{R}^3)$ *to the solution in* $H^s(\mathbb{R}^3) \times H^{s-1}(\mathbb{R}^3)$ *at time* t *is* $([\delta^s, \delta^{s-1}], \rho, [\delta^s, \delta^{s-1}])$-*computable.*

Corollary 15. *For each real number* s *and each computable real number* t *the wave propagator*

$$S_W(t) : H^s(\mathbb{R}^3) \times H^{s-1}(\mathbb{R}^3) \to H^s(\mathbb{R}^3) \times H^{s-1}(\mathbb{R}^3)$$

mapping initial data in $H^s(\mathbb{R}^3) \times H^{s-1}(\mathbb{R}^3)$ *to solution in* $H^s(\mathbb{R}^3) \times H^{s-1}(\mathbb{R}^3)$ *at time* t *is* $([\delta^s, \delta^{s-1}], [\delta^s, \delta^{s-1}])$-*computable.*

The proofs show that the Type-2 machine computing the solution of (∗) from the initial condition and the time does not depend on s and does not need a name of s as an input. Therefore, the real number s determining the Sobolev space $H^s(\mathbb{R}^3)$ does not need to be computable. It is merely part of the definition of the representation δ^s:

$$\delta^s(p) = f : \iff \delta_L(p) = (1 + |\xi|^2)^{s/2} \hat{f}.$$

5   Relation to Physical Reality

In the preceeding sections we have studied computability properties of the solution operator of the wave equation. From the variety of computability models for analysis discussed today we have chosen "Type 2 Theory of Effectivity" (TTE) which is conceptually simple, realistic and very flexible. In Section 2 we have outlined the concepts and definitions of TTE which are needed for the rest of the paper. In particular, each of our computability definitions is based on or associated with a concept of *approximation* formalized by a topology which is generated by a subbase of "atomic properties".

In Section 3 we have discussed the solution operator of the wave equation acting on k times continuously differentiable initial conditions. We have shown that it is computable on appropriate computation spaces but does not preserve the order of differentiability in general.

In particular, the wave propagator $S_1 : C^1(\mathbb{R}^3) \to C(\mathbb{R}^3)$, which sends the initial Cauchy data $u(0, \cdot) = f \in C^1(\mathbb{R}^3)$ and $u_t(0, \cdot) = g \equiv 0$ to the solution at time 1, is (δ_3^1, δ_3)-computable. Hence it is (τ_3^1, τ_3)-continuous and maps δ_3^1-computable initial data to δ_3-computable solutions. However, S_1 is not (τ_3, τ_3)-continuous. As a consequence, S_1 cannot be (δ_3, δ_3)-computable, and according to the examples by Pour-El/Richards [PER89] and Pour-El/Zhong [PEZ97] S_1 maps some δ_3-computable initial condition $f_{PR} \in C^1(\mathbb{R}^3)$ to a solution $S_1(f_{PR})$ which is not δ_3-computable. Of course, such a function $f_{PR} \in C^1(\mathbb{R}^3)$ cannot be δ_3^1-computable, i.e., it cannot have δ_3-computable partial first derivatives. In Section 4 we have considered waves from Sobolev spaces and proved that also in this very natural setting the solution operator for the Cauchy problem of the wave equation is computable.

We return to our question, whether the Pour-El/Richards counter-example induces a physical method for computing a number function which is not Turing computable. We consider a physical setting which is related to our mathematical theory as follows: (A1) The possible states of the system are 3-dimensional waves $f \in C(\mathbb{R}^3)$. (A2) Waves propagate according to the solution (3.1) of the wave equation (*). (A3) For a given wave f, the result of an observation or measurement at a given time are finitely many properties from σ_3^1 about amplitudes and amplitudes of the first partial derivarives of f. (A4) No other measurements can be performed. (A5) The properties $A_1, A_2, \ldots, A_k \in \sigma^1$ can be observed simultaneously in State f, if, and only if, $f \in A_1 \cap A_2 \cap \ldots \cap A_k$.

Can we determine all σ_3-properties of $S_1(f_{PR})$ by measurements? By assumptions A3 and A4, the initial condition f_{PR} cannot be prepared exactly at time 0. Therefore, we have to repeat experiments of the following type: Choose initial atomic properties $A_1, \ldots, A_k \in \sigma_3^1$ and a final property $B \in \sigma_3$: prepare some wave with the properties $A_1, \ldots, A_k$ at time 0 and try to observe Property B at time 1. If we could compute every finite subset of σ_3^1-properties of the function f_{PR}, we were able to determine gradually a list of all σ_3-properties of $S_1(f_{PR})$. Since $S_1(f_{PR})$ is not δ_3-computable, such a list is not computable and we would have a physical procedure to compute a number function which is not Turing computable. But since f_{PR} is not δ_3^1-computable but only δ_3-computable, we can compute only finite subsets of σ_3 (i.e., properties of amplitudes of f_{PR}). Since the operator S_1 is not (τ_3, τ_3)-continuous in f_{PR}, the properties $B \in \sigma$ which in this case can be observed at time 1 do not converge to the single function $f_{PR} \in C(\mathbb{R}^3)$.

The assumptions (A3)–(A5) about measurements are idealizing reality, since they admit arbitrarily precise measurements. Furthermore, it is not clear, whether for waves measurements of properties in σ_3 or σ_3^1 ("amplitude boxes") are realistic at all. For example, averaging energy over small cubes, which leads to L^2-topology, might be more realistic. In summary, it seems to be very unlikely that the Pour-El/Richards counter-example can be used to build a physical machine with a "wave subroutine" computing a function which is not Turing computable. We may still believe that Turing's Thesis holds.

References

[Bra97] Vasco Brattka. Computable invariance. In Tao Jiang and D.T. Lee, editors, *Computing and Combinatorics*, volume 1276 of *Lecture Notes in Computer Science*, pages 146–155, Berlin, 1997. Springer. Third Annual Conference, COCOON'97, Shanghai, China, August 1997.

[Eda95] Abbas Edalat. Domain theory and integration. *Theoretical Computer Science*, 151:163–193, 1995.

[Grz55] Andrzej Grzegorczyk. Computable functionals. *Fundamenta Mathematicae*, 42:168–202, 1955.

[Ko91] Ker-I Ko. *Complexity Theory of Real Functions*. Progress in Theoretical Computer Science. Birkhäuser, Boston, 1991.

[KW84] Christoph Kreitz and Klaus Weihrauch. Compactness in constructive analysis revisited. Informatik Berichte 49, FernUniversität Hagen, Hagen, September 1984.

[KW85] Cristoph Kreitz and Klaus Weihrauch. Theory of representations. *Theoretical Computer Science*, 38:35–53, 1985.

[Myh71] J. Myhill. A recursive function defined on a compact interval and having a continuous derivative that is not recursive. *Michigan Math. J.*, 18:97–98, 1971.

[PER89] Marian B. Pour-El and J. Ian Richards. *Computability in Analysis and Physics*. Perspectives in Mathematical Logic. Springer, Berlin, 1989.

[PEZ97] Marian Pour-El and Ning Zhong. The wave equation with computable initial data whose unique solution is nowhere computable. *Mathematical Logic Quarterly*, 43(4):499–509, 1997.

[Tur36] Alan M. Turing. On computable numbers, with an application to the "Entscheidungsproblem". *Proceedings of the London Mathematical Society*, 42(2):230–265, 1936.

[Wei] Klaus Weihrauch. *An Introduction to Computable Analysis*. (Book, to appear 1999).

[Wei87] Klaus Weihrauch. *Computability*, volume 9 of *EATCS Monographs on Theoretical Computer Science*. Springer, Berlin, 1987.

[Wei95] Klaus Weihrauch. A simple introduction to computable analysis. Informatik Berichte 171, FernUniversität Hagen, Hagen, July 1995. 2nd edition.

[Wei97] Klaus Weihrauch. A foundation for computable analysis. In Douglas S. Bridges, Cristian S. Calude, Jeremy Gibbons, Steve Reeves, and Ian H. Witten, editors, *Combinatorics, Complexity, and Logic*, Discrete Mathematics and Theoretical Computer Science, pages 66–89, Singapore, 1997. Springer. Proceedings of DMTCS'96.

[WZ98] Klaus Weihrauch and Ning Zhong. The wave propagtor is Turing computable. In Ker-I Ko, Anil Nerode, Marian B. Pour-El, Klaus Weihrauch, and Jiří Wiedermann, editors, *Computability and Complexity in Analysis*, volume 235 of *Informatik-Berichte*, pages 127–155. FernUniversität Hagen, August 1998. CCA Workshop, Brno, Czech Republik, August, 1998.

An FPTAS for Agreeably Weighted Variance on a Single Machine (Extended Abstract)

Gerhard J. Woeginger

Institut für Mathematik B, TU Graz, Graz, Austria

Abstract. We investigate the following scheduling problem: There is a single machine and a set of jobs. Every job is specified by its processing time and by its weight. The goal is to find a schedule that minimizes the sum of squared deviations from the weighted average job completion time. Jobs with small processing times have large weights, and hence the weights are agreeable.

This problem is $\mathcal{NP}$-hard. In 1995, Cai derived a fully polynomial time approximation scheme for the special case where the weights of the jobs are polynomially bounded in the number n of jobs. In this paper we completely settle the approximability status of this scheduling problem: We construct a fully polynomial time approximation scheme for the general case, without putting any restrictions on the weights of the jobs.

1 Introduction

We consider a scheduling system that consists of n jobs $J_1, \ldots, J_n$ that are to be processed without preemption on a single machine. Job J_j ($j = 1, \ldots, n$) has a positive integer processing time p_j and a positive integer weight w_j. The total weight $\sum_{j=1}^{n} w_j$ of the jobs is denoted by W. In a schedule σ, we denote by C_j the completion time of job J_j and by $\overline{C}$ the average weighted completion time of the jobs, i.e.

$$\overline{C} = \frac{1}{W} \sum_{j=1}^{n} w_j C_j. \tag{1}$$

The goal is to find a schedule σ that minimizes the *weighted variance* of the job completion times, i.e. the value

$$\text{VAR}(\sigma) = \sum_{j=1}^{n} w_j (C_j - \overline{C})^2. \tag{2}$$

This scheduling problem is called the *weighted completion time variance* problem (W-CTV, for short). A special case of W-CTV is the *agreeably weighted completion time variance* problem AW-CTV. In this special case the jobs are agreeably weighted, i.e. $p_i < p_j$ implies $w_i \geq w_j$ for all i, j. Another, even more restricted special case is the unweighted *completion time variance* problem CTV in which $w_j = 1$ holds for all j.

The agreeably weighted variant AW-CTV is an intermediate case between no weights and arbitrary weights. It captures some of the difficulties of job weights, but still it has considerably more structure than the variant with arbitrary weights. In scheduling theory, agreeably weighted variants of many other problems have been investigated in detail, e.g. for the problem of minimizing the weighted number of late jobs (Lawler [11]) or for the problem of minimizing the weighted number of late jobs with release dates and with preemption (Lawler [12]).

The weighted completion time variance problem has first been formulated by Merten & Muller [13]. They motivate the variance performance measure by computer file organization problems in which it is important to provide uniform response time to the users. In the same spirit, Kanet [9] motivates the measure as being applicable to any service and manufacturing setting where it is desirable to provide jobs or customers jobs with approximately the same service. Bagchi [1] extends the model to bicriteria problems where both the mean and the variance of the job completion times are to be minimized. Bagchi, Chang & Sullivan [2] study the problem of minimizing absolute and squared deviations of completion times from a common due date. For a comprehensive review of these types of problems, see Baker & Scudder [3].

For the unweighted problem CTV, Schrage [15] conjectures that there always exists an optimal schedule where the longest job is processed first, the second-longest job is processed last, and the third-longest job is processed as second job. Hall & Kubiak [7] prove Schrage's conjecture. De, Ghosh & Wells [5] present a pseudo-polynomial algorithm for CTV, and Cai [4] extends this pseudo-polynomial algorithm over to AW-CTV. The computational complexity of CTV was unknown for a long time until in 1993 Kubiak [10] established $\mathcal{NP}$-hardness in the ordinary sense. As a consequence, also the more general problems AW-CTV and W-CTV are $\mathcal{NP}$-hard. This completely settles the complexity status of AW-CTV and CTV: They are $\mathcal{NP}$-hard in the ordinary sense and solvable in pseudo-polynomial time. Deciding whether W-CTV is $\mathcal{NP}$-hard in the strong sense, remains an open problem.

If a problem is $\mathcal{NP}$-hard to solve to optimality, research usually turns to obtaining polynomial-time approximation algorithms, i.e. fast algorithms that construct suboptimal schedules whose objective value is not too far away from the optimal objective value. We say that a polynomial time approximation algorithm is a ρ-approximation algorithm ($\rho > 1$) if it always delivers a solution with objective value at most ρ times the optimal objective value. A family of polynomial-time $(1 + \varepsilon)$-approximation algorithms over all $\varepsilon > 0$ is called a *polynomial-time approximation scheme*, PTAS for short. If the running time of a PTAS is also polynomial in $1/\varepsilon$, then it is called a *fully polynomial-time approximation scheme*, FPTAS for short. An FPTAS is the strongest possible polynomial time approximation result that one can derive for an $\mathcal{NP}$-hard problem unless $\mathcal{P} = \mathcal{NP}$.

Cai [4] derives an FPTAS for the special case of AW-CTV where the job weights are polynomially bounded in the number n of jobs. In other words, in this special case the weights of the jobs must not differ exponentially from each other. Since the unweighted problem CTV obviously fulfills this condition, Cai's work yields an FPTAS for CTV.

In this paper, we construct an FPTAS for the general problem AW-CTV, without putting any restrictions on the weights of the jobs. Our FPTAS results from manipulating a dynamic programming formulation of AW-CTV. There are two standard approaches for transforming a dynamic program into an FPTAS; both of them go back to the 1970s. The first approach is attributed to Sahni (see e.g. [14]). The main idea is to round the input data of the instance, with the goal of bringing the running time of the dynamic program down to polynomial. The second approach is the TRIMMING-OF-THE-STATE-SPACE technique of Ibarra & Kim [8]. Here the main idea is to clean up the state space of the dynamic program, and to collapse states that are 'close' to each other, with the goal of bringing the size of the state space down to polynomial. Of course in both approaches the crucial point is how to control the error that is introduced by the rounding and simplifying and trimming of the dynamic program.

Cai [4] designs an efficient dynamic programming formulation for AW-CTV and then follows Sahni's approach to get an FPTAS for his special case with the polynomially bounded weights. Quite differently from Cai [4], we will start from a less efficient dynamic programming formulation of AW-CTV that stores and maintains some surplus information in the state space. However, it is precisely this surplus information that makes it possible to apply the technique of Ibarra & Kim and to prove that it indeed yields an FPTAS. In the analysis of the FPTAS, we have to resolve several technical difficulties which arise from the quadratic terms in the objective function and which make it hard to control the rounding errors. The FPTAS presented here can not be derived via the approach developed in Woeginger [16].

The approximability status of the general weighted problem W-CTV remains open; in fact, it is even open whether W-CTV has a polynomial time approximation algorithm with *constant* worst case ratio.

The paper is organized as follows. Section 2 contains some preliminaries on AW-CTV. Section 3 gives a dynamic programming formulation DP for AW-CTV, and Section 4 introduces some technical concepts. The results of Sections 3 and 4 are then used in Section 5 for trimming the state space of DP and for deriving the fully polynomial time approximation scheme for the general problem AW-CTV.

2 Preliminaries

In this section we collect several definitions, observations, and propositions on AW-CTV. From now on, we will assume without loss of generality that the jobs have been renumbered such that

$$p_1 \leq p_2 \leq \cdots \leq p_n \quad \text{and} \quad w_1 \geq w_2 \geq \cdots \geq w_n. \tag{3}$$

Such a numbering exists as the jobs are agreeably weighted. We denote by P the total processing time $\sum_{j=1}^{n} p_j$ of the jobs, and by W their total weight $\sum_{j=1}^{n} w_j$. The objective function of a schedule σ as formulated in (2) may be rewritten as

$$\text{VAR}(\sigma) = \sum_{j=1}^{n} w_j C_j^2 \quad W\overline{C}^2 = \sum_{j=1}^{n} w_j C_j^2 - \frac{1}{W}(\sum_{j=1}^{n} w_j C_j)^2. \tag{4}$$

Proposition 1. *For any schedule with job completion times C_j $(j = 1, \ldots, n)$ and for any subset $J \subseteq \{1, \ldots, n\}$*

$$(\sum_{j \in J} w_j C_j)^2 \leq W \sum_{j \in J} w_j C_j^2. \tag{5}$$

Proposition 2. *An optimal schedule σ^* for AW-CTV does not contain any intermediate idle time between the processing of the jobs.*

If a schedule is shifted in time (i.e. if all job completion times are increased by the same amount), then the value of the objective function does not change.

For the unweighted problem CTV, Eilon & Chowdhury [6] observe that in an optimal schedule the processing times of the jobs processed before $\overline{C}$ are in non-increasing order and the processing times of the jobs processed after $\overline{C}$ are in non-decreasing order. Cai [4] generalizes this observation as follows to AW-CTV.

Proposition 3. *(Cai [4])*
For any instance of AW-CTV that fulfills the inequalities (3), there exists an optimal schedule $\langle J_{\pi(1)}, J_{\pi(2)}, \ldots, J_{\pi(n)} \rangle$ of the following form: Let z denote the index for which $J_{\pi(z)} = J_1$.

(i) For $j = 1, \ldots, z - 1$, $\pi(j) > \pi(j + 1)$ holds.
 For $j = z, \ldots, n - 1$, $\pi(j) < \pi(j + 1)$ holds.
(ii) For $j = 1, \ldots, z - 1$, $C_{\pi(j)} \leq \overline{C} + \frac{1}{2} p_{\pi(j)}$ holds.
 For $j = z + 1, \ldots, n - 1$, $C_{\pi(j)} \geq \overline{C} + \frac{1}{2} p_{\pi(j)}$ holds.

Any schedule that fulfills the properties (i) and (ii) stated in Proposition 3 is called *V-shaped*.

Lemma 4. *Let σ^+ be an optimal V-shaped schedule in which the processing of J_1 starts at time 0. Let σ^- be the optimal schedule that results from shifting schedule σ^+ by p_1 time units to the left. For $j = 1, \ldots, n$ denote by C_j^+ and C_j^- the completion time of job J_j in schedule σ^+ and σ^-, respectively. Let VAR^* denote the optimal objective value. Then*

$$\min \{\sum_{j=1}^{n} w_j (C_j^+)^2, \sum_{j=1}^{n} w_j (C_j^-)^2\} \leq 4\,\text{VAR}^*. \tag{6}$$

3 A dynamic programming formulation

In this section we give a dynamic programming formulation for AW-CTV that relies strongly on Proposition 3.

The dynamic program goes through n phases. The k-th phase ($k = 1, \ldots, n$) takes care of job J_k; it produces a set S_k of *states*. A state in S_k is a quintuple (ℓ, r, L, R, Q) that encodes a partial schedule for the subset $\{J_1, \ldots, J_k\}$ of jobs. This partial schedule occupies a time interval around the processing of job J_1, which starts its processing either at time 0 or at time $-p_1$. The schedule decomposes into a *left part* that consists of the jobs that complete at or before time 0, and into a *right part* that consists of the jobs that complete after time 0. The precise meaning of the variables in a state is as follows.

- ℓ is the total length of the jobs in the left part of the partial schedule;
- r is the total length of the jobs in the right part of the partial schedule;
- L denotes the absolute value of the total weighted job completion time of the jobs in the left part of the partial schedule;
- R denotes the total weighted job completion time of the jobs in the right part of the partial schedule;
- Q denotes the total weighted sum of squared job completion times of all jobs in the partial schedule.

Note that $0 \le \ell, r \le P$, that $0 \le L, R \le WP$, and that $0 \le Q \le WP^2$. The dynamic programming formulation DP is given in Figure 1.

---

1 Initialize $S_1 := \{(0, p_1, 0, w_1 p_1, w_1 p_1^2), \ (p_1, 0, 0, 0, 0)\}$
2 **For** $k = 2$ **to** n **do**
3   Initialize $S_k := \emptyset$
4   **For** every $(\ell, r, L, R, Q) \in S_{k-1}$ **do**
5         $C := \ell;$ add $(\ell + p_k, r, L + w_k C, R, Q + w_k C^2)$ to S_k;
6         $C := r + p_k;$ add $(\ell, r + p_k, L, R + w_k C, Q + w_k C^2)$ to S_k;
7   **EndFor**
8   **Do nothing**
9 **EndFor**

Fig. 1. The dynamic programming formulation DP for AW-CTV.

Line 1 initializes S_1 with the two schedules for $\{J_1\}$ in which J_1 is started at time 0 and time $-p_1$, respectively. The "Do nothing" in Line 8 will be replaced by another command in the trimmed version of this dynamic program. The loop in lines 2–9 puts job J_k at the left and at the right end of every schedule for the jobs $\{J_1, \ldots, J_{k-1}\}$ in S_{k-1} and creates corresponding states in S_k. With this it is obvious that for every V-shaped schedule σ in which the processing of job J_1 starts at time 0 or at time $-p_1$, the final state set S_n contains a corresponding state that encodes σ. Then by Proposition 2, Proposition 3, and by (4),

$$\text{VAR}^* \ = \ \min \ \{Q - \frac{1}{W}(R - L)^2 \ : \ (\ell, r, L, R, Q) \in S_n\}. \tag{7}$$

In general, the running time of DP will be exponential in the input size. The running time mainly depends on the cardinalities of the state sets S_k and is proportional to $\sum_{k=1}^{n} |S_k|$.

We remark that the relation (7) would also hold true if we had simply initialized S_1 in line 1 as $S_1 := \{(0, p_1, 0, w_1 p_1, w_1 p_1^2)\}$. The value of the component r in any state $(\ell, r, L, R, Q) \in S_k$ is implicitly contained in the values of ℓ and k. Moreover, the only information that is needed in (7) from the components L and R is their difference, and these components could be merged into a single component $R - L$. Hence, DP could be simplified and its running time could be improved. However, the FPTAS that we are going to develop in the following sections will crucially depend on the formulations in Figure 1.

4 More technicalities

In this section, we introduce some definitions and concepts for five-dimensional vectors that will be used in Section 5 to trim the state space of the dynamic program. Due to space limitations, all proofs have been omitted from this section. For a real number α, $\alpha > 1$, two non-negative vectors $\mathbf{s} = (s_1, s_2, s_3, s_4, s_5)$ and $\mathbf{t} = (t_1, t_2, t_3, t_4, t_5)$ are called α-*close* to each other, if

$$\frac{1}{\alpha} s_m \ \le \ t_m \ \le \ \alpha s_m \qquad \text{for } m = 1, \dots, 4 \tag{8}$$

and

$$\frac{1}{\alpha^2} s_5 \ \le \ t_5 \ \le \ \alpha^2 s_5. \tag{9}$$

Note that α-closeness is a symmetric and reflexive relation on the vectors.

Lemma 5. *Let* $\mathbf{s}$, $\mathbf{t}$, *and* $\mathbf{u}$ *be non-negative five-dimensional vectors. Let* $\alpha, \beta > 1$. *If* $\mathbf{s}$ *is* α-*close to* $\mathbf{t}$, *and* $\mathbf{t}$ *is* β-*close to* $\mathbf{u}$, *then* $\mathbf{s}$ *is* $(\alpha\beta)$-*close to* $\mathbf{u}$.

Lemma 6. *Let* $\alpha > 1$. *Let* (ℓ, r, L, R, Q) *and* (ℓ', r', L', R', Q') *be non-negative vectors that are* α-*close to each other. Let* $p, w > 0$. *Then the following holds.*

(i) $(\ell + p, r, L + w\ell, R, Q + w\ell^2)$ *is* α-*close to* $(\ell' + p, r', L' + w\ell', R', Q' + w(\ell')^2)$.
(ii) $(\ell, r + p, L, R + w(r + p), Q + w(r + p)^2)$ *is* α-*close to*
     $(\ell', r' + p, L', R' + w(r' + p), Q' + w(r' + p)^2)$.

Lemma 7. *Let* $\alpha > 1$ *and* $\tau \ge 1$. *Let* T *be a set of five-dimensional vectors whose coordinates are integers in the range* $[0, \tau]$. *If* T *does not contain any pair of* α-*close vectors, then* $|T| \le (2 + \ln \tau / \ln \alpha)^5$ *holds.*

5 The fully polynomial time approximation scheme

In this section we apply the TRIMMING-OF-THE-STATE-SPACE technique of Ibarra & Kim [8] to the dynamic program DP from Section 3. By doing this, we will derive a fully polynomial time approximation scheme for AW-CTV.

Let $\varepsilon > 0$ be the desired precision of approximation. We fix a so-called *trimming parameter* $\Delta \doteq 1 + \varepsilon/(40n)$. It is easy to see that $\Delta^{2n} \leq 1 + \varepsilon/10$. Elementary calculations show that for values y with $1 < y \leq 1 + \varepsilon/10$, the expression $5y - 4y^{-1}$ only takes values smaller than $1 + \varepsilon$. Hence,

$$5\Delta^{2n} - 4\Delta^{-2n} \leq 1 + \varepsilon. \tag{10}$$

The formulation of the approximation scheme will be based on the parameter Δ, and in the analysis we will use inequality (10) to prove the desired performance guarantee.

In developing the approximation scheme, the main idea is to *trim down* every state set T_k in the dynamic program to a relatively small state set $T_k^\diamond$ at the end of the k-th phase, $k = 1, \ldots, n$. The resulting state set $T_k^\diamond$ will fulfill the following properties:

T1. $T_k^\diamond$ is a subset of T_k.
T2. $T_k^\diamond$ does not contain any pair of Δ-close states.
T3. For every state $\mathbf{t}$ in the untrimmed state set T_k, $T_k^\diamond$ contains some Δ-close state $\mathbf{t}^\diamond$.

One way of trimming is to apply a greedy procedure. We replace line 8 in the dynamic program in Figure 1 by the lines 8.1–8.6 as depicted in Figure 2. Clearly, the resulting set $T_k^\diamond$ fulfills properties T1–T3, and the computation of $T_k^\diamond$ only costs $O(|T_k|^2)$ time.

From now on, we will use the following conventions. The original dynamic program in Figure 1 will be abbreviated by *DP*, and the trimmed dynamic program in Figure 2 will be abbreviated by *TDP*. The state sets computed by DP are called S_k. The state sets computed by TDP are called T_k (before the trimming) and $T_k^\diamond$ (after the trimming).

Lemma 8. *The running time of TDP is polynomial in n, $\log W$, $\log P$, and $1/\varepsilon$.*

Lemma 9. *For every $k = 1, \ldots, n$ and for every state $\mathbf{s} \in S_k$ in DP, there exists a state $\mathbf{t}^\diamond \in T_k^\diamond$ in TDP that is Δ^k-close to $\mathbf{s}$.*

Proof. The proof is by induction on k. Since $S_1 = T_1^\diamond$, there is nothing to show for $k = 1$. As induction hypothesis, we assume that for every state in S_{k-1} there exists a Δ^{k-1}-close state in $T_{k-1}^\diamond$.

Consider an arbitrary state $\mathbf{s} \in S_k$ in the original DP. This state $\mathbf{s}$ originates from some state $\mathbf{s}_\# = (\ell, r, L, R, Q) \in S_{k-1}$ via line 5 or line 6 in DP, and hence either

(i) $\mathbf{s} = (\ell + p_k, r, L + w_k\ell, R, Q + w_k\ell^2)$ or

1   Initialize $T_1^\diamond := \{(0, p_1, 0, w_1 p_1, w_1 p_1^2),\ (p_1, 0, 0, 0, 0)\}$
2   **For** $k = 2$ **to** n **do**
3   Initialize $T_k := \emptyset$
4   **For** every $(\ell, r, L, R, Q) \in T_{k-1}^\diamond$ **do**
5            $C := \ell;$ add $(\ell + p_k, r, L + w_k C, R, Q + w_k C^2)$ to T_k;
6            $C := r + p_k;$add $(\ell, r + p_k, L, R + w_k C, Q + w_k C^2)$ to T_k;
7   **EndFor**
8.1   Initialize $T_k^\diamond := \emptyset$
8.2   **For** every $\mathbf{t} = (\ell, r, L, R, Q) \in T_k$ **do**
8.3   **If** $T_k^\diamond$ contains an element that is Δ-close to $\mathbf{t}$
8.4   **then** discard $\mathbf{t}$
8.5   **else** add $\mathbf{t}$ to $T_k^\diamond$
8.6   **EndFor**
9   **EndFor**

Fig. 2. The trimmed dynamic program TDP for AW-CTV.

(ii) $\mathbf{s} = (\ell, r + p_k, L, R + w_k(r + p_k), Q + w_k(r + p_k)^2)$.

We will only deal with case (i). The argument for case (ii) can be done in an analogous way with the exception that one has to apply the statement in Lemma 6(ii) instead of the statement in Lemma 6(i). Now by the induction hypothesis, in case (i) there exists a state $\mathbf{t}_\# = (\ell', r', L', R', Q') \in T_{k-1}^\diamond$ that is Δ^{k-1}-close to $\mathbf{s}_\#$. By the construction of T_k, the set T_k then contains the state $\mathbf{t} = (\ell' + p_k, r', L' + w_k \ell', R', Q' + w_k(\ell')^2)$. Finally by the construction of $T_k^\diamond$, there exists a state $\mathbf{t}^\diamond$ in $T_k^\diamond$ that is Δ-close to $\mathbf{t}$.

Since $\mathbf{s}_\#$ is Δ^{k-1}-close to $\mathbf{t}_\#$, Lemma 6(i) yields that $\mathbf{s}$ is Δ^{k-1}-close to $\mathbf{t}$. Since $\mathbf{s}$ is Δ^{k-1}-close to $\mathbf{t}$, and $\mathbf{t}$ is Δ-close to $\mathbf{t}^\diamond$, Lemma 5 yields that $\mathbf{s}$ is Δ^k-close to $\mathbf{t}^\diamond$. $\square$

Now consider an optimal V-shaped schedule σ^+ in which the processing of J_1 starts at time 0. Precisely as in the statement of Lemma 4, let σ^- be the schedule that results from shifting σ^+ by p_1 time units to the left, let C_j^+ and C_j^- ($j = 1, \ldots, n$) denote the completion time of job J_j in schedule σ^+ and σ^-, and let VAR* denote the optimal objective value. Then by Lemma 4, inequality (6) holds; without loss of generality we assume that in (6)

$$\sum_{j=1}^n w_j (C_j^+)^2 \leq 4 \,\text{VAR}^*. \tag{11}$$

By the discussion in Section 3, there exists a state $\mathbf{s} = (\ell^*, r^*, L^*, R^*, Q^*) \in S_n$ of DP that encodes schedule σ^+. Then (7) yields that

$$\text{VAR}^* = Q^* - \frac{1}{W}(R^* - L^*)^2. \tag{12}$$

Define sets $\mathcal{R} = \{j : C_j^+ > 0\}$ and $\mathcal{L} = \{j : C_j^+ \leq 0\}$. Then from Proposition 1 we get that $(R^*)^2 \leq W \sum_{j \in \mathcal{R}} w_j (C_j^+)^2$ and $(L^*)^2 \leq W \sum_{j \in \mathcal{L}} w_j (C_j^-)^2$. Adding these two inequalities and using (11) gives

$$(R^*)^2 + (L^*)^2 \leq 4W \cdot \text{Var}^*. \tag{13}$$

By Lemma 9, state set $T_n^\diamond$ of TDP contains a state $(\ell^\diamond, r^\diamond, L^\diamond, R^\diamond, Q^\diamond)$ that is Δ^n-close to $\mathbf{s}$. According to (8) and (9), then

$$\Delta^{-n} L^* \leq L^\diamond \leq \Delta^n L^* \qquad \Delta^{-n} R^* \leq R^\diamond \leq \Delta^n R^* \qquad Q^\diamond \leq \Delta^{2n} Q^*. \tag{14}$$

Consider a schedule $\sigma^\diamond$ that corresponds to state $\mathbf{t}^\diamond$. Let $\text{Var}^\diamond = Q^\diamond - (R^\diamond - L^\diamond)^2 / W$ denote the objective value of $\sigma^\diamond$. Then

$$
\begin{aligned}
W \cdot \text{Var}^\diamond &= W Q^\diamond + 2 R^\diamond L^\diamond - (R^\diamond)^2 - (L^\diamond)^2 \\
&\leq \Delta^{2n} (W Q^* + 2 R^* L^*) - \Delta^{-2n} ((R^*)^2 + (L^*)^2) \\
&= \Delta^{2n} (W Q^* + 2 R^* L^* - (R^*)^2 - (L^*)^2) + \\
&\qquad\qquad (\Delta^{2n} - \Delta^{-2n})((R^*)^2 + (L^*)^2) \\
&\leq \Delta^{2n} W \cdot \text{Var}^* + (\Delta^{2n} - \Delta^{-2n}) 4 W \cdot \text{Var}^* \\
&= (5 \Delta^{2n} - 4 \Delta^{-2n}) W \cdot \text{Var}^* \\
&\leq (1 + \varepsilon) W \cdot \text{Var}^*.
\end{aligned}
$$

In this chain of inequalities, the first inequality follows from (14), the second inequality follows from (12) and (13), and the third inequality follows from (10).

Hence, the weighted variance $\text{Var}^\diamond$ of $\sigma^\diamond$ is at most $(1 + \varepsilon) \text{Var}^*$. By Lemma 8 the value $\text{Var}^\diamond$ can be computed in time that is polynomial in n, $\log W$, $\log P$, and $1/\varepsilon$, i.e. polynomial in the size of the input and in $1/\varepsilon$. Summarizing, we have the following theorem.

Theorem 10. *There exists a fully polynomial time approximation scheme for the scheduling problem* AW-CTV, *i.e. for minimizing the weighted variance of job completion times on a single machine with job-dependent, agreeable weights.*

Acknowledgement. This work has been supported by the START program Y43-MAT of the Austrian Ministry of Science.

References

1. U. BAGCHI, 1989. Simultaneous minimization of mean and variation of flow time and waiting time in single machine systems, *Operations Research* 37, 118–125.
2. U. BAGCHI, Y.L. CHANG, AND R.S. SULLIVAN, 1987. Minimizing absolute and squared deviations of completion times with different earliness and tardiness penalties and a common due date, *Naval Research Logistics* 34, 738–751.
3. K.R. BAKER AND G.D. SCUDDER, 1990. Sequencing with earliness and tardiness penalties: a review, *Operations Research* 38, 22–36.

4. X. CAI, 1995. Minimization of agreeably weighted variance in single machine systems, *European Journal of Operational Research 85*, 576–592.

5. P. DE, J.B. GHOSH & C.E. WELLS, 1992. On the minimization of completion time variance with a bicriteria-extension, *Operations Research 40*, 1148–1155.

6. S. EILON AND I.G. CHOWDHURY, 1977. Minimizing waiting variance in the single machine problem, *Management Science 23*, 567–575.

7. N.G. HALL AND W. KUBIAK, 1991. Proof of a conjecture of Schrage about the completion time variance problem, *Operations Research Letters 10*, 467–472.

8. O. IBARRA AND C.E. KIM, 1975. Fast approximation algorithms for the knapsack and sum of subset problems, *Journal of the ACM 22*, 463–468.

9. J.J. KANET, 1981. Minimizing variation of flow time in single machine systems, *Management Science 27*, 1453–1459.

10. W. KUBIAK, 1993. Completion time variance on a single machine is difficult, *Operations Research Letters 14*, 49–59.

11. E.L. LAWLER, 1976. Sequencing to minimize the weighted number of tardy jobs, *RAIRO Recherche opérationelle S10(5)*, 27–33.

12. E.L. LAWLER, 1994. Knapsack-like scheduling problems, the Moore-Hodgson algorithm and the 'tower of sets' property, *Mathematical and Computer Modelling 20*, 91–106.

13. A.G. MERTEN AND M.E. MULLER, 1972. Variance minimization in single machine sequencing problems, *Management Science 18*, 518–528.

14. S.K. SAHNI, 1976. Algorithms for scheduling independent tasks, *Journal of the ACM 23*, 116–127.

15. L. SCHRAGE, 1975. Minimizing the time-in-system variance for a finite jobset, *Management Science 21*, 540–543.

16. G.J. WOEGINGER, 1999. When does a dynamic programming formulation guarantee the existence of an FPTAS? *Proceedings of the 10th Annual ACM-SIAM Symposium on Discrete Algorithms (SODA'99)*, 820–829.

Erratum: Bulk-Synchronous Parallel Multiplication of Boolean Matrices

A. Tiskin

Oxford University Computing Laboratory
Wolfson Building, Parks Rd., Oxford OX1 3QD, UK
email: tiskin@comlab.ox.ac.uk

Abstract. We correct an error in the analysis of local computation cost of a bulk-synchronous parallel algorithm for Boolean matrix multiplication.

In [1], we proposed a bulk-synchronous parallel (BSP) algorithm for Boolean matrix multiplication. The main contribution of the paper consists in the application of a result from extremal graph theory, the Szemerédi regularity lemma, to a problem from the seemingly unrelated area of BSP computation. The main result of [1] is Algorithm 2 in page 504. The algorithm is not practical; its main motivation is to demonstrate that the Strassen-type algorithm, when applied to Boolean matrices, is not asymptotically optimal in communication.

While the above claim still holds, the analysis of local computation involved in Algorithm 2 is erroneous. The paragraph immediately preceding the algorithm description should read:

> The number of nodes in the cluster graph of each block is $O\left(2^{2^{10}\epsilon^{-17}}\right) = O\left(2^{2^{44}p^{68}}\right)$. Therefore, each cluster graph contains $O\left(2^{2^{45}p^{68}}\right)$ edges. Each processor computes cluster graphs for p^2 blocks, therefore the total number of cluster graph edges computed by a processor is at most $O\left(2^{2^{46}p^{68}}\right)$. The cluster graphs must be exchanged between the processors. To obtain an algorithm with low communication cost, we require that this number of edges is at most $O(n^2/p)$, therefore it is sufficient to assume that $n = \Omega\left(2^{2^{45}p^{68}}\right)$.

Within the algorithm description, the cost analysis paragraph should read:

> The local computation, communication and synchronisation costs are $W = O\left(2^{2^{46}p^{68}} \cdot n^\omega\right)$, $H = O(n^2/p)$, $S = O(1)$. Hence, for any $\gamma > \omega$, and $n = \Omega\left(2^{2^{46}\cdot(\gamma-\omega)^{-1}\cdot p^{68}}\right)$, the local computation cost is $W = O(n^\gamma/p)$, and still $H = O(n^2/p)$, $S = O(1)$.

Thus, no claim of asymptotic efficiency in local computation is being made. However, the local communication cost is still polynomial in n with exponent ω. Therefore, for sufficiently large n, the algorithm improves on the asymptotic cost of any Strassen-type BSP algorithm with exponent ψ, $\omega < \psi < 3$.

References

1. A. Tiskin. Bulk-synchronous parallel multiplication of Boolean matrices. In K. G. Larsen, S. Skyum, and W. Winskel, editors, *Proceedings of ICALP '98*, volume 1443 of *Lecture Notes in Computer Science*, pages 494–506. Springer-Verlag, 1998

Author Index

Lecture Notes in Computer Science

For information about Vols. 1–1553
please contact your bookseller or Springer-Verlag

Vol. 1596: R. Poli, H.-M. Voigt, S. Cagnoni, D. Corne, G.D. Smith, T.C. Fogarty (Eds.), Evolutionary Image Analysis, Signal Processing and Telecommunications. Proceedings, 1999. X, 225 pages. 1999.

Vol. 1597: H. Zuidweg, M. Campolargo, J. Delgado, A. Mullery (Eds.), Intelligence in Services and Networks. Proceedings, 1999. XII, 552 pages. 1999.

Vol. 1598: R. Poli, P. Nordin, W.B. Langdon, T.C. Fogarty (Eds.), Genetic Programming. Proceedings, 1999. X, 283 pages. 1999.

Vol. 1599: T. Ishida (Ed.), Multiagent Platforms. Proceedings, 1998. VIII, 187 pages. 1999. (Subseries LNAI).

Vol. 1601: J.-P. Katoen (Ed.), Formal Methods for Real-Time and Probabilistic Systems. Proceedings, 1999. X, 355 pages. 1999.

Vol. 1602: A. Sivasubramaniam, M. Lauria (Eds.), Network-Based Parallel Computing. Proceedings, 1999. VIII, 225 pages. 1999.

Vol. 1603: J. Vitek, C.D. Jensen (Eds.), Secure Internet Programming. X, 501 pages. 1999.

Vol. 1605: J. Billington, M. Diaz, G. Rozenberg (Eds.), Application of Petri Nets to Communication Networks. IX, 303 pages. 1999.

Vol. 1606: J. Mira, J.V. Sánchez-Andrés (Eds.), Foundations and Tools for Neural Modeling. Proceedings, Vol. I, 1999. XXIII, 865 pages. 1999.

Vol. 1607: J. Mira, J.V. Sánchez-Andrés (Eds.), Engineering Applications of Bio-Inspired Artificial Neural Networks. Proceedings, Vol. II, 1999. XXIII, 907 pages. 1999.

Vol. 1608: S. Doaitse Swierstra, P.R. Henriques, J.N. Oliveira (Eds.), Advanced Functional Programming. Proceedings, 1998. XII, 289 pages. 1999.

Vol. 1609: Z. W. Raś, A. Skowron (Eds.), Foundations of Intelligent Systems. Proceedings, 1999. XII, 676 pages. 1999. (Subseries LNAI).

Vol. 1610: G. Cornuéjols, R.E. Burkard, G.J. Woeginger (Eds.), Integer Programming and Combinatorial Optimization. Proceedings, 1999. IX, 453 pages. 1999.

Vol. 1611: I. Imam, Y. Kodratoff, A. El-Dessouki, M. Ali (Eds.), Multiple Approaches to Intelligent Systems. Proceedings, 1999. XIX, 899 pages. 1999. (Subseries LNAI).

Vol. 1612: R. Bergmann, S. Breen, M. Göker, M. Manago, S. Wess, Developing Industrial Case-Based Reasoning Applications. XX, 188 pages. 1999. (Subseries LNAI).

Vol. 1613: A. Kuba, M. Šámal, A. Todd-Pokropek (Eds.), Information Processing in Medical Imaging. Proceedings, 1999. XVII, 508 pages. 1999.

Vol. 1614: D.P. Huijsmans, A.W.M. Smeulders (Eds.), Visual Information and Information Systems. Proceedings, 1999. XVII, 827 pages. 1999.

Vol. 1615: C. Polychronopoulos, K. Joe, A. Fukuda, S. Tomita (Eds.), High Performance Computing. Proceedings, 1999. XIV, 408 pages. 1999.

Vol. 1617: N.V. Murray (Ed.), Automated Reasoning with Analytic Tableaux and Related Methods. Proceedings, 1999. X, 325 pages. 1999. (Subseries LNAI).

Vol. 1619: M.T. Goodrich, C.C. McGeoch (Eds.), Algorithm Engineering and Experimentation. Proceedings, 1999. VIII, 349 pages. 1999.

Vol. 1620: W. Horn, Y. Shahar, G. Lindberg, S. Andreassen, J. Wyatt (Eds.), Artificial Intelligence in Medicine. Proceedings, 1999. XIII, 454 pages. 1999. (Subseries LNAI).

Vol. 1621: D. Fensel, R. Studer (Eds.), Knowledge Acquisition Modeling and Management. Proceedings, 1999. XI, 404 pages. 1999. (Subseries LNAI).

Vol. 1622: M. González Harbour, J.A. de la Puente (Eds.), Reliable Software Technologies – Ada-Europe'99. Proceedings, 1999. XIII, 451 pages. 1999.

Vol. 1625: B. Reusch (Ed.), Computational Intelligence. Proceedings, 1999. XIV, 710 pages. 1999.

Vol. 1626: M. Jarke, A. Oberweis (Eds.), Advanced Information Systems Engineering. Proceedings, 1999. XIV, 478 pages. 1999.

Vol. 1627: T. Asano, H. Imai, D.T. Lee, S.-i. Nakano, T. Tokuyama (Eds.), Computing and Combinatorics. Proceedings, 1999. XIV, 494 pages. 1999.

Col. 1628: R. Guerraoui (Ed.), ECOOP'99 - Object-Oriented Programming. Proceedings, 1999. XIII, 529 pages. 1999.

Vol. 1629: H. Leopold, N. García (Eds.), Multimedia Applications, Services and Techniques - ECMAST'99. Proceedings, 1999. XV, 574 pages. 1999.

Vol. 1631: P. Narendran, M. Rusinowitch (Eds.), Rewriting Techniques and Applications. Proceedings, 1999. XI, 397 pages. 1999.

Vol. 1632: H. Ganzinger (Ed.), Automated Deduction – Cade-16. Proceedings, 1999. XIV, 429 pages. 1999. (Subseries LNAI).

Vol. 1633: N. Halbwachs, D. Peled (Eds.), Computer Aided Verification. Proceedings, 1999. XII, 506 pages. 1999.

Vol. 1634: S. Džeroski, P. Flach (Eds.), Inductive Logic Programming. Proceedings, 1999. VIII, 303 pages. 1999. (Subseries LNAI).

Vol. 1636: L. Knudsen (Ed.), Fast Software Encryption. Proceedings, 1999. VIII, 317 pages. 1999.

Vol. 1638: A. Hunter, S. Parsons (Eds.), Symbolic and Quantitative Approaches to Reasoning and Uncertainty. Proceedings, 1999. IX, 397 pages. 1999. (Subseries LNAI).

Vol. 1639: S. Donatelli, J. Kleijn (Eds.), Application and Theory of Petri Nets 1999. Proceedings, 1999. VIII, 425 pages. 1999.

Vol. 1640: W. Tepfenhart, W. Cyre (Eds.), Conceptual Structures: Standards and Practices. Proceedings, 1999. XII, 515 pages. 1999. (Subseries LNAI).

Vol. 1644: J. Wiedermann, P. van Emde Boas, M. Nielsen (Eds.), Automata, Languages, and Programming. Proceedings, 1999. XIII, 720 pages. 1999.

Vol. 1649: R.Y. Pinter, S. Tsur (Eds.), Next Generation Information Technologies and Systems. Proceedings, 1999. IX, 327 pages. 1999.

Vol. 1650: K.-D. Althoff, R. Bergmann, L.K. Branting (Eds.), Case-Based Reasoning Research and Development. Proceedings, 1999. XII, 598 pages. 1999. (Subseries LNAI).

Vol. 1653: S. Covaci (Ed.), Active Networks. Proceedings, 1999. XIII, 346 pages. 1999.